The Legal Environment Today

Business in Its Ethical, Regulatory, and International Setting

SECOND EDITION

Roger LeRoy Miller
Institute for University Studies
Arlington, Texas

Frank B. Cross
Associate Director,
Center for Legal and Regulatory Studies,
University of Texas at Austin

WEST **West Educational Publishing Company**
an International Thomson Publishing company I(T)P®

Cincinnati • Albany • Boston • Detroit • Johannesburg • London • Madrid • Melbourne • Mexico City
New York • Pacific Grove • San Francisco • Scottsdale • Singapore • Tokyo • Toronto

PUBLISHER/TEAM DIRECTOR:	JACK CALHOUN
SENIOR ACQUISITIONS EDITOR:	ROB DEWEY
ACQUISITIONS EDITOR:	SCOTT PERSON
DEVELOPMENT EDITOR:	JAN LAMAR
PRODUCTION EDITORS:	BILL STRYKER AND
	ANN RUDRUD
PRODUCTION ASSISTANT:	MEGAN RYAN
MARKETING MANAGER:	MIKE WORLS
COVER DESIGN:	DOUG ABBOTT
INTERNAL DESIGN:	ANN B. RUDRUD
PROOFREADING:	SUZIE F. DeFAZIO
INDEX:	BOB MARSH

Library of Congress Cataloging-in-Publication Data
Miller, Roger LeRoy.
The legal environment today : business in its ethical, regulatory, and international setting / Roger LeRoy Miller, Frank B. Cross.
— 2nd ed.
    p.   cm.
  Includes index.
  ISBN 0–538–88534–3 (hard : alk. paper)
  1. Business law—United States.   2. Law—United States.
I. Cross, Frank B.   II. Title.
KF889.M536 1999
346.7307—dc21
                                         98-5809
                                         CIP

23456789 D 5432109

Printed in the United States of America

I(T)P®

International Thomson Publishing
West Educational Publishing is an ITP Company.
The ITP trademark is used under license.

Contents in Brief

Appendices A–I

Contents

Each chapter begins with a *Chapter Outline* and *Chapter Objectives*. At the end of each chapter you'll find *Key Terms, Chapter Summary, For Review, Questions and Case Problems,* and an *Interacting with the Internet* feature. Most chapters also include *International Perspective* and/or *Ethical Perspective* boxes. Topics of special features, *Landmark in the Legal Environment, Inside the Legal Environment,* and *Technology and the Legal Environment,* are listed separately, beginning on page xvi.

Appendices A-1

Special Features

Preface to the Instructor

Knowledge of the legal environment is essential for anyone contemplating a career in the business world. Changes are occurring in the legal, regulatory, ethical, and global environments more rapidly then ever before. In many instances, technology is both driving and facilitating these changes. While none of the issues regarding punitive damages, the assessment of legal fees on losing parties, cost-benefit analyses of regulations, and regulation of the Internet have been completely resolved, one thing is certain: awareness of the legal and regulatory environment of business is critical for those entering the business world.

The Legal Environment Today: Business in Its Ethical, Regulatory, and International Setting, Second Edition, has been written to satisfy the increasingly important "need to know" of today's students. Your students will learn about all of the major legal environment topics when using this text. Not only will they obtain a rock-solid foundation in the subject matter, but they will also be motivated to learn more through our use of high-interest pedagogical features, such as *Landmark in the Legal Environment* and *Inside the Legal Environment.* We believe that teaching the legal environment can be enjoyable and so, too, can learning about it.

A Complete Course in the Legal Environment

The most important aspects of the legal environment are presented in this text, which is divided into six units:

- ■ Unit One: The Foundations
- ■ Unit Two: The Public Environment
- ■ Unit Three: The Private Environment
- ■ Unit Four: The Employment Environment
- ■ Unit Five: The Regulatory Environment
- ■ Unit Six: The International Environment

Within each unit we have attempted to make the material flow both within chapters and from chapter to chapter. Nonetheless, apart from the opening chapters on the foundations, which students should read first, the text can be used in any order that you wish. In other words, virtually all chapters are self-contained, which gives you complete flexibility in using the book.

Key Features

Virtually all of the chapters in this text have one or more of the special features described below. These features are designed both to instruct and to pique the interest of your students. To continue our emphasis on critical thinking, for the Second Edition we have added to each feature a question, "For Critical Analysis." These questions, which may serve as a basis for classroom discussion, require the student to reflect on some aspect or implication of the law discussed in the features.

Technology and the Law

A number of chapters in the Second Edition of *The Legal Environment Today* contain a special feature focusing on the legal challenges presented by new developments in technology. Some examples of this feature are the following:

■ **Technology and Free Speech** (Chapter 5).
■ **Technology and Online Defamation in Cyberspace** (Chapter 9).

Landmark in the Legal Environment

Most of the chapters in this edition have a *Landmark in the Legal Environment*. These *Landmarks* discuss important cases, statutes, or other laws affecting the legal environment of business. Among the *Landmarks* are the following:

■ **Equitable Principles and Maxims** (Chapter 1).
■ *Palsgraf v. Long Island Railroad Co.* (Chapter 8).
■ **The Statute of Frauds** (Chapter 12).

Inside the Legal Environment

A special feature entitled *Inside the Legal Environment* is included in nearly all of the chapters of this text. These features present practical and instructive examples of how the law affects people in the business and/or personal world. Some of the features are as follows:

■ **Self-Critical Analysis and "Smoking Guns"** (Chapter 2).
■ **Product Liability and the Preemption Issue** (Chapter 10).

On the Web

When you visit **www.westbuslaw.com** you will find classroom material, online teaching support, updates to current law, links to other legal sources on the Web, and supplements and study aids for students, some of which you may provide yourself. Following are some of the categories into which these resources are grouped:

- ■ **Case Updates and Internet Application.** This part of the site includes updates to the law, divided by subject matter, and links to other resources on the Internet, also organized by subject.
- ■ **Hot Links.** This area of the site highlights the newest and best legal resources on the Web.
- ■ **Cyberlaw.** This link on the site includes brief answers to some of the legal questions arising in the expanding area of cyberlaw.
- ■ **Teaching Resources.** Available at this area of the site is on-line teaching support, including details on the supplements available and a link to the Faculty Center in West's Legal Studies Resource Center.
- ■ **Resources.** Students can obtain on-line support, including details about the Study Guide and other help.
- ■ **West's Legal Studies Resource Center.** This link includes legal news and case updates, categorized by topic, as well as links to West's Law Information Center, WestDoc Daily Law Highlights, and other invaluable legal reference sites.

Ethical Perspectives

In addition to a chapter on ethics, chapter-ending ethical questions, and the Ethical Considerations following many of the cases presented in this text, we have included special features called *Ethical Perspectives*. These features are closely integrated with the text so that students can read about some of the ethical implications of topics as they are covered in the text. For example, in Chapter 8, when discussing the potential liability of social hosts, we present an *Ethical Perspective* focusing on the ethical ramifications of holding social hosts liable for harms caused to others by intoxicated guests. Each *Ethical Perspective* concludes with a critical thinking question about the topic covered.

International Perspectives

As part of the greater emphasis in the Second Edition on the global legal environment, nearly every chapter also contains at least one *International Perspective*. These features, like the *Ethical Perspectives*, are closely integrated into the text material and give your students an understanding of the international dimensions of topics that are discussed in the text. For example, in Chapter 17, following a discussion of affirmative action, an *International Perspective* describes how affirmative action programs are also under attack in the European Union. Each *International Perspective* concludes with a critical thinking question about the topic covered.

Emphasis on the International Legal Environment

Because our world is becoming smaller, we feel that legal environment students must have more than a passing understanding of the international legal environment. Consequently, in addition to a general introduction to national and international laws in Chapter 1, we have included the following chapters and special features in *The Legal Environment Today*:

■ **A chapter on the Regulation of International Transactions.** In Chapter 24, your students will learn how international customs, treaties, organizations, conferences, and traditional doctrines regulate the global environment of business.

■ **A chapter on the Legal Environment in Other Nations.** All of Chapter 25 is devoted to comparative legal environments. There your students will see how different countries treat contract formation and enforceability, employment relationships, and the like.

■ **International Perspectives.** As mentioned, among the key features included in this text are the *International Perspectives*. These features help your students keep the global legal environment in view as they study particular aspects of the legal environment in the United States.

■ **Special Appendices.** The appendices include excerpts from the General Agreement on Tariffs and Trade (in Appendix R) and from the North American Free Trade Agreement (in Appendix S).

A Special Case Format

In each chapter, we present cases that have been selected to illustrate the principles of law discussed in the text. The cases are numbered sequentially for easy referencing in class discussions, homework assignments, and examinations. In choosing the case to be included in this edition, our goal has been to achieve a balance between classic cases and those from the late 1990s.

Each case is presented in a special format, which begins with the case and citation. The full citation includes the name of the court deciding the case, the date of the case, and the major parallel reporters in which the case can be found. For federal court or agency cases, the seal of the state is presented.

COMPANY PROFILES.   Many of the cases in the Second Edition of *The Legal Environment Today* are preceded by a Company Profile. These profiles give a brief history of the company involved in the particular case and give your students the real-world background to the case.

HISTORICAL AND SOCIAL SETTINGS.   A special section entitled Historical and Social Setting appears in many cases just following the case title and citation. These settings explicitly address the AACSB's curriculum requirements by focusing on the international, political, ethical, social, environmental, technological, or cultural context of each case being presented. Depending on the specific focus, the title of the section varies. For example, for one case the section title might be Historical and Social Setting; for another, it may be Historical and Political Setting or Historical and Cultural Setting.

BASIC CASE FORMAT.   Following the Historical and Social Setting, each case is summarized in the following four clearly labeled sections:

■ **Background and Facts**
■ **In the Words of the Court** (an excerpt from the court opinion)
■ **Decision and Remedy**

For those instructors who like to see the entire set of court opinions for the cases presented in the text in summarized form, we have created a book, called *Case Printouts for The Legal Environment Today*, Second Edition. This supplement contains the output from WESTLAW (without headnotes) for virtually every case that is included in each chapter. If the instructor wishes, the full set of opinions may be copied and handed out to students.

FOR CRITICAL ANALYSIS.   Each case in this edition of *The Legal Environment Today* concludes with a section entitled For Critical Analysis. This section consists of a question that requires the student to think critically about a particular issue raised by the case. The section addresses the AACSB's curriculum requirements by focusing on how particular aspects of the dispute or the court's decision relate to ethical, international, technological, cultural, or other types of issues. Each For Critical Analysis section has a subtitle indicating the type of issue to which the question relates. For example, in one case, the subtitle may be Ethical Consideration; in another, Political Consideration; and so on.

Other Special Pedagogical Devices

We have included in *The Legal Environment Today*, Second Edition, a number of additional pedagogical devices, including those discussed below.

Pedagogical Devices in the Text

■ **Chapter Objectives**
■ **Chapter Outline**
■ **Margin definitions**
■ **Quotations**
■ **Exhibits and forms**
■ **Photographs (with critical-thinking questions)**

Chapter Ending Pedagogy

■ **Key Terms** (with appropriate page references)
■ **Chapter Summary** (in graphic format with page references)
■ **For Review** (a series of brief review questions)
■ **Questions and Case Problems** (Including hypotheticals and case problems; many of the case problems are based on cases from the mid-1990s.)
■ **A Question of Ethics and Social Responsibility**
■ **Case Briefing Assignment**
■ **For Critical Analysis**

Unit Ending Cumulative Questions

New to the Second Edition are unit-ending cumulative hypothetical questions. These questions appear at the end of the Questions and Case Problems section in the final chapter of the unit. Each of these questions introduces a hypothetical business firm and then asks a series of questions about how the law applies to various actions taken by the firm. To answer the questions, the student must apply the laws discussed throughout the unit. Suggested answers to the unit-ending cumulative questions are included in the Answers Manual.

Interacting with the Internet

We have included another special new feature in the Second Edition of *The Legal Environment Today*, called *Interacting with the Internet*. These features, which appear at the ends of nearly all the chapters, indicate how you and your students can access materials relating to chapter topics via the Internet. Specific Internet addresses and "navigational" instructions are included in these features.

Appendices

To help students learn how to find and analyze case law, we have added a special appendix at the end of Chapter 1. There your students will find information, including an exhibit, on how to read citations to cases, statutes, and agency regulations. The appendix to Chapter 1 also presents an annotated sample court case to help your students understand how to read and understand the cases presented within this text.

Because the majority of students keep their business law texts as a reference source, we have included at the end of the book the following full set of appendices:

A.   Briefing Cases—Instructions and Selected Cases
B.   The Constitution of the United States
C.   The Administrative Procedure Act of 1946 (Excerpts)
D.   The Uniform Commercial Code (Excerpts)
E.   The National Labor Relations Act of 1914 (Excerpts)
F.   The Sherman Act of 1890 (Excerpts)
G.   The Clayton Act of 1914 (Excerpts)
H.   The Federal Trade Commission Act of 1914 (Excerpts)
I.   The Robinson-Patman Act of 1936 (Excerpts)
J.   Securities Act of 1933 (Excerpts)
K.   Securities Exchange Act of 1934 (Excerpts)
L.   Title VII of the Civil Rights Act of 1964 (Excerpts)
M.   Civil Rights Act of 1991(Excerpts)
N.   Americans with Disabilities Act of 1990 (Excerpts)
O.   The Uniform Partnership Act
P.   The Revised Uniform Partnership Act (Excerpts)
Q.   The Uniform Limited Liability Company Act (Excerpts)
R.   The General Agreement on Tariffs and trade of 1994 (Excerpts)
S.   The North American Free Trade Agreement of 1993 (Excerpts)
T.   The Small Business Regulatory Enforcement Fairness Act of 1996 (Excerpts)
U.   Spanish Equivalents for Important Legal Terms in English

Supplements

This edition of *The Legal Environment Today* is accompanied by an expansive number of teaching and learning supplements. For further information on *The Legal Environment Today* business teaching/learning package, contact your local West/ITP sales representative. An additional source of information, which is discussed more fully earlier in this Preface, is

www.westbuslaw.com

Printed Supplements

- *Instructor's Course Planning Guide and Media Handbook*
- *Instructor's Manual*
- *Study Guide with Quicken Business Law Partner CD-ROM* (prepared by William Eric Hollowell and text author Roger LeRoy Miller)—includes a value-added CD-ROM, Quicken Business Law Partner. Exercises based on the CD-ROM are included in the *Study Guide.*
- A comprehensive *Test Bank* (co-written by text author Roger LeRoy Miller)—Contains approximately 1,000 multiple-choice questions with answers and over 950 true-false questions with answers; also available on software.
- *Answers to Questions and Case Problems and Alternate Problem Sets with Answers*
- *Case Printouts*
- *Law and the Entrepreneur*
- *Landmark Cases in Business Law and the Legal Environment*
- *Advanced Topics and Contemporary Issues: Expanded Coverage*, Third Edition, by Frank B. Cross
- *Personal Law Handbook*
- *Handbook of Selected Statues*
- *Handbook on Critical Thinking and Writing in Business Law and Legal Environment*
- *Instructor's Manual for the Drama of the Law* video series
- *Transparency Acetates*
- *Regional Reporters*

Multimedia Supplements

- *Quicken Business Law Partner* (business forms on CD-ROM)
- Computerized *Instructor's Manual*
- *WESTEST* (computerized versions of the Test Banks)
- "The Legal Tutor on Contracts" software
- "The Legal Tutor on Sales" software
- Interactive Software—Contracts
- Interactive Software—Sales
- "You Be the Judge" software

- Case-Problem Cases on Diskette
- WESTLAW
- CD-ROM Resources for Business Law and Legal Environment
- West's Business Law and the Legal Environment Audiocassette Library
- Videocassettes including those discussed next

Court TV

New to the Second Edition of *The Legal Environment Today* are several recently acquired videos. Students can see the dynamics of a whole trial in Court TV's *Trial Stories*, chosen especially to illustrate topics for business law. Each *Trial Story* runs about one hour and tells the whole story of a case, from opening arguments to the verdict, and includes background information and interviews to help the viewer understand the facts of the case.

CNN Legal Issues Update Video

You can update your coverage of legal issues, as well as spark lively classroom discussion and deeper understanding of business law, by using the CNN Legal Issues update video. This video is produced by Turner Learning, Inc.., using the resources of CNN, the world's first twenty-four-hour, all-news network.

Additional Videos

South-Western's Business Law video series, a set of situational videos, covers a range of topics for the full legal environment course, including the Uniform Commercial Code and employment law.

For Users of the First Edition

We thought that those of you who have been using *The Legal Environment Today* would like to know some of the major changes that have been made for the Second Edition. The book is basically the same, but we think that we have improved it greatly, thanks in part to the many letters, telephone calls, and reviews that we have received.

Organizational Changes

- Tort liability, business torts, and intellectual property are now covered in Unit Three.
- The product liability chapter now appears with our coverage of torts.
- The material on contracts has been moved to follow the chapters on torts, intellectual property, and product liability.

New or Significantly Revised Chapters

- **Chapter 1 (The Legal and International Foundation).** The material covered in this chapter has been revised and streamlined to make the text flow more smoothly. The discussion of jurisprudential thought has been greatly condensed, and more coverage is given to classifications of law. Additionally, the entire discussion of how to find and analyze case law has been moved to a special appendix just following Chapter 1.

■ **Chapter 2 (Ethics and Social Responsibility).** This chapter has been revised extensively. Many sections have been rewritten to reflect today's business environment and current ethical challenges. The discussion of corporate social responsibility is given a more real-world flavor by applying the concepts discussed to a hypothetical business firm. The section on measuring social responsibility has been completely rewritten to reflect today's increased emphasis on corporate process as an important "yardstick" for measuring corporate responsibility.

■ **Chapter 7 (Criminal Wrongs).** This chapter now includes an exhibit showing the ways in which criminal law differs from civil law and a new section discussing the federal sentencing guidelines.

■ **Chapter 10 (Product Liability).** This chapter includes more detail on actions in strict product liability.

■ **Chapter 11 (Intellectual Property and Cyberlaw).** This chapter is an expanded version of material that appeared in the chapter on business torts in the previous edition. This new chapter includes coverage of electronic torts, including the electronic infringement of ownership rights in intellectual property (via the Internet, for example). An *Inside the Legal Environment* entitled "Online Copyright Infringement" highlights some of the legal challenges posed by the widespread use of the Internet for the unauthorized copying and use of others' property. A *Landmark in the Legal Environment* on the 1994 Agreement on Trade-Related Aspects of Intellectual Property Rights (TRIPS) emphasizes the growing need for intellectual property protection on a global level. A special feature on *Technology and Software Piracy* explores the ramifications for intellectual property owners of the unauthorized downloading of software from electronic bulletin boards.

■ **Chapter 12 (Introduction to Contracts).** Our coverage of contract law has been expanded into two chapters. Brief coverage of sales law has been added to the second chapter, Chapter 13, Contract Remedies and Sales.

■ **Chapter 14 (Creditors' Rights and Bankruptcy).** The section on bankruptcy has been revised to enhance understandability and to conform with the current Bankruptcy Code, as amended by the 1994 Bankruptcy Reform Act. The revisions include the 1998 changes to most of the Code's dollar amounts updated to reflect the effect of inflation.

■ **Chapter 15 (Business Organizations).** This chapter now includes expanded coverage of limited liability business forms, including limited liability companies (LLCs) and limited liability partnerships (LLPs).

■ **Chapter 16 (Employment Relationships).** This chapter contains a major new section on the Family Medical and Leave Act of 1993, and a more extensive discussion of employee privacy rights.

■ **Chapter 17 (Equal Employment Opportunities).** The section on affirmative action has been expanded and updated to include references to the most recent cases on this issue.

■ **Chapter 19 (Consumer Protection).** This chapter now discusses the most recent consumer protection laws, including the Telephone Consumer Protection Act of 1991, the Telemarketing and Consumer Fraud and Abuse Prevention Act of 1994, the FTC Telemarketing Sales Rule of 1995, the Home Ownership and Equity Protection Act of 1994, and the Truth-in-Lending Act Amendments of 1995.

■ **Chapter 23 (Investor Protection).** This chapter has been updated throughout, and the section on exemptions to registration requirements under the 1933 Securities Act has been rewritten to reflect current law. An *Inside the Legal Environment* looks at the current controversy over class-action suits and at the impact of the 1995 Private Securities Litigation Reform Act on such actions.

What Else Is New?

In addition to the changes noted above, you will find a number of other items or features in *The Legal Environment Today*, Second Edition, as listed below.

NEW FEATURES. The following features are new to the Second Edition:

■ **Chapter Objectives**
■ **Chapter Contents**
■ *Technology and the Legal Environment*
■ A greater number of *Ethical Perspectives* and *Internatonal Perspectives,* which are also presented in a new format.
■ **For Critical Analysis** questions concluding every feature and every case.
■ **Company Profiles** preceding many of the cases.
■ **Interacting with the Internet**
■ Simplified **For Review** questions placed prior to the standard end-of-the-chapter Questions and Case Problems.
■ Unit-ending **Cumulative Hypothetical Questions**

NEW EXHIBITS. We have modified exhibits contained in the Second Edition of *The Legal Environment Today* whenever necessary to achieve greater clarity or accuracy. In addition, the following entirely new exhibits have been added for the Second Edition:

■ **The Legal Systems of Nations (Exhibit 1–1)**
■ **Federal Courts and State Court Systems (Exhibit 3–2)**
■ **Tort Lawsuit and Criminal Prosecution for the Same Act (Exhibit 8–1)**
■ **Civil and Criminal Law Compared (Exhibit 7–1)**
■ **Exemptions under the 1933 Securities Act (Exhibit 23–1)**
■ **A Sample Restricted Stock Certificate (Exhibit 23–2)**

NEW CASES AND CASE PROBLEMS.   There are approximately seventy-five new cases and fifty new case problems. Additionally, there are several new hypothetical questions, ethical questions, case briefing assignments, and questions "For Critical Analysis." Of course, all of the unit-ending hypothetical questions are new.

NEW APPENDICES.

■ **Appendix Q: The Uniform Limited Liability Company Act (Excerpts)**

■ Appendix T: The Small Business Regulatory Enforcement Fairness Act of 1996 (Excerpts)

Acknowledgments

We owe a debt of extreme gratitude to the numerous individuals who worked directly with us or at West Publishing Company. We also wish to thank Lavina Leed Miller, who provided expert research, editing, and proofing services for this project. Additional proofing was done by Suzie Franklin DeFazio and Roxanna Lee. We must especially thank William Eric Hollowell, co-author of the *Instructor's Manual*, *Study Guide*, and *Test Bank*, for his excellent research efforts. We were again fortunate to have the indexing services of Bob Marsh. Our appreciation also goes to Suzanne Jasin for her many special efforts on the project.

We continue to be the fortunate recipients of an incredibly skilled and dedicated editorial and production team at West. We wish to thank Jack Calhoun, Rob Dewey, and Scott Person for their overall supervision of the project. Our long-time developmental editor, Jan Lamar, also helped us plan this project and made sure we addressed all reviewers' criticisms and suggestions. She additionally made sure that the preparation of supplements went smoothly and on time.

Our production manager at West, Bill Stryker, together with Ann Borman Rudrud and Megan Ryan, made sure that we came out with an error-free, visually appealing edition. We will always be in their debt.

We received numerous helpful comments from many users of the first edition. In addition, we thank the following reviewers who helped us make this second edition even more useful for professors and students alike.

Jane Bennett
Orange Coast College
Tom Moore
Georgia College and State University
Mark Phelps
University of Oregon
Martha Sartoris
North Hennepin Community College
Gwen Seaquist
Ithaca College

We know that we are not perfect. If you or your students find something you don't like or want us to change, write to us. That is how we can make *The Legal Environment Today* an even better book in the future.

Roger LeRoy Miller
Frank B. Cross

DEDICATION

To Jeff LeSage.
Your advice has always been right.
Thanks for being a friend, too.

R.L.M.

To my parents and sisters.

F.B.C.

The
Foundations

CHAPTER 1

The Legal and International Foundation

Contents

Chapter Objectives

After reading this chapter, you should be able to . . .

1. Explain what is generally meant by the term *law*.
2. Describe the origins and importance of the common law tradition.
3. Identify the four major sources of American law.
4. List some important classifications of law.
5. Distinguish between national law and international law.

Lord Balfour's assertion in the quotation alongside emphasizes the underlying theme of every page in this book—that law is of interest to all persons, not just to lawyers. Those entering the world of business will find themselves subject to numerous laws and government regulations. A basic knowledge of these laws and regulations is beneficial—if not essential—to anyone contemplating a successful career in the business world of today.

In this introductory chapter, we first look at the nature of law and at some concepts that have significantly influenced how jurists and scholars view the nature and function of law. We then examine the common law tradition of the United States, as well as some of the major sources and classifications of American law. The chapter concludes with a discussion of the global legal environment, which frames many of today's business transactions.

> "The law is of as much interest to the layman as it is to the lawyer."
>
> Lord Balfour, 1848–1930
> (British prime minister, 1902–1905)

The Nature of Law

There have been and will continue to be different definitions of *law*. The Greek philosopher Aristotle (384–322 B.C.E.) saw law as a "pledge that citizens of a state will do justice to one another." Aristotle's mentor, Plato (427–347 B.C.E.), believed that law was a form of social control. The Roman orator and politician Cicero (106–43 B.C.E.) contended that law was the agreement of reason and nature, the distinction between the just and the unjust. The British jurist Sir William Blackstone (1723–1780) described law as "a rule of civil conduct prescribed by the supreme power in a state, commanding what is right, and prohibiting what is wrong." In America, the eminent jurist Oliver Wendell Holmes, Jr. (1841–1935), contended that law was a set of rules that allowed one to predict how a court would resolve a particular dispute—"the prophecies of what the courts will do in fact, and nothing more pretentious, are what I mean by the law."

Although these definitions vary in their particulars, they all are based on the following general observation: **law** consists of enforceable rules governing relationships among individuals and between individuals and their society. In the study of law, often referred to as **jurisprudence,** this very broad statement concerning the nature of law is the point of departure for all legal scholars and philosophers. We look here at three of the most influential schools of legal thought, or philosophies of law: the natural law tradition, legal positivism, and legal realism.

Oliver Wendell Holmes. Does Holmes' definition of the law still apply?

Law A body of enforceable rules governing relationships among individuals and between individuals and their society.

Jurisprudence The science or philosophy of law.

The Natural Law Tradition

The oldest and one of the most significant schools of jurisprudence is the natural law tradition, which dates back to ancient Greece and Rome. **Natural law** denotes a system of moral and ethical principles that are inherent in human nature and that can be discovered by humans through the use of their natural intelligence. The Greek philosopher Aristotle distinguished between natural law (which applies universally to all humankind) and **positive law** (the conventional, or written, law of a particular society at a particular point in time).

In essence, the natural law tradition presupposes that the legitimacy of positive, or conventional, law derives from natural law. Whenever positive law conflicts with natural law, positive law loses its legitimacy and should be changed. A law prohibiting murder, for example, reflects not only the values accepted by a particular society at a particular time (positive law) but also a

Natural Law The belief that government and the legal system should reflect universal moral and ethical principles that are inherent in human nature. The natural law school is the oldest and one of the most significant schools of legal thought.

Positive Law The body of conventional, or written, law of a particular society at a particular point in time.

universally accepted precept that murder is wrong (natural law). To murder someone is thus a violation of natural law. If a law allowed persons to murder each other, that law would be wrong, because it did not accord with natural law. In a sense, the natural law tradition encourages individuals to disobey conventional, or written, laws if those individuals believe that the laws are in conflict with natural law.

Legal Positivism

Legal Positivism A school of legal thought centered on the assumption that there is no law higher than the laws created by the government. Laws must be obeyed, even if they are unjust, to prevent anarchy.

Another school of legal thought is known as **legal positivism.** Legal positivists believe that there can be no higher law than a nation's positive laws—the laws created by a particular society at a particular point in time. Essentially, from the positivist perspective, the law is the law and must be obeyed on pain of punishment. Whether a particular law is bad or good is irrelevant. The merits or demerits of a given law can be discussed, and laws can be changed in an orderly manner through a legitimate lawmaking process. As long as a law exists, however, that law must be obeyed. If people felt justified in disobeying particular laws just because they did not feel the laws were just, anarchy would ensue.

Legal Realism

Legal Realism A school of legal thought of the 1920s and 1930s that generally advocated a less abstract and more realistic approach to the law, an approach that takes into account customary practices and the circumstances in which transactions take place. The school left a lasting imprint on American jurisprudence.

Legal realism, which became a popular school of legal thought in the 1920s and 1930s, left a strong imprint on American jurisprudence. Contrary to the dominant legal thinking of their time, the legal realists believed that the law could not—and should not—be an abstract body of rules applied uniformly to cases with similar circumstances. According to the legal realists, impartial and uniform application of the law is not possible. After all, judges are human beings with unique personalities, value systems, and intellects. Given this obvious fact, it would be impossible for any two judges to engage in an identical reasoning process when evaluating the same case.

The legal realists argued that each case also involves a unique set of circumstances—no two cases, no matter how similar, are ever exactly the same. Therefore, judges should take into account the specific circumstances of each case, rather than rely on some abstract rule that might not relate to those particular circumstances. When making decisions, judges should also consider extra-legal sources, such as economic and sociological data, to the extent that such sources could illuminate the circumstances and issues involved in specific cases. In other words, the law should take social and economic realities into account.

United States Supreme Court Justice Oliver Wendell Holmes, Jr. (1841–1935), and Karl Llewellyn (1893–1962) were both influential proponents of legal realism. Llewellyn is best known for his dominant role in drafting the Uniform Commercial Code (UCC), a set of rules for commercial transactions that will be discussed later in this chapter. The UCC reflects the influence of legal realism in its emphasis on practicality, flexibility, reasonability, and customary trade practices.

> **"It is perfectly proper to regard and study the law simply as a great anthropological document."**
>
> Oliver Wendell Holmes, Jr., 1841–1935
> (Associate justice of the United States Supreme Court, 1902–1932)

The Common Law Tradition

▼ How jurists view the law is particularly important in a legal system in which judges play a paramount role, as they do in the American legal system. Because of our colonial heritage, much of American law is based on the English legal system. A knowledge of this tradition is necessary to an understanding of the nature of our legal system today.

Early English Courts of Law

In 1066, after the Normans conquered England, William the Conqueror and his successors began the process of unifying the country under their rule. One of the means they used to this end was the establishment of the king's courts, or *curia regis*. Before the Norman Conquest, disputes had been settled according to the local legal customs and traditions in various regions of the country. The king's courts sought to establish a uniform set of rules for the country as a whole. What evolved in these courts was the beginning of the **common law**— a body of general rules that prescribed social conduct and that was applied throughout the entire English realm.

Courts developed the common law rules from the principles underlying judges' decisions in actual legal controversies. Judges attempted to be consistent, and whenever possible, they based their decisions on the principles suggested by earlier cases. They sought to decide similar cases in a similar way and considered new cases with care, because they knew that their decisions would make new law. Each interpretation became part of the law on the subject and served as a legal **precedent**—that is, a decision that furnished an example or authority for deciding subsequent cases involving similar legal principles or facts.

In the early years of the common law, there was no single place or publication in which court opinions, or written decisions, could be found. In the late thirteenth and early fourteenth centuries, however, portions of the more important decisions of each year were gathered together and recorded in *Year Books*. The *Year Books* were useful references for lawyers and judges. In the

> **"It will not do to decide the same question one way between one set of litigants and the opposite way between another."**
>
> Benjamin N. Cardozo, 1870–1938
> (Associate justice of the United States Supreme Court, 1932–1938)

Common Law That body of law developed from custom or judicial decisions in English and U.S. courts, not attributable to a legislature.

Precedent A court decision that furnishes an example or authority for deciding subsequent cases involving identical or similar facts.

The Court of Chancery in the reign of George I. Early English court decisions formed the basis of what type of law?

sixteenth century, the *Year Books* were discontinued, and other reports of cases became available. (See the appendix to this chapter for a discussion of how cases are reported, or published, in the United States today.)

Stare Decisis

Stare Decisis A common law doctrine under which judges are obligated to follow the precedents established in prior decisions.

The practice of deciding new cases with reference to former decisions, or precedents, eventually became a cornerstone of the English and American judicial systems. The practice forms a doctrine called *stare decisis*[1] ("to stand on decided cases"). Under this doctrine, judges are obligated to follow the precedents established within their jurisdictions. For example, if the Supreme Court of California (that state's highest court) has ruled in a certain way on an issue, that decision will control the outcome of future cases on that issue brought before the state courts in California. Similarly, a decision on a given issue by the United States Supreme Court (the nation's highest court) is binding on all inferior courts. Controlling precedents in a jurisdiction are referred to as **binding authorities,** as are statutes or other laws that must be followed.

Binding Authority Any source of law that a court must follow when deciding a case. Binding authorities include constitutions, statutes, and regulations that govern the issue being decided, as well as court decisions that are controlling precedents within the jurisdiction.

The doctrine of *stare decisis* helps the courts to be more efficient, because if other courts have carefully reasoned through a similar case, their legal reasoning and opinions can serve as guides. *Stare decisis* also makes the law more stable and predictable. If the law on a given subject is well settled, someone bringing a case to court can usually rely on the court to make a decision based on what the law has been.

DEPARTURES FROM PRECEDENT.   Sometimes a court will depart from the rule of precedent if it decides that a given precedent should no longer be followed. If a court decides that a precedent is simply incorrect or that technological or social changes have rendered the precedent inapplicable, the court might rule contrary to the precedent.

Cases that overturn precedent often receive a great deal of publicity. In *Brown v. Board of Education of Topeka,*[2] for example, the United States Supreme Court expressly overturned precedent when it concluded that separate educational facilities for whites and blacks, which had been upheld as constitutional in numerous previous cases,[3] were inherently unequal. The Supreme Court's departure from precedent in *Brown* received a tremendous amount of publicity as people began to realize the ramifications of this change in the law.

WHEN THERE IS NO PRECEDENT.   Sometimes there is no precedent within a jurisdiction on which to base a decision, or there are conflicting precedents. A court then may look to precedents set in other jurisdictions for guidance. Such precedents, because they are not binding on the court, are referred to as **persuasive authorities.** A court may also consider a number of factors, including legal principles and policies underlying previous court decisions or existing statutes, fairness, social values and customs, public policy, and data and concepts drawn from the social sciences.

Persuasive Authority Any legal authority or source of law that a court may look to for guidance but on which it need not rely in making its decision. Persuasive authorities include cases from other jurisdictions and secondary sources of law.

---

1.   Pronounced *ster*-ay dih-*si*-ses.
2.   347 U.S. 483, 74 S.Ct. 686, 98 L.Ed. 873 (1954). (See the appendix at the end of this chapter for an explanation of how to read legal citations.)
3.   See *Plessy v. Ferguson,* 163 U.S. 537, 16 S.Ct. 1138, 41 L.Ed. 256 (1896).

Which of these sources is chosen or receives the greatest emphasis will depend on the nature of the case being considered and the particular judge hearing the case. Although judges always strive to be free of subjectivity and personal bias in deciding cases, each judge has his or her own unique personality, set of values or philosophical leanings, and intellectual attributes—all of which necessarily frame the judicial decision-making process.

Equitable Remedies and Courts of Equity

In law, a **remedy** is the means given to a party to enforce a right or to compensate for the violation of a right. For example, suppose that Shem is injured because of Rowan's wrongdoing. A court may order Rowan to compensate Shem for the harm by paying Shem a certain amount of money.

Remedy The relief given to an innocent party to enforce a right or compensate for the violation of a right.

In the early king's courts of England, the kinds of remedies that could be granted were severely restricted. If one person wronged another, the king's courts could award as compensation either money or property, including land. These courts became known as *courts of law,* and the remedies were called *remedies at law.* Even though this system introduced uniformity in the settling of disputes, when plaintiffs wanted a remedy other than economic compensation, the courts of law could do nothing, so "no remedy, no right."

REMEDIES IN EQUITY. Equity is that branch of unwritten law, founded in justice and fair dealing, that seeks to supply a fairer and more adequate remedy than any remedy available at law. In medieval England, when individuals could not obtain an adequate remedy in a court of law, they petitioned the king for relief. Most of these petitions were decided by an adviser to the king called the *chancellor.* The chancellor was said to be the "keeper of the king's conscience." When the chancellor thought that the claim was a fair one, new and unique remedies were granted. In this way, a new body of rules and remedies came into being, and eventually formal *chancery courts,* or *courts of equity,* were established. The remedies granted by these courts were called *remedies in equity.* Thus, two distinct court systems were created, each having a different set of judges and a different set of remedies.

Plaintiffs (those bringing lawsuits) had to specify whether they were bringing an "action at law" or an "action in equity," and they chose their courts accordingly. For example, a plaintiff might ask a court of equity to order a **defendant** (a person against whom a lawsuit is brought) to perform within the terms of a contract. A court of law could not issue such an order, because its remedies were limited to payment of money or property as compensation for damages. A court of equity, however, could issue a decree for *specific performance*—an order to perform what was promised. A court of equity could also issue an *injunction,* directing a party to do or refrain from doing a particular act. In certain cases, a court of equity could allow for the *rescission* (cancellation) of the contract so that the parties would be returned to the positions that they held prior to the contract's formation. Equitable remedies will be discussed in greater detail in Chapter 13.

Plaintiff One who initiates a lawsuit.

Defendant One against whom a lawsuit is brought; the accused person in a criminal proceeding.

THE MERGING OF LAW AND EQUITY. Today, in most states, the courts of law and equity are merged, and thus the distinction between the two courts has largely disappeared. A plaintiff may now request both legal and equitable remedies in the same action, and the trial court judge may grant either form—or

> **REMEMBER** Even though, in most states, courts of law and equity have merged, the principles of equity still apply.

Landmark in the Legal Environment

Equitable Principles and Maxims

In medieval England, courts of equity had the responsibility of using discretion in supplementing the common law. Even today, when the same court can award both legal and equitable remedies, such discretion is exercised. Courts often invoke equitable principles and maxims when making their decisions. Here are some of the more significant equitable principles and maxims:

1. *Whoever seeks equity must do equity.* (Anyone who wishes to be treated fairly must treat others fairly.)
2. *Where there is equal equity, the law must prevail.* (The law will determine the outcome of a controversy in which the merits of both sides are equal.)
3. *One seeking the aid of an equity court must come to the court with clean hands.* (Plaintiffs must have acted fairly and honestly.)
4. *Equity will not suffer a wrong to be without a remedy.* (Equitable relief will be awarded when there is a right to relief and there is no adequate remedy at law.)
5. *Equity regards substance rather than form.* (Equity is more concerned with fairness and justice than with legal technicalities.)
6. *Equity aids the vigilant, not those who rest on their rights.* (Equity will not help those who neglect their rights for an unreasonable period of time.)

The last maxim has become known as the *equitable doctrine of laches.* The doctrine arose to encourage people to bring lawsuits while the evidence was fresh; if they failed to do so, they would not be allowed to bring a lawsuit. What constitutes a reasonable time, of course, varies according to the circumstances of the case. Time periods for different types of cases are now usually fixed by statutes of limitations. After the time allowed under a statute of limitations has expired, no action can be brought, no matter how strong the case was originally.

For Critical Analysis: *Do you think that the government should establish, through statutes of limitations, the time limits within which different types of lawsuits can be brought?*

---

both forms—of relief. The merging of law and equity, however, does not diminish the importance of distinguishing legal remedies from equitable remedies. To request the proper remedy, one must know what remedies are available for the specific kinds of harms suffered. Today, as a rule, courts will grant an equitable remedy only when the remedy at law (money damages) is inadequate.

Equitable Principles and Maxims General propositions or principles of law that have to do with fairness (equity).

EQUITABLE PRINCIPLES AND MAXIMS. Over time, a number of **equitable principles and maxims** evolved that have since guided the courts in deciding whether plaintiffs should be granted equitable relief. Because of their importance, both historically and in our judicial system today, these principles and maxims are set forth in the above *Landmark in the Legal Environment.*

Sources of American Law

Primary Source of Law A document that establishes the law on a particular issue, such as a constitution, a statute, an administrative rule, or a court decision.

There are numerous sources of American law. **Primary sources of law,** or sources that establish the law, include the following:

- The U.S. Constitution and the constitutions of the various states.
- Statutes, or laws, passed by Congress and by state legislatures.
- Regulations created by administrative agencies, such as the federal Food and Drug Administration.
- Case law (court decisions).

We describe each of these important primary sources of law in the following pages.

Secondary sources of law are books and articles that summarize and clarify the primary sources of law. Examples are legal encyclopedias, treatises, articles in law reviews published by law schools, or other legal journals. Courts often refer to secondary sources of law for guidance in interpreting and applying the primary sources of law discussed here.

Secondary Source of Law A publication that summarizes or interprets the law, such as a legal encyclopedia, a legal treatise, or an article in a law review.

Constitutional Law

The federal government and the states have separate written constitutions that set forth the general organization, powers, and limits of their respective governments. **Constitutional law** is the law as expressed in these constitutions.

The U.S. Constitution is the supreme law of the land. As such, it is the basis of all law in the United States. A law in violation of the Constitution, no matter what its source, will be declared unconstitutional and will not be enforced. Because of its paramount importance in the American legal system, we discuss the Constitution at length in Chapter 5 and present the complete text of the U.S. Constitution in Appendix B.

The Tenth Amendment to the U.S. Constitution, which defines the powers and limitations of the federal government, reserves all powers not granted to the federal government to the states. Each state in the union has its own constitution. Unless they conflict with the U.S. Constitution or a federal law, state constitutions are supreme within their respective borders.

Constitutional Law Law based on the U.S. Constitution and the constitutions of the various states.

Statutory Law

Statutes enacted by legislative bodies at any level of government make up another source of law, which is generally referred to as **statutory law.**

FEDERAL STATUTES.   Federal statutes are laws that are enacted by the U.S. Congress. As mentioned, any law—including a federal statute—that violates the U.S. Constitution will be held unconstitutional.

Statutory Law The body of law enacted by legislative bodies (as opposed to constitutional law, administrative law, or case law).

Boy Scouts view the U.S. Constitution on display in Washington, D.C. Can a law be in violation of the Constitution and still be enforced? If not, why not?

Citation A reference to a publication in which a legal authority—such as a statute or a court decision—or other source can be found.

Examples of federal statutes that affect business operations include laws regulating the purchase and sale of securities, or corporate stocks and bonds (discussed in Chapter 23); consumer protection statutes (discussed in Chapter 19); and statutes prohibiting employment discrimination (discussed in Chapter 17). Whenever a particular statute is mentioned in this text, we usually provide a footnote showing its **citation** (a reference to a publication in which a legal authority—such as a statute or a court decision—or other source can be found). In the appendix following this chapter, we explain how you can use these citations to find statutory law.

STATE AND LOCAL STATUTES AND ORDINANCES.   State statutes are laws enacted by state legislatures. Any state law that conflicts with the U.S. Constitution, with federal laws enacted by Congress, or with the state's constitution will be deemed unconstitutional. Statutory law also includes the ordinances passed by cities and counties, none of which can violate the U.S. Constitution, the relevant state constitution, or federal or state laws.

Examples of state statutes include state criminal statutes (discussed in Chapter 7), state corporation statutes (discussed in Chapter 15), state deceptive trade practices acts (referred to in Chapter 19), and state versions of the Uniform Commercial Code (to be discussed shortly). Examples of local ordinances include zoning ordinances and local laws regulating housing construction and such things as the overall appearance of a community.

A federal statute, of course, applies to all states. A state statute, in contrast, applies only within the state's borders. State laws thus vary from state to state.

UNIFORM LAWS.   The differences among state laws were particularly notable in the 1800s, when conflicting state statutes frequently made the rapidly developing trade and commerce among the states very difficult. To counter these problems, a group of legal scholars and lawyers formed the National Conference of Commissioners (NCC) on Uniform State Laws in 1892 to draft uniform statutes for adoption by the states. The NCC still exists today and continues to issue proposed uniform statutes.

> **BE CAREFUL** Even though uniform laws are intended to be adopted without changes, states often modify them to suit their particular needs.

Adoption of a uniform law is a state matter, and a state may reject all or part of the statute or rewrite it as the state legislature wishes. Hence, even when a uniform law is said to have been adopted in many states, those states' laws may not be entirely "uniform." Once adopted by a state legislature, a uniform act, however modified, becomes a part of the statutory law of that state.

The earliest uniform law, the Uniform Negotiable Instruments Law, was completed by 1896 and was adopted in every state by the early 1920s (although not all states used exactly the same wording). Over the following decades, other acts were drawn up in a similar manner. In all, over two hundred uniform acts have been issued by the NCC since its inception. The most ambitious uniform act of all, however, was the Uniform Commercial Code.

THE UNIFORM COMMERCIAL CODE (UCC).   The Uniform Commercial Code (UCC), which was created through the joint efforts of the NCC and the American Law Institute,[4] was first issued in 1952. The UCC has been adopted in all fifty states,[5] the District of Columbia, and the Virgin Islands. The UCC

---

4.   This institute was formed in the 1920s and consists of practicing attorneys, legal scholars, and judges.
5.   Louisiana has adopted only Articles 1, 3, 4, 5, 7, 8, and 9.

facilitates commerce among the states by providing a uniform, yet flexible, set of rules governing commercial transactions. The UCC assures businesspersons that their contracts, if validly entered into, normally will be enforced.

Because of its importance in the area of commercial law, we cite the UCC frequently in this text. We also present excerpts from the latest version of the UCC in Appendix C. (For more about the UCC, see Chapter 13.)

Administrative Law

An important source of American law consists of **administrative law**—the rules, orders, and decisions of administrative agencies. An **administrative agency** is a federal, state, or local government agency established to perform a specific function. Rules issued by various administrative agencies now affect virtually every aspect of a business's operation, including the firm's capital structure and financing, its hiring and firing procedures, its relations with employees and unions, and the way it manufactures and markets its products.

At the national level, numerous **executive agencies** exist within the cabinet departments of the executive branch. The Food and Drug Administration, for example, is within the Department of Health and Human Services. Executive agencies are subject to the authority of the president, who has the power to appoint and remove officers of federal agencies. There are also major **independent regulatory agencies** at the federal level, such as the Federal Trade Commission, the Securities and Exchange Commission, and the Federal Communications Commission. The president's power is less pronounced in regard to independent agencies, whose officers serve for fixed terms and cannot be removed without just cause.

There are administrative agencies at the state and local levels as well. Commonly, a state agency (such as a state pollution-control agency) is created as a parallel to a federal agency (such as the Environmental Protection Agency). Just as federal statutes take precedence over conflicting state statutes, so do federal agency regulations take precedence over conflicting state regulations. Because the rules of state and local agencies vary widely, we focus here exclusively on federal administrative law.

AGENCY CREATION. Because Congress cannot possibly oversee the actual implementation of all the laws it enacts, it must delegate such tasks to others, particularly when the issues relate to highly technical areas, such as air and water pollution. By delegating some of its constitutional authority to make and implement laws to agencies, Congress is able to monitor indirectly a particular area in which it has passed legislation without becoming bogged down in the many details relating to enforcement—details that are often best left to specialists.

Congress creates an administrative agency by enacting **enabling legislation**, which specifies the name, composition, purpose, and powers of the agency being created. For example, the Federal Trade Commission (FTC) was created in 1914 by the Federal Trade Commission Act.[6] This act prohibits unfair and deceptive trade practices. It also describes the procedures the agency must follow to charge persons or organizations with violations of the act, and it provides for judicial review (review by the courts) of agency orders. Other

Administrative Law The body of law created by administrative agencies (in the form of rules, regulations, orders, and decisions) in order to carry out their duties and responsibilities.

Administrative Agency A federal or state government agency established to perform a specific function. Administrative agencies are authorized by legislative acts to make and enforce rules to administer and enforce the acts.

Executive Agency An administrative agency within the executive branch of government. At the federal level, executive agencies are those within the cabinet departments.

Independent Regulatory Agency An administrative agency that is not considered part of the government's executive branch and is not subject to the authority of the president. Independent agency officials cannot be removed without cause.

Enabling Legislation A statute enacted by Congress that authorizes the creation of an administrative agency and specifies the name, composition, purpose, and powers of the agency being created.

---

6. 15 U.S.C. Sections 45–58.

portions of the act grant the agency powers to "make rules and regulations for the purpose of carrying out the Act," to conduct investigations of business practices, to obtain reports from interstate corporations concerning their business practices, to investigate possible violations of the act, to publish findings of its investigations, and to recommend new legislation. The act also empowers the FTC to hold trial-like hearings and to **adjudicate** (resolve judicially) certain kinds of trade disputes that involve FTC regulations.

Note that the FTC's grant of power incorporates functions associated with the legislative branch of government (rulemaking), the executive branch (investigation and enforcement), and the judicial branch (adjudication). Taken together, these functions constitute what has been termed **administrative process,** which is the administration of law by administrative agencies.

Adjudicate To render a judicial decision. In the administrative process, the proceeding in which an administrative law judge hears and decides on issues that arise when an administrative agency charges a person or a firm with violating a law or regulation enforced by the agency.

Administrative Process The procedure used by administrative agencies in the administration of law.

Rulemaking The process undertaken by an administrative agency when formally adopting a new regulation or amending an old one. Rulemaking involves notifying the public of a proposed rule or change and receiving and considering the public's comments.

RULEMAKING.   One of the major functions of an administrative agency is **rulemaking**—creating or modifying rules, or regulations, pursuant to its enabling legislation. The Administrative Procedure Act of 1946[7] imposes strict procedural requirements that agencies must follow in their rulemaking and other functions.

The most common rulemaking procedure involves three steps. First, the agency must give public notice of the proposed rulemaking proceedings, where and when the proceedings will be held, the agency's legal authority for the proceedings, and the terms or subject matter of the proposed rule. The notice must be published in the *Federal Register,* a daily publication of the U.S. government. Second, following this notice, the agency must allow ample time for interested parties to comment in writing on the proposed rule. After the comments have been received and reviewed, the agency takes them into consideration when drafting the final version of the regulation. The third and final step is the drafting of the final version and the publication of the rule in the *Federal Register.* (See the appendix at the end of this chapter for an explanation of how to find agency regulations.)

INVESTIGATION AND ENFORCEMENT.   Agencies have both investigatory and prosecutorial powers. An agency can compel individuals or organizations to hand over specified books, papers, records, or other documents. In addition, agencies may conduct on-site inspections, although a search warrant is normally required for such inspections. Sometimes the search of a home, an office, or a factory is the only means of obtaining evidence needed to prove a regulatory violation. Agencies investigate a wide range of activities, including coal mining, automobile manufacturing, and the industrial discharge of pollutants into the environment.

Administrative Law Judge (ALJ) One who presides over an administrative agency hearing and who has the power to administer oaths, take testimony, rule on questions of evidence, and make determinations of fact.

ADJUDICATION.   After conducting its own investigation of a suspected rule violation, an agency may decide to take action against a specific party. The action may involve a trial-like hearing before an **administrative law judge (ALJ).** The ALJ may compel the charged party to pay fines or may forbid the party to carry on some specified activity. Either side may appeal the ALJ's decision to the commission or board that governs the agency. If the party fails to

---

7.   5 U.S.C. Sections 551–706.

Ethical Perspective

Combining the functions normally divided among the three branches of government into a single governmental entity, such as the FTC, creates institutional flexibility, but it also concentrates a considerable amount of power in a single organization. The broad range of authority exercised by administrative agencies sometimes poses questions of fairness.

For example, when an agency claims that a business firm's practices violate an agency rule, the firm has little recourse against the agency—even if the rule seems somewhat arbitrary. The firm normally must comply with the agency's requests (for documents, for example) during the agency's investigation, and if the dispute is adjudicated, the firm will be subject to the agency's decision. Of course,

the firm may be able to appeal the decision to a court, but as long as the agency followed proper procedures when issuing the rule and had some rational basis for the rule, a court will be reluctant to overrule the agency's decision.

The Constitution authorizes only the legislative branch to create laws. Administrative agencies, however, which are not specifically referred to in the Constitution, make rules that are as legally binding as laws passed by Congress. Although the government exercises certain controls over agency powers and functions, in many ways administrative agencies function independently.

For Critical Analysis: *Is there any way to avoid placing so much power in the hands of administrative agencies? Is there any practical alternative?*

---

get relief here, appeal can be made to a federal court. (Administrative law is discussed in more detail in Chapter 6.)

Case Law and Common Law Doctrines

The body of law that was first developed in England and that is still used today in the United States consists of the rules of law announced in court decisions. These rules of law include interpretations of constitutional provisions, of statutes enacted by legislatures, and of regulations created by administrative agencies. Today, this body of law is referred to variously as the common law, judge-made law, or **case law.**

The common law—the doctrines and principles embodied in case law—governs all areas not covered by statutory law (or agency regulations issued to implement various statutes). In disputes concerning contracts for the sale of goods, for example, the Uniform Commercial Code (statutory law) applies instead of the common law of contracts. Similarly, in a dispute concerning a particular employment practice, if a statute regulates that practice, the statute will apply rather than the common law doctrine that applied prior to the enactment of the statute.

Case Law The rules of law announced in court decisions. Case law includes the aggregate of reported cases that interpret judicial precedents, statutes, regulations, and constitutional provisions.

THE RELATIONSHIP BETWEEN THE COMMON LAW AND STATUTORY LAW.   The body of statutory law has expanded greatly since the beginning of this nation, and this expansion has resulted in a proportionate reduction in the scope and applicability of common law doctrines. Nonetheless, there is a significant overlap between statutory law and case law, and thus common law doctrines remain a significant source of legal authority.

For example, many statutes essentially codify existing common law rules, and thus the courts, in interpreting the statutes, often rely on the common law as a guide to what the legislators intended. Additionally, how the courts

> **"Statutes do not interpret themselves; their meaning is declared by the courts."**
>
> John Chipman Gray, 1839–1915 (American lawyer and teacher)

interpret a particular statute determines how that statute will be applied. If you wanted to learn about the coverage and applicability of a particular statute, for example, you would, of course, need to locate the statute and study it. You would also need to see how the courts in your jurisdiction have interpreted the statute—in other words, what precedents have been established in regard to that statute. Often, the applicability of a newly enacted statute does not become clear until a body of case law develops to clarify how, when, and to whom the statute applies.

RESTATEMENTS OF THE LAW.   The American Law Institute drafted and published compilations of the common law called Restatements of the law, which generally summarize the common law rules followed by most states. There are Restatements of the law in the areas of contracts, torts, agency, trusts, property, restitution, security, judgments, and conflict of laws. The Restatements, like other secondary sources of law, do not in themselves have the force of law but are an important source of legal analysis and opinion on which judges often rely in making their decisions.

Many of the Restatements are now in their second or third editions. We refer to the Restatements frequently in subsequent chapters of this text, indicating in parentheses the edition to which we are referring. For example, we refer to the second edition of the *Restatement of the Law of Contracts* simply as the *Restatement (Second) of Contracts.*

Classifications of Law

The huge body of the law may be broken down according to several classification systems. For example, one classification system divides law into **substantive law** (all laws that define, describe, regulate, and create legal rights and obligations) and **procedural law** (all laws that establish the methods of enforcing the rights established by substantive law).

Another classification system divides law into civil law and criminal law. **Civil law** spells out the rights and duties that exist between persons and between persons and their governments, and the relief available when a person's rights are violated. Contract law, for example, is part of civil law. The whole body of tort law (see Chapters 8 and 9), which deals with the infringement by one person on the legally recognized rights of another, is also an area of civil law. **Criminal law** has to do with a wrong committed against society for which society demands redress (see Chapter 7). Criminal acts are proscribed by local, state, or federal government statutes.

Other classification systems divide law into federal law and state law, private law (dealing with relationships between persons) and public law (addressing the relationship between persons and their governments), and so on. One of the broadest classification systems divides law into national law and international law, a topic to which we now turn.

National and International Law

Although the focus of this book is U.S. business law, increasingly businesspersons in this country are engaging in transactions that extend beyond our

Substantive Law Law that defines, describes, regulates, and creates legal rights and obligations.

Procedural Law Law that establishes the methods of enforcing the rights established by substantive law.

Civil Law The branch of law dealing with the definition and enforcement of all private or public rights, as opposed to criminal matters.

Criminal Law Law that defines and governs actions that constitute crimes. Generally, criminal law has to do with wrongful actions committed against society for which society demands redress.

Technology
and OnLine Legal Research

The world of legal research is rapidly changing. In the past, researchers painstakingly had to examine dozens, if not hundreds, of different printed volumes containing court decisions, federal statutes, state statutes, and regulations from administrative agencies. Today, most—if not all—legal research can be done online. That is to say, any student who is studying the law and any attorney or other legal practitioner can now search through the millions of pages of available legal sources in minutes.

ONLINE LEGAL RESEARCH SERVICES
One of the first and most comprehensive online legal research services is Westlaw®, which has been provided for years by West Group. Powerful computers at West Group's headquarters in Eagan, Minnesota, enable researchers to find in minutes documents that would otherwise take hours, if not days or weeks to uncover. In the last few years, individuals accessing Westlaw have been able to ask their legal research questions in plain English by using WIN (Westlaw Is Natural). A competing system, called LEXIS, is provided by Reed-Elsevier.

THE INTERNET
Finally, anybody with a computer, a modem, and a way to access the Internet can obtain certain legal documents, including cases decided by the United States Supreme Court, virtually minutes after they are released for publication. The Internet is a web of educational, corporate, and research computer networks around the world. Today, at least 100 million people are using it, and there are over 100,000 networks connected to it. Perhaps the most interesting part of the Internet is the World Wide Web, commonly called the Web, which is a vast, interlinked network of computer files all over the world. You can use the Internet to find discussion groups, news groups, and electronic publications. The most common use of the Internet is for electronic mail (e-mail).

Virtually every month a new source of authoritative legal research materials is being put on the Internet. For example, the Securities and Exchange Commission (SEC)

recently made available on the Internet, at no cost, its Electronic Data Gathering, Analysis, and Retrieval System (Internet address: http://www.sec.gov/). Plus, West Group has made the entire Westlaw legal and business service available on the WorldWide Web (http://www.westlaw. com) to any researcher.

CD-ROM LIBRARIES
Increasingly, much of the material that can be accessed online is becoming available on CD-ROM. CD stands for *compact disc.* ROM stands for *read-only memory,* meaning that the CDs cannot be erased as a videocassette can be and then reused. Literally hundreds of thousands of pages of legal research materials—cases, statutes, and so on—are recorded on CD-ROM. The equivalent of an entire encyclopedia can be put on one normal CD-ROM. Newer technologies will allow the equivalent of up to ten encyclopedias on one CD-ROM.

For Critical Analysis: *Describe what a law and legal research library might consist of in the future.*

How has technology changed the methods of legal research?

•••

national borders. In these situations, the laws of other nations or the laws governing relationships among nations may come into play. For this reason, those who pursue a career in business today should have an understanding of the global legal environment.

We examine the laws governing international business transactions in later chapters (including Chapters 24 and 25). It is worthwhile at this point, however, to summarize some important aspects of the international legal environment, because many of the topics covered in this text have international dimensions.

National Law

National Law Law that pertains to a particular nation (as opposed to international law).

National law is the law of a particular nation, such as the United States or France. National law, of course, varies from country to country, because each country's law reflects the interests, customs, activities, and values that are unique to that nation's culture. Even though the laws and legal systems of various countries differ substantially, broad similarities do exist.

Basically, there are two legal systems in today's world. One of these systems is the common law system of England and the United States, which we have already discussed. The other system is based on Roman civil law, or "code law." The term *civil law,* as used here, refers not to civil as opposed to criminal law but to *codified* law—an ordered grouping of legal principles enacted into law by a legislature or governing body. In a **civil law system,** the primary source of law is a statutory code, and case precedents are not judicially binding, as they normally are in a common law system. Although judges in a civil law system commonly refer to previous decisions as sources of legal guidance, they are not bound by precedent; in other words, the doctrine of *stare decisis* does not apply.

Civil Law System A system of law derived from that of the Roman Empire and based on a code rather than case law; the predominant system of law in the nations of continental Europe and the nations that were once their colonies. In the United States, Louisiana is the only state that has a civil law system.

Exhibit 1–1 lists the countries that today follow either the common law system or the civil law system. Generally, those countries that were once colonies of Great Britain retained their English common law heritage after they achieved their independence. Similarly, the civil law system, which is followed in most of the continental European countries, was retained in the Latin American, African, and Asian countries that were once colonies of the continental European nations. Japan and South Africa also have civil law systems, and ingredients of the civil law system are found in the Islamic courts of predominantly Muslim countries. In the United States, the state of Louisiana, because of its historical ties to France, has in part a civil law system. The legal systems of Puerto Rico, Québec, and Scotland are similarly characterized as having elements of the civil law system.

■ Exhibit 1–1
The Legal Systems of Nations

CIVIL LAW	COMMON LAW
Argentina	Australia
Austria	Bangladesh
Brazil	Canada
Chile	Ghana
China	India
Egypt	Israel
Finland	Jamaica
France	Kenya
Germany	Malaysia
Greece	New Zealand
Indonesia	Nigeria
Iran	Singapore
Italy	United Kingdom
Japan	United States
Mexico	Zambia
Poland	
South Korea	
Sweden	
Tunisia	
Venezuela	

International Law

International law can be defined as the law that governs relations among nations. The key difference between national law and international law is the fact that national law can be enforced by government authorities. What government, though, can enforce international law? By definition, a *nation* is a sovereign entity, which means that there is no higher authority to which that nation must submit. If a nation violates an international law, the most that other countries or international organizations can do (if persuasive tactics fail) is resort to coercive actions against the violating nation. Coercive actions range from severance of diplomatic relations and boycotts to, at the last resort, war.

International Law The law that governs relations among nations. National laws, customs, treaties, and international conferences and organizations are generally considered to be the most important sources of international law.

In essence, international law is the result of centuries-old attempts to reconcile the traditional need of each nation to be the final authority over its own affairs with the desire of nations to benefit economically from trade and harmonious relations with one another. Although no sovereign nation can be compelled to obey a law external to itself, nations can and do voluntarily agree to be governed in certain respects by international law for the purpose of facilitating international trade and commerce, as well as civilized discourse.

International Perspective

The ability to conduct business successfully in a foreign nation requires not only a knowledge of that nation's laws but also some familiarity with its cultural system. One obvious cultural difference among nations is language. Language differences have occasionally confounded efforts to do business abroad. For example, Parker Pen's motto, "Prevent embarrassment, use Parker Ink," was itself an embarrassment in Spanish-speaking countries because the Spanish word *embarazo* means not only "embarrassment" but also "pregnancy."

Perceptions of time, management styles, and conceptions of what kind of behavior is appropriate also vary from one culture to another. In many countries, for example, gift giving is a common practice between contracting companies or between companies and government officials. To Americans, such gift giving may look suspiciously like an unethical (and possibly illegal) bribe.

The role played by women in other countries may also present some difficulties for firms doing business internationally. Equal employment opportunity is a fundamental public policy in the United States. Some other countries, however, largely reject any role for women professionals, which may cause problems for American women who attempt to conduct business transactions in those countries.

For Critical Analysis: *Suppose that John, the president of a U.S. bank, wants to take his top vice president, Carla, with him to a meeting overseas. John is advised that he would lose respect in the eyes of the overseas company if he took Carla, a woman, with him. List some of the pros and cons of taking Carla to the meeting that John should consider in making his decision.*

International law is an intermingling of rules and constraints derived from a variety of sources. The laws of individual nations are sources of international law, as are the customs that have evolved among nations in their relations with one another. Of increasing importance in regulating international activities, however, are treaties and international organizations.

TREATIES.   A **treaty** is an agreement between two or more nations that creates rights and duties binding on the parties to the treaty, just as a private contract

Treaty An agreement formed between two or more independent nations.

Judges at a trial of Islamic extremists on charges of murder. What impact does the use of a civil law system have on rulings in the Islamic courts of predominantly Muslim countries?

creates rights and duties binding on the parties to the contract. To give effect to a treaty, the supreme power of each nation that is a party to the treaty must ratify it. For example, the U.S. Constitution requires approval by two-thirds of the Senate before a treaty executed by the president will be binding on the U.S. government.

Bilateral agreements, as the term implies, occur when only two nations form an agreement that will govern their commercial exchanges or other relations with one another. Multilateral agreements are those formed by several nations. The European Union (EU), for example, which regulates commercial activities among its fifteen European member nations, is the result of a multilateral trade agreement. The North American Free Trade Agreement (NAFTA), which regulates trade among Canada, the United States, and Mexico, is another example of a multilateral trade agreement.

One treaty of particular significance to the international legal environment of business is the United Nations 1980 Convention on Contracts for the International Sale of Goods (CISG). Essentially, the CISG is to international sales transactions what the Uniform Commercial Code is to domestic sales transactions. The CISG governs the international sale of goods between firms or individuals located in different countries, providing that the countries involved have ratified the CISG.

INTERNATIONAL ORGANIZATIONS. International organizations and conferences also play an important role in the international legal arena. International organizations and conferences adopt resolutions, declarations, and other types of standards that often require a particular behavior of nations. The General Assembly of the United Nations, for example, has adopted numerous resolutions and declarations that embody principles of international law and has sponsored conferences that have led to the formation of international agreements. The United States is a member of more than one hundred multilateral and bilateral organizations, including at least twenty through the United Nations.

Key Terms

adjudicate 12

administrative agency 11

administrative law 11

administrative law
    judge (ALJ) 12

administrative process 12

binding authority 6

case law 13

citation 10

civil law 14

civil law system 16

common law 5

constitutional law 9

criminal law 14

defendant 7

enabling legislation 11

equitable principles and
    maxims 8

executive agency 11

independent regulatory
    agency 11

international law 16

jurisprudence 3

law 3

legal positivism 4

legal realism 4

national law 16

natural law 3

persuasive authority 6

plaintiff 7

positive law 3

precedent 5

primary source of law 8

procedural law 14

remedy 7

rulemaking 12

secondary source of law 9

stare decisis 6

statutory law 9

substantive law 14

treaty 17

Chapter Summary
The Legal and International Foundation

THE NATURE OF LAW (See pages 3–4.)	Law can be defined as a body of enforceable rules governing relationships among individuals and between individuals and their society. Three important schools of legal thought, or legal philosophies, are the following: 1. **Natural law tradition**—One of the oldest and most significant schools of legal thought. Those who believe in natural law hold that there is a universal law applicable to all human beings and that this law is of a higher order than positive, or conventional, law. 2. **Legal positivism**—A school of legal thought centered on the assumption that there is no law higher than the laws created by the government. Laws must be obeyed, even if they are unjust, to prevent anarchy. 3. **Legal realism**—A popular school of legal thought during the 1920s and 1930s. Legal realists generally advocated a less abstract and more realistic approach to the law, an approach that would take into account customary practices and the circumstances in which transactions take place. The school left a lasting imprint on American jurisprudence.

THE COMMON LAW TRADITION
(See pages 4–8.)
	1. **Common law**—Law that originated in medieval England with the creation of the king's courts, or *curia regis,* and the development of a body of rules that were common to (or applied throughout) the land.
	
	2. *Stare decisis*—A doctrine under which judges "stand on decided cases"—or follow the rule of precedent—in deciding cases. *Stare decisis* is the cornerstone of the common law tradition.
	
	3. **Remedies**—
	   a. Remedies at law—Money or something else of value.
	   b. Remedies in equity—Remedies that are granted when the remedies at law are unavailable or inadequate. Equitable remedies include specific performance, an injunction, and contract rescission (cancellation).

SOURCES OF AMERICAN LAW (See pages 8–14.)	1. **Constitutional law**—The law as expressed in the U.S. Constitution and the various state constitutions. The U.S. Constitution is the supreme law of the land. State constitutions are supreme within state borders to the extent that they do not violate the U.S. Constitution or a federal law. 2. **Statutory law**—Laws or ordinances created by federal, state, and local legislatures and governing bodies. None of these laws can violate the U.S. Constitution or the relevant state constitutions. Uniform laws, when adopted by a state legislature, become statutory law in that state. 3. **Administrative law**—The rules, orders, and decisions of federal or state government administrative agencies. Federal administrative agencies are created by enabling legislation enacted by the U.S. Congress. Agency functions include rulemaking, investigation and enforcement, and adjudication. 4. **Case law and common law doctrines**—Judge-made law, including interpretations of constitutional provisions, of statutes enacted by legislatures, and of regulations created by administrative agencies. The common law—the doctrines and principles embodied in case law—governs all areas not covered by statutory law (or agency regulations issued to implement various statutes).

(Continued)

Chapter Summary, continued

CLASSIFICATIONS OF LAW (See page 14.)	The law may be broken down according to several classification systems, such as substantive or procedural law, civil or criminal law, federal or state law, and private or public law.

NATIONAL AND INTERNATIONAL LAW (See pages 14–16.)	1. **National law**—Most nations today have either a common law system or a civil law system:
	
	   a. **Common law system**—See the summary of the common law tradition above. Generally, those countries that were once colonies of Great Britain retained their English common law heritage after they achieved their independence. Today, nations with common law systems include England, the United States, Ireland, Canada, Australia, New Zealand, and India.
	
	   b. **Civil law system**—A legal system stemming from Roman "code law," in which the primary source of law is a statutory code—an ordered grouping of legal principles enacted into law by a legislature or governing body. Precedents are not binding in a civil law system. Most of the continental European countries have a civil law system, as do those African, Latin American, and Asian nations that were once colonies of those European countries. Japan and South Africa also have civil law systems.
	
	2. **International law**—A body of written and unwritten laws observed by independent nations and governing the acts of individuals as well as governments. Sources of international law include national laws, customs, treaties, and international organizations and conferences.

For Review

1. What is the common law tradition?
2. What is a precedent? When might a court depart from precedent?
3. What is the difference between remedies at law and remedies in equity?
4. What is the Uniform Commercial Code?
5. What is the difference between civil law and criminal law?

Questions and Case Problems

1–1. Philosophy of Law. After World War II, which ended in 1945, an international tribunal of judges convened at Nuremberg, Germany. The judges convicted several Nazi war criminals of "crimes against humanity." Assuming that the Nazis who were convicted had not disobeyed any law of their country and had merely been following their government's (Hitler's) orders, what law had they violated? Explain.

1–2. Legal Systems. What are the key differences between a common law system and a civil law system? Why do some countries have common law systems and others have civil law systems?

1–3. Reading Citations. Assume that you want to read the entire court opinion in the case of *White v. York International Corp.*, 45 F.3d 357 (10th Cir. 1995). The case deals with the question of whether an employer violated the Americans with Disabilities Act of 1990, a federal statute that prohibits discrimination against persons with disabilities. Read the section entitled "Finding Case Law" in the appendix that follows this chapter, and then explain specifically where you would find the court's opinion.

1–4. Sources of American Law. This chapter discussed a number of sources of American law. Which source of law takes priority in the following situations, and why?

(a) A federal statute conflicts with the U.S. Constitution.
(b) A federal statute conflicts with a state constitution.
(c) A state statute conflicts with the common law of that state.
(d) A state constitutional amendment conflicts with the U.S. Constitution.
(e) A federal administrative regulation conflicts with a state constitution.

1–5. *Stare Decisis*. In the text of this chapter, we stated that the doctrine of *stare decisis* "became a cornerstone of the English and American judicial systems." What does *stare decisis* mean, and why has this doctrine been so fundamental to the development of our legal tradition?

1–6. Court Opinions. Read through the section entitled "Case Titles and Terminology" in the appendix following this chapter. What is the difference between a concurring opinion and a majority opinion? Between a concurring opinion and a dissenting opinion? Why do judges and justices write concurring and dissenting opinions, given the fact that these opinions will not affect the outcome of the case at hand, which has already been decided by majority vote?

1–7. Common Law versus Statutory Law. Courts are able to overturn precedents and thus can change the common law. Should judges have the same authority to overrule statutory law? Explain.

1–8. Philosophy of Law. In the middle of the last century, the United States declared war on Mexico and levied taxes to support the war effort. Henry David Thoreau (author of *Walden*), who felt that the war was unjust, refused to pay taxes to support it and was subsequently imprisoned for violating the law. Thoreau maintained that obeying the law in these circumstances would be unethical. Which of the schools of legal thought discussed in this chapter would be the most sympathetic toward Thoreau's views on law? Explain.

1–9. Statute of Limitations. The equitable principle "Equity aids the vigilant, not those who rest on their rights" means that courts will not aid those who do not pursue a cause of action while the evidence is fresh and while the true facts surrounding the issue can be discovered. State statutes of limitations are based on this principle. Under Article 2 of the Uniform Commercial Code, which has been adopted by virtually all of the states, the statute of limitations governing sales contracts states that parties must bring an action for the breach of a sales contract within four years, although the parties (the seller

and the buyer) can reduce this period by agreement to only one year. Which party (the seller or the buyer) would benefit more by a one-year period, and which would benefit more by a four-year period? Discuss.

1–10. Binding versus Persuasive Authority. A county court in Illinois is deciding a case involving an issue that has never been addressed before in that state's courts. The Iowa Supreme Court, however, recently decided a case involving a very similar fact pattern. Is the Illinois court obligated to follow the Iowa Supreme Court's decision on the issue? If the United States Supreme Court had decided a similar case, would that decision be binding on the Illinois court? Explain.

A Question of Ethics and Social Responsibility

1–11. On July 5, 1884, Dudley, Stephens, and Brooks— "all able-bodied English seamen"—and an English teenage boy were cast adrift in a lifeboat following a storm at sea. They had no water with them in the boat, and all they had for sustenance were two one-pound tins of turnips. On July 24, Dudley proposed that one of the four in the lifeboat be sacrificed to save the others. Stephens agreed with Dudley, but Brooks refused to consent—and the boy was never asked for his opinion. On July 25, Dudley killed the boy, and the three men then fed upon the boy's body and blood. Four days later, the men were rescued by a passing vessel. They were taken to England and tried for the murder of the boy. If the men had not fed upon the boy's body, they would probably have died of starvation within the four-day period. The boy, who was in a much weaker condition, would likely have died before the rest. [*Regina v. Dudley and Stephens*, 14 Q.B.D. (Queen's Bench Division, England) 273 (1884)]

1. The basic question in this case is whether the survivors should be subject to penalties under English criminal law, given the men's unusual circumstances. You be the judge, and decide the issue. Give the reasons for your decision.
2. Should judges ever have the power to look beyond the written "letter of the law" in making their decisions? Why or why not?

For Critical Analysis

1–12. Courts of equity tend to follow general rules or maxims rather than common law precedents, as courts of law do. Some of these maxims were listed in this chapter's *Landmark in the Legal Environment*. Why would equity courts give credence to such general maxims rather than to a hard-and-fast body of law?

INTERACTING WITH
The Internet

■ A few years ago, only computer fanatics even knew about the Internet. Today, at least 100 million people use it, and by the end of the century it is projected that 200 million people will be using it worldwide. Today, there are over 65,000 networks connected to the Internet with about 10 million computers in 100 countries. The Internet is not a centralized system, but rather a collection of networks running the same software standards. You can think of the Internet as a web of educational, corporate, and research computer networks around the world. The Internet has many uses, including transmitting weather reports, doing library searches, and finding addresses of university students and faculty thousands of miles away. On the Internet, you will find discussion groups, news groups, electronic publications, and electronic mail (e-mail), the most common use of the Internet.

■ Your college or university is probably connected directly to the Internet and pays thousands of dollars a year for this hookup. Faculty, administrators, and students can get an e-mail address and password. The address is just like a mailbox at which you receive electronic information. Addresses differ depending on the gateway that leads from your computer through another computer to the person or address you want to reach. Many chapters of *The Legal Environment Today* end with Internet addresses and activities that you may find useful.

■ A little advice on hardware: You should use a computer with sufficient RAM (random access memory) to handle the World Wide Web (WWW) protocol, which means at least 16 megabytes, but preferably 32 megabytes. You should also use a modem that runs at least at 14.4 kilobaud, but preferably at 56 kilobaud.

Appendix to
CHAPTER 1

Finding and Analyzing the Law

Laws pertaining to business consist of both statutory law and case law. The statutes, agency regulations, and case law referred to in this text establish the rights and duties of businesspersons engaged in various types of activities. The cases presented within the chapters provide you with concise, real-life illustrations of the interpretation and application of the law by the courts. Because of the importance of knowing how to find statutory and case law, this appendix offers a brief introduction to how statutes and cases are published and to the legal "shorthand" employed in referencing these legal sources.

Finding Statutory and Administrative Law

When Congress passes laws, they are collected in a publication titled *United States Statutes at Large.* When state legislatures pass laws, they are collected in similar state publications. Most frequently, however, laws are referred to in their codified form—that is, the form in which they appear in the federal and state codes.

In these codes, laws are compiled by subject. The *United States Code* (U.S.C.) arranges all existing federal laws of a public and permanent nature by subject. Each of the fifty subjects into which the U.S.C. arranges the laws is given a title and a title number. For example, laws relating to commerce and trade are collected in Title 15, which is titled "Commerce and Trade." Titles are subdivided by sections. A citation to the U.S.C. includes title and section numbers. Thus, a reference to "15 U.S.C. Section 1" means that the statute can be found in Section 1 of Title 15. ("Section" may also be designated by the symbol §, and "Sections" by §§.)

Sometimes a citation includes the abbreviation *et seq.*—as in "15 U.S.C. Sections 1 *et seq.*" The term is an abbreviated form of *et sequitur,* which in Latin means "and the following"; when used in a citation, it refers to sections that concern the same subject as the numbered section and follow it in sequence.

State codes follow the U.S.C. pattern of arranging law by subject. The state codes may be called codes, revisions, compilations, consolidations, general statutes, or statutes, depending on the preference of the states. In some codes, subjects are designated by number. In others, they are designated by name. For example, "13 Pennsylvania Consolidated Statutes Section 1101" means the statute can be found in Title 13, Section 1101, of the Pennsylvania code. "California Commercial Code Section 1101" means the statute can be found under the subject heading "Commercial Code" of the California code in Section 1101. Abbreviations may be used. For example, "13 Pennsylvania Consolidated Statutes Section 1101" may be abbreviated "13 Pa. C.S. § 1101," and "California Commercial Code Section 1101" may be abbreviated "Cal. Com. Code § 1101."

Rules and regulations adopted by federal administrative agencies are compiled in the *Code of Federal Regulations* (C.F.R.). Like the U.S.C., the C.F.R. is divided into fifty titles. Rules within each title are assigned section numbers. A full citation to the C.F.R. includes title and section numbers. For example, a reference to "17 C.F.R. Section 230.504" means that the rule can be found in Section 230.504 of Title 17.

Commercial publications of these laws and regulations are available and are widely used. For example, WestGroup publishes the *United States Code Annotated* (U.S.C.A.). The U.S.C.A. contains the complete text of laws included in the U.S.C., as well as notes of court decisions that interpret and apply specific sections of the statutes, plus the text of presidential proclamations and executive orders. The U.S.C.A. also includes research aids, such as cross-references to related statutes, historical notes, and library references. A citation to the U.S.C.A. is similar to a citation to the U.S.C.: "15 U.S.C.A. Section 1."

Finding Case Law

▼ Before discussing the case reporting system, we need to look briefly at the court system. As will be discussed in detail in Chapter 3, there are two types of courts in the United States, federal courts and state courts. Both the federal and state court systems consist of several levels, or tiers, of courts. *Trial courts,* in which evidence is presented and testimony given, are on the bottom tier (which also includes lower courts handling specialized issues). Decisions from a trial court can be appealed to a higher court, which commonly would be an intermediate *court of appeals,* or an *appellate court.* Appellate courts are known as reviewing courts because they do not hear evidence or testimony, as trial courts do; rather, an appellate court reviews all of the records relating to a case to determine whether the trial court's decision was correct. Decisions from these intermediate courts of appeals may be appealed to an even higher court, such as a state supreme court or the United States Supreme Court.

State Court Decisions

Most state trial court decisions are not published. Except in New York and a few other states that publish selected opinions of their trial courts, decisions from the state trial courts are merely filed in the office of the clerk of the court, where the decisions are available for public inspection. Written decisions of the appellate, or reviewing, courts, however, are published and distributed. The reported appellate decisions are published in volumes called *reports* or *reporters,* which are numbered consecutively. State appellate court decisions are found in the state reporters of that particular state.

Additionally, state court opinions appear in regional units of the *National Reporter System,* published by West Group. Most lawyers and libraries have the West reporters because they report cases more quickly and are distributed more widely than the state-published reports. In fact, many states have eliminated their own reporters in favor of West's National Reporter System.

The National Reporter System divides the states into the following geographical areas: *Atlantic* (A. or A.2d), *South Eastern* (S.E. or S.E.2d), *South Western* (S.W. or S.W.2d), *North Western* (N.W. or N.W.2d), *North Eastern* (N.E. or N.E.2d), *Southern* (So. or So.2d), and *Pacific* (P. or P.2d). (The *2d* in the abbreviations refers to *Second Series.*) The states included in each of these regional divisions are indicated in Exhibit 1A–1, which illustrates West's National Reporter System.

After appellate decisions have been published, they are normally referred to (cited) by the name of the case; the volume, name, and page number of the state's official reporter (if different from West's National Reporter System); the volume, unit, and page number of the *National Reporter;* and the volume, name, and page number of any other selected reporter. This information is included in the *citation.* (Citing a reporter by volume number, name, and page number, in that order, is common to all citations.) When more than one reporter is cited for the same case, each reference is called a *parallel citation.* For example, consider the following case: *Williams v. Garraghty,* 249 Va. 224, 455 S.E.2d 209 (1995). We see that the opinion in this case may be found in Volume 249 of the official *Virginia Reports,* on page 224. The parallel citation is to Volume 455 of the *South Eastern Reporter, Second Series,* page 209. In presenting appellate opinions in this text, in addition to the reporter, we give the name of the court hearing the case and the year of the court's decision.

A few of the states—including those with intermediate appellate courts, such as California, Illinois, and New York—have more than one reporter for opinions given by courts within their states. Sample citations from these courts, as well as others, are listed and explained in Exhibit 1A–2.

Federal Court Decisions

Federal district court decisions are published unofficially in West's *Federal Supplement* (F.Supp.), and opinions from the circuit courts of appeals (federal reviewing courts) are reported unofficially in West's *Federal Reporter* (F., F.2d, or F.3d). Cases concerning federal bankruptcy law are published unofficially in West's *Bankruptcy Reporter* (Bankr.). Opinions from the United States Supreme Court are reported in the *United States Reports* (U.S.), West's *Supreme Court Reporter* (S.Ct.), the *Lawyers' Edition of the Supreme Court Reports* (L.Ed. or L.Ed.2d), and other publications.

■ **Exhibit 1A–1 National Reporter System—Regional/Federal**

Regional Reporters	Coverage Beginning	Coverage
Atlantic Reporter (A. or A.2d)	1885	Connecticut, Delaware, Maine, Maryland, New Hampshire, New Jersey, Pennsylvania, Rhode Island, Vermont, and District of Columbia.
North Eastern Reporter (N.E. or N.E.2d)	1885	Illinois, Indiana, Massachusetts, New York, and Ohio.
North Western Reporter (N.W. or N.W.2d)	1879	Iowa, Michigan, Minnesota, Nebraska, North Dakota, South Dakota, and Wisconsin.
Pacific Reporter (P. or P.2d)	1883	Alaska, Arizona, California, Colorado, Hawaii, Idaho, Kansas, Montana, Nevada, New Mexico, Oklahoma, Oregon, Utah, Washington, and Wyoming.
South Eastern Reporter (S.E. or S.E.2d)	1887	Georgia, North Carolina, South Carolina, Virginia, and West Virginia.
South Western Reporter (S.W. or S.W.2d)	1886	Arkansas, Kentucky, Missouri, Tennessee, and Texas.
Southern Reporter (So. or So.2c)	1887	Alabama, Florida, Louisiana, and Mississippi.
Federal Reporters		
Federal Reporter (F., F.2d, or F.3d)	1880	U.S. Circuit Court from 1880 to 1912; U.S. Commerce Court from 1911 to 1913; U.S. District Courts from 1880 to 1932; U.S. Court of Claims (now called U.S. Court of Federal Claims) from 1929 to 1932 and since 1960; U.S. Court of Appeals since 1891; U.S. Court of Customs and Patent Appeals since 1929; U.S. Emergency Court of Appeals since 1943.
Federal Supplement (F.Supp.)	1932	U.S. Court of Claims from 1932 to 1960; U.S. District Courts since 1932; and U.S. Customs Court since 1956.
Federal Rules Decisions (F.R.D.)	1939	U.S. District Courts involving the Federal Rules of Civil Procedure since 1939 and Federal Rules of Criminal Procedure since 1946.
Supreme Court Reporter (S.Ct.)	1882	U.S. Supreme Court since the October term of 1882.
Bankruptcy Reporter (Bankr.)	1980	Bankruptcy decisions of U.S. Bankruptcy Courts, U.S. District Courts, U.S. Courts of Appeals, and U.S. Supreme Court.
Military Justice Reporter (M.J.)	1978	U.S. Court of Military Appeals and Courts of Military Review for the Army, Navy, Air Force, and Coast Guard.

NATIONAL REPORTER SYSTEM MAP

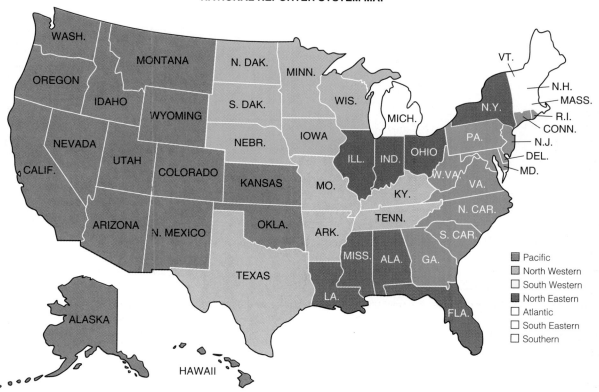

Legend:
- ■ Pacific
- North Western
- □ South Western
- ■ North Eastern
- □ Atlantic
- □ South Eastern
- □ Southern

■ **Exhibit IA–2   How to Read Case Citations**

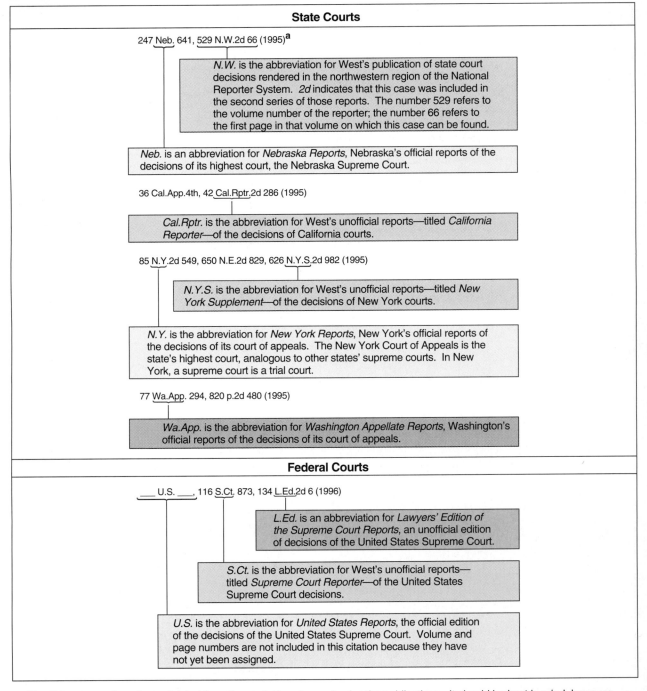

State Courts

247 Neb. 641, 529 N.W.2d 66 (1995)[a]

N.W. is the abbreviation for West's publication of state court decisions rendered in the northwestern region of the National Reporter System. *2d* indicates that this case was included in the second series of those reports. The number 529 refers to the volume number of the reporter; the number 66 refers to the first page in that volume on which this case can be found.

Neb. is an abbreviation for *Nebraska Reports*, Nebraska's official reports of the decisions of its highest court, the Nebraska Supreme Court.

36 Cal.App.4th, 42 Cal.Rptr.2d 286 (1995)

Cal.Rptr. is the abbreviation for West's unofficial reports—titled *California Reporter*—of the decisions of California courts.

85 N.Y.2d 549, 650 N.E.2d 829, 626 N.Y.S.2d 982 (1995)

N.Y.S. is the abbreviation for West's unofficial reports—titled *New York Supplement*—of the decisions of New York courts.

N.Y. is the abbreviation for *New York Reports*, New York's official reports of the decisions of its court of appeals. The New York Court of Appeals is the state's highest court, analogous to other states' supreme courts. In New York, a supreme court is a trial court.

77 Wa.App. 294, 820 p.2d 480 (1995)

Wa.App. is the abbreviation for *Washington Appellate Reports*, Washington's official reports of the decisions of its court of appeals.

Federal Courts

___ U.S. ___, 116 S.Ct. 873, 134 L.Ed.2d 6 (1996)

L.Ed. is an abbreviation for *Lawyers' Edition of the Supreme Court Reports,* an unofficial edition of decisions of the United States Supreme Court.

S.Ct. is the abbreviation for West's unofficial reports—titled *Supreme Court Reporter*—of the United States Supreme Court decisions.

U.S. is the abbreviation for *United States Reports*, the official edition of the decisions of the United States Supreme Court. Volume and page numbers are not included in this citation because they have not yet been assigned.

a. The Case names have been deleted from these citations to emphasize the publications. It should be kept in mind, however, that the name of a case is as important as the specific page numbers in the volumes in which it is found. If a citation is incorrect, the correct citation may be found in a publication's index of case names. The date of a case is also important because, in addition to providing a check on error in citations, the value of a recent case as an authority is likely to be greater than that of earlier cases.

■ **Exhibit IA–2 How to Read Case Citations (continued)**

Federal Courts (continued)

74 F.3d 613 (5th Cir. 1996)

5th Cir. is an abbreviation denoting that this case was decided in the United States Court of Appeals for the Fifth Circuit.

912 F.Supp. 663 (E.D.N.Y. 1996)

E.D.N.Y. is an abbreviation indicating that the United States District Court for the Eastern District of New York decided this case.

English Courts

9 Exch. 341, 156 Eng.Rep. 145 (1854)

Eng.Rep. is an abbreviation for *English Reports, Full Reprint,* a series of reports containing selected decisions made in English courts between 1378 and 1865.

Exch. is an abbreviation for *English Exchequer Reports*, which includes the original reports of cases decided in England's Court of Exchequer.

Statutory and Other Citations

18 U.S.C. Section 1961(1)(A)

U.S.C. denotes *United States Code*, the codification of *United States Statutes at Large*. The number 18 refers to the statute's U.S.C. title number and 1961 to its section number within that title. The number 1 refers to a subsection within the section and the letter A to a subdivision within the subsection.

UCC 2–206(1)(b)

UCC is an abbreviation for *Uniform Commercial Code*. The first number 2 is a reference to an article of the UCC and 206 to a section within that article. The number 1 refers to a subsection within the section and the letter b to a subdivision within the subsection.

Restatement (Second) of Torts, Section 568

Restatement (Second) of Torts refers to the second edition of the American Law Institute's *Restatement of the Law of Torts*. The number 568 refers to a specific section.

17 C.F.R. Section 230.505

C.F.R. is an abbreviation for *Code of Federal Regulations*, a compilation of federal administrative regulations. The number 17 is a reference to the regulation's title number and 230.505 to a specific section within that title.

The *United States Reports* is the official edition of all decisions of the United States Supreme Court for which there are written opinions. Published by the federal government, the series includes reports of Supreme Court cases dating from the August term of 1791, although originally many of the decisions were not reported in the early volumes.

West's *Supreme Court Reporter* is an unofficial edition dating from the Court's term in October 1882. Preceding each case report are a summary of the case and *headnotes* (brief editorial statements of the law involved in the case). The headnotes are given classification numbers that serve to cross-reference each headnote to other headnotes on similar points of law throughout the National Reporter System and other West publications. The numbers facilitate research of all relevant cases on a given point of law. This is important because, as may be evident from the discussion of *stare decisis* in Chapter 1, a lawyer's goal in undertaking legal research is to find an authority that cannot be factually distinguished from his or her case.

The Lawyers Cooperative Publishing Company of Rochester, New York, publishes the *Lawyers' Edition of the Supreme Court Reports,* which is an unofficial edition of the entire series of the Supreme Court reports. The *Lawyers' Edition* contains many of the decisions not reported in the early official volumes. Additionally, among other editorial features, the *Lawyers' Edition,* in its second series, precedes the report of each case with a full summary, includes excerpts from the attorneys' notes on the cases, and discusses in detail selected cases of special interest to the legal profession.

Sample citations for federal court decisions are also listed and explained in Exhibit 1A–2.

Old Case Law

On a few occasions, this text cites opinions from old, classic cases dating to the nineteenth century or earlier; some of these are from the English courts. The citations to these cases appear not to conform to the descriptions given above, because the reporters in which they were published have since been replaced. A sample citation for an English reporter is included in Exhibit 1A–2. Whenever citations to old reporters are made in this text, the citations will be explained as they are presented.

Reading and Understanding Case Law

Case law is critical to decision making in the business context because businesses must operate within the boundaries established by law. It is thus essential that businesspersons understand case law.

The cases in this text have been rewritten and condensed from the full text of the courts' opinions. For those wishing to review court cases for future research projects or to gain additional legal information, the following sections will provide useful insights into how to read and understand case law.

Case Titles and Terminology

The title of a case, such as *Adams v. Jones,* indicates the names of the parties to the lawsuit. The *v.* in the case title stands for *versus,* which means "against." In the trial court, Adams was the plaintiff—the person who filed the suit. Jones was the defendant. If the case is appealed, however, the appellate court will sometimes place the name of the party appealing the decision first, so that the case may be called *Jones v. Adams.* Because some reviewing courts retain the trial court order of names, it is often impossible to distinguish the plaintiff from the defendant in the title of a reported appellate court decision. You must carefully read the facts of each case to identify each party. Otherwise, the discussion by the appellate court will be difficult to understand.

The following terms and phrases are frequently encountered in court opinions and legal publications. Because it is important to understand what is meant by these terms and phrases, we define and discuss them here.

PLAINTIFFS AND DEFENDANTS.   As mentioned in Chapter 1, the *plaintiff* in a lawsuit is the party that initiates the action. The *defendant* is the party against which a lawsuit is brought. Lawsuits frequently involve more than one plaintiff and/or defendant.

APPELLANTS AND APPELLEES.   The *appellant* is the party that appeals a case to another court or jurisdiction from the court or jurisdiction in which the case was originally brought. Sometimes, an appellant that appeals a judgment is referred to as the *petitioner.* The *appellee* is the party against whom the appeal is taken. Sometimes, the appellee is referred to as the *respondent*.

JUDGES AND JUSTICES.   The terms *judge* and *justice* are usually synonymous and represent two designations given to judges in various courts. All members of the United States Supreme Court, for example, are referred to as justices. And justice is the formal title usually given to judges of appellate courts, although this is not always the case. In New York, a justice is a judge of the trial court (which is called the Supreme Court), and a member of the Court of Appeals (the state's highest court) is called a judge. The term *justice* is commonly abbreviated to J., and *justices* to JJ. A Supreme Court case might refer to Justice Kennedy as Kennedy, J., or to Chief Justice Rehnquist as Rehnquist, C.J.

DECISIONS AND OPINIONS.   Most decisions reached by reviewing, or appellate, courts are explained in written *opinions*. The opinion contains the court's reasons for its decision, the rules of law that apply, and the judgment.

There are four possible types of written opinions for any particular case decided by an appellate court. When all judges or justices unanimously agree on an opinion, the opinion is written for the entire court and can be deemed a *unanimous opinion*. When there is not a unanimous opinion, a *majority opinion* is written, outlining the views of the majority of the judges or justices deciding the case. Often, a judge or justice who feels strongly about making or emphasizing a point that was not made or emphasized in the unanimous or majority opinion will write a *concurring opinion*. That means the judge or justice agrees (concurs) with the judgment given in the unanimous or majority opinion but for different reasons. In other than unanimous opinions, a *dissenting opinion* is usually written by a judge or justice who does not agree with the majority. The dissenting opinion is important because it may form the basis of the arguments used years later in overruling the precedential majority opinion.

A NOTE ON ABBREVIATIONS.   In court opinions, as well as in other areas of this text, certain terms appearing in the names of firms or organizations will often be abbreviated. The terms *Company, Incorporated,* and *Limited,* for example, will frequently appear in their abbreviated forms as *Co., Inc.,* and *Ltd.,* respectively, and *Brothers* is commonly abbreviated to *Bros.* Certain organizations and legislative acts are also frequently referred to by their initials or acronyms. In all such cases, to prevent confusion we will give the complete name of the organization or act on first mentioning it in a given section of the text.

A Sample Court Case

To illustrate how to read and analyze a court opinion, we have annotated an actual case that was heard by the U.S. Court of Appeals for the First Circuit. The lawsuit was initiated by Michael Evans, who filed an employment discrimination suit, claiming that he was terminated on the basis of a disability.

You will note that triple asterisks (* * *) and quadruple asterisks (* * * *) frequently appear within the opinion. The triple asterisks indicate that we have deleted a few words or sentences from the opinion for the sake of readability or brevity. Quadruple asterisks mean that an entire paragraph (or more) has been omitted. Also, when the opinion cites another case or legal source, the citation to the referenced cases or sources has been omitted to save space and to improve the flow of the text. These editorial practices are continued in the other court opinions presented in this text. In addition, whenever a case opinion presented in this text includes a term or a phrase that may not be readily understandable, we have added a bracketed definition or paraphrase of the term or phrase. In the sample case in Exhibit 1A–3, important sections, terms, and phrases are defined or discussed in the margins.

Diagramming Case Problems

When briefing and analyzing a case problem in *The Legal Environment Today,* you may find it helpful in attempting to understand the facts of the problem to diagram those facts. You might use a square for a plaintiff (the party who files a legal action) and a triangle for a defendant (the party against whom the action is brought), for example, and arrows to indicate who is suing whom. You might also find that it saves time to use symbols in your diagrams. Many symbols are commonly used among law students and lawyers. To indicate a reference to a plaintiff, for

■ **Exhibit 1A–3   A Sample Court Case**

This section contains the case citation —the name of the case, the name of the court that heard the case, the year of the court's decision, and the reporters in which the court's opinion can be found.

The volume and page numbers of the *Federal Reporter* are blank because the opinion has not yet been published in that reporter.

This line includes the name of the judge who authored the opinion for the court.

The first paragraphs in this opinion summarize the facts that led to the lawsuit in this case.

EVANS V. FEDERAL EXPRESS CORP.
United States Court of Appeals,
First Circuit, 1998.
133 F.3d 137.

BOUDIN, Circuit Judge

Federal Express hired [Michael] Evans at the beginning of 1989 as a part-time freight handler * * * . Evans' supervisor * * * was Kenneth Pierce. In 1991, Pierce approved a four-week leave of absence for Evans to enter a residential drug-treatment program for cocaine abuse * * * .

When Evans entered the hospital * * *, he learned there about alcoholism, and when he left the hospital, he entered an Alcoholics Anonymous program. Evans says that he did not drink for approximately a year thereafter.

In late 1992, Evans was warned by Pierce that his attendance record had become unsatisfactory. Within the next six months, Evans twice failed to report and was given a written warning * * * . Then, in or around November 1993, Evans was absent from work on account of his arrest in a matter unrelated to Federal Express. On February 16, 1994, Evans was again absent from work * * * .

The following day Evans * * * told Pierce that he wanted a further leave of absence to enter an alcohol rehabilitation program. * * * Pierce refused [the request]. * * *

Evans was issued a new written warning because of his February 16 absence * * * . [I]n late February and again in early March 1994, Evans failed to show up for work * * * . This lead to a "last chance" written warning to Evans on March 10, 1994. Two days later, Evans again was absent from work without prior notice. On March 15, 1994, * * * under threat of discharge, Evans submitted a letter of resignation.

* * * *

■ **Exhibit 1A–3 A Sample Court Case (continued)**

A **complaint** is a document filed with a court by a plaintiff (the party initiating a lawsuit) alleging wrongdoing on the part of the defendant (the party against whom the lawsuit is brought).

This paragraph presents the plaintiff's charge against the defendant.

* * * Evans filed a **complaint** * * * charging that Federal Express had discriminated again him because of a handicap—alcoholism—in violation of [a Massachusetts statute] which makes it unlawful "[f]or any employer * * * to * * * discriminate against, because of his handicap, any person * * * capable of performing the essential functions of the position involved with reasonable accommodation * * * ."

* * * *

A **district court** is a federal trial court in which a lawsuit is initiated.

A **motion for summary judgment** is a request for a court to enter a judgment without proceeding to trial. The motion can be based on evidence outside the pleadings and is granted only if no facts are in dispute.

This paragraph summarizes the procedural background of this case.

* * * [T]he **district court** [hearing this case granted Federal Express's] **motion for summary judgment.** [Evans appealed. The] Massachusetts [statute] defines handicap to mean "a physical or mental impairment which substantially limits one or more major life activities of a person" * * *. [A]lcoholism constitutes a "handicap" under the Massachusetts statute.

This paragraph states the argument on whifch the plaintiff rests his charges against the defendant.

[Evans'] claim rests on the view that in his circumstances a second leave to treat alcoholism was an obligatory reasonable accommodation. * * *

These paragraphs contain the court's reasoning on the issue before it. This is the opinion of the majority of the judges or justices hearing the case. An appellate court's decision is often phrased with reference to the decision of the lower court from which the case was appealed. For example, an appellate court may "affirm" or "reverse" a lower court's ruling. A court's reasoning reflects the relevant principles that lead to the court's conclusion.

One element in the reasonableness equation is likelihood of success; and recoveries from substance abuse or addiction on one try are notoriously chancy. Here, Evans had already made one effort to deal with alcoholism at the time of his cocaine treatment and had not succeeded. It is one thing to say that further treatment made medical sense, and quite another to say that the law required the company to retain Evans through a succession of efforts.

Evans says that after he was discharged he did undergo treatment and now holds down a job; but the company is entitled to be judged on what it knew at the time or could reasonable foresee (and for all we know the shock of the discharge is what helped Evans shape up). * * *

* * * *

An appellate court will **affirm** (give legal force to) a lower court's judgment if it concludes that the lower court did not err in any way.

Affirmed.

example, the pi symbol—π—is often used, and a defendant is noted by delta—Δ—a triangle.

Diagramming the facts helps to emphasize that you should accept the facts as they are given. For example, under some circumstances, the manager of a store may have a duty to warn customers of the hazard presented by a wet floor by putting a sign near the hazard. If there is a statement in a case problem about the existence of a wet floor and the lack of a sign, you should accept that the floor was wet and there was no sign. Arguing with the statement ("Anyone can see when a floor is wet," "Maybe the floor was not too wet," "Maybe an employee was getting a sign to put up," or "Maybe someone stole the sign") only diminishes your ability to learn. When you have learned what the principle is that the case problem involves, then you can ask, "What if the facts were different?"

In analyzing and diagramming case problems, you may find the following method helpful. First, before reading a problem, read the question at the end. Does it ask you to evaluate the facts, the plaintiff's claim, or the defendant's defense? The point is to gain an understanding of the answer toward which the problem is directed. Second, read the problem, paying special attention to the facts that are directed to the question. As you read, write down the names of the plaintiff and defendant and draw different shapes around them, with an arrow to indicate who is bringing the action against whom. This illustrates the litigation and gives you a framework for answering the question.

For instance, consider the following case problem.

George Nesselrode lost his life in an airplane crash. The plane had been manufactured by Beech Aircraft Corp. and sold to Executive Beechcraft, Inc. Shortly before the crash occurred. Executive Beechcraft had conducted a routine inspection of the plane and found that some of the parts needed to be replaced. The new parts were supplied by Beech Aircraft but installed by Executive Beechcraft. These particular parts could be installed backwards, and if they were, the plane would crash. In Nesselrode's case, the

crash resulted from just such an incorrect installation of airplane parts. Nesselrode's wife Jane and three daughters sued Beech Aircraft, Executive Beechcraft, and Gerald Hultgren, the pilot who had flown the plane. Beech Aircraft claimed that it was not at fault because it had not installed the parts. Will Beech Aircraft be held liable for Nesselrode's death? [*Nesselrode v. Executive Beechcraft, Inc.,* 707 S.W.2d 371 (Mo. 1986)]

Here is how the facts in this problem might be diagrammed.

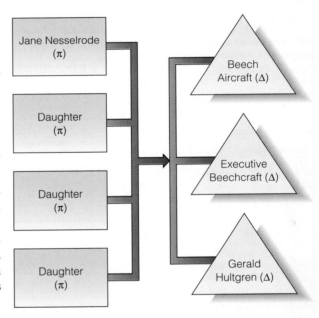

If, after diagramming the facts, you have trouble applying the principle that a problem asks you to discuss, reread the relevant section in the text. The diagramming method may also prove helpful when you are briefing and analyzing cases already analyzed and edited by the authors or cases that you are assigned or that you researched separately.

INTERACTING WITH
The Internet

■ Realize that you can obtain access to the Internet through many national or regional commercial electronic services such as America Online. In any event, once you get on the Internet, every site and every document on the Internet has a specific address described by uniform resource locators, known as URLs. You can think of URLs as the phone numbers of information on the Internet. A URL in effect tells computers where a particular site you wish to visit is located. It further tells the computer where the information at that site can be obtained. You have to type the URLs exactly as written. Here are some useful Internet addresses for you to use now:

■ Legal Information Institute:
http://www.law.cornell.edu

■ Virtual Law Library:
http://www.law.indiana.edu/

■ Yahoo:
http://www.yahoo.com/Government/Law/

■ You can also get updated information on legal sites on the Internet by contacting Nolo Press at
http://gnn.com/gnn/bus/nolo/

■ There are several other collections of law sites that you might want to access. The 'Lectric Law Library offers a large variety of legal information. Its Internet address on the Web is
http://www.lectlaw.com

A scientist updates pages on the World Wide Web (WWW or Web), a global network of computers connected by the Internet. In what ways does technology contribute to the speed of change in the law?

Ethics and Social Responsibility

Contents

Chapter Objectives

After reading this chapter, you should be able to . . .

1. Define business ethics and its relationship to personal ethics.
2. Explain the relationship between the law and ethics.
3. Compare and contrast duty-based ethics and utilitarian ethics.
4. Identify the various groups to whom corporations are perceived to owe duties.
5. Discuss some of the difficulties involved in measuring corporate social responsibility.

Business and ethics have never been a truly happy couple. This is because, as John Duke Coleridge indicated in the accompanying quotation, business "must be in a sense selfish." After all, the primary reason for going into business is to make a profit. Throughout history, there has been an underlying tension between the pursuit of profits and the welfare of those groups (employees, consumers, suppliers, creditors, communities, and others) that are affected by this pursuit.

Business owners and managers traditionally have had to ensure that their profit-making activities did not exceed the ethical boundaries established by society. In the past, though, these boundaries were often regarded as being coterminous with the law—that is, if something was legal, it was ethical. Shady business dealings were regarded as "just business" more often than not. In the last few decades, however, the ethical boundaries within which business firms must operate have narrowed significantly. In the rights-conscious world of today, a business firm that decides it has no duties other than those prescribed by law may find it difficult to survive. If a firm's behavior is perceived as unethical—even though it may be legal—that firm may suffer negative publicity, boycotts, and lost profits.

In preparing for a career in business, you will find that a background in business ethics and a commitment to ethical behavior is just as important as a knowledge of the specific laws that you will read about in this text. In this chapter, we first examine the nature of business ethics and some of the sources of ethical standards that have guided others in their business decision making. We then look at some of the obstacles to ethical behavior faced by businesspersons. In the remaining pages of the chapter, which deals with corporate social responsibility, we explore the issue mentioned in the preceding paragraph: How can businesspersons act in an ethically responsible manner and at the same time make profits for their firms or their firms' owners?

> **"It must be remembered that all trade is and must be in a sense selfish."**
>
> John Duke Coleridge, 1821–1892
> (English jurist)

The Nature of Business Ethics

To understand the nature of business ethics, we need to define what is meant by ethics generally. **Ethics** can be defined as the study of what constitutes right or wrong behavior. It is the branch of philosophy that focuses on morality and the way in which moral principles are applied to daily life. Ethics has to do with questions relating to the fairness, justness, rightness, or wrongness of an action. What is fair? What is just? What is the right thing to do in this situation?—these are essentially ethical questions.

Often, moral principles serve as the guiding force in an individual's personal ethical system. Although the terms *ethical* and *moral* are often used interchangeably, the terms refer to slightly different concepts. Whereas ethics has to do with the philosophical, rational basis for morality, morals are often defined as universal rules or guidelines (such as those rooted in religious precepts) that determine our actions and character.

Ethics Moral principles and values applied to social behavior.

Defining Business Ethics

Business ethics focuses on what constitutes ethical behavior in the world of business. Personal ethical standards, of course, play an important role in determining what is or is not ethical, or appropriate, business behavior. Business

Business Ethics Ethics in a business context; a consensus of what constitutes right or wrong behavior in the world of business and the application of moral principles to situations that arise in a business setting.

activities are just one part of the human enterprise, and the ethical standards that guide our behavior as, say, mothers, fathers, or students apply equally well to our activities as businesspersons. Businesspersons, though, often must address more complex ethical issues and conflicts in the workplace than they do in their personal lives—as you will learn in this chapter and throughout this book.

Business Ethics and the Law

Because the law reflects and codifies a society's ethical values, many of our ethical decisions are made for us—by our laws. Nevertheless, simply obeying the law does not fulfill all ethical obligations. In the interest of preserving personal freedom, as well as for practical reasons, the law does not—and cannot—codify all ethical requirements. No law says, for example, that it is *illegal* to lie to one's family, but it may be *unethical* to do so. Likewise, in the business world, numerous actions might be unethical but not necessarily illegal. Even though it may be convenient for businesspersons to satisfy themselves by mere compliance with the law, such an approach may not always yield ethical outcomes, as the *International Perspective* below indicates.

In short, the law has its limits—it cannot make all our ethical decisions for us. When it does not, ethical standards must guide the decision-making process.

International Perspective

The production of a new pharmaceutical product is both expensive and time consuming. Because the adverse side effects of a particular drug cannot always be determined in laboratory experiments—especially when symptoms may not manifest themselves for many years—a pharmaceutical company can never be completely certain about the safety of its products when it first brings them to market. Further complicating the marketing strategies of these companies is the fact that certain drug products may be banned in the United States by the Food and Drug Administration. Because U.S. drug laws are among the toughest in the world, companies with such products will naturally look elsewhere for potential customers—particularly in developing countries that do not have such extensive restrictions on consumer products.

Among the most widely distributed of these banned drugs have been several antidiarrheal products produced by companies such as G. D. Searle, Johnson & Johnson, and Wyeth. Because diarrhea kills several million children in underdeveloped countries each year, the need for effective products is evident. The World Health Organization has said that an inexpensive mixture of sugar, salt, and water can help to rehydrate children much more effectively and safely than any of the drugs available for sale. The lure of an estimated $500 million market, however, has, at least until recently, proved irresistible to many pharmaceutical companies. After a scathing British documentary revealed that a number of infants in Pakistan had died after being given the antidiarrheal drug Immodium, Johnson & Johnson agreed to withdraw its product from all developing countries.

For Critical Analysis: *Is it unethical of U.S. companies to sell banned drugs overseas? Would your answer be different if the drugs significantly benefited the health of consumers in overseas markets?*

Sources of Ethical Standards

Religious and philosophical inquiry into the nature of "the good" is an age-old pursuit. Broadly speaking, though, ethical reasoning relating to business traditionally has been characterized by two fundamental approaches. One approach defines ethical behavior in terms of *duty*. The other approach determines what is ethical in terms of the *consequences*, or *outcome*, of any given action. We examine each of these approaches here.

Duty-Based Ethics

Is it wrong to cheat on an examination, if nobody will ever know that you cheated and if it helps you get into law school so that you can eventually volunteer your legal services to the poor and needy? Is it wrong to lie to your parents if the lie harms nobody but helps to keep family relations congenial? These kinds of ethical questions implicitly weigh the "end" of an action against the "means" used to attain that end. If you believe that you have an ethical *duty* not to lie or cheat, however, then lying and cheating can never be justified by the consequences, no matter how benevolent or desirable those consequences may be. Duty-based ethics may be based on religious precepts or philosophical reasoning.

RELIGION. Duty-based ethical standards are often derived from moral principles rooted in religious sources. In the Judeo-Christian tradition, for example, the Ten Commandments of the Old Testament establish rules for moral action. Other religions have their own sources of revealed truth—such as the Koran in the Muslim world. Within the confines of their influence, moral principles are universal and *absolute*—they are not to be questioned. For example, consider one of the Ten Commandments: "Thou shalt not steal." This is an absolute mandate. Even a benevolent motive for stealing (such as Robin Hood's) cannot justify the act, because the act itself is inherently immoral and thus wrong. When an act is prohibited by religious teachings that serve as the foundation of a person's moral or ethical standards, the act is unethical for that person and should not be undertaken, regardless of its consequences.

Ethical standards based on religious teachings also may involve an element of *compassion*. Therefore, even though it might be profitable for a firm to lay off a less productive employee, if it would be difficult for that employee to find employment elsewhere and his or her family were to suffer as a result, this potential suffering would be given substantial weight by the decision makers. Compassionate treatment of others is also mandated—to a certain extent, at least—by the Golden Rule of the ancients ("Do unto others as you would have them do unto you"), which has been adopted by most religions.

KANTIAN PHILOSOPHY. Ethical standards based on a concept of duty may also be derived solely from philosophical principles. Immanuel Kant (1724–1804), for example, identified some general guiding principles for moral behavior based on what he believed to be the fundamental nature of human beings. Kant held that it is rational to assume that human beings are qualitatively different from other physical objects occupying space. Persons

Categorical Imperative A concept developed by the philosopher Immanuel Kant as an ethical guideline for behavior. In deciding whether an action is right or wrong, or desirable or undesirable, a person should evaluate the action in terms of what would happen if everybody else in the same situation, or category, acted the same way.

are endowed with moral integrity and the capacity to reason and conduct their affairs rationally. Therefore, their thoughts and actions should be respected. When human beings are treated merely as a means to an end, they are being treated as the equivalent of objects and are being denied their basic humanity.

A central postulate in Kantian ethics is that individuals should evaluate their actions in light of the consequences that would follow if *everyone* in society acted in the same way. This **categorical imperative** can be applied to any action. For example, say that you are deciding whether to cheat on an examination. If you have adopted Kant's categorical imperative, you will decide not to cheat, because if everyone cheated, the examination would be meaningless.

Outcome-Based Ethics

"Thou shalt act so as to generate the greatest good for the greatest number." This is a paraphrase of the major premise of the utilitarian approach to ethics. **Utilitarianism** is a philosophical theory first developed by Jeremy Bentham (1748–1832) and then advanced, with some modifications, by John Stuart Mill (1806–1873)—both British philosophers. In contrast to duty-based ethics, utilitarianism is outcome oriented. It focuses on the consequences of an action, not on the nature of the action itself or on any set of preestablished moral values or religious beliefs.

Utilitarianism An approach to ethical reasoning in which ethically correct behavior is not related to any absolute ethical or moral values but to an evaluation of the consequences of a given action on those who will be affected by it. In utilitarian reasoning, a "good" decision is one that results in the greatest good for the greatest number of people affected by the decision.

Under a utilitarian model of ethics, an action is morally correct, or "right," when, among the people it affects, it produces the greatest amount of good for the greatest number. When an action affects the majority adversely, it is morally wrong. Applying the utilitarian theory thus requires (1) a determination of which individuals will be affected by the action in question; (2) a **cost-benefit analysis**—an assessment of the negative and positive effects of alternative actions on these individuals; and (3) a choice among alternative actions that will produce maximum societal utility (the greatest positive benefits for the greatest number of individuals).

Cost-Benefit Analysis A decision-making technique that involves weighing the costs of a given action against the benefits of the action.

Lab workers conduct research for the development of a drug. If the drug proves beneficial to most people but adverse to a few, would it, under a utilitarian model of ethics, be marketed?

Utilitarianism is often criticized because it tends to focus on society as a whole rather than on individual human rights. For example, from a utilitarian standpoint, it might be ethically acceptable to test drugs or medicines on human beings because presumably a majority of the population would benefit from the experiments. If, however, one accepts the principle that each individual has basic human rights (to life, freedom, and the pursuit of happiness), then an action that deprives an individual or group of individuals of these rights—even for the greater good of society—is ethically unacceptable. No amount of cost-benefit analysis can justify the action.

> **BE CAREFUL** Ethical concepts about what is right and what is wrong can change.

Applying Ethical Standards

Consider the following example: A corporation that markets baby formula in developing countries has learned that mothers in those countries often mix the formula with impure water, to make the formula go further. As a result, babies are suffering from malnutrition, diarrhea, and in some instances, even death. What is the corporation's ethical responsibility in this situation? Should it withdraw the product from those markets (and lose profits), or should it conduct a cost-benefit analysis and let the decision be guided by the results?

If the corporation's decision makers felt that they had an absolute duty not to harm others, then the only ethical response would be to withdraw the product from those markets. If the decision makers approached the problem from a utilitarian perspective, they would engage in a cost-benefit analysis. The cost of the action (the suffering and death of babies) would be weighed against its benefit (the availability of the formula to mothers). Having the formula available frees mothers from the task of breastfeeding and thus allows them to earn money to help raise their incomes and standards of living. The question in a utilitarian analysis would focus on whether the benefit outweighed the cost—not the inherent rightness or wrongness of the action.

In fact, this scenario is not hypothetical. In the 1970s, the Nestlé Company concluded, on the basis of a cost-benefit analysis, that it was ethically justified in continuing to market its baby formula in developing countries. Other companies marketing infant formula in those areas, however, reached a different decision: they pulled out of those markets. Nestlé was severely criticized for its behavior. The company's opponents were outraged, not because the formula had been marketed initially but because of Nestlé's decision to continue marketing the formula based on its cost-benefit analysis.

Obstacles to Ethical Business Behavior

People sometimes behave unethically in the business context, just as they do in their private lives. Some businesspersons knowingly engage in unethical behavior because they think that they can "get away with it"—that no one will ever learn of their unethical actions. Examples of this kind of unethical behavior include padding expense accounts, casting doubts on the integrity of a rival co-worker to gain a job promotion, stealing company supplies or equipment, and so on. Obviously, these acts are unethical, and many of them are illegal as well.

In other situations, businesspersons who would choose to act ethically may be deterred from doing so because of situational circumstances or external pressures. We look here at how both the corporate environment and the

> **REMEMBER** There is a constant tension among ethics, social forces, profits, and the law.

Inside the Legal Environment
Self-Critical Analysis and "Smoking Guns"

Under the U.S. Sentencing Guidelines, which were created by the U.S. Department of Justice to provide standardized criminal sentences for federal crimes (see Chapter 7), corporate lawbreakers face sanctions and fines that can be as high as hundreds of millions of dollars. The guidelines allow judges to ease up on penalties, however, if a company can show that it has taken substantial steps to prevent, investigate, and punish wrongdoing by corporate employees. The sentencing guidelines thus provide an incentive for companies to establish ethics programs and procedures for implementing and monitoring corporate behavior. The theory is that companies that attempt to regulate their own behavior through self-critical analysis (SCA)—through internal audits or investigations of corporate conduct—should receive more favorable treatment under the law than those that do not.

Although laws promoting SCA foster ethical behavior, business owners and managers continue to face significant challenges in attempting to prevent wrongdoing within their companies. One of the problems with SCA is that it is virtually impossible to conduct a meaningful internal investigation or undertake an in-depth review process without creating a "paper trail" of some kind. Should the company have to defend itself in a lawsuit, the memos, reports, and other written evidence resulting from an investigation could be subject to discovery (see Chapter 3). If discovered by the plaintiff, these documents could be just the "smoking guns" the plaintiff is seeking—and the company may find it difficult to defend itself.

In an attempt to overcome this disincentive to undertake SCA, several states have passed laws that allow certain types of information resulting from internal audits and reviews to be privileged—that is, not admissible as evidence in a legal proceeding against the company. Some courts have also ruled that the results of a company's internal investigation of corporate conduct are protected by the "privilege of self-critical analysis." These courts hold that the SCA privilege furthers the public policy of encouraging self-evaluation on the part of companies.

In one case, for example, a plaintiff alleging gender discrimination on the part of her employer sought access to the employer's records of an investigation it had conducted on the obstacles faced by women within the company. The court, holding that the records were protected by the SCA privilege, stated that "[f]ew, if any, companies would risk commissioning a candid . . . report if these reports could later be used against the company in litigation.[a] Nonetheless, in most states, there are no real guarantees that the results of internal investigations will be kept confidential.

For Critical Analysis: *List some of the pros and cons of applying the self-critical analysis privilege.*

---

a.   *Flynn v. Goldman, Sachs & Co.* (S.D.N.Y. 1993)[1993 WL 362380]; this case is not reported in West's *Federal Supplement* reporter, but it can be retrieved on WESTLAW using the WL citation given here. See *Sheppard v. Consolidated Edison Co. of New York,* 893 F.Supp. 6 (E.D.N.Y. 1995), for another example of the application of the SCA privilege. For a discussion of the contrary view—that the SCA privilege should not be applied—see *Warren v. Legg Mason Wood Walker, Inc.,* 896 F.Supp. 540 (E.D.N.C. 1995).

---

conduct of management can sometimes act as deterrents to ethical behavior. (See the *Inside the Legal Environment* above for a discussion of another potential deterrent.)

Ethics and the Corporate Environment

Some contend that the nature of the corporate structure itself acts as a deterrent to ethically responsible behavior. We examine the corporate structure in Chapter 15. Briefly, a corporation is structured as follows: The owners of the corporation are the shareholders—those who purchase shares of stock in the company. The shareholders, however, do not run the corporation. Rather, they elect a board of directors and entrust those directors with the responsibility of directing and overseeing the corporate enterprise. The directors, in turn, hire officers and managers to handle the day-to-day business activities of the firm. A shareholder may also be a director, and a director may also be a corporate officer—the president or chief executive officer, for example.

ETHICS AND COLLECTIVE DECISION MAKING. The corporate setting complicates ethical decision making because (normally) no one person makes a corporate decision. If you are an officer or manager of a large corporation, for example, you may find that the decision as to what is right or wrong for the corporation is not yours to make. Corporate officers and managers, of course, do make decisions that affect the corporation, and your input may weigh in the decision. The ultimate decision makers, however, are the members of the board of directors, who must make decisions as a group.

Collective decision making, because it places emphasis on consensus and unity of opinion, also tends to hinder individual ethical assertiveness. For example, suppose that a director has ethical misgivings about a planned corporate venture that promises to be highly profitable. If the other directors have no such misgivings, the director who does may be swayed by the enthusiasm of the others for the project and downplay his or her own criticisms.

DIMINISHED PERSONAL ACCOUNTABILITY. To some extent, the corporate collectivity may shield corporate personnel from both personal exposure to the consequences of their decisions and personal accountability for those decisions. For example, suppose that a corporate board decides to market a new product that results in several consumers' deaths. Those who made the decision do not witness or deal directly with these consequences. Furthermore, just as normally no one individual is responsible for a corporate decision, so

Ethical Perspective

In the corporate setting, complaints by product users about the corporation's products rarely affect corporate decision makers personally. Would the decision makers' view of their ethical responsibilities change significantly if they were personally involved? At least one person, John Swanson, would answer this question in the affirmative.

Swanson was a high-ranking corporate officer at Dow Corning Corporation, which had manufactured and marketed silicone breast implants since 1963. Swanson's wife was among the implant recipients. For years, the company had been receiving complaints about silicone leakage from the implants and consequent adverse health effects. Dow

Corning took a defensive stance, maintaining that there was no convincing evidence that linked silicone to the complex of symptoms experienced by the recipients. Swanson supported Dow's position for years—until 1990, when he finally became convinced that his wife's deteriorating health condition was the result of the implants. Swanson urged the company to withdraw the implants from the market, but to no avail. The company continued to manufacture the implants until 1992. In the long run, Dow Corning was forced into bankruptcy due to litigation against the firm by implant recipients.

For Critical Analysis: *Is it likely that Swanson would have criticized Dow Corning's behavior if he had not been personally involved?*

normally no one person is held accountable for the decision. (In recent years, however, the courts have been increasingly willing to look behind the "corporate veil" and hold individual corporate actors liable, or legally responsible, for actions resulting in harm to others.)

Ethics and Management

Much unethical business behavior occurs simply because it is not always clear what ethical standards and behaviors are appropriate or acceptable in a given context. Although most firms now issue ethical policies or codes of conduct, these policies and codes are not always effective in creating an ethical workplace. At times, this is because a firm's ethical policies are not communicated clearly to employees or do not bear on the real ethical issues confronting decision makers. Additionally, particularly in a large corporation, unethical behavior in one corporate department may simply escape the attention of those in control of the corporation or the corporate officials responsible for implementing and monitoring the company's ethics program.

Another deterrent to ethical behavior exists when corporate management, by its own conduct, indicates that ethical considerations take second place. If management makes no attempt to deter unethical behavior—through reprimands or employment terminations, for example—it will be clear to employees that management is not all that serious about ethics. Likewise, if a company doles out promotions or salary increases to those who obviously engage in unethical tactics to increase the firm's profits, then employees who do not resort to such tactics will be at a disadvantage. An employee in this situation may decide that because "everyone else does it," he or she might as well do so also.

Of course, an even stronger deterrent to ethical behavior occurs when employers engage in blatantly unethical or illegal conduct and expect their employees to do so as well. An employee in this situation faces two options, neither of which is satisfactory: participate in the conduct or "blow the whistle" on (inform authorities of) the employer's actions—and, of course, risk being fired.

Corporate Social Responsibility

Corporate Social Responsibility The concept that corporations can and should act ethically and be accountable to society for their actions.

We now return to the question posed in this chapter's introduction: How can businesspersons act in an ethically responsible manner and at the same time make profits for their firms or their firms' owners? This question is at the heart of the debate surrounding the concept of **corporate social responsibility**—the idea that corporations can and should act ethically and be accountable to society for their actions. No one contests the claim that corporations have duties to their shareholders, employers, and product users (consumers). Many of these duties are written into law—that is, they are *legal* duties. The question of corporate social responsibility concerns the extent to which a corporation has ethical duties to various groups in society that go beyond its legally prescribed duties.

To understand the debate over corporate social responsibility, consider a hypothetical firm: the Farthing Company. This firm markets its products, primarily paints and glues, throughout the world. The company is facing a financial crisis and must find a way to increase its profits if it is to survive. In so doing, however, Farthing will need to take into account the ethical ramifications of any decisions it makes. In the following pages, we examine some of the problematic aspects of a corporation's responsibilities in regard to shareholders, employees, consumers, the community, and society. As you will see, corporations like the Farthing Company face difficult conflicts in trying to be ethically responsible.

> **REMEMBER** Changing ethical notions about social responsibility often motivate lawmakers to enact or repeal a law.

Duty to Shareholders

Corporate directors and officers have a duty to act in the shareholders' interest. Because of the nature of the relationship between corporate directors and officers and the shareholder-owners, the law holds directors and officers to a high standard of care in business decision making (see Chapter 15).

Traditionally, it was perceived that this duty to shareholders took precedence over all other corporate duties and that the primary goal of corporations should be profit maximization. Milton Friedman, the Nobel Prize–winning economist and a proponent of the profit-maximization view, saw "one and only one" social responsibility of a corporation: "to use its resources and engage in activities designed to increase its profits, so long as it stays within the rules of the game."[1] The "rules of the game" were the "basic rules of society, both those embodied in law and those embodied in ethical custom."[2]

Those who support the profit-maximization view of social responsibility contend that the duty to maximize profits must outweigh any other duty when duties conflict—to the extent, of course, that in maximizing shareholders' profits a firm does not violate the "basic rules of society." The question here is, What are these basic rules?

For example, suppose that our hypothetical firm, the Farthing Company, has suffered a setback because the U.S. government banned the sale of one of its paint thinners. The paint thinner, if allowed to touch the user's skin, can on rare occasions cause severe burns, and some consumers have complained of such injuries. The product is not banned in foreign markets, though, and thus Farthing faces an ethical question: Should it continue marketing the product in other countries? Certainly, it would benefit the shareholders to do so, but would such an action violate society's basic rules and ethical customs? Even if the action violated the ethical rules of even a small minority of Americans, that small minority, through activism and publicity, could harm Farthing's reputation as an ethically responsible corporation.

Duty to Employees

One of the primary concerns of every employer is the ability to control the workplace environment. After all, it is the employer who is responsible for making the business firm a success, and success requires qualified, competent, loyal employees and efficient operations. Employees, however, also have

---

1. *Capitalism and Freedom* (Chicago: University of Chicago Press, 1962), p. 133.
2. Milton Friedman, "Does Business Have Social Responsibility?" *Bank Administration,* April 1971, pp. 13–14.

Under the law, pregnant employees must be treated the same as other employees, unless they differ in their ability to perform the duties of their jobs. It is illegal for an employer to discriminate on the basis of pregnancy. Is such discrimination also unethical?

concerns. They want to earn a fair wage; they want to work in an environment free of health-endangering hazards; they want to be treated fairly and equally by their employers; and increasingly in recent years, they want employers to respect their personal integrity and privacy rights.

By law, employers are required to provide a safe workplace, to pay a minimum wage, and to provide equal employment opportunities for all potential and existing employees. Does an employer also have ethical obligations to employees that go beyond these legal duties? Additionally, what if, in fulfillment of one ethical (or legal) obligation, another duty must be violated? We look here at some employment decisions facing employers in which various ethical or legal duties come into conflict. (See Chapters 16, 17, and 18 for other ethical issues that arise in the employment context.)

EMPLOYMENT DISCRIMINATION.   As will be discussed in Chapter 17, federal laws require employers to offer equal employment opportunities to all job applicants and employees. These laws prohibit employers from discriminating against existing or potential employees on the basis of race, color, national origin, gender, religion, age, or disability. Many states have similar laws protecting employees. Sometimes, though, employers who are trying to fulfill a perceived ethical obligation to treat employees fairly and equally find themselves in a no-win situation.

The following case illustrates such a situation. Even though the employer went substantially beyond minimum legal compliance in attempting to provide a safe workplace for employees, the firm was nonetheless charged by some of its employees with having violated another ethical (and legal) duty—that of providing equal employment opportunities for women.

Case 2.1   ●   United Automobile Workers v. Johnson Controls, Inc.

Supreme Court of the United States, 1991.
499 U.S. 187,
111 S.Ct. 1196,
113 L.Ed.2d 158.

HISTORICAL AND SOCIAL SETTING   *With the industrial revolution of the nineteenth century came factories, assembly-line production, and a different way of life for workers. In those days, employees had few rights and often worked long hours in conditions that today would be inconceivable. There was no minimum wage, and the concept of overtime pay was not yet born. Over the course of the twentieth century, the government enacted numerous labor and employee laws to cure these problems. Today, employers who are insensitive to employee needs and working conditions may find themselves subject to lawsuits brought by the affected employees. In the interests of protecting female employees (and protecting their firms against potential liability), some firms have established fetal protection policies.*

BACKGROUND AND FACTS   Johnson Controls, Inc., created its Battery Division in 1978. In 1982, as part of an ongoing attempt to reduce the health hazards that might result from lead exposure, Johnson adopted a "fetal protection policy," under which women of childbearing age were prohibited from working in the Battery Division. Johnson reached this decision after scientific studies indicated that a pregnant woman's exposure to high lead levels could harm the fetus. Employees and their union, United Automobile Workers, brought a suit in a federal court against Johnson, claiming that the fetal protection policy violated Title VII of the Civil Rights Act of 1964, which prohibits discrimination in employment on the basis of gender. The trial court held for Johnson, and the union and employees appealed. The federal appellate court affirmed the trial court's ruling. The case was then appealed to the United States Supreme Court.

Case 2.1—continued

IN THE WORDS OF THE COURT . . .
Justice BLACKMUN delivered the opinion of the Court.
* * * *

Under * * * Title VII [of the Civil Rights Act of 1964], an employer may discriminate on the basis of "religion, sex, or national origin in those certain instances where religion, sex, or national origin is a bona fide occupational qualification [BFOQ][a] reasonably necessary to the normal operation of that particular business or enterprise." We therefore turn to the question whether Johnson Controls' fetal-protection policy is one of those "certain instances" that come within the BFOQ exception.
* * * *

Johnson Controls argues that its fetal-protection policy falls within the so-called safety exception to the BFOQ. * * *
* * * *

Our case law * * * makes clear that the safety exception is limited to instances in which sex or pregnancy actually interferes with the employee's ability to perform the job. This approach is consistent with the language of the BFOQ provision itself, for it suggests that permissible distinctions based on sex must relate to ability to perform the duties of the job. Johnson Controls suggests, however, that we expand the exception to allow fetal-protection policies that mandate particular standards for pregnant or fertile women. We decline to do so. Such an expansion contradicts not only the language of the BFOQ and the narrowness of its exception but the plain language and history of the Pregnancy Discrimination Act [PDA].

The PDA's amendment to Title VII contains a BFOQ standard of its own: unless pregnant employees differ from others "in their ability or inability to work," they must be "treated the same" as other employees "for all employment related purposes." * * * In other words, women as capable of doing their jobs as their male counterparts may not be forced to choose between having a child and having a job.
* * * *

We have no difficulty concluding that Johnson Controls cannot establish a BFOQ. Fertile women, as far as appears in the record, participate in the manufacture of batteries as efficiently as anyone else. * * * Title VII and the PDA simply do not allow a woman's dismissal because of her failure to submit to sterilization.

DECISION AND REMEDY The Supreme Court reversed the judgment of the appellate court and remanded the case for further proceedings. Johnson Controls' fetal protection policy was discriminatory in violation of Title VII of the Civil Rights Act and the Pregnancy Discrimination Act.

FOR CRITICAL ANALYSIS—POLITICAL CONSIDERATION *The Court deemed it inappropriate for either the courts or employers "to decide whether a woman's reproductive role is more important to herself and her family than her economic role." Congress, by passing the Pregnancy Discrimination Act, "left this choice to the woman as hers to make." Should Congress have been more concerned about the rights of the unborn?*

a. See Chapter 17 for a discussion of this defense to employment discrimination.

SEXUAL HARASSMENT VERSUS WRONGFUL DISCHARGE.

Another conflict of duties that sometimes faces employers poises the choice of being sued for sexual harassment against the choice of being sued for wrongful discharge. Lawsuits for *sexual harassment* in the workplace (discussed in Chapter 17) have climbed dramatically in number in the past decade. So have suits for *wrongful discharge*—firing an employee without good cause or for discriminatory reasons (see Chapters 16 and 17). Suppose that an employee of the Farthing Company complains to her supervisor that a co-worker is sexually harassing her—physically touching her in objectionable ways, making lewd comments about her and to her, and so on. The company immediately investigates the claim, and on finding that it is substantiated, promptly fires the harassing employee. The employee then sues the firm for wrongful discharge.

Can a court hold Farthing liable for wrongful discharge when, in firing the employee, the company was complying with a legal requirement? After all, federal law and the Equal Employment Opportunity Commission's guidelines require employers to take "immediate and appropriate corrective action" in response to an employee's complaint of sexual abuse. The answer to this question is that under some state laws and employment agreements, employers are prohibited from firing employees without a "just cause," and particular incidents of sexual harassment may or may not constitute just cause for firing the harasser.[3]

> **NOTE** A business that examines its conduct, and the conduct of its managers and employees, can prevent unethical and illegal acts.

CORPORATE RESTRUCTURING AND EMPLOYEE WELFARE.

Suppose that our hypothetical firm, the Farthing Company, decided to reduce its costs by downsizing and restructuring its operations. Among other things, this would allow Farthing to cut back on its overhead by consolidating various supervisory and managerial positions. The question for Farthing is, Which employees should be retained and which should be let go? Should the firm retain its highly paid employees who have worked for—and received annual raises from—the firm for years? Alternatively, in the interests of cutting costs, should it retain (or hire) younger, less experienced persons at lower salaries?

The firm would not necessarily be acting illegally if it pursued the second option. Unless a fired employee can prove that the employer has breached an employment contract or violated the Age Discrimination in Employment Act (ADEA) of 1967, he or she will not have a cause of action against the employer. The ADEA prohibits discrimination against workers forty years old and older on the basis of their age, but Farthing can always say that lack of performance or ability, not age, was the deciding factor. The question here is, Would such an action be ethical?

In deciding this issue, remember that Farthing must keep its eye on its profit margin. If it does not, the firm may fail, and the shareholders will lose their investments. Furthermore, why should the firm retain highly paid employees if it can obtain essentially the same work output for a lower price by retaining its less highly paid employees? Does Farthing owe an ethical duty to its employees who have served the firm loyally over a long period of time? Most people would say yes. Should this duty take precedence over Farthing's duty

One employee harasses another. If their employer discharges the harasser, could a court hold the employer liable for wrongful discharge?

---

3.   See, for example, *Chrysler Motors Corp. v. International Union, Allied Industrial Workers of America,* 959 F.2d 685 (7th Cir. 1992).

to the firm's owners to maintain or increase the profitability of the firm? Would your answer be the same if the firm faced imminent bankruptcy if it could not lower its operational costs? What if long-time employees were willing to take a slight reduction in pay to help the firm through its financial difficulties? What if they were not?

In the following case, an employer was confronted with a dwindling market and decreasing sales. The employer decided to reduce its costs of doing business by eliminating some of its obligations to its employees.

Case 2.2 ⬤ Varity Corp. v. Howe

Supreme Court of the United States, 1996.
516 U.S. 489,
116 S.Ct. 1065,
134 L.Ed.2d 130.

HISTORICAL AND ECONOMIC SETTING *Since 1950, the number of U.S. farms has declined as small farms have been driven out of business by huge corporate agribusinesses with assets that small farmers cannot match. Between 1980 and 1996, the number of farms decreased by over 14 percent, to less than two million, even as the average acreage per farm increased by 10 percent, to nearly 470 acres. Agribusinesses require fewer workers than do small farms, and thus, the total farm population also decreased by 24 percent in the 1980s. Fewer farmers means a smaller market for those who cater to it.*

BACKGROUND AND FACTS Varity Corporation manufactures and sells farm implements. In 1986, Varity set up a subsidiary, Massey Combines Corporation (MCC), to mar-

ket its self-propelled combines and four-wheel-drive tractors. The sales of both products were at an all-time low. Varity convinced current and former employees who were, or had been, involved with the products to accept a transfer to MCC of their jobs and retirement benefit plans. Varity did not tell those employees that it expected MCC to fail. Within two years, MCC failed. Among other consequences, some retirees stopped receiving benefits. The retirees and other ex-employees sued Varity in a federal district court under the Employee Retirement Income Security Act of 1974 (ERISA).[a] They claimed that Varity owed them a fiduciary duty, which it had breached.[b] The court ruled in their favor, and the U.S. Court of Appeals for the Eighth Circuit affirmed the decision. Varity then appealed to the United States Supreme Court.

---

a. 29 U.S.C. Sections 1001–1461. See Chapter 16.
b. A fiduciary is a party who, because of something that he or she has undertaken to do, has a duty to act primarily for another's benefit.

IN THE WORDS OF THE COURT . . .
Justice BREYER delivered the opinion of the Court.
* * * *

* * * ERISA requires a "fiduciary" to "discharge his duties with respect to a plan solely in the interest of the participants and beneficiaries." To participate knowingly and significantly in deceiving a plan's beneficiaries in order to save the employer money at the beneficiaries' expense, is not to act "solely in the interest of the participants and beneficiaries." As other courts have held, "[l]ying is inconsistent with the duty of loyalty owed by all fiduciaries * * * ."

DECISION AND REMEDY The United States Supreme Court affirmed the decision of the lower court. Varity breached its fiduciary duty to its employees with respect to their retirement benefits.

FOR CRITICAL ANALYSIS—ETHICAL CONSIDERATION *Should a company continue to market a slow-selling line of products for the sole purpose of employing those who work on the products?*

Duty to Consumers

Clearly, a corporation has a duty to the users of its products. This is not just an ethical duty but a legal one as well—as you will read in later chapters of this book. The issue, with respect to corporate social responsibility, is the extent to which a corporation has an ethical duty *beyond* those duties mandated by law or when the corporation is uncertain that a legal duty exists. Often, the issue turns on how a firm (or the public or a court) answers the following question: At what point does corporate responsibility for the safety of consumers end and consumer responsibility begin?

PRODUCT MISUSE.   Suppose that the Farthing Company learns that one of its products—glue—is being inhaled by some children in several Latin American countries. The health consequences of this misuse can include future kidney disease and brain damage. Consumer activists have launched a media campaign against Farthing, accusing it of being unethical by marketing its glue in those countries when such harms result. What is Farthing's responsibility in this situation? On the one hand, (1) it is not the company's fault that its product is being misused, (2) it has violated no legal duty, and (3) to cease selling the product in those areas would significantly cut into its profits. On the other hand, (1) suspending sales would reduce the suffering of some children, and (2) if Farthing ignores the public outcry, the continued adverse publicity could also cause the firm to lose sales—and thus profits. Farthing's solution will rest on the "ethical weight" it attaches to each of these factors.[4]

WHEN IS A RISK "OPEN AND OBVIOUS"?   Whenever a corporation markets a product, the law imposes a duty on the firm to warn consumers, among other things, of the harms that can result from *foreseeable* misuses. When a risk is open and obvious, however, courts tend to hold that no warning is necessary. Sharp knives, for example, can obviously injure their users. Sometimes, a business firm has no way of predicting how a court might rule in deciding whether a particular risk is open and obvious or whether consumers should be warned of the risk. Courts normally decide the issue on a case-by-case basis, and courts often disagree on whether certain types of risks are open and obvious. The following case involves an allegation that an automobile manufacturer failed to warn consumers that seat belts would not necessarily protect them from injuries in head-on collisions.

---

4.   When the H. B. Fuller Company faced this situation a few years ago, its solution was to suspend sales of its glues in some Latin American countries but not others. Fuller's critics contended that it should have suspended sales in all of the Latin American countries in which the product was being misused.

Case 2.3 ● Mazda Motor of America, Inc. v. Rogowski

Court of Special Appeals of Maryland, 1995.
105 Md.App. 318,
659 A.2d 391.

HISTORICAL AND ECONOMIC SETTING   The *first motor vehicle death in the United States was reported in*

New York City on September 14, 1899. Since then, nearly three million people have died in motor vehicle accidents, and many more have been seriously injured. The number of deaths and injuries per 100,000 vehicles has decreased considerably, however—from more than three hundred in 1912,

(Continued)

Case 2.1—continued

for example, to less than fifty today. Much of the decrease can be attributed to such safety measures as seat belts.

BACKGROUND AND FACTS   Francis Rogowski fell asleep at the wheel of his Mazda pickup truck and collided head-on with a large tree. To recover for the cost of his injuries, Rogowski sued Mazda Motor of America, Inc., and others in a Maryland state court. Rogowski claimed, among other things, that Mazda should have warned him the seat belts would not protect him from all injuries if he were in an accident. The court agreed that Mazda was liable for failure to warn and awarded damages of $601,644 to Rogowski. Mazda appealed.

IN THE WORDS OF THE COURT . . .
JOHN F. McAULIFFE, Judge.

* * * *

* * * [T]he danger not warned about was clear and obvious. It borders on the absurd to suggest that persons of ordinary intelligence would not appreciate the fact that seat belts, no matter how well designed and made, cannot be expected to protect the occupants of a vehicle from all injury, or even from serious injury, no matter how substantial the impact of a collision. * * * [T]here simply is no necessity to explain that which is obvious—that seat belts do not and cannot protect the occupants of the vehicle from injury no matter how severe the accident. Moreover, the giving of unnecessary warnings should be avoided because the presence of superfluous warnings seriously detracts from the efficacy of warnings that are needed.

* * * Bombarded with nearly useless warnings about risks that rarely materialize in harm, many consumers could be expected to give up on warnings altogether. And the few persons who might continue to take warnings seriously in an environment crowded with warnings of remote risks would probably overreact, investing too heavily in their versions of "safety." Given these limits on the capacity of consumers to react effectively to excessive risk information, the optimal, rather than the highest, levels of risk information, measured both qualitatively and quantitatively, are what is called for.

DECISION AND REMEDY   The Court of Special Appeals of Maryland held that the danger not warned about was clear and obvious, and reversed and remanded the case to the lower court.

FOR CRITICAL ANALYSIS—SOCIAL CONSIDERATION   *If the notice Rogowski claimed should have been required in his case was required for every automobile manufacturer, presumably every motor vehicle owner's manual would say the same thing. What impact would this have on such a notice?*

Duty to the Community

In some circumstances, the community in which a business enterprise is located has a substantial stake in the firm. Assume, for example, that the Farthing Company employs two thousand workers at one of its plants. If the company decides that it would be profitable to close the plant or move it to another location, the employees—and the community—would suffer as a result. Today, to be considered socially responsible, a corporation must take both employees' needs and community needs into consideration when making such a decision.

> **"A man cannot shift his misfortunes to his neighbor's shoulders."**
>
> Oliver Wendell Holmes, Jr., 1841–1935
> (Associate justice of the United States Supreme Court, 1902–1932)

Duty to Society

Perhaps the most disputed area in the controversy surrounding corporate social responsibility is the nature of a corporation's duty to society at large. Generally, the question turns less on whether corporations owe a duty to society than on how that duty can best be fulfilled.

> **"It is not from the benevolence of the butcher, the brewer, or the baker, that we expect our dinner, but from their regard to their own self-interest."**
>
> Adam Smith, 1723–1790
> (Scottish economist)

PROFIT MAXIMIZATION.   Those who contend that corporations should first and foremost attend to the goal of profit maximization would argue that it is by generating profits that a firm can best contribute to society. Society benefits by profit-making activities, because profits can only be realized when a firm markets products or services that are desired by society. These products and services enhance the standard of living, and the profits accumulated by successful business firms generate national wealth. Our laws and court decisions promoting trade and commerce reflect the public policy that the fruits of commerce (wealth) are desirable and good. Because our society values wealth as an ethical goal, corporations, by contributing to wealth, automatically are acting ethically.

Furthermore, profit maximization results in the efficient allocation of resources. Capital, labor, raw materials, and other resources are directed to the production of those goods and services most desired by society. If capital were directed toward a social goal instead of being reinvested in the corporation, the business operation would become less efficient. For example, if an automobile company contributes $1 million annually to the United Way, that contribution represents $1 million that is not reinvested in making better and safer cars.

Those arguing for profit maximization as a corporate goal also point out that it would be inappropriate to use the power of the corporate business world to fashion society's goals by promoting social causes. Determinations as

Ethical Perspective

What if a business firm moves into a community? Does it have an obligation to evaluate first the effect its presence there will have on that community? This question has surfaced recently in regard to Wal-Mart's expansion into smaller communities. Generally, most people in such communities welcome the lower prices and wider array of goods that Wal-Mart offers relative to other, smaller stores in the area. A vocal minority of people in some communities, however, claim that smaller stores often find it impossible to compete with Wal-Mart's prices and thus are forced to go out of business. Many of these smaller stores have existed for years and, according to Wal-Mart's critics, enhance the quality of community life. These critics claim that it is unethical of Wal-Mart to disregard a town's interest in the quality and character of its community life.

Recently, starting in Oklahoma, Wal-Mart has begun to consolidate some of its smaller stores into large "superstores." In the process of this consolidation, Wal-Mart is closing stores in some of the very towns in which it drove its smaller competitors out of business. This development raises yet another ethical question: Does Wal-Mart have an obligation to continue operations in a community once it has driven its competitors out of business?

For Critical Analysis: *Is it fair to blame Wal-Mart for what essentially amounts to its efficiency in supplying consumers with lower-priced products? Does Wal-Mart have an ethical obligation not to drive smaller firms out of business?*

to what exactly is in society's best interest are essentially political questions, and therefore the public, through the political process, should have a say in making those determinations. The legislature—not the corporate board-room—is thus the appropriate forum for such decisions.

CRITICS OF PROFIT MAXIMIZATION. Critics of the profit-maximization view believe that corporations should become actively engaged in seeking and fur-thering solutions to social problems. Because so much of the wealth and power of this country is controlled by business, business in turn has a responsibility to society to use that wealth and power in socially beneficial ways. Corporations should therefore promote human rights, strive for equal treatment of minorities and women in the workplace, take care to preserve the environment, and gen-erally not profit from activities that society has deemed unethical. The critics also point out that it is ethically irresponsible to leave decisions concerning social welfare up to the government, because many social needs are not being met sufficiently through the political process.

The Corporate Balancing Act

Today's corporate decision makers are, in a sense, poised on a fulcrum between profitability and ethical responsibility. If they emphasize profits at the expense of perceived ethical responsibilities, they may become the target of negative media exposure, consumer boycotts, and perhaps lawsuits. If they invest too heavily in good works or social causes, however, their profits may suffer. Striking the right balance on this fulcrum is not always easy, and usu-ally some profits must be sacrificed in the process. Instead of *maximum profits,* many firms today aim for *optimum profits*—profits that can be real-ized while staying within legal and ethical limits. Notice how PriceCostco's Code of Ethics (see the fold-out exhibit in this chapter) stresses both legal *and* ethical duties.

Measuring Corporate Social Responsibility

Measuring corporate social responsibility is difficult because depending on whose yardstick one uses, the answer differs. Traditionally, corporate philan-thropy has been used to measure social responsibility. Today, many feel that being ethically responsible involves much more than simply donating funds to charitable causes.

Corporate Philanthropy

Since the nineteenth century and the emergence of large, wealthy business enterprises in America, corporations have generally contributed some of their shareholders' wealth to meet social needs. Frequently, corporations establish separate nonprofit foundations for this purpose. For example, Honda, Inc., created the American Honda Education Corporation, through which it donated $40 million over a ten-year period to launch and support the Eagle Rock School in Estes Park, Colorado. This school and educator training center gives preference to students who have not been able to succeed in the more rigid, highly structured public school systems. Today, virtually all major corporations routinely donate to hospitals, medical research, the arts, universities, and programs that benefit society.

A related yardstick for measuring corporate social responsibility is the specific causes to which a corporation contributes. One indication of this measure was evident in a worldwide poll conducted a few years ago. Pollsters found that two-thirds of the respondents would switch brands to a manufacturer that supported a social cause that they liked.[5]

> **"The highest morality almost always is the morality of process."**
>
> Alexander M. Bickel, 1924–1974 (Rumanian-American legal scholar)

Corporate Process

Increasingly, corporations are being judged less on the basis of their philanthropic activities than on their practices, or corporate process. Corporate process, in this sense, refers to how a corporation conducts its affairs at all levels of operation. Does it establish and effectively implement ethical policies and take those policies seriously? Does it deal ethically with its shareholders? Does it consider the needs of its employees—for day-care facilities or flexible working hours, for example? Does it promote equal opportunity in the workplace for women, minority groups, and persons with disabilities? Do the corporation's suppliers, particularly those from developing countries, protect the human rights of their employees (provide for safety in the workplace or pay a decent wage, for example)? Does the corporation investigate complaints about its products promptly and, if necessary, take action to improve them?

---

5.   Justin Martin, "Good Citizenship Is Good Business," *Fortune*, March 21, 1992, pp. 15–16.

Ben and Jerry, of Ben and Jerry's Ice Cream, at the One World, One Heart Festival in New York City. According to Ben, "Business has a responsibility to give back to the community." Does giving back to the community conflict with other corporate purposes? If so, can a balance be struck? How?

strike to "bring goods to market at a lower price."

If we do these four things throughout our organization, we will realize our ultimate goal, which is to REWARD OUR SHAREHOLDERS.

If you are ever in doubt as to what course of action to take on a business matter that is open to varying ethical interpretations, take the high road and do what is right.

If you want our help, we are always available for advice and counsel. That's our job and we welcome your questions or comments.

Our continued success depends on you. We thank each of you for your contribution to our past success and for the high standards you have insisted upon in our company.

Accepting "gratuities" from a vendor might be interpreted as accepting a bribe. This can be a crime (see Chapter 7). In an international context, a bribe can be a violation of the Foreign Corrupt Practices Act. This act and other international laws are discussed in Chapter 24.

"Truth in advertising/packaging" legal standards are part of the statutes and regulations that are discussed in Chapter 19, which deals with consumer law.

If the company fails to honor one of its commitments, it may be sued for breach of contract. Breach of contract and its remedies are discussed in Chapters 12 and 13.

If the company did not provide products that comply with safety and health standards, it could be held liable in civil suits on legal grounds that are classified as torts (see Chapters 8 and 9).

Failing to pay bills when they become due could subject the company to the creditors' remedies. The company might even be forced into involuntary bankruptcy (see Chapter 14).

Disclosure of "inside information" that constitutes *trade secrets* could subject an employee to civil liability or criminal prosecution (see Chapters 7 and 11).

Promotions and other benefits of employment cannot be granted or withheld on the basis of discrimination. This is against the law. Employment discrimination is the subject of Chapter 17.

Antitrust laws apply to illegal restraints of trade—an agreement between competitors to set prices, for example, or an attempt by one company to control an entire market. Antitrust laws are discussed in Chapter 22.

Safety standards for the work environment are governed by the Occupational Safety and Health Act and other statutes. Laws regulating safety in the workplace are discussed in Chapter 16.

Failure to comply with "ecological" standards could be a violation of environmental laws (see Chapter 20).

For many, the answers to these and similar questions are the key factors in determining whether a corporation is socially responsible. From this perspective, no matter how much a corporation may contribute to worthy causes, it will not be socially responsible if it fails to observe ethical standards in its day-to-day activities.

It Pays to Be Ethical

Most corporations today have learned that it pays to be ethically responsible—even if it means less profits in the short run (and it often does). Today's corporations are subject to more intensive scrutiny—both by government agencies and the public—than they ever were in the past. If a corporation fails to conduct its operations ethically or respond quickly to an ethical crisis, its goodwill and reputation (and thus future profits) will likely suffer as a result.

There are other reasons as well for a corporation to behave ethically. Companies that demonstrate a commitment to ethical behavior—by implementing ethical programs, complying with environmental regulations, and promptly investigating product complaints, for example—often receive more lenient treatment from government agencies or the courts. Furthermore, by keeping their own houses in order, corporations may be able to avoid the necessity for the government to do so—through new laws or regulations.

Additionally, investors may shy away from a corporation's stock if the corporation is perceived to be socially irresponsible. Since the 1970s, certain investment funds have guaranteed to the purchasers of their shares that they will only invest in companies that are ethical. They did not invest in the Dow Chemical Company, for example, because it produced napalm that was used in the Vietnam War (1964–1975). They did not invest in corporations that had any dealings with South Africa because at that time, South Africa practiced *apartheid,* or complete separation of the races. Today, ethical funds base their investments on various ethical criteria. For example, some funds invest money only in corporations that are "environmentally kind."

Ethics in the Global Context

Given the varied cultures and religions of the world's nations, one might expect frequent conflicts in ethics between foreign and U.S. businesspersons. In fact, many of the most important ethical precepts are common to virtually all countries. Some important ethical differences do exist, however. In Islamic (Muslim) countries, for example, the consumption of alcohol and certain foods is forbidden by the Koran (the sayings of the prophet Mohammed, which lie at the heart of Islam and Islamic law). It would be thoughtless and imprudent to invite a Saudi Arabian business contact out for a drink.

The role played by women in other countries also may present some difficult ethical problems for firms doing business internationally. Equal employment opportunity is a fundamental public policy in the United States, and Title VII of the Civil Rights Act of 1964 prohibits discrimination against women in the employment context (see Chapter 17). Some other countries, however, largely reject any role for women professionals, which may cause difficulties for American women conducting business transactions in those countries.

Engaging in an international business deal can require different cultural courtesies, as shown here. How might cultural differences cause ethical conflicts between U.S. and foreign businesspersons?

Another ethical problem in international business dealings has to do with the legitimacy of certain side payments to government officials. In the United States, the majority of contracts are formed within the private sector. In many foreign countries, however, decisions on most major construction and manufacturing contracts are made by government officials because of extensive government regulation and control over trade and industry. Side payments to government officials in exchange for favorable business contracts are not unusual in such countries, nor are they considered to be unethical. In the past, U.S. corporations doing business in developing countries largely followed the dictum, "When in Rome, do as the Romans do."

In the 1970s, however, the U.S. press, and government officials as well, uncovered a number of business scandals involving large side payments by American corporations—such as Lockheed Aircraft—to foreign representatives for the purpose of securing advantageous international trade contracts. In response to this unethical behavior, Congress passed the Foreign Corrupt Practices Act (FCPA) in 1977, which prohibits American businesspersons from bribing foreign officials to secure advantageous contracts. The act, which is the subject of this chapter's *Landmark in the Legal Environment*, has made it difficult for American companies to compete as effectively as they otherwise might in the global marketplace.

> **"The law is not the same morning and night."**
>
> George Herbert, 1593–1633
> (English poet and minister)

The Ever-Changing Ethical Landscape

Our sense of what is ethical—what is fair or just or right in a given situation—changes over time. Conduct that might have been considered ethical ten years ago might be considered unethical today. Indeed, most of the ethical and social issues discussed in this chapter and elsewhere in this text either did not exist or were of little public concern at the turn of the twentieth century and,

andmark
in the Legal Environment
The Foreign Corrupt Practices Act of 1977

The Foreign Corrupt Practices Act (FCPA) of 1977 is divided into two major parts. The first part applies to all U.S. companies and their directors, officers, shareholders, employees, and agents. This part of the FCPA prohibits the bribery of most officials of foreign governments if the purpose of the payment is to get the official to act in his or her official capacity to provide business opportunities.

The FCPA does not prohibit payment of substantial sums to minor officials whose duties are ministerial. These payments are often referred to as "grease," or facilitating payments. They are meant to ensure that administrative services that might otherwise be performed at a slow pace are sped up. Thus, for example, if a firm makes a payment to a minor official to speed up an import licensing process, the firm has not violated the FCPA. Generally, the act, as amended, permits payments to foreign officials if such payments are lawful within the foreign country. The act also does not prohibit payments to private foreign companies or other third parties unless the American firm knows that the payments will be passed on to a foreign government in violation of the FCPA.

The second part of the FCPA is directed toward accountants, because in the past bribes were often con-

cealed in corporate financial records. All companies must keep detailed records that "accurately and fairly" reflect the company's financial activities. In addition, all companies must have an accounting system that provides "reasonable assurance" that all transactions entered into by the company are accounted for and legal. These requirements assist in detecting illegal bribes. The FCPA further prohibits any person from making false statements to accountants or false entries in any record or account.

In 1988, the FCPA was amended to provide that business firms that violated the act may be fined up to $2 million. Individual officers or directors who violate the FCPA may be fined up to $100,000 (the fine cannot be paid by the company) and may be imprisoned for up to five years.

For Critical Analysis: *The FCPA did not change international trade practices in other countries, but it effectively tied the hands of American firms trying to secure foreign contracts. In passing the FCPA, did Congress give too much weight to ethics and too little weight to international economic realities?*

---

in some cases, even as recently as a decade ago. Technological innovations, the communications revolution, pressing environmental problems, and social movements resulting in greater rights for minorities, women, and consumers have all dramatically changed the society in which we live and, consequently, the business and ethical landscape of America.

This changing ethical landscape is perhaps nowhere more evident than in the evolution of the concept of corporate social responsibility. Today's business manager must not only keep an eye on his or her firm's profit margins but also keep an "ear to the ground" to detect changing social perceptions of what constitutes ethical and socially responsible corporate behavior.

Key Terms

business ethics   35
categorical imperative   38
corporate social
   responsibility   42

cost-benefit analysis   38
ethics   35

utilitarianism   38

Chapter Summary
Ethics and Social Responsibility

▼

THE NATURE OF BUSINESS ETHICS (See pages 35–36.)	Ethics can be defined as the study of what constitutes right or wrong behavior. Business ethics focuses on how moral and ethical principles are applied in the business context. The law reflects society's convictions on what constitutes right or wrong behavior. The law has its limits, though, and some actions may be legal yet not be ethical.
SOURCES OF ETHICAL STANDARDS (See pages 37–39.)	1. **Duty-based ethics**—Ethics based on religious beliefs and philosophical reasoning, such as that of Immanuel Kant. 2. **Outcome-based ethics (utilitarianism)**—Ethics based on philosophical reasoning, such as that of John Stuart Mill.
OBSTACLES TO ETHICAL BUSINESS BEHAVIOR (See pages 39–42.)	1. **The corporate structure**— a. Collective decision making tends to deter individual ethical assertiveness. b. The corporate structure tends to shield corporate actors from personal responsibility and accountability. 2. **Management**— a. Uncertainty on the part of employees as to what kind of behavior is expected of them makes it difficult for them to behave ethically. b. Unethical conduct by management shows employees that ethical behavior is not a priority.
CORPORATE SOCIAL RESPONSIBILITY (See pages 42–51.)	Corporate social responsibility rests on the assumption that corporations should conduct their affairs in a socially responsible manner, but there is disagreement as to what constitutes socially responsible behavior. Corporations are perceived to hold duties to the following groups—duties that often come into conflict: 1. **Duty to shareholders**—Because the shareholders are the owners of the corporation, directors and officers have a duty to act in the shareholders' interest (maximize profits). 2. **Duty to employees**—Employers have numerous legal duties to employees, including providing employees with a safe workplace and refraining from discriminating against employees on the basis of race, color, national origin, gender, religion, age, or disability. These duties sometimes come into conflict. Many believe that employers hold ethical duties to their employees that go beyond those prescribed by law. 3. **Duty to consumers**—Corporate directors and officers have a legal duty to the users of their products. Most people feel that corporations also have an ethical duty that goes beyond what the law requires. Controversy exists over the point at which corporate responsibility for consumer safety ends and consumer responsibility begins. 4. **Duty to the community**—Most people hold that a corporation has a duty to the community in which it operates. The corporation should consider the needs of the community when making decisions that substantially affect the welfare of the community. 5. **Duty to society**—Most people hold that a corporation has a duty to society in general, but they differ in their ideas on how corporations can best fulfill this duty. One view is that corporations serve society's needs most effectively by

Chapter Summary, continued

CORPORATE SOCIAL RESPONSIBILITY— continued	maximizing profits because profits generally increase national wealth and social welfare. Another view holds that corporations, because they control so much of the country's wealth and power, should use their own wealth and power in socially beneficial ways and not engage in actions that society deems unethical.
THE CORPORATE BALANCING ACT (See page 51–52.)	Today's corporate decision makers must balance profitability against ethical responsibility when making their decisions. Instead of maximum profits, corporations increasingly aim for optimum profits—the maximum profits that can be realized by the firm while pursuing actions that are not only legal and profitable but also ethical.
MEASURING CORPORATE SOCIAL RESPONSIBILITY (See pages 52–53.)	It is difficult to measure corporate social responsibility because different yardsticks are used. Traditionally, corporate philanthropy has been used as a means of measuring corporate social responsibility. Increasingly, corporate process—how a corporation conducts its business on a day-to-day basis—is a key factor in determining whether a corporation is socially responsible.
ETHICS IN THE GLOBAL CONTEXT (See pages 54–55.)	Despite the cultural and religious differences among nations, the most important ethical precepts are common to virtually all countries. Two notable differences relate to the role of women in society and the practice of giving side payments to foreign officials to secure favorable contracts. The Foreign Corrupt Practices Act (FCPA) of 1977, which prohibits the bribery of foreign officials through such side payments, put U.S. businesspersons at a relative disadvantage to businesspersons from other countries who are not subject to such laws.
THE EVER-CHANGING ETHICAL LANDSCAPE (See page 55–56.)	What is considered ethical in a society may change over time as social customs change and new developments alter our social and business environment.

For Review

1. What is ethics? What is business ethics? What are some sources of ethical standards?

2. What are some of the obstacles to ethical business behavior?

3. To what groups does a corporation owe duties? Why do these duties sometimes come into conflict?

4. What is the difference between maximum profits and optimum profits?

5. What are some of the yardsticks by which corporate social responsibility is measured?

Questions and Case Problems

2–1. Business Ethics. Some business ethicists maintain that whereas personal ethics has to do with right or wrong behavior, business ethics is concerned with appropriate behavior. In other words, ethical behavior in business has less to do with moral principles than with what society deems to be appropriate behavior in the business context. Do you agree with this distinction? Do personal and business ethics ever overlap? Should personal ethics play any role in business ethical decision making?

2–2. Corporate Social Responsibility.   Assume that you are a high-level manager for a shoe manufacturer. You know that your firm could increase its profit margin by producing shoes in Indonesia, where you could hire women for $40 a month to assemble them. You also know, however, that a competing shoe manufacturer recently was accused, by human rights advocates, of engaging in exploitative labor practices because the manufacturer sold shoes made by Indonesian women for similarly low wages. You personally do not believe that paying $40 a month to Indonesian women is unethical, because you know that in that impoverished country, $40 a month is a better-than-average wage rate. Assuming that the decision is yours to make, should you have the shoes manufactured in Indonesia and make higher profits for your company? Should you instead avoid the risk of negative publicity and the consequences of that publicity for the firm's reputation and subsequent profits? Are there other alternatives? Discuss fully.

2–3. Corporate Social Responsibility.   Do you agree with Milton Friedman's conclusion that there is "one and only one responsibility of business"—to increase its profits? If so, what arguments would you use in defending this statement? If not, what arguments would you raise against it?

2–4. Duty to Consumers.   Two eight-year-old boys, Douglas Bratz and Bradley Baughn, were injured while riding a mini–trail bike manufactured by Honda Motor Co. Bratz, who was driving the bike while Baughn rode as a passenger behind him, ran three stop signs and then collided with a truck. Bratz did not see the truck because, at the time of the accident, he was looking behind him at a girl chasing them on another mini–trail bike. Bratz wore a helmet, but it flew off on impact because it was unfastened. Baughn was not wearing a helmet. The owner's manual for the mini–trail bike stated in bold print that the bike was intended for off-the-road use only and urged users to "Always Wear a Helmet." A prominent label on the bike itself also warned that the bike was for off-the-road use only and that it should not be used on public streets or highways. In addition, Bratz's father had repeatedly told the boy not to ride the bike in the street. The parents of the injured boys sued Honda, alleging that the mini–trail bike was unreasonably dangerous. Honda claimed it had sufficiently warned consumers of potential dangers that could result if the bike was not used as directed. Should Honda be held responsible for the boys' injuries? Why or why not? [*Baughn v. Honda Motor Co.*, 107 Wash.2d 127, 727 P.2d 655 (1986)]

2–5. Duty to Employees.   In 1984, General Telephone Co. of Illinois, Inc. (GTE), for reasons of efficiency, decided to consolidate its nationwide operations and eliminate unnecessary job positions. One of the positions eliminated was held by John Burnell, a fifty-two-year-old employee who had worked for GTE for thirty-four years and had always received "above average" performance ratings. GTE offered Burnell the choice of either accepting another position within the firm at the same salary or accepting early retirement with a salary continuation for a certain period of time. Burnell did not want to retire, but he was afraid that if he did accept the other position and if the other position was later eliminated, he might not then have the choice of early retirement with the same separation benefit. Because he received no assurances that the other job would be secure in the future, he accepted the early-retirement alternative. Burnell later alleged that he had been "constructively discharged"—that is, that GTE had made his working conditions so intolerable that he was forced to resign. Had GTE constructively discharged Burnell? Can GTE's actions toward Burnell be justified from an ethical standpoint? Discuss. [*Burnell v. General Telephone Co. of Illinois, Inc.*, 181 Ill.App.3d 533, 536 N.E.2d 1387, 130 Ill.Dec. 176 (1989)]

2–6. Duty to Consumers.   Beverly Landrine's infant daughter died after the baby swallowed a balloon while playing with a doll known as "Bubble Yum Baby." When a balloon was inserted into the doll's mouth and the doll's arm was pumped, thereby inflating the balloon, the doll simulated the blowing of a bubble gum bubble. The balloon was made by Perfect Product Co. and distributed by Mego Corp. Landrine brought a suit against the manufacturer and distributor, alleging that the balloon was defectively made or inherently unsafe when used by children and that Perfect had failed to warn of the danger associated with the balloon's use. Discuss whether the producer and distributor of the balloon should be held liable for the harm caused by its product. [*Landrine v. Mego Corp.*, 95 A.D.2d 759, 464 N.Y.S.2d 516 (1983)]

2–7. Duty to Consumers.   The Seven-Up Co., as part of a marketing scheme, placed two glass bottles of "Like" cola on the front entrance of the Gruenemeier residence. Russell Gruenemeier, a nine-year-old boy, began playing while holding one of the bottles. He tripped and fell, and the bottle broke, severely cutting his right eye and causing him to eventually lose his eyesight in the eye. Russell's mother brought an action against the Seven-Up Co. for damages, claiming that the cause of Russell's injury was Seven-Up's negligence. She claimed that the company was negligent because it placed potentially dangerous instrumentalities—glass bottles—within the reach of small children and that the firm should have used unbreakable bottles for its marketing scheme. Are glass bottles so potentially dangerous that the Seven-Up Co. should be held liable for the boy's harm? If you were the judge, how would you decide the issue? [*Gruenemeier v. Seven-Up Co.*, 229 Neb. 267, 426 N.W.2d 510 (1988)]

2–8. Duty to Consumers. The father of an eleven-year-old child sued the manufacturer of a jungle gym because the manufacturer had failed to warn users of the equipment that they might fall off the gym and get hurt, as the boy did in this case. The father also claimed that the jungle gym was unreasonably dangerous because, as his son began to fall and reached frantically for a bar to grasp, there was no bar within reach. The father based his argument in part on a previous case involving a plaintiff who was injured as a result of somersaulting off a trampoline. In that case [*Pell v. Victor J. Andrew High School*, 123 Ill.App.3d 423, 462 N.E.2d 858, 78 Ill.Dec. 739 (1984)], the court had held that the trampoline's manufacturer was liable for the plaintiff's injuries because it had failed to warn of the trampoline's propensity to cause severe spinal cord injuries if it was used for somersaulting. Should the court be convinced by the father's arguments? Why or why not? [*Cozzi v. North Palos Elementary School District No. 117*, 232 Ill.App.3d 379, 597 N.E.2d 683, 173 Ill.Dec. 709 (1992)]

2–9. Duty to Employees. Matt Theurer, an eighteen-year-old high school senior, worked part-time at a McDonald's restaurant in Oregon. Theurer volunteered to work an extra shift one day, in addition to his regular shifts (one preceding and one following the extra shift). After working about twelve hours during a twenty-four-hour period, Theurer told the manager that he was tired and asked to be excused from his next regularly scheduled shift so that he could rest. The manager agreed. While driving home from work, Theurer fell asleep at the wheel and crashed into a van driven by Frederic Faverty. Theurer died, and Faverty was severely injured. Faverty sued McDonald's, alleging, among other things, that McDonald's was negligent in permitting Theurer to drive a car when it should have known that Theurer was too tired to drive safely. Do employers have a duty to prevent fatigued employees from driving home from work? Should such a duty be imposed on them? How should the court decide this issue? How would you decide the issue if you were the judge? [*Faverty v. McDonald's Restaurants of Oregon, Inc.*, 133 Or.App. 514, 892 P.2d 703 (1994)]

A Question of Ethics and Social Responsibility

2–10. Hazen Paper Co. manufactured paper and paperboard for use in such products as cosmetic wrap, lottery tickets, and pressure-sensitive items. Walter Biggins, a chemist hired by Hazen in 1977, developed a water-based paper coating that was both environmentally safe and of superior quality. By the mid-1980s, the company's sales had increased dramatically as a result of its extensive use of "Biggins Acrylic." Because of this, Biggins thought he deserved a substantial raise in salary, and from 1984 to 1986, Biggins's persistent requests for a raise became a bone of contention between him and his employers. Biggins ran a business on the side, which involved cleaning up hazardous wastes for various companies. Hazen told Biggins that unless he signed a "confidentiality agreement" promising to restrict his outside activities during the time he was employed by Hazen and for a limited time afterward, he would be fired. Biggins said he would sign the agreement only if Hazen raised his salary to $100,000. Hazen refused to do so, fired Biggins, and hired a younger man to replace him. At the time of his discharge in 1986, Biggins was sixty-two years old, had worked for the company nearly ten years, and was just a few weeks away from being entitled to pension rights worth about $93,000. In view of these circumstances, evaluate and answer the following questions. [*Hazen Paper Co. v. Biggins*, 507 U.S. 604, 113 S.Ct. 1701, 123 L.Ed.2d 338 (1993)]

1. Did the company owe an ethical duty to Biggins to increase his salary, given the fact that its sales increased dramatically as a result of Biggins's efforts and ingenuity in developing the coating? If you were one of the company's executives, would you have raised Biggins's salary? Why or why not?

2. Generally, what public policies come into conflict in cases involving employers who, for reasons of cost and efficiency of operations, fire older, higher-paid workers and replace them with younger, lower-paid workers? If you were an employer facing the need to cut back on personnel to save costs, what would you do, and on what ethical premises would you justify your decision?

For Critical Analysis

2–11. If a firm engages in "ethically responsible" behavior solely for the purpose of gaining profits from the goodwill it generates, the "ethical" behavior is essentially a means toward a self-serving end (profits and the accumulation of wealth). In this situation, is the firm acting unethically in any way? Should motive or conduct carry greater weight on the ethical scales in this situation?

INTERACTING WITH
The Internet

■ The key to running an ethical business enterprise is effective and ethical management. A good source for information on management ethics is Academy of Management (AM) On-Line. AM can be accessed at

http://www.aom.pace.edu/

■ The Foundation for Enterprise Development (FED) is an organization dedicated to fostering highly productive corporate cultures. FED provides practical guidelines on how companies can integrate employees into their business decision-making processes. To access FED's home page, go to

http://www.fed.org/

■ A number of socially responsible corporations have taken up residence on the Internet. The Progressive Business Web Pages constitute a valuable source of information concerning these businesses, including information on environmentally conscious firms. To access these pages, go to

http://envirolink.org.

■ For a wealth of information on philanthropic organizations in the United States, you can access the Internet Non-Profit Center, a project of the American Institute of Philanthropy, at

http://www.nonprofits.org/

■ Because of its extensive collection of information on corporations in the United States, Hoover's Online is an invaluable resource. For data on more than 1,500 corporations, access Hoover's Online at

http://www.hoovers.com

■ If you are interested in how another country views business ethics, you should explore Ethical Business, a site originating in Great Britain. You can find this site at

http://www.arq.co.uk/ethicalbusiness

CHAPTER

3

The
American
Court System

Contents

Chapter Objectives

After reading this chapter, you should be able to . . .

1. Explain the concepts of jurisdiction and venue.
2. State the requirements for federal jurisdiction.
3. Identify the basic components of the federal and state court systems.
4. Compare and contrast the functions of trial courts and appellate courts.
5. Discuss the various steps involved in an appeal.

> "The Judicial
> Department comes
> home in its effects to
> every man's fireside:
> it passes on his
> property his
> reputation, his life,
> his all."
>
> John Marshall, 1755–1835
> (Chief Justice of the United States
> Supreme Court, 1801–1835)

As Chief Justice John Marshall remarked in the quotation alongside, ultimately, we are all affected by what the courts say and do. This is particularly true in the business world—nearly every businessperson faces either a potential or an actual lawsuit at some time or another in his or her career. For this reason, anyone contemplating a career in business will benefit from an understanding of American court systems, including the mechanics of lawsuits.

In this chapter, after examining the judiciary's overall role in the American governmental scheme, we discuss some basic requirements that must be met before a party may bring a lawsuit before a particular court. We then look at the court systems of the United States in some detail and, to clarify judicial procedures, follow a hypothetical case through a state court system. Even though there are fifty-two court systems—one for each of the fifty states, one for the District of Columbia, plus a federal system—similarities abound. Keep in mind that the federal courts are not superior to the state courts; they are simply an independent system of courts, which derives its authority from Article III, Section 2, of the U.S. Constitution.

The Judiciary's Role in American Government

▼ As you learned in Chapter 1, the body of American law is vast and complex. It includes the federal and state constitutions, statutes passed by legislative bodies, administrative law, and the case decisions and legal principles that form the common law. These laws would be meaningless, however, without the courts to interpret and apply them. This is the essential role of the judiciary—the courts—in the American governmental system: to interpret and apply the law.

Judicial Review The process by which a court decides on the constitutionality of legislative enactments and actions of the executive branch.

As the branch of government entrusted with interpreting the laws, the judiciary can decide, among other things, whether the laws or actions of the other two branches are constitutional. The process for making such a determination is known as **judicial review**. The power of judicial review enables the judicial branch to act as a check on the other two branches of government, in line with the checks and balances system established by the U.S. Constitution.

The power of judicial review is not mentioned in the Constitution, however. Rather, it was established by the United States Supreme Court's decision in *Marbury v. Madison.*[1] In that case, which was decided in 1803, the Supreme Court stated, "It is emphatically the province and duty of the Judicial Department to say what the law is. . . . If two laws conflict with each other, the courts must decide on the operation of each. . . . So if the law be in opposition to the Constitution . . . [t]he Court must determine which of these conflicting rules governs the case. This is the very essence of judicial duty." Since the *Marbury v. Madison* decision, details of which are offered in this chapter's *Landmark in the Legal Environment* on page 63, the power of judicial review has remained unchallenged. Today, this power is exercised by both federal and state courts.

Basic Judicial Requirements

▼ Before a lawsuit can be brought before a court, certain requirements must first be met. These requirements relate to jurisdiction, venue, and standing to sue. We examine each of these important concepts here.

---

1.   5 U.S. (1 Cranch) 137, 2 L.Ed. 60 (1803).

Landmark in the Legal Environment
Marbury v. Madison (1803)

In the edifice of American law, the *Marbury v. Madison* decision in 1803 can be viewed as the keystone of the constitutional arch. The facts of the case were as follows. John Adams, who had lost his bid for reelection to Thomas Jefferson in 1800, feared the Jeffersonians' antipathy toward business and toward a strong central government. Adams thus worked feverishly to "pack" the judiciary with loyal Federalists (those who believed in a strong national government) by appointing what came to be called "midnight judges" just before Jefferson took office. All of the fifty-nine judicial appointment letters had to be certified and delivered, but Adams's secretary of state (John Marshall) had only succeeded in delivering forty-two of them by the time Jefferson took over as president. Jefferson, of course, refused to order his secretary of state, James Madison, to deliver the remaining commissions.

William Marbury and three others to whom the commissions had not been delivered sought a writ of *mandamus* (an order directing a government official to fulfill a duty) from the United States Supreme Court, as authorized by Section 13 of the Judiciary Act of 1789. As fate would have it, John Marshall had stepped down as Adams's secretary of state only to become chief justice of the Supreme Court. Marshall faced a dilemma: If he ordered the commissions delivered, the new secretary of state (Madison) could simply refuse to deliver them—and the Court had no way to compel action, because it had no police force. At the same time, if Marshall simply allowed the new administration to do as it wished, the Court's power would be severely eroded.

Marshall masterfully fashioned a decision that did not require anyone to do anything but at the same time enlarged the power of the Supreme Court. He stated that the highest

James Madison. If Madison had delivered the commissions of the Federalist judges, would the U.S. Supreme Court today have the power of judicial review?

court did not have the power to issue a writ of *mandamus* in this particular case. Marshall pointed out that although the Judiciary Act of 1789 specified that the Supreme Court could issue writs of *mandamus* as part of its original jurisdiction, Article III of the Constitution, which spelled out the Court's original jurisdiction, did not mention writs of *mandamus*. Because Congress did not have the right to expand the Supreme Court's jurisdiction, this section of the Judiciary Act of 1789 was unconstitutional—and thus void. The decision still stands today as a judicial and political masterpiece.

For Critical Analysis: *What might result if the courts could not exercise the power of judicial review?*

Jurisdiction

In Latin, *juris* means "law," and *diction* means "to speak." Thus, "the power to speak the law" is the literal meaning of the term **jurisdiction**. Before any court can hear a case, it must have jurisdiction over the person against whom the suit is brought or over the property involved in the suit. The court must also have jurisdiction over the subject matter.

Jurisdiction The authority of a court to hear and decide a specific action.

JURISDICTION OVER PERSONS. Generally, a court can exercise personal jurisdiction (*in personam* jurisdiction) over residents of a certain geographical area. A state trial court, for example, normally has jurisdictional authority over

> "The power vested in the American courts of justice, of pronouncing a statute to be unconstitutional, forms one of the most powerful barriers which has ever been devised against the tyranny of political assemblies."
>
> Alexis de Tocqueville, 1805–1859
> (French historian and stateman)

Long Arm Statute A state statute that permits a state to obtain personal jurisdiction over nonresident defendants. A defendant must have certain "minimum contacts" with that state for the statute to apply.

residents of a particular area of the state, such as a county or district. A state's highest court (often called the state supreme court)[2] has jurisdictional authority over all residents within the state.

In some cases, under the authority of a state **long arm statute,** a court can exercise personal jurisdiction over nonresident defendants as well. Before a court can exercise jurisdiction over a nonresident under a long arm statute, though, it must be demonstrated that the nonresident had sufficient contacts, or *minimum contacts,* with the state to justify the jurisdiction.[3] For example, if an individual has committed a wrong within the state, such as causing an automobile accident or selling defective goods, a court can usually exercise jurisdiction even if the person causing the harm is located in another state. Similarly, a state may exercise personal jurisdiction over a nonresident defendant who is sued for breaching a contract that was formed within the state.

In regard to corporations,[4] the minimum-contacts requirement is usually met if the corporation does business within the state. Suppose that a corporation incorporated under the laws of Maine and headquartered in that state has a branch office or manufacturing plant in Georgia. Does this corporation have sufficient minimum contacts with the state of Georgia to allow a Georgia court to exercise jurisdiction over the Maine corporation? Yes, it does. If the Maine corporation advertises and sells its products in Georgia, those activities may also suffice to meet the minimum-contacts requirements. In the following case, the issue is whether an Italian corporation had sufficient minimum contacts with the state of Arizona to permit a suit against the corporation to be brought in an Arizona state court.

---

2. As will be discussed shortly, a state's highest court is often referred to as the state supreme court, but there are exceptions. For example, in New York, the supreme court is a trial court.
3. The minimum-contacts standard was established in *International Shoe Co. v. State of Washington,* 326 U.S. 310, 66 S.Ct. 154, 90 L.Ed. 95 (1945).
4. In the eyes of the law, corporations are "legal persons"—entities that can sue and be sued. See Chapter 15.

Case 3.1 ● A. Uberti and Co. v. Leonardo

Supreme Court of Arizona, 1995.
892 P.2d 1354.

HISTORICAL AND SOCIAL SETTING *Colt Industries manufactured the first Peacemaker, a six-shot, single-action revolver, in 1873. The U.S. government adopted it for service that same year, and the gun became known as "the gun that won the West." In 1892, Colt and other gun manufacturers began making safer, more reliable, and more efficient revolvers. The market for the 1873 model declined until the 1950s, when television Westerns created a new market for replica firearms.*

BACKGROUND AND FACTS Aldo Uberti and Company, an Italian corporation, manufactures a replica of the Peacemaker known as the Cattleman. Uberti sells its guns to

a U.S. distributor for sale throughout the country. Henry Pacho, a resident of Arizona, bought one of the guns, wrapped it in a towel, and put it under the seat of his car. His two-year-old niece Corrina was helping to clean the car when the gun fell out of the towel, hit the pavement, and discharged. The bullet struck Corrina in the head and killed her. Corrina's parents filed a suit in an Arizona state court against Uberti, alleging that the company was liable for the "design, manufacture, sale, and distribution of a defective and unreasonably dangerous product." Uberti asked the court to dismiss the suit on the ground that the court did not have personal jurisdiction over Uberti. The court refused, and Uberti appealed. The appellate court reversed. Corrina's parents then appealed to the Supreme Court of Arizona.

(Continued)

Case 3.1—continued

IN THE WORDS OF THE COURT . . .

FELDMAN, Chief Justice.

   *   *   *   *

   *   *   * Defendant [Uberti] knew its products, passing through its American distributor *   *   * would flow into local markets across America.

   *   *   *   *

   *   *   * Defendant's catalogs and advertising *   *   * support the conclusion that the gun, as a replica of an American frontier weapon, was originally and primarily designed and made for the American market. *   *   *

   *   *   *   *

   Defendant argues that its activities, at best, focused on the United States in general, not Arizona. Therefore, Arizona exceeds due process by asserting its jurisdiction here. Were this true, then no individual state could assert jurisdiction over Defendant simply because Defendant did not target a particular state or group of states but instead intended to sell its product to all of America. The argument turns common sense on its head. Holding that a defendant intending to sell its products to any and all citizens in the United States could not be held accountable in any jurisdiction where its products caused injury defies any sensible concept of due process. *   *   *

   *   *   * Thus, we do not believe that Plaintiffs must show Defendant's specific intent to sell in Arizona. An intent to sell across America is enough.

DECISION AND REMEDY   The Supreme Court of Arizona held that Uberti could be sued in an Arizona state court.

FOR CRITICAL ANALYSIS—ETHICAL CONSIDERATION   *The typical car dealership directs its sales efforts toward the local market in a single state. If a customer buys a car and drives it to another state, where a defect in the car causes an accident, is it fair to allow that state's courts to exercise personal jurisdiction over the dealership located in the other state?*

JURISDICTION OVER PROPERTY.   A court can also exercise jurisdiction over property that is located within its boundaries. This kind of jurisdiction is known as *in rem* jurisdiction, or "jurisdiction over the thing." For example, suppose that a dispute arises over the ownership of a boat in dry dock in Fort Lauderdale, Florida. The boat is owned by an Ohio resident, over whom a Florida court cannot normally exercise personal jurisdiction. The other party to the dispute is a resident of Nebraska. In this situation, a lawsuit concerning the boat could be brought in a Florida state court on the basis of the court's *in rem* jurisdiction.

JURISDICTION OVER SUBJECT MATTER.   Jurisdiction over subject matter is a limitation on the types of cases a court can hear. In both the federal and state court systems, there are courts of *general* (unlimited) *jurisdiction* and courts of *limited jurisdiction*. An example of a court of general jurisdiction is a state or federal trial court. An example of a state court of limited jurisdiction is a probate court. **Probate courts** are state courts that handle only matters relating to the transfer of a person's assets and obligations after that person's death, including matters relating to the custody and guardianship of children. An example of a federal court of limited subject-matter jurisdiction is a bankruptcy court. **Bankruptcy courts** handle only bankruptcy proceedings, which

Probate Court A state court of limited jurisdiction that conducts proceedings relating to the settlement of a deceased person's estate.

Bankruptcy Court A federal court of limited jurisdiction that handles only bankruptcy proceedings. Bankruptcy proceedings are governed by federal bankruptcy law.

Boat lying in dry dock. Can a state exercise jurisdiction over this boat if its owner is a resident of another state?

are governed by federal bankruptcy law (discussed in Chapter 14). In contrast, a court of general jurisdiction can decide virtually any type of case.

A court's jurisdiction over subject matter is usually defined in the statute or constitution creating the court. In both the federal and state court systems, a court's subject-matter jurisdiction can be limited not only by the subject of the lawsuit but also by the amount of money in controversy, by whether a case is a felony (a more serious type of crime) or a misdemeanor (a less serious type of crime), or by whether the proceeding is a trial or an appeal.

ORIGINAL AND APPELLATE JURISDICTION. The distinction between courts of original jurisdiction and courts of appellate jurisdiction normally lies in whether the case is being heard for the first time. Courts having original jurisdiction are courts of the first instance, or trial courts—that is, courts in which lawsuits begin, trials take place, and evidence is presented. In the federal court system, the *district courts* are trial courts. In the various state court systems, the trial courts are known by various names, as will be discussed shortly.

The key point here is that normally, any court having original jurisdiction is known as a trial court. Courts having appellate jurisdiction act as reviewing courts, or appellate courts. In general, cases can be brought before appellate courts only on appeal from an order or a judgment of a trial court or other lower court.

JURISDICTION OF THE FEDERAL COURTS. Because the federal government is a government of limited powers, the jurisdiction of the federal courts is limited. Article III of the U.S. Constitution establishes the boundaries of federal judicial power. Section 2 of Article III states that "[t]he judicial Power shall extend to all Cases, in Law and Equity, arising under this Constitution, the Laws of the United States, and Treaties made, or which shall be made, under their Authority."

Whenever a plaintiff's cause of action is based, at least in part, on the U.S. Constitution, a treaty, or a federal law, then a **federal question** arises, and the case comes under the judicial power of the federal courts. Any lawsuit involving a federal question can originate in a federal court. People who claim that their constitutional rights have been violated can begin their suits in a federal court.

Federal district courts can also exercise original jurisdiction over cases involving **diversity of citizenship**. Such cases may arise between (1) citizens of different states, (2) a foreign country and citizens of a state or of different states, or (3) citizens of a state and citizens or subjects of a foreign country. The amount in controversy must be more than $75,000 before a federal court can take jurisdiction in such cases. For purposes of diversity jurisdiction, a corporation is a citizen of both the state in which it is incorporated and the state in which its principal place of business is located. A case involving diversity of citizenship can be filed in the appropriate federal district court, or, if the case starts in a state court, it can sometimes be transferred to a federal court. A large percentage of the cases filed in federal courts each year are based on diversity of citizenship.

Note that in a case based on a federal question, a federal court will apply federal law. In a case based on diversity of citizenship, however, a federal court will apply the relevant state law (which is often the law of the state in which the court sits).

Federal Question A question that pertains to the U.S. Constitution, acts of Congress, or treaties. A federal question provides a basis for federal jurisdiction.

Diversity of Citizenship Under Article III, Section 2, of the Constitution, a basis for federal court jurisdiction over a lawsuit between (1) citizens of different states, (2) a foreign country and citizens of a state or of different states, or (3) citizens of a state and citizens or subjects of a foreign country. The amount in controversy must be more than $75,000 before a federal court can take jurisdiction in such cases.

Ethical Perspective

Diversity jurisdiction arose out of what were basically considerations of fairness. Apparently, the authors of the Constitution felt that a state might be biased toward its own citizens, and therefore, when a dispute involved citizens from different states, a federal forum should be available to protect the out-of-state party. Today, the possibility of bringing a case in a federal court when diversity jurisdiction exists is often an attractive option. For example, a California plaintiff who wants to sue a New York business firm for damages that exceed $75,000 can file the suit in a federal court located in California—the plaintiff does not have to initiate the suit in a New York court.

Diversity jurisdiction offers many advantages, but there is also a major disadvantage—the federal courts spend a good deal of their time deciding issues that arise under state law. Like the state courts, the federal courts are increasingly overburdened with cases. Some people see limiting or abolishing diversity jurisdiction as a solution to this problem. In 1994, for example, the Long Range Planning Committee of the Judicial Conference of the United States (the official organization of the federal judiciary) recommended that diversity jurisdiction be eliminated entirely except in cases involving foreigners or in cases in which local prejudice in a state court can be clearly demonstrated. This is not the first such proposal. In fact, since the 1920s bills have been introduced periodically in Congress to curtail or abolish diversity jurisdiction. So far, none of the proposals has been adopted into law.

For Critical Analysis: *Are the benefits of diversity jurisdiction worth its costs to the federal court system?*

**Exclusive
Federal Jurisdiction**
(cases involving
federal crimes,
federal antitrust law,
bankruptcy, patents,
copyrights, trademarks,
suits against the
United States, some
areas of admiralty law,
and certain other
matters specified
in federal statutes)

**Concurrent
Jurisdiction**
(cases involving
federal questions,
diversity-of-citizenship
cases)

**Exclusive
State Jurisdiction**
(cases involving
all matters not
subject to
federal jurisdiction)

■ **Exhibit 3–1
Exclusive and
Concurrent Jurisdiction**

Concurrent Jurisdiction
Jurisdiction that exists when
two different courts have the
power to hear a case.

Exclusive Jurisdiction
Jurisdiction that exists when a
case can be heard only in a
particular court or type of court.

Venue The geographical district
in which an action is tried and
from which the jury is selected.

Standing to Sue The
requirement that an individual
must have been injured or
threatened with injury to bring a
lawsuit.

Justiciable Controversy A
controversy that is not
hypothetical or academic but
real and substantial; a requirement that must be satisfied
before a court will hear a case.

EXCLUSIVE VERSUS CONCURRENT JURISDICTION.   When both federal and state courts have the power to hear a case, as is true in suits involving diversity of citizenship, **concurrent jurisdiction** exists. When cases can be tried only in federal courts or only in state courts, **exclusive jurisdiction** exists. Federal courts have exclusive jurisdiction in cases involving federal crimes, bankruptcy, patents, and copyrights; in suits against the United States; and in some areas of admiralty law (law governing transportation on the seas and ocean waters). States also have exclusive jurisdiction in certain subject matters—for example, in divorce and adoption. The concepts of concurrent and exclusive jurisdiction are illustrated in Exhibit 3–1.

Venue

Jurisdiction has to do with whether a court has authority to hear a case involving specific persons, property, or subject matter. **Venue**[5] is concerned with the most appropriate location for a trial. For example, two state courts (or two federal courts) may have the authority to exercise jurisdiction over a case, but it may be more appropriate or convenient to hear the case in one court than in the other.

Basically, the concept of venue reflects the policy that a court trying a suit should be in the geographical neighborhood (usually the county) in which the incident leading to the lawsuit occurred or in which the parties involved in the lawsuit reside. Pretrial publicity or other factors, though, may require a change of venue to another community, especially in criminal cases in which the defendant's right to a fair and impartial jury has been impaired.

For example, in 1992, when four Los Angeles police officers accused of beating Rodney King were brought to trial, the attorneys defending the police officers requested a change of venue from Los Angeles to Simi Valley, California. The attorneys argued that to try the case in a Los Angeles court would jeopardize the defendants' right to a fair trial. The court agreed and granted the request. For similar reasons, a change of venue from Oklahoma City to Denver, Colorado, was ordered for the trial of Timothy McVeigh and Terry Nichols, who had been indicted in connection with the 1995 bombing of the federal building in Oklahoma City.

Standing to Sue

Before a person can bring a lawsuit before a court, the party must have **standing to sue,** or a sufficient "stake" in a matter to justify seeking relief through the court system. In other words, a party must have a legally protected and tangible interest at stake in the litigation in order to have standing. The party bringing the lawsuit must have suffered a harm, or been threatened a harm, by the action about which he or she complained. At times, a person will have standing to sue on behalf of another person. For example, suppose that a child suffered serious injuries as a result of a defectively manufactured toy. Because the child is a minor, a lawsuit could be brought on his or her behalf by another person, such as the child's parent or legal guardian.

Standing to sue also requires that the controversy at issue be a **justiciable**[6] **controversy**—a controversy that is real and substantial, as opposed to hypothetical or academic. For example, in the above example, the child's parent

---

5.   Pronounced *ven*-yoo.
6.   Pronounced jus-*tish*-uh-bul.

Timothy McVeigh, who was convicted of bombing the federal building in Oklahoma City. What is the most important factor requiring a change of venue to another community, especially in a criminal case? What effect does television and the other media have on a court's consideration of a request for a change of venue?

could not sue the toy manufacturer merely on the ground that the toy was defective. The issue would become justiciable only if the child had actually been injured due to the defect in the toy as marketed. In other words, the parent normally could not ask the court to determine, for example, what damages *might* be obtained if the child had been injured, because this would be merely a hypothetical question.

Meeting standing requirements is not always easy. In the following case, for example, an environmental organization sued a company for allegedly discharging pollutants into waterways beyond the amount allowed by the Environmental Protection Agency. At issue in the case was whether the organization had standing to sue under federal environmental laws.

Case 3.2 ⬤ Friends of the Earth, Inc. v. Crown Central Petroleum Corp.

United States Court of Appeals, Fifth Circuit, 1996.
95 F.3d 358.

BACKGROUND AND FACTS Crown Central Petroleum Corporation does business as La Gloria Oil & Gas Company. Under a permit issued by the Environmental Protection Agency (EPA), La Gloria's oil refinery discharges storm-water run-off into Black Fork Creek. Black Fork Creek flows into Prairie Creek, which flows into the Neches River, which flows into Lake Palestine eighteen miles downstream. Friends of the Earth, Inc. (FOE), is a not-for-profit corpora-

tion dedicated to the protection of the environment. FOE filed a suit in a federal district court against La Gloria under the Federal Water Pollution Control Act.[a] FOE claimed that La Gloria had violated its EPA permit and that this conduct had directly affected "the health, economic, recreational, aesthetic, and environmental interests of FOE's members" who used the lake. La Gloria filed a motion for summary judgment, arguing that FOE lacked standing to bring the suit. The court granted the motion, and FOE appealed.

———
a. 33 U.S.C. Sections 1251–1387.

(Continued)

Case 3.2—continued

IN THE WORDS OF THE COURT . . .
PATRICK E. HIGGINBOTHAM, Circuit Judge:
* * * *

To demonstrate that FOE's members have standing, FOE must show that
* * * the injury is "fairly traceable" to the defendant's actions * * *.
* * * *

* * * FOE offered no competent evidence that La Gloria's discharges have made their way to Lake Palestine or would otherwise affect Lake Palestine. * * * FOE and its members relied solely on the truism that water flows downstream and inferred therefrom that any injury suffered downstream is "fairly traceable" to unlawful discharges upstream. At some point this common sense observation becomes little more than surmise. At that point certainly the requirements [for standing] are not met.

DECISION AND REMEDY   The U.S. Court of Appeals for the Fifth Circuit affirmed the lower court's decision. FOE lacked standing to bring a suit against La Gloria.

FOR CRITICAL ANALYSIS—ECONOMIC CONSIDERATION
What would happen if there was no requirement of standing to sue?

> **"The perfect judge fears nothing— he could go front to front before God."**
>
> Walt Whitman, 1819–1892
> (American poet)

The State and Federal Court Systems

As mentioned earlier in this chapter, each state has its own court system. Additionally, there is a system of federal courts. Although no state court system is the same, Exhibit 3–2 illustrates the basic organizational structure characteristic of the court systems in many states. The exhibit also shows how the federal court system is structured. We turn now to an examination of these court systems, beginning with the state courts.

State Court Systems

Typically a state court system will include several levels, or tiers, of courts. As indicated in Exhibit 3–2, state courts may include (1) trial courts of limited jurisdiction, (2) trial courts of general jurisdiction, (3) appellate courts, and (4) the state's highest court (often called the state supreme court). Judges in the state court system are usually elected by the voters for a specified term.

Generally, any person who is a party to a lawsuit has the opportunity to plead the case before a trial court and then, if he or she loses, before at least one level of appellate court. Finally, if a federal statute or federal constitutional issue is involved in the decision of the state supreme court, that decision may be further appealed to the United States Supreme Court.

TRIAL COURTS.   Trial courts are exactly what their name implies—courts in which trials are held and testimony taken. State trial courts have either general or limited jurisdiction. Trial courts that have general jurisdiction as to subject matter may be called county, district, superior, or circuit courts.[7] The jurisdiction of these courts is often determined by the size of the county in which the

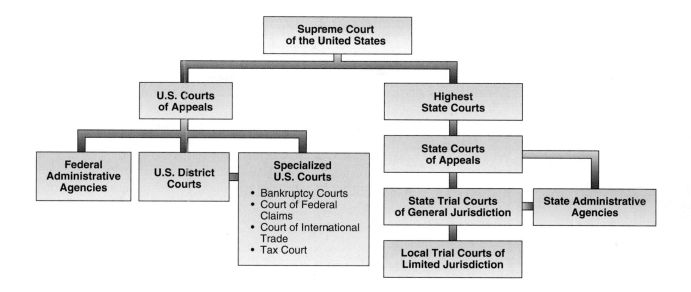

court sits. State trial courts of general jurisdiction have jurisdiction over a wide variety of subjects, including both civil disputes and criminal prosecutions. In some states, trial courts of general jurisdiction may hear appeals from courts of limited jurisdiction.

Some courts of limited jurisdiction are called special inferior trial courts or minor judiciary courts. **Small claims courts** are inferior trial courts that hear only civil cases involving claims of less than a certain amount, such as $2,500—the amount varies from state to state. Suits brought in small claims courts are generally conducted informally, and lawyers are not required. In a minority of states, lawyers are not even allowed to represent people in small claims courts for most purposes. Another example of an inferior trial court is a local municipal court that hears mainly traffic cases. Decisions of small claims courts and municipal courts may be appealed to a state trial court of general jurisdiction.

Other courts of limited jurisdiction as to subject matter include domestic relations courts, which handle only divorce actions and child custody cases, and probate courts, as mentioned earlier.

COURTS OF APPEALS. Every state has at least one court of appeals (appellate court, or reviewing court), which may be an intermediate appellate court or the state's highest court. About half of the states have intermediate appellate courts. Generally, courts of appeals do not conduct new trials, in which evidence is submitted to the court and witnesses are examined. Rather, an appellate court panel of three or more judges reviews the record of the case on appeal, which includes a transcript of the trial proceedings, and the panel determines whether the trial court committed an error.

Small Claims Courts Special courts in which parties may litigate small claims (usually, claims involving $2,500 or less). Attorneys are not required in small claims courts, and in many states attorneys are not allowed to represent the parties.

---

7. The name in Ohio is court of common pleas; the name in New York is supreme court.

Appellate courts look at *questions of law* (on which only a judge, not a jury, can rule) but usually defer to a trial court's findings on *questions of fact* (which may be decided by a judge or a jury based on evidence presented at trial). This is because the trial court judge and jury were in a better position to evaluate testimony—by directly observing witnesses' gestures, demeanor, and nonverbal behavior generally during the trial. At the appellate level, the judges review the written transcript of the trial, which does not include these nonverbal elements.

An appellate court will challenge a trial court's finding of fact only when the finding is clearly erroneous (that is, when it is contrary to the evidence presented at trial) or when there is no evidence to support the finding. For example, if a jury concluded that a manufacturer's product harmed the plaintiff but no evidence was submitted to the court to support that conclusion, the appellate court would hold that the trial court's decision was erroneous. The options exercised by appellate courts will be further discussed later in this chapter.

> **BE CAREFUL** The decisions of a state's highest court are final on questions of state law.

STATE SUPREME (HIGHEST) COURTS.   The highest appellate court in a state is usually called the supreme court but may be called by some other name. For example, in both New York and Maryland, the highest state court is called the court of appeals. The decisions of each state's highest court on all questions of state law are final. Only when issues of federal law are involved can a decision made by a state's highest court be overruled by the United States Supreme Court.

The Federal Court System

The federal court system is basically a three-tiered model consisting of (1) U.S. district courts (trial courts of general jurisdiction) and various courts of limited jurisdiction, (2) U.S. courts of appeals (intermediate courts of appeals), and (3) the United States Supreme Court.

Unlike state court judges, who are usually elected, federal court judges—including the justices of the Supreme Court—are appointed by the president of the United States, subject to the approval of the U.S. Senate. All federal judges receive lifetime appointments (because under Article III they "hold their offices during Good Behavior").

U.S. DISTRICT COURTS.   At the federal level, the equivalent of a state trial court of general jurisdiction is the district court. There is at least one federal district court in every state. The number of judicial districts can vary over time, primarily owing to population changes and corresponding caseloads. Currently, there are ninety-six federal judicial districts.

U.S. district courts have original jurisdiction in federal matters. Federal cases typically originate in district courts. There are other trial courts with original, but special (or limited), jurisdiction, such as the federal bankruptcy courts and others shown in Exhibit 3–2.

U.S. COURTS OF APPEALS.   In the federal court system, there are thirteen U.S. courts of appeals—also referred to as U.S. circuit courts of appeals. The federal courts of appeals for twelve of the circuits hear appeals from the federal district courts located within their respective judicial circuits. The Court of Appeals for the Thirteenth Circuit, called the Federal Circuit, has national appellate jurisdiction over certain types of cases, such as cases involving patent law and cases in which the U.S. government is a defendant.

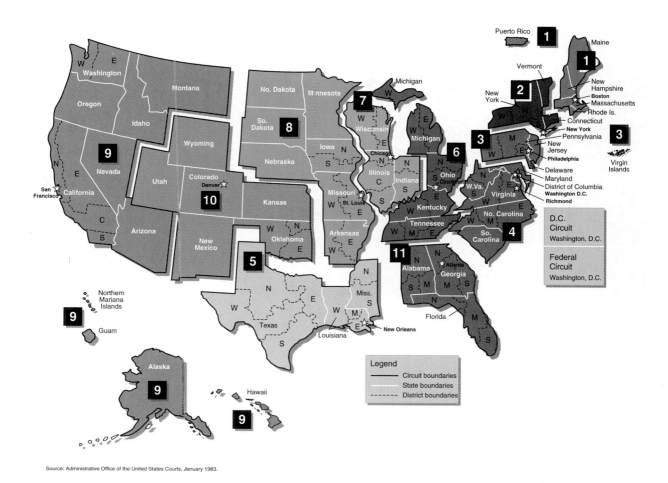

Source: Administrative Office of the United States Courts, January 1983.

The decisions of the circuit courts of appeals are final in most cases, but appeal to the United States Supreme Court is possible. Exhibit 3–3 shows the geographical boundaries of U.S. circuit courts of appeals and the boundaries of the U.S. district courts within each circuit.

THE UNITED STATES SUPREME COURT. The highest level of the three-tiered model of the federal court system is the United States Supreme Court. According to the language of Article III of the U.S. Constitution, there is only one national Supreme Court. All other courts in the federal system are considered "inferior." Congress is empowered to create other inferior courts as it deems necessary. The inferior courts that Congress has created include the second tier in our model—the U.S. courts of appeals—as well as the district courts and any other courts of limited, or specialized, jurisdiction.

The United States Supreme Court consists of nine justices. Although the United States Supreme Court has original, or trial, jurisdiction in rare instances (set forth in Article III, Section 2), most of its work is as an appeals court. The Supreme Court can review any case decided by any of the federal courts of appeals, and it also has appellate authority over some cases decided in the state courts.

■ **Exhibit 3–3**
U.S. Courts of Appeals and U.S. District Courts

> "We are not final because we are infallible, but we are infallible only because we are final."
>
> Robert H. Jackson, 1892–1954
> (Associate justice of the United States Supreme Court, 1941–1954)

The justices of the U.S. Supreme Court are: seated left to right, Antonin Scalia, John Paul Stevens, Chief Justice William H. Rehnquist, Sandra Day O'Connor, and Anthony M. Kennedy; and standing left to right, Ruth Bader Ginsburg, David H. Souter, Clarence Thomas, and Stephen Breyer. Does the fact that these justices are appointed for life have any effect on the decisions they reach in the cases they hear?

Writ of Certiorari A writ from a higher court asking the lower court for the record of a case.

Rule of Four A rule of the United States Supreme Court under which the Court will not issue a writ of *certiorari* unless at least four justices approve of the decision to issue the writ.

To bring a case before the Supreme Court, a party requests the Court to issue a writ of *certiorari*. A **writ of *certiorari***[8] is an order issued by the Supreme Court to a lower court requiring the latter to send it the record of the case for review. The Court will not issue a writ unless at least four of the nine justices approve of it. This is called the **rule of four.** Whether the Court will issue a writ of *certiorari* is entirely within its discretion. The Court is not required to issue one, and most petitions for writs are denied. (Thousands of cases are filed with the Supreme Court each year, yet it hears, on average, less than one hundred of these cases.[9]) A denial is not a decision on the merits of a case, nor does it indicate agreement with the lower court's opinion. Furthermore, denial of the writ has no value as a precedent.

Typically, the petitions granted by the Court involve cases that raise important constitutional questions or cases that conflict with other state or federal court decisions. Similarly, if federal appellate courts are rendering inconsistent opinions on an important issue, the Supreme Court may review the case and issue a decision to define the law on the matter.

Following a Case through the State Courts

To illustrate the procedures that would be followed in a civil lawsuit brought in a state court, we present a hypothetical case and follow it through the state court system. The case involves an automobile accident in which Kevin Anderson, driving a Mercedes, struck Lisa Marconi, driving a Ford Taurus. The accident occurred at the intersection of Wilshire Boulevard and Rodeo Drive in Beverly Hills, California. Marconi suffered personal injuries,

8.   Pronounced sur-*shee*-uh-*rah*-ree.
9.   From the mid-1950s through the early 1990s, the Supreme Court reviewed more cases per year than it has in the last few years. In the Court's 1982–1983 term, for example, the Court issued opinions in 151 cases. In contrast, opinions were issued in only about 90 cases during the Court's 1996–1997 term.

incurring medical and hospital expenses as well as lost wages for four months. Anderson and Marconi are unable to agree on a settlement, and Marconi sues Anderson. Marconi is the plaintiff, and Anderson is the defendant. Both are represented by lawyers.

During each phase of the **litigation** (the process of working a lawsuit through the court system), Marconi and Anderson will be required to observe strict procedural requirements. A large body of law—procedural law—establishes the rules and standards for determining disputes in courts. Procedural rules are very complex, and they vary from court to court. There is a set of federal rules of procedure and various sets of rules for state courts. Additionally, the applicable procedures will depend on whether the case is a civil or criminal case. Generally, the Marconi-Anderson litigation will involve the procedures discussed in the following subsections. Keep in mind that attempts to settle the case may be ongoing throughout the trial.

The Pleadings

The complaint and answer (and the counterclaim and reply)—all of which are discussed below—taken together are called the **pleadings**. The pleadings inform each party of the claims of the other and specify the issues (disputed questions) involved in the case.

THE PLAINTIFF'S COMPLAINT.   Marconi's suit against Anderson commences when her lawyer files a **complaint** with the appropriate court. The complaint contains a statement alleging (asserting to the court, in a pleading) the facts necessary for the court to take jurisdiction, a brief summary of the facts necessary to show that the plaintiff is entitled to a remedy, and a statement of the remedy the plaintiff is seeking. Exhibit 3–4 illustrates how the complaint might read in the Marconi-Anderson case. Complaints may be lengthy or brief, depending on the complexity of the case.

After the complaint has been filed, the sheriff, a deputy of the county, or another *process server* (one who delivers a complaint and summons) serves a **summons** and a copy of the complaint on defendant Anderson. The summons notifies Anderson that he must file an answer to the complaint with both the court and the plaintiff's attorney within a specified time period (usually twenty to thirty days). The summons also informs Anderson that failure to answer will result in a **default judgment** for the plaintiff, meaning the plaintiff will be awarded the damages alleged in her complaint.

THE DEFENDANT'S ANSWER.   The defendant's **answer** either admits the statements or allegations set forth in the complaint or denies them and outlines any defenses that the defendant may have. If Anderson admits to all of Marconi's allegations in his answer, the court will enter a judgment for Marconi. If Anderson denies any of Marconi's allegations, the litigation will go forward.

Anderson can deny Marconi's allegations and set forth his own claim that Marconi was in fact negligent and therefore owes him money for damages to his Mercedes. This is appropriately called a **counterclaim**. If Anderson files a counterclaim, Marconi will have to answer it with a pleading, normally called a **reply,** which has the same characteristics as an answer.

Anderson can also admit the truth of Marconi's complaint but raise new facts that may result in dismissal of the action. This is called raising an *affirmative*

Litigation The process of resolving a dispute through the court system.

Pleadings Statements made by the plaintiff and the defendant in a lawsuit that detail the facts, charges, and defenses involved in the litigation; the complaint and answer are part of the pleadings.

Complaint The pleading made by a plaintiff alleging wrongdoing on the part of the defendant; the document that, when filed with a court, initiates a lawsuit.

Summons A document informing a defendant that a legal action has been commenced against him or her and that the defendant must appear in court on a certain date to answer the plaintiff's complaint. The document is delivered by a sheriff or any other person so authorized.

Default Judgment A judgment entered by a court against a defendant who has failed to appear in court to answer or defend against the plaintiff's claim.

Answer Procedurally, a defendant's response to the plaintiff's complaint.

Counterclaim A claim made by a defendant in a civil lawsuit that in effect sues the plaintiff.

Reply Procedurally, a plaintiff's response to a defendant's answer.

**IN THE LOS ANGELES MUNICIPAL COURT
FOR THE LOS ANGELES JUDICIAL DISTRICT**

Lisa Marconi
_____
                Plaintif

                v.

Kevin Anderson
_____
                Defendant

CIVIL NO. 8—1026

COMPLAINT

Comes now the plaintiff and for her cause of action against the defendant alleges and states as follows:

1. The jurisdiction of this court is based on Section 86 of the California Civil Code.
2. This action is between plaintiff, a California resident living at 1434 Palm Drive, Anaheim, California, and defendant, a California resident living at 6950 Garrison Avenue, Los Angeles, California.
3. On September 10, 1997, plaintiff, Lisa Marconi, was exercising good driving habits and reasonable care in driving her car through the intersection of Rodeo Drive and Wilshire Boulevard when defendant, Kevin Anderson, negligently drove his vehicle through a red light at the intersection and collided with plaintiff's vehicle. Defendant was negligent in the operation of the vehicle as to:
    a. Speed,
    b. Lookout,
    c. Management and control.
4. As a result of the collision plaintiff suffered severe physical injury that prevented her from working and property damage to her car. The costs she incurred include $10,000 in medical bills, $9,000 in lost wages, and $5,000 for automobile repairs.

WHEREFORE, plaintiff demands judgment against the defendant for the sum of $24,000 plus interest at the maximum legal rate and the costs of this action.

By _____
Roger Harrington
Attorney for the Plaintiff
800 Orange Avenue
Anaheim, California 91426

defense. For example, Anderson could assert the running of the relevant statute of limitations (a state or federal statute that sets the maximum time period during which a certain action can be brought or rights enforced) as an affirmative defense.

Motion to Dismiss A pleading in which a defendant asserts that the plaintiff's claim fails to state a cause of action (that is, has no basis in law) or that there are other grounds on which a suit should be dismissed.

MOTION TO DISMISS.   A **motion to dismiss** requests the court to dismiss the case for stated reasons. The motion to dismiss is often made by a defendant before filing an answer to the plaintiff's complaint. Grounds for dismissal of a case include improper delivery of the complaint and summons, improper venue, and the plaintiff's failure to state a claim for which a court could grant relief (a remedy). For example, if Marconi had suffered no injuries or losses as a result of Anderson's negligence, Anderson could move to have the case dismissed because Marconi had not stated a claim for which relief could be granted.

If the judge grants the motion to dismiss, the plaintiff generally is given time to file an amended complaint. If the judge denies the motion, the suit will go forward, and the defendant must then file an answer.

Note that if Marconi wishes to discontinue the suit because, for example, an out-of-court settlement has been reached, she can likewise move for dismissal. The court can also dismiss the case on its own motion.

Pretrial Motions

Either party may attempt to get the case dismissed before trial through the use of various pretrial motions. We have already mentioned the motion to dismiss. Two other important pretrial motions are the motion for judgment on the pleadings and the motion for summary judgment.

At the close of the pleadings, either party may make a **motion for judgment on the pleadings,** or on the merits of the case. The judge will grant the motion only when there is no dispute over the facts of the case and the only issue to be resolved is a question of law. In deciding on the motion, the judge may only consider the evidence contained in the pleadings.

In contrast, in a **motion for summary judgment,** the court may consider evidence outside the pleadings, such as sworn statements (affidavits) by parties or witnesses or other documents relating to the case. A motion for summary judgment can be made by either party. As with the motion for judgment on the pleadings, a motion for summary judgment will be granted only if there are no genuine questions of fact and the only question is a question of law.

Deciding whether a certain issue presents a question of fact or a question of law is not always easy, and judges sometimes disagree on whether summary judgment is appropriate in a given case. The following case illustrates this point.

Motion for Judgment on the Pleadings A motion by either party to a lawsuit at the close of the pleadings requesting the court to decide the issue solely on the pleadings without proceeding to trial. The motion will be granted only if no facts are in dispute.

Motion for Summary Judgment A motion requesting the court to enter a judgment without proceeding to trial. The motion can be based on evidence outside the pleadings and will be granted only if no facts are in dispute.

Case 3.3 ⬤ Metzgar v. Playskool, Inc.

United States Court of Appeals,
Third Circuit, 1994.
30 F.3d 459.

COMPANY PROFILE *Hasbro, Inc., is the world's largest toy maker. Hasbro manufactures and sells many of the most famous, biggest-selling toys—including games, puzzles, and baby items—on the U.S. and world markets. Hasbro products include Cabbage Patch Kids, G.I. Joe, Lincoln Logs, Mr. Potato Head, Monopoly, Scrabble, Trivial Pursuit, Twister, and Yahtzee. Hasbro brand names include Hasbro, Kenner, Milton Bradley, Parker Brothers, Tonka, and Playskool.*

BACKGROUND AND FACTS Ronald Metzgar placed his fifteen-month-old son Matthew, awake and healthy, in his playpen.

Ronald left the room for five minutes and on his return found Matthew lifeless. A purple toy block had lodged in the boy's throat, choking him to death. Ronald called 911, but efforts to revive Matthew were to no avail. There was no warning of a choking hazard on the box containing the block. Matthew's parents sued Playskool, Inc., the manufacturer of the block, and others in a federal district court. They alleged, among other things, negligence[a] in failing to warn of the hazard of the block. Playskool filed a motion for summary judgment, arguing that the danger of a young child choking on a small block was obvious. The court entered a summary judgment in favor of Playskool. The parents appealed.

a. *Negligence* is a failure to use the standard of care that a reasonable person would exercise in similar circumstances. See Chapter 8.

(Continued)

Case 3.3—continued

IN THE WORDS OF THE COURT . . .
MANSMANN, Circuit Judge.
* * * *

* * * For a risk to be deemed obvious for purposes of a failure to warn claim, * * * there must be general consensus within the relevant community. We cannot see how the purple Playskool block can be deemed as a matter of law an obvious safety hazard in the eyes of the relevant community, when Playskool itself believed the block was safe for its intended use. Furthermore, Matthew's parents * * * testified that they did not believe that the product posed an obvious threat of asphyxiation to Matthew. Moreover, the defendant did not proffer any evidence tending to show that the danger of asphyxiation was obvious.

Under a negligence theory, although a failure to warn claim may be defeated if the risk was obvious or known, the question of obviousness is more properly submitted to a jury than disposed on motion for summary judgment. The court's role in deciding a motion for summary judgment is merely to decide whether there is a genuine issue of material fact for trial. The district court's dismissal of Metzgars' negligent claim on the basis of its determination that the danger to Matthew was obvious was tantamount to holding that no reasonable jury could conclude otherwise. Based on the evidence of record, we cannot agree.

DECISION AND REMEDY   The U.S. Court of Appeals for the Third Circuit held that the question of the obviousness in this case was not a proper subject for summary judgment and remanded the case for a trial.

FOR CRITICAL ANALYSIS—SOCIAL CONSIDERATION   *When a case requires a determination of such matters as community standards, summary judgment is not considered appropriate. Such matters are given to juries to determine. Why?*

Discovery

Discovery A phase in the litigation process during which the opposing parties may obtain information from each other and from third parties prior to trial.

Before a trial begins, each party can use a number of procedural devices to obtain information and gather evidence about the case from the other party or from third parties. The process of obtaining such information is known as **discovery**. Discovery includes gaining access to witnesses, documents, records, and other types of evidence.

The Federal Rules of Civil Procedure and similar rules in the states set forth the guidelines for discovery activity. The rules governing discovery are designed to make sure that a witness or a party is not unduly harassed, that privileged material (communications that need not be presented in court) is safeguarded, and that only matters relevant to the case at hand are discoverable.

Discovery prevents surprises at trial by giving parties access to evidence that might otherwise be hidden. This allows both parties to learn as much as they can about what to expect at a trial before they reach the courtroom. It also serves to narrow the issues so that trial time is spent on the main questions in the case. Currently, the trend is toward allowing more discovery and thus fewer surprises.[10]

DEPOSITIONS AND INTERROGATORIES. Discovery can involve the use of depositions or interrogatories, or both. **Depositions** are sworn testimony by a party to the lawsuit or any witness. The person being deposed (the deponent) answers questions asked by the attorneys, and the questions and answers are recorded by an authorized court official and sworn to and signed by the deponent. (Occasionally, written depositions are taken when witnesses are unable to appear in person.) The answers given to depositions will, of course, help the attorneys prepare their cases. They can also be used in court to impeach (challenge the credibility of) a party or a witness who changes testimony at the trial. In addition, the answers given in a deposition can be used as testimony if the witness is not available at trial.

Interrogatories are written questions for which written answers are prepared and then signed under oath. The main difference between interrogatories and written depositions is that interrogatories are directed to a party to the lawsuit (the plaintiff or the defendant), not to a witness, and the party can prepare answers with the aid of an attorney. The scope of interrogatories is broader, because parties are obligated to answer questions, even if it means disclosing information from their records and files.

OTHER INFORMATION. A party can serve a written request to the other party for an admission of the truth of matters relating to the trial. Any matter admitted under such a request is conclusively established for the trial. For example, Marconi can ask Anderson to admit that he was driving at a speed of forty-five miles an hour. A request for admission saves time at trial, because the parties will not have to spend time proving facts on which they already agree.

A party can also gain access to documents and other items not in his or her possession in order to inspect and examine them. Likewise, a party can gain "entry upon land" to inspect the premises. Anderson's attorney, for example, normally can gain permission to inspect and duplicate Marconi's car repair bills.

When the physical or mental condition of one party is in question, the opposing party can ask the court to order a physical or mental examination. If the court is willing to make the order, which it will do only if the need for the information outweighs the right to privacy of the person to be examined, the opposing party can obtain the results of the examination.

Pretrial Conference

Either party or the court can request a pretrial conference, or hearing. Usually, the hearing consists of an informal discussion between the judge and the opposing attorneys after discovery has taken place. The purpose of the hearing is to explore the possibility of a settlement without trial and, if this is not possible, to identify the matters that are in dispute and to plan the course of the trial.

Deposition The testimony of a party to a lawsuit or a witness taken under oath before a trial.

Interrogatories A series of written questions for which written answers are prepared and then signed under oath by a party to a lawsuit, usually with the assistance of the party's attorney.

---

10. This is particularly evident in the 1993 revision of the Federal Rules of Civil Procedure. The revised rules provide that each party must disclose to the other, on an ongoing basis, the types of evidence that will be presented at trial, the names of witnesses that may or will be called, and so on.

Jurors are sworn in. Why might a defendant want the facts in a case to be considered by a jury rather than a judge?

Jury Selection

A trial can be held with or without a jury. If there is no jury, the judge determines the truth of the facts alleged in the case. The Seventh Amendment to the U.S. Constitution guarantees the right to a jury trial for cases in federal courts when the amount in controversy exceeds $20. Most states have similar guarantees in their own constitutions (although the threshold dollar amount is usually higher than $20). The right to a trial by jury does not have to be exercised, and many cases are tried without a jury. In most states and in federal courts, one of the parties must request a jury, or the right is presumed to be waived.

Before a jury trial commences, a jury must be selected. The jury-selection process is known as *voir dire*[11] (a French phrase meaning "to speak the truth"). In most jurisdictions, the *voir dire* consists of oral questions that attorneys for the plaintiff and the defendant ask a group of prospective jurors (one at a time) to determine whether a potential jury member is biased or has any connection with a party to the action or with a prospective witness.

During *voir dire*, a party may challenge a certain number of prospective jurors *peremptorily*—that is, ask that an individual not be sworn in as a juror without providing any reason. Alternatively, a party may challenge a prospective juror *for cause*—that is, provide a reason why an individual should not be sworn in as a juror. If the judge grants the challenge, the individual is asked to step down. A prospective juror may not be excluded from the jury by the use of discriminatory challenges, however, such as those based on racial criteria[12] or gender.[13]

Voir Dire A French phrase meaning "to speak the truth." In jury trials, the phrase refers to the process in which the attorneys question prospective jurors to determine whether they are biased or have any connection with a party to the action or with a prospective witness.

---

11.   Pronounced vwahr deehr.
12.   *Batson v. Kentucky,* 476 U.S. 79, 106 S.Ct. 1712, 90 L.Ed.2d 69 (1986).
13.   *J.E.B. v. Alabama ex rel. T.B.,* 511 U.S. 127, 114 S.Ct. 1419, 128 L.Ed.2d 89 (1994). (*Ex rel.* is Latin for *ex relatione.* The phrase refers to an action brought on behalf of the state, by the attorney general, at the instigation of an individual who has a private interest in the matter.)

At the Trial

At the opening of the trial, the attorneys present their opening arguments, setting forth the facts that they expect to provide during the trial. Then the plaintiff's case is presented. In our hypothetical case, Marconi's lawyer would introduce evidence (relevant documents, exhibits, and the testimony of witnesses) to support Marconi's position. The defendant has the opportunity to challenge any evidence introduced and to cross-examine any of the plaintiff's witnesses.

At the end of the plaintiff's case, the defendant's attorney has the opportunity to ask the judge to direct a verdict for the defendant on the ground that the plaintiff has presented no evidence that would justify the granting of the plaintiff's remedy. This is called a **motion for a directed verdict** (known in federal courts as a *motion for judgment as a matter of law*). If the motion is not granted (it seldom is), the defendant's attorney then presents the evidence and witnesses for the defendant's case. The plaintiff's attorney can challenge any evidence introduced and cross-examine the defendant's witnesses.

After the defense concludes its presentation, the attorneys present their closing arguments, each urging a verdict in favor of his or her client. The judge instructs the jury in the law that applies to the case (these instructions are often called *charges*), and the jury retires to the jury room to deliberate a verdict. In the Marconi-Anderson case, the jury will not only decide for the plaintiff or for the defendant but, if it finds for the plaintiff, will also decide on the amount of the **award** (the money to be paid to her).

Posttrial Motions

After the jury has rendered its verdict, either party may make a posttrial motion. If Marconi wins, and Anderson's attorney has previously moved for a

> **"Proceed. You have my biased attention."**
>
> Learned Hand, 1872–1961 (American jurist)

Motion for a Directed Verdict In a jury trial, a motion for the judge to take the decision out of the hands of the jury and direct a verdict for the moving party on the ground that the other party has not produced sufficient evidence to support his or her claim.

Award The amount of money awarded to a plaintiff in a civil lawsuit as damages.

> **BE CAREFUL** A prospective juror cannot be excluded solely on the basis of his or her race or gender.

Ethical Perspective

Attorneys naturally want to exclude from the jury people who are unsympathetic to the client's position, and a flourishing new industry—jury consulting—has developed to help attorneys perform this task. Jury consultants decide, based on a demographic analysis of responses to pretrial surveys or other data, what kind of jurors (in terms of age, gender, education, religious background, and so on) would constitute the ideal jury. The consultant then creates questions for the attorney, who uses them during *voir dire* to exclude from the jury (through the use of peremptory challenges) persons who do not fit the "jury profile."

Do jury profiles work? Certainly many attorneys, including those who participated in the O. J. Simpson trial of 1994 to 1995, think they do. The defense retained Jo-Ellan Dimitrius of Los Angeles, who had helped select the jury that acquitted, in 1992, the four white police officers accused of beating Rodney King, an African American. Even before the Simpson trial began, observers were commenting that the mostly African American and female jury boded well for the defense—and Simpson, as it turned out, was acquitted. The prosecution retained Donald Vinson of DecisionQuest, Inc., in Los Angeles.

The growing use of jury consultants raises some disturbing ethical issues. For one thing, jury consultants are expensive, thus giving wealthier litigants a relative advantage in the courtroom. For another, they may be making the truly "impartial" jury a thing of the past.

For Critical Analysis: *In his dissent in the* Batson v. Kentucky *decision (see footnote 12), the late Justice Thurgood Marshall contended that peremptory challenges should be banned entirely. Do you agree?*

Motion for Judgment N.O.V.
A motion requesting the court to grant judgment in favor of the party making the motion on the ground that the jury verdict against him or her was unreasonable and erroneous.

Motion for a New Trial A motion asserting that the trial was so fundamentally flawed (because of error, newly discovered evidence, prejudice, or other reason) that a new trial is necessary to prevent a miscarriage of justice.

directed verdict, Anderson's attorney may make a **motion for judgment _n.o.v._** (from the Latin _non obstante veredicto,_ which means "notwithstanding the verdict"—called a _motion for judgment as a matter of law_ in the federal courts) in Anderson's favor on the ground that the jury verdict in favor of Marconi was unreasonable and erroneous. If the judge decides that the jury's verdict was reasonable in light of the evidence presented at trial, the motion will be denied. If the judge agrees with Anderson's attorney, then he or she will set the jury's verdict aside and enter a judgment in favor of Anderson.

Alternatively, Anderson could make a **motion for a new trial,** requesting the judge to set aside the adverse verdict and to hold a new trial. The motion will be granted if the judge is convinced, after looking at all the evidence, that the jury was in error but does not feel it is appropriate to grant judgment for the other side. A new trial may also be granted on the ground of newly discovered evidence, misconduct by the participants or the jury during the trial, or error by the judge. In the following case, the plaintiffs filed a motion for a new trial based on allegations of juror misconduct.

Case 3.4 ⬤ Powell v. Allstate Insurance Co.

Supreme Court of Florida, 1995.
652 So.2d 354.

HISTORICAL AND SOCIAL SETTING   _One of the principles on which the United States was founded is that all persons are created equal and are entitled to have their individual human dignity respected. This guarantee is in our federal and state constitutions, and there have been long-standing, continual efforts by legislative enactments and judicial decisions to purge our society of racial and other prejudices. Despite these efforts, however, such biases still appear to influence decisions by many people who would deny equal human dignity to those who differ from them in color, religion, or ethnic origin._

BACKGROUND AND FACTS   Derrick and Eugenia Powell, American citizens of Jamaican birth, were in an automobile

accident with another motorist, whose insurance liability policy limit was $10,000. Claiming damages in excess of $200,000, the Powells sued their own insurer, Allstate Insurance Company, in a Florida state court to recover the difference. A jury awarded Derrick $29,320 and Eugenia nothing. The next day, one of the jurors—all of whom were white—told the Powells' attorney and the judge that some of the jurors had made racial jokes and statements about the Powells during the trial and the jury deliberations. The Powells filed a motion for a new trial. The court denied the motion, and the appellate court affirmed. The Powells appealed to the Supreme Court of Florida.

IN THE WORDS OF THE COURT . . .
ANSTEAD, Justice.
    *   *   *   *

    *   *   * [W]hen appeals to racial bias are made openly among the jurors, they constitute overt acts of misconduct. *   *   * This [ruling] may not keep improper bias from being a silent factor with a particular juror, but, hopefully, it will act as a check on such bias and prevent the bias from being expressed so as to overtly influence others.

We also find the conduct alleged herein, if established, to be violative of the guarantees of both the federal and state constitutions which ensure all litigants a fair and impartial jury and equal protection of the law.

    *   *   * The obvious difficulty with prejudice in a judicial context is that it prevents the impartial decision-making that both the Sixth Amendment and

(Continued)

Case 3.4—continued

fundamental fair play require. A racially or religiously biased individual harbors certain negative stereotypes which, despite his [or her] protestations to the contrary, may well prevent him or her from making decisions based solely on the facts and law that our jury system requires.

DECISION AND REMEDY The Supreme Court of Florida held that explicit statements of racial bias made by jurors concerning the parties in a case constitute overt juror misconduct. The court remanded the case for a hearing to determine whether such statements were made about the Powells. If so, the Powells were entitled to a new trial.

FOR CRITICAL ANALYSIS—POLITICAL CONSIDERATION *The words "Equal Justice Under Law" are in marble over the entrance to the United States Supreme Court. Should the fact that this principle is not always perfectly implemented allow the courts to consciously ignore it sometimes? Why or why not?*

The Appeal

Assume here that any posttrial motion is denied, and Anderson appeals the case. (If Marconi wins but receives a smaller money award than she sought, she can appeal also.) A notice of appeal must be filed with the clerk of the trial court within a prescribed time. Anderson now becomes the appellant, or petitioner, and Marconi becomes the appellee, or respondent.

FILING THE APPEAL. Anderson's attorney files with the appellate court the record on appeal, which includes the pleadings, the trial transcript, the judge's ruling on motions made by the parties, and other trial-related documents. Anderson's attorney will also file with the reviewing court a condensation of the record, known as an abstract, which is filed with the reviewing court along with the brief. The **brief** is a formal legal document outlining the facts and issues of the case, the judge's rulings or jury's findings that should be reversed or modified, the applicable law, and arguments on Anderson's behalf (citing applicable statutes and relevant cases as precedents).

Marconi's attorney will file an answering brief. Anderson's attorney can file a reply to Marconi's brief, although it is not required. The reviewing court then considers the case.

APPELLATE REVIEW. As mentioned earlier, a court of appeals does not hear evidence. Rather, it reviews the record for errors of law. Its decision concerning a case is based on the record on appeal, the abstracts, and the attorneys' briefs. The attorneys can present oral arguments, after which the case is taken under advisement. In general, appellate courts do not reverse findings of fact unless the findings are unsupported or contradicted by the evidence.

If the reviewing court believes that an error was committed during the trial or that the jury was improperly instructed, the judgment will be *reversed*. Sometimes the case will be *remanded* (sent back to the court that originally heard the case) for a new trial. In most cases, the judgment of the lower court is *affirmed*, resulting in the enforcement of the court's judgment or decree.

If the reviewing court is an intermediate appellate court, the losing party normally may appeal to the state supreme court (the highest state court). Such a petition corresponds to a petition for a writ of *certiorari* in the United States Supreme Court. If the petition is granted, new briefs must be filed before the state supreme court, and the attorneys may be allowed or requested to present

Brief A formal legal document submitted by the attorney for the appellant or the appellee (in answer to the appellant's brief) to an appellate court when a case is appealed. The appellant's brief outlines the facts and issues of the case, the judge's rulings or jury's findings that should be reversed or modified, the applicable law, and the arguments on the client's behalf.

> **KEEP IN MIND** An appellate court generally will not overturn a lower court's decision unless there has been an error of law.

Technology and the Courtroom

Many perceive the courtroom as the last bastion of tradition. There you can expect to find gleaming hardwood floors and banisters, judges in somber robes, orderly procedures, and above all, decorum. Even the courts, however, can no longer ignore the benefits of technology. In the past decade, computers, modems, videocassette recorders (VCRs), and yards of electronic cable have slowly been bringing the courts into the modern age—for better or worse.

The Virtual Courtroom

Imagine this "courtroom" scene: A judge in Kansas City sits before several split-level computer screens and orders the trial to begin. The plaintiff and the plaintiff's attorney, sitting in the attorney's Los Angeles teleconferencing room, appear on one of the judge's screens. The defendant and the defendant's attorney, in the attorney's New York offices, appear on another. Both attorneys give their opening arguments. While presenting her case, the plaintiff's attorney has an expert witness located at a teleconferencing station in Albuquerque, New Mexico, give testimony on the plaintiff's behalf. The defendant's attorney cross-examines the witness, and the plaintiff's attorney then introduces several computerized documents as evidence. The documents appear on the other participants' screens.

The proceedings are being videotaped, and special software converts the spoken words into a written transcript. At any time during the trial, the judge or the attorneys can print out the transcript of the trial to that point. They can also access the pretrial pleadings, which were filed electronically and are instantly retrievable, as well as depositions, interrogatories, and other trial-related documents. The defense, for example, calls up a portion of a witness's deposition for the court to view on one of the screens. At the conclusion of the trial, the trial record is stored electronically and can be accessed immediately by anyone interested in the proceedings.

Into the Future

The scenario just described, of course, depicts the virtual courtroom. Although it may seem futuristic now, it will not be in the fairly near future. Already, much of the technology exists and is being demonstrated in an experimental courtroom in Williamsburg, Virginia. Set up by the Court Technology Laboratory at the National Center for State Courts in Williamsburg, the court serves as a demonstration center by vendors of what is possible.

Experiments in cyberspace trials are not confined to the United States. Germany, for example, recently held a test trial in which the plaintiff's lawyer was only virtually present—appearing on a television screen. Other tests are being planned, and some anticipate that the "cybertrial" will soon be adopted in German civil trials and labor tribunals—to save lawyers' time and clients' travel costs.

For Critical Analysis: *The virtual courtroom clearly offers many advantages to trial participants in terms of efficiency and lower costs. Are there any disadvantages? Explain.*

oral arguments. Like the intermediate appellate courts, the supreme court may reverse or affirm the appellate court's decision or remand the case. At this point, unless a federal question is at issue, the case has reached its end.

Key Terms

answer 75
award 81
bankruptcy court 65
brief 83
complaint 75
concurrent jurisdiction 68

counterclaim 75
default judgment 75
deposition 79
discovery 78
diversity of citizenship 67
exclusive jurisdiction 68

federal question 67
interrogatories 79
judicial review 62
jurisdiction 63
justiciable controversy 68
litigation 75

Chapter Summary

The American Court System

THE JUDICIARY'S ROLE IN AMERICAN GOVERNMENT (See page 62.)	The role of the judiciary—the courts—in the American governmental system is to interpret and apply the law. Through the process of judicial review—determining the constitutionality of laws—the judicial branch acts as a check on the executive and legislative branches of government. The power of judicial review was established by Chief Justice John Marshall in *Marbury v. Madison* (1803).
BASIC JUDICIAL REQUIREMENTS (See pages 62–70.)	1. **Jurisdiction**—Before a court can hear a case, it must have jurisdiction over the person against whom the suit is brought or the property involved in the suit, as well as jurisdiction over the subject matter. a. Limited versus general jurisdiction—Limited jurisdiction exists when a court is limited to a specific subject matter, such as probate or divorce. General jurisdiction exists when a court can hear any kind of case. b. Original versus appellate jurisdiction—Original jurisdiction exists with courts that have authority to hear a case for the first time (trial courts). Appellate jurisdiction exists with courts of appeals, or reviewing courts; generally, appellate courts do not have original jurisdiction. c. Federal jurisdiction—Arises (1) when a federal question is involved (when the plaintiff's cause of action is based, at least in part, on the U.S. Constitution, a treaty, or a federal law) or (2) when a case involves diversity of citizenship (citizens of different states, for example), and the amount in controversy exceeds \$50,000. d. Concurrent versus exclusive jurisdiction—Concurrent jurisdiction exists when two different courts have authority to hear the same case. Exclusive jurisdiction exists when only state courts or only federal courts have authority to hear a case. 2. **Venue**—Venue has to do with the most appropriate location for a trial, which is usually the geographical area in which the event leading to the dispute took place or where the parties reside. 3. **Standing to sue**—A requirement that a party must have a legally protected and tangible interest at stake sufficient to justify seeking relief through the court system. The controversy at issue must also be a justiciable controversy—one that is real and substantial, as opposed to hypothetical or academic.
THE STATE AND FEDERAL COURT SYSTEMS (See pages 70–74.)	1. **Trial courts**—Courts of original jurisdiction, in which legal actions are initiated. a. State—Courts of general jurisdiction can hear any case; courts of limited jurisdiction include divorce courts, probate courts, traffic courts, small claims courts, and so on.

Chapter Summary, continued

<table>
<tr>
<td>

THE STATE AND FEDERAL COURT SYSTEMS—continued
(See pages 70–74.)

</td>
<td>

b. Federal—The federal district court is the equivalent of the state trial court. Federal courts of limited jurisdiction include the U.S. Tax Court, the U.S. Bankruptcy Court, and the U.S. Court of Federal Claims.

2. **Intermediate appellate courts**—Courts of appeals, or reviewing courts; generally without original jurisdiction. Many states have an intermediate appellate court; in the federal court system, the U.S. circuit courts of appeals are the intermediate appellate courts.

3. **Supreme (highest) courts**—Each state has a supreme court, although it may be called by some other name, from which appeal to the United States Supreme Court is only possible if a federal question is involved. The United States Supreme Court is the highest court in the federal court system and the final arbiter of the Constitution and federal law.

</td>
</tr>
<tr>
<td>

PROCEDURAL RULES
(See pages 74–84.)

</td>
<td>

Rules of procedure prescribe the way in which disputes are handled in the courts. Rules differ from court to court, and separate sets of rules exist for federal and state courts, as well as for criminal and civil cases. A sample civil court case in a state court would involve the following procedures:

1. **The pleadings**—

   a. **Complaint**—Filed by the plaintiff with the court to initiate the lawsuit; served with a summons on the defendant.

   b. **Answer**—Admits or denies allegations made by the plaintiff; may assert a counterclaim or an affirmative defense.

   c. **Motion to dismiss**—A request to the court to dismiss the case for stated reasons, such as the plaintiff's failure to state a claim for which relief can be granted.

2. **Pretrial motions (in addition to the motion to dismiss)**—

   a. **Motion for judgment on the pleadings**—May be made by either party; will be granted if the parties agree on the facts and the only question is how the law applies to the facts. The judge bases the decision solely on the pleadings.

   b. **Motion for summary judgment**—May be made by either party; will be granted if the parties agree on the facts. The judge applies the law in rendering a judgment. The judge can consider evidence outside the pleadings when evaluating the motion.

3. **Discovery**—The process of gathering evidence concerning the case. Discovery involves depositions (sworn testimony by a party to the lawsuit or any witness), interrogatories (written questions and answers to these questions made by parties to the action with the aid of their attorneys), and various requests (for admissions, documents, medical examination, and so on).

4. **Pretrial conference**—Either party or the court can request a pretrial conference to identify the matters in dispute after discovery has taken place and to plan the course of the trial.

5. **Trial**—Following jury selection (*voir dire*), the trial begins with opening statements from both parties' attorneys. The following events then occur:

   a. The plaintiff's introduction of evidence (including the testimony of witnesses) supporting the plaintiff's position. The defendant's attorney can challenge evidence and cross-examine witnesses.

   b. The defendant's introduction of evidence (including the testimony of witnesses) supporting the defendant's position. The plaintiff's attorney can challenge evidence and cross-examine witnesses.

</td>
</tr>
</table>

Chapter Summary, continued

**PROCEDURAL RULES
continued**
(See pages 74–84.)

c. Closing arguments by attorneys in favor of their respective clients, the judge's instructions to the jury, and the jury's verdict.

6. **Posttrial motions**—

   a. Motion for judgment *n.o.v.* ("notwithstanding the verdict")—Will be granted if the judge is convinced that the jury was in error.

   b. Motion for a new trial—Will be granted if the judge is convinced that the jury was in error; can also be granted on the grounds of newly discovered evidence, misconduct by the participants during the trial, or error by the judge.

7. **Appeal**—Either party can appeal the trial court's judgment to an appropriate court of appeals. After reviewing the record on appeal, the abstracts, and the attorneys' briefs, the appellate court holds a hearing and renders its opinion.

For Review

1. What is judicial review? How and when was the power of judicial review established?

2. Before a court can hear a case, it must have jurisdiction. Over what must it have jurisdiction? In what circumstances does a federal court have jurisdiction?

3. What is the difference between a trial court and an appellate court?

4. In a lawsuit, what are the pleadings? What is discovery?

5. What are the steps involved in an appeal?

Questions and Case Problems

3–1. Courts of Appeals. Appellate courts normally see only written transcripts of trial proceedings when they are reviewing cases. Today, in some states, videotapes are being used as the official trial reports. If the use of videotapes as official reports continues, will this alter the appellate process? Should it? Discuss fully.

3–2. Discovery. In the past, the rules of discovery were very restrictive, and trials often turned on elements of surprise. For example, a plaintiff would not necessarily know until the trial what the defendant's defense was going to be. Within the last twenty-five years, however, new rules of discovery have substantially changed all this. Now each attorney can discover practically all the evidence that the other will be presenting at trial, with the exception of certain information—namely, the opposing attorney's work product. *Work product* is not a clear concept. Basically, it includes all the attorney's thoughts on

the case. Can you see any reason why such information should not be made available to the opposing attorney? Discuss fully.

3–3. Motions. When and for what purpose are each of the following motions made? Which of them would be appropriate if a defendant claimed that the only issue between the parties was a question of law and that the law was favorable to the defendant's position?

   (a) A motion for judgment on the pleadings.

   (b) A motion for a directed verdict.

   (c) A motion for summary judgment.

   (d) A motion for judgment *n.o.v.*

3–4. Peremptory Challenges. During *voir dire*, the parties or their attorneys select those persons who will serve as jurors during the trial. The parties are prohibited, however, from excluding potential jurors on the basis of race or other discriminatory criteria. An issue concerns whether the prohibition against discrimination extends to potential jurors who have physical or mental disabilities. Federal law prohibits discrimination against an otherwise qualified person with a disability when that person could be accommodated without too much difficulty. Should this law also apply to the jury-selection process? For example, should parties be prohibited from excluding blind persons, through either challenges for cause or peremptory challenges, from serving on juries? Discuss.

3–5. Jurisdiction. Marya Callais, a citizen of Florida, was walking near a busy street in Tallahassee, Florida, one day when a large crate flew off a passing truck and hit her, resulting in numerous injuries. She incurred a great deal of pain and suffering, plus significant medical expenses, and she could not work for six months. She wanted to sue the trucking firm for $300,000 in damages. The firm's headquarters were in Georgia, although the company did business in Florida. In what court might Callais bring suit—a Florida state court, a Georgia state court, or a federal court? What factors might influence her decision?

3–6. Motion to Dismiss. Martin brought a civil rights action against his employer, the New York Department of Mental Hygiene, when it failed to promote him on several occasions. His complaint stated only that the defendant had discriminated against him on the basis of race by denying him "the authority, salary, and privileges commensurate with this position." The employer made a motion to dismiss the claim for failure to state a cause of action. Discuss whether the employer could be successful. [*Martin v. New York State Department of Mental Hygiene,* 588 F.2d 371 (2d Cir. 1978)]

3–7. Jury Trials. On June 16, 1986, the director of the Administrative Office of the U.S. Courts notified all federal district courts that no civil jury trials could be initiated until the end of the fiscal year (September 30) due to lack of funds with which to pay the jurors. Armster and others claimed that the consequent delay (of three and a half months) in scheduling a jury trial violated the Seventh Amendment right to a civil jury trial. The Justice Department maintained that although the Sixth Amendment guarantees a speedy *criminal* jury trial, the Seventh Amendment does not guarantee a speedy *civil* jury trial. The Justice Department further noted that district courts have postponed civil jury trials before, although for other reasons—such as court-calendar congestion, the lack of a sufficient number of judges, and the priority accorded to trying criminal cases before civil actions. Discuss whether the suspension of civil jury trials for a period of three and a half months due to lack of funds to pay jurors violates the constitutional right to a trial by jury. Are people always entitled to a jury trial in civil lawsuits? [*Armster v. U.S. District Court for the Central District of California,* 792 F.2d 1423 (9th Cir. 1986)]

3–8. Jurisdiction. George Rush, a New York resident and columnist for the New York *Daily News,* wrote a critical column about Berry Gordy, the founder and former president of Motown Records. Gordy, a California resident, filed suit in a California state court against Rush and the newspaper (the defendants), alleging defamation (a civil wrong, or tort, that occurs when the publication of false statements harms a person's good reputation). Most of the newspaper's subscribers are in the New York area, and the paper covers mostly New York events. Thirteen copies of its daily edition are distributed to California subscribers, however, and the paper does cover events that are of nationwide interest to the entertainment industry. Because of its focus on entertainment, the newspaper also routinely sends reporters to California to gather news from California sources. Can a California state court exercise personal jurisdiction over the New York defendants in this case? What factors will the court consider in deciding this question? If you were the judge, how would you decide the issue, and why? Discuss fully. [*Gordy v. Daily News, L.P.,* 95 F.3d 829 (9th Cir. 1996)]

3–9. Motion for a New Trial. Washoe Medical Center, Inc., admitted Shirley Swisher for the treatment of a fractured pelvis. During her stay, Swisher suffered a fatal fall from her hospital bed. Gerald Parodi, the administrator of her estate, and others filed an action against Washoe in which they sought damages for the alleged lack of care in treating Swisher. During *voir dire,* when the plaintiffs' attorney returned a few minutes late from a break, the trial judge led the prospective jurors in a standing ovation. The judge joked with one of the prospective jurors, whom he had known in college, about the judge's fitness to serve as a judge and personally endorsed another prospective juror's business. After the trial, the jury returned a verdict in favor of Washoe. The plaintiffs moved for a new trial, but the judge denied the motion. The plaintiffs then appealed, arguing that the tone set by the judge during *voir dire* prejudiced their right to a fair trial. Should the appellate court agree? Why or why not? [*Parodi v. Washoe Medical Center, Inc.,* 111 Nev. 365, 892 P.2d 588 (1995)]

A Question of Ethics and Social Responsibility

3–10. The state of Alabama, on behalf of a mother (T.B.), brought a paternity suit against the alleged father (J.E.B.) of T.B.'s child. During jury selection, the state, through peremptory challenges, removed nine of the ten prospective male jurors. J.E.B.'s attorney struck the final male from the jury pool. As a result of these peremptory strikes, the final jury consisted of twelve women. When the jury returned a verdict in favor of the mother, the father appealed. The father argued that eliminating men from the jury constituted gender discrimination and violated his rights to equal protection and due process (see Chapter 5). The father requested the court to extend the principle enunciated in *Batson v. Kentucky* (cited in footnote 12 of this chapter), which prohibited peremptory strikes based solely on race, to include gender-based strikes. The appellate court refused to do so. [*J.E.B. v. Alabama ex rel. T.B.*, 511 U.S. 127, 114 S.Ct. 1419, 128 L.Ed.2d 89 (1994)]

1. Do you agree with J.E.B. that the state's exercise of its peremptory challenges violated this right to equal protection and due process? Why or why not?
2. If you were the judge, how would you rule?
3. The late Supreme Court Justice Thurgood Marshall urged, when the Court was reviewing the *Batson* case, that peremptory challenges be banned entirely. Do you agree with this proposal? Discuss.

For Critical Analysis

3–11. American courts are forums for adversarial justice, in which attorneys defend the interests of their respective clients before the court. This means that an attorney may end up claiming before a court that his or her client is innocent, even though the attorney knows that the client acted wrongfully. Is it ethical for attorneys to try to "deceive" the court in these situations? Can the adversarial system of justice really lead to "truth"?

INTERACTING WITH The Internet

■ Go to the West's Legal Studies Home Page at

http://www.westblusaw.com

There you will find a variety of legal resources. Visit us often!

■ Numerous rules of procedure and evidence frame the litigation process. If you are interested in learning more about these rules, you can look at the Federal Rules of Civil Procedure (FRCP) and the Federal Rules of Evidence (FRE), both of which are now on the Internet. The FRCP and the FRE can be found at

http://www.cornell.edu/

■ The federal district courts also have local rules that govern their procedures, although these rules are available online for only a few courts. You can access the local rules for the following federal courts by using the Internet addresses given here:

The U.S. District Court for the District of Colorado:

http://www.usa.net/cololaw/features/fedrules.htm

The U.S. District Courts for the Southern and Eastern Districts of New York (Joint Local Rules):

http://www.ljextra.com/courthouse/fedrules.html

■ Procedural rules for several of the state courts are now also online. You can access the rules for selected state courts at the following addresses:

Alaska Rules of Civil Procedure:

http://www.alaska.net/~akctlib/homepage.htm

California Code of Civil Procedure:

http://www.calbar.org/pub250/relst3.htm

Indiana Code of Civil Procedure:

http://www.law.indiana.edu/codes/in/incode.html

New York Civil Practice Law and Rules:

http://www.law.cornell.edu/ny/statutes/cplr.htm

Washington Code of Civil Procedure:

http://leginfo.leg.wa.gov/pub/rcw/title_04

Wyoming Rules of Civil Procedure:

http://courts.state.wy.us/rules.htm

■ For information on attorneys, you can look at the *Martindale-Hubbell Law Directory*, which is available online at

http://www.martindale.com

This directory lists the names, addresses, telephone numbers, areas of legal practice, and other data for more than 900,000 lawyers and law firms in the United States.

■ For an example of a typical set of state rules governing attorney conduct, you can access Idaho's Rules of Professional Conduct Governing Lawyers at

http://www.law.cornell.edu:80/lawyers/ruletable.html

CHAPTER 4

Legal Representation and Alternative Dispute Resolution

Contents

Chapter Objectives

After reading this chapter, you should be able to . . .

1. Describe the role of attorneys in the dispute-resolution process.
2. List the differences between litigation and the other forms of dispute resolution.
3. Discuss the processes of negotiation and mediation.
4. Identify the steps in the arbitration process.
5. Define summary jury trials and mini-trials.

90

Despite Bentham's sentiments to the contrary (expressed in the quotation alongside), all persons, *including* lawyers, are expected to know the law so as to conduct themselves in an appropriate manner. Laws are passed to promote the public welfare. Every law implicitly or explicitly recognizes a particular legal right or punishes a specific kind of behavior. Some laws restrict the actions of individuals, while others authorize persons to behave in a certain way. Each law necessarily involves a parceling out of rights and duties. Often the same person possesses both rights and duties, but the rights are useless unless persons who are deprived of them or who are otherwise injured can be compensated for the injury. Because there is no mechanism in our legal system that automatically transfers assets from a wrongdoer to the victim, victims must insist that their legal rights be enforced if they are to have any hope of recovering damages—usually in the form of a cash payment—for their injuries.

> **"Lawyers are the only persons in whom ignorance of the law is not punished."**
>
> Jeremy Bentham, 1748–1832 (British philosopher)

Attorneys and Dispute Resolution

When a person has suffered an injury for which he or she seeks compensation, that person may wish to seek the advice of an **attorney**. An attorney is a person who has received a law degree and has been licensed by one or more states to practice law. An attorney is often hired to represent the interests of a client in a legal proceeding or to review particular legal documents, such as a contract to purchase or lease a home. Despite the diversity of legal issues that attorneys may confront on a day-to-day basis, they share a common approach to the law because their education nearly always involves an in-depth study of basic legal principles and concepts, rather than a memorization of existing laws (which frequently change). Consequently, all attorneys use similar research and analytical techniques.

Attorney A person who has received a law degree and has been licensed by one or more states to practice law.

The Roles of an Attorney

An attorney must fulfill several different roles to represent the interests of a client effectively. Although law-school training provides a general background from which to approach a given legal matter and research the law, attorneys also research the extent to which the client's position is supported by that law. The attorney must also verify that the facts support the client's position. In a legal matter involving illegal activities, the attorney may uncover evidence that contradicts the client's position or even directly implicates the client in criminal activity. In such cases, the attorney is not required to disclose the client's complicity, but the attorney may not knowingly assist the client in any way that would facilitate the perpetration of a crime.

ADVISER.   If a client comes to an attorney for advice on how to avoid a particular problem in the future, the attorney will counsel the client as to what practices should be changed and what measures should be taken to head off potential problems. Here the attorney will find it necessary to practice **preventive law** and play the role of adviser, spotting possible legal land mines before they harm the client. Because there is more than one way to deal with most legal problems, the attorney will have to investigate the full range of possible solutions and then suggest a preferred alternative.

Preventive Law The law that an attorney practices when he or she plays the role of an adviser for a client, spotting possible legal problems and suggesting preventive measures before the problems harm the client.

For example, Primo Electronics wants to buy fifty Adco computers from Wadel Wholesalers, Inc. Wadel is willing to sell. Wadel agrees to ship the computers to Primo, but Wadel does not want to pay for any damage to the computers that may occur while they are in transit. Wadel's attorney might suggest that Wadel obtain insurance to cover the risk of any damage to the computers. The attorney might alternatively suggest that a clause be included in the contract under which Primo agrees to assume the risk of damage.

DRAFTER.   Because the attorney must handle a client's legal affairs, the attorney may be called on to draft documents and instruments ranging from leases and contracts to promissory notes and mortgages. Words are the lawyer's tools. Most attorneys will find that they must familiarize themselves with several areas of the law to draft competent documents. The form of a document, particularly the extent to which it complies with certain legal formalities, may be as important as the document's content. Yet an attorney cannot draft a document for a client without knowing something about the content and the client's goals and objectives. In the case of a corporate client, the attorney will often find that he or she can draft a more effective document by becoming familiar with the corporation's operations and future plans.

Thus, Wadel's attorney can draft a more effective contract by knowing that Wadel wishes to avoid liability for any damage to the Adco computers while they are being shipped to Primo. If the attorney knows that Wadel wishes to avoid liability in all similar future transactions, the attorney might draft a basic contract form that Wadel could use in the Primo deal and in future transactions.

NEGOTIATOR.   The attorney is often required to negotiate the terms of a particular agreement or settlement on behalf of his or her client. Negotiation is the art of persuasion. The attorney must marshal the strongest arguments in

An attorney advises her client. Can an attorney's skill as an advocate and an advisor have more effect than the facts in a client's case?

favor of the client and bring them to bear on the opposing side to produce the most favorable results. Most transactions involving significant sums of money are preceded by lengthy negotiations in which the terms of the deal and any accompanying details are hammered out. Although the client may choose to conduct certain business negotiations without the attorney present, the client will want to confer with the attorney throughout the course of the negotiations. A properly negotiated contract can avoid many legal disputes and costs in the future.

ADVOCATE.   Sometimes a lawyer must represent a client in court. If two parties are unable to resolve their dispute over a particular matter—such as whether the delivery of a defective item should obligate the buyer to pay for that item—then they may wish to solve their problem in court. Both parties will usually hire attorneys to present their respective positions to a jury. This advocacy role is perhaps the most demanding one for attorneys to fulfill because the litigation of even minor claims requires that the attorney be prepared to deal with any potential problems, ranging from witnesses who knowingly offer false testimony to a last-minute revelation of damaging evidence. A court proceeding, particularly one that involves high stakes, can be mentally and emotionally draining. The successful advocate will maintain the necessary presence of mind to deal with or minimize any problems that may arise.

The Attorney-Client Relationship

For many individuals and businesses, relationships with attorneys last for decades. Thus, it is important that clients seek attorneys who are knowledgeable in the areas of the law that are needed to address their concerns. The client and attorney should communicate well—the attorney should perceive which issues are of foremost concern to the client and address those issues. The attorney should keep the client informed of developments in the law that affect the client's concerns. Most important, the attorney should advise the client of possible actions to take and then act according to the client's choice.

SELECTING AN ATTORNEY.   In some situations, attorneys are allowed to include information about their areas of specialization in advertisements aimed at the general public. Also, a person interested in pursuing a legal claim should ask friends or relatives to recommend an attorney. If they cannot suggest an attorney who practices in the desired area of law, then the person can call the local or state bar association to obtain the names of several lawyers. If this approach proves unsatisfactory, then the local telephone directory may be scanned for possible selections. If all these steps are unsuccessful, then a professional directory should be consulted. Most libraries have copies of the *Martindale-Hubbell Law Directory*, which features professional biographies of nearly all the attorneys engaged in private practice throughout the country; the listings also include areas of concentration, as well as bank references and representative clients. *Martindale-Hubbell Law Directory* and other sources for selecting an attorney can be found on the Internet.

ESTABLISHING THE RELATIONSHIP.   Having selected an attorney, the client should make an appointment to see the attorney as soon as possible. Even a company that maintains an in-house attorney usually seeks outside counsel

> **"A lawyer's opinion is worth nothing unless paid for."**
>
> (Proverb)

when the matter involves a particular area of expertise outside the range of the company attorney. Undue delay may cost the client the opportunity of pursuing legal action or may, alternatively, increase the potential liability of the client. Although it is preferable that a client consult a lawyer before becoming involved in a legal dispute, many people put off the decision to hire a lawyer until the matter has become aggravated. In many cases, this procrastination will prevent a simple, relatively inexpensive solution to the matter.

Once the decision to hire the attorney has been made, the client must disclose any relevant information so that the attorney can formulate the strongest possible plan of attack or the best defense.

THE ATTORNEY-CLIENT PRIVILEGE.   Attorneys can best serve their clients only when they know all the relevant facts. The **attorney-client privilege** protects any relevant confidential communications from compelled disclosure—that is, courts and other government institutions cannot require that the communications be disclosed. The privilege protects communications between an attorney and client made for the purpose of furnishing or obtaining professional legal advice or assistance. Thus, as long as the client's present legal matters are being discussed, the attorney cannot reveal the contents of these discussions even if, for example, the client confesses to having committed a string of robberies in the past.

This privilege may be waived only by the client. This privilege may not be claimed if the conversation takes place in the presence of a nonessential third person, such as a janitor or courier. Even though the client's spouse may not be needed, his or her presence will not affect the attorney-client privilege. Similarly, this privilege will continue to exist if the attorney's secretary hears the conversations because the secretary will play a key role in the preparation of the case.

The Role of the Court

The adversarial nature of our legal system pits the attorneys for the opposing parties against each other; the assumption is that the search for the truth will best be facilitated by the presentation of competing arguments and evidence. The dispute must be a real one, however, in which tangible injury has been suffered or there is an immediate threat of harm; the courts will not consider hypothetical questions. For example, a court will hear a dispute between you and your neighbor over whether his weekend barbecues constitute a nuisance that should be stopped. The court will not entertain questions of law relating to nuisances from two persons who are interested purely in discussing the law's theoretical implications.

Although the courts allow attorneys great leeway in defining the issues and presenting the relevant evidence, the court itself is responsible for making sure that the trial is conducted in a proper and dignified manner. The court does not usually interview witnesses or ask many questions about particular evidence, but it will prevent the parties from straying too far from the issues being litigated. It will also monitor the methods used by the attorneys in questioning witnesses and rule on various motions made by the attorneys regarding, for example, the introduction of new evidence. Although the role of the jury is to determine the relevant facts in a case, the judge, by virtue of the instruc-

Attorney-Client Privilege
Protected communications between an attorney and client made for the purpose of furnishing or obtaining professional legal advice or assistance. Courts and other government institutions cannot require disclosure of the communications.

A judge listens as an attorney appeals to the jury during a trial. Can a judge in a jury trial influence the outcome of the case? In what way? Should an individual or a company consider such factors when deciding whether to file a lawsuit?

tions that he or she gives to the jury members before they begin deliberating a **verdict**, determines in part whether those facts support the position of the plaintiff or the defendant.

The Decision to File a Lawsuit

Before an individual or a company decides to file a complaint and thus initiate legal proceedings against a defendant, it must be determined, in consultation with an attorney, (1) whether the law provides an adequate remedy for the claim, (2) who can reasonably be expected to prevail in the lawsuit, and (3) whether the expected benefit is sufficient to compensate for any costs and expenses as well as any lost business.

In deciding whether to pursue a legal claim or right, the prospective **litigant** must consider a number of questions that relate not only to the desirability of the suit itself but also to whether such an action will help or hinder the person's long-term objectives. Filing a lawsuit may permanently rupture a long-standing personal or business relationship, so careful attention will have to be given to whether the expected gains resulting from a successful court case outweigh the potential costs. Any such cost-benefit analysis is further muddied when both parties have strong legal support for their particular positions. In such cases, the verdict may turn on a party's demeanor or some other irrelevant factor. Although an attorney will take all reasonable measures to present the strongest possible case on behalf of a client, there are other factors, such as the client's appearance or voice, that are beyond the control of even the most talented attorney.

ADEQUACY OF THE REMEDY.   The fact that a company has been adversely affected by the actions of a competitor will not necessarily give rise to a claim for **damages**, because the law grants remedies only for certain types of conduct. In general, the courts will not grant a particular type of relief simply because a company wishes to be insulated from the pressures of a competitive market. Suppose that the Sparkling Cola Company is able to convince Red Castle, a nationwide chain of fast-food restaurants, to use its cola products instead of those offered by Red Castle's long-time supplier, the Effervescent Cola Company, based on favorable consumer taste tests and Sparkling's willingness to undersell Effervescent. Effervescent will probably not be able to sue Sparkling for interfering with its contractual relationship with Red Castle simply because it lost a customer to a competitor having a better product.

In contrast, if Sparkling convinces Red Castle to stop using Effervescent's products by spreading false rumors about the quality of the products or labor problems at Effervescent's manufacturing plants, then Effervescent can seek to recover damages from Sparkling based on a variety of legal theories, including defamation and wrongful interference with a contractual relationship (discussed in Chapters 8 and 9). In such a situation, it would clearly be in Effervescent's interest to seek damages, because Sparkling might otherwise continue spreading false rumors about its products to Effervescent's remaining customers.

CHANCES OF WINNING THE SUIT.   Once Effervescent has determined that there is a remedy for the particular injury it has suffered, it must then attempt to determine the likelihood that it will be able to win the lawsuit. Although jury

Verdict A formal decision made by a jury.

Litigant A party to a lawsuit.

Damages Money sought as a remedy for a breach of contract or for a tortious act.

trials always have an element of unpredictability (jurors may disregard important facts and give undue weight to trivial facts), any assessment by Effervescent of its chances of prevailing in court will depend on the applicable laws and the outcomes of any factually similar cases. Effervescent and its attorney will also have to consider whether there is enough evidence to convince a court to rule in its favor and whether Sparkling can offer any **defenses**, or excuses, to justify its actions. Finally, Effervescent will have to consider whether its own actions could significantly reduce its chances of prevailing in court.

Defense That which a defendant offers and alleges in an action or suit as a reason why the plaintiff should not recover or establish what he or she seeks.

VALUE OF THE REMEDY.   Assuming that Effervescent and its attorney have determined that they stand a very good chance of winning their suit against Sparkling, they will then have to decide whether the relief that they would probably receive is worth the time and expense of the litigation.

Legal Fees   One factor that Effervescent must consider is, of course, the cost of the attorney's time—the legal fees that it will have to pay to collect damages from the defendant. Attorneys base their fees on such factors as the difficulty of a matter, the amount of time involved, the experience and skill of the attorney in the particular area of the law, and the cost of doing business. In the United States, legal fees range from $60 per hour to $450 per hour (the average fee per hour is between $140 and $160). Not included in attorneys' fees are such expenses as court filing charges and other costs directly related to a case.

A particular legal matter may include one or a combination of several types of fees. *Fixed fees* may be charged for the performance of such services as drafting a simple will. *Hourly fees* may be computed for matters that involve an indeterminate period of time. Any case brought to trial, for example, may involve an expenditure of time that cannot be precisely estimated in advance. *Contingent fees* are fixed as a percentage (between 25 and 40 percent) of a client's recovery in certain types of lawsuits, such as personal injury. If the lawsuit is unsuccessful, the attorney receives no fee. The client will, however, have to pay the court fees and any other expenses incurred by the attorney (such as travel expenses, copying expenses, and so on—often called out-of-pocket costs) on the client's behalf.

Many state and federal statutes allow for an award of attorneys' fees in certain legal actions, such as probate matters. In these cases, a judge sets the amount of the fee, based on such factors as the results obtained by the attorney and the fee customarily charged for similar services. In some cases, a client may receive an award of attorneys' fees as part of his or her recovery.

Settlement Considerations   A client's decision as to how much money he or she can afford to invest in the resolution of a particular legal problem is frequently the most important factor in determining the extent to which an attorney will pursue a resolution. If a client decides that he or she can afford a lengthy trial and one or more appeals, an attorney may pursue those actions. Often, once a client learns the extent of the costs involved in litigating a claim, he or she will be more willing to settle the claim instead of going to trial.

If the litigation is expected to be extremely costly, then Effervescent may wish to consider alternative approaches, such as settling with Sparkling out of court, submitting the dispute to a third party (not a member of the judiciary), or doing nothing at all. Effervescent will also have to decide whether Sparkling has the financial resources to satisfy a court judgment and whether the enforcement of the judgment will be excessively expensive.

The Decision to Defend against a Lawsuit

The plaintiff is not the only one that must consider the merits of becoming involved in a lawsuit. The defendant does not usually wish to be involved in a lawsuit, and there are a number of issues that the defendant must consider before deciding to battle the plaintiff in court. These issues include (1) whether the relationship it has with the plaintiff is too valuable to risk by becoming involved in an adversarial proceeding, (2) whether the publicity surrounding a trial would appreciably damage its reputation or image, and (3) whether the claim can be settled in a less costly manner.

VALUE OF A BUSINESS RELATIONSHIP.   In some cases, the defendant will not have to worry about the potential disruption of any business relationship because it has no commercial relationship with the plaintiff. But even in the case of a competitor, a company might be reluctant to become involved in litigation because of the effect a court battle might have on possible joint ventures or mutually beneficial research and development programs. Because Sparkling is highly competitive with Effervescent, it is not likely to place a very high value on the effect a vigorous courtroom defense will have on its relationship. Consequently, Sparkling will be more inclined to consider litigation as a viable strategy for resolving the dispute. The story might be very different if the suit were filed by Bob's Beef Wagon, a regional restaurant chain and long-time purchaser of Sparkling products. In that situation, Sparkling would consider the value of Bob's business very seriously and investigate alternative solutions before deciding to become involved in a court trial.

POTENTIAL DAMAGE TO A COMPANY'S REPUTATION.   Because trials are public proceedings, they may be covered, if the case is sufficiently noteworthy, by newspaper, magazine, radio, and television journalists. This means that any statements made by either side, as well as any testimony or evidence, may be publicized by the media. If the case between Effervescent and Sparkling involves numerous unflattering allegations regarding unethical business practices and poor product quality, then Sparkling will have to consider the likelihood that these charges will be publicized throughout the country. Sparkling's attorney may also remind the company that the charges themselves—rather than the actual truth of the charges—will dominate the media coverage. Furthermore, Sparkling will have to consider the harm to its image as a model corporate citizen that might result from a verdict for the plaintiff (Effervescent). In general, the cost of satisfying a judgment might understate the true cost of the legal dispute, because the publicity might negate the positive public image that Sparkling has achieved through its advertising campaigns.

OTHER FORMS OF RESOLUTION.   Even though Sparkling may have been served with a complaint by Effervescent's attorney, this does not preclude Sparkling from exploring alternative methods of settling the dispute. These methods include an out-of-court settlement. The attractiveness of an out-of-court settlement may be directly related to the amount of publicity given to the case and its effect on public attitudes toward the company. Because the terms of out-of-court settlements are normally not made available to the public, they provide a means by which a company may "buy" its way out of a lawsuit and avoid the attendant publicity. Of course, Sparkling's receptiveness to an out-of-court settlement would depend on its own perception about the strength of its case. If it believes that Effervescent has filed the lawsuit merely to harass it, then it might prefer to risk litigating the claims.

Alternatively, Sparkling might propose to Effervescent that they submit the matter to arbitration. In *arbitration*, which will be discussed more fully later in this chapter, the parties agree to let a neutral third party decide the issue. Both parties might prefer arbitration as a solution for avoiding the incessant delays and higher costs of courtroom litigation. Because the terms of the arbitration agreement would not be released to the public, both companies could avoid having their images sullied by the press.

The Search for Alternatives to Litigation

A number of solutions have been proposed, and some have been implemented, to reduce the congestion in our court system and to reduce the litigation costs facing all members of society. The enforcement of arbitration clauses, the use of court-referred arbitration and mediation, and the emergence of an increasing number of private forums for dispute resolution have all helped to reduce the caseload of the courts.

Another possible solution to the problem involves putting caps on damage awards, particularly for pain and suffering. Without the probability of obtaining multimillion-dollar judgments for pain and suffering, some potential litigants will be deterred from undertaking lawsuits to obtain damages. Another avenue of attack is to penalize those who bring frivolous lawsuits. Rule 11 of the Federal Rules of Civil Procedure allows for disciplinary sanctions against lawyers and litigants who bring frivolous lawsuits in federal courts.

Many courts require mediation or arbitration before a case goes to trial. There are proposals to reduce delay and expenses in federal civil cases further, and pro-

The parties to a controversy and their attorneys negotiate to resolve the dispute. When should a third party be brought in to mediate?

posals are being considered by the states as well. Some of the proposals can be viewed as case-management plans. One proposal, for example, would require each federal district court to implement procedures for placing cases on different tracks, with simple cases being handled more quickly than complex ones.

Politics and Law

Because reforms of any system affect individuals and groups differently, they seldom are accomplished easily and quickly. Reform of the court system is a prime example. At the federal level, members of Congress long have been concerned with bringing court costs and delay under control. These concerns gave rise to the enactment of legislation in the early 1990s that required the federal courts to develop a plan to cut costs and reduce delay within the federal judicial system.

New Methods and Arrangements

The search for alternative means to resolve disputes has produced several distinct methods and arrangements. These range from neighbors' sitting down over a cup of coffee to work out their differences to huge multinational corporations' agreeing to resolve a dispute through a formal hearing before a panel of experts. All of these alternatives to traditional litigation make up what is broadly termed alternative dispute resolution.

Alternative dispute resolution (ADR) describes any procedure or device for resolving disputes other than the traditional judicial process. ADR is normally a less expensive and less time-consuming process than formal litigation. In some cases, it also has the advantage of being more private. Except in cases involving court-annexed arbitration (discussed later in this chapter), no public record of ADR proceedings is created; only the parties directly involved are privy to the information presented during the process. This is a particularly important consideration in many business disputes, because such cases may involve sensitive commercial information.

Alternative Dispute Resolution (ADR) The resolution of disputes in ways other than those involved in the traditional judicial process. Negotiation, mediation, and arbitration are forms of ADR.

Negotiation and Mediation

Alternative dispute resolution methods differ in the degree of formality involved and the extent to which third parties participate in the process. Generally, negotiation is the least formal method and involves no third parties. Mediation may be similarly informal but does involve the participation of a third party.

Negotiation

In the process of negotiation, the parties come together informally, with or without attorneys to represent them. Within this informal setting, the parties air their differences and try to reach a settlement or resolution without the involvement of independent third parties. Because no third parties are involved and because of the informal setting, negotiation is the simplest form of ADR. Even if a lawsuit has been initiated, the parties may continue to negotiate their differences and settle their dispute at any time during the litigation process.

PREPARATION FOR NEGOTIATION.   Because so many disputes are settled through negotiation, in spite of the informality of this means of dispute resolution, each party must carefully prepare his or her side of the case. The elements of the dispute should be considered, documents and other evidence should be collected, and witnesses should be prepared to testify. Negotiating from a well-prepared position improves the odds of obtaining a favorable result. Even if a dispute is not resolved through negotiation, preparation for negotiation will reduce the effort required to get ready for the next step in the dispute resolution process.

"ASSISTED NEGOTIATION."   To facilitate negotiation, various forms of what might be called "assisted negotiation" have been employed. Forms of ADR associated with the negotiation process include mini-trials and early neutral case evaluation. Another form of assisted negotiation—the summary jury trial—is discussed later in this chapter.

Mini-Trial A private proceeding in which each party to a dispute argues its position before the other side and vice versa. A neutral third party may be present and act as an adviser if the parties fail to reach an agreement.

A **mini-trial** is a private proceeding in which each party's attorney briefly argues the party's case before the other party. Typically, a neutral third party, who acts as an adviser and an expert in the area being disputed, is also present. If the parties fail to reach an agreement, the adviser renders an opinion as to how a court would likely decide the issue. The proceeding assists the parties in determining whether they should negotiate a settlement of the dispute or take it to court.

Early Neutral Case Evaluation A form of alternative dispute resolution in which a neutral third party evaluates the strengths and weakness of the disputing parties' positions; the evaluator's opinion forms the basis for negotiating a settlement.

In **early neutral case evaluation,** the parties select a neutral third party (generally an expert in the subject matter of the dispute) to evaluate their respective positions. The parties explain their positions to the case evaluator however they wish. The evaluator then assesses the strengths and weaknesses of the parties' positions, and this evaluation forms the basis for negotiating a settlement.

Mediation

Mediation A method of settling disputes outside of court by using the services of a neutral third party, called a mediator. The mediator acts as a communicating agent between the parties and suggests ways in which the parties can resolve their dispute.

Mediation is similar to negotiation. In the mediation process, as in negotiation, the parties themselves must reach agreement over their dispute. The major difference between negotiation and mediation is that the latter involves a third party, called a mediator. The **mediator** assists the parties in reaching a mutually acceptable agreement. The mediator talks face to face with the parties and allows them to discuss their disagreement, usually in an informal environment. The mediator's role, however, is limited to assisting the parties. The mediator does not decide a controversy; he or she only facilitates the process by helping the parties more quickly find common ground on which they can begin to reach an agreement for themselves.

Mediator A person who attempts to reconcile the differences between two or more parties.

ADVANTAGES OF MEDIATION.   Few procedural rules are involved in the mediation process—far fewer than in a courtroom setting. The proceedings can be tailored to fit the needs of the parties—the mediator can be told to maintain a diplomatic role or be asked to express an opinion about the dispute, lawyers can be excluded from the proceedings, and the exchange of a few documents can replace the more expensive and time-consuming process of pretrial discovery. Disputes are often settled far more quickly in mediation than in formal litigation.[1]

---

1. In Florida alone, as many as fifty thousand disputes that might have ended up in court are instead resolved through mediation each year. Florida's insurance commissioner used mediation to resolve hundreds of insurance claims stemming from 1992's Hurricane Andrew.

There are other benefits. Because the parties reach agreement by mutual consent, the bitterness that often flows from the winner-take-all outcome of a formal trial decision is avoided. Hard feelings are also minimized by the less stressful environment provided by mediation; the absence of the formal rules and adversarial tone of courtroom proceedings lessens the hostility the parties may feel toward one another. Minimizing hard feelings can be very important when the parties have to go on working with one another while the controversy is being resolved or after it has been settled. This is frequently the case when two businesses—say, a supplier and a purchaser—have a long-standing, mutually beneficial relationship that they would like to preserve despite their controversy. Similar considerations are found in the context of management and labor disputes; employee disciplinary matters and grievances are subjects that invite mediation as an alternative to formal litigation.

Another important benefit of mediation is that the mediator is selected by the parties. In litigation, the parties have no control over the selection of a judge. In mediation, the parties may select a mediator on the basis of expertise in a particular field as well as for fairness and impartiality. To the degree that the mediator has these attributes, he or she will effectively aid the parties in reaching an agreement over their dispute.

DISADVANTAGES OF MEDIATION.   Mediation is not without disadvantages. A mediator is likely to charge a fee. (This can be split between the parties, though.) Informality and the absence of a third party referee can also have disadvantages. (Remember that a mediator can only help the parties reach a decision, not make a decision for them.) Without a deadline hanging over the parties' heads, and without the threat of sanctions if they fail to negotiate in good faith, they may be less willing to make concessions or otherwise strive honestly and diligently to reach a settlement. This can slow the process or even cause it to fail.

Arbitration

A third method of dispute resolution combines the advantages of third party decision making—as provided by judges and juries in formal litigation—with the speed and flexibility inherent in rules of procedure and evidence less rigid than those governing courtroom litigation. This is the process of **arbitration**—the settling of a dispute by an impartial third party (other than a court) who renders a legally binding decision. The third party who renders the decision is called an **arbitrator.**

When a dispute arises, the parties can agree to settle their differences informally through arbitration rather than formally through the court system. Alternatively, the parties may agree ahead of time that, if a dispute should arise, they will submit to arbitration rather than bring a lawsuit. Both parties are obligated to follow the arbitrator's decision regardless of whether or not they agree with it; this is what is meant by saying the decision is legally binding.

The federal government and many state governments favor arbitration over litigation. The federal policy favoring arbitration is embodied in the Federal Arbitration Act (FAA) of 1925.[2] The FAA requires that courts give deference to all voluntary arbitration agreements in cases governed by federal law. Virtually

Arbitration The settling of a dispute by submitting it to a disinterested third party (other than a court), who renders a decision. The decision may or may not be legally binding.

Arbitrator A disinterested party who, by prior agreement of the parties submitting their dispute to arbitration, has the power to resolve the dispute and (generally) bind the parties.

2. 9 U.S.C. Sections 1–15.

any dispute can be the subject of arbitration. A voluntary agreement to arbitrate a dispute normally will be enforced by the courts if the agreement does not compel an illegal act or contravene public policy.

The Federal Arbitration Act

The Federal Arbitration Act does not establish a set arbitration procedure. The parties themselves must agree on the manner of resolving their dispute. The FAA provides the means for enforcing the arbitration procedure that the parties have established for themselves.

Section 4 of the FAA allows a party to petition a federal district court for an order compelling arbitration under an agreement to arbitrate a dispute. If the judge is "satisfied that the making of the agreement for arbitration or the failure to comply therewith is not in issue, the court shall make an order directing the parties to proceed with arbitration in accordance with the terms of the agreement."

Under Section 9, the parties to the arbitration may agree to have the arbitrator's decision confirmed in a federal district court. Through confirmation, one party obtains a court order directing another party to comply with the terms of the arbitrator's decision. Section 10 establishes the grounds by which the arbitrator's decision may be set aside (canceled). The grounds for setting aside a decision are limited to misconduct, fraud, corruption, or abuse of power in the arbitration process itself; a court will not review the merits of the dispute or the arbitrator's judgment.

The FAA covers any arbitration clause in a contract that involves interstate commerce. Business activities that have even remote connections or minimal effects on commerce between two or more states are considered to be included. Thus, arbitration agreements involving transactions only slightly connected to the flow of interstate commerce may fall under the FAA. In the following case, the United States Supreme Court considered whether to apply this principle to an arbitration agreement that, at the time of contracting, the parties did not expect to involve interstate commerce.

Case 4.1 ● Allied-Bruce Terminix Companies, Inc. v. Dobson

Supreme Court of the United States, 1995.
513 U.S. 265,
115 S.Ct. 834,
130 L.Ed.2d 753.

HISTORICAL AND ENVIRONMENTAL SETTING *One of the responsibilities of home ownership is to protect the structure from the elements of nature. Those elements include termites. Termites feed chiefly on wood, such as the wood used to construct houses. The tiny insects can destroy a home that is unprotected or inadequately protected. In the United States, termites cause over $250 million in losses each year. Common methods to prevent the entry of termites into buildings include using chemically treated wood in the construction of the building or chemically treating the soil on which the building is constructed.*

BACKGROUND AND FACTS Steven Gwin signed a contract with Allied-Bruce Terminix Companies, Inc., to protect his home from termite infestation. The contract specified that any dispute would be resolved by arbitration. After Gwin sold the home to Michael Dobson, the structure became infested with termites. Dobson filed a suit against Gwin and Allied-Bruce in an Alabama state court. Allied-Bruce asked the court to compel arbitration under the Federal Arbitration Act (FAA) section making enforceable a written arbitration provision in "a contract evidencing a transaction involving commerce." The court refused, on the ground that, at the time of contracting, the parties did not expect their contract to involve interstate commerce. Allied-Bruce appealed. The state supreme court affirmed, and the company appealed again—to the United States Supreme Court.

(Continued)

Case 4.1—continued

IN THE WORDS OF THE COURT . . .
Justice BREYER delivered the opinion of the Court.
* * * *

The Federal Arbitration Act provides that a " * * * contract evidencing a transaction involving commerce to settle by arbitration a controversy thereafter arising out of such contract or transaction * * * shall be valid, irrevocable, and enforceable * * * ."

* * * Is "involving" the functional equivalent of the word "affecting"? That phrase—"affecting commerce"—normally signals a congressional intent to exercise its Commerce Clause powers to the full. * * *

After examining the statute's language, background, and structure, we conclude that the word "involving" is broad and is indeed the functional equivalent of "affecting." * * *
* * * *

[Interpreting the phrase "evidencing a transaction" to mean that the parties, at the time they entered into the contract, contemplated that it would involve substantial interstate activity] invites litigation about what was, or was not, "contemplated." Why would Congress intend a test that risks the very kind of costs and delay through litigation (about the circumstances of contract formation) that Congress wrote the Act to help the parties avoid?
* * * *

* * * [W]e * * * [read] the [FAA's] language as insisting that the "transaction" in fact "involve" interstate commerce, even if the parties did not contemplate an interstate commerce connection.

DECISION AND REMEDY   The United States Supreme Court held that the FAA extends to the limits of Congress's commerce clause power. The Court reversed the ruling of the state supreme court and remanded the case for further proceedings.

FOR CRITICAL ANALYSIS—ETHICAL CONSIDERATION   *The Federal Arbitration Act was enacted in 1925, when the commerce clause did not have the reach that it does today. Is it fair to expand the reach of the FAA with the expansion of the reach of the commerce clause?*

State Arbitration Statutes

Virtually all states follow the federal approach to voluntary arbitration. Thirty-four states and the District of Columbia have adopted the Uniform Arbitration Act, which was drafted by the National Conference of Commissioners on Uniform State Laws in 1955. Those states that have not adopted the uniform act nonetheless follow many of the practices specified in it.

Under the uniform act, the basic approach is to give full effect to voluntary agreements to arbitrate disputes between private parties. The act supplements private arbitration agreements by providing explicit procedures and remedies for enforcing arbitration agreements. The uniform act does not, however, dictate the terms of the agreement. Moreover, under both federal and state statutes, the parties are afforded considerable latitude in deciding the subject matter of the arbitration and the methods for conducting the arbitration process. In the absence of a controlling statute, the rights and duties of the parties are established and limited by their agreement.

The Arbitration Process

Submission An agreement by two or more parties to refer any disputes they may have under their contract to a disinterested third party, such as an arbitrator, who has the power to render a binding decision.

The arbitration process begins with a *submission*. **Submission** is the act of referring a dispute to an arbitrator. The next step is the *hearing*, in which evidence and arguments are presented to the arbitrator. The process culminates in an *award*, which is the decision of the arbitrator.

The right to appeal the award to a court of law is limited. If the award was made under a voluntary arbitration agreement, a court normally will not set it aside even if it was the result of an erroneous determination of fact or an incorrect interpretation of law by the arbitrator.

This limitation is based on at least two grounds. First, if an award is not treated as final, then, rather than speeding up the dispute-resolution process, arbitration would merely add one more layer to the process of litigation. Second, the basis of arbitration—the freedom of parties to agree among themselves how to settle a controversy—supports treating an award as final. Having had the opportunity to frame the issues and to set out the manner for resolving the dispute, one party should not complain if the result was not what that party had hoped it would be.

SUBMISSION. The parties may agree to submit questions of fact, questions of law, or both to the arbitrator. The parties may even agree to leave the interpretation of the arbitration agreement to the arbitrator. In the case of an existing agreement to arbitrate, the clause itself is the submission to arbitration.

The submission typically states the identities of the parties, the nature of the dispute to be resolved, the monetary amounts involved in the controversy, the place at which the arbitration is to take place, and the intention of the parties to be bound by the arbitrator's award. Exhibit 4–1 contains a sample submission form.

Most states require that an agreement to submit a dispute to arbitration be in writing. Moreover, because the goal of arbitration is speed and efficiency in resolving controversies, most states require that matters be submitted within a definite period of time, generally six months from the date on which the dispute arises.

THE HEARING. Because the parties are free to construct the method by which they want their dispute resolved, they must state the issues that will be submitted and the powers that the arbitrator will exercise. The arbitrator may be given power at the outset of the process to establish rules that will govern the proceedings. Typically, these rules are much less restrictive than those governing formal litigation. Regardless of who establishes the rules, the arbitrator will apply them during the course of the hearing.

Restrictions on the kind of evidence and the manner in which it is presented may be less rigid in arbitration, partly because the arbitrator is likely to be an expert in the subject matter involved in the controversy. Restrictions may also be less stringent because there is less fear that the arbitrator will be swayed by improper evidence.

In the typical hearing format, the parties begin as they would at trial by presenting opening arguments to the arbitrator and stating what remedies should or should not be granted. After the opening statements have been made, evidence is presented. Witnesses may be called and examined by both sides. After

American Arbitration Association

SUBMISSION TO DISPUTE RESOLUTION

Date: _____

The named parties hereby submit the following dispute for resolution under the
_____ Rules* of the American Arbitration Association:

Procedure Selected: ___Binding arbitration ____ Mediation settlement

____ Other _____
(Describe)

FOR INSURANCE CASES ONLY:

_____ _____ to _____
Policy Number   Effective Dates

_____   _____
Date of Incident   Location

Insured: _____ Claim Number:_____

Name(s) of Claimant(s)   Check if a Minor   Amount Claimed

_____   ____   _____

_____   ____   _____

Nature of Dispute and/or Injuries Alleged (attach additional sheets if necessary):

Place of Hearing: _____

We agree that, if binding arbitration is selected, we will abide by and perform any award
rendered hereunder and that a judgment may be entered on the award.

To Be Completed by the Claimant	*To Be Completed by the Respondent*
Name of Party	Name of Party
Address	Address
City, State, and ZIP Code	City, State, and ZIP Code
( ) _____ Telephone Fax	( ) _____ Telephone Fax
Signature†	Signature†
Name of Party's Attorney or Representative	Name of Party's Attorney or Representative
Address	Address
City, State, and ZIP Code	City, State, and ZIP Code
( ) _____ Telephone Fax	( ) _____ Telephone Fax
Signature†	Signature†

Please file three copies with the AAA.

* *If you have a question as to which rules apply, please contact the AAA.*

† *Signatures of all parties are required for arbitration.*   *Form G1-7/90*

■ **Exhibit 4–I
Sample Submission
Form**

all the evidence has been presented, the parties give their closing arguments. On completion of these arguments, the arbitrator closes the hearing.

THE AWARD.   After each side has had an opportunity to present evidence and to argue its case, the arbitrator reaches a decision. The final decision of the arbitrator is called an **award**, even if no money is conferred on a party as a result of the proceedings. Under most statutes, the arbitrator must render an award within thirty days of the close of the hearing.

In most states, the award need not state the arbitrator's findings regarding factual questions in the case. Nor must the award state the conclusions that the arbitrator reached on any questions of law that may have been presented. All that is required for the award to be valid is that it completely resolve the controversy.

Most states do, however, require that the award be in writing, regardless of whether any conclusions of law or findings of fact are included. If the arbitrator does state his or her legal conclusions and factual findings, then a letter or an opinion will be drafted containing the basis for the award. Even when there is no statutory requirement that the arbitrator state the factual and legal basis for the award, the parties may impose the requirement in their submission or in their pre-dispute agreement to arbitrate.

Enforcement of Agreements to Submit to Arbitration

The role of the courts in the arbitration process is limited. One important role is played at the prearbitration stage. A court may be called on to order one party to an arbitration agreement to submit to arbitration under the terms of the agreement. The court in this role is essentially interpreting a contract. The court must determine to what the parties have committed themselves before ordering that they submit to arbitration.

When a dispute arises as to whether or not the parties have agreed in an arbitration clause to submit a particular matter to arbitration, one party may file suit to compel arbitration. The court before which the suit is brought will not decide the basic controversy but must decide the issue of arbitrability—that is, whether the issue is one that must be resolved through arbitration. If the court finds that the subject matter in controversy is covered by the agreement to arbitrate, then a party may be compelled to arbitrate the dispute involuntarily.

Although the parties may agree to submit the issue of arbitrability to an arbitrator, the agreement must be explicit; a court will never *infer* an agreement to arbitrate. Unless a court finds an *explicit* agreement to have the arbitrator decide whether a dispute is arbitrable, the court will decide the issue. This is an important initial determination, because no party will be ordered to submit to arbitration unless the court is convinced that the party has consented to do so.

Should claims involving alleged violations of federal statutes protecting employees from employment discrimination be arbitrable? The United States Supreme Court answered this question in the following landmark case. (See this chapter's *Inside the Legal Environment* on page 108 for a discussion of the effects of arbitration on employee rights.)

Award In the context of litigation, the amount of money awarded to a plaintiff in a civil lawsuit as damages. In the context of arbitration, the arbitrator's decision.

REMEMBER   Litigation—even of a dispute over whether a particular matter should be submitted to arbitration—can be time consuming and expensive.

Case 4.2 ● Gilmer v. Interstate/Johnson Lane Corp.

Supreme Court of the United States, 1991.
500 U.S. 20,
111 S.Ct. 1647,
114 L.Ed.2d 26.

BACKGROUND AND FACTS Interstate/Johnson Lane Corporation required some of its employees, including Robert Gilmer, to register as securities representatives with the New York Stock Exchange (NYSE). The registration application included an agreement to arbitrate when NYSE rules required it. One of the rules requires the arbitration of any controversy arising out of a registrant's termination of employment. Interstate terminated Gilmer's employment at age sixty-two. Gilmer filed a suit in a federal district court, alleging that he had been discharged in violation of the Age Discrimination in Employment Act (ADEA) of 1967.[a] (This act attempts to prevent employers from discriminating against older employees—see Chapter 17.) Interstate asked the court to order the arbitration of Gilmer's claim, according to the agreement in Gilmer's registration application with the NYSE. The court denied the employer's request, but on appeal, the appellate court ordered the arbitration. Gilmer appealed to the United States Supreme Court.

IN THE WORDS OF THE COURT . . .
Justice WHITE delivered the opinion of the Court.
* * * *

* * * Although all statutory rights may not be appropriate for arbitration, having made the bargain to arbitrate, the party should be held to it unless Congress itself has evinced an intention to preclude a waiver of judicial remedies for the statutory rights at issue. * * * If such an intention exists, it will be discoverable in the text of the ADEA, its legislative history, or an inherent conflict between arbitration and the ADEA's underlying purposes. Throughout such an inquiry, it should be kept in mind that questions of arbitrability must be addressed with a healthy regard for the federal policy favoring arbitration.
* * * *

As Gilmer contends, the ADEA is designed not only to address individual grievances, but also to further important social policies. We do not perceive any inherent inconsistency between those policies, however, and enforcing agreements to arbitrate age discrimination claims. * * *
* * * *

Gilmer also argues that compulsory arbitration is improper because it deprives claimants of the judicial forum provided for by the ADEA. Congress, however, did not explicitly preclude arbitration or other nonjudicial resolution of claims, even in its recent amendments to the ADEA. * * * In addition, * * * arbitration agreements * * * serve to advance the objective of allowing [claimants] a broader right to select the forum for resolving disputes, whether it be judicial or otherwise.

DECISION AND REMEDY The United States Supreme Court held that the arbitration of an age discrimination claim can be compelled. The Court affirmed the order requiring the parties to arbitrate the claim.

FOR CRITICAL ANALYSIS—ETHICAL CONSIDERATION *The decision to compel arbitration may seem to contradict the public policy enunciated in such statutes as the ADEA. For what practical reason might courts favor the arbitration of disputes, even in the employment context?*

a. 29 U.S.C. Sections 621–634.

Inside the Legal Environment
ADR and Employment Discrimination

Over the last three decades, Congress has enacted statutes that give employees significant protection from employers' discriminatory practices. These statutes protect employees from employment discrimination based on race, color, national origin, gender, religion, age, and disability (see Chapter 17).

What happens to these rights, though, if an employee has agreed, in his or her employment contract, to arbitrate any claims arising from the employment relationship? For one thing, the procedural protections available in an arbitral forum can differ significantly from those available in the litigation process. For example, discovery usually is more limited in arbitration than in litigation. If a discrimination claim is arbitrated, an employee may find it difficult to gain access to company documents or other evidence of the discriminatory practice. Remedies also differ. Under Title VII of the Civil Rights Act of 1964, as amended, plaintiffs who can prove that they are victims of intentional discrimination in violation of Title VII may be awarded punitive damages—in addition to actual damages (such as

lost wages), reinstatement, and so on. In contrast, arbitration clauses may limit or prohibit entirely an award of punitive damages.

Many people today are concerned about the pitfalls of arbitration for employee rights. For example, JAMS/Endispute, a leading provider of arbitration services, claims that it is unfair of employers to require employees to sign contracts containing arbitration clauses that limit their rights to obtain punitive damages. JAMS has thus adopted a policy of taking only those cases in which an employee retains the same avenues available in court, including the right to obtain punitive damages. In a policy statement issued in 1995, the Equal Employment Opportunity Commission also expressed its disapproval of the mandatory arbitration of employment claims.

The courts, of course, are obligated to follow the precedent set by the United States Supreme Court in the *Gilmer* decision (presented in this chapter as Case 4.2), in which the Court stated that claims of employment discrimination are arbitrable. Nonetheless, courts are finding grounds not to enforce arbitration

clauses. For example, the U.S. Court of Appeals for the Ninth Circuit held that an arbitration clause will not be binding if an employee did not "knowingly" waive his or her rights to statutory remedies when signing the contract containing the clause[a] or if the clause eliminates punitive damages or other remedies provided under federal law.[b] The New Mexico Supreme Court found yet another reason not to enforce an arbitration clause: the clause limited the employee's right to appeal.[c] These and other cases may represent a countertrend against the decisions of the early 1990s, which seemed to expand continuously the scope of arbitrable issues.

For Critical Analysis: Why do people sign arbitration agreements in the first place?

---

a.   *Prudential Insurance Co. of America v. Lai,* 42 F.3d 1299 (9th Cir. 1994).
b.   *Graham Oil Co. v. ARCO Products Co.,* 43 F.3d 1244 (9th Cir. 1994).
c.   *Board of Education of Carlsbad Municipal Schools v. Harrel,* 882 P.2d 511 (N.Mex.1994).

Setting Aside an Arbitration Award

After the arbitration has been concluded, the losing party may appeal the arbitrator's award to a court, or the winning party may seek a court order compelling the other party to comply with the award. The scope of review in either situation is much more restricted than in an appellate court's review of a trial court decision. The court does not look at the merits of the underlying dispute, and the court will not add to or subtract from the remedies provided by the award. The court's role is limited to determining whether there exists a valid award. If so, the court will order the parties to comply with the terms. The general view is that because the parties were free to frame the issues and set the powers of the arbitrator at the outset, they cannot complain about the result.

International Perspective

International standards for the recognition of arbitration agreements and awards were set by the United Nations Convention on the Recognition and Enforcement of Foreign Arbitral Awards,[a] which has been signed by seventy-three countries, including the United States. Article V(2) of the convention creates an exception to enforcement of arbitration clauses that are "contrary to the public policy" of the relevant country. Thus, the resolution of a case will depend on the strength of a public policy in a given country. International organizations that handle arbitration matters include the United Nations Commission on International Trade Laws, the London Court of International Arbitration, the Euro-Arab Chamber of Commerce, the International Chamber of Commerce in Paris, and the International Trademark Association.

For Critical Analysis: *Should businesspersons evaluate the policies of different countries before deciding where to arbitrate their disputes?*

_____

a.   June 10, 1958, 21 U.S.T. 2517 (the New York Convention).

FACT FINDINGS AND LEGAL CONCLUSIONS.   The arbitrator's fact findings and legal conclusions are normally final. That the arbitrator may have erred in a ruling during the hearing or made an erroneous fact finding is normally no basis for setting aside an award: the parties agreed that the arbitrator would be the judge of the facts. Similarly, no matter how obviously the arbitrator was mistaken in a conclusion of law, the award is normally nonetheless binding: the parties agreed to accept the arbitrator's interpretation of the law. A court will not look at the merits of the dispute, the sufficiency of the evidence presented, or the arbitrator's reasoning in reaching a particular decision.

This approach is consistent with the underlying view of all voluntary arbitration—that its basis is really contract law. If the parties freely contract with one another, courts will not interfere simply because one side feels that it received a bad bargain. Any party challenging an award must face the presumption that a final award is valid. But is an award final or binding if the parties did not agree that it would be? That was the issue in the following case.

Case 4.3 ● Orlando v. Interstate Container Corp.

United States Court of Appeals,
Third Circuit, 1996.
100 F.3d 296.

BACKGROUND AND FACTS   Joseph Orlando, an employee of Interstate Container Corporation, underwent heart bypass surgery. For several months, he did not work and collected disability benefits, in part as provided by a collective bargaining agreement.[a] When his condition improved, he asked to return to work, but Interstate denied his request. He filed a complaint with the company, which, under the collective bargaining agreement, went to arbitration, culminating in an arbitrator's decision in Interstate's favor. The agreement did not state that the arbitrator's decision would be "final" or "binding," however. In Orlando's subsequent suit against Interstate, a federal district court ruled that the decision was not binding. Interstate appealed.

_____

a.   A collective bargaining agreement is a contract negotiated by employees and their employer concerning the terms and conditions of employment. See Chapter 18.

(Continued)

Case 4.3—continued

IN THE WORDS OF THE COURT . . .
WEIS, Circuit Judge.
  * * * *

[Interstate] argues that because the contract makes arbitration mandatory, it must necessarily be final as well. That argument finds support in the policy favoring arbitration as a means of resolving disputes, but fails to meet the requirement of authorization by agreement of the parties. * * *

  * * * *

* * * [W]e must give full credit to the language the parties have chosen to include—or not include—in their agreement.

Collective bargaining agreements almost invariably explain that arbitration proceedings will be "final," "binding," or "exclusive," or use other words to that effect. This agreement was drafted by parties well-versed in labor matters and cognizant [aware] of that convention. The omission of any indication that arbitration proceedings should be final and binding leads us to conclude that, if we nevertheless declared them to be so, we would not be enforcing the will of the parties, as expressed in their agreement.

DECISION AND REMEDY The U.S. Court of Appeals for the Third Circuit affirmed the lower court's decision. An arbitration award may not be final or binding unless the parties agreed that it would be.

FOR CRITICAL ANALYSIS—SOCIAL CONSIDERATION *Why might the parties to an arbitration agreement prefer that the arbitration award not be final?*

PUBLIC POLICY AND ILLEGALITY. In keeping with contract law principles, no award will be enforced if compliance with the award would result in the commission of a crime or would conflict with some greater social policy mandated by statute. A court will not overturn an award, however, simply because the arbitrator was called on to resolve a dispute involving a matter of significant public concern.[3] For an award to be set aside, it must call for some action on the part of the parties that would conflict with or in some way undermine public policy. The issue in the following case was whether enforcement of an arbitrator's award would violate public policy.

───────────

3. See, for example, *Faherty v. Faherty,* 97 N.J. 99, 477 A.2d 1257 (1984).

Case 4.4 ● Meehan v. Nassau Community College

Supreme Court, Appellate Division,
Second Department, 1996.
647 N.Y.S.2d 865.

BACKGROUND AND FACTS Nassau Community College required all faculty members in its communications department to possess a master's degree in communications. Michael DeLuca did not have the requisite degree but was nevertheless assigned to teach communications courses. The Middle States Association Commission on Higher Education told the college that its accreditation would be in jeopardy unless its assignment of faculty was based, "first and foremost," on academic credentials. The college reviewed its personnel files, discovered that DeLuca did not have the necessary credentials, and declined to assign him any more courses. DeLuca's subsequent complaint went to arbitration before the New York State Public Employee Relations Board, which ordered DeLuca's reinstatement. The college refused, and DeLuca (through John Meehan, a faculty representative) filed a suit against the college in a New York state court to confirm the award. The court denied DeLuca's request, and he appealed.

(Continued)

Case 4.4—continued

IN THE WORDS OF THE COURT . . .
MEMORANDUM BY THE COURT.
* * * *

* * * [O]nly when [an arbitrator's] award contravenes a strong public policy, almost invariably involving an important constitutional or statutory duty or responsibility, may it be set aside. * * * [H]ere, it is clear that the award the petitioner seeks to confirm contravenes strong public policy, inasmuch as it requires the College to retain DeLuca even though he is undisputably unqualified to teach in the Communications Department because of his lack of certain academic credentials.

DECISION AND REMEDY   The state appellate court affirmed the decision of the trial court setting aside the arbitrator's award. Enforcement of the award would violate public policy. The college did not have to reinstate DeLuca.

FOR CRITICAL ANALYSIS—ECONOMIC CONSIDERATION   *Why might a party insist on the enforcement of an award that is against public policy?*

DEFECTS IN THE ARBITRATION PROCESS.   There are some bases for setting aside an award when there is a defect in the arbitration process. These bases are typified by those set forth in the Federal Arbitration Act. Section 10 of the act provides four grounds on which an arbitration award may be set aside:

1. The award was the result of corruption, fraud, or other "undue means."
2. The arbitrator exhibited bias or corruption.
3. The arbitrator refused to postpone the hearing despite sufficient cause, refused to hear evidence pertinent and material to the dispute, or otherwise acted to substantially prejudice the rights of one of the parties.
4. The arbitrator exceeded his or her powers or failed to use them to make a mutual, final, and definite award.

The first three bases for setting aside the award include actions or decisions that are more than simply mistakes in judgment. Each requires some "bad faith" on the part of the arbitrator. Bad faith actions or decisions are ones that affect the integrity of the arbitration process. The honesty and impartiality, rather than the judgment, of the arbitrator are called into question.

Sometimes it is difficult to make the distinction between honest mistakes in judgment and actions or decisions made in bad faith. A bribe is clearly the kind of "undue means" included in the first basis for setting aside an award. Letting only one side argue its case is likewise a clear violation of the second basis.

Meetings between the arbitrator and one party outside the presence of the other party also taint the arbitration process. Although meetings might not involve the kind of corruption that results from taking a bribe, they do affect the integrity of the process; the third basis for setting aside an award is meant to protect against this.

Not every refusal by an arbitrator to admit certain evidence is grounds for setting aside an award under the third basis. As noted, to provide a basis for overturning an award, the arbitrator's decision must be more than an error in judgment, no matter how obviously incorrect that judgment might appear to another observer. The decision must be so obviously wrong or unfair as to imply bias or corruption. Otherwise, the decision normally cannot be a basis for setting aside an award.

The fourth basis for setting aside an award is that the arbitrator exceeded his or her powers in arbitrating the dispute. This issue involves the question of arbitrability. An arbitrator exceeds his or her powers and authority by attempting to resolve an issue that is not covered by the agreement to submit to arbitration.

WAIVER.   Although a defect in the arbitration process is sufficient grounds for setting aside an award, a party sometimes forfeits the right to challenge an award by failing to object to the defect in a timely manner. The party must object when he or she learns of the problem. After making the objection, the party can still proceed with the arbitration process and still challenge the award in court after the arbitration proceedings have concluded. If, however, a party makes no objection and proceeds with the arbitration process, then a later court challenge to the award may be denied on the ground that the party *waived* the right to challenge the award on the basis of the defect.

Frequently, this occurs when a party fails to object that an arbitrator is exceeding his or her powers in resolving a dispute because the subject matter is not arbitrable or because the party did not agree to arbitrate the dispute. The question of arbitrability is one for the courts to decide. If a party does not object on this issue at the first demand for arbitration, however, a court may consider the objection waived.

CONFLICTS OF LAW.   Parties are afforded wide latitude in establishing the manner in which their disputes will be resolved. Nevertheless, an agreement to arbitrate may be governed by the FAA or one of the many state arbitration acts, even though the parties do not refer to a statute in their agreement. Recall that the FAA covers any arbitration clause in a contract that involves interstate commerce. Frequently, however, transactions involving interstate commerce also have substantial connections to particular states, which may in turn have their own arbitration acts. In such situations, unless the FAA and state arbitration law are nearly identical, the acts may conflict. How are these conflicts to be resolved?

As a general principle, the supremacy clause and the commerce clause of the U.S. Constitution are the bases for giving federal law preeminence; when there is a conflict, state law is preempted by federal law. Thus, in cases of arbitration, the strong federal policy favoring arbitration can override a state's laws that might be more favorable to normal litigation.

CHOICE OF LAW.   Notwithstanding federal preemption of conflicting state laws, the Federal Arbitration Act has been interpreted as allowing the parties to choose a particular state law to govern their arbitration agreement. The parties may choose to have the laws of a specific state govern their agreement by including in the agreement a *choice-of-law clause*. The FAA does not mandate any particular set of rules that parties must follow in arbitration; the parties are free to agree on the manner best suited to their needs. Consistent with this view that arbitration is at heart a contractual matter between private parties, the United States Supreme Court has upheld arbitration agreements containing choice-of-law provisions.

Disadvantages of Arbitration

Arbitration has some disadvantages. The result in any particular dispute can be unpredictable, in part because arbitrators do not need to follow any previous cases in rendering their decisions. Unlike judges, arbitrators do not have to issue written opinions or facilitate a participant's appeal to a court. Arbitrators must decide disputes according to whatever rules have been provided by the parties, regardless of how unfair those rules may be. In some cases, arbitration can be nearly as expensive as litigation. In part, this is because both sides must prepare their cases for presentation before a third party decision maker, just as they would have to do to appear in court. Discovery is usually not available in arbitration, however, which means that during the hearing the parties must take the time to question witnesses whom, in a lawsuit, they might not need to call.[4]

The Integration of ADR and Formal Court Procedures

▼ Because of the congestion within the judicial system, many jurisdictions at both the state and federal levels are integrating alternative dispute resolution into the formal legal process. Utilizing methods such as arbitration and mediation within the traditional framework may relieve the logjams afflicting most of the nation's court systems.

Court-Mandated ADR

Increasingly, courts are requiring that parties attempt to settle their differences through some form of ADR before proceeding to trial. For example, several federal district courts encourage nonbinding arbitration for cases involving amounts less than $100,000. Less than 10 percent of the cases referred for arbitration ever go to trial. Today, about half of all federal courts have adopted formal rules regarding the use of ADR, and many other courts without such rules use ADR procedures.

Most states have adopted programs that allow them to refer certain types of cases for mediation or arbitration. Typically—as in California and Hawaii—court systems have adopted mandatory mediation or nonbinding arbitration programs for certain types of disputes, usually involving less than a specified threshold dollar amount.[5] Only if the parties fail to reach an agreement, or if one of the parties disagrees with the decision of a third party mediating or arbitrating the dispute, will the case be heard by a court. South Carolina was the first state to institute a voluntary arbitration program at the appellate court level. In the South Carolina system, litigants must waive a court hearing when requesting arbitration. All decisions by the arbitrators are final and binding.

Court-Annexed Arbitration

Court-annexed arbitration differs significantly from the voluntary arbitration process discussed above. There are some disputes that courts will not allow to go to arbitration. Most states, for example, do not allow court-annexed arbitration in disputes involving title to real estate or in cases in which a court's equity powers are involved.

---

4.   One notable dispute concerning computer chip technology was in arbitration for more than seven years and cost the participants more than $100 million. See *Advanced Micro Devices, Inc. v. Intel Corp.*, 9 Cal.4th 362, 885 P.2d 994, 36 Cal.Rptr.2d 581 (1994).
5.   Hawaii, for example, has a program of mandatory, nonbinding arbitration for disputes involving less than $150,000.

A FUNDAMENTAL DIFFERENCE. The fundamental difference between voluntary arbitration and court-annexed arbitration is the finality and reviewability of the award. With respect to court-annexed arbitration, either party may reject the award for any reason. In the event that one of the parties does reject the award, the case will proceed to trial, and the court will hear the case *de novo*—that is, the court will reconsider all the evidence and legal questions as though no arbitration had occurred.

Everyone who has a recognizable cause of action or against whom such an action is brought is entitled to have the issue decided in a court of law. Because court-annexed arbitration is not voluntary, there must be some safeguard against using it in a way that denies an individual his or her day in court. This safeguard is provided by permitting either side to reject the award regardless of the reason for so doing.

The party rejecting the award may be penalized, however. Many statutes providing for court-annexed arbitration impose court costs and fees on a party who rejects an arbitration award but does not improve his or her position by going to trial. Thus, for example, if a party rejects an arbitration award, and the award turns out to be more favorable to that party than the subsequent jury verdict, the party may be compelled to pay the costs of the arbitration or some fee for the costs of the trial.

In court-annexed arbitration, discovery of evidence occurs before the hearing. After the hearing has commenced, a party seeking to discover new evidence must usually secure approval from the court that mandated the arbitration. This is intended to prevent the parties from using arbitration as a means of previewing each other's cases and then rejecting the arbitrator's award.

THE ROLE OF THE ARBITRATOR. Notwithstanding the differences between voluntary and court-annexed arbitration, the role of the arbitrator is essentially the same in both types of proceedings. The arbitrator determines issues of both fact and law. The arbitrator also makes all decisions concerning applications of the rules of procedure and evidence during the hearing.

WHICH RULES APPLY. Regarding the rules of evidence, there are differences among the states. Most states impose the same rules of evidence on an arbitration hearing as on a trial. Other states, such as New Jersey, allow all evidence relevant to the dispute regardless of whether the evidence would be admissible at trial. Still other jurisdictions, such as Washington, leave it to the arbitrator to decide what evidence is admissible.

WAIVER. Once a court directs that a dispute is to be submitted to court-annexed arbitration, the parties must proceed to arbitration. As noted above, either side may reject the award that results from the arbitration for any reason. If a party fails to appear at or participate in the arbitration proceeding as directed by the court, however, that failure constitutes a waiver of the right to reject the award.

Court-Related Mediation

Mediation is proving to be more popular than arbitration as a court-related method of ADR. No federal court has adopted an arbitration program since 1991, while mediation programs continue to increase in number in both federal and state courts. Today, more court systems offer or require mediation, rather than arbitration, as an alternative to litigation. In the 1980s, there were only about 200 mediators in the United States. Today, more than 60,000 persons offer mediation services. Mediation is currently being taught in 95 percent of the accredited law schools in the country.

Mediation is often used in disputes relating to employment law, environmental law, product liability, and franchises. One of the most important business advantages of mediation is the lower cost, which can be 25 percent (or less) of the expense of litigation. Another advantage is the speed with which a dispute can go through mediation (possibly one or two days) compared with arbitration (possibly months) or litigation (possibly years).

Part of the popularity of mediation is that its goal, unlike that of litigation and some other forms of ADR, is for opponents to work out a resolution that benefits both sides. The rate of participants' satisfaction with the outcomes in mediated disputes is high. In New Hampshire, for example, where mediation is mandatory for all civil cases in most state trial courts, as many as 70 percent of the participants report satisfaction with the results.

Summary Jury Trials

Another means by which the courts have integrated alternative dispute resolution methods into the traditional court process is through the use of summary jury trials. A **summary jury trial** is a mock trial that occurs in a courtroom before a judge and jury. Evidence is presented in an abbreviated form, along with each side's major contentions. The jury then presents a verdict.

The fundamental difference between a traditional trial and a summary jury trial is that in the latter, the jury's verdict is only advisory. The goal of a summary jury trial is to give each side an idea of how it would fare in a full-blown jury trial with a more elaborate and detailed presentation of evidence and

Summary Jury Trial (SJT) A method of settling disputes in which a trial is held, but the jury's verdict is not binding. The verdict acts only as a guide to both sides in reaching an agreement during the mandatory negotiations that immediately

The participants in a jury trial and in a summary jury trial appear to be the same. To whose advantage are the differences between these types of dispute resolution?

arguments. At the end of the summary jury trial, the presiding judge meets with the parties and may encourage them to settle their dispute without going through a standard jury trial.

The U.S. Court of Appeals for the Sixth Circuit recently addressed the question of whether summary jury trials can be mandatory. The court concluded that it would be unfair to litigants to force them to undergo summary jury trials before they were permitted to have their claims heard in a federal court.[6]

ADR and Mass Torts

A *tort* is a civil wrong that does not arise from a breach of contract. (Torts are discussed in detail in Chapters 8 and 9. Breach of contract is discussed in Chapter 13.) *Mass tort* is the term applied to civil lawsuits that share such features as scientific or technological complexity and a large number of participants. Such cases often feature a high degree of emotional involvement on the part of the claimants, who may suffer from severe or life-threatening injuries, and on the part of the defendants, whose financial existence may be at stake. Examples of mass torts include litigation involving Agent Orange, the Dalkon Shield, the prescription drug DES, heart valves, and asbestos.

In the 1990s, there was an explosion in the number of mass torts. For example, more than 300,000 claims have been filed in asbestos-related litigation—in the mid-1990s, new claims were filed at the rate of 5,000 every month. Such claims are overwhelming our civil justice system. In attempts to clear the courts, some judges in mass tort cases turn to methods of alternative dispute resolution, including mediation, arbitration, mini-trials, and summary jury trials. ADR may be used to assess the validity or the value of the claims or to sort out or resolve the scientific, technological, or medical issues. ADR may be used to settle large numbers of claims in a speedy, efficient, cost-effective manner. Once a settlement is reached, a neutral third party may coordinate payments to claimants. There may even be provision for an ADR appeals process.

ADR Forums and Services

Services facilitating dispute resolution outside the courtroom are provided by both government agencies and private organizations. The major source of private arbitration services is the American Arbitration Association (AAA). Most of the largest law firms in the nation are members of this association. Founded in 1926, the AAA now settles more than 72,000 disputes a year and has offices in every state. Cases brought before the AAA are heard by an expert or a panel of experts—of whom usually about half are lawyers—in the area relating to the dispute. To cover its costs, this nonprofit organization charges a fee, paid by the party filing the claim. In addition, each party to the dispute pays a price for each hearing day, as well as a special additional fee in cases involving personal injuries or property loss.

In addition to the AAA, numerous other state and local nonprofit organizations provide arbitration services. For example, the Arbitration Association of Florida provides ADR services in that state. The Better Business Bureau (BBB) offers ADR programs to aid in the resolution of certain types of disagreements. The BBB's latest ADR process involves a mediation program

---

6. *In re NLO, Inc.,* 5 F.3d 154 (6th Cir. 1993).

International Perspective

The United States is not the only country that encourages mediation, arbitration, and other forms of ADR. Japan, for example, has recently authorized the establishment of neutral panels to act as mediators in product liability suits (suits brought by plaintiffs who have allegedly been injured by a seller's defective product—see Chapter 10). Several industries, including those manufacturing and selling housing materials, automobiles, and appliances, have set up such panels, which follow guidelines published by the Japanese Ministry of International Trade and Industry.

In 1995, China also made it simpler for disputes to be settled through ADR by passing a new arbitration law.

The law spells out what types of disputes are arbitrable, the form and content of valid arbitration clauses, and so on. Under the law, although most disputes can be arbitrated, family matters (such as those relating to marriage, adoption, and financial support) cannot be submitted for arbitration. Such disputes will continue to be handled by the relevant administrative agencies of the Chinese government.

For Critical Analysis: *Do you see any reason why certain types of disputes, such as those involving family matters, should not be decided by arbitration?*

---

called ComputerCare, through which buyers and sellers of computer equipment and software can settle their disputes. Many industries—including the insurance, automobile, and securities industries—also now have mediation or arbitration programs to facilitate timely and inexpensive settlement of claims. In all, there exist over six hundred ADR entities in the United States.

Those who seek to settle their disputes quickly can turn to private, for-profit organizations to act as mediators or arbitrators. The private system of justice includes hundreds of firms throughout the country offering dispute-resolution services by hired judges. Procedures in these private courts are fashioned to meet the desires of the clients seeking their services. For example, the parties might decide on the date of the hearing, the presiding judge, whether the judge's decision will be legally binding, and the site of the hearing—which could be a conference room, a law-school office, or a leased courtroom complete with flag and Bible. The judges may follow procedures similar to those of the federal courts and use similar rules. Each party to the dispute may pay a filing fee and a designated fee for a half-day hearing session or a special, one-hour settlement conference.

Key Terms

Chapter Summary
Legal Representation and Alternative Dispute Resolution

ATTORNEYS AND DISPUTE RESOLUTION
(See pages 91–98.)

1. **Roles of an attorney**—Adviser (advises a client on steps to take to avoid possible legal problems), drafter (writes contracts and other documents for clients), negotiator (persuades, argues, or settles with another party on a client's behalf), and advocate (presents a client's position in court).

2. **Attorney-client relationship**—A client must disclose all relevant information to his or her attorney so the attorney can determine the best course of action. The attorney must keep the information confidential—the attorney-client privilege prevents a court and other government bodies from compelling disclosure of the information.

3. **Decision to file a lawsuit**—Factors include whether the law provides a remedy, whether the person can expect to prevail, and whether the expected benefit will compensate for expenses and other costs, including any business lost as a result of the lawsuit and accompanying publicity.

4. **Decision to defend against a lawsuit**—Factors include whether the relationship with the plaintiff is too valuable to risk, whether the publicity surrounding a trial would damage the defendant's reputation or image, and whether the dispute could be resolved in a less costly manner.

ALTERNATIVE DISPUTE RESOLUTION (ADR)
(See pages 98–117.)

ADR is a less costly, less time-consuming, and increasingly attractive alternative to litigation in the courts. Forms of ADR include the following:

1. **Negotiation**—The parties come together, with or without attorneys to represent them, and try to reach a settlement without the involvement of a third party.

2. **Mediation**—The parties themselves reach an agreement with the help of a third party, called a mediator, who proposes solutions.

3. **Arbitration**—A more formal method of ADR in which the parties submit their dispute to a neutral third party, the arbitrator, who renders a decision, which may or may not be legally binding, depending on the circumstances. Some courts refer certain cases for arbitration before allowing the cases to proceed to trial; in most cases, this kind of arbitration is nonbinding on the parties.

4. **Summary jury trial**—A kind of trial in which litigants present their arguments and evidence and the jury renders a nonbinding verdict.

5. **Mini-trial**—A private proceeding in which each party's attorney argues the party's case before the other party. Often, a neutral third party acts as an adviser and renders an opinion on how a court would likely decide the issue.

6. **For-profit alternatives**—The parties rent a judge to hear their case and render a verdict to which the parties agree to be bound. Several firms now provide for this kind of private justice.

For Review

1. What roles do attorneys play in resolving disputes?

2. What are some of the similarities and differences between litigation and other forms of dispute resolution?

3. How do the processes of negotiation and mediation differ?

4. What are the steps in the arbitration process?

5. What are the differences between voluntary arbitration and court-annexed arbitration?

Questions and Case Problems

4–1. Arbitration. In an arbitration proceeding, the arbitrator need not be a judge or even a lawyer. How, then, can the arbitrator's decision have the force of law and be binding on the parties involved?

4–2. Choice of Law. Two private U.S. corporations enter into a joint-venture agreement to conduct mining operations in the newly formed Middle Eastern nation of Euphratia. As part of the agreement, the companies include an arbitration clause and a choice-of-law provision. The first states that any controversy arising out of the performance of the agreement will be settled by arbitration. The second states that the agreement is to be governed by the laws of the location of the venture, Euphratia. A dispute arises, and the parties discontinue operations. One of the parties claims sole ownership to the Euphratian mines and orders the other party to remove its equipment from the mines. The other party disputes the claim of sole ownership and seeks an order from a U.S. federal court compelling the parties to submit to arbitration over the ownership issue and alleged breaches of the joint-venture agreement. How should the court rule if the laws of Euphratia state that, whereas arbitration agreements are to be enforced generally, matters of ownership of natural resources can only be resolved in a Euphratian court of law? Does it matter that two U.S. companies engaged in international commerce would be governed by the Federal Arbitration Act?

4–3. Confirmation of Award. Two brothers, both of whom are certified public accountants (CPAs), form a professional association to provide tax-accounting services to the public. They also agree, in writing, that any disputes that arise between them over matters concerning the association will be submitted to an independent arbitrator, whom they designate to be their father, who is also a CPA. A dispute arises, and the matter is submitted to the father for arbitration. During the course of arbitration, which occurs over several weeks, the father asks the older brother, who is visiting one evening, to explain a certain entry in the brothers' association accounts. The younger brother learns of the discussion at the next meeting for arbitration; he says nothing about it, however. The arbitration is concluded in favor of the older brother, who seeks a court order compelling the younger brother to comply with the award. The younger brother seeks to set aside the award, claiming that the arbitration process was tainted by bias because "Dad always liked my older brother best." The younger brother also seeks to have the award set aside on the basis of improper conduct in that matters subject to arbitration were discussed between the father and older brother without the younger brother's being present. Should a court confirm the award or set it aside? Why?

4–4. Calculation of Award. After resolving their dispute, the two brothers encountered in Problem 4–3 decide to resume their tax-accounting practice according to the terms of their original agreement. Again a dispute arises, and again it is decided by the father (now retired except for numerous occasions on which he acts as an arbitrator) in favor of the older brother. The older brother files a petition to enforce the award. The younger brother seeks to set aside the award and offers evidence that the father, as arbitrator, made a gross error in calculating the accounts that was material to the dispute being arbitrated. If the court is convinced that the father erred in the calculations, should the award be set aside? Why?

4–5. Compelling Arbitration. In 1981, AT&T laid off seventy-nine workers in the Chicago area, purportedly because of a slowdown in economic activity. The Communications Workers of America, a union representing some AT&T workers, argued that there was no lack of work and objected to the layoffs as violations of the terms of a collective bargaining agreement between the union and AT&T. The agreement provided that "differences arising with respect to the interpretation of this contract or the performance of any obligation" under the agreement would be resolved through arbitration. The agreement reserved to AT&T the free exercise of managerial functions such as hiring and firing employees. The agreement conditioned such decision making on compliance with the terms of the contract but expressly excluded disputes over those decisions from arbitration. AT&T relied on this exclusion to avoid the union's demand for arbitration over the layoffs. The union sought a court order to compel arbitration. The court held that the issue of whether the dispute over the layoffs was subject to arbitration should be decided by the arbitrator and ordered the parties to submit the question to the arbitrator. An appellate court affirmed the holding, and AT&T appealed to the United States Supreme Court. How should the Court rule? Discuss fully. [*AT&T Technologies v. Communications Workers of America*, 475 U.S. 643, 106 S.Ct. 1415, 89 L.Ed.2d 648 (1990)]

4–6. Arbitration. Randall Fris worked as a seaman on an Exxon Shipping Co. oil tanker for eight years without incident. One night, he boarded the ship for duty while intoxicated, in violation of company policy. This policy also allowed Exxon to discharge employees who were intoxicated and thus unfit for work. Exxon discharged Fris. Under a contract with Fris's union, the discharge was submitted to arbitration. The arbitrators ordered Exxon to reinstate Fris on an oil tanker. Exxon filed a suit against the union, challenging the award as contrary to public policy, which opposes having intoxicated persons operate seagoing vessels. Can a court set aside an arbitration award on the ground that the award violates public policy? Should the court set aside the award in this case? Explain. [*Exxon Shipping Co. v. Exxon Seamen's Union*, 11 F.3d 1189 (3d Cir. 1993)]

4–7. Arbitration. Phillip Beaudry, who suffered from mental illness, worked in the Department of Income Maintenance for the state of Connecticut. Beaudry was fired from his job when it was learned that he had misappropriated approximately $1,640 in state funds. Beaudry filed a complaint with his union, Council 4 of the American Federation of State, County, and Municipal Employees (AFSCME), and eventually the dispute was submitted to an arbitrator. The arbitrator concluded that Beaudry had been dismissed without "just cause," because Beaudry's acts were caused by his mental illness and "were not willful or volitional or within his capacity to control." Because Beaudry was disabled, the employer was required, under state law, to transfer him to a position that he was competent to hold. The arbitrator awarded Beaudry reinstatement, back pay, seniority, and other benefits. The state appealed the decision to a court. What public policies must the court weigh in making its decision? How should the court rule? [*State v. Council 4, AFSCME*, 27 Conn.App. 635, 608 A.2d 718 (1992)]

4–8. Arbitrator's Authority. Hembree purchased a home from Broadway Realty and Trust Co. In the contract of sale, the buyer and seller agreed to arbitrate any claim or controversy "arising out of or relating to this contract." Hembree later claimed that the roof was defective, and the case was arbitrated. The arbitrator decided in favor of Hembree on the basis that the seller had breached an implied warranty. The seller appealed the arbitrator's decision, claiming that the arbitrator had exceeded his authority, because only claims arising out of or relating to the contract were to be arbitrated, and an implied warranty claim did not arise out of or relate to "this contract." Discuss whether the arbitrator was within his authority in addressing the implied warranty claim. [*Hembree v. Broadway Realty and Trust Co.*, 151 Ariz. 418, 728 P.2d 288 (1986)]

4–9. Arbitration. Colorado's Mandatory Arbitration Act required that all civil lawsuits involving damages of less than $50,000 be arbitrated rather than tried in court. The act affected eight judicial districts in the state. It provided for a court trial for any party dissatisfied with an arbitrator's decision. It also provided that if the trial did not result in an improvement of more than 10 percent in the position of the party who had demanded the trial, that party had to pay the costs of the arbitration proceeding. The constitutionality of the act was challenged by a plaintiff who maintained in part that the act violated litigants' rights of access to the courts and trial by jury. What will the court decide? Explain your answer. [*Firelock, Inc. v. District Court, 20th Judicial District*, 776 P.2d 1090 (Colo. 1989)]

4–10. Arbitration. New York State revised its New Car Lemon Law to allow consumers who complained of purchasing a "lemon" to have their disputes arbitrated before a professional arbitrator appointed by the New York attorney general. Before this revision, the Lemon Law allowed for arbitration of disputes, but the forum in which arbitration took place was sponsored by trade associations within the automobile industry, and consumers often complained of unfair awards. The revised law also provided that consumers could choose between two options: arbitration before a professional arbitrator and suing the manufacturer in court. Manufacturers, however, were compelled to arbitrate claims, if a consumer chose to do so, and could not resort to the courts. Trade associations representing automobile manufacturers and importers brought an action seeking a declaration that the alternative arbitration mechanism of the Lemon Law was unconstitutional because it deprived them of their right to trial by jury. How will the court decide? Discuss. [*Motor Vehicle Manufacturers Association of the United States v. State*, 75 N.Y.2d 175, 550 N.E.2d 919, 551 N.Y.S.2d 470 (1990)]

A Question of Ethics and Social Responsibility

4–11. Linda Bender, in her application for registration as a stockbroker with A. G. Edwards & Sons, Inc., agreed to submit any disputes with her employer to arbitration. Bender later sued her supervisor and employer (the defendants) for sexual harassment in violation of Title VII of the Civil Rights Act of 1964, which prohibits, among other things, employment discrimination based on gender. The defendants requested the court to compel arbitration. The district court judge refused to do so, holding that Bender could not be forced to waive her right to adjudicate Title VII claims in a federal court. The appellate court reversed, ruling that Title VII claims are arbitrable. The court held that compelling Bender to submit her claim for arbitration did not deprive her of the right to a judicial forum, because if the arbitration proceedings were somehow legally deficient, she could still take her case to a federal court for review. [*Bender v. A. G. Edwards & Sons, Inc.*, 971 F.2d 698 (11th Cir. 1992)]

1. Does the right to a postarbitration judicial forum equate to the right to initial access to a judicial forum in employment disputes?

2. Should the fact that reviewing courts rarely set aside arbitrators' awards have any bearing on the arbitrability of certain types of claims, such as those brought under Title VII?

Case Briefing Assignment

4–12. Examine Case A.1 [*Rodriguez de Quijas v. Shearson/American Express, Inc.*, 490 U.S. 477, 109 S.Ct. 1917, 104 L.Ed.2d 379 (1989)] in Appendix A. The case has been excerpted there in great detail. Review and then brief the case, making sure that your brief answers the following questions.

1. What is the legislative policy "embodied in the Arbitration Act"?

2. How did the Court reconcile the protections afforded investors under the Securities Act and the legislative policy advanced by the Arbitration Act? Did the Court believe that by submitting to arbitration, investors forgo "substantive rights" given under the Securities Act?

For Critical Analysis

4–13. The attorney-client privilege protects disclosure of communications. Therefore, a client cannot be compelled to answer such a question as, "What did you tell your attorney about the accident?" Imagine, however, that the client is asked, "Did you see that the light was red?" Should the client be allowed to refuse to answer on the ground that he or she disclosed that fact to the attorney?

Unit I Cumulative Hypothetical Problem

4–14. Korman, Inc., a toy manufacturer, has its headquarters in Minneapolis, Minnesota. It markets its toys throughout the United States, as well as in overseas markets. Korman has recently placed on the market a new line of dolls with such irreverent names as "Harass Me," "Spit on Me," "Pull My Hair," "Watch Me Scream," "Cut Me Quick," and "Abuse Me, Please." The dolls are a success commercially and have netted Korman more profits than any of its other toys. Given these "facts," answer the following questions:

1. Jan's Toy Mart, the California distributor of Korman toys, wants to sue Korman for allegedly breaching a contract. If Jan's Toy Mart brought its suit in a California state court, could that court exercise jurisdiction over Korman? Explain.

2. Suppose that in its contract with Korman, Jan's Toy Mart agreed to submit any dispute that arose between the two companies to binding arbitration. Following the arbitration hearing, the arbitrator concludes that Korman did not breach the contract. Jan's Toy Mart is unsatisfied with the arbitrator's award. Can Jan's Toy Mart appeal the arbitrator's decision to a court?

3. Parents and teachers claim that Korman's dolls encourage children to be violent and that it is unethical of Korman to continue marketing the dolls. Parent-teacher groups are organizing boycotts against Korman and the dolls and have launched a media campaign against the company. Recently, they picketed Korman's headquarters in Minneapolis, bearing such signs as "Korman Hates Kids" and "Watch Korman Scream." If you were a Korman executive, would you recommend that the company cease manufacturing the toys? What factors would Korman's directors need to consider in making this decision?

INTERACTING WITH
The Internet

■ A preeminent resource on the Internet for information on alternative dispute resolution (ADR) is the American Arbitration Association (AAA), which you can locate at

http://www.adr.org

The AAA's site offers information on ADR in a number of areas, including labor relations, employment, commerce, the construction industry, and international disputes. The site provides the text of AAA rules, samples of several AAA forms, and some useful articles on ADR.

■ ConflictNet, which describes itself as "a network of people dedicated to promoting the constructive resolution of conflict," provides information on ADR as well as links to other ADR resources on the Internet. To reach this site, go to

http://www.igc.apc.org/conflictnet

■ You can find publications pertaining to ADR by accessing the Federal Judicial Center at

http://www.fjc.gov

■ A pilot project involving online dispute resolution is the Virtual Magistrate Project, which is sponsored by several ADR organizations, including the American Arbitration Association, the Villanova Center for Information Law and Policy, and the Cyberspace Law Institute. For information on this project, including its docket and decisions, go to

http://vmag.vcilp.org

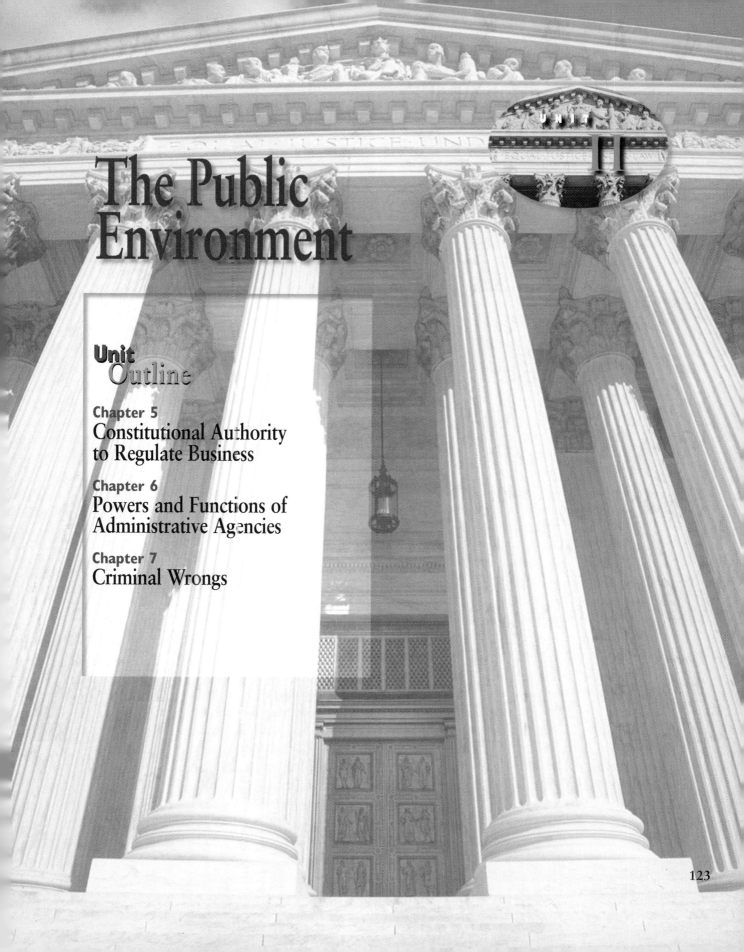

The Public Environment

123

Constitutional Authority to Regulate Business

Contents

Chapter Objectives

After reading this chapter, you should be able to . . .

1. Describe the form of government created by the U.S. Constitution.
2. Explain the relationship between the national government and state governments as set forth in the Constitution.
3. Identify the constitutional basis for the regulatory power of the federal government.
4. Summarize the fundamental rights protected by the Bill of Rights.
5. Give some examples of how the Bill of Rights affects business.

The U.S. Constitution is brief. It consists of only about seven thousand words, which is less than one-third of the number of words in the average state constitution. Perhaps its brevity explains why it has proved to be so "marvelously elastic," as Franklin Roosevelt pointed out in the quotation at the right, and why it has survived for over two hundred years—longer than any other written constitution in the world.

Laws that govern business have their origin in the lawmaking authority granted by this document, which is the supreme law in this country.[1] As mentioned in Chapter 1, neither Congress nor any state may pass a law that conflicts with the Constitution.

In this chapter, we first look at some basic constitutional concepts and clauses and their significance for business. Then we examine how certain fundamental freedoms guaranteed by the Constitution affect businesspersons and the workplace.

> **"The United States Constitution has proved itself the most marvelously elastic compilation of rules of government ever written."**
>
> Franklin D. Roosevelt, 1882–1945 (Thirty-second president of the United States, 1933–1945)

The Constitutional Powers of Government

The U.S. Constitution established a federal form of government. A **federal form of government** is one in which the states form a union and the sovereign power is divided between a central governing authority and the member states. The Constitution delegates certain powers to the national government, and the states retain all other powers. The relationship between the national government and the state governments is a partnership—neither partner is superior to the other except within the particular area of exclusive authority granted to it under the Constitution.

To prevent the possibility that the national government might use its power arbitrarily, the Constitution provided for three branches of government. The legislative branch makes the laws, the executive branch enforces the laws, and the judicial branch interprets the laws. Each branch performs a separate function, and no branch may exercise the authority of another branch.

Each branch, however, has some power to limit the actions of the other two branches. Congress, for example, can enact legislation relating to spending and commerce, but the president can veto that legislation. The executive branch is responsible for foreign affairs, but treaties with foreign governments require the advice and consent of members of the Senate. Although Congress determines the jurisdiction of the federal courts, the United States Supreme Court has the power to hold acts of the other branches of the federal government unconstitutional.[2] Thus, with this system of **checks and balances,** no one branch of government can accumulate too much power.

Federal Form of Government A system of government in which the states form a union and the sovereign power is divided between a central government and the member states.

The Commerce Clause

Article I, Section 8, of the U.S. Constitution expressly permits Congress "[t]o regulate Commerce with foreign Nations, and among the several States, and with the Indian Tribes." This clause, referred to as the **commerce clause,** has had a greater impact on business than any other provision in the Constitution.

Checks and Balances The national government is composed of three separate branches: the executive, the legislative, and the judicial branches. Each branch of the government exercises a check on the actions of the others.

Commerce Clause The provision in Article I, Section 8, of the U.S. Constitution that gives Congress the power to regulate interstate commerce.

---

1. See Appendix B for the full text of the U.S. Constitution.
2. See the *Landmark in the Legal Environment* in Chapter 3 on *Marbury v. Madison,* 5 U.S. (1 Cranch) 137, 2 L.Ed. 60 (1803), a case in which the doctrine of judicial review was clearly enunciated by Chief Justice John Marshall.

International Perspective

The U.S. Constitution, although brief, delineates the basic structure of the government, the authority of each of the three branches of the government, and the relationship between the national government and the state governments. The first ten amendments to the Constitution spell out the basic rights and liberties of Americans. In contrast, Great Britain has no single written document that serves as its constitution. Therefore, it is difficult to obtain a clear outline, in the form of a central body of constitutional rules, that indicates how the British government operates and how the rights of its citizens are protected.

In the place of one document, Britain has a collection of customs and practices, as well as judicial decisions handed down in numerous court cases. In fact, what is regarded as making up the British constitution today is actually a combination of statutes, judicial decisions, conventions, constitutional commentaries, authoritative opinions, letters, and works of scholarship. These include the Magna Carta (1215), the 1689 Bill of Rights, the Reform Act of 1832, and other laws passed by Parliament. Perhaps, then, the distinction between the British "unwritten" constitution and our own is simply that the British constitution exists in written fragments, whereas the U.S. Constitution is contained in one document.

For Critical Analysis: *What are the advantages of having a written constitution, as the United States does? Are there any disadvantages?*

> ### "We are under a Constitution, but the Constitution is what judges say it is."
>
> Charles Evans Hughes, 1862–1948 (Chief justice of the United States Supreme Court, 1930–1941)

REMEMBER Congress can regulate commerce within states as long as the commerce concerns more than one state.

This power was delegated to the federal government to ensure the uniformity of rules governing the movement of goods through the states.

For some time, the commerce power was interpreted as being limited to *interstate* commerce (commerce among the states) and not applicable to *intrastate* commerce (commerce within the states). In 1824, however, in *Gibbons v. Ogden* (see the *Landmark in the Legal Environment*), the United States Supreme Court held that commerce within states could also be regulated by the national government as long as the commerce concerned more than one state.

THE BREADTH OF THE COMMERCE CLAUSE.   As a result of Marshall's decision in *Gibbons v. Ogden*, the commerce clause allowed the national government to exercise increasing authority over all areas of economic affairs throughout the land. In a 1942 case,[3] for example, the Court held that wheat production by an individual farmer intended wholly for consumption on his own farm was subject to federal regulation. The Court reasoned that the home consumption of wheat reduced the demand for wheat and thus could have a substantial effect on interstate commerce. In *McLain v. Real Estate Board of New Orleans, Inc.*, a 1980 case, the Supreme Court acknowledged that the commerce clause had "long been interpreted to extend beyond activities actually in interstate commerce to reach other activities, while wholly local in nature, which nevertheless substantially affect interstate commerce."[4]

In 1995, however, in *United States v. Lopez*,[5] the Supreme Court held—for the first time in sixty years—that there was a limit to the reach of the commerce clause. In the *Lopez* case, the Supreme Court concluded that Congress had exceeded its constitutional authority when it passed the Gun-Free School

---

3.   See *Wickard v. Filburn*, 317 U.S. 111, 63 S.Ct. 82, 87 L.Ed. 122 (1942).
4.   444 U.S. 232, 100 S.Ct. 502, 62 L.Ed.2d 441 (1980).
5.   514 U.S. 549, 115 S.Ct. 1624, 131 L.Ed.2d 626 (1995).

Ships involved in interstate commerce are loaded with shipping containers. Why do you think Congress was given exclusive power to regulate interstate commerce?

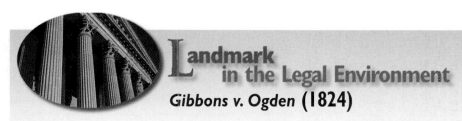

Landmark in the Legal Environment
Gibbons v. Ogden (1824)

The commerce clause, which is found in Article I, Section 8, of the U.S. Constitution, gives Congress the power "to regulate Commerce with foreign Nations, and among the several States, and with the Indian Tribes." What exactly does "to regulate commerce" mean? What does "commerce" entail? These questions came before the United States Supreme Court in 1824 in the case of *Gibbons v. Ogden.*[a]

The background of the case was as follows. Robert Fulton, inventor of the steamboat, and Robert Livingston, who was then American minister to France, secured a monopoly on steam navigation on the waters in the state of New York from the New York legislature in 1803. Fulton and Livingston licensed Aaron Ogden, a former governor of New Jersey and a U.S. senator, to operate steam-powered ferryboats between New York and New Jersey. Thomas Gibbons, who had obtained a license from the U.S. government to operate boats in interstate waters, competed with Ogden without New York's permission. Ogden sued Gibbons. The New York state courts granted Ogden an injunction, prohibiting Gibbons from operating

in New York waters. Gibbons appealed the decision to the United States Supreme Court.

Sitting as chief justice on the Supreme Court was John Marshall, an advocate of a strong national government. In his decision, Marshall defined the word *commerce* as used in the commerce clause to mean all commercial inter-course—that is, all business dealings that affect more than one state. The Court ruled against Ogden's monopoly, reversing the injunction against Gibbons. Marshall used this opportunity not only to expand the definition of commerce but also to validate and increase the power of the national legislature to regulate commerce. Said Marshall, "What is this power? It is the power . . . to prescribe the rule by which commerce is to be governed." Marshall held that the power to regulate interstate commerce was an exclusive power of the national government and that this power included the power to regulate any intrastate commerce that substantially affects interstate commerce.

For Critical Analysis: *What might have resulted if the Court had held otherwise—that the national government did not have the exclusive power to regulate interstate commerce?*

a.   22 U.S. (9 Wheat.) 1, 6 L.Ed. 23 (1824).

Zones Act in 1990. The Court stated that the act, which banned the possession of guns within one thousand feet of any school, was unconstitutional because it attempted to regulate an area that had "nothing to do with commerce, or any sort of economic enterprise." The Court held that activities regulated under the commerce clause, to be constitutional, must substantially affect interstate commerce.

The decision in the *Lopez* case was a close one (four of the nine justices dissented), and the extent to which the decision will curb the regulation of purely local business activities under the commerce clause is as yet unclear. It is notable that just a few days after the *Lopez* case was decided, the Supreme Court again declared that what appeared (to many) to be fundamentally local activities sufficiently affected interstate commerce to be subject to a federal statute. In *United States v. Robertson*,[6] the Court held that the activities of an Alaska gold miner involved interstate commerce because the miner purchased some equipment and supplies in Los Angeles for use in his mining enterprise, recruited workers from outside Alaska, and took some gold (about 15 percent of the mine's output) out of state.

Today, at least theoretically, the power over commerce authorizes the national government to regulate every commercial enterprise in the United States. The breadth of the commerce clause permits the national government to legislate in areas in which there is no explicit grant of power to Congress. In the following case, a motel owner challenged the constitutionality of the Civil Rights Act of 1964, alleging that Congress lacked the authority to regulate what the motel owner claimed was "local" business.

---

6.   514 U.S. 669, 115 S.Ct. 1732, 131 L.Ed.2d 714 (1995).

| RECALL Any law in violation of the U.S. Constitution will not be enforced. |

Case 5.1 ● Heart of Atlanta Motel v. United States

Supreme Court of the United States, 1964.
379 U.S. 241,
85 S.Ct. 348,
13 L.Ed. 2d 258.

HISTORICAL AND SOCIAL SETTING *In the first half of the twentieth century, state governments sanctioned segregation on the basis of race. In 1954, the United States Supreme Court decided that racially segregated school systems violated the Constitution. In the following decade, the Court ordered an end to racial segregation imposed by the states in other public facilities, such as beaches, golf courses, buses, parks, auditoriums, and courtroom seating. Privately owned facilities that excluded or segregated African Americans and others on the basis of race were not subject to the same constitutional restrictions, however. Congress passed the Civil Rights Act of 1964 to prohibit racial discrimination in "establishments affecting interstate commerce." These facilities included "places of public accommodation."*

BACKGROUND AND FACTS The owner of the Heart of Atlanta Motel refused to rent rooms to African Americans in violation of the Civil Rights Act of 1964. The motel owner brought an action in a federal district court to have the act declared unconstitutional, alleging that Congress had exceeded its power to regulate commerce by enacting the act. The owner argued that his motel was not engaged in interstate commerce but was "of a purely local character." The motel, however, was accessible to state and interstate highways. The owner advertised nationally, maintained billboards throughout the state, and accepted convention trade from outside the state (75 percent of the guests were residents of other states). The court sustained the constitutionality of the act and enjoined (prohibited) the owner from discriminating on the basis of race. The owner appealed. The case ultimately went to the United States Supreme Court.

(Continued)

Case 5.1—continued

IN THE WORDS OF THE COURT . . .
Mr. Justice CLARK delivered the opinion of the Court.
* * * *

While the Act as adopted carried no congressional findings, the record of its passage through each house is replete with evidence of the burdens that discrimination by race or color places upon interstate commerce * * * . This testimony included the fact that our people have become increasingly mobile with millions of all races traveling from State to State; that [African Americans] in particular have been the subject of discrimination in transient accommodations, having to travel great distances to secure the same; that often they have been unable to obtain accommodations and have had to call upon friends to put them up overnight. * * * These exclusionary practices were found to be nationwide, the Under Secretary of Commerce testifying that there is "no question that this discrimination in the North still exists to a large degree" and in the West and Midwest as well * * * . This testimony indicated a qualitative as well as quantitative effect on interstate travel by [African Americans]. The former was the obvious impairment of the [African American] traveler's pleasure and convenience that resulted when he continually was uncertain of finding lodging. As for the latter, there was evidence that this uncertainty stemming from racial discrimination had the effect of discouraging travel on the part of a substantial portion of the [African American] community * * * . We shall not burden this opinion with further details since the voluminous testimony presents overwhelming evidence that discrimination by hotels and motels impedes interstate travel.
* * * *

It is said that the operation of the motel here is of a purely local character. But, assuming this to be true, "if it is interstate commerce that feels the pinch, it does not matter how local the operation that applies the squeeze." * * * Thus the power of Congress to promote interstate commerce also includes the power to regulate the local incidents thereof, including local activities in both the States of origin and destination, which might have a substantial and harmful effect upon that commerce.

DECISION AND REMEDY The United States Supreme Court upheld the constitutionality of the Civil Rights Act of 1964. The power of Congress to regulate interstate commerce permitted the enactment of legislation that could halt even local discriminatory practices.

FOR CRITICAL ANALYSIS—POLITICAL CONSIDERATION *Suppose that only 5 percent of the motel's guests—or even 2 or 1 percent—were from out of state. In such a situation, would the Court still have been justified in regulating the motel's activities?*

THE REGULATORY POWERS OF THE STATES.   A problem that frequently arises under the commerce clause concerns a state's ability to regulate matters within its own borders. The U.S. Constitution does not expressly exclude state regulation of commerce, and there is no doubt that states have a strong interest in regulating activities within their borders. As part of their inherent sovereignty, states possess **police powers.** The term does not relate solely to criminal law enforcement but also to the right of state governments to regulate private activities to protect or promote the public order, health, safety, morals, and

Police Powers Powers possessed by states as part of their inherent sovereignty. These powers may be exercised to protect or promote the public order, health, safety, morals, and general welfare.

Hazardous waste is deposited at a burial site. Can the state in which this site is located regulate this activity? If so, and if those regulations impinge on interstate commerce, will they be held unconstitutional?

general welfare. Fire and building codes, antidiscrimination laws, parking regulations, zoning restrictions, licensing requirements, and thousands of other state statutes covering virtually every aspect of life have been enacted pursuant to a state's police powers.

When state regulations impinge on interstate commerce, courts must balance the state's interest in the merits and purposes of the regulation against the burden placed on interstate commerce. Generally, state laws enacted pursuant to a state's police powers carry a strong presumption of validity. If state laws substantially interfere with interstate commerce, however, they will be held to violate the commerce clause of the Constitution.

In *Raymond Motor Transportation, Inc. v. Rice,*[7] for example, the United States Supreme Court invalidated Wisconsin administrative regulations limiting the length of trucks traveling on its highways. The Court weighed the burden on interstate commerce against the benefits of the regulations and concluded that the challenged regulations "place a substantial burden on interstate commerce and they cannot be said to make more than the most speculative contribution to highway safety."

Because courts balance the interests involved, it is extremely difficult to predict the outcome in a particular case. The following case concerns an issue that has elicited much controversy in recent years: whether states have the power to discriminate against shipments of out-of-state waste to intrastate disposal facilities.

---

7.   434 U.S. 429, 98 S.Ct. 787, 54 L.Ed.2d 664 (1978).

Case 5.2 ● Oregon Waste Systems, Inc. v. Department of Environmental Quality of the State of Oregon

Supreme Court of the United States, 1994.
511 U.S. 93,
114 S.Ct. 1345,
128 L.Ed.2d 13.

HISTORICAL AND SOCIAL SETTING   *The treatment and disposal of waste is a major industry. The United States leads the world in the production of waste. Almost ten billion tons of waste of all types are generated in the United States every year. This waste includes everybody's garbage and sewage, as well as the by-products of industry, agriculture, mining, demolition, dredging, and energy production. Thus, large quantities of waste move in interstate commerce every day.*

BACKGROUND AND FACTS   Oregon Waste Systems, Inc., operates a waste-disposal facility in Gilliam County,

Oregon. The facility receives waste from sources in Oregon and from sources outside the state. In 1989, Oregon imposed a fee ($.85 per ton) on all of the solid waste that such facilities receive from sources in Oregon and imposed a higher fee ($2.25 per ton) on solid waste generated outside the state. Oregon Waste, other operators of waste-disposal facilities in Oregon, and Gilliam County filed a suit against the state in an Oregon court, challenging the higher fee as a violation of, among other things, the commerce clause. The court upheld the higher fee, and the plaintiffs appealed. The Oregon Supreme Court affirmed the ruling. The plaintiffs appealed to the United States Supreme Court.

IN THE WORDS OF THE COURT . . .
Justice THOMAS delivered the opinion of the Court.
* * * *

* * * [T]he first step in analyzing any law subject to judicial scrutiny under the * * * Commerce Clause is to determine whether it "regulates

(Continued)

Case 5.2—continued

evenhandedly with only 'incidental' effects on interstate commerce, or discriminates against interstate commerce." * * *

* * * Oregon's $2.25 per ton surcharge is discriminatory on its face. The surcharge subjects waste from other States to a fee almost three times greater than the $0.85 per ton charge imposed on solid in-state waste. * * *
* * * *

Respondents' principal defense of the higher surcharge on out-of-state waste is that it is a "compensatory tax" necessary to make shippers of such waste pay their "fair share" of the costs imposed on Oregon by the disposal of their waste in the State. * * *
* * * *

* * * [W]e have little difficulty concluding that the Oregon surcharge is not such a tax. * * * Respondents' failure to identify a specific charge on intrastate commerce equal to or exceeding the surcharge is fatal to their claim.

Respondents argue that * * * intrastate commerce does pay its share of the costs underlying the surcharge through general taxation. * * *

* * * [T]he very fact that in-state shippers of out-of-state waste, such as Oregon Waste, are charged the out-of-state surcharge even though they pay Oregon income taxes refutes respondents' argument * * * .

DECISION AND REMEDY The United States Supreme Court reversed the judgment of the Oregon Supreme Court and remanded the case.

FOR CRITICAL ANALYSIS—ECONOMIC CONSIDERATION *In terms of the outcome in this case, would it have mattered if the fee for out-of-state waste was only, say, 10 cents per ton higher than the fee for in-state waste?*

The Supremacy Clause

Article VI of the Constitution provides that the Constitution, laws, and treaties of the United States are "the supreme Law of the Land." This article, commonly referred to as the **supremacy clause,** is important in the ordering of state and federal relationships. When there is a direct conflict between a federal law and a state law, the state law is rendered invalid. Because some powers are concurrent (shared by the federal government and the states), however, it is necessary to determine which law governs in a particular circumstance.

When Congress chooses to act exclusively in a concurrent area, it is said to have *preempted* the area. In this circumstance, a valid federal statute or regulation will take precedence over a conflicting state or local law or regulation on the same general subject. Congress, however, rarely makes clear its intent to preempt an entire subject area against state regulation; consequently, the courts must determine whether Congress intended to exercise exclusive dominion over a given area. Consideration of **preemption** often occurs in the commerce clause context.

No single factor is decisive as to whether a court will find preemption. Generally, congressional intent to preempt will be found if the federal law is so pervasive, comprehensive, or detailed that the states have no room to supplement it. Also, when a federal statute creates an agency—such as the National Labor Relations Board—to enforce the law, matters that may come within the agency's jurisdiction will likely preempt state laws.

Supremacy Clause The provision in Article VI of the Constitution that provides that the Constitution, laws, and treaties of the United States are "the supreme Law of the Land." Under this clause, state and local laws that directly conflict with federal law will be rendered invalid.

Preemption A doctrine under which certain federal laws preempt, or take precedence over, conflicting state or local laws.

The Taxing and Spending Powers

Article I, Section 8, provides that Congress has the "Power to lay and collect Taxes, Duties, Imposts, and Excises." Section 8 further provides that "all Duties, Imposts and Excises shall be uniform throughout the United States." The requirement of uniformity refers to uniformity among the states, and thus Congress may not tax some states while exempting others.

Traditionally, if Congress attempted to regulate indirectly, by taxation, an area over which it had no authority, the tax would be invalidated by the courts. Today, however, if a tax measure bears some reasonable relationship to revenue production, it is generally held to be within the national taxing power. Moreover, the expansive interpretation of the commerce clause almost always provides a basis for sustaining a federal tax.

Under Article I, Section 8, Congress has the power "to pay the Debts and provide for the common Defence and general welfare of the United States." Through the spending power, Congress disposes of the revenues accumulated from the taxing power. Congress can spend revenues not only to carry out its enumerated powers but also to promote any objective it deems worthwhile, so long as it does not violate the Bill of Rights. For example, Congress could not condition welfare payments on the recipients' political views. The spending power necessarily involves policy choices, with which taxpayers may disagree.

Business and the Bill of Rights

The importance of a written declaration of the rights of individuals eventually caused the first Congress of the United States to submit twelve amendments to the Constitution to the states for approval. The first ten of these amendments, commonly known as the **Bill of Rights,** were adopted in 1791 and embody a series of protections for the individual against various types of interference by the federal government.[8] Some constitutional protections apply to business entities as well. For example, corporations exist as separate legal entities, or *legal persons,* and enjoy many of the same rights and privileges as *natural persons* do.

Summarized here are the protections guaranteed by these ten amendments.[9] The due process clause of the Fourteenth Amendment, which we discuss later in this chapter, applies many of the rights guaranteed by these first ten amendments to the states.

1. The First Amendment guarantees the freedoms of religion, speech, and the press and the rights to assemble peaceably and to petition the government.
2. The Second Amendment guarantees the right to keep and bear arms.
3. The Third Amendment prohibits, in peacetime, the lodging of soldiers in any house without the owner's consent.
4. The Fourth Amendment prohibits unreasonable searches and seizures of persons or property.

> "Bills of rights give assurance to the individual of the preservation of his liberty. They do not define the liberty they promise."
>
> Benjamin N. Cardozo, 1870–1938
> (Associate Justice of the United States Supreme Court, 1932–1938)

Bill of Rights The first ten amendments to the U.S. Constitution.

---

8.   One of these proposed amendments was ratified 203 years later (in 1992) and became the Twenty-seventh Amendment to the Constitution. See Appendix B.
9.   See the Constitution in Appendix B for the complete text of each amendment.

5. The Fifth Amendment guarantees the rights to indictment by grand jury (see Chapter 7), to due process of law, and to fair payment when private property is taken for public use (see Chapter 21). The Fifth Amendment also prohibits compulsory self-incrimination and double jeopardy (trial for the same crime twice).

6. The Sixth Amendment guarantees the accused in a criminal case the right to a speedy and public trial by an impartial jury and with counsel. The accused has the right to cross-examine witnesses against him or her and to solicit testimony from witnesses in his or her favor.

7. The Seventh Amendment guarantees the right to a trial by jury in a civil case involving at least twenty dollars.[10]

8. The Eighth Amendment prohibits excessive bail and fines, as well as cruel and unusual punishment.

9. The Ninth Amendment establishes that the people have rights in addition to those specified in the Constitution.

10. The Tenth Amendment establishes that those powers neither delegated to the federal government nor denied to the states are reserved for the states.

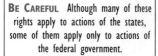

> **BE CAREFUL** Although many of these rights apply to actions of the states, some of them apply only to actions of the federal government.

The rights secured by the Bill of Rights are not absolute. Ultimately, it is the United States Supreme Court, as the interpreter of the Constitution, that both gives meaning to these constitutional rights and determines their boundaries.

Freedom of Speech

The First Amendment freedoms of religion, speech, press, assembly, and petition have all been applied to the states through the due process clause of the

---

10. Twenty dollars was forty days' pay for the average person when the Bill of Rights was written.

Ethical Perspective

As you can see in the above list, many of the rights guaranteed by the first ten amendments are described in very general terms. For example, the Fourth Amendment prohibits unreasonable searches and seizures, but it does not define what constitutes an "unreasonable" search or seizure. Similarly, the Eighth Amendment prohibits excessive bail or fines, but no definition of *excessive* is contained in that amendment. Clearly, our constitutional rights depend not only on the Constitution but also on how our institutions of government give those rights their specific form and substance. Ultimately, it is the United States Supreme Court, as the interpreter of the Constitution, that defines our rights and determines their boundaries.

Ethical convictions—perceptions of what is right and what is wrong—inevitably enter into the process of interpreting and applying the mandates expressed in the Constitution, including the Bill of Rights. These perceptions naturally change over time—and thus, so do interpretations of the nature of our constitutional rights. For example, although the Supreme Court is obligated to follow precedents it established earlier (see the discussion of *stare decisis* in Chapter 1), it can, and has on occasion, departed from precedent in the interests of serving changed perceptions of fairness and justice.

For Critical Analysis: *Supreme Court justices are not elected by the people but are appointed by the president, with the advice and consent of the Senate. Do you think that the justices exercise too much authority in shaping the rights and liberties of Americans? Can you think of a better alternative?*

A minor reviews the contents of a compact disc. Should all forms of verbal expression be protected under the First Amendment to the Constitution?

Fourteenth Amendment (discussed later in this chapter). As mentioned, however, none of these freedoms confers an absolute right.

UNPROTECTED SPEECH.   In interpreting the meaning of the First Amendment's guarantee of free speech, the United States Supreme Court has made it clear that certain types of speech will not be protected. Speech that harms the good reputation of another, or defamatory speech (see Chapter 8), will not be protected under the First Amendment. Speech that violates criminal laws (such as threatening speech, pornography, and so on) is not constitutionally protected.

Other unprotected speech includes "fighting words," or words that are likely to incite others to respond violently, and obscene speech. Numerous state and federal statutes make it a crime to disseminate obscene materials. The United States Supreme Court has grappled from time to time with the problem of trying to establish an operationally effective definition of obscene speech, but frequently this determination is left to state and local authorities. Generally, obscenity is still a constitutionally unsettled area, whether it deals with speech, printed materials, or filmed materials. In the interest of protecting against the abuse of children, however, the Supreme Court has upheld state laws prohibiting the sale and possession of child pornography.[11] In the interest of protecting women against sexual harassment in the workplace, at least one court has banned lewd speech and pornographic pinups in the workplace.[12] In recent

---

11.   See *Osborne v. Ohio,* 495 U.S. 103, 110 S.Ct. 1691, 109 L.Ed.2d 98 (1990).
12.   *Robinson v. Jacksonville Shipyards, Inc.,* 760 F.Supp. 1486 (M.D.Fla. 1991).

Ethical Perspective

Determining the point at which speech oversteps its constitutionally protected boundaries often poses troublesome ethical questions both for the courts and for society. For example, in recent years several colleges and universities have issued speech or behavioral codes in an attempt to curb the "hate speech" exchanged between members of different ethnic groups on their campuses. The University of Michigan, for instance, established a code that banned "any behavior, verbal or physical, that stigmatizes or victimizes an individual on the basis of race, ethnicity, religion, sex, sexual orientation, creed, national origin, ancestry, age, marital status, handicap or Vietnam-era veterans status." Other universities have issued similar codes. Do such codes go too far in restraining the free speech of students?

Many people contend that forcing students to engage only in "politically correct" speech violates the First

Amendment right to freedom of expression. Others argue that hate speech essentially constitutes "fighting words" and thus should not be constitutionally protected. The courts have generally been reluctant to uphold these codes on the ground that they go too far in restricting the free speech of students. The Michigan code, for example, was ruled unconstitutional, as were similar codes issued by the University of Wisconsin and Stanford University.[a]

For Critical Analysis: *Does hate speech equate with fighting words? Should colleges and universities be permitted to regulate speech on their campuses?*

---

a.   See *Doe v. University of Michigan,* 721 F.Supp. 852 (E.D.Mich. 1989); *The UWM Post v. Board of Regents of the University of Wisconsin System,* 774 F.Supp. 1163 (E.D.Wis. 1991); and "California Court Strikes Down Stanford Ban of 'Fighting Words,'" *The New York Times,* March 1, 1995, p. B8.

Technology and Free Speech

When you are talking to someone, you can say just about anything without fear of prosecution. What about a situation in which you are "talking to" someone over the Internet, though? Are there any restrictions on your freedom of speech? The courts are having a hard time dealing with this thorny issue in today's on-line world. In various World Wide Web sites on the Internet, so-called news groups have been set up to allow people to "chat" about their mutual interests. Consequently, there are news groups on virtually every topic under the sun—gardening; political candidates; numerous movie stars, such as Kevin Costner and Winona Ryder; and country-and-western stars, such as the Mavericks and Trisha Yearwood.

What about news groups that deal with pornography, however defined, or even pedophilia? Anyone with a computer and a modem can create a news group in Usenet, which overlaps with the Internet. Indeed, the name of an alternative ("alt.") Usenet news group includes "pedophile," and this news group contains digitized photos that users can download to their own computers. Child pornography violates various federal and state laws. Even if local operators somehow screened out child pornography, users could still exchange digitized photos via electronic mail

(e-mail). Moreover, American users can tap into computer systems abroad. There, U.S. obscenity laws do not apply.

Public concern over access to pornographic and obscene materials via the Internet led Congress to enact the Communications Decency Act (CDA) as part of the Telecommunications Act of 1996. The CDA made it a criminal offense to transmit "indecent" speech or images to minors or to make such speech or images available on-line to minors. Ultimately, the Supreme Court ruled that these provisions of the CDA were unconstitutional.[a] The Court held that the CDA suppressed speech that adults have a constitutional right to send and receive via the Internet, even though the government has a legitimate interest in protecting children from harmful material.

For Critical Analysis: *The CDA stated that indecent speech is to be measured by community standards, but what community standards would have applied to the Internet, which has no geographic boundaries?*

_____
a.   *Reno v. American Civil Liverties Union,___U.S.,___, 117 S.Ct. 2329, 138 L.Ed.2d 874 (1997).*

years, obscenity issues have also arisen in relation to television shows, movies, the lyrics and covers of music albums, and the content of monologues by "shock" comedians. (See this chapter's *Technology and Free Speech* for a discussion of free speech and on-line communications via the Internet.)

COMMERCIAL SPEECH—ADVERTISING.   Courts often make a distinction between "normal" speech and "commercial" speech, which is speech and communications made by business firms, such as advertising. Although commercial speech is protected by the First Amendment, its protection is not as extensive as that afforded to noncommercial speech. A state may restrict certain kinds of advertising, for example, in the interest of protecting consumers from being misled by the advertising practices. States also have a legitimate interest in the beautification of roadsides, and this interest allows states to place restraints on billboard advertising.

Generally, a restriction on commercial speech will be considered valid as long as it meets the following three criteria: (1) it must seek to implement a substantial government interest, (2) it must directly advance that interest, and (3) it must go no further than necessary to accomplish its objective. At issue in the following case is whether a law prohibiting the inclusion of the alcohol content on beer labels unconstitutionally restricts commercial speech.

Case 5.3 ⬤ Rubin v. Coors Brewing Co.

Supreme Court of the United States, 1995.
514 U.S. 476,
115 S.Ct. 1585,
131 L.Ed.2d 532.

HISTORICAL AND SOCIAL SETTING *In the United States, no federal law regulates the level of alcohol in beer. The most popular beers contain between 3 and 5 percent alcohol. Ice beers are typically between 5 and 6 percent alcohol. Malt liquors may be as much as 7 percent alcohol. Beer is a popular drink among young consumers, who sometimes prefer the more potent brands. In the 1980s, it was widely—and erroneously—believed that beer brewed by the Coors Brewing Company was less potent than other beers.*

BACKGROUND AND FACTS In 1987, Coors applied to the Bureau of Alcohol, Tobacco and Firearms (BATF), an agency of the Department of the Treasury, for approval of proposed Coors beer labels that disclosed the alcohol content of the beer. The BATF rejected the labels on the ground that the Federal Alcohol Administration Act (FAAA) of 1935[a] prohibits the disclosure of the alcohol content of beer on labels. Coors filed a suit in a federal district court against the government to block the enforcement of the FAAA, on the ground that it violated the First Amendment. The government argued that enforcement of the FAAA suppresses the threat of "strength wars" among brewers, who, without the regulation, would compete in the marketplace based on the potency of their products. The district court granted Coors relief, and the government appealed. When the appellate court affirmed, the government appealed to the United States Supreme Court.

IN THE WORDS OF THE COURT . . .
Justice THOMAS delivered the opinion of the Court.

* * * *

 * * * [T]he Government * * * has a significant interest in protecting the health, safety, and welfare of its citizens by preventing brewers from competing on the basis of alcohol strength, which could lead to greater alcoholism and its attendant social costs. * * *

* * * *

We conclude that [the FAAA] cannot directly and materially advance [this] interest * * * . [T]he laws governing labeling * * * prohibit statements of alcohol content in advertising * * * only in States that affirmatively prohibit such advertisements. As only 18 States at best prohibit disclosure of content in advertisements, brewers remain free to disclose alcohol content in advertisements, but not on labels, in much of the country. * * *

 * * * While [the FAAA] bans the disclosure of alcohol content on beer labels, it allows the exact opposite in the case of wines and spirits. * * * Further, the Government permits brewers to signal high alcohol content through use of the term "malt liquor." * * *

* * * *

[Finally] the Government's regulation of speech is not sufficiently tailored to its goal. * * * [Coors] suggests several alternatives, such as directly limiting the alcohol content of beers, prohibiting marketing efforts emphasizing high alcohol strength * * * , or limiting the labeling ban only to malt liquors * * * . We agree that the availability of these options, all of which could advance the Government's asserted interest in a manner less intrusive to [Coors'] First Amendment rights, indicates that [the FAAA] is more extensive than necessary.

DECISION AND REMEDY The Supreme Court held that the labeling ban violated the First Amendment's protection of commercial speech.

FOR CRITCAL ANALYSIS—POLITICAL CONSIDERATION *The trend in federal regulation of consumer products appears to favor greater disclosure of information. Whose interests are advanced by the disclosure of more information?*

---

a. 27 U.S.C. Sections 201–220.

POLITICAL SPEECH.   Political speech that otherwise would be within the protection of the First Amendment does not lose that protection simply because its source is a corporation. For example, in *First National Bank of Boston v. Bellotti,* national banking associations and business corporations sought United States Supreme Court review of a Massachusetts statute that prohibited corporations from making political contributions or expenditures that individuals were permitted to make. The Court ruled that the Massachusetts law was unconstitutional because it violated the right of corporations to freedom of speech.[13] Similarly, the Court has held that a law forbidding a corporation from using bill inserts to express its views on controversial issues also violates the First Amendment.[14]

Does a state law banning the distribution of anonymous political leaflets unconstitutionally restrain political speech? This question is at issue in the following case.

> **REMEMBER** The First Amendment guarantee of freedom of speech only applies to government restrictions on speech.

---

13.   435 U.S. 765, 98 S.Ct. 1407, 55 L.Ed.2d 707 (1978).
14.   *Consolidated Edison Co. v. Public Service Commission,* 447 U.S. 530, 100 S.Ct. 2326, 65 L.Ed.2d 319 (1980).

Case 5.4 ● McIntyre v. Ohio Elections Commission

Supreme Court of the United States, 1995.
514 U.S. 334,
115 S.Ct. 1511,
131 L.Ed.2d 426.

HISTORICAL AND POLITICAL SETTING   *Anonymous pamphlets, leaflets, brochures, and books have played an important role in the political life of the United States. Perhaps the most famous embodiment of this tradition is* The Federalist Papers, *a series of essays published in New York City newspapers in 1787 and 1788. Writing under the name "Publius," James Madison, Alexander Hamilton, and John Jay argued in* The Federalist Papers *for the ratification of the Constitution.*

BACKGROUND AND FACTS   In April 1988, Margaret McIntyre distributed leaflets to persons attending public meetings at the Blendon Middle School in Westerville, Ohio. The leaflets expressed opposition to a proposed school tax. Some of the leaflets did not identify an author but only purported to express the views of "CONCERNED PARENTS AND TAX PAYERS." A school official filed a complaint with the Ohio Elections Commission under a state statute that prohibits the distribution of campaign literature that does not contain the name and address of the person or official issuing it. The commission imposed a fine of $100. McIntyre appealed to an Ohio state court, arguing that the statute was unconstitutional. The court agreed and dropped the fine. An Ohio appellate court reinstated the fine, and the Ohio Supreme Court affirmed. The state supreme court concluded that the statute was reasonable in light of the state's interests in providing voters with information and in preventing fraud. McIntyre appealed to the United States Supreme Court.

IN THE WORDS OF THE COURT . . .
Justice STEVENS delivered the opinion of the Court.
*   *   *   *

*   *   * [A]n author's decision to remain anonymous, like other decisions concerning omissions or additions to the content of a publication, is an aspect of the freedom of speech protected by the First Amendment.
*   *   *   *

(Continued)

Case 5.4—continued

* * * [T]he speech in which Mrs. McIntyre engaged—handing out leaflets in the advocacy of a politically controversial viewpoint—is the essence of First Amendment expression. * * *

When a law burdens * * * political speech, we * * * uphold the restriction only if it is narrowly tailored to serve an overriding state interest.
* * * *

* * * The simple interest in providing voters with * * * information does not justify a state requirement that a writer make statements or disclosures she would otherwise omit. Moreover, in the case of a handbill written by a private citizen who is not known to the recipient, the name and address of the author adds little, if anything, to the reader's ability to evaluate the document's message. * * *

The state interest in preventing fraud and libel stands on a different footing. * * * Ohio does not, however, rely solely on [this statute] to protect that interest. Its Election Code includes detailed and specific prohibitions against making or disseminating false statements during political campaigns. * * *

As this case demonstrates, the prohibition encompasses documents that are not even arguably false or misleading. * * * We recognize that a State's enforcement interest might justify a more limited identification requirement, but Ohio has shown scant cause for inhibiting the leafletting at issue here.

DECISION AND REMEDY   The United States Supreme Court reversed the decision of the lower court, holding that the First Amendment protects the freedom to publish anonymously.

FOR CRITICAL ANALYSIS—POLITICAL CONSIDERATION   *When the source of political speech is a corporation, should the corporation be required to identify itself? Would such a requirement be constitutional?*

Freedom of Religion

Establishment Clause   The provision in the First Amendment to the Constitution that prohibits Congress from creating any law "respecting an establishment of religion."

Free Exercise Clause   The provision in the First Amendment to the Constitution that prohibits Congress from making any law "prohibiting the free exercise" of religion.

The First Amendment states that the government may neither establish any religion nor prohibit the free exercise of religious practices. The first part of this constitutional provision is referred to as the **establishment clause,** and the second part is known as the **free exercise clause.** Government action, both federal and state, must be consistent with this constitutional mandate.

Federal or state regulation that does not promote religion or place a significant burden on religion is constitutional even if it has some impact on religion. "Sunday closing laws," for example, make the performance of some commercial activities on Sunday illegal. These statutes, also known as "blue laws" (from the color of the paper on which an early Sunday law was written), have been upheld on the ground that it is a legitimate function of government to provide a day of rest. The United States Supreme Court has held that the closing laws, although originally of a religious character, have taken on the secular purpose of promoting the health and welfare of workers.[15] Even though closing laws admittedly make it easier for Christians to attend religious services, the Court has viewed this effect as an incidental, not a primary, purpose of Sunday closing laws.

---

15.   *McGowan v. Maryland*, 366 U.S. 420, 81 S.Ct. 1101, 6 L.Ed.2d 393 (1961).

Inside
the Legal Environment
Religious Symbols Go to Court

Retailers in America know the importance of the Christmas season. Some major retailers obtain 40 percent of their annual sales revenues during the holiday period. Municipalities also spend tax dollars to decorate streets and government offices. Most of these decorations are not religious and apparently offend few individuals. What about blatantly religious scenes, however? Does any government in the United States have the legal right to use public monies for the display of religious scenes or to permit the display of religious symbols on government (public) property? At issue here is the establishment clause of the First Amendment to the U.S. Constitution: "Congress shall make no law respecting an establishment of religion."

A major test of a municipality's ability to spend public funds on religious scenes during the Christmas season occurred in 1984. The city of Pawtucket in Rhode Island included a crèche—a model depicting Mary, Joseph, and others around the crib of Jesus in the stable at Bethlehem—in a larger, nonreligious Christmas display, which included reindeer, candy-striped poles, and a Christmas tree. The entire display, although it was located in a private park, was the city's official display and had been both erected and maintained by city employees. This case, known as *Lynch v. Donnelly*,[a] was decided in

favor of the municipal government. The crèche could be included as long as it was just one part of a holiday display. The presence of the crèche was deemed constitutional; it did not violate the establishment clause.

What about the simultaneous display by local governments of objects that are symbols from various religions? In *County of Allegheny v. American Civil Liberties Union*,[b] the American Civil Liberties Union (ACLU) sued Allegheny County, where Pittsburgh, Pennsylvania, is located, because of what the ACLU claimed were "frankly religious displays." Each year, the county erects a crèche in its county courthouse, and the city of Pittsburgh also displays a menorah (a nine-branched candelabrum used in celebrating Chanukah) near the annual Christmas tree on the steps of its city-county building. Although the county displays nonreligious holiday symbols in the courthouse, they are not displayed alongside the crèche, as they were in the *Lynch* case. Therefore, the Supreme Court held that the presence of the crèche was unconstitutional. Displaying the menorah, however, did not violate the First Amendment, because the menorah was situated in close proximity to the Christmas tree.

In 1995, the Supreme Court again tangled with religious symbols and the establishment clause. The issue concerned whether the Ku Klux Klan

(KKK) should be allowed to place an unattended cross in Capitol Square, the statehouse plaza in Columbus, Ohio, during the Christmas season. The Court ruled in favor of the KKK. Because the square is a forum for the discussion of public questions and for public activities, the presence of the cross would not indicate the government's endorsement of a religious belief. Neither *Allegheny* nor *Lynch*, stated the Court, "even remotely assumes that the government's neutral treatment of private religious expression can be unconstitutional."[c]

Clearly, court judges and justices do not have an easy job. In addition to their other duties, they periodically have to function as, in Justice Kennedy's words, a kind of "theology board."

For Critical Analysis: *During oral arguments before the Supreme Court in the ACLU case discussed above, Justice Scalia asked the attorney representing the city of Pittsburgh the following question: "[M]usn't the city do something for every religion in order to avoid appearing to endorse one religion over another?" How would you answer this question?*

a. 465 U.S. 668, 104 S.Ct. 1355, 79 L.Ed.2d 604 (1984).

b. 492 U.S. 573, 109 S.Ct. 3086, 106 L.Ed.2d 472 (1989).

c. *Capitol Square Review and Advisory Board v. Pinette*, 515 U.S. 753, 115 S.Ct. 2440, 132 L.Ed.2d 650 (1995).

The First Amendment does not require a complete separation of church and state. On the contrary, it affirmatively mandates *accommodation* of all religions and forbids hostility toward any.[16] As indicated in this chapter's *Inside the Legal Environment,* the courts do not have an easy task in determining the extent to which governments can accommodate a religion without appearing to promote that religion and thus violate the establishment clause. For business firms, an important issue involves the accommodation that businesses must make for the religious beliefs of their employees. We examine this issue in Chapter 17, in the context of employment discrimination.

Self-Incrimination

> **Be Aware** The Fifth Amendment protection against self-incrimination does not cover partnerships or corporations.

The Fifth Amendment guarantees that no person "shall be compelled in any criminal case to be a witness against himself." Thus, in any federal proceeding, an accused person cannot be compelled to give testimony that might subject him or her to any criminal prosecution. Nor can an accused person be forced to testify against himself or herself in state courts, because the due process clause of the Fourteenth Amendment (discussed later in this chapter) incorporates the Fifth Amendment provision against self-incrimination.

The Fifth Amendment's guarantee against self-incrimination extends only to natural persons. Because a corporation is a legal entity and not a natural person, the privilege against self-incrimination does not apply to it. Similarly, the business records of a partnership do not receive Fifth Amendment protection.[17] When a partnership is required to produce these records, it must give the information even if it incriminates the persons who constitute the business entity. Sole proprietors and sole practitioners (those who fully own their businesses) who have not incorporated cannot be compelled to produce their business records. These individuals have full protection against self-incrimination, because they function in only one capacity; there is no separate business entity.

Searches and Seizures

The Fourth Amendment protects the "right of the people to be secure in their persons, houses, papers, and effects." Before searching or seizing private property, law enforcement officers must obtain a **search warrant**—an order from a judge or other public official authorizing the search or seizure.

Search Warrant An order granted by a public authority, such as a judge, that authorizes law enforcement personnel to search particular premises or property.

Probable Cause Reasonable grounds to believe the existence of facts warranting certain actions, such as the search or arrest of a person.

SEARCH WARRANTS AND PROBABLE CAUSE.   To obtain a search warrant, the officers must convince a judge that they have reasonable grounds, or probable cause, to believe a search will reveal a specific illegality. **Probable cause** requires law enforcement officials to have trustworthy evidence that would convince a reasonable person that the proposed search or seizure is more likely justified than not. Furthermore, the Fourth Amendment prohibits *general* warrants. It requires a particular description of that which is to be searched or seized. General searches through a person's belongings are impermissible. The search cannot extend beyond what is described in the warrant.

---

16.   *Zorach v. Clauson,* 343 U.S. 306, 72 S.Ct. 679, 96 L.Ed. 954 (1952).
17.   The privilege has been applied to some small family partnerships. *See United States v. Slutsky,* 352 F.Supp. 1005 (S.D.N.Y. 1972).

There are exceptions to the requirement of a search warrant, as when it is likely that the items sought will be removed before a warrant can be obtained. For example, if a police officer has probable cause to believe an automobile contains evidence of a crime and it is likely that the vehicle will be unavailable by the time a warrant is obtained, the officer can search the vehicle without a warrant.

SEARCHES AND SEIZURES IN THE BUSINESS CONTEXT. Constitutional protection against unreasonable searches and seizures is important to businesses and professionals. As federal and state regulation of commercial activities increased, frequent and unannounced government inspections were conducted to ensure compliance with the regulations. Such inspections were at times extremely disruptive. In *Marshall v. Barlow's, Inc.,*[18] the United States Supreme Court held that government inspectors do not have the right to enter business premises without a warrant, although the standard of probable cause is not the same as that required in nonbusiness contexts. The existence of a general and neutral enforcement plan will justify issuance of the warrant.

Lawyers and accountants frequently possess the business records of their clients, and inspecting these documents while they are out of the hands of their true owners also requires a warrant. No warrant is required, however, for seizures of spoiled or contaminated food. Nor are warrants required for searches of businesses in such highly regulated industries as liquor, guns, and strip mining. General manufacturing is not considered to be one of these highly regulated industries, however.

Of increasing concern to many government employers is how to maintain a safe and efficient workplace without jeopardizing the Fourth Amendment rights of employees "to be secure in their persons." Requiring government employees to undergo random drug tests, for example, may be held to violate the Fourth Amendment.

> **"What is due process of law depends on circumstances. It varies with the subject matter and necessities of the situation."**
>
> Oliver Wendell Holmes, Jr., 1841–1935
> (Associate justice of the United States Supreme Court, 1902–1932)

A person undergoing a drug test. Should government employers be permitted to require all their employees to take random drug tests?

Other Constitutional Protections

▼ Two other constitutional guaranties of great significance to Americans are mandated by the *due process clauses* of the Fifth and Fourteenth Amendments and the *equal protection clause* of the Fourteenth Amendment.

Due Process

Both the Fifth and the Fourteenth Amendments provide that no person shall be deprived "of life, liberty, or property, without due process of law." The **due process clause** of these constitutional amendments has two aspects—procedural and substantive.

PROCEDURAL DUE PROCESS. *Procedural* due process requires that any government decision to take life, liberty, or property must be made fairly. For example, fair procedures must be used in determining whether a person will be subjected to punishment or have some burden imposed on him or her. Fair

Due Process Clause The provisions of the Fifth and Fourteenth Amendments to the Constitution that guarantee that no person shall be deprived of life, liberty, or property without due process of law. Similar clauses are found in most state constitutions.

18. 436 U.S. 307, 98 S.Ct. 1816, 56 L.Ed.2d 305 (1978).

procedure has been interpreted as requiring that the person have at least an opportunity to object to a proposed action before a fair, neutral decision maker (which need not be a judge). Thus, for example, if a driver's license is construed as a property interest, some sort of opportunity to object to its suspension or termination by the state must be provided.

SUBSTANTIVE DUE PROCESS.   *Substantive* due process focuses on the content, or substance, of legislation. If a law or other governmental action limits a *fundamental right*, it will be held to violate substantive due process unless it promotes a *compelling or overriding* state interest. Fundamental rights include interstate travel, privacy, voting, and all First Amendment rights. Compelling state interests could include, for example, the public's safety. Thus, laws designating speed limits may be upheld even though they affect interstate travel, if they are shown to reduce highway fatalities, because the state has a compelling interest in protecting the lives of its citizens.

In all other situations, a law or action does not violate substantive due process if it rationally relates to any legitimate governmental end. It is almost impossible for a law or action to fail the "rationality" test. Under this test, virtually any business regulation will be upheld as reasonable—the United States Supreme Court has sustained insurance regulations, price and wage controls, banking controls, and controls of unfair competition and trade practices against substantive due process challenges.

To illustrate, if a state legislature enacted a law imposing a fifteen-year term of imprisonment without a trial on all businesspersons who appeared in their own television commercials, the law would be unconstitutional on both substantive and procedural grounds. Substantive review would invalidate the legislation because it abridges freedom of speech. Procedurally, the law is unfair because it imposes the penalty without giving the accused a chance to defend his or her actions. The lack of procedural due process will cause a court to invalidate any statute or prior court decision. Similarly, a denial of substantive due process requires courts to overrule any state or federal law that violates the Constitution. In the following case, the court considered whether the retroactive application of a statute violated a defendant's due process rights.

Case 5.5 ● Shadburne-Vinton v. Dalkon Shield Claimants Trust

United States Court of Appeals,
Fourth Circuit, 1995.
60 F.3d 1071.

HISTORICAL AND TECHNOLOGICAL SETTING   *An intrauterine device (IUD) is a contraceptive device made of plastic and sometimes containing copper. Today, IUDs are generally reliable, although some women experience painful periods, and there is a risk of pelvic infection. In the 1980s, however, the Dalkon Shield IUD, manufactured by the A. H.*

Robins Company, was believed to have caused much more serious injuries to many of the women who used it.

BACKGROUND AND FACTS   Susan Shadburne-Vinton used a Dalkon Shield IUD from 1974 through 1976. Claiming that the IUD had rendered her infertile and caused her to develop multiple sclerosis, Shadburne-Vinton filed suit against the A. H. Robins Company in a federal district court in 1983. The court dismissed her suit under an Oregon statute that limited the time for filing such suits to "not later than eight years" after the date on which a prod-

(Continued)

Case 5.5—continued

uct was purchased. Shadburne-Vinton appealed, but the appeal was suspended when Robins filed for bankruptcy. During the suspension, the Oregon legislature amended the statute to exclude IUD manufacturers. The amendment expressly stated that it applied retroactively. When Shadburne-Vinton's case went forward, the Dalkon Shield Claimants Trust (which substituted for Robins as a result of the bankruptcy proceeding) argued that retroactive application of the amendment to the statute would violate the trust's due process rights. The court agreed and issued a judgment in favor of the trust. Shadburne-Vinton appealed.

IN THE WORDS OF THE COURT . . .
CHAPMAN, Senior Circuit Judge:

* * * *

* * * [T]he Due Process Clause of the Fifth Amendment allows retroactive application of either federal or state statutes as long as the statute serves a legitimate legislative purpose that is furthered by rational means.

* * *

* * * *

* * * [W]e must determine whether the Oregon statute * * * , which expressly states that it applies retroactively, serves a legitimate legislative purpose that is furthered by rational means. After extensive hearings on the legislation, the Oregon legislature determined that retroactive application of the Special IUD Statute was fair and equitable to all parties involved. Because many of the women suffered injuries from the IUD in the early to mid-1970s, and the link between the IUD and the injuries it caused was not discovered until the early 1980s, the unamended statute * * * barred the claims of many women. The Oregon Legislature determined that the Special IUD Statute was necessary to provide these claimants with a fair opportunity to litigate their claims.

DECISION AND REMEDY The U.S. Court of Appeals for the Fourth Circuit concluded that the statute did not violate the due process clause of the Fifth Amendment and reversed the lower court's ruling.

FOR CRITICAL ANALYSIS—POLITICAL CONSIDERATION *In whose best interest is it to set a time limit within which a lawsuit must be brought?*

Equal Protection

Under the Fourteenth Amendment, a state may not "deny to any person within its jurisdiction the equal protection of the laws." The United States Supreme Court has used the due process clause of the Fifth Amendment to make the **equal protection clause** applicable to the federal government. Equal protection means that the government must treat similarly situated individuals in a similar manner.

Both substantive due process and equal protection require review of the substance of the law or other governmental action rather than review of the procedures used. When a law or action limits the liberty of all persons to do something, it may violate substantive due process; when a law or action limits the liberty of some persons but not others, it may violate the equal protection clause. Thus, for example, if a law prohibits all persons from buying contraceptive devices, it raises a substantive due process question; if it prohibits only unmarried persons from buying the same devices, it raises an equal protection issue.

Equal Protection Clause The provision in the Fourteenth Amendment to the Constitution that guarantees that no state will "deny to any person within its jurisdiction the equal protection of the laws." This clause mandates that the state governments treat similarly situated individuals in a similar manner.

Basically, in determining whether a law or action violates the equal protection clause, a court will consider questions similar to those previously noted as applicable in a substantive due process review. Under an equal protection inquiry, when a law or action distinguishes between or among individuals, the basis for the distinction—that is, the *classification*—is examined.

STRICT SCRUTINY.   If the law or action inhibits some persons' exercise of a fundamental right, the law or action will be subject to "strict scrutiny" by the courts. Under this standard, the classification must be necessary to promote a compelling state interest. Also, if the classification is based on a *suspect trait*—such as race, national origin, or citizenship status—the classification must be necessary to promote a compelling state interest. Compelling state interests include remedying past unconstitutional or illegal discrimination but do not include correcting the general effects of "society's" discrimination. Thus, for example, if a city gives preference to minority applicants in awarding construction contracts, the city normally must identify the past unconstitutional or illegal discrimination against minority construction firms that it is attempting to correct.

INTERMEDIATE SCRUTINY.   Another standard, that of "intermediate scrutiny," is applied in cases involving discrimination based on gender or legitimacy. Laws using these classifications must be *substantially related to important government objectives*. For example, an important government objective is preventing illegitimate teenage pregnancies. Because males and females are not similarly situated in this circumstance—only females can become pregnant—a law that punishes men but not women for statutory rape will be upheld. A state law requiring illegitimate children to bring paternity suits within six years of their births, however, will be struck down if legitimate children are allowed to seek support from their parents at any time.

THE "RATIONAL BASIS" TEST.   In matters of economic or social welfare, the classification will be considered valid if there is any conceivable *rational basis* on which the classification might relate to any legitimate government interest. It is almost impossible for a law or action to fail the rational basis test. Thus, for example, a city ordinance that in effect prohibits all pushcart vendors except a specific few from operating in a particular area of the city will be upheld if the city proffers a rational basis—perhaps regulation and reduction of traffic in the particular area—for the ordinance. In contrast, a law that provides unemployment benefits only to people over six feet tall would violate the guarantee of equal protection. There is no rational basis for determining the distribution of unemployment compensation on the basis of height. Such a distinction could not further any legitimate government objective.

Privacy Rights

Today, virtually all institutions with which an individual has dealings—including schools, doctors and dentists, insurance companies, mail-order houses, banking institutions, credit-card companies, and mortgage firms—obtain information about that individual and store it in their computer files. In addition, numerous government agencies, such as the Census Bureau, the Social Security Administration, and the Internal Revenue Service, collect and store data concerning individuals' incomes, expenses, marital status, and other per-

A businessperson works with data on a computer. When such data consists of personal information about individuals, is there sufficient legal protection against the invasion of those individuals' privacy?

sonal history and habits. Any time an individual applies for a driver's license, a credit card, or even telephone service, information concerning that individual is gathered and stored. Frequently, this personal information finds its way to credit bureaus, marketing departments and firms, or other organizations without the permission or even the knowledge of the individuals concerned.

A personal right to privacy is held to be so fundamental as to be applicable at both the state and the federal levels. Although there is no specific guarantee of a right to privacy in the Constitution, such a right has been derived from guarantees found in the First, Third, Fourth, Fifth, and Ninth Amendments. Invasion of another's privacy is also a civil wrong (see Chapter 8), and over the last several decades legislation has been passed at the federal level to protect the privacy of individuals in several areas of concern (see Exhibit 5–1). In the business context, issues of privacy often arise in the employment context.

Constitutional Law in Cyberspace

▼ The growing use of the Internet for both personal and business communications has created new legal challenges in virtually every area of the law, including many of the areas discussed in this text. Here we examine selected legal issues relating to constitutional law.

Regulating Online Obscenity

As discussed earlier in this chapter, obscene speech is not protected by the First Amendment. In 1996, in response to public concern over access to pornographic and obscene materials via the Internet, Congress enacted the Communications Decency Act (CDA). This act, which was part of the Telecommunications Act of 1996, made it a criminal offense to transmit "indecent" speech or images to minors (those under the age of eighteen) or to make such speech or images available online to minors. The act defined indecent speech as any communication that depicts or describes sexual or excretory activities or organs in a way that is

TITLE	PROVISIONS CONCERNING PRIVACY
Freedom of Information Act (1966)	Provides that individuals have a right to obtain access to information about them collected in government files.
Fair Credit Reporting Act (1970)	Provides that consumers have the right to be informed of the nature and scope of a credit investigation, the kind of information that is being compiled, and the names of the firms or individuals who will be receiving the report.
Crime Control Act (1973)	Safeguards the confidentiality of information amassed for certain state criminal systems.
Family and Educational Rights and Privacy Act (1974)	Limits access to computer-stored records of education-related evaluations and grades in private and public colleges and universities.
Privacy Act (1974)	Protects the privacy of individuals about whom the federal government has information. Specifically, the act provides as follows: 1. Agencies originating, using, disclosing, or otherwise manipulating personal information must ensure the reliability of the information and provide safeguards against its misuse. 2. Information compiled for one purpose cannot be used for another without the concerned individual's permission. 3. Individuals must be able to find out what data concerning them are being compiled and how the data will be used. 4. Individuals must be given a means by which to correct inaccurate data.
Tax Reform Act (1976)	Preserves the privacy of personal financial information.
Right to Financial Privacy Act (1978)	Prohibits financial institutions from providing the federal government with access to a customer's records unless the customer authorizes the disclosure.
Electronic Fund Transfer Act (1978)	Requires financial institutions to notify an individual if a third party gains access to the individual's account.
Counterfeit Access Device and Computer Fraud and Abuse Act (1984)	Prohibits the use of a computer without authorization to retrieve data in a financial institution's or consumer reporting agency's files.
Cable Communications Policy Act (1984)	Regulates access to information collected by cable service operators on subscribers to cable services.
Electronic Communications Privacy Act (1986)	Prohibits the interception of information communicated by electronic means.

■ **Exhibit 5–1**
Federal Legislation
Relating to Privacy

"patently offensive," as measured by current community standards. Violators of the act could be fined up to $250,000 or imprisoned for up to two years.

A major legal issue raised by the language of the act was that there is no national standard by which to measure "indecent" or "patently offensive" speech. The CDA's definition of these terms followed the traditional practice of measuring obscenity by current community standards. Generally, the United States Supreme Court has held that in a legal action concerning obscene

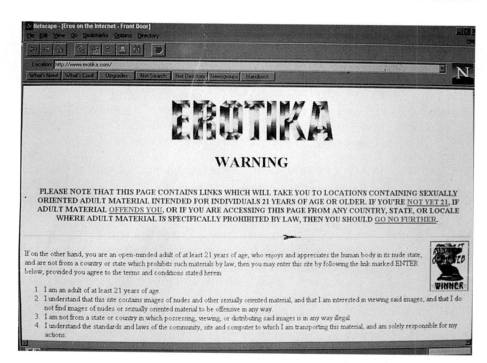

A warning on the Internet regarding the appropriateness of certain materials for minors. What standards should apply to materials as easily available as these on the Internet?

speech, the relevant standard is that of the community in which the information is accessed or the jury sits. With respect to Internet transmissions, however, obscene materials can be accessed by virtually anyone in any community in the United States (as well as globally). In effect, this means that any Internet transmission that is "patently offensive" by even the most restrictive community standards would be illegal under the CDA.

The American Civil Liberties Union (ACLU) and other organizations immediately challenged the constitutionality of the CDA in a lawsuit against the U.S. attorney general, Janet Reno, and the Justice Department. The plaintiffs alleged that the CDA's definition of indecency was unconstitutionally vague and subjected persons to criminal penalties without specifically identifying crimes to which these penalties attach. In *American Civil Liberties Union v. Reno*,[19] a federal district court in Pennsylvania agreed with the plaintiffs and issued a temporary restraining order prohibiting the government from enforcing the section of the CDA pertaining to indecent materials. Shortly thereafter, another federal district court held that the act was unconstitutional because it was overbroad and impermissibly regulated constitutionally protected communications between adults.[20]

In 1997, the United States Supreme Court held that the CDA's provisions regarding "indecent" and "patently offensive" transmissions violated the First Amendment because of their "unprecedented" breadth: although the government has an interest in protecting children from potentially harmful materials, the CDA suppressed a large amount of speech that adults have a constitutional right to send and receive.[21]

---

19.   929 F.Supp. 824 (E.D.Pa. 1996).
20.   *Shea v. Reno*, 930 F.Supp. 916 (S.D.N.Y. 1996).
21.   *Reno v. American Civil Liberties Union*, ___ U.S. ___, 117 S.Ct. 2329, 138 L.Ed.2d 874 (1997).

Cryptography and Constitutional Protections

One of the foremost concerns of the business community today is the security of electronic proprietary and commercial information. To protect electronic data from being accessed by unauthorized persons, many companies use hardware or software with encryption capabilities. When data is *encrypted,* the access codes are scrambled to protect against unauthorized use. The widespread practice of encrypting data has created some interesting legal issues.

ENCRYPTED DATA AND CRIMINAL LAW.   One issue has to do with the Fourth Amendment protection against unreasonable searches and seizures. Suppose that law enforcement personnel obtain a search warrant to search an individual's office or home for certain information. If this information consists of encrypted data stored on a computer's hard drive or on external storage devices, how can it be accessed? A law enforcement agent might succeed in decrypting the data, but whether it would be lawful would depend on whether the information, once known, fell properly within the search warrant's description of the material to be searched and seized.

If law enforcement personnel could not "break" the code and decrypt the data, another issue would arise: Could the owner or possessor of the data be compelled to provide the encryption code? Under the Fifth Amendment, no person can be compelled to give evidence if that evidence would be self-incriminating. Traditionally, persons have been compelled to produce certain types of physical evidence, such as fingerprints, but whether a person can be compelled to use his or her *mind* to assist law enforcement personnel in obtaining incriminating evidence is not clear.

ENCRYPTION SOURCE CODES AND FREE SPEECH.   A constitutional issue that has recently come before the courts is whether computer source codes used in encryption software constitute "speech" protected by the First Amendment. The issue arose in the context of a controversy over government restrictions on the export of encryption software.

Under the International Traffic in Arms Regulations (ITAR),[22] administered by the U.S. Department of State, any firm that wishes to export encryption software or products containing encryption components must first obtain a license from the government to do so. In the past, it was difficult, if not impossible, to obtain such a license. In 1996, however, the government began to relax the regulations somewhat. Firms are now allowed to sell certain types of high-level encryption software for commercial purposes only. Software manufacturers complain that any restrictions unfairly place them at a disadvantage in the international marketplace. The government, however, contends that restrictions on the export of encryption software are necessary to prevent the software from falling into the hands of terrorists or others who could use it in ways that could threaten national security.

The constitutional issue currently before the courts is whether encryption software—more specifically, the source codes used to encrypt data—constitute speech. If so, then the government's regulation of this speech may be challenged on constitutional grounds. Whether cryptography qualifies as speech falling under the protection of the First Amendment is at issue in the following case.

---

22.   22 C.F.R. Sections 120–130.

Case 5.6 ● Bernstein v. U.S. Department of State

United States District Court,
Northern District of California, 1996.
922 F.Supp. 1426.

BACKGROUND AND FACTS As a graduate student at the University of California at Berkeley in the field of cryptography, Daniel Bernstein developed an encryption system he called "Snuffle." Bernstein asked the U.S. Department of State whether he needed a license to "export" Snuffle—that is, to teach and discuss its source code at conferences, in journals, and in on-line discussion groups. A license to disclose certain technical data to "foreign person[s]" is required under the Arms Export Control Act (AECA)[a] and the International Traffic in Arms Regulations (ITAR). The State Department said that Bernstein did need a license. Bernstein filed a suit in a federal district court against the State Department, contending in part that the AECA and the ITAR were unconstitutional as applied to Snuffle. He asked the court to, among other things, block their enforcement until his claim could be heard. The State Department filed a motion to dismiss, arguing in part that the Snuffle source code was not "speech" and thus was not protected by the First Amendment to the Constitution.

IN THE WORDS OF THE COURT . . .
PATEL, District Judge.
    *   *   *   *

    *   *   * According to defendants, the source code, a functioning cryptograpic product, is not intended to convey a particular message. It cannot be speech, they say, because its purpose is functional rather than communicative.
    *   *   *   *

    *   *   * Contrary to defendants' suggestion, the functionality of a language does not make it any less like speech. * * * [E]ven if Snuffle source code, which is easily compiled into object code for the computer to read and easily used for encryption, is essentially functional, that does not remove it from the realm of speech. Instructions, do-it-yourself manuals, recipes, even technical information about hydrogen bomb construction, are often purely functional; they are also speech.

DECISION AND REMEDY The court held that a cryptographic code is speech protected by the First Amendment. The court denied the State Department's motion to dismiss and granted Bernstein's request to temporarily block enforcement of the AECA and the ITAR.

FOR CRITICAL ANALYSIS—POLITICAL CONSIDERATION *What might have happened if the court had held that the computer code was not protected by the First Amendment?*

———
a. 22 U.S.C. Section 2278.

Free Speech and Unwanted Electronic Mail

Many First Amendment cases involve the question of whether the government can prohibit persons from distributing political, religious, or other leaflets or printed materials in public forums. Normally, any law that restricts or prohibits *speech* (that is, the political, religious, or other *message* communicated in the leaflets or other printed materials) must relate to one of the categories of punishable speech (such as "fighting words," obscenity, defamation, and so on) or be justified by a *compelling state interest*.

    Any law concerning speech-related conduct (that is, the distribution of leaflets or other printed materials) may reasonable restrict the time, place, or manner in which the conduct takes place. To be constitutional, however, the law must (1) be *content neutral,* (2) be *narrowly tailored* to serve a significant government interest, and (3) leave open sufficient *alternative channels of communication.* Recall that the Bill of Rights, including the First Amendment, protects persons from *government* actions, not actions taken by private parties. The rules just stated, however, apply even to certain privately owned facilities, such as shopping malls, because such areas are deemed to be community business centers and thus serve a public function.

ELECTRONIC LEAFLETS.   What about the transmission of "electronic leaflets" over the Internet? Should the same principles apply? Is the transmission of such material—often referred to as "junk mail" or "spam"—over the Internet significantly different from the distribution of leaflets in a shopping mall or on a public street? This issue arose in a recent dispute between America Online (AOL), the well-known Internet service provider, and Cyber Promotions (CP). CP transmits electronic ads to thousands of E-mail addresses, including AOL subscribers. In response to complaints from its subscribers, AOL blocked all E-mail from CP. AOL also gathered all of CP's E-mail messages together and returned them to CP in an "E-mail bomb" that brought down the computer system of CP's Internet service provider. CP sued AOL, claiming, among other things, that its electronic messages were protected speech under the First Amendment.

AOL claimed that the First Amendment, which prohibits the government from restraining speech-related conduct, does not apply to AOL, which is a private company. Therefore, AOL can block E-mail transmissions directed to its subscribers without violating the First Amendment. CP contended that because the Internet was initially subsidized by the government, speech over the Internet should be constitutionally protected. In CP's suit against AOL, a federal district court declared that CP did not have a constitutional right, under the First Amendment, to send unsolicited E-mail advertisements to AOL subscribers and that AOL was entitled to block CP's attempt to do so.[23]

OTHER ISSUES.   Some questions raised in this case relate to other areas of the law. For example, in regard to intellectual property law (discussed in Chapter 11), are the E-mail addresses of AOL's subscribers AOL's property, or are they more like the addresses in a telephone book, which anybody can access and use? Additionally, should the government regulate unwanted E-mail just as it does unwanted faxes (see Chapter 19)? After all, recipients of ads and leaflets distributed through the mails or shopping malls do not have to pay for those materials. In contrast, some subscribers of on-line service providers pay an hourly fee for service, which shifts the cost of e-mail ads to the customer.

---

23.   *Cyber Promotions, Inc. v. America Online, Inc.,* 948 F.Supp. 436 (E.D.Pa. 1966). Note that in a similar case brought against CP by CompuServe in 1997, a federal district court held that CP's sending unsolicited e-mail advertisements to CompuServe's proprietary network, after CompuServe had repeatedly demanded CP to cease transmitting such materials, was actionable as a trespass to personal property (a tort, or wrongful act, discussed in Chapter 8). See *Compuserve, Inc. v. Cyber Promotions, Inc.,* 962 F.Supp. 1015 (S.D. Ohio 1997).

Key Terms

Bill of Rights 132
checks and balances 125
commerce clause 125
due process clause 141
equal protection clause 143

establishment clause 138
federal form of
  government 125
free exercise clause 138
police powers 129

preemption 131
probable cause 140
search warrant 140
supremacy clause 131

Chapter Summary

Constitutional Authority to Regulate Business

CONSTITUTIONAL POWERS OF GOVERNMENT (See pages 125–132.)	The U.S. Constitution established a federal form of government, in which government powers are shared by the national government and the state governments. At the national level, government powers are divided among the legislative, executive, and judicial branches.
COMMERCE CLAUSE (See pages 125–131.)	1. **The breadth of the commerce clause**—The commerce clause expressly permits Congress to regulate commerce. Over time, courts expansively interpreted this clause, and today the commerce power authorizes the national government, at least theoretically, to regulate virtually every commercial enterprise in the United States. 2. **The regulatory powers of the states**—Under their police powers, state governments may regulate private activities to protect or promote the public order, health, safety, morals, and general welfare. If state regulations substantially interfere with interstate commerce, they will be held to violate the commerce clause of the U.S. Constitution.
SUPREMACY CLAUSE (See page 131.)	The U.S. Constitution provides that the Constitution, laws, and treaties of the United States are "the supreme Law of the Land." Whenever a state law directly conflicts with a federal law, the state law is rendered invalid.
TAXING AND SPENDING POWERS (See page 132.)	The U.S. Constitution gives Congress the power to impose uniform taxes throughout the United States and to spend revenues accumulated from the taxing power. Congress can spend revenues to promote any objective it deems worthwhile, so long as it does not violate the Bill of Rights.
BUSINESS AND THE BILL OF RIGHTS (See pages 132–141.)	The Bill of Rights, which consists of the first ten amendments to the U.S. Constitution, was adopted in 1791 and embodies a series of protections for individuals—and in most cases, business entities—against various types of interference by the federal government. Freedoms guaranteed by the Bill of Rights include the following: 1. **Freedom of speech**—Types of speech protected under the First Amendment include commercial speech and political speech. Certain types of speech, such as defamatory speech and lewd or obscene speech, are not protected under the First Amendment.

(Continued)

Chapter Summary, continued

BUSINESS AND THE BILL OF RIGHTS—continued
(See pages 132–141.)

2. **Freedom of religion**—Under the First Amendment, the government may neither establish any religion (the establishment clause) nor prohibit the free exercise of religion (the free exercise clause).

3. **Self-incrimination**—The Fifth Amendment guarantees that no person "shall be compelled in any criminal case to be a witness against himself." This Fifth Amendment protection against self-incrimination does not apply to corporations or partnerships.

4. **Searches and seizures**—The Fourth Amendment prohibits unreasonable searches and seizures. Normally, law enforcement personnel must obtain a search warrant before they can legitimately conduct a search or seizure.

OTHER CONSTITUTIONAL PROTECTIONS
(See pages 141–146.)

1. **Due process**—Both the Fifth and the Fourteenth Amendments provide that no person shall be deprived of "life, liberty, or property, without due process of law." Procedural due process requires that any government decision to take life, liberty, or property must be made fairly, using fair procedures. Substantive due process focuses on the content of legislation. Generally, a law that is not compatible with the Constitution violates substantive due process unless the law promotes a compelling state interest, such as public safety.

2. **Equal protection**—Under the Fourteenth Amendment, a state may not "deny to any person within its jurisdiction the equal protection of the laws." A law or action that limits the liberty of some persons but not others may violate the equal protection clause. Such a law may be deemed valid, however, if there is a rational basis for the discriminatory treatment of a given group or if the law substantially relates to an important government objective.

3. **Privacy rights**—There is no specific guarantee of a right to privacy in the Constitution, but such a right has been derived from guarantees found in other constitutional amendments.

For Review

1. What is the basic structure of the American government?
2. What constitutional clause gives the federal government the power to regulate commercial activities among the various states?
3. What constitutional clause allows laws enacted by the federal government to take priority over conflicting state laws?
4. What is the Bill of Rights? What rights and liberties does this document establish?
5. Where in the Constitution can the due process clause be found?

Questions and Case Problems

5–1. Government Powers. The framers of the Constitution feared the twin evils of tyranny and anarchy. Discuss how specific provisions of the Constitution and the Bill of Rights reflect these fears and protect against both of these extremes.

5–2. Commercial Speech. A mayoral election is about to be held in a large U.S. city. One of the candidates is Luis Delgado, and his campaign supporters wish to post campaign signs on lampposts and utility posts throughout the city. A city ordinance, however, prohibits the posting of any signs on public property. Delgado's supporters contend that the city ordinance is unconstitutional, because it violates their rights to free speech. What factors might a court consider in determining the constitutionality of this ordinance?

5–3. Commerce Clause. Suppose that Georgia enacts a law requiring the use of contoured rear-fender mudguards on trucks and trailers operating within its state lines. The statute further makes it illegal for trucks and trailers to use straight mudguards. In thirty-five other states, straight mudguards are legal. Moreover, in the neighboring state of Florida, straight mudguards are explicitly required by law. There is some evidence suggesting that contoured mudguards might be a little safer than straight mudguards. Discuss whether this Georgia statute would violate the commerce clause of the U.S. Constitution.

5–4. Freedom of Religion. A business has a backlog of orders, and to meet its deadlines, management decides to run the firm seven days a week, eight hours a day. One of the employees, Marjorie Tollens, refuses to work on Saturday on religious grounds. Her refusal to work means that the firm may not meet its production deadlines and may therefore suffer a loss of future business. The firm fires Tollens and replaces her with an employee who is willing to work seven days a week. Tollens claims that her employer, in terminating her employment, violated her constitutional right to the free exercise of her religion. Do you agree? Why or why not?

5–5. Equal Protection. In 1988, the Nebraska legislature enacted a statute that required any motorcycle operator or passenger on Nebraska's highways to wear a protective helmet. Eugene Robotham, a licensed motorcycle operator, sued the state of Nebraska to block enforcement of the law. Robotham asserted, among other things, that the statute violated the equal protection clause, because it placed requirements on motorcyclists that were not imposed on other motorists. Will the court agree with Robotham that the law violates the equal protection clause? Why or why not? [*Robotham v. State,* 241 Neb. 379, 488 N.W.2d 533 (1992)]

5–6. Freedom of Religion. A 1988 Minnesota statute required all operators of slow-moving vehicles to display on their vehicles a fluorescent orange-red triangular emblem. Although during the daytime an alternative (a black triangle with a white reflective border and red reflective tape) could be used, at night all slow-moving vehicles had to display the orange-red emblem. Hershberger and the other defendants, who were Amish, claimed that the statute violated their First Amendment freedom of religion because displaying the "loud" colors and "worldly symbols" on their vehicles (black, boxlike buggies) compromised their religious belief that they should remain separate and apart from the modern world. They would not object to displaying a sign similar to the

alternative symbol if they could use silver, instead of red, reflective tape and if they did not have to display the "regular" emblem at night. The state argued that although the silver tape was as effective as the red in terms of visibility, the red tape was customarily associated with slow-moving vehicles, and therefore the Amish should comply with the statute as written. What will the court hold? Discuss. [*State v. Hershberger,* 444 N.W.2d 282 (Minn. 1989)]

5–7. Commerce Clause. Taylor owned a bait business in Maine and arranged to have live baitfish imported into the state. The importation of the baitfish violated a Maine statute. Taylor was charged with violating a federal statute that makes it a crime to transport fish in interstate commerce in violation of state law. Taylor moved to dismiss the charges on the ground that the Maine statute unconstitutionally burdened interstate commerce. Maine intervened to defend the validity of its statute, arguing that the law legitimately protected the state's fisheries from parasites and nonnative species that might be included in shipments of live baitfish. Were Maine's interests in protecting its fisheries from parasites and nonnative species sufficient to justify the burden placed on interstate commerce by the Maine statute? Discuss. [*Maine v. Taylor,* 477 U.S. 131, 106 S.Ct. 2440, 91 L.Ed.2d 110 (1986)]

5–8. Freedom of Speech. The Allstate Insurance Co. agreed to refer its policyholders to members of the USA-GLAS Network for automobile glass repair and replacement. In response to the concerns of independent glass businesses over the loss of revenue caused by the arrangement, the South Dakota legislature passed a statute prohibiting an insurance company from requiring or recommending that a policyholder "use a particular company or location for the providing of automobile glass replacement or repair services or products." Allstate filed a suit against the state, challenging the validity of the statute as, among other things, an unconstitutional restriction on commercial speech. Will the court agree with Allstate? Why or why not? [*Allstate Insurance Co. v. State of South Dakota,* 871 F.Supp. 355 (D.S.D. 1994)]

5–9. Commerce Clause. South Dakota Disposal Systems, Inc. (SDDS), applied to the South Dakota Department of Water and Natural Resources (DWNR) for a permit to operate a solid-waste–disposal facility (Lonetree). It was estimated that 90 to 95 percent of the waste would come from out of state. The DWNR determined that Lonetree would be environmentally safe and issued a permit. Later, a public referendum was held. The state attorney general issued a pamphlet to accompany the referendum that urged the public to vote against "the out-of-state dump" because "South Dakota is not the nation's dumping grounds." SDDS filed a suit against the state, challenging the referendum as a violation of, among other things, the commerce clause. Was the referendum unconstitutional? Why or why not? [*SDDS, Inc. v. State of South Dakota,* 47 F.3d 263 (8th Cir. 1995)]

5–10. Freedom of Religion. Isaiah Brown was the director of the information services department for Polk County, Iowa. During department meetings in his office, he allowed occasional prayers and, in addressing one meeting, referred to Bible passages related to sloth and "work ethics." There was no apparent disruption of the work routine, but the county administrator reprimanded Brown. Later, the administrator ordered Brown to re-move from his office all items with a religious connotation. Brown sued the county, alleging that the reprimand and the order violated, among other things, the free exercise clause of the First Amendment. Could the county be held liable for violating Brown's constitutional rights? Discuss. [*Brown v. Polk County, Iowa,* 61 F.3d 650 (8th Cir. 1995)]

A Question of Ethics and Social Responsibility

5–11. Agnes and John Donahue refused to rent an apartment to an unmarried couple, Verna Terry and Robert Wilder. The Donahues were devout Roman Catholics and firmly believed, in accordance with the church's teachings, that engaging in sexual relations outside of marriage was a mortal sin. Renting an apartment to an unmarried couple would, in Agnes Donahue's mind, be aiding the couple in the commission of a sin, and therefore she refused to rent the apartment to Terry and Wilder. Terry and Wilder filed a complaint with the California Fair Employment and Housing Commission, alleging that the Donahues' refusal to rent them an apartment violated a state statute prohibiting discrimination on the basis of marital status. Eventually, the case was heard by a California appellate court. The question before the court was whether the state's interest in prohibiting discrimination based on marital status outweighed the Donahues' state constitutional right to the free exercise of their religion. [*Donahue v. Fair Employment and Housing Commission,* 7 Cal.App.4th 1498, 2 Cal.Rptr.2d 32 (1991)]

1. In your opinion, should the court make an exception to the applicability of the state statute prohibiting discrimination on the basis of marital status in the Donahues' case? Why or why not?
2. What if a landlord's religious convictions led him or her to refuse to rent premises to certain prospective tenants for other reasons—because of their race or national origin, for example?

Case Briefing Assignment

5–12. Examine Case A.2 [*Austin v. Berryman,* 878 F.2d 786 (4th Cir. 1989)] in Appendix A. The case has been excerpted there in great detail. Review and then brief the case, making sure that you include answers to the following questions in your brief.

1. Who were the plaintiff and defendant in this action?
2. Why did Austin claim that she had been forced to leave her job?
3. Why was Austin refused state unemployment benefits?
4. Did the state's refusal to give Austin unemployment compensation violate her rights under the free exercise clause of the First Amendment?
5. What logic or reasoning did the court employ in arriving at its conclusion?

For Critical Analysis

5–13. In recent years, many people have criticized the film and entertainment industries for promoting violence by exposing the American public, and particularly American youth, to extremely violent films and song lyrics. Do you think that the right to free speech can (or should) be traded off to reduce violence in America?

INTERACTING WITH The Internet

■ The World Wide Web version of the Constitution provides hypertext links to amendments and other changes. Go to

http://www.law.cornell.edu/constitution/constitution. overview.html

■ The home page of Emory University School of Law offers access to a number of early American documents, including scanned originals of the Constitution and the Bill of Rights. This page is located at

http://www.law.emory.edu/FEDERAL/

■ You can obtain all of the decisions of the United States Supreme Court relating to constitutional issues by using a site developed by Cornell University Law School at

http://supct.law.cornell.edu/supct

■ Summaries and the full text of constitutional law decisions by the United States Supreme Court are included at the OYEZ site referred to in the *Interacting with the Internet* section at the end of Chapter 1. The address for this site is

http://oyez.nwu.edu/oyez.html

■ For information on the effect of new computer and communications technologies on the constitutional rights and liberties of Americans, go to the Center for Democracy and Technology at

http://www.cdt.org/

■ The Cyberspace Law Institute (CLI) also focuses on law and communications technology. According to the CLI, it is devoted to studying and helping to develop "the new forms of law and lawmaking required by the growth of global communications networks and online communities." By using the CLI site, you can find articles and information on such topics as privacy, flaming, obscenity, and other issues relating to constitutional law. Go to

http://www.cli.org

■ The constitutions of almost all of the states are now on line. You can find them at

http://www.findlaw.com/11stategov/

■ If you would like to see constitutions of various other countries in the world, go to

http://www.eur.nl/iacl/const.html

CHAPTER 6

Powers and Functions of Administrative Agencies

Contents

Chapter Objectives

After reading this chapter, you should be able to . . .

1. Explain the rulemaking function of administrative agencies.
2. Describe the investigation and adjudication functions of agencies.
3. Identify how agency authority is held in check.
4. List laws that make agencies more accountable to the public.
5. Discuss the relationship between state and federal agencies.

As the opening quotation suggests, government agencies established to administer the law have a tremendous impact on the day-to-day operation of the government and the economy. In its early years, the United States had a relatively simple, nonindustrial economy that required little regulation. Thus, comparatively few administrative agencies were created. Today, however, there are rules covering virtually every aspect of a business's operation. Consequently, agencies have multiplied. For example, at the federal level, the Securities and Exchange Commission regulates the firm's capital structure and financing, as well as its financial reporting. The National Labor Relations Board oversees relations between the firm and any unions with which it may deal. The Equal Employment Opportunity Commission also regulates employment relationships. The Environmental Protection Agency and the Occupational Safety and Health Administration affect the way the firm manufactures its products. The Federal Trade Commission affects the way it markets these products.

Added to this layer of federal regulation is a second layer of state regulation that, when not preempted by federal legislation, may cover many of the same activities or regulate independently those activities not covered by federal regulation. Finally, agency regulations at the county or municipal level also affect certain types of business activities.

Administrative agencies issue rules, orders, and decisions. These regulations make up the body of *administrative law.* You were introduced briefly to some of the main principles of administrative law in Chapter 1. In the following pages, these principles are presented in much greater detail.

> "[P]erhaps more values today are affected by [administrative] decisions than by those of all the courts."
>
> Robert H. Jackson, 1892–1954 (Associate justice of the United States Supreme Court, 1941–1954)

Agency Creation and Powers

▼ Congress creates federal administrative agencies. Because Congress cannot possibly oversee the actual implementation of all the laws it enacts, it must delegate such tasks to others, particularly when the issues relate to highly technical areas, such as air and water pollution. By delegating some of its authority to make and implement laws, Congress can monitor indirectly a particular area in which it has passed legislation without becoming bogged down in the details relating to enforcement—details that are often best left to specialists.

Enabling Legislation

To create an administrative agency, Congress passes enabling legislation, which specifies the name, purposes, functions, and powers of the agency being created. Federal administrative agencies may exercise only those powers that Congress has delegated to them in enabling legislation. Through similar enabling acts, state legislatures create state administrative agencies.

Congress created the Federal Trade Commission (FTC), for example, in the Federal Trade Commission Act of 1914.[1] The act prohibits unfair and deceptive trade practices. It also describes the procedures that the agency must follow to charge persons or organizations with violations of the act, and it provides for judicial review of agency orders. The act grants the FTC the power to do the following:

---

1. 15 U.S.C. Sections 41–58.

Workers are required to follow health and safety regulations on the job. Some persons contend that federal agencies have issued too many regulations. Why are administrative regulations so much more detailed than, for example, the provisions of the Constitution?

- Create "rules and regulations for the purpose of carrying out the Act."
- Conduct investigations of business practices.
- Obtain reports from interstate corporations concerning their business practices.
- Investigate possible violations of federal antitrust statutes.[2]
- Publish findings of its investigations.
- Recommend new legislation.
- Hold trial-like hearings to resolve certain kinds of trade disputes that involve FTC regulations or federal antitrust laws.

The commission that heads the FTC is composed of five members, each of whom the president appoints, with the advice and consent of the Senate, for a term of seven years. The president designates one of the commissioners to be chair. Various offices and bureaus of the FTC undertake different administrative activities for the agency. The organization of the FTC is illustrated in Exhibit 6–1.

Types of Agencies

There are two basic types of administrative agencies: executive agencies and independent regulatory agencies. Federal executive agencies include the cabinet departments of the executive branch, which were formed to assist the president in carrying out executive functions, and the subagencies within the cabinet departments. The Occupational Safety and Health Administration, for example, is a subagency within the Department of Labor. Exhibit 6–2 lists the cabinet departments and their most important subagencies.

---

2.   The FTC shares this task with the Antitrust Division of the U.S. Department of Justice.

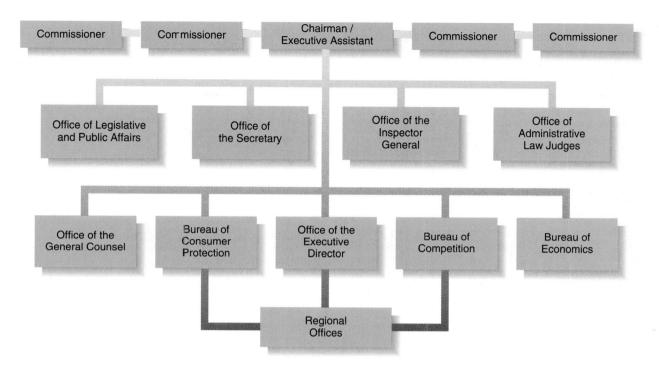

All administrative agencies are part of the executive branch of government, but independent regulatory agencies are outside the major executive departments. The Federal Trade Commission and the Securities and Exchange Commission are examples of independent regulatory agencies. These and other selected independent regulatory agencies, as well as their principal functions, are listed in Exhibit 6–3.

The significant difference between the two types of agencies lies in the accountability of the regulators. Agencies that are considered part of the executive branch are subject to the authority of the president, who has the power to appoint and remove federal officers. In theory, this power is less pronounced in regard to independent agencies, whose officers serve for fixed terms and cannot be removed without just cause. In practice, however, the president's power to exert influence over independent agencies is often considerable.

For both types of agencies, standard federal administrative regions were established to attain uniformity in the location and jurisdiction of agency offices. Standard regions also promote the coordination of the activities of agencies at all levels of government. Agencies whose regional divisions do not currently conform to the standard regions are expected to adopt the system when they change their organization or set up new offices. The standard federal regions are identified in Exhibit 6–4.

Agency Powers and the Constitution

Administrative agencies occupy an unusual niche in the American legal scheme, because they exercise powers that are normally divided among the three branches of government. Notice that in the FTC's enabling legislation discussed above, the FTC's grant of power incorporates functions associated

■ **Exhibit 6–1**
Organization of the
Federal Trade Commission

DEPARTMENT	DATE FORMED	IMPORTANT SUBAGENCIES
State	1789	Passport Office, Bureau of Diplomatic Security; Foreign Service; Bureau of Human Rights and Humanitarian Affairs; Bureau of Consular Affairs; Bureau of Intelligence and Research
Treasury	1789	Internal Revenue Service; Bureau of Alchohol, Tobacco, and Firearms; U.S. Secret Service; U.S. Mint; Customs Service
Interior	1849	U.S. Fish and Wildlife Service; National Park Service; Bureau of Indian Affairs; Bureau of Land Management
Justice	1870[a]	Federal Bureau of Investigation; Drug Enforcement Administration; Bureau of Prisons; U.S. Marshals Service; Immigration and Naturalization Service
Agriculture	1889	Soil Conservation Service; Agricultural Research Service; Food Safety and Inspection Service; Federal Crop Insurance Corporation ; Farmers Home Administration
Commerce	1913[b]	Bureau of the Census; Bureau of Economic Analysis; Minority Business Development Agency; Patent and Trademark Office; National Oceanic and Atmospheric Administration; U.S. Travel and Tourism Administration
Labor	1913[b]	Occupational Safety and Health Administration; Bureau of Labor Statistics; Employment Standards Administration; Office of Labor-Management Standards; Employment and Training Administration
Defense	1949[c]	National Guard; Defense Investigative Service; National Security Agency; Joint Chiefs of Staff; Departments of the Air Force, Navy, Army
Housing and Urban Development	1965	Assistant Secretary for Community Planning and Development; Government National Mortgage Association; Assistant Secretary for Housing—Federal Housing Commissioner; Assistant Secretary for Fair Housing and Equal Opportunity
Transportation	1967	Federal Aviation Administration; Federal Highway Administration; National Highway Traffic Safety Administration; U.S. Coast Guard; Federal Transit Administration
Energy	1977	Office of Civilian Radioactive Waste Management; Bonneville Power Administration; Office of Nuclear Energy; Energy Information Administration; Office of Conservation and Renewable Energy
Health and Human Services	1980[d]	Food and Drug Administration; Health Care Financing Administration; Public Health Service
Education	1980[e]	Office of Special Education and Rehabilitation Services; Office of Elementary and Secondary Education; Office of Postsecondary Education; Office of Vocational and Adult Education
Veterans' Affairs	1989	Veterans Health Administration; Veterans Benefits Administration: National Cemetery System

a. Formed from the Office of the Attorney General (created in 1789).
b. Formed from the Department of Commerce and Labor (created in 1903).
c. Formed from the Department of War (created in 1789) and the Department of the Navy (created in 1798).
d. Formed from the Department of Health, Education, and Welfare (created in 1953).
e. Formed from the Department of Health, Education, and Welfare (created in 1953).

■ **Exhibit 6–2**
**Executive Departments
and Important
Subagencies**

NAME	DATE FORMED	PRINCIPAL DUTIES
Federal Reserve System Board of Governors (Fed)	1913	Determines policy with respect to interest rates, credit availability, and the money supply.
Federal Trade Commission (FTC)	1914	Prevents businesses from engaging in unfair trade practices; stops the formation of monopolies in the business sector; protects consumer rights.
Securities and Exchange Commission (SEC)	1934	Regulates the nation's stock exchanges, in which shares of stock are bought and sold; enforces the securities laws, which require full disclosure of the financial profiles of companies that wish to sell stocks and bonds to the public.
Federal Communications Commission (FCC)	1934	Regulates all communications by telegraph, cable, telephone, radio, satellite, and television.
National Labor Relations Board (NLRB)	1935	Protects employees' rights to join unions and bargain collectively with employers; attempts to prevent unfair labor practices by both employers and unions.
Equal Employment Opportunity Commission (EEOC)	1964	Works to eliminate discrimination in employment based on religion, sex, race, color, disability, national origin, or age; investigates claims of discrimination.
Environmental Protection Agency (EPA)	1970	Undertakes programs aimed at reducing air and water pollution; works with state and local agencies to help fight environmental hazards. (It has been suggested recently that its status be elevated to that of a department.)
Nuclear Regulatory Commission (NRC)	1975	Ensures that electricity-generating nuclear reactors in the United States are built and operated safely; regularly inspects operations of such reactors.

with the legislature (rulemaking), the executive branch (enforcement of the rules), and the courts (adjudication, or the formal resolution of disputes).

The constitutional principle of *checks and balances* allows each branch of government to act as a check on the actions of the other two branches. Furthermore, the Constitution authorizes only the legislative branch to create laws. Yet administrative agencies, to which the Constitution does not specifically refer, make **legislative rules,** or *substantive rules,* that are as legally binding as laws that Congress passes.

Courts generally hold that Article I of the U.S. Constitution authorizes delegating such powers to administrative agencies. In fact, courts generally hold that Article I is the basis for all administrative law. Section 1 of that article grants all legislative powers to Congress and requires Congress to oversee the implementation of all laws. Article I, Section 8, gives Congress the power to make all laws necessary for executing its specified powers. The courts interpret these passages, under what is known as the **delegation doctrine,** as granting Congress the power to establish administrative agencies that can create rules for implementing those laws.

The three branches of government exercise certain controls over agency powers and functions, as is discussed later in this chapter, but in many ways

■ **Exhibit 6–3 Selected Independent Regulatory Agencies**

Legislative Rule An administrative agency rule that carries the same weight as a congressionally enacted statute.

Delegation Doctrine A doctrine based on Article I, Section 8, of the U.S. Constitution, which has been construed to allow Congress to delegate some of its power to make and implement laws to administrative agencies.

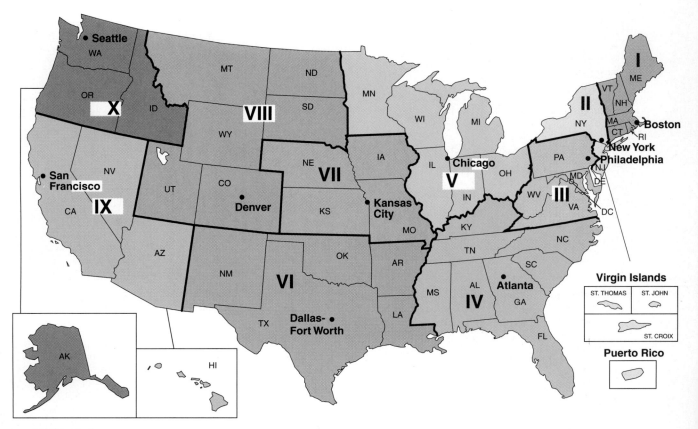

■ **Exhibit 6–4**
Standard Federal
Administrative Regions

Bureaucracy The organizational structure, consisting of government bureaus and agencies, through which the government implements and enforces the laws.

administrative agencies function independently. For this reason, administrative agencies, which constitute the **bureaucracy,** are sometimes referred to as the "fourth branch" of theAmerican government.

Administrative Process

▼ The three functions mentioned previously—rulemaking, enforcement, and adjudication—make up what is called the administrative process. Administrative process involves the administration of law by administrative agencies, in contrast to judicial process, which involves the administration of law by the courts.

The Administrative Procedure Act (APA) of 1946[3] imposes procedural requirements that all federal agencies must follow in their rulemaking, adjudication, and other functions. The APA is such an integral part of the administrative process that its application will be examined as we go through the basic functions carried out by administrative agencies.

---

3.   5 U.S.C. Sections 551–706.

Rulemaking

A major function of an administrative agency is rulemaking—the formulation of new regulations. In an agency's enabling legislation, Congress confers the agency's power to make rules. For example, the Occupational Safety and Health Act of 1970 authorized the Occupational Health and Safety Administration (OSHA) to develop and issue rules governing safety in the workplace. In 1991, OSHA deemed it in the public interest to issue a new rule regulating the health-care industry to prevent the spread of such diseases as acquired immune deficiency syndrome (AIDS). OSHA created a rule specifying various standards—on how contaminated instruments should be handled, for example—with which employers in that industry must comply.

In formulating its rule, OSHA had to follow specific rulemaking procedures required under the APA. We look here at the most common rulemaking procedure, called **notice-and-comment rulemaking.** This procedure involves three basic steps: notice of the proposed rulemaking, a comment period, and the final rule.

NOTICE OF THE PROPOSED RULEMAKING.   When a federal agency decides to create a new rule, the agency publishes a notice of the proposed rulemaking proceedings in the *Federal Register,* a daily publication of the executive branch that prints government orders, rules, and regulations. The notice states where and when the proceedings will be held, the agency's legal authority for making the rule (usually its enabling legislation), and the terms or subject matter of the proposed rule.

COMMENT PERIOD.   Following the publication of the notice of the proposed rulemaking proceedings, the agency must allow ample time for persons to comment in writing on the proposed rule. The purpose of this comment period is to give interested parties the opportunity to express their views on the proposed rule in an effort to influence agency policy. The comments may be in writing or, if a hearing is held, may be given orally. The agency need not respond to all comments, but it must respond to any significant comments that bear directly on the proposed rule. The agency responds by either modifying its final rule or explaining, in a statement accompanying the final rule, why it did not make any changes. In some circumstances, an agency may accept comments after the comment period is closed. The agency should summarize these *ex parte* comments for possible review.

THE FINAL RULE.   After the agency reviews the comments, it drafts the final rule and publishes it in the *Federal Register.* Exhibit 6–5 shows a sample page from a rule published in the *Federal Register.* The final rule is later compiled with the rules and regulations of other federal administrative agencies in the *Code of Federal Regulations* (CFR). Final rules have binding legal effect unless the courts later overturn them.

In the following case, the American Dental Association and other health-care providers asked a court to overturn an OSHA rule created in 1991 to contain the spread of blood-borne diseases in the health-care industry. The court discussed some of the considerations that OSHA took into account before formulating its rule. These considerations are illustrative of the factors that any agency must consider in the rulemaking process.

Notice-and-Comment Rulemaking A procedure in agency rulemaking that requires (1) notice, (2) opportunity for comment, and (3) a published draft of the final rule.

■ **Exhibit 6–5 —A Page from the *Federal Register***

64004   Federal Register / Vol. 56, No. 235 / Friday, December 6, 1991 / Rules and Regulations

DEPARTMENT OF LABOR

Occupational Safety and Health Administration

29 CFR Part 1910.1030

[Docket No. H-370]

Occupational Exposure to Bloodborne Pathogens

AGENCY: Occupational Safety and Health Administration (OSHA), Labor
ACTION: Final rule.

SUMMARY: The Occupational Safety and Health Administration hereby promulgates a standard under section 6(b) of the Occupational Safety and Health Act of 1970 (the Act), 29 U.S.C. 655 to eliminate or minimize occupational exposure to Hepatitis B Virus (HBV), Human Immunodeficiency Virus (HIV) and other bloodborne pathogens. Based on a review of the information in the rulemaking record, OSHA has made a determination that employees face a significant health risk as the result of occupational exposure to blood and other potentially infectious materials because they may contain bloodborne pathogens, including Hepatitis B virus which causes Hepatitis B, a serious liver disease, and human immunodeficiency virus, which causes Acquired Immunodeficiency Syndrome (AIDS). The Agency further concludes that this exposure can be minimized or eliminated using a combination of engineering and work practice controls, personal protective clothing and equipment, training, medical surveillance, Hepatitis B vaccination, signs and labels, and other provisions.

DATES: This standard shall become effective on March 6, 1992.

Any petitions for review must be filed not later than the 59th day following the promulgation of the standard. See Section 6(f) of the OSH Act; 29 CFR 1911.18(d) and *United Mine Workers of America* v. *Mine Safety and Health Administration,* **900 F.2d 384** (D.C. Cir. 1990).

ADDRESSES: For additional copies of this standard, contact: OSHA Office of Publications; U.S. Department of Labor, room N3101, 200 Constitution Ave., NW., Washington, DC 20210, Telephone (202) 523-9667.

For copies of materials in the docket, contact: OSHA Docket Office, Docket No. H-370, room N2625, U.S. Department of Labor, 200 Constitution Ave, NW., Washington, DC 20210, Telephone (202) 523-7894. The hours of operation of the Docket Office are 10 a.m. until 4 p.m.

In compliance with 28 U.S.C. 2112(a), the Agency designates for receipt of

petitions for review of the standard, the Associate Solicitor for Occupational Safety and Health, Office of the Solicitor, room S–4004, U.S. Department of Labor, 200 Constitution Avenue, NW., Washington, DC 20210.
FOR FURTHER INFORMATION CONTACT:
Mr. James F. Foster, OSHA, U.S. Department of Labor, Office of Public Affairs, Room N3647, 200 Constitution Avenue, NW., Washington, DC 20210, telephone (202) 523-8151.
SUPPLEMENTARY INFORMATION:

Table of Contents

I. Introduction
II. Pertinent Legal Authority
III. Events Leading to the Standard
IV. Health Effects
V. Quantitative Risk Assessment
VI. Significance of Risk
VII. Regulatory Impact Analysis and Regulatory Flexibility Analysis
VIII. Environmental Impact
IX. Summary and Explanation of the Standard
X. Authority and Signature
XI. The Standard

References to the rulemaking record are in the text of the preamble. References are given as "Ex." followed by a number to designate the reference in the docket. For example, "Ex.1" means exhibit 1 in the docket H–370. This document is a copy of the Advance Notice of Proposed Rulemaking for Bloodborne Pathogens that was published in the **Federal Register** on November 27, 1987 (52 FR 45438). References to the transcripts of the public hearings are given as "Tr." followed by the date and page. For example, "Mr. Clyde R. Bragdon, Jr. Tr. 9/14/89, p. 100" refers to the first page of the testimony of Mr. Clyde A. Bragdon, Jr., Administrator of the U.S. Fire Administration, given at the public hearing on September 14, 1989. A list of the exhibits, copies of the exhibits, and copies of the transcripts are available in the OSHA Docket Office.

I. Introduction

The preamble to the Final Standard for Occupational Exposure to Bloodborne Pathogens discusses the events leading to the promulgation of final standard, health effects of exposure, degree and significance of the risk, an analysis of the technological and economic feasibility of the standard's implementation, regulatory impact and regulatory flexibility analysis, and the rationale behind the specific provisions of the standard.

The public was invited to comment on these matters following publication of the Advance Notice of Proposed Rulemaking on November 27, 1987 (52 FR 45436) And following publication of

the Proposed Standard on May 30, 1989 (54 FR 23042).

The Agency recognizes the unique nature of both the healthcare industry and other operations covered by this standard. The Agency concludes the employee protection can be provided in a manner consistent with a high standard of patient care.

Hazardous Waste Operations and Emergency Response Standard

The Hazardous Waste Operations and Emergency Response (HAZWOPER) Standard (29 CFR 1910.120) covers three groups of employees: workers at uncontrolled hazardous waste remediation sites; workers at Resource Conservation Recovery Act (RCRA) permitted hazardous waste treatment, storage, and disposal facilities; and those workers expected to respond to emergencies caused by the uncontrolled release of hazardous substances.

The definition of hazardous substance includes any biological agent or infectious material which may cause disease or death. There are three potential scenarios where the bloodborne and hazardous waste operations and emergency response standard may interface. These scenarios include: workers involved in cleanup operations at hazardous waste sites involving regulated waste; workers at RCRA permitted incinerators that burn infectious waste; and workers responding to an emergency caused by the uncontrolled release of regulated waste (e.g., a transportation accident).

Employers of employees engaged in these three activities must comply with the requirements in 29 CFR 1910.120 as well as the Bloodborne Pathogens Standard. If there is a conflict or overlap, the provision that is more protective of employee health and safety applies.

Information Collection Requirements

5 CFR part 1320 sets forth procedures or agencies to follow in obtaining OMB clearance for information collection requirements under the Paperwork Reduction Act of 1980, 44 U.S.C. 3501 et seq. The final bloodborne pathogen standard requires the employer to allow OSHA access to the exposure control plan, medical and training records. In accordance with the provisions of the Paperwork Reduction Act and the regulations issued pursuant thereto, OSHA certifies that it has submitted the information collection to OBM for review under section 3504(h) of that Act.

Public reporting burden for this collection of information is estimated to average five minutes per response to

Case 6.1 ● American Dental Association v. Martin

United States Court of Appeals,
Seventh Circuit, 1993.
984 F.2d 823.

HISTORICAL AND SOCIAL SETTING *Health-care workers are always at risk of being infected with their patients' diseases. For example, viruses, such as those causing acquired immune-deficiency syndrome (AIDS) and hepatitis B (a serious liver disease), can be transmitted in the blood of patients. The human immunodeficiency virus (HIV) causes AIDS. Although HIV cannot survive exposure to air, it can be transmitted if, for example, a health-care worker accidentally sticks himself or herself with a needle on which there is the fresh blood of an HIV carrier. AIDS appears to be fatal in all cases. The hepatitis B virus (HBV), by contrast, is rarely fatal—only about 1 percent of those infected die—but it is more easily transmitted.*

BACKGROUND AND FACTS In 1991, the Occupational Safety and Health Administration (OSHA) promulgated a rule to protect health-care workers from viruses that can be transmitted in the blood of patients. The rule requires employers in the health-care industry to take certain precautions relating to the handling of contaminated instruments (such as needles), the disposal of contaminated waste, and the use of protective clothing (such as gloves, masks, and gowns). The rule also requires employers to provide vaccinations for hepatitis B for their employees and confidential blood testing of workers following accidental exposures (such as being stuck with a contaminated needle). The American Dental Association (ADA) and two other groups asked a federal court to review the rule. The ADA argued, among other things, that OSHA failed to establish that dental workers were sufficiently at risk to benefit from the rule. Furthermore, the rule would unnecessarily burden consumers with increased medical costs and, hence, diminished care.

IN THE WORDS OF THE COURT . . .
POSNER, Circuit Judge.

* * * *

In deciding to impose this extensive array of restrictions on the practice of medicine, nursing, and dentistry, OSHA did not (indeed is not authorized to) compare the benefits with the costs and impose the restrictions on finding that the former exceeded the latter. Instead it asked whether the restrictions would materially reduce a significant workplace risk to human health without imperiling the existence of, or threatening massive dislocation to, the health care industry. * * *

* * * *

OSHA cannot impose onerous requirements on an industry that does not pose substantial hazards to the safety or health of its workers * * * . But neither is the agency required to proceed workplace by workplace, which * * * would require it to promulgate hundreds of thousands of separate rules. It is not our business to pick the happy medium between these extremes. It is OSHA's business. If it provides a rational explanation for its choice, we are bound. * * *

* * * *

* * * [T]he dental association's argument that OSHA's rule is likely to cause a deterioration in dental care as dental patients flee the higher prices resulting from the industry's efforts to shift some of the costs of compliance with the rule to its customers [is untenable]. There are some [costs omitted in OSHA's analysis] * * * but not enough to make a decisive difference * * * .

DECISION AND REMEDY The U.S. Court of Appeals for the Seventh Circuit denied the ADA's petition to review the rule.

FOR CRITICAL ANALYSIS—POLITICAL CONSIDERATION *Why doesn't an administrative agency simply weigh the costs and benefits of a proposed rule and act according to the result?*

Investigation

Administrative agencies conduct investigations of the entities that they regulate. Agencies investigate a wide range of activities, including coal mining, automobile manufacturing, and the industrial discharge of pollutants into the environment. A typical agency investigation occurs during the rulemaking process to obtain information about a certain individual, firm, or industry. The purpose of such an investigation is to avoid issuing a rule that is arbitrary and capricious and instead is based on a consideration of relevant factors. After final rules are issued, agencies conduct investigations to monitor compliance with those rules. A typical agency investigation of this kind might begin when a citizen reports a possible violation.

INSPECTIONS AND TESTS.   Many agencies gather information through on-site inspections. Sometimes, inspecting an office, a factory, or some other business facility is the only way to obtain the evidence needed to prove a regulatory violation. At other times, an inspection or test is used in place of a formal hearing to correct or prevent an undesirable condition. Administrative inspections and tests cover a wide range of activities, including safety inspections of underground coal mines, safety tests of commercial equipment and automobiles, and environmental monitoring of factory emissions. An agency may also ask a firm or individual to submit certain documents or records to the agency for examination.

Normally, business firms comply with agency requests to inspect facilities or business records, because it is in any firm's interest to maintain a good relationship with regulatory bodies. In some instances, however, such as when a

Warehouse employees work in potentially hazardous conditions. Should government officers be allowed unlimited access to private property to check for compliance with agency regulations?

firm thinks an agency's request is unreasonable and may be detrimental to the firm's interest, the firm may refuse to comply with the request. In such situations, an agency may resort to the use of a subpoena or a search warrant.

SUBPOENAS. There are two basic types of subpoenas. The subpoena *ad testificandum* ("to testify") is the technical term for an ordinary subpoena. It is a writ, or order, compelling a witness to appear at an agency hearing. The subpoena *duces tecum* ("bring it with you") compels an individual or organization to hand over books, papers, records, or documents to the agency. An administrative agency may use either type of subpoena to obtain testimony or documents.

There are limits on what an agency can demand. To determine whether an agency is abusing its discretion in its pursuit of information as part of an investigation, a court may consider such factors as the following:

- The purpose of the investigation. An investigation must have a legitimate purpose. An improper purpose is, for example, harassment.
- The relevancy of the information being sought. Information is relevant if it reveals that the law is being violated or if it assures the agency that the law is not being violated.
- The specificity of the demand for testimony or documents. A subpoena must, for example, adequately describe the material being sought.
- The burden of the demand on the party from whom the information is sought. In responding to a request for information, a party must bear the costs of, for example, copying the documents that must be handed over, but a business is generally protected from revealing information such as trade secrets.

In the following case, former bank directors challenged the right of an administrative agency to subpoena their personal financial records. The court considered the extent of the agency's investigative powers.

Case 6.2 ● Federal Deposit Insurance Corp. v. Wentz

United States Court of Appeals,
Third Circuit, 1995.
55 F.3d 905.

HISTORICAL AND SOCIAL SETTING *Congress created the Federal Deposit Insurance Corporation (FDIC) in 1933 to help prevent commercial bank failures and to protect bank customers' accounts. In 1992, nearly five hundred banks failed. More than half of all bank failures can be attributed to agricultural loans, when the failure of farms leads to default on the loans. Fraud also often plays a role, particularly in nonagricultural states. When a bank fails, the FDIC covers each account loss up to $100,000 and then sells the bank's assets, or takes other steps, to regain some of those funds.*

BACKGROUND AND FACTS Sidney Wentz and Natalie Koether were directors of the Howard Savings Bank of Livingston, New Jersey, when it was declared insolvent in October 1992. The Federal Deposit Insurance Corporation (FDIC) was appointed receiver. In April 1993, the FDIC issued subpoenas *duces tecum* to Wentz, Koether, and others, seeking, among other things, their personal financial records. The directors refused to comply. The FDIC asked a federal district court to enforce the subpoenas, arguing that the records were needed to assess any bank losses that might be due to any breach of the directors' fiduciary duties. The court ordered the directors to produce only those records showing additions to or reductions in their assets. The directors appealed, contending that this order intruded on their privacy.

(Continued)

Case 6.2—continued

IN THE WORDS OF THE COURT . . .
WEIS, Circuit Judge.
    * * * *

When personal documents of individuals, as contrasted with business records of corporations, are the subject of an administrative subpoena, privacy concerns must be considered. * * * [R]elevant factors [include] such matters as the type of record requested, the information that it might contain, the potential for harm and subsequent nonconsensual disclosure, the adequacy of safeguards to prevent unauthorized disclosure, the degree of need for access, * * * and the presence of recognizable public interests justifying access.
    * * * *

In applying [these] factors * * * , there is a significant public interest in promptly resolving the affairs of insolvent banks on behalf of their creditors and depositors, many of whom have lost significant sums of money and are often left with little hope for recovery. * * *

The FDIC has shown a reasonable need for gaining access to the directors' records in order to determine whether they reveal breaches of fiduciary duties through the improper channeling of bank funds for personal benefit. Moreover, the directors have not produced any evidence to show that the information contained in their personal financial records "is of such a high degree of sensitivity that the intrusion could be considered severe or that the [directors] are likely to suffer any adverse effects from disclosure to [FDIC] personnel." Finally, we observe that regulatory provisions have been promulgated to guard against subsequent unauthorized disclosure of the subpoenaed information.

DECISION AND REMEDY   The U.S. Court of Appeals for the Third Circuit affirmed the district court's order.

FOR CRITICAL ANALYSIS—ECONOMIC CONSIDERATION   *If the FDIC covers most of the customers' losses, why would anyone care whether the bank directors channeled some bank funds for their personal benefit?*

SEARCH WARRANTS.   The Fourth Amendment protects against unreasonable searches and seizures by requiring that in most instances a physical search for evidence must be conducted under the authority of a search warrant. An agency's search warrant is an order directing law enforcement officials to search a specific place for a specific item and present it to the agency. Although it was once thought that administrative inspections were exempt from the warrant requirement, the United States Supreme Court held in *Marshall v. Barlow's, Inc.*,[4] that the requirement does apply to the administrative process.

Agencies can conduct warrantless searches in several situations. Warrants are not required to conduct searches in highly regulated industries. Firms that sell firearms or liquor, for example, are automatically subject to inspections without warrants. Sometimes, a statute permits warrantless searches of certain

---

4.   436 U.S. 307, 98 S.Ct. 1816, 56 L.Ed.2d 305 (1978).

types of hazardous operations, such as coal mines. Also, a warrantless inspection in an emergency situation is normally considered reasonable.

Adjudication

After conducting an investigation of a suspected rule violation, an agency may begin to take administrative action against an individual or organization. Most administrative actions are resolved through negotiated settlements at their initial stages, without the need for formal **adjudication** (the resolution of the dispute through a hearing conducted by the agency).

NEGOTIATED SETTLEMENTS. Depending on the agency, negotiations may take the form of a simple conversation or a series of informal conferences. Whatever form the negotiations take, their purpose is to rectify the problem to the agency's satisfaction and eliminate the need for additional proceedings.

Settlement is an appealing option to firms for two reasons. First, firms in regulated industries often do not want to appear to the regulating agency to be uncooperative. Second, litigation can be very expensive. To conserve their own resources and avoid formal actions, administrative agencies devote a great deal of effort to giving advice and negotiating solutions to problems.

FORMAL COMPLAINTS. If a settlement cannot be reached, the agency may issue a formal *complaint* against the suspected violator. If the Environmental Protection Agency (EPA), for example, finds that a factory is polluting groundwater in violation of federal pollution laws, the EPA will issue a complaint against the violator in an effort to bring the plant into compliance with federal regulations. This complaint is a public document, and a press release may accompany it. The factory charged in the complaint will respond by filing an answer to the EPA's allegations. If the factory and the EPA cannot agree on a settlement, the case is heard in a trial-like setting before an administrative law judge (ALJ). The adjudication process is described below and illustrated graphically in Exhibit 6–6.

THE ROLE OF AN ADMINISTRATIVE LAW JUDGE. The ALJ presides over the hearing and has the power to administer oaths, take testimony, rule on questions of evidence, and make determinations of fact. Although formally the ALJ works for the agency prosecuting the case (in our example, the EPA), the law requires an ALJ to be an unbiased adjudicator (judge).

Certain safeguards prevent bias on the part of the ALJ and promote fairness in the proceedings. For example, the Administrative Procedure Act requires that the ALJ be separate from the EPA's investigative and prosecutorial staff. The APA also prohibits *ex parte* communications—that is, communications between the ALJ and any party to an agency proceeding, such as the EPA or the factory, without the participation of the other party and without making a record of the communication. Finally, provisions of the APA protect the ALJ from agency disciplinary actions unless the agency can show good cause for such actions.

HEARING PROCEDURES. Hearing procedures vary widely from agency to agency. Administrative agencies generally can exercise substantial discretion over the type of hearing procedures that they will use. Frequently, disputes are

Adjudication The act of rendering a judicial decision. In administrative process, the proceeding in which an administrative law judge hears and decides on issues that arise when an administrative agency charges a person or a firm with violating a law or regulation enforced by the agency.

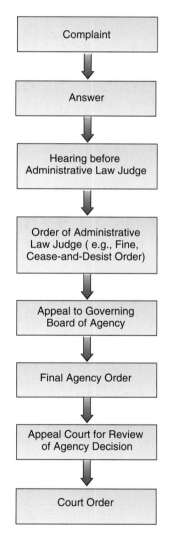

■ **Exhibit 6–6**
The Process of Formal Administrative Adjudication

resolved through informal adjudication proceedings. For example, the parties, their counsel, and the ALJ may simply meet at a table in a conference room for the dispute-settlement proceedings.

A formal adjudicatory hearing, in contrast, resembles a trial in many respects. Prior to the hearing, the parties are permitted to undertake extensive discovery proceedings (involving depositions, interrogatories, and requests for documents or other information, as described in Chapter 3). During the hearing, the parties may give testimony, present other evidence, and cross-examine adverse witnesses.

A significant difference between a trial and an administrative agency hearing, though, is that normally much more information, including hearsay (secondhand information offered for its truth), can be introduced as evidence during an administrative hearing.

Initial Order In the context of administrative law, an agency's disposition in a matter other than a rulemaking. An administrative law judge's initial order becomes final unless it is appealed.

Final Order The final decision of an administrative agency on an issue. If no appeal is taken, or if the case is not reviewed or considered anew by the agency commission, the administrative law judge's initial order becomes the final order of the agency.

AGENCY ORDERS.   Following a hearing, the ALJ renders an **initial order,** or decision, on the case. Either party may appeal the ALJ's decision to the board or commission that governs the agency. If the factory is dissatisfied with the ALJ's decision, for example, it may appeal the decision to the commission that governs the EPA. If the factory is dissatisfied with the commission's decision, it may appeal the decision to a federal court of appeals. If no party appeals the case, the ALJ's decision becomes the **final order** of the agency. If a party does appeal the case, the final order comes from the commission's decision or that of the reviewing court. If a party appeals and the commission and the court decline to review the case, the ALJ's decision also becomes final. This point, as well as the role of common sense in an administrative decision, is illustrated in the following case.

Case 6.3 ● Buck Creek Coal, Inc. v. Federal Mine Safety and Health Administration

United States Court of Appeals,
Seventh Circuit, 1995.
52 F.3d 133.

HISTORICAL AND SOCIAL SETTING   *Historically, three fossil fuels—coal, oil, and natural gas—have accounted for the bulk of U.S. energy production. Of those three fuels, coal accounted for the largest share of energy production in the 1980s. It is estimated that U.S. coal production could be sustained at present levels for more than two hundred years. Some of the richest U.S. coal deposits are in the Appalachian Mountains and in the southern half of Indiana.*

BACKGROUND AND FACTS   Buck Creek Coal, Inc., operates a coal mine in Sullivan County, Indiana. When James

Holland, an inspector for the Mine Safety and Health Administration (MSHA), inspected the mine, he noted an accumulation of loose coal and coal dust in the feeder area, where mined coal is transferred from mine shuttle cars to conveyor belts. Holland issued a citation that charged Buck Creek with violations of federal regulations that require mine operators to keep feeder areas clean. After hearing evidence from both sides, an ALJ found that the evidence supported Holland's conclusions and fined Buck Creek $2,000. Buck Creek asked the Federal Mine Safety and Health Review Commission to review the ALJ's conclusions. When the commission declined, Buck Creek sought review in the courts.

IN THE WORDS OF THE COURT . . .
ILANA DIAMOND ROVNER, Circuit Judge.
    * * * *

    * * * [The ALJ] made these findings, based primarily on the testimony of Inspector Holland: "[T]here were substantial accumulations of loose coal,

(Continued)

Case 6.3—continued

coal fines and float coal dust, in the feeder area * * * . A heated roller turning in that combustible material could easily be an ignition source which could in turn cause a fire. * * * [I]n the event of a fire, smoke and gas inhalation by miners in the area would cause a reasonably serious injury requiring medical attention." * * * [N]o further evidence was necessary to support the ALJ's conclusion. First, * * * Inspector Holland [is] a federal mine inspector with 32 years of mining experience who specializes in mine ventilation. Nor was anything more than Inspector Holland's opinion necessary to support the common sense conclusion that a fire burning in an underground coal mine would present a serious risk of smoke and gas inhalation to miners who are present. * * * [F]ire is one of the primary safety concerns that has motivated federal regulation of the coal mining industry.

Nor has Buck Creek identified any evidence that tends to undermine the ALJ's conclusion. * * * Buck Creek has relied mainly on * * * testimony [that] pertained to Buck Creek's fire safety systems. * * * The fact that Buck Creek has safety measures in place * * * does not mean that fires do not pose a serious safety risk to miners. Indeed, the precautions are * * * in place * * * precisely because of the significant dangers associated with coal mine fires.

DECISION AND REMEDY The U.S. Court of Appeals for the Seventh Circuit denied Buck Creek's petition for review. The ALJ's conclusions became the final order for the agency.

FOR CRITICAL ANALYSIS—SOCIAL CONSIDERATION *What role does common sense play in the application and review of administrative rulings?*

Limitations on Agency Powers

Combining the functions normally divided among the three branches of government into an administrative agency concentrates considerable power in a single organization. Because of this concentration of authority, one of the major policy objectives of the government is to control the risks of arbitrariness and overreaching by administrative agencies without hindering the effective use of agency power to deal with those particular problem areas that caused the agency's original creation by Congress.

The judicial branch of the government exercises control over agency powers through the courts' review of agency actions. The executive and legislative branches of government also exercise control over agency authority.

> **"[A]bsolute discretion . . . is more destructive of freedom than any of man's other inventions."**
>
> William O. Douglas, 1898–1980
> (Associate justice of the United States Supreme Court, 1939–1975)

Judicial Controls

The APA provides for judicial review of most agency decisions. If the factory in the above example is dissatisfied with the agency's order, it can appeal the decision to a federal appeals court. Agency actions are not automatically subject to judicial review, however. Parties seeking review must demonstrate that they meet certain requirements, including those listed here:

■ The action must be *reviewable* by the court. The APA creates a presumption that agency actions are reviewable, making this requirement easy to satisfy.

Inside the Legal Environment
Business Opportunity Scams

This is how it starts: a promise of big income for a few hours of easy work—"No Experience Necessary!" The promise appears in an ad in a newspaper or a magazine, or in a commercial on television or radio, urging you to "Act Now!" The work may be said to take "only a little of your spare time" and may involve tending video games or pay phones, or stocking vending machines or display racks for anything from car wax and cookies to herbal pills and pizza. It sounds too good to be true—and it is. Such deals cost innocent investors more than millions of dollars a year.

If you agree to take advantage of one of these so-called opportunities, it may end up taking advantage of you. To obtain the display racks and inventory, for example, you may be asked to make a large down payment or to buy a large amount of start-up product. To convince you of the "Easy Money!" claims, a seller may cite a government report or include testimonials from "satisfied dealers." The promises of profitability are usually empty—the report may not exist, and the testimonials will be hand picked for what they say.

One item that a scam artist will not provide is the document that the Federal Trade Commission (FTC) requires under its business opportunity disclosure rule.[a] Basically, this rule applies to deals that cost an investor $500 or more in the first six months and in which the seller agrees to handle such matters as finding locations. The document must include an audited financial statement and must cover, among other things, the seller's business history. If an ad claims that a product will be profitable, a prospective buyer is entitled to written proof. The document must also state the following: "To protect you, we've required your [seller] to give you this information. We haven't checked it, and don't know if it's correct. * * * If you find anything you think may be wrong or anything important that's been left out, you should let us know about it. It may be against the law."

Such information might have helped the individual who invested $12,000 in popcorn vending machines that return less than $30 per month. It might have helped the person who invested more than $13,000 in video games that broke down in less than ninety days, or the two investors who lost $72,000 in hot-pizza vending machines. Other buyers have lost as much as $40,000 each in display-rack frauds involving such items as greeting cards and CD-ROMs.

In response to an astounding increase in these bogus money-making schemes, the FTC initiated Project Telesweep in 1995. A team of FTC employees, pretending to be potential entrepreneurs, began answering the ads that boasted big returns on business "opportunities" like those listed above. After identifying the frauds and accumulating evidence, the FTC joined the U.S. Department of Justice, the North American Securities Administrators Association, and the attorneys general of twenty states to bring legal actions against more than one hundred business opportunity scams for violations of state and federal law, including the FTC disclosure rule.

For Critical Analysis: *What should a potential entrepreneur do to protect himself or herself from fraudulent business opportunities?*

---

a. 16 C.F.R. Section 436.1.

- The party must have *standing to sue* the agency (the party must have a direct stake in the outcome of the judicial proceeding).
- The party must have *exhausted all possible administrative remedies.* Each agency has its "chain of review," and the party must follow agency appeal procedures before a court will deem that administrative remedies have been exhausted.
- There must be an *actual controversy* at issue. Courts will not review cases before it is necessary to decide them.

Recall from Chapter 3 that appellate courts normally defer to the decisions of trial courts on questions of fact. In reviewing administrative actions, the courts are similarly reluctant to review the factual findings of agencies. In most cases, the courts accept the facts as found in the agency proceedings. Normally, when a court reviews an administrative agency decision, the court considers the following types of issues:

- Whether the agency has exceeded its authority under the Congress's enabling legislation.
- Whether the agency has properly interpreted laws applicable to the agency action under review.
- Whether the agency has violated any constitutional provisions.
- Whether the agency has acted in accordance with procedural requirements of the law.
- Whether the agency's actions were arbitrary, capricious, or an abuse of discretion.
- Whether any conclusions drawn by the agency are not supported by substantial evidence.

The court in the following case considered whether the Federal Communications Commission acted arbitrarily or capriciously in rejecting a particular complaint.

Case 6.4 ● American Message Centers v. Federal Communications Commission

United States Court of Appeals, District of Columbia Circuit, 1995. 50 F.3d 35.

HISTORICAL AND TECHNOLOGICAL SETTING *AT&T Corporation had a monopoly on telephone service until the early 1980s, when, as part of the settlement in a U.S. government lawsuit, the firm agreed to divide its local telephone services into seven independent companies. AT&T retained its long distance operations. Today, there are approximately four hundred companies that compete in the long distance and local telephone service markets. They generate nearly $200 billion in total revenues. Telephone use—fueled by such technological changes as cellular networks, fax machines, and 800 and 900 numbers—is expanding at more than three times the rate of population growth. AT&T, MCI Communications Corporation, and Sprint Corporation hold about 90 percent of the long distance market.*

BACKGROUND AND FACTS American Message Centers (AMC) provides answering services to retailers. Calls to a retailer are automatically forwarded to AMC, which pays for the calls. AMC obtains telephone service at a discount from major carriers, including Sprint. Sprint's tariff (a public document setting out rates and rules relating to Sprint's services) states that the "subscriber shall be responsible for the payment of all charges for service." When AMC learned that computer hackers had obtained the access code for AMC's lines and had made nearly $160,000 in long distance calls, it asked Sprint to absorb the cost. Sprint refused. AMC filed a complaint with the Federal Communications Commission (FCC), claiming in part that Sprint's tariff was vague and ambiguous, in violation of the Communications Act of 1934 and FCC rules. These laws require that a carrier's tariff "clearly and definitely" specify any "exceptions or conditions which in any way affect the rates named in the tariff." The FCC rejected AMC's complaint. AMC petitioned for review.

IN THE WORDS OF THE COURT . . .
TATEL, Circuit Judge.
* * * *

* * * On its face, Sprint's tariff establishes a general obligation to pay "all charges for service provided." This is "clear" and "definite." If Sprint "provides" the service—in other words, if the call goes through—the customer has to pay for the call. According to AMC, only a tariff stating

(Continued)

Case 6.4—continued

that subscribers are responsible for all charges, including charges for toll fraud [fraudulently made long distance telephone calls], would be sufficiently clear and definite to allow a carrier to charge consumers for unauthorized calls. * * * [N]othing in the [Communications Act of 1934] or the [FCC's] rules compels it to adopt such a rigid requirement. While carriers must identify any exceptions or conditions affecting their tariffs, charging subscribers for unauthorized but completed calls is not an exception or condition to Sprint's general payment obligation. Instead, it falls under the general rule that the customer pays for all completed calls.

DECISION AND REMEDY   The U.S. Court of Appeals for the District of Columbia Circuit concluded that the FCC's decision was not arbitrary or capricious.

FOR CRITICAL ANALYSIS—TECHNOLOGICAL CONSIDERATION
Under what circumstances might a telephone service provider such as Sprint have the responsibility to protect its customers from computer hackers?

Executive Controls

The executive branch of government exercises control over agencies both through the president's powers to appoint federal officers and through the president's veto powers. The president may veto enabling legislation presented by Congress or congressional attempts to modify an existing agency's authority.

Legislative Controls

> **"Law . . . is a human institution, created by human agents to serve human ends."**
>
> Harlan F. Stone, 1872–1946
> (Chief Justice of the United States Supreme Court, 1941–1946)

Congress also exercises authority over agency powers. Through enabling legislation, Congress gives power to an agency. Of course, an agency may not exceed the power that Congress delegates to it. Through subsequent legislation, Congress can take away that power or even abolish an agency altogether. Legislative authority is required to fund an agency, and enabling legislation usually sets certain time and monetary limits relating to the funding of particular programs. Congress can always revise these limits.

In addition to its power to create and fund agencies, Congress has the authority to investigate the implementation of its laws and the agencies that it has created. Individual legislators may also affect agency policy through their "casework" activities, which involve attempts to help their constituents deal with agencies.

Other legislative checks on agency actions include the Administrative Procedure Act, discussed earlier in this chapter, and the laws discussed in the next section.

Public Accountability

▼   As a result of growing public concern over the powers exercised by administrative agencies, Congress passed several laws to make agencies more accountable through public scrutiny. We discuss here the most significant of these laws.

Freedom of Information Act

Enacted in 1966, the Freedom of Information Act (FOIA)[5] requires the federal government to disclose certain "records" to "any person" on request, even without any reason being given for the request. The FOIA exempts certain types of records. For other records, though, a request that complies with the FOIA procedures need only contain a reasonable description of the information sought (see Exhibit 6–7). An agency's failure to comply with a request may be challenged in

---

5. 5 U.S.C. Section 552.

Date

Agency Head or FOIA Officer
Title
Name of Agency
Address of Agency
City, State, Zip

Re: Freedom of Information Act Request

Dear _____ :

Under the provisions of the Freedom of Information Act, 5, U.S.C. 552, I am requesting access to _____ **[identify the records as clearly as possible]**.

If there are any fees for searching for, or copying, the records I have requested, please inform me before you fill the request. **[Or:]** please supply the records without informing me if the fees do not exceed $ _____ .

[Optional:] I am requesting this information because _____
_____
[State the reason for your request if you think it will assist you in obtaining the information.]

[Optional:] As you know, the act permits you to reduce or waive fees when the release of the information is considered as "primarily benefiting the public." I believe that this request fits that category, and I therefore ask that you waive any fees.

If all or any part of this request is denied, please cite the specific exemption(s) that you think justifies your refusal to release the information, and inform me of the appeal procedures available to me under the law.

I would appreciate your handling this request as quickly as possible, and I look forward to hearing from you within 10 days, as the law stipulates.

Sincerely,

[Signature]

Name
Address
City, State, Zip

■ **Exhibit 6–7**
Sample Letter Requesting Information from an Executive Department or Agency

SOURCE: U.S. Congress, House Committee on Government Operations, *A Citizen's Guide on How to Use the Freedom of Information Act and the Privacy Act Requesting Government Documents*, 95th Congress, 1st Session (1977).

a federal district court. The media, industry trade associations, public-interest groups, and even companies seeking information about competitors rely on these FOIA provisions to obtain information from government agencies.

Government-in-the-Sunshine Act

Congress passed the Government-in-the-Sunshine Act,[6] or open meeting law, in 1976. It requires that "every portion of every meeting of an agency" be open to "public observation." The act also requires procedures to ensure that the public is provided with adequate advance notice of the agency's scheduled meeting and agenda. As with the FOIA, the Sunshine Act contains certain exceptions. Closed meetings are permitted when (1) the subject of the meeting concerns accusing any person of a crime, (2) open meetings would frustrate implementation of future agency actions, or (3) the subject of the meeting involves matters relating to future litigation or rulemaking. Courts interpret these exceptions to allow open access whenever possible.

Regulatory Flexibility Act

Concern over the effects of regulation on the efficiency of businesses, particularly smaller ones, led Congress to pass the Regulatory Flexibility Act in 1980.[7] Under this act, whenever a new regulation will have a "significant impact upon a substantial number of small entities," the agency must conduct a regulatory flexibility analysis. The analysis must measure the cost that the rule would impose on small businesses and must consider less burdensome alternatives. The act also contains provisions to alert small businesses about forthcoming regulations. The act relieved some record-keeping burdens for small businesses, especially with regard to hazardous waste management.

State Administrative Agencies

Although much of this chapter deals with federal administrative agencies, state agencies also play a significant role in regulating activities within the states. Many of the factors that encouraged the proliferation of federal agencies also fostered the growing presence of state agencies. For example, the reasons for the growth of administrative agencies at all levels of government include the inability of Congress and state legislatures to oversee the actual implementation of their laws and the greater technical competence of the agencies.

Parallel Agencies

Commonly, a state creates an agency as a parallel to a federal agency to provide similar services on a more localized basis. Such parallel agencies include the federal Social Security Administration and the state welfare agency, the Internal Revenue Service and the state revenue department, and the Environmental Protection Agency and the state pollution-control agency. Not

6.   5 U.S.C. Section 552b.
7.   5 U.S.C. Sections 601–612.

State pollution control workers check for levels of contaminants that may pose a threat to human health or the environment. Some observers believe that regulations of such substances contributes to an attempt by administrative agencies to control businesses too tightly. Are such regulations a proper use of the government's administrative power?

all federal agencies have parallel state agencies, however. For example, the Federal Bureau of Investigation and the Nuclear Regulatory Commission have no parallel agencies at the state level.

Conflicts between Parallel Agencies

If the actions of parallel state and federal agencies conflict, the actions of the federal agency will prevail. For example, if the Federal Aviation Administration specifies the hours during which airplanes may land at and depart from airports, a state or local government cannot issue inconsistent laws or regulations governing the same activities. The priority of federal law over conflicting state laws is based on the supremacy clause of the U.S. Constitution. This clause, which is found in Article VI of the Constitution, states that the Constitution and "the Laws of the United States which shall be made in Pursuance thereof . . . shall be the supreme Law of the Land."

Key Terms

adjudication 169
bureaucracy 162
delegation doctrine 161

final order 170
initial order 170
legislative rule 161

notice-and-comment
rulemaking 163

Chapter Summary
Powers and Functions of Administrative Agencies   ▼

CREATION AND POWERS OF ADMINISTRATIVE AGENCIES (See pages 157–162.)	1. Under the U.S. Constitution, Congress may delegate the task of implementing its laws to government agencies. By delegating the task, Congress may indirectly monitor an area in which it has passed legislation without becoming bogged down in the details relating to enforcement of the legislation.
	2. Administrative agencies are created by enabling legislation, which usually specifies the name, composition, and powers of the agency.
	3. Administrative agencies exercise rulemaking, enforcement, and adjudicatory powers.
ADMINISTRATIVE PROCESS—RULEMAKING (See pages 163–165.)	1. Agencies are authorized to create new regulations—their rulemaking function. This power is conferred on an agency in the enabling legislation, and these rules are as important as formal acts of Congress.
	2. **Notice-and-comment rulemaking**—The most common rulemaking procedure. Begins with the publication of the proposed regulation in the *Federal Register*. Publication of the notice is followed by a comment period to allow private parties to comment on the proposed rule.
ADMINISTRATIVE PROCESS—INVESTIGATION (See pages 166–169.)	1. Administrative agencies investigate the entities that they regulate. They conduct investigations during the rulemaking process to obtain information and after rules are issued to monitor compliance.
	2. The most important investigative tools available to an agency are the following:
	a. Inspections and tests—Used to gather information and to correct or prevent undesirable conditions.
	b. Subpoenas—Orders that direct individuals to appear at a hearing or to hand over specified documents.
	3. Limits on administrative investigations include the following:
	a. The investigation must be for a legitimate purpose.
	b. The information sought must be relevant, and the investigative demands must be specific and not unreasonably burdensome.
	c. The Fourth Amendment protects companies and individuals from unreasonable searches and seizures by requiring search warrants in most instances.
ADMINISTRATIVE PROCESS—ADJUDICATION (See pages 169–171.)	1. After a preliminary investigation, an agency may initiate an administrative action against an individual or organization by filing a complaint. Most such actions are resolved at this stage, before they go through the formal adjudicatory process.
	2. If there is no settlement, the case is presented to an administrative law judge (ALJ) in a proceeding similar to a trial.
	3. After a case is concluded, the ALJ renders an initial order, which may be appealed by either party to the agency and ultimately to a federal appeals court. If no appeal is taken or the case is not reviewed, then the order becomes the final order of the agency.
LIMITATIONS ON AGENCY POWERS (See pages 171–174.)	1. **Judicial controls**—Administrative agencies are subject to the judicial review of the courts. A court may review whether—
	a. An agency has exceeded the scope of its enabling legislation.

(Continued)

Chapter Summary, continued

LIMITATIONS ON AGENCY POWERS—continued (See pages 171–174.)	**b.** An agency has properly interpreted the laws.
	c. An agency has violated the U.S. Constitution.
	d. An agency has complied with all applicable procedural requirements.
	e. An agency's actions are arbitrary or capricious, or an abuse of discretion.
	f. An agency's conclusions are not supported by substantial evidence.
	2. Executive controls—The president can control administrative agencies through appointments of federal officers and through vetoes of legislation creating or affecting agency powers.
	3. Legislative controls—Congress can give power to an agency, take it away, increase or decrease the agency's finances, or abolish the agency. The Administrative Procedure Act of 1946 also limits agencies.
PUBLIC ACCOUNTABILITY (See pages 174–177.)	**1. Freedom of Information Act of 1966**—Requires the government to disclose records to "any person" on request.
	2. Government-in-the-Sunshine Act of 1976—Requires the following:
	a. "[E]very portion of every meeting of an agency" must be open to "public observation."
	b. Procedures must be implemented to ensure that the public is provided with adequate advance notice of the agency's scheduled meeting and agenda.
	3. Regulatory Flexibility Act of 1980—Requires a regulatory flexibility analysis whenever a new regulation will have a "significant impact upon a substantial number of small entities."
STATE ADMINISTRATIVE AGENCIES (See page 177.)	**1.** States create agencies that parallel federal agencies to provide similar services on a more localized basis.
	2. If the actions of parallel state and federal agencies conflict, the actions of the federal agency will prevail.

For Review

1. How are federal administrative agencies created?
2. What are the three operations that make up the basic functions of most administrative agencies?
3. What sequence of events must normally occur before an agency rule becomes law?
4. How do administrative agencies enforce their rules?
5. How do the three branches of government limit the power of administrative agencies?

Questions and Case Problems

6–1. Rulemaking Procedures. Assume that the Securities and Exchange Commission (SEC) has a policy not to enforce rules prohibiting insider trading except when the insiders make monetary profits for themselves. Then the SEC modifies this policy by a determination that the agency has the statutory authority to bring an enforcement action against an individual even if he or she does not personally profit from the insider trading. In modifying the policy, the SEC does not conduct a rulemaking but simply announces its new decision. A securities organization objects and says that the policy was unlawfully developed without opportunity for public comment. In a lawsuit challenging the new policy, should the policy be overruled under the Administrative Procedure Act? Discuss.

6–2. Rulemaking Procedures.   Assume that the Food and Drug Administration (FDA), using proper procedures, adopts a rule describing its future investigations. This new rule covers all future cases in which the FDA wants to regulate food additives. Under the new rule, the FDA says that it will not regulate food additives without giving food companies an opportunity to cross-examine witnesses. Some time later, the FDA wants to regulate methylisocyanate, a food additive. In doing so, the FDA undertakes an informal rulemaking procedure, without cross-examination, and regulates methylisocyanate. Producers protest, saying that the FDA promised cross-examination. The FDA responds that the Administrative Procedure Act does not require such cross-examination and that it could freely withdraw the promise made in its new rule. If the producers challenge the FDA in a court, on what basis would the court rule in their favor?

6–3. Rulemaking and Adjudication Powers.   For decades, the Federal Trade Commission (FTC) resolved fair trade and advertising disputes through individual adjudications. In the 1960s, the FTC began promulgating rules that defined fair and unfair trade practices. In cases involving violations of these rules, the due process rights of participants were more limited and did not include cross-examination. This was because, although anyone found violating a rule would receive a full adjudication, the legitimacy of the rule itself could not be challenged in the adjudication. Any party charged with violating a rule was almost certain to lose the adjudication. Affected parties complained to a court, arguing that their rights before the FTC were unduly limited by the new rules. What will the court examine to determine whether to uphold the new rules?

6–4. Rulemaking Procedures.   The Department of Commerce issued a flammability standard that required all mattresses, including crib mattresses, to pass a test that involved contact with a burning cigarette. The manufacturers of crib mattresses petitioned the department to exempt their product from the test procedure, but the department refused to do so. The crib manufacturers sued the department and argued that applying such a rule to crib mattresses was arbitrary and capricious, because infants do not smoke. On what basis might the court hold that the rule is not arbitrary and capricious? [*Bunny Bear, Inc. v. Peterson,* 473 F.2d 1002 (1st Cir. 1973)]

6–5. Rulemaking Procedures.   The Atomic Energy Commission (AEC) was engaged in rulemaking proceedings for nuclear reactor safety. An environmental group sued the commission, arguing that its proceedings were inadequate. The commission had carefully complied with all requirements of the Administrative Procedure Act (APA). The environmentalists argued, however, that the very hazardous and technical nature of the reactor safety issue required elaborate procedures above and beyond those of the act. A federal appellate court agreed and overturned the AEC rules. The commission appealed the case to the United States Supreme Court. Under what circumstances should an agency have to do more than comply with the APA? [*Vermont Yankee Nuclear Power Corp. v. Natural Resources Defense Council, Inc.,* 435 U.S. 519, 98 S.Ct. 1197, 55 L.Ed.2d 460 (1978)]

6–6. Executive Controls.   In 1982, the president of the United States appointed Matthew Chabal, Jr., to the position of U.S. marshal. U.S. marshals are assigned to the federal courts. In the fall of 1985, Chabal received an unsatisfactory annual performance rating, and the president fired him shortly thereafter. Given that U.S. marshals are assigned to the federal courts, are these appointees members of the executive branch? Did the president have the right to fire Chabal without consulting Congress about the decision? [*Chabal v. Reagan,* 841 F.2d 1216 (3d Cir. 1988)]

6–7. Agency Investigations.   A state statute required vehicle dismantlers—persons whose business includes dismantling automobiles and selling the parts—to be licensed and to keep records regarding the vehicles and parts in their possession. The statute also authorized warrantless administrative inspections; that is, without first obtaining a warrant, agents of the state department of motor vehicles or police officers could inspect a vehicle dismantler's license and records, as well as vehicles on the premises. Pursuant to this statute, police officers entered an automobile junkyard and asked to see the owner's license and records. The owner replied that he did not have the documents. The officers inspected the premises and discovered stolen vehicles and parts. The junkyard owner, who was charged with possession of stolen property and unregistered operation as a vehicle dismantler, argued that the warrantless inspection statute was unconstitutional under the Fourth Amendment. The trial court disagreed, reasoning that the junkyard business was a highly regulated industry. On appeal, the highest state court concluded that the statute had no truly administrative purpose and impermissibly authorized searches only to discover stolen property. The state appealed to the United States Supreme Court. Should the Court uphold the statute? Discuss. [*New York v. Burger,* 482 U.S. 691, 107 S.Ct. 2636, 96 L.Ed.2d 601 (1987)]

6–8. Rulemaking Process.   In 1976, the Environmental Protection Agency (EPA) proposed a rule establishing new pollution-control standards for coal-fired steam generators. The agency gave notice and received comments in the manner prescribed by the Administrative Procedure Act. After the public comments had been received, the EPA received informal suggestions from members of Congress and other federal officials. In 1979, the EPA published its final standards. Several environmental groups protested these standards, arguing that they were too lax. As part of this protest, the groups complained that political influence from Congress and other federal officials had encouraged the EPA to relax the proposed standards. The groups went on to argue that these *ex parte* comments were themselves illegal or that such comments at least should have been summarized in the record. What will the court decide? Discuss fully. [*Sierra Club v. Costle*, 657 F.2d 298 (D.C.Cir. 1981)]

6–9. Arbitrary and Capricious Test. In 1977, the Department of Transportation (DOT) adopted a passive-restraint standard (known as Standard 208) that required new cars to have either air bags or automatic seat belts. By 1981, it had become clear that all the major auto manufacturers would install automatic seat belts to comply with this rule. The DOT determined that most purchasers of cars would detach their automatic seat belts, thus making them ineffective. Consequently, the department repealed the regulation. State Farm Mutual Automobile Insurance Co. and other insurance companies sued in the District of Columbia Circuit Court of Appeals for a review of the DOT's repeal of the regulation. That court held that the repeal was arbitrary and capricious, because the DOT had reversed its rule without sufficient support. The motor vehicle manufacturers then appealed this decision to the United States Supreme Court. What will result? Discuss. [*Motor Vehicle Manufacturers Association v. State Farm Mutual Automobile Insurance Co.*, 463 U.S. 29, 103 S.Ct. 2856, 77 L.Ed.2d 443 (1983)]

A Question of Ethics and Social Responsibility

6–10. The Marine Mammal Protection Act was enacted in 1972 to reduce incidental killing and injury of marine mammals during commercial fishing operations. Under the act, commercial fishing vessels are required to allow an employee of the National Oceanic and Atmospheric Administration (NOAA) to accompany the vessels to conduct research and observe operations. In December 1986, after NOAA had adopted a new policy of recruiting female as well as male observers, NOAA notified Caribbean Marine Services Co. that female observers would be assigned to accompany two of the company's fishing vessels on their next voyages. The owners and crew members of the ships (the plaintiffs) moved for an injunction against the implementation of the NOAA directive. The plaintiffs contended that the presence of a female on board a fishing vessel would be very awkward, because the female would have to share the crew's quarters, and crew members enjoyed little or no privacy with respect to bodily functions. Further, the plaintiffs alleged that the presence of a female would be disruptive to fishing operations, because some of the crew members were "crude" men with little formal education who might harass or sexually assault a female observer, and the officers would therefore have to devote time to protecting the female from the crew. Finally, the plaintiffs argued that the presence of a female observer could destroy morale and distract the crew, thus affecting the crew's efficiency and decreasing the vessel's profits. [*Caribbean Marine Services Co. v. Baldrige*, 844 F.2d 668 (9th Cir. 1988)]

1. In general, do you think that the public policy of promoting equal employment opportunity should override the concerns of the vessel owners and crew? If you were the judge, would you grant the injunction? Why or why not?

2. The plaintiffs pointed out that fishing voyages could last three months or longer. Would the length of a particular voyage affect your answer to the preceding question?

3. The plaintiffs contended that even if the indignity of sharing bunk rooms and toilet facilities with a female observer could be overcome, the observer's very presence in the common areas of the vessel, such as the dining area, would unconstitutionally infringe on the crew members' right to privacy in these areas. Evaluate this claim.

For Critical Analysis

6–11. Does Congress delegate too much power to federal administrative agencies? Do the courts defer too much to Congress in its grant of power to those agencies? What are the alternatives?

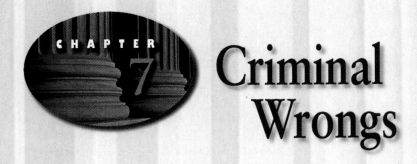

Criminal Wrongs

CHAPTER 7

Contents

Chapter Objectives

After reading this chapter, you should be able to . . .

1. Explain the difference between criminal offenses and other types of wrongful conduct.
2. Indicate the essential elements of criminal liability.
3. Describe the constitutional safeguards that protect the rights of persons accused of crimes.
4. Identify and define the crimes that affect business.
5. Summarize the defenses to criminal liability.

Various sanctions are used to bring about a society in which individuals engaging in business can compete and flourish. These sanctions include damages for various types of tortious conduct (as discussed in the preceding chapters), damages for breach of contract (to be discussed in Chapter 13), and the equitable remedies discussed in Chapter 1. Additional sanctions are imposed under criminal law. Many statutes regulating business provide for criminal as well as civil sanctions. Therefore, criminal law joins civil law as an important element in the legal environment of business.

In this chapter, following a brief summary of the major differences between criminal and civil law, we look at how crimes are classified and what elements must be present for criminal liability to exist. We then examine criminal procedural law, which attempts to ensure that a criminal defendant's right to "due process of law" (see the quotation at right) is enforced. In the remainder of the chapter, we focus on crimes affecting business and the defenses that can be raised to avoid liability for criminal actions.

> "No state shall make or enforce any law which shall abridge the privileges or immunities of citizens of the United States; nor shall any State deprive any person of life, liberty, or property without due process of law, nor deny to any person within its jurisdiction the equal protection of the laws."
>
> Fourteenth Amendment to the U.S. Constitution, July 28, 1868

Civil Law and Criminal Law

Civil law spells out the duties that exist between persons or between citizens and their governments, excluding the duty not to commit crimes. Contract law, for example, is part of civil law. The whole body of tort law, which deals with the infringement by one person on the legally recognized rights of another, is also an area of civil law. The right of people engaged in business to compete and flourish is sustained by the civil law, which imposes damages for various types of tortious conduct (as discussed in the preceding chapters) and damages for breach of contract (to be discussed in Chapter 13).

Criminal law, in contrast, has to do with crime. A **crime** can be defined as a wrong against society proclaimed in a statute and, if committed, punishable by society through fines and/or imprisonment—and, in some cases, death. Because crimes are *offenses against society as a whole,* they are prosecuted by a public official, not by victims. Exhibit 7–1 on page 184 presents additional ways in which criminal and civil law differ.

Crime A wrong against society proclaimed in a statute and, if committed, punishable by society through fines and/or imprisonment—and, in some cases, death.

Classification of Crimes

Depending on their degree of seriousness, crimes are classified as felonies or misdemeanors. **Felonies** are serious crimes punishable by death or by imprisonment in a federal or state penitentiary for more than a year. The Model Penal Code[1] provides for four degrees of felony: (1) capital offenses, for which the maximum penalty is death; (2) first degree felonies, punishable by a maximum penalty of life imprisonment; (3) second degree felonies, punishable by a maximum of ten years' imprisonment; and (4) third degree felonies, punishable by a maximum of five years' imprisonment.

Felony A crime—such as arson, murder, rape, or robbery—that carries the most severe sanctions, usually ranging from one year in a state or federal prison to the forfeiture of one's life.

---

1. The American Law Institute issued the Official Draft of the Model Penal Code in 1962. The Model Penal Code is not a uniform code. Uniformity of criminal law among the states is not as important as uniformity in other areas of the law. Types of crimes vary with local circumstances, and it is appropriate that punishments vary accordingly. The Model Penal Code contains four parts: (1) general provisions, (2) definitions of special crimes, (3) provisions concerning treatment and corrections, and (4) provisions on the organization of correction.

■ **Exhibit 7–1**
Civil and Criminal Law Compared

ISSUE	CIVIL LAW	CRIMINAL LAW
Area of concern	Rights and duties between individuals	Offenses against society as a whole
Wrongful act	Harm to a person	Violation of a statute that prohibits some type of activity
Party who brings suit	Person who suffered harm	The state
Standard of proof	Preponderance of the evidence	Beyond a reasonable doubt
Remedy	Damages to compensate for the harm	Punishment (fine or imprisonment)

Misdemeanor A lesser crime than a felony, punishable by a fine or imprisonment for up to one year in other than a state or federal penitentiary.

Under federal law and in most states, any crime that is not a felony is considered a **misdemeanor**. Misdemeanors are crimes punishable by a fine or by confinement for up to a year. If incarcerated (imprisoned), the guilty party goes to a local jail instead of a penitentiary. Disorderly conduct and trespass are common misdemeanors. Some states have different classes of misdemeanors. For example, in Illinois misdemeanors are either Class A (confinement for up to a year), Class B (not more than six months), or Class C (not more than thirty days). Whether a crime is a felony or a misdemeanor can also determine whether the case is tried in a magistrate's court (for example, by a justice of the peace) or a general trial court.

Petty Offense In criminal law, the least serious kind of criminal offense, such as a traffic or building-code violation.

In most jurisdictions, **petty offenses** are considered to be a subset of misdemeanors. Petty offenses are minor violations, such as violations of building codes. Even for petty offenses, however, a guilty party can be put in jail for a few days, fined, or both, depending on state law.

Criminal Liability

Two elements must exist simultaneously for a person to be convicted of a crime: (1) the performance of a prohibited act and (2) a specified state of mind or intent on the part of the actor. Every criminal statute prohibits certain behavior. Most crimes require an act of *commission*; that is, a person must *do* something in order to be accused of a crime.[2] In some cases, an act of *omission* can be a crime, but only when a person has a legal duty to perform the omitted act. Failure to file a tax return is an example of an omission that is a crime.

The *guilty act* requirement is based on one of the premises of criminal law—that a person is punished for harm done to society. Thinking about killing someone or about stealing a car may be wrong, but the thoughts do no harm until they are translated into action. Of course, a person can be punished for attempting murder or robbery, but normally only if he or she took substantial steps toward the criminal objective.

---

2.   Called the *actus reus* (pronounced *ak*-tuhs *ray*-uhs), or "guilty act."

A wrongful mental state[3] is as necessary as a wrongful act in establishing criminal liability. What constitutes such a mental state varies according to the wrongful action. For murder, the act is the taking of a life, and the mental state is the intent to take life. For theft, the guilty act is the taking of another person's property, and the mental state involves both the knowledge that the property belongs to another and the intent to deprive the owner of it. Without the mental state required by law for a particular crime, there is no crime, as the following case illustrates.

> **"A man may have as bad a heart as he chooses, if his conduct is within the rules."**
>
> Oliver Wendell Holmes, Jr., 1841–1935
> (Associate justice of the United States Supreme Court, 1902–1932)

3. Called the *mens rea* (pronounced mehns *ray*-uh), or "evil intent."

Case 7.1 ⬤ Johnson v. State

SUPREME COURT OF FLORIDA, 1992.
597 So.2d 798.

HISTORICAL AND SOCIAL SETTING *During the early days of the development of crimes at common law, judges often held an act to be criminal even if the perpetrator had no criminal intent. Starting in the early seventeenth century, judges began to require, in addition to the commission of a criminal act, some sort of criminal intent. Today, criminal liability still generally requires criminal intent.*

BACKGROUND AND FACTS Raymond Johnson allegedly snatched a purse left in an unattended car at a gas station. Because the purse contained both money and a firearm, among other items, the state trial court convicted and sentenced Johnson for burglary of a conveyance (vehicle), grand theft of property (cash and payroll checks), and grand theft of a firearm. On appeal, Johnson claimed that he could not be guilty of grand theft of a firearm because he did not know that the purse contained a firearm. In other words, intent to commit the latter crime was lacking, and therefore that crime had not been committed.

IN THE WORDS OF THE COURT . . .
PER CURIAM [by the whole court].
  * * * *

May a defendant be separately convicted and sentenced for grand theft of cash and grand theft of a firearm accomplished by means of snatching a purse that contained both cash and a firearm when the defendant did not know the nature of the purse's contents?
  * * * We answer the * * * question in the negative and remand for further proceedings.
  * * * *

The theft occurred when Johnson wrongfully took the property of another. He did this in one swift motion. * * * A separate crime occurs only when there are separate distinct acts of seizing the property of another.
  * * * In this case there was one intent and one act of taking the handbag.
  * * * Accordingly, there could be only one theft conviction in this case.

DECISION AND REMEDY The Supreme Court of Florida held that Johnson could not be separately convicted for grand theft of cash and grand theft of a firearm accomplished by the single act of snatching a purse when he did not know the contents of the purse. The court remanded the case.

FOR CRITICAL ANALYSIS—SOCIAL CONSIDERATION *Why didn't the court conclude that because Johnson intended to steal the purse, he therefore intended to steal everything contained in the purse?*

> "Our procedure has been always haunted by the ghost of the innocent man convicted."
>
> Learned Hand, 1872–1961
> (American jurist)

Procedure in Criminal Law

Criminal law brings the force of the state, with all its resources, to bear against the individual. Criminal procedures are designed to protect the constitutional rights of individuals and to prevent the arbitrary use of power on the part of the government.

Constitutional Safeguards

The U.S. Constitution provides specific safeguards for those accused of crimes. The United States Supreme Court has ruled that most of these safeguards apply not only in federal but also in state courts by virtue of the due process clause of the Fourteenth Amendment. These safeguards include the following:

1. The Fourth Amendment protection from unreasonable searches and seizures.
2. The Fourth Amendment requirement that no warrants for a search or an arrest can be issued without probable cause.
3. The Fifth Amendment requirement that no one can be deprived of "life, liberty, or property without due process of law."
4. The Fifth Amendment prohibition against **double jeopardy** (trying someone twice for the same criminal offense).[4]
5. The Fifth Amendment requirement that no person can be required to be a witness against (incriminate) himself or herself.
6. The Sixth Amendment guarantees of a speedy trial, a trial by jury, a public trial, the right to confront witnesses, and the right to a lawyer at various stages of criminal proceedings.
7. The Eighth Amendment prohibitions against excessive bail and fines and cruel and unusual punishment.

Double Jeopardy A situation occurring when a person is tried twice for the same criminal offense; prohibited by the Fifth Amendment to the Constitution.

Exclusionary Rule In criminal procedure, a rule under which any evidence that is obtained in violation of the accused's constitutional rights guaranteed by the Fourth, Fifth, and Sixth Amendments, as well as any evidence derived from illegally obtained evidence, will not be admissible in court.

THE EXCLUSIONARY RULE.   Under what is known as the **exclusionary rule**, all evidence obtained in violation of the constitutional rights spelled out in the Fourth, Fifth, and Sixth Amendments normally must be excluded, as well as all evidence derived from the illegally obtained evidence. Evidence derived from the illegally obtained evidence is known as the "fruit of the poisonous tree." For example, if a confession is obtained after an illegal arrest, the arrest would be "the poisonous tree," and the confession, if "tainted" by the arrest, would be the "fruit."

The purpose of the exclusionary rule is to deter police from conducting warrantless searches and other misconduct. The rule is sometimes criticized because it can lead to injustice. Many a defendant has "gotten off on a technicality" because law enforcement personnel failed to observe procedural requirements based on the above-mentioned constitutional amendments. Even

NOTE   A person may be convicted despite police misconduct, because knowledge of facts obtained independently of the misconduct are admissible.

---

4.   The prohibition against double jeopardy means that once a criminal defendant is acquitted (found "not guilty") or convicted of a particular crime, the government may not reindict the person and retry him or her for the same crime. The prohibition against double jeopardy does not preclude the crime victim from bringing a civil suit against the same person to recover damages. For example, a person found "not guilty" of assault and battery in a criminal case may be sued by the victim in a civil tort case for damages. Additionally, a state's prosecution of a crime will not prevent a separate federal prosecution of the same crime, and vice versa. For example, a defendant found "not guilty" of violating a federal law can be tried in a state court for the same act, if the act is defined as a crime under state law.

Police search a crack house in Florida. Do the owners and occupants of such houses receive protection from unreasonable searches and seizures under the Constitution? Should they?

though a defendant may be obviously guilty, if the evidence of that guilt is obtained improperly (without a valid search warrant, for example), it normally cannot be used against the defendant in court.

The courts, however, can exercise a certain amount of discretion in determining whether evidence is obtained improperly, thus balancing the scales somewhat. For example, in a 1995 case heard by the U.S. Court of Appeals for the Ninth Circuit, the judges had to decide whether evidence obtained from a legally conducted wiretap surveillance operation overseas violated the defendant's Fourth Amendment rights. If it did, the evidence would be inadmissible under the exclusionary rule. The court held that even though the wiretapping would have been illegal in the United States, the evidence legally obtained overseas was admissible. The court stated that the extent to which an American is protected from surveillance in another country is determined by the law of that country.[5]

The following case presents another interesting issue: Does the exclusionary rule require the suppression of evidence obtained during an arrest that was made on the basis of an erroneous computer record?

---

5.   *United States v. Barona,* 56 F.3d 1087 (9th Cir. 1995).

Case 7.2 ● Arizona v. Evans

Supreme Court of the United States, 1995.
514 U.S. 1,
115 S.Ct. 1185,
131 L.Ed.2d 34.

HISTORICAL AND ETHICAL SETTING   *For centuries, U.S. courts allowed the introduction of relevant evidence in criminal trials even if the evidence had been acquired unlawfully. Beginning at the end of the nineteenth century, however, some federal courts thought that to protect the integrity of the judicial process, unlawfully acquired evidence should not be used in criminal trials. In 1914, the United States Supreme Court agreed that a federal court*

(Continued)

Case 7.2—continued

should not be a party to a wrong by allowing prosecutors to use the "fruits" of a police violation of the Fourth Amendment.[a] *Over the last thirty years, there has been a steady attack on this rule, in part on the ground that evidence should not be excluded, even if it was seized illegally, when it clearly shows the guilt of the person charged.*

BACKGROUND AND FACTS   During a routine traffic stop in Phoenix, Arizona, a police officer arrested Isaac Evans when the police computer indicated that there was an outstanding warrant for his arrest. In fact, the warrant had been quashed (voided) more than two weeks earlier, but court employees had wrongly failed to remove the warrant from the computer. The police searched Evans's car and discovered marijuana. Evans was charged, in an Arizona state court, with possession of marijuana. He moved to suppress the evidence (marijuana), on the ground that the arrest was unlawful because the warrant had already been quashed. The court granted Evans's motion, but on appeal, the state appellate court reversed. The state supreme court vacated (set aside) the appellate court's ruling, and the case was appealed to the United States Supreme Court.

IN THE WORDS OF THE COURT . . .
Chief Justice REHNQUIST delivered the opinion of the Court.

* * * *

* * * [T]he [exclusionary] rule's application has been restricted to those instances where its remedial objectives are thought most efficaciously served.

* * *

* * * *

* * * [T]he exclusionary rule was historically designed as a means of deterring police misconduct, not mistakes by court employees. * * * [Evans] offers no evidence that court employees are inclined to ignore or subvert the Fourth Amendment or that lawlessness among these actors requires application of the extreme sanction of exclusion. To the contrary, the Chief Clerk of the Justice Court testified * * * that this type of error occurred [only] once every three or four years.

* * * [M]ost important, there is no basis for believing that application of the exclusionary rule in these circumstances will have a significant effect on court employees responsible for informing the police that a warrant has been quashed. * * * [C]ourt clerks * * * have no stake in the outcome of particular criminal prosecutions. * * *

* * * [A]pplication of the exclusionary rule also could not be expected to alter the behavior of the arresting officer. * * * There is no indication that the arresting officer was not acting * * * reasonably when he relied upon the police computer record.

DECISION AND REMEDY   The United States Supreme Court held that evidence seized in violation of the Fourth Amendment as a result of errors of court employees, causing an incorrect computer record, is admissible in a criminal trial. The Court reversed and remanded the case.

FOR CRITICAL ANALYSIS—SOCIAL CONSIDERATION   *What if police department personnel (instead of court employees) had been responsible for the computer error? How would this circumstance affect the Court's reasoning?*

a.   *Weeks v. United States,* 232 U.S. 383, 34 S.Ct. 341, 58 L.Ed. 652 (1914).

THE *MIRANDA* RULE.   In *Miranda v. Arizona,* the United States Supreme Court established the rule that individuals who are arrested must be informed of certain constitutional rights, including their right to remain silent and their right to counsel. If the arresting officers fail to inform a criminal suspect of these constitutional rights, any statements the suspect makes will not be admissible in court. Because of its importance in criminal procedure, the *Miranda* case is presented as this chapter's *Landmark in the Legal Environment.*

THE EROSION OF THE *MIRANDA* RULE. The Supreme Court and lower courts have enforced the *Miranda* rule hundreds of times since the *Miranda* decision. Over time, however, several exceptions to the rule have been created. Congress in 1968 passed the Omnibus Crime Control and Safe Streets Act, which provided—among other things—that in federal cases a voluntary confession could be used in evidence even if the accused was not informed of his or her rights. The United States Supreme Court has carved out other exceptions. In 1984, for example, the Court recognized a "public safety" exception to the *Miranda* rule. The need to protect the public warranted the admissibility of statements made by the defendant (in this case, indicating where he placed the gun) as evidence in a trial, even when the defendant had not been informed of

> **REMEMBER** Once a suspect has been informed of his or her rights, anything he or she says can be used as evidence in a trial.

Landmark in the Legal Environment
Miranda v. Arizona (1966)

The United States Supreme Court's decision in Miranda v. Arizona[a] has been cited in more court decisions than any other case in the history of American law. Through television shows and other media, the case has also become familiar to most of America's adult population. The case arose after Ernesto Miranda was arrested in his home, on March 13, 1963, for the kidnapping and rape of an eighteen-year-old woman. Miranda was taken to a Phoenix, Arizona, police station and questioned by two police officers. Two hours later, the officers emerged from the interrogation room with a written confession signed by Miranda. The confession was admitted into evidence at the trial, and Miranda was convicted and sentenced to prison for twenty to thirty years.

Miranda appealed the decision, claiming that he had not been informed of his constitutional rights. He did not claim that he was innocent of the crime or that his confession was false or made under duress. He only claimed that he would not have confessed to the crime if he had been advised of his right to remain silent and to have an attorney. Nonetheless, the Supreme Court of Arizona held that Miranda's constitutional rights had not been violated and affirmed his conviction. In forming its decision, the court emphasized the fact that Miranda had not specifi-

cally requested an attorney. The Miranda case was subsequently consolidated with three other cases involving similar issues and reviewed by the United States Supreme Court.

In its decision, the Supreme Court stated that whenever an individual is taken into custody, "the following measures are required: He must be warned prior to any questioning that he has the right to remain silent, that anything he says can be used against him in a court of law, that he has the right to the presence of an attorney, and that if he cannot afford an attorney one will be appointed for him prior to any questioning if he so desires." If the accused waives his or her rights to remain silent and to have counsel present, the government must be able to demonstrate that the waiver was made knowingly, intelligently, and voluntarily.

Today, both on television and in the real world, police officers routinely advise suspects of their "Miranda rights" upon arrest. When Ernesto Miranda himself was later murdered, the suspected murderer was "read his Miranda rights."

For Critical Analysis: *Should illegally seized evidence be excluded from a criminal trial even if the evidence clearly shows the guilt of the person charged? Why should defendants who have admitted that they are guilty be allowed to avoid criminal liability because of procedural violations?*

a. 384 U.S. 436, 86 S.Ct. 1602, 16 L.Ed.2d 694 (1966).

International Perspective

The right to remain silent is rooted in the Fifth Amendment prohibition against self-incrimination (no person "shall be compelled in any criminal case to be a witness against himself"). This protection against self-incrimination is a fundamental element in U.S. criminal procedure. For example, as will be discussed shortly, in a criminal trial a defendant need not say anything in his or her defense; rather, the burden is on the state to prove that the defendant committed the crime with which he or she is charged. Juries are not permitted to infer that a defendant is guilty simply because he or she remains silent.

The right to remain silent has long been a legal hallmark in Great Britain also. Until recently, a British police officer, upon arresting a suspect, was required to tell the suspect, "You do not have to say anything unless you wish to do so, but what you say may be given in evidence." In 1994, however, the British Parliament passed an act that provides that a criminal defendant's silence may be interpreted as evidence of the defendant's guilt. British police officers are now required, when making arrests, to inform the suspects, "You do not have to say anything. But if you do not mention now something which you later use in your defense, the court may decide that your failure to mention it now strengthens the case against you. A record will be made of everything you say, and it may be given in evidence if you are brought to trial."

For Critical Analysis: *Should U.S. judges and juries be allowed to make inferences from a defendant's silence?*

---

his *Miranda* rights.[6] Today, juries can even accept confessions without being convinced of their voluntariness.

Criminal Process

As mentioned, a criminal prosecution differs significantly from a civil case in several respects. These differences reflect the desire to safeguard the rights of the individual against the state. Exhibit 7–2 summarizes the major steps in processing a criminal case. We discuss below in more detail three phases of the criminal process—arrest, indictment or information, and trial.

ARREST.   Before a warrant for arrest can be issued, there must be probable cause for believing that the individual in question has committed a crime. As discussed in Chapter 5, *probable cause* can be defined as a substantial likelihood that the person has committed or is about to commit a crime. Note that probable cause involves a likelihood, not just a possibility. Arrests may sometimes be made without a warrant if there is no time to get one, but the action of the arresting officer is still judged by the standard of probable cause.

Indictment A charge by a grand jury that a named person has committed a crime.

Grand Jury A group of citizens called to decide, after hearing the state's evidence, whether a reasonable basis (probable cause) exists for believing that a crime has been committed and whether a trial ought to be held.

INDICTMENT OR INFORMATION.   Individuals must be formally charged with having committed specific crimes before they can be brought to trial. If issued by a grand jury, this charge is called an **indictment**.[7] A **grand jury** usually consists of a greater number of jurors than the ordinary trial jury. A grand jury does not determine the guilt or innocence of an accused party; rather, its func-

---

6.   *New York v. Quarles,* 467 U.S. 649, 104 S.Ct. 2626, 81 L.Ed.2d 550 (1984).
7.   Pronounced in-*dyte*-ment.

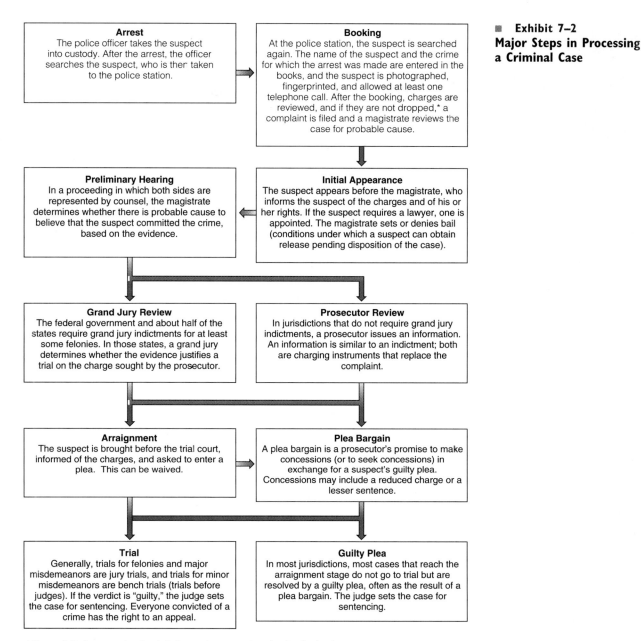

■ **Exhibit 7–2**
Major Steps in Processing a Criminal Case

Arrest
The police officer takes the suspect into custody. After the arrest, the officer searches the suspect, who is then taken to the police station.

Booking
At the police station, the suspect is searched again. The name of the suspect and the crime for which the arrest was made are entered in the books, and the suspect is photographed, fingerprinted, and allowed at least one telephone call. After the booking, charges are reviewed, and if they are not dropped,* a complaint is filed and a magistrate reviews the case for probable cause.

Preliminary Hearing
In a proceeding in which both sides are represented by counsel, the magistrate determines whether there is probable cause to believe that the suspect committed the crime, based on the evidence.

Initial Appearance
The suspect appears before the magistrate, who informs the suspect of the charges and of his or her rights. If the suspect requires a lawyer, one is appointed. The magistrate sets or denies bail (conditions under which a suspect can obtain release pending disposition of the case).

Grand Jury Review
The federal government and about half of the states require grand jury indictments for at least some felonies. In those states, a grand jury determines whether the evidence justifies a trial on the charge sought by the prosecutor.

Prosecutor Review
In jurisdictions that do not require grand jury indictments, a prosecutor issues an information. An information is similar to an indictment; both are charging instruments that replace the complaint.

Arraignment
The suspect is brought before the trial court, informed of the charges, and asked to enter a plea. This can be waived.

Plea Bargain
A plea bargain is a prosecutor's promise to make concessions (or to seek concessions) in exchange for a suspect's guilty plea. Concessions may include a reduced charge or a lesser sentence.

Trial
Generally, trials for felonies and major misdemeanors are jury trials, and trials for minor misdemeanors are bench trials (trials before judges). If the verdict is "guilty," the judge sets the case for sentencing. Everyone convicted of a crime has the right to an appeal.

Guilty Plea
In most jurisdictions, most cases that reach the arraignment stage do not go to trial but are resolved by a guilty plea, often as the result of a plea bargain. The judge sets the case for sentencing.

* At any point in the processing of a criminal case, charges may be reduced or dismissed.

tion is to determine, after hearing the state's evidence, whether a reasonable basis (probable cause) exists for believing that a crime has been committed and whether a trial ought to be held.

Usually, grand juries are called in cases involving serious crimes, such as murder. For lesser crimes, an individual may be formally charged with a crime by what is called an **information,** or criminal complaint. An information will be issued by a magistrate (a public official vested with judicial authority) if the magistrate determines that there is sufficient evidence to justify bringing the individual to trial.

Information A formal accusation or complaint (without an indictment) issued in certain types of actions (usually criminal actions involving lesser crimes) by a law officer, such as a magistrate.

Ethical Perspective

Criminal suspects may waive their *Miranda* rights (see this chapter's *Landmark in the Legal Environment*), but the waiver must be made voluntarily. Evidence that the accused was tricked into waiving his or her rights will show that the rights were not voluntarily waived. What happens, though, if a suspect is tricked into confessing to a crime *after* the suspect has waived his or her rights?

Lying to criminal suspects to induce them to confess to crimes has occurred. In one case, for example, a police officer told a suspect accused of stabbing a person that the suspect's fingerprints had been found on the knife (which was not true). The suspect then confessed to the crime.[a] In another case, a suspect was told that a co-defendant had said something that, in fact, the co-defendant had not said.[b] In both of these cases, the courts held that the confessions induced by the lies were admissible. Coercion was not involved, no threats of harm were made, no bribes were tendered, and generally, in each case, the defendant's will was not "overcome" by the police. The central question remains, however: Where does society draw the line between trickery and coercion? Other kinds of police actions, such as "reverse sting" operations carried out by undercover agents, raise similar ethical questions.

For Critical Analysis: *Trickery may lead to more guilty criminal defendants being convicted. What cost is nonetheless imposed on society by such actions?*

_____
a.   *State v. Barner,* 486 N.W.2d 1 (Minn.App. 1992).

b.   *Frazier v. Cupp,* 394 U.S. 731, 89 S.Ct. 1420, 22 L.Ed.2d 684 (1969).

Beyond a Reasonable Doubt
The standard of proof used in criminal cases. If there is any reasonable doubt that a criminal defendant did not commit the crime with which he or she has been charged, then the verdict must be "not guilty."

> **NOTE**   Reasonable doubt is, as its name implies, doubt based on reason. It is not doubt based on wishes, or imagination, or a desire to avoid doing something unpleasant.

TRIAL.   At a criminal trial, the accused person does not have to prove anything; the entire burden of proof is on the prosecutor (the state). The prosecution must show that, based on all the evidence presented, the defendant's guilt is established **beyond a reasonable doubt**. If there is any reasonable doubt that a criminal defendant did not commit the crime with which he or she has been charged, then the verdict must be "not guilty." Note that giving a verdict of "not guilty" is not the same as stating that the defendant is innocent; it merely means that not enough evidence was properly presented to the court to prove guilt beyond all reasonable doubt.

The requirement that a defendant's guilt be proved beyond a reasonable doubt is a stricter standard of proof than the standard normally used in civil proceedings, in which a defendant's liability is usually decided based on a preponderance of the evidence. A *preponderance of the evidence* means that the evidence offered in support of a certain claim outweighs the evidence offered to negate the claim. The higher standard of proof in criminal cases reflects a fundamental social value—a belief that it is worse to convict an innocent individual than to let a guilty person go free.

Courts have complex rules about what types of evidence may be presented and how the evidence may be brought out in criminal cases, especially in jury trials. These rules are designed to ensure that evidence in trials is relevant, reliable, and not prejudicial against the defendant.

Federal Sentencing Guidelines

In 1984, Congress enacted the Sentencing Reform Act. This act created the U.S. Sentencing Commission, which was charged with the task of standardizing sentences for federal crimes. The commission fulfilled its task, and in 1987 its

Ethical Perspective

Jurors in a criminal case must find the defendant guilty "beyond a reasonable doubt." What, though, does "reasonable doubt" mean? Traditionally in the United States, judges have told jurors that guilt beyond a reasonable doubt equates to a "moral certainty" that a defendant is guilty. Some defendants have claimed, however, that the "moral certainty" test of guilt is too subjective and invites the jurors to ignore objective evidence presented at trial—thus violating the defendants' constitutional rights to due process of law.

In a 1994 case, the United States Supreme Court held otherwise, stating that "so long as the court instructs the jury on the necessity that the defendant's guilt be proven beyond a reasonable doubt, the Constitution does not require that any particular form of words be used in advising the jury of the government's burden of proof." After delving into modern dictionaries, Justice Sandra Day O'Connor concluded that although the phrase "moral certainty," standing alone, "might not be recognized by mod-

ern jurors as a synonym for 'proof beyond a reasonable doubt,' its use in conjunction with the abiding conviction language" did not invite "conviction on less than the constitutionally required proof."[a]

Justice Ruth Bader Ginsburg, in a separate opinion, suggested that courts adopt a model jury instruction devised by the Federal Judicial Center, which defines reasonable doubt as "proof that leaves you firmly convinced of the defendant's guilt." Clearly, the debate over reasonable doubt indicates that law is not yet an exact science.

For Critical Analysis: *Judges are often reluctant to explain to juries what the phrase "reasonable doubt" means, fearing that the more they explain it, the less clear it will be. Do you think that judges should explain to juries what "reasonable doubt" means? Or should the definition of this phrase be left to the jurors?*

a. *Victor v. Nebraska,* 511 U.S. 1, 114 S.Ct. 1239, 127 L.Ed.2d 583 (1994).

---

sentencing guidelines for all federal crimes became effective. The guidelines establish a range of possible penalties for each federal crime. Depending on the defendant's criminal record, the seriousness of the offense, and other factors specified in the guidelines, federal judges must select a sentence from within this range when sentencing criminal defendants.

The commission also created specific guidelines for the punishment of crimes committed by corporate employees (white-collar crimes). These guidelines, which went into effect in 1991, established stiffer penalties for criminal violations of securities laws (see Chapter 23), antitrust laws (see Chapter 22), employment laws (see Chapters 16, 17, and 18), mail and wire fraud, commercial bribery, and kickbacks and money laundering (all discussed later in this chapter). The guidelines allow federal judges to take into consideration a number of factors when selecting from the range of possible penalties for a specified crime. These factors include the defendant company's history of past violations, the extent of management's cooperation with federal investigators, and the extent to which the firm has undertaken specific programs and procedures to prevent criminal activities by its employees.

Criminal cases are sometimes appealed on the ground that the sentence imposed was too severe. In the following case, for example, the defendant, because of a check-kiting scheme, had been charged with bank fraud. Obtaining the property—including money—of a financial institution such as a bank is a federal crime. The issue before the appellate court is whether the defendant's sentence should be reduced in light of the fact that he immediately repaid the amount that he obtained through the fraudulent scheme.

Police officers take a suspect into custody. Why must a criminal suspect be informed of his or her legal rights?

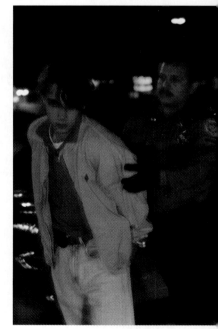

Case 7.3   ● United States v. Asher

United States Court of Appeals,
Seventh Circuit, 1995.
59 F.3d 622.

HISTORICAL AND POLITICAL SETTING *At one time, the Interstate Commerce Commission regulated the routes and rates of trucking companies. Congress deregulated the industry in 1980, allowing truckers to ship freight anywhere and charge whatever they wanted. The immediate effect was a huge number of small, start-up companies—more than twelve thousand in the first few years. The most successful of the truckers, however, were the large national companies that could carry freight anywhere. Most of the new, small outfits failed.*

BACKGROUND AND FACTS   Asher Truck & Trailer, Inc., had facilities in Evansville, Indiana, and Mount Vernon, Illinois. Guy Asher, the company's owner and operator, kept separate bank accounts for the two facilities. When the business began to have cash flow problems, Asher began to write checks on the Evansville account and deposit them in the Mount Vernon account, and vice versa, knowing that the accounts on which the checks were drawn did not have sufficient funds to cover the checks. When the scheme was discovered, the Mount Vernon account was overdrawn by $160,000, which Asher promptly repaid. Asher was charged in a federal district court with bank fraud, and he pleaded guilty to the charge. Asher argued, however, that his sentence should be reduced because he had immediately repaid the bank. The court refused to reduce his sentence, and Asher appealed.

IN THE WORDS OF THE COURT . . .
ESCHBACH, Circuit Judge.
    * * * *

    * * * [W]hile Asher's decision to repay the amount of loss that existed at the time the * * * scheme was discovered may indicate that he accepted responsibility for his fraudulent practices, it does not indicate that his fraudulent practices created no loss to the bank * * * . [I]n fraud cases, "[a]s in theft cases, loss is the value of the money, property or services unlawfully taken * * * ." The time to determine that loss * * * is the moment the loss is detected.
    * * * Asher's argument that there was no loss to the bank because he promptly repaid the full amount of his overdrafts does not carry the day.
    * * * The mere fortuity that he had the financial resources available to him to repay the victim bank in full after his * * * scheme was discovered does not negate the fact that he engaged in fraudulent conduct which resulted in the loss of $160,000.

DECISION AND REMEDY   The U.S. Court of Appeals for the Seventh Circuit held that for purposes of sentencing in bank fraud cases, the amount of loss should be measured at the time a crime is discovered. The appellate court affirmed the district court's judgment.

FOR CRITICAL ANALYSIS—ECONOMIC CONSIDERATION   *Do you think that the court's decision in this case will discourage criminals from repaying their victims?*

Crimes Affecting Business

White-Collar Crime Nonviolent crime committed by individuals or corporations to obtain a personal or business advantage.

▼   Many of the crimes that occur in the business context and that are discussed in the following pages are commonly referred to as **white-collar crimes.** Although there is no official definition of white-collar crime, the term is popularly used to mean an illegal act or series of acts committed by an individual or business entity using some nonviolent means to obtain a personal or business advantage. Usually, this kind of crime is committed in the course of a legitimate occupation. Corporate crimes, which are not treated here, also fall under the category of white-collar crimes.

Forgery

The fraudulent making or altering of any writing in a way that changes the legal rights and liabilities of another is **forgery**. If, without authorization, Severson signs Bennett's name to the back of a check made out to Bennett, Severson is committing forgery. Forgery also includes changing trademarks, falsifying public records, counterfeiting, and altering a legal document.

Forgery The fraudulent making or altering of any writing in a way that changes the legal rights and liabilities of another.

Robbery

At common law, **robbery** was defined as forcefully and unlawfully taking personal property of any value from another. The use of force or intimidation is usually necessary for an act of theft to be considered a robbery. Thus, picking pockets is not robbery, because the action is unknown to the victim. Typically, states have more severe penalties for *aggravated* robbery—robbery with the use of a deadly weapon.

Robbery The act of forcefully and unlawfully taking personal property of any value from another; force or intimidation is usually necessary for an act of theft to be considered a robbery.

Burglary

At common law, **burglary** was defined as breaking and entering the dwelling of another at night with the intent to commit a felony. Originally, the definition was aimed at protecting an individual's home and its occupants. Most state statutes have eliminated some of the requirements found in the common law definition. The time at which the breaking and entering occurs, for example, is usually immaterial. State statutes frequently omit the element of breaking, and some states do not require that the building be a dwelling. Aggravated burglary, which is defined as burglary with the use of a deadly weapon, burglary of a dwelling, or both, incurs a greater penalty.

Burglary The unlawful entry into a building with the intent to commit a felony. (Some state statutes expand this to include the intent to commit any crime.)

Larceny

Any person who wrongfully or fraudulently takes and carries away another person's personal property is guilty of **larceny**. Larceny includes the fraudulent intent to deprive an owner permanently of property. Many business-related larcenies entail fraudulent conduct. Whereas robbery involves force or fear, larceny does not. Therefore, picking pockets is larceny, not robbery.

As society becomes more complex, the question often arises as to what is property. In most states, the definition of property that is subject to larceny statutes has expanded. Stealing computer programs may constitute larceny even though the "property" consists of magnetic impulses. Stealing computer time can also constitute larceny. So, too, can the theft of natural gas. Trade secrets can be subject to larceny statutes. Intercepting cellular phone calls to obtain another's phone card number—and then using that number to place long-distance calls, often overseas—is a form of property theft. These types of larceny are covered by "theft of services" statutes in many jurisdictions.

Larceny The wrongful taking and carrying away of another person's personal property with the intent to permanently deprive the owner of the property. Some states classify larceny as either grand or petit, depending on the property's value.

The common law distinction between grand and petit larceny depends on the value of the property taken. Many states have abolished this distinction, but in those that have not, grand larceny is a felony and petit larceny, a misdemeanor.

Obtaining Goods by False Pretenses

It is a criminal act to obtain goods by means of false pretenses—for example, buying groceries with a check, knowing that one has insufficient funds to cover it. Statutes dealing with such illegal activities vary widely from state to state.

Receiving Stolen Goods

It is a crime to receive stolen goods. The recipient of such goods need not know the true identity of the owner or the thief. All that is necessary is that the recipient knows or should have known that the goods are stolen, which implies an intent to deprive the owner of those goods.

Embezzlement

Embezzlement The fraudulent appropriation of money or other property by a person to whom the money or property has been entrusted.

When a person entrusted with another person's property or money fraudulently appropriates it, **embezzlement** occurs. Typically, embezzlement involves an employee who steals money. Banks face this problem, and so do a number of businesses in which corporate officers or accountants "jimmy" the books to cover up the fraudulent conversion of money for their own benefit. Embezzlement is not larceny, because the wrongdoer does not physically take the property from the possession of another, and it is not robbery, because force or fear is not used.

It does not matter whether the accused takes the money from the victim or from a third person. If, as the financial officer of a large corporation, Saunders pockets a certain number of checks from third parties that were given to her to deposit into the corporate account, she is embezzling.

Ordinarily, an embezzler who returns what has been taken will not be prosecuted, because the owner usually will not take the time to make a complaint, give depositions, and appear in court. That the accused intended eventually to return the embezzled property, however, does not constitute a sufficient defense to the crime of embezzlement. The role of intention in establishing whether embezzlement has occurred is emphasized in the following case.

Case 7.4 ● United States v. Faulkner

United States Court of Appeals, Ninth Circuit, 1981.
638 F.2d 129.

HISTORICAL AND POLITICAL SETTING *At one time, the law generally divided theft into three separate crimes—larceny, false pretenses, and embezzlement. Statutes prohibiting embezzlement often listed the kinds of persons who might have lawful possession of another's property (store clerks, bank employees, merchants, and so on) and provided that any such person who fraudulently converted the property to his or her own use was guilty of embezzlement. Today, in those jurisdictions that have enacted new criminal codes, the three separate crimes have been replaced*

with a single crime. With regard to the once-separate crime of embezzlement, these statutes may simply provide that one who is in lawful possession of another's property and intends to convert it to his or her own use is guilty.

BACKGROUND AND FACTS Faulkner, a truck driver, was hauling a load of refrigerators from San Diego to New York for the trucking company that employed him. He departed from his assigned route and stopped in Las Vegas, where he attempted to display and sell some of the refrigerators to a firm. Although the refrigerators never left the truck, to display them he had to break the truck's seals, enter the cargo department, and open two refrigerator cartons. The store owner refused to purchase the appliances,

(Continued)

Case 7.4—continued

and when Faulkner left the store, he was arrested. He was later convicted under federal law for the embezzlement of an interstate shipment. Faulkner appealed, claiming that there were no grounds for the charge, because he had never removed any equipment from the truck.

IN THE WORDS OF THE COURT ...
SKOPIL, Circuit Judge.
* * * *

The stealing or unlawful taking contemplated by the statute consists of taking over possession and control with intent to convert to the use of the taker. The statute does not require physical removal of the goods, nor even asportation [carrying away] in the common law larceny sense.

The felonious intent required by the statute consists of the intent to appropriate or convert the property of the owner. An intent to return the property does not exculpate the defendant.

We hold that there was sufficient evidence establishing the requisite act and intent. Faulkner exercised dominion and control over the refrigerators by leaving his assigned route to go to Urbauer's store and negotiate a sale. * * * The jury could therefore find that Faulkner had assumed possession and control of the goods. These facts also permitted the jury to conclude that Faulkner intended to convert the goods to his own use. It was not necessary that Faulkner remove the goods from the truck, nor complete the sale.

DECISION AND REMEDY The U.S. Court of Appeals for the Ninth Circuit affirmed the judgment of the trial court.

FOR CRITICAL ANALYSIS—SOCIAL CONSIDERATION *By definition, a crime involves both intent and a criminal act. What criminal act did Faulkner commit?*

Arson

The willful and malicious burning of a building (and in some states, personal property) owned by another is the crime of **arson**. At common law, arson applied only to burning down another person's house. The law was designed to protect human life. Today, arson statutes have been extended to cover the destruction of any building, regardless of ownership, by fire or explosion.

Every state has a special statute that covers a person's burning a building for the purpose of collecting insurance. If Smith owns an insured apartment building that is falling apart and sets fire to it himself or pays someone else to do so, he is guilty not only of arson but also of defrauding insurers, which is an attempted larceny. Of course, the insurer need not pay the claim when insurance fraud is proved.

Arson The malicious burning of another's dwelling. Some statutes have expanded this to include any real property regardless of ownership and the destruction of property by other means—for example, by explosion.

> **"A large number of houses deserve to be burnt."**
>
> H. G. Wells, 1866–1946
> (English author)

Mail and Wire Fraud

One of the most potent weapons against white-collar criminals is the Mail Fraud Act of 1990.[8] Under this act, it is a federal crime to use the mails to defraud the public. Illegal use of the mails must involve (1) mailing or causing

8. 18 U.S.C. Sections 1341–1342.

A businessperson places a call with a cellular phone. If this call is intercepted to obtain the phone number and that number is used without permission to place long-distance calls, what crime is committed?

Computer Crime Any act that is directed against computers and computer parts, that uses computers as instruments of crime, or that involves computers and constitutes abuse.

BE AWARE   Technological change is one of the primary factors that lead to new types of crime.

someone else to mail a writing—something written, printed, or photocopied—for the purpose of executing a scheme to defraud and (2) a contemplated or an organized scheme to defraud by false pretenses. If, for example, Johnson advertises by mail the sale of a cure for cancer that he knows to be fraudulent because it has no medical validity, he can be prosecuted for fraudulent use of the mails.

Federal law also makes it a crime to use wire, radio, or television transmissions to defraud.[9] Violators may be fined up to $1,000, imprisoned for up to five years, or both. If the violation affects a financial institution, the violator may be fined up to $1 million, imprisoned for up to thirty years, or both.

Computer Crime

The American Bar Association defines **computer crime** as any act that is directed against computers and computer parts, that uses computers as instruments of crime, or that involves computers and constitutes abuse. Frequently our laws are inadequate to deal with the various types of computer crimes that are committed. As mentioned earlier, larceny statutes were originally passed to prohibit the taking and carrying away of physical property belonging to another.

Computer crimes, however, such as those involving the theft of computer data or services, frequently do not require a physical "taking and carrying away" of another's property. Some states have expanded their definitions of property to allow computer crimes to fall within their larceny statutes, but in other states prosecutors have to rely on other criminal statutes. People committing computer crimes often receive lenient punishments, which has led lawmakers to put forth various proposals to deal with this type of crime.

A variety of different types of crime can be committed with or against computers. We look here at some of the ways in which computers have been involved in criminal activity, as well as at some of the difficulties involved in prosecuting computer crime.

FINANCIAL CRIMES.   Many computer crimes fall into the broad category of financial crimes. In addition to using computers for information storage and retrieval, businesses commonly use computers to conduct financial transactions. This is equally true of the government, which handles virtually all of its transactions via computer. These circumstances provide opportunities for employees and others to commit crimes that can involve serious economic losses. For example, employees of accounting and computer departments can transfer monies among accounts with little effort and without the risk involved in transactions evidenced by paperwork. Thus, not only is the potential for crime in the area of financial transactions great, but also most monetary losses from computer crime are suffered in this area.

SOFTWARE PIRACY.   Given the expense of software, many individuals and businesses have been tempted to steal software by decoding and making unauthorized copies of software programs. Under most state laws, software piracy is classified as a crime. At the federal level, the traditional laws protecting intellectual property (such as patent and copyright laws) have been amended in the last decade or so to extend coverage to computer programs (see Chapter

---

9.   18 U.S.C. Section 1343.

11). In 1990, in an attempt to control further the unauthorized copying of computer programs, the federal government passed a law that prohibits, with some exceptions, the renting, leasing, or lending of computer software without the express permission of the copyright holder.

PROPERTY THEFT. Computer crimes can also involve property theft. One type is the theft of computer equipment (hardware), which has become easier in recent years as computer components have become smaller and more readily transportable. Another type of property theft is the theft of computer-related property, which may involve taking goods that are controlled and accounted for by means of a computer application program. For example, an employee in a company's accounting department could manipulate inventory records to conceal unauthorized shipments of goods. The theft of computer equipment and the theft of goods with the aid of computers are subject to the same criminal and tort laws covering thefts of other physical property.

VANDALISM AND DESTRUCTIVE PROGRAMMING. Another form of computer crime is the intentional destruction of computer hardware or software. In one instance, an individual erased a company's records merely by walking past computer storage banks with an electromagnet. Other destructive acts have required greater technical awareness and facility. A knowledgeable individual, such as an angry employee whose job has just been terminated, can do a considerable amount of damage to computer data and files. One ongoing problem for businesspersons and other computer users today is guarding against computer "viruses"—computer programs that are designed to rearrange, replace, or destroy data. This form of vandalism is difficult to combat because of the difficulty of locating and prosecuting those responsible for "unleashing" such programs.

THEFT OF DATA OR SERVICES. Many people would agree that when an individual uses another's computer or computer information system without authorization, the individual is stealing. For example, an employee who used a computer system or data stored in a computer system for private gain and without the employer's authorization would likely be considered a thief, as would a politician who used a government computer to send out campaign brochures. Under an increasing number of revised criminal codes and broad judicial interpretations of existing statutes, the unauthorized use of computer data or services is considered larceny. The following case illustrates how one court interpreted a statute to cover the theft of computer time and storage.

Case 7.5 ● United States v. Collins

United States Court of Appeals, District of Columbia Circuit, 1995. 56 F.3d 1416.

HISTORICAL AND TECHNOLOGICAL SETTING

Early computers used vacuum tubes. The Electronic Numerical Integrator and Calculator (ENIAC) required 18,000 vacuum tubes to operate in 1946. The ENIAC took up 2,000 square feet and weighed 50 tons. It could perform approximately 10,000 calculations per second but had an internal memory capacity of only 20 words. By comparison, in the early 1990s a single silicon chip less than ¼ inch across was more than a million times as fast and could store 800,000 words. If cars had become as efficient, a Rolls Royce would cost $1 and get one million miles per gallon.

(Continued)

Case 7.5—continued

BACKGROUND AND FACTS   Peter Collins worked for the U.S. Defense Intelligence Agency (DIA) and had access to the DIA's classified computer system. Collins was also involved in amateur ballroom dancing through the U.S. Amateur Ballroom Dance Association. Over a five-year period, Collins used the DIA's computer system to create hundreds of documents, including newsletters, mailing lists, and calendars, relating to his ballroom dance activities. Collins was subsequently prosecuted and convicted in a federal district court of, among other things, converting to his own use government computer time and storage. Collins appealed to the U.S. Court of Appeals for the District of Columbia Circuit. He argued in part that his conviction should be reversed on the ground that the statute under which he was convicted for the conversion of computer time and storage does not cover intangible property (property that, like computer data and services, does not have a physical existence).

IN THE WORDS OF THE COURT . . .
PER CURIAM [by the whole court].
* * * *

   The statute renders criminally liable any person who "knowingly converts to his use or the use of another * * * any * * * thing of value of the United States or of any * * * agency thereof." * * *
   * * * Congress did not limit those things which could be converted to "tangible property," but rather any "thing of value." * * * [T]he language chosen by Congress could not have been broader. * * * [W]e refuse to ignore the plain meaning of the provision.
   * * * Congress intended to enact a broad prohibition against the misappropriation of anything belonging to the national government, unrestrained by * * * fine and technical distinctions * * * . Congressional intent * * * clearly confirms our * * * analysis that * * * [the statute] covers the misappropriation of intangible property.

DECISION AND REMEDY   The U.S. Court of Appeals for the District of Columbia Circuit affirmed the district court's judgment.

FOR CRITICAL ANALYSIS—TECHNOLOGICAL CONSIDERATION
When computer time is stolen, it may never affect others' use of the computer. Why, then, is such an action prosecuted?

PROSECUTING COMPUTER CRIME.   In attempting to control computer crime, governments at both the federal and state levels have undertaken protective measures. The Counterfeit Access Device and Computer Fraud and Abuse Act of 1984, as amended, prohibits unauthorized access to certain types of information, such as restricted government information, information contained in a financial institution's financial records, and information contained in a consumer reporting agency's files on consumers. Penalties for violations include up to five years' imprisonment and a fine of up to $250,000 or twice the amount that was gained by the thief or lost by the victim as a result of the crime. Several states have also passed legislation specifically addressing the problem of computer crime.

   One of the major problems in attempting to control computer crime is that it cannot be prosecuted if it is not reported. It seems clear to many people that the reason computer crimes often go unreported is because business firms are reluctant to disclose the vulnerability of their systems. Companies adversely affected by such crime do not want to publicize the fact, because they are afraid customers will doubt the accuracy and security of computer-generated material. Cases involving computer crimes are thus often settled out of court to avoid publicity. (See this chapter's *Technology and Prosecuting Computer Crime* on page 203 for a discussion of the problems faced by prosecutors in trying to control the alleged crimes committed via the Internet.)

Bribery

Basically, three types of bribery are considered crimes: bribery of public officials, commercial bribery, and bribery of foreign officials.

BRIBERY OF PUBLIC OFFICIALS.   The attempt to influence a public official to act in a way that serves a private interest is a crime. As an element of this crime, intent must be present and proved. The bribe can be anything the recipient considers to be valuable. It is important to realize that *the commission of the crime of bribery occurs when the bribe is offered*. The recipient does not have to agree to perform whatever action is desired by the person offering the bribe, nor does the recipient have to accept the bribe, for the crime of bribery to occur.

COMMERCIAL BRIBERY.   Typically, people make commercial bribes to obtain proprietary information, cover up an inferior product, or secure new business. Industrial espionage sometimes involves commercial bribes. For example, a person in one firm may offer an employee in a competing firm some type of payoff in exchange for trade secrets and pricing schedules. So-called kickbacks or payoffs for special favors or services are a form of commercial bribery in some situations.

BRIBERY OF FOREIGN OFFICIALS.   Bribing foreign officials to obtain favorable business contracts is a crime. This crime and the Foreign Corrupt Practices Act of 1977, which was passed to curb the practice of bribery by American businesspersons in securing foreign contracts.

Bankruptcy Fraud

Today, federal bankruptcy law (see Chapter 14) allows individuals and businesses to be relieved of oppressive debt through bankruptcy proceedings. Numerous white-collar crimes may be committed during the many phases of a bankruptcy proceeding. A creditor, for example, may file a false claim against the debtor, which is a crime. Also, a debtor may fraudulently transfer assets to favored parties before or after the petition for bankruptcy is filed. For example, a company-owned automobile may be "sold" at a bargain price to a trusted friend or relative. Closely related to the crime of fraudulent transfer of property is the crime of fraudulent concealment of property, such as hiding gold coins.

Money Laundering

The profits from illegal activities amount to billions of dollars a year, particularly the profits from illegal drug transactions and, to a lesser extent, from racketeering, prostitution, and gambling. Under federal law, banks, savings and loan associations, and other financial institutions are required to report currency transactions of over $10,000. Consequently, those who engage in illegal activities face difficulties in placing their cash profits from illegal transactions.

As an alternative to simply placing cash from illegal transactions in bank deposits, wrongdoers and racketeers have invented ways to launder "dirty"

A businessperson works with a computer. If the work being done is copied by another employee without permission and given to a business competitor, what crime has been committed?

"[It is] very much better to bribe a person than kill him."

Sir Winston Churchill, 1874–1965
(British prime minister, 1940–1945, 1951–1955)

Technology and Prosecuting Computer Crime

Technology has always been just a few steps ahead of the law. This is particularly true in respect to the Internet, the use of which has given rise to perplexing legal issues. Consider, for example, a case brought by the government against David LaMacchia. LaMacchia, a student at the Massachusetts Institute of Technology (MIT), used MIT's computer network to gain entry to the Internet. Using pseudonyms and an encrypted address, LaMacchia set up an electronic bulletin board, which he called Cynosure, and encouraged his correspondents to upload popular software applications and computer games onto it. He then transferred the software to a second encrypted address (Cynosure II), where it could be downloaded by other users with access to the Cynosure password.

Eventually, the worldwide traffic generated by LaMacchia's offer of free software came to the attention of federal authorities, who arrested LaMacchia for conspiring with "persons unknown" to violate the federal law prohibiting wire fraud. The government alleged that LaMacchia's scheme facilitated, on an international scale, the "illegal copying and distribution of copyrighted software" and that the scheme caused losses of more than a million dollars to software copyright holders.

The problem in LaMacchia's case, however, was that the court could not find that he had committed any crime. The court held that for wire fraud to exist, LaMacchia would have had to defraud people of money. If LaMacchia had sold the software, he would have committed a criminal act. LaMacchia also had not violated the Copyright Act, which imposes criminal penalties only when copyrighted products are copied without authorization "willfully and for purposes of commercial advantage or private financial gain." LaMacchia's actions, however, had not resulted in any "commercial advantage or private gain" for LaMacchia.

The court concluded that in arriving at its decision, it did not mean "to suggest that there is anything edifying about what LaMacchia is alleged to have done . . . . [O]ne might at best describe [LaMacchia's] actions as heedlessly irresponsible, and at worst as nihilistic, self-indulgent, and lacking in any fundamental sense of values. Criminal as well as civil penalties should probably attach to willful, multiple infringements of copyrighted software even absent a commercial motive on the part of the infringer. One can envision ways that the copyright law could be modified to permit such prosecution. But, '[i]t is the legislature, not the Court which is to define a crime, and ordain its punishment.'"[a]

This is but one example of how ill-equipped existing criminal laws are to handle new kinds of issues emerging in an on-line era. The problem will become even greater as the use of the Internet grows.

For Critical Analysis: *Do you think that the easy pirating of software via the Internet will eventually stifle innovation on the part of software manufacturers?*

---

a.   *United States v. LaMacchia,* 871 F.Supp. 535 (D.Mass. 1994).

Money Laundering Falsely reporting income that has been obtained through criminal activity as income obtained through a legitimate business enterprise—in effect, "laundering" the "dirty money."

money to make it "clean." This **money laundering** is done through legitimate businesses. For example, a successful drug dealer might become a partner with a restaurateur. Little by little, the restaurant shows an increasing profit. As a shareholder or partner in the restaurant, the wrongdoer is able to report the "profits" of the restaurant as legitimate income on which federal and state taxes are paid. The wrongdoer can then spend those monies without worrying about whether his or her lifestyle exceeds the level possible with his or her reported income. The Federal Bureau of Investigation estimates that organized crime alone has invested tens of billions of dollars in as many as a hundred thousand business establishments in the United States for the purpose of money laundering.

Insider Trading

An individual who obtains "inside information" about the plans of large corporations can often make stock-trading profits by using such information to guide decisions relating to the purchase or sale of corporate securities. **Insider trading** is a violation of securities law and will be considered more fully in Chapter 23. At this point, it may be said that one who possesses inside information and who has a duty not to disclose it to outsiders may not profit from the purchase or sale of securities based on that information until the information is available to the public.

Insider Trading The purchase or sale of securities on the basis of "inside information" (information that has not been made available to the public) in violation of a duty owed to the company whose stock is being traded.

Criminal RICO Violations

The Racketeer Influenced and Corrupt Organizations Act (RICO) was passed in an attempt to prevent the use of legitimate business enterprises as shields for racketeering activity and to prohibit the purchase of any legitimate business interest with illegally obtained funds (see the discussion of RICO in Chapter 9).

Most of the criminal RICO offenses have little, if anything, to do with normal business activities, for they involve gambling, arson, and extortion. Securities fraud (involving the sale of stocks and bonds), as well as mail fraud, wire fraud, welfare fraud, embezzlement, and numerous other crimes defined by state or federal statutes, however, are also criminal RICO violations, and RICO has become an effective tool in attacking these white-collar crimes in recent years. Under criminal provisions of RICO, any individual found guilty of a violation is subject to a fine of up to $25,000 per violation, imprisonment for up to twenty years, or both.

Defenses to Crimes

There are numerous defenses that the law deems sufficient to excuse a defendant's criminal behavior. Among the most important defenses to criminal liability are infancy, intoxication, insanity, mistake, consent, duress, justifiable use of force, entrapment, and the statute of limitations. Also, in some cases, defendants are given *immunity* and thus relieved, at least in part, of criminal liability for crimes they committed. We look at each of these defenses here.

Note that procedural violations (such as obtaining evidence without a valid search warrant) may operate as defenses also—because evidence obtained in violation of a defendant's constitutional rights may not be admitted in court. If the evidence is suppressed, then there may be no basis for prosecuting the defendant.

Infancy

The term *infant,* as used in the law, refers to any person who has not yet reached the age of majority (see Chapter 12). Exhibit 7–3 indicates the relationship between age and responsibility for criminal acts under the common law.

In all states, certain courts handle cases involving children who are alleged to have violated the law. In some states, juvenile courts handle children's cases exclusively. In most states, however, courts that handle children's cases also have jurisdiction over other matters, such as traffic offenses. Originally, juvenile court hearings were informal, and lawyers were rarely present. Since 1967, however, when the United States Supreme Court ordered that a child charged with delinquency must be allowed to consult with an attorney before being committed to a state institution,[10] juvenile court hearings have become more formal. In some states, a

---

10. *In re Gault,* 387 U.S.1, 87 S.Ct. 1428, 18 L.Ed.2d 527 (1967).

■ **Exhibit 7–3**
Responsibility of Infants for Criminal Acts under the Common Law

Age 0–7	Absolute presumption of incompetence.
Age 7–14	Presumption of incompetence, but government may oppose.
Age 14+	Presumption of competence, but infant may oppose.

child will be treated as an adult and tried in a regular court if he or she is above a certain age (usually fourteen) and is guilty of a felony, such as rape or murder.

Intoxication

The law recognizes two types of intoxication, whether from drugs or from alcohol: *involuntary* and *voluntary*. Involuntary intoxication occurs when a person either is physically forced to ingest or inject an intoxicating substance or is unaware that a substance contains drugs or alcohol. Involuntary intoxication is a defense to a crime if its effect was to make a person incapable of understanding that the act committed was wrong or incapable of obeying the law.

Using voluntary drug or alcohol intoxication as a defense is based on the theory that extreme levels of intoxication may negate the state of mind that a crime requires. Many courts are reluctant to allow voluntary intoxication as a defense to a crime, however. After all, the defendant, by definition, voluntarily chose to put himself or herself into an intoxicated state. Voluntary intoxication as a defense may be effective in cases in which the defendant was *extremely* intoxicated when committing the wrong.

Insanity

> **"Insanity is often the logic of an accurate mind overtaxed."**
>
> Oliver Wendell Holmes, Jr., 1841–1935 (Associate justice of the United States Supreme Court, 1902–1932)

Just as a child is often judged incapable of the state of mind required to commit a crime, so also may be someone suffering from a mental illness. Thus, insanity may be a defense to a criminal charge. The courts have had difficulty deciding what the test for legal insanity should be, and psychiatrists as well as lawyers are critical of the tests used. Almost all federal courts and some states use the relatively liberal standard set forth in the Model Penal Code:

A person is not responsible for criminal conduct if at the time of such conduct as a result of mental disease or defect he lacks substantial capacity either to appreciate the wrongfulness of his conduct or to conform his conduct to the requirements of the law.

Some states use the *M'Naghten* test,[11] under which a criminal defendant is not responsible if, at the time of the offense, he or she did not know the nature and quality of the act or did not know that the act was wrong. Other states use the irresistible-impulse test. A person operating under an irresistible impulse may know an act is wrong but cannot refrain from doing it.

Mistake

Everyone has heard the saying, "Ignorance of the law is no excuse." Ordinarily, ignorance of the law or a mistaken idea about what the law requires is not a

---

11.   A rule derived from *M'Naghten's Case*, 8 Eng.Rep. 718 (1843).

valid defense. In some states, however, that rule has been modified. People who claim that they honestly did not know that they were breaking a law may have a valid defense if (1) the law was not published or reasonably made known to the public or (2) the people relied on an official statement of the law that was erroneous.

A *mistake of fact*, as opposed to a *mistake of law*, operates as a defense if it negates the mental state necessary to commit a crime. If, for example, Oliver Wheaton mistakenly walks off with Julie Tyson's briefcase because he thinks it is his, there is no theft. Theft requires knowledge that the property belongs to another.

Consent

What if a victim consents to a crime or even encourages the person intending a criminal act to commit it? The law allows **consent** as a defense if the consent cancels the harm that the law is designed to prevent. In each case, the question is whether the law forbids an act that was committed against the victim's will or forbids the act without regard to the victim's wish. The law forbids murder, prostitution, and drug use whether the victim consents to it or not. Also, if the act causes harm to a third person who has not consented, there is no escape from criminal liability. Consent or forgiveness given after a crime has been committed is not really a defense, though it can affect the likelihood of prosecution. Consent operates as a defense most successfully in crimes against property.

Consent Voluntary agreement to a proposition or an act of another. A concurrence of wills.

Duress

Duress exists when the *wrongful threat* of one person induces another person to perform an act that he or she would not otherwise perform. In such a situation, duress is said to negate the mental state necessary to commit a crime. For duress to qualify as a defense, the following requirements must be met:

1. The threat must be of serious bodily harm or death.
2. The harm threatened must be greater than the harm caused by the crime.
3. The threat must be immediate and inescapable.
4. The defendant must have been involved in the situation through no fault of his or her own.

One crime that cannot be excused by duress is murder. It is difficult to justify taking a life even if one's own life is threatened.

Duress Unlawful pressure brought to bear on a person, causing the person to perform an act that he or she would not otherwise perform.

Justifiable Use of Force

Probably the most well-known defense to criminal liability is **self-defense.** Other situations, however, also justify the use of force: the defense of one's dwelling, the defense of other property, and the prevention of a crime. In all of these situations, it is important to distinguish between the use of deadly and nondeadly force. Deadly force is likely to result in death or serious bodily harm. Nondeadly force is force that reasonably appears necessary to prevent the imminent use of criminal force.

Generally speaking, people can use the amount of nondeadly force that seems necessary to protect themselves, their dwellings, or other property or to prevent the commission of a crime. Deadly force can be used in self-defense if there is a *reasonable belief* that imminent death or grievous bodily harm will otherwise result, if the attacker is using unlawful force (an example of lawful

Self-Defense The legally recognized privilege to protect one's self or property against injury by another. The privilege of self-defense protects only acts that are reasonably necessary to protect one's self or property.

force is that exerted by a police officer), and if the defender has not initiated or provoked the attack. Deadly force normally can be used to defend a dwelling only if the unlawful entry is violent and the person believes deadly force is necessary to prevent imminent death or great bodily harm or—in some jurisdictions—if the person believes deadly force is necessary to prevent the commission of a felony (such as arson) in the dwelling.

Entrapment

Entrapment In criminal law, a defense in which the defendant claims that he or she was induced by a public official—usually an undercover agent or police officer—to commit a crime that he or she would otherwise not have committed.

Entrapment is a defense designed to prevent police officers or other government agents from encouraging crimes in order to apprehend persons wanted for criminal acts. In the typical entrapment case, an undercover agent *suggests* that a crime be committed and somehow pressures or induces an individual to commit it. The agent then arrests the individual for the crime.

For entrapment to be considered a defense, both the suggestion and the inducement must take place. The defense is intended not to prevent law enforcement agents from setting a trap for an unwary criminal but rather to prevent them from pushing the individual into it. The crucial issue is whether a person who committed a crime was predisposed to commit the crime or did so because the agent induced it.

An interesting variation of the entrapment defense is "sentencing entrapment." This occurs when undercover police officers induce a criminal suspect to commit a more serious crime than the crime contemplated by the suspect, thus causing the person, if convicted, to receive a harsher penalty under the federal sentencing guidelines discussed earlier. In the following case, the defendants claimed that they had been the victims of this form of entrapment.

Case 7.6 ● United States v. Cannon

United States District Court,
District of North Dakota, 1995.
886 F.Supp. 705.

HISTORICAL AND POLITICAL SETTING *The Bureau of Alcohol, Tobacco, and Firearms (BATF) was established in 1972. Among its criminal enforcement objectives is the suppression of illegal trafficking, possession, and use of firearms. During the 1990s, the BATF came under fire for overzealousness in the pursuit of some of its criminal enforcement activities. Although this criticism was sometimes interpreted as rhetoric on the part of antigovernment radicals, Congress initiated hearings into BATF conduct, and it was proposed that perhaps the agency should be dissolved and its duties transferred to other government agencies.*

BACKGROUND AND FACTS Keith and Stephanie Cannon sold crack cocaine to a deputy sheriff, who was operating undercover as a drug buyer. The Cannons asked the under-cover officer to help them procure some handguns. He arranged for an agent of the BATF to pose as an illegal gun seller. The BATF agent, on his own initiative, brought a machine gun to the meeting with the Cannons. At that meeting, the Cannons again sold crack to the sheriff and bought three handguns from the agent. After the undercover officers exercised some persuasive sales tactics, the Cannons also bought the machine gun. They were promptly arrested and charged with using firearms during and in relation to drug trafficking. The Cannons were tried in a federal district court and convicted. Because one of the weapons was a machine gun, their convictions required prison sentences of thirty years. At their sentencing hearing, the Cannons argued in part that they should receive a different minimum term (five years—the minimum mandatory sentence for the use of a firearm generally), on the ground of sentencing entrapment.

(Continued)

Case 7.6—continued

IN THE WORDS OF THE COURT . . .
WEBB, Chief Judge.
* * * *

* * * [This court determines] based on all the evidence * * * that in the context of a sentencing entrapment analysis, the defendants have met their burden of proving * * * that the defendants were not predisposed to purchase a machine gun and that they were induced to do so by the government. Therefore, * * * the court * * * holds that the government conduct in this case constitutes sentencing entrapment, and excludes the tainted conduct and the statutory mandatory sentence from consideration in sentencing.

DECISION AND REMEDY The federal district court ordered that the Cannons be sentenced as though no machine gun had been present during their offense.

FOR CRITICAL ANALYSIS—ECONOMIC CONSIDERATION *Should there be any legal limits on the degree of temptation to which law enforcement officers can subject persons who are under investigation? Why or why not?*

Statute of Limitations

With some exceptions, such as for the crime of murder, statutes of limitations apply to crimes just as they do to civil wrongs. In other words, criminal cases must be prosecuted within a certain number of years. If a criminal action is brought after the statutory time period has expired, the accused person can raise the statute of limitations as a defense.

Immunity

At times, the state may wish to obtain information from a person accused of a crime. Accused persons are understandably reluctant to give information if it will be used to prosecute them, and they cannot be forced to do so. The privilege against self-incrimination is granted by the Fifth Amendment to the Constitution, which reads, in part, "nor shall [any person] be compelled in any criminal case to be a witness against himself." In cases in which the state wishes to obtain information from a person accused of a crime, the state can grant *immunity* from prosecution or agree to prosecute for a less serious offense in exchange for the information. Once immunity is given, the person can no longer refuse to testify on Fifth Amendment grounds, because he or she now has an absolute privilege against self-incrimination.

Often a grant of immunity from prosecution for a serious crime is part of the **plea bargaining** between the defendant and the prosecuting attorney. The defendant may be convicted of a lesser offense, while the state uses the defendant's testimony to prosecute accomplices for serious crimes carrying heavy penalties.

Plea Bargaining The process by which a criminal defendant and the prosecutor in a criminal case work out a mutually satisfactory disposition of the case, subject to court approval; usually involves the defendant's pleading guilty to a lesser offense in return for a lighter sentence.

Key Terms

arson 197
beyond a reasonable doubt
 192

burglary 195
computer crime 198
consent 205

crime 183
double jeopardy 186
duress 205

Chapter Summary
Criminal Wrongs

CIVIL LAW AND CRIMINAL LAW (See page 183.)	1. **Civil law**—Spells out the duties that exist between persons or between citizens and their governments, excluding the duty not to commit crimes. In a civil case, damages are awarded to compensate those harmed by others' wrongful acts, or equitable remedies may be granted.
	2. **Criminal law**—Has to do with crimes, which are defined as wrongs against society proclaimed in statutes and, if committed, punishable by society through fines and/or imprisonment—and, in some cases, death. Because crimes are offenses against society as a whole, they are prosecuted by a public official, not by victims. (See Exhibit 7–1 for a summary of how criminal and civil laws differ.)
CLASSIFICATION OF CRIMES (See pages 183–184.)	1. **Felonies**—Serious crimes punishable by death or by imprisonment in a penitentiary for more than a year.
	2. **Misdemeanors**—Under federal law and in most states, any crime that is not a felony.
CRIMINAL LIABILITY (See pages 184–185.)	1. **Guilty act**—In general, some form of harmful act must be committed for a crime to exist.
	2. **Intent**—An intent to commit a crime, or a wrongful mental state, is required for a crime to exist.
PROCEDURE IN CRIMINAL LAW (See pages 186–194.)	1. **Constitutional safeguards**—The rights of accused persons are protected under the Constitution, particularly by the Fourth, Fifth, Sixth, and Eighth Amendments. Under the exclusionary rule, evidence obtained in violation of the constitutional rights of the accused will not be admissible in court. In *Miranda v. Arizona*, the United States Supreme Court ruled that individuals must be informed of their constitutional rights (such as their rights to counsel and to remain silent) on being taken into custody.
	2. **Criminal process**—Procedures governing arrest, indictment, and trial for a crime are designed to safeguard the rights of the individual against the state. See Exhibit 7–2 for the steps involved in prosecuting a criminal case.
FEDERAL SENTENCING GUIDELINES (See pages 192–194.)	Guidelines established by the U.S. Sentencing Commission indicating a range of penalties for each federal crime; federal judges must abide by these guidelines when imposing sentences on those convicted of federal crimes.

(Continued)

Chapter Summary, continued

CRIMES AFFECTING BUSINESS
(See pages 194–203.)

1. **Forgery**—The fraudulent making or altering of any writing in a way that changes the legal rights and liabilities of another.

2. **Robbery**—The forceful and unlawful taking of personal property of any value from another.

3. **Burglary**—At common law, defined as breaking and entering the dwelling of another at night with the intent to commit a felony. State statutes now vary in their definitions of burglary.

4. **Larceny**—The wrongful or fraudulent taking and carrying away of another's personal property with the intent to deprive the owner permanently of the property.

5. **Obtaining goods by false pretenses**—Such as cashing a check knowing that there are insufficient funds in the bank to cover it.

6. **Receiving stolen goods**—A crime if the recipient knew or should have known that the goods were stolen.

7. **Embezzlement**—The fraudulent appropriation of another person's property or money by a person to whom the property or money was entrusted.

8. **Arson**—The willful and malicious burning of a building or (in some states) personal property owned by another.

9. **Mail and wire fraud**—Using the mails, wires, radio, or television to defraud the public.

10. **Computer crime**—Any act that is directed against computers and computer parts, that uses computers as instruments of crime, or that involves computers and constitutes abuse. Computer crime includes financial crimes that involve computers; theft of computer software, equipment, data, or services; and vandalism and destructive programming of computers.

11. **Bribery**—Includes bribery of public officials, commercial bribery, and bribery of foreign officials. The crime of bribery is committed when the bribe is tendered.

12. **Bankruptcy fraud**—Encompasses crimes committed in connection with bankruptcy proceedings, including false claims of creditors and fraudulent transfers of assets by debtors.

13. **Money laundering**—Establishing legitimate enterprises through which "dirty" money (obtained through criminal activities) can be "laundered."

14. **Insider trading**—The buying or selling of corporate securities by a person in possession of material nonpublic information in violation of securities laws.

15. **Criminal RICO violations**—Include the use of legitimate business enterprises to shield racketeering activity, securities fraud, and mail fraud.

DEFENSES TO CRIMINAL LIABILITY
(See pages 203–207.)

1. Infancy.
2. Intoxication.
3. Insanity.
4. Mistake.
5. Consent.
6. Duress.
7. Justifiable use of force.
8. Entrapment.
9. Statute of limitations.
10. Immunity.

For Review

1. How are crimes distinguished from other wrongful acts?

2. What two elements must exist before a person can be held liable for a crime?

3. What constitutional safeguards exist to protect persons accused of crimes?

4. List and describe five crimes affecting business.

5. What defenses might be raised by criminal defendants to avoid liability for criminal acts?

Questions and Case Problems

7–1. Criminal versus Civil Trials. In criminal trials, the defendant must be proved guilty beyond a reasonable doubt, whereas in civil trials, the defendant need only be proved guilty by a preponderance of the evidence. Discuss why a higher standard of proof is required in criminal trials.

7–2. Types of Crimes. Determine from the facts below what type of crime has been committed in each situation.

(a) Carlos is walking through an amusement park when his wallet, with $2,000 in it, is "picked" from his pocket.

(b) Carlos walks into a camera shop. Without force and without the owner's noticing, Carlos walks out of the store with a camera.

7–3. Types of Crimes. The following situations are similar (all involve the theft of Makoto's television set), yet they represent three different crimes. Identify the three crimes, noting the differences among them.

(a) While passing Makoto's house one night, Sarah sees a portable television set left unattended on Makoto's lawn. Sarah takes the television set, carries it home, and tells everyone she owns it.

(b) While passing Makoto's house one night, Sarah sees Makoto outside with a portable television set. Holding Makoto at gunpoint, Sarah forces him to give up the set. Then Sarah runs away with it.

(c) While passing Makoto's house one night, Sarah sees a portable television set in a window. Sarah breaks the front-door lock, enters, and leaves with the set.

7–4. Types of Crimes. Which, if any, of the following crimes necessarily involve illegal activity on the part of more than one person?

(a) Bribery.

(b) Forgery.

(c) Embezzlement.

(d) Larceny.

(e) Receiving stolen property.

7–5. Double Jeopardy. Armington, while robbing a drugstore, shot and seriously injured a drugstore clerk, Jennings. Armington was subsequently convicted in a criminal trial of armed robbery and assault and battery. Jennings later brought a civil tort suit against Armington for damages. Armington contended that he could not be tried again for the same crime, as that would constitute double jeopardy, which is prohibited by the Fifth Amendment to the Constitution. Is Armington correct? Explain.

7–6. Receiving Stolen Property. Rafael stops Laura on a busy street and offers to sell her an expensive wristwatch for a fraction of its value. After some questioning by Laura, Rafael admits that the watch is stolen property, although he says he was not the thief. Laura pays for and receives the wristwatch. Has Laura committed any crime? Has Rafael? Explain.

7–7. Embezzlement. Slemmer, who had been a successful options trader, gave lectures to small groups about stock options. Several persons who attended his lectures decided to invest in stock options and have Slemmer advise them. They formed an investment club called Profit Design Group (PDG). Slemmer set up an account for PDG with a brokerage firm. Slemmer had control of the PDG account and could make decisions on which stock options to buy or sell. He was not authorized to withdraw money from the account for his own benefit. Nonetheless, he withdrew money from the PDG account to make payments on real estate that he owned. Slemmer made false representations to the members of PDG, and he eventually lost all the money in their account. A jury found him guilty of first degree theft by embezzlement. Slemmer objected to the trial court's failure to instruct the jury that an intent to permanently deprive was an element of the crime charged. Is intent to permanently deprive another of property a required element for the crime of embezzlement? Explain. [*State v. Slemmer,* 48 Wash.App. 48, 738 P.2d 281 (1987)]

7–8. Self-Defense. Bernardy came to the defense of his friend Harrison in a fight with Wilson. Wilson started the fight, and after Harrison knocked Wilson down, Bernardy (who was wearing tennis shoes) kicked Wilson several times in the head. Bernardy stated that he did so because he believed an onlooker, Gowens, would join forces with Wilson against Harrison. Bernardy maintained that his use of force was justifiable because he was protecting another (Harrison) from injury. Discuss whether Bernardy's use of force to protect Harrison from harm was justified. [*State v. Bernardy,* 25 Wash.App. 146, 605 P.2d 791(1980)]

7–9. Criminal Liability. In January 1988, David Ludvigson was hired as chief executive officer of Leopard Enterprises, a group of companies that owned funeral homes and cemeteries in Iowa and sold "pre-need" funeral contracts. Under Iowa law, 80 percent of monies obtained under such a contract must be set aside in trust until the death of the person for whose benefit the funds were paid. Shortly after Ludvigson was hired, the firm began having financial difficulties. Ludvigson used money from these contracts to pay operating expenses until the company went bankrupt and was placed in receivership. Ludvigson was charged and found guilty on five counts of second degree theft stemming from the misappropriation of these funds. He appealed, alleging, among other things, that because none of the victims whose trust funds were used to cover operating expenses was denied services, no injury was done and thus no crime was committed. Will the court agree with Ludvigson? Explain. [*State v. Ludvigson,* 482 N.W.2d 419 (Iowa 1992)]

7–10. Defenses to Criminal Liability. The Child Protection Act of 1984 makes it a crime to receive knowingly through the mails sexually explicit depictions of children. After this act was passed, government agents found Keith Jacobson's name on a bookstore's mailing list. (Jacobson previously had ordered and received from a bookstore two *Bare Boys* magazines containing photographs of nude preteen and teenage boys.) To test Jacobson's willingness to break the law, government agencies sent mail to him, through five fictitious organizations and a bogus pen pal, over a period of two and a half years. Many of these "organizations" claimed that they had been founded to protect sexual freedom, freedom of choice, and so on. Jacobson eventually ordered a magazine. He testified at trial that he ordered the magazine because he was curious about "all the trouble and the hysteria over pornography and I wanted to see what the material was." When the magazine was delivered, he was arrested for violating the 1984 act. What defense dis-

cussed in this chapter might Jacobson raise to avoid criminal liability under the act? Explain fully. [*Jacobson v. United States,* 503 U.S. 540, 112 S.Ct. 1535, 118 L.Ed.2d 174 (1992)]

7–11. Entrapment. When Sharon Shepherd attempted to sell cocaine powder to an undercover law enforcement officer, the officer insisted that she first convert the powder to crack cocaine—which she did by "cooking" the powder in a microwave for a few minutes. The agent then purchased the cocaine in its converted state. The agent's purpose in requesting Shepherd to convert the powder to crack was to cause Shepherd to receive a more severe sentence. Under the federal sentencing guidelines, the mandatory sentence for the sale of crack cocaine is from 120 to 135 months in prison, whereas the sentence for the sale of cocaine powder is only 60 months. Was Shepherd a victim of "sentencing entrapment"? What factors should the court consider in deciding this issue? Discuss fully. [*United States v. Shepherd,* 857 F.Supp. 105 (D.C. 1994)]

A Question of Ethics and Social Responsibility

7–12. A troublesome issue concerning the constitutional privilege against self-incrimination has to do with "jail plants"—that is, placing undercover police officers in cells with criminal suspects to gain information from the suspects. For example, in one case the police placed an undercover agent, Parisi, in a jail cellblock with Lloyd Perkins, who had been imprisoned on charges unrelated to the murder that Parisi was investigating. When Parisi asked Perkins if he had ever killed anyone, Perkins made statements implicating himself in the murder. Perkins was then charged with the murder. [*Illinois v. Perkins,* 496 U.S. 914, 110 S.Ct. 2394, 110 L.Ed.2d 243 (1990)]

1. Review the discussion of *Miranda v. Arizona* in this chapter's *Landmark in the Legal Environment.* Should Perkins's statements be suppressed—that is, not be treated as admissible evidence at trial—because he was not "read his rights," as required by the *Miranda* decision, prior to making his self-incriminating statements? Does *Miranda* apply to Perkins's situation?

2. Do you think that it is fair for the police to resort to trickery and deception to bring those who have committed crimes to justice? Why or why not? What rights or public policies must be balanced in deciding this issue?

For Critical Analysis

7–13. Do you think that criminal procedure in this country is weighted too heavily in favor of accused persons? Can you think of a fairer way to balance the constitutional rights of accused persons against the right of society to be protected against criminal behavior? Explain.

Unit II Cumulative
Hypothetical Problem

7–14. Korman, Inc., a toy manufacturer, has its headquarters in Minneapolis, Minnesota. Korman has recently placed on the market a new line of dolls with such irreverent names as "Harass Me," "Spit on Me," "Pull My Hair," "Watch Me Scream," "Cut Me Quick," and "Abuse Me, Please." The dolls are a success commercially and have netted Korman more profits than any of its other toys. Given these "facts," answer the following questions:

1. Suppose that Korman does business only within the state of Minnesota. A Korman employee claims that the company has violated a federal employment law. Korman argues that it is not liable because the law applies only to employees of companies that are engaged in interstate commerce. What might a court decide? Discuss fully.

2. The Occupational Safety and Health Administration (OSHA) has proposed a new safety rule governing the handling of certain materials in the workplace, including those used by Korman in its manufacturing operations. Korman concludes that the rule, which will involve substantial compliance costs, will not significantly increase workplace safety. Korman sends a letter to OSHA indicating its objections to the proposed rule and enclosing research reports and other data supporting those objections. Does OSHA have any obligation to consider these objections? What procedures must OSHA follow when it makes new rules, such as this one?

3. The head of Korman's accounting department, Roy Olson, has to pay his daughter's college tuition within a week, or his daughter will not be able to continue taking classes. The payment due is over $20,000. Roy would be able to make the payment in two months, but cannot do so until then. The college refuses to wait that long. In desperation, Roy—through a fictitious bank account and some clever accounting—"borrows" funds from Korman. Before Roy can pay back the borrowed funds, an auditor discovers what Roy did. Korman's president alleges that Roy has "stolen" company funds and informs the police of the theft. Has Roy committed a crime? If so, what crime did he commit? Explain.

INTERACTING WITH
The Internet

■ A good starting place to find information on criminal law on the Internet is

http://www.fsu.edu/~crimdo/cj.html

This site, which is updated regularly, offers the most extensive collection of criminal law links on the Internet, including links to local, state, federal, and international resources, as well as to other crime-related Web sites.

■ Another site with a large number of links to crime-related topics is

http://dpa.state.ky.us:80/

■ If you are interested in looking at the text of the *U.S. Sentencing Guidelines Manual,* go to

http://www.ussc.gov

■ The Justice Information Center is an excellent source for information on criminal and juvenile justice throughout the world. To access this information, go to

http://www.ncjrs.org

■ The Federal Bureau of Investigation (FBI) offers abundant information and statistics on crime, including information concerning FBI investigations, international crime, wiretapping, electronic surveillance, and economic espionage. You can locate the FBI's home page at

http://www.fbi.gov

■ One of the goals of the National Institute of Justice, the research arm of the U.S. Department of Justice, is "to prevent and reduce crime and to improve the criminal justice system." To learn about the institute's research and its various projects (in such areas as community policing, violence against women, and drug courts), go to

http://www.ojp.usdoj.gov/nij

The Private Environment

Unit
Outline

Torts and Strict Liability

Contents

Chapter Objectives

After reading this chapter, you should be able to . . .

1. Explain how torts and crimes differ.

2. State the purpose of tort law.

3. Identify some intentional torts against persons and property.

4. Name the four elements of negligence.

5. Define strict liability, and list some circumstances in which it will be applied.

As Scott Turow's statement in the quotation on the right indicates, **torts** are wrongful actions.[1] Through tort law, society compensates those who have suffered injuries as a result of the wrongful conduct of others. Although some torts, such as assault and trespass, originated in the English common law, the field of tort law continues to expand as new ways to commit wrongs are discovered and new conceptions of what is right and wrong in a social or business context emerge.

Tort law covers a wide variety of injuries. Society recognizes an interest in personal physical safety, and tort law provides remedies for acts that cause physical injury or that interfere with physical security and freedom of movement. Society recognizes an interest in protecting personal property, and tort law provides remedies for acts that cause destruction or damage to property. Society also recognizes an interest in protecting certain intangible interests, such as personal privacy, family relations, reputation, and dignity, and tort law provides remedies for invasion of these protected interests.

Certain torts normally occur only in the business context. The important area of business torts will be treated in Chapter 9. In this chapter, we discuss torts that can occur in any context, including the business environment. In fact, as you will see in later chapters of this book, many of the lawsuits brought by or against business firms are based on the tort theories discussed in this chapter.

The Basis of Tort Law

Two notions serve as the basis of all torts: wrongs and compensation. Tort law recognizes that some acts are wrong because they cause injuries to others. Of course, a tort is not the only type of wrong that exists in the law; crimes also involve wrongs. A crime, however, is an act so reprehensible that it is considered a wrong against the state or against society as a whole, as well as against the individual victim. Therefore, the *state* prosecutes and punishes (through fines and/or imprisonment—and possibly death) persons who commit criminal acts. A tort action, in contrast, is a civil action in which one person brings a personal suit against another to obtain compensation (money damages) or other relief for the harm suffered.

Some torts, such as assault and battery (to be discussed shortly), provide a basis for a criminal prosecution as well as a tort action. For example, Joe is walking down the street, minding his own business, when suddenly a person attacks him. In the ensuing struggle, the attacker stabs Joe several times, seriously injuring Joe. A police officer restrains and arrests the wrongdoer. In this situation, the attacker may be subject both to criminal prosecution by the state and to a tort lawsuit brought by Joe. Exhibit 8–1 on page 216 illustrates how the same wrongful act can result in both civil (tort) and criminal actions against the wrongdoer.

Intentional Torts against Persons

An **intentional tort**, as the term implies, requires *intent*. The **tortfeasor** (the one committing the tort) must intend to commit an act, the consequences of

---

1. The term *tort* is French for "wrong."

> **"'Torts' more or less means 'wrongs' . . . . One of my friends [in law school] said that Torts is the course which proves that your mother was right."**
>
> Scott Turow, 1949–
> (American lawyer and author)

Tort A civil wrong not arising from a breach of contract. A breach of a legal duty that proximately causes harm or injury to another.

Intentional Tort A wrongful act knowingly committed.

Tortfeasor One who commits a tort.

■ **Exhibit 8–1**
Tort Lawsuit and Criminal Prosecution for the Same Act

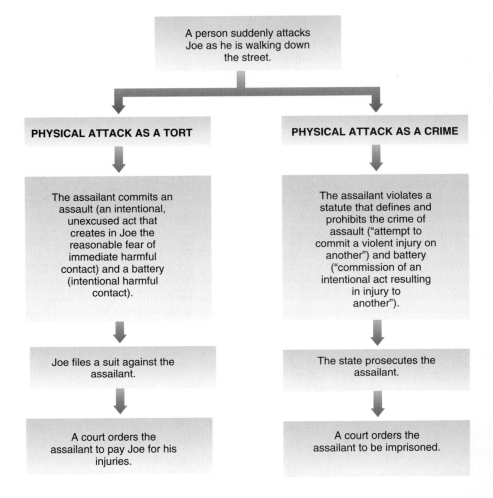

A person suddenly attacks Joe as he is walking down the street.

PHYSICAL ATTACK AS A TORT	**PHYSICAL ATTACK AS A CRIME**
The assailant commits an assault (an intentional, unexcused act that creates in Joe the reasonable fear of immediate harmful contact) and a battery (intentional harmful contact).	The assailant violates a statute that defines and prohibits the crime of assault ("attempt to commit a violent injury on another") and battery ("commission of an intentional act resulting in injury to another").
Joe files a suit against the assailant.	The state prosecutes the assailant.
A court orders the assailant to pay Joe for his injuries.	A court orders the assailant to be imprisoned.

which interfere with the personal or business interests of another in a way not permitted by law. An evil or harmful motive is not required—in fact, the tort-feasor may even have a beneficial motive for committing what turns out to be a tortious act. In tort law, intent only means that the actor intended the consequences of his or her act or knew with substantial certainty that certain consequences would result from the act. The law generally assumes that individuals intend the *normal* consequences of their actions. Thus, forcefully pushing another—even if done in jest and without any evil motive—is an intentional tort (if injury results), because the object of a strong push can ordinarily be expected to fall down or to be knocked backward.

This section discusses intentional torts against persons, which include assault and battery, false imprisonment, infliction of emotional distress, defamation, invasion of privacy, and misrepresentation.

Assault and Battery

Assault Any word or action intended to make another person fearful of immediate physical harm; a reasonably believable threat.

Any intentional, unexcused act that creates in another person a reasonable apprehension or fear of immediate harmful or offensive contact is an **assault**. Apprehension is not the same as fear. If a contact is such that a reasonable person would want to avoid it, and if there is a reasonable basis for believing that the contact will occur, then the plaintiff suffers apprehension whether or not he or she is afraid. The interest protected by tort law concerning assault is the freedom from having to expect harmful or offensive contact. The occurrence of apprehension is enough to justify compensation.

The *completion* of the act that caused the apprehension, if it results in harm to the plaintiff, is a **battery,** which is defined as an unexcused and harmful or offensive physical contact *intentionally* performed. For example, Ivan threatens Jean with a gun, then shoots her. The pointing of the gun at Jean is an assault; the firing of the gun (if the bullet hits Jean) is a battery. The interest protected by tort law concerning battery is the right to personal security and safety. The contact can be harmful, or it can be merely offensive (such as an unwelcome kiss). Physical injury need not occur. The contact can involve any part of the body or anything attached to it—for example, a hat or other item of clothing, a purse, or a chair or an automobile in which one is sitting. Whether the contact is offensive or not is determined by the *reasonable person standard.*[2] The contact can be made by the defendant or by some force the defendant sets in motion—for example, a rock thrown, food poisoned, or a stick swung.

Battery The unprivileged, intentional touching of another.

COMPENSATION. With respect to battery, if the plaintiff shows that there was contact and the jury agrees that the contact was offensive, the plaintiff has a right to compensation. There is no need to show that the defendant acted out of malice; the person could have just been joking or playing around. The underlying motive does not matter, only the intent to bring about the harmful or offensive contact to the plaintiff. In fact, proving a motive is never necessary (but is sometimes relevant). A plaintiff may be compensated for the emotional harm or loss of reputation resulting from a battery, as well as for physical harm.

DEFENSES TO ASSAULT AND BATTERY. A number of legally recognized defenses (reasons why plaintiffs should not obtain what they are seeking) can be raised by a defendant who is sued for assault or battery, or both:

1. *Consent.* When a person consents to the act that damages him or her, there is generally no liability (legal responsibility) for the damage done.
2. *Self-defense.* An individual who is defending his or her life or physical well-being can claim self-defense. In situations of both *real* and *apparent* danger, a person may use whatever force is *reasonably* necessary to prevent harmful contact.
3. *Defense of others.* An individual can act in a reasonable manner to protect others who are in real or apparent danger.
4. *Defense of property.* Reasonable force may be used in attempting to remove intruders from one's home, although force that is likely to cause death or great bodily injury normally cannot be used just to protect property.

BE AWARE Some of these same defenses can be raised by a defendant who is sued for other torts.

---

2. The reasonable person standard is an objective test of how a reasonable person would have acted under the same circumstances. See "The Duty of Care and Its Breach" later in this chapter.

A shoplifter attempts to conceal his theft of a store's merchandise. Could the owner of the store detain him but avoid liability for false imprisonment?

Actionable Capable of serving as the basis of a lawsuit.

Defamation Anything published or publicly spoken that causes injury to another's good name, reputation, or character.

Slander Defamation in oral form.

Libel Defamation in written form.

False Imprisonment

False imprisonment is defined as the intentional confinement or restraint of another person's activities without justification. False imprisonment interferes with the freedom to move without restraint. The confinement can be accomplished through the use of physical barriers, physical restraint, or threats of physical force. Moral pressure or threats of future harm do not constitute false imprisonment. It is essential that the person being restrained not comply with the restraint willingly.

Businesspersons are often confronted with suits for false imprisonment after they have attempted to confine a suspected shoplifter for questioning. Under the privilege to detain granted to merchants in some states, a merchant can use the defense of *probable cause* to justify delaying a suspected shoplifter. Probable cause exists when the evidence to support the belief that a person is guilty outweighs the evidence against that belief. The detention, however, must be conducted in a *reasonable* manner and for only a *reasonable* length of time.

Infliction of Emotional Distress

The tort of *infliction of emotional distress* can be defined as an intentional act that amounts to extreme and outrageous conduct resulting in severe emotional distress to another.[3] For example, a prankster telephones an individual and says that the individual's spouse has just been in a horrible accident. As a result, the individual suffers intense mental pain or anxiety. The caller's behavior is deemed to be extreme and outrageous conduct that exceeds the bounds of decency accepted by society and is therefore **actionable** (capable of serving as the ground for a lawsuit). Another example of this tort is "stalking" a person, thus causing that person to experience emotional distress from the fear of possible harm. Stalking is a crime, but courts in many states have concluded that it also constitutes the tort of intentional infliction of emotional distress.

Defamation

Defamation of character involves wrongfully hurting a person's good reputation. The law has imposed a general duty on all persons to refrain from making false, defamatory statements about others. Breaching this duty orally involves the tort of **slander**; breaching it in writing involves the tort of **libel**. The tort of defamation also arises when a false statement is made about a person's product, business, or title to property. We deal with these torts in the following chapter.

The common law defines four types of false utterances that are considered torts *per se* (meaning no proof of injury or harm is required for these false utterances to be actionable):

1. A statement that another has a loathsome communicable disease.
2. A statement that another has committed improprieties while engaging in a profession or trade.
3. A statement that another has committed or has been imprisoned for a serious crime.
4. A statement that an unmarried woman is unchaste.

---

3.   *Restatement (Second) of Torts*, Section 46, Comment d. The *Restatement (Second) of Torts* is a compilation of the law of torts by the American Law Institute.

THE PUBLICATION REQUIREMENT. The basis of the tort of defamation is the publication of a statement or statements that hold an individual up to contempt, ridicule, or hatred. *Publication* here means that the defamatory statements are communicated to persons other than the defamed party. If Thompson writes Andrews a private letter accusing him of embezzling funds, the action does not constitute libel. If Peters calls Gordon dishonest, unattractive, and incompetent when no one else is around, the action does not constitute slander. In neither case was the message communicated to a third party.

The courts have generally held that even dictating a letter to a secretary constitutes publication, although the publication may be privileged (privileged communications will be discussed shortly). Moreover, if a third party overhears defamatory statements by chance, the courts usually hold that this also constitutes publication. Defamatory statements made via the Internet are also actionable (see *Technology and Defamation in Cyberspace* below).

> **"Reputation, reputation, reputation! Oh, I have lost my reputation! I have lost the immortal part of myself, and what remains is bestial."**
>
> William Shakespeare, 1564–1616
> (English dramatist and poet)

Technology and Defamation in Cyberspace

The widespread use of the Internet for personal and business communications has given rise to a new kind of tort—the "cybertort." Internet users may, without realizing it, commit various wrongs online. Here we look at just one wrongful act that may occur in cyberspace—the tort of defamation.

ONLINE DEFAMATION

Any defamatory statement that is communicated to a third party is considered "published" under defamation law and thus actionable (capable of providing the basis for a lawsuit). What about defamatory statements made via the Internet? Suppose, for example, that a couple of friends are exchanging thoughts online in a chat group. One of them accuses her boss of sexual misconduct. Does this statement constitute defamation? Yes. This is because what may seem like a private online "conversation" between just two persons is, in fact, a very public exchange, possibly accessible to millions of people. The fact that those people are unseen at the time a defamatory statement is made makes no difference. The person defamed (the boss, in this example) could suffer serious harm from the statement—loss of reputation and perhaps even the loss of a job. The person who made the defamatory statement could be sued in tort for damages.

FREE SPEECH VERSUS DEFAMATION

As mentioned in Chapter 5, the freedom of speech guaranteed by the First Amendment to the Constitution is not absolute. Speech that harms another person's good name and reputation may be the basis for a defamation suit, and this is true whether the statement is communicated over the radio or television, in a printed publication, or via the Internet.

In one case, for example, an anthropologist, Gilbert Hardwick, posted a message on a worldwide academic network accusing another anthropologist, David Rindos, of engaging in sexual misconduct. According to the judge hearing the case, Hardwick's statements suggested that Rindos engaged in sexual misconduct and that his "professional career and reputation has not been based on appropriate academic research but on 'his ability to berate and bully all and sundry.'" Rindos succeeded in winning a $40,000 judgment against Hardwick for these remarks.[a]

Generally, in determining whether statements are defamatory, the courts distinguish between statements of *fact* and statements of *opinion*. For example, suppose that someone posts a message on an electronic bulletin board accusing a seller of motorcycles of being a "sleazy jerk." In terms of legal liability, the message sender is probably in safe waters. If, however, the message accused the seller of being a "sleazy jerk who sells stolen motorbikes," that statement alleges a fact—that the seller is engaging in criminal behavior. Unless the statement is true, the message sender could be liable in a defamation suit for substantial damages.

For Critical Analysis: *What precautions should Internet users take to avoid liability for defamation?*

a. As discussed in Deborah Branscum, "Cyberspace Lawsuits," *MacWorld*, May 1995, pp. 149–150.

Note further that any individual who republishes or repeats defamatory statements is liable even if that person reveals the source of such statements.

The following case raises an interesting issue concerning the publication requirement: Can a plaintiff establish the publication of defamatory statements without the testimony of a third person regarding what he or she heard or understood?

Case 8.1 ● Food Lion, Inc. v. Melton

Supreme Court of Virginia, 1995.
250 Va. 144,
458 S.E.2d 580.

HISTORICAL AND ETHICAL SETTING *In 1992, on ABC's PrimeTime Live, reporters claimed that grocery stores owned by Food Lion, Inc., sold contaminated goods and repackaged out-of-date food. The company denied the charges. At the same time, the U.S. government was investigating Food Lion for violations of child labor laws (see Chapter 16), and shareholders in the company had filed a suit alleging that the firm reported misleading information about its financial standing. Meanwhile, Food Lion employees filed their own suits, claiming that the company forced them to work overtime without compensating them for it. In 1994, Food Lion also faced a possible class-action suit alleging racial discrimination.*

BACKGROUND AND FACTS In April 1991, after shopping at a Food Lion grocery store, sixty-eight-year-old Christine Melton was walking out of the store when a Food Lion security guard stopped her in the parking lot. The guard accused her of leaving with meat belonging to the store in her purse. According to Melton, the guard questioned her repeatedly, loudly, and in an accusatory manner, and "there were people stopping to listen and see what was going on." Finally, Melton allowed the guard to search her purse. No meat was found. Melton filed a suit against Food Lion in a Virginia state court, in part on the ground of defamation. Food Lion in effect denied that the incident ever happened. Melton was not able to identify any of the people who "stopped to listen" and could not offer proof as to what they heard. On the defamation claim, the court entered a judgment in favor of Food Lion, and Melton appealed to the Virginia Supreme Court.

IN THE WORDS OF THE COURT . . .
KEENAN, Justice.
     * * * *

     * * * [T]o establish *prima facie* evidence of publication, a plaintiff is not required to present testimony from a third party regarding what that person heard and understood, or to identify the person to whom the defamatory words were published. Instead, a plaintiff may prove publication of defamatory remarks by * * * evidence that the remarks were heard by a third party who understood these remarks as referring to the plaintiff in a defamatory sense.

     * * * Melton testified that the security guard stood very close to her and made his accusations in a "very loud tone" of voice * * * . She also testified that, during this time, people were close by, and they stopped "to listen and see what was going on." We hold that, when considered in the light most favorable to Melton, this evidence was sufficient to permit a reasonable inference that the accuser's words were heard and understood by a third party as referring to Melton and as imputing the commission of a crime.

DECISION AND REMEDY The Virginia Supreme Court held that a plaintiff does not need to present testimony from any third person, or even to identify any such person, to prove publication of defamatory remarks. The court reversed the judgment of the lower court and remanded the case.

FOR CRITICAL ANALYSIS—SOCIAL CONSIDERATION *Under what circumstances should a court require testimony from third parties in order to prove that a statement was "published" for defamation purposes?*

DEFENSES AGAINST DEFAMATION.   Truth is normally an absolute defense against a defamation charge. In other words, if the defendant in a defamation suit can prove that his or her allegedly defamatory statements were true, the defendant will not be liable.

Another defense that is sometimes raised is that the statements were **privileged** communications, and thus the defendant is immune from liability. Privileged communications are of two types: absolute and qualified. Only in judicial proceedings and certain legislative proceedings is *absolute* privilege granted. For example, statements made by attorneys and judges during a trial are absolutely privileged. So are statements made by legislators during congressional floor debate, even if the legislators make such statements maliciously—that is, knowing them to be untrue. An absolute privilege is granted in these situations because judicial and legislative personnel deal with matters that are so much in the public interest that the parties involved should be able to speak out fully and freely without restriction.

In other situations, a person will not be liable for defamatory statements because he or she has a *qualified,* or conditional, privilege. For example, statements made in recommendation letters or in written evaluations of employees are qualifiedly privileged. Generally, if the communicated statements are made in good faith and the publication is limited to those who have a legitimate interest in the communication, the statements fall within the area of qualified privilege. The concept of conditional privilege rests on the common law assumption that in some situations, the right to know or speak is of equal importance with the right not to be defamed.

In general, false and defamatory statements that are made about *public figures* (those who exercise substantial governmental power and any persons in the public limelight) and that are published in the press are privileged if they are made without **actual malice.**[4] To be made with actual malice, a statement must be made *with either knowledge of falsity or a reckless disregard of the truth.* Statements made about public figures, especially when they are made via a public medium, are usually related to matters of general public interest; they are made about people who substantially affect all of us. Furthermore, public figures generally have some access to a public medium for answering disparaging (belittling, discrediting) falsehoods about themselves; private individuals do not. For these reasons, public figures have a greater burden of proof in defamation cases (they must prove actual malice) than do private individuals.

Invasion of Privacy

A person has a right to solitude and freedom from prying public eyes—in other words, to privacy. Four acts qualify as an invasion of that privacy:

1. The use of a person's name, picture, or other likeness for commercial purposes without permission. This tort, which is usually referred to as the tort of *appropriation,* will be examined in the next chapter.
2. Intrusion in an individual's affairs or seclusion in an area in which the person has a reasonable expectation of privacy.
3. Publication of information that places a person in a false light. This could be a story attributing to the person ideas not held or actions not taken by the person. (Publishing such a story could involve the tort of defamation as well.)

Privilege In tort law, the ability to act contrary to another person's right without that person's having legal redress for such acts. Privilege may be raised as a defense to defamation.

> **"Truth is generally the best vindication against slander."**
>
> Abraham Lincoln, 1809–1865
> (Sixteenth president of the United States, 1861–1865)

Actual Malice Real and demonstrable evil intent. In a defamation suit, a statement made about a public figure normally must be made with actual malice (with either knowledge of its falsity or a reckless disregard of the truth) for liability to be incurred.

---

4.   *New York Times Co. v. Sullivan,* 376 U.S. 254, 84 S.Ct. 710, 11 L.Ed.2d 686 (1964).

4. Public disclosure of private facts about an individual that an ordinary person would find objectionable.

Misrepresentation—Fraud (Deceit)

A misrepresentation leads another to believe in a condition that is different from the condition that actually exists. This is often accomplished through a false or incorrect statement. Misrepresentations may be innocently made by someone who is unaware of the existing facts, but the tort of **fraudulent misrepresentation,** or **fraud,** involves intentional deceit, usually for personal gain. The tort includes several elements:

1. Misrepresentation of facts or conditions with knowledge that they are false or with reckless disregard for the truth.
2. Intent to induce another to rely on the misrepresentation.
3. Justifiable reliance by the deceived party.
4. Damages suffered as a result of reliance.
5. Causal connection between the misrepresentation and the injury suffered.

Fraudulent Misrepresentation (Fraud) Any misrepresentation, either by misstatement or omission of a material fact, knowingly made with the intention of deceiving another and on which a reasonable person would and does rely to his or her detriment.

For fraud to occur, more than mere **puffery,** or *seller's talk,* must be involved. Fraud exists only when a person represents as a fact something he or she knows is untrue. For example, it is fraud to claim that a roof does not leak when one knows it does. Facts are objectively ascertainable, whereas seller's talk is not. "I am the best accountant in town" is seller's talk. The speaker is not trying to represent something as fact, because the term *best* is a subjective, not an objective, term.[5]

Puffery A salesperson's often exaggerated claims concerning the quality of property offered for sale. Such claims involve opinions rather than facts and are not considered to be legally binding promises or warranties.

Normally, the tort of misrepresentation or fraud occurs only when there is reliance on a *statement of fact.* Sometimes, however, reliance on a *statement of opinion* may involve the tort of misrepresentation if the individual making the statement of opinion has a superior knowledge of the subject matter. For example, when a lawyer makes a statement of opinion about the law, a court would construe reliance on such a statement to be equivalent to reliance on a statement of fact. We examine fraudulent misrepresentation again in Chapter 12, in the context of contract law.

Intentional Torts against Property

Intentional torts against property include trespass to land, trespass to personal property, and conversion. These torts are wrongful actions that interfere with individuals' legally recognized rights with regard to their land or personal property. The law distinguishes real property from personal property. *Real property* is land and things "permanently" attached to the land. *Personal property* consists of all other items, which are basically movable. Thus, a house and lot are real property, whereas the furniture inside a house is personal property. Money and securities are also personal property.

---

5. In contracts for the sale of goods, Article 2 of the Uniform Commercial Code distinguishes, for warranty purposes, between statements of opinion ("puffery") and statements of fact. See Chapter 13 for a further discussion of the Uniform Commercial Code.

Trespass to Land

A **trespass to land** occurs whenever a person, without permission or legal authorization, enters onto, above, or below the surface of land that is owned by another; causes anything to enter onto the land; remains on the land; or permits anything to remain on it. Actual harm to the land is not an essential element of this tort, because the tort is designed to protect the right of an owner to exclusive possession of his or her property. Common types of trespass to land include walking or driving on the land, shooting a gun over the land, throwing rocks at a building that belongs to someone else, building a dam across a river and thus causing water to back up on someone else's land, and placing part of one's building on an adjoining landowner's property.

TRESPASS CRITERIA, RIGHTS, AND DUTIES.   Before a person can be a trespasser, the owner of the real property (or other person in actual and exclusive possession of the property) must establish that person as a trespasser. For example, "posted" trespass signs expressly establish as a trespasser a person who ignores these signs and enters onto the property. A guest in your home is not a trespasser—unless he or she has been asked to leave but refuses. Any person who enters onto your property to commit an illegal act (such as a thief entering a lumberyard at night to steal lumber) is established impliedly as a trespasser, without posted signs.

At common law, a trespasser is liable for damages caused to the property. In addition, a trespasser generally cannot hold the owner liable for injuries sustained on the premises. This common law rule is being abandoned in many jurisdictions in favor of a "reasonable duty of care" rule that varies depending on the status of the parties. For example, a landowner may have a duty to post a notice that the property is patrolled by guard dogs. Furthermore, under the "attractive nuisance" doctrine, children do not assume the risks of the premises if they are attracted to the premises by some object, such as an unfenced swimming pool, abandoned building, or sand pile. Trespassers normally can be removed from the premises through the use of reasonable force without the owner's being liable for assault and battery.

DEFENSES AGAINST TRESPASS TO LAND.   Trespass to land involves wrongful interference with another person's real property rights. If it can be shown that the trespass was warranted, however, as when a trespasser enters to assist someone in danger, a defense exists. Another defense is to show that the purported owner did not actually have the right to possess the land in question.

Trespass to Personal Property

Whenever any individual unlawfully harms the personal property of another or otherwise interferes with the personal property owner's right to exclusive possession and enjoyment of that property, **trespass to personal property**— also called *trespass to personalty*[6]—occurs. If a student takes another student's business law book as a practical joke and hides it so that the owner is unable to find it for several days prior to a final examination, the student has engaged in a trespass to personal property.

A sign warns trespassers. Should a trespasser be allowed to recover from a landowner for injuries sustained on the premises?

Trespass to Land The entry onto, above, or below the surface of land owned by another without the owner's permission or legal authorization.

Trespass to Personal Property The unlawful taking or harming of another's personal property; interference with another's right to the exclusive possession of his or her personal property.

---

6. Pronounced *per*-sun-ul-tee.

If it can be shown that trespass to personal property was warranted, then a complete defense exists. Most states, for example, allow automobile repair shops to hold a customer's car (under what is called an *artisan's lien,* discussed in Chapter 14) when the customer refuses to pay for repairs already completed.

Conversion

Conversion The wrongful taking, using, or retaining possession of personal property that belongs to another.

Whenever personal property is wrongfully taken from its rightful owner or possessor and placed in the service of another, the act of **conversion** occurs. Conversion is defined as any act depriving an owner of personal property without that owner's permission and without just cause. When conversion occurs, the lesser offense of trespass to personal property usually occurs as well. If the initial taking of the property was unlawful, there is trespass; retention of that property is conversion. If the initial taking of the property was permitted by the owner or for some other reason is not a trespass, failure to return it may still be conversion. Conversion is the civil side of crimes related to theft. A store clerk who steals merchandise from the store commits a crime and engages in the tort of conversion at the same time.

> **KEEP IN MIND** In tort law, the underlying motive does not matter— what matters is the intent to do the act that results in the tort.

Even if a person mistakenly believed that he or she was entitled to the goods, a tort of conversion may occur. In other words, good intentions are not a defense against conversion; in fact, conversion can be an entirely innocent act. Someone who buys stolen goods, for example, commits the tort of conversion even if he or she does not know that the goods were stolen. If the true owner brings a tort action against the buyer, the buyer must either return the property to the owner or pay the owner the full value of the property, despite having already paid money to the thief.

A successful defense against the charge of conversion is that the purported owner does not in fact own the property or does not have a right to possess it that is superior to the right of the holder. Necessity is another possible defense against conversion. If Abrams takes Mendoza's cat, Abrams is guilty of conversion. If Mendoza sues Abrams, Abrams must return the cat or pay damages. If, however, the cat has rabies and Abrams took the cat to protect the public, Abrams has a valid defense—necessity (and perhaps even self-defense, if he can prove that he was in danger because of the cat).

Unintentional Torts (Negligence)

Negligence The failure to exercise the standard of care that a reasonable person would exercise in similar circumstances.

The tort of **negligence** occurs when someone suffers injury because of another's failure to live up to a required *duty of care.* In contrast to intentional torts, in torts involving negligence, the tortfeasor neither wishes to bring about the consequences of the act nor believes that they will occur. The actor's conduct merely creates a *risk* of such consequences. If no risk is created, there is no negligence.

Many of the actions discussed in the section on intentional torts constitute negligence if the element of intent is missing. For example, if Juarez intentionally shoves Natsuyo, who falls and breaks an arm as a result, Juarez will have committed an intentional tort. If Juarez carelessly bumps into Natsuyo, however, and she falls and breaks an arm as a result, Juarez's action will constitute negligence. In either situation, Juarez has committed a tort.

In examining a question of negligence, one should ask four questions:

1. Did the defendant owe a duty of care to the plaintiff?
2. Did the defendant breach that duty?
3. Did the plaintiff suffer a legally recognizable injury as a result of the defendant's breach of the duty of care?
4. Did the defendant's breach cause the plaintiff's injury?

Each of these elements of neligence is discussed below.

The Duty of Care and Its Breach

The concept of a **duty of care** arises from the notion that if we are to live in society with other people, some actions can be tolerated and some cannot; some actions are right and some are wrong; and some actions are reasonable and some are not. The basic principle underlying the duty of care is that people are free to act as they please so long as their actions do not infringe on the interests of others.

When someone fails to comply with the duty of exercising reasonable care, a potentially tortious act may have been committed. Failure to live up to a standard of care may be an act (setting fire to a building) or an omission (neglecting to put out a campfire). It may be an intentional act, a careless act, or a carefully performed but nevertheless dangerous act that results in injury. Courts consider the nature of the act (whether it is outrageous or commonplace), the manner in which the act is performed (cautiously versus heedlessly), and the nature of the injury (whether it is serious or slight) in determining whether the duty of care has been breached.

THE REASONABLE PERSON STANDARD.   Tort law measures duty by the **reasonable person standard.** In determining whether a duty of care has been breached, the courts ask how a reasonable person would have acted in the same circumstances. The reasonable person standard is said to be (though in an absolute sense it cannot be) objective. It is not necessarily how a particular person would act. It is society's judgment on how people *should* act. If the so-called reasonable person existed, he or she would be careful, conscientious, even tempered, and honest. This hypothetical reasonable person is frequently used by the courts in decisions relating to other areas of law as well.

That individuals are required to exercise a reasonable standard of care in their activities is a pervasive concept in business law, and many of the issues dealt with in subsequent chapters of this text have to do with this duty. What constitutes reasonable care varies, of course, with the circumstances.

DUTY OF LANDOWNERS.   Landowners are expected to exercise reasonable care to protect from harm persons coming onto their property. As mentioned earlier, in some jurisdictions, landowners are held to owe a duty to protect even trespassers against certain risks. Landowners who rent or lease premises to tenants are expected to exercise reasonable care to ensure that the tenants and their guests are not harmed in common areas, such as stairways, entryways, laundry rooms, and the like.

Retailers and other firms that explicitly or implicitly invite persons to come onto their premises are usually charged with a duty to exercise reasonable care

> **"There is a duty if the court says there is a duty."**
>
> William Lloyd Prosser, 1898–1972
> (American legal scholar)

Duty of Care The duty of all persons, as established by tort law, to exercise a reasonable amount of care in their dealings with others. Failure to exercise due care, which is normally determined by the "reasonable person standard," constitutes the tort of negligence.

Reasonable Person Standard The standard of behavior expected of a hypothetical "reasonable person." The standard against which negligence is measured and that must be observed to avoid liability for negligence.

Ethical Perspective

Does a person's duty of care include a duty to come to the aid of a stranger in peril? For example, assume that you are walking down a city street and notice that a pedestrian is about to step directly in front of an oncoming bus. Do you have a legal duty to warn that individual? No. Although most people would probably concede that, in this situation the observer has an *ethical* duty to warn the other, tort law does not impose a general duty to rescue others in peril.

People involved in special relationships, however, have been held to have a duty to rescue other parties within the relationship. A married person, for example, has a duty to rescue his or her child or spouse if either is in danger.

Other special relationships, such as those between teachers and students or hiking and hunting partners, may also give rise to a duty to rescue. In addition, if a person who has no duty to rescue undertakes to rescue another, then the rescuer is charged with a duty to follow through with due care on the rescue attempt.

In regard to the duty to rescue, the distinction between legal and ethical duties is clearly evident. Although the law might not require a passerby to save a drowning toddler in a wading pool, society expects that people will aid others who are in danger and cannot help themselves.

For Critical Analysis: *Should the law impose a general duty to rescue others in peril?*

Business Invitees Those people, such as customers or clients, who are invited onto business premises by the owner of those premises for business purposes.

to protect those persons, who are considered to be **business invitees.** For example, if you entered a supermarket, slipped on a wet floor, and sustained injuries as a result, the owner of the supermarket would be liable for damages if when you slipped there was no sign warning that the floor was wet. A court would hold that the business owner was negligent because the owner failed to exercise a reasonable degree of care in protecting the store's customers against foreseeable risks about which the owner knew or *should have known.* That a patron might slip on the wet floor and be injured as a result was a foreseeable risk, and the owner should have taken care to avoid this risk or to warn the

A safety cone warns that a floor could be slippery. If someone slips on this floor, falls, and is injured, should this warning allow the property owner to avoid liability?

customer of it. The landowner also has a duty to discover and remove any hidden dangers that might injure a customer or other invitee.

Some risks, of course, are so obvious that the owner need not warn of them. For example, a business owner does not need to warn customers to open a door before attempting to walk through it. Other risks, however, even though they may seem obvious to a business owner, may not be so in the eyes of another, such as a child. For example, a hardware store owner may not think it is necessary to warn customers that a stepladder leaning against the back wall of the store could fall down and harm them. It is possible, though, that a child could tip the ladder over and be hurt as a result and that the store could be held liable. In the following case, the court has to decide whether a supermarket owner should be held liable for a customer's injuries on the premises.

Case 8.2 ● Dumont v. Shaw's Supermarkets, Inc.

Supreme Judicial Court of Maine, 1995.
664 A.2d 846.

HISTORICAL AND POLITICAL SETTING *For more than two decades, the states have been changing their tort laws to reduce what some consider to be excessive advantages given to plaintiffs. In the mid-1970s, for example, some states set limits on the amounts of recovery allowed in medical malpractice cases. In the 1980s, the focus was on reducing liability in cases involving product liability (see Chapter 10). In the 1990s, the debate has concerned other liability issues, lawyers' fees, and the "loser pays" concept. Due in part to these efforts by the states, the number of filings of tort lawsuits has decreased by 6 percent since 1991.*

BACKGROUND AND FACTS At Shaw's Supermarkets, Inc., chocolate-covered peanuts are sold in bulk with other

unpackaged, unwrapped candy in bins next to the produce section. Shaw's is aware that self-serve, small, loose, slippery items create a hazard for customers, who may slip and fall if they step on them. Shaw's places mats next to some of the produce and in other locations, but Shaw's does not place mats on the floor next to the candy bins. While shopping at Shaw's, Shirley Dumont slipped on a chocolate-covered peanut, fell, and was injured. Dumont sued Shaw's in a Maine state court, alleging negligence. The court ruled that Dumont could recover only if she proved that Shaw's caused the candy to be on the floor, that Shaw's knew that the candy was on the floor, or that the candy was on the floor for such a length of time that Shaw's should have known it was there. Because Dumont proved none of these things, the court entered a judgment in favor of Shaw's. Dumont appealed to the state's highest court, the Supreme Judicial Court of Maine.

IN THE WORDS OF THE COURT . . .
GLASSMAN, Justice.
* * * *

* * * [T]he plaintiff presented evidence * * * that there existed a foreseeable risk of a recurrent condition and that Shaw's did not exercise reasonable care in failing to place mats next to the bulk candy display. Shaw's was aware that items with similar characteristics to the chocolate-covered peanuts created an increased hazard to customers and had placed mats on the floor to mitigate the risk.

* * * In those circumstances, a store owner may be chargeable with constructive notice[a] of the existence of the specific condition at issue.

* * * [A] store owner who is aware of the existence of a recurrent condition that poses a potential danger to invitees may not ignore that knowledge and fail reasonably to respond to the foreseeable danger of the likelihood of a recurrence of the condition.

---

a. Notice that is implied or imposed by law, as opposed to actual notice.

(Continued)

Case 8.2—continued

DECISION AND REMEDY The Supreme Judicial Court of Maine held that it is not necessary to prove that a store owner had actual notice of a specific condition giving rise to an injury. The court vacated the lower court's judgment and remanded the case for further proceedings.

FOR CRITICAL ANALYSIS—SOCIAL CONSIDERATION *Does the principle applied in this case make a store owner the "absolute insurer" of the store's customers? In other words, is a store owner liable for injuries to customers on the premises even if the owner has taken precautions that are reasonably necessary to protect those customers?*

Professionals review plans at a construction site. Could they successfully defend against a lawsuit for negligence by claiming that they were not familiar with certain principles of their profession?

Malpractice Professional misconduct or the lack of the requisite degree of skill as a professional. Negligence—the failure to exercise due care—on the part of a professional, such as a physician or an attorney, is commonly referred to as malpractice.

Compensatory Damages A money award equivalent to the actual value of injuries or damages sustained by the aggrieved party.

Punitive Damages Money damages that may be awarded to a plaintiff to punish the defendant and deter future similar conduct.

DUTY OF PROFESSIONALS.   If an individual has knowledge, skill, or intelligence superior to that of an ordinary person, the individual's conduct must be consistent with that status. Professionals—including doctors, dentists, psychiatrists, architects, engineers, accountants, lawyers, and others—are required to have a standard minimum level of special knowledge and ability. Therefore, in determining what constitutes reasonable care in cases involving professionals, their training and expertise is taken into account. In other words, an accountant cannot defend against a lawsuit for negligence by stating, "But I was not familiar with that principle of accounting."

If a professional violates his or her duty of care toward a client, the professional may be sued for **malpractice.** For example, a patient might sue a physician for *medical malpractice.* A client might sue an attorney for *legal malpractice.*

The Injury Requirement and Damages

For a tort to have been committed, the plaintiff must have suffered a *legally recognizable* injury. To recover damages (receive compensation), the plaintiff must have suffered some loss, harm, wrong, or invasion of a protected interest. Essentially, the purpose of tort law is to compensate for legally recognized injuries resulting from wrongful acts. If no harm or injury results from a given negligent action, there is nothing to compensate—and no tort exists. For example, if you carelessly bump into a passerby, who stumbles and falls as a result, you may be liable in tort if the passerby is injured in the fall. If the person is unharmed, however, there normally could be no suit for damages, because no injury was suffered. Although the passerby might be angry and suffer emotional distress, few courts recognize negligently inflicted emotional distress as a tort unless it results in some physical disturbance or dysfunction.

As already mentioned, the purpose of tort law is not to punish people for tortious acts but to compensate the injured parties for damages suffered. Occasionally, however, damages awarded in tort lawsuits include both **compensatory damages** (which are intended to reimburse a plaintiff for actual losses—to make the plaintiff whole) and **punitive damages** (which are intended to punish the wrongdoer and deter others from similar wrongdoing). Few negligent acts, however, are so reprehensible that punitive damages are available. (See this chapter's *Inside the Legal Environment* on page 23 for a further discussion of punitive damages awards in tort litigation.) Unlike in some other nations, in the United States the damages awarded do not depend on whether the tort was intentional or negligent.

In recent years, tort litigation has often resulted in high punitive damages awards. In some cases, these awards have been hundreds of times higher than the compensatory damages awarded to the plaintiffs. Some defendants have claimed that such awards violate the Eighth Amendment's prohibition against excessive fines or the defendants' constitutional rights to due process. The constitutionality of a high punitive damages award is at issue in the following case.

Case 8.3 ⬤ BMW of North America, Inc. v. Gore

Supreme Court of the United States, 1996.
517 U.S. 559,
116 S.Ct. 1589,
134 L.Ed.2d 809.

BACKGROUND AND FACTS After Dr. Ira Gore bought a new BMW from an authorized dealer, he discovered that the car had been damaged by acid rain and repainted before its delivery to him. Gore filed a suit in an Alabama state court against BMW of North America, Inc., the car's distributor, and others, based on the failure to disclose the damage and repair. BMW admitted that its policy was not to tell customers of damage to new cars if the cost of repairing the damage was not more than 3 percent of the car's price. After a trial, the jury awarded Gore $4,000 in compensatory damages and $4 million in punitive damages. On appeal, the Alabama Supreme Court reduced the punitive damages award to $2 million. The defendants appealed to the United States Supreme Court, arguing that the award was grossly excessive in violation of the due process clause of the Fourteenth Amendment.

IN THE WORDS OF THE COURT . . .
Justice STEVENS delivered the opinion of the Court.
 * * * *

Elementary notions of fairness * * * dictate that a person receive fair notice * * * of the severity of the penalty that a State may impose. Three guideposts, each of which indicates that BMW did not receive adequate notice * * *, lead us to the conclusion that the $2 million award against BMW is grossly excessive: the degree of reprehensibility of the nondisclosure; the disparity between the harm or potential harm suffered by Dr. Gore and his punitive damages award; and the difference between this remedy and the civil penalties authorized or imposed in comparable cases. * * *
 * * * *

In this case, none of the aggravating factors associated with particularly reprehensible conduct is present. * * * BMW's conduct evinced no indifference to or reckless disregard for the health and safety of others. * * *
 * * * *

The $2 million in punitive damages * * * is 500 times the amount of [Gore's] actual harm * * * . [T]here is no suggestion that [he] * * * was threatened with any additional potential harm * * * .
 * * * *

 * * * [The] sanction imposed on BMW is substantially greater than the statutory fines * * * for similar malfeasance [misconduct].

DECISION AND REMEDY The United States Supreme Court held that the award of $2 million in punitive damages was grossly excessive. The Court reversed the state court's ruling and remanded the case.[a]

FOR CRITICAL ANALYSIS—ECONOMIC CONSIDERATION *What would be the result if companies such as BMW were held liable for any and all amounts of punitive damages?*

---

a. On remand, the Alabama Supreme Court reduced the punitive damages to $50,000. See *BMW of North America, Inc. v. Gore,* 701 So.2d 507 (Ala. 1997).

Inside the Legal Environment
The High Cost of Tort Litigation

Americans like to sue, or at least that's what it looks like if you examine the number of lawsuits occurring in this country. We have more than 750,000 lawyers in the United States. Both totally and on a per capita basis, that is more lawyers than most other nations claim. Furthermore, the percentage of total national income devoted to tort costs is higher in the United States than anywhere else. It is five times what it is in Canada, France, Germany, Britain, or Japan. And while tort costs in other nations have remained relatively stable, they have been on the rise in the United States. Currently, the estimated cost of tort litigation in this country exceeds $130 billion annually.

Not surprisingly, if you are in the business world, you should be insured against the possibility of tort litigation. Businesspersons and professionals are potentially subject to a wide array of tort lawsuits brought by clients, customers and consumers, and others. Manufacturers and sellers, for example, are frequently the targets of product *liability* lawsuits— that is, lawsuits brought by con-

sumers who are harmed by a faulty or defective product. To protect against having to pay millions of dollars in damages, manufacturers and sellers purchase liability insurance. The cost of high damages awards and insurance protection against them is borne not just by business but by society in general. This is because those costs are passed on to customers, clients, and consumers in the form of higher prices. Today, about 20 percent of the cost of a $35 stepladder goes to insurance.

High punitive damages awards, which in some cases are hundreds of times higher than the compensatory damages awarded to the plaintiffs, have led some defendants to claim that these awards violate the Eighth Amendment's prohibition against excessive fines or the defendants' constitutional rights to due process. In *BMW of North America v. Gore*,[a] for example, a jury awarded $4,000 in compensatory damages and one thousand times that amount ($4 million) in punitive damages. The

Alabama Supreme Court reduced the punitive damages award to $2 million. When the case was appealed to the United States Supreme Court, the Court held that the $2 million award was "grossly excessive" and violated the defendant's due process rights.

Attempts at reducing the number and size of damages awards fall under the rubric of tort reform. Efforts at tort reform in many states are aimed at capping, or putting a ceiling on, high awards. Some states limit the size of punitive awards. New Jersey requires a finding of actual malice or wanton and willful disregard of rights before granting punitive damages. Some states have limited awards for such noneconomic harm as emotional distress. In all, at least thirty states have changed their rules relating to the availability of punitive damages. For some time, members of Congress have been trying to achieve consensus on a tort reform bill, but to date, they have not succeeded.

For Critical Analysis: *Who ultimately pays for extremely large punitive damages awards?*

a.   517 U.S. 559, 116 S.Ct. 1589, 134 L.Ed.2d 809 (1996). See Case 8.3.

> "There's no limit to how complicated things can get, on account of one thing always leading to another."
>
> E. B. White, 1899–1985
> (American author)

Causation

Another element necessary to a tort is *causation*. If a person fails in a duty of care and someone suffers injury, the wrongful activity must have caused the harm for a tort to have been committed.

CAUSATION IN FACT AND PROXIMATE CAUSE.   In deciding whether there is causation, the court must address two questions:

1. *Is there causation in fact?* Did the injury occur because of the defendant's act, or would it have occurred anyway? If an injury would not have occurred without the defendant's act, then there is causation in fact.

International Perspective

Among national tort laws, there are many differences—and many different approaches to the calculation of damages. For example, Swiss and Turkish law permit a court to reduce damages if an award of full damages would cause undue hardship to a party who was found negligent. Also, in some nations of northern Africa, different amounts of damages are awarded depending on the type of tortious action committed, whether the tort was intentional or negligent, and so on.

For Critical Analysis: *Should courts in the United States consider, when awarding damages, whether the awards would cause undue hardship to the defendants?*

Causation in fact can usually be determined by the use of the *but for* test: "but for" the wrongful act, the injury would not have occurred. Theoretically, causation in fact is limitless. One could claim, for example, that "but for" the creation of the world, a particular injury would not have occurred. Thus, as a practical matter, the law has to establish limits, and it does so through the concept of proximate cause.

2. *Was the act the proximate cause of the injury?* **Proximate cause,** or legal cause, exists when the connection between an act and an injury is strong enough to justify imposing liability. Consider an example. Ackerman carelessly leaves a campfire burning. The fire not only burns down the forest but also sets off an explosion in a nearby chemical plant that spills chemicals into a river, killing all the fish for a hundred miles downstream and ruining the economy of a tourist resort. Should Ackerman be liable to the resort owners? To the tourists whose vacations were ruined? These are questions of proximate cause that a court must decide.

Probably the most cited case on proximate cause is the *Palsgraf* case discussed in the *Landmark in the Legal Environment* on page 233. The question before the court was as follows: Does a defendant's duty of care extend only to those who may be injured as a result of a foreseeable risk, or does it extend also to a person whose injury could not reasonably be foreseen?

FORESEEABILITY. Since the *Palsgraf* case, (see page 233) the courts have used *foreseeability* as the test for proximate cause. The railroad guards were negligent, but the railroad's duty of care did not extend to Palsgraf, because her injury was unforeseeable. If the victim of the harm or the consequences of the harm done are unforeseeable, there is no proximate cause. Of course, it is foreseeable that people will stand on railroad platforms and that objects attached to the platforms will fall as the result of explosions nearby; however, this is not a chain of events against which a reasonable person would usually guard. It is difficult to predict when a court will say that something is foreseeable and when it will say that something is not. How far a court stretches foreseeability is determined in part by the extent to which the court is willing to stretch the defendant's duty of care. In the following case, the court considered whether, under the circumstances, the harm caused by arson is a reasonably foreseeable risk.

Causation in Fact An act or omission without which an event would not have occurred.

Proximate Cause Legal cause; exists when the connection between an act and an injury is strong enough to justify imposing liability.

NOTE Proximate cause can be thought of as a question of social policy: Should the defendant be made to bear the loss instead of the plaintiff?

Case 8.4 ⬤ Addis v. Steele

Appeals Court of Massachusetts, 1995.
38 Mass.App.Ct. 433,
648 N.E.2d 773.

HISTORICAL AND ECONOMIC SETTING *Of major crimes, arson is the easiest to commit, the most difficult to detect, and the hardest to prove. Every year, arson kills as many as a thousand people and injures thousands more. Property worth more than a billion dollars is destroyed, and millions of dollars in jobs and property taxes are lost. One common motive for arson is profit: people in serious financial trouble sometimes burn their own buildings to collect insurance money. Predictably, arson thus causes a significant increase in the price of fire insurance.*

BACKGROUND AND FACTS On the morning of October 2, 1989, a fire started by an arsonist broke out in the Red Inn in Provincetown, Massachusetts. The inn had a smoke detector, sprinkler, and alarm system, which alerted the guests, but there were no emergency lights or clear exits. Attempting to escape, Deborah Addis and James Reed, guests at the inn, found the first-floor doors and windows locked. Ultimately, they forced open a second-floor window and jumped out. To recover for their injuries, they filed a suit in a Massachusetts state court against Tamerlane Corporation, which operated the inn under a lease, and others (including Duane Steele, who worked for the owner of the inn). Addis and Reed contended in part that Tamerlane was negligent. Tamerlane responded that harm caused by arson is not a reasonably foreseeable risk. The court entered a judgment against Tamerlane, and Tamerlane appealed. The appellate court affirmed the lower court's judgment. Tamerlane then appealed to a higher state court.

IN THE WORDS OF THE COURT . . .
GILLERMAN, Justice.
    *   *   *   *

   The corporation [Tamerlane] concedes that "the possibility of fire was foreseen and guarded against with * * * smoke detector, sprinkler and alarm system[s]." Given the foreseeability of a fire at the inn, the corporation gains no benefit from the fact that the fire was set. "The duty to protect the other against unreasonable risk of harm extends to * * * risks arising from * * * acts of third persons, whether they be innocent, negligent, intentional, or even criminal." * * * [T]he corporation's failure to provide adequate lighting and egress created a foreseeable risk that a fire, however started —innocently, negligently, or by a criminal act—would cause harm to its guests * * * .

DECISION AND REMEDY The Appeals Court of Massachusetts held that the harm caused by the fire, even though it had been set by an arsonist, was a reasonably foreseeable risk, and affirmed the lower courts' judgments against Tamerlane.

FOR CRITICAL ANALYSIS—ECONOMIC CONSIDERATION *Does a business always have a duty to protect its patrons from the harm caused by the criminal activity of third persons? In other words, is the harm caused by all crimes reasonably foreseeable under* all *circumstances? If not, under what circumstances is harm caused by crime foreseeable?*

> **COMPARE** The concept of superseding intervening force is not a question of physics, but is, like proximate cause, a question of responsibility.

SUPERSEDING INTERVENING FORCES.   An independent intervening force may break the connection between a wrongful act and an injury to another. If so, it acts as a *superseding cause*—that is, the intervening force or event sets aside, or replaces, the original wrongful act as the cause of the injury. For example, suppose that Derrick keeps a can of gasoline in the trunk of his car. The presence of the gasoline creates a foreseeable risk and is thus a negligent act. If Derrick's car skids and crashes into a tree, causing the gasoline can to explode,

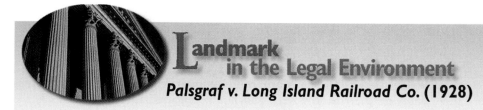

Landmark in the Legal Environment
Palsgraf v. Long Island Railroad Co. (1928)

In 1928, the New York Court of Appeals (that state's highest court) issued its decision in *Palsgraf v. Long Island Railroad Co.*,[a] a case that has become a landmark in negligence law with respect to proximate cause.

The facts of the case were as follows. The plaintiff, Palsgraf, was waiting for a train on a station platform. A man carrying a small package wrapped in newspaper was rushing to catch a train that had begun to move away from the platform. As the man attempted to jump aboard the moving train, he seemed unsteady and about to fall. A railroad guard on the train car reached forward to grab him, and another guard on the platform pushed him from behind to help him board the train. In the process, the man's package fell on the railroad tracks and exploded, because it contained fireworks. The repercussions of the explosion caused scales at the other end of the train platform to fall on Palsgraf, who was injured as a result. She sued the railroad company for damages in a New York state court.

At the trial, the jury found that the railroad guards were negligent in their conduct. On appeal, the question before the New York Court of Appeals was whether the conduct of the railroad guards was the proximate cause of Palsgraf's injuries. In other words, did the guards' duty of care extend to Palsgraf, who was outside the zone of danger and whose injury could not reasonably have been foreseen?

The court stated that the question of whether the guards were negligent *with respect to Palsgraf* depended on whether her injury was *reasonably foreseeable* to the railroad guards. Although the guards may have acted negligently with respect to the man boarding the train, this has no bearing on the question of their negligence with respect to Palsgraf. This is not a situation in which a person commits an act so potentially harmful (for example, firing a gun at a building) that he or she would be held responsible for any harm that resulted. The court stated that here, "by concession, there was nothing in the situation to suggest to the most cautious mind that the parcel wrapped in newspaper would spread wreckage through the station." The court thus concluded that the railroad guards were not negligent with respect to Palsgraf and not liable for her injuries.

For Critical Analysis: *If the guards knew that the package contained fireworks, would the court have ruled otherwise? Would it matter that the guards were motivated by a desire to help the man board the train and not by a desire to harm anyone?*

[a]248 N.Y. 339, 162 N.E. 99 (1928).

Derrick would be liable for injuries sustained by passing pedestrians because of his negligence. If the explosion had been caused by lightning striking the car, however, the lightning would supersede Derrick's original negligence as a cause of the damage, because the lightning was not foreseeable.

In negligence cases, the negligent party will often attempt to show that some act has intervened after his or her action and that this second act was the proximate cause of injury. Typically, in cases in which an individual takes a defensive action, such as swerving to avoid an oncoming car, the original wrongdoer will not be relieved of liability even if the injury actually resulted from the attempt to escape harm. The same is true under the "danger invites rescue" doctrine. Under this doctrine, if Lemming commits an act that endangers Salter and Yokem sustains an injury trying to protect Salter, then Lemming will be liable for Yokem's injury, as well as for any injuries Salter may sustain. Rescuers can injure themselves, or the person rescued, or even a stranger, but the original wrongdoer will still be liable.

A bungee jumper leaps from a platform. If the jumper is injured and sues the operator of the jump for negligence, what defenses might the operator use to avoid liability?

Defenses to Negligence

The basic defenses in negligence cases are (1) assumption of risk, (2) contributory negligence, and (3) comparative negligence.

ASSUMPTION OF RISK.   A plaintiff who voluntarily enters into a risky situation, knowing the risk involved, will not be allowed to recover. This is the defense of assumption of risk. The requirements of this defense are (1) knowledge of the risk and (2) voluntary assumption of the risk. For example, a driver entering a race knows there is a risk of being killed or injured in a crash. The driver has assumed the risk of injury.

The risk can be assumed by express agreement, or the assumption of risk can be implied by the plaintiff's knowledge of the risk and subsequent conduct. Of course, the plaintiff does not assume a risk different from or greater than the risk normally carried by the activity. In our example, the race car driver assumes the risk of being injured in the race but not the risk that the banking in the curves of the racetrack will give way during the race because of a construction defect.

Risks are not deemed to be assumed in situations involving emergencies. Neither are they assumed when a statute protects a class of people from harm and a member of the class is injured by the harm. For example, employees are protected by statute from harmful working conditions and therefore do not assume the risks associated with the workplace. If an employee is injured, he or she will generally be compensated regardless of fault under state workers' compensation statutes (discussed in Chapter 16).

In the following case, the plaintiff suffered an injury to his pitching arm in a simulated baseball game during a tryout for a major league team. The issue before the court was whether the plaintiff had assumed the risk of the injury, thus precluding him from recovery.

Case 8.5 ● Wattenbarger v. Cincinnati Reds, Inc.

California Court of Appeal,
Third District, 1994.
28 Cal.App.4th 746,
33 Cal.Rptr.2d 732.

HISTORICAL AND CULTURAL SETTING

Despite the legend of Abner Doubleday's invention of baseball, most sports historians agree that the game was not the invention of just a single person. Instead, baseball evolved in the nineteenth century from a number of ball-and-stick games (including a game called "base ball") that had been popular earlier in England and colonial America. Segregated until John (Jackie) Robinson integrated the Brooklyn Dodgers in 1947, baseball teams today can include players of all ethnic, cultural, and national backgrounds.

BACKGROUND AND FACTS In June 1990, in Lodi, California, seventeen-year-old Jeffrey Wattenbarger tried out for the position of pitcher for the Cincinnati Reds.

During the tryouts, Wattenbarger's shoulder popped. It occurred on his third pitch to a batter during a simulated game. He stepped off the mound and told the representatives of the Reds. Hearing no response, Wattenbarger stepped back onto the mound and threw another pitch. He immediately experienced severe pain. Later, it was discovered that a portion of the bone and tendons had pulled away sometime during Wattenbarger's pitching, and he underwent an operation on the arm. Seeking damages for the injury, Wattenbarger brought an action in a California state court against the Reds, claiming they had been negligent in allowing him to throw the fourth pitch. The Reds asserted, among other things, the defense of assumption of risk—that is, that Wattenbarger, by participating in the tryout, had assumed the risk of injury—and filed a motion for summary judgment. The court granted the motion, and Wattenbarger appealed to a state appellate court.

(Continued)

Case 8.5—continued

IN THE WORDS OF THE COURT . . .
PUGLIA, Presiding Justice.

* * * *

* * * [A]ssumption of risk occurs where a plaintiff voluntarily participates in a sporting event or activity involving certain inherent risks. * * *

* * * *

Had plaintiff stopped after his third pitch of the simulated game, we would have no difficulty finding * * * assumption of risk a bar to recovery.

* * *

However, the incident did not end with the third pitch. * * * [W]hen plaintiff * * * informed the Reds' personnel his arm had "popped," he was seeking guidance as to how to proceed. Hearing nothing to countermand the original instruction to pitch, * * * plaintiff threw another pitch, thereby causing further injury.

* * * *

* * * [D]efendants were not co-participants in the sport or activity but were instead in control of it. Defendants decided what would be done and when. They controlled the simulated game * * *.

Under these circumstances, defendants owed a duty to plaintiff and the other participants not to increase the risks * * *.

DECISION AND REMEDY   Concluding that there were factual issues to be resolved at trial, the California Court of Appeal remanded the case to the lower court for further proceedings.

FOR CRITICAL ANALYSIS—CULTURAL CONSIDERATION   *Baseball team managers are aware that young potential players, such as Wattenbarger, sometimes face significant cultural pressure to succeed in the sport. How does this knowledge affect baseball managers' duty of care during tryouts?*

CONTRIBUTORY NEGLIGENCE.   All individuals are expected to exercise a reasonable degree of care in looking out for themselves. In a few jurisdictions, recovery for injury resulting from negligence is prevented if the plaintiff was also negligent (failed to exercise a reasonable degree of care). This is the defense of **contributory negligence.** Under the doctrine of contributory negligence, no matter how insignificant the plaintiff's negligence is relative to the defendant's negligence, the plaintiff will be precluded from recovering any damages.

An exception to the doctrine of contributory negligence may apply if the defendant failed to take advantage of an opportunity to avoid causing the damage. Under the "last clear chance" rule, the plaintiff may recover full damages despite his or her own negligence. For example, if Murphy walks across the street against the light, and Lewis, a motorist, sees her in time to avoid hitting her but hits her anyway, Lewis (the defendant) is not permitted to use Murphy's (the plaintiff's) prior negligence as a defense. The defendant negligently missed the opportunity to avoid injuring the plaintiff. In those states that have adopted the comparative negligence rule, discussed next, the last clear chance doctrine does not apply.

COMPARATIVE NEGLIGENCE.   The majority of states now allow recovery based on the doctrine of **comparative negligence.** This doctrine enables both the

Contributory Negligence A theory in tort law under which a complaining party's own negligence contributed to or caused his or her injuries. Contributory negligence is an absolute bar to recovery in a minority of jurisdictions.

Comparative Negligence A theory in tort law under which the liability for injuries resulting from negligent acts is shared by all parties who were negligent (including the injured party), on the basis of each person's proportionate negligence.

plaintiff's and the defendant's negligence to be computed and the liability for damages distributed accordingly. Some jurisdictions have adopted a "pure" form of comparative negligence that allows the plaintiff to recover, even if the extent of his or her fault is greater than that of the defendant. For example, if the plaintiff was 80 percent at fault and the defendant 20 percent at fault, the plaintiff may recover 20 percent of his or her damages. Many states' comparative negligence statutes, however, contain a "50 percent" rule by which the plaintiff recovers nothing if he or she was more than 50 percent at fault. In the following case, the court had to determine the meaning of a particular state's comparative negligence statute.

Case 8.6 ⬤ Rodgers v. American Honda Motor Co.

United States Court of Appeals,
First Circuit, 1995.
46 F.3d 1.

HISTORICAL AND INTERNATIONAL SETTING
Since the nineteenth century, many civil law jurisdictions—including Austria, China, France, Germany, Japan, Portugal, Spain, Switzerland, and Turkey—have apportioned damages in accident cases according to a comparative fault doctrine. In 1945, Great Britain, a common law jurisdiction, began to apply comparative negligence in its accident cases. Britain's law has been followed in Australia, Canada, New Zealand, and Northern Ireland. In the United States, the first state to adopt a comparative negligence doctrine was Mississippi, in 1910. The doctrine has since been adopted in most of the states.

BACKGROUND AND FACTS   Brian Rodgers, an experienced all-terrain-vehicle (ATV) rider, helped a friend repair a three-wheel ATV. Without putting on a helmet, Rodgers gave the ATV a trial run. It flipped, and Rodgers struck his head, causing injuries to his brain. Rodgers's wife, Debra, and his other guardian filed a suit in a Maine state court against the American Honda Motor Company, the manufacturer of the ATV. During the trial, the plaintiffs asked the court to exclude testimony that Rodgers had not been wearing a helmet. The court ruled that the testimony was admissible, and the plaintiffs appealed to the U.S. Court of Appeals for the First Circuit.

IN THE WORDS OF THE COURT . . .
    BAILEY ALDRICH, Senior Circuit Judge.
        * * * *
    Analysis of the statute persuades us that the [state] court was correct. It provides, in relevant part,
        * * * Where damages are recoverable by any person by virtue of this section, * * * the court shall * * * reduce the total damages * * * to the extent deemed just and equitable, having regard to the claimant's share in the responsibility for the damages * * * .
    If such claimant is found by the jury to be equally at fault, the claimant shall not recover.
        * * * The first consideration that struck us was the rigidity of the final, all-important cut-off paragraph as against the sensitivity of the language preceding it. * * * The change in tone was apparently felt by the Maine court as well. It observed, "This paragraph was not found in the original draft of the Bill considered by the Legislature and is quite obviously the result of a political compromise." Striking "at fault," and substituting "responsible for the damage sustained," the court proceeded to interpret the paragraph as saying, "If in the apportionment process such claimant is found by the jury to be equally responsible for the damage sustained or more responsible for the damage sustained than the defendant, the claimant shall not recover."

(Continued)

Case 8.6—continued

DECISION AND REMEDY   The U.S. Court of Appeals for the First Circuit affirmed the ruling of the trial court. The appellate court added that because "the uncontradicted evidence that plaintiff's failure to wear a helmet was responsible for essentially all the damage sustained, this reading of the statute is fatal to his case."

FOR CRITICAL ANALYSIS—INTERNATIONAL CONSIDERATION
When the plaintiff lives in one country and the defendant in another, and the respective countries use different formulas for measuring comparative negligence, which formula should be applied?

Special Negligence Doctrines and Statutes

There are a number of special doctrines and statutes relating to negligence. We examine a few of them here.

RES IPSA LOQUITUR.   Generally, in lawsuits involving negligence, the plaintiff has the burden of proving that the defendant was negligent. In certain situations, when negligence is very difficult or impossible to prove, the courts may infer that negligence has occurred, in which case the burden of proof rests on the defendant—to prove he or she was *not* negligent. The inference of the defendant's negligence is known as the doctrine of *res ipsa loquitur,* which translates as "the facts speak for themselves." This doctrine is applied only when the event creating the damage or injury is one that ordinarily does not occur in the absence of negligence. *Res ipsa loquitur* has been applied to such events as trains derailing, wheels falling off moving vehicles, and bricks or windowpanes falling from a defendant's premises. For the doctrine to apply, the event must have been within the defendant's power to control, and it must not have been due to any voluntary action or contribution on the part of the plaintiff. Some courts will add still another condition—that the evidence available to explain the event be more accessible to the defendant than to the plaintiff.

Res Ipsa Loquitur A doctrine under which negligence may be inferred simply because an event occurred, if it is the type of event that would not occur in the absence of negligence. Literally, the term means "the facts speak for themselves."

NEGLIGENCE PER SE.   Certain conduct, whether it consists of an action or a failure to act, may be treated as **negligence** *per se* ("in or of itself"). Negligence *per se* may occur if an individual violates a statute or an ordinance providing for a criminal penalty and that violation causes another to be injured. The injured person must prove (1) that the statute clearly sets out what standard of conduct is expected, when and where it is expected, and of whom it is expected; (2) that he or she is in the class intended to be protected by the statute; and (3) that the statute was designed to prevent the type of injury that he or she suffered. The standard of conduct required by the statute is the duty that the defendant owes to the plaintiff, and a violation of the statute is the breach of that duty.

Negligence *Per Se* An act (or failure to act) in violation of a statutory requirement.

For example, a statute may require a landowner to keep a building in a safe condition and may also subject the landowner to a criminal penalty, such as a fine, if the building is not kept safe. The statute is meant to protect those who are rightfully in the building. Thus, if the owner, without a sufficient excuse, violates the statute and a tenant is thereby injured, then a majority of courts will hold that the owner's unexcused violation of the statute conclusively establishes negligence—that is, that the owner's violation is negligence *per se.*

SPECIAL NEGLIGENCE STATUTES.   A number of states have enacted statutes prescribing duties and responsibilities in certain circumstances, the violation of which will impose civil liability. For example, most states now have what are

Good Samaritan Statute A state statute that provides that persons who rescue or provide emergency services to others in peril—unless they do so recklessly, thus causing further harm—cannot be sued for negligence.

Dram Shop Act A state statute that imposes liability on the owners of bars and taverns, as well as those who serve alcoholic drinks to the public, for injuries resulting from accidents caused by intoxicated persons when the sellers or servers of alcoholic drinks contributed to the intoxication.

Strict Liability Liability regardless of fault. In tort law, strict liability may be imposed on defendants in cases involving abnormally dangerous activities, dangerous animals, or defective products.

called **Good Samaritan statutes.** Under these statutes, persons who are aided voluntarily by others cannot turn around and sue the "Good Samaritans" for negligence. These laws were passed largely to protect physicians and medical personnel who voluntarily render their services in emergency situations to those in need, such as individuals hurt in car accidents.

Many states have also passed **dram shop acts,** under which a tavern owner or bartender may be held liable for injuries caused by a person who became intoxicated while drinking at the bar or who was already intoxicated when served by the bartender. In some states, statutes impose liability on *social hosts* (persons hosting parties) for injuries caused by guests who became intoxicated at the hosts' homes. Under these statutes, it is unnecessary to prove that the tavern owner, bartender, or social host was negligent.

Strict Liability

Another category of torts is called **strict liability,** or *liability without fault.* Intentional torts and torts of negligence involve acts that depart from a reasonable standard of care and cause injuries. Under the doctrine of strict liability, liability for injury is imposed for reasons other than fault. Strict liability for damages proximately caused by an abnormally dangerous or exceptional activity is one application of this doctrine. Courts apply the doctrine of strict liability in such cases because of the extreme risk of the activity. For example, even if blasting with dynamite is performed with all reasonable care, there is still a risk of injury. Balancing that risk against the potential for harm, it is fair to ask the person engaged in the activity to pay for injury caused by that activ-

Ethical Perspective

Many people question the fairness of state statutes that impose liability on social hosts for injuries caused by guests' intoxication. The trend has been to permit such suits, and currently nearly half of the states allow plaintiffs injured in car accidents to sue social hosts—those who served alcoholic beverages to the defendants. Sometimes, the definition of a "social host" is fashioned broadly. For example, in one case, a person who hosted a "bring your own bottle" party was held liable for injuries caused by a drunken guest.[a] In another case, a passenger in a car who gave the driver an alcoholic beverage was held liable, even though the driver was sober at that time.[b]

The Illinois Supreme Court recently "went against the wind" on this issue when it affirmed the long-established

precedent in that state of not permitting social hosts to be liable for their guests' harmful behavior. The court stated that allowing such suits would open a "Pandora's Box of unlimited liability" in which plaintiffs' attorneys could "drag into court any and all adults who may qualify as a social host." According to the Illinois court, the victims of drunk driving "have always had, and will continue to have, a civil remedy. They can sue the drunk driver, who is undoubtedly at fault. We have not been presented with any evidence to suggest that this civil remedy is insufficient."[c]

For Critical Analysis: *Explain the differences in the number of lawsuits brought and their outcomes under the "social host" doctrine as opposed to the rule stated by the Illinois court.*

a.   *Dower v. Gamba,* 276 N.J.Super. 319, 647 A.2d 1364 (1994).
b.   *Wheeler v. Murphy,* 452 S.E.2d 416 (W.Va. 1994).

c.   *Charles v. Seigfried,* 165 Ill.2d 482, 651 N.E.2d 154, 209 Ill.Dec. 226 (1995).

A building is torn down by a demolition crew. If a passerby is injured by falling debris, would the doctrine of strict liability apply? Why or why not?

ity. Although there is no fault, there is still responsibility because of the dangerous nature of the undertaking.

There are other applications of the strict liability principle. Persons who keep dangerous animals, for example, are strictly liable for any harm inflicted by the animals. A significant application of strict liability is in the area of *product liability*—liability of manufacturers and sellers for harmful or defective products. Liability here is a matter of social policy and is based on two factors: (1) the manufacturing company can better bear the cost of injury, because it can spread the cost throughout society by increasing prices of goods and services, and (2) the manufacturing company is making a profit from its activities and therefore should bear the cost of injury as an operating expense. We will discuss product liability in greater detail in Chapter 10.

In the following case, the issue before the court is whether a fumigation company should be held strictly liable for injuries caused by the Vikane gas that the company used during the fumigation of a condominium complex.

> **REMEMBER** A business may be considered to have an ethical duty to consumers that goes beyond its legal duty.

Case 8.7 ● Old Island Fumigation, Inc. v. Barbee

District Court of Appeal of Florida, Third District, 1992.
604 So.2d 1246.

HISTORICAL AND SOCIAL SETTING *The early law of torts was not primarily concerned with whether a wrongdoer was at fault but rather with keeping the peace—providing a remedy in lieu of private vengeance. At that time, a person who hurt another by accident, or even in self-defense, was required to pay for the injury or damage. The rule was "he who breaks must*

pay." Gradually, the law came to recognize fault as the basis for imposing liability, and it was suggested that there should be no liability without fault. In the late nineteenth century, however, the law began to accept that in some cases, a defendant may be liable not only in the absence of fault but even if he or she has followed a standard of reasonable care. In the context of abnormally dangerous activities, the courts recognized a new doctrine: in the event of harm for which no one is at fault, the party who can best bear the loss will be held liable.

(Continued)

Case 8.7—continued

BACKGROUND AND FACTS Old Island Fumigation, Inc., fumigated Buildings A and B of a condominium complex. Residents in Buildings A and B were evacuated during the procedure, but occupants of Building C were not. Shortly after the fumigation, which involved the use of Vikane gas, several residents of Building C became ill and were treated for sulfuryl fluoride poisoning. Sulfuryl fluoride is the active ingredient of Vikane gas. Several months later, an architect discovered that the fire wall between Buildings B and C was defective and contained an open space measuring four feet by eighteen inches, through which the gas had entered Building C. The defect was visible only from within the crawl space, and thus it had been missed by various building inspectors, as well as by the fumigating company. Residents of Building C sued Old Island in a Florida state court, alleging that fumigation was an ultrahazardous activity and that Old Island was therefore strictly liable for their injuries. The company asserted that it should not be responsible for injuries caused by the negligence of others—the original architect and contractors for the condominiums, who had failed to note and repair the defect in the fire wall. The trial court granted the plaintiffs' motion for summary judgment against Old Island, and Old Island appealed.

IN THE WORDS OF THE COURT . . .
PER CURIAM [by the whole court].
* * * *

Old Island Fumigation, Inc., is strictly liable for damages caused to the plaintiffs by its fumigation of the condominium complex. Fumigation is an ultrahazardous activity as it "necessarily involves a risk of serious harm * * * which cannot be eliminated by the exercise of the utmost care, and is not a matter of common usage." [F]actors to be considered in determining whether [the] activity is [an] ultrahazardous activity are: whether [the] activity involves [a] high degree of risk of harm to property of others; whether [the] potential harm is likely to be great; whether [the] risk can be eliminated by exercise of reasonable care; whether [the] activity is [a] matter of common usage; whether [the] activity is appropriate to [the] place where [the activity is] conducted; [and] whether [the] activity has substantial value to [the] community. Old Island Fumigation is thus liable regardless of the level of care exercised in carrying out this activity.

Any alleged negligence by a third party does not free the fumigation company from liability.

DECISION AND REMEDY The District Court of Appeal of Florida affirmed the trial court's judgment.

FOR CRITICAL ANALYSIS—SOCIAL CONSIDERATION *Do you agree that business firms should bear the cost of injuries, even though the firms were not at fault, simply because the firms can spread the cost throughout society by increasing the prices of their goods or services?*

Key Terms

actionable 218
actual malice 221
assault 216
battery 217
business invitee 226
causation in fact 231
comparative negligence 235
compensatory damages 228

contributory negligence 235
conversion 224
defamation 218
dram shop act 238
duty of care 225
fraudulent misrepresentation (fraud) 222
Good Samaritan statute 238

intentional tort 215
libel 218
malpractice 228
negligence 224
negligence *per se* 237
privilege 221
proximate cause 231
puffery 222

Chapter Summary
Torts and Strict Liability

INTENTIONAL TORTS AGAINST PERSONS (See pages 215–222.)	1. **Assault and battery**—An assault is an unexcused and intentional act that causes another person to be apprehensive of immediate harm. A battery is an assault that results in physical contact.
	2. **False imprisonment**—The intentional confinement or restraint of another person's movement without justification.
	3. **Infliction of emotional distress**—An intentional act that amounts to extreme and outrageous conduct resulting in severe emotional distress to another.
	4. **Defamation (libel or slander)**—A false statement of fact, not made under privilege, that is communicated to a third person and that causes damage to a person's reputation. For public figures, the plaintiff must also prove actual malice.
	5. **Invasion of privacy**—The use of a person's name or likeness for commercial purposes without permission, wrongful intrusion into a person's private activities, publication of information that places a person in a false light, or disclosure of private facts that an ordinary person would find objectionable.
	6. **Misrepresentation—fraud (deceit)**—A false representation made by one party, through misstatement of facts or through conduct, with the intention of deceiving another and on which the other reasonably relies to his or her detriment.
INTENTIONAL TORTS AGAINST PROPERTY (See pages 222–224.)	1. **Trespass to land**—The invasion of another's real property without consent or privilege. Specific rights and duties apply once a person is expressly or impliedly established as a trespasser.
	2. **Trespass to personal property**—Unlawfully damaging or interfering with the owner's right to use, possess, or enjoy his or her personal property.
	3. **Conversion**—A wrongful act in which personal property is taken from its rightful owner or possessor and placed in the service of another.
UNINTENTIONAL TORTS—NEGLIGENCE (See pages 224–238.)	1. **Negligence**—The careless performance of a legally required duty or the failure to perform a legally required act. Elements that must be proved are that a legal duty of care exists, that the defendant breached that duty, and that the breach caused damage or injury to another.
	2. **Defenses to negligence**—The basic defenses in negligence cases are (a) assumption of risk, (b) contributory negligence, and (c) comparative negligence.
	3. **Special negligence doctrines and statutes**— a. *Res ipsa loquitur*—A doctrine under which a plaintiff need not prove negligence on the part of the defendant because "the facts speak for

(Continued)

Chapter Summary, continued

UNINTENTIONAL TORTS—NEGLIGENCE— CONTINUED (See pages 224–238.)	themselves." *Res ipsa loquitur* has been applied to such events as trains derailing, wheels falling off moving vehicles, and elevators falling. b. **Negligence *per se*—**A type of negligence that may occur if a person violates a statute or an ordinance providing for a criminal penalty and the violation causes another to be injured. c. **Special negligence statutes—**State statutes that prescribe duties and responsibilities in certain circumstances, the violation of which will impose civil liability. Dram shop acts and Good Samaritan statutes are examples of special negligence statutes.
STRICT LIABILITY (See pages 238–240.)	Under the doctrine of strict liability, a person may be held liable, regardless of the degree of care exercised, for damages or injuries caused by his or her product or activity. Strict liability includes liability for harms caused by abnormally dangerous activities, by wild animals, and by defective products (product liability).

For Review

1. What is the function of tort law?
2. What must a public figure prove to succeed in a defamation suit?
3. What are the four elements of negligence?
4. What defenses are available in an action for negligence?
5. What is strict liability? In what circumstances might this doctrine be applied?

Questions and Case Problems

8–1. Defenses to Negligence. Corinna was riding her bike on a city street. While she was riding, she frequently looked behind her to verify that the books that she had fastened to the rear part of her bike were still attached. On one occasion while she was looking behind her, she failed to notice a car that was entering an intersection just as she was crossing it. The car hit her, causing her to sustain numerous injuries. Three witnesses stated that the driver of the car had failed to stop at the stop sign before entering the intersection. Corinna sued the driver of the car for negligence. What defenses might the defendant driver raise in this lawsuit? Discuss fully.

8–2. Liability to Business Invitees. Kim went to Ling's Market to pick up a few items for dinner. It was a rainy, windy day, and the wind had blown water through the door of Ling's Market each time the door opened. As Kim entered through the door, she slipped and fell in the approximately one-half inch of rainwater that had accumulated on the floor. The manager knew of the weather conditions but had not posted any sign to warn customers of the water hazard. Kim injured her back as a result of the fall and sued Ling's for damages. Can Ling's be held liable for negligence in this situation? Discuss.

8–3. Negligence. In which of the following situations will the acting party be liable for the tort of negligence? Explain fully.

(a) Mary goes to the golf course on Sunday morning, eager to try out a new set of golf clubs she has just purchased. As she tees off on the first hole, the head of her club flies off and injures a nearby golfer.

(b) Mary's doctor gives her some pain medication and tells her not to drive after she takes it, as the medication induces drowsiness. In spite of the doctor's warning, Mary decides to drive to the store while on the medication. Owing to her lack of alertness, she fails to stop at a traffic light and crashes into another vehicle, in which a passenger is injured.

8–4. Causation. Ruth carelessly parks her car on a steep hill, leaving the car in neutral and failing to engage the parking brake. The car rolls down the hill, knocking down an electric line. The sparks from the broken line ignite a grass fire. The fire spreads until it reaches a barn one mile away. The barn houses dynamite, and the burning barn explodes, causing part of the roof to fall on and injure a passing motorist, Jim. Can Jim recover from Ruth? Why or why not?

8–5. Trespass to Land. During a severe snowstorm, Yoshiko parked his car in a privately owned parking lot. The car was later towed from the lot, and Yoshiko had to pay $100 to the towing company to recover his car. Yoshiko sued the owner of the parking lot, Icy Holdings, Inc., to get back the $100 he had paid. Icy Holdings claimed that notwithstanding the severe snowstorm, Yoshiko's parking of his car on its property constituted trespass, and therefore Icy Holdings did not act wrongfully in having the car towed off the lot. Discuss whether Yoshiko can recover his $100.

8–6. Tort Theories. The Yommers operated a gasoline station. In December 1967, the McKenzies, their neighbors, noticed a smell in their well water, which proved to be caused by gasoline in the water. McKenzie complained to the Yommers, who arranged to have one of their underground storage tanks replaced. Nevertheless, the McKenzies were unable to use their water for cooking or bathing until they had a filter and water softener installed. At the time of the trial, in December 1968, they were still bringing in drinking water from an outside source. The McKenzies sued the Yommers for damages. The Yommers claimed that the McKenzies had not proved that there was any intentional wrongdoing or negligence on the part of the Yommers, and therefore they should not be held liable. Under what theory might the McKenzies recover damages even in the absence of any negligence on the Yommers' part? Explain. [*Yommer v. McKenzie*, 255 Md. 220, 257 A.2d 138 (1969)]

8–7. Defenses to Negligence. George Giles was staying at a Detroit hotel owned by the Pick Hotels Corp. While a hotel employee was removing luggage from the back seat of Giles's car, Giles reached into the front seat to remove his briefcase. As he did so, he supported himself by placing his left hand on the center pillar to which the rear door was hinged, with his fingers in a position to be injured if the rear door was closed. The hotel employee closed the rear door, and a part of Giles's left index finger was amputated. Giles sued the hotel for damages. What defense or defenses against negligence discussed in this chapter might relieve the hotel, partially or totally, from liability for Giles's injury? Explain fully. [*Giles v. Pick Hotels Corp.*, 232 F.2d 887 (6th Cir. 1956)]

8–8. Strict Liability. Danny and Marion Klein were injured when an aerial shell at a public fireworks exhibit went astray and exploded near them. They sued the Pyrodyne Corp., the pyrotechnic company that was hired to set up and discharge the fireworks, alleging, among other things, that the company should be strictly liable for damages caused by the fireworks display. Will the court agree with the Kleins? What factors will the court consider in making its decision? Discuss fully. [*Klein v. Pyrodyne Corp.*, 117 Wash.2d 1, 810 P.2d 917 (1991)]

8–9. Duty to Business Invitees. George Ward entered a K-Mart department store in Champaign, Illinois, through a service entrance near the home improvements department. After purchasing a large mirror, Ward left the store through the same door. On his way out the door, carrying the large mirror in front and somewhat to the side of him, he collided with a concrete pole located just outside the door about a foot and a half from the outside wall. The mirror broke, and the broken glass cut Ward's right cheek and eye, resulting in reduced vision in that eye. He later stated that he had not seen the pole, had not realized what was happening, and only knew that he felt "a bad pain, and then saw stars." Ward sued K-Mart Corp. for damages, alleging that the store was negligent. What was the nature of K-Mart's duty of care to Ward? Did it breach that duty by placing the concrete pole just outside the door? What factors should the court consider when deciding whether K-Mart should be held liable for Ward's injuries? Discuss fully. [*Ward v. K-Mart Corp.*, 136 Ill.2d 132, 554 N.E.2d 223, 143 Ill.Dec. 288 (1990)]

8–10. Duty of Care. As pedestrians exited at the close of an arts and crafts show, Jason Davis, an employee of the show's producer, stood near the exit. Suddenly and without warning, Davis turned around and collided with Yvonne Esposito, an eighty-year-old woman. Esposito was knocked to the ground, fracturing her hip. After hip-replacement surgery, she was left with a permanent physical impairment. Esposito filed a suit in a federal district court against Davis and others, alleging negligence. What are the factors that indicate whether or not Davis owed Esposito a duty of care? What do those factors indicate in these circumstances? [*Esposito v. Davis*, 47 F.3d 164 (5th Cir. 1995)]

8–11. Negligence *Per Se.* A North Carolina Department of Transportation regulation prohibits the placement of telephone booths within public rights of way. Despite this regulation, GTE South, Inc., placed a booth in the right of way near the intersection of Hillsborough and Sparger Roads in Durham County. Laura Baldwin was using the booth when an accident at the intersection caused a dump truck to cross the right of way and smash into the booth. To recover for her injuries, Baldwin filed a suit in a North Carolina state court against GTE and others. Was Baldwin within the class of persons protected by the regulation? If so, did GTE's placement of the booth constitute negligence *per se*? [*Baldwin v. GTE South, Inc.*, 335 N.C. 544, 439 S.E.2d 108 (1995)]

A Question of Ethics and Social Responsibility

8–12.   Ernesto Parra choked to death on a piece of food while eating at a restaurant. The administrator of Parra's estate sued the restaurant, claiming, among other things, that the restaurant breached its duty to rescue Parra while he was choking. The court stressed that under the common law, there is no general duty to aid a person in peril. If Parra had been injured by a dangerous condition in the restaurant, such as a slippery floor, then the restaurant would have had a duty to come to Parra's assistance and ensure that he received any medical treatment necessary. The restaurant, however, had not been responsible for placing Parra in danger; the fact that Parra choked was totally personal to Parra. According to the court, "As a general rule, a restaurateur is not an insurer of his customers' safety against all personal injuries. He has no duty as to 'conditions or risks which are ordinary and are, or should be, known or obvious to the patrons.'" [*Parra v. Tarasco, Inc.*, 230 Ill.App.3d 819, 595 N.E.2d 1186, 172 Ill.Dec. 516 (1992)]

1. Do you agree with the court's decision that the restaurant had no duty to rescue Parra? Why or why not?

2. Do you think that the law should impose a duty on all persons to rescue others in distress? What would be some of the implications of such a law for society? Discuss fully.

Case Briefing Assignment

8–13.   Examine Case A.3 [*Burlingham v. Mintz*, 891 P.2d 527 (Mont. 1995)] in Appendix A. The case has been excerpted there in great detail. Review and then brief the case, making sure that you include answers to the following questions in your brief.

1. Who were the plaintiff and defendant in this action?
2. Describe the events that led up to this lawsuit.
3. What was the central issue on appeal?
4. How did the state supreme court rule on this issue and dispose of the case?

For Critical Analysis

8–14.   What general principle underlies the common law doctrine that business owners have a duty of care toward their customers? Does the duty of care unfairly burden business owners? Why or why not?

INTERACTING WITH
The Internet

■ Within the legal interest group on the commercial service America Online, there is a subcategory on torts and contracts. If you subscribe to America Online, the key word is

LEGAL

■ Standards established by professional associations play an important role in determining the minimum standard of care expected of the members of those professions—and thus are an important factor in negligence cases. You can locate the professional standards for various professional organizations at the following Internet site:

http://www.lib.uwaterloo.ca/society/standards.html

■ Cornell Law School also provides business and professional codes for a number of states. To find these, go to

http://www.law.cornell.edu/statutes.html#state

CHAPTER 9

Basic Business Torts

Contents

Chapter Objectives

After reading this chapter, you should be able to . . .

1. Identify the circumstances in which a party will be held liable for the tort of wrongful interference.

2. Explain how the tort of appropriation occurs.

3. State when the tort of disparagement of property occurs.

4. List activities prohibited by RICO.

5. Describe civil liability under RICO.

Business Tort The wrongful interference with another's business rights.

Our economic system of free enterprise is predicated on the ability of businesspersons to compete for customers and for sales. Unfettered competitive behavior has been shown to lead to economic efficiency and economic progress. Businesses may, generally speaking, engage in whatever is *reasonably* necessary to obtain a fair share of a market or to recapture a share that has been lost. They are not allowed to use the motive of completely eliminating competition to justify certain business activities, however. Thus, an entire area of what is called business torts has arisen.

As the opening quotation indicates, businesspersons need to know what the law is if they are to obey it. Remember that a tort is a breach of a duty owed to an individual or to a group. As mentioned in Chapter 8, many of the torts discussed there also occur in the business context. In Chapter 10, we will look at product liability, which also involves tort actions. Certain other torts that relate to business will be treated in Chapter 11. The torts examined here, in Chapter 9, traditionally have been referred to as **business torts,** which are defined as wrongful interferences with the business rights of others. Included in business torts are such vaguely worded concepts as *unfair competition* and *wrongfully interfering with the business relations of others.*

We restrict our discussion in this chapter to the following causes of action:

1. Wrongful interference with another's business rights.
2. Appropriation of another's name or likeness without permission.
3. Disparagement of business property or reputation.
4. Business defamation in cyberspace.

Following our discussion of these torts, we consider the application of the Racketeer Influenced and Corrupt Organizations Act (known more popularly as RICO) to fraudulent and other unlawful business activities.

Wrongful Interference

Torts involving wrongful interference with another's business rights generally fall into two categories—interference with a contractual relationship and interference with a business relationship.

Wrongful Interference with a Contractual Relationship

The body of tort law relating to *wrongful interference with a contractual relationship* has increased greatly in recent years. A landmark case in this area involved an opera singer, Joanna Wagner, who was under contract to sing for a man named Lumley for a specified period of years.[1] A man named Gye, who knew of this contract, nonetheless "enticed" Wagner to refuse to carry out the agreement, and Wagner began to sing for Gye. Gye's action constituted a tort, because it interfered with the contractual relationship between Wagner and Lumley. (Of course, Wagner's refusal to carry out the agreement also entitled Lumley to sue Wagner for breach of contract.)

In principle, any lawful contract can be the basis for an action of this type. The plaintiff must prove that the defendant actually knew of the contract's existence and intentionally *induced* the breach of the contractual relationship,

---

1. *Lumley v. Gye,* 118 Eng.Rep. 749 (1853).

not merely that the defendant reaped the benefits of a broken contract. For example, suppose that Kharkhin has a contract with Sutton that calls for Sutton to do gardening work on Kharkhin's large estate every week for fifty-two weeks at a specified price per week. Minnick, who needs gardening services, contacts Sutton and offers to pay Sutton a wage that is substantially higher than that offered by Kharkhin—although Minnick knows nothing about the Sutton-Kharkhin contract. Sutton breaches his contract with Kharkhin so that he can work for Minnick. Kharkhin cannot sue Minnick, because Minnick knew nothing of the Sutton-Kharkhin contract and was totally unaware that the higher wage he offered induced Sutton to breach that contract.

Three elements are necessary for wrongful interference with a contractual relationship to occur:

1. A valid, enforceable contract must exist between two parties.
2. A third party must *know* that this contract exists.
3. This third party must *intentionally* cause one of the two parties to the contract to break the contract, and the interference must be for the purpose of advancing the economic interest of the third party.

The contract may be between a firm and its employees or a firm and its customers, suppliers, competitors, or other parties. Sometimes a competitor of a firm draws away a key employee. If the original employer can show that the competitor induced the breach of the employment contract—that is, that the employee would not normally have broken the contract—damages can be recovered. In a famous case in the 1980s, Texaco, Inc., was found to have wrongfully interfered with an agreement between the Pennzoil Company and the Getty Oil Company. After Pennzoil had agreed to purchase a portion of Getty Oil, Texaco made an offer to purchase Getty Oil, and Getty Oil accepted Texaco's offer. Pennzoil then successfully sued Texaco for wrongful interference with Pennzoil's contractual relationship with Getty Oil.[2]

Wrongful Interference with a Business Relationship

Individuals devise countless schemes to attract business, but they are forbidden by the courts to interfere unreasonably with another's business in their attempts to gain a share of the market. There is a difference between *competition* and *predatory behavior*. The distinction usually depends on whether a business is attempting to attract customers in general or to solicit only those customers who have already shown an interest in the similar product or service of a specific competitor. If a shopping center contains two shoe stores, an employee of Store A cannot be positioned at the entrance of Store B for the purpose of diverting customers to Store A. This type of activity constitutes the tort of wrongful interference with a business relationship, often referred to as interference with a prospective (economic) advantage, and it is commonly considered to be an unfair trade practice. If this type of activity were permitted, Store A would reap the benefits of Store B's advertising.

McDonald's golden arches. Would it be a tort for a competitor to advertise so effectively that this business's usual patrons are diverted to the competitor's location?

2. *Texaco, Inc. v. Pennzoil Co.,* 725 S.W.2d 768 (Tex.App.—Houston [1st Dist.] 1987), writ ref'd n.r.e.). (Generally, a complete Texas Court of Appeals citation includes a writ-of-error history showing the Texas Supreme Court's disposition of the case. In this case, "writ ref'd n.r.e." is an abbreviation for "writ refused, no reversible error," which means that Texas's highest court refused to grant the appellant's request to review the case, because the court did not consider there to be any reversible error.)

> **REMEMBER** What society and the law consider permissible often depends on the circumstances.

"Anyone can win unless there happens to be a second entry."

George Ade, 1866–1944 (American humorist)

Generally, a plaintiff must prove the following elements to recover damages for the tort of wrongful interference with a business relationship:

1. There was an established business relationship.
2. The tortfeasor (one who causes a tort), by use of predatory methods, intentionally caused this business relationship to end.
3. The plaintiff suffered damages as a result of the tortfeasor's actions.

Defenses to Wrongful Interference

A person will not be liable for the tort of wrongful interference with a contractual or business relationship if it can be shown that the interference was justified, or permissible. Bona fide competitive behavior is a permissible interference even if it results in the breaking of a contract. If Jerrod's Meats advertises so effectively that it induces Sam's Restaurant to break its contract with Burke's Meat Company, Burke's Meat Company will be unable to recover against Jerrod's Meats on a wrongful interference theory. After all, the public policy that favors free competition in advertising definitely outweighs any possible instability that such competitive activity might cause in contractual relations. Therefore, although luring customers away from a competitor through aggressive marketing and advertising strategies obviously interferes with the competitor's relationship with his or her customers, such activity is permitted by the courts.

In the following case, two drugstore owners sued Wal-Mart Stores, Inc., alleging that Wal-Mart's sales tactics (selling products below cost, holding frequent sales, and so on) amounted to predatory behavior. Wal-Mart contended that its activities were not predatory and in fact promoted competition.

Case 9.1 ● Wal-Mart Stores, Inc. v. American Drugs, Inc.

Supreme Court of Arkansas, 1995.
319 Ark. 214,
891 S.W.2d 30.

BACKGROUND AND FACTS   Wal-Mart Stores, Inc., prices some of its products below cost. This is known as a loss-leader strategy. Wal-Mart—or any seller who uses this strategy—hopes that the low prices will attract customers who will then buy other, higher-priced products. Part of Wal-Mart's strategy is to change which products it offers below cost in response to competitors' prices for those same products. American Drugs, Inc., and two other competitors of the Conway Wal-Mart Store in Faulkner County, Arkansas, filed a suit in an Arkansas state court against Wal-Mart, alleging that its loss-leader strategy violated the Arkansas Unfair Practices Act.[a] This act prohibits below-cost pricing that is used "for the purpose of injuring competitors and destroying competition." The court ordered Wal-Mart to stop its below-cost sales. Wal-Mart appealed to the Arkansas Supreme Court.

a.   Arkansas Code Sections 4-75-201 *et seq.*

IN THE WORDS OF THE COURT . . .
    BROWN, Justice.
        *   *   *   *

    *   *   *   A firm that cuts its prices or substantially reduces its profit margin is not necessarily engaging in predatory pricing. *   *   * Indeed, there is a real danger in mislabeling such practices as predatory, because consumers

(Continued)

Case 9.1—continued

generally benefit from the low prices resulting from aggressive price competition.

* * * *

* * * [T]he loss-leader strategy employed by Conway Wal-Mart is readily justifiable as a tool to foster competition and to gain a competitive edge as opposed to simply being viewed as a stratagem to eliminate rivals altogether. * * * Certainly legitimate competition in the market place can, and often does, result in economic injury to competitors. A competitor that has been injured by legitimate competitive pricing, though, should not be permitted to use the Arkansas [Unfair Practices] Act as a fountain for recouping its losses. In short, the circumstances of this case are not sufficiently egregious [outstandingly bad] to prove that Conway Wal-Mart crossed the line with regard to predatory prices and purposeful destruction of competition.

DECISION AND REMEDY   The Arkansas Supreme Court held that the use of a loss-leader strategy is not enough to show an intent to destroy competition. The court reversed the order of the lower court and dismissed the suit against Wal-Mart.

FOR CRITICAL ANALYSIS—ETHICAL CONSIDERATION   *Is it fair to absolve Wal-Mart of liability in these circumstances? Why or why not?*

Appropriation

The use of another person's name, likeness, or other identifying characteristic, without permission and for the benefit of the user, is the tort of **appropriation.** Under the law, normally an individual's right to privacy includes the right to the exclusive use of his or her identity. For example, in a case involving a Ford Motor Company television commercial in which a Bette Midler "sound-alike" sang a song that Midler had made famous, the court held that Ford "for their own profit in selling their product did appropriate part of her identity."[3]

A court ruled similarly in a case brought by Vanna White, the hostess of the popular television game show *Wheel of Fortune,* against Samsung Electronics America, Inc. Without White's permission, Samsung included in an advertisement for Samsung videocassette recorders a depiction of a robot dressed in a wig, gown, and jewelry, posed in a setting that resembled the *Wheel of Fortune* set, in a stance for which White is famous. The court held in White's favor, holding that the tort of appropriation does not require the use of a celebrity's name or likeness. The court stated that Samsung's robot ad left "little doubt" as to the identity of the celebrity that the ad was meant to depict.[4]

Often, cases alleging appropriation require the courts to balance a celebrity's right to the exclusive use of his or her identity against the First Amendment right to freedom of speech. For example, in one case, a California newspaper reproduced in poster form pages from various issues that contained photographs and an artist's renditions of Joe Montana, who was at that time a well-known professional quarterback. In Montana's suit against the newspaper for the commercial misappropriation of his name, photograph, and

Appropriation   In tort law, the use by one person of another person's name, likeness, or other identifying characteristic without permission and for the benefit of the user.

An actor impersonates television talk show host Sally Jesse Raphael. Is this exploitation of the celebrity's identity? If so, is this an invasion of a right for which the law provides relief?

---

3.   *Midler v. Ford Motor Co.,* 849 F.2d 460 (9th Cir. 1988).
4.   *White v. Samsung Electronics America, Inc.,* 971 F.2d 1395 (9th Cir. 1992).

likeness, however, the court held that the defendant newspaper's reproduction and sale of the posters was protected speech under the First Amendment.[5]

Other sports-related commercial misappropriation cases have involved the rights of those who invest time and money in the creation and broadcast of sports events. In the following case, the court considered whether the transmission of real-time information about National Basketball Association games in progress via America Online constituted commercial misappropriation.

_____

5.   *Montana v. San Jose Mercury News, Inc.*, 34 Cal.App.4th, 40 Cal.Rptr.2d 639 (1995).

Case 9.2 ● National Basketball Association v. Motorola, Inc.

United States Court of Appeals,
Second Circuit, 1997.
105 F.3d 841.

HISTORICAL AND ECONOMIC SETTING   *The commercial value and appeal of National Basketball Association (NBA) games can be attributed to years of successful promotion. NBA games reach the peak of their value while they are being played. In the mid-1990s, 80 percent of NBA revenues were derived from the sale of broadcast distribution licenses and admission fees to the arenas. The NBA licenses rights to real-time game data to select local, regional, and national media, including television and radio broadcasters, a satellite service, and a company that provides audio descriptions of games via an 800 number.*

BACKGROUND AND FACTS   Sports Team Analysis and Tracking Systems, Inc. (Stats), provides information about sports to the media—including ESPN and NBC Sports—and to the public. One of Stats's methods is to disseminate real-time information about NBA games in progress via its site on America Online, Inc. (AOL). Users who access the site see point-by-point changes in scores, game time remaining, and such player and team statistics as field goals, free throws, rebounds, three-point shots, total points, and minutes played. The information is updated as frequently as every fifteen seconds. Stats does not have the NBA's permission to transmit this information, however. The NBA and NBA Properties, Inc., filed a suit in a federal district court against Stats and others (including Motorola, Inc., which sells pagers that display similar information), alleging, in part, commercial misappropriation. The defendants argued that because they did not replicate entire broadcasts of NBA games, they were doing nothing wrong. The court ruled in favor of the NBA, and the defendants appealed.

IN THE WORDS OF THE COURT . . .
WINTER, Circuit Judge:
    * * * *

We conclude that Motorola and Stats have not engaged in unlawful misappropriation * * * .
    * * * *

With regard to the NBA's primary products—producing basketball games with live attendance and licensing copyrighted broadcasts of those games—there is no evidence that anyone regards [Motorola's pagers] or the AOL site as a substitute for attending NBA games or watching them on television. * * *
    * * * *

* * * The use of pagers to transmit real-time information about NBA games requires: (i) the collecting of facts about the games; (ii) the transmission of these facts on a network; (iii) the assembling of them by the particular service; and (iv) the transmission of them to pagers or an on-line computer site. * * * Motorola and Stats expend their own resources to collect purely factual information generated in NBA games * * * . They have their own network and assemble and transmit data themselves.

(Continued)

Case 9.2—continued

DECISION AND REMEDY The court held that Stats's transmission of real-time NBA game information on AOL did not constitute commercial misappropriation.

FOR CRITICAL ANALYSIS—SOCIAL CONSIDERATION *What would have been the effect on television and radio coverage of sports events if the court had held Stats liable for misappropriation?*

Defamation in the Business Context

As discussed in Chapter 8, the tort of defamation occurs when an individual makes a false statement that injures another's reputation. Defamation may take the form of libel (defamatory statements in written or printed form) or slander (defamatory statements made orally). Defamation becomes a business tort when the defamatory matter injures someone in a profession, business, or trade or when it adversely affects a business entity in its credit rating and other dealings.

Recently, questions have arisen about the potential liability of on-line computer information services, such as CompuServe and Prodigy, for defamatory statements made in sources included in their databases. This chapter's *Inside the Legal Environment* on page 252 focuses on this important issue.

> **"Hurl your calumnies boldly; something is sure to stick."**
>
> Francis Bacon, 1561–1626
> (English philosopher and statesman)

Disparagement of Property

Disparagement of property occurs when economically injurious falsehoods are made not about another's reputation but about another's *product* or *property*. *Disparagement of property* is a general term for torts that can be more specifically referred to as *slander of quality* or *slander of title*.

Slander of Quality

Publishing false information about another's product, alleging it is not what its seller claims, constitutes the tort of **slander of quality**. This tort has also been given the name **trade libel**. The plaintiff must prove that actual damages proximately resulted from the slander of quality. That is, it must be shown not only that a third person refrained from dealing with the plaintiff because of the improper publication but also that the plaintiff suffered damages because the third person refrained from dealing with him or her. The economic calculation of such damages—they are, after all, conjectural—is often extremely difficult.

It is possible for an improper publication to be both a slander of quality and a defamation. For example, a statement that disparages the quality of a product may also, by implication, disparage the character of a person who would sell such a product. In one case, for instance, claiming that a product that was marketed as a sleeping aid contained "habit-forming drugs" was held to constitute defamation.[6]

Disparagement of Property
An economically injurious falsehood made about another's product or property. A general term for torts that are more specifically referred to as slander of quality or slander of title.

Slander of Quality (Trade Libel) The publication of false information about another's product, alleging that it is not what its seller claims.

---

6. *Harwood Pharmacal Co. v. National Broadcasting Co.*, 9 N.Y.2d 460, 174 N.E.2d 602, 214 N.Y.S.2d 725 (1961).

Inside the Legal Environment
Liability for Online Defamation

In today's online world, one of the most significant legal issues regarding defamation in the business context concerns the liability of online service providers (OSPs), such as America Online, CompuServe, and Prodigy. Should OSPs be liable for speech generated by the third party users of their services? The answer to this question depends, in large part, on whether an OSP is classified as a publisher or a distributor.

Traditionally, the courts have held that bookstores, newsstands, and other distributors of books and periodicals have no duty to monitor every book or periodical that they distribute. This would be an unreasonable demand on the seller and a restriction on the public's access to reading matter.[a] Therefore, *distributors* of defamatory materials are not themselves liable for the defamation—unless they happened to know or had reason to know of the defamatory contents. A *publisher*, in contrast, *can* be held liable for defamatory contents in books and periodicals. This is because, under tort law governing defamation, one who repeats or otherwise republishes a defamatory statement is subject to liability as if he or she had originally published it.

THE STATUS OF OSPs

Should OSPs be considered distributors or publishers of information? Two significant cases decided in the 1990s addressed this question. In the first case, *Cubby, Inc. v. CompuServe, Inc.,*[b] the plaintiffs alleged that CompuServe should be held liable for defamatory statements made against them on one of CompuServe's information sources. The court held that CompuServe was a distributor and thus could not be held liable for the defamatory statements *unless* there was a showing that it knew or had reason to know of the statements.

In the second case, *Stratton Oakmont, Inc. v. Prodigy Services Co.,*[c] the court held that Prodigy was a publisher and thus could be held liable for defamatory statements posted on its "Money Talk" bulletin board by an unidentified Prodigy user. The court reached this conclusion largely because Prodigy had held itself out—in its policy statements and in national newspaper articles—as an online service that exercised editorial control over the content of messages posted on it. Prodigy expressly differentiated itself from its competition and likened itself to a newspaper. Prodigy also instructed "board leaders" to monitor bulletin board postings and delete notes from its boards if they were offensive or in "bad taste."

THE COMMUNICATIONS DECENCY ACT

As discussed in Chapter 5, the Communications Decency Act (CDA) was passed in 1996 to regulate the transmission of obscene and pornographic materials. Although the "indecency" provisions of the act have been declared unconstitutional, other provisions have not. Among the CDA's other provisions are those relating to the liability of online service providers.

Section 230(c) of the CDA reads as follows: "No provider or user of an interactive computer service shall be treated as the publisher or speaker of any information provided by another information content provider." Section 230(c) also states that providers and users of interactive computer services are not subject to civil liability "on account of any action taken voluntarily in good faith to restrict access to or availability of" any materials online that the provider deems "objectionable." In other words, an online service provider may not be held liable as a publisher simply because it attempts to exercise editorial control over the content of transmitted materials. The specific purpose of this section of the CDA was to overrule the decision in the *Stratton Oakmont* case.

Section 230(c) does not distinguish between online service providers that have knowledge of defamatory content being transmitted online and providers that do not. Thus, if the words of this section are taken literally, online service providers now have absolute immunity with respect to defamatory statements by third party users of their services.

For Critical Analysis: *What are some of the pros and cons of defining online information services as distributors? As publishers?*

---

a.   *Smith v. California,* 361 U.S. 147, 80 S.Ct. 215, 4 L.Ed.2d 205 (1959).
b.   776 F.Supp. 135 (S.D.N.Y. 1991).
c.   No. 31063/94, Supreme Court of New York, May 24, 1995. This decision is not published in a printed reporter, but may be accessed on WESTLAW by keying in the cite 1995 WL 323710.

A used-car lot. Would this dealer be entitled to damages if its competitors published a false notice that the dealer's stock consisted of stolen autos? If so, how might a court determine the amount?

Slander of Title

When a publication falsely denies or casts doubt on another's legal ownership of property, and when this results in financial loss to the property's owner, the tort of **slander of title** may exist. Usually, this is an intentional tort in which someone knowingly publishes an untrue statement about another's ownership of certain property with the intent of discouraging a third person from dealing with the person slandered. For example, it would be difficult for a car dealer to attract customers after competitors published a notice that the dealer's stock consisted of stolen autos.

Slander of Title The publication of a statement that denies or casts doubt on another's legal ownership of any property, causing financial loss to that property's owner.

RICO

Businesses have often been sued for fraudulent or other tortious activities under the Racketeer Influenced and Corrupt Organizations Act.[7] The act, which is commonly known as RICO, was passed by Congress in 1970 as part of the Organized Crime Control Act. The purpose of the act was to curb the apparently increasing entry of organized crime into the legitimate business world.

Activities Prohibited by RICO

Under RICO, it is a federal crime (1) to use income obtained from racketeering activity to purchase any interest in an enterprise, (2) to acquire or maintain an interest in an enterprise through racketeering activity, (3) to conduct or participate in the affairs of an enterprise through racketeering activity, or (4) to conspire to do any of the preceding activities.

---

7. 18 U.S.C. Sections 1961–1968.

Racketeering activity is not a new type of substantive crime created by RICO; rather, RICO incorporates by reference twenty-six separate types of federal crimes and nine types of state felonies[8] and states that if a person commits two of these offenses, he or she is guilty of "racketeering activity." The act provides for both criminal liability (discussed in Chapter 7) and civil liability.

Civil Liability under RICO

The penalties for violations of the RICO statute are harsh. In the event of a violation, the statute permits the government to seek civil penalties, including the divestiture of a defendant's interest in a business (called forfeiture) or the dissolution of the business. Perhaps the most controversial aspect of RICO is that in some cases, private individuals are allowed to recover three times their actual losses (treble damages), plus attorneys' fees, for business injuries caused by a violation of the statute.

The broad language of RICO has allowed it to be applied in cases that have little or nothing to do with organized crime, and an aggressive trial attorney may attempt to show that any business fraud constitutes "racketeering activity." In its 1985 decision in *Sedima, S.P.R.L. v. Imrex Co.,*[9] the United States Supreme Court interpreted RICO broadly and set a significant precedent for subsequent applications of the act. Plaintiffs have used the RICO statute in numerous commercial fraud cases because of the inviting prospect of being awarded treble damages if they win. The most frequent targets of civil RICO lawsuits are insurance companies, employment agencies, commercial banks, and stockbrokerage firms.

One of the requirements of RICO is that there be more than one offense—there must be a "pattern of racketeering activity." What constitutes a "pattern" has been the subject of much litigation. According to the interpretation of some courts, a pattern must involve, among other things, continued criminal activity. This is known as the "continuity" requirement. Part of this requirement is that the activity occur over a "substantial" period of time. The court in the following case considered whether the actions of the defendants met this requirement.

---

8.   See 18 U.S.C. Section 1961(1)(A).
9.   473 U.S. 479, 105 S.Ct. 3275, 87 L.Ed.2d 346 (1985).

Case 9.3 ● Tabas v. Tabas

United States
Court of Appeals,
Third Circuit, 1995.
47 F.3d 1280.

BACKGROUND AND FACTS Charles and Daniel Tabas formed a partnership to conduct real estate and other business ventures. They agreed that if either partner died, the other would distribute the partnership income equally to

himself and to the estate of the deceased partner. When Charles died, Daniel agreed to mail monthly partnership income checks to Charles's widow, Harriette. Daniel mailed monthly checks in the same amount to himself. In addition, Daniel drew a salary and paid a variety of personal expenses from partnership income. When Harriette and the executors of Charles's estate learned of Daniel's activities, they confronted him, and he agreed to dissolve the partnership and sell the assets. Continuing dissatisfac-

(Continued)

Case 9.3—continued

tion with Daniel's conduct prompted Harriette and the executors (the plaintiffs) to file a suit in a federal district court against Daniel and others (the defendants), alleging, among other things, that acts of fraud over the previous three and a half years constituted violations of RICO.

Daniel filed a motion for summary judgment, which the court granted. The court found no "continuity," reasoning that as soon as the partnership assets were sold, all of the alleged fraud would stop. The plaintiffs appealed.

IN THE WORDS OF THE COURT . . .
ROTH, Circuit Judge:
* * * *

* * * Each time defendants misrepresented the business nature of an expense, made a questionable charge, or received compensation to which they were not entitled, they lessened the income available to the Estate. Plaintiffs have provided evidence that these activities, which implemented defendants' purported scheme to defraud the Estate, lasted more than three and a half years * * * . We conclude that a scheme lasting over three years extends over a "substantial" period of time and therefore constitutes the type of "long-term criminal conduct" that RICO was enacted to address. Accordingly, we find, from the strictly durational aspect of the scheme, that plaintiffs in the present case have made a sufficient showing to survive summary judgment on the "continuity" prong of the pattern analysis.

DECISION AND REMEDY   The U.S. Court of Appeals for the Third Circuit reversed the district court's ruling and remanded the case for further proceedings.

FOR CRITICAL ANALYSIS—ETHICAL CONSIDERATION   *Would it have been fair not to hold the defendants liable under RICO in this case? Why or why not?*

Key Terms

appropriation 249
business tort 246
disparagement of property
  251

slander of quality 253
slander of title 253

trade libel 253

Chapter Summary
Basic Business Torts

WRONGFUL INTERFERENCE (See pages 246–249.)	1. **Wrongful interference with a contractual relationship**—The intentional interference with a valid, enforceable contract by a third party.
	2. **Wrongful interference with a business relationship**—The unreasonable interference by one party with another's business relationship.
APPROPRIATION (See pages 249–251.)	The use by one person of another's name, likeness, or other identifying characteristic, without permission and for the benefit of the user.

(Continued)

Chapter Summary, continued

DEFAMATION IN THE BUSINESS CONTEXT (See pages 251 and 252.)	A false statement that injures someone in a profession, business, or trade or that adversely affects a business entity in its credit rating and other dealings.
DISPARAGEMENT OF PROPERTY (See pages 251 and 253.)	Slanderous or libelous statements made about another's product or property; more specifically referred to as slander of quality (trade libel) or slander of title.
RICO (See pages 253–255.)	The Racketeer Influenced and Corrupt Organizations Act (RICO) of 1970 makes it a federal crime (1) to use income obtained from racketeering activity to purchase any interest in an enterprise, (2) to acquire or maintain an interest in an enterprise through racketeering activity, (3) to conduct or participate in the affairs of an enterprise through racketeering activity, or (4) to conspire to do any of the preceding activities. The broad language of RICO has allowed it to be applied in cases that have little or nothing to do with organized crime.

For Review

1. What elements are necessary to establish the existence of wrongful interference with a contractual or business relationship?
2. What is the tort of appropriation?
3. How might the tort of defamation occur in the business context?
4. What is disparagement of property? When does it occur?
5. What is RICO? What activities are prohibited by this act?

Questions and Case Problems

9–1. Wrongful Interference.   Lothar owns a bakery. He has been trying to obtain a long-term contract with the owner of Martha's Tea Salons for some time. Lothar starts a local advertising campaign on radio and television and in the newspaper. This advertising campaign is so persuasive that Martha decides to break the contract she has had with Harley's Bakery so that she can patronize Lothar's bakery. Is Lothar liable to Harley's Bakery for the tort of wrongful interference with a contractual relationship? Is Martha liable for this tort? For anything?

9–2. Wrongful Interference.   Katrina was stranded in Alaska as the result of a union strike against the airline. She had purchased a round-trip ticket before leaving her home in Dallas. She was forced to return to Dallas on another airline and incurred additional expense for her return ticket. She sued the union for tortious interference with her contract with the airline and sought to recover the additional expense. Should the union be liable to Katrina for damages? Why or why not?

9–3. Business Tort Theories.   Red Stripe Airlines negotiates a lease at an airport for gates on the same concourse as Green Top Airlines. In fact, for passengers to get to Green Top's gates, they must walk past Red Stripe's gates. Red Stripe puts up a large sign that states, "Passengers of other airlines—turn in your tickets or cancel your reservations, and we will give you 25 percent off the price of your trip if you fly on Red Stripe Airlines." In addition, Red Stripe's ticket agents solicit business from travelers on their way to Green Top's gates. At this time, only Red Stripe and Green Top have operative gates on the concourse. Discuss fully any business tort theories under which Green Top can recover against Red Stripe for the latter's actions. (Remember: A ticket is a contract.)

9–4. Business Tort Theories.   Luigi owns and operates a famous Italian restaurant in New York City. Luigi hires chef Toni to prepare the pasta and other dishes on his menu. Toni also contributes a column to *Gourmet Eating* magazine in which he discusses Italian food and restaurants in the area and rates all restaurants with stars. The ratings range from one star (the lowest rating) to five stars (the highest rating). Toni is prohibited from discussing or rating Luigi's restaurant in his column as long as he is employed by Luigi. One day, Luigi and Toni have a dispute over Toni's salary, and Toni, in front of a substantial number of regular customers who are well known in New York society, accuses Luigi of watering his house wine and of not making his own pasta. Luigi has on occasion purchased some pasta from a pasta shop in the neighborhood, but he has never watered his wine. Toni quits on the spot and later, in *Gourmet Eating*, rates Luigi's restaurant with only one star, adding a notation that Luigi's wine and pasta are inferior to the wine and pasta offered by other restaurants. Under what tort theories, if any, can Luigi file suit against Toni? Discuss fully.

9–5. Wrongful Interference. Lehigh Corp., a developer of real estate, obtained a restraining order (which is similar to an injunction) against one of its former sales representatives, Leroy Azar. Lehigh brought prospective customers to its development, Lehigh Acres, and provided accommodations at its company-owned motel. Azar pursued a practice of following Lehigh purchasers as they entered the motel and persuading them to rescind (cancel) their contracts with Lehigh and purchase less expensive property from him. Lehigh sued Azar, asserting that Azar was tortiously interfering with the advantageous business relationship between Lehigh and its customers. Azar contended that Lehigh's customers had a right under federal law to rescind their contracts within three days and that he was merely providing them with an opportunity to be relieved of their contracts and to obtain comparable property for lower prices. What should the court decide? Discuss fully. [*Azar v. Lehigh Corp.*, 364 So.2d 860 (Fla.App.2d 1978)]

9–6. Wrongful Interference. Duggin entered into a contract to purchase certain land from Williams. The contract specified that if the property was not rezoned by June 15, 1981, either party could cancel. Duggin invested a great deal of time and money in engineering studies and surveys that increased the value of the property. Before the June 15 rezoning deadline, Duggin made an agreement to assign the contract to Centennial Development Corp. at a profit. The land was not rezoned as of June 15, but Centennial was prepared to purchase the land without the rezoning. Williams's attorney, Adams, learned of Duggin's deal and convinced Williams to cancel on July 30, 1981, in accordance with the provision in the agreement. Adams also convinced Williams to transfer the property to Adams, after which he sold the land to Centennial. Adams claimed that he was merely working on behalf of his client, Williams. Does Duggin have a claim against Adams for wrongful interference with contract rights even though Williams had the right to termi-

nate the contract at will? Explain your answer. [*Duggin v. Adams*, 234 Va. 221, 360 S.E.2d 832 (1987)]

9–7. Wrongful Interference. DBI Services, Inc., provided oil-field trucking services, brine water, and drilling mud to oil producers in the Seminole area of Texas. From 1983 to 1986, the major oil producer in the area, Amerada Hess Corp. (AH), regularly contracted with DBI for its services. AH learned in a 1986 audit of its contractors that DBI had engaged in lavish entertainment of certain AH employees who were responsible for awarding job contracts. Disturbed by this discovery, AH thereafter refused to deal with DBI. AH also refused to accept contract bids from any firms that planned to subcontract work out to DBI, even if the firms had submitted the lowest bids for the contracts. DBI sued AH for tortious interference with its contractual relationships with these other firms. AH claimed that it was not obligated to accept the lowest bids for contracts and that it had a right to determine with whom it would do business. How will the court decide the issue? Discuss. [*DBI Services, Inc. v. Amerada Hess Corp.*, 907 F.2d 506 (5th Cir. 1990)]

9–8. Wrongful Interference. Bombardier Capital, Inc., provides financing to boat and recreational vehicle dealers. Bombardier's credit policy requires dealers to forward immediately to Bombardier the proceeds of boat sales. When Howard Mulcahey, Bombardier's vice president of sales and marketing, learned that a dealer was not complying with this policy, he told Frank Chandler, Bombardier's credit director, of his concern. Before Chandler could obtain the proceeds, Mulcahey falsely told Jacques Gingras, Bombardier's president, that Chandler was, among other things, trying to hide the problem. On the basis of Mulcahey's statements, Gingras fired Chandler and put Mulcahey in charge of the credit department. Under what business tort theory discussed in this chapter might Chandler recover damages from Mulcahey? Explain. [*Chandler v. Bombardier Capital, Inc.*, 44 F.3d 80 (2d Cir. 1994)]

9–9. RICO. During the 1980s, Mutual Trading Corp. (MTC) bought and sold tires made by Uniroyal Goodrich Tire Co. In the 1990s, Uniroyal discovered that MTC had perpetrated at least four separate schemes to swindle money from Uniroyal. As part of one scheme, for example, MTC had submitted fraudulent claims for reimbursement for amounts it had refunded to customers in Saudi Arabia. As part of another scheme, MTC had obtained from Uniroyal twice as much for its advertising costs in Nigeria as the parties had previously agreed on. Uniroyal filed a suit against MTC and others in a federal district court, alleging, among other things, that these schemes violated RICO. MTC responded in part that the allegations depicted only a single scheme perpetrated on a single victim and that thus there was no "pattern of racketeering activity." What constitutes a pattern of activity to satisfy RICO? Is RICO satisfied in this case? [*Uniroyal Goodrich Tire Co. v. Mutual Trading Corp.*, 63 F.3d 516 (7th Cir. 1995)]

A Question of Ethics and Social Responsibility

9–10.   Pennzoil Co. agreed to buy control of Getty Oil Co. Both companies announced the news on January 5, 1984, although details of the agreement remained unsettled. While a formal written document was being negotiated, Texaco, Inc., made a higher bid for Getty, and on January 6, Getty's board of directors accepted it. As part of the deal, Getty insisted that Texaco assume responsibility for any claims brought by Pennzoil against Getty, and Getty's major shareholders insisted on a guaranteed price of at least "the price Pennzoil had agreed to pay." Pennzoil sued Texaco in a Texas state court, alleging wrongful interference with its contract with Getty. The court found that (1) Getty had agreed to Pennzoil's offer; (2) Texaco knowingly interfered with this agreement; (3) as a result, Pennzoil suffered damages of $7.53 billion; (4) Texaco's actions were intentional and in disregard of

Pennzoil's rights; and (5) Pennzoil was entitled to additional punitive damages of $3 billion. Texaco appealed. The Court of Appeals of Texas accepted the findings of the jury and affirmed the lower court's decision. [*Texaco, Inc. v. Pennzoil Co.*, 729 S.W.2d 768 (Tex.App.— Houston [1st Dist.] 1987), writ ref'd n.r.e.]

1. Texaco argued that its offer was merely in response to a campaign of active solicitation by the Getty entities, who were dissatisfied with the terms of Pennzoil's offer. Is it fair to hold Texaco liable in these circumstances? Why or why not?

2. What public policies must be balanced in considering the issues in this case?

For Critical Analysis

9–11.   Civil actions under RICO have been brought almost entirely against "respected businesses allegedly engaged in a pattern of specifically identified criminal conduct" rather than against "the archetypal, intimidating mobster," according to the United States Supreme Court. If this is an inappropriate use of RICO, who is responsible for correcting the situation?

Product Liability

Contents

Chapter Objectives

After reading this chapter, you should be able to . . .

1. Discuss how negligence can provide a basis for a product liability action.

2. Describe how misrepresentation can serve as a basis for product liability.

3. List the requirements for an action in strict liability.

4. Identify who may be liable for defects caused by defective products.

5. Summarize the defenses that can be raised against product liability claims.

259

> **"If the nature of a thing is such that it is reasonably certain to place life and limb in peril when negligently made, it is then a thing of danger."**
>
> Benjamin N. Cardozo, 1870–1938
> (Associate justice of the United States Supreme Court, 1932–1938)

Product Liability The legal liability of manufacturers, sellers, and lessors of goods to consumers, users, and bystanders for injuries or damages that are caused by the goods.

Express Warranty A promise, ancillary to an underlying sales agreement, that is included in the written or oral terms of the sales agreement under which the promisor assures the quality, description, or performance of the goods.

Implied Warranty of Merchantability A presumed promise by a merchant seller of goods that the goods are reasonably fit for the general purpose for which they are sold, are properly packaged and labeled, and are of proper quality.

Implied Warranty of Fitness for a Particular Purpose A presumed promise made by a merchant seller of goods that the goods are fit for the particular purpose for which the buyer will use the goods. The seller must know the buyer's purpose and know that the buyer is relying on the seller's skill and judgment to select suitable goods.

Product liability refers to the liability incurred by manufacturers and sellers of products when product defects cause injury or property damages to consumers, users, or bystanders (people in the vicinity of the product). Product liability encompasses the tort theories of negligence, misrepresentation, and strict liability—all of which were discussed in Chapter 8. For example, as indicated in the quotation alongside, if a product is defective because of the manufacturer's negligence, an injured user of the product can sue the manufacturer for negligence in a product liability suit. If a user is injured by a product as a result of the seller's fraudulent misrepresentation of the nature of that product, the basis of the product liability suit is fraud. In the last several decades, the doctrine of strict liability often has been applied in product liability suits.

In this chapter, we examine each of these bases for product liability. Note that product liability can also be based on warranty law.

Warranty Law

Today, warranty law is an important part of the entire spectrum of laws relating to product liability. Most goods are covered by some type of warranty designed to protect consumers. The concept of warranty is based on the seller's assurance to the buyer that the goods will meet certain standards. Because a warranty imposes a duty on the seller, a breach of the warranty is a breach of the seller's promise.

The Uniform Commercial Code (UCC) designates five types of warranties that can arise in a contract for the sale of goods. These include express and implied warranties. A seller can create an **express warranty** by making a representation concerning the quality, condition, description, or performance potential of goods at such a time that the buyer could have relied on the representation when he or she agreed to the contract. These representations may be made in advertisements or by a salesperson. An **implied warranty of merchantability** that goods are "reasonably fit for the ordinary purposes for which such goods are used" arises automatically in a sale of goods by a merchant who deals in such goods. An **implied warranty of fitness for a particular purpose** arises when any seller—merchant or nonmerchant—knows the particular purpose for which a buyer will use the goods and knows that the buyer is relying on the seller's skill and judgment to select suitable goods.

Consumers, purchasers, and even users of goods can recover *from any seller* for losses resulting from breach of implied and express warranties. A manufacturer is a *seller*. Therefore, a person who purchases goods from a retailer can recover from the retailer or the manufacturer if the goods are not merchantable, because in most states *privity of contract* (the legal connection that exists between contracting parties) is no longer a prerequisite for recovery for personal injuries for a breach of warranty. That is, a product purchaser may sue not only the firm from which he or she purchased a product but also a third party—the manufacturer of the product—in product liability.

Negligence

Chapter 8 defined *negligence* as the failure to exercise the degree of care that a reasonable, prudent person would have exercised under the circumstances. If a manufacturer fails to exercise "due care" to make a product safe, then a person who is injured by the product may sue the manufacturer for negligence.

Due care must be exercised in designing the product, in selecting the materials, in using the appropriate production process, in assembling and testing the product, and in placing adequate warnings on the label informing the user of dangers of which an ordinary person might not be aware. The duty of care also extends to the inspection and testing of any purchased products that are used in the final product sold by the manufacturer.

A product liability action based on negligence does not require **privity of contract** between the injured plaintiff and the negligent defendant-manufacturer. Section 395 of the *Restatement (Second) of Torts* states as follows:

> A manufacturer who fails to exercise reasonable care in the manufacture of a chattel [movable good] which, unless carefully made, he should recognize as involving an unreasonable risk of causing physical harm to those who lawfully use it for a purpose for which the manufacturer should expect it to be used and to those whom he should expect to be endangered by its probable use, is subject to liability for physical harm caused to them by its lawful use in a manner and for a purpose for which it is supplied.

In other words, a manufacturer is liable for its failure to exercise due care to any person who sustained an injury proximately caused by a negligently made (defective) product, regardless of whether the injured person is in privity of contract with the negligent defendant-manufacturer or lessor. Relative to the long history of the common law, this exception to the privity requirement is a fairly recent development, dating to the early part of the twentieth century. A leading case in this respect is *MacPherson v. Buick Motor Co.*, which is presented as this chapter's *Landmark in the Legal Environment*.

Misrepresentation

When a fraudulent misrepresentation has been made to a user or consumer, and that misrepresentation ultimately results in an injury, the basis of liability may be the tort of fraud. Examples are the intentional mislabeling of packaged cosmetics and the intentional concealment of a product's defects.

Strict Liability

Under the doctrine of strict liability (discussed in Chapter 8), people may be liable for the results of their acts regardless of their intentions or their exercise of reasonable care. Under this doctrine, liability does not depend on privity of contract. The injured party does not have to be the buyer or a third party beneficiary, as required under contract warranty theory. Indeed, this type of liability in law is not governed by the provisions of the UCC because it is a tort doctrine, not a principle of contract law.

The *Restatement (Second) of Torts* designates how the doctrine of strict liability should be applied. It is a precise and widely accepted statement of the liabilities of sellers of goods (including manufacturers, processors, assemblers, packagers, bottlers, wholesalers, distributors, retailers, and lessors) and

---

RECALLL The elements of negligence include a duty of care, a breach of the duty, and an injury to the plaintiff proximately caused by the breach.

Privity of Contract The relationship that exists between the promisor and the promisee of a contract.

"One may smile, and smile, and be a villain."

William Shakespeare, 1564–1616
(English dramatist and poet)

Landmark in the Legal Environment
MacPherson v. Buick Motor Co. (1916)

In the landmark case of *MacPherson v. Buick Motor Co.,*[a] the New York Court of Appeals—New York's highest court—dealt with the liability of a manufacturer that failed to exercise reasonable care in manufacturing a finished product. The case was brought by Donald MacPherson, who suffered injuries while riding in a Buick automobile that suddenly collapsed because one of the wheels was made of defective wood. The spokes crumbled into fragments, throwing MacPherson out of the vehicle and injuring him.

MacPherson had purchased the car from a Buick dealer, but he brought suit against the manufacturer, Buick Motor Company. The wheel itself had not been made by Buick; it had been bought from another manufacturer. There was evidence, though, that the defects could have been discovered by reasonable inspection by Buick and that no such inspection had taken place. MacPherson charged Buick with negligence for putting a human life in imminent danger. The major issue before the court was whether Buick owed a duty of care to anyone except the immediate purchaser of the car (that is, the Buick dealer).

In deciding the issue, Justice Benjamin Cardozo stated that "[i]f the nature of a thing is such that it is reasonably

certain to place life and limb in peril when negligently made, it is then a thing of danger. . . . If to the element of danger there is added knowledge that the thing will be used by persons other than the purchaser, and used without new tests, then, irrespective of contract, the manufacturer of this thing of danger is under a duty to make it carefully." The court concluded that "[b]eyond all question, the nature of an automobile gives warning of probable danger if its construction is defective. This automobile was designed to go 50 miles an hour. Unless its wheels were sound and strong, injury was almost certain."

Although Buick had not manufactured the wheel itself, the court held that Buick had a duty to inspect the wheels and that Buick "was responsible for the finished product." Therefore, Buick was liable to MacPherson for the injuries he sustained when he was thrown from the car.

For Critical Analysis: *To what extent, if any, have technological developments contributed to the courts' placing less emphasis on the doctrine of* caveat emptor *("let the buyer beware") and more emphasis on the doctrine of* caveat venditor *("let the seller beware")?*

a.   217 N.Y. 382, 111 N.E. 1050 (1916).

---

deserves close attention. Section 402A of the *Restatement (Second) of Torts* states as follows:

1. One who sells any product in a defective condition unreasonably dangerous to the user or consumer or to his property is subject to liability for physical harm thereby caused to the ultimate user or consumer or to his property, if
   a. the seller is engaged in the business of selling such a product, and
   b. it is expected to and does reach the user or consumer without substantial change in the condition in which it is sold.
2. The rule stated in Subsection (1) applies although
   a. the seller has exercised all possible care in the preparation and sale of his product, and
   b. the user or consumer has not bought the product from or entered into any contractual relation with the seller.

Strict liability is imposed by law as a matter of public policy. This policy rests on the threefold assumption that (1) consumers should be protected against unsafe products; (2) manufacturers and distributors should not escape liability for faulty products simply because they are not in privity of contract

> **"The assault upon the citadel of privity [of contract] is proceeding in these days apace."**
>
> Benjamin Cardozo, 1870–1938
> (Associate justice of the United States Supreme Court, 1932–1938)

with the ultimate user of those products; and (3) manufacturers, sellers, and lessors of products are in a better position to bear the costs associated with injuries caused by their products—costs that they can ultimately pass on to all consumers in the form of higher prices.

California was the first state to impose strict liability in tort on manufacturers. In the landmark decision that follows, the California Supreme Court sets out the reason for applying tort law rather than contract law to cases in which consumers are injured by defective products.

Case 10.1 ● Greenman v. Yuba Power Products, Inc.

Supreme Court of California, 1962.
59 Cal.2d 57,
377 P.2d 897,
27 Cal.Rptr. 697.

HISTORICAL AND SOCIAL SETTING *From the earliest days of the common law, English courts applied a doctrine of strict liability. Often, persons whose conduct resulted in the injury of another were held liable for damages, even if they had not intended to injure anyone and had exercised reasonable care. This approach was abandoned around 1800 in favor of the* fault *approach, in which an action was considered tortious only if it was wrongful or blameworthy in some respect. Strict liability began to be reapplied to manufactured goods in several landmark cases in the 1960s, a decade during which many traditional assumptions were being challenged.*

BACKGROUND AND FACTS The plaintiff, Greenman, wanted a Shopsmith—a combination power tool that could be used as a saw, drill, and wood lathe—after seeing a Shopsmith demonstrated by a retailer and studying a brochure prepared by the manufacturer. The plaintiff's wife bought and gave him one for Christmas. More than a year later, a piece of wood flew out of the lathe attachment of the Shopsmith while the plaintiff was using it, inflicting serious injuries on him. About ten and a half months later, the plaintiff filed suit in a California state court against both the retailer and the manufacturer for breach of warranties and negligence. The trial court jury found for the plaintiff. The case was ultimately appealed to the Supreme Court of California.

IN THE WORDS OF THE COURT . . .
TRAYNOR, Justice.
        * * * *

Plaintiff introduced substantial evidence that his injuries were caused by defective design and construction of the Shopsmith. * * * The jury could therefore reasonably have concluded that the manufacturer negligently constructed the Shopsmith. The jury could also reasonably have concluded that statements in the manufacturer's brochure were untrue, that they constituted express warranties, and that plaintiff's injuries were caused by their breach.
        * * * *

[But] to impose strict liability on the manufacturer under the circumstances of this case, it was not necessary for plaintiff to establish an express warranty * * * . A manufacturer is strictly liable in tort when an article he places on the market, knowing that it is to be used without inspection for defects, proves to have a defect that causes injury to a human being. * * *
        * * * *

* * * The purpose of such liability is to insure that the costs of injuries resulting from defective products are borne by the manufacturers * * * rather than by the injured persons who are powerless to protect themselves.

(Continued)

Case 10.1—continued

DECISION AND REMEDY   The Supreme Court of California upheld the jury verdict for the plaintiff. The manufacturer was held strictly liable in tort for the harm caused by its unsafe product.

FOR CRITICAL ANALYSIS—ETHICAL CONSIDERATION   *What UCC rule did the manufacturer refer to when it argued that the plaintiff had "waited too long" to give notice of the breach of warranty? What ethical doctrine underlies this rule?*

Unreasonably Dangerous Product   In product liability, a product that is defective to the point of threatening a consumer's health and safety. A product will be considered unreasonably dangerous if it is dangerous beyond the expectation of the ordinary consumer or if a less dangerous alternative was economically feasible for the manufacturer, but the manufacturer failed to produce it.

If a child is injured by a toy, should the manufacturer be held liable regardless of the circumstances? Why or why not?

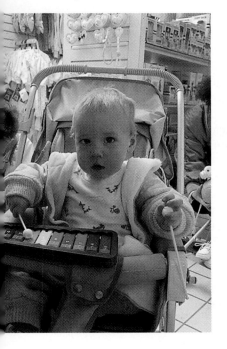

Requirements of Strict Product Liability—Summarized

The bases for an action in strict liability as set forth in Section 402A of the *Restatement (Second) of Torts* and as the doctrine is commonly applied can be summarized as a series of six requirements, which are listed here. If these requirements are met, the manufacturer's liability to an injured party may be virtually unlimited.[1]

1. The product must be in a defective condition when the defendant sells it.
2. The defendant must normally be engaged in the business of selling (or otherwise distributing) that product.
3. The product must be unreasonably dangerous to the user or consumer because of its defective condition (in most states).
4. The plaintiff must incur physical harm to self or property by use or consumption of the product.
5. The defective condition must be the proximate cause of the injury or damage.
6. The goods must not have been substantially changed from the time the product was sold to the time the injury was sustained.

Thus, in any action against a manufacturer, seller, or lessor, the plaintiff does not have to show why or in what manner the product became defective. To recover damages, however, the plaintiff must show that the product was so defective as to be unreasonably dangerous; that the product caused the plaintiff's injury; and that at the time the injury was sustained, the condition of the product was essentially the same as when it left the hands of the defendant manufacturer, seller, or lessor.

Product Defect and Strict Liability Claims

A court may consider a product so defective as to be an **unreasonably dangerous product** if either (1) the product was dangerous beyond the expectation of the ordinary consumer or (2) a less dangerous alternative was economically feasible for the manufacturer, but the manufacturer failed to produce it. Generally, claims that a product is so defective as to be unreasonably dangerous fall into the three categories discussed here.

FLAW IN THE MANUFACTURING PROCESS.   A plaintiff may allege that a product was unreasonably dangerous because of a flaw in the manufacturing

---

1.   Some states have enacted what are called *statutes of repose*. Basically, these statutes provide that after a specific statutory period of time from the date of manufacture or sale, a plaintiff is precluded from pursuing a cause of action for injuries or damages sustained from a product, even though the product is defective. The states of Illinois, Indiana, Alabama, Tennessee, Florida, Texas, and Nebraska are illustrative.

process. As discussed earlier, manufacturers are required to use due care in the manufacture, assembly, and testing of the goods they produce. A manufacturer that fails to exercise proper care in manufacturing a product may be liable in strict liability for harms suffered by users of the product.

DESIGN DEFECT.   A product, although perfectly manufactured, may nonetheless be unreasonably dangerous because of a defect in design. Generally, a plaintiff claiming a design defect must show that a safer alternative was available and economically feasible for the manufacturer, but the manufacturer failed to produce it. When determining whether a less dangerous alternative was economically feasible for the manufacturer, courts will consider a number of factors, including the product's social utility and desirability, the availability of—and economic feasibility of producing—a safer alternative, the obviousness of the danger posed by the product, the probability of injury and its likely seriousness, and the possibility of eliminating the danger without appreciably impairing the product's function.

People often cut themselves on knives, but because there is no way to avoid injuries without making the product useless and because the danger is obvious to users, a court normally would not find a knife to be unreasonably dangerous and would not hold a supplier of knives liable. In contrast, a court may consider a snowblower without a safety guard over the opening through which the snow is blown to be in a condition that is unreasonably dangerous, even if the snowblower carries warnings to stay clear of the opening. The danger may be within the users' expectations, but the court will also consider the likelihood of injury and its probable seriousness, as well as the cost of putting a guard over the opening and the guard's effect on the blower's operation.

Some products are safe when used as their manufacturers and distributors intend but not safe when used in other ways. Suppliers are generally required to expect reasonably foreseeable misuses and to design products that are either safe when misused or marketed with some protective device—for example, a childproof cap. The following case required the court to determine whether a misuse of a product was reasonably foreseeable.

Case 10.2 ● Lutz v. National Crane Corp.

Supreme Court of Montana, 1994.
884 P.2d 455.

HISTORICAL AND TECHNOLOGICAL SETTING
Industrial cranes are often used in close proximity to power lines. Operators must take extreme care to avoid contact with the lines. Sideloading (dragging) with a crane causes the crane cable to extend its slack in unpredictable ways, increasing the risk of contact with one of the lines. If this happens, electricity can be conducted through the crane and electrocute anyone who is touching it. There are 2,300 crane/power line contacts in the United States each year, and crane/power line electrocutions are
the fifth leading cause of work-related deaths in the United States. For this reason, insulated links, which stop the conduction of electricity, are available to crane manufacturers.

BACKGROUND AND FACTS   Gerald Lutz and another employee of Montana Ready-Mix were using a crane to retrieve drilling pipe from beneath power lines when the crane cable touched one of the lines. The cable did not have an insulated link and thus conducted electricity from the line to the pipe, electrocuting Lutz. Lutz's widow, Lori Lutz, filed a suit in a Montana state court against the National Crane Corporation, which manufactured the crane, and others, alleging, among other things, that the crane—

(Continued)

Case 10.2—continued

without an insulated link—was defectively designed and unreasonably dangerous. National Crane argued, among other things, that the employees had been using the crane to sideload and that sideloading was an unreasonable misuse. The court awarded Lori Lutz $815,400, less 20 percent, which it attributed, in part, to Gerald Lutz's unreasonable misuse. Both parties appealed. Lori Lutz sought the full $815,400. She admitted that sideloading was a misuse but claimed that it was reasonably foreseeable.

IN THE WORDS OF THE COURT . . .
HARRISON, Justice.
    *   *   *   *
    *   *   * [C]ranes are often operated in close proximity to live electrical lines and *   *   * sideloading is not an uncommon, albeit improper, practice of crane operators and groundcrews. *   *   *
        *   *   *   *
National Crane admits that the cranes which it manufactures can be misused through sideloading. National Crane also knows that if sideloading occurs in the vicinity of power lines, the possibility exists that its crane cables might contact power lines. It is undisputed that a crane/power line contact was foreseeable to National Crane. *   *   *
    It being admitted that the alleged misuse of the crane through sideloading was reasonably foreseeable to National Crane, we hold that, as a matter of law, the *   *   * defense of unreasonable misuse is unavailable to National Crane.

DECISION AND REMEDY   The Supreme Court of Montana remanded the case to the lower court with the instruction to reinstate the full award.

FOR CRITICAL ANALYSIS—SOCIAL CONSIDERATION   *Who would bear the consequences if the law did not allow for reasonably foreseeable misuses?*

> **NOTE**   Although a failure to exercise due care can result in strict liability, proof of such a failure is not required, as it is in an action based on negligence.

INADEQUATE WARNING.   A plaintiff in a strict liability action may claim that a product is unreasonably dangerous because it lacks adequate warnings or instructions. Manufacturers and other suppliers of products have a duty to warn product users of product-associated risks and dangers, unless the risks and dangers are commonly known. (As will be discussed later in this chapter, an assertion that a danger is commonly known can be used as a defense to product liability.) A pharmaceutical company, for example, must warn of possible side effects of its drugs or of the risks associated with using a certain drug in conjunction with other medications.

Generally, a manufacturer must warn those who purchase its product of the harms that can result from the misuse of the product as well. If a particular misuse of a product is foreseeable, a court normally will hold that the manufacturer had a duty to warn of the dangers associated with such misuse.

Market-Share Liability

Generally, in all cases involving product liability, a plaintiff must prove that the defective product that caused his or her injury was the product of a specific defendant. In the last decade or so, in cases in which plaintiffs could not prove which of many distributors of a harmful product supplied the particular product that caused the plaintiffs' injuries, courts have dropped this requirement.

Ethical Perspective

Cases alleging inadequate warnings often present thorny issues for the courts to decide. For example, should a manufacturer of an opaque windshield sunscreen have to warn a consumer not to drive his or her car without first removing the sunscreen? Should a manufacturer of swimming pools have to warn swimmers not to dive into the shallow end of the pool? These and similar questions raise the issue addressed in Chapter 2: At what point does the manufacturer's responsibility for consumer safety end and the consumer's responsibility for his or her own safety begin?

In deciding cases involving this issue, the courts generally try to balance the policy of protecting consumers against harmful products with the policy that manufacturers cannot be absolute insurers of the safety of all products on the market. Sometimes, though, common sense seems to give way to the principle that consumers should be warned of *all* foreseeable harms associated with products, even if those harms are obvious. When this happens, other plaintiffs are encouraged to bring suits for injuries for which, at least in the minds of many (including many courts), the sellers should not be held responsible.

For Critical Analysis: *Why weren't issues of product liability and strict liability important a hundred years ago?*

This has occurred, for example, in several cases involving DES (diethylstilbestrol), a drug administered in the past to prevent miscarriages. DES's harmful character was not realized until, a generation later, daughters of the women who had taken DES developed health problems, including vaginal carcinoma, that were linked to the drug. Partly because of the passage of time, a plaintiff-daughter often could not prove which pharmaceutical company—out of as many as three hundred—had marketed the DES her mother had ingested. In these cases, some courts applied **market-share liability,** holding that all firms that manufactured and distributed DES during the period in question were liable for the plaintiffs' injuries in proportion to the firms' respective shares of the market.[2]

Market-share liability has also been applied in other situations. In one case, for example, a plaintiff who was a hemophiliac received injections of a blood protein known as antihemophiliac factor (AHF) concentrate. The plaintiff later tested positive for the AIDS (acquired immune deficiency syndrome) virus. Because it was not known which manufacturer was responsible for the particular AHF received by the plaintiff, the court held that all of the manufacturers of AHF could be held liable under a market-share theory of liability.[3] In another case, the New York Court of Appeals (that state's highest court) held that even if a firm can prove that it did not manufacture the particular product that caused injuries to the plaintiff, the firm can be held liable based on the firm's share of the national market.[4]

Market-Share Liability A method of sharing liability among several firms that manufactured or marketed a particular product that may have caused a plaintiff's injury.

Other Applications of Strict Liability

Although the drafters of the *Restatement (Second) of Torts,* Section 402A, did not take a position on bystanders, all courts extend the strict liability of manufacturers and other sellers to injured bystanders. For example, in one case, an automobile manufacturer was held liable for injuries caused by the explosion

---

2. See, for example, *Martin v. Abbott Laboratories,* 102 Wash.2d 581, 689 P.2d 368 (1984).
3. *Smith v. Cutter Biological, Inc.,* 72 Haw. 416, 823 P.2d 717 (1991).
4. *Hymowitz v. Eli Lilly and Co.,* 73 N.Y.2d 487, 539 N.E.2d 1069, 541 N.Y.S.2d 941 (1989).

of a car's motor. A cloud of steam that resulted from the explosion caused multiple collisions because other drivers could not see well.[5]

The rule of strict liability also applies to suppliers of component parts. Thus, if General Motors buys brake pads from a subcontractor and puts them in Chevrolets without changing their composition, and those pads are defective, both the supplier of the brake pads and General Motors will be held strictly liable for the damages caused by the defects.

Defenses to Product Liability

There are several defenses that manufacturers, sellers, or lessors can raise to avoid liability for harms caused by their products. We look at some of these defenses here.

Assumption of Risk

Assumption of risk can sometimes be used as a defense in a product liability action. To establish such a defense, the defendant must show that

1. the plaintiff knew and appreciated the risk created by the product defect and
2. the plaintiff voluntarily assumed the risk, even though it was unreasonable to do so.

(See Chapter 8 for a more detailed discussion of assumption of risk.)

BE CAREFUL A defendant cannot successfully claim that the plaintiff assumed a risk different from or greater than the risk normally associated with a product.

Product Misuse

Product Misuse A defense against product liability that may be raised when the plaintiff used a product in a manner not intended by the manufacturer.

Similar to the defense of voluntary assumption of risk is that of **product misuse**. Here, the injured party *does not know that the product is dangerous for a particular use* (contrast this with assumption of risk), but the use is not the one for which the product was designed. The courts have severely limited this defense, however. Even if the injured party does not know about the inherent danger of using the product in a wrong way, if the misuse is foreseeable, the seller must take measures to guard against it.

Comparative Negligence

Developments in the area of comparative negligence (discussed in Chapter 8) have even affected the doctrine of strict liability—the most extreme theory of product liability. Whereas previously the plaintiff's conduct was not a defense to strict liability, today many jurisdictions consider the negligent or intentional actions of both the plaintiff and the defendant in the apportionment of liability and damages. This means that even if a product was misused by the plaintiff, the plaintiff may nonetheless be able to recover at least some damages for injuries caused by the defendant's defective product.

Commonly Known Dangers

The dangers associated with certain products (such as sharp knives and guns) are so commonly known that manufacturers need not warn users of those dangers. If a defendant succeeds in convincing the court that a plaintiff's injury resulted from a *commonly known danger,* the defendant will not be liable.

5.   *Giberson v. Ford Motor Co.,* 504 S.W.2d 8 (Mo. 1974).

An injured individual sits near the scene of an accident. Under what circumstances might a person who drives or rides in a car be liable for his or her own injuries?

A classic case on this issue involved a plaintiff who was injured when an elastic exercise rope that she had purchased slipped off her foot and struck her in the eye, causing a detachment of the retina. The plaintiff claimed that the manufacturer should be liable because it had failed to warn users that the exerciser might slip off a foot in such a manner. The court stated that to hold the manufacturer liable in these circumstances "would go beyond the reasonable dictates of justice in fixing the liabilities of manufacturers." After all, stated the court, "[a]lmost every physical object can be inherently dangerous or potentially dangerous in a sense. . . . A manufacturer cannot manufacture a knife that will not cut or a hammer that will not mash a thumb or a stove that will not burn a finger. The law does not require [manufacturers] to warn of such common dangers."[6]

A related defense is the *knowledgeable user* defense. If a particular danger (such as electrical shock) is or should be commonly known by particular users of the product (such as electricians), the manufacturer of electrical equipment need not warn these users of the danger. The following case illustrates this concept.

---

6. *Jamieson v. Woodward & Lothrop*, 247 F.2d 23, 101 D.C.App. 32 (1957).

Case 10.3 ⬤ Travelers Insurance Co. v. Federal Pacific Electric Co.

Supreme Court of New York,
Appellate Division, First Department, 1995.
211 A.D.2d 40,
625 N.Y.S.2d 121.

COMPANY PROFILE *The Federal Pacific Electric Company makes electrical equipment, including Stab-Lok circuit*

breakers. The Reliance Electric Company bought Federal from UV Industries Liquidating Trust, Inc., in 1979. In 1980, Federal revealed that it had obtained Underwriters Laboratories (UL) certification for its Stab-Lok circuit breakers by cheating on UL tests. Reliance sued UV Industries. A cash settlement ended the lawsuit in 1984. Two

(Continued)

Case 10.3—continued

years later, Reliance sold Federal to the Challenger Electric Equipment Corporation. The federal Consumer Product Safety Commission later concluded that the Stab-Lok circuit breakers "did not present a serious risk of injury."

BACKGROUND AND FACTS   A water pipe burst, flooding a switchboard at the offices of RCA Global Communications, Inc. This tripped the switchboard circuit breakers. RCA employees assigned to reactivate the switchboard included an electrical technician with twelve years of on-the-job training, a licensed electrician, and an electrical engineer with twenty years of experience who had studied power engineering in college. The employees attempted to switch one of the circuit breakers back on without testing for short circuits, which they later admitted they knew how to do and should have done. The circuit breaker failed to engage but ignited an explosive fire. RCA filed a claim with its insurer, the Travelers Insurance Company. Travelers paid the claim and filed a suit in a New York state court against, among others, the Federal Pacific Electric Company, the supplier of the circuit breakers. Travelers alleged that Federal had been negligent in failing to give RCA adequate warnings and instructions regarding the circuit breakers. The court apportioned 15 percent of the responsibility for the fire to Federal. Federal appealed.

IN THE WORDS OF THE COURT . . .
NARDELLI, Justice.
    * * * *
    * * * [T]here is "no necessity to warn a customer already aware— through common knowledge or learning—of a specific hazard" and, in the proper case, the court can decide as a matter of law that there is no duty to warn or that the duty has been discharged. * * *
        * * * *
    Given the * * * common knowledge of the minimal accepted practices in the field and the level of expertise, training and experience of the RCA electricians which encompassed the specific situation they faced, the * * * court should have found that there was no necessity on the part of Federal to warn RCA, which was already aware of the specific hazard, and the court should have granted Federal's motion entering judgment in its favor * * * .

DECISION AND REMEDY   The Supreme Court of New York, Appellate Division, reversed the judgment of the lower court and dismissed the complaint against Federal.

FOR CRITICAL ANALYSIS—TECHNOLOGICAL CONSIDERATION   *What might have been the result in this case if the training, experience, and expertise of the employees dispatched to check the circuit breakers had been with a different, out-of-date technology?*

Other Defenses

A defendant can also defend against product liability by showing that there is no basis for the plaintiff's claim. For example, in a product liability case based on negligence, a defendant who can show that the plaintiff has not met the requirements (such as causation) for an action in negligence will not be liable. In regard to strict liability, a defendant could claim that the plaintiff failed to meet one of the requirements for an action in strict liability. For example, if the defendant establishes that the goods have been subsequently altered, the defendant will not be held liable. (See this chapter's *Inside the Legal Environment* on the next page for a discussion of how federal preemption of state law claims can, in effect, serve as a defense to liability in some situations.)

Inside the Legal Environment
Product Liability and the Preemption Issue

If a manufacturer, such as an automobile manufacturer, complies with federal safety standards in manufacturing its products, can it nonetheless be held liable under state product liability laws? The answer to this question, which has significant implications for businesses and consumers alike, depends on whether the federal standards are held to preempt relevant state laws. When Congress chooses to act exclusively in an area in which the federal government and the states have concurrent (shared) powers, Congress is said to have *preempted* the area, thus precluding claims brought under a conflicting state or local law on the same subject.

A leading case on this issue, *Cipollone v. Liggett Group, Inc.,*[a] was decided by the United States Supreme Court in 1992. In that case, the Court held that the Federal Cigarette Labeling and Advertising Act of 1965, which requires specific warnings to be included on cigarette packages, preempted state laws requiring cigarette manufacturers to sufficiently warn consumers of the potential dangers associated with cigarette smoking. The Court stated, however, that there was no indication that Congress intended to preempt state laws that fall *outside* the scope of the federal law, such as laws governing fraudulent misrepresentation.

In *Cipollone* and other cases involving preemption issues, the courts must decide whether Congress, when enacting a particular statute, *intended* to preempt state law claims. In determining congressional intent, courts

look at the wording of the statute itself, as well as at the legislative history of the statute (such as congressional committee reports on the topic). For example, in *Tebbetts v. Ford Motor Co.,*[b] a plaintiff alleged that a 1988 Ford Escort was defectively designed because it did not contain an air bag on the driver's side. The defendant-manufacturer contended that it had complied with federal safety regulations authorized by the National Traffic and Motor Vehicle Safety Act of 1966 and that those regulations preempted recovery under state product-safety laws. The court interpreted House and Senate reports on the issue, as well as a clause included in the act itself, to mean that all state law claims were not preempted by the federal regulations. (The relevant clause stated that "[c]ompliance with any Federal motor vehicle safety standard issued under this [act] does not exempt any person from any liability under common law.")

Generally, manufacturers should be wary in assuming that just because they comply with federally mandated product-safety standards they will not be subject to liability under state laws. Courts differ in their interpretations of congressional intent, and the outcomes in cases involving similar facts can thus also differ. For example, numerous cases have been brought by plaintiffs who have suffered injuries from the use of certain pesticides or herbicides. Some courts have held that the Federal Insecticide, Fungicide, and Rodenticide Act (FIFRA) of 1947, which imposes labeling requirements on manufacturers of these products,

preempts actions under state laws.[c] Other courts, however, have held that FIFRA does not preempt all state law claims—for example, those based on negligence or misrepresentation.[d]

For Critical Analysis: *Does the trend toward giving states more authority to regulate their own affairs and away from federal regulation further argue against federal preemption of state law claims?*

c. See, for example, *TaylorAg Industries v. Pure-Gro,* 54 F.3d 555 (9th Cir. 1995).
d. See, for example, *Gorton v. American Cyanamid Co.,* 533 N.W.2d 746 (Wisc. 1995).

An air bag deployed in a car. If, in an accident, this air bag failed to deploy and the driver suffered injuries that could be attributed to that failure, could the manufacturer of the car be held liable?

a. 505 U.S. 504, 112 S.Ct. 2608, 120 L.Ed.2d 407 (1992).

b. 665 A.2d 345 (N.H. 1995).

International Perspective

American manufacturers have discovered that just about anything they produce can result in a product liability lawsuit, even if the consumer has used the product incorrectly or in violation of the manufacturer's printed instructions. The fear of huge liability lawsuits may discourage companies from engaging in the kind of research and development necessary to be internationally competitive in certain markets thought to have unusually high product liability claims. Some manufacturers feel that they cannot afford to produce any product that is not completely risk free, because they may face excessive liability.

Americans are among the most litigious people in the world. Although other industrialized countries are developing more stringent consumer product laws, thus affording injured parties greater opportunities to sue manufacturers for injuries caused by defective products, most of these countries do not hold their manufacturers to standards of strict liability (discussed later in this chapter). Consequently, foreign companies are able to undertake research programs and produce products that American companies, fearful of potential liability, may not consider economically justifiable. Of course, foreign producers that sell their products in the United States must abide by U.S. liability rules.

For Critical Analysis: *How do expansive product liability laws and court decisions affect the growth of small businesses?*

Key Terms

express warranty 260
implied warranty of fitness
    for a particular purpose
    260

implied warranty of
    merchantability 260
market-share liability 267
privity of contract 261

product liability 260
product misuse 268
unreasonably dangerous
    product 264

Chapter Summary
Product Liability

WARRANTY LAW (See page 260.)	Under the Uniform Commercial Code, certain warranties can arise in a contract for a sale of goods. These include express warranties, an implied warranty of merchantability, and an implied warranty of fitness for a particular purpose. Consumers and others can recover from any seller for losses resulting from a breach of these warranties.
LIABILITY BASED ON NEGLIGENCE (See pages 260–261.)	1. Due care must be used by the manufacturer in designing the product, selecting materials, using the appropriate production process, assembling and testing the product, and placing adequate warnings on the label or product. 2. Privity of contract is not required. A manufacturer is liable for failure to exercise due care to any person who sustains an injury proximately caused by a negligently made (defective) product.

(Continued)

Chapter Summary, continued

LIABILITY BASED ON MISREPRESENTATION (See page 261.)	Fraudulent misrepresentation of a product may result in product liability based on the tort of fraud.
STRICT LIABILITY— REQUIREMENTS (See pages 261–264.)	1. The defendant must sell the product in a defective condition. 2. The defendant must normally be engaged in the business of selling that product. 3. The product must be unreasonably dangerous to the user or consumer because of its defective condition (in most states). A court may consider a product so defective as to be unreasonably dangerous if either (a) the product was dangerous beyond the expectation of the ordinary consumer or (b) a less dangerous alternative was economically feasible for the manufacturer, but the manufacturer failed to produce it. 4. The plaintiff must incur physical harm to self or property by use or consumption of the product. (Courts will also extend strict liability to include injured bystanders.) 5. The defective condition must be the proximate cause of the injury or damage. 6. The goods must not have been substantially changed from the time the product was sold to the time the injury was sustained.
STRICT LIABILITY— PRODUCT DEFECT (See pages 264–266.)	Claims that a product is so defective as to be unreasonably dangerous generally allege that the product is unreasonably dangerous for one of the following reasons: 1. Because of a flaw in the manufacturing process. 2. Because of a design defect. 3. Because the manufacturer failed to warn adequately of harms associated with the product's use.
MARKET-SHARE LIABILITY (See pages 266–267.)	In cases in which plaintiffs cannot prove which of many distributors of a harmful product supplied the particular product that caused the plaintiffs' injuries, some courts have applied market-share liability. All firms that manufactured and distributed the harmful product during the period in question are then held liable for the plaintiffs' injuries in proportion to the firms' respective shares of the market, as directed by the court.
OTHER APPLICATIONS OF STRICT LIABILITY (See pages 267–268.)	1. Manufacturers and other sellers are liable for harms suffered by injured bystanders due to defective products. 2. Suppliers of component parts are strictly liable for defective parts that, when incorporated into a product, cause injuries to users.
DEFENSES TO PRODUCT LIABILITY (See pages 268–272.)	1. **Assumption of risk**—The user or consumer knew of the risk of harm and voluntarily assumed it. 2. **Product misuse**—The user or consumer misused the product in a way unforeseeable by the manufacturer. 3. **Comparative negligence**—Liability may be distributed between plaintiff and defendant under the doctrine of comparative negligence. 4. **Commonly known dangers**—If a defendant succeeds in convincing the court that a plaintiff's injury resulted from a commonly known danger, such as the danger associated with using a sharp knife, the defendant will not be liable. 5. **Other defenses**—A defendant can also defend against a strict liability claim by showing that there is no basis for the plaintiff's claim (that the plaintiff has not met the requirements for an action in negligence or strict liability, for example).

For Review

1. Can a manufacturer be held liable to *any* person who suffers an injury proximately caused by the manufacturer's negligently made product?

2. What are the elements of a cause of action in strict product liability?

3. Who may be held liable for injuries caused by defective products?

4. In what circumstance might a plaintiff not have to prove that a specific product was the product of a particular defendant?

5. What defenses to liability can be raised in a product liability lawsuit?

Questions and Case Problems

10–1. Product Liability. Under what contract theory can a seller be held liable to a consumer for physical harm or property damage that is caused by the goods sold? Under what tort theories can the seller be held liable?

10–2. Product Liability. Carmen buys a television set manufactured by AKI Electronics. She is going on vacation, so she takes the set to her mother's house for her mother to use. Because the set is defective, it explodes, causing considerable damage to her mother's house. Carmen's mother sues AKI for the damages to her house. Discuss the theories under which Carmen's mother can recover from AKI.

10–3. Product Liability. George Nesselrode lost his life in an airplane crash. The plane had been manufactured by Beech Aircraft Corp. and sold to Executive Beechcraft, Inc. Shortly before the crash occurred, Executive Beechcraft had conducted a routine inspection of the plane and found that some of the parts needed to be replaced. The new parts were supplied by Beech Aircraft but installed by Executive Beechcraft. These particular airplane parts could be installed backward, and if they were, the plane would crash. Nesselrode's crash resulted from just such an incorrect installation of the airplane parts. Nesselrode's wife, Jane, and three daughters sued Executive Beechcraft, Beech Aircraft, and Gerald Hultgren, the pilot who had flown the plane, for damages. Beech Aircraft claimed that it was not at fault because it had not installed the parts. Will Beech Aircraft be held liable for Nesselrode's death? Discuss. [*Nesselrode v. Executive Beechcraft, Inc.,* 707 S.W.2d 371 (Mo. 1986)]

10–4. Strict Liability. Embs was buying some groceries at Stamper's Cash Market. Unnoticed by her, a carton of 7-Up was sitting on the floor at the edge of the produce counter about one foot from where she was standing. Several of the 7-Up bottles exploded. Embs's leg was injured severely enough that she had to be taken to the hospital by a managing agent of the store. Embs sued the manufacturer of 7-Up, Pepsi-Cola Bottling Co. of Lexington, Kentucky, Inc., claiming that the manufacturer should be held strictly liable for the harm caused by its products. The trial court dismissed her claim. On appeal, what will the court decide? Discuss fully. [*Embs v. Pepsi-Cola Bottling Co. of Lexington, Kentucky, Inc.,* 528 S.W.2d 703 (Ky.App. 1975)]

10–5. Duty to Warn. William Mackowick, who had worked as an electrician for thirty years, was installing high-voltage capacitors in a switchgear room in a hospital when he noticed that a fellow electrician had removed the cover from an existing capacitor manufactured by Westinghouse Electric Corp. A warning label that Westinghouse had placed inside the cover of the metal box containing the capacitor instructed users to ground the electricity before handling. Nothing was said on the label about the propensity of electricity to arc. (Arcing occurs when electricity grounds itself by "jumping" to a nearby object or instrument.) Mackowick, while warning the other electrician of the danger, pointed his screwdriver toward the capacitor box. The electricity flowing through the fuses arced to the screwdriver and sent a high-voltage electric current through Mackowick's body. As a result, he sustained severe burns and was unable to return to work for three months. Should Westinghouse be held liable because it failed to warn users of arcing—a principle of electricity? Discuss. [*Mackowick v. Westinghouse Electric Corp.,* 575 A.2d 100 (Pa. 1990)]

10–6. Strict Liability. David Jordon, a ten-year-old boy, lost control of his sled, hit a tree, and was injured. The sled was a plastic toboggan-like sled that had been purchased from K-Mart. David's parents brought suit against K-Mart, alleging that the sled was defective and unreasonably dangerous because (1) the sled contained design defects (the molded runners on the sled rendered the sled unsteerable, and the sled lacked any independent steering or braking mechanisms), and (2) there were no warnings of the dangers inherent in the use of the sled. K-Mart moved for summary judgment. Should the court grant K-Mart's motion? Discuss fully. [*Jordon v. K-Mart Corp.*, 416 Pa.Super. 186, 611 A.2d 1328 (1992)]

10–7. Defenses to Product Liability. The Campbell Soup Co. manufactured, sold, and shipped packages of chicken-flavored Campbell's Ramen Noodle Soup to a distributor. The distributor sold and shipped the packages to Associated Grocers. Associated Grocers shipped the packages to Warehouse Foods, a retail grocer. Six weeks after Campbell first shipped the soup to the distributor, Warehouse Foods sold it to Kathy Jo Gates. Gates prepared the soup. Halfway through eating her second bowl, she discovered beetle larvae in the noodles. She filed a product liability suit against Campbell and others. Gates argued, in effect, that the mere presence of the bugs in the soup was sufficient to hold Campbell strictly liable. How might Campbell defend itself? [*Campbell Soup Co. v. Gates,* 319 Ark. 54, 889 S.W.2d 750 (1994)]

10–8. Product Liability. John Whitted bought a Chevrolet Nova from General Motors Corp. (GMC). Six years later, Whitted crashed the Nova into two trees. During the impact, the seat belt broke, and Whitted was thrust against the steering wheel, which broke, and the windshield, which shattered. He suffered fractures in his left arm and cuts to his forehead. Whitted sued GMC and the manufacturer, asserting, among other things, that because the seat belt broke, the defendants were strictly liable for his injuries. What does Whitted have to show in order to prove his case? [*Whitted v. General Motors Corp.,* 58 F.3d 1200 (7th Cir. 1995)]

A Question of Ethics and Social Responsibility

10–9. Three-year-old Randy Welch, the son of Steve and Teresa Griffith, climbed up to a shelf and obtained a disposable butane cigarette lighter. Randy then used the lighter to ignite a flame, which set fire to his pajama top. Welch and his parents sued the lighter's manufacturer, Scripto-Tokai Corp., for damages, alleging that the lighter was defective and unreasonably dangerous because it was not child resistant. In view of this factual background, consider the following questions. [*Welch v. Scripto-Tokai Corp.,* 651 N.E.2d 810 (Ind.App. 1995)]

1. One of the questions raised in this case was whether the risks attending the lighter were sufficiently "open and obvious" that the manufacturer did not need to warn of those risks. If you were the judge, how would you decide this issue? Explain your reasoning.
2. If a product is not dangerous to an extent beyond that contemplated by the ordinary consumer, should the manufacturer nonetheless be held liable if it could have made the product safer? Explain.
3. How can a court decide what kinds of risks should be open and obvious for the ordinary consumer?

For Critical Analysis

10–10. The United States has the strictest product liability laws in the world today. Why do you think many other countries, particularly developing countries, are more lax with respect to holding manufacturers liable for product defects?

CHAPTER 11

Intellectual Property and Cyberlaw

Contents

Chapter Objectives

After reading this chapter, you should be able to . . .

1. Identify the law governing trademarks and related property.
2. Explain how the law protects copyrights.
3. State what a patent is and when patent infringement occurs.
4. Define a trade secret and the law that protects it.
5. Describe international protection for intellectual property rights.

Most people think of wealth in terms of houses, land, cars, stocks, and bonds. Wealth, however, also includes **intellectual property**, which consists of the products of individuals' minds—products that result from intellectual, creative processes. Although it is an abstract term for an abstract concept, intellectual property is nonetheless wholly familiar to virtually everyone. *Trademarks, service marks, copyrights,* and *patents* are all forms of intellectual property. The book you are reading is copyrighted. Undoubtedly, the personal computer you use at home is trademarked. The study of intellectual property law is valuable because intellectual property has taken on an increasing importance, not only within the United States but globally as well. Today, ownership rights in intangible intellectual property are more important to the prosperity of many U.S. companies than are their tangible assets.

The need to protect creative works was voiced by the framers of the U.S. Constitution over two hundred years ago, as stated in the accompanying quotation. Laws protecting patents, trademarks, and copyrights are explicitly designed to protect and reward inventive and artistic creativity. Although intellectual property law limits the economic freedom of some individuals, it does so to protect the freedom of others to enjoy the fruits of their labors—in the form of profits.

In the first part of this chapter, we examine trademark, patent, and copyright laws, as well as the legal protection available for intellectual property that consists of *trade secrets*. We then examine an issue of increasing significance to businesspersons: the protection of intellectual property rights in today's online environment.

Intellectual Property
Property resulting from intellectual, creative processes.

"To promote the Progress of Science and useful Arts, by securing for limited Times to Authors and Inventors the exculsive Right to their respective Writings and Discoveries."

Article I, Section 8, of the U.S. Constitution

Trademarks and Related Property

A **trademark** is a distinctive mark, motto, device, or implement that a manufacturer stamps, prints, or otherwise affixes to the goods it produces so that they may be identified on the market and their origin vouched for. Statutory protection of trademarks and related property is provided at the federal level by the Lanham Trademark Act of 1946.[1] The Lanham Act was enacted in part to protect manufacturers from losing business to rival companies that used confusingly similar trademarks. The Lanham Act incorporates the common law of trademarks and provides remedies for owners of trademarks who wish to enforce their claims in federal court. Many states also have trademark statutes.

At common law, the person who used a symbol or mark to identify a business or product was protected in the use of that trademark. Clearly, if one used the trademark of another, it would lead consumers to believe that one's goods were made by the other. The law seeks to avoid this kind of confusion. In the following famous case concerning Coca-Cola, the defendants argued that the Coca-Cola trademark was entitled to no protection under the law, because the term did not accurately represent the product.

Trademark A distinctive mark, motto, device, or implement that a manufacturer stamps, prints, or otherwise affixes to the goods it produces so that they may be identified on the market and their origins made known. Once a trademark is established (under the common law or through registration), the owner is entitled to its exclusive use.

---

1. 15 U.S.C. Sections 1051–1127.

Case 11.1 ● The Coca-Cola Co. v. The Koke Co. of America

Supreme Court of the United States, 1920.
254 U.S. 143,
41 S.Ct. 113,
65 L.Ed. 189.

COMPANY PROFILE *John Pemberton, an Atlanta pharmacist, invented a caramel-colored, carbonated soft drink in 1886. His bookkeeper, Frank Robinson, named the beverage Coca-Cola after two of the ingredients, coca leaves and kola nuts. Asa Candler bought the Coca-Cola Company in 1891, and within seven years, he made the soft drink available in all of the United States, as well as in parts of Canada and Mexico. Candler continued to sell Coke aggressively and to open up new markets, reaching Europe before 1910. In doing so, however, he attracted numerous competitors, some of whom tried to capitalize directly on the Coke name.*

BACKGROUND AND FACTS The Coca-Cola Company sought to enjoin (prevent) the Koke Company of America and other beverage companies from, among other things, using the word Koke for their products. The Koke Company of America and other beverage companies contended that the Coca-Cola trademark was a fraudulent representation and that Coca-Cola was therefore not entitled to any help from the courts. The Koke Company and the other defendants alleged that the Coca-Cola Company, by its use of the Coca-Cola name, represented that the beverage contained cocaine (from coca leaves), which it no longer did. The trial court granted the injunction against the Koke Company, but the appellate court reversed the lower court's ruling. Coca-Cola then appealed to the United States Supreme Court.

IN THE WORDS OF THE COURT . . .

Mr. Justice HOLMES delivered the opinion of the Court.

* * * *

* * * Before 1900 the beginning of [Coca-Cola's] good will was more or less helped by the presence of cocaine, a drug that, like alcohol or caffeine or opium, may be described as a deadly poison or as a valuable item of the pharmacopeia according to the rhetorical purposes in view. The amount seems to have been very small,[a] but it may have been enough to begin a bad habit and after the Food and Drug Act of June 30, 1906, if not earlier, long before this suit was brought, it was eliminated from the plaintiff's compound. * * *

* * * Since 1900 the sales have increased at a very great rate corresponding to a like increase in advertising. The name now characterizes a beverage to be had at almost any soda fountain. It means a single thing coming from a single source, and well known to the community. It hardly would be too much to say that the drink characterizes the name as much as the name the drink. In other words Coca-Cola probably means to most persons the plaintiff's familiar product to be had everywhere rather than a compound of particular substances. * * * [B]efore this suit was brought the plaintiff had advertised to the public that it must not expect and would not find cocaine, and had eliminated everything tending to suggest cocaine effects except the name and the picture of [coca] leaves and nuts, which probably conveyed little or nothing to most who saw it. It appears to us that it would be going too far to deny the plaintiff relief against a palpable fraud because possibly here and there an ignorant person might call for the drink with the hope for incipient cocaine intoxication. The plaintiff's position must be judged by the facts as they were when the suit was begun, not by the facts of a different condition and an earlier time.

DECISION AND REMEDY The district court's injunction was allowed to stand. The competing beverage companies were enjoined from calling their products Koke.

FOR CRITICAL ANALYSIS—SOCIAL CONSIDERATION *How can a court determine when a particular nickname for a branded product has entered into common use?*

---

a.   In reality, until 1903 the amount of active cocaine in each bottle of Coke was equivalent to one "line" of cocaine.

Trademark Registration

Trademarks may be registered with the state or with the federal government. To register for protection under federal trademark law, a person must file an application with the U.S. Patent and Trademark Office in Washington, D.C. Under current law, a mark can be registered (1) if it is currently in commerce or (2) if the applicant intends to put it into commerce within six months.

Under extenuating circumstances, the six-month period can be extended by thirty months, giving the applicant a total of three years from the date of notice of trademark approval to make use of the mark and file the required use statement. Registration is postponed until the mark is actually used. Nonetheless, during this waiting period, any applicant can legally protect his or her trademark against a third party who previously has neither used the mark nor filed an application for it. Registration is renewable between the fifth and sixth years after the initial registration and every ten years thereafter (every twenty years for trademarks registered before 1990).

Registration of a trademark with the U.S. Patent and Trademark Office gives notice on a nationwide basis that the trademark belongs exclusively to the registrant. The registrant is also allowed to use the symbol ® to indicate that the mark has been registered. Whenever that trademark is copied to a substantial degree or used in its entirety by another, intentionally or unintentionally, the trademark has been infringed (used without authorization). When a trademark has been infringed, the owner of the mark has a cause of action against the infringer. A person need not have registered a trademark in order to sue for trademark infringement, but registration does furnish proof of the date of inception of the trademark's use.

> "The protection of trademarks is the law's recognition of the psychological function of symbols. If it is true that we live by symbols, it is no less true that we purchase goods by them."
>
> Felix Frankfurter, 1882–1965 (Associate justice of the United States Supreme Court, 1939–1962)

Distinctiveness of Mark

A central objective of the Lanham Act is to reduce the likelihood that registered marks will be so similar to one another that consumers cannot distinguish among them. The Lanham Act states, "No trademark by which the goods of the applicant may be distinguished from the goods of others shall be refused registration."[2]

Only those trademarks that are deemed sufficiently distinctive from all competing trademarks will be protected, however. The trademarks must be sufficiently distinct to enable consumers to identify the manufacturer of the goods easily and to differentiate among competing products.

STRONG MARKS.   Fanciful, arbitrary, or suggestive trademarks are generally considered to be the most distinctive (strongest) trademarks, because they are normally taken from outside the context of the particular product and thus provide the best means of distinguishing one product from another.

Fanciful trademarks include invented words, such as Xerox for one manufacturer's copiers and Kodak for another company's photographic products. Arbitrary trademarks include actual words used with products that have no literal connection to the words, such as English Leather used as a name for an after-shave lotion (and not for leather processed in England). Suggestive trademarks are those that suggest something about a product without describing the product directly. For example, the trademark Dairy Queen suggests an association between the products and milk, but it does not directly describe ice cream.

---

2.   15 U.S.C. Section 1052.

SECONDARY MEANING.   Descriptive terms, geographical terms, and personal names are not inherently distinctive and do not receive protection under the law until they acquire a secondary meaning. A secondary meaning may arise when customers begin to associate a specific term or phrase (such as London Fog) with specific trademarked items (coats with London Fog labels). Whether a secondary meaning becomes attached to a term or name usually depends on how extensively the product is advertised, the market for the product, the number of sales, and other factors. Once a secondary meaning is attached to a term or name, a trademark is considered distinctive and is protected. Even a shade of color can qualify for trademark protection, once customers associate the color with the product.[3]

GENERIC TERMS.   Generic terms, such as *bicycle* and *computer*, receive no protection, even if they acquire secondary meanings. A particularly thorny problem arises when a trademark acquires generic use. For example, *aspirin* and *thermos* were originally the names of trademarked products, but today the words are used generically. Other examples are *escalator, trampoline, raisin bran, dry ice, lanolin, linoleum, nylon,* and *corn flakes.* Even so, the courts will not allow another firm to use those marks in such a way as to deceive a potential consumer.

The Federal Trademark Dilution Act of 1995

In 1995, Congress amended the Lanham Act by passing the Federal Trademark Dilution Act.[4] Until the passage of this amendment, federal trademark law only prohibited the unauthorized use of the same mark on competing (or on noncompeting but "related") goods or services when such use would likely confuse consumers as to the origin of those goods and services. Trademark dilution laws, which about half of the states have enacted, protect "distinctive" or "famous" trademarks (such as Jergens, McDonald's, RCA, and Macintosh) from certain unauthorized uses of the marks *regardless* of a showing of competition or a likelihood of confusion. The Federal Trademark Dilution Act extended the protection available to trademark owners by creating a federal cause of action for trademark dilution.

In one of the first cases to be decided under the 1995 act's provisions, a federal court held that a famous mark may be diluted not only by the use of an *identical* mark but also by the use of a *similar* mark. The case was brought by Ringling Bros.-Barnum & Bailey, Combined Shows, Inc., against the state of Utah. Ringling Bros. claimed that Utah's use of the slogan "The Greatest Snow on Earth"—to attract visitors to the state's recreational and scenic resorts— diluted the distinctiveness of the circus's famous trademark, "The Greatest Show on Earth." Utah moved to dismiss the suit, arguing that the 1995 provisions only protect owners of famous trademarks against the unauthorized use of identical marks. The court disagreed and refused to grant Utah's motion to dismiss the case.[5]

Brand names for popular soft drinks. Why are such names given protection under trademark law?

---

3.   *Qualitex Co. v. Jacobson Products Co.,* 514 U.S. 159, 115 S.Ct. 1300, 131 L.Ed.2d 248 (1995).
4.   15 U.S.C. Section 1125.
5.   *Ringling Bros.–Barnum & Bailey, Combined Shows, Inc. v. Utah Division of Travel Development,* 935 F.Supp. 736 (E.D.Va. 1996).

Trade Dress

The term **trade dress** refers to the image and overall appearance of a product—for example, the distinctive decor, menu, layout, and style of service of a particular restaurant. Basically, trade dress is subject to the same protection as trademarks. In cases involving trade dress infringement, as in trademark infringement cases, a major consideration is whether consumers are likely to be confused by the allegedly infringing use. The issue in the following case was whether a golf course owner was liable for trade dress infringement for replicating on its course, without permission, the most prominent feature of a different, famous golf course.

Trade Dress The image and overall appearance of a product—for example, the distinctive decor, menu, layout, and syle of service of a particular restaurant.

Case 11.2 ● Pebble Beach Co. v. Tour 18 I, Ltd.

United States
District Court,
Southern District of Texas, 1996.
942 F.Supp. 1513.

BACKGROUND AND FACTS   Sea Pines Company, Inc., operates Harbour Town Golf Links—one of the most famous golf courses in the United States—on Hilton Head Island, South Carolina. Tour 18 I, Limited, operates golf courses in Texas. For its courses, Tour 18 intentionally copied golf holes from famous courses, including Harbour Town's Hole 18, without the permission of the owners. Tour 18 even built replicas of the Harbour Town lighthouse, which is the distinctive feature of the Harbour Town course. Tour 18 markets its courses aggressively, featuring especially the replicas of the lighthouse. Sea Pines and others, including Pebble Beach Company, filed a suit in federal district court against Tour 18. The plaintiffs alleged, among other things, that Tour 18's use of the replica lighthouses constituted trade dress infringement.

IN THE WORDS OF THE COURT . . .
HITTNER, District Judge.
        * * * *

* * * Tour 18 is liable for trade dress infringement if there is a likelihood of confusion generated by Tour 18's replication and use of [Sea Pines's] trade dress.

* * * [T]hat there is an identity of customers, identity of advertising, and similarity between the parties' goods and services * * * support a finding of likelihood of confusion. Additionally, * * * the trade dress of the lighthouse is a strong, distinctive identifier * * * for Harbour Town Golf Links. Tour 18's intent in copying the trade dress of the lighthouse and Harbour Town Hole 18 also weighs in favor of a likelihood of confusion.

* * * [M]any golfers [have been] confused into believing Tour 18 received permission or approval from plaintiffs to replicate their golf holes. * * * Therefore, in this Court's view, Tour 18's adoption of Sea Pines' trade dress creates confusion among golfers as to whether Tour 18 sought and received assistance, approval, or permission from Sea Pines to replicate the Harbour Town lighthouse and 18th Hole.

DECISION AND REMEDY   The federal district court held that Tour 18 was liable for trade dress infringement. The court ordered Tour 18 to remove its replicas of the Harbour Town lighthouse from its courses and to disclaim prominently, in all of its marketing, "any association, affiliation, sponsorship, or permission from" Sea Pines.

FOR CRITICAL ANALYSIS—*Why did the court require the defendant to stop its infringement and disclaim any association with Sea Pines?*

Service Mark A mark used in the sale or the advertising of services, such as to distinguish the services of one person from the services of others. Titles, character names, and other distinctive features of radio and television programs may be registered as service marks.

Certification Mark A mark used by one or more persons, other than the owner, to certify the region, materials, mode of manufacture, quality, or accuracy of the owner's goods or services.

Collective Mark A mark used by members of a cooperative, association, or other organization to certify the region, materials, mode of manufacture, quality, or accuracy of the specific goods or services.

Trade Name A term that is used to indicate part or all of a business's name and that is directly related to the business's reputation and goodwill. Trade names are protected under the common law (and under trademark law, if the name is the same as the firm's trademarked property).

Service, Certification, and Collective Marks

A **service mark** is similar to a trademark but is used to distinguish the services of one person or company from those of another. For example, each airline has a particular mark or symbol associated with its name. Titles and character names used in radio and television are frequently registered as service marks.

Other marks protected by law include certification marks and collective marks. A **certification mark** is used by one or more persons other than the owner to certify the region, materials, mode of manufacture, quality, or accuracy of the owner's goods or services. When used by members of a cooperative, association, or other organization, it is referred to as a **collective mark**. Examples of certification marks are the phrases "Good Housekeeping Seal of Approval" and "UL Tested." Collective marks appear at the ends of the credits of movies to indicate the various associations and organizations that participated in the making of the movies. The union marks found on the tags of certain products are also collective marks.

Trade Names

Trademarks apply to *products*. The term **trade name** is used to indicate part or all of a business's name, whether the business is a sole proprietorship, a partnership, or a corporation. Generally, a trade name is directly related to a business and its goodwill. A trade name may be protected as a trademark if the trade name is the same as the name of the company's trademarked product—for example, Coca-Cola. Unless also used as a trademark or service mark, a trade name cannot be registered with the federal government. Trade names are protected under the common law, however. As with trademarks, words must be unusual or fancifully used if they are to be protected as trade names. The word *Safeway*, for example, was held by the courts to be sufficiently fanciful to obtain protection as a trade name for a foodstore chain.[6]

Patents

A **patent** is a grant from the government that gives an inventor the exclusive right to make, use, and sell an invention for a period of twenty years from the date of filing the application for a patent. Patents for a fourteen-year period are given for designs, as opposed to inventions. For either a regular patent or a design patent, the applicant must demonstrate to the satisfaction of the U.S. Patent and Trademark Office that the invention, discovery, process, or design is genuine, novel, useful, and not obvious in light of current technology. A patent holder gives notice to all that an article or design is patented by placing on it the word *Patent* or *Pat.* plus the patent number.

Patent Infringement

If a firm makes, uses, or sells another's patented design, product, or process without the patent owner's permission, the tort of patent infringement occurs. Patent infringement may occur even though not all features or parts of an

---

6. *Safeway Stores v. Suburban Foods*, 130 F.Supp. 249 (E.D.Va. 1955).

invention are copied. (With respect to a patented process, however, all steps or their equivalents must be copied in order for infringement to occur.) Often, litigation for patent infringement is so costly that the patent holder will instead offer to sell to the infringer a license to use the patented design, product, or process. Indeed, in many cases, the costs of detection, prosecution, and monitoring are so high that patents are valueless to their owners, because the owners cannot afford to protect them.

Until recently, parties involved in patent litigation also faced another problem: it was often hard to predict the outcome of litigation because jurors found it difficult to understand the issues in dispute. This was particularly true when the claims involved patents on complicated products—such as sophisticated technological or biotechnological products. In a significant case decided in 1996, *Markman v. Westview Instruments, Inc.,*[7] the United States Supreme Court held that it is the responsibility of judges, not juries, to interpret the scope and nature of patent claims. In other words, before a case goes to the jury, the judge must interpret the nature of the claim and give the jury instructions based on that interpretation.

Determining the nature and scope of a patent claim is a key element in most patent cases. Many observers thus predict that the likely result of the Supreme Court's decision will be that the majority of patent cases will be decided on motions for summary judgment. Many also predict that the Court's decision will also lead to greater clarity and uniformity in the case law in this area.

Patent A government grant that gives an inventor the exclusive right or privilege to make, use, or sell his or her invention for a limited time period. The word patent usually refers to some invention and designates either the instrument by which patent rights are evidenced or the patent itself.

> **"The patent system . . . added the fuel of interest to the fire of genius."**
>
> Abraham Lincoln, 1809–1865
> (Sixteenth president of the United States, 1861–1865)

---

7. 517 U.S. 370, 116 S.Ct. 1384, 134 L.Ed.2d 577 (1996).

International Perspective

In the United States, if someone sells a counterfeit product that infringes on another's patent, the patent owner can bring a suit against the infringer for damages. What happens, though, if counterfeit products are sold in countries that do not offer much protection for those holding patent rights to the products under U.S. law? In such situations, not only do U.S. patent holders lose revenues from the sales of the fake products, but also, at least in some instances, consumers may suffer from the counterfeit products.

Certainly, the growing trade in counterfeit drugs has not appreciably benefited consumers in developing countries, because such products may consist of inert or even harmful chemicals. The death in 1990 of more than a hundred children in Nigeria after they were given a counterfeit medicine that contained an industrial solvent is just one of the more obvious examples of the dangers posed by these products. Unfortunately, drug counterfeiters are so skilled at duplicating the packaging of the legitimate products that a chemical analysis of the product itself is often necessary to uncover the fraud.

Although U.S. pharmaceutical companies lose billions of dollars in revenues each year to the counterfeiters, the companies have generally been reluctant to acknowledge that such a problem even exists. The fact that developing countries often do not offer any significant legal protection for drugs patented in the United States further complicates efforts to stop the production and sale of phony drugs.

For Critical Analysis: *Why would U.S. pharmaceutical companies be reluctant to acknowledge the fact that counterfeit versions of their drugs are harming consumers?*

Patents for Software

At one time, it was difficult for developers and manufacturers of software to obtain patent protection because many software products simply automate procedures that can be performed manually. In other words, the computer programs do not meet the "novel" and "not obvious" requirements previously mentioned. Also, the basis for software is often a mathematical equation or formula, which is not patentable. In 1981, however, the United States Supreme Court held that it is possible to obtain a patent for a process that incorporates a computer program—providing, of course, that the process itself is patentable.[8] Subsequently, many patents have been issued for software-related inventions.

Another obstacle to obtaining patent protection for software is the procedure for obtaining patents. The process can be expensive and slow. The time element is a particularly important consideration for someone wishing to obtain a patent on software. In light of the rapid changes and improvements in computer technology, the delay could undercut the product's success in the marketplace.

Despite these difficulties, patent protection is used in the computer industry. If a patent is infringed, the patent holder may sue for an injunction, damages, and the destruction of all infringing copies, as well as attorneys' fees and court costs.

Copyrights

A **copyright** is an intangible property right granted by federal statute to the author or originator of a literary or artistic production of a specified type. Currently, copyrights are governed by the Copyright Act of 1976,[9] as amended. Works created after January 1, 1978, are automatically given statutory copyright protection for the life of the author plus 70 years. For copyrights owned by publishing houses, the copyright expires 95 years from the date of publication or 120 years from the date of creation, whichever is first. For works by more than one author, the copyright expires 70 years after the death of the last surviving author.

Copyrights can be registered with the U.S. Copyright Office in Washington, D.C. A copyright owner no longer needs to place the symbol © or the term *Copr.* or *Copyright* on the work, however, to have the work protected against infringement. Chances are that if somebody created it, somebody owns it.

What Is Protected Expression?

Works that are copyrightable include books, records, films, artworks, architectural plans, menus, music videos, product packaging, and computer software. To obtain protection under the Copyright Act, a work must be original and fall into one of the following categories: (1) literary works; (2) musical works; (3) dramatic works; (4) pantomimes and choreographic works; (5) pictorial, graphic, and sculptural works; (6) films and other audiovisual works; and (7) sound recordings. To be protected, a work must be "fixed in a durable

Patent application documents. What does an applicant need to prove about his or her invention to obtain a patent?

Copyright The exclusive right of "authors" to publish, print, or sell an intellectual producton for a statutory period of time. A copyright has the same monopolistic nature as a patent or trademark, but it differs in that it applies exclusively to works of art, literature, and other works of authorship (including computer programs).

---

8.   *Diamond v. Diehr*, 450 U.S. 175, 101 S.Ct. 1048, 67 L.Ed.2d 155 (1981).
9.   17 U.S.C. Sections 101 et seq.

medium" from which it can be perceived, reproduced, or communicated. Protection is automatic. Registration is not required.

Section 102 of the Copyright Act specifically excludes copyright protection for any "idea, procedure, process, system, method of operation, concept, principle, or discovery, regardless of the form in which it is described, explained, illustrated, or embodied." Note that it is not possible to copyright an *idea*. The underlying ideas embodied in a work may be freely used by others. What is copyrightable is the particular way in which an idea is *expressed*. Whenever an idea and an expression are inseparable, the expression cannot be copyrighted. Generally, anything that is not an original expression will not qualify for copyright protection. Facts widely known to the public are not copyrightable. Page numbers are not copyrightable, because they follow a sequence known to everyone. Mathematical calculations are not copyrightable.

Compilations of facts, however, are copyrightable. Section 103 of the Copyright Act defines a compilation as "a work formed by the collection and assembling of preexisting materials or data that are selected, coordinated, or arranged in such a way that the resulting work as a whole constitutes an original work of authorship." The key requirement in the copyrightability of a compilation is originality. Thus, the White Pages of a telephone directory do not qualify for copyright protection when the information that makes up the directory (names, addresses, and telephone numbers) is not selected, coordinated, or arranged in an original way.[10] In one case, even the Yellow Pages of a telephone directory did not qualify for copyright protection.[11]

Copyright law protects song lyrics as literary works. When recording a song, notice of copyright must be included, and royalties must be paid. In addition, the lyrics cannot be published without permission. These principles are not in doubt. What is sometimes in doubt is how they apply to new technology. At issue in the following case was how they applied to a new development in the karaoke industry.

---

10. *Feist Publications, Inc. v. Rural Telephone Service Co.*, 499 U.S. 340, 111 S.Ct. 1282, 113 L.Ed.2d 358 (1991).
11. *Bellsouth Advertising & Publishing Corp. v. Donnelley Information Publishing, Inc.*, 999 F.2d 1436 (11th Cir. 1993).

Case 11.3 ● ABKCO Music Inc. v. Stellar Records, Inc.

United States
Court of Appeals,
Second Circuit, 1996.
96 F.3d 60.

BACKGROUND AND FACTS ABKCO Music, Inc., owns the copyrights to seven songs by Mick Jagger and Keith Richards. Performance Tracks, Inc., is in the karaoke industry. Using new technology, Tracks encodes the audio rendition of a song with a simultaneous video display of the lyrics on "compact discs + graphics" (CD+Gs).[a] Tracks and Stellar Records, Inc., distributed their versions of

ABKCO's Jagger-Richards tunes on CD+Gs, including, without ABKCO's permission, the songs' lyrics. ABKCO filed a suit in a federal district court against the distributors, alleging in part copyright infringement. The court ordered Tracks to stop "publishing" the lyrics. In effect, this prohibited Tracks from distributing its discs. Tracks appealed.

---

a. The primary difference between CD+Gs and other karaoke discs is that CD+Gs display only the lyrics. Other discs include other images, such as a picture of a beach.

(Continued)

Case 11.3—continued

IN THE WORDS OF THE COURT . . .
OWEN, * * * Judge.
    * * * *

    A time-honored method of facilitating singing along with music has been to furnish the singer with a printed copy of the lyrics. Copyright holders have always enjoyed exclusive rights over such copies. While projecting lyrics on a screen and producing printed copies of the lyrics, of course, have their differences, there is no reason to treat them differently for purposes of the Copyright Act.
    * * * *

    Tracks * * * contends that the Copyright Act has not kept pace with new technology, and that Congress * * * would include [CD+Gs] within the definition of "phonorecords" if it were to redefine "phonorecord" today. It would, however, seem to be a sufficient answer to Tracks' contention to observe that Tracks' product is not within the statutory definition of "phonorecord," and what Congress may or may not do in the future to redefine the term is not for us to speculate.

DECISION AND REMEDY   The U.S. Court of Appeals for the Second Circuit affirmed the lower court's order.

FOR CRITICAL ANALYSIS—ETHICAL CONSIDERATION   *Is it fair for one person to realize profits by "publishing" another's copyrighted material?*

Copyright Infringement

Whenever the form or expression of an idea is copied, an infringement of copyright has occurred. The reproduction does not have to be exactly the same as the original, nor does it have to reproduce the original in its entirety. If a substantial part of the original is reproduced, there is copyyright infringement.

    Those who infringe copyrights may be liable for damages or criminal penalties. These range from actual damages or statutory damages, imposed at the court's discretion, to criminal proceedings for willful violations. Actual damages are based on the harm caused to the copyright holder by the infringement, while statutory damages, not to exceed $100,000, are provided for under the Copyright Act. Criminal proceedings may result in fines and/or imprisonment.

    An exception to liability for copyright infringement is made under the "fair use" doctrine. In certain circumstances, a person or organization can reproduce copyrighted material without paying royalties (fees paid to the copyright holder for the privilege of reproducing the copyrighted material). Section 107 of the Copyright Act provides as follows:

> [T]he fair use of a copyrighted work, including such use by reproduction in copies or phonorecords or by any other means specified by [Section 106 of the Copyright Act], for purposes such as criticism, comment, news reporting, teaching (including multiple copies for classroom use), scholarship, or research, is not an infringement of copyright. In determining whether the use made of a work in any particular case is a fair use the factors to be considered shall include—
>
> (1) the purpose and character of the use, including whether such use is of a commercial nature or is for nonprofit educational purposes;
> (2) the nature of the copyrighted work;

(3) the amount and substantiality of the portion used in relation to the copyrighted work as a whole; and

(4) the effect of the use upon the potential market for or value of the copyrighted work.

Because these guidelines are very broad, the courts determine whether a particular use is fair on a case-by-case basis. Thus, anyone reproducing copyrighted material may still be subject to a violation. In determining whether a use is fair, courts have often considered the fourth factor to be the most important.

A question that sometimes comes up is the extent to which copying material for classroom use is a fair use. That was the question in the following case.

Case 11.4 ● Princeton University Press v. Michigan Document Services, Inc.

United States
Court of Appeals,
Sixth Circuit, 1996.
99 F.3d 1381.

HISTORICAL AND SOCIAL SETTING   *To previous generations of students, the coursepack was a rare educational tool. Because of advances in technology, however, coursepacks have become almost as common as textbooks. Coursepacks are produced by commercial copyshops, which typically obtain permission before including copyrighted materials. Profits from coursepack sales can be high, and copyshops often compete intensely for business.*

BACKGROUND AND FACTS   James Smith, the owner of Michigan Document Services, Inc. (MDS), a commercial copyshop, concluded that it was unnecessary to obtain the copyright owners' permission to reproduce copyrighted materials in coursepacks. Smith publicized his conclusion, claiming that professors would not have to worry about any delay in production at his shop. MDS then compiled, bound, and sold coursepacks to students at the University of Michigan without obtaining the permission of copyright owners. Princeton University Press and two other publishers filed a suit in a federal district court against MDS, alleging copyright infringement. MDS claimed that its coursepacks were covered under the fair use doctrine. The court ruled in favor of the copyright owners, and MDS appealed.

IN THE WORDS OF THE COURT . . .
DAVID A. NELSON, Circuit Judge.
    *   *   *   *

    *   *   * To negate fair use, one need only show that if the challenged use should become widespread, it would adversely affect the potential market for the copyrighted work. Under this test, *   *   * it is reasonably clear that the plaintiff publishers have succeeded in negating fair use.

    *   *   * [M]ost of the copyshops that compete with MDS in the sale of coursepacks pay permission fees for the privilege of duplicating and selling excerpts from copyrighted works. The three plaintiffs together have been collecting permission fees at a rate approaching $500,000 a year. If copyshops across the nation were to start doing what [MDS has] been doing here, this revenue stream would shrivel and the potential value of the copyrighted works of scholarship published by the plaintiffs would be diminished accordingly.

DECISION AND REMEDY   The U.S. Court of Appeals for the Sixth Circuit held in part that MDS's practice of preparing coursepacks without obtaining the copyright owners' permission was not a fair use and ordered MDS to stop.

FOR CRITICAL ANALYSIS—SOCIAL CONSIDERATION   *Does the ruling in this case mean that copyshops can no longer copy and sell copyrighted material for classroom use?*

Copyright Protection for Software

In 1980, Congress passed the Computer Software Copyright Act, which amended the Copyright Act of 1976 to include computer programs in the list of creative works protected by federal copyright law. The 1980 statute, which classifies computer programs as "literary works," defines a computer program as a "set of statements or instructions to be used directly or indirectly in a computer in order to bring about a certain result."

Because of the unique nature of computer programs, the courts have had many problems in applying and interpreting the 1980 act. In a series of cases decided in the 1980s, the courts held that copyright protection extended not only to those parts of a computer program that can be read by humans, such as the "high-level" language of a source code, but also to the binary-language object code of a computer program, which is readable only by the computer.[12] Additionally, such elements as the overall structure, sequence, and organization of a program were deemed copyrightable.[13]

By the early 1990s, the issue had evolved into whether the "look and feel"—the general appearance, command structure, video images, menus, windows, and other screen displays—of computer programs should also be protected by copyright. Although the courts have disagreed on this issue, the tendency has been not to extend copyright protection to look-and-feel aspects of computer programs. For example, in 1992 a federal district court held that the user interface of Apple's Macintosh computer is not protected under a look-and-feel theory and that Apple's use of windows, icons, and menus—and generally the series of images that Apple calls a "desktop metaphor"—is an unprotectible "idea."[14] Similarly, in 1995, the Court of Appeals for the First Circuit held that Lotus Development Corporation's menu command hierarchy for its Lotus 1-2-3 spreadsheet is not protectable under the Copyright Act. The court deemed that the menu command hierarchy is a "method of operation," and Section 102 of the Copyright Act specifically excludes methods of operation from copyright protection.[15] The decision was affirmed by the United States Supreme Court in 1996.[16]

The No Electronic Theft Act of 1997

The No Electronic Theft Act (NETA) of 1997 provides some protection under the federal criminal copyright statute for copyrighted works, especially computer software, on the Internet. Previously, to be convicted of criminal copyright infringement, the law required that a party make a profit from the infringement. Piracy of computer software occurred on the Internet not for money, however, but one of a malicious intent or a desire for notoriety. The NETA provides that intentionally taking and distributing pirated, copyrighted

---

12.   See *Stern Electronics, Inc. v. Kaufman*, 669 F.2d 852 (2d Cir. 1982); and *Apple Computer, Inc. v. Franklin Computer Corp.*, 714 F.2d 1240 (3d Cir. 1983).
13.   *Whelan Associates, Inc. v. Jaslow Dental Laboratory, Inc.*, 797 F.2d 1222 (3d Cir. 1986).
14.   *Apple Computer, Inc. v. Microsoft Corp.*, 799 F.Supp. 1006 (D.N.Cal. 1992). The district court's ruling was not upset on appeal.
15.   *Lotus Development Corp. v. Borland International, Inc.*, 49 F.3d 807 (1st Cir. 1995).
16.   *Lotus Development Corp. v. Borland International, Inc.*, 517 U.S. 843, 116 S.Ct. 804, 113 L.Ed.2d 610 (1996). This issue may again come before the Supreme Court for a decision, because only eight justices heard the case, and there was a tied vote; the effect of the tie was to affirm the lower court's decision.

Technology and Software Piracy

Highly skilled programmers must expend thousands of hours of labor to create a commercially successful software program. Each copy of the program may sell for hundreds of dollars. Consequently, there is a tremendous incentive for individuals and companies to purchase a single copy of the program and then make duplicates—to give or sell to others or to distribute to employees within the company. The popularity of such practices in companies throughout Europe and Asia has proved particularly costly for U.S. software manufacturers.

Because U.S. companies lead the world in the production and sale of computer software, they also suffer the greatest losses (billions of dollars annually) from the unauthorized copying of computer programs, referred to as *software piracy*. Over 90 percent of the software in Pakistan, Russia, and China, for example, consists of illegal copies. For Brazil, Malaysia, and Mexico, the figures are slightly lower, but they still exceed 80 percent. In the United States, an estimated 35 percent of the software in use has been pirated.

The development of electronic networks makes it even easier to copy software illegally. Anyone with a computer and a modem can now transmit copies of computer programs to others over the Internet, to which more than 150 countries are now connected. What this means is that a program that retails for, say, $100 can be transmitted via the Internet to someone on the far side of the globe—and that person can sell copies of the program for only a few dollars per copy. Unlike unauthorized copies of videos and musical recordings, pirated software programs are not second-rate versions of the originals. A $2 copy of a computer program often performs as efficiently as the original, which may sell for $100 or more. Of course, the pirated version is not accompanied by a user's manual, which can diminish the usefulness and application of the software.

The ease with which software programs can be duplicated leaves U.S. companies with little choice except to pursue aggressively any available legal remedies in the courts and to pressure the U.S. government to push for protection against software piracy in its trade agreements with other countries. In 1994, for example, a U.S. trade agreement with China provided that the Chinese government would enforce its intellectual property laws more strictly to reduce the high rate of illegal software duplication in that country. For other measures taken against international software piracy, see this chapter's *Landmark in the Legal Environment*.

For Critical Analysis: *Is there any practical way to prevent software piracy via the Internet?*

works to others over the Internet is theft, even if there is no intent to profit personally.

Specifically, the NETA prohibits "willfully infringing a copyright by reproducing or distributing, including by electronic means, during any 180-day period, one or more copies of one or more copyrighted works with a total retail value of more than $1,000." Penalties for violations include fines of up to $250,000 and five years imprisonment. The NETA also extended the statute of limitations for prosecutions of criminal copyright infringement to five years.

Trade Secrets

Some business processes and information that are not, or cannot be, patented, copyrighted, or trademarked are nevertheless protected against appropriation by competitors as trade secrets. **Trade secrets** consist of customer lists, plans, research and development, pricing information, marketing techniques, production techniques, and generally anything that makes an individual company unique and that would have value to a competitor. Unlike copyright and trademark protection, protection of trade secrets extends both

Trade Secrets Information or processes that give a business an advantage over competitors who do not know the information or processes.

to ideas and to their expression. (For this reason, and because a trade secret involves no registration or filing requirements, trade secret protection may be well suited for software.)

The most widely used definition of a trade secret is found in the *Restatement of Torts*, Section 757(b):

> A trade secret may consist of any formula, pattern, device, or compilation of information which is used in one's business, and which gives him an opportunity to obtain an advantage over competitors who do not know or use it. It may be a formula for a chemical compound, a process of manufacturing, treating or preserving materials, . . . or a list of customers.

Of course, the secret formula, process, or other information must be disclosed to some persons, particularly to key employees. Businesses generally attempt to protect their trade secrets by having all employees who use the process or information agree in their contracts never to divulge it. (Such agreements are called *nondisclosure agreements*.) Thus, if a salesperson tries to solicit the company's customers for noncompany business, or if an employee copies the employer's unique method of manufacture, he or she has appropriated a trade secret and has also broken a contract—two separate wrongs. Theft of confidential business data by industrial espionage, as when a business taps into a competitor's computer, is a theft of trade secrets without any contractual violation and is actionable in itself.

Under Section 757 of the *Restatement of Torts*, "One who discloses or uses another's trade secret, without a privilege to do so, is liable to the other if (1) he discovered the secret by improper means, or (2) his disclosure or use constitutes a breach of confidence reposed in him by the other in disclosing the secret to him."

The Economic Espionage Act of 1996 made the theft of trade secrets a federal crime. The act also makes it a federal crime to buy or possess trade secrets of another person, knowing that the trade secrets were stolen or otherwise acquired without the owner's authorization. An individual who violates the act can be imprisoned for up to ten years and fined up to $500,000. If a corporation or other organization violates the act, it can be fined up to $5 million. Any property acquired as a result of the violation and any property used in the commission of the violation is subject to criminal forfeiture—meaning that the government can take the property.

Conducting research on the Internet. How can an owner of intellectual property protect against the infringement of his or her rights on the Internet?

∷ Cyberlaw: Protecting Intellectual Property in Cyberspace

▼ Not surprisingly, because of the unique nature of the Internet, its use creates unique legal questions and issues—particularly with respect to intellectual property rights. What exactly constitutes an infringing use of another's intellectual property rights in the online environment? How can the owners of intellectual property rights know when, and by whom, those rights are being infringed in this context? Should online service providers bear legal responsibility for infringing actions by users of their services? These are just a few of the questions raised by the presence of intellectual property in cyberspace.

The emerging body of law governing cyberspace is often referred to as *cyberlaw*. We have already examined, in previous chapters, cyberlaw as it relates to court jurisdiction, constitutional issues, and the tort of defamation.

Here we look at cyberlaw as it applies to the types of intellectual property discussed in this chapter.

Trademark Protection on the Internet—Domain Names

One of the initial trademark issues involving intellectual property in cyberspace has been whether **domain names** (Internet addresses) should be treated as trademarks or simply as a means of access, similar to street addresses in the physical world. Increasingly, the courts are holding that the principles of trademark law should apply to domain names on the Internet. Before looking at trademark infringement and dilution issues, we need to briefly discuss some of the special characteristics of domain names and how they are registered.

Domain Name The series of letters and symbols used to identify site operators on the Internet; Internet "addresses."

Domain Names

A domain name consists of a series of "domains" separated by periods. A business's domain name typically consists of two domains. The top-level domain indicates the type of organization that is using the name—such as ".com" for a commercial entity (although noncommercial entities also use this name); ".net" for a network; ".edu" for an educational organization; or ".gov" for a government organization. The second-level domain usually consists of the name of the firm that maintains the site. Companies that do business on the Internet often use their names as domain names because this allows customers to access their sites without extensive searching. Consumers who want to locate those companies' World Wide Web sites also benefit from this practice.

Domain Name Registration

The entity responsible for registering domain names is Network Solutions, Inc. (NSI), which is funded by the U.S. National Science Foundation. NSI acts on behalf of the Internet Network Information Center (InterNIC), which, in turn, handles the daily administration of the domain name system in the United States. The top-level domains handled by the NSI apply worldwide. A new organization has developed an additional set of top-level domain names that may be in effect by the time you read this book.

Initially, domain names were handed out on a first-come, first-served basis, with few questions asked. Since 1995, however, the NSI has required any party seeking to register a domain name to state that the party's use of the name will not infringe on the intellectual property rights of any other party, that the party intends to use the name on "a regular basis on the Internet" (NSI may require a party that does not use the name for more than ninety days to relinquish the name), and that the party's use of the name will not be unlawful. If the party violates these representations made in the application, the NSI may cancel the domain name.

TRADEMARK INFRINGEMENT. One of the problems in applying trademark law to Internet domain names is that trademark law allows multiple parties to use the same mark—as long as the mark is used for different goods or services and will not cause customer confusion. On the Internet as it is currently structured, however, only one party can use a particular domain name, regardless of the type of goods or services offered. In other words, although two or more businesses can own the trademark Acme, only one business can operate on the

Internet with the domain name "acme.com." Because of this restrictive feature of domain names, there is a question as to whether domain names should function as trademarks.

To date, the courts that have considered this question have held that the unauthorized use of another's mark in a domain name may constitute trademark infringement. In one case, for example, a publishing company, the Comp Examiner Agency (CEA), used "juris.com" as its domain name. Juris, Inc., contended that CEA's use of the domain name infringed on its trademark Juris, which it used in connection with software, because the use would likely cause customer confusion. The court agreed and granted an injunction against CEA's further use of the "juris.com" domain name.[17]

TRADEMARK DILUTION.   Owners of famous trademarks also have succeeded in preventing others from using their marks as domain names under the Federal Trademark Dilution Act of 1995. For example, in one case, Hasbro, Inc., the maker of the famous children's board game Candy Land, sued a company that used the domain name "candyland.com." Hasbro contended that the company's commercial use of its mark diluted the mark's distinctiveness in violation of the federal dilution law. The court agreed and issued a preliminary injunction requiring the other party to relinquish the domain name.[18]

The 1995 act exempts from its coverage certain conduct, including noncommercial uses of marks. Thus, if a party registers another's famous mark as a domain name for a Web site that is not used for commercial purposes (to advertise or sell products and services), the owner of the famous mark will have no federal cause of action for trademark dilution. One of the significant questions concerning this exemption is whether "cybersquatting" constitutes a commercial use of a domain name. Cybersquatting occurs when a party registers another party's famous mark as a domain name and then holds the other party hostage—that is, the first party offers to forfeit its rights to the domain name to the owner of the famous mark in exchange for a sum of money. In the following case, the court addressed this issue.

---

17.   *Comp Examiner Agency, Inc. v. Juris, Inc.* (C.D.Cal. 1996)[1996 WL 376600]. This decision, which is not reported in West's *Federal Supplement*, can be accessed by use of the WESTLAW (WL) citation.
18.   *Hasbro, Inc. v. Internet Entertainment Group, Ltd.* (W.D.Wash. 1996)[1996 WL 84853]. This decision, which is not reported in West's *Federal Supplement*, can be accessed by use of the WESTLAW (WL) citation.

Case 11.5 ● Panavision International, L.P. v. Toeppen

United States
District Court,
Central District of California, 1996.
945 F.Supp. 1296.

BACKGROUND AND FACTS   Panavision International, Limited Partnership, is a supplier of photographic equipment. Panavision owns several famous trademarks, including Panavision, which it advertises to the public and to movie and television studios, networks, and production companies. Panavision's "Filmed with Panavision" credit appears at the end of many movies and television shows. Dennis Toeppen registered "panavision.com" as a domain name, precluding Panavision from using the name to identify its own Web site. Toeppen told Panavision that he would sell the name for $13,000. Panavision filed a suit in a federal district court against Toeppen, charging in part that he was in violation of the Federal Trademark Dilution Act of 1995.

(Continued)

Case 11.5—continued

IN THE WORDS OF THE COURT . . .
PREGERSON, District Judge.
* * * *

Registration of a trademark as a domain name, without more, is not a commercial use of the trademark and therefore is not within the prohibitions of the [Federal Trademark Dilution] Act. In the case before the Court, however, Toeppen has made a commercial use of the Panavision marks.

Toeppen's "business" is to register trademarks as domain names and then to sell the domain names to the trademarks' owners. * * * His "business" is premised on the desire of the companies to use their trademarks as domain names and the calculation that it will be cheaper to pay him than to sue him. * * *

* * * *

* * * As a result of the current state of Internet technology, Toeppen was able * * * to eliminate the capacity of the Panavision marks to identify and distinguish Panavision's goods and services on the Internet. * * * Toeppen's conduct, which prevented Panavision from using its marks in a new and important business medium, has diluted Panavision's marks within the meaning of the statute.

DECISION AND REMEDY   The court ordered Toeppen to, among other things, transfer the registration of "panavision.com" to Panavision.

FOR CRITICAL ANALYSIS—SOCIAL CONSIDERATION   *Should a business have more right to a domain name than it does to a specific street address or telephone number? Why or why not?*

Patents for Cyberproducts

Almost every day, we hear of some innovation in communications technology, particularly Internet technology. It therefore is not surprising that new cyberproducts to meet the needs of Internet users and online service providers are being developed and patented at an unprecedented rate. Cyberproducts include data-compression software, encryption programs, software facilitating information linking and retrieval systems, and other forms of network software.

The problem faced by the developers of cyberproducts, who normally invest substantial time and money resources in the research and development of those products, is how to protect their exclusive rights to the use of the products.

A patent owner whose product is featured on the Internet may find it particularly difficult to prevent the unauthorized use of the patented property. For example, a video game maker might agree to provide part of a game on the Internet, through a third party's Web site, to give potential purchasers a sample of the product. How can the game maker prevent the third party from using, or letting others use, the product for other purposes (such as making and selling illegal copies of the game)?

Licensing the use of a product has proved to be one of the best ways to protect intellectual property on the Internet. In the context of a patent, a *license* is permission granted by the patent owner to another (the *licensee*) to make, sell, or use the patented item. Any license that a patent holder grants can be restricted to certain specified purposes and can be limited to the licensee only. Of course, because the Internet does not have any geographical boundaries, a licensing agreement should be made only in consideration of all U.S., foreign, and international laws. These same principles apply to the owners and licensees of other intellectual property, including copyrights and trademarks.

Copyrights in Cyberspace

Uploading, downloading, browsing—any of these activities conducted in cyberspace can infringe on a copyright owner's rights. The following subsections identify some of the many copyright issues that arise in cyberspace and discuss the liability of online providers for copyright infringement.

ONLINE ISSUES.   The rights granted to copyright owners in the Copyright Act include the right to make copies of a copyrighted work, the right to publicly distribute those copies, and the right to perform or display copyrighted works. How those rights apply in cyberspace is still being debated.

A copyright owner might argue that the right to make copies of a work is infringed each time the work is stored in a computer's memory. Does software stored in a computer constitute a copy in this sense? A few courts have held that it does.[19] What about the digital storage of photographs, music, and other works? A few courts have held that these are also copies.[20]

Does the online transmission of a copyrighted work without permission violate the right to publicly distribute the work? Some might claim that no right is violated because no physical copy is transferred. Others might argue that there is a violation if the recipient downloads what is transmitted to the hard disk drive of his or her computer.[21]

Some of the most controversial questions concern the right to perform copyrighted works. Does downloading a copy of a musical recording constitute a performance? What about playing it back after downloading? Questions also arise in relation to the right to publicly display a work. Is a work publicly displayed when it is visually browsed online? Most observers would agree that it is. Probably most would also agree that browsing is a "fair use," particularly if it is a noncommercial use and there is no downloading.

ONLINE LIABILITY.   One current controversy is whether online providers—including Internet access services, bulletin board service (BBS) operators, and others—should be liable for the unauthorized copying, distribution, and performance or display of copyrighted work.

The most significant factor seems to be whether a provider is directly involved in the unauthorized use. An important case concerned the unauthorized uploading of literary works through an Internet access service.[22] The

---

19.   See, for example, *MAI Systems Corp. v. Peak Computer, Inc.*, 991 F.2d 511 (9th Cir. 1993).
20.   See, for example, *Religious Technology Center v. Netcom On-Line Communications Services, Inc.*, 907 F.Supp. 1361 (N.D.Cal. 1995).
21.   See *Agee v. Paramount Communications, Inc.*, 59 F.3d 317 (2d Cir. 1995), for a further discussion of this issue. The court recommended that the Copyright Act be amended to answer the question.
22.   *Religious Technology Center v. Netcom On-Line Communications Services, Inc.*, 907 F.Supp. 1361 (N.D.Cal. 1995).

Inside the Legal Environment
Online Copyright Infringement

Intellectual property is big business. Indeed, some researchers estimate that the market value of intellectual property—copyrights, trademarks, patents, and the like—exceeds the value of physical property in the world today. Most intellectual property does not sell for the cost of production plus a normal profit. Rather, intellectual property is sold at a price that reflects heavy research costs for ingenious ideas. Any property that involves high development costs and low production costs is vulnerable to "piracy"— the unauthorized copying and use of the property.

In the past, copying intellectual products was time consuming, and the pirated copies were worse than the originals. Think about copying software today, though, via the Internet. The pirated copy of software obtained via the Internet is exactly the same as the original— after all, it is digitized. The only difference may be that the pirated version is not accompanied by a user's manual, the lack of which can diminish the usefulness and application of the software.

How Big Is the Problem?

The Business Software Alliance estimates that half of the global market for software is supplied today by pirated products. The International Federation of the Phonographic Industry believes that 20 percent of recorded music is pirated. Much of the piracy of intellectual property, especially software and music, is deemed "altruistic." People illegally give intellectual property away not to make any money but because they want to be generous. There is also a problem with respect to copyright law, which makes a distinction between reproduction for public use (which requires the copyright holder's permission) and reproduction for private use (which, within limits, does not require the copyright holder's permission). The difficulty here is distinguishing between private and public use.

Current copyright law also only controls the first sale of a particular work. It applies to your new textbook but not to any subsequent sales of the textbook as a used piece of intellectual property. In the digital world, an initial copy can be perfectly copied again and again.

Finally, current copyright law is based on national boundaries. A right to distribute copies of a CD in one country does not automatically include the right to distribute the CD in another country. The Internet, however, knows no national boundaries.

How Can the Problem Be Solved?

Is there any current solution to the increasing problem of the piracy of intellectual property via the Internet? The simple answer is no. Efforts to find such a solution are underway, nonetheless. A technological effort is being made to develop pirate-proof ways of transmitting materials. For example, IBM has developed so-called secure "packaging" for sending digital information over the Internet. In the digital world, however, every time someone comes up with a new technology, experts (often hackers) soon manage to get around it.

Many argue that the government should crack down more on piracy. It is relatively easy to discover piracy on the Internet by using one of the powerful search engines that exist today. By keying in a couple of sentences from a copyrighted work, for example, and then searching online databases, you can quickly find out what Web sites contain pirated copies of the article. It takes resources to do such research, however, and many nations are unwilling to invest their resources in efforts to reduce online piracy. Furthermore, even if the source is tracked down, it is difficult to determine who is liable. Perhaps the only long-term solution is to make the "real thing"—the original—more valuable than the pirated version. One way to do this is to continually update works that are online—most individuals will not pirate a financial newsletter that is updated every day. Alternatively, some companies will attempt to figure out different ways to make money from their intellectual property. This is certainly true on the Internet, where many services are provided free of charge, and the provider obtains revenues by selling advertising on the particular Web site.

For Critical Analysis: *Can the distribution through the Internet of intellectual property be regulated by copyright laws? Should it?*

Reading a publication on the Internet. Should the online provider of access to such publications be liable for everything that they contain?

court held that the service was not liable for copyright infringement because, like a self-service photocopier, it only provided the system that permitted unauthorized copying.

In a second case, a BBS operator's customers uploaded and downloaded copyrighted photos, to and from the bulletin board, without the copyright owner's permission. The court held the operator liable for infringement of the owner's rights, in part because some of the photos were altered to include ads for the bulletin board.[23] In a third case, a bulletin board service encouraged its users to upload unauthorized copies of video game software. The court held the service liable because it knew that the copies were unauthorized and were being uploaded into its storage media.[24]

Many online providers believe that the Copyright Act needs to be amended to impose liability only when a provider knows that a use of its service is infringing on a copyright owner's rights and does nothing about it. Copyright owners favor imposing liability in *all* circumstances. The debate continues.

International Protection for Intellectual Property

For many years, the United States has been a party to various international agreements relating to intellectual property rights. For example, the Paris Convention of 1883, to which about ninety countries are signatory, allows parties in one country to file for patent and trademark protection in any of the other member countries. Other international agreements in this area include the Berne Convention and the TRIPS agreement.

---

23. *Playboy Enterprises, Inc. v. Frena*, 839 F.Supp. 1552 (M.D.Fla. 1993).
24. *Sega Enterprises, Ltd. v. MAPHIA*, 857 F.Supp. 679 (N.D.Cal. 1994).

The Berne Convention

Under the Berne Convention of 1886, an international copyright agreement, if an American writes a book, his or her copyright in the book must be recognized by every country that has signed the convention. Also, if a citizen of a country that has not signed the convention first publishes a book in a country that has signed, all other countries that have signed the convention must recognize that author's copyright. Copyright notice is not needed to gain protection under the Berne Convention for works published after March 1, 1989.

The Berne Convention and other international agreements have given some protection to intellectual property on a worldwide level. None of them, however, has been as significant and far reaching in scope as the Trade-Related Aspects of Intellectual Property Rights—or, more simply, TRIPS—agreement.

The TRIPS Agreement

The TRIPS agreement was signed by representatives from over one hundred nations in 1994, following the eighth and final round (called the Uruguay Round) of negotiations among nations that were signatory to the General Agreement on Tariffs and Trade, or GATT.[25] The TRIPS agreement was one of several documents that were annexed to the agreement that created the World Trade Organization, or WTO, which replaced GATT as of 1995. The TRIPS agreement is the subject of the *Landmark in the Legal Environment* on page 298.

Cyberspace Issues

Because cyberspace has no national boundaries, the Internet is an international communications medium. For this reason, intellectual property in cyberspace may be subject to the laws of many countries, including the United States, and to international law.

Currently, the laws of many countries and international laws are being updated to reflect changes in technology and the spread of the Internet. Copyright holders and other owners of intellectual property generally agree that changes in the law are needed to stop the increasing international piracy of their property (see this chapter's *Inside the Legal Environment* on page 295). The World Intellectual Property Organization (WIPO) is attempting to update international law by suggesting proposals for its member countries to ratify, although widespread ratification and implementation could take a decade or more.

Among the WIPO proposals for protecting copyrights in cyberspace are provisions that could extend the rights that exist under current U.S. copyright law to the distribution and performance of their works to copyright holders in other countries. Other proposals concern issues that are discussed elsewhere in this chapter—fair use in cyberspace, temporary digital copying, and the liability of online providers—as well as technological copy protection methods.

---

25. GATT was originally negotiated in 1947 to minimize trade barriers among nations. Between 1947 and 1994, the GATT nations undertook seven more rounds of negotiations relating to tariffs and trade.

Landmark in the Legal Environment
The 1994 Agreement on Trade-Related Aspects of Intellectual Property Rights (TRIPS)

The 1994 agreement on Trade-Related Aspects of Intellectual Property Rights (TRIPS) established, for the first time, standards for the international protection of intellectual property rights, including patents, trademarks, and copyrights for movies, computer programs, books, and music.

Prior to the agreement, one of the difficulties faced by U.S. sellers of intellectual property in the international market was either the lack of protection of intellectual property rights under other countries' laws or the lack of enforcement of those laws that do exist. To address this problem, the TRIPS agreement provides that each member country must include in its domestic laws broad intellectual property rights and effective remedies (including civil and criminal penalties) for violations of those rights. Generally, the TRIPS agreement provides that each member nation must not discriminate (in terms of the administration, regulation, or adjudication of intellectual property rights) against foreign owners of such rights. In other words, a member nation cannot give its own nationals (citizens) favorable treatment without offering the same treatment to nationals of all member countries. For example, if a U.S. software manufacturer brings a suit for the infringement of intellectual property rights under a mem-

ber nation's national laws, the U.S. manufacturer is entitled to receive the same treatment as a domestic manufacturer. Each member nation must also ensure that legal procedures are available for parties who wish to bring actions for infringement of intellectual property rights. Additionally, in a related document, the Uruguay Round of GATT established a mechanism for settling disputes among member nations.

Particular provisions of the TRIPS agreement refer to patent, trademark, and copyright protection for intellectual property. The agreement specifically provides copyright protection for computer programs by stating that compilations of data, databases, or other materials are "intellectual creations" and that they are to be protected as copyrightable works. Other provisions relate to trade secrets and the rental of computer programs and cinematographic works.

For Critical Analysis: *U.S. companies currently hold a 75 percent share of the international market for prepackaged software and a 60 percent share of the international market for other software and related services. How might the TRIPS agreement affect this market share?*

Key Terms

certification mark 282
collective mark 282
copyright 284
domain name 291

intellectual property 277
patent 283
service mark 282
trade dress 281

trade name 282
trade secret 289
trademark 277

Chapter Summary
Intellectual Property and Cyberlaw

| **TRADEMARK INFRINGEMENT AND INFRINGEMENT OF RELATED PROPERTY** (See pages 277–282.) | Occurs when one uses the protected trademark, service mark, or trade name of another without permission when marketing goods or services. |

Chapter Summary, continued

PATENT INFRINGEMENT (See pages 282–284.)	Occurs when one uses or sells another's patented design, product, or process without the patent owner's permission. Computer software may be patented.
COPYRIGHT INFRINGEMENT (See pages 284–289.)	Occurs whenever the form or expression of an idea is copied without the permission of the copyright holder. An exception applies if the copying is deemed a "fair use." The Computer Software Copyright Act of 1980 specifically includes software among the kinds of intellectual property covered by copyright law.
TRADE SECRETS (See pages 289–290.)	Customer lists, plans, research and development, pricing information, and so on are protected under the common law and, in some states, under statutory law against misappropriation by competitors.
INTERNATIONAL PROTECTION (See pages 296–298.)	International protection for intellectual property exists under various international agreements. A landmark agreement is the 1994 agreement on Trade-Related Aspects of Intellectual Property Rights (TRIPS), which provides for the enforcement of intellectual property rights and the establishment of enforcement procedures in all countries signatory to the agreement.

For Review

1. What is intellectual property?

2. How are trademarks protected by law? What is the most important factor in determining whether a trademark has been infringed?

3. What kinds of intellectual property are protected by copyright law?

4. What is a trade secret? How are trade secrets protected by law?

5. What international protection is available for intellectual property?

Questions and Case Problems

11–1. Fair Use Doctrine. Professor Wise is teaching a summer seminar in business torts at State University. Several times during the course, he makes copies of relevant sections from business law texts and distributes them to his students. Wise does not realize that the daughter of one of the textbook authors is a member of his seminar. She tells her father about Wise's copying activities, which have been done without her father's or his publisher's permission. Her father sues Wise for copyright infringement. Wise claims protection under the fair use doctrine. Who will prevail? Explain.

11–2. Trademarks. Otro, Inc., has been doing business since 1962 in more than fifty locations throughout the United States. Otro manufactures and distributes a wide variety of electronic products, which prominently bear the Otro trademark. Otro advertises its products nationally. Paul is not affiliated with Otro. Without Otro's per-

mission, Paul registers the domain name "Otro.com," intending to profit by reselling or licensing it to Otro. Paul then sets up a Web site at the Otro.com address featuring a picture of himself. When Otro learns that it cannot register its mark as a domain name, Otro asks a court to order Paul to assign his registration of the name to Otro. Will the court give Otro what it wants? Why or why not?

11–3. Copyright Infringement. In which of the following situations would a court likely hold Ursula liable for copyright infringement?

   a. From a scholarly journal at the library, Ursula photocopies ten pages relating to a topic on which she is writing a term paper.

   b. Ursula makes blouses, dresses, and other clothes and sells them in her small shop. She advertises some of the outfits as Guest items, hoping that customers might mistakenly assume that they were made by Guess, the well-known maker of clothing.

c. Ursula operates a bulletin board on the Internet. She encourages the board's customers to upload scanned copies of magazines and add their own comments. With each magazine displayed on her board, she includes her board's Internet address in place of the title of the publication.

d. Ursula teaches Latin American history at a small university. She has a VCR and frequently tapes television programs relating to Latin America. She then takes the videos to her classroom so that her students can watch them.

11–4. Copyright Protection. One day during algebra class, Diedra, an enterprising fourteen-year-old student, began drawing designs on her shoelaces. By the end of the class, Diedra had decorated her shoelaces with the name of the school, Broadson Junior High, written in blue and red (the school colors) and with pictures of bears, the school's mascot. After class, Mrs. Laxton, Diedra's teacher, reprimanded Diedra for not paying attention in class and asked Diedra what she had been doing during the lecture. Diedra showed Mrs. Laxton her shoelaces. When Diedra got home that night, she wrote about the day's events in her diary. She also drew her shoelace design in the diary. Mrs. Laxton had been trying to think of how she could build school spirit. She thought about Diedra's shoelaces and decided to go into business for herself. She called her business Spirited Shoelaces and designed shoelaces for each of the local schools, decorating the shoelaces in each case with the school's name, mascot, and colors. The business became tremendously profitable. Even though Diedra never registered her idea with the patent or copyright office, does she nonetheless have intellectual property rights in the shoelace design? Will her diary account be sufficient proof that she created the idea? Discuss fully.

11–5. Fair Use Doctrine. Original Appalachian Artworks, Inc. (OAA), makes and distributes the very successful product called Cabbage Patch Kids—soft, sculptured dolls that were in great demand in the early 1980s. The dolls are unique in appearance, and the name is registered as a trademark to OAA. The design, too, is protected under a copyright registration. In 1986, Topps Chewing Gum, Inc., had an artist copy many of the features of the dolls for Topps's new product—stickers that depicted obnoxious cartoon characters called Garbage Pail Kids. The stickers, along with another product line that Topps developed, proved very lucrative; in fact, Topps expanded the product line to include T-shirts, balloons, and school notebooks. Topps claimed that its product was actually a satire of (critical comment on) OAA's product and therefore a fair use of a protected work. Did Topps's use of OAA's product constitute a fair use of the product, or did it constitute trademark and copyright infringement? [*Original Appalachian Artworks, Inc. v. Topps Chewing Gum, Inc.,* 642 F.Supp. 1031 (N.D.Ga. 1986)]

11–6. Trademark Infringement. In 1987, Quality Inns International, Inc., announced a new chain of economy hotels to be marketed under the name McSleep Inns. McDonald's wrote Quality Inns a letter stating that the use of this name infringed on the McDonald's family of trademarks characterized by the prefix Mc attached to a generic term. Quality Inns claimed that *Mc* had come into generic use as a prefix and therefore McDonald's had no trademark rights to the prefix itself. Quality Inns filed an action seeking a declaratory judgment from the court that the mark McSleep Inns did not infringe on McDonald's federally registered trademarks or common law rights to its marks and would not constitute an unfair trade practice. What factors must the court consider in deciding this issue? What will be the probable outcome of the case? Explain. [*Quality Inns International, Inc. v. McDonald's Corp.,* 695 F.Supp. 198 (D.Md. 1988)]

11–7. Trademark Infringement. CBS, Inc., owns and operates Television City, a television production facility in Los Angeles that is home to many television series. The name Television City is broadcast each week in connection with each show. CBS sells T-shirts, pins, watches, and so on emblazoned with "CBS Television City." CBS registered the name Television City with the U.S. Patent and Trademark Office as a service mark "for television production services." David and William Liederman wished to open a restaurant in New York City using the name Television City. Besides food, the restaurant would sell television memorabilia such as T-shirts, sweatshirts, and posters. When CBS learned of the Liedermans' plans, it asked a federal district court to order them not to use the name Television City in connection with their restaurant. Does CBS's registration of the Television City mark ensure its exclusive use in all markets and for all products? If not, what factors might the court consider to determine whether the Liedermans can use the name Television City in connection with their restaurant? [*CBS, Inc. v. Liederman,* 866 F.Supp. 763 (S.D.N.Y. 1994)]

11–8. Trade Secrets. William Redmond, as the general manager for PepsiCo, Inc., in California, had access to the company's inside information and trade secrets. In 1994, Redmond resigned to become chief operating officer for the Gatorade and Snapple Company, which makes and markets Gatorade and Snapple and is a subsidiary of the Quaker Oats Company. PepsiCo brought an action in a federal district court against Redmond and Quaker Oats, seeking to prevent Redmond from disclosing PepsiCo's secrets. The court ordered Redmond not to assume new duties that were likely to trigger disclosure of those secrets. The central issue on appeal was whether a plaintiff can obtain relief for trade secret misappropriation on showing that an ex-employee's new employment will *inevitably* lead him or her to rely on the plaintiff's trade secrets. How should the court rule on this issue? Discuss fully. [*PepsiCo v. Redmond*, 54 F.3d 1262 (7th Cir. 1995)]

11–9. Trademarks. Sara Lee Corp. manufactures pantyhose under the L'eggs trademark. Originally, L'eggs were sold in egg-shaped packaging, a design that Sara Lee continues to use with its product. Sara Lee's only nation-wide competitor in the same pantyhose markets is Kayser-Roth Corp. When Kayser-Roth learned of Sara Lee's plan to introduce L'eggs Everyday, a new line of hosiery, Kayser-Roth responded by simultaneously introducing a new product, Leg Looks. Sara Lee filed a complaint in a federal district court against Kayser-Roth, asserting that the name Leg Looks infringed on the L'eggs mark. Does Kayser-Roth's Leg Looks infringe on Sara Lee's L'eggs? Why or why not? [*Sara Lee Corp. v. Kayser-Roth Corp.*, 81 F.3d 455 (4th Cir. 1996)]

A Question of Ethics and Social Responsibility

11–10. Texaco, Inc., conducts research to develop new products and technology in the petroleum industry. As part of the research, Texaco employees routinely photocopy articles from scientific and medical journals without the permission of the copyright holders. The publishers of the journals brought a copyright infringement action against Texaco in a federal district court. The court ruled that the copying was not fair use. The U.S. Court of Appeals for the Second Circuit affirmed this ruling "primarily because the dominant purpose of the use is 'archival'—to assemble a set of papers for future reference, thereby serving the same purpose for which additional subscriptions are normally sold, or . . . for which photocopying licenses may be obtained." [*American Geophysical Union v. Texaco, Inc.*, 37 F.3d 881(2d Cir. 1994)]

1. Do you agree with the court's decision that the copying was not a fair use? Why or why not?
2. Do you think that the law should impose a duty on every person to obtain permission to photocopy or reproduce any article under any circumstance? What would be some of the implications of such a duty for society? Discuss fully.

For Critical Analysis

11–11. Patent protection in the United States is granted to the first person to invent a given product or process, even though another person might be the first to file for a patent on the same product or process. What are the advantages of this patenting procedure? Can you think of any disadvantages? Explain.

INTERACTING WITH The Internet

■ Go to the West's Legal Studies Home Page at

http://www.westbuslaw.com

There you will find a variety of legal resources. Visit us often!

■ Information on intellectual property law is available at the following site:

http://www.legal.net/intellct.htm

■ To perform patent searches and to access information on the patenting process, go to

http://sunsite.unc.edu/patents/intropat.html

■ You can find answers to frequently asked questions about patents at

http://www.sccsi.com/DaVinci/patentfaq.html

■ The U.S. Patent and Trademark Office provides online access to a broad range of U.S. and international trademark resources, including forms, links to relevant statutes, recent regulations, trademark registration forms, and links to international patent and trademark offices in such places as Japan, New Zealand, and Sweden. You can even order a trademark registration by e-mail using this site, which is located at

http://www.uspto.gov/

■ You can also access information on patent law at the following Internet site:

http://www.patents.com

■ Another online magazine that deals, in part, with intellectual property issues is *Law Technology Product News.* The address for this publication is

http://www.ljextra.com/ltpn/

■ The Cyberspace Law Institute (CLI) offers articles and information on topics such as copyright infringement, privacy and trade secrets, trademarks, and domain names. Find this site at

http://www.cli.org

Introduction to Contracts

Contents

Chapter Objectives

After reading this chapter, you should be able to . . .

1. Define the term *contract*, and list the basic elements that are required for contract formation.

2. State the requirements of an offer.

3. Explain the contractual rights and obligations of minors.

4. Identify the types of contracts that must be in writing to be enforceable.

5. Differentiate between complete and substantial performance of a contract, and indicate when a breach of contract occurs.

As Roscoe Pound—an eminent jurist—observed in the quotation on the right, "keeping promises" is important to a stable social order. Contract law deals with, among other things, the formation and keeping of promises. A promise is a declaration that something either will or will not happen in the future.

Like other types of law, contract law reflects our social values, interests, and expectations at a given point in time. It shows, for example, what kinds of promises our society thinks should be legally binding. It shows what excuses our society accepts for breaking such promises. Additionally, it shows what promises are considered to be contrary to public policy and therefore legally void. If a promise goes against the interests of society as a whole, it will be invalid. Also, if it was made by a child or a mentally incompetent person, or on the basis of false information, a question will arise as to whether the promise should be enforced. Resolving such questions is the essence of contract law.

In business law and the legal environment of business, questions and disputes concerning contracts arise daily. Although aspects of contract law vary from state to state, much of it is based on the common law. In 1932, the American Law Institute compiled the *Restatement of the Law of Contracts*. This work is a nonstatutory, authoritative exposition of the present law on the subject of contracts and is presently in its second edition (although a third edition is in the process of being drafted). Throughout the following chapters on contracts, we will refer to the second edition of the *Restatement of the Law of Contracts* as simply the *Restatement (Second) of Contracts*.

The Uniform Commercial Code (UCC), which governs contracts and other transactions relating to the sale of goods, occasionally departs from common law contract rules. Generally, the different treatment of contracts falling under the UCC stems from the general policy of encouraging commerce. Some of the ways in which the UCC changes common law contract rules are discussed in this chapter and in Chapter 13. In this chapter, we indicate briefly or in footnotes which common law rules have been altered by the UCC for sales contracts.

> "The social order rests upon the stability and predictability of conduct, of which keeping promises is a large item."
>
> Roscoe Pound, 1870–1964 (American jurist)

Promise A declaration that something either will or will not happen in the future.

The Function of Contracts

Contract law assures the parties to private agreements that the promises they make will be enforceable. Clearly, many promises are kept because of a moral obligation to do so or because keeping a promise is in the mutual self-interest of the parties involved, not because the **promisor** (the person making the promise) or the **promisee** (the person to whom the promise is made) is conscious of the rules of contract law. Nevertheless, the rules of contract law are often followed in business agreements to avoid potential problems.

A **contract** is an agreement that can be enforced in court. It is formed by two or more parties who agree to perform or to refrain from performing some act now or in the future. Generally, contract disputes arise when there is a promise of future performance. If the contractual promise is not fulfilled, the party who made it is subject to the sanctions of a court (see Chapter 13). That party may be required to pay money damages for failing to perform; in limited instances, the party may be required to perform the promised act.

Promisor A person who makes a promise.

Promisee A person to whom a promise is made.

Contract An agreement that can be enforced in court; formed by two or more parties who agree to perform or to refrain from performing some act now or in the future.

Types of Contracts

There are numerous types of contracts. The categories into which contracts are placed involve legal distinctions as to formation, enforceability, or performance.

Is it possible to enter into a contract over the phone? If so, what would make such a contract a bilateral contract rather than a unilateral contract?

The best method of explaining each type of contract is to compare one type with another.

Bilateral versus Unilateral Contracts

Offeror A person who makes an offer.

Offeree A person to whom an offer is made.

Every contract involves at least two parties. The **offeror** is the party making the offer. The **offeree** is the party to whom the offer is made. The offeror always promises to do or not to do something and thus is also a promisor. Whether the contract is classified as *unilateral* or *bilateral* depends on what the offeree must do to accept the offer and to bind the offeror to a contract.

Bilateral Contract A type of contract that arises when a promise is given in exchange for a return promise.

BILATERAL CONTRACTS.   If to accept the offer the offeree must only *promise* to perform, the contract is a **bilateral contract.** Hence, a bilateral contract is a "promise for a promise." An example of a bilateral contract is a contract in which one person agrees to buy another person's automobile for a specified price. No performance, such as the payment of money or delivery of goods, need take place for a bilateral contract to be formed. The contract comes into existence at the moment the promises are exchanged.

Unilateral Contract A contract that results when an offer can only be accepted by the offeree's performance.

UNILATERAL CONTRACTS.   If the offer is phrased so that the offeree can accept only by completing the contract performance, the contract is a **unilateral contract.** Hence, a unilateral contract is a "promise for an act."

A classic example of a unilateral contract is as follows: Joe says to Celia, "If you walk across the Brooklyn Bridge, I'll give you $10." Joe promises to pay only if Celia walks the entire span of the bridge. Only on Celia's complete crossing does she fully accept Joe's offer to pay $10. If she chooses not to undertake the walk, there are no legal consequences. Contests, lotteries, and other competitions in which prizes are awarded are also examples of offers for unilateral contracts. If a person complies with the rules of the contest—such as by submitting the right lottery number at the right place and time—a unilateral contract is formed, binding the organization offering the prize to a contract to perform as promised in the offer.

REVOCATION OF OFFERS FOR UNILATERAL CONTRACTS. A problem arises in unilateral contracts when the promisor attempts to *revoke* (cancel) the offer after the promisee has begun performance but before the act has been completed. For example, suppose that Roberta offers to buy Ed's sailboat, moored in San Francisco, on delivery of the boat to Roberta's dock in Newport Beach, three hundred miles south of San Francisco. Ed rigs the boat and sets sail. Shortly before his arrival at Newport Beach, Ed receives a radio message from Roberta withdrawing her offer. Roberta's offer is an offer for a unilateral contract, and only Ed's delivery of the sailboat at her dock is an acceptance.

In contract law, offers are normally *revocable* (capable of being taken back, or canceled) until accepted. Under the traditional view of unilateral contracts, Roberta's revocation would terminate the offer. Because of the harsh effect on the offeree of the revocation of an offer to form a unilateral contract, the modern-day view is that once performance has been substantially undertaken, the offeror cannot revoke the offer. Thus, in our example, even though Ed has not yet accepted the offer by complete performance, Roberta is prohibited from revoking it. Ed can deliver the boat and bind Roberta to the contract.

Express versus Implied Contracts

An **express contract** is one in which the terms of the agreement are fully and explicitly stated in words, oral or written. A signed lease for an apartment or a house is an express written contract. If a classmate calls you on the phone and agrees to buy your textbooks from last semester for $50, an express oral contract has been made.

Express Contract A contract in which the terms of the agreement are fully and explicitly stated in words, oral or written.

What determines whether a contract for accounting, tax preparation, or any other service is an express contract or an implied-in-fact contract?

Implied-in-Fact Contract A contract formed in whole or in part from the conduct of the parties (as opposed to an express contract).

A contract that is implied from the conduct of the parties is called an **implied-in-fact contract,** or an implied contract. This type of contract differs from an express contract in that the *conduct* of the parties, rather than their words, creates and defines the terms of the contract.

Quasi Contracts—Contracts Implied in Law

Quasi Contract A fictional contract imposed on parties by a court in the interests of fairness and justice; usually, quasi contracts are imposed to avoid the unjust enrichment of one party at the expense of another.

Quasi contracts, or contracts *implied in law,* are wholly different from actual contracts. Express contracts and implied-in-fact contracts are actual, or true, contracts. Quasi contracts, as the term suggests, are not true contracts. They do not arise from any agreement, express or implied, between the parties themselves. Rather, quasi contracts are fictional contracts imposed on parties by courts in the interests of fairness and justice. Quasi contracts are therefore equitable, rather than contractual, in nature. Usually, quasi contracts are imposed to avoid the *unjust enrichment* of one party at the expense of another.

> REMEMBER Quasi contract is an equitable concept, but most courts can apply the doctrine, because in most states, courts of law and equity have merged.

Executed versus Executory Contracts

Executed Contract A contract that has been completely performed by both parties.

Executory Contract A contract that has not as yet been fully performed.

Contracts are also classified according to their state of performance. A contract that has been fully performed on both sides is called an **executed contract.** A contract that has not been fully performed on either side is called an **executory contract.** If one party has fully performed but the other has not, the contract is said to be executed on the one side and executory on the other, but the contract is still classified as executory.

For example, assume that you agree to buy ten tons of coal from the Western Coal Company. Further assume that Western has delivered the coal to your steel mill, where it is now being burned. At this point, the contract is an executory contract—it is executed on the part of Western and executory on your part. After you pay Western for the coal, the contract will be executed on both sides.

Valid, Void, Voidable, and Unenforceable Contracts

Valid Contract A contract that results when elements necessary for contract formation (agreement, consideration, legal purpose, and contractual capacity) are present.

Void Contract A contract having no legal force or binding effect.

A **valid contract** has the elements necessary for contract formation. Those elements consist of (1) an agreement (offer and an acceptance) (2) supported by legally sufficient consideration (3) for a legal purpose and (4) made by parties who have the legal capacity to enter into the contract. We will discuss each of these elements in this chapter.

A **void contract** is no contract at all. The terms *void* and *contract* are contradictory. A void contract produces no legal obligations on the part of any of the parties. For example, a contract can be void because one of the parties was adjudged by a court to be legally insane (and thus lacked the legal capacity to enter into a contract) or because the purpose of the contract was illegal.

Voidable Contract A contract that may be legally avoided (canceled, or annulled) at the option of one of the parties.

A **voidable contract** is a *valid* contract but one that can be avoided at the option of one or both of the parties. The party having the option can elect either to avoid any duty to perform or to *ratify* (make valid) the contract. If the contract is avoided, both parties are released from it. If it is ratified, both parties must fully perform their respective legal obligations.

As a general rule, contracts made by minors are voidable at the option of the minor. Contracts entered into under fraudulent conditions are voidable at the option of the defrauded party. In addition, contracts entered into under legally defined duress or undue influence are voidable.

An **unenforceable contract** is one that cannot be enforced because of certain legal defenses against it. It is not unenforceable because a party failed to satisfy a legal requirement of the contract; rather, it is a valid contract rendered unenforceable by some statute or law. For example, certain contracts must be in writing, and if they are not, they will not be enforceable except in certain exceptional circumstances.

Unenforceable Contract A valid contract rendered unenforceable by some statute or law.

Requirements of a Contract

The four requirements that constitute what are known as the elements of a contract are (1) agreement, (2) consideration, (3) capacity, and (4) legality. We discuss the element of agreement first.

Agreement

An essential element for contract formation is **agreement**—the parties must agree on the terms of the contract. Ordinarily, agreement is evidenced by two events: an *offer* and an *acceptance*. One party offers a certain bargain to another party, who then accepts that bargain.

Because words often fail to convey the precise meaning intended, the law of contracts generally adheres to the *objective theory of contracts*. Under this theory, a party's words and conduct are held to mean whatever a reasonable person in the offeree's position would think they meant. The court will give words their usual meanings even if "it were proved by twenty bishops that [the] party . . . intended something else."[1]

Agreement A meeting of two or more minds in regard to the terms of a contract; usually broken down into two events—an offer by one party to form a contract, and an acceptance of the offer by the person to whom the offer is made.

REQUIREMENTS OF THE OFFER. An **offer** is a promise or commitment to perform or refrain from performing some specified act in the future. Three elements are necessary for an offer to be effective:

1. There must be a *serious, objective intention* by the offeror.
2. The terms of the offer must be reasonably *certain,* or *definite,* so that the parties and the court can ascertain the terms of the contract.
3. The offer must be communicated to the offeree.

Once an effective offer has been made, the offeree has the power to accept the offer. If the offeree accepts, the offer is translated into an agreement (and into a contract, if other essential elements are present).

Offer A promise or commitment to perform or refrain from performing some specified act in the future.

Intention The first requirement for an effective offer to exist is a serious, objective intention on the part of the offeror. Intent is not determined by the *subjective* intentions, beliefs, or assumptions of the offeror. Rather, it is determined by what a reasonable person in the offeree's position would conclude the offeror's words and actions meant. Offers made in obvious anger, jest, or undue excitement do not meet the serious-and-objective-intent test. Because these offers are not effective, an offeree's acceptance does not create an agreement.

"[Contracts] must not be the sports of an idle hour, mere matters of pleasantry and badinage, never intended by the parties to have any serious effect whatever."

William Stowell, 1745–1836 (English jurist)

---

1. Judge Learned Hand in *Hotchkiss v. National City Bank of New York,* 200 F. 287 (2d Cir. 1911), aff'd 231 U.S. 50, 34 S.Ct. 20 58 L.Ed. 115 (1913). (The term *aff'd* is an abbreviation for *affirmed*; an appellate court can affirm a lower court's judgment, decree, or order, thereby declaring that it is valid and must stand as rendered.)

> **BE CAREFUL** An opinion is not an offer and not a contract term. Goods or services can be "perfect" in one party's opinion and "poor" in another's.

An expression of opinion is not an offer. It does not evidence an intention to enter into a binding agreement. In *Hawkins v. McGee,*[2] for example, Hawkins took his son to McGee, a doctor, and asked McGee to operate on the son's hand. McGee said that the boy would be in the hospital three or four days and that the hand would *probably* heal a few days later. The son's hand did not heal for a month, but nonetheless the father did not win a suit for breach of contract. The court held that McGee did not make an offer to heal the son's hand in three or four days. He merely expressed an opinion as to when the hand would heal.

Similarly, a *statement of intention* is not an offer. If Ari says "I *plan* to sell my stock in Novation, Inc., for $150 per share," a contract is not created if John "accepts" and tenders the $150 per share for the stock. Ari has merely expressed his intention to enter into a future contract for the sale of the stock. If John accepts and tenders the $150 per share, no contract is formed, because a reasonable person would conclude that Ari was only *thinking about* selling his stock, not promising to sell it.

Preliminary negotiations must also be distinguished from an offer. A request or invitation to negotiate is not an offer; it only expresses a willingness to discuss the possibility of entering into a contract. Examples are statements such as "Will you sell Forest Acres?" and "I wouldn't sell my car for less than $1,000." A reasonable person in the offeree's position would not conclude that such a statement evidenced an intention to enter into a binding obligation. Likewise, when the government and private firms need to have construction work done, contractors are invited to submit bids. The *invitation* to submit bids is not an offer, and a contractor does not bind the government or private firm by submitting a bid. (The bids that the contractors submit are offers, however, and the government or private firm can bind the contractor by accepting the bid.) In general, mail-order catalogues, price lists, and circular letters (meant for the general public) are treated not as offers to contract but as invitations to negotiate.[3] On rare occasions, though, courts have construed advertisements to be offers because the ads contained such definite terms.

In the following case, the court addressed the question of whether a letter informing several people that a cottage was for sale was an offer or merely a preliminary negotiation.

---

2. *Hawkins v. McGee,* 84 N.H. 114, 146 A. 641 (1929).
3. *Restatement (Second) of Contracts,* Section 26, Comment b.

Case 12.1 ● Mellen v. Johnson

Supreme Judicial Court of
Massachusetts, 1948.
322 Mass. 236,
76 N.E.2d 658.

HISTORICAL AND ENVIRONMENTAL SETTING *Nahant, Massachusetts, is one of the small communities on the*

North Shore of Greater Boston Harbor. An area of rugged coast and ocean beaches, the North Shore has been a desirable place to live since the Puritans landed in Salem in 1628. The area's many rivers and marshes supply the region with drinking water. Plum Island includes an important wildlife refuge. The fish population has been deci-

(Continued)

Case 12.1—continued

mated, but lobsters and clams abound. Residents say no place is as perfect or as pristine. As for Nahant, even in years in which other North Shore communities saw declines in the prices of housing, Nahant saw increases.*

BACKGROUND AND FACTS   Johnson, who owned a three-bedroom cottage in Nahant, Massachusetts, sent a letter to Mellen saying that he was putting the cottage on the market. Earlier, Mellen had expressed an interest in purchasing the cottage. The letter indicated that several other people,

who had also expressed an interest in purchasing the property, were being informed by letter of its availability at the same time. Mellen, interpreting the letter as an offer, promptly accepted. Johnson sold the property to a higher bidder, and Mellen sued Johnson in a Massachusetts state court. The court found that the letter was an offer and ordered Johnson to convey the property to Mellen on Mellen's payment of the purchase price. Johnson appealed.

IN THE WORDS OF THE COURT . . .
WILKINS, Justice.
 * * * *

The letter of March 27 was not an offer. It expressed "a desire to dispose of" the property. It announced that the agent was "writing the several people, including yourself, who have previously expressed an interest in the property." Its conclusion, in part, was, "I will be interested in hearing further from you if you have any interest in this property, for as I said before, I am advising those who have asked for an opportunity to consider it." The recipient could not reasonably understand this to be more than an attempt at negotiation. It was a mere request or suggestion that an offer be made to the defendant.

DECISION AND REMEDY   The Supreme Judicial Court of Massachusetts reversed the decision of the trial court and dismissed Mellen's complaint.

FOR CRITICAL ANALYSIS—SOCIAL CONSIDERATION   *How can the kind of confusion that arose in this case be prevented? Is it enough to say to prospective purchasers that other parties have also been informed that certain property is for sale?*

a.   Beth Daley, "South vs. North," *The Boston Globe,* September 3, 1995, p. 1.

Definiteness   The second requirement for an effective offer involves the definiteness of its terms. An offer must have reasonably definite terms so that a court can determine if a breach has occurred and give an appropriate remedy.[4]

An offer may invite an acceptance to be worded in such specific terms that the contract is made definite. For example, suppose that Marcus Business Machines contacts your corporation and offers to sell "from one to ten MacCool copying machines for $1,600 each; state number desired in acceptance." Your corporation agrees to buy two copiers. Because the quantity is specified in the acceptance, the terms are definite, and the contract is enforceable.

Definiteness is also required when a contract is modified. The terms of a contract as modified must be reasonably definite so that a court can determine if there has been a breach. The following case illustrates this point.

---

4.   *Restatement (Second) of Contracts,* Section 33. The UCC has relaxed the requirements regarding the definiteness of terms in contracts for the sale of goods. See UCC 2–204(3).

Case 12.2 ● Ruud v. Great Plains Supply, Inc.

Supreme Court of Minnesota, 1995.
526 N.W.2d 369.

COMPANY PROFILE *Michael Wigley bought Great Plains Supply, Inc. (GPS), a building materials supplier, in 1989. GPS had suffered losses in nine of the previous ten years. To turn GPS around, Wigley closed unprofitable stores and concentrated business on contractors. By 1994, sales exceeded $100 million—up more than 40 percent over 1993—and sales from GPS's truss manufacturing facilities doubled for the fifth straight year. GPS plants, lumberyards, and distribution centers are located primarily in the Midwest. Successful salespersons are promoted to management, and managers are compensated according to their performance.*

BACKGROUND AND FACTS The corporate manual of Great Plains Supply, Inc., states that employees can be discharged at any time for any reason. This manual constitutes an employment contract between GPS and its employees. Kevin Ruud was a store manager for GPS. Before accepting an offer to transfer to an unprofitable store, he expressed worries about job security to Michael Wigley, GPS's owner, and Ronald Nelson, a GPS vice president. Wigley and Nelson each responded, "Good employees are taken care of." Ruud accepted the transfer, but when the store closed as he had feared, he was offered only lesser jobs at lower pay. Ruud quit his job and filed a suit in a Minnesota state court against GPS, Wigley, and Nelson for, among other things, breach of contract. Ruud alleged that their statements modified the terms of his contract with GPS to include permanent employment. The court dismissed the claims against Wigley and Nelson and granted GPS's motion for summary judgment. Ruud appealed, and the appellate court reversed the trial court's summary judgment on the issue. The case was then appealed to the state supreme court.

IN THE WORDS OF THE COURT . . .
GARDEBRING, Justice.

＊ ＊ ＊ ＊

＊ ＊ ＊ We conclude that Wigley and Nelson did not intend that GPS offer Kevin Ruud a "permanent" job, but rather were simply making policy statements as to the general goodwill of the company toward Kevin Ruud and its other employees. Furthermore, even if there was an intention to modify the [terms of Ruud's employment] contract, the statements of Wigley and Nelson are so vague as to leave undeterminable the nature of that modification. Therefore, we conclude that as a matter of law, the statements of Nelson and Wigley are not sufficiently definite to create an offer of permanent employment.

DECISION AND REMEDY The Supreme Court of Minnesota reinstated the order for summary judgment in favor of GPS.

FOR CRITICAL ANALYSIS—SOCIAL CONSIDERATION *Are there any circumstances under which an employer would intend to make a promise of permanent employment to any prospective or actual employee?*

Communication A third requirement for an effective offer is communication, resulting in the offeree's knowledge of the offer. Suppose that Tolson advertises a reward for the return of her lost cat. Dirlik, not knowing of the reward, finds the cat and returns it to Tolson. Ordinarily, Dirlik cannot recover the reward, because an essential element of a reward contract is that the one who claims the reward must have known it was offered. A few states would allow recovery of the reward, but not on contract principles—Dirlik would be allowed to recover on the basis that it would be unfair to deny him the reward just because he did not know about it.

TERMINATION OF THE OFFER.   The communication of an effective offer to an offeree gives the offeree the power to transform the offer into a binding, legal obligation (a contract) by an acceptance. This power of acceptance, however, does not continue forever. It can be terminated by *action of the parties* or by *operation of law.*

Termination by Action of the Parties   An offer can be terminated by the action of the parties in any of three ways: by revocation, by rejection, or by counteroffer. The offeror's act of withdrawing an offer is referred to as **revocation.** Unless an offer is irrevocable, the offeror usually can revoke the offer (even if he or she has promised to keep the offer open), as long as the revocation is communicated to the offeree before the offeree accepts. Revocation may be accomplished by express repudiation of the offer (for example, with a statement such as "I withdraw my previous offer of October 17") or by performance of acts inconsistent with the existence of the offer, which are made known to the offeree.

The offer may be rejected by the offeree, in which case the offer is terminated. Any subsequent attempt by the offeree to accept will be construed as a new offer, giving the original offeror (now the offeree) the power of acceptance. A rejection is ordinarily accomplished by words or by conduct evidencing an intent not to accept the offer. As with revocation, rejection of an offer is effective only when it is actually received by the offeror or the offeror's agent.

A **counteroffer** is a rejection of the original offer and the simultaneous making of a new offer. Suppose that Burke offers to sell his home to Lang for $170,000. Lang responds, "Your price is too high. I'll offer to purchase your house for $165,000." Lang's response is termed a counteroffer because it rejects Burke's offer to sell at $170,000 and creates a new offer by Lang to purchase the home at a price of $165,000. At common law, the **mirror image rule** requires that the offeree's acceptance match the offeror's offer exactly. In other words, the terms of the acceptance must "mirror" those of the offer. If the acceptance materially changes or adds to the terms of the original offer, it will be considered not an acceptance but a counteroffer—which, of course, need not be accepted. The original offeror can, however, accept the terms of the counteroffer and create a valid contract.[5]

Termination by Operation of Law   The offeree's power to transform an offer into a binding, legal obligation can be terminated by operation of the law if any of four conditions occur: lapse of time, destruction of the subject matter, death or incompetence of the offeror or offeree, or supervening illegality of the proposed contract.

An offer terminates automatically by law when the period of time specified in the offer has passed. For example, Jane offers to sell her boat to Jonah if he accepts within twenty days. Jonah must accept within the twenty-day period, or the offer will lapse (terminate).

If no time for acceptance is specified in the offer, the offer terminates at the end of a *reasonable* period of time. A reasonable period of time is determined

Revocation In contract law, the withdrawal of an offer by an offeror; unless the offer is irrevocable, it can be revoked at any time prior to acceptance without liability.

> **BE CAREFUL** The way in which a response to an offer is phrased can determine whether the offer is accepted or rejected.

Counteroffer An offeree's response to an offer in which the offeree rejects the original offer and at the same time makes a new offer.

Mirror Image Rule A common law rule that requires, for a valid contractual agreement, that the terms of the offeree's acceptance adhere exactly to the terms of the offeror's offer.

---

5.   The mirror image rule has been greatly modified in regard to contracts for the sale of goods. Section 2–207 of the UCC provides that a contract is formed if the offeree makes a definite expression of acceptance (such as signing the form in the appropriate location), even though the terms of the acceptance modify or add to the terms of the original offer.

by the subject matter of the contract, business and market conditions, and other relevant circumstances. An offer to sell farm produce, for example, will terminate sooner than an offer to sell farm equipment, because farm produce is perishable and subject to greater fluctuations in market value.

An offer is automatically terminated if the specific subject matter of the offer is destroyed before the offer is accepted. For example, if Bekins offers to sell his cow to Yatsen, but the cow dies before Yatsen can accept, the offer is automatically terminated.

An offeree's power of acceptance is terminated when the offeror or offeree dies or is deprived of legal capacity to enter into the proposed contract, unless the offer is irrevocable.[6] An offer is personal to both parties and normally cannot pass to the decedent's heirs, guardian, or estate. This rule applies whether or not the one party had notice of the death or incompetence of the other party.

A statute or court decision that makes an offer illegal will automatically terminate the offer. If Acme Finance Corporation offers to lend Jack $20,000 at 15 percent annually, and a state statute is enacted prohibiting loans at interest rates greater than 12 percent before Jack can accept, the offer is automatically terminated. (If the statute is enacted after Jack accepts the offer, a valid contract is formed, but the contract may still be unenforceable.)

ACCEPTANCE.   An **acceptance** is a voluntary act by the offeree that shows assent, or agreement, to the terms of an offer. The offeree's act may consist of words or conduct. Generally, a third person cannot substitute for the offeree and effectively accept the offer. After all, the identity of the offeree is as much a condition of a bargaining offer as any other term contained therein. Thus, except in special circumstances, only the person to whom the offer is made or that person's agent can accept the offer and create a binding contract. For example, Lottie makes an offer to Paul. Paul is not interested, but Paul's friend José accepts the offer. No contract is formed.

Unequivocal Acceptance   To exercise the power of acceptance effectively, the offeree must accept unequivocally. This is the *mirror image rule* previously discussed. If the acceptance is subject to new conditions or if the terms of the acceptance materially change the original offer, the acceptance may be deemed a counteroffer that implicitly rejects the original offer.

Certain terms, when added to an acceptance, will not qualify the acceptance sufficiently to constitute rejection of the offer. Suppose that in response to a person offering to sell a painting by a well-known artist, the offeree replies, "I accept; please send a written contract." The offeree is requesting a written contract but is not making it a condition for acceptance. Therefore, the acceptance is effective without the written contract. If the offeree replies, "I accept if you send a written contract," however, the acceptance is expressly conditioned on the request for a writing, and the statement is not an acceptance but a counteroffer. (Notice how important each word is!)[7]

Acceptance A voluntary act by the offeree that shows assent, or agreement, to the terms of an offer; may consist of words or conduct.

DON'T FORGET When an offer is rejected, it is terminated.

---

6.   *Restatement (Second) of Contracts,* Section 48. If the offer is irrevocable, it is not terminated when the offeror dies. Also, if the offer is such that it can be accepted by the performance of a series of acts, and those acts began before the offeror died, the offeree's power of acceptance is not terminated.

7.   As noted in footnote 5, in regard to sales contracts, the UCC provides that an acceptance may still be valid even if some terms are added. The new terms are simply treated as proposals for additions to the contract, or become part of the contract. See UCC 2–207(2).

Communication of Acceptance   Whether the offeror must be notified of the acceptance depends on the nature of the contract. In a bilateral contract, communication of acceptance is necessary, because acceptance is in the form of a promise (not performance), and the contract is formed when the promise is made (rather than when the act is performed). The offeree must communicate the acceptance to the offeror. Communication of acceptance is not necessary, however, if the offer dispenses with the requirement. Also, if the offer can be accepted by silence, no communication is necessary.[8]

Because in a unilateral contract the full performance of some act is called for, acceptance is usually evident, and notification is therefore unnecessary. Exceptions do exist, however. When the offeror requests notice of acceptance or has no adequate means of determining whether the requested act has been performed, or when the law requires such notice of acceptance, then notice is necessary.[9]

Mode and Timeliness of Acceptance   The general rule is that acceptance in a bilateral contract is timely if it is effected within the duration of the offer. Problems arise, however, when the parties involved are not dealing face to face. In such cases, the offeree may use an authorized mode of communication. Acceptance takes effect, thus completing formation of the contract, at the time the offeree sends the communication via the mode expressly or impliedly authorized by the offeror. This is the so-called **mailbox rule**, also called the "deposited acceptance rule," which the majority of courts uphold. Under this rule, if the authorized mode of communication is the mail, then an acceptance becomes valid when it is dispatched—not when it is received by the offeror.

Consideration

In every legal system, some promises will be enforced, and some promises will not be enforced. The simple fact that a party has made a promise, then, does not mean the promise is enforceable. Under the common law, a primary basis for the enforcement of promises is consideration. **Consideration** is usually defined as the value given in return for a promise. Often, consideration is broken down into two parts: (1) something of *legally sufficient value* must be given in exchange for the promise, and (2) there must be a *bargained-for* exchange.

LEGAL VALUE.   The "something of legally sufficient value" may consist of (1) a promise to do something that one has no prior legal duty to do (to pay money on receipt of certain goods, for example), (2) the performance of an action that one is otherwise not obligated to undertake (such as providing accounting services), or (3) the refraining from an action that one has a legal right to undertake. Generally, to be legally sufficient, consideration must be either *detrimental to the promisee* or *beneficial to the promisor.* Note that legal detriment (creating, modifying, or giving up a legal right) is not the same as economic, or actual, detriment (paying money or suffering economic losses).

What if, in return for a promise to pay, a person forbears to pursue harmful habits, such as the use of tobacco and alcohol? Does such forbearance represent

If an offeror expressly authorizes acceptance of his or her offer by first-class mail or express delivery, can the offeree accept by a faster means, such as a fax?

Mailbox Rule A rule providing that an acceptance of an offer becomes effective on dispatch (on being placed in a mailbox), if mail is, expressly or impliedly, an authorized means of communication of acceptance to the offeror.

Consideration Generally, the value given in return for a promise. The consideration, which must be present to make the contract legally binding, must result in a detriment to the promisee (something of legally sufficient value and bargained for) or a benefit to the promisor.

---

8.   Under the UCC, an order or other offer to buy goods that are to be promptly shipped may be treated as either a bilateral or a unilateral offer and can be accepted by a promise to ship or by actual shipment. See UCC 2–206 (1)(b).

9.   UCC 2–206(2).

Technology and the Mailbox Rule

The world of offer and acceptance has changed in recent years. To a certain extent, this change has been brought about by the emergence of express delivery services. When an offer is sent via Federal Express (or some other express delivery service), for example, express delivery is the impliedly authorized means of acceptance. The "mailbox rule," which states that an acceptance is effective on dispatch, does not come into play, because mail (other than express mail) is not an impliedly authorized means of acceptance in this situation. Electronic communications systems have even more significantly altered the ways in which offers and acceptances are exchanged by businesspersons today.

Faxed Offers and Acceptances

What happens when an offer or acceptance is faxed, rather than mailed? In effect, because of the nearly instantaneous sending and receiving of faxes, the mailbox rule becomes irrelevant. Another legal issue raised by the use of faxes is whether faxed documents are valid in light of the fact that faxed signatures are not "original." To date, courts that have addressed this issue generally have held that signatures on faxed documents are legally binding unless an "original" signature is specifically required. Usually, in cases involving faxed documents, the courts simply assume that they are valid.[a]

What happens when an acceptance is faxed to the offeror's office but for some reason is not received by the

offeror in a timely fashion? This is similar to a situation in which a letter goes astray because of an incorrect address. In such a situation, the mailbox rule that an acceptance is "effective on dispatch" does not apply, and the acceptance will not be effective until received by the offeror. Very likely, if a fax transmitted to the offeror failed to reach the offeror for some reason, a court would look closely at the circumstances. For example, if the offeror did not receive the fax because her fax machine was out of paper, and the offeree had reason to suspect or know that the offeror did not receive the fax, then the court might hold that the faxed acceptance was not effective.

Digital Signatures

A current issue presented by technology in regard to contracts (as well as other areas of the law) is how to create and verify "digital signatures" for use in electronic communications via computer networks, including those on the Internet. The Science and Technology section of the American Bar Association is currently preparing digital signature guidelines, as well as a Model Digital Signature Act. These efforts are in response to the growing need for certainty in regard to how traditional legal principles apply to electronically communicated documents. Among other things, such transmissions will require some kind of "CyberNotary" to provide legal authentication and certification of electronic documents. Efforts are already under way to create this new "legal specialization."

For Critical Analysis: What other types of issues, other than signature problems, might arise when transmitting offers and acceptances via the Internet?

---

a.   See, for example, *Bazak v. Mast Industries*, 73 N.Y.2d 113, 535 N.E.2d 633, 538 N.Y.S. 503 (1989); and *Hessenthaler v. Farzin*, 388 Pa.Super., 564 A.2d 990 (1989).

> **"It is the essence of a consideration, that, by the terms of the agreement, it is given and accepted as the motive or inducement of the promise."**
>
> Oliver Wendell Holmes, Jr., 1841–1935 (Associate justice of the United States Supreme Court, 1902–1932)

a legal detriment to the promisee and thus create consideration for the contract, or does it in fact benefit the promisee and thus *not* create consideration for the contract? This was the issue before the court in *Hamer v. Sidway*, a classic case concerning consideration, which we present in this chapter's *Landmark in the Legal Environment.*

BARGAINED-FOR EXCHANGE.   The second element of consideration is that it must provide the basis for the bargain struck between the contracting parties. The consideration given by the promisor must induce the promisee to incur a legal detriment either now or in the future, and the detriment incurred must induce the promisor to make the promise. This element of bargained-for exchange distinguishes contracts from gifts.

Landmark in the Legal Environment
Hamer v. Sidway (1891)

In *Hamer v. Sidway*,[a] the issue before the court arose from a contract created in 1869 between William Story, Sr., and his nephew, William Story II. The uncle promised his nephew that if the nephew refrained from drinking alcohol, using tobacco, and playing billiards and cards for money until he reached the age of twenty-one, the uncle would pay him $5,000. The nephew, who indulged occasionally in all of these "vices," agreed to refrain from them and did so for the next six years. Following his twenty-first birthday in 1875, the nephew wrote to his uncle that he had performed his part of the bargain and was thus entitled to the promised $5,000. A few days later, the uncle wrote the nephew a letter stating, "[Y]ou shall have the five thousand dollars, as I promised you." The uncle said that the money was in the bank, and that the nephew could "consider this money on interest."

The nephew left the money in the care of his uncle, who held it for the next twelve years. When the uncle died in 1887, however, the executor of the uncle's estate refused to pay the $5,000 claim brought by Hamer, a third party to whom the promise had been *assigned*. (The law allows

parties to assign, or transfer, rights in contracts to third parties.) The executor, Sidway, contended that the contract was invalid because there was insufficient consideration to support it. He argued that neither a benefit to the promisor (the uncle) nor a detriment to the promisee (the nephew) existed in this case. The uncle had received nothing, and the nephew had actually benefited by fulfilling the uncle's wishes. Therefore, no contract existed.

Although a lower court upheld Sidway's position, the New York Court of Appeals reversed and ruled in favor of the plaintiff, Hamer. "The promisee used tobacco, occasionally drank liquor, and he had a legal right to do so," the court stated. "That right he abandoned for a period of years upon the strength of the promise of the testator [one who makes a will] that for such forbearance he would give him $5,000. We need not speculate on the effort which may have been required to give up the use of those stimulants. It is sufficient that he restricted his lawful freedom of action within certain prescribed limits upon the faith of his uncle's agreement."

For Critical Analysis: *How might one argue that this contract also benefited the promisor (Story, Sr.)?*

a. 124 N.Y. 538, 27 N.E. 256 (1891).

ADEQUACY. Legal sufficiency of consideration involves the requirement that consideration be something of value in the eyes of the law. Adequacy of consideration involves "how much" consideration is given. Essentially, adequacy of consideration concerns the fairness of the bargain. On the surface, fairness would appear to be an issue when the values of items exchanged are unequal. In general, however, courts do not question the adequacy of consideration if the consideration is legally sufficient.

PREEXISTING DUTY. Under most circumstances, a promise to do what one already has a legal duty to do does not constitute legally sufficient consideration, because no legal detriment is incurred.[10] The preexisting legal duty may be imposed by law or may arise out of a previous contract. A sheriff, for example, cannot collect a reward for information leading to the capture of a criminal if the sheriff already has a legal duty to capture the criminal. Likewise, if a party is already bound by contract to perform a certain duty, that duty cannot serve as consideration for a second contract.[11]

10. See *Foakes v. Beer*, 9 App.Cas. 605 (1884).
11. Note that under the UCC, any agreement modifying a contract within Article 2 on Sales needs no consideration to be binding. See UCC 2–209(1).

Past Consideration An act done before the contract is made, which ordinarily, by itself, cannot be consideration for a later promise to pay for the act.

Promissory Estoppel A doctrine that applies when a promisor makes a clear and definite promise on which the promisee justifiably relies; such a promise is binding if justice will be better served by the enforcement of the promise.

> "To break an oral agreement which is not legally binding is morally wrong."
>
> The Talmud,
> *Bava Metzi'a*

Contractual Capacity The threshold mental capacity required by the law for a party who enters into a contract to be bound by that contract.

PAST CONSIDERATION.   Promises made in return for actions or events that have already taken place are unenforceable. These promises lack consideration in that the element of bargained-for exchange is missing. In short, you can bargain for something to take place now or in the future but not for something that has already taken place. Therefore, **past consideration** is no consideration.

ILLUSORY PROMISES.   If the terms of the contract express such uncertainty of performance that the promisor has not definitely promised to do anything, the promise is said to be *illusory*—without consideration and unenforceable. For example, suppose that the president of Tuscan Corporation says to his employees, "All of you have worked hard, and if profits continue to remain high, a 10 percent bonus at the end of the year will be given—if management thinks it is warranted." This is an *illusory promise,* or no promise at all, because performance depends solely on the discretion of the president (the management). There is no bargained-for consideration. The statement declares merely that management may or may not do something in the future.

PROMISSORY ESTOPPEL.   Sometimes individuals rely on promises, and such reliance may form a basis for contract rights and duties. Under the doctrine of **promissory estoppel** (also called *detrimental reliance*), a person who has reasonably relied on the promise of another can often hope to obtain some measure of recovery. For the doctrine of promissory estoppel to be applied, the following elements are required:

1. There must be a clear and definite promise.
2. The promisee must justifiably rely on the promise.
3. The reliance normally must be of a substantial and definite character.
4. Justice will be better served by the enforcement of the promise.

Capacity

The third element required for the formation of a contract (after agreement and consideration) is **contractual capacity**—the legal ability to enter into a contractual relationship. Courts generally presume the existence of contractual capacity, but there are some situations in which capacity is lacking or may be questionable. A person *adjudged by a court* to be mentally incompetent, for example, cannot form a legally binding contract with another party. In other situations, a party may have the capacity to enter into a valid contract but also have the right to avoid liability under it. For example, minors usually are not legally bound by contracts.

Ethical Perspective

Quasi contracts, or contracts implied in law, arise to establish justice and fairness. The term *quasi contract* is misleading, because a quasi contract is not really a contract at all. It does not arise from any agreement between two individuals. Rather, a court imposes a quasi contract on the parties when justice so requires to prevent unjust enrichment. The doctrine of unjust enrichment is based on the theory that individuals should not be allowed to profit or enrich themselves inequitably at the expense of others. This belief is fundamental in our society and is clearly inspired by ethical considerations.

For Critical Analysis: *Why is the term* contract *used in situations involving quasi-contractual recovery, in view of the fact that no agreement between the parties exists?*

MINORS.   Today, in virtually all states, the *age of majority* (when a person is no longer a minor) for contractual purposes is eighteen years for both sexes.[12] In addition, some states provide for the termination of minority on marriage. Subject to certain exceptions, the contracts entered into by a minor are voidable at the option of that minor.

The general rule is that a minor can enter into any contract an adult can, provided that the contract is not one prohibited by law for minors (for example, the sale of alcoholic beverages). Although minors have the right to avoid their contracts, there are exceptions.

Disaffirmance   For a minor to exercise the option to avoid a contract, he or she need only manifest an intention not to be bound by it. The minor "avoids" the contract by disaffirming it. The technical definition of **disaffirmance** is the legal avoidance, or setting aside, of a contractual obligation. Words or conduct may serve to express this intent. The contract can ordinarily be disaffirmed at any time during minority or for a reasonable time after the minor comes of age. In some states, however, when there is a contract for the sale of land by a minor, the minor cannot disaffirm the contract until he or she reaches the age of majority. When a minor disaffirms a contract, all property that he or she has transferred to the adult as consideration can be recovered, even if it is then in the possession of a third party.[13]

Note that an adult who enters into a contract with a minor cannot avoid his or her contractual duties on the ground that the minor can do so. Unless the minor exercises the option to disaffirm the contract, the adult party normally is bound by it.

Minor's Obligations on Disaffirmance   All state laws permit minors to disaffirm contracts (with certain exceptions—to be discussed shortly), including executed contracts. States differ, however, on the extent of a minor's obligations on disaffirmance. Courts in a majority of states hold that the minor need only return the goods (or other consideration) subject to the contract, provided the goods are in the minor's possession or control. For example, suppose that Jim

> **Disaffirmance** The legal avoidance, or setting aside, of a contractual obligation.

---

12.   The age of majority may still be twenty-one for other purposes, such as the purchase and consumption of alcohol. The word *infant* is usually used synonymously with the word *minor*.
13.   The Uniform Commercial Code, in Section 2–403(1), allows an exception if the third party is a "good faith purchaser for value."

International Perspective

Like courts in the United States, courts in Great Britain may permit minors' contracts to be avoided on the ground that minors lack contractual capacity. Great Britain, however, has no single, fixed age limit for lack of capacity. British courts deal with contracts on a case-by-case basis. In deciding whether a minor can avoid a particular contract, a British court will consider a number of factors, including the specific circumstances of the case, the nature of the item contracted for, and the psychological maturity of the minor.

For Critical Analysis: *What benefit is there to the U.S. system, which lacks flexibility with respect to the contractual capacity of minors?*

When a minor disaffirms a contract, such as a contract to buy a computer, most states require the minor to return whatever consideration he or she received, if it is within his or her control. Why do some states require more?

Garrison, a seventeen-year-old, purchases a computer from Radio Shack. While transporting the computer to his home, Garrison, through no fault of his own, is involved in a car accident. As a result of the accident, the plastic casing of the computer is broken. The next day, he returns the computer to Radio Shack and disaffirms the contract. Under the majority view, this return fulfills Garrison's duty even though the computer is now damaged.

A minor who enters into a contract for necessaries may disaffirm the contract but remains liable for the reasonable value of the goods. **Necessaries** are basic needs, such as food, clothing, shelter, and medical services. In some cases, however, courts have not limited necessaries to items required for physical existence but have interpreted the term to include whatever is believed to be necessary to maintain a person's standard of living or financial and social status. Thus, what will be considered a necessary for one person may be a luxury for another.

In the following case, a minor's father brought an action on behalf of his son to disaffirm the minor's purchase of an automobile and to recover the money paid for the car from a seller who knew that the purchaser was a minor when the contract was made.

Necessaries Necessities required for life, such as food, shelter, clothing, and medical attention; may include whatever is believed to be necessary to maintain a person's standard of living or financial and social status.

Case 12.3 ● Quality Motors, Inc. v. Hays

Supreme Court of Arkansas, 1949.
216 Ark. 264,
225 S.W.2d 326.

HISTORICAL AND ECONOMIC SETTING *In 1949, a business recession produced a decline in the cost of living. United Automobile Workers at General Motors plants accepted a slight wage cut, after they had obtained a wage increase the year before. Unemployment jumped more than two percentage points, while prices of shares on the stock market fell more than 10 percent. The cost of housing and health care rose, while other consumer prices fell. A gallon of gasoline cost 21 cents. A new Cadillac cost*

(Continued)

Case 12.3—continued

$5,000. The average steelworker, after taxes, made $3,000 a year, and the average high school teacher made $4,700 a year. The typical car salesperson made, after taxes, $8,000 annually.

BACKGROUND AND FACTS Sixteen-year-old Johnny Hays went to Quality Motors, Inc., to purchase a car. The salesperson refused to sell the car unless the purchase was made by an adult, so Johnny left and later returned with a young man of twenty-three. Hays paid for the car, and a bill of sale was made out to the twenty-three-year-old. The salesperson then drove the two boys into town to a notary public, the young man transferred the title to the car to Johnny, and the salesperson delivered the car to Johnny. Johnny's father attempted to return the car to Quality Motors for a full refund, but Quality Motors refused it. Subsequently, Johnny wrecked the car in an accident. Johnny, through his father, brought suit in an Arkansas state court to disaffirm the contract and recover the purchase price. The trial court ordered the purchase price to be refunded to Hays on his return of the car to Quality Motors. Quality Motors appealed.

IN THE WORDS OF THE COURT . . .
DUNAWAY, Justice.

* * * *

The law is well settled in Arkansas that an infant may disaffirm his contracts, except those made for necessaries, without being required to return the consideration received, except such part as may remain in specie in his hands. * * *

* * * *

Appellant knowingly and through a planned subterfuge sold an automobile to a minor. It then refused to take the car back. Even after the car was wrecked once, it was in appellant's place of business, and appellant was still resisting disaffirmance of the contract. The loss which appellant has suffered is the first result of its own acts.

DECISION AND REMEDY The Supreme Court of Arkansas affirmed the lower court's decree. Hays was allowed to disaffirm the contract and return the car without liability for damages.

FOR CRITICAL ANALYSIS—CULTURAL CONSIDERATION *What societal values have led to laws governing disaffirmance that weigh so heavily in favor of minors?*

Ratification In contract law, **ratification** is the act of accepting and giving legal force to an obligation that previously was not enforceable. A minor who has reached the age of majority can ratify a contract expressly or impliedly.

Express ratification occurs when the minor expressly states, orally or in writing, that he or she intends to be bound by the contract. Implied ratification exists when the conduct of the minor is inconsistent with disaffirmance (as when the minor enjoys the benefits of the contract) or when the minor fails to disaffirm an executed (fully performed) contract within a reasonable time after reaching the age of majority. If the contract is still executory (not yet performed or only partially performed), however, failure to disaffirm the contract will not necessarily imply ratification.

Generally, the courts base their determination on whether the minor, after reaching the age of majority, has had ample opportunity to consider the nature of the contractual obligations he or she entered into as a minor and the extent to which the adult party to the contract has performed.

INTOXICATED PERSONS. Another situation in which contractual capacity becomes an issue is when a contract is formed by a person who claims to have

Ratification The act of accepting and giving legal force to an obligation that previously was not enforceable.

been intoxicated at the time the contract was made. The general rule is that if a person who is sufficiently intoxicated to lack mental capacity enters into a contract, the contract is voidable at the option of the intoxicated person. This is true even if the intoxication was purely voluntary. For the contract to be voidable, it must be proved that the intoxicated person's reason and judgment were impaired to the extent that he or she did not comprehend the legal consequences of entering into the contract. If the person was intoxicated but understood these legal consequences, the contract is enforceable.

Simply because the terms of the contract are foolish or are obviously favorable to the other party does not mean the contract is voidable (unless the other party fraudulently induced the person to become intoxicated). Problems often arise in determining whether a party was sufficiently intoxicated to avoid legal duties. Generally, contract avoidance on the ground of intoxication is rarely permitted.

The following case involves an unusual business transaction in which boasts and dares "after a few drinks" resulted in a contract to sell certain property. The issue before the court is whether the seller was sufficiently intoxicated to render the contract voidable at the seller's option.

> **BE CAREFUL** A contract will almost always be enforced if both parties knew what they were signing.

Case 12.4 ● Lucy v. Zehmer

Supreme Court of Appeals of Virginia, 1954.
196 Va. 493,
84 S.E.2d 516.

HISTORICAL AND SOCIAL SETTING *In part because intoxication is usually self-induced, the emphasis in cases that concern lack of capacity on the ground of intoxication is sometimes different from the emphasis in cases that concern lack of capacity on other grounds. Particularly in older cases, there is often a discussion of the parties' morals. Rather than focusing on whether the person was sober enough to understand what he or she was doing, the issue was whether the law should allow someone who becomes intoxicated voluntarily to avoid the consequences of his or her behavior. At least one court at the turn of the century held that intoxication is never a defense.*[a]

BACKGROUND AND FACTS Lucy and Zehmer had known each other for fifteen or twenty years. For some time, Lucy

had been wanting to buy Zehmer's farm. Zehmer had always told Lucy that he was not interested in selling. One night, Lucy stopped in to visit with the Zehmers at a restaurant they operated. Lucy said to Zehmer, "I bet you wouldn't take $50,000 for that place." Zehmer replied, "Yes, I would, too; you wouldn't give fifty." Throughout the evening, the conversation returned to the sale of the farm. At the same time, the parties were drinking whiskey. Eventually, Zehmer wrote up an agreement, on the back of a restaurant check, for the sale of the farm, and he asked his wife to sign it—which she did. When Lucy brought an action in a Virginia state court to enforce the agreement, Zehmer argued that he had been "high as a Georgia pine" at the time and that the offer had been made in jest: "two doggoned drunks bluffing to see who could talk the biggest and say the most." Lucy claimed that he had not been intoxicated and did not think Zehmer had been, either, given the way Zehmer handled the transaction. The trial court ruled in favor of the Zehmers, and Lucy appealed.

---

a. *Cook v. Bagnell Timber Co.,* 78 Ark. 47, 94 S.W. 695 (1906).

IN THE WORDS OF THE COURT . . .
BUCHANAN, J. [Justice] delivered the opinion of the court.
* * * *

The appearance of the contract, the fact that it was under discussion for forty minutes or more before it was signed; Lucy's objection to the first draft because it was written in the singular, and he wanted Mrs. Zehmer to sign it

(Continued)

Case 12.4—continued

also; the rewriting to meet that objection and the signing by Mrs. Zehmer; the discussion of what was to be included in the sale, the provision for the examination of the title, the completeness of the instrument that was executed, the taking possession of it by Lucy with no request or suggestion by either of the defendants that he give it back, are facts which furnish persuasive evidence that the execution of the contract was a serious business transaction rather than a casual, jesting matter as defendants now contend.

    * * * *

In the field of contracts, as generally elsewhere, "*We must look to the outward expression of a person as manifesting his intention rather than to his secret and unexpressed intention. 'The law imputes to a person an intention corresponding to the reasonable meaning of his words and acts.'* " [Emphasis added.]

DECISION AND REMEDY The Supreme Court of Virginia determined that the writing was an enforceable contract and reversed the ruling of the lower court. The Zehmers were required by court order to carry through with the sale of the Ferguson Farm to the Lucys.

FOR CRITICAL ANALYSIS—CULTURAL CONSIDERATION *Should the policy considerations in cases involving intoxication be different from those in cases involving other capacity issues? Why or why not?*

MENTALLY INCOMPETENT PERSONS. If a person has been adjudged mentally incompetent by a court of law and a guardian has been appointed, any contract made by the mentally incompetent person is *void*—no contract exists. Only the guardian can enter into a binding contract on behalf of the mentally incompetent person.

If a mentally incompetent person not previously so adjudged by a court enters into a contract, the contract may be *voidable* if the person does not know he or she is entering into the contract or lacks the mental capacity to comprehend its nature, purpose, and consequences. A contract entered into by a mentally incompetent person (but not previously so adjudged by a court) may also be deemed valid and enforceable if the contract was formed during a lucid interval. For such a contract to be valid, it must be shown that the person was able to comprehend the nature, purpose, and consequences of the contract *at the time the contract was formed.*

Legality

To this point, we have discussed three of the requirements for a valid contract to exist—agreement, consideration, and contractual capacity. Now we examine a fourth—legality. For a contract to be valid and enforceable, it must be formed for a legal purpose. A contract to do something that is prohibited by federal or state statutory law is illegal and, as such, void from the outset and thus unenforceable. Additionally, a contract to commit a tortious act or to commit an action that is contrary to public policy is illegal and unenforceable.

CONTRACTS CONTRARY TO STATUTE. Statutes sometimes prescribe the terms of contracts. In some instances, the laws are specific, even providing for the inclusion of certain clauses and their wording. Other statutes prohibit certain contracts on the basis of their subject matter, the time at which they are entered into, or the status of the contracting parties. We examine here several ways in which contracts may be contrary to a statute and thus illegal.

Usury   Vitually every state has a statute that sets the maximum rate of interest that can be charged for different types of transactions, including ordinary loans. A lender who makes a loan at an interest rate above the lawful maximum commits **usury**. The maximum rate of interest varies from state to state.

Usury Charging an illegal rate of interest.

Gambling   In general, gambling contracts are illegal and thus void. All states have statutes that regulate gambling—defined as any scheme that involves the distribution of property by chance among persons who have paid valuable consideration for the opportunity (chance) to receive the property.[14] Gambling is the creation of risk for the purpose of assuming it. In some states, such as Nevada and New Jersey, casino gambling is legal. In other states, certain other forms of gambling are legal. California, for example, has not defined draw poker as a crime, although criminal statutes prohibit numerous other types of gambling games. Several states allow horse racing, and about half of the states have recognized the substantial revenues that can be obtained from gambling and have legalized state-operated lotteries, as well as lotteries (such as bingo) arranged for charitable purposes. Many states also allow gambling on Indian reservations.

Sabbath (Sunday) Laws   Statutes called Sabbath (Sunday) laws prohibit the formation or performance of certain contracts on a Sunday. Under the common law, such contracts are legal in the absence of this statutory prohibition. Under some state and local laws, all contracts entered into on a Sunday are illegal. Laws in other states or municipalities prohibit only the sale of certain types of merchandise, such as alcoholic beverages, on a Sunday.

Blue Laws State or local laws that prohibit the performance of certain types of commercial activities on Sunday.

These laws, which date back to colonial times, are often called **blue laws.** Blue laws get their name from the blue paper on which New Haven, Connecticut, printed its new town ordinance in 1781. The ordinance prohibited all work on Sunday and required all shops to close on the "Lord's Day." A number of states and municipalities enacted laws forbidding the carrying on of "all secular labor and business on the Lord's Day." Exceptions to Sunday laws permit contracts for necessities (such as food) and works of charity. A fully performed (executed) contract that was entered into on a Sunday normally cannot be rescinded (canceled).

Sunday laws are often not enforced, and some of these laws have been held to be unconstitutional on the ground that they are contrary to the freedom of religion. Nonetheless, as a precaution, business owners contemplating doing business in a particular locality should check to see if any Sunday statutes or ordinances will affect their business activities.

RECALL Under the First Amendment, the government cannot promote or place a significant burden on religion.

Licensing Statutes   All states require that members of certain professions obtain licenses allowing them to practice. Physicians, lawyers, real estate brokers, architects, electricians, and stockbrokers are but a few of the people who must be licensed. Some licenses are obtained only after extensive schooling and examinations, which indicate to the public that a special skill has been acquired. Others require only that the particular person be of good moral character.

---

14.   See *Wishing Well Club v. Akron,* 66 Ohio Law Abs. 406, 112 N.E.2d 41 (1951).

Some states expressly provide that the lack of a license in certain occupations bars the enforcement of work-related contracts. If the statute does not expressly state this, one must look to the underlying purpose of the licensing requirements for a particular occupation. If the purpose is to protect the public from unauthorized practitioners, a contract involving an unlicensed individual is illegal and unenforceable. If, however, the underlying purpose of the statute is to raise government revenues, a contract with an unlicensed practitioner is enforceable—although the unlicensed person is usually fined.

CONTRACTS CONTRARY TO PUBLIC POLICY.   Although contracts involve private parties, some are not enforceable because of the negative impact they would have on society. These contracts are said to be *contrary to public policy*. Examples include a contract to commit an immoral act (such as a surrogate-parenting contract, which several courts and state statutes equate with "baby selling") and a contract that prohibits marriage. As an example of the latter, suppose that Everett offers a young man $500 if he refrains from marrying Everett's daughter. If the young man accepts, no contract is formed (the contract is void) because it is contrary to public policy. Thus, if the man marries Everett's daughter, Everett cannot sue him for breach of contract. Business contracts that may be contrary to public policy include contracts in restraint of trade and unconscionable contracts or clauses.

Contracts in Restraint of Trade   Contracts in restraint of trade (anticompetitive agreements) usually adversely affect the public, which favors competition in the economy. Typically, such contracts also violate one or more federal or state statutes.[15] An exception is recognized when the restraint is reasonable and it is *ancillary* to (is a subsidiary part of) a contract, such as a contract for the sale of a business or an employment contract. Many such exceptions involve a type of restraint called a *covenant not to compete,* or a restrictive covenant.

Covenants not to compete are often contained in contracts concerning the sale of an ongoing business. A covenant not to compete is created when a seller agrees not to open a new store in a certain geographical area surrounding the old store. Such an agreement, when it is ancillary to a sales contract and reasonable in terms of time and geographic area, enables the seller to sell, and the purchaser to buy, the "goodwill" and "reputation" of an ongoing business. If, for example, a well-known merchant sells his or her store and opens a competing business a block away, many of the merchant's customers will likely do business at the new store. This renders valueless the good name and reputation sold to the other merchant for a price. If a covenant not to compete was not ancillary to a sales agreement, however, it would be void, because it unreasonably restrains trade and is contrary to public policy.

Unconscionable Contracts or Clauses   Ordinarily, a court does not look at the fairness or equity of a contract; in other words, it does not inquire into the adequacy of consideration. Persons are assumed to be reasonably intelligent, and the court does not come to their aid just because they have made unwise or foolish bargains. In certain circumstances, however, bargains are so oppressive that the courts relieve innocent parties of part or all of their duties. Such a bargain is called an **unconscionable contract** (or **unconscionable clause**). Both the Uniform Commercial Code (UCC) and the Uniform Consumer Credit

> "Public policy is in its nature so uncertain and fluctuating, varying with the habits of the day, . . . that it is difficult to determine its limits with any degree of exactness."
>
> Joseph Story, 1779–1845
> (Associate Justice of the United States Supreme Court, 1811–1845)

Unconscionable Contract (or Unconscionable Clause) A contract or clause that is void on the basis of public policy because one party, as a result of his or her disproportionate bargaining power, is forced to accept terms that are unfairly burdensome and that unfairly benefit the dominating party.

15.   Such as the Sherman Antitrust Act, the Clayton Act, and the Federal Trade Commission Act (see Chapter 22).

Code (UCCC) embody the unconscionability concept—the former with regard to the sale of goods and the latter with regard to consumer loans and the waiver of rights.[16]

Contracts entered into because of one party's vastly superior bargaining power may be deemed unconscionable. These situations usually involve an **adhesion contract,** which is a contract drafted by the dominant party and then presented to the other—the adhering party—on a "take it or leave it" basis.[17]

Often closely related to the concept of unconscionability are **exculpatory clauses,** defined as clauses that release a party from liability in the event of monetary or physical injury, *no matter who is at fault*. Indeed, some courts refer to such clauses in terms of unconscionability. Suppose, for example, that Madison Manufacturing Company hires a laborer and has him sign a contract containing the following clause:

> Said employee hereby agrees with employer, in consideration of such employ-
> ment, that he will take upon himself all risks incident to his position and will in
> no case hold the company liable for any injury or damage he may sustain, in his
> person or otherwise, by accidents or injuries in the factory, or which may result
> from defective machinery or carelessness or misconduct of himself or any other
> employee in service of the employer.

This contract provision attempts to remove Madison's potential liability for injuries occurring to the employee, and it would usually be held contrary to public policy.[18]

Exculpatory clauses may be enforced, however, when the parties seeking their enforcement are not involved in businesses considered important to the public interest. These businesses have included health clubs, amusement parks, horse-rental concessions, golf-cart concessions, and skydiving organizations. Because these services are not essential, the firms offering them are sometimes considered to have no relative advantage in bargaining strength, and anyone contracting for their services is considered to do so voluntarily.

THE EFFECT OF ILLEGALITY.   In general, an illegal contract is void: the contract is deemed never to have existed, and the courts will not aid either party. In most illegal contracts, both parties are considered to be equally at fault—*in pari delicto*. If the contract is executory (not yet fulfilled), neither party can enforce it. If it is executed, there can be neither contractual nor quasi-contractual recovery.

There are exceptions to the general rule that neither party to an illegal bargain can sue for breach and neither can recover for performance rendered. We look at these exceptions here.

Justifiable Ignorance of the Facts   When one of the parties to a contract is relatively innocent (has no knowledge or any reason to know that the contract is illegal), that party can often obtain restitution or recovery of benefits conferred in a partially executed contract. The courts do not enforce the contract but do allow the parties to return to their original positions. It is also possible

---

Adhesion Contract A "standard form" contract, such as that between a large retailer and a consumer, in which the stronger party dictates the terms.

Exculpatory Clause A clause that releases a contractual party from liability in the event of monetary or physical injury, no matter who is at fault.

---

16.   See, for example, UCC Sections 2–302 and 2–719 (and UCCC Sections 5.108 and 1.107).
17.   See, for example, *Henningsen v. Bloomfield Motors, Inc.,* 32 N.J. 358, 161 A.2d 69 (1960).
18.   For a case with similar facts, see *Little Rock & Fort Smith Railway Co. v. Eubanks,* 48 Ark. 460, 3 S.W. 808 (1887). In such a case, the exculpatory clause may also be illegal on the basis of a violation of a state workers' compensation law.

for an innocent party who has fully performed under the contract to enforce the contract against the guilty party.

Members of Protected Classes   When a statute protects a certain class of people, a member of that class can enforce an illegal contract even though the other party cannot. For example, there are statutes that prohibit certain employees (such as flight attendants) from working more than a specified number of hours per month. These employees thus constitute a class protected by statute. An employee who is required to work more than the maximum can recover for those extra hours of service.

Fraud, Duress, or Undue Influence   Whenever a plaintiff has been induced to enter into an illegal bargain as a result of fraud, duress, or undue influence, he or she can either enforce the contract or recover for its value.

Defenses to Contract Formation or Enforceability

▼   A contract has been entered into by two parties, each with full legal capacity and for a legal purpose. The contract is also supported by consideration. Nonetheless, the contract may be unenforceable if the parties have not genuinely assented to the terms. Lack of genuine assent is a defense to the enforcement of a contract.

A contract that is otherwise valid may also be unenforceable if it is not in the proper form. For example, if a contract is required by law to be in writing, and there is no written evidence of the contract, it may not be enforceable.

Genuineness of Assent

Genuineness of assent may be lacking because of mistake, fraudulent misrepresentation, undue influence, or duress. Generally, a party who demonstrates that he or she did not genuinely assent to the terms of a contract can choose either to carry out the contract or to rescind (cancel) it, and thus avoid the entire transaction.

MISTAKES.   Generally, courts distinguish between *mistakes as to judgment of market value or conditions* and *mistakes as to fact*. Only the latter normally have legal significance.

Suppose, for example, that Jud Wheeler contracts to buy ten acres of land because he believes that he can resell the land at a profit to Bart. Can Jud escape his contractual obligations if it later turns out that he was mistaken? Not likely. Jud's overestimation of the value of the land or of Bart's interest in it is an ordinary risk of business for which a court will not normally provide relief. Now suppose that Jud purchases a painting of a landscape from Roth's Gallery. Both Jud and Roth believe that the painting is by the artist Van Gogh. Jud later discovers that the painting is a very clever fake. Because neither Jud nor Roth was aware of this fact when they made their deal, Jud can rescind the contract and recover the purchase price of the painting.

Mistakes occur in two forms—*unilateral* and *bilateral (mutual)*. A unilateral mistake is made by only one of the contracting parties; a mutual mistake is made by both.

Unilateral Mistakes   A unilateral mistake involves some *material fact*—that is, a fact important to the subject matter of the contract. In general, a unilateral

> **"Mistakes are the inevitable lot of mankind."**
>
> Sir George Jessel, 1824–1883
> (English jurist)

> **BE CAREFUL** What a party to a contract knows or should know can determine whether the contract is enforceable.

mistake does not afford the mistaken party any right to relief from the contract. In other words, the contract normally is enforceable.[19] For example, Ellen intends to sell her motor home for $17,500. When she learns that Chin is interested in buying a used motor home, she faxes him an offer to sell her vehicle to him, but when typing the fax, she mistakenly keys in the price of $15,700. Chin writes back, accepting Ellen's offer. Even though Ellen intended to sell her motor home for $17,500, she has made a unilateral mistake and is bound by contract to sell the vehicle to Chin for $15,700.

Mutual Mistakes   When both parties are mistaken about the same material fact, the contract can be rescinded by either party.[20] Note that, as with unilateral mistakes, the mistake must be about a *material fact* (one that is important and central to the contract). If, instead, a mutual mistake concerns the later market value or quality of the object of the contract, the contract normally can be enforced by either party. This rule is based on the theory that both parties assume certain risks when they enter into a contract. Without this rule, almost any party who did not receive what he or she considered a fair bargain could argue bilateral mistake. In essence, this would make adequacy of consideration a factor in determining whether a contract existed, and as discussed previously, the courts normally do not inquire into the adequacy of the consideration.

A word or term in a contract may be subject to more than one reasonable interpretation. In that situation, if the parties to the contract attach materially different meanings to the term, their mutual misunderstanding may allow the contract to be rescinded. The following classic case on mutual misunderstanding involved a ship named *Peerless* that was to sail from Bombay with certain cotton goods on board. More than one ship named *Peerless* sailed from Bombay that winter, however.

---

19.   *The Restatement (Second) of Contracts,* Section 153, liberalizes the general rule to take into account the modern trend of allowing avoidance in some circumstances even though only one party has been mistaken.
20.   *Restatement (Second) of Contracts,* Section 152.

Case 12.5 ⬤ Raffles v. Wichelhaus

Court of Exchequer, England, 1864.
159 Eng.Rep. 375.

HISTORICAL AND POLITICAL SETTING   *Before the Civil War, the states in the southern United States were largely agricultural. By the mid-nineteenth century, the staple of this agricultural area had become cotton. Cotton was important to the economy of the South and to the economy of the European textile industry, which by 1860 was booming. In the 1860s, when the southern states seceded from the United States to form the Confederate States, the United States announced a blockade of southern ports. The states of the Confederacy knew that cotton was*

important to the European economy, and they were confident that Europe would exert pressure on the United States to lift the blockade. Instead, to obtain cotton, European merchants turned to other sources, including India.

BACKGROUND AND FACTS   Wichelhaus purchased a shipment of cotton from Raffles to arrive on a ship called the *Peerless* from Bombay, India. Wichelhaus meant a ship called the *Peerless* sailing from Bombay in October; Raffles meant another ship called the *Peerless* sailing from Bombay in December. When the goods arrived on the December *Peerless,* Raffles delivered them to Wichelhaus. By that time, however, Wichelhaus was no longer willing to accept them.

(Continued)

Case 12.5—continued

IN THE WORDS OF THE COURT . . .
PER CURIAM [by the whole court].
* * * *

There is nothing on the face of the contract to show that any particular ship called the "Peerless" was meant; but the moment it appears that two ships called the "Peerless" were about to sail from Bombay there is a latent ambiguity * * * . That being so, there was no consensus * * * , and therefore no binding contract.

DECISION AND REMEDY   The judgment was for the defendant, Wichelhaus. The court held that no mutual assent existed, because each party attached a materially different meaning to an essential term of the written contract—that is, a mutual mistake of fact had occurred.

FOR CRITICAL ANALYSIS—SOCIAL CONSIDERATION   *What policy considerations underlie the general rule that contracts involving mutual mistakes of fact may be rescinded, whereas contracts involving unilateral mistakes of fact (with the exceptions discussed earlier) may not be?*

FRAUDULENT MISREPRESENTATION.   Although fraud is a tort, the presence of fraud also affects the genuineness of the innocent party's consent to a contract. When an innocent party consents to a contract with fraudulent terms, the contract usually can be avoided, because he or she has not *voluntarily* consented to the terms.[21] Normally, the innocent party can either rescind (cancel) the contract and be restored to his or her original position or enforce the contract and seek damages for injuries resulting from the fraud.

Typically, there are three elements of fraud:

1. A misrepresentation of a material fact must occur.
2. There must be an intent to deceive.
3. The innocent party must justifiably rely on the misrepresentation.

Additionally, to collect damages, a party must have been injured as a result of the misrepresentation.

Ordinarily, neither party to a contract has a duty to come forward and disclose facts, and a contract normally will not be set aside because certain pertinent information has not been volunteered. Generally, however, if a *serious* defect or a *serious* potential problem is known to the seller but cannot reasonably be suspected to be known by the buyer, the seller may have a duty to speak.

> **"It was beautiful and simple as all truly great swindles are."**
>
> O. Henry, 1862–1910
> (American author)

> **REMEMBER** To collect damages in almost any lawsuit, there must be some sort of injury.

UNDUE INFLUENCE.   Undue influence arises from relationships in which one party can greatly influence another party, thus overcoming that party's free will. Minors and elderly people, for example, are often under the influence of guardians. If a guardian induces a young or elderly *ward* (a person placed by a court under the care of a guardian) to enter into a contract that benefits the guardian, the guardian may have exerted undue influence.

Undue influence can arise from a number of confidential relationships or relationships founded on trust, including attorney-client, doctor-patient, guardian-ward, parent-child, husband-wife, and trustee-beneficiary relationships. The essential feature of undue influence is that the party being taken advantage of does not, in reality, exercise free will in entering into a contract.

> **CONTRAST** Even when there is no undue influence, a minor can avoid a contract.

---

21.   *Restatement (Second) of Contracts*, Sections 163 and 164.

Inside the Legal Environment
"Silent Fraud" in the Employment Context

The "silent fraud" doctrine dates back to at least 1886. In that year, the Michigan Supreme Court held that "[a] fraud arising from the suppression of the truth is as prejudicial as that which springs from the assertion of a falsehood, and courts have not hesitated to sustain recoveries where the truth has been suppressed with the intent to defraud."[a]

One of the problems with claims of silent fraud is that it is not always clear what information a party to a contract is required to disclose to the other party. For example, does a company have a duty to disclose to prospective employees information concerning the financial health of the company? That question arose in a recent case brought by Karen Clement-Rowe against the Michigan Health Care Corporation.[b] The corporation hired Clement-Rowe as a health nurse in 1990. On accepting

the job, Clement-Rowe sold her home in Saginaw, Michigan, and moved to Detroit. About a month after she was hired, the company fired 150 of its employees, including Clement-Rowe, in response to a severe financial crisis.

In her lawsuit, Clement-Rowe alleged, among other things, silent fraud. She claimed that the corporation had a duty to disclose its adverse financial condition when it hired her and that she would not have taken a job with the company if such information had been disclosed. According to Clement-Rowe, the nondisclosure was intentional—the corporation intended to induce her to rely on the nondisclosure in accepting employment. In evaluating the case, the Court of Appeals of Michigan held that Clement-Rowe had met the requirements for a claim of silent fraud; therefore the trial court's decision to grant the defendant corporation's request for summary judgment on this issue was in error.

The final words of the appellate court's opinion contain an important message for any company that seeks to hire new personnel while facing serious financial difficulties: "Today's

employment market is both tenuous and difficult. Nearly all employment is at-will.[c] The economic well-being and financial stability of a potential employer is an important factor in accepting a job offer. Consequently, an employer who succeeds in asserting its economic health to attract qualified employees knowing the assertions are untrue may not later hide behind an at-will employment contract. Neither may it be permitted to avoid liability after omitting to disclose, when asked, known economic instability which later leads to economically-based layoffs."

For Critical Analysis: *If employers were required to disclose adverse financial conditions to prospective employees, how would employers be able to induce qualified personnel (who may be able to help the companies recover financially) to come to work for their companies?*

a.   *Tompkins v. Hollister,* 60 Mich. 470, 27 N.W. 651 (1886).
b.   *Clement-Rowe v. Michigan Health Care Corp.,* 212 Mich.App. 503, 538 N.W.2d 20 (1995).

c.   Under the common law doctrine of employment at will, an employer can fire employees "at will"—that is, with or without cause.

A contract entered into under excessive or undue influence lacks genuine assent and is therefore voidable.[22]

Duress

Assent to the terms of a contract is not genuine if one of the parties is *forced* into the agreement. Forcing a party to enter into a contract because of the fear created by threats is legally defined as *duress.*[23] In addition, blackmail or extortion to induce consent to a contract constitutes duress. Duress is both a defense to the enforcement of a contract and a ground for rescission, or cancellation, of a contract. Therefore, a party who signs a contract under duress can choose to

22.   *Restatement (Second) of Contracts,* Section 177.
23.   *Restatement (Second) of Contracts,* Sections 174 and 175.

carry out the contract or to avoid the entire transaction. (The wronged party usually has this choice in cases in which assent is not real or genuine.)

The Statute of Frauds—Requirement of a Writing

Today, almost every state has a statute that stipulates what types of contracts must be in writing. In this text, we refer to such statutes as the **Statute of Frauds.** The primary purpose of the statute is to ensure that there is reliable evidence of the existence and terms of certain classes of contracts deemed historically to be important or complex.

Statute of Frauds A state statute under which certain types of contracts must be in writing to be enforceable.

CONTRACTS INVOLVING INTERESTS IN LAND. Land is real property, which includes not only land but all physical objects that are permanently attached to the soil, such as buildings plants, trees, and the soil itself. Under the Statute of Frauds, a contract involving an interest in land, to be enforceable, must be evidenced by a writing.[24] If Carol, for example, contracts orally to sell Seaside Shelter to Axel but later decides not to sell, Axel cannot enforce the contract. Similarly, if Axel refuses to close the deal, Carol cannot force Axel to pay for the land by bringing a lawsuit. The Statute of Frauds is a *defense* to the enforcement of this type of oral contract.

A contract for the sale of land ordinarily involves the entire interest in the real property, including buildings, growing crops, vegetation, minerals, timber, and anything else affixed to the land. Therefore, a *fixture* (personal property so affixed or so used as to become a part of the realty) is treated as real property.

The Statute of Frauds requires written contracts not just for the sale of land but also for the transfer of other interests in land, such as mortgages and leases.

THE ONE-YEAR RULE. Contracts that cannot, *by their own terms*, be performed within one year from the day after the contract is formed must be in writing to be enforceable. Because disputes over such contracts are unlikely to occur until some time after the contracts are made, resolution of these disputes is difficult unless the contract terms have been put in writing. The one-year period begins to run *the day after the contract is made.*[25] Exhibit 12–1 illustrates the one-year rule.

The test for determining whether an oral contract is enforceable under the one-year rule of the statute is not whether the agreement is *likely* to be performed

---

24. In some states, the contract will be enforced, however, if each party admits to the existence of the oral contract in court or admits to its existence during discovery before trial (see Chapter 3).
25. Arthur Corbin, *Corbin on Contracts* (St. Paul: West Publishing Co., 1952), Section 444.

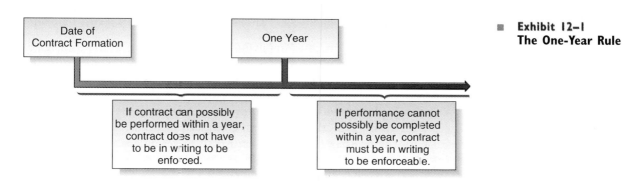

■ **Exhibit 12–1 The One-Year Rule**

within one year from the date of contract formation but whether performance within a year is *possible*. When performance of a contract is objectively impossible during the one-year period, the oral contract will be unenforceable.

COLLATERAL PROMISES.   A **collateral promise,** or secondary promise, is one that is ancillary (subsidiary) to a principal transaction or primary contractual relationship. In other words, a collateral promise is one made by a third party to assume the debts or obligations of a primary party to a contract if that party does not perform. Any collateral promise of this nature falls under the Statute of Frauds and therefore must be in writing to be enforceable.

Collateral Promise A secondary promise that is ancillary (subsidiary) to a principal transaction or primary contractual relationship, such as a promise made by one person to pay the debts of another if the latter fails to perform. A collateral promise normally must be in writing to be enforceable.

There is an exception. An oral promise to answer for the debt of another is covered by the Statute of Frauds *unless* the guarantor's main purpose in accepting secondary liability is to secure a personal benefit. Under the "main purpose" rule, this type of contract need not be in writing.[26] The assumption is that a court can infer from the circumstances of a case whether the "leading objective" of the promisor was to secure a personal benefit and thus, in effect, to answer for his or her own debt.

PROMISES MADE IN CONSIDERATION OF MARRIAGE.   A unilateral promise to pay a sum of money or to give property in consideration of a promise to marry must be in writing. If Mr. Baumann promises to pay Joe Villard $10,000 if Villard promises to marry Baumann's daughter, the promise must be in writing. The same rule applies to **prenuptial agreements**—agreements made before marriage (also called *antenuptial agreements*) that define each partner's ownership rights in the other partner's property. For example, a prospective wife may wish to limit the amount her prospective husband could obtain if the marriage ended in divorce. Prenuptial agreements made in consideration of marriage must be in writing to be enforceable.

Prenuptial Agreement An agreement made before marriage that defines each partner's ownership rights in the other partner's property. Prenuptial agreements must be in writing to be enforceable.

CONTRACTS FOR THE SALE OF GOODS.   The Uniform Commercial Code (UCC) contains several Statute of Frauds provisions that require written evidence of a contract. Section 2–201 contains the major provision, which generally requires a writing or memorandum for the sale of goods priced at $500 or more. A writing that will satisfy the UCC requirement need only state the quantity term; other terms agreed on need not be stated "accurately" in the writing, as long as they adequately reflect both parties' intentions. The contract will not be enforceable, however, for any quantity greater than that set forth in the writing. In addition, the writing must be signed by the person against whom enforcement is sought. Beyond these two requirements, the writing need not designate the buyer or the seller, the terms of payment, or the price.

EXCEPTIONS TO THE STATUTE OF FRAUDS.   Exceptions to the applicability of the Statute of Frauds are made in certain situations. We describe those situations here.

Partial Performance   In cases involving contracts relating to the transfer of interests in land, if the purchaser has paid part of the price, taken possession, and made permanent improvements to the property, and if the parties cannot be returned to their status quo prior to the contract, a court may grant *specific performance* (performance of the contract according to its precise terms). Whether the courts will enforce an oral contract for an interest in land when partial performance has taken place is usually determined by the degree of

---

26. *Restatement (Second) of Contracts,* Section 116.

International Perspective

Recall from Chapter 1 that the Convention on Contracts for the International Sale of Goods (CISG) provides rules that govern international sales contracts between countries that have ratified the convention, or agreement. Article 11 of the CISG does not incorporate any Statute of Frauds provisions. Rather, it states that a "contract for sale need not be concluded in or evidenced by writing and is not subject to any other requirements as to form."

Article 11 accords with the legal customs of most nations, in which contracts no longer need to meet certain formal or writing requirements to be enforceable. Ironically, even England, the nation that created the original Statute of Frauds in 1677, has repealed all of it except the provisions relating to collateral promises and to transfers of interests in land. Many other countries that once had such statutes have also repealed all or parts of them. Civil law countries, such as France, never have required certain types of contracts to be in writing.

For Critical Analysis: *If there were no Statute of Frauds and if a dispute arose concerning an oral agreement, how would the parties substantiate their respective positions?*

---

injury that would be suffered if the court chose *not* to enforce the oral contract. In some states, mere reliance on certain types of oral contracts is enough to remove them from the Statute of Frauds.

Under the UCC, an oral contract is enforceable to the extent that a seller accepts payment or a buyer accepts delivery of the goods.[27] For example, if Ajax Corporation ordered by telephone twenty crates of bleach from Cloney, Inc., and repudiated the contract after ten crates had been delivered and accepted, Cloney could enforce the contract to the extent of the ten crates accepted by Ajax.

Admissions In some states, if a party against whom enforcement of an oral contract is sought "admits" in pleadings, testimony, or otherwise in court proceedings that a contract for sale was made, the contract will be enforceable.[28] A contract subject to the UCC will be enforceable, but only to the extent of the quantity admitted.[29] Thus, if the president of Ajax Corporation admits under oath that an oral agreement was made with Cloney, Inc., for twenty crates of bleach, the agreement will be enforceable to that extent.

Promissory Estoppel In some states, an oral contract that would otherwise be unenforceable under the Statute of Frauds may be enforced under the doctrine of promissory estoppel, or detrimental reliance. As explained earlier in this chapter, if a promisor makes a promise on which the promisee justifiably relies to his or her detriment, a court may *estop* (prevent) the promisor from denying that a contract exists. Section 139 of the *Restatement (Second) of Contracts* provides that in these circumstances, an oral promise can be enforceable notwithstanding the Statute of Frauds if the reliance was foreseeable to the person making the promise and if injustice can be avoided only by enforcing the promise.

Special Exceptions under the UCC Special exceptions to the applicability of the Statute of Frauds apply to sales contracts. Oral contracts for customized goods may be enforced in certain circumstances. Oral contracts *between merchants* that have been confirmed in writing may also be enforceable.

---

27. UCC 2–201(3)(c).
28. *Restatement (Second) of Contracts*, Section 133.
29. UCC 2–201(3)(b).

Ethical Perspective

Ethical standards certainly underlie the doctrine of promissory estoppel, under which a person who has reasonably relied on the promise of another can often obtain some measure of recovery. Essentially, promissory estoppel allows a variety of promises to be enforced despite the fact that they lack what is formally regarded as consideration.

In the business world, a person who relies to his or her detriment on the promise of another can often recover damages, particularly when justice is better served by estopping the other party from denying that a contractual promise was made. An oral promise made by an insurance agent to a business owner, for example, may be binding if the owner relies on that promise to his or her detriment. Employees who rely to their detriment on an employer's promise may be able to recover under the doctrine of promissory estoppel. A contractor who, when bidding for a job, relies on a subcontractor's promise to perform certain construction work at a certain price may be able to recover any damages sustained by the subcontractor's failure to perform on the basis of promissory estoppel. These are but a few examples of the many ways in which the courts, in the interests of fairness and justice, have estopped a promisor from denying that a contract existed.

For Critical Analysis: *Can you think of any other contract doctrine under which, to ensure justice, courts will allow a party to recover based on detrimental reliance?*

Third Party Rights

Because a contract is a private agreement between the parties who have entered into it, it is fitting that these parties alone should have rights and liabilities under the contract. This concept is referred to as privity of contract, and it establishes the basic principle that third parties have no rights in contracts to which they are not parties.

There are two important exceptions to the rule of privity of contract. One exception allows a party to a contract to transfer the rights arising from the contract to another or to free himself or herself from the duties of a contract by having another person perform them. Legally, the first of these actions is referred to as an *assignment of rights* and the second, as a *delegation of duties.* A second exception to the rule of privity of contract involves a *third party beneficiary* contract. Here, the rights of a third party against the promisor arise from the original contract, as the parties to the original contract normally make it with the intent to benefit the third party.

Assignments

Assignment The act of transferring to another all or part of one's rights arising under a contract.

In a bilateral (mutual) contract, the two parties have corresponding rights and duties. One party has a right to require the other to perform some task, and the other has a duty to perform it. The transfer of *rights* to a third person is known as an **assignment.** When rights under a contract are assigned unconditionally, the rights of the *assignor* (the party making the assignment) are extinguished.[30] The third party (the *assignee,* or party receiving the assignment) has a right to demand performance from the other original party to the contract (the *obligor*). The assignee takes only those rights that the assignor originally had.

As a general rule, all rights can be assigned. Exceptions are made, however, in special circumstances. If a statute expressly prohibits assignment, the

---

30. *Restatement (Second) of Contracts,* Section 317.

particular right in question cannot be assigned. When a contract is *personal* in nature, the rights under the contract cannot be assigned unless all that remains is a money payment.[31] A right cannot be assigned if assignment will materially increase or alter the risk or duties of the obligor.[32] If a contract stipulates that the right cannot be assigned, then *ordinarily* it cannot be assigned.

There are several exceptions to the fourth restriction. These exceptions are as follows:

1. A contract cannot prevent an assignment of the right to receive money. This exception exists to encourage the free flow of money and credit in modern business settings.
2. The assignment of rights in real estate often cannot be prohibited, because such a prohibition is contrary to public policy. Prohibitions of this kind are called restraints against **alienation** (transfer of land ownership).
3. The assignment of *negotiable instruments* (checks and certain other items) cannot be prohibited.
4. In a contract for the sale of goods, the right to receive damages for breach of contract or for payment of an account owed may be assigned even though the sales contract prohibits such assignment.[33]

In the following case, the central issue was whether a covenant not to compete contained in an employment contract could be assigned.

> **Alienation** A term used to define the process of transferring land out of one's possession (thus "alienating" the land from oneself).

---

31. *Restatement (Second) of Contracts*, Sections 317 and 318.
32. See UCC 2–210(2).
33. See UCC 2–210(2).

Case 12.6 ● Reynolds and Reynolds Co. v. Hardee

United States District Court,
Eastern District of Virginia, 1996.
932 F.Supp. 149.

BACKGROUND AND FACTS   Thomas Hardee worked for Jordan Graphics, Inc., as a sales representative under an employment contract that included a covenant not to compete. Reynolds and Reynolds Company contracted to buy most of Jordan's assets. On the day of the sale, Jordan terminated Hardee's employment. Reynolds offered Hardee a new contract that contained a more restrictive covenant not to compete. Hardee rejected the offer and began selling in competition with Reynolds. Reynolds filed a suit in a federal district court against Hardee, seeking, among other things, to enforce the covenant not to compete that was in the contract between Hardee and Jordan. Hardee filed a motion to dismiss the case, asserting that Reynolds was not an assignee of that contract and could not enforce it.

IN THE WORDS OF THE COURT . . .
REBECCA BEACH SMITH, District Judge.
    * * * *

* * * [C]ontracts for personal services are not assignable, unless both parties agree to the assignment. Defendant's [Hardee's] Employment Agreement with Jordan [was] clearly a contract for personal services, based on trust and confidence. Defendant's position involved direct sales to clients; he acted as Jordan's agent in its dealings with customers. A person in such a position must necessarily obtain the trust and confidence of his or her employer. Defendant also placed considerable trust in Jordan by even agreeing to the non-compete clause, namely trusting that Jordan would not fire him and then invoke the covenant not to compete.

(Continued)

Case 12.6—continued

* * * *

* * * Without question, an employment contract of the sort involved in this case is not assignable * * * .

DECISION AND REMEDY   The court found that Reynolds was not an assignee of the contract between Hardee and Jordan and thus could not enforce it. The court dismissed this part of Reynolds's claim.

FOR CRITICAL ANALYSIS—SOCIAL CONSIDERATION   *What interests must a court balance when deciding whether a covenant not to compete is assignable?*

Delegations

Delegation of Duties The act of transferring to another all or part of one's duties arising under a contract.

Just as a party can transfer rights to a third party through an assignment, a party can also transfer duties. Duties are not assigned, however; they are *delegated.* Normally, a **delegation of duties** does not relieve the party making the delegation (the *delegator*) of the obligation to perform in the event that the party to whom the duty has been delegated (the *delegatee*) fails to perform. No special form is required to create a valid delegation of duties. As long as the delegator expresses an intention to make the delegation, it is effective; the delegator need not even use the word *delegate.*

As a general rule, any duty can be delegated. There are, however, some exceptions to this rule. Delegation is prohibited in the following circumstances:

1. When performance depends on the *personal* skill or talents of the obligor.
2. When special trust has been placed in the obligor.
3. When performance by a third party will vary materially from that expected by the obligee (the one to whom performance is owed) under the contract.
4. When the contract expressly prohibits delegation.

COMPARE In an assignment, the assignor's original contract rights are extinguished after assignment. In a delegation, the delegator remains liable for performance under the contract if the delegatee fails to perform.

If a delegation of duties is enforceable, the *obligee* (the one to whom performance is owed) must accept performance from the delegatee (the one to whom the duties are delegated). The obligee can legally refuse performance from the delegatee only if the duty is one that cannot be delegated. A valid delegation of duties does not relieve the delegator of obligations under the contract.[34] Thus, if the delegatee fails to perform, the delegator is still liable to the obligee.

Third Party Beneficiaries

Third Party Beneficiary One for whose benefit a promise is made in a contract but who is not a party to the contract.

Intended Beneficiary A third party for whose benefit a contract is formed; an intended beneficiary can sue the promisor if such a contract is breached.

Incidental Beneficiary A third party who incidentally benefits from a contract but whose benefit was not the reason the contract was formed; an incidental beneficiary has no rights in a contract and cannot sue to have the contract enforced.

To have contractual rights, a person normally must be a party to the contract. In other words, privity of contract must exist. As mentioned earlier in this chapter, an exception to the doctrine of privity exists when the original parties to the contract intend at the time of contracting that the contract performance directly benefit a third person. In this situation, the third person becomes a **third party beneficiary** of the contract. As an **intended beneficiary** of the contract, the third party has legal rights and can sue the promisor directly for breach of the contract.

The benefit that an **incidental beneficiary** receives from a contract between two parties is unintentional. Therefore, an incidental beneficiary cannot

---

34. *Crane Ice Cream Co. v. Terminal Freezing & Heating Co.,* 147 Md. 588, 128 A. 280 (1925).

enforce a contract to which he or she is not a party. For example, Ed contracts with Ona to build a recreational facility on Ona's land. Once the facility is constructed, it will greatly enhance the property values in the neighborhood. If Ed subsequently refuses to build the facility, Tandy, Ona's neighbor, cannot enforce the contract against Ed.

Contract Discharge

The most common way to **discharge,** or terminate, one's contractual duties is by the **performance** of those duties. The duty to perform under a contract may be *conditioned* on the occurrence or nonoccurrence of a certain event, or the duty may be *absolute*. In addition to performance, there are numerous other ways in which a contract can be discharged, including discharge by agreement of the parties and discharge based on impossibility of performance.

Discharge by Performance

The contract comes to an end when both parties fulfill their respective duties by performance of the acts they have promised. Performance can also be accomplished by tender. **Tender** is an unconditional offer to perform by a person who is ready, willing, and able to do so. Therefore, a seller who places goods at the disposal of a buyer has tendered delivery and can demand payment according to the terms of the agreement. A buyer who offers to pay for goods has tendered payment and can demand delivery of the goods. Once performance has been tendered, the party making the tender has done everything possible to carry out the terms of the contract. If the other party then refuses to perform, the party making the tender can consider the duty discharged and sue for **breach of contract.**

COMPLETE VERSUS SUBSTANTIAL PERFORMANCE. Normally, conditions expressly stated in the contract must fully occur in all aspects for *complete performance* (strict performance) of the contract to occur. Any deviation breaches the contract and discharges the other party's obligations to perform. Although in most contracts the parties fully discharge their obligations by complete performance, sometimes a party fails to fulfill all of the duties or completes the duties in a manner contrary to the terms of the contract. The issue then arises as to whether the performance was nonetheless sufficiently substantial to discharge the contractual obligations.

To qualify as *substantial performance*, the performance must not vary greatly from the performance promised in the contract, and it must create substantially the same benefits as those promised in the contract. If performance is substantial, the other party's duty to perform remains absolute (less damages, if any, for the minor deviations).[35]

PERFORMANCE TO THE SATISFACTION OF ANOTHER. When the subject matter of the contract is personal, a contract to be performed to the satisfaction of one of the parties is conditioned, and performance must actually satisfy that party. For example, contracts for portraits, works of art, and tailoring are

Discharge The termination of an obligation. In contract law, discharge occurs when the parties have fully performed their contractual obligations or when events, conduct of the parties, or operation of the law releases the parties from performance.

Performance In contract law, the fulfillment of one's duties arising under a contract with another; the normal way of discharging one's contractual obligations.

Tender An unconditional offer to perform an obligation by a person who is ready, willing, and able to do so.

Breach of Contract The failure, without legal excuse, of a promisor to perform the obligations of a contract.

> **"The law is not exact upon the subject, but leaves it open to a good man's judgment."**
>
> Hugo Grotius, 1583–1645 (Dutch jurist, political leader, and theologian)

---

35. For a classic case on substantial performance, see *Jacobs & Young, Inc. v. Kent*, 230 N.Y. 239, 129 N.E. 889 (1921).

considered personal. Therefore, only the personal satisfaction of the party fulfills the condition—unless a jury finds the party is expressing dissatisfaction only to avoid payment or otherwise is not acting in good faith.

MATERIAL BREACH OF CONTRACT.   When a breach of contract is *material*[36]—that is, when performance is not deemed substantial—the nonbreaching party is excused from the performance of contractual duties and has a cause of action to sue for damages caused by the breach. If the breach is *minor* (not material), the nonbreaching party's duty to perform can sometimes be suspended until the breach is remedied, but the duty is not entirely excused. Once the minor breach is cured, the nonbreaching party must resume performance of the contractual obligations undertaken.

A breach entitles the nonbreaching party to sue for damages, but only a material breach discharges the nonbreaching party from the contract. The policy underlying these rules is that contracts should go forward when only minor problems occur, but contracts should be terminated if major problems arise.[37]

ANTICIPATORY REPUDIATION OF A CONTRACT.   Before either party to a contract has a duty to perform, one of the parties may refuse to perform his or her contractual obligations. This is called **anticipatory repudiation.**[38] When anticipatory repudiation occurs, it is treated as a material breach of contract, and the nonbreaching party is permitted to bring an action for damages immediately, even though the scheduled time for performance under the contract may still be in the future.[39] Until the nonbreaching party treats this early repudiation as a breach, however, the breaching party can retract his or her anticipatory repudiation by proper notice and restore the parties to their original obligations.[40]

There are two reasons for treating an anticipatory repudiation as a present, material breach. First, the nonbreaching party should not be required to remain ready and willing to perform when the other party has already repudiated the contract. Second, the nonbreaching party should have the opportunity to seek a similar contract elsewhere and should have the duty to do so to minimize his or her loss.

Quite often, an anticipatory repudiation occurs when a sharp fluctuation in market prices creates a situation in which performance of the contract would be extremely unfavorable to one of the parties. For example, Shasta Manufacturing Company contracts to manufacture and sell 100,000 personal computers to New Age, Inc., a computer retailer with 500 outlet stores. Delivery is to be made eight months from the date of the contract. One month later, three suppliers of computer parts raise their prices to Shasta. Because of these higher prices, Shasta stands to lose $500,000 if it sells the computers to New Age at the contract price. Shasta writes to New Age, informing New Age that it cannot deliver the 100,000 computers at the agreed-on contract price.

> "Men do less than they ought, unless they do all that they can."
>
> Thomas Carlyle, 1795–1881 (Scottish historian and essayist)

Anticipatory Repudiation An assertion or action by a party indicating that he or she will not perform an obligation that the party is contractually obligated to perform at a future time.

REMEMBER The risks that prices will fluctuate and values will change are ordinary business risks for which the law does not provide relief.

---

36. *Restatement (Second) of Contracts*, Section 241.
37. See UCC 2–612, which provides that an installment contract for the sale of goods is breached only when one or more nonconforming installments *substantially impairs* the value of the *whole* contract.
38. *Restatement (Second) of Contracts*, Section 253, and UCC 2–610.
39. The doctrine of anticipatory repudiation first arose in the landmark case of *Hochster v. De La Tour*, 2 Ellis and Blackburn Reports 678 (1853), when the English court recognized the delay and expense inherent in a rule requiring a nonbreaching party to wait until the time of performance before suing on an anticipatory repudiation.
40. See UCC 2–611.

Even though you might sympathize with Shasta, its letter is an anticipatory repudiation of the contract, allowing New Age the option of treating the repudiation as a material breach and proceeding immediately to pursue remedies, even though the actual contract delivery date is still seven months away.[41]

Discharge by Agreement

Any contract can be discharged by the agreement of the parties. The agreement can be contained in the original contract, or the parties can form a new contract for the express purpose of discharging the original contract.

DISCHARGE BY RESCISSION. Rescission is the process in which the parties cancel the contract and are returned to the positions they occupied prior to the contract's formation. For *mutual rescission* to take place, the parties must make another agreement that also satisfies the legal requirements for a contract—there must be an *offer*, an *acceptance*, and *consideration*. Ordinarily, if the parties agree to rescind the original contract, their promises *not* to perform those acts promised in the original contract will be legal consideration for the second contract.

Mutual rescission can occur in this manner when the original contract is executory on both sides (that is, neither party has completed performance). The agreement to rescind an executory contract is generally enforceable, even if it is made orally and even if the original agreement was in writing.[42] When one party has fully performed, however, an agreement to rescind the original contract is not usually enforceable. Because the performing party has received no consideration for the promise to call off the original bargain, additional consideration is necessary.[43]

DISCHARGE BY NOVATION. The process of **novation** substitutes a third party for one of the original parties. Essentially, the parties to the original contract and one or more new parties all get together and agree to the substitution. The requirements of a novation are as follows:

1. The existence of a previous, valid obligation.
2. Agreement by all of the parties to a new contract.
3. The extinguishing of the old obligation (discharge of the prior party).
4. A new, valid contract.

Discharge by Accord and Satisfaction In an *accord and satisfaction*, the parties agree to accept performance different from the performance originally promised. An *accord* is defined as an executory contract (one that has not yet been performed) to perform some act in order to satisfy an existing contractual duty that is not yet discharged.[44] A *satisfaction* is the performance of the accord agreement. An *accord* and its *satisfaction* discharge the original contractual obligation.

"Agreement makes law."

(Legal maxim)

Rescission A remedy whereby a contract is canceled and the parties are returned to the positions they occupied before the contract was made; may be effected through the mutual consent of the parties, by their conduct, or by court decree.

Novation The substitution, by agreement, of a new contract for an old one, with the rights under the old one being terminated. Typically, there is a substitution of a new person who is responsible for the contract and the removal of the original party's rights and duties under the contract.

---

41. Another illustration can be found in *Reliance Cooperage Corp. v. Treat*, 195 F.2d 977 (8th Cir. 1952).
42. Agreements to rescind contracts involving transfers of realty, however, must be evidenced by a writing. Another exception has to do with the sale of goods under the UCC, when the sales contract requires written rescission.
43. Under UCC 2–209(1), however, no consideration is needed to modify a contract for a sale of goods. See UCC 1–107.
44. *Restatement (Second) of Contracts*, Section 281.

When Performance Is Impossible

Impossibility of Performance
A doctrine under which a party to a contract is relieved of his or her duty to perform when performance becomes impossible or totally impracticable (through no fault of either party).

After a contract has been made, performance may become impossible in an objective sense. This is known as **impossibility of performance** and may discharge a contract.[45] *Objective impossibility* ("It can't be done") must be distinguished from *subjective impossibility* ("I'm sorry, I simply can't do it"). Examples of subjective impossibility include contracts in which goods cannot be delivered on time because of a freight car shortage[46] and contracts in which money cannot be paid on time because the bank is closed.[47] In effect, the nonperforming party is saying, "It is impossible for *me* to perform," not "It is impossible for *anyone* to perform." Accordingly, such excuses do not discharge a contract, and the nonperforming party is normally held in breach of contract.

COMMERCIAL IMPRACTICABILITY. The discharge of contractual obligations based on impossibility of performance may occur when performance becomes *commercially impracticable*—that is, much more difficult or expensive than anticipated. In such situations, courts may excuse parties from their performance obligations under the doctrine of *commercial impracticability*. For example, in one case, a court held that a contract could be discharged because a party would have to pay ten times more than the original estimate to excavate a certain amount of gravel.[48]

TEMPORARY IMPOSSIBILITY. An occurrence or event that makes performance temporarily impossible operates to *suspend* performance until the impossibility ceases. Then, ordinarily, the parties must perform the contract as originally planned. If, however, the lapse of time and the change in circumstances surrounding the contract make it substantially more burdensome for the parties to perform the promised acts, the contract is discharged.

The leading case on the subject, *Autry v. Republic Productions*,[49] involved an actor who was drafted into the army in 1942. Being drafted rendered the actor's contract temporarily impossible to perform, and it was suspended until the end of the war. When the actor got out of the army, the value of the dollar had so changed that performance of the contract would have been substantially burdensome to him. Therefore, the contract was discharged.

> **"Law is a practical matter."**
>
> Roscoe Pound, 1870–1964
> (American jurist)

---

45. *Restatement (Second) of Contracts*, Section 261.
46. *Minneapolis v. Republic Creosoting Co.*, 161 Minn. 178, 201 N.W. 414 (1924).
47. *Ingham Lumber Co. v. Ingersoll & Co.*, 93 Ark. 447, 125 S.W. 139 (1910).
48. *Mineral Park Land Co. v. Howard*, 172 Cal. 289, 156 P. 458 (1916).
49. 30 Cal.2d 144, 180 P.2d 888 (1947).

Key Terms

acceptance 312
adhesion contract 324
agreement 307
alienation 333
anticipatory repudiation 336
assignment 332
bilateral contract 304

blue law 322
breach of contract 335
collateral promise 330
consideration 313
contract 304
contractual capacity 316
counteroffer 311

delegation of duties 334
disaffirmance 317
discharge 335
exculpatory clause 324
executed contract 306
executory contract 306
express contract 305

Chapter Summary
Introduction to Contracts

THE FUNCTION OF CONTRACTS (See page 304.)	Contract law establishes what kinds of promises will be legally binding and supplies procedures for enforcing legally binding promises, or agreements.
TYPES OF CONTRACTS (See pages 304–307.)	1. **Bilateral**—A promise for a promise. 2. **Unilateral**—A promise for an act (acceptance is the completed—or substantial—performance of the act). 3. **Express**—Formed by words (oral, written, or a combination). 4. **Implied in fact**—Formed by the conduct of the parties. 5. **Quasi contract (contract implied in law)**—Imposed by law to prevent unjust enrichment. 6. **Executed**—A fully performed contract. 7. **Executory**—A contract not yet fully performed. 8. **Valid**—The contract has the necessary contractual elements of offer and acceptance, consideration, parties with legal capacity, and having been made for a legal purpose. 9. **Void**—No contract exists, or there is a contract without legal obligations. 10. **Voidable**—One party has the option of avoiding or enforcing the contractual obligation. 11. **Unenforceable**—A contract exists, but it cannot be enforced because of a legal defense.
	AGREEMENT
REQUIREMENTS OF THE OFFER (See pages 307–310.)	1. **Intent**—There must be a serious, objective intention by the offeror to become bound by the offer. Nonoffer situations include (a) expressions of opinion; (b) statements of intention; (c) preliminary negotiations; and (d) generally, advertisements, catalogues, and circulars. 2. **Definiteness**—The terms of the offer must be sufficiently definite to be ascertainable by the parties or by a court. 3. **Communication**—The offer must be communicated to the offeree.

(Continued)

Chapter Summary, continued

TERMINATION OF THE OFFER (See pages 311–312.)	1. **By action of the parties**—An offer can be revoked or rejected at any time before acceptance without liability. A counteroffer is a rejection of the original offer and the making of a new offer. 2. **By operation of law**—An offer can terminate by (a) lapse of time, (b) destruction of the specific subject matter of the offer, (c) death or incompetence of the parties, or (d) supervening illegality.
ACCEPTANCE (See pages 312–313.)	1. Can be made only by the offeree or the offeree's agent. 2. Must be unequivocal. Under the common law (mirror image rule), if new terms or conditions are added to the acceptance, it will be considered a counteroffer.

CONSIDERATION

ELEMENTS OF CONSIDERATION (See pages 313–315.)	Consideration is broken down into two parts: (1) something of *legally sufficient value* must be given in exchange for the promise, and (2) there must be a *bargained-for exchange*. To be legally sufficient, consideration must involve a legal detriment to the promisee, a legal benefit to the promisor, or both. One incurs a legal detriment by doing (or refraining from doing) something that one had no prior legal duty to do (or to refrain from doing).
ADEQUACY OF CONSIDERATION (See page 315.)	Adequacy of consideration relates to "how much" consideration is given and whether a fair bargain was reached. Courts will inquire into the adequacy of consideration (if the consideration is legally sufficient) only when fraud, undue influence, duress, a gift, or unconscionability may be involved.
PROMISSORY ESTOPPEL (See page 316.)	When a promisor reasonably expects a promise to induce definite and substantial action or forbearance by the promisee, and the promisee does act in reliance on the promise, the promise is binding if injustice can be avoided only by enforcement of the promise.

CAPACITY

MINORS (See pages 317–319.)	Contracts with minors are voidable at the option of the minor. When disaffirming executed contracts, the minor has a duty to return received goods if they are still in the minor's control or (in some states) to pay their reasonable value.
INTOXICATED PERSONS (See pages 319–320.)	1. A contract entered into by an intoxicated person is voidable at the option of the intoxicated person if the person was sufficiently intoxicated to lack mental capacity, even if the intoxication was voluntary. 2. A contract with an intoxicated person is enforceable if, despite being intoxicated, the person understood the legal consequences of entering into the contract.
MENTALLY INCOMPETENT PERSONS (See page 320.)	1. A contract made by a person adjudged by a court to be mentally incompetent is void. 2. A contract made by a mentally incompetent person not adjudged by a court to be mentally incompetent is voidable at the option of the mentally incompetent person.

LEGALITY

CONTRACTS CONTRARY TO STATUTE (See pages 320–323.)	1. **Usury**—Occurs when a lender makes a loan at an interest rate above the lawful maximum. The maximum rate of interest varies from state to state. 2. **Gambling**—Gambling contracts that contravene (go against) state statutes are deemed illegal and thus void.

(Continued)

Chapter Summary, continued

CONTRACTS CONTRARY TO STATUTE—continued (See pages 320–323.)	3. **Sabbath (Sunday) laws**—Laws prohibiting the formation or the performance of certain contracts on Sunday. Such laws vary widely from state to state, and many states do not enforce them.
	4. **Licensing statutes**—Contracts entered into by persons who do not have a license, when one is required by statute, will not be enforceable *unless* the underlying purpose of the statute is to raise government revenues (and not to protect the public from unauthorized practitioners).
CONTRACTS CONTRARY TO PUBLIC POLICY (See pages 323–325.)	1. **Contracts in restraint of trade**—Contracts to reduce or restrain free competition are illegal. An exception is a *covenant not to compete.* It is usually enforced by the courts if the terms are ancillary to a contract (such as a contract for the sale of a business or an employment contract) and are reasonable as to time and area of restraint.
	2. **Unconscionable contracts and clauses**—When a contract or contract clause is so unfair that it is oppressive to one party, it can be deemed unconscionable; as such, it is illegal and cannot be enforced.
	3. **Exculpatory clauses**—An exculpatory clause is a clause that releases a party from liability in the event of monetary or physical injury, no matter who is at fault. In certain situations, exculpatory clauses may be contrary to public policy and thus unenforceable.

DEFENSES TO CONTRACT FORMATION OR ENFORCEABILITY

GENUINENESS OF ASSENT (See pages 325–329.)	1. **Mistakes**—
	a. **Unilateral**—Generally, the mistaken party is bound by the contract.
	b. **Bilateral**—When both parties are mistaken about the same material fact, such as identity, either party can avoid the contract. If the mistake concerns value or quality, either party can enforce the contract.
	2. **Fraudulent misrepresentation**—When fraud occurs, usually the innocent party can enforce or avoid the contract. For damages, the innocent party must suffer an injury.
	3. **Undue influence**—Undue influence arises from special relationships, such as fiduciary or confidential relationships, in which one party's free will has been overcome by the undue influence exerted by the other party. Usually, the contract is voidable.
	4. **Duress**—Duress is defined as forcing a party to enter a contract under the fear of a threat—for example, the threat of violence or serious economic loss. The party forced to enter the contract can rescind the contract.
FORM (See pages 329–332.)	1. **Applicability**—The following types of contracts fall under the Statute of Frauds and must be in writing to be enforceable: (1) contracts involving interests in land, (2) contracts whose terms cannot be performed within one year, (3) collateral promises, (4) promises made in consideration of marriage, and (5) contracts for the sale of goods priced at $500 or more.
	2. **Exceptions**—Partial performance, admissions, and promissory estoppel.

THIRD PARTY RIGHTS

ASSIGNMENT (See pages 332–334.)	1. An assignment is the transfer of rights under a contract to a third party. The party assigning the rights is the *assignor,* and the party to whom the rights are

(Continued)

Chapter Summary, continued

ASSIGNMENT—continued (See pages 332–334.)	assigned is the *assignee*. The assignee has a right to demand performance from the other original party to the contract. 2. Generally, all rights can be assigned, except in the following circumstances: a. When assignment is expressly prohibited by statute (for example, workers' compensation benefits).
DELEGATION (See page 334.)	A delegation is the transfer of duties under a contract to a third party (the delegatee), who then assumes the obligation of performing the contractual duties previously held by the one making the delegation (the delegator). A valid delegation of duties does not relieve the delegator of obligations under the contract. If the delegatee fails to perform, the delegator is still liable to the obligee.
THIRD PARTY BENEFICIARY CONTRACT (See pages 334–335.)	A third party beneficiary contract is one made for the purpose of benefiting a third party. 1. **Intended beneficiary**—One for whose benefit a contract is created. When the promisor (the one making the contractual promise that benefits a third party) fails to perform as promised, the third party can sue the promisor directly. Examples of third party beneficiaries are creditor beneficiaries and donee beneficiaries. 2. **Incidental beneficiary**—A third party who indirectly (incidentally) benefits from a contract but for whose benefit the contract was not specifically intended. Incidental beneficiaries have no rights to the benefits received and cannot sue to have the contract enforced.

WAYS TO DISCHARGE A CONTRACT

PERFORMANCE (See pages 335–337.)	A contract may be discharged by complete (strict) or by substantial performance. In some cases, performance must be to the satisfaction of another. Totally inadequate performance constitutes a material breach of contract. An anticipatory repudiation of a contract allows the other party to sue immediately for breach of contract.
AGREEMENT (See page 337.)	Parties may agree to discharge their contractual obligations in several ways: 1. **By rescission**—The parties mutually agree to rescind (cancel) the contract. 2. **By novation**—A new party is substituted for one of the primary parties to a contract. 3. **By accord and satisfaction**—The parties agree to render performance different from that originally agreed on.
OBJECTIVE IMPOSSIBILITY OF PERFORMANCE (See page 338.)	Parties' obligations under contracts may be discharged by objective impossibility of performance or commercial impracticability of performance.

For Review

1. What are the four basic elements necessary to the formation of a valid contract?
2. What elements are necessary for an effective offer? What are some examples of nonoffers?
3. What is consideration? What is required for consideration to be legally sufficient?

4. Generally, a minor can disaffirm any contract. What are some exceptions to this rule?
5. What contracts must be in writing to be enforceable?
6. How are most contracts discharged?

Questions and Case Problems

12–1. Contractual Promises. Rosalie, a wealthy widow, invited an acquaintance, Jonathan, to her home for dinner. Jonathan accepted the offer and, eager to please her, spent lavishly in preparing for the evening. His purchases included a new blazer, new shoes, an expensive floral arrangement, and champagne. On the appointed evening, Jonathan arrived at Rosalie's house only to find that she had left for the evening. Jonathan wants to sue Rosalie to recover some of his expenses. Can he? Why or why not?

12–2. Consideration. Ben hired Lewis to drive his racing car in a race. Tuan, a friend of Lewis, promised to pay Lewis $3,000 if he won the race. Lewis won the race, but Tuan refused to pay the $3,000. Tuan contended that no legally binding contract had been formed, because he had received no consideration from Lewis for his promise to pay the $3,000. Lewis sued Tuan for breach of contract, arguing that winning the race was the consideration given in exchange for Tuan's promise to pay the $3,000. What rule of law discussed in this chapter supports Tuan's claim? Explain.

12–3. Acceptance. On Saturday, Arthur mailed Tanya an offer to sell his car to her for $2,000. On Monday, having changed his mind and not having heard from Tanya, Arthur sent her a letter revoking his offer. On Wednesday, before she had received Arthur's letter of revocation, Tanya mailed a letter of acceptance to Arthur. When Tanya demanded that Arthur sell his car to her as promised, Arthur claimed that no contract existed because he had revoked his offer prior to Tanya's acceptance. Is Arthur correct? Explain.

12–4. Contracts by Minors. Kalen is a seventeen-year-old minor who has just graduated from high school. He is attending a university two hundred miles from home and has contracted to rent an apartment near the university for one year at $500 per month. He is working at a convenience store to earn enough money to be self-supporting. After living in the apartment and paying monthly rent for four months, a dispute arises between him and the landlord. Kalen, still a minor, moves out and returns the key to the landlord. The landlord wants to hold Kalen liable for the balance of the payments due under the lease. Discuss fully Kalen's liability in this situation.

12–5. Impossibility of Performance. Millie contracted to sell Frank 1,000 bushels of corn to be grown on Millie's farm. Owing to drought conditions during the growing season, Millie's yield was much less than anticipated, and she could deliver only 250 bushels to Frank. Frank accepted the lesser amount but sued Millie for breach of contract. Can Millie defend successfully on the basis of objective impossibility of performance? Explain.

12–6. Offers versus Nonoffers. The Olivers were planning to sell some of their ranch land and mentioned this fact to Southworth, a neighbor. Southworth expressed interest in purchasing the property and later notified the Olivers that he had the money available to buy it. The Olivers told Southworth they would let him know shortly about the details concerning the sale. The Olivers later sent a letter to Southworth—and (unknown to Southworth) to several other neighbors—giving information about the sale, including the price, the location of the property, and the amount of acreage involved. When Southworth received the letter, he sent a letter to the Olivers "accepting" their offer. The Olivers stated that the information letter had not been intended as an "offer" but merely as a starting point for negotiations. Southworth brought suit against the Olivers to enforce the "contract." Did a contract exist? Why or why not? Explain fully. [*Southworth v. Oliver*, 284 Or. 361, 587 P.2d 994 (1978)]

12–7. Gambling Contracts. No law prohibits citizens in a state that does not sponsor a state-operated lottery from purchasing lottery tickets in a state that does have such a lottery. Because Georgia did not have a state-operated lottery, Talley and several other Georgia residents allegedly agreed to purchase a ticket in a lottery sponsored by Kentucky and to share the proceeds if they won. They did win, but apparently Talley had difficulty collecting his share of the proceeds. In Talley's suit to obtain his share of the funds, a Georgia trial court held that the "gambling contract" was unenforceable because it was contrary to Georgia's public policy. On appeal, how should the court rule on this issue? Discuss. [*Talley v. Mathis*, 265 Ga. 179, 453 S.E.2d 704 (1995)]

12–8. Genuineness of Assent. Linda Lorenzo purchased Lurlene Noel's home in 1988 without having it inspected. The basement started leaking in 1989. In 1991, Lorenzo had the paneling removed from the basement walls and discovered that the walls were bowed inward and cracked. Lorenzo then had a civil engineer inspect the basement walls, and he found that the cracks had been caulked and painted over before the paneling was installed. He concluded that the "wall failure" had existed "for at least thirty years" and that the basement walls were "structurally unsound." Does Lorenzo have a cause of action against Noel? If so, on what ground? Discuss. [*Lorenzo v. Noel*, 206 Mich.App. 682, 522 N.W.2d 724 (1994)]

12–9. One-Year Rule. Adam Curry worked as a videodisc jockey for MTV Networks (MTVN). In discussions during 1993, Curry and MTVN executives orally agreed that Curry could develop, at his own expense, an Internet site address ("mtv.com") and that MTVN would not interfere with Curry's development of the site. By early 1994, Curry's mtv.com address had been accessed by millions of Internet users, in part because of a computer bulletin board (developed by Curry) that facilitated communication between performers and other music professionals. In the meantime, MTVN decided to offer on-line services through America On-Line. These services were to include a bulletin board similar to that developed by Curry. In mid-January 1994, MTVN requested that Curry cease using the mtv.com address. A dispute ensued, and eventually MTVN sued Curry on several grounds. Curry counterclaimed that MTVN had breached its oral contract with him. MTVN argued that because the contract could not be performed within one year, the Statute of Frauds barred its enforcement. How should the court decide this issue? Explain. [*MTV Networks, A Division of Viacom International, Inc. v. Curry*, 867 F.Supp. 202 (S.D.N.Y. 1994)]

12–10. Third Party Beneficiaries. When Charles and Judy Orr were divorced in 1970, their divorce agreement included a provision that Charles would pay for the college or professional school education of the couple's two children, then minors. In 1990, when Charles's daughter Jennifer was attending college, Charles refused to pay her college tuition. Can Jennifer, who was not a party to her parents' divorce agreement, bring a court action to compel her father to pay her college expenses? Discuss fully.

[*Orr v. Orr*, 228 Ill.App.3d 234, 592 N.E.2d 553, 170 Ill.Dec. 117 (1992)]

A Question of Ethics and Social Responsibility

12–11. Mark Van Wagoner, an attorney experienced in real estate transactions, and his wife, Kathryn, were interested in buying certain property being sold by Carol Klas for her former husband, John Klas. When the Van Wagoners asked Carol Klas if there had been any appraisals of the property, she replied that there had been several appraisals, ranging from $175,000 to $192,000. (At trial, Carol claimed that she understood the term appraisal to mean any opinion as to the market value of the house.) The Van Wagoners did not request a written *appraisal* of the property until after signing an agreement to purchase the property for $175,000. Carol Klas then provided them with a written appraisal that listed the house's value as $165,000. When the Van Wagoners refused to go through with the deal, John Klas brought suit to recover the difference between the agreement price and the price for which the house was later sold. In view of these facts, answer the following questions. [*Klas v. Van Wagoner*, 829 P.2d 135 (Utah App.1992)]

1. The Van Wagoners claimed that the contract should be rescinded on the basis of their mistaken assumption as to the value of the house. What kind of mistake was made in this situation (mutual or unilateral, mistake of value or mistake of fact)? How should the court rule on this issue?

2. Mark Van Wagoner was an attorney experienced in real estate transactions. Should the court take this fact into consideration when making its decision?

3. Generally, what ethical principles, as expressed in public policies, are in conflict here and in similar situations in which parties enter into a contract with mistaken assumptions?

For Critical Analysis

12–12. Review the list of basic requirements for contract formation given at the beginning of this chapter. In view of those requirements, analyze the relationship entered into when a student enrolls in a college or university. Has a contract been formed? If so, is it a bilateral contract or a unilateral contract? Discuss.

INTERACTING WITH
The Internet

■ Within the legal interest group on the commercial service America Online, there is a subcategory on torts and contracts. If you subscribe to America Online the key word is:

legal

■ The 'Lectric Law Library provides information on contract law, including a definition of a contract, the elements required for a contract, and so on. Go to

http://www.lectlaw.com

Then go to the Laypeople's Law Lounge, and scroll down to Contracts.

■ Findlaw's directory of law-related Web sites offers numerous links to aspects of contract law. Findlaw's URL is

http://findlaw.com/

Look in their index of legal subjects for Contracts, and you will find information ranging from a "Layman's Guide to Drafting and Signing Contracts" to contract law in cyberspace to sample contract forms.

■ The Law Office's URL is

http://www.thelawoffice.com/

Select the topic of Business Law from the USA Legal Topics list in the left-hand column. Go to Guide to Business Law and then to Contracts.

■ Law Guru, which allows you to access more than 160 legal search engines and indexes from a single location, can lead you to other sources on contract law. Go to

http://lawguru.com/lawlinks.html

■ Cornell University's School of Law provides links to online sources of law, including contract law, at

http://www.law.cornell.edu/topics/contracts.html

■ The Library of Congress offers online links to an extensive menu of topics concerning contract law at

http://www.1oc.gov/

■ You can find a research project report on the nature and enforceability of electronic contracts at

http://www.uchastings.edu/plri/fall94/whipple.html

The report discusses critical issues with respect to satisfying the writing requirements of the Statute of Frauds.

Contract Remedies and Sales

Contents

Chapter Objectives

After reading this chapter, you should be able to . . .

1. Define the different types of damages that may be obtainable on the breach of a contract.
2. Describe the usual measure of damages for breach of various types of contracts.
3. Distinguish between liquidated damages and penalties.
4. List the equitable remedies that may be granted by courts, and indicate when they will be granted.
5. Identify which contracts are subject to the Uniform Commerical Code.

As the Athenian political leader Solon instructed centuries ago, a contract will not be broken so long as "it is to the advantage of both" parties not to break it. Normally, the reason a person enters into a contract with another is to secure an advantage. When it is no longer advantageous for a party to fulfill his or her contractual obligations, breach of contract may result. As discussed in Chapter 12, a *breach of contract* occurs when a party fails to perform part or all of the required duties under a contract.[1] Once a party fails to perform or performs inadequately, the other party—the nonbreaching party—can choose one or more of several remedies.

The most common remedies available to a nonbreaching party include damages, rescission and restitution, specific performance, and reformation. As discussed in Chapter 1, courts distinguish between *remedies at law* and *remedies in equity*. Today, the remedy at law is normally money damages. We discuss this remedy in the first part of this chapter. Equitable remedies include rescission and restitution, specific performance, and reformation, all of which we examine later in the chapter. Usually a court will not award an equitable remedy unless the remedy at law is inadequate. In this chapter, we look at some special legal doctrines and concepts relating to remedies. Finally, we conclude the chapter with a look at sales of goods subject to the Uniform Commercial Code.

> "Men keep their engagements when it is to the advantage of both not to break them."
>
> Solon, sixth century B.C.E.
> (Athenian legal reformer)

Damages

A breach of contract entitles the nonbreaching party to sue for money damages. As you read in Chapter 8, damages are designed to compensate a party for harm suffered as a result of another's wrongful act. In the context of contract law, damages are designed to compensate the nonbreaching party for the loss of the bargain. Often, courts say that innocent parties are to be placed in the position they would have occupied had the contract been fully performed.[2]

> REMEMBER The terms of a contract must be sufficiently definite for a court to determine the amount of damages to award.

Types of Damages

There are basically four kinds of damages: compensatory, consequential, punitive, and nominal damages.

COMPENSATORY DAMAGES. As discussed in Chapter 8, *compensatory damages* compensate an injured party for injuries or damages actually sustained by that party. The nonbreaching party must prove that the actual damages arose directly from the loss of the bargain caused by the breach of contract. The amount of compensatory damages is the difference between the value of the breaching party's promised performance under the contract and the value of his or her actual performance. This amount is reduced by any loss that the injured party has avoided, however.

Suppose that you contract with Marinot Industries to perform certain personal services exclusively for Marinot during August for a payment of $3,500. Marinot cancels the contract and is in breach. You are able to find another job during August but can only earn $1,000. You normally can sue Marinot for

---

1. *Restatement (Second) of Contracts,* Section 235(2).
2. *Restatement (Second) of Contracts,* Section 347, and UCC 1–106(1).

breach and recover $2,500 as compensatory damages. You may also recover from Marinot the amount you spent to find the other job. Expenses or costs that are caused directly by a breach of contract—such as those incurred to obtain performance from another source—are *incidental damages*.

The measurement of compensatory damages varies by type of contract. Certain types of contracts deserve special mention—contracts for the sale of goods, contracts for the sale of land, and construction contracts.

Sale of Goods   In a contract for the sale of goods, the usual measure of compensatory damages is an amount equal to the difference between the contract price and the market price.[3] Suppose that MediQuick Laboratories contracts with Cal Computer Industries to purchase ten Model X-15 computer workstations for $8,000 each. If Cal Computer fails to deliver the ten workstations, and the current market price of the workstations is $8,150, MediQuick's measure of damages is $1,500 (10 × $150). In cases in which the buyer breaches and the seller has not yet produced the goods, compensatory damages normally equal the lost profits on the sale, not the difference between the contract price and the market price.

Sale of Land   The measure of damages in a contract for the sale of land is ordinarily the same as it is for contracts involving the sale of goods—that is, the difference between the contract price and the market price of the land. The majority of states follow this rule regardless of whether it is the buyer or the seller who breaches the contract.

A minority of states, however, follow a different rule when the seller breaches the contract and the breach is not deliberate. An example of a non-

---

3.   That is, the difference between the contract price and the market price at the time and place at which the goods were to be delivered or tendered. See UCC 2–708 and 2–713.

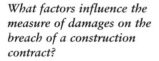

What factors influence the measure of damages on the breach of a construction contract?

■ Exhibit 13–1
Measurement of
Damages—Breach of
Construction
Contracts

PARTY IN BREACH	TIME OF BREACH	MEASUREMENT OF DAMAGES
Owner	Before construction begins	Profits (contract price less cost of materials and labor)
Owner	After construction begins	Profits plus costs incurred up to time of breach
Owner	After construction is completed	Contract price
Contractor	Before construction is completed	Generally, all costs incurred by owner to complete construction

deliberate breach of a contract to sell land occurs when a previously unknown easement (a right of use over the property of another) is discovered and renders title to the land unmarketable. (In real property law, *title* means the right to own property or the evidence of that right.) In such a situation, these states allow the prospective purchaser to recover any down payment plus any expenses incurred (such as fees for title searches or attorneys). This minority rule effectively places a purchaser in the position that he or she occupied prior to the contract of sale.

Construction Contracts   With construction contracts, the measure of damages often varies depending on which party breaches and at what stage the breach occurs. See Exhibit 13–1 for illustrations. In the following case, the issue centers on the proper measure of damages in a breached construction contract.

Case 13.1 ● Shadow Lakes, Inc. v. Cudlipp Construction and Development Co.

District Court of Appeal of Florida,
Second District, 1995.
658 So.2d 116.

HISTORICAL AND ECONOMIC SETTING   *In the last half of the twentieth century, the housing industry has experienced extraordinary growth. Since 1960, nearly sixty million units (including single-family houses, apartments, and mobile homes) have been built—twenty million more than in the previous forty years. Since 1920, however, the population has increased by only about 150 million. In other words, between 1920 and 1995, a new unit was built for every one and a half persons. Much of this growth has occurred in Florida, which is now the fourth most populous state.*

BACKGROUND AND FACTS   Cudlipp Construction and Development Company agreed to build up to 375 houses for Shadow Lakes, Inc., near Tampa, Florida. Under the contract, the parties were bound to complete fourteen of the houses, but either party had the right to terminate the agreement with regard to future houses if prices could not be mutually agreed on by the parties. For each house, Shadow Lakes agreed to pay a fixed price, which included the costs of construction and a fee for Cudlipp's services. The contract indicated that the fee covered "off-site and on-site supervision, office overhead and general support," as well as Cudlipp's profit—which, according to Cudlipp's testimony at trial—was to be $10,000 per house. Problems developed between the parties after Cudlipp had begun to

(Continued)

Case 13.1—continued

construct eight houses. Cudlipp filed a suit in a Florida state court against Shadow Lakes, alleging, among other things, breach of contract. The damages Cudlipp sought included lost profits of $3,670,000 ($10,000 for 367 houses—375 houses less the 8 houses already under construction). The jury awarded Cudlipp $3,670,000 in lost profits, and Shadow Lakes appealed.

IN THE WORDS OF THE COURT . . .
QUINCE, Judge.
         * * * *

    * * * Whether or not the parties would have come to a meeting of the minds regarding other houses beyond the original fourteen is pure speculation and conjecture. Not only did the parties have to agree on price, but the acreage needed for the project had to be purchased by Shadow Lakes.

    * * * [T]he total amount of profit to be realized on each home is * * * speculative. Although Mr. Cudlipp initially stated the $10,000 for each house was to be pure profit, he later acknowledged certain overhead and other expenses should be subtracted from that figure. The contract itself indicated the figure included off-site and on-site supervision, office overhead and general support. Moreover, Mr. Cudlipp stated * * * that the $10,000 figure also included possible upgrades to the houses by the ultimate purchasers.

DECISION AND REMEDY   The District Court of Appeal of Florida reversed the award and remanded for a new trial on the amount.

FOR CRITICAL ANALYSIS—ECONOMIC CONSIDERATION
What might be an appropriate measure of damages if in fact a contractor was realizing no profit, or was even actually losing money, on a contract?

Consequential Damages
Special damages that compensate for a loss that is not direct or immediate (for example, lost profits). The special damages must have been reasonably foreseeable at the time the breach or injury occurred in order for the plaintiff to collect them.

CONSEQUENTIAL DAMAGES.   Foreseeable damages that result from a party's breach of contract are referred to as **consequential damages**, or *special damages*. Consequential damages differ from compensatory damages in that they are caused by special circumstances beyond the contract itself. When a seller does not deliver goods, *knowing* that a buyer is planning to resell those goods immediately, consequential damages are awarded for the loss of profits from the planned resale. For example, Gilmore contracts to have a specific item shipped to her—one that she desperately needs to repair her printing press. In contracting with the shipper, Gilmore tells him that she must receive the item by Monday or she will not be able to print her paper and will lose $750. If the shipper is late, Gilmore normally can recover the consequential damages caused by the delay (that is, the $750 in losses).

    For a nonbreaching party to recover consequential damages, the breaching party must know (or have reason to know) that special circumstances will cause the nonbreaching party to suffer an additional loss.[4] This rule was enunciated in *Hadley v. Baxendale*, a case decided in England in 1854 and presented in this chapter's *Landmark in the Legal Environment*. Today, the rule still applies. When damages are awarded, compensation is given only for those

NOTE A seller who does not wish to take on the risk of consequential damages can limit the buyer's remedies.

_____
4.   UCC 2–715(2).

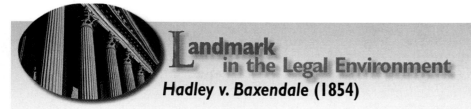

Landmark in the Legal Environment
Hadley v. Baxendale (1854)

A landmark case in establishing the rule that notice of special ("consequential") circumstances must be given if consequential damages are to be recovered is *Hadley v. Baxendale*,[a] decided in 1854. This case involved a broken crankshaft used in a flour mill run by the Hadley family in Gloucester, England. The crankshaft attached to the steam engine in the mill broke, and the shaft had to be sent to a foundry located in Greenwich so that a new shaft could be made to fit the other parts of the engine. The Hadleys hired Baxendale, a common carrier, to transport the shaft from Gloucester to Greenwich. Baxendale received payment in advance and promised to deliver the shaft the following day. It was not delivered for several days, however. As a consequence, the mill was closed during those days because the Hadleys had no extra crankshaft on hand to use. The Hadleys sued Baxendale to recover the profits they lost during that time. Baxendale contended that the loss of profits was "too remote."

In the mid-1800s, it was normal for large mills, such as that run by the Hadleys, to have more than one crankshaft in case the main one broke and had to be repaired, as it did in this case. Also, in those days it was common knowledge that flour mills did indeed have spares. It is against this background that the parties argued their respective

positions on whether the damages resulting from loss of profits while the crankshaft was out for repair were "too remote" to be recoverable.

The crucial issue before the court was whether the Hadleys had informed the carrier, Baxendale, of the special circumstances surrounding the crankshaft's repair, particularly of the fact that the mill would have to shut down while the crankshaft was being repaired. If Baxendale had been notified of this circumstance at the time the contract was formed, then the remedy for breaching the contract would have been the amount of damages that would reasonably follow from the breach—including the Hadleys' lost profits. In the court's opinion, however, the only circumstances communicated by the Hadleys to Baxendale at the time the contract was made were that the item to be transported was a broken crankshaft of a mill and that the Hadleys were the owners and operators of that mill. The court concluded that these circumstances did not reasonably indicate that the mill would have to stop operations if the delivery of the crankshaft was delayed.

For Critical Analysis: *If it had not been the custom in the mid-1800s for mills to have extra crankshafts on hand, how would this circumstance have affected the court's ruling?*

---

a. 9 Exch. 341, 156 Eng.Rep. 145 (1854).

• •

injuries that the defendant *could reasonably have foreseen* as a probable result of the usual course of events following a breach. If the injury complained of is outside the usual and foreseeable course of events, the plaintiff must show specifically that the defendant had reason to know the facts and foresee the injury.

PUNITIVE DAMAGES. Recall from Chapter 8 that *punitive damages* are designed to punish a wrongdoer and set an example to deter similar conduct in the future. Punitive damages, which are also referred to as *exemplary damages*, are generally not recoverable in an action for breach of contract. Such damages have no legitimate place in contract law because they are, in essence, penalties, and a breach of contract is not unlawful in a criminal sense. A contract is simply a civil relationship between the parties. The law may compensate one party for the loss of the bargain—no more and no less.

In a few situations, a person's actions can cause both a breach of contract and a tort. For example, the parties can establish by contract a certain reasonable

> **"The duty to keep a contract at common law means a prediction that you must pay damages if you do not keep it—and nothing else."**
>
> Oliver Wendell Holmes, Jr., 1841–1935
> (Associate justice of the United States Supreme Court, 1902–1932)

Ethical Perspective

The reason punitive damages are awarded in tort actions while they normally are not in contract actions has to do with the different purposes of tort and contract law. The social policies reflected in each body of law are particularly evident in the different remedies available under tort and contract law. Tort damages are awarded to compensate a victim for harms proximately caused by a tortious act, regardless of whether the full extent of those harms could have been anticipated. Because intentional torts are generally viewed as morally wrongful actions, punitive damages are sometimes awarded to deter particularly egregious conduct.

Contract damages, in contrast, are generally limited to those damages that could be reasonably foreseen when the parties entered into the contract. This limitation on contract damages allows parties to estimate in advance the risks they assume in entering into contracts and thus furthers the public policy of encouraging commerce. Unlike an intentional tort, an intentional breach of contract is often viewed as morally neutral (unless the breach also involves a tort). This is because a breach of contract can sometimes create a net gain for society. For example, a businessperson may be economically more productive by breaching a contract (and paying damages for the breach) for the purpose of performing another contract that will yield higher benefits to the breaching party.

For Critical Analysis: *Can a breach of contract ever be viewed as "morally neutral" by the nonbreaching party to that contract?*

---

standard or duty of care. Failure to live up to that standard is a breach of contract, and the act itself may constitute negligence. An intentional tort (such as fraud) may also be tied to a breach of contract. In such a situation, it is possible for the nonbreaching party to recover punitive damages for the tort in addition to compensatory and consequential damages for the breach of contract.

NOMINAL DAMAGES.   Damages that are awarded to an innocent party when only a technical injury is involved and no actual damage (no financial loss) has been suffered are called **nominal damages**. Nominal damage awards are often small, such as one dollar, but they do establish that the defendant acted wrongfully.

For example, suppose that Parrott contracts to buy potatoes at fifty cents a pound from Lentz. Lentz breaches the contract and does not deliver the potatoes. Meanwhile, the price of potatoes falls. Parrott is able to buy them in the open market at half the price he agreed to pay Lentz. Parrott is clearly better off because of Lentz's breach. Thus, in a suit for breach of contract, Parrott may be awarded only nominal damages for the technical injury he sustained, as no monetary loss was involved. Most lawsuits for nominal damages are brought as a matter of principle under the theory that a breach has occurred and some damages must be imposed regardless of actual loss.

Mitigation of Damages

In most situations, when a breach of contract occurs, the injured party is held to a duty to mitigate, or reduce, the damages that he or she suffers. Under this doctrine of **mitigation of damages**, the required action depends on the nature of the situation. For example, in the majority of states, wrongfully terminated employees have a duty to mitigate damages suffered by their employers' breach. The damages they will be awarded are their salaries less the incomes they would have received in similar jobs obtained by reasonable means. It is the employer's burden to prove the existence of such jobs and to prove that the employee could have been hired. An employee is, of course, under no duty to

Nominal Damages A small monetary award (often one dollar) granted to a plaintiff when no actual damage was suffered.

Mitigation of Damages A rule requiring a plaintiff to have done whatever was reasonable to minimize the damages caused by the defendant.

> "Nominal damages are, in effect, only a peg to hang costs on."
>
> Sir William Henry Maule, 1788–1858 (British jurist)

take a job that is not of the same type and rank. This is illustrated in the following case.

Case 13.2 ● Parker v. Twentieth Century-Fox Film Corp.

Supreme Court of California, 1970.
3 Cal.3d 176,
474 P.2d 689,
89 Cal.Rptr. 737.

COMPANY PROFILE *Daryl Zanuck and Joseph Schenk formed the Twentieth Century Company in 1933 to make movies. Two years later, they merged with the Fox Film Company, which had been founded by William Fox, and became Twentieth Century-Fox Film Corporation. Today, Twentieth Century-Fox produces movies and television shows as part of the News Corporation Limited, which is headquartered in Australia. The News Corporation also has interests in the production and distribution of newspapers, magazines, books, television programs, and films in Great Britain, Hong Kong, New Zealand, and other countries.*

BACKGROUND AND FACTS Twentieth Century-Fox Film Corporation planned to produce a musical, *Bloomer Girl*,

and contracted with Shirley MacLaine Parker to play the leading female role. According to the contract, Fox was to pay Parker $53,571.42 per week for fourteen weeks, for a total of $750,000. Fox later decided not to produce *Bloomer Girl* and tried to substitute another contract for the existing contract. Under the terms of this second contract, Parker would play the leading role in a Western movie for the same amount of money guaranteed by the first contract. Fox gave Parker one week in which to accept the new contract. Parker filed suit in a California state court against Fox to recover the amount of compensation guaranteed in the first contract because, she maintained, the two roles were not at all equivalent. The *Bloomer Girl* production was a musical, to be filmed in California, and it could not be compared with a "western-type" production that Fox tentatively planned to produce in Australia. When the trial court held for Parker, Fox appealed. Ultimately, the California Supreme Court reviewed the case.

IN THE WORDS OF THE COURT . . .
BURKE, Justice.
* * * *

The general rule is that the measure of recovery by a wrongfully discharged employee is the amount of salary agreed upon for the period of service, less the amount which the employer affirmatively proves the employee has earned or with reasonable effort might have earned from other employment. However, before projected earnings from other employment opportunities not sought or accepted by the discharged employee can be applied in mitigation, the employer must show that the other employment was comparable, or substantially similar, to that of which the employee has been deprived * * * .
* * * *

* * * The mere circumstance that *Bloomer Girl* was to be a musical review calling upon plaintiff's talents as a dancer as well as an actress, and was to be produced in the City of Los Angeles, whereas *Big Country* was a straight dramatic role in a "Western Type" story taking place in an opal mine in Australia, demonstrates the difference in kind between the two employments; the female lead as a dramatic actress in a western style motion picture can by no stretch of imagination be considered the equivalent of or substantially similar to the lead in a song-and-dance production.

DECISION AND REMEDY The Supreme Court of California affirmed the trial court's ruling. Parker could not be required to accept Fox's offer of the western-movie contract to mitigate the damages she incurred as a result of the breach of contract.

FOR CRITICAL ANALYSIS—INTERNATIONAL CONSIDERATION *Many legal systems, including that of France, have no clear requirement that damages must be mitigated. Can justice be better served by requiring that damages be mitigated? If so, how?*

Liquidated Damages versus Penalties

Liquidated Damages An amount, stipulated in the contract, that the parties to a contract believe to be a reasonable estimation of the damages that will occur in the event of a breach.

Penalty A sum inserted into a contract, not as a measure of compensation for its breach but rather as punishment for a default. The agreement as to the amount will not be enforced, and recovery will be limited to actual damages.

A **liquidated damages** provision in a contract specifies that a certain amount of money is to be paid in the event of a future default or breach of contract. (*Liquidated* means determined, settled, or fixed.) Liquidated damages differ from penalties. A **penalty** specifies a certain amount to be paid in the event of a default or breach of contract and is designed to penalize the breaching party. Liquidated damages provisions normally are enforceable; penalty provisions are not.[5]

To determine whether a particular provision is for liquidated damages or for a penalty, the court must answer two questions: First, at the time the contract was formed, was it difficult to estimate the potential damages that would be incurred if the contract was not performed on time? Second, was the amount set as damages a reasonable estimate of those potential damages and not excessive?[6] If the answers to both questions are yes, the provision will be enforced. If either answer is no, the provision will normally not be enforced. In a construction contract, it is difficult to estimate the amount of damages that might be caused by a delay in completing construction, so liquidated damages clauses are often used.

The following case involved a contract clause that required a client to pay an attorney substantial damages if the client terminated its relationship with the attorney. The issue before the court was whether the clause was a liquidated damages clause or a penalty clause.

---

5. This is also the rule under the Uniform Commercial Code. See UCC 2–718(1).
6. *Restatement (Second) of Contracts*, Section 356(1).

Case 13.3 ● AFLAC, Inc. v. Williams

Supreme Court of Georgia, 1994.
264 Ga. 351,
444 S.E.2d 314.

HISTORICAL AND SOCIAL SETTING *Historically, lawyers and law firms concentrated their efforts on the practice of law, but they also traditionally held a position as general counselor to their clients. In the 1980s and 1990s, according to some observers, lawyers began to focus too narrowly on legal issues. Consequently, attorneys lost ground, in their traditional role as general counselors, to financial advisers, accounting firms, banks, actuaries, and other consultants who were looking for new areas in which to do business when they found their own traditional markets shrinking.*

BACKGROUND AND FACTS AFLAC, Inc., hired Peter Williams, an attorney, under a seven-year contract to give the company legal advice as needed. The contract provided that if AFLAC terminated the relationship, it would pay Williams 50 percent of whatever amount was due for the remaining term. After four years, AFLAC terminated the contract with Williams and asked a Georgia state court to determine the enforceability of the termination payment provision. The court declared the provision unenforceable, and Williams appealed. The state appellate court reversed this decision, and AFLAC appealed.

IN THE WORDS OF THE COURT . . .
FLETCHER, Justice.
  *   *   *   *
  * * * [The contract] requires AFLAC to pay an unreasonably high sum as damages, requires payment without considering Williams' duty to mitigate

(Continued)

Case 13.3—continued

his damages, and obligates AFLAC to pay even if Williams is discharged for cause. * * * [The] provision is not a reasonable estimate of Williams' damages and instead is a penalty imposed to punish AFLAC * * * .

DECISION AND REMEDY The Supreme Court of Georgia held that the provision was an unenforceable, liquidated damages clause and reversed the decision of the intermediate appellate court.

FOR CRITICAL ANALYSIS—ETHICAL CONSIDERATION *Why shouldn't parties to a contract be allowed to agree to the imposition of whatever penalty they wish in the event of a breach?*

Rescission and Restitution

As discussed in Chapter 12, *rescission* is essentially an action to undo, or cancel, a contract—to return nonbreaching parties to the positions that they occupied prior to the transaction. When fraud, mistake, duress, or failure of consideration is present, rescission is available. The failure of one party to perform under a contract entitles the other party to rescind the contract.[7] The rescinding party must give prompt notice to the breaching party. Furthermore, both parties must make **restitution** to each other by returning goods, property, or money previously conveyed.[8] If the goods or property can be restored *in specie*—that is, if they can be returned—they must be. If the goods or property have been consumed, restitution must be made in an equivalent amount of money.

Essentially, restitution refers to the recapture of a benefit conferred on the defendant through which the defendant has been unjustly enriched. For example, Andrea pays $10,000 to Miles in return for Miles's promise to design a house for her. The next day Miles calls Andrea and tells her that he has taken a position with a large architectural firm in another state and cannot design the house. Andrea decides to hire another architect that afternoon. Andrea can get restitution of $10,000, because she conferred an unjust benefit of $10,000 on Miles. (See this chapter's *Inside the Legal Environment* for a further discussion of restitution and the distinction between restitution and damages.)

Restitution An equitable remedy under which a person is restored to his or her original position prior to loss or injury, or placed in the position he or she would have been in had the breach not occurred.

Specific Performance

The equitable remedy of **specific performance** calls for the performance of the act promised in the contract. This remedy is often attractive to a nonbreaching party, because it provides the exact bargain promised in the contract. It also avoids some of the problems inherent in a suit for money damages. First, the nonbreaching party need not worry about collecting the judgment.[9] Second,

Specific Performance An equitable remedy requiring *exactly* the performance that was specified in a contract; usually granted only when money damages would be an inadequate remedy and the subject matter of the contract is unique (for example, real property).

7. The rescission discussed here refers to *unilateral* rescission, in which only one party wants to undo the contract. In *mutual* rescission, both parties agree to undo the contract. Mutual rescission discharges the contract; unilateral rescission is generally available as a remedy for breach of contract.
8. *Restatement (Second) of Contracts,* Section 370.
9. Courts dispose of cases, after trials, by entering judgments. A judgment may order the losing party to pay money damages to the winning party. Collection of judgments, however, poses problems—such as when the judgment debtor is insolvent (cannot pay his or her bills when they become due) or has only a small net worth, or when the debtor's assets cannot be seized, under exemption laws, by a creditor to satisfy a debt (see Chapter 14).

Inside the Legal Environment
Restitution versus Damages

The remedy of rescission and restitution, which attempts to restore the parties to their pre-contractual status, rests on the equitable principle that a person should not be unjustly enriched. Whereas damages are measured by the amount of the plaintiff's loss, restitution is measured by the amount of the defendant's gain. In some cases, this distinction has little practical effect, because the plaintiff's loss is equal to the defendant's gain. In other cases, however, the defendant's gain is greater than the plaintiff's loss.

Suppose, for example, that Andrea gives Miles $10,000 in return for Miles's promise to design a house for her. The next day, Miles uses the $10,000 to purchase an old Ferrari, which he immediately sells to another person for $12,000. He then notifies Andrea that he cannot perform the contract. If Andrea sued for damages, she could obtain $10,000. If she sues to rescind the contract and obtain restitution, however, the question arises as to whether the $2,000 profit Miles made on the purchase and sale of the Ferrari should be included as restitution (and be given to Andrea) or be retained by Miles.

This thorny issue came before the Colorado Supreme Court in a case brought by Hydrosphere Resource Consultants, Inc., against EarthInfo, Inc., for breach of contract. Under the contract, EarthInfo was obligated to package and market CD-ROM players and software that had been developed by Hydrosphere and to pay Hydrosphere a percentage of its net sales as royalties. A dispute arose, and EarthInfo refused to pay Hydrosphere any royalties after June 30, 1990. Hydrosphere sued EarthInfo for rescission and restitution, and the court had to decide whether the amount of restitution should include just Hydrosphere's unpaid royalties on sales made after the breach or all of EarthInfo's profits made on those sales.

The court noted that in similar cases, some courts have refused to award the breaching party's profits to the nonbreaching party under the theory that a breach of contract is not a "wrong." Other courts, however, have concluded that the breaching party should be stripped of the profits—they should go to the non-breaching party. The Colorado court adopted neither approach, concluding that the question should be decided on a case-by-case basis. The outcome should depend on "the nature of the defendant's wrong, the relative extent of his or her contribution, and the feasibility of separating this from the contribution traceable to the plaintiff's interest."

The court stated that if "the defendant's wrongdoing is intentional or substantial, or there are no other means of measuring the wrongdoer's enrichment, recovery of profits must be granted." Because EarthInfo intentionally breached the contract, the breach was substantial, and damages were difficult to assess, the court held that the amount of restitution should include EarthInfo's profits from the sale of Hydrosphere's products—less the costs incurred by EarthInfo in packaging and marketing the products.[a]

For Critical Analysis: *Is there any reason why a nonbreaching party would seek rescission and restitution as a remedy, instead of damages, if the amount of restitution would be equal to the damages sought?*

a. *EarthInfo, Inc. v. Hydrosphere Resource Consultants, Inc.*, 900 P.2d 113 (Colo. 1995).

the nonbreaching party need not look around for another contract. Third, the actual performance may be more valuable than the money damages. Although the equitable remedy of specific performance is often preferable to other remedies, normally it is not granted unless the party's legal remedy (money damages) is inadequate.[10]

For example, contracts for the sale of goods that are readily available on the market rarely qualify for specific performance. Money damages ordinarily are adequate in such situations, because substantially identical goods can be bought or sold in the market. If the goods are unique, however, a court of

---

10. *Restatement (Second) of Contracts*, Section 359.

A collection of antique coins and other artifacts. When is specific performance the appropriate remedy for a breach of contract?

equity will decree specific performance. For example, paintings, sculptures, and rare books and coins are often unique, and money damages will not enable a buyer to obtain substantially identical substitutes in the market. The same principle applies to contracts relating to sales of land or interests in land, because each parcel of land is unique by legal description.

Courts normally refuse to grant specific performance of contracts for personal services. Sometimes the remedy at law may be adequate if substantially identical services are available from other persons (as with lawn-mowing services). Even for individually tailored personal-service contracts, courts are very hesitant to order specific performance by a party, because public policy strongly discourages involuntary servitude.[11] Moreover, the courts do not want to monitor a personal-service contract. For example, if you contract with a brain surgeon to perform brain surgery on you and the surgeon refuses to perform, the court would not compel (and you certainly would not want) the surgeon to perform under these circumstances. There is no way the court can assure meaningful performance in such a situation.[12]

> "Specific performance is a remedy of grace and not a matter of right, and the test of whether or not it should be granted depends on the particular circumstances of each case."
>
> George Bushnell, 1887–1965 (American jurist)

Reformation

When the parties have imperfectly expressed their agreement in writing, the equitable remedy of *reformation* allows the contract to be rewritten to reflect the parties' true intentions. This remedy applies most often when fraud or

---

11.   The Thirteenth Amendment to the U.S. Constitution prohibits involuntary servitude, but negative injunctions (that is, prohibiting rather than ordering certain conduct) are possible. Thus, you may not be able to compel a person to perform under a personal-service contract, but you may be able to restrain that person from engaging in similar contracts with others for a period of time.

12.   Similarly, courts often refuse to order specific performance of construction contracts, because courts are not set up to operate as construction supervisors or engineers.

International Perspective

In the United States, the general rule is that the equitable remedy of specific performance will be granted only if the remedy at law (money damages) is inadequate. In Germany, however, the typical remedy for a breach of contract is specific performance. In other words, a German court normally would order the breaching party to go forward and perform the contract. German courts will award damages for breach of contract in some circumstances, but damages are available only after notice and other procedures have been employed to seek performance.

For Critical Analysis: If U.S. courts commonly granted the remedy of specific performance, as German courts do, would parties be less likely to breach their contracts?

---

mutual mistake (for example, a clerical error) has occurred. If Keshan contracts to buy a certain piece of equipment from Shelley but the written contract refers to a different piece of equipment, a mutual mistake has occurred. Accordingly, a court could reform the contract so that the writing conforms to the parties' original intention as to which piece of equipment is being sold.

Two other examples deserve mention. The first involves two parties who have made a binding oral contract. They further agree to reduce the oral contract to writing, but in doing so, they make an error in stating the terms. Universally, the courts allow into evidence the correct terms of the oral contract, thereby reforming the written contract.

The second example has to do with written covenants not to compete. As discussed in Chapter 12, if a covenant not to compete is for a valid and legitimate purpose (such as the sale of a business), but the area or time restraints of the covenant are unreasonable, some courts reform the restraints by making them reasonable and enforce the entire contract as reformed. Other courts throw the entire restrictive covenant out as illegal.

Recovery Based on Quasi Contract

DON'T FORGET The function of a quasi contract is to impose a legal obligation on parties who made no actual promises.

Recall from Chapter 12 that a quasi contract is not a true contract but a fictional contract that is imposed on the parties to obtain justice and prevent unjust enrichment. Hence, a quasi contract becomes an equitable basis for relief. Generally, when one party confers a benefit on another, justice requires that the party receiving the benefit pay a reasonable value for it so as not to be unjustly enriched at the other party's expense.

Quasi-contractual recovery is useful when one party has *partially* performed under a contract that is unenforceable. It can be an alternative to suing for damages, and it allows the party to recover the reasonable value of the partial performance. For quasi-contractual recovery to occur, the party seeking recovery must show the following:

1. A benefit was conferred on the other party.
2. The party conferring the benefit did so with the expectation of being paid.
3. The party seeking recovery did not act as a volunteer in conferring the benefit.

4. Retaining the benefit without paying for it would result in an unjust enrichment of the party receiving the benefit.

For example, suppose that Ericson contracts to build two oil derricks for Petro Industries. The derricks are to be built over a period of three years, but the parties do not create a written contract. Enforcement of the contract will therefore be barred by the Statute of Frauds.[13] Ericson completes one derrick, and then Petro Industries informs him that it will not pay for the derrick. Ericson can sue in quasi contract because (1) a benefit (one oil derrick) has been conferred on Petro Industries; (2) Ericson conferred the benefit (built the derrick) expecting to be paid; (3) Ericson did not volunteer to build the derrick but built it under an unenforceable oral contract; and (4) allowing Petro Industries to retain the derrick without paying would enrich the company unjustly. Therefore, Ericson should be able to recover the reasonable value of the oil derrick (under the theory of *quantum meruit*[14]—"as much as he deserves"). The reasonable value is ordinarily equal to the fair market value.

Election of Remedies

In many cases, a nonbreaching party has several remedies available. Because the remedies may be inconsistent with one another, the common law of contract requires the party to choose which remedy to pursue. This is called *election of remedies*.

The purpose of the doctrine of election of remedies is to prevent double recovery. Suppose that Jefferson agrees to sell his land to Adams. Then Jefferson changes his mind and repudiates the contract. Adams can sue for compensatory damages or for specific performance. If she receives damages as a result of the breach, she should not also be granted specific performance of the sales contract, because that would mean she would end up with both the land *and* damages, which would be unfair. In effect, she would recover twice for the same breach of contract. The doctrine of election of remedies requires Adams to choose the remedy she wants, and it eliminates any possibility of double recovery.

Unfortunately, the doctrine has been applied in a rigid and technical manner, leading to some harsh results. For example, in a Wisconsin case, a man named Carpenter was fraudulently induced to buy a piece of land for $100. He spent $140 moving onto the land and then discovered the fraud. Instead of suing for damages, Carpenter sued to rescind the contract. The court denied recovery of the $140 because the seller, Mason, had not received the $140 and was therefore not required to reimburse Carpenter for his moving expenses. So Carpenter suffered a net loss of $140 on the transaction. If Carpenter had sued for damages, he could have recovered the $100 purchase price and the $140.[15]

In the following case, the frustrated sellers of a house were apparently attempting to avoid the doctrine of election of remedies in order to, as the old saying goes, "have their cake and eat it, too."

> **BE AWARE** Which remedy a plaintiff elects depends on the subject of the contract, the defenses of the breaching party, the advantages that might be gained in terms of tactics against the defendant, and what the plaintiff can prove with respect to the remedy sought.

---

13. Contracts that by their terms cannot be performed within one year must be in writing to be enforceable. See Chapter 12.
14. Pronounced *kwahn*-tuhm *mehr*-oo-wuht.
15. See *Carpenter v. Mason*, 181 Wis. 114, 193 N.W. 973 (1923). Because of the harsh results of the doctrine of election of remedies, the Uniform Commercial Code expressly rejects it. Remedies under the UCC are essentially *cumulative* in nature (see UCC 2–703 and 2–711).

Case 13.4 ● Palmer v. Hayes

Court of Appeals of Utah, 1995.
892 P.2d 1059.

HISTORICAL AND ECONOMIC SETTING   *Real estate transactions have long involved the same steps as those that shape a deal today. A transaction starts with a seller who wants to sell and a buyer who wants to buy. The buyer makes a bid on the property. This bid usually takes the form of a proposed contract of sale and includes a deposit of 1 or 2 percent of the price offered for the property. In transactions involving single-family homes, unsophisticated buyers often do not realize how binding their bids can be. If a seller accepts a buyer's proposal, the buyer is bound to it.*

BACKGROUND AND FACTS   Kenneth and Rebecca Palmer wanted to sell their house. Edward and Stephanie Hayes signed a proposed contract of sale, under which they agreed to give the Palmers' real estate agent, Maple Hills Realty, $2,000 as a deposit on the house. The agreement provided that in the event of default, the Palmers could either keep the deposit or sue to enforce their rights. The Palmers accepted the Hayeses' offer and signed the contract. Before the property changed hands, however, the Hayeses changed their minds and asked for the return of their deposit. The Palmers refused and filed a suit against the Hayeses in a Utah state court, seeking damages. The Hayeses filed a motion for summary judgment on the ground that, by not releasing the deposit, the Palmers had elected their remedy. The court ruled in favor of the Hayeses on this point, and the Palmers appealed.

IN THE WORDS OF THE COURT . . .
BENCH, Judge:
* * * *
* * * [A] seller's failure to offer to return earnest money deposits precludes the seller from pursuing other remedies.
* * * [B]efore a seller may pursue a remedy other than liquidated damages, the seller must release any claim to the deposit money.
* * * The Palmers therefore needed only to indicate to Maple Hills Realty, in writing, that they released the deposit money to the Hayeses. Then they could have proceeded with their suit for damages. * * *
* * * [B]y failing to release the deposit money, the Palmers elected to retain it as liquidated damages.

DECISION AND REMEDY   The Court of Appeals of Utah, concluding that the Palmers had elected the remedy of liquidated damages, affirmed the lower court's ruling.

FOR CRITICAL ANALYSIS—INTERNATIONAL CONSIDERATION
What are the reasons for applying the doctrine of election of remedies to preclude sellers who keep deposits from suing for damages?

Provisions Limiting Remedies

> **RECALL** Exculpatory clauses are often held unconscionable, depending on the relative bargaining positions of the parties and the importance to the public interest of the business seeking to enforce the clause.

A contract may include provisions stating that no damages can be recovered for certain types of breaches or that damages must be limited to a maximum amount. The contract may also provide that the only remedy for breach is replacement, repair, or refund of the purchase price. Provisions stating that no damages can be recovered are called *exculpatory clauses* (see Chapter 12). Provisions that affect the availability of certain remedies are called *limitation-of-liability clauses.*

Whether these contract provisions and clauses will be enforced depends on the type of breach that is excused by the provision. For example, a provision excluding liability for fraudulent or intentional injury will not be enforced. Likewise, a clause excluding liability for illegal acts or violations of law will not be enforced. A clause excluding liability for negligence may be enforced in some cases. When an exculpatory clause for negligence is contained in a contract made between parties who have roughly equal bargaining positions, the clause usually will be enforced.

The UCC provides that in a contract for the sale of goods, remedies can be limited.

The Sale of Goods

▼ When we turn to sales contracts, we move away from common law principles and into the area of statutory law. State statutory law governing sales and lease transactions is based on the Uniform Commercial Code (UCC). Article 2 of the UCC governs **sales contracts**, or contracts for the sale of goods. To facilitate commercial transactions, Article 2 modifies some of the common law contract requirements that were discussed in this chapter and the previous chapter. To the extent that it has not been modified by the UCC, however, the common law of contracts also applies to sales contracts. For example, the common law requirements for a valid contract—agreement (offer and acceptance), consideration, capacity, and legality—are applicable to sales contracts as well. Thus, you should reexamine these common law principles when studying sales. In general, the rule is that whenever there is a conflict between a common law contract rule and the UCC, the UCC controls. In other words, when a UCC provision addresses a certain issue, the UCC governs; when the UCC is silent, the common law governs.

In regard to Article 2, you should keep in mind two things. First, Article 2 deals with the sale of *goods*; it does not deal with real property (real estate), services, or intangible property such as stocks and bonds. Thus, if the subject matter of a dispute is goods, the UCC governs. If it is real estate or services, the common law applies. The relationship between general contract law and the law governing sales of goods is illustrated in Exhibit 13–2. Second, in some

Sales Contract A contract for the sale of goods under which the ownership of goods is transferred from a seller to a buyer for a price.

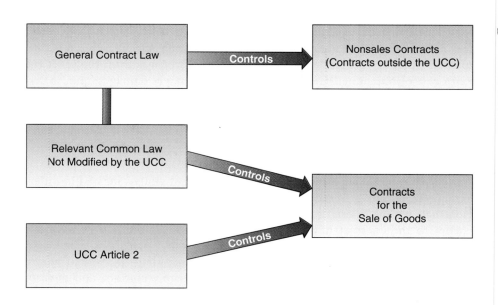

▪ **Exhibit 13–2 Law Governing Contracts** This exhibit graphically illustrates the relationship between general contract law and the law governing contracts for the sale of goods. Sales contracts are not governed exclusively by Article 2 of the Uniform Commerical Code but also by general contract law whenever it is relevant and has not been modified by the UCC.

cases, the rules may vary quite a bit, depending on whether the buyer or the seller is a *merchant*.

Performance of a Sales Contract

In the performance of a sales contract, the basic obligation of the seller is to transfer and deliver conforming goods. The basic obligation of the buyer is to accept and pay for conforming goods in accordance with the contract [UCC 2–301]. Overall performance of a sales contract is controlled by the agreement between the parties. When the contract is unclear and disputes arise, the courts look to the UCC.

Remedies for Breach of Sales Contracts

Sometimes circumstances make it difficult for a person to carry out the performance promised in a contract, in which case the contract may be breached. When breach occurs, the aggrieved party looks for remedies. These remedies range from retaining the goods to requiring the breaching party's performance under the contract. The general purpose of these remedies is to put the aggrieved party "in as good a position as if the other party had fully performed." Remedies under the Uniform Commercial Code (UCC) are *cumulative* in nature. In other words, an innocent party to a breached sales or lease contract is not limited to one, exclusive remedy. (Of course, a party still may not recover twice for the same harm.)

REMEDIES OF THE SELLER. A buyer breaches a sales contract by any of the following actions: (1) wrongfully rejecting tender of the goods; (2) wrongfully revoking acceptance of the goods; (3) failing to make payment on or before delivery of the goods; or (4) repudiating the contract. On the buyer's breach, the seller is afforded several distinct remedies under the UCC. These include the right to stop or withhold delivery of the goods and the right to recover damages or to recover the purchase price of the goods.

REMEDIES OF THE BUYER. A seller breaches a sales contract by failing to deliver conforming goods or repudiating the contract prior to delivery. On the breach, the buyer has a choice of several remedies under the UCC. These remedies include the right to reject nonconforming or improperly delivered goods; to *cover* (that is, to buy the goods elsewhere and recover from the seller the extra cost of obtaining the substitute goods); to recover damages; and, in certain circumstances, to obtain specific performance of the contract.

International currency. The values of different types of currencies fluctuate. What other variables should a party consider when entering into an international sales contract?

Contracts for the International Sale of Goods

International sales contracts between firms or individuals located in different countries are governed by the 1980 United Nations Convention on Contracts for the International Sale of Goods (CISG)—if the countries of the parties to the contract have ratified the CISG (and if the parties have not agreed that some other law will govern their contract). As of 1996, thirty-eight countries had ratified or acceded to the CISG, including the United States, Canada, Mexico, some Central and South American countries, and most of the European nations. Four other nations have signed the CISG and indicated their intent to ratify it. Essentially, the CISG is to international sales contracts what Article 2 of the UCC is to domestic sales contracts.

Businesspersons must take special care when drafting international sales contracts to avoid problems caused by distance, including language differences and different national laws. The fold-out exhibit contained within this chapter, which shows an actual international sales contract used by Starbucks Coffee Company, illustrates many of the special terms and clauses that are typically contained in international contracts for the sale of goods. Annotations in the exhibit explain the meaning and significance of specific clauses in the contract. (See Chapter 24 for a discussion of other laws that frame global business transactions.)

Key Terms

consequential damages 350
liquidated damages 354
mitigation of damages 352

nominal damages 352
penalty 354
restitution 354

sales contract 361
specific performance 355

Chapter Summary
Contract Remedies and Sales

COMMON REMEDIES AVAILABLE TO THE NONBREACHING PARTY

DAMAGES
(See pages 347–355.)

The legal remedy of damages is designed to compensate the nonbreaching party for the loss of the bargain. By awarding money damages, the court tries to place the parties in the positions that they would have occupied had the contract been fully performed. The nonbreaching party frequently has a duty to *mitigate* (lessen or reduce) the damages incurred as a result of the contract's breach. There are five broad categories of damages:

1. Compensatory damages—Damages that compensate the nonbreaching party for injuries actually sustained and proved to have arisen directly from the loss of the bargain resulting from the breach of contract.

   a. In breached contracts for the sale of goods, the usual measure of compensatory damages is an amount equal to the difference between the contract price and the market price.

   b. In breached contracts for the sale of land, the measure of damages is ordinarily the same as in contracts for the sale of goods.

   c. In breached construction contracts, the measure of damages depends on which party breaches and at what stage of construction the breach occurs.

2. Consequential damages—Damages resulting from special circumstances beyond the contract itself; the damages flow only from the consequences of a breach. For a party to recover consequential damages, the damages must be the foreseeable result of a breach of contract, and the breaching party must have known at the time the contract was formed that special circumstances existed and that the nonbreaching party would incur additional loss on breach of the contract. Also called *special damages*.

(Continued)

Chapter Summary, continued

DAMAGES—continued (See pages 347–355.)	3. **Punitive damages**—Damages awarded to punish the breaching party. Usually not awarded in an action for breach of contract unless a tort is involved. 4. **Nominal damages**—Damages small in amount (such as one dollar) that are awarded when a breach has occurred but no actual damages have been suffered. Awarded only to establish that the defendant acted wrongfully. 5. **Liquidated damages**—Damages that may be specified in a contract as the amount to be paid to the nonbreaching party in the event the contract is later breached. Clauses providing for liquidated damages are enforced if the damages were difficult to estimate at the time the contract was formed and if the amount stipulated is reasonable. If construed to be a penalty, the clause will not be enforced.
RESCISSION AND RESTITUTION (See page 355.)	1. **Rescission**—A remedy whereby a contract is canceled and the parties are restored to the original positions that they occupied prior to the transaction. Available when fraud, a mistake, duress, or failure of consideration is present. The rescinding party must give prompt notice of the rescission to the breaching party. 2. **Restitution**—When a contract is rescinded, both parties must make restitution to each other by returning the goods, property, or money previously conveyed. Restitution prevents the unjust enrichment of the defendant.
SPECIFIC PERFORMANCE (See pages 355–357.)	An equitable remedy calling for the performance of the act promised in the contract. Specific performance is only available in special situations—such as those involving contracts for the sale of unique goods or land—and when monetary damages would be an inadequate remedy. Specific performance is not available as a remedy in breached contracts for personal services.
REFORMATION (See pages 357–358.)	An equitable remedy allowing a contract to be "reformed," or rewritten, to reflect the parties' true intentions. Available when an agreement is imperfectly expressed in writing.
RECOVERY BASED ON QUASI CONTRACT See pages 358–359.)	An equitable theory imposed by the courts to obtain justice and prevent unjust enrichment in a situation in which no enforceable contract exists. The party seeking recovery must show the following: 1. A benefit was conferred on the other party. 2. The party conferring the benefit did so with the expectation of being paid. 3. The benefit was not volunteered. 4. Retaining the benefit without paying for it would result in the unjust enrichment of the party receiving the benefit.
CONTRACT DOCTRINES RELATING TO REMEDIES	
ELECTION OF REMEDIES (See pages 359–360.)	A common law doctrine under which a nonbreaching party must choose one remedy from those available. This doctrine prevents double recovery.
PROVISIONS LIMITING REMEDIES (See pages 360–361.)	A contract may provide that no damages (or only a limited amount of damages) can be recovered in the event the contract is breached. Clauses excluding liability for fraudulent or intentional injury or for illegal acts cannot be enforced. Clauses excluding liability for negligence may be enforced if both parties hold roughly equal bargaining power. Under the UCC, in contracts for the sale of goods, remedies may be limited.
CONTRACTS FOR SALES OF GOODS	
THE SCOPE OF ARTICLE 2— SALES (See pages 361–362.)	Article 2 governs contracts for the sale of goods (tangible, movable personal property). The common law of contracts also applies to sales contracts to the extent that the common law has not been modified by the UCC.

Continued

Chapter Summary, continued

OBLIGATIONS OF THE SELLER AND BUYER (See page 362.)	The seller or lessor must tender *conforming* foods to the buyer. On tender of delivery by the seller, the buyer or lessor must pay for the goods.
REMEDIES FOR BREACH (See page 362.)	When the buyer breaches a contract for the sale of goods, the seller may stop or withhold delivery of the goods, or recover damages or the purchase price of the goods. When the seller breaches a sales contract, the buyer may reject the goods, recover damages, obtain specific performance, or cover (buy replacement goods) and obtain from the seller the extra cost of the cover.
CONTRACTS FOR THE INTERNATIONAL SALE OF GOODS (See pages 362–363.)	International sales contracts are governed by the United Nations Convention on Contracts for the International Sale of Goods (CISG)—if the countries of the parties to the contract have ratified the CISG (and if the parties have not agreed that some other law will govern their contract). Essentially, the CISG is to international sales contracts what Article 2 of the UCC is to domestic sales contracts.

For Review

1. What is the difference between compensatory damages and consequential damages? What are nominal damages, and when might they be awarded by a court?

2. What is the usual measure of damages on a breach of contract for a sale of goods?

3. Under what circumstances will the remedy of rescission and restitution be available?

4. When might specific performance be granted as a remedy?

5. Describe the scope and coverage of Article 2 of the UCC.

Questions and Case Problems

13–1. Liquidated Damages. Carnack contracts to sell his house and lot to Willard for $100,000. The terms of the contract call for Willard to pay 10 percent of the purchase price as a deposit toward the purchase price, or as a down payment. The terms further stipulate that should the buyer breach the contract, the deposit will be retained by Carnack as liquidated damages. Willard pays the deposit, but because her expected financing of the $90,000 balance falls through, she breaches the contract. Two weeks later Carnack sells the house and lot to Balkova for $105,000. Willard demands her $10,000 back, but Carnack refuses, claiming that Willard's breach and the contract terms entitle him to keep the deposit. Discuss who is correct.

13–2. Election of Remedies. Perez contracts to buy a new Oldsmobile from Central City Motors, paying $2,000 down and agreeing to make twenty-four monthly payments of $350 each. He takes the car home and, after making one payment, learns that his Oldsmobile has a Chevrolet engine in it rather than the famous Olds Super V-8 engine. Central City never informed Perez of this fact. Perez immediately notifies Central City of his dissatisfaction and returns the car to Central City. Central City accepts the car and returns to Perez the $2,000 down payment plus the one $350 payment. Two weeks later Perez, without a car and feeling angry, files a suit against Central City, seeking damages for breach of warranty and fraud. Discuss the effect of Perez's actions.

13–3. Specific Performance. In which of the following situations might a court grant specific performance as a remedy for the breach of contract?

   a. Tarrington contracts to sell her house and lot to Rainier. Then, on finding another buyer willing to pay a higher purchase price, she refuses to deed the property to Rainier.

b. Marita contracts to sing and dance in Horace's nightclub for one month, beginning June 1. She then refuses to perform.

c. Juan contracts to purchase a rare coin from Edmund, who is breaking up his coin collection. At the last minute, Edmund decides to keep his coin collection intact and refuses to deliver the coin to Juan.

d. There are three shareholders of Astro Computer Corp.: Coase, who owns 48 percent of the stock; De Valle, who owns 48 percent; and Cary, who owns 4 percent. Cary contracts to sell his 4 percent to De Valle but later refuses to transfer the shares to him.

13–4. Measure of Damages. Johnson contracted to lease a house to Fox for $700 a month, beginning October 1. Fox stipulated in the contract that before he moved in, the interior of the house had to be completely repainted. On September 9, Johnson hired Keever to do the required painting for $1,000. He told Keever that the painting had to be finished by October 1 but did not explain why. On September 28, Keever quit for no reason, having completed approximately 80 percent of the work. Johnson then paid Sam $300 to finish the painting, but Sam did not finish until October 4. Fox, when the painting had not been completed as stipulated in his contract with Johnson, leased another home. Johnson found another tenant who would lease the property at $700 a month, beginning October 15. Johnson then sued Keever for breach of contract, claiming damages of $650. This amount included the $300 Johnson paid Sam to finish the painting and $350 for rent for the first half of October, which Johnson had lost as a result of Keever's breach. Johnson had not yet paid Keever anything for Keever's work. Can Johnson collect the $650 from Keever? Explain.

13–5. Measure of Damages. Ben owns and operates a famous candy store. He makes most of the candy sold in the store, and business is particularly heavy during the Christmas season. Ben contracts with Sweet, Inc., to purchase ten thousand pounds of sugar, to be delivered on or before November 15. Ben informs Sweet that this particular order is to be used for the Christmas season business. Because of production problems, the sugar is not tendered to Ben until December 10, at which time Ben refuses the order because it is so late. Ben has been unable to purchase the quantity of sugar needed to meet the Christmas orders and has had to turn down numerous regular customers, some of whom have indicated that they will purchase candy elsewhere in the future. The sugar that Ben has been able to purchase has cost him ten cents per pound above Sweet's price. Ben sues Sweet for breach of contract, claiming as damages the higher price paid for the sugar from others, lost profits from this year's lost Christmas sales, future lost profits from customers who have indicated that they will discontinue

doing business with him, and punitive damages for failure to meet the contracted-for delivery date. Sweet claims Ben is limited to compensatory damages only. Discuss who is correct and why.

13–6. Consequential Damages. Kerr Steamship Co. delivered to Radio Corp. of America (RCA) a twenty-nine-word, coded message to be sent to Kerr's agent in Manila. The message included instructions on loading cargo onto one of Kerr's vessels. Kerr's profits on the carriage of the cargo were to be about $6,600. RCA mislaid the coded message, and it was never sent. Kerr sued RCA for the $6,600 in profits that it lost because RCA failed to send the message. Can Kerr recover? Explain. [*Kerr Steamship Co. v. Radio Corp. of America*, 245 N.Y. 284, 157 N.E. 140 (1927)]

13–7. Liquidated Damages versus Penalties. Dewerff was a teacher and basketball coach for Unified School District No. 315. The employment contract included a clause that read, in part: "Penalty for breaking contracts: . . . In all cases where a teacher under contract fails to honor the full term of his or her contract, a lump sum of $400 is to be collected if the contract is broken before August 1." Dewerff resigned on June 28, 1978, and he was told that the school would accept his resignation on his payment of the $400 stipulated in the contract. When Dewerff refused to make the $400 payment, the school district sued for $400 as "liquidated damages" on the basis of the contract clause. Dewerff argued that the contract provision was a "penalty" clause and unenforceable in this situation. Is Dewerff correct? Discuss. [*Unified School District No. 315, Thomas County v. Dewerff*, 6 Kan.App.2d 77, 626 P.2d 1206 (1981)]

13–8. Limitation of Liability. Westinghouse Electric Corp. entered into a contract with New Jersey Electric to manufacture and install a turbine generator for producing electricity. The contract price was over $10 million. The parties engaged in three years of negotiations and bargaining before they agreed on a suitable contract. The ultimate contract provided, among other things, that Westinghouse would not be liable for any injuries to the property belonging to the utility or to its customers or employees. Westinghouse warranted only that it would repair any defects in workmanship and materials appearing within one year of installation. After installation, part of New Jersey Electric's plant was damaged, and several of its employees were injured because of a defect in the turbine. New Jersey Electric sued Westinghouse, claiming that Westinghouse was liable for the damages because the exculpatory provisions in the contract were unconscionable. What was the result? [*Royal Indemnity Co. v. Westinghouse Electric Corp.*, 385 F.Supp. 520 (S.D.N.Y. 1974)]

13–9. Liquidated Damages versus Penalties. The Ivanovs, who were of Russian origin, agreed to purchase the Sobels' home for $300,000. A $30,000 earnest money deposit was placed in the trust account of Kotler Realty, Inc., the broker facilitating the transaction. Tiasia Buliak, one of Kotler's salespersons, negotiated the sale because she spoke fluent Russian. To facilitate the closing without the Ivanovs' having to be present, Buliak suggested they form a Florida corporation, place the cash necessary to close the sale in a corporate account, and give her authority to draw checks against it. The Ivanovs did as Buliak had suggested. Before the closing date of the sale, Buliak absconded with all of the closing money, which caused the transaction to collapse. Subsequently, because the Ivanovs had defaulted, Kotler Realty delivered the $30,000 earnest money deposit in its trust account to the Sobels. The Ivanovs then sued the Sobels, seeking to recover the $30,000. Was the clause providing that the seller could retain the earnest money if the buyer defaulted an enforceable liquidated damages clause or an unenforceable penalty clause? Discuss. [*Ivanov v. Sobel*, 654 So.2d 991 (Fla.App.3d 1995)]

13–10. Mitigation of Damages. Charles Kloss had worked for Honeywell, Inc., for over fifteen years when Honeywell decided to transfer the employees at its Ballard facility to its Harbour Pointe facility. Honeywell planned to hire a medical person at the Harbour Pointe facility and promised Kloss that if he completed a nursing program and became a registered nurse (RN), the company would hire him for the medical position. When Kloss graduated from his RN program, however, Honeywell did not assign him to a nursing or medical position. Instead, the company gave Kloss a job in its maintenance department. Shortly thereafter, Kloss left the company and eventually sued Honeywell for damages (lost wages) resulting from Honeywell's breach of the employment contract. One of the issues facing the court was whether Kloss, by voluntarily leaving the maintenance job at Honeywell, had failed to mitigate his damages. How should the court rule on this issue? Discuss. [*Kloss v. Honeywell, Inc.*, 77 Wash.App. 294, 890 P.2d 480 (1995)]

A Question of Ethics and Social Responsibility

13–11. In 1984, Robert Ryan, a widower with a ninth-grade education, fell behind in his mortgage payments and faced foreclosure. Norman Weiner told Ryan that he could loan him money to help him keep his house if Ryan signed over the deed to the house as "security" for the loan. When Weiner left, he took Ryan's deed to the property with him for "safekeeping." The next day, Ryan signed several papers without reading them, believing

that he was signing loan documents, because he trusted Weiner. In fact, he had signed documents that conveyed ownership of his house to Weiner. Weiner brought the mortgage payments up to date, continued to make the payments on the house, and paid for utilities and services necessary to maintain the house. Ryan continued to live in the house and made monthly payments to Weiner. The payments steadily increased from $100 to $310 a month. During that time, the mortgage payments increased also, from $93 in 1984 to $120 in 1991. In May 1991, Ryan concluded that he had paid off his mortgage and also his "loan" from Weiner and refused to make further payments. When Weiner initiated legal proceedings to evict Ryan, Ryan sought to rescind his transfer of the property to Weiner. Based on these facts, answer the following questions. [*Ryan v. Weiner*, 610 A.2d 1377 (Del. 1992)]

1. In view of the fact that Ryan voluntarily signed a document (contract) conveying his property to Weiner, should he be allowed to rescind that contract? What public policies are in conflict here?
2. When the equitable remedy of rescission and restitution is granted, the parties are restored to their status quo prior to the contract's formation. Is it possible in this case to restore the parties to their status quo prior to the 1984 transaction? Discuss.

Case Briefing Assignment

13–12. Examine Case A.4 [*Potter v. Oster*, 426 N.W.2d 148 (Iowa 1988)] in Appendix A. The case has been excerpted there in great detail. Review and then brief the case, making sure that you include answers to the following questions in your brief.

1. Why was Oster appealing the trial court's decision?
2. Why did Oster assert that allowing the remedy of rescission and restitution in this case would lead to an inequitable result?
3. According to the court, what three requirements must be met before rescission will be granted?
4. Did the Potters meet these three requirements, and if so, why?
5. What reasons did the court give for its conclusion that remedies at law were inadequate in this case?
6. Why are remedies at law presumed to be inadequate for breach of real estate contracts?

For Critical Analysis

13–13. Review the discussion of the doctrine of election of remedies in this chapter. What are some of the advantages and disadvantages of this doctrine?

INTERACTING WITH
The Internet

■ The following sites offer information on contract law, including breach of contract and remedies:

http://www.nolo.com/Chunkcm/CM9.html

http://www.law.cornell.edu/topics/contracts.html

■ For the most updated information on the Uniform Commercial Code, including drafts of revised articles, go to

http://www.law.cornell.edu/ucc/ucc.table.html

Or go to

http://www.kentlaw.edu/

■ Cornell Law School's Legal Information Institute offers online access to the Uniform Commercial Code as enacted in several of the states at

http://www.law.cornell.edu/statutes.html#state

Creditors' Rights and Bankruptcy

Contents

Chapter Objectives

After reading this chapter, you should be able to . . .

1. Summarize the various remedies available to creditors, and indicate how and when creditors use these remedies to collect debts.

2. Differentiate between suretyship and guaranty arrangements.

3. Outline the typical steps in a bankruptcy proceeding.

4. Describe what property constitutes a debtor's estate in a bankruptcy proceeding and what property is exempt.

5. Compare and contrast the types of relief available under Chapter 7, Chapter 11, Chapter 12, and Chapter 13 of the Bankruptcy Code.

America's font of practical wisdom, Benjamin Franklin, observed a truth known to all debtors—that creditors do observe "set days and times" and will expect to recover their money at the agreed-on times. Historically, debtors and their families have been subjected to punishment, including involuntary servitude and imprisonment, for their inability to pay debts. The modern legal system, however, has moved away from a punishment philosophy in dealing with debtors. In fact, many observers say that it has moved too far in the other direction, to the detriment of creditors.

Normally, creditors have no problem collecting the debts owed to them. When disputes arise over the amount owed, however, or when the debtor simply cannot or will not pay, what happens? What remedies are available to creditors when debtors default? In the first part of this chapter, we focus on other laws that assist the debtor and creditor in resolving their disputes without the debtor's having to resort to bankruptcy. The second part of this chapter discusses bankruptcy as a last resort in resolving debtor-creditor problems.

Laws Assisting Creditors

▼   Both the common law and statutory laws other than Article 9 of the UCC create various rights and remedies for creditors. We discuss here some of these rights and remedies.

Liens

As discussed earlier in this text, a *lien* is an encumbrance on property to satisfy a debt or protect a claim for the payment of a debt. Creditors' liens include the mechanic's lien, the artisan's lien, the innkeeper's lien, and judicial liens.

MECHANIC'S LIEN.   When a person contracts for labor, services, or materials to be furnished for the purpose of making improvements on real property (land and things attached to the land, such as buildings and trees—see Chapter 21) but does not immediately pay for the improvements, the creditor can file a **mechanic's lien** on the property. This creates a special type of debtor-creditor relationship in which the real estate itself becomes security for the debt.

For example, a painter agrees to paint a house for a homeowner for an agreed-on price to cover labor and materials. If the homeowner refuses to pay for the work or pays only a portion of the charges, a mechanic's lien against the property can be created. The painter is the lienholder, and the real property is encumbered with a mechanic's lien for the amount owed. If the homeowner does not pay the lien, the property can be sold to satisfy the debt. Notice of the *foreclosure* (the process by which the creditor deprives the debtor of his or her property) and sale must be given to the debtor in advance, however. Note that state law governs mechanic's liens. The time period within which a mechanic's lien must be filed is usually 60 to 120 days from the last date labor or materials were provided.

ARTISAN'S LIEN.   An **artisan's lien** is a security device created at common law through which a creditor can recover payment from a debtor for labor and materials furnished in the repair or improvement of personal property.

Mechanic's Lien A statutory lien on the real property of another, created to ensure payment for work performed and materials furnished in the repair or improvement of real property, such as a building.

Artisan's Lien A possessory lien given to a person who has made improvements and added value to another person's personal property as security for payment for services performed.

Making improvements on real property. Under what circumstances does the property become security for the cost of the improvements?

For example, Cindy leaves her diamond ring at the jeweler's to be repaired and to have her initials engraved on the band. In the absence of an agreement, the jeweler can keep the ring until Cindy pays for the services that the jeweler provides. Should Cindy fail to pay, the jeweler has a lien on Cindy's ring for the amount of the bill and normally can sell the ring in satisfaction of the lien.

In contrast to a mechanic's lien, an artisan's lien is *possessory*. The lienholder ordinarily must have retained possession of the property and have expressly or impliedly agreed to provide the services on a cash, not a credit, basis. Usually, the lienholder retains possession of the property. When this occurs, the lien remains in existence as long as the lienholder maintains possession, and the lien is terminated once possession is voluntarily surrendered—unless the surrender is only temporary. If it is a temporary surrender, there must be an agreement that the property will be returned to the lienholder. Even with such an agreement, if a third party obtains rights in that property while it is out of the possession of the lienholder, the lien is lost. The only way that a lienholder can protect a lien and surrender possession at the same time is to record notice of the lien (if state law so permits) in accordance with state lien and recording statutes.

Modern statutes permit the holder of an artisan's lien to foreclose and sell the property subject to the lien to satisfy payment of the debt. As with the mechanic's lien, the holder of an artisan's lien is required to give notice to the owner of the property prior to foreclosure and sale. The sale proceeds are used to pay the debt and the costs of the legal proceedings, and the surplus, if any, is paid to the former owner.

In the following case, a creditor with a purchase-money security interest (PMSI) in an automobile tried to repossess the property but failed to do so because an artisan's lien had also been placed on the car.

> **"Creditor: One of a tribe of savages dwelling beyond the Financial Straits and dreaded for their desolating incursions."**
>
> Ambrose Bierce, 1842–1914
> (American writer)

Case 14.1 ● National Bank of Joliet v. Bergeron Cadillac, Inc.

Appellate Court of Illinois, 1977.
66 Ill.2d 140,
361 N.E.2d 116,
5 Ill.Dec. 588.

HISTORICAL AND SOCIAL SETTING   *Before the UCC, there was generally no specific statutory rule concerning the priority of artisan's or mechanic's liens over other security interests (except for Section 11 of the Uniform Trust Receipts Act of 1933). Under the case law existing at that time, some courts ruled that the priority of the liens turned on whether the secured party had "title." The drafters of the UCC clarified the law in respect to the priority of liens. Article 9 provides that liens securing claims that arise from work intended to enhance or preserve the value of collateral take priority over earlier security interests, even if the earlier interests have been perfected [UCC 9–310]. The work must have been performed in the ordinary course of the lienholder's business, and the lienholder must possess the collateral. Of course, another state statute may make the lien subordinate to an earlier, perfected security interest. If there is a state statute creating artisan's or mechanic's liens but the statute is silent regarding priorities, UCC 9–310 provides that an artisan's or mechanic's lien takes priority.*

BACKGROUND AND FACTS   In February 1973, Gladys Schmidt borrowed $4,120 from the National Bank of Joliet to finance the purchase of a Cadillac. The bank held a security interest in the automobile and had perfected this interest by filing in the office of the secretary of state. In August 1973, Schmidt took the car to Bergeron Cadillac, Inc., for repairs, which cost approximately $2,000. When Schmidt failed to pay for the repairs, Bergeron Cadillac retained possession of the car and placed an artisan's lien on it. In September, Schmidt defaulted on her payments to the bank, and the bank later filed an action in an Illinois state court to gain possession of the Cadillac from Bergeron. The trial court held for Bergeron Cadillac, and the bank appealed.

IN THE WORDS OF THE COURT . . .
WARD, Chief Justice:
        * * * *

The plain language of [UCC] 9–310 gives the lien of persons furnishing services or materials upon goods in their possession priority over a perfected security interest unless the lien is created by statute and the statute expressly provides otherwise.
        * * * *

We cannot accept the plaintiff's contention that the General Assembly's enactment of the two statutes creating liens in favor of repairmen with respect to personal property evidenced an intent to supersede the artisan's common law lien. Both of the statutes expressly provide that the liens created shall be in addition to, and shall not exclude, any lien existing by virtue of the common law.

DECISION AND REMEDY   The Illinois appellate court affirmed the judgment of the trial court.

FOR CRITICAL ANALYSIS—ETHICAL CONSIDERATION   *Is the fact that artisan's liens "arise from work intended to enhance or preserve the value of collateral" a sufficient reason to give artisan's liens priority over perfected security interests?*

Innkeeper's Lien A possessory lien placed on the luggage of hotel guests for hotel charges that remain unpaid.

INNKEEPER'S LIEN.   An **innkeeper's lien** is another security device created at common law. An innkeeper's lien is placed on the baggage of guests for the agreed-on hotel charges that remain unpaid. If no express agreement has been made on the amount of those charges, then the lien will be for the reasonable value of the accommodations furnished. The innkeeper's lien is terminated either by the guest's payment of the hotel charges or by the innkeeper's surrender of the baggage to the guest, unless the surrender is temporary.

Additionally, the lien is terminated by the innkeeper's foreclosure and sale of the property.

JUDICIAL LIENS. When a debt is past due, a creditor can bring a legal action against the debtor to collect the debt. If a creditor is successful in the action, the court awards the creditor a judgment against the debtor (usually for the amount of the debt plus any interest and legal costs incurred in obtaining the judgment). Frequently, however, the creditor is unable to collect the awarded amount.

To ensure that a judgment in the creditor's favor will be collectible, creditors are permitted to request that certain nonexempt property of the debtor be seized to satisfy the debt. (As will be discussed later in this chapter, under state or federal statutes, certain property is exempt from attachment by creditors.) If the court orders the debtor's property to be seized prior to a judgment in the creditor's favor, the court's order is referred to as a *writ of attachment*. If the court orders the debtor's property to be seized following a judgment in the creditor's favor, the court's order is referred to as a *writ of execution*.

Attachment **Attachment** is a court-ordered seizure and taking into custody of property prior to the securing of a judgment for a past-due debt. Attachment rights are created by state statutes. Attachment is a *prejudgment* remedy, because it occurs either at the time of or immediately after the commencement of a lawsuit and before the entry of a final judgment. By statute, the restrictions and requirements for a creditor to attach before judgment are specific and limited. The due process clause of the Fourteenth Amendment to the Constitution limits the courts' power to authorize seizure of a debtor's property without notice to the debtor or a hearing on the facts.

To use attachment as a remedy, the creditor must have an enforceable right to payment of the debt under law, and the creditor must follow certain procedures. Otherwise, the creditor can be liable for damages for wrongful attachment. He or she must file with the court an *affidavit* (a written or printed statement, made under oath or sworn to) stating that the debtor is in default and stating the statutory grounds under which attachment is sought. The creditor must also post a

Attachment In the context of judicial liens, a court-ordered seizure and taking into custody of property prior to the securing of a judgment for a past-due debt.

International Perspective

Under the principle of comity (discussed in Chapter 24), a court in one country may enforce a judgment rendered by a court in another country. For example, suppose that a German court enters a judgment ordering the attachment of a debtor's assets that are located in the United States. A U.S. court will give full effect to that judgment unless the procedures underlying the German court's judgment seem too unfair. For example, in one case, a U.S. court refused to enforce a pretrial writ of attachment issued by a Spanish court. The U.S. court refused to "tie up all the assets of an enterprise in Illinois," because the defendant had no opportunity to appear before the Spanish court to contest the order.[a]

For Critical Analysis: *What criteria should a U.S. court use to determine the fairness of a foreign court's writ of attachment?*

a. *Carezo v. Babson Brothers Co.*, No. 91 C 7622 (N.D.Ill. 1992).

Writ of Attachment A court's order, prior to a trial to collect a debt, directing the sheriff or other officer to seize nonexempt property of the debtor; if the creditor prevails at trial, the seized property can be sold to satisfy the judgment.

Writ of Execution A court's order, after a judgment has been entered against the debtor, directing the sheriff to seize (levy) and sell any of the debtor's nonexempt real or personal property. The proceeds of the sale are used to pay off the judgment, accrued interest, and costs of the sale; any surplus is paid to the debtor.

Garnishment A legal process used by a creditor to collect a debt by seizing property of the debtor (such as wages) that is being held by a third party (such as the debtor's employer).

bond to cover at least court costs, the value of the loss of use of the good suffered by the debtor, and the value of the property attached. When the court is satisfied that all the requirements have been met, it issues a **writ of attachment,** which directs the sheriff or other officer to seize nonexempt property. If the creditor prevails at trial, the seized property can be sold to satisfy the judgment.

Writ of Execution If the debtor will not or cannot pay the judgment, the creditor is entitled to go back to the court and obtain a court order, directing the sheriff to seize (levy) and sell any of the debtor's nonexempt real or personal property that is within the court's geographical jurisdiction (usually the county in which the courthouse is located). This order is called a **writ of execution.** The proceeds of the sale are used to pay off the judgment, accrued interest, and the costs of the sale. Any excess is paid to the debtor. The debtor can pay the judgment and redeem the nonexempt property any time before the sale takes place. Because of exemption laws and bankruptcy laws, however, many judgments are virtually uncollectible.

Garnishment

Garnishment occurs when a creditor is permitted to collect a debt by seizing property of the debtor that is being held by a third party. Typically, a garnishment judgment is served on a debtor's employer so that part of the debtor's usual paycheck will be paid to the creditor. As a result of a garnishment proceeding, the court orders the debtor's employer to turn over a portion of the debtor's wages to pay the debt.

The legal proceeding for a garnishment action is governed by state law, and garnishment operates differently from state to state. According to the laws in some states, the creditor needs to obtain only one order of garnishment, which will then continuously apply to the debtor's weekly wages until the entire debt is paid. In other states, the creditor must go back to court for a separate order of garnishment for each pay period.

Both federal laws and state laws limit the amount of money that can be garnished from a debtor's weekly take-home pay.[1] Federal law provides a minimal framework to protect debtors from losing all their income in order to pay judgment debts.[2] State laws also provide dollar exemptions, and these amounts are often larger than those provided by federal law. Under federal law, garnishment of an employee's wages for any one indebtedness cannot be a ground for dismissal of an employee.

One of the questions courts have faced in recent years has to do with whether a debtor's pension fund can be attached by creditors, through garnishment or other proceedings, to satisfy a debt. Under federal law, certain types of pension funds may not be attached. The law is less clear, however, on whether pension funds, *after* they have been received by a retiree, can be subject to attachment by creditors. This issue is before the court in the following case.

---

1.   Some states (for example, Texas) do not permit garnishment of wages by private parties except under a child-support order.
2.   For example, the federal Consumer Credit Protection Act of 1968, 15 U.S.C. Sections 1601–1693r, provides that a debtor can retain either 75 percent of the disposable earnings per week or the sum equivalent to thirty hours of work paid at federal minimum wage rates, whichever is greater.

Case 14.2 ● United States v. Smith

United States Court of Appeals,
Fourth Circuit, 1995.
47 F.3d 681.

HISTORICAL AND SOCIAL SETTING *Pension plans have a significant financial impact on the lives of millions of Americans. At one time, some employees with long years of service were deprived of their pension benefits through a variety of purportedly unethical methods. For these and other reasons, Congress enacted the Employee Retirement Income Security Act of 1974 (ERISA).*[a] *ERISA provides that certain pension benefits "may not be alienated [transferred]." Some courts have interpreted this to mean that even after a retiree has received his or her bene-*

fit, the amount received cannot be subject to any court-ordered transfer.

BACKGROUND AND FACTS For nine years, Charles Smith asked his friends and acquaintances to invest their money in his business schemes. Smith used most of the money—estimated to be more than $350,000—for personal expenses. Smith was indicted for criminal fraud and pleaded guilty to that crime in a federal district court. The court imposed a prison sentence and ordered Smith to repay his victims as much as possible by turning over, each month, the entire amount of his pension benefits. Smith appealed the order, claiming that it violated the "anti-alienation" provision of ERISA.

IN THE WORDS OF THE COURT . . .
ERVIN, Chief Judge
* * * *

This court has long recognized a "strong public policy against the alienability of * * * ERISA [pension] benefits." The Supreme Court, as well, has found that it is not "appropriate to approve any * * * exception * * * ."
* * * *

* * * The government * * * cannot require Smith to turn over his pension benefits * * * . Understandably, there may be a natural distaste for the result we reach here. The statute, however, is clear. Congress has made a policy decision to protect the ERISA income of retirees, even if that decision prevents others from securing relief for the wrongs done them.

DECISION AND REMEDY The U.S. Court of Appeals for the Fourth Circuit vacated the lower court's order and remanded the case. The appellate court ordered the lower court to redetermine the amount that Smith pay to his victims, based on "a balance of the victims' interest in compensation and Smith's other financial resources."

FOR CRITICAL ANALYSIS—ETHICAL CONSIDERATION *Why does the law protect certain pension benefits from court-ordered transfers?*

———————
a. 29 U.S.C. Sections 1001–1461.

Creditors' Composition Agreements

Creditors may contract with the debtor for discharge of the debtor's liquidated debts (debts that are definite, or fixed, in amount) on payment of a sum less than that owed. These agreements are called **creditors' composition agreements** or *composition agreements* and are usually held to be enforceable.

Mortgage Foreclosure

Mortgage holders have the right to foreclose on mortgaged property in the event of a debtor's default. The usual method of foreclosure is by judicial sale of the property, although the statutory methods of foreclosure vary from state

Creditors' Composition Agreement An agreement formed between a debtor and his or her creditors in which the creditors agree to accept a lesser sum than that owed by the debtor in full satisfaction of the debt.

Mortgagee Under a mortgage agreement, the creditor who takes a security interest in the debtor's property.

Mortgagor Under a mortgage agreement, the debtor who gives the creditor a security interest in the debtor's property in return for a mortgage loan.

to state. If the proceeds of the foreclosure sale are sufficient to cover both the costs of the foreclosure and the mortgaged debt, the debtor receives any surplus. If the sale proceeds are insufficient to cover the foreclosure costs and the mortgaged debt, however, the **mortgagee** (the creditor-lender) can seek to recover the difference from the **mortgagor** (the debtor) by obtaining a *deficiency judgment* representing the difference between the mortgaged debt and the amount actually received from the proceeds of the foreclosure sale. The mortgagee obtains a deficiency judgment in a separate legal action that he or she pursues subsequent to the foreclosure action. The deficiency judgment entitles the mortgagee to recover the amount of the deficiency from other property owned by the debtor.

Suretyship and Guaranty

When a third person promises to pay a debt owed by another in the event the debtor does not pay, either a *suretyship* or a *guaranty* relationship is created. Suretyship and guaranty have a long history under the common law and provide creditors with the right to seek payment from the third party if the primary debtor defaults on his or her obligations. Exhibit 14–1 illustrates the relationship between a suretyship or guaranty party and the creditor.

Suretyship An express contract in which a third party to a debtor-creditor relationship (the surety) promises to be primarily responsible for the debtor's obligation.

Surety A person, such as a cosigner on a note, who agrees to be primarily responsible for the debt of another.

SURETY.   A contract of strict **suretyship** is a promise made by a third person to be responsible for the debtor's obligation. It is an express contract between the **surety** (the third party) and the creditor. The surety in the strictest sense is *primarily* liable for the debt of the principal. The creditor need not exhaust all legal remedies against the principal debtor before holding the surety responsible for payment. The creditor can demand payment from the surety from the moment the debt is due.

For example, Robert Delmar wants to borrow money from the bank to buy a used car. Because Robert is still in college, the bank will not lend him the funds unless his father, Joseph Delmar, who has dealt with the bank before, will cosign the note (add his signature to the note, thereby becoming a surety and thus jointly liable for payment of the debt). When Joseph Delmar cosigns

■ **Exhibit 14–1 Suretyship and Guaranty Parties**

In a suretyship or guaranty arrangement, a third party promises to be responsible for a debtor's obligations. A third party who agrees to be responsible for the debt even if the primary debtor does not default is known as a surety; a third party who agrees to be *secondarily* responsible for the debt only if the primary debtor defaults is known as a guarantor. As noted in Chapter 12, normally a promise of guaranty (a collateral, or secondary, promise) must be in writing to be enforceable.

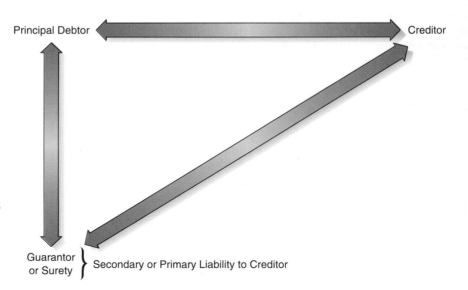

Principal Debtor — Creditor

Guarantor or Surety   } Secondary or Primary Liability to Creditor

the note, he becomes primarily liable to the bank. On the note's due date, the bank has the option of seeking payment from either Robert or Joseph Delmar, or both jointly.

GUARANTY.   A guaranty contract is similar to a suretyship contract in that it includes a promise to answer for the debt or default of another. With a guaranty arrangement, the **guarantor**—the third person making the guaranty—is *secondarily* liable. The guarantor can be required to pay the obligation *only after the principal debtor defaults,* and default usually takes place only after the creditor has made an attempt to collect from the debtor.

For example, a small corporation, BX Enterprises, needs to borrow funds to meet its payroll. The bank is skeptical about the creditworthiness of BX and requires Dawson, its president, who is a wealthy businessperson and the owner of 70 percent of BX Enterprises, to sign an agreement making himself personally liable for payment if BX does not pay off the loan. As a guarantor of the loan, Dawson cannot be held liable until BX Enterprises is in default.

The Statute of Frauds requires that a guaranty contract between the guarantor and the creditor must be in writing to be enforceable unless the *main purpose* exception applies. As discussed in Chapter 12, this exception provides that if the main purpose of the guaranty agreement is to benefit the guarantor, then the contract need not be in writing to be enforceable.

Guarantor A person who agrees to satisfy the debt of another (the debtor) only after the principal debtor defaults; a guarantor's liability is thus secondary.

DEFENSES OF THE SURETY AND THE GUARANTOR.   The defenses of the surety and the guarantor are basically the same. Therefore, the following discussion applies to both, although it refers only to the surety.

Certain actions will release the surety from the obligation. For example, any binding material modification in the terms of the original contract made between the principal debtor and the creditor—including the awarding of a binding extension of time for making payment—without first obtaining the consent of the surety will discharge a gratuitous surety completely and a compensated surety to the extent that the surety suffers a loss. (An example of a gratuitous surety is a father who agrees to assume responsibility for his daughter's obligation; an example of a compensated surety is a venture capitalist who will profit from a loan made to the principal debtor.)

Naturally, if the principal obligation is paid by the debtor or by another person on behalf of the debtor, the surety is discharged from the obligation. Similarly, if valid tender of payment is made, and the creditor rejects it with knowledge of the surety's existence, then the surety is released from any obligation on the debt.

Generally, the surety can use any defenses available to a principal debtor to avoid liability on the obligation to the creditor. Defenses available to the principal debtor that the surety *cannot* use include the principal debtor's incapacity or bankruptcy and the statute of limitations. The ability of the surety to assert any defenses the debtor may have against the creditor is the most important concept in suretyship, because most of the defenses available to the surety are also those of the debtor.

Obviously, a surety may also have his or her own defenses—for example, incapacity or bankruptcy. If the creditor fraudulently induced the surety to guarantee the debt of the debtor, the surety can assert fraud as a defense. In most states, the creditor has a legal duty to inform the surety, prior to the formation of the suretyship contract, of material facts known by the creditor that would substantially increase the surety's risk. Failure to do so is fraud and makes the suretyship obligation voidable. In addition, if a creditor surrenders the collateral to the debtor or impairs the collateral while knowing of the surety and without the surety's consent, the surety is released to the extent of any loss suffered from the creditor's actions. The primary reason for this requirement is to protect the surety who agreed to become obligated only because the debtor's collateral was in the possession of the creditor.

RIGHTS OF THE SURETY AND THE GUARANTOR.   The rights of the surety and the guarantor are basically the same. Therefore, again, the following discussion applies to both.

When the surety pays the debt owed to the creditor, the surety is entitled to certain rights. First, the surety has the legal **right of subrogation.** Simply stated, this means that any right the creditor had against the debtor now becomes the right of the surety. Included are creditor rights in bankruptcy, rights to collateral possessed by the creditor, and rights to judgments secured by the creditor. In short, the surety now stands in the shoes of the creditor and may pursue any remedies that were available to the creditor against the debtor.

Second, the surety has the **right of reimbursement** from the debtor. Basically, the surety is entitled to receive from the debtor all outlays made on behalf of the suretyship arrangement. Such outlays can include expenses incurred as well as the actual amount of the debt paid to the creditor.

Third, in the case of **co-sureties** (two or more sureties on the same obligation owed by the debtor), a surety who pays more than his or her proportionate share on a debtor's default is entitled to recover from the co-sureties the amount paid above the surety's obligation. This is the **right of contribution.** Generally, a co-surety's liability either is determined by agreement or, in the absence of agreement between the co-sureties, can be specified in the suretyship contract itself.

For example, assume that two co-sureties are obligated under a suretyship contract to guarantee the debt of a debtor. Together, the sureties' maximum liability is $25,000. As specified in the suretyship contract, surety A's maximum liability is $15,000, and surety B's is $10,000. The debtor owes $10,000 and is in default. Surety A pays the creditor the entire $10,000. In the absence of any agreement between the two co-sureties, surety A can recover $4,000 from surety B [($10,000/$25,000) × $10,000 = $4,000].

Laws Assisting Debtors

▼   The law protects debtors as well as creditors. Certain property of the debtor, for example, is exempt from creditors' actions. Probably the most familiar of these exemptions is the **homestead exemption.** Each state permits the debtor to retain the family home, either in its entirety or up to a specified dollar amount, free from the claims of unsecured creditors or trustees in bankruptcy. The purpose of the homestead exemption is to ensure that the debtor will retain some form of shelter.

Suppose that Van Cleave owes Acosta $40,000. The debt is the subject of a lawsuit, and the court awards Acosta a judgment of $40,000 against Van Cleave. The homestead of Van Cleave is valued at $50,000, and the state exemption on homesteads is $25,000. There are no outstanding mortgages or

Right of Subrogation The right of a person to stand in the place of (be substituted for) another, giving the substituted party the same legal rights that the original party had.

Right of Reimbursement The legal right of a person to be restored, repaid, or indemnified for costs, expenses, or losses incurred or expended on behalf of another.

Co-surety A joint surety; a person who assumes liability jointly with another surety for the payment of an obligation.

Right of Contribution The right of a co-surety who pays more than his or her proportionate share on a debtor's default to recover the excess paid from other co-sureties.

Homestead Exemption A law permitting a debtor to retain the family home, either in its entirety or up to a specified dollar amount, free from the claims of unsecured creditors or trustees in bankruptcy.

other liens on his homestead. To satisfy the judgment debt, Van Cleave's family home is sold at public auction for $45,000. The proceeds of the sale are distributed as follows:

1. Van Cleave is given $25,000 as his homestead exemption.
2. Acosta is paid $20,000 toward the judgment debt, leaving a $20,000 deficiency judgment that can be satisfied from any other nonexempt property (personal or real) that Van Cleave may have, if allowed by state law.

State exemption statutes usually include both real and personal property. Personal property that is most often exempt from satisfaction of judgment debts includes the following:

1. Household furniture up to a specified dollar amount.
2. Clothing and certain personal possessions, such as family pictures or a Bible.
3. A vehicle (or vehicles) for transportation (at least up to a specified dollar amount).
4. Certain classified animals, usually livestock but including pets.
5. Equipment that the debtor uses in a business or trade, such as tools or professional instruments, up to a specified dollar amount.

Consumer protection statutes (see Chapter 19) also protect debtors' rights. Of course, bankruptcy laws, which are discussed in the next section, are designed specifically to assist debtors in need of relief from their debts.

Bankruptcy and Reorganization

▼ At one time, debtors who could not pay their debts as they came due faced harsh consequences, including imprisonment and involuntary servitude. Today, in contrast, debtors have numerous rights. Some of these rights have already been mentioned. We now look at another significant right of debtors: the right to petition for bankruptcy relief under federal law.

Bankruptcy law in the United States has two goals—to protect a debtor by giving him or her a fresh start, free from creditors' claims; and to ensure equitable treatment to creditors who are competing for a debtor's assets. Bankruptcy law is federal law, but state laws on secured transactions, liens, judgments, and exemptions also play a role in federal bankruptcy proceedings.

Current bankruptcy law is based on the Bankruptcy Reform Act of 1978, as amended. In this chapter, we refer to this act, as amended, as the Bankruptcy Code (or, more simply, the Code). On page 380, the *Landmark in the Legal Environment* traces the historical evolution of bankruptcy law and the importance of the 1978 Bankruptcy Reform Act.

Bankruptcy Courts

Bankruptcy proceedings are held in federal bankruptcy courts. A bankruptcy court's primary function is to hold *core proceedings*[3] dealing with the

> "How often have I been able to trace bankruptcies and insolvencies to some lawsuit, . . . the costs of which have mounted up to large sums."
>
> Henry Peter Brougham, 1778–1868 (English politician)

---

3. Core proceedings are procedural functions, such as allowance of claims, decisions on preferences, automatic-stay proceedings, confirmation of bankruptcy plans, discharge of debts, and so on. These terms and procedures are defined and discussed in the following sections of this chapter.

Landmark in the Legal Environment
The Bankruptcy Reform Act of 1978

Article I, Section 8, of the U.S. Constitution gives Congress the power to establish "uniform Laws on the subject of Bankruptcies throughout the United States." Congress initially exercised this power in 1800, when the first bankruptcy law was enacted as a result of the business crisis created by restraints imposed on American trade by the British and French. In 1803, the law was repealed, and during the rest of the century—always in response to some crisis—Congress periodically enacted (and later repealed) other bankruptcy legislation. The National Bankruptcy Act of 1898, however, was not repealed, and since that time the United States has had ongoing federal statutory laws concerning bankruptcy. The 1898 act allowed only for *liquidation* in bankruptcy proceedings (which occurs when the debtor's assets are sold and the proceeds distributed to creditors). Some relief through reorganization was first allowed by amendments to the 1898 act in the 1930s.

Modern bankruptcy law is based on the Bankruptcy Reform Act of 1978, which repealed the 1898 act and represented a major overhaul of federal bankruptcy law. The 1978 act attempted to remedy previous abuses of bankruptcy law, introduced more clarity into bankruptcy procedures, and generally made it easier for debtors to obtain bankruptcy relief. A major organizational change in the 1978 act was the establishment of a new system of bankruptcy courts, in which each federal judicial district would

have an adjunct bankruptcy court with exclusive jurisdiction over bankruptcy cases. The act also specified that, in contrast to the lifetime terms of judges in other federal courts, bankruptcy court judges would have a fourteen-year term.

The 1978 act, referred to now simply as the Bankruptcy Code, has been amended several times since its passage. Amendments to the Code have created additional bankruptcy judgeships, placed bankruptcy court judges under the authority of the U.S. district courts, extended the bankruptcy trustee system nationally, granted more power to bankruptcy trustees in the handling of bankruptcy matters, and added a new chapter to the Bankruptcy Code (Chapter 12) to aid financially troubled farmers. The most significant amendments to the Bankruptcy Code were made by the Bankruptcy Reform Act of 1994. Among the many important changes of the 1994 act was the creation of a "fast-track" procedure for small-business debtors (those not involved in owning or managing real estate and with debts of less than $2 million) under Chapter 11 of the Code.

For Critical Analysis: *The Code no longer refers to persons who file for bankruptcy as "bankrupts" but simply as "debtors." What does this change in terminology signify, if anything?*

> **RECALL** Congress regulates the jursidiction of the federal courts, within the limits set by the Constitution. Congress can expand or reduce the number of federal courts at any time.

procedures required to administer the estate of the debtor in bankruptcy. Bankruptcy courts are under the authority of U.S. district courts (see Exhibit 3–2 on the federal court system in Chapter 3), and rulings from bankruptcy courts can be appealed to the district courts. Fundamentally, a bankruptcy court fulfills the role of an administrative court for the district court concerning matters in bankruptcy. A bankruptcy court can conduct a jury trial if the appropriate district court has authorized it and if the parties to the bankruptcy consent to a jury trial.

Types of Bankruptcy Relief

The Bankruptcy Code is contained in Title 11 of the U.S. Code (U.S.C.). Chapters 1, 3, and 5 of the Code include general definitional provisions and provisions governing case administration and procedures, creditors, the debtor, and the estate. These three chapters of the Code apply generally to all types of bankruptcies. The next five chapters set forth the different types of relief that debtors may seek. Chapter 7 provides for **liquidation** proceedings (the selling of all nonexempt assets and the distribution of the proceeds to the debtor's creditors). Chapter 9 governs the adjustment of the debts of municipalities. Chapter 11 governs reorganizations. Chapter 12 (for family farmers) and Chapter 13 (for individuals) provide for adjustment of the debts of parties with regular income.[4]

In the following pages, we deal first with liquidation proceedings under Chapter 7 of the Code. We then examine the procedures required for Chapter 11 reorganizations and for Chapter 12 and Chapter 13 plans.

Chapter 7—Liquidation

Liquidation is the most familiar type of bankruptcy proceeding and is often referred to as an *ordinary,* or *straight, bankruptcy.* Put simply, debtors in straight bankruptcies state their debts and turn their assets over to trustees. The trustees sell the assets and distribute the proceeds to creditors. With certain exceptions, the remaining debts are then discharged (extinguished), and the debtors are relieved of the obligation to pay the debts.

Any "person"—defined as including individuals, partnerships, and corporations—may be a debtor under Chapter 7. Railroads, insurance companies, banks, savings and loan associations, investment companies licensed by the Small Business Administration, and credit unions *cannot* be Chapter 7 debtors, however. Other chapters of the Code or other federal or state statutes apply to them. A husband and wife may file jointly for bankruptcy under a single petition.

Filing the Petition

A straight bankruptcy may be commenced by the filing of either a voluntary or an involuntary **petition in bankruptcy**—the document that is filed with a bankruptcy court to initiate bankruptcy proceedings.

VOLUNTARY BANKRUPTCY. A voluntary petition is brought by the debtor, who files official forms designated for that purpose in the bankruptcy court. A **consumer-debtor** (defined as an individual whose debts are primarily consumer debts) who has selected Chapter 7 must state in the petition, at the time of filing, that he or she understands the relief available under other chapters and has chosen to proceed under Chapter 7. If the consumer-debtor is represented by an attorney, the attorney must file an affidavit stating that he or she has informed the debtor of the relief available under each chapter. Any debtor who is liable on a claim held by a creditor can file a voluntary petition. The debtor does not even have to be insolvent to do so.[5] The voluntary petition contains the following schedules:

Liquidation The sale of all of the nonexempt assets of a debtor and the distribution of the proceeds to the debtor's creditors. Chapter 7 of the Bankruptcy Code provides for liquidation bankruptcy proceedings.

Salesperson in a snow-board shop. If this shop files for bankruptcy, could it continue in business?

Petition in Bankruptcy The document that is filed with a bankruptcy court to initiate bankruptcy proceedings. The official forms required for a petition in bankruptcy must be completed accurately, sworn to under oath, and signed by the debtor.

Consumer-Debtor An individual whose debts are primarily consumer debts (debts for purchases made primarily for personal or household use).

---

4. There are no Chapters 2, 4, 6, 8, or 10 in Title 11. Such "gaps" are not uncommon in the U.S.C. This is because chapter numbers (or other subdivisional unit numbers) are sometimes reserved for future use when a statute is enacted. (A gap may also appear if a law has been repealed.)

5. The inability to pay debts as they become due is known as *equitable* insolvency. A *balance-sheet* insolvency, which exists when a debtor's liabilities exceed assets, is not the test. Thus, it is possible for debtors to petition voluntarily for bankruptcy even though their assets far exceed their liabilities. This situation may occur when a debtor's cash flow problems become severe.

1. A list of both secured and unsecured creditors, their addresses, and the amount of debt owed to each.
2. A statement of the financial affairs of the debtor.
3. A list of all property owned by the debtor, including property claimed by the debtor to be exempt.
4. A listing of current income and expenses.

Order for Relief A court's grant of assistance to a complainant. In bankruptcy proceedings, the order relieves the debtor of the immediate obligation to pay the debts listed in the bankruptcy petition.

The official forms must be completed accurately, sworn to under oath, and signed by the debtor. To conceal assets or knowingly supply false information on these schedules is a crime under the bankruptcy laws. If the voluntary petition for bankruptcy is found to be proper, the filing of the petition will itself constitute an order for relief. An **order for relief** relieves the debtor of the immediate obligation to pay the debts listed in the petition. Once a consumer-debtor's voluntary petition has been filed, the clerk of the court (or person directed) must give the trustee and creditors mailed notice of the order for relief not more than twenty days after the entry of the order.

As mentioned previously, debtors do not have to be insolvent to file for voluntary bankruptcy. Debtors do not have unfettered access to Chapter 7 bankruptcy proceedings, however. Section 707(b) of the Bankruptcy Code allows a bankruptcy court to dismiss a petition for relief under Chapter 7 if the granting of relief would constitute "substantial abuse" of Chapter 7.

For example, the court might determine, after evaluating the debtor's schedule listing current income and expenses, that the debtor would be able to pay creditors a reasonable amount from future income. In this situation, the court might conclude that it would be a substantial abuse of Chapter 7 to allow the debtor to have his or her debts completely discharged. The court might dismiss the consumer-debtor's Chapter 7 petition after a hearing and encourage the debtor to file a repayment plan under Chapter 13 of the Code, when that would result in a substantial improvement in a creditor's receipt of payment. In the following case, the court had to decide whether granting a Chapter 7 discharge to the debtor would constitute substantial abuse.

Case 14.3   ● Matter of Blair

United States Bankruptcy Court, Northern District of Alabama, Eastern Division, 1995. 180 Bankr. 656.

HISTORICAL AND POLITICAL SETTING   *In the early 1980s, retailers and consumer lenders complained to Congress of an increasing number of Chapter 7 discharges being granted to debtors who creditors felt could actually afford to pay their debts. In response, Congress enacted the substantial abuse provision. The provision illustrates the tension between two principles underlying bankruptcy law: to give debtors the opportunity for a fresh start and to help*

creditors thwart the abuse of consumer credit. An indication of this tension is the fact that Congress did not define "substantial abuse" but left the task to the courts.

BACKGROUND AND FACTS   James Blair, Jr., owed primarily consumer debts of less than $7,000, and his income exceeded his living expenses by more than $200 a month. When he filed a petition for relief under Chapter 7, the court concluded that if he were to file a repayment plan under Chapter 13, his debts would be paid off in forty months. The bankruptcy administrator filed a motion to dismiss Blair's petition.

(Continued)

Case 14.3—continued

IN THE WORDS OF THE COURT . . .
JAMES S. SLEDGE, Bankruptcy Judge.

* * * *

* * * [T]he substantial abuse determination must be made on a case by case basis, in light of the totality of the circumstances. * * * [F]actors [that] should be considered * * * [include:] (1) Whether the bankruptcy petition was filed because of sudden illness, calamity, disability, or unemployment; (2) Whether the debtor incurred cash advances and made consumer purchases far in excess of his ability to pay; (3) Whether the debtor's proposed family budget is excessive or unreasonable; (4) Whether the debtor's schedules and statement of current income and expenses reasonably and accurately reflect the true financial condition; and (5) Whether the petition was filed in good faith.

* * * *

* * * [T]his Court concludes that granting this debtor relief under Chapter 7 would be a substantial abuse of the provisions of the chapter as well as perverting the purpose of the Bankruptcy Code: to give a fresh start to the honest but unfortunate debtor.

DECISION AND REMEDY The court dismissed Blair's petition.

FOR CRITICAL ANALYSIS—ECONOMIC CONSIDERATION *The court also stated that granting Blair relief under Chapter 7 would be "perverting the purpose of the Bankruptcy Code." What did the court mean by this statement?*

INVOLUNTARY BANKRUPTCY. An involuntary bankruptcy occurs when the debtor's creditors force the debtor into bankruptcy proceedings. An involuntary case cannot be commenced against a farmer[6] or a charitable institution (or those entities not eligible for Chapter 7 relief—mentioned earlier), however. For an involuntary action to be filed against other debtors, the following requirements must be met: If the debtor has twelve or more creditors, three or more of those creditors having unsecured claims totaling at least $10,775 must join in the petition. If a debtor has fewer than twelve creditors, one or more creditors having a claim of $10,775 may file.

If the debtor challenges the involuntary petition, a hearing will be held, and the bankruptcy court will enter an order for relief if it finds either of the following:

1. That the debtor is generally not paying debts as they become due.
2. That a general receiver, custodian, or assignee took possession of, or was appointed to take charge of, substantially all of the debtor's property within 120 days before the filing of the petition.

If the court grants an order for relief, the debtor will be required to supply the same information in the bankruptcy schedules as in a voluntary bankruptcy.

6. *Farmers* are defined as persons who receive more than 80 percent of their gross income from farming operations, such as tilling the soil; dairy farming; ranching; or the production or raising of crops, poultry, or livestock. Corporations and partnerships, as well as individuals, can be farmers.

An involuntary petition should not be used as an everyday debt-collection device, and the Code provides penalties for the filing of frivolous (unjustified) petitions against debtors. Judgment may be granted against the petitioning creditors for the costs and attorneys' fees incurred by the debtor in defending against an involuntary petition that is dismissed by the court. If the petition is filed in bad faith, damages can be awarded for injury to the debtor's reputation. Punitive damages may also be awarded.

Automatic Stay

Automatic Stay In bankruptcy proceedings, the suspension of virtually all litigation and other action by creditors against the debtor or the debtor's property; the stay is effective the moment the debtor files a petition in bankruptcy.

The filing of a petition, either voluntary or involuntary, operates as an **automatic stay** on (suspension of) virtually all litigation and other action by creditors against the debtor or the debtor's property. In other words, once a petition is filed, creditors cannot commence or continue most legal actions against the debtor to recover claims or to repossess property in the hands of the debtor. A secured creditor, however, may petition the bankruptcy court for relief from the automatic stay in certain circumstances. Additionally, the automatic stay does not apply to paternity, alimony, or family maintenance and support debts.

A creditor's failure to abide by an automatic stay imposed by the filing of a petition can be costly. If a creditor *knowingly* violates the automatic-stay provision (a willful violation), any party injured is entitled to recover actual damages, costs, and attorneys' fees and may also be entitled to recover punitive damages.

Creditors' Meeting and Claims

BE AWARE In most cases, creditors' meetings take only five or ten minutes. But a debtor who lies, commits bribery, conceals assets, uses a false name, or makes false claims is subject to a $5,000 fine and up to five years in prison.

Within a reasonable time after the order of relief is granted (not less than ten days or more than thirty days), the bankruptcy court must call a meeting of the creditors listed in the schedules filed by the debtor. The bankruptcy judge does not attend this meeting. The debtor must attend this meeting (unless excused by the court) and submit to an examination under oath. Failure to appear or making false statements under oath may result in the debtor's being denied a discharge of bankruptcy. At the meeting, the trustee ensures that the debtor is advised of the potential consequences of bankruptcy and of his or her ability to file under a different chapter.

In a bankruptcy case in which the debtor has no assets (called a "no-asset" case), creditors are notified of the debtor's petition for bankruptcy but are instructed not to file a claim. In such a situation, the creditors will receive no payment, and most, if not all, of the debtor's debts will be discharged. If there are sufficient assets to be distributed to creditors, however, each creditor must normally file a *proof of claim* with the bankruptcy court clerk within ninety days of the creditors' meeting to be entitled to receive a portion of the debtor's estate. The proof of claim lists the creditor's name and address, as well as the amount that the creditor asserts is owed to the creditor by the debtor. If a creditor fails to file a proof of claim, the bankruptcy court or trustee may file the proof of claim on the creditor's behalf but is not obligated to do so. If a claim is for a disputed amount, the bankruptcy court will set the value of the claim.

Creditors' claims are automatically allowed unless contested by the trustee, the debtor, or another creditor. The Code, however, does not allow claims for breach of employment contracts or real estate leases for terms longer than one year. These claims are limited to one year's wages or rent, despite the remaining length of either contract in breach.

Property of the Estate

On the commencement of a liquidation proceeding under Chapter 7, an **estate in property** is created. The estate consists of all the debtor's legal and equitable interests in property presently held, wherever located, together with certain jointly owned property, property transferred in transactions voidable by the trustee, proceeds and profits from the property of the estate, and certain after-acquired property. Interests in certain property—such as gifts, inheritances, property settlements (resulting from divorce), or life insurance death proceeds—to which the debtor becomes entitled *within 180 days after filing* may also become part of the estate. Thus, the filing of a bankruptcy petition generally fixes a dividing line: property acquired prior to the filing becomes property of the estate, and property acquired after the filing, except as just noted, remains the debtor's.

Estate in Property In bankruptcy proceedings, all of the debtor's legal and equitable interests in property presently held, wherever located, together with certain jointly owned property, property transferred in transactions voidable by the trustee, proceeds and profits from the property of the estate, and certain property interests to which the debtor becomes entitled within 180 days after filing for bankruptcy.

Exempted Property

Any individual debtor is entitled to exempt certain property from the property of the estate. The Bankruptcy Code establishes a federal exemption scheme under which the following property is exempt:[7]

1. Up to $16,150 in equity in the debtor's residence and burial plot (the homestead exemption).
2. Interest in a motor vehicle up to $2,575.
3. Interest in household goods and furnishings, wearing apparel, appliances, books, animals, crops, and musical instruments up to $425 in a particular item but limited to $8,625 in total.
4. Interest in jewelry up to $1,075.
5. Any other property worth up to $850, plus any unused part of the $16,150 homestead exemption up to an amount of $8,075.
6. Interest in any tools of the debtor's trade, up to $1,625.
7. Certain life insurance contracts owned by the debtor.
8. Certain interests in accrued dividends or interests under life insurance contracts owned by the debtor.
9. Professionally prescribed health aids.
10. The right to receive Social Security and certain welfare benefits, alimony and support payments, and certain pension benefits.
11. The right to receive certain personal injury and other awards, up to $16,150.

Individual states have the power to pass legislation precluding debtors in their states from using the federal exemptions. At least thirty-five states have done this. In those states, debtors may use only state (not federal) exemptions. In the rest of the states, an individual debtor (or husband and wife who file jointly) may choose between the exemptions provided under state law and the federal exemptions. State laws may provide significantly greater protection for debtors than federal law. For example, Florida and Texas traditionally have provided for generous exemptions for homeowners. State laws may also define the property coming within an exemption differently than the federal law.

---

7. The dollar amounts stated in the Bankruptcy Code are adjusted automatically every three years based on changes in the Consumer Price Index.

The Trustee's Role

U.S. Trustee A government
official who performs certain
administrative tasks that a
bankruptcy judge would
otherwise have to perform.

Promptly after the order for relief has been entered, an interim, or provisional, trustee is appointed by the **U.S. trustee** (a government official who performs certain administrative tasks that a bankruptcy judge would otherwise have to perform). The interim trustee administers the debtor's estate until the first meeting of creditors, at which time either a permanent trustee is elected or the interim trustee becomes the permanent trustee. Trustees are entitled to compensation for services rendered, plus reimbursement for expenses.

The basic duty of the trustee is to collect the debtor's available estate and reduce it to money for distribution, preserving the interests of *both* the debtor and unsecured creditors. In other words, the trustee is accountable for administering the debtor's estate. To enable the trustee to accomplish this duty, the Code gives him or her certain powers, stated in both general and specific terms.

TRUSTEE'S POWERS.   The trustee has the power to require persons holding the debtor's property at the time the petition is filed to deliver the property to the trustee. To enable the trustee to implement this power, the Code provides that the trustee occupies a position equivalent in rights to that of certain other parties. For example, in some situations, the trustee has the same rights as creditors and can obtain a judicial lien or levy execution on the debtor's property. This means that a trustee has priority over an unperfected secured party to the debtor's property. The trustee also has rights equivalent to those of the debtor.

In addition, the trustee has the power to avoid (cancel) certain types of transactions, including those transactions that the debtor could rightfully avoid, *preferences,* certain statutory *liens,* and *fraudulent transfers* by the debtor. Avoidance powers must be exercised within two years of the order for relief (the period runs even if a trustee has not been appointed). These powers of the trustee are discussed in more detail in the following subsections.

VOIDABLE RIGHTS.   A trustee steps into the shoes of the debtor. Thus, any reason that a debtor can use to obtain the return of his or her property can be used by the trustee as well. These grounds (for recovery) include fraud, duress, incapacity, and mutual mistake.

For example, Rob sells his boat to Inga. Inga gives Rob a check, knowing that there are insufficient funds in her bank account to cover the check. Inga has committed fraud. Rob has the right to avoid that transfer and recover the boat from Inga. Once an order for relief has been entered for Rob, the trustee can exercise the same right to recover the boat from Inga. If the trustee does not take action to enforce one of his or her rights, the debtor in a Chapter 7 bankruptcy will nevertheless be able to enforce that right.[8]

PREFERENCES.   A debtor is not permitted to transfer property or to make a payment that favors—or gives a **preference** to—one creditor over others. The trustee is allowed to recover payments made both voluntarily and involuntarily to one creditor in preference over another.

Preference In bankruptcy
proceedings, property transfers
or payments made by the debtor
that favor (give preference to)
one creditor over others. The
bankruptcy trustee is allowed to
recover payments made both
voluntarily and involuntarily to
one creditor in preference over
another.

---

8.   In a Chapter 11 reorganization (to be discussed later), for which generally no trustee is appointed, the debtor has the same avoiding powers as a trustee in a Chapter 7 liquidation. In repayment plans under Chapters 12 and 13 (also to be discussed later), a trustee must be appointed.

To have made a preferential payment that can be recovered, an *insolvent* debtor generally must have transferred property, for a *preexisting* debt, within *ninety days* of the filing of the petition in bankruptcy. The transfer must give the creditor more than the creditor would have received as a result of the bankruptcy proceedings. The trustee does not have to prove insolvency, as the Code provides that the debtor is presumed to be insolvent during this ninety-day period.

Sometimes the creditor receiving the preference is an insider—an individual, a partner, a partnership, or an officer or a director of a corporation (or a relative of one of these) who has a close relationship with the debtor. If this is the case, the avoidance power of the trustee is extended to transfers made within *one year* before filing; however, the *presumption* of insolvency is confined to the ninety-day period. Therefore, the trustee must prove that the debtor was insolvent at the time of an earlier transfer.

Not all transfers are preferences. To be a preference, the transfer must be made for something other than current consideration. Therefore, it is generally assumed by most courts that payment for services rendered within ten to fifteen days prior to the payment of the current consideration is not a preference. If a creditor receives payment in the ordinary course of business, such as payment of last month's telephone bill, the payment cannot be recovered by the trustee in bankruptcy. To be recoverable, a preference must be a transfer for an antecedent (preexisting) debt, such as a year-old printing bill. In addition, the Code permits a consumer-debtor to transfer any property to a creditor up to a total value of $600, without the transfer's constituting a preference. Also, payment of paternity, alimony, maintenance, and support debts is not a preference.

If a preferred creditor has sold the property to an innocent third party, the trustee cannot recover the property from the innocent party. The creditor, however, generally can be held accountable for the value of the property.

LIENS ON DEBTOR'S PROPERTY.   The trustee is permitted to avoid the fixing of certain statutory liens, such as a mechanic's lien, on property of the debtor. Liens that first become effective at the time of the bankruptcy or insolvency of the debtor are voidable by the trustee. Liens that are not perfected or enforceable against a good faith purchaser on the date of the petition are also voidable.

> **NOTE** What the trustee does with property recovered as a preference, in most cases, is to sell it and distribute the proceeds to the debtor's creditors.

FRAUDULENT TRANSFERS.   The trustee may avoid fraudulent transfers or obligations if they were made within one year of the filing of the petition or if they were made with actual intent to hinder, delay, or defraud a creditor. Transfers made for less than a reasonably equivalent consideration are also vulnerable if the debtor thereby became insolvent, was left engaged in business with an unreasonably small amount of capital, or intended to incur debts that would be beyond his or her ability to pay. When a fraudulent transfer is made outside the Code's one-year limit, creditors may seek alternative relief under state laws. State laws often allow creditors to recover for transfers made up to three years prior to the filing of a petition.

The court in the following case had to determine whether the debtors' contributions to their church, in the year preceding their filing of a Chapter 7 petition, could be recovered as "fraudulent transfers."

Case 14.4 ● In Re Newman

United States Bankruptcy Court,
District of Kansas, 1995.
183 Bankr. 239.

HISTORICAL AND POLITICAL SETTING
Commercial and religious laws have coexisted for at least as long as humans have attempted to write down either. English bankruptcy law can trace its origin to early Jewish customs and medieval Jewish commercial and bankruptcy law. Bankruptcy courts descend from English religious courts. U.S. bankruptcy law derives from English practices. Over the centuries, the recovery of fraudulent transfers has become a central tenet of bankruptcy law.

BACKGROUND AND FACTS Paul and Myrtle Newman filed a Chapter 7 petition. They listed their monthly income as

$1,556 and monthly expenses as $2,458. Their debts totaled more than $25,000, consisting mostly of credit-card and medical bills. Despite the Newmans' circumstances, within the year preceding their petition, they had donated more than $2,400 to the Midway Southern Baptist Church. The donations were pursuant to their "sincere and firmly held belief in tithing."[a] In return for most of the donations, the Newmans received "spiritual benefits" but nothing tangible. Michael Morris, the Newmans' bankruptcy trustee, filed a suit in a federal bankruptcy court against the church to recover the money that the Newmans had donated in the preceding year.

---

a. *Tithing* means contributing part of one's income (the term tithe means "one-tenth") to a church to support the clergy and church administration costs.

IN THE WORDS OF THE COURT ...
JOHN K. PEARSON, Bankruptcy Judge.

* * * *

* * * No fraud is required to recover transfers made gratuitously on the eve of bankruptcy. * * *

* * * [T]he trustee must show the following: (1) A transfer of an interest of the debtor in property occurred; (2) The transfer occurred within one year of the bankruptcy filing; (3) The debtor received less than equivalent value in exchange for the transfer; and (4) The debtor was insolvent on the date of the transfer. * * *

* * * [T]he transfers in question involved interests of the debtors in property, occurred within one year of the debtors' bankruptcy filing, and * * * the debtors were insolvent on the dates of the various transfers. * * *

* * * *

* * * [T]he focus is on whether the debtors received reasonably equivalent value in exchange for their transfers to the defendant. * * *

* * * *

"Reasonably equivalent" value in bankruptcy has long meant tangible benefit or economic value. * * *

* * * *

* * * Such economic benefit is clearly lacking in this case.

DECISION AND REMEDY The court granted the trustee's request.

FOR CRITICAL ANALYSIS—ETHICAL CONSIDERATION *What is the policy behind allowing for the recovery of certain transfers made prior to bankruptcy? Who benefits from this recovery?*

Property Distribution

Creditors are either secured or unsecured. A *secured* creditor has a security interest in collateral that secures the debt. An *unsecured* creditor does not have any security interest.

SECURED CREDITORS. The Code provides that a consumer-debtor, within thirty days of the filing of a Chapter 7 petition or before the date of the first meeting of the creditors (whichever is first), must file with the clerk a statement of intention with respect to the secured collateral. The statement must indicate whether the debtor will retain the collateral or surrender it to the secured party. Additionally, if applicable, the debtor must specify whether the collateral will be claimed as exempt property and whether the debtor intends to redeem the property or reaffirm the debt secured by the collateral. The trustee is obligated to enforce the debtor's statement within forty-five days after the statement is filed.

If the collateral is surrendered to the perfected secured party, the secured creditor can enforce the security interest either by accepting the property in full satisfaction of the debt or by foreclosing on the collateral and using the proceeds to pay off the debt. Thus, the secured party has priority over unsecured parties to the proceeds from the disposition of the secured collateral. Indeed, the Code provides that if the value of the secured collateral exceeds the secured party's claim, the secured party also has priority to the proceeds in an amount that will cover reasonable fees (including attorneys' fees, if provided for in the security agreement) and costs incurred because of the debtor's default. Any excess over this amount is used by the trustee to satisfy the claims of unsecured creditors. Should the secured collateral be insufficient to cover the secured debt owed, the secured creditor becomes an unsecured creditor for the difference.

UNSECURED CREDITORS. Bankruptcy law establishes an order or priority for classes of debts owed to unsecured creditors, and they are paid in the order of their priority. Each class of debt must be fully paid before the next class is entitled to any of the proceeds—if there are sufficient funds to pay the entire class. If not, the proceeds are distributed *proportionately* to each creditor in the class, and all classes lower in priority on the list receive nothing. The order of priority among classes of unsecured creditors is as follows:

1. Administrative expenses—including court costs, trustee fees, and bankruptcy attorneys' fees.
2. In an involuntary bankruptcy, expenses incurred by the debtor in the ordinary course of business from the date of the filing of the petition up to the appointment of the trustee or the issuance by the court of an order for relief.
3. Unpaid wages, salaries, and commissions earned within ninety days of the filing of the petition, limited to $4,300 per claimant. Any claim in excess of $4,300 is treated as a claim of a general creditor (listed as number 9 below).
4. Unsecured claims for contributions to be made to employee benefit plans, limited to services performed during 180 days prior to the filing of the bankruptcy petition and $4,300 per employee.
5. Claims by farmers and fishers, up to $4,300, against debtor operators of grain storage or fish storage or processing facilities.
6. Consumer deposits of up to $1,950 given to the debtor before the petition was filed in connection with the purchase, lease, or rental of property or the purchase of services that were not received or provided. Any claim in excess of $1,950 is treated as a claim of a general creditor (listed as number 9 below).

7. Paternity, alimony, maintenance, and support debts.
8. Certain taxes and penalties due to government units, such as income and property taxes.
9. Claims of general creditors.

If any amount remains after the priority classes of creditors have been satisfied, it is turned over to the debtor.

Discharge

From the debtor's point of view, the purpose of a liquidation proceeding is to obtain a fresh start through the discharge of debts.[9] Certain debts, however, are not dischargeable in a liquidation proceeding. Also, certain debtors may not qualify—because of their conduct—to have all debts discharged in bankruptcy.

EXCEPTIONS TO DISCHARGE.   Claims that are not dischargeable under Chapter 7 include the following:

1. Claims for back taxes accruing within three years prior to bankruptcy.
2. Claims for amounts borrowed by the debtor to pay federal taxes.
3. Claims against property or money obtained by the debtor under false pretenses or by false representations.
4. Claims by creditors who were not notified of the bankruptcy; these claims did not appear on the schedules the debtor was required to file.
5. Claims based on fraud or misuse of funds by the debtor while he or she was acting in a fiduciary capacity or claims involving the debtor's embezzlement or larceny.
6. Alimony, child support, and (with certain exceptions) property settlements.
7. Claims based on willful or malicious conduct by the debtor toward another or the property of another.
8. Certain government fines and penalties.
9. Certain student loans, unless payment of the loans imposes an undue hardship on the debtor and the debtor's dependents.
10. Consumer debts of more than $1,000 for luxury goods or services owed to a single creditor incurred within sixty days of the order for relief. This denial of discharge is a rebuttable presumption (that is, the denial may be challenged by the debtor), however, and any debts reasonably incurred to support the debtor or dependents are not classified as luxuries.
11. Cash advances totaling more than $1,000 that are extensions of open-end consumer credit obtained by the debtor within sixty days of the order for relief. A denial of discharge of these debts is also a rebuttable presumption.
12. Judgments or consent decrees against a debtor as a result of the debtor's operation of a motor vehicle while intoxicated.

In the following case, the debtor sought to have her student loans discharged in bankruptcy. The question before the court was whether payment of the loan would constitute an "undue hardship" for the debtor. (See this chapter's *Inside the Legal Environment* on page 392 for more detail on the Code's provisions on the nondischargeability of certain student loans.)

---

9. Discharges are granted under Chapter 7 only to *individuals,* not to corporations or partnerships. The latter may use Chapter 11, or they may terminate their existence under state law.

Case 14.5 ● In Re Baker

United States Bankruptcy Court,
Eastern District of Tennessee, 1981.
10 Bankr. 870.

HISTORICAL AND SOCIAL SETTING *In 1980, about 53 percent of married women in the United States were working, compared with about 41 percent ten years earlier. More than 60 percent of wives who were separated from their husbands worked outside the home in 1980, compared with about 52 percent in 1970; for divorced women, the figures were about 74 percent and 72 percent, respectively. On average, however, in 1980, women earned only 62 cents for every dollar that men earned. In American families, husbands averaged nearly $21,000 in earnings and wives, $8,600. At the same time, of mothers who were entitled to child support, less than 75 percent actually received any payments. Of mothers living below the poverty line, more than 60 percent received nothing at all.*

BACKGROUND AND FACTS Mary Lou Baker attended three different institutions of higher learning. At these three schools, she received educational loans totaling $6,635. After graduation, she was employed, but her monthly take-home pay was less than $650. Monthly expenses for herself and her three children were approximately $925. Her husband had left town and provided no child or other financial support. She received no public aid and had no other income. In January 1981, just prior to this action, Baker's church paid her gas bill so that she and her children could have heat in their home. One child had reading difficulty, and another required expensive shoes. Baker had not been well and had been unable to pay her medical bills. She filed for bankruptcy. In her petition, she sought a discharge of her educational loans based on the hardship provision.

IN THE WORDS OF THE COURT . . .
RALPH H. KELLEY, Bankruptcy Judge.

     *   *   *   *

     *   *   * The restriction [against discharge of student loans] was designed to remedy an abuse by students who, immediately upon graduation, would file bankruptcy to secure a discharge of educational loans. These students often had no other indebtedness and could easily pay their debts from future wages.

     *   *   *   *

     The court concludes that under the circumstances of this case, requiring the debtor to repay the debts * * * would impose upon her and her dependents an undue hardship. In passing [the restriction against discharge of student loans], Congress intended to correct an abuse. It did not intend to deprive those who have truly fallen on hard times of the "fresh start" policy of the new Bankruptcy Code.

DECISION AND REMEDY The debtor's student loans were discharged. Given the fact that she had "truly fallen on hard times," Baker should be allowed to have her debts discharged in bankruptcy to avoid undue hardship.

FOR CRITICAL ANALYSIS—ETHICAL CONSIDERATION *Why does the Bankruptcy Code generally prohibit the discharge of student loans, such as those obtained through government-guaranteed educational loan programs?*

OBJECTIONS TO DISCHARGE. In addition to the exceptions to discharge previously listed, the following circumstances (relating to the debtor's *conduct* and not the debt) will cause a discharge to be denied:

1. The debtor's concealment or destruction of property with the intent to hinder, delay, or defraud a creditor.
2. The debtor's fraudulent concealment or destruction of financial records.

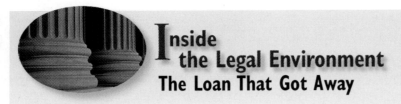

Inside the Legal Environment
The Loan That Got Away

Section 523(a)(8) of the Bankruptcy Code provides that certain educational debts are not dischargeable in bankruptcy—unless paying the debt causes "undue hardship" for the debtor (see, for example, Case 14.5). This section of the Code is designed to deter students from financing their education with funds borrowed through government-guaranteed loan programs or nonprofit scholarship programs and then, once they have graduated, filing for bankruptcy to discharge the educational debt.

Student loans come in many forms, and thus Section 523(a)(8) of the Code attempts to define fairly specifically the types of student loans that are not dischargeable. The Code states that a nondischargeable student debt is any debt "for an educational benefit overpayment or loan made, insured or guaranteed by a governmental unit, or made under any program funded in whole or in part by a governmental unit or nonprofit institution, or for an obligation to repay funds received as an educational benefit, scholarship or stipend." Given this lengthy definition, is it possible for a dispute to arise over whether a particular loan qualifies as a nondischargeable student loan?

Yes, it is, as evidenced by a case decided by the U.S. Court of Appeals for the Third Circuit in 1995. The case involved a $200,000 loan made by Santa Fe Medical Services, Inc., to a physician, Dr. Elizabeth Crowe, to entice Crowe to accept a job offer. Crowe needed the money to pay off an educational loan she had received through the U.S. National Health Service Corps (NHSC) Scholarship Program while she was in medical school. Crowe used the $200,000 to pay her debt to the NHSC, but then, a few years later—after she had repaid Santa Fe only about $5,000—she declared bankruptcy. During the bankruptcy proceedings, Santa Fe claimed that the debt was not dischargeable because it was an educational loan. When the bankruptcy court discharged the debt, Santa Fe appealed.

On appeal, Santa Fe urged the court to consider the purpose of the loan—which was to pay off an educational debt. The court, however, concluded that the real reason Santa Fe loaned the money to Crowe was not to facilitate her education, "which had long since been completed," but rather to induce Crowe to accept employment with Santa Fe

"by providing her with a means to repay her obligation to the NHSC." Furthermore, stated the court, the purpose of this section of the Code was "principally to protect government entities and nonprofit institutions of higher education—places which lend money or guarantee loans to individuals for educational purposes—from bankruptcy discharge." If Crowe did not repay Santa Fe, neither the federal Treasury nor the solvency of the NHSC would be affected.

In sum, the court held that this section of the Code simply "does not reach the particular type of loan at issue in this case." Loans made "pursuant to the terms of an employment contract" that are used to repay educational debts are not dischargeable in bankruptcy.[a]

For Critical Analysis: *If a student, after graduating from college, took out a loan from a bank to pay off an educational debt, should that loan be dischargeable in bankruptcy? Why does this issue rarely come before the courts?*

---

a. *In re Segal,* 57 F.3d 342 (3d Cir. 1995).

---

3. The granting of a discharge to the debtor within six years of the filing of the petition.[10]

When a discharge is denied under these circumstances, the assets of the debtor are still distributed to the creditors, but the debtor remains liable for the unpaid portions of all claims.

---

10.   A discharge under Chapter 13 of the Code within six years of the filing of the petition does not bar a subsequent Chapter 7 discharge when a good faith Chapter 13 plan paid at least 70 percent of all allowed unsecured claims and was the debtor's "best effort."

Ethical Perspective

The obvious effect of a discharge in bankruptcy is that the individual debtor is given a "fresh start" financially and can go forward without worrying about old debts that cannot be paid. The other consequences of a discharge in bankruptcy may not be so immediately apparent, however. The most notable of these consequences is the fact that the debtor's credit rating may be affected for years to come. A poor credit rating, in turn, may foreclose future opportunities for the debtor, including job opportunities.

There is no law prohibiting private employers from discriminating against job applicants on the basis of the applicants' prior bankruptcy status. The Bankruptcy Code does provide that the *government* may not "deny employment to, terminate the employment of, or discriminate with respect to employment against" a person who has been a bankruptcy debtor. In the parallel provision concerning private employers, however, the Code omits the phrase "deny employment to." Therefore, although a private employer may not fire an employee who has filed for bankruptcy protection, the employer may refuse to hire a job applicant who has done so. The courts provide little relief for job applicants who encounter such experiences, generally holding that the wording of the Code's provisions in these respects reflects the specific intentions of legislators who drafted those provisions.[a]

For Critical Analysis: *Can an employer's discrimination against job applicants on the basis of their history of bankruptcy ever be justified?*

a. See, for example, *Pastore v. Medford Savings Bank*, 186 Bankr. 553 (D.Mass. 1995).

EFFECT OF DISCHARGE. The primary effect of a discharge is to void, or set aside, any judgment on a discharged debt and prohibit any action to collect a discharged debt. A discharge does not affect the liability of a co-debtor.

REVOCATION OF DISCHARGE. The Code provides that a debtor's discharge may be revoked. On petition by the trustee or a creditor, the bankruptcy court may, within one year, revoke the discharge decree if it is discovered that the debtor was fraudulent or dishonest during the bankruptcy proceedings. The revocation renders the discharge void, allowing creditors not satisfied by the distribution of the debtor's estate to proceed with their claims against the debtor.

REAFFIRMATION OF DEBT. A debtor may voluntarily agree to pay off a debt—for example, a debt owed to a family member, close friend, or some other party—notwithstanding the fact that the debt could be discharged in bankruptcy. An agreement to pay a debt dischargeable in bankruptcy is referred to as a *reaffirmation agreement.* To be enforceable, reaffirmation agreements must be made before a debtor is granted a discharge, and they must be filed with the court. If the debtor is represented by an attorney, court approval is not required if the attorney files a declaration or affidavit stating that (1) the debtor has been fully informed of the consequences of the agreement (and a default under the agreement), (2) the agreement is made voluntarily, and (3) the agreement does not impose undue hardship on the debtor or the debtor's family. If the debtor is not represented by an attorney, court approval is required, and the agreement will be approved only if the court finds that the agreement will result in no undue hardship to the debtor and is in the best interest of the debtor.

The agreement must contain a clear and conspicuous statement advising the debtor that reaffirmation is not required. The debtor can rescind, or cancel, the agreement at any time prior to discharge or within sixty days of filing the agreement, whichever is later. This rescission period must be stated *clearly* and *conspicuously* in the reaffirmation agreement.

Chapter 11—Reorganization

> **"Debt rolls a man over and over, binding him hand and foot, and letting him hang upon the fatal mesh until the long-legged interest devours him."**
>
> Henry Ward Beecher, 1813–1887
> (American clergyman, writer, and abolitionist)

Workout An out-of-court agreement between a debtor and his or her creditors in which the parties work out a payment plan or schedule under which the debtor's debts can be discharged.

The type of bankruptcy proceeding used most commonly by a corporate debtor is the Chapter 11 *reorganization*. In a reorganization, the creditors and the debtor formulate a plan under which the debtor pays a portion of his or her debts and is discharged of the remainder. The debtor is allowed to continue in business. Although this type of bankruptcy is commonly a corporate reorganization, any debtor (except a stockbroker or a commodities broker) who is eligible for Chapter 7 relief is eligible for relief under Chapter 11.[11] Railroads are also eligible.

The same principles that govern the filing of a liquidation petition apply to reorganization proceedings. The case may be brought either voluntarily or involuntarily. The same principles govern the entry of the order for relief. The automatic-stay provision is also applicable in reorganizations.

In some instances, creditors may prefer private, negotiated debt-adjustment agreements, also known as **workouts,** to bankruptcy proceedings. Often these out-of-court workouts are much more flexible and thus more conducive to a speedy settlement. Speed is critical, because delay is one of the most costly elements in any bankruptcy proceeding. Another advantage of workouts is that they avoid the various administrative costs of bankruptcy proceedings.

A bankruptcy court, after notice and a hearing, may dismiss or suspend all proceedings in a case at any time if dismissal or suspension would better serve the interests of the creditors. The Code also allows a court, after notice and a hearing, to dismiss a case under reorganization "for cause." *Cause* includes the absence of a reasonable likelihood of rehabilitation, the inability to effect a plan, and an unreasonable delay by the debtor that is prejudicial to (may harm the interests of) creditors.[12] In the following widely publicized case, creditors of Johns-Manville Corporation sought to dismiss a voluntary Chapter 11 petition filed by Manville.

---

11.   *Toibb v. Radloff,* 501 U.S. 157, 111 S.Ct. 2197, 115 L.Ed.2d 145 (1991).
12.   See 11 U.S.C. Section 1112(b).

Case 14.6 ● In Re Johns-Manville Corp.

United States Bankruptcy Court, Southern District of New York, 1984. 36 Bankr. 727.

HISTORICAL AND ENVIRONMENTAL SETTING

In the late 1970s and early 1980s, the number of claims for injuries caused by asbestos in the products manufactured and sold by Johns-Manville Corporation was mounting.

Studies projected runaway asbestos-related health costs for the company within the foreseeable future. The accounting firm of Price Waterhouse advised the company that at least $1.9 billion would be needed as a reserve fund to meet those costs. This figure took into account only the moderate to severe asbestos disease cases, assumed that Manville's insurance companies would pay many of the costs, and did not include punitive damages. As the num-

(Continued)

Case 14.6—continued

ber of claims accelerated, Manville's insurance companies disavowed their liability. Asbestos-related property damage claims began to present another source of liability. Schools sought damages for their unknowing use of asbestos products in ceilings, walls, piping, ductwork, and boilers in school buildings. Manville estimated that it could need another $500 million to $1.4 billion to cover this liability. In addition, Manville had debts in the amount of approximately $700 million not related to the asbestos problem.

BACKGROUND AND FACTS On August 26, 1982, Johns-Manville Corporation, a highly successful industrial enterprise, filed for protection under Chapter 11 of the Bankruptcy Code. This filing came as a surprise to some of Manville's creditors, as well as to some of the other corporations that were also being sued, along with Manville, for injuries caused by asbestos exposure. Manville asserted that the approximately sixteen thousand lawsuits pending as of the filing date and the potential lawsuits of people who had been exposed but who would not manifest the asbestos-related diseases until sometime in the future necessitated its filing. Manville's creditors, on motion to the bankruptcy court, contended that Manville did not file in good faith, that Manville was not insolvent, and that therefore the voluntary Chapter 11 petition should be dismissed.

IN THE WORDS OF THE COURT . . .
BURTON R. LIFLAND, Bankruptcy Judge.
* * * *

In determining whether to dismiss [a Chapter 11 case], a court is not necessarily required to consider whether the debtor has filed in "good faith" because that is not a specified predicate under the Code for filing. Rather * * * good faith emerges as a requirement for the confirmation of a plan.
* * *

A "principal goal" of the Bankruptcy Code is to provide "open access" to the "bankruptcy process." * * *

Accordingly, the drafters of the Code envisioned that a financially beleaguered debtor with real debt and real creditors should not be required to wait until the economic situation is beyond repair in order to file a reorganization petition. * * * This philosophy not only comports with the elimination of an insolvency requirement, but also is a corollary of the key aim of Chapter 11 of the Code, that of avoidance of liquidation. * * *

In the instant case, not only would liquidation be wasteful and inefficient in destroying the utility of valuable assets of the companies as well as jobs, but, more importantly, liquidation would preclude just compensation of some present asbestos victims and all future asbestos claimants. This unassailable reality represents all the more reason for this Court to adhere to this basic potential liquidation avoidance aim of Chapter 11 and deny the motions to dismiss. Manville must not be required to wait until its economic picture has deteriorated beyond salvation to file for reorganization.

DECISION AND REMEDY The motions to dismiss the Manville petition were denied. The court concluded that a bankruptcy proceeding was appropriate in this situation.

FOR CRITICAL ANALYSIS—ETHICAL CONSIDERATION *In view of the fact that Manville was a solvent corporation, did it deserve the "fresh start" it achieved through Chapter 11 proceedings?*

Debtor in Possession

On entry of the order for relief, the debtor generally continues to operate his or her business as a **debtor in possession (DIP)**. The court, however, may appoint a trustee (often referred to as a *receiver*) to operate the debtor's business if gross

Debtor in Possession (DIP) In Chapter 11 bankruptcy proceedings, a debtor who is allowed to continue in possession of the estate in property (the business) and to continue business operations.

mismanagement of the business is shown or if appointing a trustee is in the best interests of the estate.

The DIP's role is similar to that of a trustee in a liquidation. The DIP is entitled to avoid preferential payments made to creditors and fraudulent transfers of assets that occurred prior to the filing of the Chapter 11 petition. The DIP has the power to decide whether to cancel or assume obligations under executory contracts (contracts that have not yet been performed) that were made prior to the petition.

Creditors' Committees

As soon as practicable after the entry of the order for relief, a creditors' committee of unsecured creditors is appointed. The committee may consult with the trustee or the DIP concerning the administration of the case or the formulation of the reorganization plan. Additional creditors' committees may be appointed to represent special interest creditors. Orders affecting the estate generally will not be entered without either the consent of the committee or a hearing in which the judge hears the position of the committee.

Businesses with debts of less than $2 million that do not own or manage real estate can avoid creditors' committees. In these cases, orders can be entered without a committee's consent.

The Reorganization Plan

A reorganization plan to rehabilitate the debtor is a plan to conserve and administer the debtor's assets in the hope of an eventual return to successful operation and solvency. The plan must be fair and equitable and must do the following:

1. Designate classes of claims and interests.
2. Specify the treatment to be afforded the classes. (The plan must provide the same treatment for each claim in a particular class.)
3. Provide an adequate means for execution.

Ethical Perspective

Chapter 11 reorganizations have become the target of substantial criticism. One of the arguments against Chapter 11 is that it allows the very managers who "bankrupted" a firm to continue to manage the firm as debtors in possession while the firm is in Chapter 11 proceedings. According to some critics, the main beneficiaries of Chapter 11 corporate reorganizations are not the shareholder-owners of the corporations but attorneys and current management. Basically, these critics argue that reorganizations do not preserve companies' assets, because large firms must pay millions of dollars for attorneys and accountants during the reorganization process, which can take years to complete.

Because of the expenses associated with reorganization proceedings, the chance that any one company will survive Chapter 11 proceedings is less than 7 percent. Only the very largest corporations seem to have a real chance of emerging from Chapter 11 proceedings as viable business entities.

For Critical Analysis: *Should Chapter 11 be scrapped, as some critics recommend? Should it be amended to set time limits on reorganization proceedings?*

FILING THE PLAN.   Only the debtor may file a plan within the first 120 days after the date of the order for relief. If the debtor does not meet the 120-day deadline, however, or if the debtor fails to obtain the required creditor consent (see below) within 180 days, any party may propose a plan. The plan need not provide for full repayment to unsecured creditors. Instead, unsecured creditors receive a percentage of each dollar owed to them by the debtor. If a small-business debtor chooses to avoid creditors' committees, the time for the debtor's filing is shortened to 100 days, and any other party's plan must be filed within 160 days.

ACCEPTANCE AND CONFIRMATION OF THE PLAN.   Once the plan has been developed, it is submitted to each class of creditors for acceptance. Each class must accept the plan unless the class is not adversely affected by the plan. A class has accepted the plan when a majority of the creditors, representing two-thirds of the amount of the total claim, vote to approve it. Even when all classes of claims accept the plan, the court may refuse to confirm it if it is not "in the best interests of the creditors." A spouse or child of the debtor can block the plan if it does not provide for payment of his or her claims in cash.

Even if only one class of claims has accepted the plan, the court may still confirm the plan under the Code's so-called **cram-down provision**. In other words, the court may confirm the plan over the objections of a class of creditors. Before the court can exercise this right of cram-down confirmation, it must be demonstrated that the plan "does not discriminate unfairly" against any creditors and that the plan is "fair and equitable."

The plan is binding on confirmation. The debtor is given a reorganization discharge from all claims not protected under the plan. This discharge does not apply to any claims that would be denied discharge under liquidation.

Chapter 13—Repayment Plan

▼ Chapter 13 of the Bankruptcy Code provides for the "Adjustment of Debts of an Individual with Regular Income." Individuals (not partnerships or corporations) with regular income who owe fixed unsecured debts of less than $269,250 or fixed secured debts of less than $807,750 may take advantage of bankruptcy repayment plans. This includes salaried employees; individual proprietors; and individuals who live on welfare, Social Security, fixed pensions, or investment income. Many small-business debtors have a choice of filing under either Chapter 11 or Chapter 13. There are several advantages to repayment plans. One advantage is that they are less expensive and less complicated than reorganization proceedings or liquidation proceedings.

A Chapter 13 case can be initiated only by the filing of a voluntary petition by the debtor. Certain liquidation and reorganization cases may be converted to Chapter 13 cases with the consent of the debtor. A Chapter 13 case may be converted to a Chapter 7 case at the request of either the debtor or, under certain circumstances, a creditor. A Chapter 13 case also may be converted to a Chapter 11 case after a hearing. On the filing of a petition under Chapter 13, a trustee must be appointed. The automatic stay previously discussed also takes effect. Although the stay applies to all or part of a consumer debt, it does not apply to any business debt incurred by the debtor.

Credit cards. Should debtors be allowed to discharge all credit-card debts in bankruptcy?

Cram-down Provision A provision of the Bankruptcy Code that allows a court to confirm a debtor's Chapter 11 reorganization plan even though only one class of creditors has accepted it. To exercise the court's right under this provision, the court must demonstrate that the plan does not discriminate unfairly against any creditors and is fair and equitable.

REMEMBER A secured debt is a debt in which a security interest in personal property or fixtures assures payment of the obligation.

The Repayment Plan

Shortly after the petition is filed, the debtor must file a repayment plan. This plan may provide either for payment of all obligations in full or for payment of a lesser amount. A plan of rehabilitation by repayment provides for the turnover to the trustee of such future earnings or income of the debtor as is necessary for execution of the plan. The time for payment under the plan may not exceed three years unless the court approves an extension. The term, with extension, may not exceed five years.

The Code requires the debtor to make "timely" payments, and the trustee is required to ensure that the debtor commences these payments. The debtor must begin making payments under the proposed plan within thirty days after the plan has been filed with the court. If the plan has not been confirmed, the trustee is instructed to retain the payments until the plan is confirmed and then distribute them accordingly. If the plan is denied, the trustee will return the payments to the debtor less any costs. Failure of the debtor to make timely payments or to begin payments within the thirty-day period will allow the court to convert the case to a liquidation bankruptcy or to dismiss the petition.

CONFIRMATION OF THE PLAN.   After the plan is filed, the court holds a confirmation hearing, at which interested parties may object to the plan. The court will confirm a plan with respect to each claim of a secured creditor under any of the following circumstances:

1. If the secured creditors have accepted the plan.
2. If the plan provides that creditors retain their claims against the debtor's property and if the value of the property to be distributed to the creditors under the plan is not less than the secured portion of their claims.
3. If the debtor surrenders the property securing the claim to the creditors.

OBJECTION TO THE PLAN.   Unsecured creditors do not have a vote to confirm a repayment plan, but they can object to it. The court can approve a plan over the objection of the trustee or any unsecured creditor only in either of the following situations:

1. When the value of the property to be distributed under the plan is at least equal to the amount of the claims.
2. When all the debtor's projected disposable income to be received during the three-year plan period will be applied to making payments. Disposable income is all income received *less* amounts needed to support the debtor and dependents and/or amounts needed to meet ordinary expenses to continue the operation of a business.

MODIFICATION OF THE PLAN.   Prior to the completion of payments, the plan may be modified at the request of the debtor, the trustee, or an unsecured creditor. If any interested party has an objection to the modification, the court must hold a hearing to determine approval or disapproval of the modified plan.

Discharge

After the completion of all payments, the court grants a discharge of all debts provided for by the repayment plan. Except for allowed claims not provided for by the plan, certain long-term debts provided for by the plan, and claims

BE CAREFUL Courts, trustees, and creditors carefully monitor Chapter 13 debtors. If payments are not made, a court can require a debtor to explain why and may allow a creditor to take back his or her property.

for alimony and child support, all other debts are dischargeable. A discharge of debts under a Chapter 13 repayment plan is sometimes referred to as a "superdischarge." One of the reasons for this is that the law allows a Chapter 13 discharge to include fraudulently incurred debt and claims resulting from malicious or willful injury. Therefore, a discharge under Chapter 13 may be much more beneficial to some debtors than a liquidation discharge under Chapter 7 might be.

Even if the debtor does not complete the plan, a hardship discharge may be granted if failure to complete the plan was due to circumstances beyond the debtor's control and if the value of the property distributed under the plan was greater than creditors would have received in a liquidation proceeding. A discharge can be revoked within one year if it was obtained by fraud.

A farmer prepares a field for planting a crop. If the farmer is forced to petition for bankruptcy relief under Chapter 12, what happens to the crop?

Chapter 12—Family-Farmer Plan

The Bankruptcy Code defines a *family farmer* as one whose gross income is at least 50 percent farm dependent and whose debts are at least 80 percent farm related. The total debt must not exceed $1.5 million. A partnership or closely held corporation that is at least 50 percent owned by the farm family can also take advantage of Chapter 12.

The procedure for filing a family-farmer bankruptcy plan is very similar to the procedure for filing a repayment plan under Chapter 13. The farmer-debtor must file a plan not later than ninety days after the order for relief. The filing of the petition acts as an automatic stay against creditors' actions against the estate.

The content of a family-farmer plan is basically the same as that of a Chapter 13 repayment plan. The plan can be modified by the farmer-debtor but, except for cause, must be confirmed or denied within forty-five days of the filing of the plan.

Court confirmation of the plan is the same as for a repayment plan. In summary, the plan must provide for payment of secured debts at the value of the collateral. If the secured debt exceeds the value of the collateral, the remaining debt is unsecured. For unsecured debtors, the plan must be confirmed if either the value of the property to be distributed under the plan equals the amount of the claim or the plan provides that all of the farmer-debtor's disposable income to be received in a three-year period (or longer, by court approval) will be applied to making payments. Completion of payments under the plan discharges all debts provided for by the plan.

A farmer who has already filed a reorganization or repayment plan may convert the plan to a family-farmer plan. The farmer-debtor may also convert a family-farmer plan to a liquidation plan.

Key Terms

artisan's lien 370
attachment 373
automatic stay 384
consumer-debtor 381

co-surety 378
cram-down provision 397
creditors' composition
  agreement 375

debtor in possession (DIP)
  395
estate in property 385
garnishment 374

Chapter Summary
Creditors' Rights and Bankruptcy

	LAWS ASSISTING CREDITORS
LIENS (See pages 370–374.)	1. **Mechanic's lien**—A nonpossessory, filed lien on an owner's real estate for labor, services, or materials furnished to or made on the realty. 2. **Artisan's lien**—A possessory lien on an owner's personal property for labor performed or value added. 3. **Innkeeper's lien**—A possessory lien on a hotel guest's baggage for hotel charges that remain unpaid. 4. **Judicial Liens**— a. **Attachment**—A court-ordered seizure of property prior to a court's final determination of the creditor's rights to the property. Attachment is available only on the creditor's posting of a bond and in strict compliance with the applicable state statutes. b. **Writ of execution**—A court order directing the sheriff to seize (levy) and sell a debtor's nonexempt real or personal property to satisfy a court's judgment in the creditor's favor.
GARNISHMENT (See pages 374–375.)	A collection remedy that allows the creditor to attach a debtor's money (such as wages owed) and property that are held by a third person.
CREDITORS' COMPOSITION AGREEMENT (See page 375.)	A contract between a debtor and his or her creditors by which the debtor's debts are discharged by payment of a sum less than the sum that is actually owed.
MORTGAGE FORECLOSURE (See pages 375–376.)	On the debtor's default, the entire mortgage debt is due and payable, allowing the creditor to foreclose on the realty by selling it to satisfy the debt.
SURETYSHIP OR GUARANTY (See pages 376–378.)	Under contract, a third person agrees to be primarily or secondarily liable for the debt owed by the principal debtor. A creditor can turn to this third person for satisfaction of the debt.
	LAWS ASSISTING DEBTORS
EXEMPTIONS (See pages 378–379.)	Numerous laws, including consumer protection statutes, assist debtors. Additionally, state laws exempt certain types of real and personal property from levy of execution or attachment. 1. **Real property**—Each state permits a debtor to retain the family home, either in its entirety or up to a specified dollar amount, free from the claims of unsecured creditors or trustees in bankruptcy (homestead exemption).

(Continued)

Chapter Summary, continued

EXEMPTIONS—continued (See pages 378–379.)	2. Personal property—Personal property that is most often exempt from satisfaction of judgment debts includes the following: a. Household furniture up to a specified dollar amount. b. Clothing and certain personal possessions. c. Transportation vehicles up to a specified dollar amount. d. Certain classified animals, such as livestock and pets. e. Equipment used in a business or trade up to a specified dollar amount.

BANKRUPTCY—A COMPARISON OF CHAPTERS 7, 11, 12, AND 13
(See pages 379–399.)

ISSUE	Chapter 7	Chapter 11	Chapters 12 and 13
PURPOSE	Liquidation.	Reorganization.	Adjustment.
WHO CAN PETITION	Debtor (voluntary) or creditors (involuntary).	Debtor (voluntary) or creditors (involuntary).	Debtor (voluntary) only.
WHO CAN BE A DEBTOR	Any "person" (including partnerships and corporations) except railroads, insurance companies, banks, savings and loan institutions, investment companies licensed by the Small Business Administration, and credit unions. Farmers and charitable institutions cannot be involuntarily petitioned.	Any debtor eligible for Chapter 7 relief; railroads are also eligible.	Chapter 12—Any family farmer (one whose gross income is at least 50 percent farm dependent and whose debts are at least 80 percent farm related) or any partnership or closely held corporation at least 50 percent owned by a farm family, when total debt does not exceed $1.5 million. Chapter 13—Any individual (not partnerships or corporations) with regular income who owes fixed unsecured debts of less than $269,250 or fixed secured debts of less than $807,750.
PROCEDURE LEADING TO DISCHARGE	Nonexempt property is sold with proceeds to be distributed (in order) to priority groups. Dischargeable debts are terminated.	Plan is submitted; if it is approved and followed, debts are discharged.	Plan is submitted and must be approved if the debtor turns over disposable income for a three-year period; if the plan is followed, debts are discharged.
ADVANTAGES	On liquidation and distribution, most debts are discharged, and the debtor has an opportunity for a fresh start.	Debtor continues in business. Creditors can either accept the plan, or it can be "crammed down" on them. The plan allows for the reorganization and liquidation of debts over the plan period.	Debtor continues in business or possession of assets. If the plan is approved, most debts are discharged after a three-year period.

For Review

1. What is a prejudgment attachment? What is a writ of execution? How does a creditor use these remedies?

2. What is garnishment? When might a creditor undertake a garnishment proceeding?

3. In a bankruptcy proceeding, what constitutes the debtor's estate in property? What property is exempt from the estate under federal bankruptcy law?

4. What is the difference between an exception to discharge and an objection to discharge?

5. In a Chapter 11 reorganization, what is the role of the debtor in possession?

Questions and Case Problems

14–1. Creditors' Remedies. In what circumstances would a creditor resort to each of the following remedies when trying to collect on a debt?

(a) Mechanic's lien.
(b) Artisan's lien.
(c) Innkeeper's lien.
(d) Writ of attachment.
(e) Writ of execution.
(f) Garnishment.

14–2. Rights of the Surety. Meredith, a farmer, borrowed $5,000 from Farmer's Bank and gave the bank $4,000 in bearer bonds to hold as collateral for the loan. Meredith's neighbor, Peterson, who had known Meredith for years, signed as a surety on the note. Because of a drought, Meredith's harvest that year was only a fraction of what it normally was, and he was forced to default on his payments to Farmer's Bank. The bank did not immediately sell the bonds but instead requested $5,000 from Peterson. Peterson paid the $5,000 and then demanded that the bank give him the $4,000 in securities. Can Peterson enforce this demand? Explain.

14–3. Rights of the Guarantor. Sabrina is a student at Sunnyside University. In need of funds to pay for tuition and books, she attempts to secure a short-term loan from University Bank. The bank agrees to make a loan if Sabrina will have someone financially responsible guarantee the loan payments. Abigail, a well-known businessperson and a friend of Sabrina's family, calls the bank and agrees to pay the loan if Sabrina cannot. Because of Abigail's reputation, the bank makes the loan. Sabrina makes several payments on the loan, but because of illness she is not able to work for one month. She requests that University Bank extend the loan for three months. The bank agrees and raises the interest rate for the extended period. Abigail has not been notified of the

extension (and therefore has not consented to it). One month later, Sabrina drops out of school. All attempts to collect from Sabrina have failed. University Bank wants to hold Abigail liable. Will the bank succeed? Explain.

14–4. Distribution of Property. Runyan voluntarily petitions for bankruptcy. He has three major claims against his estate. One is by Calvin, a friend who holds Runyan's negotiable promissory note for $2,500; one is by Kohak, an employee who is owed three months' back wages of $4,500; and one is by the First Bank of Sunny Acres on an unsecured loan of $5,000. In addition, Martinez, an accountant retained by the trustee, is owed $500, and property taxes of $1,000 are owed to Micanopa County. Runyan's nonexempt property has been liquidated, with the proceeds totaling $5,000. Discuss fully what amount each party will receive, and why.

14–5. Creditors' Remedies. Orkin owns a relatively old home valued at $45,000. He notices that the bathtubs and fixtures in both bathrooms are leaking and need to be replaced. He contracts with Pike to replace the bathtubs and fixtures. Pike replaces them and submits her bill of $4,000 to Orkin. Because of financial difficulties, Orkin does not pay the bill. Orkin's only asset is his home, which under state law is exempt up to $40,000 as a homestead. Discuss fully Pike's remedies in this situation.

14–6. Writ of Attachment. Topjian Plumbing and Heating, Inc., the plaintiff, sought prejudgment writs of attachment to satisfy an anticipated judgment in a contract action against Bruce Topjian, Inc., the defendant. The plaintiff did not petition the court for permission to effect the attachments but merely completed the forms, served them on the defendant and on the Fencers (the owners of a parcel of land that had previously belonged to the defendant), and recorded them at the registry of deeds. On what grounds might the court invalidate the attachments? [*Topjian Plumbing and Heating, Inc. v. Bruce Topjian, Inc.*, 129 N.H. 481, 529 A.2d 391 (1987)]

14–7. Rights of the Guarantor. Hallmark Cards, Inc., sued Edward Peevy, who had guaranteed an obligation owed to Hallmark by Garry Peevy. At the time of Edward Peevy's guaranty, Hallmark had in its possession property pledged as security by Garry Peevy. Before the suit was filed, Hallmark sold the pledged property without giving notice to Edward Peevy. Because the property sold did not cover the loan balance, Hallmark sued for the balance, seeking a deficiency judgment. Edward Peevy contended that because Hallmark had sold the property pledged by Garry Peevy as security for the obligation without notifying him (Edward Peevy), Hallmark was not entitled to a deficiency judgment against him. Hallmark contended that Edward Peevy was not entitled to notice of the sale of the collateral and was not required to give consent. Which party will prevail in court? Discuss. [*Hallmark Cards, Inc. v. Peevy*, 293 Ark. 594, 739 S.W.2d 691 (1987)]

14–8. Preferences. Fred Currey purchased cattle from Itano Farms, Inc. As payment for the cattle, Currey gave Itano Farms worthless checks in the amount of $50,250. Currey was later convicted of passing bad checks, and the state criminal court ordered him to pay Itano Farms restitution in the amount of $50,250. About four months after this court order, Currey and his wife filed for Chapter 7 bankruptcy protection. During the ninety days prior to the filing of the petition, Currey had made three restitution payments to Itano, totaling $14,821. The Curreys sought to recover these payments as preferences. What should the court decide? Explain. [*In re Currey*, 144 Bankr. 490 (D.Ida. 1992)]

14–9. Dismissal of Chapter 7 Case. Ellis and Bonnie Jarrell filed a Chapter 7 petition. The petition was not filed due to a calamity, sudden illness, disability, or unemployment—both Jarrells were employed. Their petition was full of inaccuracies that understated their income and overstated their obligations. For example, they declared as an expense a monthly contribution to an investment plan. The truth was that they had monthly income of $3,197.45 and expenses of $2,159.44. They were attempting to discharge a total of $15,391.64 in unsecured debts. Most of these were credit-card debts, at least half of which had been taken as cash advances. Should the court dismiss the petition? If so, why? Discuss. [*In re Jarrell*, 189 Bankr. 374 (M.D.N.C. 1995)]

A Question of Ethics and Social Responsibility

14–10. In September 1986, Edward and Debora Davenport pleaded guilty in a Pennsylvania court to welfare fraud and were sentenced to probation for one year. As a condition of their probation, the Davenports were ordered to make monthly restitution payments to the county probation department, which would forward the payments to the Pennsylvania Department of Public Welfare, the victim of the Davenports' fraud. In May 1987, the Davenports filed a petition for Chapter 13 relief and listed the restitution payments among their debts. The bankruptcy court held that the restitution obligation was a dischargeable debt. Ultimately, the United States Supreme Court reviewed the case. The Court noted that under the Bankruptcy Code, a debt is defined as a liability on a claim, and a claim is defined as a right to payment. Because the restitution obligations clearly constituted a right to payment, the Court held that the obligations were dischargeable in bankruptcy. [*Pennsylvania Department of Public Welfare v. Davenport*, 495 U.S. 552, 110 S.Ct. 2126, 109 L.Ed.2d 588 (1990)]

1. Critics of this decision contend that the Court adhered to the letter, but not the spirit, of bankruptcy law in arriving at its conclusion. In what way, if any, did the Court not abide by the "spirit" of bankruptcy law?

2. Do you think that Chapter 13 plans, which allow nearly all types of debts to be discharged, tip the scales of justice too far in favor of debtors?

Case Briefing Assignment

14–11. Examine Case A.5 [*Hawley v. Cement Industries, Inc.*, 51 F.3d 246 (11th Cir. 1995)] in Appendix A. The case has been excerpted there in great detail. Review and then brief the case, making sure that you include answers to the following questions in your brief.

1. How did the case originate, and who are the parties?
2. What was the central issue to be decided?
3. What law governs the issue?
4. How did the lower court decide the case?
5. What was the appellate court's decision on the matter?

For Critical Analysis

14–12. Since the reform of bankruptcy law in 1978, the number of annual bankruptcy filings has increased significantly. Just in the last decade, for example, the number of filings has more than tripled. By the mid-1990s, more than 900,000 bankruptcy petitions were being filed each year. Has the Bankruptcy Code made it too easy for debtors to avoid their obligations by filing for bankruptcy? What are the implications of the increased number of bankruptcy filings for future potential debtors who seek to obtain credit?

INTERACTING WITH
The Internet

■ The Legal Information Institute at Cornell University offers a collection of law materials concerning debtor-creditor relationships, including federal statutes and recent Supreme Court decisions on this topic, at

http://www.law.cornell.edu/topics/debtor_creditor.html

■ The U.S. Bankruptcy Code is online at

http://www.law.cornell.edu:80/uscode/11

■ Cornell Law School's Legal Information Institute provides a general introduction to bankruptcy law and links to related Internet resources at

http://www.law.cornell.edu/topics/bankruptcy.html

■ You can find links to an extensive number of bankruptcy resources on the Internet by accessing the Bankruptcy Lawfinder at

http://www.agin.com/lawfind/

■ The American Bankruptcy Institute (ABI) is also a good resource for bankruptcy information. The ABI site includes a collection of selected bankruptcy court decisions, daily and weekly summaries of important bankruptcy news, legislative updates, and so on. You can access the site at

http://www.abiworld.org

■ For a discussion of alternatives to bankruptcy, go to

http://apocalypse.berkshire.net/~mkb/

The site includes information on the following alternatives: Debt Workout, Do Nothing, and Pay Creditors.

Business Organizations

Contents

Chapter Objectives

After reading this chapter, you should be able to . . .

1. Identify and describe the three major traditional forms of business organization.

2. Summarize the advantages and disadvantages of doing business as a partnership and as a corporation, respectively.

3. Specify how the limited liability company addresses needs that are not met by traditional forms of business.

4. Define the term *franchise,* and indicate how a franchising relationship arises.

5. Describe the roles of corporate directors, officers, and shareholders.

405

> **"[E]veryone thirsteth after gaine."**
>
> Sir Edward Coke, 1552–1634
> (English jurist and politician)

Entrepreneur One who initiates and assumes the financial risks of a new enterprise and undertakes to provide or control its management.

Many Americans would agree with Sir Edward Coke that most people, at least, "thirsteth after gaine." Certainly, an entrepreneur's primary motive for undertaking a business enterprise is to make profits. An **entrepreneur** is by definition one who initiates and *assumes the financial risks* of a new enterprise and undertakes to provide or control its management.

One of the questions faced by any entrepreneur who wishes to start up a business is what form of business organization he or she should choose for the business endeavor. In this chapter, we first examine the basic features of the three major traditional business forms—sole proprietorships, partnerships, and corporations. We then look at a relatively new, but significant, business form: the limited liability company, or LLC. The LLC is rapidly becoming an attractive alternative to the traditional corporate form. The limited liability partnership, or LLP, is a variation of the LLC. We also discuss private franchises and touch on the roles, rights, and duties of corporate directors, officers, and shareholders, and ways in which conflicts among these corporate participants are resolved.

Major Traditional Business Forms

Traditionally, entrepreneurs have used three major forms to structure their business enterprises: the sole proprietorship, the partnership, and the corporation.

Sole Proprietorships

Sole Proprietorship The simplest form of business, in which the owner is the business; the owner reports business income on his or her personal income tax return and is legally responsible for all debts and obligations incurred by the business.

The simplest form of business is a **sole proprietorship.** In this form, the owner is the business; thus, anyone who does business without creating a separate business organization has a sole proprietorship. Sole proprietorships constitute over two-thirds of all American businesses. They are also usually small enterprises—about 1 percent of the sole proprietorships existing in the United States have revenues that exceed $1 million per year. Sole proprietors can own

A manager checks a shipment of the products that his firm sells. What form of organization would this firm likely find to be best for doing business and why?

and manage any type of business from an informal, home-office undertaking to a large restaurant or construction firm.

A major advantage of the sole proprietorship is that the proprietor receives all of the profits (because he or she assumes all of the risk). In addition, it is often easier and less costly to start a sole proprietorship than to start any other kind of business, as few legal forms are involved. This type of business organization also entails more flexibility than does a partnership or a corporation. The sole proprietor is free to make any decision he or she wishes to concerning the business—whom to hire, when to take a vacation, what kind of business to pursue, and so on. A sole proprietor pays only personal income taxes on profits, which are reported as personal income on the proprietor's personal income tax form. Sole proprietors are also allowed to establish certain tax-exempt retirement accounts such as in the form of Keogh plans.[1]

The major disadvantage of the sole proprietorship is that, as sole owner, the proprietor alone bears the burden of any losses or liabilities incurred by the business enterprise. In other words, the sole proprietor has unlimited liability, or legal responsibility, for all obligations incurred in doing business. This unlimited liability is a major factor to be considered in choosing a business form. Another disadvantage is that the proprietor's opportunity to raise capital is limited to personal funds and the funds of those who are willing to make loans. The sole proprietorship also has the disadvantage of lacking continuity upon the death of the proprietor. When the owner dies, so does the business— it is automatically dissolved. If the business is transferred to family members or other heirs, a new proprietorship is created.

What are the advantages of operating a bakery as a sole proprietorship?

Partnerships

Traditionally, partnerships have been classified as either general partnerships or limited partnerships. The two forms of partnership differ considerably in regard to legal requirements and the rights and liabilities of partners. We look here at the basic characteristics of each of these forms.

GENERAL PARTNERSHIPS. A **partnership** arises from an agreement, express or implied, between two or more persons to carry on a business for profit. Partners are co-owners of a business and have joint control over its operation and the right to share in its profits. No particular form of partnership agreement is necessary for the creation of a partnership, but for practical reasons, the agreement should be in writing. Basically, the partners may agree to almost any terms when establishing the partnership so long as they are not illegal or contrary to public policy.

A partnership is a legal entity only for limited purposes, such as the partnership name and title of ownership and property. A key advantage of the partnership is that the firm itself does not pay federal income taxes, although the firm must file an information return with the Internal Revenue Service (IRS). A partner's profit from the partnership (whether distributed or not) is taxed as individual income to the individual partner. The main disadvantage of the partnership is that the partners are subject to personal liability for partnership obligations. In other words, if the partnership cannot pay its debts, the personal assets of the partners are subject to creditors' claims.

Partnership An agreement by two or more persons to carry on, as co-owners, a business for profit.

---

1. A *Keogh plan* is a retirement program designed for self-employed persons through which a certain percentage of their income can be contributed tax free to the plan, and principal and interest earnings will not be taxed until funds are withdrawn from the plan.

Limited Partnership A partnership consisting of one or more general partners (who manage the business and are liable to the full extent of their personal assets for debts of the partnership) and of one or more limited partners (who contribute only assets and are liable only up to the amount contributed by them).

General Partner In a limited partnership, a partner who assumes responsibility for the management of the partnership and liability for all partnership debts.

Limited Partner In a limited partnership, a partner who contributes capital to the partnership but has no right to participate in the management and operation of the business. The limited partner assumes no liability for partnership debts beyond the capital contributed.

Corporation A legal entity formed in compliance with statutory requirements. The entity is distinct from its shareholders-owners.

S Corporation A close business corporation that has met certain requirements as set out by the Internal Revenue Code and thus qualifies for special income-tax treatment. Essentially, an S corporation is taxed the same as a partnership, but its owners enjoy the privilege of limited liability.

LIMITED PARTNERSHIPS.   A special and quite popular form of partnership is the **limited partnership,** which consists of at least one general partner and one or more limited partners. A limited partnership is a creature of statute, because it does not come into existence until a *certificate of partnership* is filed with the appropriate state office. A **general partner** assumes responsibility for the management of the partnership and liability for all partnership debts. A **limited partner** has no right to participate in the general management or operation of the partnership and assumes no liability for partnership debts beyond the amount of capital he or she has contributed. Thus, one of the major benefits of becoming a limited partner is this limitation on liability, both with respect to lawsuits brought against the partnership and the amount of money placed at risk.

Corporations

A third and very widely used type of business organizational form is the **corporation.** Corporations are owned by *shareholders*—those who have purchased ownership shares in the business. A *board of directors,* elected by the shareholders, manages the business. The board of directors normally employs *officers* to oversee day-to-day operations.

The corporation, like the limited partnership, is a creature of statute. The corporation's existence as a legal entity, which can be perpetual, depends generally on state law.

One of the key advantages of the corporate form of business is that the liability of its owners (shareholders) is limited to their investments. The shareholders usually are not personally liable for the obligations of the corporation. Another advantage is that a corporation can raise capital by selling shares of corporate stock to investors. A key disadvantage of the corporate form is that any distributed corporate income is taxed twice. The corporate entity pays taxes on the firm's income, and when income is distributed to shareholders, the shareholders again pay taxes on that income.

Some small corporations are able to avoid this double-taxation feature of the corporation by electing to be treated, for tax purposes, as an **S corporation.** Subchapter S of the Internal Revenue Code allows qualifying corporations to be taxed in a way similar to the way a partnership is taxed. In other words, an S corporation is not taxed at the corporate level. As in a partnership, the income is taxed only once—when it is distributed to the shareholder-owners, who pay personal income taxes on their respective shares of the profits.

International Perspective

Many nations permit businesspersons to establish limited partnerships. Often, as in the United States, limited partnerships must comply with statutory requirements. In Argentina, for example, the limited partnership (called a *sociedad en comandita*) is closely regulated by the government. Additionally, as in the United States, other nations commonly provide that in a limited partnership, the limited partners cannot partic-

ipate in management. In Argentina, for example, limited partners are known as "sleeping partners" and have limited liability so long as they do not actively participate in management.

For Critical Analysis: *The right to participate in management is an important right of partners in an ordinary partnership. Why are limited partners in a limited partnership prohibited from exercising this right?*

Major Traditional Business Forms Compared

▼ Exhibit 15–1 lists the essential advantages and disadvantages of each of the three major traditional forms of business organization. We select for discussion here four important concerns for anyone starting a business—the ease of creation, the liability of the owners, tax features, and the need for capital.

Ease of Creation

No formalities are required in starting a business as a sole proprietorship. A general partnership can be organized easily and inexpensively. A corporation must be organized according to specific statutory procedures, must have sufficient capitalization, and must pay other costs of formal incorporation. In fact, throughout its life, a corporation is subject to more governmental supervision and reporting requirements than a partnership or a sole proprietorship normally is.

Liability of Owners

Generally, sole proprietors and general partners have personal liability, whereas the liability of limited partners and shareholders of corporations is limited to their investments. The issue of liability is an important one for the firm's owners, who may not want to place their personal assets at risk in the event the business cannot meet its obligations. The form of the organization does not always in and of itself determine the liability of the owners, however. For example, a court may "pierce the corporate veil" in certain circumstances and hold corporate shareholders personally liable for corporate obligations.

Furthermore, creditors may not be willing to extend credit to a newly formed or small corporation precisely because of the limited liability of corporate owners. Typically, if a corporation has relatively few shareholders, a bank or other lender will require the shareholders to cosign or guarantee personally any loans made to the corporation. That is, the shareholders agree to become personally liable for the loan if the corporation cannot meet its debts or goes bankrupt. In essence, the shareholders become guarantors for the corporation's debt. Hence, the corporate form of business does not prevent the shareholders from having personal liability in such a situation, because they have assumed the liability voluntarily.

Tax Considerations

Various tax considerations must be taken into account when one decides how best to organize a business. As discussed earlier, income earned by a sole proprietor is simply taxed as personal income. Tax aspects of partnerships and corporations are summarized in Exhibit 15–2 on page 411.

The Need for Capital

One of the most common reasons for changing from a sole proprietorship to a partnership or a corporation is the need for additional capital to finance expansion. A sole proprietor can seek partners who will bring capital with them. The partnership might be able to secure more funds from potential lenders than could the sole proprietor.

> **"What is the difference between a taxidermist and a tax collector? The taxidermist takes only your skin."**
>
> Samuel Clemens (Mark Twain), 1835–1910 (American author and humorist)

CHARACTERISTIC	SOLE PROPRIETORSHIP	PARTNERSHIP	CORPORATION
Method of Creation	Created at will by the owner.	Created by agreement of the parties.	Charter issued by the state—created by statutory authorization.
Legal Position	Not a separate entity; the owner is the business.	Not a separate legal entity in some states.	Always a legal entity separate and distinct from its owners—a legal fiction for the purposes of owning property and being party to litigation.
Liability	Unlimited liability.	Unlimited liability.	Limited liability of shareholders—shareholders are not liable for the debts of the corporation
Duration	Determined by the owner; automatically dissolved on the owner's death.	Terminated by agreement of the partners, by the death of one or more of the partners, by withdrawal of a partner, by bankruptcy, and so on.	Can have perpetual existence.
Transferability of Interest	Interest can be transferred, but the individual's proprietorship then ends.	Although a partnership interest can be assigned, the assignee normally does not have the full rights of a partner.	Shares of stock can be transferred.
Management	Completely at the owner's discretion.	Each general partner has a direct and equal voice in management unless expressly agreed otherwise in the partnership agreement.	Shareholders elect directors, who set policy and appoint officers.
Taxation	The owner pays personal taxes on business income.	Each partner pays income taxes based on a pro rata share of net profits, whether or not they are distributed.	Double taxation—the corporation pays income tax on net profits, with no deduction for dividends, and shareholders pay income tax on disbursed dividends they receive.
Organizational Fees, Annual License Fees, and Annual Reports	None.	None.	All required.
Transaction of Business in Other States	Generally no limitation.	Generally no limitation.[a]	Normally must qualify to do business and obtain a certificate of authority.

[a]A few states have enacted statutes requiring that foreign (out-of-state) partnerships qualify to do business there—for example, 3 N.H.Rec.Stat. Ann. Chapter 305-A in New Hampshire.

■ **Exhibit 15–1**
Major Business Forms Compared

TAX ASPECT	PARTNERSHIP	CORPORATION
Federal Income Tax	Partners are taxed on proportionate shares of partnership income, even if not distrubted; the partnership files information returns only.	The income of the corporation is taxed; stockholders are also taxed on distributed dividends. The corporation files corporate income tax forms.
Accumulation	Partners are taxed on accumulated as well as distributed earnings.	Corporate stockholders are not taxed on accumulated earnings. There is, however, a penalty tax, in some instances, that the corporation must pay for "unreasonable" accumulations of income.
Captial Gains	Partners are taxed on their proportionate shares of capital gains, which are taxed at the ordinary income rate.	The corporation is taxed on captial gains and losses.
Exempt Income	Partners are not taxed on their proportionate shares of capital gains, which are taxed at the ordinary income rate.	Any exempt income distributed by a corporation is fully taxable income to the stockholders.
Pension Plan	Partners can adopt a Keogh plan, an Individual Retirement Account (IRA), or a 401-K plan.	Employees and officers who are also stockholders can be beneficiaries of a pension trust. The corporation can deduct its payments to the trust.
Social Security	Partners must pay a self-employment tax (in 1998, 12.4 percent on income up to $68,400, plus 2.9 percent Medicare tax on all income).	All compensation to officers and employee-stockholders is subject to Social Security taxation up to the maximum.
Death Benefits (excluding those provided by insurance)	There is no exemption for payments to partners' beneficiaries.	Benefits up to $5,000 can be recieved tax-free by employee's' beneficiaries.
State Taxes	The partnership is not subject to taxes. State income taxes are paid by each partner.	The corporation is subject to state income taxes (although these taxes can be deducted on federal returns).

When a firm wants to expand greatly, however, simply increasing the number of partners can result in too many partners and make it difficult for the firm to operate effectively. Therefore, incorporation might be the best choice for an expanding business organization because a corporation can obtain more capital by issuing shares of stock. The original owners will find that, although their proportionate ownership of the company is reduced, they are able to expand much more rapidly by selling shares in the company.

■ **Exhibit 15–2**
Tax Aspects of Partnerships and Corporations

S Corporations

The Subchapter S Revision Act of 1982 was passed "to permit the incorporation and operation of certain small businesses without the incidence of

Technology and The Entrepreneur

Technology via the Internet has allowed those with relatively small capital needs to access, easily and inexpensively, a large number of potential investors. Today, there are several on-line "matching services." These services specialize in matching potential investors with companies seeking investors. A small company seeking capital investment could pay a fee to a service provider, which would then include a description of the company in a list that it makes available to investors—also for a fee.

For example, one on-line service provider, American Venture, charges each company $150 for a six-month listing that includes a one-page summary of the company's business. Investors, for a fee of $95, can have access to American Venture's list of companies for a year. If an investor is interested in a particular company, he or she can contact the company directly. Other on-line providers offer even more services for entrepreneurs, including franchising opportunities.

Matching services are not new. For decades, several companies have provided such services by using computerized databases to match business firms' investment needs with potential investors. What is new is that many of these service providers are now going on-line and expanding the geographical scope of their operations.

For Critical Analysis: *How can an investor who uses on-line matching services protect himself or herself against fraud?*

income taxation at both the corporate and shareholder level."[2] Additionally, Congress divided corporations into two groups: S corporations, which have elected Subchapter S treatment, and *C corporations,* which are all other corporations. Certain close corporations can choose to qualify under Subchapter S of the Internal Revenue Code to avoid the imposition of income taxes at the corporate level while retaining many of the advantages of a corporation, particularly limited liability.

Qualification Requirements for S Corporations

Among the numerous requirements for S corporation status, the following are the most important:

1. The corporation must be a domestic corporation.
2. The corporation must not be a member of an affiliated group of corporations.
3. The shareholders of the corporation must be individuals, estates, or certain trusts. Partnerships and nonqualifying trusts cannot be shareholders. Corporations can be shareholders under certain circumstances.
4. The corporation must have seventy-five or fewer shareholders.
5. The corporation must have only one class of stock, although not all shareholders need have the same voting rights.
6. No shareholder of the corporation may be a nonresident alien.

Benefits of S Corporations

At times, it is beneficial for a regular corporation to elect S corporation status. Benefits include the following:

---

2.   Senate Report No. 640, 97th Congress, 1st Session (1981).

1. When the corporation has losses, the S election allows the shareholders to use the losses to offset other income.
2. When the shareholder's tax bracket is lower than the corporation's tax bracket, the S election causes the corporation's pass-through net income to be taxed in the shareholder's bracket. This is particularly attractive when the corporation wants to accumulate earnings for some future business purpose.
3. As mentioned, a single tax on corporate income is imposed at individual income tax rates at the shareholder level. (The income is taxable to shareholders whether or not it is actually distributed.)

> **"The art of taxation consists in so plucking the goose as to obtain the largest amount of feathers with the smallest possible amount of hissing."**
>
> Jean Baptiste Colbert, 1619–1683 (French politician and financial reformer)

Limited Liability Companies

The two most common forms of business organization selected by two or more persons entering into business together are the partnership and the corporation. As already explained—and summarized in Exhibits 15–1 and 15–2—each form has distinct advantages and disadvantages. For partnerships, the advantage is that partnership income is taxed only once (all income is "passed through" the partnership entity to the partners themselves, who are taxed only as individuals); the disadvantage is the personal liability of the partners. For corporations, the advantage is the limited liability of shareholders; the disadvantage is the double taxation of corporate income. For many entrepreneurs and investors, the ideal business form would combine the tax advantages of the partnership form of business with the limited liability of the corporate enterprise.

The limited partnership and the S corporation partially address these needs. The limited liability of limited partners, however, is conditional: limited liability exists only so long as the limited partner does *not* participate in management. The problem with S corporations is that only small corporations (those with seventy-five or fewer shareholders) may acquire S corporation status. Furthermore, with few exceptions, only *individuals* may be shareholders in an S corporation; partnerships and corporations cannot be shareholders. Finally, no nonresident alien can be a shareholder in an S corporation. This means that if, say, a European investor wanted to purchase shares in an S corporation, it would not be permissible.

> **CONTRAST** A partnership must have at least two partners. In many states, an LLC can be created with only one shareholder-member.

Since 1977, an increasing number of states have authorized a new form of business organization called the **limited liability company** (LLC). The LLC is a hybrid form of business enterprise that offers the limited liability of the corporation but the tax advantages of a partnership. The origins and characteristics of this increasingly significant form of business organization are discussed in the following *Landmark in the Legal Environment* on page 414. State statutes also now provide for limited liability partnerships (LLPs), which are similar in structure to limited liability companies.

Limited Liability Company (LLC) A hybrid form of business enterprise that offers the limited liability of the coporation but the tax advantages of a partnership.

Private Franchises

Times have changed dramatically since Ray Kroc, the late founder of McDonald's, launched the franchising boom more than thirty-five years ago. Today, over a third of all retail sales and an increasing part of the total annual national output of the United States are generated by private franchises.

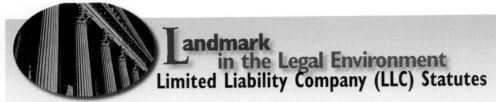

Landmark in the Legal Environment
Limited Liability Company (LLC) Statutes

In 1977, the state of Wyoming passed legislation authorizing the creation of a limited liability company (LLC). Interest in LLCs mushroomed after a 1988 ruling by the Internal Revenue Service that Wyoming LLCs would be taxed as partnerships instead of as corporations. Before that ruling, the only other state to enact a statute authorizing LLCs was Florida, in 1982. By 1996, all but a few states had enacted LLC statutes. The various state LLC statutes are far from uniform, but generally they are based on the Wyoming act's provisions, with variations based on the corporate and partnership laws of whatever state is enacting the LLC statute.

A major advantage of the LLC is that, like the partnership and the S corporation, the LLC does not pay taxes as an entity; rather, profits are "passed through" the LLC and paid personally by the members of the company. Another advantage is that the liability of members is limited to the amount of their investments. In an LLC, members are allowed to participate fully in management activities, and under at least one state's statute, the firm's managers need not even be members of the LLC. Yet another advantage is that corporations and partnerships, as well as foreign investors, can be LLC members, whereas these entities cannot be shareholders in S corporations. Also in contrast to S corporations, there is no limit on the number of shareholder-members of the LLC.

The disadvantages of the LLC are relatively few. Perhaps the greatest disadvantage is that LLC statutes differ from state to state, and thus any firm engaged in multistate operations may face difficulties. In an attempt to promote some uniformity among the states in respect to LLC statutes, the National Conference of Commissioners on Uniform State Laws drafted a uniform limited liability company statute for submission to the states to consider for adoption. Until all of the states have adopted the uniform law, however, an LLC in one state will have to check the rules in the other states in which the firm does business to ensure that it retains its limited liability.

Although LLCs emerged in the United States only in 1977, they have been in existence for over a century in other areas, including several European and South American nations. Part of the impetus behind creating LLCs in this country is that foreign investors are allowed to become LLC members. Generally, in an era increasingly characterized by global business efforts and investments, the LLC offers U.S. firms and potential investors from other countries flexibility and opportunities greater than those available through partnerships or corporations.

For Critical Analysis: *Given the fact that the tax and liability characteristics of partnerships and corporations have long been in existence, why is it that LLC statutes have emerged only recently?*

Franchise Any arrangement in which the owner of a trademark, trade name, or copyright licenses another to use that trademark, trade name, or copyright, under specified conditions or limitations, in the selling of goods and services.

Franchisee One receiving a license to use another's (the franchisor's) trademark, trade name, or copyright in the sale of goods and services.

Franchisor One licensing another (the franchisee) to use his or her trademark, trade name, or copyright in the sale of goods or services.

A **franchise** is defined as any arrangement in which the owner of a trademark, a trade name, or a copyright licenses others to use the trademark, trade name, or copyright in the selling of goods or services. A **franchisee** (a purchaser of a franchise) is generally legally independent of the **franchisor** (the seller of the franchise). At the same time, the franchise is economically dependent on the franchisor's integrated business system. In other words, a franchisee can operate as an independent businessperson but still obtain the advantages of a regional or national organization. Well-known franchises include McDonald's, KFC, and Burger King.

Types of Franchises

Because the franchising industry is so extensive (at least sixty-five types of distinct businesses sell franchises), it is difficult to summarize the many types of franchises that now exist. Generally, though, the majority of franchises fall into one of the following three classifications: distributorships, chain-style business operations, or manufacturing or processing-plant arrangements. We briefly describe these types of franchises here.

DISTRIBUTORSHIP.   A *distributorship* arises when a manufacturing concern (franchisor) licenses a dealer (franchisee) to sell its product. Often, a distributorship covers an exclusive territory. An example of this type of franchise is an automobile dealership.

CHAIN-STYLE BUSINESS OPERATION.   A *chain-style business operation* exists when a franchise operates under a franchisor's trade name and is identified as a member of a select group of dealers that engages in the franchisor's business. Often, the franchisor requires that the franchisee maintain certain standards of operation. In addition, sometimes the franchisee is obligated to deal exclusively with the franchisor to obtain materials and supplies. Examples of this type of franchise are McDonald's and most other fast-food chains.

MANUFACTURING OR PROCESSING-PLANT ARRANGEMENT.   A *manufacturing or processing-plant arrangement* exists when the franchisor transmits to the franchisee the essential ingredients or formula to make a particular product. The franchisee then markets the product either at wholesale or at retail in accordance with the franchisor's standards. Examples of this type of franchise are Coca-Cola and other soft-drink bottling companies.

Familiar franchises compete for business. What laws govern the relationship between franchisors and franchisees?

Laws Governing Franchising

Because a franchise relationship is primarily a contractual relationship, it is governed by contract law. If the franchise exists primarily for the sale of products manufactured by the franchisor, the law governing sales contracts as expressed in Article 2 of the Uniform Commercial Code applies (see Chapter 13). Additionally, the federal government and most states have enacted laws governing certain aspects of franchising. Generally, these laws are designed to protect prospective franchisees from dishonest franchisors and to prohibit franchisors from terminating franchises without good cause.

> **KEEP IN MIND** Because a franchise involves the licensing of a trademark, a trade name, or a copyright, the law governing intellectual property may apply in some cases.

FEDERAL REGULATION OF FRANCHISING.   Automobile dealership franchisees are protected from automobile manufacturers' bad faith termination of their franchises by the Automobile Dealers' Franchise Act[3]—also known as the Automobile Dealers' Day in Court Act—of 1965. If a manufacturer-franchisor terminates a franchise because of a dealer-franchisee's failure to comply with unreasonable demands (for example, failure to attain an unrealistically high sales quota), the manufacturer may be liable for damages.

Another federal statute is the Petroleum Marketing Practices Act (PMPA)[4] of 1979, which prescribes the grounds and conditions under which a franchisor may terminate or decline to renew a gasoline station franchise. Federal antitrust laws (discussed in Chapter 22), which prohibit certain types of anticompetitive agreements, may also apply in certain circumstances.

In 1979, the Federal Trade Commission (FTC) issued regulations that require franchisors to disclose material facts necessary to a prospective franchisee's making an informed decision concerning the purchase of a franchise.

---

3.   15 U.S.C. Sections 1221 *et seq.*
4.   15 U.S.C. Sections 2801 *et seq.*

Ethical Perspective

A franchising relationship is based on a contract, and contract law thus applies. Why, then, has the government deemed it necessary to enact laws to protect franchisees from the consequences of contracts into which they have voluntarily entered? One reason is that a franchisee often relies heavily on information about the business provided by the franchisor when deciding to purchase a franchise. Disclosure laws, such as the FTC rule and disclosure requirements under state statutes, help to ensure that prospective franchisees have accurate information when deciding whether to enter into a franchise contract.

Another reason is that many franchise contracts are essentially adhesion contracts—in the sense that the purchaser of a franchise often has little bargaining power relative to the franchisor and little say in the contract provisions. Additionally, franchise contracts are typically lengthy documents, consisting of perhaps fifty pages (McDonald's eleven-page contract is an exception). A franchisee who is relatively inexperienced in business may not realize the economic and legal consequences of particular clauses in the contract or of the absence of certain clauses—such as a clause granting the franchisee exclusive rights to sell the franchisor's products in a particular territory.

For Critical Analysis: *Are lengthy franchise contracts necessarily disadvantageous to franchisees? Explain.*

> **REMEMBER** Unfair contracts between a party with a great amount of bargaining power and another with little power are generally not enforced. This is part of the freedom *from* contract.

STATE REGULATION OF FRANCHISING.   State legislation tends to be similar to federal statutes and the FTC regulations. For example, to protect franchisees, a state law might require the disclosure of information that is material to making an informed decision regarding the purchase of a franchise. This could include such information as the actual costs of operation, recurring expenses, and profits earned, along with facts substantiating these figures. State deceptive trade practices acts may also prohibit certain types of actions on the part of franchisors.

In response to the need for a uniform franchise law, the National Conference of Commissioners on Uniform State Laws drafted a model law that standardizes the various state franchise regulations. Because the uniform law represents a compromise of so many diverse interests, it has met with little success in being adopted as law by the various states.

The Franchise Contract

The franchise relationship is defined by a contract between the franchisor and the franchisee. The franchise contract specifies the terms and conditions of the franchise and spells out the rights and duties of the franchisor and the franchisee. If either party fails to perform the contractual duties, that party may be subject to a lawsuit for breach of contract. (If a franchisee is induced to enter into a franchise contract by the franchisor's fraudulent misrepresentation, the franchisor may also be liable for damages. See, for example, the case discussed in this chapter's *Inside the Legal Environment.*)

Because each type of franchise relationship has its own characteristics, it is difficult to describe the broad range of details a franchising contract may include. In the remaining pages of this chapter, we look at some of the major issues that typically are addressed in a franchise contract.

PAYMENT FOR THE FRANCHISE.   The franchisee ordinarily pays an initial fee or lump-sum price for the franchise license (the privilege of being granted a fran-

Inside the Legal Environment
A Case of Nondisclosure

Franchisors usually have numerous statistics and market studies available for prospective franchisees to examine. These data enable prospective franchisees to evaluate the likely return on their investments and to make an informed decision. What if a franchisor does not disclose certain data to a prospective franchisee—data that might dissuade the prospective franchisee from purchasing the franchise? Ford Motor Company learned the answer to this question when it was ordered to pay over $7.5 million in damages (including $6 million in punitive damages) to its franchisees who sued it for fraudulent misrepresentation.

In 1988, the plaintiffs, Samuel Foster II and Dee-Witt Sperau, had acquired a Ford dealership in Selma, Alabama. Foster was an African American, and he and Sperau had purchased the dealership pursuant to Ford's minority dealership program. Since the 1960s, Ford had actively recruited minority dealers and provided them with a number of special benefits, including training and financial assistance. In 1987, Cornelius Willingham, an employee in Ford's district sales office in Charlotte,

North Carolina, discussed the minority program with Foster. Foster later testified that Willingham had told him that the vast majority of African American dealers participating in the program were making profits and receiving a good return on their investments. Other Ford representatives with whom Foster dealt confirmed Willingham's representations.

In fact, the Ford representatives knew from studies of the minority program that the failure rate of minority dealers during the first two years was extremely high. None of the Ford representatives disclosed this information to either Foster or Sperau, however. If they had disclosed the information, Foster and Sperau probably would not have invested $1 million in the business—which went bankrupt after three years of operation.

When Foster and Sperau sued Ford for fraud, the trial court awarded damages to the plaintiffs. On appeal, the Alabama Supreme Court affirmed the trial court's judgment. The state's highest court held that "[t]here was evidence from which the jury could find, by a clear and convincing standard, that Ford defrauded the Plaintiffs by using sales

and profit forecasts and capitalization requirements which were deceptive based upon facts known to Ford." The court emphasized that "at the same time that it was aggressively recruiting African American dealer candidates, including Samuel Foster, with high sales and profits forecasts, Ford management was telling its board of directors that it expected these same new minority dealer candidates to be 'loss dealers.'"[a]

For Critical Analysis: *Ford argued that providing negative information to African American dealer candidates would discourage their participation in Ford's minority program. If you were the judge, how would you respond to this argument?*

---

a. *Sperau v. Ford Motor Co.*, 674 S.2d. 24 (Ala. 1995) The damages awarded in this case will likely be reduced substantially. In 1996, the United States Supreme Court remanded the case to the Alabama Supreme Court for further consideration in light of the Court's ruling on the issue of excessive damages in *BMW of North America, Inc. v. Gore*, 517 U.S. 559, 116 S.Ct. 1589, 134 L.Ed.2d 809 (1996)—see the *Inside the Legal Environment* in Chapter 3.

chise). This fee is separate from the various products that the franchisee purchases from or through the franchisor. In some industries, the franchisor relies heavily on the initial sale of the franchise for realizing a profit. In other industries, the continued dealing between the parties brings profit to both. In most situations, the franchisor will receive a stated percentage of the annual sales or annual volume of business done by the franchisee. The franchise agreement may also require the franchisee to pay a percentage of advertising costs and certain administrative expenses.

LOCATION AND BUSINESS ORGANIZATION OF THE FRANCHISE. Typically, the franchisor will determine the territory to be served. The franchise agreement may specify whether the premises for the business must be leased or purchased outright. In some cases, construction of a building is necessary to meet the terms of the agreement. Often, the franchise contract will indicate whether the franchisee has exclusive rights, or "territorial rights," to a certain geographical area.

Certainly the agreement will specify whether the franchisor supplies equipment and furnishings for the premises or whether this is the responsibility of the franchisee. When the franchise is a service operation, such as a motel, the contract often provides that the franchisor will establish certain standards for the facility and will make inspections to ensure that the standards are being maintained in order to protect the franchise's name and reputation.

The business organization of the franchisee is of great concern to the franchisor. Depending on the terms of the franchise agreement, the franchisor may specify particular requirements for the form and capital structure of the business. The franchise agreement can provide that standards of operation—relating to such aspects of the business as sales quotas, quality, and record keeping—be met by the franchisee. Furthermore, a franchisor may wish to retain stringent control over the training of personnel involved in the operation and over administrative aspects of the business. Although the day-to-day operation of the franchise business is normally left up to the franchisee, the franchise agreement may provide for the amount of supervision and control agreed on by the parties.

PRICE AND QUALITY CONTROLS OF THE FRANCHISE.   Franchises provide the franchisor with an outlet for the firm's goods and services. Depending on the nature of the business, the franchisor may require the franchisee to purchase certain supplies from the franchisor at an established price.[5]

As a general rule, the validity of a provision permitting the franchisor to enforce certain quality standards is unquestioned. Because the franchisor has a legitimate interest in maintaining the quality of the product or service to protect its name and reputation, it can exercise greater control in this area than would otherwise be tolerated. Increasingly, however, franchisors are finding that if they exercise too much control over the operations of their franchisees, they may incur liability, as principals, for the torts of their franchisees' employees.

TERMINATION OF THE FRANCHISE.   The duration of the franchise is a matter to be determined between the parties. Generally, a franchise will start out for a short period, such as a year, so that the franchisee and the franchisor can determine whether they want to stay in business with one another. Usually, the franchise agreement will specify that termination must be "for cause," such as death or disability of the franchisee, insolvency of the franchisee, breach of the franchise agreement, or failure to meet specified sales quotas. Most franchise contracts provide that notice of termination must be given. If no set time for termination is specified, then a reasonable time, with notice, will be implied. A franchisee must be given reasonable time to wind up the business—that is, to do the accounting and return the copyright or trademark or any other property of the franchisor.

---

5.   Although a franchisor can require franchisees to purchase supplies from it, requiring a franchisee to purchase exclusively from the franchisor may violate federal antitrust laws (see Chapter 22). For two landmark cases in these areas, see *United States v. Arnold, Schwinn & Co.*, 388 U.S. 365, 87 S.Ct. 1956, 18 L.Ed.2d (1967); and *Fortner Enterprises, Inc. v. U.S. Steel Corp.*, 394 U.S. 495, 89 S.Ct. 1252, 22 L.Ed.2d 495 (1969).

Because a franchisor's termination of a franchise often has adverse consequences for the franchisee, much franchise litigation involves claims of wrongful termination. Generally, the termination provisions of contracts are more favorable to the franchisor. This means that the franchisee, who normally invests a substantial amount of time and money in the franchise operation to make it successful, may receive little or nothing for the business on termination. The franchisor owns the trademark and hence the business.

It is in this area that statutory and case law become important. The federal and state laws discussed earlier attempt, among other things, to protect franchisees from the arbitrary or unfair termination of their franchises by the franchisors. Generally, both statutory and case law emphasize the importance of good faith and fair dealing in terminating a franchise relationship.

In determining whether a franchisor has acted in good faith when terminating a franchise agreement, the courts generally try to balance the rights of both parties. If a court perceives that a franchisor has arbitrarily or unfairly terminated a franchise, the franchisee will be provided with a remedy for wrongful termination. If a franchisor's decision to terminate a franchise was made in the normal course of the franchisor's business operations, however, and reasonable notice of termination was given to the franchisee, normally a court would not consider such a termination wrongful. At issue in the following case is whether Domino's Pizza, Inc., had acted wrongfully when it terminated one of its franchises.

Case 15.1 ● Bennett Enterprises, Inc. v. Domino's Pizza, Inc.

United States Court of Appeals,
District of Columbia Circuit, 1995.

HISTORICAL AND SOCIAL SETTING *Pizza was originally an Italian dish, but its popularity exploded in the United States as part of the fast-food revolution that began in the 1950s. Today, the American appetite for pizza is more than eight pounds per person per year. U.S. pizza franchisors have spread their operations overseas to open pizza stores and restaurants in more than fifty countries. Pizza Hut, Inc., is the leader in sales in pizza restaurants. Domino's Pizza, Inc., is number one in pizza delivery sales.*

BACKGROUND AND FACTS   Bennett Enterprises, Inc., entered into a franchise agreement with Domino's Pizza, Inc., to operate a Domino's pizza store. The agreement stated that Domino's had the right to terminate the franchise if Bennett failed to comply with any provision, including a promise to comply with "all applicable laws." For most of its first year in business, Bennett did not turn a profit and did not pay any taxes. Domino's told Bennett that if it did not resolve its tax problems, Domino's would terminate the franchise. Bennett did not pay the taxes or work out a payment plan with the government, but instead sold the franchise and filed a suit against Domino's in a federal district court. Bennett charged Domino's with, among other things, breach of contract, on the ground that the franchise agreement did not entitle Domino's to declare Bennett in default on the basis of unpaid taxes. The court ruled in Bennett's favor. Domino's appealed.

IN THE WORDS OF THE COURT . . .
SENTELLE, Circuit Justice.
* * * *

The language of [the franchise agreement] is not ambiguous * * * because it is not reasonably or fairly susceptible to an interpretation that does not encompass compliance with state and federal tax laws. * * *

(Continued)

Case 15.1—continued

[A]ny reasonable construction of the language "all applicable laws" in a business franchise agreement must include tax statutes at the very minimum. To that extent the contract is unambiguous, and that is the only extent with which we are concerned. * * * Under the franchise agreement Domino's had the right to place Bennett in default for failure to pay taxes.

DECISION AND REMEDY   The U.S. Court of Appeals for the District of Columbia Circuit reversed the lower court's judgment.

FOR CRITICAL ANALYSIS—ECONOMIC CONSIDERATION   *Would violations of other laws, such as parking ordinances or speed limits, have been sufficient grounds for Domino's to terminate Bennett's franchise?*

The Nature of the Corporation

> "A corporation is an artificial being, invisible, intangible, and existing only in contemplation of law."
>
> John Marshall, 1755–1835 (Chief Justice of the United States Supreme Court, 1801–1835)

The corporation is a creature of statute. Its existence depends generally on state law. Each state has its own body of corporate law, and these laws are not entirely uniform. The Model Business Corporation Act (MBCA) is a codification of modern corporation law that has been influential in the drafting and revision of state corporation statutes. Today, the majority of state statutes are guided by the revised version of the MBCA, known as the Revised Model Business Corporation Act (RMBCA).

A *corporation* can consist of one or more *natural* persons (as opposed to the artificial "person" of the corporation) identified under a common name. The primary document needed to incorporate (that is, form the corporation according to state law) is the **articles of incorporation,** which include such information about the corporation as its functions and the structure of its organization. As soon as a corporation is formed, an organizational meeting is held to adopt **bylaws** (rules for managing the firm) and to elect a board of directors.

Articles of Incorporation The document filed with the appropriate governmental agency, usually the secretary of state, when a business is incorporated; state statutes usually prescribe what kind of information must be contained in the articles of incorporation.

Bylaws A set of governing rules adopted by a corporation or other association.

The corporation substitutes itself for its shareholders in conducting corporate business and in incurring liability, yet its authority to act and the liability for its actions are separate and apart from the individuals who own it. (In certain limited situations, the "corporate veil" can be pierced; that is, liability for the corporation's obligations can be extended to shareholders, a topic to be discussed later in this chapter.)

Corporate Personnel

Responsibility for the overall management of the corporation is entrusted to a *board of directors,* which is elected by the shareholders. The board of directors hires *corporate officers* and other employees to run the daily business operations of the corporation.

When an individual purchases a share of stock in a corporation, that person becomes a *shareholder* and an owner of the corporation. Unlike the members in a partnership, the body of shareholders can change constantly without affecting the continued existence of the corporation. A shareholder can sue the corporation, and the corporation can sue a shareholder. Additionally, under certain circumstances, a shareholder can sue on behalf of a corporation.

Corporate Taxation

Corporate profits are taxed by state and federal governments. Corporations can do one of two things with corporate profits—retain them or pass them on to shareholders in the form of **dividends.** The corporation receives no tax deduction for dividends distributed to shareholders. Dividends are again taxable (except when they represent distributions of capital) as ordinary income to the shareholder receiving them. This double-taxation feature of the corporation is one of its major disadvantages.

Profits not distributed are retained by the corporation. These **retained earnings,** if invested properly, will yield higher corporate profits in the future and thus normally cause the price of the company's stock to rise. Individual shareholders can then reap the benefits of these retained earnings in the capital gains they receive when they sell their shares.

The consequences of a failure to pay corporate taxes can be severe. The state may dissolve a corporation for this reason. Alternatively, corporate status may be suspended until the taxes are paid. In the following case, the state had suspended a corporation's **corporate charter** (the document issued by a state agency or authority—usually the secretary of state—that grants a corporation legal existence and the right to function) because of the corporation's failure to pay certain taxes. The issue before the court is whether a shareholder who was unaware of the suspension could be held personally liable on a corporate contract.

Dividend A distribution to corporate shareholders of corporate profits or income, disbursed in proportion to the number of shares held.

Retained Earnings The portion of a corporation's profits that has not been paid out as dividends to shareholders.

Corporate Charter The document issued by a state agency or authority (usually the secretary of state) that grants a corporation legal existence and the right to function.

Case 15.2 ⬤ Charles A. Torrence Co. v. Clary

Court of Appeals of North Carolina, 1995. 464 S.E.2d 502.

HISTORICAL AND POLITICAL SETTING *At one time, opening a small business was relatively simple in terms of the obli-gations to the government. Today, however, many businesspersons feel that there is an ocean of federal, state, and local laws that threatens to swamp even the least regulated of small businesses. For example, all states require proof of financial responsibility and compliance with other requirements before they issue a license to engage in certain businesses or occupations. Even a business that is exempt from state regulations may be required to obtain a county or city permit or license. Every level of government also imposes taxes and penalties for not paying them.*

BACKGROUND AND FACTS In 1989, the architectural firm of Clary, Martin, McMullen & Associates, Inc. (CMMA, Inc.), failed to pay its North Carolina franchise taxes,[a] and the state suspended its corporate charter. Between April 1991 and March 1992, the Charles A. Torrence Company provided graphics services for the firm. In September 1992, Moodye Clary—a shareholder, the president, and the director of marketing of CMMA, Inc.—learned that his firm's corporate charter had been suspended. When CMMA, Inc., failed to pay Torrence's bill, Torrence filed a suit in a North Carolina state court against CMMA, Inc., as well as against Moodye Clary personally, for the money. The court dismissed the claim against Moodye Clary, and Torrence appealed.

IN THE WORDS OF THE COURT . . .
GREENE, Judge.

* * * *

* * * [T]he suspension was only designed to put "additional bite" into the collection of franchise taxes, but not to deprive the shareholders of the normal protection of limited liability. * * * [D]irectors and officers are

(Continued)

Case 15.2—continued

personally liable for corporate obligations incurred by them on behalf of the corporation, or by others with their acquiescence, if at that time they were aware that the corporate charter was suspended. * * *

In this case, the evidence is that the defendant * * * had no knowledge, at the time the debt was incurred on behalf of the Corporation, that the corporate charter was suspended.

DECISION AND REMEDY   The Court of Appeals of North Carolina affirmed the lower court's decision.

FOR CRITICAL ANALYSIS—SOCIAL CONSIDERATION *Why wouldn't a court permit a shareholder who knows that the charter of his or her firm has been suspended to retain limited liability for corporate debts?*

---

a.   A *franchise tax* is an annual tax imposed for the privilege of doing business in a state.

Constitutional Rights of Corporations

A corporation is recognized under state and federal law as a "person," and it enjoys many of the same rights and privileges that U.S. citizens enjoy. The Bill of Rights guarantees a person, as a citizen, certain protections, and corporations are considered persons in most instances. Accordingly, a corporation has the same right as a natural person to equal protection of the laws under the Fourteenth Amendment. It has the right of access to the courts as an entity that can sue or be sued. It also has the right of due process before denial of life, liberty, or property, as well as freedom from unreasonable searches and seizures and from double jeopardy.

Under the First Amendment, corporations are entitled to freedom of speech. As we pointed out in Chapter 5, however, commercial speech (such as advertising) and political speech (such as contributions to political causes or candidates) receive significantly less protection than noncommercial speech.

Only the corporation's individual officers and employees possess the Fifth Amendment right against self-incrimination.[6] Additionally, the privileges and immunities clause of the Constitution (Article IV, Section 2) does not protect corporations.[7] This clause requires each state to treat citizens of other states equally with respect to access to courts, travel rights, and so forth.

> **"Did you expect a corporation to have a conscience, when it has no soul to be damned and no body to be kicked?"**
>
> Edward Thurlow, 1731–1806
> (English jurist)

Torts and Criminal Acts

A corporation is liable for the torts committed by its agents or officers within the course and scope of their employment. This principle applies to a corporation exactly as it applies to the ordinary agency relationships discussed in Chapter 16. It follows the doctrine of *respondeat superior.*

Under modern criminal law, a corporation can sometimes be held liable for the criminal acts of its agents and employees, provided the punishment is one that can be applied to the corporation. Corporate criminal prosecutions were at one time relatively rare, but in the past decade they have increased significantly in number. Obviously, corporations cannot be imprisoned, but they can be fined. Of course, corporate directors and officers can be imprisoned, and in

---

6.   *In re Grand Jury No. 86–3 (Will Roberts Corp.),* 816 F.2d 569 (11th Cir. 1987).
7.   *W. C. M. Window Co. v. Bernardi,* 730 F.2d 486 (7th Cir. 1984).

recent years, many have faced criminal penalties for their own actions or for the actions of employees under their supervision.

Recall from Chapter 7 that the U.S. Sentencing Commission, which was established by the Sentencing Reform Act of 1984, created standardized sentencing guidelines for federal crimes. These guidelines went into effect in 1987. The commission subsequently created specific sentencing guidelines for crimes committed by corporate employees (white-collar crimes). The net effect of the guidelines has been a fivefold to tenfold increase in criminal penalties for crimes committed by corporate personnel.

Classification of Corporations

The classification of a corporation depends on its purpose, ownership characteristics, and location. A corporation is referred to as a **domestic corporation** by its home state (the state in which it incorporates). A corporation formed in one state but doing business in another is referred to in that other state as a **foreign corporation**. A corporation formed in another country—say, Mexico—but doing business in the United States is referred to in the United States as an **alien corporation**.

A corporation does not have an automatic right to do business in a state other than its state of incorporation. It normally must obtain a *certificate of authority* in any state in which it plans to do business. Once the certificate has been issued, the powers conferred on a corporation by its home state generally can be exercised in the other state.

Domestic Corporation In a given state, a corporation that does business in, and is organized under the law of, that state.

Foreign Corporation In a given state, a corporation that does business in the state without being incorporated therein.

Alien Corporation A designation in the United States for a corporation formed in another country but doing business in the United States.

Corporate Management—Shareholders

The acquisition of a share of stock makes a person an owner and shareholder in a corporation. Shareholders thus own the corporation. Although

BMW automobiles are inspected at a plant in the United States. BMW is classified as an alien corporation. What is the difference between an alien corporation and a foreign corporation?

they have no legal title to corporate property, such as buildings and equipment, they do have an *equitable* (ownership) interest in the firm.

As a general rule, shareholders have no responsibility for the daily management of the corporation, although they are ultimately responsible for choosing the board of directors, which does have such control. Ordinarily, corporate officers and other employees owe no direct duty to individual shareholders. Their duty is to the corporation as a whole. A director, however, is in a fiduciary relationship to the corporation and therefore serves the interests of the shareholders. Generally, there is no legal relationship between shareholders and creditors of the corporation. Shareholders can, in fact, be creditors of the corporation and thus have the same rights of recovery against the corpo-ration as any other creditor.

In this section, we look at the powers and voting rights of shareholders, which are generally established in the articles of incorporation and under the state's general incorporation law.

> **BE AWARE** Shareholders are not normally agents of their corporation.

Shareholders' Powers

Shareholders must approve fundamental corporate changes before the changes can be effected. Hence, shareholders are empowered to amend the articles of incorporation (charter) and bylaws, approve a merger or the dissolution of the corporation, and approve the sale of all or substantially all of the corporation's assets. Some of these powers are subject to prior board approval.

Directors are elected to (and removed from) the board of directors by a vote of the shareholders. The first board of directors is either named in the articles of incorporation or chosen by the incorporators to serve until the first shareholders' meeting. From that time on, the selection and retention of directors are exclusively shareholder functions.

Directors usually serve their full terms; if they are unsatisfactory, they are simply not reelected. Shareholders have the inherent power, however, to remove a director from office *for cause* (breach of duty or misconduct) by a majority vote.[8] Some state statutes (and some corporate charters) even permit removal of directors *without cause* by the vote of a majority of the holders of outstanding shares entitled to vote.

Shareholders' Meetings

Shareholders' meetings must occur at least annually, and additional, special meetings can be called as needed to take care of urgent matters. Because it is usually not practical for owners of only a few shares of stock of publicly traded corporations to attend shareholders' meetings, such stockholders normally give third parties written authorization to vote their shares at the meeting. This authorization is called a **proxy** (from the Latin *procurare*, "to manage, take care of"). Proxies are often solicited by management, but any person can solicit proxies to concentrate voting power.

> **Proxy** In corporation law, a written agreement between a stockholder and another under which the stockholder authorizes the other to vote the stockholder's shares in a certain manner.

SHAREHOLDER VOTING. For shareholders to act during a meeting, a quorum must be present. Generally, a quorum exists when shareholders holding more than 50 percent of the outstanding shares are present. Corporate business matters are presented in the form of *resolutions,* which shareholders vote to approve or disapprove. Some state statutes have set forth specific voting

---

8. A director can often demand court review of removal for cause.

requirements, and corporations' articles or bylaws must abide by these statutory requirements. Some states provide that the unanimous written consent of shareholders is a permissible alternative to holding a shareholders' meeting. Once a quorum is present, a majority vote of the shares represented at the meeting is usually required to pass resolutions.

At times, a greater-than-majority vote will be required either by a statute or by the corporate charter. Extraordinary corporate matters, such as a merger, consolidation, or dissolution of the corporation, require a higher percentage of the representatives of all corporate shares entitled to vote, not just a majority of those present at that particular meeting.

> **BE CAREFUL** Once a quorum is present, a vote can be taken even if some shareholders leave without casting their votes.

CUMULATIVE VOTING.   Most states permit or even require shareholders to elect directors by cumulative voting, a method of voting designed to allow minority shareholders representation on the board of directors.[9] When cumulative voting is allowed or required, the number of members of the board to be elected is multiplied by the total number of voting shares. The result equals the number of votes a shareholder has, and this total can be cast for one or more nominees for director. All nominees stand for election at the same time. When cumulative voting is not required either by statute or under the articles, the entire board can be elected by a simple majority of shares at a shareholders' meeting.

Cumulative voting can best be understood by an example. Suppose that a corporation has 10,000 shares issued and outstanding. One group of shareholders (the minority shareholders) holds only 3,000 shares, and the other group of shareholders (the majority shareholders) holds the other 7,000 shares. Three members of the board are to be elected. The majority shareholders' nominees are Acevedo, Barkley, and Craycik. The minority shareholders' nominee is Drake. Can Drake be elected by the minority shareholders?

If cumulative voting is allowed, the answer is yes. The minority shareholders have 9,000 votes among them (the number of directors to be elected times the number of shares held by the minority shareholders equals 3 times 3,000, which equals 9,000 votes). All of these votes can be cast to elect Drake. The majority shareholders have 21,000 votes (3 times 7,000 equals 21,000 votes), but these votes have to be distributed among their three nominees. The principle of cumulative voting is that no matter how the majority shareholders cast their 21,000 votes, they will not be able to elect all three directors if the minority shareholders cast all of their 9,000 votes for Drake, as illustrated in Exhibit 15–3.

---

9.   See, for example, California Corporate Code Section 708. Under RMBCA 7.28, however, no cumulative voting rights exist unless the articles of incorporation so provide.

Ballot	Majority Share Holder's Votes			Minority Share Holder's Votes	Directors Elected
	Acevedo	Barkley	Craycik	Drake	
1	10,000	10,000	1,000	9,000	Acevedo/Barkley/Drake
2	9,001	9,000	2,999	9,000	Acevedo/Barkley/Drake
3	6,000	7,000	8,000	9,000	Barkley/Craycik/Drake

■ **Exhibit 15–3 Results of Cumulative Voting**
This exhibit illustrates how cumulative voting gives minority shareholders a greater chance of electing a director of their choice. By casting all of their 9,000 votes for one candidate (Drake), the minority shareholders will succeed in electing Drake to the board of directors.

Corporate Management—Directors

▼ A corporation typically is governed by a board of directors. Subject to statutory limitations, the number of directors is set forth in the corporation's articles or bylaws.

Election of Directors

The first board of directors is normally appointed by the incorporators on the creation of the corporation, or directors are named by the corporation itself in the articles. The first board serves until the first annual shareholders' meeting. Subsequent directors are elected by a majority vote of the shareholders.

The term of office for a director is usually one year—from annual meeting to annual meeting. Longer and staggered terms are permissible under most state statutes. A common practice is to elect one-third of the board members each year for a three-year term. In this way, there is greater management continuity.

Directors' Qualifications and Compensation

Few legal requirements exist concerning directors' qualifications. Only a handful of states impose minimum age and residency requirements. A director is sometimes a shareholder, but this is not a necessary qualification—unless, of course, statutory provisions or corporate articles or bylaws require ownership.

Compensation for directors is ordinarily specified in the corporate articles or bylaws. Because directors have a fiduciary relationship to the shareholders and to the corporation, an express agreement or provision for compensation often is necessary for them to receive money from the funds that they control and for which they have responsibilities.

Board of Directors' Meetings

The board of directors conducts business by holding formal meetings with recorded minutes. The date on which regular meetings are held is usually established in the articles or bylaws or by board resolution, and no further notice is customarily required. Special meetings can be called, with notice sent to all directors.

Quorum requirements can vary among jurisdictions. (A **quorum** is the minimum number of members of a body of officials or other group that must be present in order for business to be validly transacted.) Many states leave the decision as to quorum requirements to the corporate articles or bylaws. In the absence of specific state statutes, most states provide that a quorum is a majority of the number of directors authorized in the articles or bylaws. Voting is done in person (unlike voting at shareholders' meetings, which can be done by proxy, as discussed earlier in this chapter).[10] The rule is one vote per director. Ordinary matters generally require a simple majority vote; certain extraordinary issues may require a greater-than-majority vote.

Quorum The number of members of a decision-making body that must be present before business may be transacted.

---

10.   Except in Louisiana, which allows a director to vote by proxy under certain circumstances. Some states, such as Michigan and Texas, and Section 8.20 of the RMBCA permit telephone conferences for board of directors' meetings.

Directors' Management Responsibilities

Directors have responsibility for all policymaking decisions necessary to the management of corporate affairs. Just as shareholders cannot act individually to bind the corporation, the directors must act as a body in carrying out routine corporate business. One director has one vote, and generally the majority rules. The general areas of responsibility of the board of directors include the following:

1. Declaration and payment of corporate dividends to shareholders.
2. Authorization for major corporate policy decisions—for example, the initiation of proceedings for the sale or lease of corporate assets outside the regular course of business, the determination of new product lines, and the overseeing of major contract negotiations and major management-labor negotiations.
3. Appointment, supervision, and removal of corporate officers and other managerial employees and the determination of their compensation.
4. Financial decisions, such as the issuance of authorized shares and bonds.

The board of directors can delegate some of its functions to an executive committee or to corporate officers. In doing so, the board is not relieved of its overall responsibility for directing the affairs of the corporation, but corporate officers and managerial personnel are empowered to make decisions relating to ordinary, daily corporate affairs within well-defined guidelines.

Role of Officers and Directors

A director occupies a position of responsibility unlike that of other corporate personnel. Directors are sometimes inappropriately characterized as *agents* because they act on behalf of the corporation. No *individual* director,

> **CONTRAST** Shareholders own a corporation and directors make policy decisions, but officers who run the daily business of the corporation often have significant decision-making power.

Corporate executives discuss the business of their firm. How do the rights and duties of corporate officers differ from those of corporate directors?

> "It is not the crook in modern business that we fear but the honest man who does not know what he is doing."

Owen D. Young, 1874–1962
(American corporate executive and public official)

Fiduciary As a noun, a person having a duty created by his or her undertaking to act primarily for another's benefit in matters connected with the undertaking. As an adjective, a relationship founded on trust and confidence.

however, can act as an agent to bind the corporation; and as a group, directors collectively control the corporation in a way that no agent is able to control a principal. Directors are often incorrectly characterized as *trustees* because they occupy positions of trust and control over the corporation. Unlike trustees, however, they do not own or hold title to property for the use and benefit of others.

The officers and other executive employees are hired by the board of directors or, in rare instances, by the shareholders. In addition to carrying out the duties articulated in the bylaws, corporate and managerial officers act as agents of the corporation, and the ordinary rules of agency (discussed in Chapter 16) normally apply to their employment. The qualifications required of officers and executive employees are determined at the discretion of the corporation and are included in the articles or bylaws. In most states, a person can hold more than one office and can be both an officer and a director of the corporation.

Directors and officers are deemed **fiduciaries** of the corporation, because their relationship with the corporation and its shareholders is one of trust and confidence. The fiduciary duties of the directors and officers include the duty of care and the duty of loyalty. The duty of care requires directors and officers to be honest and use prudent business judgment in the conduct of corporate affairs. Directors and officers must carry out their responsibilities in an informed, businesslike manner. The duty of loyalty requires the subordination of the self-interest of the directors and officers to the interest of the corporation. In general, it prohibits directors and officers from using corporate funds or confidential corporate information for personal advantage. Directors and officers can be held liable to the corporation and to the shareholders for breach of either of these duties.

A breach of the duty of loyalty occurs when an officer or director, for his or her personal gain, takes advantage of a business opportunity that is financially within the corporation's reach, is in line with the firm's business, is to the firm's practical advantage, and is one in which the corporation has an interest. Whether buying certain stock constitutes the usurping of a corporate opportunity is at issue in the following case.

Case 15.3 ● Yiannatsis v. Stephanis

Supreme Court of Delaware, 1995.
653 A.2d 275.

HISTORICAL AND SOCIAL SETTING   *More than 90 percent of all U.S. corporations have ten or fewer shareholders. Many of these corporations are family-owned firms organized to own and operate relatively small businesses. A close corporation can ignore some of the formalities that a more widely owned corporation must observe. In regard to board meetings and shareholder votes, however, a close corporation cannot avoid some requirements, particularly those mandated by an agreement among the shareholders.*

BACKGROUND AND FACTS   Demos and Stella Yiannatsis and Demos's cousins John and Costas Stephanis were the directors of the Sunview Corporation. Demos, John, and Costas were also Sunview's shareholders. In 1975, the three shareholders agreed that if any shareholder—or after the shareholder's death, the executor of his or her estate—wished to sell Sunview stock, the stock must be offered to the corporation first. If the shareholders could not agree on a price, they would hire appraisers to determine the value. The purpose of this agreement was to prevent the stock from being sold to a fourth party. In 1984, Costas died. At the next Sunview board meeting, Costas's executor offered to sell Costas's stock for $150,000 cash plus $55,000 payable

(Continued)

Case 15.3—continued

over time. The directors (Demos, Stella, and John) voted to refuse the offer. The next day, Stella offered to buy the stock, on slightly different terms. The executor agreed. John filed a suit in a Delaware state court against Stella and Demos, alleging that they had usurped a corporate opportunity. The court ruled in John's favor, and the defendants appealed.

IN THE WORDS OF THE COURT . . .
VEASEY, Chief Justice:
* * * *

* * * Sunview's opportunity to purchase the Costas Stock was never properly presented to Sunview, and * * * Demos and Stella acted without regard for the 1975 Agreement or the fiduciary duties they owed to Sunview and John. * * * [T]he minutes of the * * * 1984 Sunview Annual Board of Directors' Meeting reflect that the Costas Stock price was determined at the meeting where Stella agreed to purchase the Costas Stock. Given this fact, it would be impossible for Sunview to explore adequately the possibility of purchasing the relevant stock before Stella decided to buy it herself. * * * Demos' and Stella's actions are classic examples of the acts of faithless fiduciaries, and they should not benefit from their wrongful actions.

DECISION AND REMEDY   The Supreme Court of Delaware affirmed the judgment of the lower court.

FOR CRITICAL ANALYSIS—ETHICAL CONSIDERATION   *How could Stella and Demos have met their fiduciary obligations to the corporation?*

Conflicts of Interest

The duty of loyalty also requires officers and directors to disclose fully to the board of directors any possible conflict of interest that might occur in conducting corporate transactions. The various state statutes contain different standards, but a contract will generally *not* be voidable if it was fair and reasonable to the corporation at the time it was made, if there was a full disclosure of the interest of the officers or directors involved in the transaction, and if the contract was approved by a majority of the disinterested directors or shareholders.

For example, Southwood Corporation needs office space. Lambert Alden, one of its five directors, owns the building adjoining the corporation's main office building. He negotiates a lease with Southwood for the space, making a full disclosure to Southwood and the other four board directors. The lease arrangement is fair and reasonable, and it is unanimously approved by the corporation's board of directors. In this situation, Alden has not breached his duty of loyalty to the corporation, and the contract is thus valid. The rule is one of reason. If it were otherwise, directors would be prevented from ever giving financial assistance to the corporations they serve.

The Business Judgment Rule

Directors and officers are expected to exercise due care and to use their best judgment in guiding corporate management, but they are not insurers of business success. Honest mistakes of judgment and poor business decisions on their part do not make them liable to the corporation for resulting damages.

> **"All business proceeds on beliefs, or judgments of probabilities, and not on certainties."**
>
> Charles Eliot, 1834–1936 (American educator and editor)

Business Judgment Rule A rule that immunizes corporate management from liability for actions that result in corporate losses or damages if the actions are undertaken in good faith, and are within both the power of the corporation and the authority of management to make.

This is the **business judgment rule.** The rule generally immunizes directors and officers from liability for the consequences of a decision that is within managerial authority, as long as the decision complies with management's fiduciary duties and as long as acting on the decision is within the powers of the corporation. Consequently, if there is a reasonable basis for a business decision, it is unlikely that the court will interfere with that decision, even if the corporation suffers as a result.

To benefit from the rule, directors and officers must act in good faith, in what they consider to be the best interests of the corporation, and with the care that an ordinarily prudent person in a similar position would exercise in similar circumstances. This requires an informed decision, with a rational basis, and with no conflict between the decision maker's personal interest and the interest of the corporation. To be informed the director or officer must do what is necessary to become informed: attend presentations, ask for information from those who have it, read reports, review other written materials such as contracts—in other words, carefully study a situation and its alternatives. To be free of conflicting interests, the director must not engage in self-dealing. For instance, a director should not oppose a *tender offer* (an offer to purchase shares in the company made by another company directly to the shareholders) that is in the corporation's best interest simply because its acceptance may cost the director her or his position. For a decision to have an apparently rational basis, the decision itself must appear to have been made reasonably. For example, a director should not accept a tender offer with only a moment's consideration based solely on the market price of the corporation's shares.

Rights and Duties of Officers and Managers

The rights of corporate officers and other high-level managers are defined by employment contracts, because these persons are employees of the company. Corporate officers normally can be removed by the board of directors at any time with or without cause and regardless of the terms of the employment contracts—although in so doing, the corporation may be liable for breach of contract. The duties of corporate officers are the same as those of directors, because both groups are involved in decision making and are in similar positions of control. Hence, officers are viewed as having the same fiduciary duties of care and loyalty in their conduct of corporate affairs as directors have.

Rights of Shareholders

Shareholders possess numerous rights. A significant right—the right to vote their shares—has already been discussed. We now look at some additional rights of shareholders.

Stock Certificates

Stock Certificate A certificate issued by a corporation evidencing the ownership of a specified number of shares in the corporation.

A **stock certificate** is a certificate issued by a corporation that evidences ownership of a specified number of shares in the corporation. Stock is intangible personal property, and the ownership right exists independently of the certificate itself. A stock certificate may be lost or destroyed, but ownership is not destroyed with it. A new certificate can be issued to replace one that has been lost or destroyed.[11] Notice of shareholders' meetings, dividends, and operational and financial reports are all distributed according to the recorded ownership listed in the corporation's books, not on the basis of possession of the certificate.

Preemptive Rights

A **preemptive right** is a common law concept under which a preference is given to shareholders over all other purchasers to subscribe to or purchase shares of a *new issue* of stock in proportion to the percentage of total shares they already hold. This allows each shareholder to maintain his or her portion of control, voting power, or financial interest in the corporation. Most statutes either (1) grant preemptive rights but allow them to be negated in the corporation's articles or (2) deny preemptive rights except to the extent that they are granted in the articles. The result is that the articles of incorporation determine the existence and scope of preemptive rights. Generally, preemptive rights apply only to additional, newly issued stock sold for cash, and the preemptive rights must be exercised within a specified time period (usually thirty days).

Preemptive Rights
Rights held by shareholders that entitle them to purchase newly issued shares of a corporation's stock, equal in percentage to shares presently held, before the stock is offered to any outside buyers. Preemptive rights enable shareholders to maintain their proportionate ownership and voice in the corporation.

Dividends

As mentioned earlier in this chapter, a *dividend* is a distribution of corporate profits or income ordered by the directors and paid to the shareholders in proportion to their respective shares in the corporation. Dividends can be paid in cash, property, stock of the corporation that is paying the dividends, or stock of other corporations.[12]

State laws vary, but each state determines the general circumstances and legal requirements under which dividends are paid. State laws also control the sources of revenue to be used; only certain funds are legally available for paying dividends.

ILLEGAL DIVIDENDS. A dividend paid while the corporation is insolvent is automatically an illegal dividend, and shareholders may be liable for returning the payment to the corporation or its creditors. Furthermore, as just discussed, dividends are generally required by statute to be distributed only from certain authorized corporate accounts. Sometimes dividends are improperly paid from an unauthorized account, or their payment causes the corporation to become insolvent. Generally, in such cases, shareholders must return illegal dividends only if they knew that the dividends were illegal when they received them. Whenever dividends are illegal or improper, the board of directors can be held personally liable for the amount of the payment. When directors can show that a shareholder knew that a dividend was illegal when it was received, however, the directors are entitled to reimbursement from the shareholder.

DIRECTORS' FAILURE TO DECLARE A DIVIDEND. When directors fail to declare a dividend, shareholders can ask a court to compel the directors to meet and

---

11. For a lost or destroyed certificate to be reissued, a shareholder normally must furnish an indemnity bond to protect the corporation against potential loss should the original certificate reappear at some future time in the hands of a bona fide purchaser [UCC 8–302, 8–405(2)].
12. Technically, dividends paid in stock are not dividends. They maintain each shareholder's proportional interest in the corporation. On one occasion, a distillery declared and paid a "dividend" in bonded whiskey.

to declare a dividend. For the shareholders to succeed, they must show that the directors have acted so unreasonably in withholding the dividend that the directors' conduct is an abuse of their discretion.

Often, large money reserves are accumulated for a bona fide purpose, such as expansion, research, or other legitimate corporate goals. The mere fact that sufficient corporate earnings or surplus is available to pay a dividend is not enough to compel directors to distribute funds that, in the board's opinion, should not be paid. The courts are circumspect about interfering with corporate operations and will not compel directors to declare dividends unless abuse of discretion is clearly shown. In the following classic case, the shareholders brought a court action to compel Ford Motor Company to declare a dividend.

Case 15.4 ● Dodge v. Ford Motor Co.

Supreme Court of Michigan, 1919.
204 Mich. 459,
170 N.W. 668.

HISTORICAL AND SOCIAL SETTING *Corporations are owned by shareholders but run by directors and officers. Practical and ethical problems are inevitable. Directors are supposed to act in the best interests of the corporation, which is presumed to be the same as the best interests of the shareholders. Directors and shareholders may have different views about the corporation's best interests, however. Directors who look toward long-term growth and future profitability may want to reinvest profits in the firm. Shareholders may be more interested in receiving those profits as current dividends.*

BACKGROUND AND FACTS Henry Ford was the president and major shareholder of Ford Motor Company. In the

company's early years, business expanded rapidly, and in addition to regular quarterly dividends, special dividends were often paid. By 1916, surplus above capital was still $111,960,907. That year, however, Henry Ford declared that the company would no longer pay special dividends but would put back into the business all the earnings of the company above the regular dividend of 5 percent. According to the court, Ford stated as follows: "My ambition is to employ still more men, to spread the benefits of this industrial system to the greatest possible number, to help them build up their lives and their homes. To do this, we are putting the greatest share of our profits back into the business." The minority shareholders, who owned 10 percent of the stock filed a lawsuit in a Michigan state court against Ford and others to force the declaration of a dividend. The court ordered the Ford directors to declare a dividend, and the plaintiffs appealed.

IN THE WORDS OF THE COURT . . .
OSTRANDER, Chief Justice.
* * * *

* * * Courts of equity will not interfere in the management of the directors unless it is clearly made to appear that they are guilty of fraud or misappropriation of the corporate funds, or refuse to declare a dividend when the corporation has a surplus of net profits which it can, without detriment to its business, divide among its stockholders, and when a refusal to do so would amount to such an abuse of discretion as would constitute a fraud, or breach of that good faith which they are bound to exercise towards the stockholders.
* * * *

Defendants say, and it is true, that a considerable cash balance must be at all times carried by such a concern [as Ford]. But * * * there was a large daily, weekly, monthly, receipt of cash. The output was practically

(Continued)

Case 15.4—continued

continuous and was continuously, and within a few days, turned into cash.
Moreover, the contemplated expenditures were not to be immediately made.
* * * So that, without going further, it would appear that, accepting and
approving the plan of the directors, it was their duty to distribute * * *
a very large sum of money to stockholders.

DECISION AND REMEDY   The Supreme Court of Michigan
ordered the Ford Motor Company to declare a dividend.
The court held that, in view of the firm's large capital surplus, to withhold a dividend would violate the directors'
duty to the shareholders.

FOR CRITICAL ANALYSIS—SOCIAL CONSIDERATION   *Generally,
how can a court determine when directors should pay
dividends?*

Inspection Rights

Shareholders in a corporation enjoy both common law and statutory inspection rights.[13] The shareholder's right of inspection is limited, however, to the
inspection and copying of corporate books and records for a *proper purpose,*
provided the request is made in advance. The shareholder can inspect in person, or an attorney, agent, accountant, or other type of assistant can do so.

Transfer of Shares

Stock certificates generally are negotiable and freely transferable by indorsement and delivery. Transfer of stock in closely held corporations, however,
usually is restricted by the bylaws, by a restriction stamped on the stock certificate, or by a shareholder agreement. The existence of any restrictions on
transferability must always be noted on the face of the stock certificate, and
these restrictions must be reasonable.

Sometimes, corporations or their shareholders restrict transferability by
reserving the option to purchase any shares offered for resale by a shareholder.
This **right of first refusal** remains with the corporation or the shareholders for
only a specified time or a reasonable time. Variations on the purchase option
are possible. For example, a shareholder might be required to offer the shares
to other shareholders first or to the corporation first.

When shares are transferred, a new entry is made in the corporate stock
book to indicate the new owner. Until the corporation is notified and the entry
is complete, the current record owner has the right to be notified of (and
attend) shareholders' meetings, the right to vote the shares, the right to receive
dividends, and all other shareholder rights.

Right of First Refusal The
right to purchase personal or
real property—such as corporate
shares or real estate—before the
property is offered for sale to
others.

Shareholder's Derivative Suit

When those in control of a corporation—the corporate directors—fail to sue in
the corporate name to redress a wrong suffered by the corporation, shareholders are permitted to do so "derivatively" in what is known as a **shareholder's
derivative suit.** Some wrong must have been done to the corporation, and
before a derivative suit can be brought, the shareholders must first state their

Shareholder's Derivative Suit
A suit brought by a shareholder
to enforce a corporate cause of
action against a third person.

---

13. See, for example, *Schwartzman v. Schwartzman Packing Co.,* 99 N.M. 436, 659 P.2d 888
(1983).

complaint to the board of directors. Only if the directors fail to solve the problem or take appropriate action can the derivative suit go forward.

The right of shareholders to bring a derivative action is especially important when the wrong suffered by the corporation results from the actions of corporate directors or officers. This is because the directors and officers would probably want to prevent any action against themselves.

The shareholder's derivative suit is singular in that those suing are not pursuing rights or benefits for themselves personally but are acting as guardians of the corporate entity. Therefore, any damages recovered by the suit normally go into the corporation's treasury, not to the shareholders personally.

Liability of Shareholders

▼   One of the hallmarks of the corporate organization is that shareholders are not personally liable for the debts of the corporation. If the corporation fails, shareholders can lose their investments, but that is generally the limit of their liability. In certain instances of fraud, undercapitalization, or careless observance of corporate formalities, a court will pierce the corporate veil (disregard the corporate entity) and hold the shareholders individually liable. These situations are the exception, however, not the rule. Although they are rare, certain other instances arise where a shareholder can be personally liable. One relates to illegal dividends, which were discussed previously. Two others relate to *stock subscriptions* and *watered stock*, which we discuss here.

Sometimes stock-subscription agreements—written contracts by which one agrees to buy capital stock of a corporation—exist prior to incorporation. Normally, these agreements are treated as continuing offers and are irrevocable (for up to six months under RMBCA 6.20). Once the corporation has been formed, it can sell shares to shareholder investors. In either situation, once the subscription agreement or stock offer is accepted, a binding contract is formed. Any refusal to pay constitutes a breach resulting in the personal liability of the shareholder.

Shares of stock can be paid for by property or by services rendered instead of cash. They cannot be purchased with promissory notes, however. The general rule is that for **par-value shares** (shares that have a specific face value, or formal cash-in value, written on them, such as one penny or one dollar), the corporation must receive a value at least equal to the par-value amount. For **no-par shares** (shares that have no face value—no specific amount printed on their face), the corporation must receive the value of the shares as determined by the board or the shareholders when the stock was issued. When the corporation issues shares for less than these stated values, the shares are referred to as **watered stock**.[14] Usually, the shareholder who receives watered stock must pay the difference to the corporation (the shareholder is personally liable). In some states, the shareholder who receives watered stock may be liable to creditors of the corporation for unpaid corporate debts.

Par-Value Shares Corporate shares that have a specific face value, or formal cash-in value, written on them, such as one dollar.

No-Par Shares Corporate shares that have no face value—that is, no specific dollar amount is printed on their face.

Watered Stock Shares of stock issued by a corporation for which the corporation receives, as payment, less than the stated value of the shares.

---

14.   The phrase *watered stock* was originally used to describe cattle that—kept thirsty during a long drive—were allowed to drink large quantities of water just prior to their sale. The increased weight of the "watered stock" allowed the seller to reap a higher profit.

Duties of Majority Shareholders

In some cases, a majority shareholder is regarded as having a fiduciary duty to the corporation and to the minority shareholders. This occurs when a single shareholder (or a few shareholders acting in concert) owns a sufficient number of shares to exercise *de facto* control over the corporation. In these situations, majority shareholders owe a fiduciary duty to the minority shareholders when they sell their shares, because such a sale would be, in fact, a transfer of control of the corporation. Whether the controlling majority of shareholders owed a fiduciary duty to a minority shareholder was at issue in the following case.

Case 15.5 ⬤ Pedro v. Pedro

Court of Appeals of Minnesota, 1992.
489 N.W.2d 798.

HISTORICAL AND SOCIAL SETTING *The purchase of a minority shareholder's shares in a corporation by the majority shareholders is termed a buyout. In litigation, when fashioning relief involving the buyout of shareholders in a close corporation, trial courts have broad equitable powers. For example, Minnesota Statutes Section 302A.751(3a) allows courts to look to a shareholder's reasonable expectations when awarding damages. Besides the shareholder's ownership interest in the corporation, "[t]he reasonable expectations of such a shareholder are a job, salary, a significant place in management, and economic security for his family."*[a]

BACKGROUND AND FACTS Alfred, Carl, and Eugene Pedro each owned a one-third interest in The Pedro Companies (TPC), a close corporation that manufactured and sold lug-gage and leather products. All of the brothers had worked for the corporation for most of their adult lives. The relationship between Alfred and the other two brothers began to deteriorate in 1987 after Alfred discovered a discrepancy between the internal accounting records and the TPC checking account. At Alfred's insistence, two different accountants examined the records, but neither could identify the source of a $140,000 discrepancy, and one accountant said that he was denied access to numerous documents during the investigation. Alfred stated that his brothers told him that if he did not forget about the discrepancy, they would fire him—which they did in December 1987. Alfred filed suit in a Minnesota state court against his brothers, alleging that they had breached their fiduciary duties and that he had been wrongfully discharged. The trial court held for Alfred and awarded him over $1.8 million in damages, plus interest, for the value of his shares, lost wages, and attorneys' fees. The brothers appealed.

IN THE WORDS OF THE COURT . . .
NORTON, Judge.
     * * * *

The relationship among shareholders in closely held corporations is analogous to that of partners. Shareholders in closely held corporations owe one another a fiduciary duty. In a fiduciary relationship "the law imposes upon them highest standards of integrity and good faith in their dealings with each other." Owing a fiduciary duty includes dealing "openly, honestly and fairly with other shareholders."

The court's findings of fact contain many examples where appellants did not act openly, honestly, and fairly with * * * Alfred Pedro. * * *

(Continued)

Case 15.5—continued

* * * *

The unique facts in the record support the trial court's finding of an agreement to provide lifetime employment to respondent. Carl Pedro, Sr. worked at the corporation until his death. Eugene Pedro, who worked for over 50 years at TPC, testified that he intended to always work for the company. Carl Pedro, Jr. worked at TPC for over 34 years. Alfred Pedro testified of his expectation of a lifetime job like his father. He had already been employed by TPC for 45 years. Even the corporate accountant testified regarding Carl's and Eugene's expectations that they would work for the corporation as long as they wanted. Based upon this evidence it was reasonable for the trial court to determine that the parties did in fact have a contract that was not terminable at will.

DECISION AND REMEDY The Minnesota appellate court affirmed the trial court's judgment.

FOR CRITICAL ANALYSIS—ECONOMIC CONSIDERATION *Is there anything Alfred could have done to ensure that he would be employed "for life" by the corporation?*

---

a. Joseph Olson, "A Statutory Elixir for the Oppression Malady," 36 *Mercer Law Review* 627 (1985).

Key Terms

alien corporation   423
articles of incorporation   420
business judgment rule   430
bylaws   420
corporate charter   421
corporation   408
dividend   421
domestic corporation   423
entrepreneur   406
fiduciary   428
foreign corporation   423

franchise   414
franchisee   414
franchisor   414
general partner   408
limited liability
    company (LLC)   413
limited partner   408
limited partnership   408
no-par share   434
par-value share   434
partnership   407

preemptive right   431
proxy   424
quorum   426
retained earnings   421
right of first refusal   433
S corporation   408
shareholder's derivative
    suit   433
sole proprietorship   406
stock certificate   430
watered stock   434

Chapter Summary
Business Organizations

MAJOR TRADITIONAL BUSINESS FORMS (See pages 406–413.)	1. **Sole proprietorships**—The simplest form of business; used by anyone who does business without creating an organization. The owner is the business. The owner pays personal income taxes on all profits and is personally liable for all business debts.

(Continued)

Chapter Summary, continued

MAJOR TRADITIONAL BUSINESS FORMS—continued (See pages 406–413.)	**2. Partnerships—** a. General partnerships—Created by agreement of the parties; not treated as an entity except for limited purposes. Partners have unlimited liability for partnership debts, and each partner normally has an equal voice in management. Income is "passed through" the partnership to the individual partners, who pay personal taxes on the income. b. Limited partnerships—Must be formed in compliance with statutory requirements. A limited partnership consists of one or more general partners, who have unlimited liability for partnership losses, and one or more limited partners, who are liable only to the extent of their contributions. Only general partners can participate in management. **3. Corporations—**A corporation is formed in compliance with statutory requirements, is a legal entity separate and distinct from its owners, and can have perpetual existence. The shareholder-owners elect directors, who set policy and hire officers to run the day-to-day business of the corporation. Shareholders normally are not personally liable for the debts of the corporation. The corporation pays income tax on net profits; shareholders pay income tax on disbursed dividends.
LIMITED LIABILITY COMPANIES (See pages 413–414.)	The limited liability company (LLC) is a hybrid form of business organization that offers the limited liability feature of corporations but the tax benefits of partnerships. Unlike limited partners, LLC members participate in management. Unlike shareholders in S corporations, members of LLCs may be corporations or partnerships, are not restricted in number, and may be residents of other countries.
PRIVATE FRANCHISES (See pages 413–420.)	**1. Types of franchises—** a. Distributorship (for example, automobile dealerships). b. Chain-style operation (for example, fast-food chains). c. Manufacturing/processing-plant arrangement (for example, soft-drink bottling companies, such as Coca-Cola). **2. Laws governing franchising—**Franchises are governed by contract law, occasionally by agency law, and by federal and state statutory and regulatory laws. **3. The franchise contract—** a. Ordinarily requires the franchisee (purchaser) to pay a price for the franchise license. b. Specifies the territory to be served by the franchisee's firm. c. May require the franchisee to purchase certain supplies from the franchisor at an established price. d. May require the franchisee to abide by certain standards of quality relating to the product or service offered but cannot set retail resale prices. e. Usually provides for the date and/or conditions of termination of the franchise arrangement. Both federal and state statutes attempt to protect certain franchisees from franchisors who unfairly or arbitrarily terminate franchises.
THE NATURE OF THE CORPORATION (See pages 420–423.)	The corporation is a legal entity distinct from its owners. Formal statutory requirements, which vary somewhat from state to state, must be followed in forming

(Continued)

Chapter Summary, continued

THE NATURE OF THE CORPORATION—continued
(See pages 420–423.)

a corporation. The corporation can have perpetual existence or be chartered for a specific period of time.

1. **Corporate personnel**—The shareholders own the corporation. They elect a board of directors to govern the corporation. The board of directors hires corporate officers and other employees to run the daily business of the firm.

2. **Corporate taxation**—The corporation pays income tax on net profits; shareholders pay income tax on the disbursed dividends that they receive from the corporation (double-taxation feature).

3. **Torts and criminal acts**—The corporation is liable for the torts committed by its agents or officers within the course and scope of their employment (under the doctrine of *respondeat superior*). In some circumstances, a corporation can be held liable (and be fined) for the criminal acts of its agents and employees. In certain situations, corporate officers may be held personally liable for corporate crimes.

CLASSIFICATION OF CORPORATIONS
(See page 423.)

A corporation is referred to as a *domestic corporation* within its home state (the state in which it incorporates). A corporation is referred to as a *foreign corporation* by any state that is not its home state. A corporation is referred to as an *alien corporation* if it originates in another country but does business in the United States.

DIRECTORS AND OFFICERS
(See pages 420 and 426–430.)

1. **Election of directors**—The first board of directors is usually appointed by the incorporators; thereafter, directors are elected by the shareholders. Directors usually serve a one-year term, although longer and staggered terms are permitted under most state statutes.

2. **Directors' qualifications and compensation**—Few qualifications are required; a director can be a shareholder but is not required to be. Compensation is usually specified in the corporate articles or bylaws.

3. **Board of directors' meetings**—The board of directors conducts business by holding formal meetings with recorded minutes. The date of regular meetings is usually established in the corporate articles or bylaws; special meetings can be called, with notice sent to all directors. Quorum requirements vary from state to state; usually, a quorum is the majority of the corporate directors. Voting must usually be done in person, and in ordinary matters only a majority vote is required.

4. **Directors' management responsibilities**—Directors are responsible for declaring and paying corporate dividends to shareholders; authorizing major corporate decisions; appointing, supervising, and removing corporate officers and other managerial employees; determining employees' compensation; making financial decisions necessary to the management of corporate affairs; and issuing authorized shares and bonds. Directors may delegate some of their responsibilities to executive committees and corporate officers and executives.

5. **Duties**—Directors are obligated to act in good faith, to use prudent business judgment in the conduct of corporate affairs, and to act in the corporation's best interests. Directors have a fiduciary duty to subordinate their own interests to those of the corporation in matters relating to the corporation. If a director fails to exercise these duties, he or she can be answerable to the corporation and to the shareholders for breaching the duties.

6. **Business judgment rule**—This rule immunizes a director from liability for a corporate decision as long as the decision was within the powers of the

Chapter Summary, continued

DIRECTORS AND OFFICERS—continued— (See pages 420 and 426–430.)	corporation and the authority of the director to make and was an informed, reasonable, and loyal decision.

SHAREHOLDERS
(See pages 423–425 and 430–436.)
	1. **Shareholders' meetings**—Shareholders' meetings must occur at least annually; special meetings can be called when necessary. Notice of the date, time, and place of the meeting (and its purpose, if it is specially called) must be sent to shareholders. Shareholders may vote by proxy (authorizing someone else to vote their shares) and may submit proposals to be included in the company's proxy materials sent to shareholders before meetings.
	
	2. **Shareholder voting**—Shareholder voting requirements and procedures are as follows:
	
	    a. A minimum number of shareholders (a quorum—generally, more than 50 percent of shares held) must be present at a meeting for business to be conducted; resolutions are passed (usually) by simple majority vote.
	
	    b. Cumulative voting may or may not be required or permitted. Cumulative voting gives minority shareholders a better chance to be represented on the board of directors.
	
	    c. A shareholder may appoint a proxy (substitute) to vote his or her shares.
	
	3. **Shareholders' rights**—Shareholders have numerous rights, which may include the following:
	
	    a. The right to a stock certificate and preemptive rights.
	
	    b. The right to obtain a dividend (at the discretion of the directors).
	
	    c. Voting rights.
	
	    d. The right to inspect the corporate records.
	
	    e. The right to sue on behalf of the corporation (bring a shareholder's derivative suit) when the directors fail to do so.
	
	4. **Shareholders' liability**—Shareholders may be liable for the retention of illegal dividends, for breach of a stock-subscription agreement, and for the value of watered stock.
	
	5. **Duties of majority shareholders**—In certain situations, majority shareholders may be regarded as having a fiduciary duty to minority shareholders and will be liable if that duty is breached.

For Review

1. Which form of business organization is the simplest?

2. Under what circumstances might a limited partner or a shareholder be held liable for the obligations of his or her partnership or corporation?

3. What is a franchise? What are the most common types of franchises?

4. What are the duties of the directors and officers of a corporation?

5. If a group of shareholders perceives that the corporation has suffered a wrong and the directors refuse to take action, can the shareholders compel the directors to act? If so, how?

Questions and Case Problems

15–1. Forms of Business Organization. In each of the following situations, determine whether Georgio's Fashions is a sole proprietorship, a partnership, a limited partnership, or a corporation.

(a) Georgio's defaults on a payment to supplier Dee Creations. Dee sues Georgio's and each of the owners of Georgio's personally for payment of the debt.

(b) Georgio's raises $200,000 through the sale of shares of its stock.

(c) At tax time, Georgio's files a tax return with the IRS and pays taxes on the firm's net profits.

(d) Georgio's is owned by three persons, two of whom are not allowed to participate in the firm's management.

15–2. Choice of Business Form. Jorge, Marta, and Jocelyn are college graduates, and Jorge has come up with an idea for a new product that he believes could make the three of them very rich. His idea is to manufacture soft-drink dispensers for home use and market them to consumers throughout the Midwest. Jorge's personal experience qualifies him to be both first-line supervisor and general manager of the new firm. Marta is a born salesperson. Jocelyn has little interest in sales or management but would like to invest a large sum of money that she has inherited from her aunt. What factors should Jorge, Marta, and Jocelyn consider in deciding which form of business organization to adopt?

15–3. Rights of Shareholders. Dmitri has acquired one share of common stock of a multimillion-dollar corporation with over 500,000 shareholders. Dmitri's ownership is so small that he is questioning what his rights are as a shareholder. For example, he wants to know whether this one share entitles him to attend and vote at shareholders' meetings, inspect the corporate books, and receive periodic dividends. Discuss Dmitri's rights in these matters.

15–4. Duties of Directors. Overland Corp. is negotiating with Wharton Construction Co. for the renovation of Overland's corporate headquarters. Wharton, the owner of Wharton Construction, is also one of the five members of the board of directors of Overland. The contract terms are standard for this type of contract. Wharton has previously informed two of the other Overland directors of his interest in the construction company. Overland's board approves the contract on a three-to-two vote, with Wharton voting with the majority. Discuss whether this contract is binding on the corporation.

15–5. Franchise Termination. Ormsby Motors, Inc. (OMI), was a General Motors Corp. (GM) dealership. Their agreement provided for termination if OMI submitted "false . . . claims for any payment." Larry Kain

was in charge of OMI's warranty claims. After several years of excessive claims, GM complained to OMI. When nothing changed, GM conducted a dealer audit. The audit uncovered, among other things, over eighty claims in one ten-day period for paint repair work that was never done. OMI denied knowledge of Kain's activities. GM terminated its dealership agreement with OMI. OMI asked a federal district court to stop the termination, arguing in part that GM did not have good cause. Did GM have good cause? Explain. [*Ormsby Motors, Inc. v. General Motors Corp.*, 842 F.Supp. 344 (N.D.Ill. 1994)]

15–6. Good Faith in Franchise Relations. Barn-Chestnut, Inc. (BCI), entered into a franchise agreement with Grocers Development Corp. (GDC) for a Convenient Food Mart "for as long as [BCI] . . . shall have a good and valid lease" to the property. GDC sold its interest in the franchise and the property to CFM Development Corp. When the lease was about to expire, CFM offered to enter into a new lease and franchise agreement with BCI at a significantly higher price. BCI refused. When CFM refused to make another deal, BCI filed a suit against CFM in a West Virginia state court on the ground that CFM had to offer BCI a lease because the franchise was contingent on a lease. The court did not agree. BCI then argued that the implied obligation of good faith required CFM to offer to renew the lease. Essentially, the question on appeal was whether a franchisor had an obligation to renew a franchise even though there was no clause in the contract requiring that the lease/franchise be renewed. Is BCI correct in contending that the franchisor does have such an obligation? Explain. [*Barn-Chestnut, Inc. v. CFM Development Corp.*, 193 W.Va. 565, 457 S.E.2d 502 (1995)]

15–7. Duties of Directors. Midwest Management Corp. was looking for investment opportunities. Morris Stephens, one of Midwest's directors and the chairman of the investment committee, proposed that Midwest provide financing for Stephens's son and his business colleagues, who were in need of financing to open a broker-dealer business. Midwest agreed to propose to the shareholders for their approval an investment of $250,000 in the new business on the condition that Stephens would manage the business and would purchase 100,000 shares of stock in the new firm. At each of two shareholders' meetings, the directors informed the shareholders that Stephens had agreed to the condition. Stephens was present at both meetings and did not deny that he had agreed to purchase the 100,000 shares of stock and manage the new corporation. On the shareholders' approval, the $250,000 investment was made, and later another $150,000 was invested when the new business suffered losses. About a year after it had opened, the business closed, and Midwest ended up losing over $325,000. Midwest then learned that Stephens had not kept his agreement to purchase stock in and manage the corporation. Midwest sued Stephens for breaching his fiduciary duties and asked for compensatory and punitive damages. Did Midwest succeed? Explain. [*Midwest Management Corp. v. Stephens,* 353 N.W.2d 76 (Iowa 1984)]

15–8. Rights of Shareholders. Jacob Schachter and Herbert Kulik, the founders of Ketek Electric Corp., each owned 50 percent of the corporation's shares and served as the corporation's only officers. Arnold Glenn, as trustee, and Kulik brought a shareholder's derivative suit in a New York state court against Schachter, alleging that Schachter had diverted Ketek assets and opportunities to Hoteltron Systems, Inc., a corporation wholly owned by Schachter. The trial court held for Glenn and Kulik, and it awarded damages to Kulik, not to Ketek. On appeal, the appellate court ruled that the damages should be awarded to the injured corporation, Ketek, rather than to the innocent shareholder, Kulik. Kulik appealed to the state supreme court, arguing that awarding damages to the corporation was inequitable because Schachter, as a shareholder of Ketek, would ultimately share in the proceeds of the award. How should the state supreme court rule, and why? [*Glenn v. Hoteltron Systems, Inc.,* 74 N.Y.2d 386, 547 N.E.2d 71, 547 N.Y.S.2 816 (1989)]

15–9. Business Judgment Rule. William Bear was the president of the William R. Bear Agency, Inc. (Bear Agency). Timothy Schirmer was a shareholder. In 1990, the YMCA was an important client of Bear Agency, and Bear spent company funds for family memberships in the YMCA. The same year, Bear put his wife on the payroll because, at the time, she was the only one in the office with computer experience. He decided not to declare a bonus for the employees in 1990, in part to invest the money in computers for the firm. The next April, Bear bought a BMW with company funds to use as a company car. Disapproving these actions, Schirmer filed a suit against Bear, Bear Agency, and others in an Illinois state court, asking the court to dissolve the corporation, among other things. Discuss how the decision not to dissolve Bear Agency might be supported by the business judgment rule. [*Schirmer v. Bear,* 271 Ill.App.3d 778, 648 N.E.2d 1131, 208 Ill.Dec. 209 (1994)]

A Question of Ethics and Social Responsibility

15–10. McQuade was the manager of the New York Giants baseball team. McQuade and John McGraw purchased shares in the National Exhibition Co., the corporation that owned the Giants, from Charles Stoneham, who owned a majority of National Exhibition's stock. As part of the transaction, each of the three agreed to use his best efforts to ensure that the others continued as directors and officers of the organization. Stoneham and McGraw, however, subsequently failed to use their best efforts to ensure that McQuade continued as the treasurer and a director of the corporation, and McQuade sued to compel specific performance of the agreement. A court reviewing the matter noted that McQuade had been "shabbily" treated by the others but refused to grant specific performance on the ground that the agreement was void because it interfered with the duty of the others as directors to do what was best for all the shareholders. Although shareholders may join to elect corporate directors, they may not join to limit the directors' discretion in managing the business affairs of an organization; the directors must retain their independent judgment. Consider the implications of the case, and address the following questions. [*McQuade v. Stoneham,* 263 N.Y. 323, 189 N.E. 234 (1934)]

1. Given that even the court sympathized with McQuade, was it ethical to put the business judgment of the directors ahead of an otherwise valid promise they had made?
2. Are there practical considerations that support the court's decision? How can directors perform the tasks dictated to them if their judgment is constrained by earlier agreements with some of the shareholders?
3. Can you think of any circumstances in which it would be fair to the shareholders, as a group, to interfere with the directors' business judgment by holding some of the directors to a similar prior agreement with some or all of the other directors?

Case Briefing Assignment

15–11. Examine Case A.6 [*Maschmeier v. Southside Press, Ltd.,* 435 N.W.2d 377 (Iowa App. 1989)] in Appendix A. The case has been excerpted there in great detail. Review and then brief the case, making sure that you include answers to the following questions in your brief.

1. What was the primary reason for this lawsuit?
2. What restriction did the corporate bylaws place on the transfer of corporate shares? On transfer, how was the price of shares to be determined?
3. How did the majority shareholders (the parents) effectively "freeze out" or "squeeze out" the minority shareholders (the sons)?
4. Why was it necessary for the court to determine the fair value of shares, as the shareholders had agreed in the bylaws on a method for accomplishing this?
5. Why was it necessary to establish that the majority shareholders had acted oppressively toward the minority shareholders or wasted corporate assets before the court could fashion its particular remedy in this case?

For Critical Analysis

15–12. As indicated in this chapter, the law permits individuals to exercise the option of organizing their business enterprises in many different forms. What policy interests are served by granting entrepreneurs these options? Would it be better if the law required that everyone organize his or her business in the same form? Discuss.

Unit III Cumulative Hypothetical Problem

15–13. Samuel Polson has an idea for a new software application. Polson hires an assistant and invests a considerable amount of his own time and money developing the application. To develop other software, and to manufacture and market his applications, Polson needs capital.

1. Polson borrows $5,000 from his friend, Michael Brant. Polson promises to repay Brant the $5,000 in three weeks. Brant, in urgent need of money, borrows $5,000 from his friend Mary Viva and assigns his rights to the $5,000 Polson owes him to Viva in return for the loan. Viva notifies Polson of the assignment. Polson pays Brant the $5,000 on the date stipulated in their contract. Brant refuses to give the money to Viva, and Viva sues Polson. Is Polson obligated to pay Viva $5,000 also? Discuss.

2. Polson learns that a competitor, Trivan, Inc., has already filed for a patent on a nearly identical program and has manufactured and sold the software to some customers. Polson learns from a reliable source that Trivan paid Polson's assistant a substantial sum of money to obtain a copy of the program. What legal recourse does Polson have against Trivan? Discuss fully.

3. While Polson is developing his idea and founding his business, he has no income. He continues to have living expenses, however, as well as payments due on his mortgage, various credit-card debts, and some loans that he took out to pay for his son's college tuition. As his business begins to make money. Polson files for Chapter 7 liquidation to be rid of his personal debts entirely, even though he believes he could probably pay them off over a four-year period if he scrimped and used every cent available to pay his creditors. Are all of Polson's personal debts dischargeable under Chapter 7, including the debts incurred for his son's education? Given the fact that Polson could foreseeably pay off his debts over a four-year period, will the court allow Polson to obtain relief under Chapter 7? Why or why not?

4. Polson is the sole owner of the business and pays no business income taxes. What is the form of Polson's business organization? What other options, in terms of business organizational forms, does Polson have? What are the advantages and disadvantages of each option? If Polson decides to incorporate the business under the name Polson Software, Inc., what steps will he need to take to do so?

INTERACTING WITH The Internet

■ The Web site of the law firm of Reinhart *et al.* provides extensive information about business organizations. The URL for this site is

http://www.rbvdnr.com/

■ For information on limited liability companies, go to

http://www.mgovg.com/

■ You can find the full text of the Internet Revenue Service rule concerning the taxation of limited liability companies and limited liability partnerships by accessing the Treasure Chest of Important Documents at the following site:

http://www.LWeekly.com

■ To learn how the U.S. Small Business Administration assists in forming, financing, and operating businesses, go to

http://www.sbaonline.sba.gov/

■ For daily news on the world of business, you can access Money Online at

http://www.money.com/

The Employment Environment

443

Employment Relationships

Contents

Chapter Objectives

After reading this chapter, you should be able to . . .

1. Distinguish between employees and independent contractors.
2. Outline the ways in which an agency relationship can arise.
3. Specify the duties that agents and principals owe to each other.
4. Describe the liability of the principal and the agent with respect to third parties.
5. Describe the major laws relating to health and safety in the workplace.

Employment relationships are agency relationships. Indeed, one of the most common, important, and pervasive legal relationships is that of **agency**. In an agency relationship between two parties, one of the parties, called the *agent,* agrees to represent or act for the other, called the *principal.* The principal has the right to control the agent's conduct in matters entrusted to the agent, and the agent must exercise his or her powers "for the benefit of the principal only," as Justice Joseph Story indicated in the quotation alongside. By using agents, a principal can conduct multiple business operations simultaneously in various locations. Thus, for example, contracts that bind the principal can be made at different places with different persons at the same time.

A familiar example of an agent is a corporate officer who serves in a representative capacity for the owners of the corporation. In this capacity, the officer has the authority to bind the principal (the corporation) to a contract. Indeed, agency law is essential to the existence and operation of a corporate entity, because only through its agents can a corporation function and enter into contracts. Because agency relationships permeate the business world, an understanding of the law of agency is crucial to understanding the legal environment of business.

Also important to the framework of the legal environment of business are employment statutes. For most of this century, the relationship of employer and employee has been the subject of federal and state legislation. Many of these statutes are discussed in the last part of this chapter.

> **"[It] is a universal principle in the law of agency, that the powers of the agent are to be exercised for the benefit of the principal only, and not of the agent or of third parties."**
>
> Joseph Story, 1779–1845
> (Associate justice of the United States Supreme Court, 1811–1844)

Agency A relationship between two parties in which one party (the agent) agrees to represent or act for the other (the principal).

Agency Relationships

Section 1(1) of the *Restatement (Second) of Agency*[1] defines *agency* as "the fiduciary relation which results from the manifestation of consent by one person to another that the other shall act in his behalf and subject to his control, and consent by the other so to act." The term **fiduciary** is at the heart of agency law. The term can be used both as a noun and as an adjective. When used as a noun, it refers to a person having a duty created by his or her undertaking to act primarily for another's benefit in matters connected with the undertaking. When used as an adjective, as in "fiduciary relationship," it means that the relationship involves trust and confidence.

In a principal-agent relationship, the parties have agreed that the agent will act *on behalf and instead of* the principal in negotiating and transacting business with third persons. Agency relationships commonly exist between employers and employees. A salesperson in a department store, for example, is an agent of the store's owner (the principal) and acts on the owner's behalf. Any sale of goods made by the salesperson to a customer is binding on the principal. Similarly, most representations of fact made by the salesperson with respect to the goods sold are binding on the principal. Agency relationships may sometimes also exist between employers and independent contractors who are hired to perform special tasks or services.

Fiduciary As a noun, a person having a duty created by his or her undertaking to act primarily for another's benefit in matters connected with the undertaking. As an adjective, a relationship founded on trust and confidence.

---

1. The *Restatement (Second) of Agency* is an authoritative summary of the law of agency and is often referred to by jurists in their decisions and opinions.

Employer-Employee Relationships

Normally, all employees who deal with third parties are deemed to be agents. All employment laws (state and federal) apply only to the employer-employee relationship. Statutes governing Social Security, withholding taxes, workers' compensation, unemployment compensation, workplace safety laws, employment discrimination, and the like are applicable only if there is an employer-employee status. *These laws do not apply to the independent contractor.*

Because employees who deal with third parties are normally deemed agents of their employers, agency law and employment law overlap considerably. Agency relationships, though, as will become apparent, can exist outside an employee-employer relationship and thus have a broader reach than employment laws do. Additionally, bear in mind that agency law is based on the common law. In the employment realm, many common law doctrines have been displaced by statutory law and government regulations governing employment relationships.

Employer–Independent Contractor Relationships

Independent Contractor One who works for, and receives payment from, an employer but whose working conditions and methods are not controlled by the employer. An independent contractor is not an employee but may be an agent.

Independent contractors are not employees, because by definition, those who hire them have no control over the details of their physical performance. Section 2 of the *Restatement (Second) of Agency* defines an **independent contractor** as follows:

> [An independent contractor is] a person who contracts with another to do something for him but who is not controlled by the other nor subject to the other's right to control with respect to his physical conduct in the performance of the undertaking. He may or may not be an agent.

Building contractors and subcontractors are independent contractors, and a property owner does not control the acts of either of these professionals. Truck drivers who own their equipment and hire out on a per-job basis are independent contractors, but truck drivers who drive company trucks on a regular basis are usually employees.

The relationship between a person or firm and an independent contractor may or may not involve an agency relationship. To illustrate: An owner of real estate who hires a real estate broker to negotiate a sale of his or her property not only has contracted with an independent contractor (the real estate broker) but also has established an agency relationship for the specific purpose of assisting in the sale of the property. Another example is an insurance agent, who is both an independent contractor and an agent of the insurance company for which he or she sells policies. (Note that an insurance *broker,* in contrast to an insurance agent, normally is not an agent of the insurance company but of the person obtaining insurance.)

A truck driver shakes hands with his employer. What are the factors for determining whether the driver is an employee or an independent contractor?

Criteria for Determining Employee Status

A question the courts frequently face in determining liability under agency law is whether a person hired by another to do a job is an employee or an independent contractor (see, for example, this chapter's *Inside the Legal Environment*). Because employers are normally held liable as principals for the

Inside the Legal Environment
Who Owns "Works for Hire"?

Under the Copyright Act of 1976, any copyrighted work created by an *employee* during the scope of his or her employment at the request of the employer is called a "work for hire." The employer owns and holds the copyright to such a work. What happens, though, when a firm hires independent contractors—freelance artists, writers, or computer programmers, for example—to create a work? In this situation, the freelancer/independent contractor will be the owner of the work created *unless* the parties agree in writing that the work is "for hire" *and if* the work falls into one of nine categories stipulated by the act, such as audiovisual works, translations, supplementary works, and others.

As might be expected, when disputes arise between firms and freelancers over copyright ownership, the firms often argue that the freelancers are not really independent contractors but employees. It is not always easy, though, for a court to make this determination. When the United States Supreme Court decided a case involving this issue in 1989, the Court set out thirteen factors that should be considered in determining the worker's status.[a] The Court did not indicate, however, the relative weight that should be attached to each factor. Therefore, it is still difficult to predict with accuracy when a freelancer will or will not be deemed an employee for copyright purposes.

Consider a case that came before the U.S. Court of Appeals for the Sixth Circuit in 1995. The case

involved a claim of copyright infringement brought by Hi-Tech Video Productions, Inc., against Capital Cities/ABC, Inc. (ABC). Hi-Tech, which had produced a travel video entitled *Mackinac Island: The Mackinac Video,* claimed that ABC had infringed Hi-Tech's copyright in the video when ABC featured parts of the video on ABC's television program *Good Morning America* without Hi-Tech's permission. ABC claimed that Hi-Tech had no valid copyright in the video, because the video had been created by independent contractors hired by Hi-Tech and with whom Hi-Tech had no written agreement stating that the video was a "work for hire."

The issue thus turned on whether Hi-Tech's hired workers (two videographers and a scriptwriter/narrator) were employees or independent contractors. The federal district court, applying the Supreme Court precedent mentioned above to the circumstances of this case, determined that the workers were employees; thus, Hi-Tech had a valid copyright in the video. In arriving at its conclusion, the district court gave substantial weight to the control factor—the fact that Hi-Tech exercised substantial control over the workers' activities. On appeal, however, the federal appellate court stressed other factors, including the parties' perception of their relationship. The appellate court concluded that the workers were not employees; thus, the video was not a "work for hire," and Hi-Tech had no copyright in the work.[b]

Picasso sculpture displayed in front of the Daley Civic Arts Center in Chicago. Who owns the copyright on commissioned art?

Clearly courts can disagree on whether a worker should be classified as an employee or an independent contractor. Therefore, a firm that wishes to own the copyright in a work created by a freelancer should make sure that it has a written agreement with the freelancer specifying that the work is a "work for hire."

For Critical Analysis: *What policy is served by the law that employers do not have copyright ownership in works created by independent contractors (unless there is a written "work for hire" agreement)?*

a. *Community for Creative Non-Violence v. Reid,* 490 U.S. 730, 109 S.Ct. 2166, 104 L.Ed.2d 811 (1989).

b. *Hi-Tech Video Productions, Inc. v. Capital Cities/ABC, Inc.,* 58 F.3d 1093 (6th Cir. 1995).

actions taken by their employee-agents within the scope of employment (as will be discussed later in this chapter), the court's decision as to employee versus independent-contractor status can be significant for the parties. In making this determination, courts often consider the following questions:

1. How much control can the employer exercise over the details of the work? (If an employer can exercise considerable control over the details of the work, this would indicate employee status.)
2. Is the worker engaged in an occupation or business distinct from that of the employer? (If so, this would point to independent-contractor status, not employee status.)
3. Is the work usually done under the employer's direction or by a specialist without supervision? (If the work is usually done under the employer's direction, this would indicate employee status.)
4. Does the employer supply the tools at the place of work? (If so, this would indicate employee status.)
5. For how long is the person employed? (If the person is employed for a long period of time, this would indicate employee status.)
6. What is the method of payment—by time period or at the completion of the job? (Payment by time period, such as once every two weeks or once a month, would indicate employee status.)
7. What degree of skill is required of the worker? (If a great degree of skill is required, this may indicate that the person was an independent contractor who was hired for a specialized job and not an employee.)

Often, the criteria for determining employee status are established by a statute or administrative agency regulation. The Internal Revenue Service (IRS), for example, establishes its own criteria for determining whether a worker is an independent contractor or an employee. In the past, these criteria consisted of a list of twenty factors. In 1996, however, these twenty factors were abolished in favor of rules that essentially encourage IRS examiners to look more closely at just one of the factors—the degree of control the business exercises over the worker.

The IRS tends to scrutinize closely a firm's classification of a worker as an independent contractor rather than an employee, because independent contractors can avoid certain tax liabilities by taking advantage of business organizational forms available to small businesses (see Chapter 15). Regardless of the firm's classification of a worker's status as an independent contractor, if the IRS decides that the worker should be classified as an employee, then the employer will be responsible for paying any applicable Social Security, withholding, and unemployment taxes.

Sometimes, it is advantageous to have independent-contractor status—for tax purposes, for example. At other times, employee status may confer desirable benefits on the worker. In the following case, for example, an insurance broker who lost her job wanted to take advantage of the protection against discrimination offered to employees under a state statute. Because that statute governed only employer-employee relationships, the plaintiff tried to convince the court that she was an employee rather than an independent contractor.

Case 16.1 ● Scott v. Massachusetts Mutual Life Insurance Co.

Court of Appeals of New York, 1995.
86 N.Y.2d 429,
657 N.E.2d 769,
633 N.Y.S.2d 754.

HISTORICAL AND SOCIAL SETTING *As recently as thirty-five years ago, some types of discrimination in employment were almost routine. Positions were filled, promotions were granted, and workers were terminated on the basis of gender, age, ethnicity, marital status, or some other irrelevant characteristic. Today, U.S. workers enjoy substantial employment rights, among the most significant of which is the right of equality in employment opportunity (see Chapter 17). The right of employees to be free from discriminatory employment practices has affected employees in virtually all workplaces.*

BACKGROUND AND FACTS James Blatt hired Marilyn Scott to sell insurance for the Massachusetts Mutual Life Insurance Company. Their contract stated, "Nothing in this contract shall be construed as creating the relationship of employer and employee," and that the contract was terminable at will by either party. Scott hired and trained other agents according to Massachusetts Mutual's guidelines, but she financed her own office and staff, was paid according to performance, had no taxes withheld from her checks, and could sell products of Massachusetts Mutual's competitors. When Blatt terminated their contract, Scott filed a suit in a New York state court against him and Massachusetts Mutual. Scott claimed that she had been discriminated against on the basis of her gender, age, and marital status in violation of a state law prohibiting employment discrimination. The defendants filed a motion for summary judgment on the ground that the law applied only to employees and Scott was an independent contractor. The court granted the motion, which an appellate court upheld. Scott appealed to New York's highest state court.

IN THE WORDS OF THE COURT . . .
TITONE, Judge.
 * * * *

 * * * [P]laintiff was responsible for financing her own operating expenses and support staff, was paid by performance rather than a salary, did not have Federal, State or local taxes withheld from her pay, could sell competitors' products and had agreed by contract to operate as an independent contractor. Although plaintiff alleges that she was required to recruit and train agents according to defendant Massachusetts Mutual's guidelines, that was true only for agents whose hiring was financed by defendant and not by plaintiff, and, in any event, reflects only minimal control over plaintiff's own work. Additionally, the fact that plaintiff was compelled to attend regular company meetings and was asked to draw up a job description for her position are not inconsistent with her status as an independent contractor. * * * [A]t most, * * * defendants exercised minimal control over plaintiff's own daily work product.

 The only conclusion to be drawn from these facts is that plaintiff operated her office with a high degree of independence not found in a traditional employer/employee relationship.

DECISION AND REMEDY The Court of Appeals of New York dismissed Scott's claim.

FOR CRITICAL ANALYSIS—SOCIAL CONSIDERATION *Which factor seems to have most influenced the court to rule that Scott was an independent contractor?*

Agency Formation

Agency relationships are *consensual;* that is, they come about by voluntary consent and agreement between the parties. Generally, the agreement need not be in writing,[2] and consideration is not required.

A principal must have contractual capacity. A person who cannot legally enter into contracts directly should not be allowed to do so indirectly through an agent. Because an agent derives the authority to enter into contracts from the principal and because a contract made by an agent is legally viewed as a contract of the principal, it is immaterial whether the agent personally has the legal capacity to make that contract. Thus, a minor can be an agent but in some states cannot be a principal appointing an agent.[3] (When a minor is permitted to be a principal, however, any resulting contracts will be voidable by the minor principal but not by the adult third party.) In sum, any person can be an agent, regardless of whether he or she has the capacity to contract. Even a person who is legally incompetent can be appointed an agent.

An agency relationship can be created for any legal purpose. An agency relationship created for an illegal purpose or contrary to public policy is unenforceable. If Sharp (as principal) contracts with Blesh (as agent) to sell illegal narcotics, the agency relationship is unenforceable, because selling illegal narcotics is a felony and is contrary to public policy. It is also illegal for medical doctors and other licensed professionals to employ unlicensed agents to perform professional actions.

Generally, there are four ways in which an agency relationship can arise: by agreement of the parties, by ratification, by estoppel, and by operation of law. We look here at each of these possibilities.

Agency by Agreement

Because an agency relationship is, by definition, consensual, normally it must be based on an express or implied agreement that the agent will act for the principal and the principal agrees to have the agent so act. An agency agreement can take the form of an express written contract. For example, Renato enters into a written agreement with Troy, a real estate agent, to sell Renato's house. An agency relationship exists between Renato and Troy for the sale of the house and is detailed in a document that both parties sign.

Many express agency agreements are oral. If Renato asks Cary, a gardener, to contract with others for the care of his lawn on a regular basis, and Cary agrees, an agency relationship exists between Renato and Cary for the lawn care.

An agency agreement can also be implied by conduct. For example, a hotel expressly allows only Boris Koontz to park cars, but Boris has no employment

---

2.   There are two main exceptions to the statement that agency agreements need not be in writing: (1) Whenever agency authority empowers the agent to enter into a contract that the Statute of Frauds requires to be in writing, then the agent's authority from the principal must likewise be in writing (this is called the *equal dignity rule*). (2) A power of attorney, which confers authority to an agent, must be in writing.

3.   Some courts have granted exceptions to allow a minor to appoint an agent for the limited purpose of contracting for the minor's necessities of life. See *Casey v. Kastel,* 237 N.Y. 305, 142 N.E. 671 (1924).

Salesperson assists a customer in a clothing store. Under what circumstances might a clothing importer be considered to act as an agent for the store?

contract there. The hotel's manager tells Boris when to work, as well as where and how to park the cars. The hotel's conduct amounts to a manifestation of its willingness to have Boris park its customers' cars, and Boris can infer from the hotel's conduct that he has authority to act as a parking valet. It can be inferred that Boris is an agent for the hotel, his purpose being to provide valet parking services for hotel guests.

Agency by Ratification

On occasion, a person who is in fact not an agent (or who is an agent acting outside the scope of his or her authority) may make a contract on behalf of another (a principal). If the principal approves or affirms that contract by word or by action, an agency relationship is created by ratification. Ratification is a question of intent, and intent can be expressed by either words or conduct. The basic requirements for ratification are discussed later in this chapter.

Agency by Estoppel

When a principal causes a third person to believe that another person is his or her agent, and the third person deals with the supposed agent, the principal is "estopped to deny" the agency relationship. In such a situation, the principal's actions create the *appearance* of an agency that does not in fact exist.

Suppose that Andrew accompanies Charles, a seed sales representative, to call on a customer, Steve, the proprietor of the General Seed Store. Andrew has done independent sales work but has never signed an employment agreement with Charles at this time. Charles boasts to Steve that he wishes he had three more assistants "just like Andrew." Steve has reason to believe from Charles's statements that Andrew is an agent for Charles. Steve then places seed orders with Andrew. If Charles does not correct the impression that Andrew is an agent, Charles will be bound to fill the orders just as if Andrew were really Charles's agent. Charles's representation to Steve created the impression that Andrew was Charles's agent and had authority to solicit orders.

The acts or declarations of a purported *agent* in and of themselves do not create an agency by estoppel. Rather, it is the deeds or statements of the *principal* that create an agency by estoppel. Suppose that Olivia walks into Dru's Dress Boutique and claims to be a sales agent for an exclusive Paris dress designer, Pierre Lapage. Dru has never had business relations with Pierre Lapage. Based on Olivia's claim, however, Dru gives Olivia an order and pre-pays 15 percent of the sales price. Olivia is not an agent, and the dresses are never delivered. Dru cannot hold Pierre Lapage liable. Olivia's acts and declarations alone do not create an agency by estoppel.

In addition, to assert the creation of an agency by estoppel, the third person must prove that he or she *reasonably* believed that an agency relationship existed and that the agent had authority. Facts and circumstances must show that an ordinary, prudent person familiar with business practice and custom would have been justified in concluding that the agent had authority.

The court in the following case considered whether an agency existed by estoppel between the owner of a jewelry cart in a mall and the seller of "The Only Completely Safe, Sterile Ear Piercing Method."

Case 16.2 ● Williams v. Inverness Corp.

Supreme Judicial Court of Maine, 1995.
664 A.2d 1244.

COMPANY PROFILE *Inverness Corporation is the world's largest maker of body-piercing equipment. Sam Mann founded Inverness in 1975 with a design for piercing equipment that was more sterile and less threatening than the products then in use. The first year's sales totaled more than $750,000. Today, the company makes disposable ear-piercing kits, skin-care products, hair-removal waxes, electrolysis kits, and jewelry dips. Based in Fair Lawn, New Jersey, Inverness sells its products in fifty-two countries.*

BACKGROUND AND FACTS The Inverness Corporation markets the Inverness Ear Piercing System, which includes a training course, an "eye-catching assortment of selling aids" such as counter displays, and release forms that tout the system as "The Only Completely Safe, Sterile Ear Piercing Method." Margaret Barrera, the owner of a jewelry cart in a mall, bought the system, took the course, and set up the displays. Seventeen-year-old Angela Williams paid Barrera to pierce Williams's ear. The ear became infected, which led to complications. Williams's mother filed a suit on Angela's behalf in a Maine state court against Inverness and Barrera, claiming in part that Inverness was liable on a theory of agency by estoppel. When the court issued a judgment in Williams's favor, Inverness appealed to Maine's highest court.

IN THE WORDS OF THE COURT . . .
DANA, Justice.
        * * * *
    * * * There are critical pieces of evidence in the record that can fairly be interpreted as leading to an inference that Inverness did hold Barrera out as its agent. Most important, a jury reasonably could infer that Inverness knew, or should have known, that Barrera distributed Inverness's release forms * * * .

(Continued)

Case 16.2—continued

* * * A jury reasonably could infer * * * that Inverness knew, or should have known, that Barrera was using the Inverness Ear Piercing System, that she displayed Inverness's "eye-catching assortment of selling aids," and that she used Inverness's training program.

Finally, there was evidence that Angela believed that Barrera was Inverness's agent, that Angela relied on Inverness's manifestations of agency, and that Angela's reliance on Barrera's care and skill was justifiable. * * * The release form and display promote the Inverness Ear Piercing System as "The Only Completely Safe, Sterile Ear Piercing Method."

DECISION AND REMEDY The Supreme Judicial Court of Maine affirmed the lower court's judgment.

FOR CRICITAL ANALYSIS—SOCIAL CONSIDERATION *What are the policy reasons for holding a firm liable on a theory of agency by estoppel?*

Agency by Operation of Law

There are other situations also in which the courts will find an agency relationship in the absence of a formal agreement. This may occur in family relationships. For example, suppose one spouse purchases certain basic necessaries and charges them to the other spouse's charge account. The courts will often rule that the latter is liable for payment of the necessaries, either because of a social policy of promoting the general welfare of the spouse or because of a legal duty to supply necessaries to family members.

Agency by operation of law may also occur in emergency situations, when the agent's failure to act outside the scope of his or her authority would cause the principal substantial loss. If the agent is unable to contact the principal, the courts will often grant this emergency power. For example, a railroad engineer may contract on behalf of his or her employer for medical care for an injured motorist hit by the train.

Duties of Agents and Principals

▼ Once the principal-agent relationship has been created, both parties have duties that govern their conduct. As discussed previously, the principal-agent relationship is *fiduciary*—one of trust. In a fiduciary relationship, each party owes the other the duty to act with the utmost good faith.

We now examine the various duties of agents and principals. In general, for every duty of the principal, the agent has a corresponding right, and vice versa. When one party to the agency relationship violates his or her duty to the other party, the remedies available to the party not in breach arise out of contract and tort law. These remedies include monetary damages, termination of the agency relationship, injunction, and required accountings.

> "I am 'in a fiduciary position'—which is always a _____ uncomfortable position."
>
> Frederic W. Maitland, 1850–1906
> (English jurist and historian)

Agent's Duties to the Principal

Generally, the agent owes the principal five duties—performance, notification, loyalty, obedience, and accounting.

PERFORMANCE.   An implied condition in every agency contract is the agent's agreement to use reasonable diligence and skill in performing the work. When an agent fails to perform his or her duties entirely, liability for breach of contract normally will result. The degree of skill or care required of an agent is usually that expected of a reasonable person under similar circumstances. Generally, this is interpreted to mean ordinary care. An agent may, however, have represented himself or herself as possessing special skills (such as those that an accountant or attorney possesses). In these situations, the agent is expected to exercise the skill or skills claimed. Failure to do so constitutes a breach of the agent's duty.

Not all agency relationships are based on contract. In some situations, an agent acts gratuitously—that is, not for money. A gratuitous agent cannot be liable for breach of contract, as there is no contract; he or she is subject only to tort liability. Once a gratuitous agent has begun to act in an agency capacity, he or she has the duty to continue to perform in that capacity in an acceptable manner and is subject to the same standards of care and duty to perform as other agents. For example, Peterson's friend, Stendhof, is a real estate broker. Stendhof gratuitously offers to sell Peterson's farm. If Stendhof never attempts to sell the farm, Peterson has no legal cause of action to force Stendhof to do so. If Stendhof does find a buyer, however, but fails to provide a sales contract within a reasonable period of time, thus causing the buyer to seek other property, then Peterson has a cause of action in tort for negligence.

NOTIFICATION.   There is a maxim in agency law that notice to the agent is notice to the principal. An agent is thus required to notify the principal of all matters that come to his or her attention concerning the subject matter of the agency. This is the duty of notification. The law assumes that the principal knows of any information acquired by the agent that is relevant to the agency—regardless of whether the agent actually passes on this information to the principal.

LOYALTY.   Loyalty is one of the most fundamental duties in a fiduciary relationship. Basically stated, the agent has the duty to act solely for the benefit of his or her principal and not in the interest of the agent or a third party. For example, an agent cannot represent two principals in the same transaction unless both know of the dual capacity and consent to it. The duty of loyalty also means that any information or knowledge acquired through the agency relationship is considered confidential. It would be a breach of loyalty to disclose such information either during the agency relationship or after its termination. Typical examples of confidential information are trade secrets and customer lists compiled by the principal.

In short, the agent's loyalty must be undivided. The agent's actions must be strictly for the benefit of the principal and must not result in any secret profit for the agent. For example, suppose that Ryder contracts with Alton, a real estate agent, to sell Ryder's property. Alton knows that he can find a buyer who will pay substantially more for the property than Ryder is asking. If Alton secretly purchased Ryder's property, however, and then sold it at a profit to another buyer, Alton would breach his duty of loyalty as Ryder's agent. Alton has a duty to act in Ryder's best interests and can only become the purchaser in this situation with Ryder's knowledge and approval.

> **BE AWARE** An agent's disclosure of confidential information could constitute the business tort of misappropriation of trade secrets.

Ethical Perspective

The duty of loyalty to one's employer-principal is fundamentally an ethical duty that has been written into law. The duty is rooted in the principle that a person cannot serve two masters at the same time. In an agency relationship, the agent's loyalty must be undivided. There are times, however, when the ethical duty of loyalty may come into conflict with another duty, such as one's duty to society. For example, consider the situation faced by employees of Firestone in regard to faulty tires produced by that company in the early 1980s. The employees who knew of the defective tires presumably could have divulged that information to the public (at the risk of losing their jobs, of course). Some scholars have argued that many of the greatest "evils" in the past twenty-five years have been accomplished in the name of "duty" to the principal. Duty in this context means placing the well-being of the principal above that of the public.

For Critical Analysis: *Agency law does not impose on the principal a duty of loyalty to the agent. Why is this? What would result if the law did not impose a duty of loyalty on agents?*

OBEDIENCE. When an agent is acting on behalf of the principal, a duty is imposed on that agent to follow all lawful and clearly stated instructions of the principal. Any deviation from such instructions is a violation of this duty. During emergency situations, however, when the principal cannot be consulted, the agent may deviate from such instructions without violating this duty. Whenever instructions are not clearly stated, the agent can fulfill the duty of obedience by acting in good faith and in a manner reasonable under the circumstances.

ACCOUNTING. Unless an agent and a principal agree otherwise, the agent has the duty to keep and make available to the principal an account of all property and money received and paid out on behalf of the principal. This includes gifts from third persons in connection with the agency. For example, a gift from a customer to a salesperson for prompt deliveries made by the salesperson's firm belongs to the firm. The agent has a duty to maintain separate accounts for the principal's funds and for the agent's personal funds, and no intermingling of these accounts is allowed. Whenever a licensed professional (such as an attorney) violates this duty to account, he or she may be subject to disciplinary proceedings carried out by the appropriate regulatory institution (such as the state bar association) in addition to being liable to the principal (the professional's client) for failure to account.

Principal's Duties to the Agent

The principal also has certain duties to the agent. These duties relate to compensation, reimbursement and indemnification, cooperation, and safe working conditions.

COMPENSATION. In general, when a principal requests certain services from an agent, the agent reasonably expects payment. The principal therefore has a duty to pay the agent for services rendered. For example, when an accountant or an attorney is asked to act as an agent, an agreement to compensate the agent for such service is implied. The principal also has a duty to pay that compensation in a timely manner. Except in a gratuitous agency relationship, in which an agent does not act for money, the principal must pay the agreed-on value for an agent's services. If no amount has been expressly agreed on, then the principal owes the agent the customary compensation for such services.

REIMBURSEMENT AND INDEMNIFICATION.   Whenever an agent disburses sums of money to fulfill the request of the principal or to pay for necessary expenses in the course of a reasonable performance of his or her agency duties, the principal has the duty to reimburse the agent for these payments. Agents cannot recover for expenses incurred by their own misconduct or negligence, however.

Subject to the terms of the agency agreement, the principal has the duty to compensate, or *indemnify*, an agent for liabilities incurred because of authorized and lawful acts and transactions. For example, if the agent, on the principal's behalf, forms a contract with a third party, and the principal fails to perform the contract, the third party may sue the agent for damages. In this situation, the principal is obligated to compensate the agent for any costs incurred by the agent as a result of the principal's failure to perform the contract. Additionally, the principal must indemnify (pay) the agent for the value of benefits that the agent confers on the principal. The amount of indemnification is usually specified in the agency contract. If it is not, the courts will look to the nature of the business and the type of loss to determine the amount.

COOPERATION.   A principal has a duty to cooperate with the agent and to assist the agent in performing his or her duties. The principal must do nothing to prevent such performance. For example, when a principal grants an agent an exclusive territory, creating an *exclusive agency*, the principal cannot compete with the agent or appoint or allow another agent to so compete in violation of the exclusive agency. If the principal did so, he or she would be exposed to liability for the agent's lost sales or profits.

SAFE WORKING CONDITIONS.   The common law requires the principal to provide safe working premises, equipment, and conditions for all agents and employees. The principal has a duty to inspect working conditions and to warn agents and employees about any unsafe areas. When the agency is one of employment, the employer's liability and the safety standards with which the employer must comply normally are covered by federal and state statutes and regulations.

Liability for Agent's Torts

An agent is liable for his or her own torts. A principal may also be liable for an agent's torts under the doctrine of *respondeat superior*,[4] a Latin term meaning "let the master respond." This doctrine, which is discussed in the following *Landmark in the Legal Environment*, is similar to the theory of strict liability discussed in Chapter 8. The doctrine imposes vicarious (indirect) lia-

> **REMEMBER** An agent who signs a negotiable instrument on behalf of a principal may be personally liable on the instrument. Liability depends in part on whether the identity of the principal is disclosed and whether the parties intend the agent to be bound.

Respondeat Superior In Latin, "Let the master respond." A doctrine under which a principal or an employer is held liable for the wrongful acts committed by agents or employees while acting within the scope of their agency or employment.

---

4.   Pronounced ree-*spahn*-dee-uht soo-*peer*-ee-your.

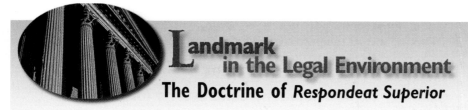

Landmark in the Legal Environment
The Doctrine of *Respondeat Superior*

The idea that a master (employer) must respond to third persons for losses negligently caused by the master's servant (employee) first appeared in Lord Holt's opinion in *Jones v. Hart* (1698).[a] By the early nineteenth century, this maxim had been adopted by most courts and was referred to as the doctrine of *respondeat superior.*

The vicarious (indirect) liability of the master for the acts of the servant has been supported primarily by two theories. The first theory rests on the issue of *control*, or *fault*: the master has control over the acts of the servant and is thus responsible for injuries arising out of such service. The second theory is economic in nature: because the master takes the benefits or profits of the servant's service, he or she should also suffer the losses; moreover, the master is better able than the servant to absorb such losses.

The *control* theory is clearly recognized in the *Restatement (Second) of Agency,* in which the master is defined as "a principal who employs an agent to perform service in his affairs and who controls, or has the right to control, the physical conduct of the other in the performance of the service." Accordingly, a servant is defined as "an agent employed by a master to perform service in his affairs

whose physical conduct in his performance of the service is controlled, or is subject to control, by the master."

There are limitations on the master's liability for the acts of the servant, however. An employer (master) is only responsible for the wrongful conduct of an employee (servant) that occurs in "the scope of the employment." The criteria used by the courts in determining whether an employee is acting within the scope of employment are stated in the *Restatement (Second) of Agency.* Generally, the act must be of a kind the servant was employed to do; must have occurred within "authorized time and space limits"; and must have been "activated, at least in part, by a purpose to serve the master."

The courts have accepted the doctrine of *respondeat superior* for nearly two centuries. This theory of vicarious liability is laden with practical implications in all situations in which a principal-agent (master-servant, employer-employee) relationship exists. The small-town grocer with one clerk and the multinational corporation with thousands of employees are equally subject to the doctrinal demand of "let the master respond."

For Critical Analysis: *How does the doctrine of* respondeat superior *relate to the doctrine of strict product liability?*

_____
a. K.B. [King's Bench] 642, 90 Eng. Reprint 1255 (1698).

• •

bility on the employer without regard to the personal fault of the employer for torts committed by an employee in the course or scope of employment.

The key to determining whether a principal may be liable for the torts of the agent under the doctrine of *respondeat superior* is whether the torts are committed within the scope of the agency or employment. The *Restatement (Second) of Agency,* Section 229, indicates the factors that courts will consider in determining whether or not a particular act occurred within the course and scope of employment. These factors are as follows:

1. Whether the act was authorized by the employer.
2. The time, place, and purpose of the act.
3. Whether the act was one commonly performed by employees on behalf of their employers.
4. The extent to which the employer's interest was advanced by the act.
5. The extent to which the private interests of the employee were involved.
6. Whether the employer furnished the means or instrumentality (for example, a truck or a machine) by which the injury was inflicted.

> **NOTE** An employee going to or from work or meals is not usually considered to be within the scope of employment. An employee whose job requires travel, however, is considered to be within the scope of employment for the entire trip, including the return.

7. Whether the employer had reason to know that the employee would do the act in question and whether the employee had ever done it before.

8. Whether the act involved the commission of a serious crime.

Liability for Independent Contractor's Torts

▼   Generally, the principal is not liable for physical harm caused to a third person by the negligent act of an independent contractor in the performance of the contract. This is because the employer does not have the *right to control* the details of an independent contractor's performance. An exception to this doctrine is made when exceptionally hazardous activities are involved, such as blasting operations, the transportation of highly volatile chemicals, or the use of poisonous gases. In these situations, a principal cannot be shielded from liability merely by using an independent contractor. Strict liability is imposed on the principal as a matter of law and, in some states, by statute. In the following case, one of the issues before the court was whether the "self-help" repossession of collateral is an inherently dangerous activity, in which case the secured creditor could be held liable for damages caused by the independent contractor's tortious actions.

Case 16.3 ● Sanchez v. MBank of El Paso

Court of Appeals of Texas—El Paso, 1990. 792 S.W.2d 530.

HISTORICAL AND SOCIAL SETTING *Under uniform laws that predated the Uniform Commercial Code (UCC), a secured party could take possession of collateral on a debtor's default without judicial process. The drafters of the UCC followed these provisions in UCC 9–503. Taking possession of collateral on default must be done without a breach of the peace, however. Among the acts that have been considered to be peaceable, in connection with repossession, is the removal of an automobile from the debtor's driveway without the debtor's knowledge. Acts that have been considered to constitute a breach of the peace, in connection with repossession, include the removal of an automobile over the debtor's objection and the removal of an automobile after a threat of violence.*

BACKGROUND AND FACTS MBank of El Paso contracted with El Paso Recovery Service (El Paso) to have El Paso repossess Yvonne Sanchez's 1978 Pontiac Trans Am, which had been purchased through MBank financing. Two men

hired by El Paso went to Sanchez's home with a tow truck and proceeded to hook the tow truck to the car, which was in the driveway. Sanchez, who was in the yard cutting the grass at the time, asked them their purpose and demanded that they cease their attempt to take the automobile and leave the premises. When they ignored her, she entered and locked herself in the car in an effort to stall them until the police or her husband could arrive. It was only after they got the automobile in the street that they identified their purpose and told her to get out of the car, which she refused to do. They then took the vehicle, with Sanchez locked in it, on a high-speed ride from her home to the repossession lot and parked the car in a fenced and locked yard with a loose guard dog. She was rescued some time later by her husband and the police. Sanchez filed suit in a Texas state court against MBank for damages, alleging that El Paso and its employees were MBank's agents and that they had willfully breached the peace in violation of UCC 9–503. The trial court granted the bank's motion for summary judgment, holding that the bank could not be liable, because El Paso was an independent contractor and not an employee or agent of MBank. Sanchez appealed.

(Continued)

Case 16.3—continued

IN THE WORDS OF THE COURT . . .
KOEHLER, Justice.
    *   *   *   *

    *   *   * [T]wo of the exceptions to the general rule that an employer is not liable for the negligent or tortious acts of an independent contractor are (1) where the employer is by statute *   *   * under a duty to provide specific safeguards for the safety of others *   *   * and (2) where the employer employs an independent contractor to do work involving a special or inherent danger to others *   *   * .
    *   *   *   *

    Our analysis of [UCC 9–503] leads us to conclude that the statute does impose a nondelegable duty on a secured party who wishes to repossess the collateral property without resorting to judicial process *   *   * to do so in a manner as to avoid a breach of the peace. *   *   *

    *   *   * [Such] a repossession, always bordering on the edge of illegality if not carried out carefully, is *   *   * inherently dangerous.

DECISION AND REMEDY The Texas appellate court reversed the trial court's decision and remanded the case for trial.

FOR CRITICAL ANALYSIS—ECONOMIC CONSIDERATION *In determining liability for a breach of the peace under UCC 9–503, should the court take into consideration the behavior of the person from whom the collateral was possessed (in this case, Sanchez)?*

Wage-Hour Laws

▼ In the 1930s, Congress enacted several laws regulating the wages and working hours of employees. In 1931, Congress passed the Davis-Bacon Act,[5] which requires the payment of "prevailing wages" to employees of contractors and subcontractors working on government construction projects. In 1936, the Walsh-Healey Act[6] was passed. This act requires that a minimum wage, as well as overtime pay of time and a half, be paid to employees of manufacturers or suppliers entering into contracts with agencies of the federal government.

In 1938, Congress passed the Fair Labor Standards Act[7] (FLSA). This act extended wage-hour requirements to cover all employers engaged in interstate commerce or engaged in the production of goods for interstate commerce, plus selected types of businesses. We examine here the FLSA's provisions in regard to child labor, maximum hours, and minimum wages.

Child Labor

The FLSA prohibits oppressive child labor. Children under fourteen years of age are allowed to do certain types of work, such as deliver newspapers, work for their parents, and work in the entertainment and (with some exceptions) agricultural areas. Children who are fourteen or fifteen years of age are

---

5. 40 U.S.C. Sections 276a–276a-5.
6. 41 U.S.C. Sections 35–45.
7. 29 U.S.C. Sections 201–260.

A restaurant worker takes a customer's order. Persons under eighteen years of age often work in restaurants. What restrictions do employers face in employing teenagers?

RECALL Special provisions also cover minors in the areas of tort law, contract law, agency law, and the law governing negotiable instruments.

allowed to work, but not in hazardous occupations. There are also numerous restrictions on how many hours per day and per week they can work. For example, they cannot work during school hours, for more than three hours on a school day (or eight hours on a nonschool day), for more than eighteen hours during a school week (or forty hours during a nonschool week), or before 7 A.M. or after 7 P.M. (9 P.M. during the summer). Most states require persons under sixteen years of age to obtain work permits.

Persons between the ages of sixteen and eighteen do not face such restrictions on working times and hours, but they cannot be employed in hazardous jobs or in jobs detrimental to their health and well-being. Persons over the age of eighteen are not affected by any of the above-mentioned restrictions.

Hours and Wages

Under the FLSA, any employee who agrees to work more than forty hours per week must be paid no less than one and a half times his or her regular pay for all hours over forty. Certain employees are exempt from the overtime provisions of the act. Exempt employees fall into four categories: executives, administrative employees, professional employees, and outside salespersons. Generally, to fall into one of these categories, an employee must earn more than a specified amount of income per week and devote a certain percentage of work time to the performance of specific types of duties, as determined by the FLSA. To qualify as an outside salesperson, the employee must regularly engage in sales work away from the office and spend no more than 20 percent of work time per week performing duties other than sales.

Minimum Wage The lowest wage, either by government regulation or union contract, that an employer may pay an hourly worker.

The FLSA provides that a **minimum wage** of a specified amount must be paid to employees in covered industries. Congress periodically revises such minimum wages. For example, the current minimum wage is $5.15 an hour. Under the FLSA, the term *wages* includes the reasonable cost of the employer in furnishing employees with board, lodging, and other facilities if they are customarily furnished by that employer.

Worker Health and Safety

▼ Under the common law, employees injured on the job had to rely on tort law or contract law theories in suits they brought against their employers. Additionally, workers had some recourse under the common law governing agency relationships, which imposes a duty on a principal-employer to provide a safe workplace for his or her agent-employee. Today, numerous state and federal statutes protect employees and their families from the risk of accidental injury, death, or disease resulting from their employment. This section discusses the primary federal statute governing health and safety in the workplace, along with state workers' compensation acts.

The Occupational Safety and Health Act

At the federal level, the primary legislation for employee health and safety protection is the Occupational Safety and Health Act of 1970.[8] Congress passed this act in an attempt to ensure safe and healthful working conditions for practically every employee in the country. The act provides for specific standards that employers must meet, plus a general duty to keep workplaces safe.

ENFORCEMENT AGENCIES. Three federal agencies develop and enforce the standards set by the Occupational Safety and Health Act. The Occupational Safety and Health Administration (OSHA) is part of the Department of Labor and has the authority to promulgate standards, make inspections, and enforce the act. OSHA has safety standards governing many workplace details, such as the structural stability of ladders and the requirements for railings. OSHA also establishes standards that protect employees against exposure to substances that may be harmful to their health.

The National Institute for Occupational Safety and Health is part of the Department of Health and Human Services. Its main duty is to conduct research on safety and health problems and to recommend standards for OSHA to adopt. Finally, the Occupational Safety and Health Review Commission is an independent agency set up to handle appeals from actions taken by OSHA administrators.

PROCEDURES AND VIOLATIONS. OSHA compliance officers may enter and inspect facilities of any establishment covered by the Occupational Safety and Health Act.[9] Employees may also file complaints of violations. Under the act, an employer cannot discharge an employee who files a complaint or who, in good faith, refuses to work in a high-risk area if bodily harm or death might result.

Employers with eleven or more employees are required to keep occupational injury and illness records for each employee. Each record must be made available for inspection when requested by an OSHA inspector. Whenever a work-related injury or disease occurs, employers must make reports directly to

> **BE CAREFUL** To check for compliance with safety standards without being cited for violations, an employer can often obtain advice from an insurer, a trade association, or a state agency.

---

8. 29 U.S.C. Sections 553, 651–678.
9. In the past, warrantless inspections were conducted. In 1978, however, the United States Supreme Court held that warrantless inspections violated the warrant clause of the Fourth Amendment to the Constitution. See *Marshall v. Barlow's, Inc.*, 436 U.S. 307, 98 S.Ct. 1816, 56 L.Ed.2d 305 (1978).

OSHA. Whenever an employee is killed in a work-related accident or when five or more employees are hospitalized in one accident, the employer must notify the Department of Labor within forty-eight hours. If the company fails to do so, it will be fined. Following the accident, a complete inspection of the premises is mandatory.

Criminal penalties for willful violation of the Occupational Safety and Health Act are limited. Employers may be prosecuted under state laws, however. In other words, the act does not preempt state and local criminal laws.[10] In the following case, an employer argued that it should not be penalized by OSHA for violating a regulation of which the employer was ignorant.

---

10.   *Pedraza v. Shell Oil Co.*, 942 F.2d 48 (1st Cir. 1991); cert. denied, *Shell Oil Co. v. Pedraza*, 502 U.S. 1082, 112 S.Ct. 993, 117 L.Ed.2d 154 (1992).

Case 16.4 ● Valdak Corp. v. Occupational Safety and Health Review Commission

United States Court of Appeals,
Eighth Circuit, 1996.
73 F.3d 1466.

HISTORICAL AND SOCIAL SETTING   *Since the Occupational Safety and Health Act was enacted in 1970, the rates of deaths and injuries in the workplace have been cut in half. In 1970, for example, eighteen of every one hundred thousand workers were killed on the job. In 1996, the rate was eight per one hundred thousand. To prevent accidental injuries and deaths, employers often impose safety measures. Such measures are particularly important when an employer's work force is young and inexperienced, as in many restaurants, retail establishments, and car washes.*

BACKGROUND AND FACTS   The Valdak Corporation operates a car wash that uses an industrial dryer to spin-dry towels. The dryer was equipped with a device that was supposed to keep it locked while it spun, but the device often did not work. An employee reached into the dryer while it was spinning, and his arm was cut off above the elbow. OSHA cited Valdak for, among other things, a willful violation of a machine-guarding regulation and assessed a $28,000 penalty. Valdak appealed to the Occupational Safety and Health Review Commission, which upheld the penalty. Valdak appealed to the U.S. Court of Appeals for the Eighth Circuit, arguing in part that it did not know about the specific regulation.

IN THE WORDS OF THE COURT . . .
JOHN R. GIBSON, Circuit Judge.
   *   *   *   *

   Valdak's claimed ignorance of the OSHA standard does not negate a finding of willfulness. Willfulness can be proved by "plain indifference" to the [Occupational Safety and Health Act's] requirements. Plain indifference to the machine guarding requirement is amply demonstrated by the facts that the dryer was equipped with an interlocking device, the interlocking device did not work, and Valdak continued to use the dryer with the broken interlock device. *   *   *

DECISION AND REMEDY   The U.S. Court of Appeals for the Eighth Circuit upheld the agency's finding.

FOR CRITICAL ANALYSIS—ETHICAL CONSIDERATION   *For what policy reasons might an employer set up a formal safety program or issue a written safety manual?*

Workers' Compensation

State **workers' compensation laws** establish an administrative procedure for compensating workers injured on the job. Instead of suing, an injured worker files a claim with the administrative agency or board that administers the local workers' compensation claims.

Most workers' compensation statutes are similar. No state covers all employees. Typically excluded are domestic workers, agricultural workers, temporary employees, and employees of common carriers (companies that provide transportation services to the public). Typically, the statutes cover minors. Usually, the statutes allow employers to purchase insurance from a private insurer or a state fund to pay workers' compensation benefits in the event of a claim. Most states also allow employers to be *self-insured*—that is, employers who show an ability to pay claims do not need to buy insurance.

In general, the right to recover benefits is predicated wholly on the existence of an employment relationship and the fact that the injury was *accidental* and *occurred on the job* or *in the course of employment*, regardless of fault. Intentionally inflicted self-injury, for example, would not be considered accidental and hence would not be covered. If an injury occurred while an employee was commuting to or from work, it would not usually be considered to have occurred on the job or in the course of employment and hence would not be covered.

An employee must notify his or her employer promptly (usually within thirty days) of an injury. Generally, an employee also must file a workers' compensation claim with the appropriate state agency or board within a certain period (sixty days to two years) from the time the injury is first noticed, rather than from the time of the accident.

An employee's acceptance of workers' compensation benefits bars the employee from suing for injuries caused by the employer's negligence. By barring lawsuits for negligence, workers' compensation laws also bar employers from raising common law defenses to negligence, such as contributory negligence or assumption of risk. A worker may sue an employer who *intentionally* injures the worker, however.

Workers' Compensation Laws State statutes establishing an administrative procedure for compensating workers' injuries that arise out of—or in the course of—their employment, regardless of fault.

Income Security

Federal and state governments participate in insurance programs designed to protect employees and their families by covering the financial impact of retirement, disability, death, hospitalization, and unemployment. The key federal law on this subject is the Social Security Act of 1935.[11]

Social Security and Medicare

The Social Security Act provides for old age (retirement), survivors, and disability insurance. The act is therefore often referred to as OASDI. Both employers and employees must "contribute" under the Federal Insurance Contributions Act (FICA)[12] to help pay for the employees' loss of income on retirement. The

BE AWARE Social Security currently covers almost all jobs in the United States. Nine out of ten workers contribute to this protection for themselves and their families.

---

11. 42 U.S.C. Sections 301–1397e.
12. 26 U.S.C. Sections 3101–3125.

basis for the employee's and the employer's contribution is the employee's annual wage base—the maximum amount of the employee's wages that are subject to the tax. The employer withholds the employee's FICA contribution from the employee's wages and then matches this contribution. (In 1998, employers were required to withhold 6.2 percent of each employee's wages, up to a maximum wage base of $68,400, and to match this contribution.)

Retired workers are then eligible to receive monthly payments from the Social Security Administration, which administers the Social Security Act. Social Security benefits are fixed by statute but increase automatically with increases in the cost of living.

Medicare, a health-insurance program, is administered by the Social Security Administration for people sixty-five years of age and older and for some under the age of sixty-five who are disabled. It has two parts, one pertaining to hospital costs and the other to nonhospital medical costs, such as visits to doctors' offices. People who have Medicare hospital insurance can also obtain additional federal medical insurance if they pay small monthly premiums, which increase as the cost of medical care increases. As with Social Security contributions, both the employer and the employee contribute to Medicare. Currently, 2.9 percent of the amount of all wages and salaries paid to employees goes toward financing Medicare. Unlike Social Security contributions, there is no cap on the amount of wages subject to the Medicare tax.

Private Pension Plans

There has been significant legislation to regulate employee retirement plans set up by employers to supplement Social Security benefits. The major federal act covering these retirement plans is the Employee Retirement Income Security Act (ERISA) of 1974.[13] This act empowers the Labor Management Services Administration of the Department of Labor to enforce its provisions governing employers who have private pension funds for their employees. ERISA does not require an employer to establish a pension plan. When a plan exists, however, ERISA establishes standards for its management.

Vesting The creation of an absolute or unconditional right or power.

A key provision of ERISA concerns **vesting**. Vesting gives an employee a legal right to receive pension benefits at some future date when he or she stops working. Before ERISA was enacted, some employees who had worked for companies for as long as thirty years received no pension benefits when their employment terminated, because those benefits had not vested. ERISA establishes complex vesting rules. Generally, however, all employee contributions to pension plans vest immediately, and employee rights to employer pension-plan contributions vest after five years of employment.

In an attempt to prevent mismanagement of pension funds, ERISA has established rules on how they must be invested. Pension managers must be cautious in their investments and refrain from investing more than 10 percent of the fund in securities of the employer. ERISA also contains detailed record-keeping and reporting requirements.

Unemployment Insurance

The United States has a system of unemployment insurance in which employers pay into a fund, the proceeds of which are paid out to qualified unem-

---

13.   29 U.S.C. Sections 1001 *et seq.*

ployed workers. The Federal Unemployment Tax Act of 1935[14] created a state system that provides unemployment compensation to eligible individuals. Employers that fall under the provisions of the act are taxed at regular intervals. Taxes are typically paid by the employers to the states, which then deposit them with the federal government. The federal government maintains an unemployment insurance fund, in which each state has an account.

> **WATCH OUT** A state government can place a lien on the property of an employer who does not pay unemployment taxes.

COBRA

Federal legislation also addresses the issue of health insurance for workers whose jobs have been terminated—and who are thus no longer eligible for group health-insurance plans. The Consolidated Omnibus Budget Reconciliation Act (COBRA) of 1985[15] prohibits the elimination of a worker's medical, optical, or dental insurance coverage on the voluntary or involuntary termination of the worker's employment. Employers, with some exceptions, must comply with COBRA if they employ twenty or more workers and provide a benefit plan to those workers.

The employer is relieved of the responsibility to provide benefit coverage if it completely eliminates its group benefit plan. An employer is also relieved of responsibility when the worker becomes eligible for Medicare, falls under a spouse's health plan, becomes insured under a different plan (with a new employer, for example), or fails to pay the premium. An employer that fails to comply with COBRA risks substantial penalties, such as a tax of up to 10 percent of the annual cost of the group plan or $500,000, whichever is less.

> **"It is the job of the legislature to follow the spirit of the nation, provided it is not contrary to the principles of government."**
>
> Charles-Louis de Secondat, Baron de Montesquieu, 1689–1755 (French philosopher and jurist)

Family and Medical Leave

In 1993, Congress passed the Family and Medical Leave Act (FMLA)[16] to assist employees who need time off work for family or medical reasons. A majority of the states also have legislation allowing for a leave from employment for family or medical reasons, and many employers maintain private family-leave plans for their workers.

The FMLA requires employers who have fifty or more employees to provide employees with up to twelve weeks of family or medical leave during any twelve-month period. During the employee's leave, the employer must continue the worker's health-care coverage and guarantee employment in the same position or a comparable position when the employee returns to work. An important exception to the FMLA, however, allows the employer to avoid reinstatement of a *key employee*—defined as an employee whose pay falls within the top 10 percent of the firm's work force. Additionally, the act does not apply to employees who have worked less than one year or less than twenty-five hours a week during the previous twelve months.

Remedies for violations of the FMLA include damages for unpaid wages (or salary), lost benefits, denied compensation, actual monetary losses (such as the

Family members welcome their newborn baby. Under federal law, how much leave can a parent take from his or her job to care for the family?

---

14. 26 U.S.C. Sections 3301–3310.
15. 29 U.S.C. Sections 1161–1169.
16. 29 U.S.C. Sections 2601, 2611–2619, 2651–2654.

cost of providing for care) up to an amount equivalent to the employee's wages for twelve weeks, job reinstatement, and promotion. The successful plaintiff is entitled to court costs; attorneys' fees; and in cases involving bad faith on the part of the employer, double damages.

Key Terms

agency 445	minimum wage 460	workers' compensation
fiduciary 445	*respondeat superior* 456	laws 463
independent contractor 446	vesting 464	

Chapter Summary
Employment Relationships

AGENCY RELATIONSHIPS (See pages 445–449.)	In a *principal-agent* relationship, an agent acts on behalf of and instead of the principal, using a certain degree of his or her own discretion. An employee who deals with third parties is normally an agent. An independent contractor is not an employee, and the employer has no control over the details of physical performance. The independent contractor is not usually an agent.
AGENCY FORMATION (See pages 450–453.)	1. **By agreement**—Through express consent (oral or written) or implied by conduct. 2. **By ratification**—The principal, either by act or agreement, ratifies the conduct of an agent who acted outside the scope of authority or the conduct of a person who is in fact not an agent. 3. **By estoppel**—When the principal causes a third person to believe that another person is his or her agent, and the third person deals with the supposed agent, the principal is "estopped to deny" the agency relationship. 4. **By operation of law**—Based on a social duty (such as the need to support family members) or created in emergency situations when the agent is unable to contact the principal.

DUTIES OF AGENTS AND PRINCIPALS
(See pages 453–456.)
	1. Duties of the agent—
	  a. Performance—The agent must use reasonable diligence and skill in performing his or her duties.
	  b. Notification—The agent is required to notify the principal of all matters that come to his or her attention concerning the subject matter of the agency.
	  c. Loyalty—The agent has a duty to act solely for the benefit of his or her principal and not in the interest of the agent or a third party.
	  d. Obedience—The agent must follow all lawful and clearly stated instructions of the principal.
	  e. Accounting—The agent has a duty to make available to the principal records of all property and money received and paid out on behalf of the principal.
	
	2. Duties of the principal—
	  a. Compensation—Except in a gratuitous agency relationship, the principal must pay the agreed-on value (or reasonable value) for an agent's services.

(Continued)

Chapter Summary, continued

DUTIES OF AGENTS AND PRINCIPALS— continued (See pages 453–456.)	**b.** Reimbursement and indemnification—The principal must reimburse the agent for all sums of money disbursed at the request of the principal and for all sums of money the agent disburses for necessary expenses in the course of reasonable performance of his or her agency duties. **c.** Cooperation—A principal must cooperate with and assist an agent in performing his or her duties. **d.** Safe working conditions—A principal must provide safe working conditions for the agent-employee.
LIABILITY IN AGENCY RELATIONSHIPS (See pages 456–459.)	**1. Liability for agent's torts**—Under the doctrine of *respondeat superior,* the principal is liable for any harm caused to another through the agent's torts if the agent was acting within the scope of his or her employment at the time the harmful act occurred. The principal is also liable for an agent's misrepresentation, whether made knowingly or by mistake. **2. Liability for independent contractor's torts**—A principal is not liable for harm caused by an independent contractor's negligence, unless hazardous activities are involved (in which situation the principal is strictly liable for any resulting harm). **3. Liability for agent's crimes**—An agent is responsible for his or her own crimes, even if the crimes were committed while the agent was acting within the scope of authority or employment. A principal will be liable for an agent's crime only if the principal participated by conspiracy or other action or (in some jurisdictions) if the agent violated certain government regulations in the course of employment.
WAGE-HOUR LAWS (See pages 459–460.)	**1. Davis-Bacon Act (1931)**—Requires the payment of "prevailing wages" to employees of contractors and subcontractors working on government construction projects. **2. Walsh-Healey Act (1936)**—Requires that a minimum wage and overtime pay be paid to employees of firms that contract with federal agencies. **3. Fair Labor Standards Act (1938)**—Extended wage-hour requirements to cover all employers whose activities affect interstate commerce. The act has specific requirements in regard to child labor, maximum hours, and minimum wages.
WORKER HEALTH AND SAFETY (See pages 461–463.)	**1.** The Occupational Safety and Health Act of 1970 requires employers to meet specific safety and health standards that are established and enforced by the Occupational Safety and Health Administration (OSHA). **2.** State workers' compensation laws establish an administrative procedure for compensating workers who are injured in accidents that occur on the job, regardless of fault.
INCOME SECURITY (See pages 463–465.)	**1. Social Security and Medicare**—The Social Security Act of 1935 provides for old age (retirement), survivors, and disability insurance. Both employers and employees must make contributions under the Federal Insurance Contributions Act (FICA) to help pay for the employees' loss of income on retirement. The Social Security Administration administers Medicare, a health-insurance program for older or disabled persons. **2. Private pension plans**—The federal Employee Retirement Income Security Act (ERISA) of 1974 establishes standards for the management of employer-provided pension plans. **3. Unemployment insurance**—The Federal Unemployment Tax Act of 1935 created a system that provides unemployment compensation to eligible individuals. Covered employers are taxed to help cover the costs of unemployment compensation.

(Continued)

Chapter Summary, continued

COBRA (See page 465.)	The Consolidated Omnibus Budget Reconciliation Act (COBRA) of 1985 requires employers to give employees, on termination of employment, the option of continuing their medical, optical, or dental insurance coverage for a certain period.
FAMILY AND MEDICAL LEAVE (See pages 465–466.)	The Family and Medical Leave Act (FMLA) of 1993 requires employers with fifty or more employees to provide their employees (except for key employees) with up to twelve weeks of unpaid family or medical leave during any twelve-month period.

For Review

1. What formalities are required to create an agency relationship?

2. What duties does the agent owe to the principal? What duties does the principal owe to the agent?

3. Under what doctrine can a principal-employer be held liable for the torts committed by an agent-employee?

4. What federal statute governs working hours and wages? What federal statutes govern labor unions and collective bargaining?

5. What federal act was enacted to protect the health and safety of employees? What are workers' compensation laws?

Questions and Case Problems

16–1. Agency Formation. Pete Gaffrey is a well-known, wealthy financier living in the city of Takima. Alan Winter, Gaffrey's friend, tells Til Borge that he (Winter) is Gaffrey's agent for the purchase of rare coins. Winter even shows Borge a local newspaper clipping mentioning Gaffrey's interest in coin collecting. Borge, knowing of Winter's friendship with Gaffrey, contracts with Winter to sell to Gaffrey a rare coin valued at $25,000. Winter takes the coin and disappears with it. On the date of contract payment, Borge seeks to collect from Gaffrey, claiming that Winter's agency made Gaffrey liable. Gaffrey does not deny that Winter was a friend, but he claims that Winter was never his agent. Discuss fully whether an agency was in existence at the time the contract for the rare coin was made.

16–2. Agent's Duties to Principal. Iliana is a traveling sales agent. Iliana not only solicits orders but also delivers the goods and collects payments from her customers. Iliana places all payments in her private checking account and at the end of each month draws sufficient cash from her bank to cover the payments made. Giberson Corp., Iliana's employer, is totally unaware of this procedure. Because of a slowdown in the economy, Giberson tells all its sales personnel to offer 20 percent discounts on orders. Iliana solicits orders, but she offers only 15 percent discounts, pocketing the extra 5 percent paid by customers. Iliana has not lost any orders by this practice, and she is rated as one of Giberson's top salespersons. Giberson now learns of Iliana's actions. Discuss fully Giberson's rights in this matter.

16–3. Health and Safety Regulations. Denton and Carlo were employed at an appliance plant. Their job required them to do occasional maintenance work while standing on a wire mesh twenty feet above the plant floor. Other employees had fallen through the mesh, one of whom had been killed by the fall. When Denton and Carlo were asked by their supervisor to do work that would likely require them to walk on the mesh, they refused due to their fear of bodily harm or death. Because of their refusal to do the requested work, the two employees were fired from their jobs. Was their discharge wrongful? If so, under what federal employment law? To what federal agency or department should they turn for assistance?

16–4. Workers' Compensation. Galvin Strang worked for a tractor company in one of its factories. Near his work station there was a conveyor belt that ran through a large industrial oven. Sometimes, the workers would use the oven to heat their meals. Thirty-inch-high flasks containing molds were fixed at regular intervals on the conveyor and were transported into the oven. Strang had to walk between the flasks to get to his work station. One day, the conveyor was not moving, and Strang used the oven to cook a frozen pot pie. As he was removing the pot pie from the oven, the conveyor came on. One of the flasks struck Strang and seriously injured him. Strang sought recovery under the state workers' compensation law. Should he recover? Why or why not?

16–5. Agent's Duties to Principal. Sam Kademenos was about to sell a $1 million life insurance policy to a prospective customer when he resigned from his position with Equitable Life Assurance Society. Before resigning from the company, he had expended substantial amounts of company money and had utilized Equitable's medical examiners to procure the $1 million sale. After resigning, Kademenos joined a competing insurance firm, Jefferson Life Insurance Co., and made the sale through it. Has he breached any duty to Equitable? Explain. [*Kademenos v. Equitable Life Assurance Society*, 513 F.2d 1073 (3d Cir. 1975)]

16–6. Respondeat Superior. Richard Lanno worked for Thermal Equipment Corp. as a project engineer. Lanno was allowed to keep a company van and tools at his home because he routinely drove to work sites directly from his home and because he was often needed for unanticipated business trips during his off hours. The arrangement had been made for the convenience of Thermal Equipment, even though Lanno's managers permitted him to make personal use of the van. Lanno was involved in a collision with Lazar while driving the van home from work one day. At the time of the accident, Lanno had taken a detour in order to stop at a store—he had intended to purchase a few items and then go home. Lazar sued Thermal Equipment, claiming that Lanno had acted within the scope of his employment. Discuss whether Lazar was able to recover from Thermal Equipment. Can employees act on behalf of their employers and themselves at the same time? Discuss. [*Lazar v. Thermal Equipment Corp.*, 148 Cal.App.3d 458, 195 Cal.Rptr. 890 (1983)]

16–7. Health and Safety Regulations. At an REA Express, Inc., shipping terminal, a conveyor belt was inoperative because an electrical circuit had shorted out. The manager called a licensed electrical contractor. When the contractor arrived, REA's maintenance supervisor was in the circuit breaker room. The floor was wet, and the maintenance supervisor was using sawdust to try to soak up the water. While REA's maintenance supervisor was standing on the wet floor and attempting to fix the short circuit, he was electrocuted. Simultaneously the licensed electrical contractor, who was standing on a wooden platform, was burned and knocked unconscious. The

Occupational Safety and Health Administration (OSHA) sought to fine REA Express $1,000 for failure to furnish a place of employment free from recognized hazards. Will the court uphold OSHA's decision? Discuss fully. [*REA Express, Inc. v. Brennan*, 495 F.2d 822 (2d Cir. 1974)]

16–8. Respondeat Superior. Justin Jones suffered from genital herpes and sought treatment from Dr. Steven Baisch of Region West Pediatric Services. A nurse's assistant, Jeni Hallgren, who was a Region West employee, told her friends and some of Jones's friends about Jones's condition. This was a violation of the Region West employee handbook, which required employees to maintain the confidentiality of patients' records. Jones filed a suit in a federal district court against Region West, among others, alleging that Region West should be held liable for its employee's actions on the basis of *respondeat superior*. On what basis might the court hold that Region West is not liable for Hallgren's acts? Discuss fully. [*Jones v. Baisch, M.D.*, 40 F.3d 252 (8th Cir. 1994)]

16–9. Employee versus Independent Contractor. Stephen Hemmerling was a driver for the Happy Cab Co. Hemmerling paid certain fixed expenses and abided by a variety of rules relating to the use of the cab, the hours that could be worked, the solicitation of fares, and so on. Rates were set by the state. Happy Cab did not withhold taxes from Hemmerling's pay. While driving a cab, Hemmerling was injured in an accident and filed a claim against Happy Cab in a Nebraska state court for workers' compensation benefits. Such benefits are not available to independent contractors. On what basis might the court hold that Hemmerling is an employee? Explain. [*Hemmerling v. Happy Cab Co.*, 247 Neb. 919, 530 N.W.2d 916 (1995)]

16–10. Workers' Compensation. Linda Burnett Kidwell, employed as a state traffic officer by the California Highway Patrol (CHP), suffered an injury at home, off duty, while practicing the standing long jump. The jump is part of a required test during the CHP's annual physical performance program fitness test. Kidwell filed a claim for workers' compensation benefits. The CHP and the California workers' compensation appeals board denied her claim. Kidwell appealed to a state appellate court. What is the requirement for granting a workers' compensation claim? Should Kidwell's claim be granted? [*Kidwell v. Workers' Compensation Appeals Board*, 33 Cal.App.4th 1130, 39 Cal.Rptr.2d 540 (1995)]

A Question of Ethics and Social Responsibility

16–11. Kimberly Sierra, suffering from a severe asthma attack, went to Southview Hospital & Family Health

Center. She was treated in the emergency room by Dr. Thomas Mucci. At the time, as a result of statements by Southview administrators, brochures, and ads, Sierra believed that the physicians at Southview were "hospital doctors." In fact, however, Mucci's contract with Southview stated, "The relationship between [Southview and Mucci] shall be that of independent contractor." Within a few hours, Sierra was pronounced dead. Sierra's mother, Edna Clark, filed a suit in an Ohio state court against Southview and others, alleging, in part, negligent medical care. Southview argued that it was not responsible for the acts of its independent contractors. Ultimately, the Supreme Court of Ohio heard the case and held that Southview was liable, under the doctrine of agency by estoppel, based primarily on its "hold[ing] itself out to the public as a provider of medical services." [*Clark v. Southview Hospital & Family Health Center,* 68 Ohio St.3d 435, 628 N.E.2d 46 (1994)]

1. Could Southview have avoided liability if Sierra had known that Mucci was an independent contractor? If so, would a sign in the emergency room have been enough? If not, how might Southview have avoided liability? Is it ethical for a hospital to attempt to avoid such responsibility?

2. Some department stores rent space in their stores to vendors of individual lines of products, such as cosmetics. In doing so, does a department store hold itself out to the public as a "provider" of cosmetics, subjecting itself to liability for the negligent acts of the independent contractors on its premises? Should the holding in the *Southview* case be applied in such contexts?

For Critical Analysis

16–12. When a worker is injured on the job, normally the sole remedy is provided through state workers' compensation statutes, regardless of fault or the employer's negligence. On average, recoveries under these statutes are less than half what recoveries in tort lawsuits would be. In view of the law's increasing concern with compensating injured parties, why are these statutes retained? What policy considerations underlie their retention?

INTERACTING WITH The Internet

■ The 'Lectric Law Library's Lawcopedia contains a summary of agency laws at

http://www.lectlaw.com/d-a.htm

Scroll down through the A's and select the link to Agent for useful information on this area of the law.

■ If you are interested in learning more about "intelligent agents," you can read the article entitled "Can Programs Bind Humans to Contracts?" at

http://www.ljx.com/internet/0113shrink.html

■ The Institute of Labor Relations at Cornell University and *Human Resource Executive* magazine have compiled an extensive index of resources on labor law. You can find these resources at

http://www.workindex.com

■ BenefitsLink offers extensive information on employee benefits, including the full text of the Employee Retirement Income Security Act (ERISA) and links to other benefits resources on the Internet. You can access BenefitsLink at

http://www.benefitslink.com/index

■ A site that offers information on health-care benefits for employees can be accessed at

http://www.rbvdnr.com/eb/eb-main.htm

■ The Web site of the Occupational Safety and Health Administration (OSHA) offers information related to workplace health and safety, including the text of the Occupational Safety and Health Act of 1970, information on how and where to file an OSHA complaint, OSHA standards and regulations, OSHA directives, and more. You can access the site at

http://www.osha-slc.gov

■ The Bureau of Labor Statistics offers a wide variety of data on employment, including data on employment compensation, working conditions, and productivity. Go to

http://stats.bls.gov/blshome.html

■ To read the Fair Labor Standards Act, go to:

http://www.law.cornell.edu/uscode/29/ch8.html

■ If you want to review proposed OSHA rules, you can access the *Federal Register* at

http://ssdc.ucsd.edu/gpo/

■ To learn more about Social Security, access the Social Security Administration's home page at

http://www.ssa.gov/

■ Go to West's Legal Studies Home Page at

http://www.westbuslaw.com

There you will find a variety of legal resources. Visit us often!

CHAPTER 17

Equal Employment Opportunities

Contents

Chapter Objectives

After reading this chapter, you should be able to . . .

1. Indicate what types of discrimination are prohibited by federal laws.

2. List and describe the three major federal statutes that prohibit employment discrimination.

3. Distinguish between disparate-treatment discrimination and disparate-impact discrimination.

4. Summarize the remedies available to victims of employment discrimination.

5. Discuss how employers can defend against claims of employment discrimination.

> **"Nor shall any State . . . deny to any person within its jurisdiction the equal protection of the laws."**
>
> The Fourteenth Amendment to the U.S. Constitution

During the early 1960s we, as a nation, focused our attention on the civil rights of all Americans, including our rights under the Fourteenth Amendment to the equal protection of the laws. Out of this movement to end racial and other forms of discrimination grew a body of law protecting workers against discrimination in the workplace. This protective legislation further eroded the employment-at-will doctrine, which was discussed in the previous chapter. In the past several decades, judicial decisions, administrative agency actions, and legislation have restricted the ability of employers, as well as unions, to discriminate against workers on the basis of race, color, religion, national origin, gender, age, or disability. A class of persons defined by one or more of these criteria is known as a *protected class.*

Several federal statutes prohibit discrimination in the employment context against members of protected classes. The most important statute is Title VII of the Civil Rights Act of 1964.[1] Title VII prohibits discrimination on the basis of race, color, religion, national origin, and gender. Discrimination on the basis of age and disability are prohibited by the Age Discrimination in Employment Act of 1967[2] and the Americans with Disabilities Act of 1990,[3] respectively.

The focus of this chapter is on the kinds of discrimination prohibited by these federal statutes. Note, however, that discrimination against employees on the basis of any of the above-mentioned criteria may also violate state human rights statutes or other state laws prohibiting discrimination.

Title VII of the Civil Rights Act of 1964

Employment Discrimination
Treating employees or job applicants unequally on the basis of race, color, national origin, religion, gender, age, or disability; prohibited by federal statutes.

Title VII of the Civil Rights Act of 1964 and its amendments prohibit **employment discrimination** against employees, applicants, and union members on the basis of race, color, national origin, religion, and gender at any stage of employment. Title VII applies to employers with fifteen or more employees, labor unions with fifteen or more members, labor unions that operate hiring halls (to which members go regularly to be rationed jobs as they become available), employment agencies, and state and local governing units or agencies. A special section of the act prohibits discrimination in most federal government employment.

Compliance with Title VII is monitored by the Equal Employment Opportunity Commission (EEOC). A victim of alleged discrimination, before bringing a suit against the employer, must first file a claim with the EEOC. The EEOC may investigate the dispute and attempt to obtain the parties' voluntary consent to an out-of-court settlement. If voluntary agreement cannot be reached, the EEOC may then file a suit against the employer on the employee's behalf. If the EEOC decides not to investigate the claim, the victim may bring his or her own lawsuit against the employer.

Until recently, the EEOC investigated every claim of employment discrimination, regardless of the merits of the claim. In 1996, however, in its "National Enforcement Plan," the EEOC stated that it will investigate only "priority cases." The plan contains a list of the types of cases that the EEOC wants to investigate and take to litigation and those that it does not. Generally, priority

---

1.   42 U.S.C. Sections 2000e–2000e-17.
2.   29 U.S.C. Sections 621–634.
3.   42 U.S.C. Sections 12102–12118.

cases are cases that affect many workers, cases involving retaliatory discharge (firing an employee in retaliation for submitting a claim to the EEOC), and cases involving types of discrimination that are of particular concern to the EEOC.

Types of Discrimination

Title VII prohibits both intentional and unintentional discrimination. Intentional discrimination by an employer against an employee is known as **disparate-treatment discrimination.** Because intent may sometimes be difficult to prove, courts have established certain procedures for resolving disparate-treatment cases. Suppose that a woman applies for employment with a construction firm and is rejected. If she sues on the basis of disparate-treatment discrimination in hiring, she must show that (1) she is a member of a protected class, (2) she applied and was qualified for the job in question, (3) she was rejected by the employer, and (4) the employer continued to seek applicants for the position or filled the position with a person not in a protected class.

If the woman can meet these relatively easy requirements, she makes out a *prima facie* case of illegal discrimination. Making out a *prima facie* case of discrimination means that the plaintiff has met her initial burden of proof and will win in the absence of a legally acceptable employer defense (defenses to claims of employment discrimination will be discussed later in this chapter). The burden then shifts to the employer-defendant, who must articulate a legal reason for not hiring the plaintiff. For example, the employer might say that the plaintiff was not hired because she lacked sufficient experience or training. To prevail, the plaintiff must then show that the employer's reason is a *pretext* (not the true reason) and that discriminatory intent actually motivated the employer's decision.

Employers often find it necessary to use interviews and testing procedures to choose from among a large number of applicants for job openings. Minimum educational requirements are also common. Employer practices, such as those involving educational requirements, may have an unintended discriminatory impact on a protected class. **Disparate-impact discrimination** occurs when, as a result of educational or other job requirements or hiring procedures, an employer's work force does not reflect the percentage of nonwhites, women, or members of other protected classes that characterizes qualified individuals in the local labor market. If a person challenging an employment practice having a discriminatory effect can show a connection between the practice and the disparity, he or she makes out a *prima facie* case, and no evidence of discriminatory intent needs to be shown. Disparate-impact discrimination can also occur when an educational or other job requirement or hiring procedure excludes members of a protected class from an employer's work force at a substantially higher rate than nonmembers, regardless of the racial balance in the employer's work force.

Discrimination Based on Race, Color, and National Origin

If a company's standards or policies for selecting or promoting employees have the effect of discriminating against employees or job applicants on the basis of race, color, or national origin, they are illegal—unless (except for race) they have a substantial, demonstrable relationship to realistic qualifications for the job in question. Discrimination against these protected classes in regard to employment conditions and benefits is also illegal.

Disparate-Treatment Discrimination A form of employment discrimination that results when an employer intentionally discriminates against employees who are members of protected classes.

Prima Facie Case A case in which the plaintiff has produced sufficient evidence of his or her conclusion that the case can go to a jury; a case in which the evidence compels the plaintiff's conclusion if the defendant produces no evidence to disprove it.

Disparate-Impact Discrimination A form of employment discrimination that results from certain employer practices or procedures that, although not discriminatory on their face, have a discriminatory effect.

Ethical Perspective

Clearly, employers have an interest in the appearance of their employees, because the appearance of the employees affects the company's image in the eyes of the public. For this reason, many employers have dress or grooming policies for their employees. What if these policies result in disparate-impact discrimination? For example, suppose that a dress code requires that men may not wear ponytails, whereas women are allowed to do so. Is this an illegal form of disparate-impact gender discrimination?

Generally, the courts have held that employers have a right to establish and enforce dress and grooming require-

ments. In other words, even though the requirements may result in disparate-impact discrimination, the discrimination is not illegal—so long as there is no discrimination in the enforcement of the policy. If an employer enforces dress codes for men more strictly than it enforces dress codes for women, for example, then a male employee may succeed in a suit for unlawful disparate-impact discrimination based on gender.

For Critical Analysis: *How do dress codes affect employees' free speech (expression) rights under the First Amendment to the Constitution?*

In such cases, there are two basic questions—whether a standard or policy has a discriminatory impact and, if it does, whether the standard or policy nevertheless has a substantial, demonstrable relationship to the job. These were the questions in the following case.

Case 17.1 ● Fickling v. New York State Department of Civil Service

United States District Court,
Southern District of New York, 1995.

HISTORICAL AND POLITICAL SETTING *Two principles form the core of Americans' beliefs about the workplace: all of us deserve equal opportunities, and hard work—not privilege, race, or gender—should determine who succeeds. In the early 1990s, the public debate about the role of race in the workplace became angrier and more divisive than at any time since the 1960s. Perhaps the real root of the discontent was the slow-growing economy, stagnant middle-class incomes, and corporate downsizing, all of which inflamed the debate over who should be hired and fired.*

BACKGROUND AND FACTS Job applicants for the position of Social Welfare Eligibility Examiner for Westchester County, New York, must pass a New York State Department of Civil Service examination. In 1989 and 1990, the exam tested mainly reading comprehension and arithmetic, skills that were of relatively little importance to the job. When it was revealed that fewer than two African Americans and about one Hispanic passed the exam for every three whites who passed, Juliette Fickling and seven other minority members who failed the test (the plaintiffs) filed a suit in a federal district court against the state and the county. The plaintiffs alleged violations of, among other things, Title VII.

IN THE WORDS OF THE COURT . . .
PARKER, District Judge.
 * * * *

 * * * A selection rate for any race, sex, or ethnic group which is less than four-fifths (4/5) (or eighty percent) of the rate for the group with the highest rate

(Continued)

Case 17.1—continued

will generally be regarded * * * as evidence of adverse impact * * * . Here, the disparate racial impact * * * was far below the 80% standard. * * *

* * * *

* * * [T]he examination tested mainly reading comprehension. In addition, 38% of the questions required arithmetic. The ability to do arithmetic, however was found to be unimportant to successful job performance * * * . The examinations did not test written expression or oral expression, except the ability to describe eligibility requirements in a comprehensible manner, despite the fact that these abilities were found to be very important to successful job performance * * * .

DECISION AND REMEDY   The federal district court ruled in favor of the plaintiffs, and ordered the parties to submit briefs on what remedies are appropriate.

FOR CRITICAL ANALYSIS—SOCIAL CONSIDERATION   *What are reasons, other than equal opportunity under Title VII, for insisting that a job test have a "substantial, demonstrable relationship" to the job?*

Discrimination Based on Religion

Title VII of the Civil Rights Act of 1964 also prohibits government employers, private employers, and unions from discriminating against persons because of their religion. An employer must "reasonably accommodate" the religious practices of its employees, unless to do so would cause undue hardship to the employer's business. For example, if an employee's religion prohibits him or her from working on a certain day of the week or at a certain type of job, the employer must make a reasonable attempt to accommodate these religious requirements. Employers must reasonably accommodate an employee's religious belief even if the belief is not based on the tenets or dogma of a particular church, sect, or denomination. The only requirement is that the belief be sincerely held by the employee.[4]

Discrimination Based on Gender

Under Title VII, as well as other federal acts, employers are forbidden to discriminate against employees on the basis of gender. Employers are prohibited from classifying jobs as male or female and from advertising in help-wanted columns that are designated male or female unless the employer can prove that the gender of the applicant is essential to the job. Furthermore, employers cannot have separate male and female seniority lists. Generally, to succeed in a suit for gender discrimination, a plaintiff must demonstrate that gender was a determining factor in the employer's decision to hire, fire, or promote him or her. Typically, this involves looking at all of the surrounding circumstances.

The Pregnancy Discrimination Act of 1978,[5] which amended Title VII, expanded the definition of gender discrimination to include discrimination based on pregnancy. Women affected by pregnancy, childbirth, or related medical conditions must be treated—for all employment-related purposes, including the receipt of benefits under employee benefit programs—the same as

> "A sign that says 'men only' looks very different on a bathroom door than a courthouse door."
>
> Thurgood Marshall, 1908–1993
> (Associate justice of the United States Supreme Court, 1967–1991)

---

4.   *Frazee v. Illinois Department of Employment Security,* 489 U.S. 829, 109 S.Ct. 1514, 103 L.Ed.2d 914 (1989).
5.   42 U.S.C. Section 2000e(k).

other persons not so affected but similar in ability to work. An employer is required to treat an employee temporarily unable to perform her job owing to a pregnancy-related condition in the same manner as the employer would treat other temporarily disabled employees. The employer must change work assignments, grant paid disability leaves, or grant leaves without pay if that is how it would treat other temporarily disabled employees. Policies concerning an employee's return to work, accrual of seniority, pay increases, and so on must also result in equal treatment.[6]

Sexual Harassment

Sexual Harassment In the employment context, the granting of job promotions or other benefits in return for sexual favors, or language or conduct that is so sexually offensive that it creates a hostile working environment.

Title VII also protects employees against **sexual harassment** in the workplace. Sexual harassment can take two forms: *quid pro quo* harassment and hostile-environment harassment. *Quid pro quo* is a Latin phrase that is often translated to mean "something in exchange for something else." *Quid pro quo* harassment occurs when job opportunities, promotions, salary increases, and so on are given in return for sexual favors.

Hostile-environment harassment occurs when an employee is subjected to sexual conduct or comments that he or she perceives as offensive. The EEOC's guidelines on harassment state that the following types of verbal or physical conduct constitute hostile-environment harassment:

1. Conduct that has the purpose or effect of creating an intimidating, hostile, or offensive working environment.
2. Conduct that has the purpose or effect of unreasonably interfering with an individual's work performance.
3. Conduct that otherwise adversely affects an individual's employment opportunities.

HARASSMENT BY SUPERVISORS AND CO-WORKERS. What if an employee is harassed by a manager or supervisor of a large firm, and the firm itself (the "employer") is not aware of the harassment? Does the employee nonetheless have a cause of action against the employer? The answer to this question is often yes. Employers are generally liable for Title VII violations by the firm's managerial or supervisory personnel. Usually, in *quid pro quo* harassment cases, the courts hold employers strictly liable for the harassment. In other words, the employer will be held liable regardless of whether the employer knew about the harassment. In hostile-environment cases, however, the majority of courts tend to hold employers liable only if the employer knew or should have known of the harassment and failed to take prompt remedial action. (Note that if the employer takes reasonable steps to discover and remedy acts of sexual harassment, these actions may shield the employer from liability— see this chapter's *Inside the Legal Environment* on this topic.)

One co-worker harasses another. What determines whether their employer will be held liable for harassment in this situation?

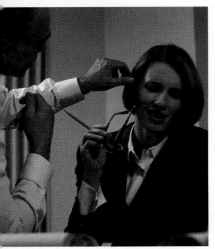

In some cases, high-level supervisors and managers have been held personally liable for harassment under the theory that the supervisors exercised sufficient control to be deemed "employers." There is a growing consensus

---

6. A cause of action under the Pregnancy Discrimination Act is not limited to women—a man may also have standing to sue for discrimination under the act. In *Nicol v. Imagematrix, Inc.,* 773 F.Supp. 802 (E.D.Va. 1991), the court held that the husband of a pregnant woman had standing to sue his former employer. The husband alleged that he had been fired because his wife (who worked for the same employer and was also fired) was pregnant.

Inside the Legal Environment
Harassment Policies May Shield Employers from Liability

The courts do not look kindly on employers that fail to take prompt remedial action when learning of sexual-harassment complaints (see, for example, Case 17.2). Employers that do take prompt action to remedy the problem, however, often can avoid liability for the harassment. Even more significantly, employers that provide specific guidelines for their employees on sexual harassment—guidelines that indicate how to report incidents of harassment—may not be held liable if employees fail to complain of the harassment through the "proper channels."

The case of *Baskerville v. Culligan International Co.*[a] is illustrative in this respect. In that case, an employee, Valerie Baskerville, complained that she was being sexually harassed by her supervisor, Michael Hall. Baskerville alleged that Hall had harassed her over a period of seven months through such incidents as the following: he had called her "pretty girl" on several occasions; once, when she was wearing a leather skirt, he made a grunting sound that sounded like "um um um" as she turned to leave his office; another time, when she commented on how hot his office

a. 50 F.3d 428 (7th Cir. 1995).

was, he raised his eyebrows and said, "Not until you stepped your foot in here."

The federal district court held that these actions constituted sexual harassment in violation of Title VII and awarded damages to Baskerville. On appeal, the U.S. Court of Appeals for the Seventh Circuit reversed the district court's judgment. The appellate court pointed out that Hall had never touched the plaintiff and had never invited her—explicitly or implicitly—to have sex with him or even to go on a date together. The court held that "Mr. Hall, whatever his qualities as a sales manager, is not a man of refinement; but neither is he a sexual harasser."

It is interesting that the appellate court also stated that even if Hall's actions had created a hostile environment—that is, if they did give rise to a cause of action for harassment—the company could still avoid liability for Hall's actions. The reason is that Baskerville did not follow the company's established guidelines, well known to her, for reporting incidents of sexual harassment. Instead of immediately going through proper channels and reporting the problem to the human resources department, as required by the company, Baskerville first complained to Hall's supervisor.

The supervisor reprimanded Hall, but the purported harassing actions continued. Eventually, Baskerville reported the problem to the company's human resources department, and the company took prompt action. The matter was promptly investigated, Hall was told to cease his offensive behavior immediately, and he was placed on probation for several months. Hall got the point, and there was no recurrence of the offensive behavior.

Clearly, employers who wish to avoid liability for harassment would be wise to establish and implement effective harassment policies and grievance procedures. Employers are charged with a duty to discover and rectify acts of sexual harassment in the workplace, and the employer's negligence is often the key factor in hostile-environment cases. Effective harassment guidelines and procedures can be used as evidence that the employer was not negligent in this duty.

For Critical Analysis: *In what circumstances might a court not allow an employer to avoid liability for harassment simply because the employee failed to complain through the "proper channels"?*

among the courts, however, that supervisors cannot be held liable, as employers, under Title VII.[7]

Often, employees alleging harassment complain that the actions of co-workers, not supervisors, are responsible for creating a hostile working environment. In such cases, the employee still has a cause of action against the

7. See, for example, *Williams v. Banning*, 72 F.3d 552 (7th Cir. 1995); and *Sheridan v. E. I. du Pont de Nemours and Co.*, 74 F.3d 1439 (3d Cir. 1996).

employer. Normally, though, the employer will be held liable only if it knew, or should have known, about the harassment and failed to take immediate remedial action.

The following case raises the issue of whether an employer can be held responsible for doing nothing in a situation involving harassment even though the harassing employee had voluntarily ceased the harassment.

Case 17.2 ⬤ Fuller v. City of Oakland, California

United States Court of Appeals, Ninth Circuit, 1995. 47 F.3d 1522.

HISTORICAL AND SOCIAL SETTING *At one time, a fear of false reporting limited the testimony of women in the prosecution of rape cases. In the 1970s, this same fear of false reporting was one of the reasons some observers initially opposed the recognition of sexual harassment as discrimination on the basis of gender. Others believed that harassment reflects a conflict between personalities, or that it is based on sexual attractiveness, not gender. Some felt that even if some conduct was harassment, once it stopped, the employer should not be held responsible for it.*

BACKGROUND AND FACTS Patricia Fuller and Antonio Romero were police officers with the city of Oakland, California, when they had a brief romantic relationship. When Fuller broke it off, Romero—who was promoted to a supervisory position—began to harass her on and off duty. Fuller complained to their superiors. Romero stopped harassing her, and the superiors took no action, except to officially call Fuller's complaint "[u]nfounded." Fuller resigned and filed a suit against the city in a federal district court under Title VII. The city argued that when the harassment stopped, its own responsibility ceased. The court agreed. Fuller appealed to the U.S. Court of Appeals for the Ninth Circuit.

IN THE WORDS OF THE COURT . . .
POOLE, Circuit Judge:
* * * *

* * * Once an employer knows or should know of harassment, a remedial obligation kicks in. That obligation will not be discharged until action—prompt, effective action—has been taken. Effectiveness will be measured by the twin purposes of ending the current harassment and deterring future harassment—by the same offender or others. * * *

* * * Title VII does not permit employers to stand idly by once they learn that sexual harassment has occurred. To do so amounts to a ratification of the prior harassment. * * *

DECISION AND REMEDY The U.S. Court of Appeals for the Ninth Circuit reversed the judgment of the lower court and remanded the case.

FOR CRITICAL ANALYSIS—SOCIAL CONSIDERATION *What steps should an employer take, once harassment has ceased, to deter future misconduct?*

HARASSMENT BY NONEMPLOYEES.   Employers may also be liable for harassment by *nonemployees* in certain circumstances. For example, if a restaurant owner or manager knows that a certain customer repeatedly harasses a waitress and permits the harassment to continue, the restaurant owner may be liable under Title VII even though the customer is not an employee of the restaurant. The issue turns on the control that the employer exerts over a nonemployee. In the situation just described, a court would likely conclude that the restaurant manager or owner could have taken action to prevent the customer from harassing the waitress.

PROVING SEXUAL HARASSMENT. One of the major problems faced by employees who are sexually harassed is that such harassment can be very difficult to prove. Often, there are no third parties who have witnessed the harassment and no written evidence of it. The question thus comes down to who is more believable, the alleged victim or the alleged offender.

Even if an employee can prove that sexually offensive conduct occurred, at what point does such conduct result in an "intimidating, hostile, or offensive working environment" or otherwise qualify as hostile-environment harassment under the EEOC's guidelines? Courts have had to struggle with such questions and usually render their decisions on a case-by-case basis. At least one court has concluded that even one incident of sexually offensive conduct can result in a hostile, offensive working environment.[8]

In *Harris v. Forklift Systems, Inc.,*[9] the United States Supreme Court addressed another controversial issue relating to hostile-environment claims. Prior to this decision, many jurisdictions had held that a worker claiming to be a victim of hostile-environment harassment must establish that he or she suffered serious psychological effects as a result of the offensive conduct. In the *Harris* case, the Supreme Court held that "Title VII bars conduct that would seriously affect a reasonable person's psychological well-being, but the statute is not limited to such conduct. So long as the environment would reasonably be perceived, and is perceived, as hostile or abusive, there is no need for it also to be psychologically injurious."

In *Harris,* the Court also attempted to settle disagreements among the courts on the standard to be applied in harassment cases. Should a neutral and objective "reasonable person" standard apply, or should a more subjective "reasonable female" or "reasonable male" standard be used? The Court adopted a broad standard by holding that in cases of alleged sexual harassment, the conduct at issue must be abusive both objectively (as perceived by a reasonable person) and subjectively (as perceived by the victim).

SAME-GENDER HARASSMENT. Recently, the courts have had to address the issue of whether men who are harassed by other men, or women who are harassed by other women, are also protected by laws that prohibit gender-based discrimination in the workplace. For example, what if the male president of a firm demands sexual favors from a male employee? Does this action qualify as sexual harassment? The United States Supreme Court has held that plaintiffs may bring actions under Title VII for same-gender harassment.[10] (The U.S. Court of Appeals for the Fifth Circuit had held that same gender sexual harrassment was not covered by Title VII.[11])

Remedies under Title VII

Employer liability under Title VII may be extensive. If the plaintiff successfully proves that unlawful discrimination occurred, he or she may be awarded reinstatement, back pay, retroactive promotions, and damages. Prior to the Civil

---

8. See *Radtke v. Everett,* 442 Mich. 368, 501 N.W.2d 155 (1993).
9. 510 U.S. 17, 114 S.Ct. 367, 126 L.Ed.2d 295 (1993).
10. *Oncale v. Sundowner Offshore Services, Inc.,* ___ U.S., ___ 118 S. Ct. 998, ___ L.Ed.2d ___ (1998).
11. *Oncale v. Sundowner Offshore Services, Inc.,* 83 F.3d 118 (5th Cir. 1996).

Rights Act of 1991, damages were not available under Title VII. Plaintiffs alleging racial discrimination therefore often brought actions under 42 U.S.C. Section 1981. Section 1981, which was enacted as part of the Civil Rights Act of 1866, prohibits discrimination on the basis of race or ethnicity in the formation or enforcement of contracts. Until the 1991 Civil Rights Act, however, damages were not available for victims of intentional employment discrimination based on sex, religion, age, or disability. The 1991 act, however, allowed compensatory damages to be awarded in cases brought under other employment laws, such as Title VII, thus significantly broadening the rights of victims of employment discrimination.

Under the 1991 act, compensatory damages are available only in cases of intentional discrimination. The statute also stipulates that compensatory damages shall not include back pay, interest on back pay, or other relief already available under Title VII. Punitive damages may be recovered against a private employer only if the employer acted with malice or reckless indifference to an individual's rights. The sum of the amount of compensatory and punitive damages is limited by the statute to specific amounts against specific employers—ranging from $50,000 against employers with one hundred or fewer employees to $300,000 against employers with more than five hundred employees.

Equal Pay Act of 1963

> **RECALL** The Fair Labor Standards Act of 1938 extends wage-hour requirements to nearly all employers.

The Equal Pay Act of 1963 was enacted as an amendment to the Fair Labor Standards Act of 1938. Basically, the act prohibits gender-based discrimination in the wages paid for equal work on jobs when their performance requires equal skill, effort, and responsibility under similar conditions. It is job content

Ethical Perspective

Title VII was not intended to be the sole remedy for employment discrimination based on race, color, national origin, religion, or gender. Plaintiffs who suffer from employment discrimination on these bases may also bring actions under other laws. In fact, it is often advantageous for some plaintiffs to do so. For example, a plaintiff alleging racial discrimination may choose to sue under Section 1981, because there are no caps on damages available under that law. Plaintiffs may also bring suits under state laws prohibiting discrimination, if the state laws allow for greater recovery than Title VII. For example, a plaintiff may recover damages for emotional distress (which are not available under Title VII) under a state statute.[a] (See also Case 17.5 later in this chapter for other advantages of bringing a discrimination suit under state law.)

Some employees may opt to sue under the equal protection clause of the Fourteenth Amendment (discussed in Chapter 5). For example, in *Beardsley v. Webb*,[b] a former deputy sheriff sued her supervisor and the sheriff, alleging sexual harassment and employment discrimination. The court held that the equal protection clause confers a right to be free from gender discrimination that is not substantially related to important governmental objectives. Furthermore, the court held that standards developed in Title VII litigation could be applied to similar litigation under the equal protection clause.

For Critical Analysis: *Can you think of any other reasons why plaintiffs might want to bring discrimination suits under laws other than Title VII?*

---

a. *Luciano v. Olsten Corp.*, 912 F.Supp. 663 (E.D.N.Y. 1996).

b. 30 F.3d 524 (4th Cir. 1994).

rather than job description that controls in all cases. To determine whether the Equal Pay Act has been violated, a court will thus look to the primary duties of the two jobs. The jobs of a barber and a beautician, for example, are considered essentially "equal." So, too, are those of a tailor and a seamstress. For the equal pay requirements to apply, the act requires that male and female employees must work at the same establishment.

A wage differential for equal work is justified if it is shown to be because of (1) seniority, (2) merit, (3) a system that pays according to quality or quantity of production, or (4) any factor other than gender. Small differences in job content, however, do not justify higher pay for one gender.

Discrimination Based on Age

Age discrimination is potentially the most widespread form of discrimination, because anyone—regardless of race, color, national origin, or gender—could be a victim at some point in life. The Age Discrimination in Employment Act (ADEA) of 1967, as amended, prohibits employment discrimination on the basis of age against individuals forty years of age or older. An amendment to the act prohibits mandatory retirement for nonmanagerial workers. For the act to apply, an employer must have twenty or more employees, and the employer's business activities must affect interstate commerce.

The burden-shifting procedure under the ADEA is similar to that under Title VII. If a plaintiff can establish that he or she (1) was a member of the protected age group, (2) was qualified for the position from which he or she was discharged, and (3) was discharged under circumstances that give rise to an inference of discrimination, the plaintiff has established a *prima facie* case of unlawful age discrimination. The burden then shifts to the employer, who must articulate a legitimate reason for the discrimination. If the plaintiff can

A worker reviews documents at his desk. Why did Congress prohibit employment discrimination based on age?

prove that the employer's reason is only a pretext and that the plaintiff's age was a determining factor in the employer's decision, the employer will be held liable under the ADEA.

Numerous cases of alleged age discrimination have been brought against employers who, to cut costs, replaced older, higher-salaried employees with younger, lower-salaried workers. Whether a firing is discriminatory or simply part of a rational business decision to prune the company's ranks is not always clear. Companies generally defend a decision to discharge a worker by asserting that the worker could no longer perform his or her duties or that the worker's skills were no longer needed. The employee must prove that the discharge was motivated, at least in part, by age bias. Proof that qualified older employees are generally discharged before younger employees or that co-workers continually made unflattering age-related comments about the discharged worker may be enough.

In the past, courts had sometimes held that to establish a *prima facie* case of age discrimination, the plaintiff must also prove that he or she was replaced by a person outside the protected class—that is, by a person under the age of forty years. In 1996, however, in *O'Connor v. Consolidated Coin Caterers Corp.*,[12] the United States Supreme Court held that a cause of action for age discrimination under the ADEA does not require the replacement worker to be outside the protected class. Rather, the issue in all ADEA cases turns on whether age discrimination has, in fact, occurred, regardless of the age of the replacement worker. In the following case, the court had to decide whether there was sufficient evidence to support a jury's finding of discrimination on the basis of age.

----

12.   517 U.S. 308, 116 S.Ct. 1307, 134 L.Ed.2d 433 (1996).

Case 17.3 ● Rhodes v. Guiberson Oil Tools

United States Court of Appeals,
Fifth Circuit, 1996.
75 F.3d 989.

HISTORICAL AND ECONOMIC SETTING *Exploring and drilling for oil is an expensive operation; drills, pipes, pumps, testing and measuring equipment, trucks, tankers, helicopters, and a variety of services are utilized. Suppliers of these products and services depend entirely on the activities of oil companies in the field. If no one is drilling for oil, the suppliers are out of business. In 1986, the oil industry was in the throes of a severe economic downturn.*

BACKGROUND AND FACTS   Calvin Rhodes sold oil field equipment for Guiberson Oil Tools. When he was dis-

charged in 1986 at age fifty-six, he was told that the discharge was part of a reduction in the work force (RIF), and that he would be considered for reemployment. Within six weeks, Guiberson hired a forty-two-year-old person to do the same job. Rhodes filed a suit in a federal district court against Guiberson under the Age Discrimination in Employment Act. At the trial, Guiberson officials testified that they had not told Rhodes the truth about why they discharged him and that they had intended to replace him. Guiberson offered as a defense Rhodes's "poor work performance" but did not present any company sales records or goals. Rhodes countered with customers' testimony about his expertise and diligence. The jury found that Rhodes was discharged because of his age. Guiberson appealed to the U.S. Court of Appeals for the Fifth Circuit.

IN THE WORDS OF THE COURT . . .
W. EUGENE DAVIS and DUHE, Circuit Judges:
* * * *

(Continued)

Case 17.3—continued

Based on this evidence, the jury was entitled to find that the reasons given for Rhodes' discharge were pretexts for age discrimination. The jury was entitled to find that Guiberson's stated reason for discharging Rhodes—RIF—was false. Additionally, the reason for discharge that Guiberson Oil proffered in court * * * was countered with evidence from which the jury could have found that Rhodes was an excellent salesman who met Guiberson Oil's legitimate productivity expectations. * * * [A] reasonable jury could have found that Guiberson Oil discriminated against Rhodes on the basis of his age.

DECISION AND REMEDY   The U.S. Court of Appeals for the Fifth Circuit affirmed the jury's finding.

FOR CRITICAL ANALYSIS—SOCIAL CONSIDERATION   *If age is not the sole reason for an adverse employment decision, how significant a factor do you think it should be to support a finding of discrimination?*

Discrimination Based on Disability

The Americans with Disabilities Act (ADA) of 1990 is designed to eliminate discriminatory employment practices that prevent otherwise qualified workers with disabilities from fully participating in the national labor force. Prior to 1990, the major federal law providing protection to those with disabilities was the Rehabilitation Act of 1973. That act covered only federal government employees and those employed under federally funded programs. The ADA extends federal protection against disability-based discrimination to all workplaces with fifteen or more workers. Basically, the ADA requires that employers "reasonably accommodate" the needs of persons with disabilities unless to do so would cause the employer to suffer an "undue hardship."

To prevail on a claim under the ADA, a plaintiff must show that he or she (1) has a disability, (2) is otherwise qualified for the employment in question, and (3) was excluded from the employment solely because of the disability. As in Title VII cases, a claim alleging violation of the ADA may be commenced only after the plaintiff has pursued the claim through the EEOC. Plaintiffs may sue for many of the same remedies available under Title VII. They may seek reinstatement, back pay, a limited amount of compensatory and punitive damages (for intentional discrimination), and certain other forms of relief. Repeat violators may be ordered to pay fines of up to $100,000.

> "[I]n order to treat some persons equally, we must treat them differently."
> Harry A. Blackmun, 1908– (Associate justice of the United States Supreme Court, 1970–1994)

> **REMEMBER** Remedies under Title VII include job reinstatement, back pay, retroactive promotions, and, in cases of intentional discrimination, limited compensatory and punitive damages.

What Is a Disability?

The ADA is broadly drafted to define persons with disabilities as persons with a physical or mental impairment that "substantially limits" their everyday activities. More specifically, the ADA defines *disability* as "(1) a physical or mental impairment that substantially limits one or more of the major life activities of such individuals; (2) a record of such impairment; or (3) being regarded as having such an impairment."

Generally, the determination of whether an individual has a disability as defined by the ADA is made on a case-by-case basis. Unlike plaintiffs in cases

Co-workers discuss business matters. Which workers with disabilities are protected from employment discrimination by the Americans with Disabilities Act?

brought under Title VII or the ADEA, who clearly either are or are not members of the classes protected by those acts, a plaintiff suing under the ADA must *prove* that he or she has a disability—and thus falls under the protection of the ADA. Meeting this first requirement for a case of disability-based discrimination is often difficult.

Health conditions that have been considered disabilities under federal law include blindness, alcoholism, heart disease, cancer, muscular dystrophy, cerebral palsy, paraplegia, diabetes, acquired immune deficiency syndrome (AIDS), and morbid obesity (defined as existing when an individual's weight is two times that of the normal person).[13] The ADA excludes from coverage certain conditions, including homosexuality and kleptomania.

Reasonable Accommodation

The ADA does not require that *unqualified* applicants with disabilities be hired or retained. Therefore, employers are not obligated to accommodate the needs of job applicants or employees with disabilities who are not otherwise qualified for the work. If a job applicant or an employee with a disability, with reasonable accommodation, can perform essential job functions, however, then the employer must make the accommodation. Required modifications may include installing ramps for a wheelchair, establishing more flexible working hours, creating or modifying job assignments, and creating or improving training materials and procedures.

Generally, employers should give primary consideration to employees' preferences in deciding what accommodations should be made. What happens if a job applicant or employee does not indicate to the employer how his or her disability can be accommodated so that the employee can perform essential job functions? In this situation, the employer may avoid liability for failing to hire or retain the individual on the ground that the applicant or employee has failed to meet the "otherwise qualified" requirement.[14]

Employers who do not accommodate the needs of persons with disabilities must demonstrate that the accommodations will cause "undue hardship." Generally, the law offers no uniform standards for identifying what is an undue hardship other than the imposition of a "significant difficulty or expense" on the employer. Usually, the courts decide whether an accommodation constitutes an undue hardship on a case-by-case basis. In one case, the court decided that paying for a parking space near the office for an employee with a disability was not an undue hardship.[15] In another case, the court held that accommodating the request of an employee with diabetes for indefinite leave until his disease was under control would create an undue hardship for the employer, because the employer would not know when the employee was returning to work. The court stated that reasonable accommodation under the ADA means accommodation so that the employee can perform the job now or "in the immediate future" rather than at some unspecified distant time.[16]

We now look at some specific requirements of the ADA in regard to the extent to which employers must reasonably accommodate the needs of employees with disabilities.

---

13. *Cook v. Rhode Island Department of Mental Health*, 10 F.3d 17 (1st Cir. 1993).
14. See, for example, *Beck v. University of Wisconsin Board of Regents*, 75 F.3d 1130 (7th Cir. 1996); and *White v. York International Corp.*, 45 F.3d 357 (10th Cir. 1995).
15. See *Lyons v. Legal Aid Society*, 68 F.3d 1512 (2d Cir. 1995).
16. *Myers v. Hase*, 50 F.3d 278 (4th Cir. 1995).

JOB APPLICATIONS AND PREEMPLOYMENT PHYSICAL EXAMS.   Employers must modify their job-application process so that those with disabilities can compete for jobs with those who do not have disabilities. A job announcement that only has a phone number, for example, would discriminate against potential job applicants with hearing impairments. Thus, the job announcement must also provide an address.

Employers are restricted in the kinds of questions they may ask on job-application forms and during preemployment interviews. Furthermore, they cannot require persons with disabilities to submit to preemployment physicals unless such exams are required of all other applicants. Employers can condition an offer of employment on the employee's successfully passing a medical examination, but disqualifications must result from the discovery of problems that render the applicant unable to perform the job for which he or she is to be hired.

> **DON'T FORGET**
> Preemployment screening procedures must be applied carefully in regard to all job applicants.

DANGEROUS WORKERS.   Employers are not required to hire or retain workers who, because of their disabilities, pose a "direct threat to the health or safety" of their co-workers. This danger must be substantial and immediate; it cannot be speculative. In the wake of the AIDS epidemic, many employers are concerned about hiring or continuing to employ a worker who has AIDS under the assumption that the worker might pose a direct threat to the health or safety of others in the workplace. Courts have generally held, however, that AIDS is not so contagious as to disqualify employees in most jobs. Therefore, employers must reasonably accommodate job applicants or employees who have AIDS or who test positive for the human immunodeficiency virus (HIV), the virus that causes AIDS.[17]

As mentioned, the ADA does not require that *unqualified* disabled applicants be hired or retained. Employers sometimes argue that persons with AIDS are not "otherwise qualified" for particular positions because they pose a direct threat to the health or safety of others that cannot be eliminated or reduced by reasonable accommodation. This was the employer's argument in the following case.

---

17.   Courts have disagreed on whether HIV-positive persons who do not have any symptoms of AIDS have a disability under the ADA. See *Doe v. Kohn Nast & Graf, P.C.*, 866 F.Supp. 190 (E.D.Pa. 1994); and *Ennis v. National Association of Business and Educational Radio, Inc.*, 53 F.3d 55 (4th Cir. 1995) for two views on this issue.

Case 17.4 ● Mauro v. Borgess Medical Center

United States District Court, Western District of Michigan, Southern Division, 1995. 886 F.Supp. 1349.

HISTORICAL AND SOCIAL SETTING   *Acquired immune deficiency syndrome (AIDS) was unknown until the first cases were reported in the United States in 1981. AIDS, which is fatal and for which there is no known cure, is caused by the human immunodeficiency virus (HIV). HIV can be transmitted from one person to another by contact of the infected blood of one person with an open wound of another. A person infected with HIV remains infected for the rest of his or her life. Although an infected person may not show any symptoms for years, he or she can still infect others.*

BACKGROUND AND FACTS   William Mauro was an operating room surgical technician for the Borgess Medical Center. Surgical technicians must occasionally place their hands into a patient's surgical incision. Borgess officials had reason to believe that Mauro was infected with HIV. When Borgess asked Mauro to be tested for HIV, however,

(Continued)

Case 17.4—continued

Mauro refused. He also refused to accept a job outside the operating room and, as a consequence, was laid off. Mauro filed a suit in a federal district court against Borgess, alleging, among other things, discrimination in violation of the Americans with Disabilities Act (ADA). Borgess filed a motion for summary judgment. Mauro argued that the probability of transmission of HIV is small and that a reasonable accommodation would be to add a person to the surgical team to work in or near a patient's incision.

IN THE WORDS OF THE COURT . . .
McKEAGUE, District Judge.

* * * *

* * * Because there is a real possibility of transmission, however small, and because the consequence of transmission is invariably death, the threat to patient safety posed by plaintiff's presence in the operating room performing the functions of a surgical technician is direct and significant. * * * A cognizable risk of permanent duration with lethal consequences suffices to make a surgical technician * * * not "otherwise qualified."

* * * *

* * * [Furthermore] to require Borgess to * * * add another person to the surgical team is not reasonable. The accommodation plaintiff demands would entail a job restructuring in the operating room, a burden the law does not impose on the employer.

DECISION AND REMEDY   The federal district court granted Borgess's motion for summary judgment.

FOR CRITICAL ANALYSIS—ETHICAL CONSIDERATION   *Some people believe that AIDS is as contagious as an influenza virus. Are employers justified in taking such fears into account in making employment-related decisions?*

HEALTH-INSURANCE PLANS.   Workers with disabilities must be given equal access to any health insurance provided to other employees. Employers can exclude from coverage preexisting health conditions and certain types of diagnostic or surgical procedures, however. An employer can also put a limit, or cap, on health-care payments in its particular group-health policy—as long as such caps are "applied equally to all insured employees" and do not "discriminate on the basis of disability." Whenever a group health-care plan makes a disability-based distinction in its benefits, the plan violates the ADA. The employer must then be able to justify the distinction by proving one of the following:

1. That limiting coverage of certain ailments is required to keep the plan financially sound.
2. That coverage of certain ailments would cause a significant increase in premium payments or their equivalent such that the plan would be unappealing to a significant number of workers.
3. That the disparate treatment is justified by the risks and costs associated with a particular disability.

THE ADA AND SUBSTANCE ABUSERS.   Drug addiction is a disability under the ADA, because drug addiction is a substantially limiting impairment. Those who are currently using illegal drugs are not protected by the act. The ADA only protects persons with *former* drug addictions—those who have completed a supervised drug-rehabilitation program or who are currently in a supervised rehabilitation program. Individuals who have used drugs casually in the past are not protected under the act. They are not considered addicts and therefore do not have a disability (addiction).

People recovering from alcoholism are protected by the ADA. Employers cannot legally discriminate against employees simply because they are suffering from alcoholism and must treat them in the same way as they treat other employees. In other words, an employee suffering from alcoholism cannot be disciplined any differently than anyone else simply because he or she was drinking the night before and came to work late. Of course, employers have the right to prohibit the use of alcohol in the workplace and can require that employees not be under the influence of alcohol while working. Employers can also fire or refuse to hire a person suffering from alcoholism if he or she poses a substantial risk of harm to either himself or herself or to others and the risk cannot be reduced by reasonable accommodation.

Defenses to Employment Discrimination

▼ The first line of defense for an employer charged with employment discrimination is, of course, to assert that the plaintiff has failed to meet his or her initial burden of proof—proving that discrimination in fact occurred. As noted, plaintiffs bringing cases under the ADA often find it difficult to meet this initial burden, because they must prove that their alleged disabilities are disabilities covered by the ADA. Furthermore, plaintiffs in ADA cases must prove that they were otherwise qualified for the job and that the reason they were not hired or were fired was solely because of their disabilities.

Once a plaintiff succeeds in proving that discrimination occurred, then the burden shifts to the employer to justify the discriminatory practice. Often, employers attempt to justify the discrimination by claiming that it was a result of a business necessity, a bona fide occupational qualification, or a seniority system. As mentioned in this chapter's *Inside the Legal Environment* on page 477, an effective anti-harassment policy and prompt remedial action when harassment occurs also may shield employers from liability under Title VII for sexual harassment in some cases.

Business Necessity

An employer may defend against a claim of discrimination by asserting that a practice that has a discriminatory effect is a business necessity. If requiring a high school diploma, for example, is shown to have a discriminatory effect, an employer might argue that a high school education is required for workers to perform the job at a required level of competence. If the employer can demonstrate to the court's satisfaction that there exists a definite connection between a high school education and job performance, then the employer will succeed in this **business necessity** defense.

Bona Fide Occupational Qualification

Another defense applies when discrimination against a protected class is essential to a job—that is, when a particular trait is a **bona fide occupational qualification (BFOQ)**. For example, a men's fashion magazine might legitimately hire only male models. Similarly, the Federal Aviation Administration can legitimately impose age limits for airline pilots. Race, however, can never

Business Necessity A defense to allegations of employment discrimination in which the employer demonstrates that an employment practice that discriminates against members of a protected class is related to job performance.

Bona Fide Occupational Qualification (BFOQ) Identifiable characteristics reasonably necessary to the normal operation of a particular business. These characteristics can include gender, national origin, and religion, but not race.

be a BFOQ. Generally, courts have restricted the BFOQ defense to instances in which the employee's gender is essential to the job. In 1991, the United States Supreme Court held that even a fetal protection policy that was adopted to protect the unborn children of female employees from the harmful effects of exposure to lead was an unacceptable BFOQ.[18]

Seniority Systems

An employer with a history of discrimination may have no members of protected classes in upper-level positions. Even if the employer now seeks to be unbiased, it may face a lawsuit seeking an order that minorities be promoted ahead of schedule to compensate for past discrimination. If no present intent to discriminate is shown, and promotions or other job benefits are distributed according to a fair **seniority system** (in which workers with more years of service are promoted first, or laid off last), however, the employer has a good defense against the suit.

Seniority System In regard to employment relationships, a system in which those who have worked longest for the company are first in line for promotions, salary increases, and other benefits; they are also the last to be laid off if the work force must be reduced.

After-Acquired Evidence Is No Defense

In some situations, employers have attempted to avoid liability for employment discrimination on the basis of "after-acquired evidence" of an employee's misconduct. For example, suppose that an employer fires a worker, and the employee sues the employer for employment discrimination. During pretrial investigation, the employer learns that the employee made material misrepresentations on his or her employment application—misrepresentations that, had the employer known about them, would have served as a ground to fire the individual. Can this after-acquired evidence be used as a defense?

The United States Supreme Court addressed this question in *McKennon v. Nashville Banner Publishing Co.*,[19] a case decided in 1995. The Court stated that both Title VII and the ADEA share a common purpose: "the elimination of discrimination in the workplace." The Court held that allowing employers to avoid liability for discrimination on the basis of after-acquired evidence did "not accord" with this purpose. After-acquired evidence of wrongdoing should not operate, "in every instance, to bar all relief for an earlier violation of the Act." Since this decision, the courts have generally held that after-acquired evidence cannot be used to shield employers from liability for employment discrimination, although it may be a factor in determining the amount of damages awarded to plaintiffs.

Affirmative Action

▼ Federal statutes and regulations providing for equal opportunity in the workplace were designed to reduce or eliminate discriminatory practices with respect to hiring, retaining, and promoting employees. **Affirmative action** programs go a step further and attempt to "make up" for past patterns of discrimination by giving members of protected classes preferential treatment in hiring or promotion.

Affirmative Action Job-hiring policies that give special consideration to members of protected classes in an effort to overcome present effects of past discrimination.

18.   *United Automobile Workers v. Johnson Controls, Inc.*, 499 U.S. 187, 111 S.Ct. 1196, 113 L.Ed.2d 158 (1991). (This case is presented in Chapter 2 as Case 2.1.)
19.   513 U.S. 352, 115 S.Ct. 879, 130 L.Ed.2d 852 (1995).

Affirmative action programs have caused much controversy, particularly when they result in what is frequently called "reverse discrimination"—discrimination against "majority" workers, such as white males (or discrimination against other minority groups that may not be given preferential treatment under a particular affirmative action program). At issue is whether affirmative action programs, because of their inherently discriminatory nature, violate the equal protection clause of the Fourteenth Amendment to the Constitution.

The *Bakke* Case

An early case addressing this issue, *Regents of the University of California v. Bakke,*[20] involved an affirmative action program implemented by the University of California at Davis. Allan Bakke, who had been turned down for medical school at the Davis campus, sued the university for reverse discrimination after he discovered that his academic record was better than those of some of the minority applicants who had been admitted to the program.

The United States Supreme Court held that affirmative action programs were subject to "intermediate scrutiny." Recall from the discussion of the equal protection clause in Chapter 5 that any law or action evaluated under a standard of intermediate scrutiny, to be constitutionally valid, must be substantially related to important government objectives. Applying this standard, the Court held that the university could give favorable weight to minority applicants as part of a plan to increase minority enrollment so as to achieve a more culturally diverse student body. The Court stated, however, that the use of a quota system, in which a certain number of places is explicitly reserved for minority applicants, violated the equal protection clause of the Fourteenth Amendment.

> **REMEMBER** The Fourteenth Amendment prohibits any state from denying any person "the equal protection of the laws." This prohibition applies to the *federal* government through the due process clause of the Fifth Amendment.

The *Adarand* Case and Subsequent Developments

Although the *Bakke* case and later court decisions alleviated the harshness of the quota system, today's courts are going even further in questioning the constitutional validity of affirmative action programs. For example, in *Adarand Constructors, Inc. v. Peña,*[21] the plaintiff (Adarand Constructors, Inc.) was not awarded a federal highway construction project even though it had submitted the lowest bid. Instead, the project went to an Hispanic-owned firm pursuant to a federal program designed to give at least 5 percent of highway construction projects to disadvantaged business enterprises. Adarand sued Federico Peña, the secretary of the Transportation Department, alleging that the federal program violated the equal protection clause.

The Supreme Court held that any federal, state, or local affirmative action program that uses racial or ethnic classifications as the basis for making decisions is subject to "strict scrutiny" by the courts. As discussed in Chapter 5, under a strict-scrutiny analysis, to be constitutional, a discriminatory law or action must be narrowly tailored to meet a *compelling* government interest. In effect, the Court's opinion in *Adarand* means that an affirmative action program cannot make use of quotas or preferences for unqualified persons, and once the program has succeeded, it must be changed or dropped.

A handshake at the end of a business deal. To what degree should race or gender be a factor in determining with whom to do business?

20.   438 U.S. 265, 98 S.Ct. 2733, 57 L.Ed.2d 750 (1978).
21.   515 U.S. 200, 115 S.Ct. 2097, 132 L.Ed.2d 158 (1995).

Since the *Adarand* decision, the lower courts have followed the Supreme Court's lead in subjecting affirmative action programs to strict scrutiny. In several cases, the lower courts have held that the affirmative action programs being challenged do violate the equal protection clause. The first federal appellate ruling on the issue, in *Hopwood v. State of Texas,*[22] involved two white law-school applicants who sued the University of Texas School of Law in Austin, alleging that they were denied admission because of the school's affirmative action program. The program allowed admitting officials to take racial and other factors into consideration when determining which students would be admitted. The Court of Appeals for the Fifth Circuit held that the program violated the equal protection clause because it discriminated in favor of minority applicants. Significantly, the court directly challenged the *Bakke* decision by stating that the use of race even as a means of achieving diversity on college campuses "undercuts the Fourteenth Amendment."

Although the cases just discussed do not directly relate to affirmative action programs in the workplace, clearly they indicate a trend that will affect employers' affirmative action programs as well. Additionally, in 1996, by a voters' initiative known as Proposition 209, California voters amended their state constitution to ban affirmative action policies in state employment, education, and contracting.[23] Similar movements are currently under way in other states. The question in the following case is whether an employer's voluntary affirmative action policy of "racial diversity" violated Title VII of the Civil Rights Act of 1964.

---

22.   84 F.3d. 720 (5th Cir. 1996).
23.   The constitutionality of this amendment was upheld in *Coalition for Economic Equity v. Wilson,* 110 F.3d 1431 (9th Cir. 1997).

Case 17.5 ● Taxman v. Board of Education of the Township of Piscataway

United States Court of Appeals,
Third Circuit, 1996.
91 F.3d 1547.

HISTORICAL AND SOCIAL SETTING   *By the mid-1990's, affirmative action plans remained controversial, although they had not yet been held illegal. The courts had held instead that a plan must be "narrowly tailored" to meet a "compelling interest."[a] Such a plan cannot include racial quotas. In other words, race might be a factor in circumstances designed to remedy discrimination, but it cannot be used as the sole determinant in other situations.*

---

a.   See, for example, *Claus v. Duquesne Light Co.,* 46 F.3d 1115 (3rd Cir. 1994), cert. denied by *Duquesne Light Co. v. Claus,* 514 U.S. 1067, 115 S.Ct. 1700, 131 L.Ed.2d 562 (1995).

BACKGROUND AND FACTS   The Board of Education of the Township of Piscataway, New Jersey, decided to reduce the teaching staff at Piscataway High School by one. Between two teachers of equal seniority and qualifications but different races, the board chose to lay off the white teacher, Sharon Taxman. Minority teachers were not underrepresented in the school district work force. The board based its decision on an affirmative action policy that was designed not to remedy discrimination but to promote "racial diversity." Taxman and others filed a suit in a federal district court against the board, challenging the policy as a violation of Title VII. The court granted a summary judgment in favor of the plaintiffs. The case was appealed to the U.S. Court of Appeals for the Third Circuit.

(Continued)

Case 17.5—continued

IN THE WORDS OF THE COURT . . .
MANSMANN, Circuit Judge.

* * * *

Title VII was enacted to further two primary goals: to end discrimination on the basis of race, color, religion, sex or national origin, thereby guaranteeing equal opportunity in the workplace, and to remedy the segregation and underrepresentation of minorities that discrimination has caused in our Nation's work force.

* * * *

* * * [T]he Board's sole purpose in applying its affirmative action policy in this case was to obtain an educational benefit which it believed would result from a racially diverse faculty. While the benefits flowing from diversity in the educational context are significant * * * , the Board does not even attempt to show that its affirmative action plan was adopted to remedy past discrimination or as the result of a manifest imbalance in the employment of minorities * * * .

* * * *

* * * [T]he Board's policy, devoid of goals and standards, is governed entirely by the Board's whim, leaving the Board free, if it so chooses, to grant racial preferences that do not promote even the policy's claimed purpose. Indeed, under the terms of this policy, the Board, in pursuit of a "racially diverse" work force, could use affirmative action to discriminate against those whom Title VII was enacted to protect.

DECISION AND REMEDY The U.S. Court of Appeals for the Third Circuit affirmed the lower court's judgment in favor of the plaintiffs and awarded Taxman 100 percent of her back pay. The case was appealed to the United States Supreme Court, but the parties agreed to an out-of-court settlement before the Supreme Court could rule on the case.

FOR CRITICAL ANALYSIS—ETHICAL CONSIDERATION *Are affirmative action plans justifiable from an ethical point of view?*

State Statutes

Although the focus of this chapter is on federal legislation, most states also have statutes that prohibit employment discrimination. Generally, the kinds of discrimination prohibited under federal legislation are also prohibited by state laws. In addition, state statutes often provide protection for certain individuals, such as homosexuals, who are not protected under Title VII. Furthermore, state laws prohibiting discrimination may provide additional damages, such as damages for emotional distress, that are not provided for under Title VII. Finally, in some cases, a court has allowed a plaintiff to recover damages for wrongful discharge on the ground that the employer's discriminatory practices were contrary to the state's public policy against discrimination.[24]

---

24. See, for example, *Molesworth v. Brandon*, 341 Md. 621, 672 A.2d 608 (1996).

International Perspective

Affirmative action programs are under attack not only in the United States but also in Europe. In 1995, the European Court of Justice delivered a landmark ruling on government-imposed affirmative action programs that give women preference in jobs and promotions. The rulings of the court, which is located in Luxembourg, are not necessarily binding on the fifteen member nations of the European Union (EU), but the court's ruling in this case is likely to have significant implications for affirmative action programs throughout the EU.

The case was brought by Eckhard Kalanke, a landscaper who works for the Parks Department in the city of Bremen, Germany. Kalanke alleged that a promotion he sought was given to a woman because of an affirmative action law requiring public agencies to give preference to qualified women for positions in which women were underrepresented. When the case reached the European Court of Justice, the court held that the Bremen affirma-

tive action policy violated a 1976 directive of the European Economic Community (EEC), which has since become the EU. The directive barred "discrimination on the grounds of sex either directly or indirectly." The court concluded that although the 1976 directive allows countries to remove barriers to employment opportunities for women, the Bremen program went too far. The court stated that "[n]ational rules which guarantee women absolute and unconditional priority for appointment or promotion go beyond promoting equal opportunities and overstep the limits of EU law."[a]

For Critical Analysis: *How can the goal of equal employment opportunities for women be achieved without affirmative action programs?*

---

a. *The New York Times International,* October 18, 1995, p. A11.

Key Terms

affirmative action 488
bona fide occupational
    qualification (BFOQ) 487
business necessity 487
disparate-impact
    discrimination 473

disparate-treatment
    discrimination 473
employment discrimination
    472
prima facie case 473

seniority system 488
sexual harassment 476

Chapter Summary
Equal Employment Opportunities

TITLE VII OF THE CIVIL RIGHTS ACT OF 1964 (See pages 472–481.)	Title VII prohibits employment discrimination based on race, color, national origin, religion, or gender. 1. **Procedures**—Employees must file a claim with the Equal Employment Opportunity Commission (EEOC). The EEOC may sue the employer on the employee's behalf; if not, the employee may sue the employer directly. 2. **Intentional versus unintentional discrimination**—Title VII prohibits both intentional (disparate-treatment) and unintentional (disparate-impact)

(Continued)

Chapter Summary, continued

TITLE VII OF THE CIVIL RIGHTS ACT OF 1964—continued (See pages 472–481.)	discrimination. Disparate-impact discrimination occurs when an employer's practice, such as hiring only persons with a certain level of education, has the effect of discriminating against a class of persons protected by Title VII. 3. **Remedies for discrimination under Title VII**—If a plaintiff proves that unlawful discrimination occurred, he or she may be awarded reinstatement, back pay, and retroactive promotions. Damages (both compensatory and punitive) may be awarded for intentional discrimination.
DISCRIMINATION BASED ON AGE (See pages 481–483.)	The Age Discrimination in Employment Act (ADEA) of 1967 prohibits employment discrimination on the basis of age against individuals forty years of age or older. Procedures for bringing a case under the ADEA are similar to those for bringing a case under Title VII.
DISCRIMINATION BASED ON DISABILITY (See pages 483–487.)	The Americans with Disabilities Act (ADA) of 1990 prohibits employment discrimination against persons with disabilities who are otherwise qualified to perform the essential functions of the jobs for which they apply. 1. **Procedures and remedies**—To prevail on a claim under the ADA, the plaintiff must show that he or she has a disability, is otherwise qualified for the employment in question, and was excluded from the employment solely because of the disability. Procedures under the ADA are similar to those required in Title VII cases; remedies are also similar to those under Title VII. 2. **Definition of disability**—The ADA defines the term *disability* as a physical or mental impairment that substantially limits one or more major life activities; a record of such impairment; or being regarded as having such an impairment. 3. **Reasonable accommodation**—Employers are required to reasonably accommodate the needs of persons with disabilities. Reasonable accommodations may include altering job-application procedures, modifying the physical work environment, and permitting more flexible work schedules. Employers are not required to accommodate the needs of all workers with disabilities. For example, employers need not accommodate workers who pose a definite threat to health and safety in the workplace or those who are not otherwise qualified for their jobs.
DEFENSES TO EMPLOYMENT DISCRIMINATION (See pages 487–488.)	If a plaintiff proves that employment discrimination occurred, employers may avoid liability by successfully asserting certain defenses. Employers may assert that the discrimination was required for reasons of business necessity, to meet a bona fide occupational qualification, or to maintain a legitimate seniority system. Evidence of prior employee misconduct acquired after the employee has been fired is not a defense to discrimination.
AFFIRMATIVE ACTION (See pages 488–491.)	Affirmative action programs attempt to "make up" for past patterns of discrimination by giving members of protected classes preferential treatment in hiring or promotion. Increasingly, such programs are being strictly scrutinized by the courts.
STATE STATUTES (See page 491.)	Generally, the kinds of discrimination prohibited by federal statutes are also prohibited by state laws. State laws may provide for more extensive protection and remedies than federal laws.

For Review

1. Generally, what kind of conduct is prohibited by Title VII of the Civil Rights Act of 1964, as amended?

2. What is the difference between disparate-treatment discrimination and disparate-impact discrimination?

3. What remedies are available under Title VII of the 1964 Civil Rights Act, as amended?

4. What federal acts prohibit discrimination based on age and discrimination based on disability?

5. Name three defenses to claims of employment discrimination.

Questions and Case Problems

17–1. Title VII Violations.   Discuss fully whether any of the following actions would constitute a violation of Title VII of the 1964 Civil Rights Act, as amended:

   a. Tennington, Inc., is a consulting firm and has ten employees. These employees travel on consulting jobs in seven states. Tennington has an employment record of hiring only white males.

   b. Novo Films, Inc., is making a film about Africa and needs to employ approximately one hundred extras for this picture. Novo advertises in all major newspapers in southern California for the hiring of these extras. The ad states that only African Americans need apply.

17–2. Discrimination Based on Age.   Tavo Jones had worked since 1974 for Westshore Resort, where he maintained golf carts. During the first decade, he received positive job evaluations and numerous merit pay raises. He was promoted to the position of supervisor of golf-cart maintenance at three courses. Then a new employee, Ben Olery, was placed in charge of the golf courses. He demoted Jones, who was over the age of forty, to running only one of the three cart facilities, and he froze Jones's salary indefinitely. Olery also demoted five other men over the age of forty. Another cart facility was placed under the supervision of Blake Blair. Later, the cart facilities for the three courses were again consolidated, but Blair—not Jones—was put in charge. At the time, Jones was still in his forties, and Blair was in his twenties. Jones overheard Blair say that "we are going to have to do away with these . . . old and senile" men. Jones quit and sued Westshore for employment discrimination. Should he prevail? Explain.

17–3. Disparate-Impact Discrimination.   Several African American employees of the Connecticut Department of Income Maintenance who sought promotion to supervisory positions took the required written examination but failed to pass it. Of all who took the examination, 54 percent of the African American employees passed it, whereas nearly 80 percent of the white employees passed. Following the examination, the state of Connecticut promoted eleven African Americans (representing 23 percent of all African American employees) and thirty-five white employees (representing 14 percent of all white employees). Teal and three other African American employees who failed the test sued the state of Connecticut and the Department of Income Maintenance. The employees asserted that the written test excluded a disproportionate number of African American employees from promotion to supervisory positions and therefore violated Title VII of the Civil Rights Act. The state argued that because a greater percentage of African American employees had been promoted, relative to white employees, the test was not discriminatory. Which party was correct?

17–4. Disparate-Impact Discrimination.   Chinawa, a major processor of cheese sold throughout the United States, employs one hundred workers at its principal processing plant. The plant is located in Heartland Corners, which has a population that is 50 percent white and 25 percent African American, with the balance Hispanic American, Asian American, and others. Chinawa requires a high school diploma as a condition of employment for its cleaning crew. Three-fourths of the white population complete high school, compared with only one-fourth of those in the minority groups. Chinawa has an all-white cleaning crew. Has Chinawa violated Title VII of the Civil Rights Act of 1964? Explain.

17–5. Discrimination Based on Gender.   Beginning in June 1966, Corning Glass Works started to open up jobs on the night shift to women. The previously separate male and female seniority lists were consolidated, and the women became eligible to exercise their seniority on the same basis as men and to bid for higher-paid night inspection jobs as vacancies occurred. On January 20, 1969, however, a new collective bargaining agreement went into effect; it established a new job evaluation system for setting wage rates. This agreement abolished (for the future) separate base wages for night-shift and day-shift inspectors and imposed a uniform base wage for inspectors that exceeded the wage rate previously in effect for the night shift. The agreement, though, did allow for a higher "red circle" rate for employees hired prior to January 20, 1969, when they were working as inspectors on the night shift. This "red circle" wage served essentially to perpetuate the differential in base wages between day and night inspectors. Had Corning violated Title VII of the Civil Rights Act of 1964? Discuss. [*Corning Glass Works v. Brennan,* 417 U.S. 188, 94 S.Ct. 2223, 41 L.Ed.2d 1 (1974)]

17–6. Burden of Proof. Melvin Hicks, an African American, was a shift supervisor at St. Mary's Honor Center, a halfway house operated by the Missouri Department of Corrections and Human Resources. After being demoted and eventually terminated from his job, Hicks brought an action under Title VII, alleging racial discrimination. Hicks successfully presented a *prima facie* case: he was a member of a protected class, he was qualified for the job of shift commander, he was demoted and then discharged, and the position he vacated was filled by a white man. St. Mary's Honor Center asserted that it had demoted and fired Hicks for legitimate, nondiscriminatory reasons—Hicks had violated procedures and threatened his supervisor. The district court found the claims to be a mere pretext (a fabricated reason for dismissing Hicks). The court nonetheless held for the center, because Hicks had failed to prove that the center's actions were motivated by any racial bias—in other words, Hicks had not been discriminated against on the basis of race, as he had contended. The appellate court reversed, holding that once the district court had found that the center's reasons were pretextual, Hicks was entitled to judgment as a matter of law. The case was appealed to the United States Supreme Court. Discuss how the Supreme Court should decide this case, and why. [*St. Mary's Honor Center v. Hicks,* 509 U.S. 502, 113 S.Ct. 2742, 125 L.Ed.2d 407 (1993)]

17–7. Defenses to Employment Discrimination. Dorothea O'Driscoll had worked as a quality control inspector for Hercules, Inc., for six years when her employment was terminated in 1986. O'Driscoll, who was over forty years of age, sued Hercules for age discrimination in violation of the Age Discrimination in Employment Act of 1967. While preparing for trial, Hercules discovered evidence of misconduct on the part of O'Driscoll that it had been unaware of when it terminated her employment. Among other things, Hercules learned that O'Driscoll had misrepresented her age on both her employment application and her application for a government security clearance (necessary to handle confidential information). She also did not disclose a previous employer, falsely represented that she had never applied for work with Hercules before, and falsely stated that she had completed two quarters of study at a technical college. Additionally, on her application for group insurance coverage, she misrepresented the age of her son, who would otherwise have been ineligible for coverage as her dependent. Hercules defended against O'Driscoll's claim of age discrimination by stating that

had it known of this misconduct, it would have terminated her employment anyway. What should the court decide? Discuss fully. [*O'Driscoll v. Hercules, Inc.,* 12 F.3d 176 (10th Cir. 1994)]

17–8. Discrimination Based on National Origin. Phanna Xieng was sent by the Cambodian government to the United States in 1974 for "advanced military training." When the Cambodian government fell in 1975, Xieng remained in the United States and eventually was employed by Peoples National Bank of Washington in 1979. In performance appraisals from 1980 through 1985, Xieng was rated by his supervisors as "capable of dealing effectively with customers" and qualified for promotion, although in each appraisal it was noted that Xieng might improve his communication skills to maximize his possibilities for future advancement. Xieng sought job promotions on numerous occasions but was never promoted. In 1986, he filed a complaint against the bank, alleging employment discrimination based on national origin. The employer argued that its refusal to promote Xieng because of his accent or communication skills did not amount to discrimination based on national origin. Is it possible to separate discrimination based on an employee's accent and communication skills from discrimination based on national origin? How should the court rule on this issue? [*Xieng v. Peoples National Bank of Washington,* 120 Wash.2d 512, 844 P.2d 389 (1993)]

17–9. Disparate-Impact Discrimination. Local 1066 of the Steamship Clerks Union accepted only new members who were sponsored by existing members. All of the existing members were white. During a six-year period, the local admitted thirty new members, all of whom were relatives of present members and also white. The Equal Employment Opportunity Commission filed a suit in a federal district court against the union, alleging that this practice constituted disparate-impact discrimination under Title VII. The union argued that it was only continuing a family tradition. What does each party have to prove to win its case? Should the union be required to change its practice? [*EEOC v. Steamship Clerks Union, Local 1066,* 48 F.3d 594 (1st Cir. 1995)]

17–10. Discrimination Based on Disability. When the University of Maryland Medical System Corp. learned that one of its surgeons was HIV positive, the university offered him transfers to positions that did not involve surgery. The surgeon refused, and the university terminated him. The surgeon filed a suit in a federal district court against the university, alleging in part a violation of the Americans with Disabilities Act. The surgeon claimed that he was "otherwise qualified" for his former position. What does he have to prove to win his case? Should he be reinstated? [*Doe v. University of Maryland Medical System Corp.,* 50 F.3d 1261 (4th Cir. 1995)]

A Question of Ethics and Social Responsibility

17–11. Luz Long and three other Hispanic employees (the plaintiffs) worked as bank tellers for the Culmore branch of the First Union Corp. of Virginia. The plaintiffs often conversed with one another in Spanish, their native language. In 1992, the Culmore branch manager adopted an "English-only" policy, which required all employees to speak English during working hours unless they had to speak another language to assist customers. The plaintiffs refused to cooperate with the new policy and were eventually fired. In a suit against the bank, the plaintiffs alleged that the English-only policy discriminated against them on the basis of their national origin. The court granted the bank's motion for summary judgment, concluding that "[t]here is nothing in Title VII which . . . provides that an employee has a right to speak his or her native tongue while on the job." [*Long v. First Union Corp. of Virginia,* 894 F.Supp. 933 (E.D.Va. 1995)]

1. The bank argued that the policy was implemented in response to complaints made by fellow employees that the Spanish-speaking employees were creating a hostile environment by speaking Spanish among themselves in the presence of other employees. From an ethical perspective, is this a sufficient reason to institute an English-only policy?
2. Is it ever ethically justifiable for employers to deny bilingual employees the opportunity to speak their native language while on the job?
3. Might there be situations in which English-only policies are necessary to promote worker health and safety?
4. Generally, what are the pros and cons of English-only policies in the workplace?

For Critical Analysis

17–12. The Equal Employment Opportunity Commission (EEOC) decided, pursuant to its "National Employment Policy" of 1996, not to investigate every complaint of discrimination, as it once did. In the same policy statement, the EEOC stated that it will place more emphasis on the mediation and arbitration of employee-employer disputes. Who will benefit more from this policy, employers or employees?

CHAPTER 18

Labor-Management Relations

Contents

Chapter Objectives

After reading this chapter, you should be able to . . .

1. Describe the process behind union elections and collective bargaining.
2. Explain which strikes are legal and whch strikes are illegal.
3. List unfair employer practices.
4. Identify unfair employee practices.
5. Define the rights of nonunion employees.

> **"Experience has proved that protection by law of the right of employees to organize and bargain collectively . . . promotes the flow of commerce."**
>
> National Labor Relations Act of 1935, Section 1

An employer's rules. How do federal labor laws influence the adoption of such rules?

Yellow Dog Contract An agreement under which an employee promises his or her employer, as a condition of employment, not to join a union.

Through the first half of the nineteenth century, most Americans were self-employed, often in agriculture. For those who were employed by others, the employers generally set the terms of employment. The nature of employment changed with the growth of the industrial revolution, which had begun about 1760. Fewer Americans were self-employed. Terms of employment were sometimes set through bargaining between employees and employers. Most industrial enterprises were in their infancies, however, and to encourage their development, the government gave employers considerable freedom to hire, fire, and determine other employment standards in response to changing conditions in the marketplace.

With increasing industrialization, the size of workplaces and the number of workplace hazards increased. Workers came to believe that to counter the power and freedom of their employers and to protect themselves, they needed to organize into unions. Employers discouraged—sometimes forcibly—collective activities such as unions. In support of unionization, Congress enacted such legislation as the Railway Labor Act of 1926.[1] These laws were often restricted to particular industries. Beginning in 1932, Congress enacted a number of statutes that increased employees' rights in general. As the opening quotation indicates, at the heart of these rights is the right to join unions and engage in collective bargaining with management to negotiate working conditions, salaries, and benefits for a group of workers.

This chapter describes the development of labor law and legal recognition of the right to form unions. The laws that govern the management-union relationship are set forth in historical perspective. Then we discuss the process of unionizing a company, the collective bargaining required of a unionized employer, the "industrial war" of strikes and lockouts that may result if bargaining fails, and the labor practices that are considered unfair under federal law.

Federal Labor Law

Federal labor laws governing union-employer relations have developed considerably since the first law was enacted in 1932. Initially, the laws were concerned with protecting the rights and interests of workers. Subsequent legislation placed some restraints on unions and granted rights to employers. This section summarizes the four major federal labor law statutes.

Norris-LaGuardia Act

Congress protected peaceful strikes, picketing, and boycotts in 1932 in the Norris-LaGuardia Act.[2] The statute restricted federal courts in their power to issue injunctions against unions engaged in peaceful strikes. The act also provided that contracts limiting an employee's right to join a union are unlawful. Such contracts are known as **yellow dog contracts.** (In the early part of the twentieth century, "yellow dog" meant "coward.") In effect, this act declared a national policy permitting employees to organize.

---

1. 45 U.S.C. Sections 151–188.
2. 29 U.S.C. Sections 101–115.

National Labor Relations Act

The National Labor Relations Act of 1935 (NLRA),[3] also called the Wagner Act, established the right of employees to form unions, the right of those unions to engage in collective bargaining (negotiate contracts for their members), and the right to strike. The act also created the National Labor Relations Board (NLRB) to oversee union elections and to prevent employers from engaging in unfair labor union activities and unfair labor practices. Details of the NLRA are provided in the *Landmark in the Legal Environment* on page 501.

To be protected under the NLRA, an individual must be an "employee," as that term is defined in the statute.[4] Courts have long held that job applicants fall within the definition (otherwise, the NLRA's ban on discrimination in regard to hiring would mean nothing). In the following case, the United States Supreme Court considered whether an individual can be a company's "employee" if, at the same time, a union pays the individual to organize the company.

3. 29 U.S.C. Sections 151–169.
4. 29 U.S.C. Section 152(3).

Case 18.1 ● NLRB v. Town & Country Electric, Inc.

Supreme Court of the United States, 1995
516 U.S. 85,
116 S.Ct. 450,
133 L.Ed.2d 371.

HISTORICAL AND SOCIAL SETTING *Over the last two decades, the percentage of private-sector workers who are union members has declined. Perhaps this is due, at least in part, to a popular belief that unions represent only a level of interference between a company's making profits and the workers' getting paid. In the public sector, however, unions are becoming more popular and are growing in force. Unions themselves are consolidating and still attempting to organize workers.*

BACKGROUND AND FACTS Town & Country Electric, Inc., advertised for job applicants but refused to interview ten of eleven applicants who were members of a union, the International Brotherhood of Electrical Workers. The applicants were union "salts"—persons paid by the union to apply for a job with a company and then, when hired, to unionize the company (in this case, Town & Country's work force). The applicants filed a complaint with the National Labor Relations Board (NLRB), alleging that the company had committed an unfair labor practice by discriminating against the applicants on the basis of union membership. The issue turned on whether job applicants paid by a union to organize a company could be considered employees under the National Labor Relations Act (NLRA). The NLRB determined that the applicants were employees and ruled in their favor. Town & Country appealed, and the U.S. Court of Appeals for the Eighth Circuit reversed. The applicants appealed to the United States Supreme Court.

IN THE WORDS OF THE COURT . . .
Justice BREYER delivered the opinion of the Court.
* * * *

* * * [T]he Board's decision is consistent with the broad language of the [NLRA] * * * . The ordinary dictionary definition of "employee" includes any "person who works for another in return for financial or other compensation." The phrasing of the [NLRA] seems to reiterate the breadth of the ordinary dictionary definition, for it says "[t]he term 'employee' shall include any employee." * * *

(Continued)

Case 18.1—continued

For another thing, the Board's broad, literal interpretation of the word "employee" is consistent with several of the [NLRA's] purposes, such as protecting "the right of employees to organize for mutual aid without employer interference" * * * .

DECISION AND REMEDY   The United States Supreme Court reversed the decision of the appellate court and remanded the case. The Court held that the applicants were employees and thus could not be discriminated against.

FOR CRITICAL ANALYSIS—SOCIAL CONSIDERATION   *How would the relationship between labor and management be affected if job applicants did not have rights under the NLRA?*

Labor-Management Relations Act

The Labor-Management Relations Act of 1947 (LMRA, or the Taft-Hartley Act)[5] was passed to proscribe certain union practices. The Taft-Hartley Act contained provisions protecting employers as well as employees. The act was bitterly opposed by organized labor groups. It provided a detailed list of unfair labor activities that unions as well as management were now forbidden to practice. In addition, the law gave the president the authority to intervene in labor disputes and delay strikes that would "imperil the national health or safety."

An important provision of the LMRA concerned the **closed shop**—a firm that requires union membership of its workers as a condition of obtaining employment. Closed shops were made illegal under the Taft-Hartley Act. The act preserved the legality of the **union shop,** which does not require membership as a prerequisite for employment but can, and usually does, require that workers join the recognized union after a specified amount of time on the job. The act also allowed individual states to pass their own **right-to-work laws—** laws making it illegal for union membership to be required for *continued* employment in any establishment. Thus, union shops are technically illegal in states with right-to-work laws.

Closed Shop A firm that requires union membership by its workers as a condition of employment. The closed shop was made illegal by the Labor-Management Relations Act of 1947.

Union Shop A place of employment in which all workers, once employed, must become union members within a specified period of time as a condition of their continued employment.

Right-to-Work Law A state law providing that employees are not to be required to join a union as a condition of obtaining or retaining employment.

Labor-Management Reporting and Disclosure Act

The Labor-Management Reporting and Disclosure Act of 1959 (the Landrum-Griffin Act)[6] established an employee bill of rights, as well as reporting requirements for union activities to prevent corruption. The Landrum-Griffin Act strictly regulated internal union business procedures.

Union elections, for example, are regulated by the Landrum-Griffin Act, which requires that regularly scheduled elections of officers occur and that secret ballots be used. Ex-convicts and Communists are prohibited from holding union office. Moreover, union officials are made accountable for union property and funds. Members have the right to attend and to participate in union meetings, to nominate officers, and to vote in most union proceedings.

Coverage and Procedures

Coverage of the federal labor laws is broad and extends to all employers whose business activity either involves or affects interstate commerce. Some

---

5. 29 U.S.C. Sections 141, 504.
6. 29 U.S.C. Sections 153, 1111.

Landmark in the Legal Environment
The National Labor Relations Act (1935)

The National Labor Relations Act of 1935 is often referred to as the Wagner Act because it was sponsored by Senator Robert Wagner. (Appendix E presents excerpts from the National Labor Relations Act.) During the 1930s, Wagner sponsored several pieces of legislation, particularly in the field of labor law. Until the early 1930s, employers had been free to establish the terms and conditions of employment. Collective activities by employees, such as participation in unions, were discouraged by employers. In 1934, when Wagner introduced the bill subsequently enacted as the National Labor Relations Act (NLRA), he saw it as a vehicle through which the disparate balance of power between employers and employees could be corrected.

Section 1 of the NLRA justifies the act under the commerce clause of the Constitution. Section 1 states that unequal bargaining power between employees and employers leads to economic instability, and refusals of employers to bargain collectively lead to strikes. These disturbances impede the flow of interstate commerce. It is declared to be the policy of the United States, under the authority given to the federal government under the commerce clause, to ensure the free flow of commerce by encouraging collective bargaining and unionization.

The pervading purpose of the NLRA was to protect interstate commerce by securing for employees the rights established by Section 7 of the act: to organize, to bargain collectively through representatives of their own choosing, and to engage in concerted activities for that and other purposes. In Section 8, the act specifically defined a number of employer practices as unfair to labor:

1. Interference with the efforts of employees to form, join, or assist labor organizations or to engage in concerted activities for their mutual aid or protection [Section 8(a)(1)].

2. Domination of a labor organization or contribution of financial or other support to it [Section 8(a)(2)].
3. Discrimination in the hiring or awarding of tenure to employees because of union affiliation [Section 8(a)(3)].
4. Discrimination against employees for filing charges under the act or giving testimony under the act [Section 8(a)(4)].
5. Refusal to bargain collectively with the duly designated representative of the employees [Section 8(a)(5)].

Another purpose of the act was to promote fair and just settlements of disputes by peaceful processes and to avoid industrial warfare. The act created the National Labor Relations Board (NLRB) to oversee elections and to prevent employers from engaging in unfair and illegal union activities and unfair labor practices. The board was granted investigatory powers and was authorized to issue and serve complaints against employers in response to employee charges of unfair labor practices. The board was further empowered to issue cease-and-desist orders—which could be enforced by a federal court of appeals if necessary—when violations were found.

Employers viewed the Wagner Act as a drastic piece of legislation, and the bill elicited a great deal of opposition. Those who opposed the act claimed that it did not come under the commerce clause of the U.S. Constitution and therefore Congress had no power to act. Those who were willing to admit that it did fall under the commerce clause claimed that it created an undue burden, which therefore rendered it unconstitutional. The constitutionality of the act was tested in 1937 in *National Labor Relations Board v. Jones & Laughlin Steel Corp.*[a] In its decision, the United States Supreme Court held that the act and its application were constitutionally valid.

_____

a.   301 U.S. 1, 57 S.Ct. 615, 81 L.Ed. 893 (1937).

workers are specifically excluded from these laws. Railroads and airlines are not covered by the NLRA but are covered by a separate act, the Railway Labor Act, which closely parallels the NLRA. Other types of workers, such as agricultural workers and domestic servants, are excluded from the NLRA and have no coverage under separate legislation.

When a union or employee believes that the employer has violated federal labor law (or vice versa), the union or employee files a charge with a regional office of the NLRB. The form for an employee to use to file an unfair labor practice charge against an employer is shown in Exhibit 18–1. The charge is

■ **Exhibit 18–1   Unfair Labor Practice Complaint Form**

FORM EXEMPT UNDER 44 U.S.C. 3512

FORM NLRB-501 (8-83)	UNITED STATES OF AMERICA NATIONAL LABOR RELATIONS BOARD **CHARGE AGAINST EMPLOYER**	**DO NOT WRITE IN THIS SPACE**	
		Case	Date Filed

INSTRUCTIONS: File an original and 4 copies of this charge with NLRB Regional Director for the region in which the alleged unfair labor practice occurred or is occurring.

1. EMPLOYER AGAINST WHOM CHARGE IS BROUGHT

a. Name of Employer	b. Number of workers employed

c. Address (*street, city, state, ZIP code*)	d. Employer Representative	e. Telephone No.

f. Type of Establishment (*factory, mine, wholesaler, etc.*)	g. Identify principal product or service

h. The above-named employer has engaged in and is engaging in unfair labor practices within the meaning of section 8(a). subsections (1) and (list subsections) _____ of the National Labor Relations Act. and these unfair labor practices are unfair practices affecting commerce within the meaning of the Act.

2. Basis of the Charge (*be specific as to facts, names, addresses, plants involved, dates, places, etc.*)

By the above and other acts, the above-named employer has interfered with, restrained, and coerced employees in the exercise of the rights guaranteed in Section 7 of the Act

3. Full name of party filing charge (*if labor organization, give full name, including local name and number*)

4a. Address (*street and number, city, state, and ZIP code*)	4b. Telephone No.

5. Full name of national or international labor organization of which it is an affiliate or constituent unit (*to be filled in when charge is filed by a labor organization*)

6. DECLARATION

I declare that I have read the above charge and that the statements are true to the best of my knowledge and belief.

By _____   _____
(*signature of representative or person making charge*)   (*title if any*)

Address _____   _____   _____
(*Telephone No.*)   (*date*)

WILLFUL FALSE STATEMENTS ON THIS CHARGE CAN BE PUNISHED BY FINE AND IMPRISONMENT
(U.S. CODE, TITLE 18, SECTION 1001)

investigated, and if it is found worthy, the regional director files a complaint. An administrative law judge (ALJ) initially hears the complaint and rules on it (see Chapter 6). The board reviews the ALJ's findings and decision. If the NLRB finds a violation, it may issue remedial orders (including requiring rehiring of discharged workers). The NLRB decision may be appealed to a U.S. court of appeals.

The Decision to Form or Select a Union

▼ The key starting point for labor relations law is the decision by a company's employees to form a union, which is usually referred to in the law as their bargaining representative. Many workplaces have no union, and workers bargain individually with the employer. If the workers decide that they want the added power of collective union representation, they must follow certain steps to have a union certified. Usually, the employer will fight these efforts to unionize.

Preliminary Organizing

Suppose that a national union, such as the American Federation of Labor and Congress of Industrial Organizations (AFL-CIO), wants to organize workers who produce semiconductor chips. The union would visit a manufacturing plant of a company—SemiCo in this example. If some SemiCo workers are interested in joining the union, they must begin organizing. An essential part of the process is to decide exactly which workers will be covered in the planned union. Will all manufacturing workers be covered or just those engaged in a single step in the manufacturing process?

The first step in forming a union is to get the relevant workers to sign **authorization cards.** These cards usually state that the worker desires to have a certain union, such as the AFL-CIO, represent the work force. If those in favor of the union can obtain authorization cards from a majority of workers, they may present the cards to the employer and ask the employer, SemiCo, to recognize the union formally. SemiCo is not required to do so, however.

More frequently, authorization cards are obtained to justify an election among workers for unionization. If SemiCo refuses to recognize the union based on authorization cards, an election is necessary to determine whether unionization has majority support among the workers. After the unionizers obtain authorization cards from at least 30 percent of the workers to be represented, the unionizers present these cards to the NLRB regional office with a petition for an election.

This 30 percent support is generally considered a sufficient showing of interest to justify an election on union representation. Union backers are not required to employ authorization cards but generally must have some evidence that at least 30 percent of the relevant work force supports a union or an election on unionization.

Appropriate Bargaining Unit

The NLRB considers the employees' petition as a basis for calling an election. In addition to a sufficient showing of interest in unionization, the proposed union must represent an **appropriate bargaining unit.**

Authorization Card A card signed by an employee that gives a union permission to act on his or her behalf in negotiations with management once a majority of the employees has signed such cards.

Appropriate Bargaining Unit A designation based on job duties, skill levels, and so on, of the proper entity that should be covered by a collective bargaining agreement.

Not every group of workers can form together into a single union. One key requirement of an appropriate bargaining unit is a *mutuality of interest* among all the workers to be represented. Groups of workers with significantly conflicting interests may not be represented in a single union.

JOB SIMILARITY.   One factor in determining the mutuality of interest is the *similarity of the jobs* of all the workers to be unionized. The NLRB considers factors such as similar levels of skill and qualifications, similar levels of wages and benefits, and similar working conditions. If represented workers have vastly different working conditions, they are unlikely to have the mutuality of interest necessary to bargain as a single unit with their employer.

One issue of job similarity has involved companies that employ both general industrial workers and craft workers (those with specialized skills, such as electricians). On many occasions, the NLRB has found that industrial and craft workers should be represented by different unions, although this is not an absolute rule.

WORK-SITE PROXIMITY.   A second important factor in determining the appropriate bargaining unit is *geographical*. If workers at only a single manufacturing plant are to be unionized, the geographical factor is not a problem. Even if the workers desire to join a national union, such as the AFL-CIO, they can join together in a single "local" division of that union. Geographical disparity may become a problem if a union is attempting to join workers at many different manufacturing sites together into a single union.

NONMANAGEMENT EMPLOYEES.   A third factor to be considered is the rule against unionization of *management* employees. The labor laws differentiate between labor and management and preclude members of management from being part of a union. There is no clear-cut definition of management, but supervisors are considered management and may not be included in worker unions. A supervisor is an individual who has the discretionary authority, as a representative of the employer, to make decisions such as hiring, suspending, promoting, firing, or disciplining other workers.[7] Professional employees, including legal and medical personnel, may be considered labor rather than management.

Moving toward Certification

A union, then, becomes certified through a procedure that begins with petitioning the NLRB. The proposed union must present authorization cards or other evidence showing an employee interest level of at least 30 percent. The organization must also show that the proposed union represents an appropriate bargaining unit. If the workers are under the NLRA's jurisdiction and if no other union has been certified within the past twelve months for these workers, the NLRB will schedule an election.

Union Election

Labor law provides for an election to determine whether employees choose to be represented by a union and, if so, which union. The NLRB supervises

7. *Waldau v. Merit Systems Protection Board*, 19 F.3d 1395 (Fed.Cir. 1994).

this election, ensuring secret voting and voter eligibility. The election is usually held about a month after the NLRB orders the vote (although it may be much longer, if management disputes the composition of an appropriate bargaining unit). If the election is a fair one, and if the proposed union receives majority support, the board certifies the union as the bargaining representative. Otherwise, the board will not certify the union.

Sometimes, a plant with an existing union may attempt to *decertify* the union (de-unionize). Although this action may be encouraged by management, it must be conducted by the employees. This action also requires a petition to the NLRB, with a showing of 30 percent employee support and no certification within the past year. The NLRB may grant this petition and call for a decertification election.

Union Election Campaign

Union organizers may campaign among workers to solicit votes for unionization. Considerable litigation has arisen over the rights of workers and outside union supporters to conduct such campaigns.

The employer retains great control over any activities, including unionization campaigns, that take place on company property and company time. Employers may lawfully use this authority to limit the campaign activities of union supporters. For example, management may prohibit all solicitations and distribution of pamphlets on company property as long as it has a legitimate business reason for doing so (such as to ensure safety or to prevent interference with business). The employer may also reasonably limit the places where solicitation occurs (for example, limit it to the lunchroom), limit the times during which solicitation can take place, and prohibit all outsiders from access to the workplace. All these actions are lawful.

Suppose that a union seeks to organize clerks at a department store. Courts have found that an employer can prohibit all solicitation in areas of the store open to the public. Union campaign activities in these circumstances could seriously interfere with the store's business.

There are some legal restrictions on management regulation of union solicitation. The key restriction is the *nondiscrimination* rule. An employer may prohibit all solicitation during work time or in certain places but may not selectively prohibit union solicitation during work time. If the employer permits political candidates to campaign on the employer's premises, for example, it also must permit union solicitation.[8]

Workers have a right to some reasonable opportunity to campaign. For example, the Supreme Court held that employees have a right to distribute a pro-union newsletter in nonworking areas on the employer's property during nonworking time. In this case, management had the burden to show some material harm from this action and could not do so.[9]

Management Election Campaign

Management may also campaign among its workers against the union (or for decertification of an existing union). Campaign tactics, however, are carefully

8. *Nonemployee* union organizers do not have the right to trespass on an employer's property to organize employees, however. See *Lechmere, Inc. v. NLRB,* 502 U.S. 527, 112 S.Ct. 841, 117 L.Ed.2d 79 (1992).
9. *Eastex, Inc. v. NLRB,* 437 U.S. 556, 98 S.Ct. 2505, 57 L.Ed.2d 428 (1978).

monitored and regulated by the NLRB. Otherwise, the economic power of management might allow coercion of the workers.

Management still has many advantages in the campaign. For example, management is allowed to call all workers together during work time and make a speech against unionization. Management need not give the union supporters an equal opportunity for rebuttal. The NLRB does restrict what management may say in such a speech, however.

NO THREATS.   In campaigning against the union, the employer may not make threats of reprisals if employees vote to unionize. A supervisor may not state, "If the union wins, you'll all be fired." This would be a threat. Employers must be very careful on this issue. For example, suppose an employer says, "Our competitor's plant in town unionized, and half the workers lost their jobs." The NLRB might consider this to be a veiled threat and therefore unfair.

An interesting controversy arose over a film that employers showed during union campaigns, *And Women Must Weep*. This film was prepared to help employers fight unionization efforts. The film dramatizes union misconduct during a strike, including vandalism, bomb threats, and attacks on neutral individuals such as a minister and an infant, who is shot and killed. Although this film is arguably inaccurate, courts have found it legal. One court wrote that "the film is a one-sided brief against unionism, devoid of significant rational content perhaps, but nevertheless not reasonably to be construed as threatening retaliation or force."[10]

"LABORATORY CONDITIONS."   Obviously, union election campaigns are not like national political campaigns, when a political party can make almost any claim. The NLRB tries to maintain "laboratory conditions" for a fair election that is unaffected by pressure. In establishing such conditions, the board considers the totality of circumstances in the campaign. The NLRB is especially strict about promises (or threats) made by the employer at the last minute, immediately before the election, because the union lacks an opportunity to respond effectively to these last-minute statements.

There is even a specific rule that prohibits an employer from making any election speech on company time, to massed assemblies of workers, within twenty-four hours of the time for voting. Such last-minute speeches are permitted only if employees attend voluntarily and on their own time.[11]

The employer is also prohibited from taking actions that might intimidate its workers. Employers may not undertake certain types of surveillance of workers or even create the impression of observing workers to identify union sympathizers. Management also is limited in its ability to question individual workers about their positions on unionization. These actions are deemed to contain implicit threats.

NLRB OPTIONS.   If the employer issues threats or engages in other unfair labor practices and then wins the election, the NLRB may invalidate the results. The NLRB may certify the union, even though it lost the election, and direct the employer to recognize the union as the employees' exclusive bargaining representative. Or the NLRB may ask a court to order a new election.

---

10. *Luxuray of New York v. NLRB,* 447 F.2d 112 (2d Cir. 1971).
11. Political party–like electioneering on behalf of a union, on the day of a union election, however, has been held acceptable and does not invalidate the election. See *Overnite Transportation Co. v. NLRB,* 104 F.3d 109 (7th Cir. 1997).

Not every statement that an employer makes against a union during a unionization campaign constitutes an unfair labor practice, however. In the following case, the NLRB argued that certain employer statements contained threats, but the employer contended that the statements were only expressions of opinion about the prospect of unionization.

Case 18.2 ● NLRB v. Pentre Electric, Inc.

United States Court of Appeals,
Sixth Circuit, 1993.
998 F.2d 363

BACKGROUND AND FACTS Pentre Electric, Inc., was an electrical contracting company co-owned by its president, Phil Luff, and its vice president, Pat Meehan. Pentre had nineteen employees. In November 1989, the International Brotherhood of Electrical Workers began a campaign to unionize the employees. At a company meeting in July 1990, Luff told the employees that most of Pentre's customers did not employ union contractors. Luff predicted that Pentre would likely have to build a new customer base in the event of the union's election but that "Pat and I would probably succeed." Later, Meehan met with about ten of the employees individually. Among other things, Meehan said that "if we were a union contractor, we'd have to establish new customers" and "I'm not prepared to do that." The election was held August 20. A majority of the employees voted against union representation. The NLRB and the union charged Pentre with unfair labor practices. After a hearing, an administrative law judge agreed, construing Meehan's statement that he was "not prepared" to face the difficulties of rebuilding a customer base as a threat to close Pentre in retaliation for a pro-union vote. The judge ordered a new election. The NLRB applied to a court for enforcement of the order. Pentre argued that its officers' statements did not constitute an unfair labor practice.

IN THE WORDS OF THE COURT . . .
BOYCE F. MARTIN, Jr., Circuit Judge.

* * * *

* * * [A]ny statement or prediction by an employer about the effects of unionization * * * must be carefully phrased on the basis of objective fact to convey an employer's belief as to demonstrably probable consequences beyond his control or to convey a management decision already arrived at to close the plant in case of unionization. If there is any implication that an employer may or may not take action solely on his own initiative for reasons unrelated to economic necessities and known only to him, the statement is no longer a reasonable prediction based on available facts but a threat of retaliation based on misrepresentation and coercion. * * *

* * * *

* * * [N]othing in [Luff's] statements intimated that he or Meehan would close the plant as a result of anti-union *animus* [animosity]. Luff's speech conveyed nothing more than his analysis of the likely economic consequences of unionization of Pentre, in light of his knowledge of Pentre's customers and competitors. * * *

* * * Like Luff, Meehan made his predictions about the effect of unionization on Pentre based upon his experience in the electrical contracting industry and his knowledge about the nature of Pentre's customer base. His statement conveyed that the probable consequences of unionization were beyond his control. * * * No employee could reasonably have come away from either speech with the belief that anti-union sentiment on the part of the company could lead to closure if the employees voted in favor of the union.

(Continued)

Case 18.2—continued

DECISION AND REMEDY   The court concluded that the statements did not constitute unfair labor practices and denied the NLRB's request for enforcement of the order for a new election.

FOR CRITICAL ANALYSIS—ECONOMIC CONSIDERATION
Why aren't union election campaigns like other political campaigns?

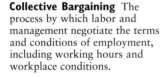 Collective Bargaining

If a fair election is held and the union wins, the NLRB will certify the union as the *exclusive bargaining representative* of the workers polled. Unions may provide a variety of services to their members, but the central legal right of a union is to serve as the sole representative of the group of workers in bargaining with the employer over the workers' rights.

The concept of bargaining is at the heart of the federal labor laws. When a union is officially recognized, it may make a demand to bargain with the employer. The union then sits at the table opposite the representatives of management to negotiate contracts for its workers. The terms of employment that result from the negotiations apply to all workers in the bargaining unit, even those who do not choose to belong to the union. This process is known as **collective bargaining.** Such bargaining is like most other business negotiations, and each side uses its economic power to pressure or persuade the other side to grant concessions.

Bargaining is a somewhat vague term. Bargaining does not mean that either side must give in on demands or even that the sides must always compromise. It does mean that a demand must be taken seriously and considered as part of a package to be negotiated. Importantly, both sides must bargain in "good faith."

Collective Bargaining The process by which labor and management negotiate the terms and conditions of employment, including working hours and workplace conditions.

Subjects of Bargaining

A common issue in collective bargaining concerns the subjects over which the parties can bargain. The law makes certain subjects mandatory for collective bargaining. These topics cannot be "taken off the table" unilaterally but must be discussed and bargained over.

TERMS AND CONDITIONS OF EMPLOYMENT.   The NLRA provides that employers may bargain with workers over wages, hours of work, and other terms and

International Perspective

In Great Britain, a union that has been recognized by an employer for collective bargaining purposes has certain rights. These rights include the right to receive information related to collective bargaining issues, the right to time off, the right to appoint a representative to handle safety matters, and the right to be consulted before an employer relocates its place of business.

For Critical Analysis: *Do you think employees have rights that should apply in all countries around the world under all circumstances?*

conditions of employment. These are broad terms that cover many employment issues. Suppose that a union wants a contract provision granting all workers four weeks of paid vacation. The company need not give in to this demand but must at least consider it and bargain over it.

Many other employment issues are also considered appropriate subjects for collective bargaining. These include safety rules, insurance coverage, pension and other employee benefits plans, procedures for employee discipline, and procedures for employee grievances against the company. The Supreme Court has held that an employer must bargain even over the price of food sold in the company cafeteria.[12]

A few subjects are illegal in collective bargaining. Management need not bargain over a provision that would be illegal if included in a contract. Thus, if a union presents a demand for **featherbedding** (the hiring of unnecessary excess workers) or for an unlawful closed shop, management need not respond to these demands.

CLOSING OR RELOCATING A PLANT. Management need not bargain with a union over the decision to close a particular facility. Similarly, management need not bargain over a decision to relocate a plant if the move involves a basic change in the nature of the employer's operation.[13] Management may choose to bargain over such decisions, however, to obtain concessions on other bargaining subjects.

Management must bargain over the economic consequences of such decisions. Thus, issues such as **severance pay** (compensation for the termination of employment) in the event of a plant shutdown are appropriate for collective bargaining. Also, if a relocation does *not* involve a basic change in the nature of an operation, management must bargain over the decision unless it can show (1) that the work performed at the new location varies significantly from the work performed at the former plant; (2) that the work performed at the former plant is to be discontinued entirely and not moved to the new location; (3) that the move involves a change in the scope and direction of the enterprise; (4) that labor costs were not a factor in the decision; or (5) that even if labor costs were a factor, the union could not have offered concessions that would have changed the decision to relocate. The following case involves a decision to relocate a significant part of an employer's operations.

---

12. *Ford Motor Co. v. NLRB*, 441 U.S. 488, 99 S.Ct. 1842, 60 L.Ed.2d 420 (1979).
13. *Dubuque Packing Co.*, 303 N.L.R.B. No. 386 (1991).

> **"I see an America where the workers are really free and through their great unions . . . can take their proper place in the council tables with the owners and managers of business."**
>
> Franklin D. Roosevelt, 1882–1945
> (Thirty-second president of the United States, 1932–1945)

Featherbedding A requirement that more workers be employed to do a particular job than are actually needed.

Severance Pay Funds in excess of normal wages or salaries paid to an employee on termination of his or her employment with a company.

Case 18.3 ● United Food and Commercial Workers International Union v. NLRB

United States Court of Appeals,
District of Columbia Circuit, 1993.
1 F.3d 24.

HISTORICAL AND CULTURAL SETTING *In the late 1970s, the consumption of meat began to drop in the United States. This was due in large part to concerns about the possible harmful effect of meat consumption on human health. By the beginning of the 1980s, Americans were buying less beef and pork and more chicken and fish. Added to the price instability of the livestock that serve as the source for the products, the decline in the consumption of beef and pork caused many companies in the meat-packing industry to look for ways to cut their costs. By the mid-1980s,*

(Continued)

Case 18.3—continued

Americans' consumption of chicken and turkey had surpassed that of beef and pork.

BACKGROUND AND FACTS   In the late 1970s, Dubuque Packing Company, a processor of beef and pork, began losing money at its plant in Dubuque, Iowa. The company and the United Food and Commercial Workers International Union (UFCW), which represented the employees, negotiated concessions to keep the plant open. In March 1981, the company announced that it planned to close the plant's hog kill and cut operations. Negotiations began again. The UFCW rejected the company's proposal to freeze wages. In June, the company announced that it might relocate—rather than close—the hog department. To assess the situation, the UFCW requested financial information, which the company refused to provide. The com-

pany said that the employees could save their jobs by approving the wage freeze proposal, which the union recommended be rejected until the company opened its books. The workers voted against the proposal. Three days later, the company announced that its decision to close the hog department was "irrevocable." On October 1, the company opened a hog operation at a new plant in Rochelle, Illinois, and two days later cut more than five hundred hog jobs at the Dubuque plant. The UFCW complained to the NLRB, claiming that the company had refused to bargain in good faith over the relocation. The NLRB agreed and ordered the company to pay back wages to all employees terminated as a result of the move. The company asked a court to review the case.

IN THE WORDS OF THE COURT . . .
BUCKLEY, Circuit Judge.
        *   *   *   *

Dubuque objects, first, to the [National Labor Relations] Board's finding that its relocation did not constitute a change in the scope and direction of its business.*   *   *

The Board's position enjoys ample support in the record.   *   *   *
Dubuque used the Rochelle facility to substantially replace the Dubuque facility. As production in Rochelle increased, there was a corresponding reduction at Dubuque until the hog kill and cut processing departments and related operations there were completely phased out. Larry J. Tangeman, general plant superintendent at Dubuque, became superintendent of the Rochelle facility and about 13 members of Dubuque management also were transferred to Rochelle, as was certain production equipment. The purposes of the Rochelle plant, to slaughter hogs, dress carcasses, and to process pork into hams, bacon, and sausage, were the same as at the Dubuque plant.   *   *   *

Dubuque's second contention is that because "the record   *   *   * is very clear that the union would not offer labor concessions," bargaining would have been futile; hence it was not required.   *   *   *

    *   *   * [T]hat principle has no bearing here.   *   *   * [T]he UFCW could, would, and did accept concessions   *   *   * all in a vain attempt to keep the Dubuque facility open. Indeed, the vote that led to Dubuque's "irrevocable" decision to relocate was not a vote to categorically refuse Dubuque's overtures, but a vote to insist on financial disclosure as a prelude to bargaining. The Board's finding that good-faith bargaining between Dubuque and the UFCW might not have been futile was substantially supported by the record.

DECISION AND REMEDY   The court upheld the NLRB's determination that the employer had refused to bargain in good faith over the relocation and enforced the order for the payment of back wages.

FOR CRITICAL ANALYSIS—ETHICAL CONSIDERATION   *Is it fair to require management to bargain over* any *decision to close a particular facility?*

Good Faith Bargaining

Parties engaged in collective bargaining often claim that the other side is not bargaining in good faith, as required by labor law. Although good faith is a matter of subjective intent, a party's actions are used to evaluate the finding of good or bad faith in bargaining.

Obviously, the employer must be willing to meet with union representatives. Excessive delaying tactics may be proof of bad faith, as is insistence on obviously unreasonable contract terms. Suppose that a company makes a single overall contract offer on a "take-it-or-leave-it" basis and refuses to consider modifications of individual terms. This also is considered bad faith in bargaining.

While bargaining is going on, management may not make unilateral changes in important working conditions, such as wages or hours of employment. These changes must be bargained over. Once bargaining reaches an impasse, management may make such unilateral changes. The law also includes an exception permitting unilateral changes in cases of business necessity.

A series of decisions have found other actions to constitute bad faith in bargaining, including the following:

- Engaging in a campaign among workers to undermine the union.
- Constantly shifting positions on disputed contract terms.
- Sending bargainers who lack authority to commit the company to a contract.

If an employer (or a union) refuses to bargain in good faith without justification, it has committed an unfair labor practice, and the other party may petition the NLRB for an order requiring good faith bargaining. Except in extreme cases, the NLRB does not have authority to require a party to accede to any specific contract terms. The NLRB may require a party to reimburse the other side for its litigation expenses.

A party to collective bargaining may be excused from bargaining when the other party refuses to bargain. The following case illustrates this situation.

Case 18.4 ● Stroehmann Bakeries, Inc. v. NLRB

United States Court of Appeals, Second Circuit, 1996. 95 F.3d 218.

BACKGROUND AND FACTS Stroehmann Bakeries, Inc., operated a distribution center for its baked goods in Syracuse, New York, where employees—known as shippers—loaded the goods onto local delivery trucks. The shippers were represented by a union. When their collective bargaining agreement expired, Stroehmann proposed eliminating their positions. In subsequent negotiations, the company admitted that it could obtain the capital to keep the Syracuse center open and proposed cutting only half of the positions. The union asked Stroehmann for extensive financial information, including lists of customers and sales accounts, accounts payable journals, supplier invoices, production reports, employee compensation, and employee pension plans. The company refused to comply with the request and, when the union did not return to the negotiations, declared that bargaining was at an impasse. Ten days later, Stroehmann eliminated the shippers' jobs. The National Labor Relations Board ordered the company to reinstate the shippers. Stroehmann asked the U.S. Court of Appeals for the Second Circuit to deny enforcement of the order.

(Continued)

Case 18.4—continued

IN THE WORDS OF THE COURT . . .
WINTER, Circuit Judge.
* * * *

Once Stroehmann conceded that it had access to capital sufficient to continue the Syracuse shipping unit, the Union's need for financial information to bargain intelligently was virtually non-existent. * * * Stroehmann did not enter the negotiations with a closed mind but rather offered proposals in response to the Union's request for ways to save jobs. It was the Union that refused to bargain after it made a request for financial information [that was denied].

The comprehensive and detailed information requested by the Union had virtually no relevance to the issues at stake in bargaining * * * . We conclude, therefore, that Stroehmann was under no obligation to respond to the voluminous requests for information submitted by the Union.

Because Stroehmann's refusal to furnish the information was permissible, it was entitled to declare an impasse when the Union refused to return to the bargaining table. The unilateral decision to close the shipping unit was, therefore, lawful.

DECISION AND REMEDY The U.S. Court of Appeals for the Second Circuit denied enforcement of the NLRB's order. The company acted within its rights in eliminating the shippers' jobs.

FOR CRITICAL ANALYSIS—POLITICAL CONSIDERATION *Why might a union (or an employee) make "voluminous requests for information" and refuse to bargain if the requests are not met?*

Strikes

The law does not require parties to reach a contract agreement in collective bargaining. Even when parties have bargained in good faith, they may be unable to reach a final agreement. When extensive collective bargaining has been conducted and the parties still cannot agree, an impasse has been reached.

When bargaining has reached an impasse, the union may call a strike against the employer to pressure it into making concessions. A strike occurs when the unionized workers leave their jobs and refuse to work. The workers also typically picket the plant, standing outside the facility with signs that complain of management's unfairness.

A strike is an extreme action. Striking workers lose their right to be paid. Management loses production and may lose customers, whose orders cannot be filled. Labor law regulates the circumstances and conduct of strikes. Most strikes are "economic strikes," which are initiated because the union wants a better contract. A union may also strike when the employer has engaged in unfair labor practices.

The right to strike is guaranteed by the NLRA, within limits, and strike activities, such as picketing, are protected by the free speech guarantee of the First Amendment to the Constitution. Nonworkers have a right to participate in picketing an employer. The NLRA also gives workers the right to refuse to cross a picket line of fellow workers who are engaged in a lawful strike. Not all strikes are lawful, however.

Striking workers picket to publicize their labor dispute. Why is the right to strike important to unions?

Illegal Strikes

An otherwise lawful strike may become illegal because of the conduct of the strikers. Violent strikes (including the threat of violence) are illegal. The use of violence against management employees or substitute workers is illegal. Certain forms of "massed picketing" are also illegal. If the strikers form a barrier and deny management or other nonunion workers access to the plant, the strike is illegal. Similarly, "sit-down" strikes, in which employees simply stay in the plant without working, are illegal.

SECONDARY BOYCOTTS. A strike directed against someone other than the strikers' employer, such as the companies that sell materials to the employer, is a **secondary boycott**. Suppose that the unionized workers of SemiCo (our hypothetical semiconductor company) go out on strike. To increase their economic leverage, the workers picket the leading suppliers and customers of SemiCo in an attempt to hurt the company's business. SemiCo is considered the primary employer, and its suppliers and customers are considered secondary employers. Picketing of the suppliers or customers is a secondary boycott, which was made illegal by the Taft-Hartley Act.

Common Situs Picketing A controversy may arise in a strike when both the primary employer and a secondary employer occupy the same job site. In this case, it may be difficult to distinguish between lawful picketing of the primary employer and an unlawful strike against a secondary employer. The law permits a union to picket a site occupied by both primary and secondary employers, an act called **common situs picketing**. If evidence indicates that the strike is directed against the secondary employer, however, it may become illegal. For example, if a union sends a threatening letter to the secondary employer about the strike, that fact may show that the picketing includes an illegal secondary boycott.

Secondary Boycott A union's refusal to work for, purchase from, or handle the products of a secondary employer, with whom the union has no dispute, for the purpose of forcing that employer to stop doing business with the primary employer, with whom the union has a labor dispute.

Common Situs Picketing The illegal picketing of a primary employer's site by workers who are involved in a labor dispute with a secondary employer.

Hot-Cargo Agreement An agreement in which employers voluntarily agree with unions not to handle, use, or deal in non-union-produced goods of other employers; a type of secondary boycott explicitly prohibited by the Labor-Management Reporting and Disclosure Act of 1959.

Hot-Cargo Agreements   In what is called a **hot-cargo agreement**, employers voluntarily agree with unions not to handle, use, or deal in non-union-produced goods of other employers. This particular type of secondary boycott was *not* made illegal by the Taft-Hartley Act, because that act only prevented unions from inducing *employees* to strike or otherwise act to force employers not to handle these goods. The Landrum-Griffin Act addressed this problem:

> It shall be [an] unfair labor practice for any labor organization and any employer to enter into any contract or any agreement . . . whereby such employer . . . agrees to refrain from handling, using, selling, transporting or otherwise dealing in any of the products of any other employer, or to cease doing business with any other person.

Hot-cargo agreements are therefore illegal. Parties injured by an illegal hot-cargo agreement or other secondary boycott may sue the union for damages.

A union may legally urge consumer boycotts of the primary employer, even at the site of a secondary employer. Suppose that a union is on strike against SemiCo, which manufactures semiconductors that are bought by Intellect, Inc., a distributor of electronic components. Intellect sells SemiCo's semiconductors to computer manufacturers. The striking workers can urge the manufacturers not to buy SemiCo's products. The workers cannot urge a total boycott of Intellect, as that would constitute a secondary boycott.

Wildcat Strike A strike that is not authorized by the union that ordinarily represents the striking employees.

WILDCAT STRIKES.   A **wildcat strike** occurs when a minority group of workers, perhaps dissatisfied with a union's representation, calls its own strike. The union is the exclusive bargaining representative of a group of workers, and only the union can call a strike. A wildcat strike, unauthorized by the certified union, is illegal.

In one case, several concrete workers left their jobs because it was raining and went on "strike." The court found the strike illegal because it was not preceded by a demand on the employer for action and because the employer had made shelter available for the workers and paid them for waiting time.

STRIKES THAT THREATEN NATIONAL HEALTH OR SAFETY.   The law also places some restrictions on strikes that threaten national health or safety. The law does not prohibit such strikes, nor does it require the settlement of labor disputes that threaten the national welfare. The Taft-Hartley Act simply provides time to encourage the settlement of these disputes, called the "cooling-off period."

Eighty-Day Cooling-Off Period A provision of the Taft-Hartley Act that allows federal courts to issue injunctions against strikes that might create a national emergency.

One of the most controversial aspects of the Taft-Hartley Act was the establishment of this **eighty-day cooling-off period**—a provision allowing federal courts to issue injunctions against strikes that would create a national emergency. The president of the United States can obtain a court injunction that will last for eighty days, and presidents have occasionally used this provision. During these eighty days, the president and other government officials can work with the employer and the union to produce a settlement and avoid a strike that may cause a national emergency.

No-Strike Clause Provision in collective bargaining agreement that states the employees will not strike for any reason and labor disputes will be resolved by arbitration.

STRIKES THAT CONTRAVENE NO-STRIKE CLAUSES.   A strike may also be illegal if it contravenes a **no-strike clause**. The previous collective bargaining agreement between a union and an employer may have contained a clause in which the union agreed not to strike (a no-strike clause). The law permits the employer to enforce this no-strike clause and obtain an injunction against the strike in some circumstances.

The Supreme Court held that a no-strike clause could be enforced with an injunction if the contract contained a clause providing for arbitration of unresolved disputes.[14] The Court held that the arbitration clause was an effective substitute for the right to strike. In the absence of an applicable arbitration provision, however, an employer cannot enjoin (forbid) a strike, even if the contract contains a no-strike clause.

Replacement Workers

Suppose that SemiCo's workers go out on strike. SemiCo is not required to shut down its operations but may find substitute workers to replace the strikers, if possible. These substitute workers are often called "scabs" by union supporters. An employer may even give the replacement workers permanent positions with the company.

In the 1930s and 1940s, strikes were powerful in part because employers often had difficulty finding trained replacements to keep their businesses running during strikes. Since the illegal air traffic controller strike in 1981, when President Ronald Reagan successfully hired replacement workers, employers have increasingly used this strategy, with considerable success. Even the National Football League (NFL), when struck by the players in 1987, found replacements to play for the NFL teams. Although some scoffed at the ability of the replacement players, the tactic was largely successful for management, as the strike was called off after only three weeks. An employer can even use an employment agency to recruit replacement workers.[15]

Rights of Strikers after the Strike

An important issue concerns the rights of strikers after the strike ends. In a typical economic strike over working conditions, the strikers have no right to return to their jobs. If satisfactory replacement workers have been found, the strikers may find themselves out of work. The law does prohibit the employer from discriminating against former strikers. Even if the employer fires all the strikers and retains all the replacement workers, former strikers must be rehired to fill any new vacancies. Former strikers who are rehired retain their seniority rights.

Different rules apply when a union strikes because the employer has engaged in unfair labor practices. If an employer is discriminating against a union's workers, they may go out on an unfair labor practice strike. Furthermore, an economic strike may become an unfair labor practice strike if the employer refuses to bargain in good faith. In the case of an unfair labor practice strike, the employer may still hire replacements but must give the strikers back their jobs once the strike is over. An employer may, however, refuse to rehire unfair labor practice strikers if the strike was deemed unlawful or if there is simply no longer any work for them to do.

Lockouts

▼ Lockouts are the employer's counterpart to the worker's right to strike. A **lockout** occurs when the employer shuts down to prevent employees from

Lockout The closing of a plant to employees by an employer to gain leverage in collective bargaining negotiations.

---

14. *Boys Markets, Inc. v. Retail Clerks Local 770*, 398 U.S. 235, 90 S.Ct. 1583, 26 L.Ed.2d 199 (1970).
15. *Professional Staff Nurses Association v. Dimensions Health Corp.*, 110 Md.App. 270, 677 A.2d 87 (1996).

working. Lockouts are usually used when the employer believes that a strike is imminent.

Lockouts may be a legal employer response. In the leading Supreme Court case on this issue, a union and an employer had reached a stalemate in collective bargaining. The employer feared that the union would delay a strike until the busy season and thereby cause the employer to suffer more greatly from the strike. The employer called a lockout before the busy season to deny the union this leverage, and the Supreme Court held that this action was legal.[16]

Some lockouts are illegal, however. An employer may not use its lockout weapon as a tool to break the union and pressure employees into decertification. Consequently, an employer must show some economic justification for instituting a lockout.

Unfair Labor Practices

▼   The preceding sections have discussed unfair labor practices in the significant acts of union elections, collective bargaining, and strikes. Many unfair labor practices may occur within the normal working relationship as well. The most significant of these practices are discussed below. Exhibit 18–2 lists the basic unfair labor practices.

Employer's Refusal to Recognize the Union and to Negotiate

As noted above, once a union has been certified as the exclusive representative of a bargaining unit, an employer must recognize and bargain in good faith with the union over issues affecting all employees who are within the bargaining unit. Failure to do so is an unfair labor practice. Because the National Labor Relations Act embraces a policy of majority rule, certification of the union as the bargaining unit's representative binds *all* of the employees in that bargaining unit. Thus, the union must fairly represent all the members of the bargaining unit.[17]

---

16. *American Ship Building Co. v. NLRB*, 380 U.S. 300, 85 S.Ct. 955, 13 L.Ed.2d 855 (1965).
17. Thus, when an employee has a grievance against the employer, the union cannot arbitrarily ignore it or handle it perfunctorily, although a union does not have to pursue all employee grievances to arbitration. See *Vaca v. Sipes,* 386 U.S. 171, 87 S.Ct. 903, 17 L.Ed.2d 842 (1967).

■ **Exhibit 18–2**
Basic Unfair Labor Practices

Employers *It is unfair to . . .*	Unions *It is unfair to . . .*
1. Refuse to recognize a union and refuse to bargain in good faith.	1. Refuse to bargain in good faith.
2. Interfere with, restrain, or coerce employees in their efforts to form a union and bargain collectively.	2. Picket to coerce unionization without the majority's support of the employees.
3. Dominate a union.	3. Demand the hiring of unnecessary excess workers.
4. Discriminate against union workers.	4. Discriminate against nonunion workers.
5. Agree to participate in a secondary boycott.	5. Agree to participate in a secondary boycott.
6. Punish employees for engaging in concerted activity.	6. Engage in an illegal strike.
	7. Charge excessive membership fees.

PRESUMPTION OF EMPLOYEE SUPPORT. Certification does not mean that a union will continue indefinitely as the exclusive representative of the bargaining unit. If the union loses the majority support of those it represents, an employer is not obligated to continue recognition of, or negotiation with, the union. As a practical matter, a newly elected representative needs time to establish itself among the workers and to begin to formulate and implement its programs. Therefore, as a matter of labor policy, a union is immune from attack by employers and from repudiation by the employees for a period of one year after certification. During this period, it is *presumed* that the union enjoys majority support among the employees; the employer cannot refuse to deal with the union as the employees' exclusive representative, even if the employees prefer not to be represented by that union.

Beyond the one-year period, the presumption of majority support continues, but it is *rebuttable*. An employer may rebut (refute) the presumption with objective evidence that a majority of employees do not wish to be represented by the union. If the evidence is sufficient to support a *good faith* belief that the union no longer enjoys majority support among the employees, the employer may refuse to continue to recognize and negotiate with the union.[18]

QUESTIONS OF MAJORITY SUPPORT. A delicate question arises during a strike in which an employer hires replacement workers. Specifically, should it be *assumed* that the replacement workers do not support the union? If they do not, and if as a result the union no longer has majority support, the employer need not continue negotiating with the union.

Another question arises when two companies merge or consolidate, when one company buys the assets or stock of another, or when, under any other circumstances, one employer steps into the shoes of another. Is a collective bargaining agreement between a union and a predecessor employer binding on the union and the successor employer? This is the issue in the following case.

---

18. An employer cannot agree to a collective bargaining agreement and later refuse to abide by it, however, on the ground of a good faith belief that the union did not have majority support when the agreement was negotiated. See *Auciello Iron Works, Inc. v. NLRB*, 517 U.S. 781, 116 S.Ct. 1754, 135 L.Ed.2d 64 (1996).

Case 18.5 ● Canteen Corp. v. NLRB

United States Court of Appeals,
Seventh Circuit, 1997.
103 F.3d 1355.

BACKGROUND AND FACTS The food service employees at the Medical College of Wisconsin were represented by the Hotel Employees and Restaurant Employees Union. When Canteen Corporation took over the food service, it agreed to negotiate a new contract with the union. Meanwhile, without informing the union, Canteen told the employees that their wages would be cut 20 to 25 percent. The employees resigned. Canteen then recruited employees from other sources and refused to negotiate with the union on the ground that it no longer represented the employees. The union filed an unfair labor practice charge with the National Labor Relations Board (NLRB). The NLRB ordered Canteen to reinstate the employees at their previous wage rates until a new contract could be negotiated. Canteen asked the U.S. Court of Appeals for the Seventh Circuit to review the order.

(Continued)

Case 18.5—continued

IN THE WORDS OF THE COURT . . .
RIPPLE, Circuit Judge.

* * * *

* * * A new employer must consult with the union when it is clear that the employer intends to hire the employees of its predecessor as the initial workforce. * * *

* * * *

* * * The totality of Canteen's conduct demonstrated that it was perfectly clear that Canteen planned to retain the predecessor employees. * * *

* * * Canteen's intention to retain the * * * employees was backed by an expectation so strong that it neglected to take serious steps to recruit from other sources until it was informed that they had rejected job offers. * * * Canteen intended from the outset to hire all of the predecessor employees and did not mention in [its] discussions [with the union] the possibility of any other changes in its initial terms and conditions of employment.

DECISION AND REMEDY   The U.S. Court of Appeals for the Seventh Circuit ordered that the NLRB's order be enforced. The employer was required to reinstate the employees at their previous wage rates until a new contract could be negotiated.

FOR CRITICAL ANALYSIS—SOCIAL CONSIDERATION   *Why should an employer be forced to honor a collective bargaining agreement between a union and the employer's predecessor?*

Employer's Interference in Union Activities

The NLRA declares it to be an unfair labor practice for an employer to interfere with, restrain, or coerce employees in the exercise of their rights to form a union and bargain collectively. Unlawful employer interference may take a variety of forms.

Courts have found it an unfair labor practice for an employer to make threats that may interfere with an employee's decision to join a union. Even asking employees about their views on the union may be considered coercive. Employees responding to such questioning must be able to remain anonymous and must receive assurances against employer reprisals. Employers also may not prohibit certain forms of union activity in the workplace. If an employee has a grievance with the company, the employer cannot prevent the union's participation in support of the employee, for example.

If an employer has unlawfully interfered with the operation of a union, the NLRB or a reviewing court may issue a cease-and-desist order halting the practice. The company typically is required to post the order on a bulletin board and renounce its past unlawful conduct.

Employer's Domination of Union

In the early days of unionization, employers fought back by forming employer-sponsored unions to represent employees. These "company unions" were seldom more than the puppets of management. The NLRA outlawed company unions and any other form of employer domination of workers' unions.

A number of acts are considered unfair labor practices under the law against employer domination. For example, an employer can have no say in which employees belong to the union or which employees serve as union officers. Nor may supervisors or other management personnel participate in union meetings.

Company actions that support a union may be considered improper potential domination. For this reason, a company cannot give union workers pay for time spent on union activities, because this is considered undue support for the union. The company may not provide financial aid to a union and may not solicit workers to join a union.

Employer's Discrimination against Union Employees

The NLRA prohibits employers from discriminating against workers because they are union officers or are otherwise associated with a union. When workers must be laid off, the company cannot consider union participation as a criterion for deciding whom to fire.

The antidiscrimination provisions also apply to hiring decisions. Suppose that certain employees of SemiCo are represented by a union, but the company is attempting to weaken the union's strength. The company is prohibited from requiring potential new hires to guarantee that they will not join the union.

Discriminatory punishment of union members or officers can be difficult to prove. The company will claim to have good reasons for its action. The NLRB has specified a series of factors to be considered in determining whether an action had an unlawful, discriminatory motivation. These include giving inconsistent reasons for the action, applying rules inconsistently and more strictly against union members, failing to give an expected warning prior to discharge or other discipline, and acting contrary to worker seniority.

In one case, an employer, Wright Line, fired an employee, Bernard Lamoureux, for knowingly altering time reports and payroll records. Lamoureux conceded that he had not worked the precise hours he reported on his time card but claimed that he had worked an equivalent number of hours at other times. Lamoureux had been a leading union advocate. The NLRB found that the company had shown particular dislike for Lamoureux because it considered him to be the "union kingpin" in the company. In addition, the company had never before discharged a worker for this type of violation. The NLRB found that this was sufficient evidence of discrimination to shift the burden of proof to the company to demonstrate that it had not had a discriminatory motive. The company could not meet this burden, and the discharge was held unlawful.[19]

The decision to close a facility cannot be made with a discriminatory motive. If a company has several facilities and only one is unionized, the company cannot shut down the union plant simply because of the union. The company could shut down the union plant if it were demonstrably less efficient than the other facilities, however.

Union's Unfair Labor Practices

Certain union activities are declared to be unfair labor practices by the Taft-Hartley Act. Secondary boycotts, discussed above, are one such union unfair labor practice.

COERCION. Another significant union unfair labor practice is coercion or restraint on an employee's decision to participate in or refrain from participating

---

19. *Wright Line, a Division of Wright Line, Inc.,* 251 N.L.R.B. No. 150 (1980).

in union activities. Obviously, it is unlawful for a union to threaten an employee or a family with violence for failure to join the union. The law's prohibition includes economic coercion as well. Suppose that a union official declares, "We have a lot of power here; you had better join the union, or you may lose your job." This threat is an unfair labor practice.

The NLRA provides unions with the authority to regulate their own internal affairs, which includes disciplining union members. This discipline cannot be used in an improperly coercive fashion, however. Suppose a disaffected union member feels that the union is no longer providing proper representation for employees and starts a campaign to decertify the union. The union may expel the employee from membership but may not fine or otherwise discipline the worker.

DISCRIMINATION.   Another significant union unfair labor practice is discrimination. A union may not discriminate against workers because they refuse to join. This provision also prohibits a union from using its influence to cause an employer to discriminate against workers who refuse to join the union. A union cannot force an employer to deny promotions to workers who fail to join the union.

OTHER UNFAIR PRACTICES.   Other union unfair labor practices include featherbedding, participation in picketing to coerce unionization without majority employee support, and refusal to engage in good faith bargaining with employer representatives.

Unions are allowed to bargain for certain "union security clauses" in contracts. Although closed shops are illegal, a union can bargain for a provision that requires workers to contribute to the union within thirty days after they are hired. This is typically called an agency shop, or union shop, clause.

The union shop clause can compel workers to begin paying dues to the certified union but cannot require the worker to "join" the union. Dues payment can be required to prevent workers from taking the benefits of union bargaining without contributing to the union's efforts. The clause cannot require workers to contribute their efforts to the union, however, or to go out on strike.

Even a requirement of dues payment has its limits. Excessive initiation fees or dues may be illegal. Unions often use their revenues to contribute to causes or to lobby politicians. A nonunion employee subject to a union shop clause who must pay dues cannot be required to contribute to this sort of union expenditure.[20]

Rights of Nonunion Employees

▼   Most of labor law involves the formation of unions and associated rights. Even nonunion employees have some similar rights, however. Most workers do not belong to unions, so this issue is significant. The NLRA protects concerted employee action, for example, and does not limit its protection to certified unions.

Concerted Activity

Data from the NLRB indicate that growing numbers of nonunion employees are challenging employer barriers to their **concerted action.** Protected con-

Concerted Action Action by employees, such as a strike or picketing, with the purpose of furthering their bargaining demands or other mutual interests.

20. *Communication Workers of America v. Beck,* 487 U.S. 735, 108 S.Ct. 2641, 101 L.Ed.2d 634 (1988).

certed action is that taken by employees for their mutual benefit regarding wages, hours, or terms and conditions of employment.

Even an action by a single employee may be protected concerted activity, if that action is taken for the benefit of other employees and if the employee has at least discussed the action with other approving workers. If only a single worker engages in a protest or walkout, the employer will not be liable for an unfair labor practice if it fires the worker unless the employer is aware that this protest or walkout is concerted activity taken with the assent of other workers. Sometimes the mutual interest of other workers should be obvious to the employer, however.

Safety

A common circumstance for nonunion activity is concern over workplace safety. The Labor-Management Relations Act authorizes an employee to walk off the job if he or she has a good faith belief that the working conditions are abnormally dangerous. The employer cannot lawfully discharge the employee under these conditions.

Suppose that Knight Company operates a plant building mobile homes. A large ventilation fan at the plant blows dust and abrasive materials into the faces of workers. The workers have complained, but Knight Company has done nothing. The workers finally refuse to work until the fan is modified, and Knight fires them. The NLRB will find that the walkout is a protected activity and can command Knight to rehire the workers with back pay.

To be protected under federal labor law, a safety walkout must be *concerted* activity. If a single worker walks out over a safety complaint, other workers must be affected by the safety issue for the walkout to be protected under the LMRA.

Employee Committees

Personnel specialists note that worker problems are often attributable to a lack of communication between labor and management. In a nonunion work force, a company may wish to create some institution to communicate with workers and act together with them to improve workplace conditions.

This institution, generally called an **employee committee**, is composed of representatives from both management and labor. The committee meets periodically and has some authority to create rules. The committee gives employees a forum to voice their dissatisfaction with certain conditions and gives management a conduit to inform workers fully of policy decisions.

The creation of an employee committee may be entirely well motivated on the company's part and may serve the interests of workers as well as management. Nevertheless, employee committees are fraught with potential problems under federal labor laws, and management must be aware of these problems.

The central problem with employee committees is that they may become the functional equivalent of unions dominated by management, in violation of the NLRA. Thus, these committees cannot perform union functions. For example, the employee representatives on such a committee should not present a package of proposals on wages and terms of employment, because this is the role of a union negotiating committee.

In the following case, a union complained that an employer had committed an unfair labor practice by maintaining an employee committee.

> "In general, to find an employee's activity to be 'concerted,' we shall require that it be engaged in with or on the authority of other employees, and not solely by and on behalf of the employee himself."
>
> National Labor Relations Board, in *Meyers Industries, Inc. (Meyers I)*, 268 N.L.R.B. No. 73 (January 6, 1984)

Employee Committee
Committee created by an employer and composed of representatives of management and nonunion employees to act together to improve workplace conditions.

Case 18.6 ● In re Simmons Industries, Inc.

National Labor Relations Board, 1996.
321 N.L.R.B. No. 32

HISTORICAL AND SOCIAL SETTING *In the 1930s and 1940s, after Congress enacted the first laws protecting unions, union membership as a percentage of the work force grew rapidly, until about a third of all workers belonged to unions. As the size of the work force continued to grow, however, the number of workers belonging to unions did not increase proportionately. By the mid-1990s, union members made up only about 15 percent of the work force. Unions, which have sometimes been frustrated by employees' reluctance to organize, often blame unsuccessful attempts to unionize a particular employer's work force on the employer.*

BACKGROUND AND FACTS Simmons Industries, Inc., operated chicken processing plants. One of Simmons's customers was Kentucky Fried Chicken (KFC). To satisfy KFC's concerns with quality, Simmons formed at each plant a total quality management (TQM) committee. Simmons appointed managers and employees from a cross section of the plants to serve on the committees and set the committees' agendas, which included such topics as employee bonuses and absences. Later, the United Food and Commercial Workers Union attempted unsuccessfully to organize the employees. The union filed a complaint with the National Labor Relations Board (NLRB), alleging that Simmons had committed unfair labor practices by, among other things, maintaining a TQM committee at its plant in Jay, Oklahoma. The union argued that the committee was a "labor organization" dominated by management in violation of the National Labor Relations Act (NLRA).

IN THE WORDS OF THE COURT . . .
DECISION AND ORDER

* * * *

* * * [T]he concept of "labor organization" * * * includes very loose, informal, unstructured, and irregular meeting groups. Such a loose organization will meet the [NLRA] definition if: (1) employees participate, (2) the organization exists, at least in part, for the purpose of dealing with employers, and (3) these dealings concern conditions of work or concern other statutory subjects such as grievances, labor disputes, wages, rates of pay, or hours of employment.

* * * *

* * * [E]mployee members [of the TQM committee] were representative of each * * * grouping of employees. * * * [T]he Committee discussed and made proposals solicited by [Simmons] with respect to the formulation and implementation of an incentive bonus pay program, clearly a mandatory bargaining subject. [Simmons] accepted some of the committee's proposal and guided itself by others in formulating the bonus plan. * * * Furthermore, the * * * Committee continued * * * to discuss and make proposals with respect to employee discipline, attendance and punctuality problems and employee courtesy breaks. On recommendations based in large part on employee member complaints, the plant manager issued a set of rules that clearly affected these conditions of employment and mandatory bargaining subjects. Thus the * * * Committee * * * effectively constituted a representational employee committee, in effect a labor organization, which was unlawfully dominated, interfered with in operation and administration, and rendered unlawful assistance to by [Simmons] in violation of [the NLRA].

(Continued)

Case 18.6—continued

DECISION AND REMEDY The NLRB ordered Simmons to, among other things, "[i]mmediately disestablish and cease giving assistance or any other support" to its TQM committee.[a]

---

a. This decision was an application of the principle declared in the leading case in this area, *Electromation, Inc.,* 309 N.L.R.B. 990 (1992).

FOR CRITICAL ANALYSIS—TECHNOLOGICAL CONSIDERATION *How might an employer give employees a forum to voice their dissatisfaction with certain conditions without forming an illegal employee committee?*

Key Terms

appropriate bargaining
  unit 503
authorization card 503
closed shop 500
collective bargaining 508
common situs picketing 513
concerted action 520

eighty-day cooling-off
  period 514
employee committee 521
featherbedding 509
hot-cargo agreement 514
lockout 515
no-strike clause 514

right-to-work law 500
secondary boycott 513
severance pay 509
union shop 500
wildcat strike 514
yellow dog contract 498

Chapter Summary
Labor-Management Relations

LABOR LAWS
(See pages 498–503.)

1. **Norris-LaGuardia Act of 1932**—Extended legal protection to peaceful strikes, picketing, and boycotts. Restricted the power of the courts to issue injunctions against unions engaged in peaceful strikes.

2. **National Labor Relations Act of 1935 (Wagner Act)**—Established the rights of employees to engage in collective bargaining and to strike. Created the National Labor Relations Board (NLRB) to oversee union elections and prevent employers from engaging in unfair labor practices (such as refusing to recognize and negotiate with a certified union or interfering in union activities).

3. **Labor-Management Relations Act of 1947 (Taft-Hartley Act)**—Extended to employers protections already enjoyed by employees. Provided a list of activities prohibited to unions (secondary boycotts, use of coercion or discrimination to influence employees' decisions to participate or refrain from union activities) and allowed employers to propagandize against unions before any NLRB election. Prohibited closed shops (which require that all workers belong to a union as a condition of employment), allowed states to pass right-to-work laws, and provided for an eighty-day cooling-off period.

4. **Labor-Management Reporting and Disclosure Act of 1959 (Landrum-Griffin Act)**—Regulated internal union business procedures and union elections. Imposed restrictions on the types of persons who may serve as union officers and outlawed hot-cargo agreements.

(Continued)

Chapter Summary, continued

UNION ORGANIZING
(See pages 503–508.)

1. **Authorization cards**—Before beginning an organizing effort, a union will attempt to assess worker support for unionization by obtaining signed authorization cards from the employees. It can then ask the employer to recognize the union, or it can submit the cards with a petition to the National Labor Relations Board.

2. **Appropriate bargaining unit**—In determining whether workers constitute an appropriate bargaining unit, the NLRB will consider whether the skills, tasks, and jobs of the workers are sufficiently similar so that they can all be adequately served by a single negotiating position.

3. **Union election campaign**—The NLRB is charged with monitoring union elections. During an election campaign, an employer may legally limit union activities as long as it can offer legitimate business justifications for those limitations. In regulating the union's presence on the business premises, the employer must treat the union in the same way it would treat any other entity having on-site contact with its workers. The NLRB is particularly sensitive to any threats in an employer's communications to workers, such as declarations that a union victory will result in the closing of the plant. The NLRB will also closely monitor sudden policy changes regarding compensation, hours, or working conditions that the employer makes before the election.

4. **Union certification**—Certification by the NLRB means that the union is the exclusive representative of a bargaining unit and that the employer must recognize the union and bargain in good faith with it over issues affecting all employees who are within the bargaining unit.

COLLECTIVE BARGAINING
(See pages 508–512.)

Once a union is elected, its representatives will engage in collective bargaining with the employer. Each side tries to use its economic power to persuade or pressure the other side to grant concessions. Topics such as wages, hours of work, and other conditions of employment are discussed during collective bargaining sessions. Other topics, such as college scholarships for the children of union members, may also be brought up for consideration. Some demands, such as a demand for featherbedding or for a closed shop, are illegal. If the parties reach an impasse, the union may call a strike against the employer to bring additional economic pressure to bear. This is one way in which the union can offset the superior bargaining power possessed by management.

STRIKES
(See pages 512–516.)

1. **Right to strike**—The right to strike is protected by the U.S. Constitution. During a strike, an employer is no longer obligated to pay union members, and union members are no longer required to show up for work.

2. **Secondary boycott**—Strikers are not permitted to engage in a secondary boycott by picketing the suppliers of an employer. Similarly, striking employees are not permitted to coerce the employer's customers into agreeing not to do business with it.

3. **Wildcat strike**—A wildcat strike occurs when a small group of union members engages in a strike against the employer without the permission of the union.

4. **Replacement workers**—An employer may hire permanent replacement employees in the event of an economic strike. If the strike is called by the union to protest the employer's unwillingness to engage in good faith negotiations, then the employer must rehire the striking workers after the strike is settled, even if it has since replaced them with other workers.

5. **Lockouts**—Employers may respond to threatened employee strikes by shutting down the plant altogether to prevent employees from working. Lockouts are used when the employer believes a strike is imminent.

(Continued)

Chapter Summary, continued

RIGHTS OF NONUNION EMPLOYEES (See pages 520–523.)	The National Labor Relations Act protects concerted action on the part of nonunion employees. Protected concerted action includes walkouts and other activities regarding wages, hours, workplace safety, or other terms or conditions of employment.

For Review

1. What federal statutes govern labor unions and collective bargaining?

2. How does the way in which a union election is conducted protect the rights of employees and employers?

3. What type of strikes are illegal?

4. What activities are prohibited as unfair employer practices?

5. What are the rights of nonunion employees?

Questions and Case Problems

18–1. Preliminary Organizing. A group of employees at the Briarwood Furniture Company's manufacturing plant were interested in joining a union. A representative of the American Federation of Labor and Congress of Industrial Organizations (AFL-CIO) told the group that her union was prepared to represent the workers and suggested that the group members begin organizing by obtaining authorization cards from their fellow employees. After obtaining 252 authorization cards from among Briarwood's 500 nonmanagement employees, the organizers requested that the company recognize the AFL-CIO as the official representative of the employees. The company refused. Has the company violated federal labor laws? What should the organizers do?

18–2. Appropriate Bargaining Unit. The Briarwood Furniture Company, discussed in the preceding problem, employs 400 unskilled workers and 100 skilled workers in its plant. The unskilled workers operate the industrial machinery used in processing Briarwood's line of standardized plastic office furniture. The skilled workers, who work in an entirely separate part of the plant, are experienced artisans who craft Briarwood's line of expensive wood furniture products. Do you see any problems with a single union's representing all the workers at the Briarwood plant? Explain. Would your answers to Problem 18–1 change if you knew that 51 of the authorization cards had been signed by the skilled workers, with the remainder signed by the unskilled workers?

18–3. Unfair Labor Practices. Suppose that Consolidated Stores is undergoing a unionization cam-

paign. Prior to the election, management says that the union is unnecessary to protect workers. Management also provides bonuses and wage increases to the workers during this period. The employees reject the union. Union organizers protest that the wage increases during the election campaign unfairly prejudiced the vote. Should these wage increases be regarded as an unfair labor practice? Discuss.

18–4. Unfair Labor Practices. SimpCo was engaged in ongoing negotiations over a new labor contract with the union representing the company's employees. As the deadline for expiration of the old labor contract drew near, several employees who were active in union activities were disciplined for being late to work. The union claimed that other employees had not been dealt with as harshly and that the company was discriminating on the basis of union activity. When the negotiations failed to prove fruitful and the old contract expired, the union called a strike. The company claimed the action was an economic strike to press the union's demands for higher wages. The union contended the action was an unfair labor practice strike because of the alleged discrimination. What importance does the distinction have for the striking workers and the company?

18–5. Appropriate Bargaining Unit. Westvaco operated plants that manufactured printed folding cartons, and its production and maintenance employees were represented by a union. The company hired four new technicians to work at the facility. The union argued that the technicians should be part of the unionized work force. Westvaco disputed this argument, claiming that the technicians, because of their greater skills, were not properly part of the same bargaining unit as the existing production and maintenance employees—the technicians had previously been put through an extensive and specialized training course that lasted about four months. The National Labor Relations Board agreed with the union and added the new technicians to the bargaining unit. Westvaco appealed to the court. How should the court rule? Explain fully. [*Westvaco, Virginia, Folding Box Division v. NLRB,* 795 F.2d 1171 (4th Cir. 1986)]

18–6. Secondary Boycotts. For many years, grapefruit was shipped to Japan from Fort Pierce and Port Canaveral, Florida. In 1990, Coastal Stevedoring Co. in Fort Pierce and Port Canaveral Stevedoring, Ltd., in Port Canaveral—nonunion firms—were engaged in a labor dispute with the International Longshoremen's Association (ILA). The ILA asked the National Council of Dockworkers' Unions of Japan to prevent Japanese shippers from using nonunion stevedores in Florida, and the council warned Japanese firms that their workers would not unload fruit loaded in the United States by nonunion labor. The threat caused all citrus shipments from Florida to Japan to go through Tampa, where they were loaded by stevedores represented by the ILA. Coastal, Canaveral, and others complained to the National Labor Relations Board (NLRB), alleging that the ILA's request of the Japanese unions was an illegal secondary boycott. How should the NLRB rule? [*International Longshoremen's Association, AFL-CIO,* 313 N.L.R.B. No. 53 (1993)]

18–7. Unfair Labor Practices. The Teamsters Union represented twenty-seven employees of Curtin Matheson Scientific, Inc. When a collective bargaining agreement between the union and the company expired, the company made an offer for a new agreement, which the union rejected. The company locked out the twenty-seven employees, and the union began an economic strike. The company hired replacement workers. When the union ended its strike and offered to accept the company's earlier offer, the company refused. The company also refused to bargain further, asserting doubt that the union was supported by a majority of the employees. The union sought help from the National Labor Relations Board (NLRB), which refused to presume that the replacement workers did not support the union. On the company's appeal, a court overturned the NLRB's ruling. The union appealed to the United States Supreme Court. How should the Court rule? [*NLRB v. Curtin Matheson Scientific, Inc.,* 494 U.S. 775, 110 S.Ct. 1542, 108 L.Ed.2d 801 (1990)]

18–8. Good Faith Bargaining. American Commercial Barge Line Co. was an affiliation made up of a number of barge and towing companies. The Seafarers International Union of North America (SIU) represented workers for Inland Tugs (IT), a separate corporate division of American Commercial Barge Line. When SIU and IT began negotiating a new collective bargaining agreement, SIU demanded that the bargaining unit include all the employees of American Commercial Barge Line. SIU also demanded that any contract include a pledge by other American Commercial Barge Line companies to continue their contributions to SIU funds, which provided for union activities. Unable to agree on these issues, the parties continued to meet for several years. Meanwhile, on the basis of an employee poll, IT changed its system of calculating wages. SIU filed a complaint with the NLRB, claiming that these changes were an unfair labor practice. IT responded that SIU was not bargaining in good faith. How should the NLRB rule? Explain. [*Inland Tugs, A Division of American Commercial Barge Line Co. v. NLRB,* 918 F.2d 1299 (7th Cir. 1990)]

18–9. Employee Committees. Electromation, Inc., a manufacturer of electrical components and related products, cut wages, bonuses, and incentive pay and tightened attendance and leave policies. When the employees complained, Electromation set up "action committees," each consisting of employees and management representatives. No employee was involved in drafting the goals of the committees. The committees were told to suggest solutions, which would be implemented if management "believed they were within budget concerns" and "would be acceptable to the employees." Employee committee members were expected to discuss suggestions with their co-workers. The Teamsters Union, which had been seeking to organize the employees, challenged the establishment of the committees as an unfair labor practice and asked the NLRB to order that they be dissolved. On what basis might the NLRB grant the union's request? [*Electromation, Inc.,* 309 N.L.R.B. 990 (1992)]

A Question of Ethics and Social Responsibility

18–10. Salvatore Monte was president of Kenrich Petrochemicals, Inc. Helen Chizmar had been Kenrich's office manager since 1963. Among the staff that Chizmar supervised were her sister, daughter, and daughter-in-law. In 1987, Chizmar's relatives and four other staff members designated the Oil, Chemical, and Atomic Workers International Union as their bargaining representative. Chizmar was not involved, but when Monte was notified that his office was unionizing, he told Chizmar that someone else could do her job for "$20,000 less" and fired her. He told another employee that one of his reasons for firing Chizmar was that he "was not going to put up with any union bullsh—." During negotiations with the union, Monte said that he planned to "get rid of the whole family." Chizmar's family complained to the

National Labor Relations Board (NLRB) that the firing was an unfair labor practice. The NLRB agreed and ordered that Chizmar be reinstated with back pay. Kenrich appealed. In view of these facts, consider the following questions. [*Kenrich Petrochemicals, Inc. v. NLRB*, 907 F.2d 400 (3d Cir. 1990)]

1. The National Labor Relations Act does not protect supervisors who engage in union activities. Should the appellate court affirm the NLRB's order nonetheless?
2. If the appellate court does not affirm the NLRB's order, what message will be sent to the supervisors and employees of Kenrich?
3. Is there anything Kenrich could (legally) do to avoid the unionization of its employees? Would it be ethical to counter the wishes of the employees to unionize?
4. What are the advantages of unionization for employees? Are there any disadvantages?

For Critical Analysis

18–11. Although the law continues to evolve in response to changes in the workplace and in society, no significant labor legislation has been passed since the 1950s, and labor law issues have declined in importance in recent years. Why is this?

Unit IV—Cumulative Hypothetical Problem

18–12. Falwell Motors, Inc., is a large corporation that manufactures automobile batteries.

1. One of Falwell's salespersons, Loren, puts in long hours every week. He spends most of his time away from the office generating sales. Less than 10 percent of his work time is devoted to other duties. Usually, he receives a substantial bonus at the end of each year from his employer, and Loren now relies on this supplement to his annual salary and commission. One year, the employer does not give any of its employees year-end bonuses. Loren calculates the amount of hours he had worked during the year beyond the required forty hours a week. Then he tells Falwell's president that if he is not paid for these overtime hours, he will sue the company for the overtime pay he has "earned." Falwell's president tells Loren that Falwell is not obligated to pay Loren overtime because Loren is a salesperson. What federal statute governs this dispute? Under this statute, is Falwell required to pay Loren for the "overtime hours"? Why or why not?
2. One day Barry, one of the salespersons, anxious to make a sale, intentionally quotes a price to a customer that is $500 lower than Falwell has authorized for that particular product. The customer purchases the product at the quoted price. When Falwell learns of the deal, it claims that it is not legally bound to the sales contract because it did not authorize Barry to sell the product at that price. Is Falwell bound by the contract? Discuss fully.
3. One day Gina, a Falwell employee, suffered a serious burn when she accidentally spilled some acid on her hand. The accident occurred because another employee, who was suspected of using illegal drugs, carelessly bumped into her. The hand required a series of skin grafting operations before it healed sufficiently to allow Gina to return to work. Gina wants to obtain compensation for her lost wages and medical expenses. Can she do so? If so, how?
4. After Gina's injury, Falwell decides to conduct random drug tests on all of its employees. Several employees claim that the testing violates their privacy rights. If the dispute is litigated, what factors will the court consider in deciding whether the random drug testing is legally permissible?
5. Aretha, a Falwell employee, is disgusted by the sexually offensive behavior of several male employees. She has complained to her supervisor on several occasions about the offensive behavior, but the supervisor merely laughs at her concerns. Aretha decides to bring a legal action against the company for sexual harassment. Does Aretha's complaint concern *quid pro quo* harassment or hostile-environment harassment? What federal statute protects employees from sexual harassment? What remedies are available under that statute? What procedures must Aretha follow in pursuing her legal action?

INTERACTING WITH The Internet

■ The Institute of Labor Relations at Cornell University and *Human Resource Executive* magazine have complied an extensive index of resources on labor law. You can find these resources at

http://www.workindex.com

■ The site of the American Federation of Labor–Congress of Industrial Organizations (AFL-CIO) provides links to a broad variety of labor-related resources. Go to

http://www.aflcio.org/

■ The National Labor Relations Board is now online at the following URL:

http://www.nlrb.gov

The Regulatory Environment

Unit
Outline

Consumer Protection

Contents

Chapter Objectives

After reading this chapter, you should be able to . . .

1. Summarize the major consumer protection laws.
2. Indicate some specific ways in which consumers are protected against deceptive advertising and sales practices.
3. Explain how the government protects consumers who are involved in credit transactions.
4. List and describe the major statutes that protect consumer health and safety.
5. Identify state consumer protection laws.

The "public interest" referred to by Justice William O. Douglas in the accompanying quotation was evident during the 1960s and 1970s in what has come to be known as the consumer movement. Some have labeled the 1960s and 1970s "the age of the consumer," because so much legislation was passed to protect consumers against purportedly unfair practices and unsafe products of sellers. Since the 1980s, the impetus driving the consumer movement has lessened, to a great extent because so many of its goals have been achieved.

All statutes, agency rules, and common law judicial decisions that serve to protect the interest of consumers are classified as **consumer law.** Consumer transactions take a variety of forms but broadly include those that involve an exchange of value for the purpose of acquiring goods, services, land, or credit for personal or family use.

Traditionally, in disputes involving consumers, it was assumed that the freedom to contract carried with it the obligation to live by the deal made. Therefore, the watchword in most such transactions was *caveat emptor*—"let the buyer beware." Over time, this attitude has changed considerably. Today, myriad federal and state laws protect consumers from unfair trade practices, unsafe products, discriminatory or unreasonable credit requirements, and other problems related to consumer transactions. Nearly every agency and department of the federal government has an office of consumer affairs, and most states have one or more such offices to assist consumers. Also, typically the attorney general's office assists consumers at the state level.

Because of the wide variation among state consumer protection laws, our primary focus in this chapter is on federal legislation—specifically, on legislation governing advertising practices, labeling and packaging, sales, health protection, product safety, and credit protection. Realize, though, that state laws often provide more sweeping and significant protections for the consumer than do federal laws. State consumer protection laws are discussed later in this chapter.

Deceptive Advertising

▼ One of the earliest—and still one of the most important—federal consumer protection laws was the Federal Trade Commission Act of 1914.[1] The act created the Federal Trade Commission (FTC) to carry out the broadly stated goal of preventing unfair and deceptive trade practices, including deceptive advertising.[2]

Deceptive Advertising Defined

Advertising will be deemed deceptive if a consumer would be misled by the advertising claim. Vague generalities and obvious exaggerations are permissible. These claims are known as *puffing.* When a claim takes on the appearance of literal authenticity, however, it may create problems. Advertising that would *appear* to be based on factual evidence but that in fact is not will be deemed deceptive. A classic example is provided by a 1944 case in which the claim that a skin cream would restore youthful qualities to aged skin was deemed deceptive.[3]

> **"Subject to specific constitutional limitations, when the legislature has spoken, the public interest has been declared in terms well nigh conclusive."**
>
> William O. Douglas, 1898–1980
> (Associate justice of the United States Supreme Court, 1939–1975)

Consumer Law The body of statutes, agency rules, and judicial decisions protecting consumers of goods and services from dangerous manufacturing techniques, mislabeling, unfair credit practices, deceptive advertising, and so on.

An ad for a "diet pill." What determines whether such ads are deceptive?

---

1. 15 U.S.C. Sections 41–58.
2. 15 U.S.C. Section 45.
3. *Charles of the Ritz Distributing Corp. v. Federal Trade Commission,* 143 F.2d 676 (2d Cir. 1944).

Some advertisements contain "half-truths," meaning that the presented information is true but incomplete, and it leads consumers to a false conclusion. For example, the makers of Campbell's soups advertised that "most" Campbell's soups were low in fat and cholesterol and thus were helpful in fighting heart disease. What the ad did not say was that Campbell's soups are high in sodium, and high-sodium diets may increase the risk of heart disease. The FTC ruled that Campbell's claims were thus deceptive. Advertising that contains an endorsement by a celebrity may be deemed deceptive if the celebrity actually makes no use of the product.

Bait-and-Switch Advertising

Bait-and-Switch Advertising Advertising a product at a very attractive price (the "bait") and then informing the consumer, once he or she is in the store, that the advertised product is either not available or is of poor quality; the customer is then urged to purchase ("switched" to) a more expensive item.

The FTC has promulgated specific rules to govern advertising techniques. One of the most important rules is contained in the FTC's "Guides Against Bait Advertising,"[4] issued in 1968. The rule seeks to prevent **bait-and-switch advertising**—that is, advertising a very low price for a particular item that will likely be unavailable to the consumer, who will then be encouraged to purchase a more expensive item. The low price is the "bait" to lure the consumer into the store. The salesperson is instructed to "switch" the consumer to a different, more expensive item. Under the FTC guidelines, bait-and-switch advertising occurs if the seller refuses to show the advertised item, fails to have in stock a reasonable quantity of the item, fails to promise to deliver the advertised item within a reasonable time, or discourages employees from selling the item.

FTC Actions against Deceptive Advertising

Cease-and-Desist Order An administrative or judicial order prohibiting a person or business firm from conducting activities that an agency or court has deemed illegal.

Counteradvertising New advertising that is undertaken pursuant to a Federal Trade Commission order for the purpose of correcting earlier false claims that were made about a product.

Multiple Product Order An order issued by the Federal Trade Commission to a firm that has engaged in deceptive advertising by which the firm is required to cease and desist from false advertising not only in regard to the product that was the subject of the action but also in regard to all the firm's other products.

The FTC receives complaints from many sources, including competitors of alleged violators, consumers, consumer organizations, trade associations, Better Business Bureaus, government organizations, and state and local officials. If enough consumers complain and the complaints are widespread, the FTC will investigate the problem and perhaps take action. If, after its investigations, the FTC believes that a given advertisement is unfair or deceptive, it drafts a formal complaint, which is sent to the alleged offender. The company may agree to settle the complaint without further proceedings.

If the company does not agree to settle the complaint, the FTC can conduct a hearing in which the company can present its defense. As discussed in Chapter 6, a hearing conducted by an administrative agency is held before an administrative law judge instead of a federal district court judge. If the FTC succeeds in proving that an advertisement is unfair or deceptive, it usually issues a **cease-and-desist order** requiring that the challenged advertising be stopped. It might also impose a sanction known as **counteradvertising** by requiring the company to advertise anew—in print, on radio, and on television—to inform the public about the earlier misinformation. The FTC may institute **multiple product orders,** which require a firm to cease and desist from false advertising not only in regard to the product that was the subject of the action but also in regard to all of the firm's other products.

Is it false or misleading to advertise a product as effective when its only effectiveness results from users' belief that it works? The court addresses this issue in the following case.

---

4.   16 C.F.R. Part 238.

Case 19.1 ⬤ Federal Trade Commission v. Pantron I Corp.

United States Court of Appeals,
Ninth Circuit, 1994.
33 F.3d 1088.

HISTORICAL AND SOCIAL SETTING *Hair has been part of people's self-image since primitive men and women first adorned it with clay, trophies, and badges. Sometimes, an abundance of hair is interpreted as characteristic of virility. At other times, a bald pate is seen as indicating masculinity. Regardless of how it is viewed, male-pattern baldness (the loss of hair from the upper scalp) results from an individual's genetic background and hormone levels. There is no "cure," and even hair transplants may have no lasting effect.*

BACKGROUND AND FACTS Pantron I Corporation sold the Helsinki Formula as a "cure" for baldness. Pantron claimed that the product reduced hair loss and promoted hair growth. The Federal Trade Commission filed a suit in a federal district court against Pantron and its owner, Hal Lederman, alleging that these claims constituted an unfair or deceptive trade practice. The court concluded in part that the product had a "placebo effect"—that is, that it worked when its users believed it would. The court issued an order that, among other things, allowed Pantron to continue claiming its product "works some of the time for a lot of people." The FTC appealed this order.

IN THE WORDS OF THE COURT . . .
REINHARDT, Circuit Judge.

* * * *

* * * Where, as here, a product's effectiveness arises solely as a result of the placebo effect, a representation that the product is effective constitutes a false advertisement even though some consumers may experience positive results. In such circumstances, the efficacy claim is misleading because the [product] is not inherently effective, its results being attributable to the psychosomatic effect produced by * * * advertising * * * .

* * * Under the evidence in the record before us, it appears that massaging vegetable oil on one's head would likely produce the same positive results as using the Helsinki Formula. * * * [A] court should not allow a seller to rely on such a placebo effect in supporting a claim of effectiveness * * * . [W]ere we to hold otherwise, advertisers would be encouraged to foist unsubstantiated claims on an unsuspecting public in the hope that consumers would believe the ads and the claims would be self-fulfilling.

DECISION AND REMEDY The U.S. Court of Appeals for the Ninth Circuit reversed this part of the lower court's order and remanded the case. Pantron could not continue to claim that its product "works some of the time for a lot of people."

FOR CRITICAL ANALYSIS—POLITICAL CONSIDERATION *What other government agencies might have taken action against Pantron and the Helsinki Formula, which is classified as a drug and sold through the mail?*

Telemarketing and Electronic Advertising

The pervasive use of the telephone to market goods and services to homes and businesses led to the passage in 1991 of the Telephone Consumer Protection Act (TCPA).[5] The act prohibits telephone solicitation using an automatic

---

5. 47 U.S.C. Sections 227 *et seq.*

telephone dialing system or a prerecorded voice. Most states also have laws regulating telephone solicitation.[6]

Not surprisingly, the widespread use of facsimile (fax) machines has led to the use of faxes as a tool for direct marketing. Advertising by fax is less expensive than mailing letters, and faxes normally receive greater attention than "junk mail." At the same time, unsolicited fax messages tie up the recipient's fax machine and impose a cost on the recipient, who must pay for fax paper and other supplies. The TCPA also makes it illegal to transmit ads via fax without first obtaining the recipient's permission.

The act is enforced by the Federal Communications Commission and also provides for a private right of action. Consumers can recover any actual monetary loss resulting from a violation of the act or receive $500 in damages for each violation, whichever is greater. If a court finds that a defendant willfully or knowingly violated the act, the court has the discretion to treble the damages awarded.

The Telemarketing and Consumer Fraud and Abuse Prevention Act[7] of 1994 directed the FTC to establish rules governing telemarketing and to bring actions against fraudulent telemarketers. The FTC's Telemarketing Sales Rule[8] of 1995 requires a telemarketer, before making a sales pitch, to inform the recipient that the call is a sales call and to identify the seller's name and the product being sold. The rule makes it illegal for telemarketers to misrepresent information (including facts about their goods or services, earnings potential, profitability, the risk attending an investment, or the nature of a prize). Additionally, telemarketers must inform the people they call of the total cost of the goods being sold, any restrictions on obtaining or using them, and whether a sale will be considered to be final and nonrefundable.

A telemarketer waits for a consumer's response. Should telemarketing be prohibited?

Labeling and Packaging Laws

A number of federal and state laws deal specifically with the information given on labels and packages. The restrictions are designed to ensure that labels and packages provide accurate information about products and warn about possible dangers from the products' use or misuse. In general, labels must be accurate. That is, they must use words as those words are understood by the ordinary consumer. For example, a box of cereal cannot be labeled "giant" if that would exaggerate the amount of cereal contained in the box. In some instances, labels must specify the raw materials used in the product, such as the percentage of cotton, nylon, or other fiber used in a garment. In other instances, the product must carry a warning. Cigarette packages and advertising, for example, must include one of several warnings about the health hazards associated with smoking.[9]

---

6.   For a discussion of the constitutionality of the TCPA, which some plaintiffs have alleged goes too far in restricting free speech, see *Moser v. Federal Communications Commission*, 46 F.3d 970 (9th Cir. 1995); *cert.* denied 515 U.S. 1161, 115 S.Ct. 2615, 132 L.Ed.2d 857 (1995).

7.   15 U.S.C. Sections 6101–6108.

8.   16 C.F.R. Sections 310.1–310.8.

9.   15 U.S.C. Sections 1331–1341.

Federal laws regulating the labeling and packaging of products include the Wool Products Labeling Act of 1939,[10] the Fur Products Labeling Act of 1951,[11] the Flammable Fabrics Act of 1953,[12] the Fair Packaging and Labeling Act of 1966,[13] the Smokeless Tobacco Health Education Act of 1986,[14] and the Nutrition Labeling and Education Act of 1990.[15] The Smokeless Tobacco Health Education Act, for example, requires that producers, packagers, and importers of smokeless tobacco label their product with one of several warnings about the health hazards associated with the use of smokeless tobacco; the warnings are similar to those contained on other tobacco product packages.

The Fair Packaging and Labeling Act requires that products carry labels that identify the product; the net quantity of the contents, as well as the quantity of servings, if the number of servings is stated; the manufacturer; and the packager or distributor. The act also authorizes requirements concerning words used to describe packages, terms that are associated with savings claims, information disclosures for ingredients in nonfood products, and standards for the partial filling of packages. Food products must bear labels detailing nutritional content, including how much fat a product contains and what kind of fat it is. These restrictions are enforced by the Department of Health and Human Services, as well as the Federal Trade Commission. The Nutrition Labeling and Education Act of 1990 requires standard nutrition facts (including fat content) on food labels; regulates the use of such terms as *fresh* and *low-fat;* and, subject to the federal Food and Drug Administration's approval, authorizes certain health claims. (See this chapter's *Inside the Legal Environment* for an overview of consumer protection on the Internet.)

Sales

Many of the laws that protect consumers concern the disclosure of certain terms in sales transactions and provide rules governing the various forms of sales, such as door-to-door sales, mail-order sales, referral sales, and the unsolicited receipt of merchandise. Much of the federal regulation of sales is conducted by the FTC under its regulatory authority to curb unfair trade practices. Other federal agencies, however, are involved to various degrees. For example, the Federal Reserve Board of Governors has issued **Regulation Z**,[16] which governs credit provisions associated with sales contracts. Many states have also enacted laws governing consumer sales transactions. Moreover, states have provided a number of consumer protection provisions through the adoption of the Uniform Commercial Code and, in those states that have adopted it, the Uniform Consumer Credit Code.

Regulation Z A set of rules promulgated by the Federal Reserve Board to implement the provisions of the Truth-in-Lending Act.

10. 15 U.S.C. Section 68.
11. 15 U.S.C. Section 69.
12. 15 U.S.C. Section 1191.
13. 15 U.S.C. Sections 1451–1461.
14. 15 U.S.C. Sections 4401–4408.
15. 21 U.S.C. Section 343-1.
16. 12 C.F.R. Sections 226.1–226.30.

Inside the Legal Environment
Consumer Protection on the Internet

According to Jodie Bernstein, head of the Federal Trade Commission's Bureau of Consumer Protection, "The Internet will not achieve its commercial potential if [it] becomes the Wild West of fraudulent schemes."[a] Because so much fraud has occurred on the Internet recently, a growing group of concerned individuals and consumer advocacy groups are calling for federal regulations to impose order on the electronic frontier. In opposition are those who fear that any regulation could stunt the growth of the Internet. They argue that the reason the Internet has grown so fast is that it has not been regulated.

ENTER THE FTC
Since the beginning of 1996, the Federal Trade Commission (FTC) has filed dozens of cases, under existing consumer protection statutes, concerning use of the Internet. Many of these cases involve so-called pyramid schemes, in which the early-round participants profit to the detriment of later-round members. In general, then, until now federal government agencies have fought online fraud by looking for violations of existing laws on the Internet. Some

states, though, have enacted specific Internet-directed laws. Additionally, the Council of Better Business Bureaus, or BBB, now provides for the online filing of complaints. The BBB also now offers an online seal of approval for online advertising.

The FTC is currently considering whether to regulate the collection of information about visitors to Web sites. The FTC's privacy initiative is available at the FTC's Web site listed in the *Interacting with the Internet* feature at the end of this chapter.

DECEPTIVE ADVERTISING IN CYBERSPACE
For years, the FTC has fought deceptive advertising in printed materials and in radio and television broadcasts. In the future, it will spend more of its resources to monitor deceptive advertising on the Internet. In the last few months of 1996, for example, it brought eight enforcement actions against entities that apparently had made false or unsubstantiated claims in their Internet ads. During that year, it brought over two dozen cases in all involving online fraud and deceptive advertising.

The FTC has moved particularly quickly on commercial Internet fraud schemes. It has even provided "hot links" on Web sites that it has targeted. A hot link takes the user to the FTC's own Web site, on which the complaint, restraining order, and other documents in the case can be read and downloaded.

OTHER AGENCIES FIGHT ONLINE FRAUD AND FALSE ADVERTISING
The Securities and Exchange Commission (SEC) also has been active in prosecuting online scams. One fraudulent scheme involved twenty thousand investors, who lost in all more than $3 million. Other cases have involved false claims about the earnings potential of home business programs, such as the claim that one could "earn $4,000 or more each month." Others have involved claims for "guaranteed credit repair."

The Department of Transportation (DOT), as well as the Food and Drug Administration (FDA), have also brought actions against purported online violators of advertising and disclosure laws. The DOT fined Virgin Airlines for failing to disclose the true price of a flight that it advertised on the Web. The FDA has not yet brought any actions against apparent online violators of regulations governing drug advertising, however. One issue that the FDA has yet to resolve is the distinction between advertising and labeling.

For Critical Analysis: *How might online industries regulate themselves? How can a set of guidelines for online advertising be developed, given that the technology is changing so rapidly?*

a. As quoted in Albert R. Karr. "Critics of Internet Clamor for More Controls," *The Wall Street Journal Europe,* October 2, 1996, p. 4.

Door-to-Door Sales

Door-to-door sales are singled out for special treatment in the laws of most states, in part because of the nature of the sales transaction. Repeat purchases are not as likely as they are in stores, and thus the seller has less incentive to cultivate the goodwill of the purchaser. Furthermore, the seller is unlikely to present alternative products and their prices. Thus, a number of states have passed "cooling-off" laws that permit the buyers of goods sold door-to-door to cancel their contracts within a specified period of time, usually two to three days after the sale.

An FTC regulation also requires sellers to give consumers three days to cancel any door-to-door sale. Because this rule applies in addition to the relevant state statutes, consumers are given the most favorable benefits of the FTC rule and their own state statutes. In addition, the FTC rule requires that consumers be notified of this right in a different language if the oral negotiations for the sale were in that language.

Telephone and Mail-order Sales

Sales made by either telephone or mail order are the greatest source of complaints to the nation's Better Business Bureaus. Many mail-order firms are far removed from most of their buyers, thus making it more burdensome for buyers to bring complaints against them. To a certain extent, consumers are protected under federal laws prohibiting mail fraud and under state consumer protection laws that parallel and supplement the federal laws.

The FTC Mail or Telephone Order Merchandise Rule of 1993, which amended the FTC Mail-Order Rule of 1975,[17] provides specific protections for consumers who purchase goods via phone lines or through the mails. The 1993 rule extended the 1975 rule to include sales in which orders are transmitted by computer, fax machine, or some similar means involving telephone lines. Among other things, the rule requires mail-order merchants to ship orders within the time promised in their catalogues or advertisements, to notify consumers when orders cannot be shipped on time, and to issue a refund within a specified period of time when a consumer cancels an order.

In addition, the Postal Reorganization Act of 1970[18] provides that *unsolicited* merchandise sent by U.S. mail may be retained, used, discarded, or disposed of in any manner deemed appropriate, without the recipient's incurring any obligation to the sender.

FTC Regulation of Specific Industries

Over the last decade, the FTC has begun to target certain sales practices on an industry-wide basis. Two examples involve the used-car business and the funeral-home trade. In 1984, the FTC enacted the Used Motor Vehicle Regulation Rule,[19] which is more commonly known as the used-car rule. This rule requires used-car dealers to affix a buyer's guide label to all cars sold on their lots. The label must disclose the following information: (1) the car's warranty or a statement that the car is being sold "as is," (2) information regarding any service contract or promises being made by the dealer, and (3) a suggestion that the purchaser obtain both an inspection of the car and a written statement of any promises made by the dealer.

> **DON'T FORGET** A seller's puffery—his or her opinion about the goods—is not a legally binding warranty or promise.

---

17. 16 C.F.R. Sections 435.1–435.2.
18. 39 U.S.C. Section 3009.
19. 16 C.F.R. Sections 455.1–455.5.

In 1984, the FTC also enacted rules requiring that funeral homes provide customers with itemized prices of all charges incurred for a funeral.[20] In addition, the regulations prohibit funeral homes from requiring specific embalming procedures or specific types of caskets for bodies that are to be cremated.

Real Estate Sales

Various federal and state laws apply to consumer transactions involving real estate. These laws are designed to prevent fraud and to provide buyers with certain types of information. In some cases, these protections mirror those provided in non–real estate sales. The disclosure requirements of the Truth-in-Lending Act apply to a number of real estate transactions, as will be discussed shortly.

INTERSTATE LAND SALES FULL DISCLOSURE ACT.   The Interstate Land Sales Full Disclosure Act[21] was passed by Congress in 1968, and it is administered by the Department of Housing and Urban Development (HUD). The purpose of the act is to ensure disclosure of certain information to consumers so that they can make reasoned decisions about land purchases. The act is similar to the Securities Act of 1933 in both purpose and design. The act requires anyone proposing to sell or lease one hundred or more lots of unimproved land, if the sale or lease is to be part of a common promotional plan, to file an initial statement of record with HUD's Office of Interstate Land Sales Registration.

The act only applies if the promotional plan can be deemed part of interstate commerce. As in cases involving securities, this is generally an easy requirement to meet. For example, even strictly local sales might be considered interstate commerce if transacted in part over the phone; although the calls might be local, the phone lines traverse state boundaries. For the same reason, use of the mail system is likely to ensure that a promotional plan is in the stream of interstate commerce.

Once the initial statement is filed, it must be approved by HUD before the developer can begin to offer the land for sale or lease. The act also provides purchasers with a private right of action for the land promoter's fraud, misrepresentation, or noncompliance with pertinent provisions of the act. Criminal penalties are provided under the act, and HUD is given certain rights with regard to inspections, injunctions, and prosecution of offenses. Three provisions of the act give purchasers rights of rescission (cancellation).

REAL ESTATE SETTLEMENT PROCEDURES ACT.   For many individuals, purchasing a home involves a bewildering array of procedures and requirements. Settlement (finalizing a real estate transaction) may require title insurance, attorneys' fees, appraisal fees, taxes, insurance, and brokers' fees. To aid home buyers, federal legislation requires specific disclosures regarding settlement procedures. The 1976 revisions of the Real Estate Settlement Procedures Act of 1974[22] make the following stipulations:

1. Within three business days after a person applies for a mortgage loan, the lender must send a booklet prepared by HUD that explains the settlement

---

20.   16 C.F.R. Section 453.2.
21.   15 U.S.C. Sections 1701–1720.
22.   12 U.S.C. Sections 2601–2617.

procedures, describes the costs to the potential buyer, and outlines the applicant's legal rights.

2. Within the three-day period, the lender must give an estimate of most of the settlement costs.
3. The lender must clearly identify individuals or firms that the applicant is required to use for legal or other services, including title search and insurance.
4. If the loan is approved, the lender must provide a truth-in-lending statement that shows the annual percentage rate on the mortgage loan.
5. Lenders, title insurers, and others involved in the transaction cannot pay kickbacks for business referred to them.

Credit Protection

Because of the extensive use of credit by American consumers, credit protection has become an especially important area regulated by consumer protection legislation. One of the most significant statutes regulating the credit and credit-card industry is Title I of the Consumer Credit Protection Act (CCPA),[23] which was passed by Congress in 1968 and is commonly referred to as the Truth-in-Lending Act (TILA).

The Truth-in-Lending Act

The TILA is basically a *disclosure law*. It is administered by the Federal Reserve Board and requires sellers and lenders to disclose credit terms or loan terms so that individuals can shop around for the best financing arrangements. TILA requirements apply only to persons who, in the ordinary course of business, lend money, sell on credit, or arrange for the extension of credit. Thus, sales or loans made between two consumers do not come under the protection of the act. Additionally, only debtors who are *natural* persons (as opposed to the artificial "person" of the corporation) are protected by this law; other legal entities are not.

The disclosure requirements are contained in Regulation Z, which, as mentioned earlier in this chapter, was promulgated by the Federal Reserve Board. If the contracting parties are subject to the TILA, the requirements of Regulation Z apply to any transaction involving an installment sales contract in which payment is to be made in more than four installments. Transactions subject to Regulation Z typically include installment loans, retail and installment sales, car loans, home improvement loans, and certain real estate loans if the amount of financing is less than $25,000.

Under the provisions of the TILA, all of the terms of a credit instrument must be clearly and conspicuously disclosed. The TILA provides for contract rescission (cancellation) if a creditor fails to follow *exactly* the procedures required by the act.[24] TILA requirements are strictly enforced.

NOTE The Federal Reserve Board is part of the Federal Reserve System, which influences the lending and investing activities of commercial banks and the cost and availability of credit.

23. 15 U.S.C. Sections 1601–1693r.
24. Note, however, that amendments to the TILA enacted in 1995 prevent borrowers from rescinding loans for minor clerical errors in closing documents [15 U.S.C. Sections 1605, 1631, 1635, 1640, and 1641].

In the following case, a consumer sued a lender, alleging TILA violations. The lender claimed that the consumer was not entitled to relief because she had lied on her credit application.

Case 19.2   ●   Purtle v. Eldridge Auto Sales, Inc.

United States Court of Appeals,
Sixth Circuit, 1996.
91 F.3d 797.

BACKGROUND AND FACTS   Renee Purtle bought a 1986 Chevrolet Blazer from Eldridge Auto Sales, Inc. To finance the purchase through Eldridge, Purtle filled out a credit application on which she misrepresented her employment status. Based on the misrepresentation, Eldridge extended credit. In the credit contract, Eldridge did not disclose the finance charge, the annual percentage rate, or the total sales price or use the term "amount financed," as the TILA and its regulations require. Purtle defaulted on the loan, and Eldridge repossesed the vehicle. Purtle filed a suit in a federal district court against Eldridge, alleging violations of the TILA. The court awarded Purtle $1,000 in damages, plus attorneys' fees and costs. Eldridge appealed, arguing in part that Purtle was not entitled to damages because she had committed fraud on her credit application.

IN THE WORDS OF THE COURT . . .
FORESTER, District Judge.

* * * *

* * * [T]he TILA imposes mandatory disclosure requirements on those who extend credit to consumers. * * * In the event that a creditor fails to disclose any of the credit terms required under the TILA and its regulations, a consumer may bring a civil action against the creditor. If a violation is proven, the consumer may recover twice the amount of the finance charge (but not less than $100.00 nor more than $1,000.00). The purpose of the statutory recovery is "to encourage lawsuits by individual consumers as a means of enforcing creditor compliance with the Act." The TILA also permits recovery of reasonable attorney's fees and costs. * * *

* * * *

* * * [O]nce a court finds a violation of the TILA, no matter how technical, the court has no discretion as to the imposition of civil liability. * * * Based on the unambiguous statutory language, it is clear that * * * the district court appropriately awarded Purtle the statutory penalty set out above.

DECISION AND REMEDY   The U.S. Court of Appeals for the Sixth Circuit affirmed the lower court's award. The lender was required to pay damages based on its violation of the TILA, despite the borrower's fraud.

FOR CRITICAL ANALYSIS—SOCIAL CONSIDERATION   *Do you think that the greatest number of consumers are protected by strict enforcement of consumer laws?*

EQUAL CREDIT OPPORTUNITY.   In 1974, the Equal Credit Opportunity Act (ECOA)[25] was enacted as an amendment to the TILA. The ECOA prohibits the denial of credit solely on the basis of race, religion, national origin, color, sex, marital status, or age. The act also prohibits credit discrimination on the basis of whether an individual receives certain forms of income, such as public-

---

25.   15 U.S.C. Section 1691–1691f.

Ethical Perspective

In some cases, consumers have taken unfair advantage of the TILA's requirements to avoid genuine obligations that they voluntarily assumed. For example, under the TILA, borrowers are allowed three business days to rescind, without penalty, a consumer loan that uses their principal dwelling as security. The lender must state specifically the last day on which the borrower can rescind the agreement. If the lender fails to do so, the borrower can rescind the loan within three years after it was made. This is true even if the lender inadvertently (unintentionally) failed to comply with the TILA's requirements.

Is it fair to hold creditors liable for TILA violations regardless of whether the violations were intentional or unintentional? According to the courts, the answer to this question is yes. The courts reason that, overall, consumers will benefit from strict compliance requirements, even though some consumers may abuse the act. In essence, the TILA is a "strict liability" statute (this is generally true of most consumer protection statutes). In other words, intention normally is irrelevant in determining whether a consumer protection statute has been violated.

For Critical Analysis: *In your opinion, should the courts give more weight to the circumstances surrounding a transaction and the intent factor in deciding cases involving alleged TILA violations? Why or why not?*

---

assistance benefits. Under the ECOA, a creditor may not require the signature of an applicant's spouse, other than as a joint applicant, on a credit instrument if the applicant qualifies under the creditor's standards of creditworthiness for the amount and terms of the credit request.

Creditors are permitted to request any information from a credit applicant except that which would be used for the type of discrimination covered in the act or its amendments. In the following case, the issue concerns whether a creditor violated the ECOA by requiring the signature of an applicant's spouse on a loan guaranty.

Case 19.3 ● Federal Deposit Insurance Corp. v. Medmark, Inc.

United States District Court,
District of Kansas, 1995.
897 F.Supp. 511.

BACKGROUND AND FACTS Bruce Shalberg was a director of Medmark, Inc., a small medical equipment supply company. As a condition of a loan to Medmark, the Merchants Bank asked Shalberg—whom the bank found to be independently creditworthy—to sign a guaranty of repayment. Later, for another loan, the bank required Shalberg's wife, Mary—who had nothing to do with Medmark—to sign the guaranty. When the bank failed, the Federal Deposit Insurance Corporation (FDIC) took over its assets. The FDIC filed a suit in a federal district court against Medmark and the Shalbergs to recover the amount of the loans. Mary Shalberg filed a motion for summary judgment, contending that the bank, in requiring her to sign the guaranty, had violated the Equal Credit Opportunity Act (ECOA).

IN THE WORDS OF THE COURT . . .
VRATIL, District Judge.
* * * *

[A regulation issued under the ECOA] specifically provides that a creditor may not require the signature of an applicant's spouse if the applicant qualifies under the creditor's standards of creditworthiness for the amount

(Continued)

Case 19.3—continued

and terms of the credit requested. The FDIC argues that the Bank "obviously" did not believe Mr. Shalberg to be independently creditworthy * * * . [But the] record contains no evidence that Mr. Shalberg was not creditworthy, in his own right, in the Bank's eyes. Summary judgment in favor of Mrs. Shalberg is therefore appropriate.

DECISION AND REMEDY   The federal district court issued a summary judgment in favor of Mary Shalberg, relieving her from any obligation on the loans. The creditor violated the ECOA by requiring Shalberg's signature on the loan guaranty.

FOR CRITICAL ANALYSIS—POLITICAL CONSIDERATION   *Why does the ECOA prohibit lenders from requiring a spouse's signature on a credit application if the applicant independently qualifies for the credit?*

> COMPARE The Electronic Fund Transfer Act also limits, under certain circumstances, the liability of a consumer to $50 for unauthorized transfers made before the issuer of an access card is notified that the card is lost.

CREDIT-CARD RULES.   The TILA also contains provisions regarding credit cards. One provision limits the liability of a cardholder to $50 per card for unauthorized charges made before the creditor is notified that the card has been lost. Another provision prohibits a credit-card company from billing a consumer for any unauthorized charges if the credit card was improperly issued by the company. For example, if a consumer receives an unsolicited credit card in the mail and the card is later stolen and used by the thief to make purchases, the consumer to whom the card was sent will not be liable for the unauthorized charges.

Further provisions of the act concern billing disputes related to credit-card purchases. If a debtor thinks that an error has occurred in billing or wishes to withhold payment for a faulty product purchased by credit card, the act outlines specific procedures for both the consumer and the credit-card company to follow in settling the dispute.

CONSUMER LEASES.   The Consumer Leasing Act (CLA) of 1988[26] amended the TILA to provide protection for consumers who lease automobiles and other goods. The CLA applies to those who lease or arrange to lease consumer goods in the ordinary course of their business. The act only applies if the goods are priced at $25,000 or less and if the lease term exceeds four months. The CLA and its implementing regulation, Regulation M,[27] require lessors to disclose in writing all of the material terms of the lease.

The Fair Credit Reporting Act

In 1970, to protect consumers against inaccurate credit reporting, Congress enacted the Fair Credit Reporting Act (FCRA).[28] The act provides that consumer credit reporting agencies may issue credit reports to users only for specified purposes, including the extension of credit, the issuance of insurance policies, compliance with a court order, and compliance with a consumer's request for a copy of his or her own credit report. The act further provides that any time a consumer is denied credit or insurance on the basis of the consumer's credit report, or is charged more than others ordinarily would be for credit or

---

26.   15 U.S.C. Sections 1667–1667e.
27.   12 C.F.R. Part 213.
28.   15 U.S.C. Sections 1681–1681t.

insurance, the consumer must be notified of that fact and of the name and address of the credit reporting agency that issued the credit report.

Under the act, consumers may request the source of any information being given out by a credit agency, as well as the identity of anyone who has received an agency's report. Consumers are also permitted to have access to the information contained about them in a credit reporting agency's files. If a consumer discovers that a credit reporting agency's files contain inaccurate information about the consumer's credit standing, the agency, on the consumer's written request, must investigate the matter and delete any unverifiable or erroneous information within a reasonable period of time.

An agency that fails to comply with the act is liable for actual damages, plus additional damages not to exceed $1,000 and attorneys' fees.[29] Damages are also available against anyone who uses a credit report for an improper purpose, as well as banks, credit-card companies, and other businesses that report information to credit agencies and do not respond adequately to customer complaints.

The following case illustrates the liability exposure of companies that maintain credit reports and ratings.

---

29. 15 U.S.C. Section 1681n.

Case 19.4   Guimond v. Trans Union Credit Information Co.

United States Court of Appeals,
Ninth Circuit, 1995.
45 F.3d 1329.

HISTORICAL AND ECONOMIC SETTING *A credit report reflects a consumer's bill-paying history. It lists the consumer's creditors and whether he or she has made payments on time. Inaccurate information can keep an individual from obtaining credit, because lenders rely on credit reports when deciding whether to extend credit. The major credit reporting agencies include the Trans Union Credit Information Company.*

BACKGROUND AND FACTS Renie Guimond learned of inaccuracies that Trans Union Credit Information Company had in its file on her. She notified Trans Union, which told her the file would be corrected; however, it was not corrected for a year. Guimond filed a suit in a federal district court against Trans Union, in part to recover damages under the Fair Credit Reporting Act (FCRA) for the company's failure to correct the information more quickly. Trans Union countered that Guimond had no claim, because she had not been denied credit before the information was corrected. The court ruled in favor of Trans Union, and Guimond appealed.

IN THE WORDS OF THE COURT . . .
FONG, District Judge:
* * * *

[The FCRA] states: Whenever a consumer reporting agency prepares a consumer report it shall follow reasonable procedures to assure maximum possible accuracy of the information * * * .
* * * *

Liability * * * is predicated on the reasonableness of the credit reporting agency's procedures * * * .
* * * [T]he focus should not have been on Guimond's damage claims. Rather the inquiry should have centered on whether Trans Union's procedures

(Continued)

Case 19.4—continued

for preparing Guimond's file contained reasonable procedures to prevent inaccuracies. Guimond has made out a *prima facie* case under [the FCRA] by showing that there were inaccuracies in her credit report. The district court was then required to consider whether Trans Union was liable under [the FCRA] before it determined that Guimond had suffered no recoverable damages.

DECISION AND REMEDY   The U.S. Court of Appeals for the Ninth Circuit reversed this part of the lower court's ruling and remanded the case for trial. The agency could be held liable if its procedures to assure the accuracy of its information were not reasonable.

FOR CRITICAL ANALYSIS—SOCIAL CONSIDERATION   *How do the policies underlying the FCRA support the court's interpretation of the statute in Guimond's case?*

Fair Debt Collection Practices Act

In 1977, Congress enacted the Fair Debt Collection Practices Act (FDCPA)[30] in an attempt to curb what were perceived to be abuses by collection agencies. The act applies only to specialized debt-collection agencies that regularly attempt to collect debts on behalf of someone else, usually for a percentage of the amount owed. Creditors attempting to collect debts are not covered by the act unless, by misrepresenting themselves, they cause debtors to believe they are collection agencies. The act explicitly prohibits a collection agency from using any of the following tactics:

1. Contacting the debtor at the debtor's place of employment if the debtor's employer objects.
2. Contacting the debtor during inconvenient or unusual times (for example, calling the debtor at three o'clock in the morning) or at any time if the debtor is being represented by an attorney.
3. Contacting third parties other than the debtor's parents, spouse, or financial adviser about payment of a debt unless a court authorizes such action.
4. Using harassment or intimidation (for example, using abusive language or threatening violence) or employing false or misleading information (for example, posing as a police officer).
5. Communicating with the debtor at any time after receiving notice that the debtor is refusing to pay the debt, except to advise the debtor of further action to be taken by the collection agency.

Validation Notice An initial notice to a debtor from a collection agency informing the debtor that he or she has thirty days to challenge the debt and request verification.

The FDCPA also requires a collection agency to include a **validation notice** whenever it initially contacts a debtor for payment of a debt or within five days of that initial contact. The notice must state that the debtor has thirty days within which to dispute the debt and to request a written verification of the debt from the collection agency. The debtor's request for debt validation must be in writing.

The enforcement of the FDCPA is primarily the responsibility of the Federal Trade Commission. The act provides that a debt collector that fails to comply

---

30.   15 U.S.C. Section 1692.

with the act is liable for actual damages, plus additional damages not to exceed $1,000[31] and attorneys' fees. In the following case, the United States Supreme Court considered whether lawyers engaged in consumer debt-collection litigation were exempt from the FDCPA.

---

31. According to the U.S. Court of Appeals for the Sixth Circuit, the $1,000 limit on damages applies to each lawsuit, not to each violation. See *Wright v. Finance Service of Norwalk, Inc.,* 22 F.3d 647 (6th Cir. 1994).

Case 19.5 ● Heintz v. Jenkins

Supreme Court of the United States, 1995.
514 U.S. 291,
115 S.Ct. 1489,
131 L.Ed.2d 395.

BACKGROUND AND FACTS Darlene Jenkins borrowed money from Gainer Bank to buy a car. The terms of the loan required her to keep the car insured. When she let her insurance expire, the bank bought a policy. Jenkins defaulted on the loan, and the bank asked George Heintz, a lawyer, to recover its money. Heintz began legal proceedings against Jenkins to recover the amount due on the loan, plus the cost of the insurance. Jenkins filed a suit in a federal district court against Heintz under the Fair Debt Collection Practices Act (FDCPA), claiming that Heintz was trying to collect an amount that was not part of the loan agreement. The court dismissed the suit, holding that the FDCPA does not apply to lawyers engaging in litigation. Jenkins appealed, and the U.S. Court of Appeals for the Seventh Circuit reversed. Heintz appealed to the United States Supreme Court.

IN THE WORDS OF THE COURT . . .
Justice BREYER delivered the opinion of the Court.
     * * * *

There are two rather strong reasons for believing that the [FDCPA] applies to the litigating activities of lawyers. First, the [FDCPA] defines the "debt collector[s]" to whom it applies as including those who "regularly collec[t] or attemp[t] to collect, directly or indirectly, [consumer] debts owed * * * another." In ordinary English, a lawyer who regularly tries to obtain payment of consumer debts through legal proceedings is a lawyer who regularly "attempts" to "collect" those consumer debts.

Second, in 1977, Congress enacted an earlier version of this statute, which contained an express exemption for lawyers. That exemption said that the term "debt collector" did not include "any attorney-at-law collecting a debt as an attorney on behalf of and in the name of a client." In 1986, however, Congress repealed this exemption * * * .

DECISION AND REMEDY The United States Supreme Court upheld the decision of the appellate court. The Court held that the FDCPA does apply to lawyers engaged in consumer debt-collection litigation.

FOR CRITICAL ANALYSIS—POLITICAL CONSIDERATION *Why do you think Congress repealed the FDCPA exemption for lawyers collecting debts?*

Garnishment of Wages

Despite the increasing number of protections afforded debtors, creditors are not without means of securing payment on debts. One of these is the right to garnish a debtor's wages after the debt has gone uncollected for a prolonged period. Recall from Chapter 14 that *garnishment* is the legal procedure by which a creditor may collect on a debt by directly attaching, or seizing, a portion of the debtor's assets (such as wages) that are in the possession of a third party (such as an employer).

State law provides the basis for a process of garnishment, but the law varies among the states as to how easily garnishment can be obtained. Indeed, a few states, such as Texas, prohibit garnishment of wages altogether except for child support. In addition, constitutional due process and federal legislation under the TILA provide further protections against abuse.[32] In general, the debtor is entitled to notice and an opportunity to be heard in a process of garnishment. Moreover, wages cannot be garnished beyond 25 percent of the debtor's after-tax earnings, and the garnishment must leave the debtor with at least a specified minimum income.

Consumer Health and Safety

Laws discussed earlier regarding the labeling and packaging of products go a long way toward promoting consumer health and safety. But there is a significant distinction between regulating the information dispensed about a product and regulating the content of the product. The classic example is tobacco products. Tobacco products have not been altered by regulation or banned outright despite their obvious hazards. What has been regulated are the warnings that producers are required to give consumers about the hazards of tobacco.[33] This section focuses on laws that regulate the actual products made available to consumers.

The Federal Food, Drug and Cosmetic Act

BE AWARE The Food and Drug Administration is authorized to obtain, among other things, orders for the recall and seizure of certain products.

The first federal legislation regulating food and drugs was enacted in 1906 as the Pure Food and Drugs Act. That law, as amended in 1938, exists presently as the Federal Food, Drug and Cosmetic Act (FFDCA).[34] The act protects consumers against adulterated and misbranded foods and drugs. More recent amendments have added substantive and procedural requirements to the act. In its present form, the act establishes food standards, specifies safe levels of potentially hazardous food additives, and sets classifications of food and food advertising.

Most of these statutory requirements are monitored and enforced by the Food and Drug Administration (FDA). Under an extensive set of procedures established by the FDA, drugs must be shown to be effective as well as safe before they may be marketed to the public, and the use of some food additives suspected of being carcinogenic is prohibited. A 1976 amendment to the FFDCA[35] authorizes the FDA to regulate medical devices, such as pacemakers and other health devices and equipment, and to withdraw from the market any such device that is mislabeled.

---

32.   15 U.S.C. Sections 1671–1677.
33.   We are ignoring recent civil litigation concerning the liability of tobacco product manufacturers for injuries that arise from the use of tobacco.
34.   21 U.S.C. Sections 301–393.
35.   21 U.S.C. Sections 352(o), 360(j), 360(k), and 360c–360k.

A warning appears on a package of cigarettes, as required by federal law. Why is Congress concerned with protecting consumers against purportedly unsafe products?

The Consumer Product Safety Act

Consumer product safety legislation began in 1953 with enactment of the Flammable Fabrics Act, which prohibits the sale of highly flammable clothing or materials. Over the next two decades, Congress enacted legislation regarding the design or composition of specific classes of products. Then, in 1972, Congress, by enacting the Consumer Product Safety Act,[36] created a comprehensive scheme of regulation over matters of consumer safety. The act also established far-reaching authority over consumer safety under the Consumer Product Safety Commission (CPSC).

The CPSC conducts research on the safety of individual products, and it maintains a clearinghouse of information on the risks associated with various consumer products. The Consumer Product Safety Act authorizes the CPSC to set standards for consumer products and to ban the manufacture and sale of any product that it deems to be potentially hazardous to consumers. The CPSC also has authority to remove from the market any products it believes to be imminently hazardous and to require manufacturers to report on any products already sold or intended for sale if the products have proved to be hazardous. The CPSC also has authority to administer other product safety legislation, such as the Child Protection and Toy Safety Act of 1969[37] and the Federal Hazardous Substances Act of 1960.[38]

The CPSC's authority is sufficiently broad to allow it to ban any product that it believes poses an "unreasonable risk" to consumers. Some of the products that the CPSC has banned include various types of fireworks, cribs, and toys, as well as many products containing asbestos or vinyl chloride.

State Consumer Protection Laws

▼ Thus far, our primary focus has been on federal legislation. As mentioned, however, state laws often provide more sweeping and significant protections

36. 15 U.S.C. Sections 2051–2083.
37. This act consists of amendments to 15 U.S.C. Sections 1261, 1262, and 1274.
38. 15 U.S.C. Sections 1261–1277.

for the consumer than do federal laws. The warranty and unconscionability provisions of the Uniform Commercial Code (discussed in Chapter 13) offer important protections for consumers against unfair practices on the part of sellers and lessors. The Magnuson-Moss Warranty Act of 1975[39] supplements the UCC provisions in cases involving both a consumer transaction of at least $10 and an express written warranty.

Far less widely adopted than the UCC is the Uniform Consumer Credit Code (UCCC). The UCCC has provisions concerning truth in lending, maximum credit ceilings, door-to-door sales, fine-print clauses, and other practices affecting consumer transactions.

Virtually all states have specific consumer protection acts, often titled "deceptive trade practices acts." Although state consumer protection statutes vary widely in their provisions, a common thread runs through most of them. Typically, state consumer protection laws are directed at deceptive trade practices, such as a seller's providing false or misleading information to consumers. As just mentioned, some of the legislation provides broad protection for consumers. A prime example is the Texas Deceptive Trade Practices Act of 1973, which forbids a seller from selling to a buyer anything that the buyer does not need or cannot afford.

---

39.   15 U.S.C. Sections 2301–2312.

Key Terms

bait-and-switch advertising 532

cease-and-desist order 532

consumer law 531
counteradvertising 532
multiple product orders 532

Regulation Z 535
validation notice 544

Chapter Summary
Consumer Protection

DECEPTIVE ADVERTISING
(See pages 531–533.)

1. **Definition of deceptive advertising**—Generally, an advertising claim will be deemed deceptive if it would mislead a reasonable consumer.

2. **Bait-and-switch advertising**—Advertising a lower-priced product (the "bait") when the intention is not to sell the advertised product but to lure consumers into the store and convince them to buy a higher-priced product (the "switch") is prohibited by the FTC.

3. **FTC actions against deceptive advertising**—

   a. Cease-and-desist orders—Requiring the advertiser to stop the challenged advertising.

   b. Counteradvertising—Requiring the advertiser to advertise to correct the earlier misinformation.

(Continued)

Chapter Summary, continued

TELEMARKETING AND ELECTRONIC ADVERTISING (See pages 533–534.)	The Telephone Consumer Protection Act of 1991 prohibits telephone solicitation using an automatic telephone dialing system or a prerecorded voice, as well as the transmission of advertising materials via fax without first obtaining the recipient's permission to do so.
LABELING AND PACKAGING (See pages 534–535.)	Manufacturers must comply with labeling or packaging requirements for their specific products. In general, all labels must be accurate and not misleading.
SALES (See pages 535–539.)	1. **Door-to-door sales**—The FTC requires all door-to-door sellers to give consumers three days (a "cooling-off" period) to cancel any sale. States also provide for similar protection. 2. **Telephone and mail-order sales**—Federal and state statutes and regulations govern certain practices of sellers who solicit over the telephone or through the mails and prohibit the use of the mails to defraud individuals. 3. **Regulations affecting specific industries**—The FTC has regulations that apply to specific industries, such as the used-car business and funeral homes. 4. **Real estate sales**—Various federal and state laws apply to consumer transactions involving real estate.
HEALTH AND SAFETY PROTECTION (See pages 546–547.)	1. **Food and drugs**—The Federal Food, Drug and Cosmetic Act of 1938, as amended, protects consumers against adulterated and misbranded foods and drugs. The act establishes food standards, specifies safe levels of potentially hazardous food additives, and sets classifications of food and food advertising. 2. **Consumer product safety**—The Consumer Product Safety Act of 1972 seeks to protect consumers from risk of injury from hazardous products. The Consumer Product Safety Commission has the power to remove products that are deemed imminently hazardous from the market and to ban the manufacture and sale of hazardous products.
CREDIT PROTECTION (See pages 539–546.)	1. **Consumer Credit Protection Act, Title I (Truth-in-Lending Act, or TILA)**—A disclosure law that requires sellers and lenders to disclose credit terms or loan terms in certain transactions, including retail and installment sales and loans, car loans, home improvement loans, and certain real estate loans. Additionally, the TILA provides for the following: 　a. Equal credit opportunity—Creditors are prohibited from discriminating on the basis of race, religion, marital status, gender, and so on. 　b. Credit-card protection—Credit-card users may withhold payment for a faulty product sold, or for an error in billing, until the dispute is resolved; liability of cardholders for unauthorized charges is limited to $50, providing notice requirements are met; consumers are not liable for unauthorized charges made on unsolicited credit cards. 　c. Consumer leases—The Consumer Leasing Act (CLA) of 1988 protects consumers who lease automobiles and other goods priced at $25,000 or less if the lease term exceeds four months. 2. **Fair Credit Reporting Act**—Entitles consumers to request verification of the accuracy of a credit report and to have unverified information removed from their files. 3. **Fair Debt Collection Practices Act**—Prohibits debt collectors from using unfair debt-collection practices, such as contacting the debtor at his or her place of *(Continued)*

Chapter Summary, continued

CREDIT PROTECTION—continued (See pages 539–546.)	employment if the employer objects or at unreasonable times, contacting third parties about the debt, harassing the debtor, and so on.
STATE CONSUMER PROTECTION LAWS (See pages 547–548.)	State laws often provide for greater consumer protection against deceptive trade practices than do federal laws. In addition, the warranty and unconscionability provisions of the Uniform Commercial Code protect consumers against sellers' deceptive practices. The Uniform Consumer Credit Code, which has not been widely adopted by the states, provides credit protection for consumers.

For Review

1. When will advertising be deemed deceptive?
2. How does the Federal Food, Drug and Cosmetic Act protect consumers?
3. What are the major federal statutes providing for consumer protection in credit transactions?
4. How does the Consumer Product Safety Act protect consumers?
5. What are the major state statutes that protect consumers?

Questions and Case Problems

19–1. Unsolicited Merchandise. Andrew, a California resident, received a flyer in the U.S. mail announcing a new line of regional cookbooks distributed by the Every-Kind Cookbook Co. Andrew was not interested and threw the flyer away. Two days later, Andrew received in the mail an introductory cookbook entitled *Lower Mongolian Regional Cookbook,* as announced in the flyer, on a "trial basis" from Every-Kind. Andrew was not interested but did not go to the trouble to return the cookbook. Every-Kind demanded payment of $20.95 for the *Lower Mongolian Regional Cookbook.* Discuss whether Andrew can be required to pay for the cookbook.

19–2. Consumer Protection. Fireside Rocking Chair Co. advertised in the newspaper a special sale price of $159 on machine-caned rocking chairs. In the advertisement was a drawing of a natural-wood rocking chair with a caned back and seat. The average person would not be able to tell from the drawing whether the rocking chair was machine caned or hand caned. Hand-caned rocking chairs sold for $259. Lowell and Celia Gudmundson went to Fireside because they had seen the ad for the machine-caned rocking chair and were very interested in purchasing one. The Gudmundsons arrived on the morning the

sale began. Fireside's agent said the only machine-caned rocking chairs he had were painted lime green and were priced at $159. He immediately turned the Gudmundsons' attention to the hand-caned rocking chairs, praising their quality and pointing out that for the extra $100, the hand-caned chairs were surely a good value. The Gudmundsons, preferring the natural-wood machine-caned rocking chair for $159 as pictured in the advertisement, said they would like to order one. The Fireside agent said he could not order a natural-wood, machine-caned rocking chair. Discuss fully whether Fireside has violated any consumer protection laws.

19–3. Door-to-Door Sales. On June 28, a sales representative for Renowned Books called on the Gonchars at their home. After a very persuasive sales pitch on the part of the sales agent, the Gonchars agreed in writing to purchase a twenty-volume set of historical encyclopedias from Renowned Books for a total of $299. An initial down payment of $35 was required, with the remainder of the price to be paid in monthly payments over a one-year period. Two days later the Gonchars, having second thoughts, contacted the book company and stated that they had decided to rescind the contract. Renowned

Books said this would be impossible. Has Renowned Books violated any consumer law by not allowing the Gonchars to rescind their contract? Explain.

19–4. Truth in Lending. Michael and Patricia Jensen purchased a new 1989 Ford Tempo from Ray Kim Ford, Inc. The Jensens signed a retail installment contract that provided for an estimated trade-in value of $800 for their old car. When the traded-in car turned out to be worth $1,388.08, Ray Kim prepared a second retail installment contract without the Jensens' knowledge. The second contract, although it credited the increased trade-in value of the car, compensated for this credit by increasing the interest rate, increasing the sales price of the car, and making other adjustments so that the second contract basically called for future cash payments by the Jensens of about the same amount as the first contract. In effect, the second contract gave the Jensens almost no benefit for the increased value of their traded-in car. The Jensens made payments under the contract until they noticed the minor difference in monthly payments, asked for a copy of the contract, and realized that it was not the contract that they had signed. The Jensens sued Ray Kim, alleging that the second contract was a forgery and that Ray Kim had violated the Truth-in-Lending Act (TILA) by not disclosing to them the credit terms of the second contract. Has Ray Kim violated the TILA? If the Jensens choose to adopt the terms of the second contract, despite the forgery, has the act been violated? Discuss fully. [*Jensen v. Ray Kim Ford, Inc.,* 920 F.2d 3 (7th Cir. 1990)]

19–5. Deceptive Advertising. Thompson Medical Co. marketed a new cream called Aspercreme that was supposed to help arthritis victims and others suffering from minor aches. Aspercreme contained no aspirin. Thompson's television advertisements stated that the product provided "the strong relief of aspirin right where you hurt" and showed the announcer holding up aspirin tablets as well as a tube of Aspercreme. The Federal Trade Commission held that the advertisements were misleading, because they led consumers to believe that Aspercreme contained aspirin. Thompson Medical Co. appealed this decision and argued that the advertisements never actually stated that the product contained aspirin. How should the court rule? Discuss. [*Thompson Medical Co. v. Federal Trade Commission,* 791 F.2d 189 (D.C. Cir. 1986)]

19–6. Deceptive Advertising. Dennis and Janice Geiger saw an advertisement in a newspaper for a Kimball Whitney spinet piano on sale for $699 at the McCormick Piano & Organ Co. Because the style of the piano drawn in the advertisement matched their furniture, the Geigers were particularly interested in the Kimball. When they went to McCormick Piano & Organ, however, they learned that the drawing closely resembled another, more expensive Crest piano and that the Kimball spinet looked quite different from the piano sketched in the drawing. The

salesperson told the Geigers that she was unable to order a spinet piano of the style they requested. When the Geigers asked for the names of other customers who had purchased the advertised pianos, the salesperson became extremely upset and said she would not, under any circumstances, sell the Geigers a piano. The Geigers then brought suit against the piano store, alleging that the store had engaged in deceptive advertising in violation of Indiana law. Was the McCormick Piano & Organ Co. guilty of deceptive advertising? Explain. [*McCormick Piano & Organ Co. v. Geiger,* 412 N.E.2d 842 (Ind.App. 1980)]

19–7. Fair Debt Collection. Josephine Rutyna was a sixty-year-old widow who, in late 1976 and early 1977, incurred a debt for medical treatment of her high blood pressure and epilepsy. She assumed that the cost of the services was paid by either Medicare or her private insurance company. In July 1978, however, she was contacted by an agent of Collection Accounts Terminal, Inc., who stated that Rutyna still owed a debt of $56 for those services. She denied that she owed the debt, and the following month she received a letter from the collection agency threatening to contact her neighbors and employer concerning the debt if the $56 was not paid immediately. Discuss fully whether the collection agency's letter violates any consumer protection law. [*Rutyna v. Collection Accounts Terminal, Inc.,* 478 F.Supp. 980 (N.D.Ill. 1979)]

19–8. Equal Credit Opportunity. The Riggs National Bank of Washington, D.C., lent more than $11 million to Samuel Linch and Albert Randolph. To obtain the loan, Linch and Randolph provided personal financial statements. Linch's statement included substantial assets that he owned jointly with his wife, Marcia. As a condition of the loan, Riggs required that Marcia, as well as Samuel and Albert, sign a personal guaranty for repayment. When the borrowers defaulted, Riggs filed a suit in a federal district court to recover its money, based on the personal guaranties. The court ruled against the borrowers, who appealed. On what basis might the borrowers argue that Riggs violated the Equal Credit Opportunity Act? [*Riggs National Bank of Washington, D.C. v. Linch,* 36 F.3d 370 (4th Cir. 1994)]

19–9. Debt Collection. Equifax A.R.S., a debt-collection agency, sent Donna Russell a notice about one of her debts. The front of the notice stated that "[i]f you do not dispute this claim (see reverse side) and wish to pay it within the next 10 days we will not post this collection to your file." The reverse side set out Russell's rights under the Fair Debt Collection Practices Act (FDCPA), including that she had thirty days to decide whether to contest the claim. Russell filed a suit in a federal district court against Equifax. The court ruled against Russell, who appealed. On what basis might Russell argue that Equifax violated the FDCPA? Did Equifax violate the FDCPA? [*Russell v. Equifax A.R.S.,* 74 F.3d 30 (2d Cir. 1996)]

A Question of Ethics and Social Responsibility

19–10. On July 16, 1982, the Semars signed a loan contract with Platte Valley Federal Savings & Loan Association, offering a second mortgage on their home as collateral. Under the Truth-in-Lending Act (TILA), borrowers are allowed three business days to rescind, without penalty, a consumer loan that uses their principal dwelling as security. The TILA requires lenders in such situations to state specifically the last date on which the borrower can rescind the loan agreement, and if they fail to include this date, the borrower may rescind the loan within three years after it was made. Platte Valley's form omitted the exact expiration date of the three-day period, although it stated that the rescission right expired three business days after July 16. The Semars ceased making monthly payments on the loan in September 1983 and sent a Notice of Rescission to Platte Valley on February 15, 1984. The Semars claimed that Platte Valley had violated the TILA by failing to specify in the loan contract the exact date of the expiration of the three-day rescission period. Because of this violation, the Semars maintained they had three years in which to rescind the contract. Although the court found the Semars to be "unsympa-

thetic plaintiffs," it nevertheless held that rescission was appropriate for the technical violation of the TILA. [*Semar v. Platte Valley Federal Savings & Loan Association*, 791 F.2d 699 (9th Cir. 1986)]

1. Do you think that the court, by adhering so strictly to the letter of the law, violated the spirit of the law?
2. When deciding issues involving alleged violations of consumer protection legislation, such as the TILA, should courts balance the equities of the cases? That is, should the ethical (or unethical) behavior of the parties to a particular transaction be taken into consideration?
3. How might you justify, on ethical grounds, the court's decision in this case?

For Critical Analysis

19–11. In some cases, the federal government has named corporate officers as defendants in prosecutions for violations of the Federal Food, Drug and Cosmetic Act. The liability of these officers does not depend on their knowledge of, or personal participation in, a criminal act. On what, then, does their liability depend? With the answer to the previous question in mind, what might a manager plead in his or her defense to avoid liability?

INTERACTING WITH The Internet

■ To view the FTC's Web site, go to

http://www.ftc.gov/

■ The Nolo Press has a section called Money and Consumer Matters at

http://www.nolo.com/

■ The Web site of the Consumer Product Safety Commission (CPSC) provides information on the CPSC as well as online versions of CPSC publications, such as its *Consumer Product Safety Review*. To access the CPSC's site, go to

http://www.cpsc.gov/

■ For information on the advertising guidelines and enforcement policy of the Federal Trade Commission (FTC), go to the Advertising Law Internet Site at

http://www.webcom.com/~lewrose/home.html

■ For information on the Food and Drug Administration, access

http://www.fda.gov/

■ The goal of the Better Business Bureau (BBB) is to provide information to consumers so they can make informed buying decisions. To access the BBB's home page, go to

http://www.bbb.org/

■ The Better Business Bureau now has a special online site, called BBBOnLine, to help consumers who shop the Internet locate reliable online businesses. You can access this site at

http://www.bbbonline.org/

■ If you subscribe to the commercial service CompuServe, you have access to its Consumer Forum. once on CompuServe, type in

Go legal

Then select

Consumer Forum

From the Library Menu, choose

Browse

CHAPTER 20

Protecting the Environment

Contents

Chapter Objectives

After reading this chapter, you should be able to . . .

1. Identify common law actions available against polluters.
2. Describe the National Environmental Policy Act.
3. Explain how the government regulates air and water pollution.
4. List and describe the major statutes that regulate toxic chemicals.
5. Identify the purpose and functions of Superfund.

> "Man, however much he may like to pretend the contrary, is part of nature."
>
> Rachel Carson, 1907–1964
> (American writer and conservationist)

Environmental Law The body of statutory, regulatory, and common law relating to the protection of the environment.

We now turn to a discussion of the various ways in which businesses are regulated by the government in the interest of protecting the environment. Concern over the degradation of the environment has increased over time in response to the environmental effects of population growth, urbanization, and industrialization. Society's generation of waste threatens not only the quality of the environment but also—as indicated by the connection made in the opening quotation—the quality of human life. Environmental protection is not without a price, however. For many businesses, the costs of complying with environmental regulations are high, and for some they are too high. There is constant tension between the desirability of increasing profits and productivity and the need to attain higher quality in the environment.

Environmental law—all law pertaining to environmental protection—is not new. Indeed, the federal government began to regulate some activities, such as those involving the pollution of navigable waterways, in the late 1800s. In the last few decades, however, the body of environmental law has expanded substantially as government has attempted to control industrial waste and to protect certain natural resources and endangered species.

In this chapter, we first discuss the common law actions that can be brought against business firms and individuals for damages caused by polluting activities. The remainder of the chapter examines the various statutes and regulations that have been created to protect the environment.

Common Law Actions

Common law remedies against environmental pollution originated centuries ago in England. Those responsible for operations that created dirt, smoke, noxious odors, noise, or toxic substances were sometimes held liable under common law theories of nuisance or negligence. Today, injured individuals continue to rely on the common law to obtain damages and injunctions against business polluters. (Statutory remedies are also available, a topic that we treat later.)

Nuisance

Nuisance A common law doctrine under which persons may be held liable for using their property in a manner that unreasonably interferes with others' rights to use or enjoy their own property.

Under the common law doctrine of **nuisance**, persons may be held liable if they use their property in a manner that unreasonably interferes with others' rights to use or enjoy their own property. In these situations, it is common for courts to balance the equities between the harm caused by the pollution and the costs of stopping it.

Courts have often denied injunctive relief on the ground that the hardships to be imposed on the polluter and on the community are greater than the hardships to be suffered by the plaintiff. For example, a factory that causes neighboring landowners to suffer from smoke, dirt, and vibrations may be left in operation if it is the core of a local economy. The injured parties may be awarded only money damages. These damages may include compensation for the decreased value of their property that results from the factory's operation.

A property owner may be given relief from pollution in situations in which he or she can identify a distinct harm separate from that affecting the general public. This harm is referred to as a "private" nuisance. Under the common law, citizens were denied standing (access to the courts—see Chapter 3) unless they suffered a harm distinct from the harm suffered by the public at large. Some states still require this. Therefore, a group of citizens who wished to stop a new development that would cause significant water pollution was denied access to the courts on the ground that the harm to them did not differ from the harm to the general public.[1] A public authority (such as a state's attorney general) can sue to abate a "public" nuisance.

In the following case, landowners sued their neighbor, the operator of a gravel pit, under the common law doctrine of nuisance. The landowners contended that the operator's excavation in the gravel pit resulted in the drying up of a spring running under their property.

> **"A nuisance may be merely a right thing in the wrong place, like a pig in the parlor instead of the barnyard."**
>
> George Sutherland, 1862–1942
> (American jurist)

1. *Save the Bay Committee, Inc. v. Mayor of City of Savannah*, 227 Ga. 436, 181 S.E.2d 351 (1971).

Case 20.1 ● Maddocks v. Giles

Supreme Judicial Court of Maine, 1996. 686 A.2d 1069.

BACKGROUND AND FACTS Sewall and Janice Maddocks owned property next to a gravel pit owned and operated by Elbridge Giles, doing business as E. A. Giles & Son. Below the surface of the Maddockses' property was a subterranean spring that produced large quantities of high-quality water. Giles's exca-

vation in the gravel pit caused the spring to dry up. The Maddockses filed a suit against Giles in a Maine state court, seeking damages on the ground that the excavation was a nuisance because the excavation caused a disruption of the flow of the spring. The court dismissed the complaint, and the Maddockses appealed to the state's highest court, the Supreme Judicial Court of Maine.

IN THE WORDS OF THE COURT . . .
GLASSMAN, Justice.
* * * *

Although we recognize the general principle that a property owner may use his land as he pleases for all lawful purposes, there is a long standing limitation of this rule preventing a landowner from drastically altering the flow of a watercourse. * * * A watercourse cannot be stopped up or diverted to the injury of other[s]. There is a public or natural [right] in such a stream, belonging to all persons whose lands are benefitted by it. * * * Application of these principles to the facts of this case leads us to conclude that the trial court erred when it dismissed the Maddockses' complaint.

The complaint alleges that Giles' excavation activities created a nuisance that caused a disruption of the flow of a subterranean spring from aquifers beneath Giles' property into the Maddockses' property. * * * [W]e conclude that the complaint sufficiently alleges a nuisance by the disruption of a watercourse * * * .

DECISION AND REMEDY The Supreme Judicial Court of Maine vacated (set aside) the lower court's dismissal of the Maddockses' complaint. Disruption of the flow of a subterranean spring may constitute a nuisance. The case could proceed to trial.

FOR CRITICAL ANALYSIS—ECONOMIC CONSIDERATION *What are the competing considerations in pollution cases that might operate to allow pollution to continue?*

Negligence and Strict Liability

An injured party may sue a business polluter in tort under the negligence and strict liability theories discussed in Chapter 8. The basis for a negligence action is a business's alleged failure to use reasonable care toward a party whose injury was foreseeable and, of course, caused by the lack of reasonable care. For example, employees might sue an employer whose failure to use proper pollution controls contaminated the air, causing the employees to suffer respiratory illnesses. A developing area of tort law involves **toxic torts**—actions against toxic polluters.

Toxic Tort Failure to use or to clean up properly toxic chemicals that cause harm to a person or society.

Businesses that engage in ultrahazardous activities—such as the transportation of radioactive materials—are strictly liable for whatever injuries the activities cause. In a strict liability action, the injured party does not need to prove that the business failed to exercise reasonable care.

Federal Regulation

▼   Congress has passed a number of statutes to control the impact of human activities on the environment. Exhibit 20–1 lists and summarizes the major federal environmental statutes discussed in this chapter. Some of these statutes were passed in an attempt to improve the quality of air and water. Some of them specifically regulate toxic chemicals—including pesticides, herbicides, and hazardous wastes. Some are concerned with radiation.

Environmental Regulatory Agencies

Much of the body of federal law governing business activities consists of the regulations issued and enforced by administrative agencies. The most well known of the agencies regulating environmental law is, of course, the Environmental Protection Agency (EPA), which was created in 1970 to coordinate federal environmental responsibilities. Other federal agencies with authority for regulating specific environmental matters include the Department of the Interior, the Department of Defense, the Department of Labor, the Food and Drug Administration, and the Nuclear Regulatory Commission. These regulatory agencies—and all other agencies of the federal government—must take environmental factors into consideration when making significant decisions.

Assessment of the Impact of Agency Actions on the Environment

The National Environmental Policy Act (NEPA) of 1969[2] requires that for every major federal action that significantly affects the quality of the environment, an **environmental impact statement** (EIS) must be prepared. An action qualifies as "major" if it involves a substantial commitment of resources (monetary or otherwise). An action is "federal" if a federal agency has the power to control it. Construction by a private developer of a ski resort on federal land, for example, may require an EIS.[3] Building or operating a nuclear plant, which

Environmental Impact Statement (EIS) A statement required by the National Environmental Policy Act for any major federal action that will significantly affect the quality of the environment. The statement must analyze the action's impact on the environment and explore alternative actions that might be taken.

---

2. 42 U.S.C. Sections 4321–4370d.
3. *Robertson v. Methow Valley Citizens' Council*, 490 U.S. 332, 109 S.Ct. 1835, 104 L.Ed.2d 351 (1989).

■ **Exhibit 20–I Federal Environmental Statutes**

POPULAR NAME	PURPOSE	STATUTE REFERENCE
Rivers and Harbors Appropriations Act (1899)	To prohibit ships and manufacturers from discharging and depositing refuse in navigable waterways.	33 U.S.C. Sections 401–418.
Federal Insecticide, Fungicide, and Rodenticide Act (FIFRA) (1947)	To control the use of pesticides and herbicides.	7 U.S.C. Sections 136–136y.
Federal Water Pollution Control Act (FWPCA) (1948)	To eliminate the discharge of pollutants from major sources into navigable waters.	33 U.S.C. Sections 1251–1387.
Atomic Energy Act (1954)	To eliminate evironmental harm from the private nuclear industry.	42 U.S.C. Sections 2011 to 2297g-4.
Clean Air Act (1963)	To control air pollution from mobile and stationary sources.	42 U.S.C. Sections 7401–7671q.
National Environmental Policy Act (NEPA) (1969)	To limit environmental harm from federal government activities.	42 U.S.C. Sections 4321–4370d.
Marine Protection, Research, and Sanctuaries Act (Ocean Dumping Act) of 1972	To regulate the transporting and dumping of material into ocean waters.	16 U.S.C. Sections 1401–1445.
Noise Control Act (1972)	To regulate noise pollution from transportation and nontransportation sources.	42 U.S.C. Sections 4901–4918.
Endangered Species Act (1973)	To protect species that are threatened with extinction.	16 U.S.C. Sections 1531–1544.
Safe Drinking Water Act (1974)	To regulate pollutants in public drinking water systems.	42 U.S.C. Sections 300f to 300j-25.
Resource Conservation and Recovery Act (RCRA) (1976)	To establish standards for hazardous waste disposal.	42 U.S.C. Sections 6901–6986.
Toxic Substances Control Act (1976)	To regulate toxic chemicals and chemical compounds.	15 U.S.C. Sections 2601–2692.
Comprehensive Environmental Response, Compensation, and Liability Act (CERCLA) (Superfund) (1980)	To regulate the clean-up of hazardous waste–disposal sites.	42 U.S.C. Sections 9601–9675.
Low Level Radioactive Waste Policy Act (1980)	To assign to the states responsibility for nuclear power plants' low-level radioactive waste.	42 U.S.C. Sections 2021b–2021j.
Nuclear Waste Policy Act (1982)	To provide for the designation of a permanent radioactive waste–disposal site.	42 U.S.C. Sections 10101–10270.
Oil Pollution Act (1990)	To establish liability for the clean-up of nagivable waters after oil-spill disasters.	33 U.S.C. Sections 2701–2761.

requires a federal permit,[4] or constructing a dam as part of a federal project would require an EIS.[5] If an agency decides that an EIS is unnecessary, it must issue a statement supporting this conclusion.

An EIS must analyze (1) the impact on the environment that the action will have, (2) any adverse effects on the environment and alternative actions that might be taken, and (3) irreversible effects the action might generate. EISs have become instruments for private citizens, consumer interest groups, businesses, and others to challenge federal agency actions on the basis that the actions improperly threaten the environment.

Other federal laws also require that environmental values be considered in agency decision making. Among the most important of these laws are those that have been enacted to protect fish and wildlife. Under the Fish and Wildlife Coordination Act of 1958,[6] federal agencies proposing to approve the impounding or diversion of the waters of a stream must consult with the Fish and Wildlife Service with a view to preventing the loss of fish and wildlife resources. Also important is the Endangered Species Act of 1973.[7] Under this act, all federal agencies are required to take steps to ensure that their actions "do not jeopardize the continued existence of endangered species" or the habitat of an endangered species. An action may jeopardize the continued existence

4. *Calvert Cliffs Coordinating Committee v. Atomic Energy Commission,* 449 F.2d 1109 (D.C. Cir. 1971).
5. *Marsh v. Oregon Natural Resources Council,* 490 U.S. 360, 109 S.Ct. 1851, 104 L.Ed.2d 377 (1989).
6. 16 U.S.C. Sections 661–666c.
7. 16 U.S.C. Sections 1531–1544.

International Perspective

Today's business managers can no longer afford to ignore the effect of their decisions on the environment. This is true not only in the United States but in other countries around the globe as well. As discussed in Chapter 2, those companies that engage in activities harmful to the environment may be subject to negative sanctions (criticism in the press, boycotts, and so on) for their "ethically irresponsible" behavior.

To guide companies in their attempts to be environmentally responsible, the Geneva-based International Organization for Standardization has created fourteen thousand universally applicable standards for the development of environmental management systems. The standards are the outgrowth of the nine thousand quality management and quality assurance standards published by the organization in 1987. The nine thousand standards

achieved wide acceptance in the United States, Europe, and Asia.

The standards are not regulatory in nature and do not impose any restrictions on polluting activities. Rather, they offer a variety of management tools and devices to help companies perform their environmental obligations. Essentially, the standards set forth a series of recommendations on how a company can establish an effective and totally integrated environmental management system. The standards reflect the commercial reality that firms doing business internationally, because they are subject to different national environmental laws, need a consistent set of environmental standards to guide them.

For Critical Analysis: *Why don't the standards impose restrictions on polluting activities?*

of a species if it sets in motion a chain of events that reduces the chances that the species will survive.

Air Pollution

Federal involvement with air pollution goes back to the 1950s, when Congress authorized funds for air-pollution research. In 1963, the federal government passed the Clean Air Act,[8] which focused on multistate air pollution and provided assistance to states. Various amendments, particularly in 1970, 1977, and 1990, strengthened the government's authority to regulate the quality of air. These laws provide the basis for issuing regulations to control pollution coming primarily from mobile sources (such as automobiles) and stationary sources (such as electric utilities and industrial plants).

Mobile Sources

Regulations governing air pollution from automobiles and other mobile sources specify pollution standards and time schedules for meeting the standards. For example, the 1970 Clean Air Act required a reduction of 90 percent in the amount of carbon monoxide and other pollutants emitted by automobiles by 1975. (This did not happen, however, and the 1977 amendments extended the deadline to 1983. Generally, automobile manufacturers met the 90 percent reduction goal by installing catalytic converters on automobiles.)

Under the 1990 amendments, automobile manufacturers must cut new automobiles' exhaust emission of nitrogen oxide by 60 percent and emission

---

8. 42 U.S.C. Sections 7401–7671q.

Who suffers the harm when automobiles pollute? Who pays the price to reduce automobile pollution? Who should pay?

of other pollutants by 35 percent. By 1998, all new automobiles had to meet these standards. Another set of emission controls may be ordered after 2000. To ensure compliance, the EPA certifies the prototype of a new automobile whose emission controls are effective up to 50,000 miles. The EPA may also inspect production models. If a vehicle does not meet the standards in actual driving, the EPA can order a recall and the repair or replacement of pollution-control equipment at the manufacturer's expense.

Service stations are also subject to environmental regulations. The 1990 amendments require service stations to sell gasoline with a higher oxygen content in forty-one cities that experience carbon monoxide pollution in the winter. Service stations are required to sell even cleaner-burning gasoline in Los Angeles and another eight of the most polluted urban areas.

The EPA attempts to update pollution-control standards when new scientific information becomes available. In light of purported evidence that very small particles (2.5 microns, or millionths of a meter) of soot affect our health as significantly as larger particles, the EPA issued new particulate standards for motor vehicle exhaust systems and other sources of pollution. The EPA also decreased the acceptable standard for ozone, which is formed when sunlight combines with pollutants from cars and other sources. Ozone is the basic ingredient of smog.[9]

Stationary Sources

The Clean Air Act authorizes the EPA to establish air-quality standards for stationary sources (such as manufacturing plants) but recognizes that the primary responsibility for preventing and controlling air pollution rests with state and local governments. The EPA sets primary and secondary levels of ambient standards—that is, the maximum levels of certain pollutants—and the states formulate plans to achieve those standards. The plans are to provide for the attainment of primary standards within three years and secondary standards within a reasonable time. For economic, political, and technological reasons, however, the deadlines are often subject to change.

Different standards apply to sources of pollution in clean areas and sources in polluted areas. Different standards also apply to existing sources of pollution and major new sources. Major new sources include existing sources modified by a change in a method of operation that increases emissions. Performance standards for major sources require use of the *maximum achievable control technology*, or MACT, to reduce emissions from the combustion of fossil fuels (coal and oil). The EPA issues guidelines as to what equipment meets this standard.

Under the 1990 amendments to the Clean Air Act, 110 of the oldest coal-burning power plants in the United States must cut their emissions by 40 percent by the year 2001 to reduce acid rain. Utilities were granted "credits" to emit certain amounts of sulfur dioxide, and those that emit less than the allowed amounts can sell their credits to other polluters. Controls on other factories and businesses are intended to reduce ground-level ozone pollution in ninety-six cities to healthful levels by 2005 (except Los Angeles, which has until 2010). Industrial emissions of 189 hazardous air pollutants must be reduced by 90 percent by 2000. By 2002, the production of chlorofluorocarbons (such as Freon), carbon tetrachloride, and methyl chloroform—used in

---

9. In 1997, President Clinton approved these regulations.

air conditioning, refrigeration, and insulation and linked to depletion of the ozone layer—must stop.

Hazardous Air Pollutants

Hazardous air pollutants are those likely to cause an increase in mortality or in serious irreversible or incapacitating illness. As noted, there are 189 of these pollutants, including asbestos, benzene, beryllium, cadmium, mercury, and vinyl chloride. These pollutants may cause cancer as well as neurological and reproductive damage. They are emitted from stationary sources by a variety of business activities, including smelting, dry cleaning, house painting, and commercial baking. Instead of establishing specific emissions standards for each hazardous air pollutant, the 1990 amendments to the Clean Air Act require industry to use pollution-control equipment that represents the maximum achievable control technology, or MACT, to limit emissions. The EPA issues guidelines as to what equipment meets this standard.

In recent years, the EPA has become increasingly concerned with the hazardous air pollutants emitted by landfills. In the past, when environmental regulators considered the pollution caused by landfilling, they generally focused only on groundwater contamination. By the 1990s, however, it had become apparent that emissions (such as toxic gases) from landfills, including hazardous air pollutants, constituted a significant source of air pollution. In 1996, the EPA issued a new rule to regulate these emissions. The rule requires landfills constructed after May 30, 1991, that emit more than a specified amount of pollutants to install landfill gas collection and control systems. The rule also requires the states to impose the same requirements on landfills constructed before May 30, 1991, if they accepted waste after November 8, 1987.[10]

Violations of the Clean Air Act

For violations of emission limits under the Clean Air Act, the EPA can assess civil penalties of up to $25,000 per day. Additional fines of up to $5,000 per day can be assessed for other violations, such as failing to maintain the required records. To penalize those for whom it is more cost effective to violate the act than to comply with it, the EPA is authorized to obtain a penalty equal to the violator's economic benefits from noncompliance. Persons who provide information about violators may be paid up to $10,000. Private citizens can also sue violators.

Those who knowingly violate the act may be subject to criminal penalties, including fines of up to $1 million and imprisonment for up to two years (for false statements or failures to report violations). Corporate officers are among those who may be subject to these penalties.

⬤ Water Pollution

▼ Federal regulations governing the pollution of water can be traced back to the Rivers and Harbors Appropriations Act of 1899.[11] These regulations prohibited

> "Among the treasures of our land is water—fast becoming our most valuable, most prized, most critical resource."
>
> Dwight D. Eisenhower, 1890–1969 (Thirty-fourth president of the United States, 1953–1961)

---

10. 40 C.F.R. Sections 60.750–759.
11. 33 U.S.C. Sections 401–418.

ships and manufacturers from discharging or depositing refuse in navigable waterways.

Navigable Waters

Once limited to waters actually used for navigation, the term *navigable waters* is today interpreted to include coastal and freshwater wetlands (how the EPA defines wetlands will be discussed shortly), as well as intrastate lakes and streams used by interstate travelers and industries. In 1948, Congress passed the Federal Water Pollution Control Act (FWPCA),[12] but its regulatory system and enforcement proved inadequate. In 1972, amendments to the FWPCA—known as the Clean Water Act—established the following goals: (1) make waters safe for swimming, (2) protect fish and wildlife, and (3) eliminate the discharge of pollutants into the water. The amendments required that municipal and industrial polluters apply for permits before discharging wastes into navigable waters.

They also set forth specific time schedules, which were extended by amendment in 1977 and by the Water Quality Act of 1987.[13] Under these schedules, the EPA establishes limitations for discharges of types of pollutants based on the technology available for controlling them. Regulations, for the most part, specify that the *best available control technology*, or BACT, be installed. The EPA issues guidelines as to what equipment meets this standard, which essentially requires the most effective pollution-control equipment available. New sources must install BACT equipment before beginning operations. Existing sources are subject to timetables for installation of BACT equipment. These sources must immediately install equipment that utilizes the *best practical control technology*, or BPCT. The EPA also issues guidelines as to what equipment meets this standard.

---

12. 33 U.S.C. Sections 1251–1387.
13. This act amended 33 U.S.C. Section 1251.

A scientist tests water from an industrial source that has been cleaned of pollutants. How "clean" should such water be before it is released into the environment?

WETLANDS. The Clean Water Act prohibits the filling or dredging of **wetlands** unless a permit is obtained from the Army Corps of Engineers. The EPA defines wetlands as "those areas that are inundated or saturated by surface or ground water at a frequency and duration sufficient to support, and that under normal circumstances do support, a prevalence of vegetation typically adapted for life in saturated soil conditions." In recent years, federal regulatory policy in regard to wetlands has elicited substantial controversy because of the broad interpretation of what constitutes a wetland subject to the regulatory authority of the federal government. The following case is illustrative.

Wetlands Areas of land designated by government agencies (such as the Army Corps of Engineers or the Environmental Protection Agency) as protected areas that support wildlife and that therefore cannot be filled in or dredged by private contractors or parties.

Case 20.2 ● Hoffman Homes, Inc. v. Administrator, United States Environmental Protection Agency

United States Court of Appeals, Seventh Circuit, 1993.
999 F.2d 256.

COMPANY PROFILE *Sam and Jack Hoffman started F&S Construction in 1947. Over the next few years, the company—renamed the Hoffman Group—built thousands of low-priced houses throughout the United States, becoming the nation's third largest builder by 1955. Norman Hassinger, a residential marketing expert, became president of the Hoffman Group in 1982 and gradually took over the firm. In 1987, the Hoffman Group became the Hassinger Companies. Hassinger created Hoffman Homes, Inc., as a home-building subsidiary.*

BACKGROUND AND FACTS Hoffman Homes, Inc., in preparation for the construction of a housing subdivision, filled and graded a 0.8-acre, bowl-shaped depression ("Area A"). Before Hoffman filled Area A, rainwater periodically collected there. The EPA issued an order stating that Hoffman had filled wetlands without a permit in violation of the Clean Water Act and ordered Hoffman to, among other things, cease its filling activities and pay a fine of $50,000 for violating the act. Hoffman protested that the EPA had no regulatory authority over Area A because the area in no way affected interstate commerce. The EPA stated that it had authority to regulate discharges of fill materials into intrastate wetlands that have a "minimal, potential effect" on interstate commerce and that Area A had such an effect because migratory birds could potentially use the area. Hoffman appealed the decision to the Seventh Circuit Court of Appeals.

IN THE WORDS OF THE COURT . . .
HARLINGTON WOOD, Senior Circuit Judge.

* * * *

* * * It is true, of course, that migratory birds can alight most anywhere. As [a witness] testified, he has seen mallards in parking lot puddles. The ALJ [administrative law judge of the EPA], however, was in the unique position to view the evidence, to hear the testimony, and to judge the credibility of the witnesses. He concluded that the evidence did not support the conclusion that Area A had characteristics whose use by and value to migratory birds is well established. We agree. The migratory birds are better judges of what is suitable for their welfare than are we [or anyone at the EPA]. Having avoided Area A the migratory birds have thus spoken and submitted their own evidence. We see no need to argue with them. No justification whatsoever is seen from the evidence to interfere with private ownership based on what appears to be no more than a well intentioned effort in these particular factual circumstances to expand government control beyond reasonable or practical limits. After April showers not every temporary wet spot necessarily becomes subject to government control.

(Continued)

Case 20.2—continued

DECISION AND REMEDY   The court, holding that Area A was not subject to regulation under the Clean Water Act, vacated the EPA's order requiring Hoffman Homes to pay a $50,000 administrative penalty for the filling of Area A.

FOR CRITICAL ANALYSIS—POLITICAL CONSIDERATION   *In evaluating cases concerning wetlands, does it matter that the EPA, and not Congress, defines specifically what constitutes a "wetland"?*

VIOLATIONS OF THE CLEAN WATER ACT.   Under the Clean Water Act, violators are subject to a variety of civil and criminal penalties. Civil penalties for each violation range from a maximum of $10,000 per day, and not more than $25,000 per violation, to as much as $25,000 per day. Criminal penalties range from a fine of $2,500 per day and imprisonment for up to one year to a fine of $1 million and fifteen years' imprisonment. Injunctive relief and damages can also be imposed. The polluting party can be required to clean up the pollution or pay for the cost of doing so. Criminal penalties apply only if a violation was intentional.

Drinking Water

Another statute governing water pollution is the Safe Drinking Water Act.[14] Passed in 1974, this act requires the EPA to set maximum levels for pollutants in public water systems. Operators of public water supply systems must come as close as possible to meeting the EPA's standards by using the best available technology that is economically and technologically feasible. The EPA is particularly concerned with contamination from underground sources. Pesticides and wastes leaked from landfills or disposed of in underground injection wells are among the more than two hundred pollutants known to exist in groundwater used for drinking in at least thirty-four states. Many of these substances are associated with cancer and damage to the central nervous system, liver, and kidneys.

The act was amended in 1996 to give the EPA greater flexibility in setting regulatory standards governing drinking water. Prior to the 1996 amendments, the EPA had to set standards for twenty-five different drinking water contaminants every three years, which it had largely failed to do. Under the 1996 amendments, the EPA can move at whatever rate it deems necessary to control contaminants that are of greatest concern to the public health. The 1996 amendments also imposed new requirements on suppliers of drinking water. Each supplier must send to every household it supplies with water an annual statement describing the source of its water, the level of any contaminants contained in the water, and any possible health concerns associated with the contaminants.

Ocean Dumping

The Marine Protection, Research, and Sanctuaries Act of 1972[15] (known popularly as the Ocean Dumping Act) regulates the transportation and dumping of material into ocean waters. (The term *material* is synonymous with the term *pollutant* as used in the Federal Water Pollution Control Act.) The Ocean

---

14. 42 U.S.C. Sections 300f to 300j-25.
15. 16 U.S.C. Sections 1401–1445.

Dumping Act prohibits entirely the ocean dumping of radiological, chemical, and biological warfare agents and high-level radioactive waste. The act establishes a permit program for transporting and dumping other materials. There are specific exemptions—materials subject to the permit provisions of other pollution legislation, wastes from structures regulated by other laws (for example, offshore oil exploration and drilling platforms), sewage, and other wastes. The Ocean Dumping Act also authorizes the designation of marine sanctuaries for "preserving or restoring such areas for their conservation, recreational, ecological, or esthetic values."

Each violation of any provision or permit may result in a civil penalty of not more than $50,000 or revocation or suspension of the permit. A knowing violation is a criminal offense that may result in a $50,000 fine, imprisonment for not more than a year, or both. An injunction may also be imposed.

Oil Pollution

In 1989, the supertanker *Exxon Valdez* caused the worst oil spill in North American history in the waters of Alaska's Prince William Sound. A quarter of a million barrels of crude oil—more than ten million gallons—leaked out of the ship's broken hull. In response to the *Exxon Valdez* oil-spill disaster, Congress passed the Oil Pollution Act of 1990.[16] Any onshore or offshore oil facility, oil shipper, vessel owner, or vessel operator that discharges oil into navigable waters or onto an adjoining shore may be liable for clean-up costs, as well as damages. The act created a $1 billion oil clean-up and economic compensation fund and decreed that by the year 2011, oil tankers using U.S. ports must be double hulled to limit the severity of accidental spills.

Under the act, damage to natural resources, private property, and the local economy, including the increased cost of providing public services, is compensable. The act provides for civil penalties of $1,000 per barrel spilled or $25,000 for each day of the violation. The party held responsible for the clean-up costs can bring a civil suit for contribution from other potentially liable parties.

Noise Pollution

Regulations concerning noise pollution include the Noise Control Act of 1972.[17] This act requires the EPA to establish noise emission standards (maximum noise levels below which no harmful effects occur from interference with speech or other activity)—for example, for railroad noise emissions. The standards must be achievable by the best available technology, and they must be economically within reason.

The act prohibits, among other things, distributing products manufactured in violation of the noise emission standards and tampering with noise control devices. Either of these activities can result in an injunction or whatever other remedy "is necessary to protect the public health and welfare." Illegal product distribution can also result in a fine and imprisonment. Violations of provisions of the Noise Control Act can result in penalties of not more than $50,000 per day and imprisonment for not more than two years.

---

16. 33 U.S.C. Sections 2701–2761.
17. 42 U.S.C. Sections 4901–4918.

> "All property in this country is held under the implied obligation that the owner's use of it shall not be injurious to the community."
>
> John Harlan, 1899–1971
> (Associate justice of the United States Supreme Court, 1955–1971)

Toxic Chemicals

Originally, most environmental clean-up efforts were directed toward reducing smog and making water safe for fishing and swimming. Over time, however, control of toxic chemicals has become an important part of environmental law.

Pesticides and Herbicides

The first toxic chemical problem to receive widespread public attention was that posed by pesticides and herbicides. Using these chemicals to kill insects and weeds has increased agricultural productivity, but their residue remains in the environment. In some instances, accumulations of this residue have killed animals, and scientists have identified potential long-term effects that are detrimental to people.

FEDERAL INSECTICIDE, FUNGICIDE, AND RODENTICIDE ACT (FIFRA).   The federal statute regulating pesticides and herbicides is the Federal Insecticide, Fungicide, and Rodenticide Act (FIFRA) of 1947.[18] Under FIFRA, pesticides and herbicides must be (1) registered before they can be sold, (2) certified and used only for approved applications, and (3) used in limited quantities when applied to food crops. If a substance is identified as harmful, the EPA can cancel its registration after a hearing. If the harm is imminent, the EPA can suspend registration pending the hearing. The EPA, or state officers or employees, may also inspect factories in which these chemicals are manufactured.

Under 1996 amendments to the Federal Food, Drug and Cosmetic Act, for a pesticide to remain on the market, there must be a "reasonable certainty of no harm" to people from exposure to the pesticide.[19] This means that there must be no more than a one-in-a-million risk to people of developing cancer from exposure in any way, including eating food that contains residues from the pesticide. Pesticide residues are in nearly all fruits and vegetables and processed foods. Under the 1996 amendments, the EPA must distribute to grocery stores brochures on high-risk pesticides that are in food, and the stores must display these brochures for consumers.

VIOLATIONS OF FIFRA.   It is a violation of FIFRA to sell a pesticide or herbicide that is unregistered, a pesticide or herbicide with a registration that has been canceled or suspended, or a pesticide or herbicide with a false or misleading label. For example, it is an offense to sell a substance that is adulterated (that has a chemical strength different from the concentration declared on the label). It is also an offense to destroy or deface any labeling required under the act. The act's labeling requirements include directions for the use of the pesticide or herbicide, warnings to protect human health and the environment, a statement of treatment in the case of poisoning, and a list of the ingredients.

A private party can petition the EPA to suspend or cancel the registration of a pesticide or herbicide. If the EPA fails to act, the private party can petition a federal court to review the EPA's failure. Penalties for registrants and

---

18. 7 U.S.C. Sections 136–136y.
19. 21 U.S.C. Section 346a.

producers for violating FIFRA include imprisonment for up to one year and a fine of no more than $50,000. Penalties for commercial dealers include imprisonment for up to one year and a fine of no more than $25,000. Farmers and other private users of pesticides or herbicides who violate the act are subject to a $1,000 fine and imprisonment for up to thirty days.

Toxic Substances

The first comprehensive law covering toxic substances was the Toxic Substances Control Act of 1976.[20] The act was passed to regulate chemicals and chemical compounds that are known to be toxic—such as asbestos and polychlorinated biphenyls, popularly known as PCBs—and to institute investigation of any possible harmful effects from new chemical compounds. The regulations authorize the EPA to require that manufacturers, processors, and other organizations planning to use chemicals first determine their effects on human health and the environment. The EPA can regulate substances that may pose an imminent hazard or an unreasonable risk of injury to health or the environment. The EPA may require special labeling, limit the use of a substance, set production quotas, or prohibit the use of a substance altogether.

Hazardous Wastes

Some industrial, agricultural, and household wastes pose more serious threats than others. If not properly disposed of, these toxic chemicals may present a substantial danger to human health and the environment. If released into the environment, they may contaminate public drinking water resources.

RESOURCE CONSERVATION AND RECOVERY ACT.   In 1976, Congress passed the Resource Conservation and Recovery Act (RCRA)[21] in reaction to an ever-increasing concern with the effects of hazardous waste materials on the environment. The RCRA required the EPA to establish regulations to monitor and control hazardous waste disposal and to determine which forms of solid waste should be considered hazardous and thus subject to regulation. The act authorized the EPA to promulgate various technical requirements for some types of facilities for storage and treatment of hazardous waste. The act also requires all producers of hazardous waste materials to label and package properly any hazardous waste to be transported.

> **BE CAREFUL** Under the Resource Conservation and Recovery Act, anyone who generates, treats, stores, or transports hazardous waste must obtain a permit.

The RCRA was amended in 1984 and 1986 to decrease the use of land containment in the disposal of hazardous waste and to require compliance with the act by some generators of hazardous waste—such as those generating less than 1,000 kilograms (2,200 pounds) a month—that had previously been excluded from regulation under the RCRA.

Under the RCRA, a company may be assessed a civil penalty based on the seriousness of the violation, the probability of harm, and the extent to which the violation deviates from RCRA requirements. The assessment may be up to $25,000 for each violation. Criminal penalties include fines up to $50,000 for each day of violation, imprisonment for up to two years (in most instances), or both. Criminal fines and the time of imprisonment can be doubled for certain repeat offenders.

---

20. 15 U.S.C. Sections 2601–2692.
21. 42 U.S.C. Sections 6901–6986.

SUPERFUND. In 1980, Congress passed the Comprehensive Environmental Response, Compensation, and Liability Act (CERCLA),[22] commonly known as Superfund. The basic purpose of Superfund is to regulate the clean-up of disposal sites in which hazardous waste is leaking into the environment. A special federal fund was created for that purpose. Because of its impact on the business community, the act is presented as this chapter's *Landmark in the Legal Environment.*

---

22. 42 U.S.C. Sections 9601–9675.

Landmark in the Legal Environment
Superfund

The origins of the Comprehensive Environmental Response, Compensation, and Liability Act (CERCLA) of 1980, which is commonly referred to as Superfund, can be traced to drafts that the Environmental Protection Agency (EPA) started to circulate in 1978. EPA officials emphasized the political necessity of new legislation by pointing to what they thought were "ticking time bombs"—dump sites around the country that were ready to explode and injure the public with toxic fumes.

The popular press also gave prominence to hazardous waste dump sites at the time. The New York Love Canal disaster began to make the headlines in 1978 after residents in the area complained about health problems, contaminated sludge oozing into their basements, and chemical "volcanoes" erupting in their yards as a result of Hooker Chemical's dumping of approximately 21,000 tons of chemicals into the canal from 1942 to 1953. The Love Canal situation made the national news virtually every day from the middle of May to the middle of June in 1980.

The basic purpose of CERCLA, which was amended in 1986 by the Superfund Amendments and Reauthorization Act, is to regulate the clean-up of leaking hazardous waste–disposal sites. The act has four primary elements:

A warning to trespassers is posted at a hazardous waste site. Who should pay the cost of cleaning up the site?

- It established an information-gathering and analysis system that allows federal and state governments to characterize chemical dump sites and to develop priorities for appropriate action.
- It authorized the EPA to respond to hazardous substance emergencies and to clean up leaking sites directly through contractors or through cooperative agreements with the states if the persons responsible for the problem fail to clean up the site.
- It created a Hazardous Substance Response Trust Fund (Superfund) to pay for the clean-up of hazardous sites.

Monies for the fund are obtained through taxes on certain businesses, including those processing or producing petroleum and chemical feed stock.
- It allowed the government to recover the cost of clean-up from the persons who were (even remotely) responsible for hazardous substance releases.

For Critical Analysis: *Must all of the contamination be removed from a hazardous waste site to ensure that it no longer poses any threat of harm to life? Would some lesser amount satisfy a reasonable degree of environmental quality?*

Potentially Responsible Parties   Superfund provides that when a release or a threatened release of hazardous chemicals from a site occurs, the EPA can clean up the site and recover the cost of the clean-up from the following persons: (1) the person who generated the wastes disposed of at the site, (2) the person who transported the wastes to the site, (3) the person who owned or operated the site at the time of the disposal, or (4) the current owner or operator. A person falling within one of these categories is referred to as a **potentially responsible party (PRP)**.

Liability under Superfund is usually joint and several—that is, a PRP who generated only a fraction of the hazardous waste disposed of at the site may nevertheless be liable for all of the clean-up costs. CERCLA authorizes a party who has incurred clean-up costs to bring a "contribution action" against any other person who is liable or potentially liable for a percentage of the costs.

Courts often focus on the meaning of the words "owner or operator" to determine who is a PRP. In one case, a parent company was held liable as an "operator" for clean-up costs for a chemical spill at a plant owned by its subsidiary. The court pointed out that the parent company controlled the subsidiary's finances, real estate transactions, and contact with the government and that the parent company's personnel held most of the subsidiary's officer and director positions.[23] In other cases, courts have held officers and shareholders liable based on their authority to exercise control over their corporations.[24] In the following case, the court considers whether a corporation can be held liable under CERCLA.

Potentially Responsible Party (PRP) A liable party under the Comprehensive Environmental Response, Compensation, and Liability Act (CERCLA). Any person who generated the hazardous waste, transported the hazardous waste, owned or operated a waste site at the time of disposal, or currently owns or operates a site may be responsible for some or all of the clean-up costs involved in removing the hazardous chemicals.

---

23. *United States v. Kayser-Roth Corp.*, 910 F.2d 24 (1st Cir. 1990).
24. See, for example, *State of New York v. Shore Realty Corp.*, 759 F.2d 1032 (2d Cir. 1985).

Case 20.3 ● B. F. Goodrich Co. v. Betkoski

United States Court of Appeals, Second Circuit, 1996.
99 F.3d 505.

BACKGROUND AND FACTS   Terrance and Harold Murtha owned and operated two landfill sites used for the disposal of hazardous substances. The EPA and the state of Connecticut cleaned up the sites and then filed suits in a federal district court to recover the costs from the Murthas and other potentially responsible parties who gen-erated or transported hazardous substances to the sites. Many of the parties, including the Murthas and B. F. Goodrich Company, agreed to, among other things, pay a share of the costs. These parties joined the EPA and the state of Connecticut in a suit against John Betkoski and eighty-seven other defendants who refused to pay. The defendants filed motions for summary judgment, which the court granted, in part based on its decisions concerning successor liability. The plaintiffs appealed.

IN THE WORDS OF THE COURT . . .
CARDAMONE, Circuit Judge:
* * * *

[CERCLA's] broad remedial purpose would be sharply curtailed if the Act did not encompass successor liability. * * * [A]bsent successor liability, a predecessor could benefit from the illegal disposal of hazardous substances and later evade responsibility for remediation simply by changing the form in which it does business, thereby subverting the Act's purpose of holding responsible parties liable for cleanup costs. * * *

(Continued)

Case 20.3—continued

* * * The traditional common law rule states that a corporation acquiring the assets of another corporation * * * takes on its liabilities if * * * the successor is a "mere continuation" of the predecessor * * * .

The [defendants] contend that when determining whether there is a "mere continuation," we should not use the common law test * * * , which requires the existence of a single corporation after the transfer of assets, with an identity of stock, stockholders, and directors between the successor and predecessor corporations. Rather, they urge that we employ the "continuity of enterprise" approach, * * * [under which liability depends on whether] the successor maintains the same business, with the same employees doing the same jobs, under the same supervisors, working conditions, and production processes, and produces the same products for the same customers.

* * * [T]he substantial continuity test is more consistent with the Act's goals * * * . We therefore adopt the substantial continuity test as the appropriate legal test for successor liability under CERCLA.

DECISION AND REMEDY   The U.S. Court of Appeals for the Second Circuit reversed the trial court's grant of summary judgment to those defendants who were successor corporations. The plaintiffs could proceed with their case.

FOR CRITICAL ANALYSIS—POLITICAL CONSIDERATION   *Why are there* any *limits as to who may be liable under CERCLA?*

Liability of Lending Institutions and Fiduciaries   In recent years, courts have wrestled with the question of whether lending institutions can be held liable for toxic waste on property they hold as collateral for their loans. Some courts followed the lead of the Court of Appeals for the Eleventh Circuit, which held in 1990 that a bank can be held liable as a PRP if the bank has the "capacity to influence" a borrower's decisions about toxic waste.[25] Other courts held to the contrary. In one case, the court held that to impose liability on a bank for involving itself in the debtor's affairs would be to "punish the Bank for engaging in its normal course of business."[26] To clarify this issue, Congress amended CERCLA in 1996 to provide that banks and other lenders can be held liable under CERCLA for property they hold as collateral only if they actually participate in the management or operational affairs of the borrower.[27]

Another issue on which the courts disagreed was whether certain fiduciaries, such as trustees and executors of estates, could be held liable as PRPs. In at least one case, a federal court held that a trustee could be personally liable for those costs of cleaning up a hazardous waste site that exceeded the value of the trust's assets.[28] The 1996 amendments also addressed this issue by stating that a fiduciary can only be held personally liable as a PRP in limited circumstances—such as when the hazardous waste pollution is caused by the fiduciary's own negligence.[29]

---

25. *United States v. Fleet Factors Corp.*, 901 F.2d 1550 (11th Cir. 1990).
26. *Z & Z Leasing, Inc. v. Graying Reel, Inc.*, 873 F.Supp. 51 (E.D.Mich. 1995).
27. 42 U.S.C. Section 9601.
28. *Phoenix v. Garbage Services Co.*, 816 F.Supp. 564 (D.Ariz. 1993).
29. 42 U.S.C. Section 9607.

Radiation

Nuclear power plants are built and operated by private industry. The nuclear industry is regulated almost exclusively by the federal government under the Atomic Energy Act of 1954.[30] The Nuclear Regulatory Commission (NRC) is the federal agency responsible for regulating the private nuclear industry. The NRC reviews the plans for each proposed nuclear plant and issues a construction permit only after preparing an environmental impact statement that considers the impact of an accidental release of radiation. After construction, the NRC licenses the plant's operation.

The Environmental Protection Agency sets standards for radioactivity in the overall environment and for the disposal of some radioactive waste. Low-level radioactive waste generated by private facilities is the responsibility of each state under the Low Level Radioactive Waste Policy Act of 1980.[31] The NRC regulates the use and disposal of other nuclear materials and radioactive waste. Some radioactive waste is buried, burned, or dumped in the ocean. Currently, however, most of it is stored at the plants in which it is produced. Under the Nuclear Waste Policy Act of 1982,[32] the government is looking for a permanent disposal site scheduled to be opened in the year 2000.

A common law theory may serve as the basis for liability for harms caused by radiation. For example, in one case, the court held that the party creating a radiation hazard is strictly liable in tort for its clean-up and any damages.[33] Liability for injury resulting from radiation may also arise under one of the statutes discussed elsewhere in this chapter. For example, the release of radioactive materials into the environment may violate the Clean Water Act, the RCRA, or the CERCLA.[34]

State and Local Regulation

Many states regulate the degree to which the environment may be polluted. Thus, for example, even when state zoning laws permit a business's proposed development, the proposal may have to be altered to change the development's impact on the environment. State laws may restrict a business's discharge of chemicals into the air or water or regulate its disposal of toxic wastes. States may also regulate the disposal or recycling of other wastes, including glass, metal, and plastic containers and paper. Additionally, states may restrict the emissions from motor vehicles.

City, county, and other local governments control some aspects of the environment. For instance, local zoning laws control some land use. These laws may be designed to inhibit or direct the growth of cities and suburbs or to protect the natural environment. Other aspects of the environment may be subject to local regulation for other reasons. Methods of waste and garbage removal and disposal, for example, can have a substantial impact on a community. The

---

30. 42 U.S.C. Sections 2011 to 2297g-4.
31. 42 U.S.C. Sections 2021b–2021j.
32. 42 U.S.C. Sections 10101–10270.
33. *T&E Industries, Inc. v. Safety Light Corp.*, 123 N.J. 371, 587 A.2d 1249 (1991).
34. See, for example, *Ohio v. Department of Energy*, 904 F.2d 1058 (6th Cir. 1990).

appearance of buildings and other structures, including advertising signs and billboards, may affect traffic safety, property values, or local aesthetics. Noise generated by a business or its customers may be annoying, disruptive, or damaging to its neighbors. The location and condition of parks, streets, and other public uses of land subject to local control affect the environment and can also affect business.

Key Terms

environmental impact
    statement (EIS) 556
environmental law 554
nuisance 554

potentially responsible party
    (PRP) 569

toxic tort 556
wetlands 563

Chapter Summary
Protecting the Environment

COMMON LAW ACTIONS (See pages 554–556.)	1. **Nuisance**—A common law doctrine under which actions against pollution-causing activities may be brought. An action is permissible only if an individual suffers a harm separate and distinct from that of the general public.
	2. **Negligence and strict liability**—Parties may recover damages for injuries sustained as a result of pollution-causing activities of a firm if it can be demonstrated that the harm was a foreseeable result of the firm's failure to exercise reasonable care (negligence); businesses engaging in ultrahazardous activities are liable for whatever injuries the activities cause, regardless of whether the firms exercise reasonable care.
STATE AND LOCAL REGULATION (See pages 571–572.)	Activities affecting the environment are controlled at the local and state levels through regulations relating to land use, the disposal and recycling of garbage and waste, and pollution-causing activities in general.
FEDERAL REGULATION (See pages 556–571.)	The National Environmental Policy Act of 1969 imposes environmental responsibilities on all federal agencies and requires for every major federal action the preparation of an environmental impact statement (EIS). An EIS must analyze the action's impact on the environment, its adverse effects and possible alternatives, and its irreversible effects on environmental quality. The Environmental Protection Agency was created in 1970 to coordinate federal environmental programs; it administers most federal environmental policies and statutes. Important areas regulated by the federal government include the following:
	1. **Air pollution**—Regulated under the authority of the Clean Air Act of 1963 and its amendments, particularly those of 1970, 1977, and 1990.
	2. **Water pollution**—Regulated under the authority of the Rivers and Harbors Appropriations Act of 1899, as amended, and the Federal Water Pollution Control Act of 1948, as amended by the Clean Water Act of 1972.
	3. **Noise pollution**—Regulated by the Noise Control Act of 1972.

(Continued)

Chapter Summary, continued

**FEDERAL REGULATION—
continued**
(See pages 556–571.)

4. **Toxic chemicals**—Pesticides and herbicides, toxic substances, and hazardous waste are regulated under the authority of the Federal Insecticide, Fungicide, and Rodenticide Act of 1947, the Toxic Substances Control Act of 1976, and the Resource Conservation and Recovery Act of 1976, respectively. The Comprehensive Environmental Response, Compensation, and Liability Act (CERCLA) of 1980, as amended, regulates the clean-up of hazardous waste-disposal sites.

5. **Radiation**—The private nuclear industry is regulated under the Atomic Energy Act of 1954. Low-level radioactive waste generated by private facilities is the responsibility of each state under the Low Level Radioactive Waste Policy Act of 1980. Under the Nuclear Waste Policy Act of 1982, the government is looking for a permanent disposal site for nuclear materials and radioactive waste.

For Review

1. Under what common law theories may polluters be held liable?

2. What is an environmental impact statement, and who must file one?

3. What does the Environmental Protection Agency do?

4. What major federal statutes regulate air and water pollution?

5. What is Superfund? To what categories of persons does liability under Superfund extend?

Questions and Case Problems

20–1. Clean Air Act. The Environmental Protection Agency (EPA) has set ambient standards for several pollutants, including sulfur dioxide, specifying the maximum concentration allowable in the outdoor air. One way to meet these standards is to reduce emissions. Companies discovered, however, that they could also meet the standards at less cost by building very high smokestacks. When emitted from such high stacks, pollutants were more widely dispersed and remained below the concentration level specified by the ambient standards. Environmental groups claimed that the Clean Air Act was designed to reduce pollution, not to disperse it, and argued that industry should not be allowed to rely on tall stacks. Are the environmental groups correct, or should industry be allowed to use the less expensive dispersal method? Discuss.

20–2. Clean Air Act. Some scientific knowledge indicates that there is no safe level of exposure to a cancer-causing agent. In theory, even one molecule of such a substance has the potential for causing cancer. Section 112 of

the Clean Air Act requires that all cancer-causing substances be regulated to ensure a margin of safety. Some environmental groups have argued that all emissions of such substances must be eliminated in order for such a margin of safety to be reached. A total elimination would likely shut down many major U.S. industries. Should the Environmental Protection Agency totally eliminate all emissions of cancer-causing chemicals? Discuss.

20–3. Environmental Laws. Moonbay is a real estate development corporation that primarily develops retirement communities. Farmtex owns a number of feedlots in Sunny Valley. Moonbay purchased twenty thousand acres of farmland in the same area and began building and selling retirement homes on this acreage. In the meantime, Farmtex continued to expand its feedlot business, and eventually only five hundred feet separated the two operations. Because of the odor and flies from the feedlots, Moonbay found it difficult to sell the homes in its development. Moonbay wants to enjoin Farmtex from operating its feedlots in the vicinity of the retirement home development. Discuss under what theory Moonbay would file this action. Discuss fully whether Farmtex has violated any federal environmental laws.

20–4. Environmental Laws. Fruitade, Inc., is a processor of a soft drink called Freshen Up. Fruitade uses returnable bottles, as well as a special acid to clean its bottles for further beverage processing. The acid is diluted by water and then allowed to pass into a navigable stream. Fruitade crushes its broken bottles and throws the crushed glass into the stream. Discuss fully any environmental laws that Fruitade has violated.

20–5. Pesticide Regulation. The Environmental Protection Agency (EPA) canceled the registration of the pesticide Diazinon for use on golf courses and sod farms because of concern about the effects of Diazinon on birds. The Federal Insecticide, Fungicide, and Rodenticide Act authorizes cancellation of the registration of products that "generally cause unreasonable adverse effects on the environment." The statute further defines "unreasonable adverse effects on the environment" to mean "any unreasonable risk to man or the environment, taking into account the . . . costs and benefits." Thus, in determining whether a pesticide should continue to be used, one must balance the risks and benefits of the use of the pesticide. Does this mean that the pesticide must be found to kill birds more often than not before its use can be prohibited? [*CIBA-Geigy Corp. v. Environmental Protection Agency,* 874 F.2d 277 (5th Cir. 1989)]

20–6. Common Law Nuisance. Taylor Bay Protective Association is a nonprofit corporation established for the purpose of restoring and improving the water quality of Taylor Bay. Local water districts began operating a flood control project in the area. As part of the project, a pumping station was developed. Testimony at trial revealed that the pumps were operated contrary to the instructions provided in the operation and maintenance manual. The pumps acted as vacuums, sucking up increased amounts of silt and depositing the silt in Taylor Bay. Thus, the project resulted in sedimentation and turbidity problems in the downstream watercourse of Taylor Bay. The association sued the local water districts, alleging that the pumping operations created a nuisance. Do the pumping operations qualify as a common law nuisance? Who should be responsible for the clean-up costs? Discuss both questions fully. [*Taylor Bay Protective Association v. Environmental Protection Agency,* 884 F.2d 1073 (8th Cir. 1989)]

20–7. Water Pollution. The Environmental Protection Agency (EPA) promulgated water-pollution discharge limits for several mining industries. These standards authorized variances exempting mining operations from coverage by the standards if the operations could show that they used special processes or facilities that made the standards inapplicable. Cost was not a consideration in

granting the variances. An industry trade association sued, claiming that the EPA should consider costs in granting variances, and the Fourth Circuit Court of Appeals agreed. Discuss whether the United States Supreme Court should overturn this decision or affirm it and let costs be considered in the granting of variances under the Clean Water Act. [*Environmental Protection Agency v. National Crushed Stone Association,* 449 U.S. 64, 101 S.Ct. 295, 66 L.Ed.2d 268 (1980)]

20–8. Superfund. During the 1970s, a number of chemical companies disposed of their wastes at a facility maintained by South Carolina Recycling and Disposal, Inc. Hazardous chemical wastes were stored rather haphazardly; some leaked into the ground, and fires occurred on several occasions. Eventually, the Environmental Protection Agency (EPA) conducted clean-up operations under Superfund and sued companies that had used the site for the costs of the clean-up. Five of the defendant companies claimed that they should not be liable for the clean-up costs because there was no evidence that their waste materials had contributed in any way to the leakage problem or to any other hazard posed by the site. The EPA asserted that causation was not required for the companies' liability, only evidence that the companies had sent waste to the site. Will the EPA succeed in its claim? Discuss. [*United States v. South Carolina Recycling and Disposal, Inc.,* 653 F.Supp. 984 (D.S.C. 1986)]

20–9. Common Law Nuisance. In 1987, John and Jean Zarlenga purchased a new home in Bloomingdale, Illinois. Bloomingdale Partners (BP) then built an eight-story apartment complex across the street from the Zarlenga home. Each of the 168 apartments had an air conditioner weighing about nine hundred pounds. Over sixty air conditioners were on the side of the complex that faced the Zarlenga home. The Zarlengas testified that the noise from these air conditioners during the summer was a "loud rumbling sound" that was "continuous and monotonous." The machines disrupted their sleep. Jean Zarlenga suffered from headaches and irritability. In her testimony, she stated, "It's made my life miserable. I cannot use my deck. I cannot have company over . . . I can't open my windows in my bedroom. I toss and turn all night." The Zarlengas sued BP for creating a nuisance, claiming that the apartment complex substantially interfered with the use and enjoyment of their home. The Zarlengas sought damages from BP for the devaluation of their home caused by the noise and for their suffering. How should the court decide this case? Discuss fully. [*In re Bloomingdale Partners,* 160 Bankr. 101 (N.D.Ill. 1993)]

20–10. Clean Water Act. Attique Ahmad owned the Spin-N-Market, a convenience store and gas station. The gas pumps were fed by underground tanks, one of which had a leak at its top that allowed water to enter. Ahmad emptied the tank by pumping its contents into a storm drain and a sewer system. Through the storm drain, gasoline flowed into a creek, forcing the city to clean the water. Through the sewer system, gasoline flowed into a sewage treatment plant, forcing the city to evacuate the plant and two nearby schools. Ahmad was charged with discharging a pollutant without a permit, which is a criminal violation of the Clean Water Act. The act provides that a person who "knowingly violates" the act commits a felony. Ahmad claimed that he had believed he was discharging only water. Did Ahmad commit a felony? Why or why not? Discuss fully. [*U.S. v. Ahmad*, 101 F.3d 386 (5th Cir. 1996)]

A Question of Ethics and Social Responsibility

20–11. The Endangered Species Act of 1973 makes it unlawful for any person to "take" endangered or threatened species. The act defines take to mean to "harass, harm, pursue," "wound," or "kill." The secretary of the interior (Bruce Babbitt) issued a regulation that further defined harm to include "significant habitat modification or degradation where it actually kills or injures wildlife." A group of businesses and individuals involved in the timber industry brought an action against the secretary of the interior and others. The group complained that the application of the "harm" regulation to the red-cockaded woodpecker and the northern spotted owl had injured the group economically, because it prevented logging operations (habitat modification) in Pacific Northwest forests containing these species. The group challenged the regulation's validity, contending that Congress did not intend the word *take* to include habitat modification. The case ultimately reached the United States Supreme Court,

which held that the secretary had reasonably construed Congress's intent when he defined harm to include habitat modification. [*Babbitt v. Sweet Home Chapter of Communities for a Great Oregon*, 515 U.S. 687, 115 S.Ct. 2407, 132 L.Ed.2d 597 (1995)]

1. Traditionally, the term *take* has been used to refer to the capture or killing of wildlife, usually for private gain. Is the secretary's regulation prohibiting habitat modification consistent with this definition?

2. One of the issues in this case was whether Congress intended to protect existing generations of species or future generations. How do the terms *take* and *habitat modification* relate to this issue?

3. Three dissenting Supreme Court justices contended that construing the act as prohibiting habitat modification "imposes unfairness to the point of financial ruin—not just upon the rich, but upon the simplest farmer who finds his land conscripted to national zoological use." Should private parties be required to bear the burden of preserving habitats for wildlife?

4. Generally, should the economic welfare of private parties be taken into consideration when environmental statutes and regulations are created and applied?

For Critical Analysis

20–12. It has been estimated that for every dollar spent cleaning up hazardous waste sites, administrative agencies spend seven dollars in overhead. Can you think of any way to trim the administrative costs associated with the clean-up of contaminated sites?

INTERACTING WITH
The Internet

■ The Virtual Law Library of the Indiana University School of Law provides numerous links to online environmental law resources. Go to

http://www.law.indiana.edu/

■ Cornell Law School's Legal Information Institute provides access to the *U.S. Code,* which contains the environmental laws discussed in this chapter. Go to

http://www.law.cornell.edu/uscode

■ Environmental Policy Related Resources offers links to an extensive number of Internet sites dealing with environmental issues. You can access this site at

http://student.ecok.edu/~polsci/resource/environ.html

■ For information on the standards, guidelines, and regulations of the Environmental Protection Agency, go to

http://www.epa.gov/

■ Envirofacts is an EPA site that combines data from various EPA programs. Here you can find information on Superfund, the release and transfer of more than 300 toxic chemicals, more than 75,000 water-discharge permits, and much more. To access this site, go to

http://www.epa.gov/enviro/html/ef_home.html

■ Environmental Information Resources, a site jointly created by the EPA and George Washington University, provides extensive links to environmental resources on the Internet, organized by subject, name, or country. Go to

http://www.gwu.edu/~greenu/index2.html

■ The site of the Chicago law firm of Ross & Hardies offers a broad overview of existing environmental laws, proposed environmental legislation, and EPA actions, as well as articles on environmental law and an online discussion forum. The URL for this site is

http://www.webcom.com/~staber

■ Another site with useful information about environmental law is provided by the McCutchen Environmental Group at

http://www.mccutchen.com/env

■ The environmental law page of *Law Journal Extra!* is a wide-ranging site with a number of useful resources. Access this site at

http://www.ljx.com/practice/environment/index.html

■ For a catalogue of books about environmental law, go to Cameron May, Environmental Publications, at

http://neon.airtime.co.uk/C-May

■ For information on the federal Office of Ocean and Coastal Resource Management, go to

http://wave.nos.noaa.gov/ocrm/

■ For similar information on the U.S. Fish and Wildlife Service, go to

http://www.fws.gov/

■ You might want to see what is happening at the National Resources Defense Council by accessing

http://www.nrdc.org/nrdc

■ A useful site with links to environmental law resources worldwide is provided by the International Environmental Liability Management Association at

http://www.actuarius.magic.ca/ielma.home.html

Land-Use Control and Real Property

Contents

Chapter Objectives

After reading this chapter, you should be able to . . .

1. Distinguish among different types of possessory ownership interests in real property.

2. Identify three types of nonpossessory interests in real property.

3. Discuss how ownership interests in real property can be transferred.

4. Indicate what a leasehold estate is and how a landlord-tenant relationship comes into existence.

5. Outline the rights of property owners concerning the use of their property.

> **"The right of property is the most sacred of all the rights of citizenship."**
>
> Jean-Jacques Rousseau, 1712–1778
> (French writer and philosopher)

From earliest times, property has provided a means for survival. Primitive peoples lived off the fruits of the land, eating the vegetation and wildlife. Later, as the wildlife was domesticated and the vegetation cultivated, property provided pasturage and farmland. In the twelfth and thirteenth centuries, the power of feudal lords was determined by the amount of land that they held; the more land they held, the more powerful they were. After the age of feudalism passed, property continued to be an indicator of family wealth and social position. In the Western world, the protection of an individual's right to his or her property has become, in the words of Jean-Jacques Rousseau, one of the "most sacred of all the rights of citizenship."

In this chapter, we first examine closely the nature of real property. We then look at the various ways in which real property can be owned and at how ownership rights in real property are transferred from one person to another. We also include a discussion of leased property and landlord-tenant relationships and conclude with a look at how the use of land is controlled.

The Nature of Real Property

Real property consists of land and the buildings, plants, and trees that it contains. Real property also includes subsurface and air rights, as well as personal property that has become permanently attached to real property. Whereas personal property is movable, real property—also called *real estate* or *realty*—is immovable.

Land

Land includes the soil on the surface of the earth and the natural or artificial structures that are attached to it. It further includes all the waters contained on or under the surface and much, but not necessarily all, of the airspace above it. The exterior boundaries of land extend down to the center of the earth and up to the farthest reaches of the atmosphere (subject to certain qualifications).

Air and Subsurface Rights

The owner of real property has relatively exclusive rights to the airspace above the land, as well as to the soil and minerals underneath it.

AIR RIGHTS.   Early cases involving air rights dealt with matters such as the right to run a telephone wire across a person's property when the wire did not touch any of the property[1] and whether a bullet shot over a person's land constituted trespass.[2] Today, disputes concerning air rights may involve the right of commercial and private planes to fly over property and the right of individuals and governments to seed clouds and produce artificial rain. Flights over private land do not normally violate the property owners' rights unless the flights are low and frequent enough to cause a direct interference with the enjoyment and use of the land.[3] Leaning walls or buildings and projecting eave spouts or roofs may also violate the air rights of an adjoining property owner.

---

1.   *Butler v. Frontier Telephone Co.,* 186 N.Y. 486, 79 N.E. 716 (1906).
2.   *Herrin v. Sutherland,* 74 Mont. 587, 241 P. 328 (1925). Shooting over a person's land constitutes trespass.
3.   *United States v. Causby,* 328 U.S. 256, 66 S.Ct. 1062, 90 L.Ed. 1206 (1946).

SUBSURFACE RIGHTS.   In many states, the owner of the surface of a piece of land is not the owner of the subsurface, and hence the land ownership may be separated. Subsurface rights can be extremely valuable, as these rights include the ownership of minerals and, in most states, oil and natural gas. Water rights are also extremely valuable, especially in the West. When the ownership is separated into surface and subsurface rights, each owner can pass title to what he or she owns without the consent of the other owner. Each owner has the right to use the land owned, and in some cases a conflict arises between a surface owner's use and the subsurface owner's need to extract minerals, oil, and natural gas. When this occurs, one party's interest may become subservient to the other party's interest, either by statute or case decision.

Significant limitations on either air rights or subsurface rights normally have to be indicated on the deed transferring title at the time of purchase. (Deeds and the types of warranties they contain are discussed later in this chapter.)

> BE AWARE If, during an excavation, a subsurface owner causes the land to subside, he or she may be liable to the owner of the surface.

Plant Life and Vegetation

Plant life, both natural and cultivated, is also considered to be real property. In many instances, the natural vegetation, such as trees, adds greatly to the value of the realty. When a parcel of land is sold and the land has growing crops on it, the sale includes the crops, unless otherwise specified in the sales contract. When crops are sold by themselves, however, they are considered to be personal property or goods. Consequently, the sale of crops is a sale of goods, and therefore it is governed by the Uniform Commercial Code rather than by real property law.[4]

Fixtures

Certain personal property can become so closely associated with the real property to which it is attached that the law views it as real property. Such property is known as a **fixture**—a thing *affixed* to realty, meaning it is attached to it by roots; embedded in it; or permanently attached by means of cement, plaster, bolts, nails, or screws. The fixture can be physically attached to real property, be attached to another fixture, or even be without any actual physical attachment to the land (such as a statue). As long as the owner *intends* the property to be a fixture, normally it will be a fixture.

Fixtures are included in the sale of land if the sales contract does not provide otherwise. The sale of a house includes the land and the house and the garage on the land, as well as the cabinets, plumbing, and windows. Because these are permanently affixed to the property, they are considered to be a part of it. Unless otherwise agreed, however, the curtains and throw rugs are not included. Items such as drapes and window-unit air conditioners are difficult to classify. Thus, a contract for the sale of a house or commercial realty should indicate which items of this sort are included in the sale.

Fixture A thing that was once personal property but that has become attached to real property in such a way that it takes on the characteristics of real property and becomes part of that real property.

Ownership of Real Property

Ownership of property is an abstract concept that cannot exist independently of the legal system. No one can actually possess or *hold* a piece of land,

> "The institution called property guards the troubled boundary between [the] individual . . . and the state."
>
> Charles A. Reich, 1928–
> (American legal scholar)

---

4. See UCC 2–107(2).

the air above it, the earth below it, and all the water contained on it. The legal system therefore recognizes certain rights and duties that constitute ownership interests in real property.

Property ownership is often viewed as a bundle of rights. One who possesses the entire bundle of rights is said to hold the property in *fee simple,* which is the most complete form of ownership. When only some of the rights in the bundle are transferred to another person, the effect is to limit the ownership rights of both the one transferring the rights and the one receiving them.

Ownership in Fee Simple

Fee Simple Absolute An ownership interest in land in which the owner has the greatest possible aggregation of rights, privileges, and power. Ownership in fee simple absolute is limited absolutely to a person and his or her heirs.

The most common type of property ownership today is the fee simple. Generally, the term *fee simple* is used to designate a **fee simple absolute,** in which the owner has the greatest possible aggregation of rights, privileges, and power. The fee simple is limited absolutely to a person and his or her heirs and is assigned forever without limitation or condition. The rights that accompany a fee simple include the right to use the land for whatever purpose the owner sees fit, subject to laws that prevent the owner from unreasonably interfering with another person's land and subject to applicable zoning laws. Furthermore, the owner has the rights of *exclusive* possession and use of the property. A fee simple is potentially infinite in duration and can be disposed of by deed or by will (by selling or giving away). When there is no will, the fee simple passes to the owner's legal heirs.

Fee Simple Defeasible An ownership interest in real property that can be taken away (by the prior grantor) upon the occurrence or nonoccurrence of a specified event.

Conveyance The transfer of a title to land from one person to another by deed; a document (such as a deed) by which an interest in land is transferred from one person to another.

Ownership in fee simple may become limited whenever the property is transferred to another *conditionally.* When this occurs, the fee simple is known as a **fee simple defeasible** (the word *defeasible* means capable of being terminated or annulled). For example, a **conveyance,** or transfer of real property, "to A and his heirs as long as the land is used for charitable purposes" creates a fee simple defeasible, because ownership of the property is conditioned on the land's being used for charitable purposes. The original owner retains a *partial* ownership interest, because if the specified condition does not occur (if the land ceases to be used for charitable purposes), then the land reverts, or returns, to the original owner. If the original owner is not living at the time, the land passes to his or her heirs.

Life Estates

Life Estate An interest in land that exists only for the duration of the life of some person, usually the holder of the estate.

A **life estate** is an estate that lasts for the life of some specified individual. A conveyance "to A for his life" creates a life estate.[5] In a life estate, the life tenant has fewer rights of ownership than the holder of a fee simple defeasible, because the rights necessarily cease to exist on the life tenant's death. The life tenant has the right to use the land, provided that he or she commits no waste (injury to the land). In other words, the life tenant cannot injure the land in a manner that would adversely affect its value. The life tenant can use the land to harvest crops or, if mines and oil wells are already on the land, can extract minerals and oil from it, but the life tenant cannot exploit the land by creating new wells or mines. The life tenant has the right to mortgage the life estate and create liens, easements, and leases; but none can extend beyond the life of the tenant. In addition, with few exceptions, the owner of a life estate has an exclusive right to possession during his or her life.

---

5.   A less common type of life estate is created by the conveyance "to A for the life of B." This is known as an estate *pur autre vie,* or an estate for the duration of the life of another.

Along with these rights, the life tenant also has some duties—to keep the property in repair and to pay property taxes. In short, the owner of the life estate has the same rights as a fee simple owner except that he or she must maintain the value of the property during his or her tenancy, less the decrease in value resulting from the normal use of the property allowed by the life tenancy.

Future Interests

When an owner in fee simple absolute conveys the estate conditionally to another (such as with a fee simple defeasible) or for a limited period of time (such as with a life estate), the original owner still retains an interest in the land. The owner retains the right to repossess ownership of the land if the conditions of the fee simple defeasible are not met or when the life of the life-estate holder ends. The residuary (or leftover) interest in the property that the owner retains is called a **future interest,** because if it arises, it will only arise in the future.

If the owner retains ownership of the future interest, then the future interest is described as a **reversionary interest,** because the property will *revert* to the original owner if the condition specified in a fee simple defeasible fails or when a life tenant dies. If, however, the owner of the future interest transfers ownership rights in that future interest to another, the future interest is described as a **remainder.** For example, a conveyance "to A for life, then to B" creates a life estate for A and a remainder (future interest) for B. An **executory interest** is a type of future interest very similar to a remainder, the difference being that an executory interest does not take effect immediately on the expiration of another interest, such as a life estate. For example, a conveyance "to A and his (or her) heirs, as long as the premises are used for charitable purposes, and if not so used for charitable purposes, then to B" creates an executory interest in the property for B.

Nonpossessory Interests

In contrast to the types of property interests just described, some interests in land do not include any rights to possess the property. These interests are thus known as *nonpossessory interests.* Two forms of nonpossessory interests are easements and profits. A license to come onto property is also a nonpossessory interest. Because easements and profits are similar and the same rules apply to both, they are discussed together.

EASEMENTS AND PROFITS. An **easement** is the right of a person to make limited use of another person's real property without taking anything from the property. An easement, for example, can be the right to travel over another's property. In contrast, a **profit**[6] is the right to go onto land in possession of another and take away some part of the land itself or some product of the land. For example, Akmed, the owner of Sandy View, gives Carmen the right to go there and remove all the sand and gravel that she needs for her cement business. Carmen has a profit. Easements and profits can be classified as either *appurtenant* or *in gross.*

LICENSE. A **license** is the revocable right of a person to come onto another person's land. It is a personal privilege that arises from the consent of the

Future Interest An interest in real property that is not at present possessory but will or may become possessory in the future.

Reversionary Interest A future interest in property retained by the original owner.

Remainder A future interest in property held by a person other than the original owner.

Executory Interest A future interest, held by a person other than the grantor, that begins after the termination of the preceding estate.

Easement A nonpossessory right to use another's property in a manner established by either express or implied agreement.

Profit In real property law, the right to enter on and remove things from the property of another (for example, the right to enter onto a person's land and remove sand and gravel therefrom).

License A revocable right or privilege of a person to come on another person's land.

---

6. The term *profit,* as used here, does not refer to the "profits" made by a business firm. Rather, it means a gain or an advantage.

owner of the land and that can be revoked by the owner. A ticket to attend a movie at a theater is an example of a license. Assume that a Broadway theater owner issues to Carla a ticket to see a play. If Carla is refused entry into the theater because she is improperly dressed, she has no right to force her way into the theater. The ticket is only a revocable license, not a conveyance of an interest in property.

Transfer of Ownership

Ownership of real property can pass from one person to another in a number of ways. Commonly, ownership interests in land are transferred by sale, in which case the terms of the transfer are specified in a real estate sales contract. When real property is sold or transferred as a gift, title to the property is conveyed by means of a **deed**—the instrument of conveyance of real property. We look here at transfers of real property by deed, as well as some other ways in which ownership rights in real property can be transferred.

Deed A document by which title to property (usually real property) is passed.

Deeds

A valid deed must contain the following elements:

1. The names of the buyer (grantee) and seller (grantor).
2. Words evidencing an intent to convey the property (for example, "I hereby bargain, sell, grant, or give").
3. A legally sufficient description of the land.
4. The grantor's (and usually the spouse's) signature.

Additionally, to be valid, a deed must be delivered to the person to whom the property is being conveyed or to his or her agent.

WARRANTY DEEDS.   Different types of deeds provide different degrees of protection against defects of title. A **warranty deed** warrants the greatest number of things and thus provides the greatest protection for the buyer, or grantee. In most states, special language is required to make a deed a general warranty deed; normally, the deed must include a written promise to protect the buyer against all claims of ownership of the property. A sample warranty deed is shown in Exhibit 21–1. Warranty deeds commonly include a number of *covenants,* or promises, that the grantor makes to the grantee.

Warranty Deed A deed in which the grantor guarantees to the grantee that the grantor has title to the property conveyed in the deed, that there are no encumbrances on the property other than what the grantor has represented, and that the grantee will enjoy quiet possession of the property; a deed that provides the greatest amount of protection for the grantee.

A *covenant of seisin*[7] and a *covenant of the right to convey* warrant that the seller has title to the estate that the deed describes and the power to convey the estate, respectively. The covenant of seisin specifically assures the buyer that the grantor has the property in the purported quantity and quality.

A *covenant against encumbrances* is a covenant that the property being sold or conveyed is not subject to any outstanding rights or interests that will diminish the value of the land, except as explicitly stated. Examples of common encumbrances include mortgages, liens, profits, easements, and private deed restrictions on the use of the land.

A *covenant of quiet enjoyment* guarantees that the buyer will not be disturbed in his or her possession of the land by the seller or any third persons. For example, assume that Julio sells a two-acre lot and office building by war-

---

7.   Pronounced *see*-zuhn.

Date: May 31, 1998
Grantor: GAYLORD A. JENTZ AND WIFE, JOANN H. JENTZ

Grantor's Mailing Address (including county):
      4106 North Loop Drive
      Austin, Travis County, Texas

Grantee: DAVID F. FRIEND AND WIFE, JOAN E. FRIEND AS JOINT TENANTS
      WITH RIGHT OF SURVIVORSHIP
Grantee's Mailing Address (including county):
      5929 Fuller Drive
      Austin, Travis County, Texas

Consideration:
For and in consideration of the sum of Ten and No/100 Dollars ($10.00) and other
valuable consideration to the undersigned paid by the grantees herein named, the
receipt of which is hereby acknowledged, and for which no lien is retained, either
express or implied.

Property (including any improvements):
Lot 23, Block "A", Northwest Hills, Green Acres Addition, Phase 4, Travis County,
Texas, according to the map or plat of record in volume 22, pages 331-336 of the
Plat Records of Travis County, Texas.

Reservations from and Exceptions to Conveyance and Warranty:

This conveyance with its warranty is expressly made subject to the following:

Easements and restrictions of record in Volume 7863, Page 53, Volume 8430,
Page 35, Volume 8133, Page 152 of the Real Property Record of Travis County,
Texas; Volume 22, Pages 335-339, of the Plat Records of Travis County, Texas;
and to any other restrictions and easements affecting said property which are
of record in Travis County, Texas.

   Grantor, for the consideration and subject to the reservations from and exceptions to conveyance and warranty, grants, sells,
and conveys to Grantee the property, together with all and singular the rights and appurtenances thereto in any wise belonging, to
have and hold it to Grantee, Grantee's heirs, executors, administrators, successors, or assigns forever. Grantor binds Grantor
and Grantor's heirs, executors, administrators, and successors to warrant and forever defend all and singular the property to
Grantee and Grantee's heirs, executors, administrators, successors, and assigns against every person whomsoever lawfully
claiming or to claim the same or any part thereof, except as to the reservations from and exceptions to conveyance and warranty.

   When the context requires, singular nouns and pronouns include the plural.

BY: *Gaylord A. Jentz*
      Gaylord A. Jentz

BY: *Joann H. Jentz*
      JoAnn H. Jentz

(Acknowledgment)

STATE OF TEXAS
COUNTY OF TRAVIS

   This instrument was acknowledged before me on the   31st day of   May **1998**

Rosemary Potter

Notary Seal   **Notary Public, State of Texas**
              Notary's name (printed): Rosemary Potter

              Notary's commission expires: 1/31/2002

■ **Exhibit 21–1**
A Sample Warranty Deed

ranty deed. Subsequently, a third person shows better title than Julio had and proceeds to evict the buyer. Here, the covenant of quiet enjoyment has been breached, and the buyer can recover the purchase price of the land plus any other damages incurred as a result of the eviction.

QUITCLAIM DEEDS.   A **quitclaim deed** offers the least amount of protection against defects in the title. Basically, a quitclaim deed conveys to the grantee whatever interest the grantor had; so if the grantor had no interest, then the grantee receives no interest. Quitclaim deeds are often used when the seller, or grantor, is uncertain as to the extent of his or her rights in the property.

RECORDING STATUTES.   Every jurisdiction has **recording statutes,** which allow deeds to be recorded. Recording a deed gives notice to the public that a certain person is now the owner of a particular parcel of real estate. Thus, prospective buyers can check the public records to see whether there have been earlier transactions creating interests or rights in specific parcels of real property. Placing everyone on notice as to the identity of the true owner is intended to prevent the previous owners from fraudulently conveying the land to other purchasers. Deeds are recorded in the county in which the property is located. Many state statutes require that the grantor sign the deed in the presence of two witnesses before it can be recorded.

Will or Inheritance

Property that is transferred on an owner's death is passed either by will or by state inheritance laws. If the owner of land dies with a will, the land passes in accordance with the terms of the will. If the owner dies without a will, state inheritance statutes prescribe how and to whom the property will pass.

Adverse Possession

Adverse possession is a means of obtaining title to land without delivery of a deed. Essentially, when one person possesses the property of another for a certain statutory period of time (three to thirty years, with ten years being most common), that person, called the *adverse possessor,* acquires title to the land and cannot be removed from it by the original owner. The adverse possessor is vested with good title just as if there had been a conveyance by deed.

For property to be held adversely, four elements must be satisfied:

1. Possession must be actual and exclusive; that is, the possessor must take sole physical occupancy of the property.
2. The possession must be open, visible, and notorious, not secret or clandestine. The possessor must occupy the land for all the world to see.
3. Possession must be continuous and peaceable for the required period of time. This requirement means that the possessor must not be interrupted in the occupancy by the true owner or by the courts.
4. Possession must be hostile and adverse. In other words, the possessor must claim the property as against the whole world. He or she cannot be living on the property with the permission of the owner.

There are a number of public-policy reasons for the adverse possession doctrine. These reasons include society's interest in resolving boundary disputes and determining ownership rights when title to property is in question and in

---

Quitclaim Deed A deed intended to pass any title, interest, or claim that the grantor may have in the property but not warranting that such title is valid. A quitclaim deed offers the least amount of protection against defects in the title.

Recording Statutes Statutes that allow deeds, mortgages, and other real property transactions be recorded so as to provide notice to future purchasers or creditors of an existing claim on the property.

Adverse Possession The acquisition of title to real property by occupying it openly, without the consent of the owner, for a period of time specified by a state statute. The occupation must be actual, open, notorious, exclusive, and in opposition to all others, including the owner.

assuring that real property remains in the stream of commerce. More fundamentally, policies behind the doctrine include not rewarding owners who sit on their rights too long and rewarding possessors for putting land to productive use. In the following case, the question before the court was whether a couple had obtained title to a certain portion of land by adverse possession.

Case 21.1 ● Klos v. Molenda

Superior Court of Pennsylvania, 1986.
355 Pa.Super. 399,
513 A.2d 490.

HISTORICAL AND CULTURAL SETTING   *After World War II ended in 1945, members of the armed forces returned to their families or began families, and the birthrate increased dramatically each year for a time. Many of the former servicepeople went to college, but even those who did not go back to school needed relatively low-cost housing. In 1947, a builder, Abraham Levitt, and his sons developed Levittown—a community on Long Island consisting of inexpensive houses and a playground, shops, and other amenities. Over the next few years, other builders began to imitate Levitt's idea, and by 1950, suburban developments were sprawling across the American landscape.*

BACKGROUND AND FACTS   In September 1950, Michael and Albina Klos purchased part of some property in Pennsylvania owned by John and Anne Molenda. The Kloses' lot was 50 feet wide and 135 feet deep. Rather than surveying the property, the seller and buyer paced off the lot and placed stakes in the ground as boundary markers. The Kloses built a house on the lot in 1952 and put in a sidewalk along the full front. They also put in a driveway thirty inches from the stake line. They planted grass in that thirty inches and maintained it until 1984. In 1983, John Molenda died, and his widow hired a surveyor to inventory the landholdings. The survey located the rightful property line between the Molendas' and the Kloses' land as being thirty inches closer to the Kloses' house than the line established earlier. This placed the property line right along the Kloses' driveway, instead of thirty inches to the side of the driveway. On learning this, Anne Molenda erected a fence right along the Kloses' driveway to mark the property line. The Kloses brought an action in a Pennsylvania state court challenging Anne Molenda's conduct, claiming that they held title to the land by adverse possession. The trial court held that the Kloses had title to the land. Anne Molenda appealed.

IN THE WORDS OF THE COURT . . .
WIEAND, Judge.

*   *   *   *

*   *   *   "[O]ne who claims title by adverse possession must prove that he had actual, continuous, exclusive, visible, notorious, distinct, and hostile possession of the land for twenty-one years *   *   * ." "An adverse possessor must intend to hold the land for himself, and that intention must be made manifest by his acts. He must keep his flag flying and present a hostile front to all adverse pretensions."

*   *   *   *

The hostile nature of the Klos possession was not destroyed because the stake line may have been placed along a property line mistakenly located by the adjoining landowners. *   *   * The parties intended that the Kloses should have title to that line, and thereafter the Kloses kept their flag flying continuously on the thirty (30) inch strip of land. Their possession, open, notorious and exclusive for more than twenty-one years, presented a hostile front to any person or persons intending to make a conflicting pretension of ownership.

(Continued)

Case 21.1—continued

DECISION AND REMEDY   The Kloses held rightful title to the land. The Pennsylvania appellate court affirmed the trial court's decision.

FOR CRITICAL ANALYSIS—ETHICAL CONSIDERATION   *If the Kloses had known from the outset that the Molendas actually owned the thirty-inch strip of land, would this have affected the outcome in this case?*

Leasehold Estates

Lease In real property law, a contract by which the owner of real property (the landlord, or lessor) grants to a person (the tenant, or lessee) an exclusive right to use and possess the property, usually for a specified period of time, in return for rent or some other form of payment.

Leasehold Estate An estate in realty held by a tenant under a lease. In every leasehold estate, the tenant has a qualified right to possess and/or use the land.

Tenancy for Years A type of tenancy under which property is leased for a specified period of time, such as a month, a year, or a period of years.

Often, real property is used by those who do not own it. A **lease** is a contract by which the owner of real property (the landlord, or lessor) grants to a person (the tenant, or lessee) an exclusive right to use and possess the property, usually for a specified period of time, in return for rent or some other form of payment. Property in the possession of a tenant is referred to as a **leasehold estate.**

The respective rights and duties of the landlord and tenant that arise under a lease agreement will be discussed shortly. Here we look at the types of leasehold estates, or tenancies, that can be created when real property is leased.

Tenancy for Years

A **tenancy for years** is created by an express contract by which property is leased for a specified period of time, such as a month, a year, or a period of years. For example, signing a one-year lease to occupy an apartment creates a tenancy for years. At the end of the period specified in the lease, the lease ends (without notice), and possession of the apartment returns to the lessor. If the tenant dies during the period of the lease, the lease interest passes to the tenant's heirs as personal property. Often, leases include renewal or extension provisions.

Periodic Tenancy A lease interest in land for an indefinite period involving payment of rent at fixed intervals, such as week to week, month to month, or year to year.

Periodic Tenancy

A **periodic tenancy** is created by a lease that does not specify how long it is to last but does specify that rent is to be paid at certain intervals. This type of tenancy is automatically renewed for another rental period unless properly terminated. For example, a periodic tenancy is created by a lease that states, "Rent is due on the tenth day of every month." This provision creates a tenancy from month to month. This type of tenancy can also extend from week to week or from year to year.

Under the common law, to terminate a periodic tenancy, the landlord or tenant must give one period's notice to the other party. If the tenancy extends from month to month, for example, one month's notice must be given. State statutes may require a different period for notice of termination in a periodic tenancy, however.

Tenancy at Will A type of tenancy under which either party can terminate the tenancy without notice; usually arises when a tenant who has been under a tenancy for years retains possession, with the landlord's consent, after the tenancy for years has terminated.

Tenancy at Will

Suppose that a landlord rents an apartment to a tenant "for as long as both agree." In such a situation, the tenant receives a leasehold estate known as a **tenancy at will.** Under the common law, either party can terminate the tenancy without notice (that is, "at will"). This type of estate usually arises when a tenant who has been under a tenancy for years retains possession after the termination date of that tenancy with the landlord's consent. Before the tenancy has been converted into a periodic tenancy (by the periodic payment of rent), it is a tenancy at will, terminable by either party without notice. Once the tenancy is treated as a periodic tenancy, termination notice must conform to the one already discussed for that type of tenancy. The death of either party or the voluntary commission of waste by the tenant will terminate a tenancy at will.

Tenancy at Sufferance

The mere possession of land without right is called a **tenancy at sufferance.** It is not a true tenancy. A tenancy at sufferance is not an estate, because it is created when a tenant *wrongfully* retains possession of property. Whenever a tenancy for years, periodic tenancy, or tenancy at will ends and the tenant continues to retain possession of the premises without the owner's permission, a tenancy at sufferance is created.

Landlord-Tenant Relationships

▼ In the past several decades, landlord-tenant relationships have become much more complex than they were before, as has the law governing them. Generally, the law has come to apply contract doctrines, such as those providing for implied warranties and unconscionability, to the landlord-tenant relationship. Increasingly, landlord-tenant relationships have become subject to specific state and local statutes and ordinances as well. In 1972, in an effort to create more uniformity in the law governing landlord-tenant relationships, the National Conference of Commissioners on Uniform State Laws issued the Uniform Residential Landlord and Tenant Act (URLTA). We look now at how a landlord-tenant relationship is created and at the respective rights and duties of landlords and tenants.

Creating the Landlord-Tenant Relationship

A landlord-tenant relationship is established by a lease contract. As mentioned, a lease contract arises when a property owner (landlord) agrees to give another party (the tenant) the exclusive right to possess the property—usually for a price and for a specified term.

FORM OF THE LEASE.   A lease contract may be oral or written. Under the common law, an oral lease is valid. As with most oral contracts, however, a party who seeks to enforce an oral lease may have difficulty proving its existence. In most states, statutes mandate that leases be in writing for some tenancies (such as those exceeding one year). To ensure the validity of a lease agreement, it should therefore be in writing and do the following:

1. Express an intent to establish the relationship.
2. Provide for the transfer of the property's possession to the tenant at the beginning of the term.
3. Provide for the landlord's reversionary interest, which entitles the property owner to retake possession at the end of the term.
4. Describe the property—for example, give its street address.
5. Indicate the length of the term, the amount of the rent, and how and when it is to be paid.

How does a leasehold estate differ from ownership in fee simple, from a life estate, and from such nonpossessory interests as easements and profits?

NOTE Sound business practice dictates that a lease for commercial property should be written carefully and should clearly define the parties' rights and obligations.

Tenancy at Sufferance A type of tenancy under which one who, after rightfully being in possession of leased premises, continues (wrongfully) to occupy the property after the lease has been terminated. The tenant has no rights to possess the property and occupies it only because the person entitled to evict the tenant has not done so.

Ethical Perspective

Because lease contracts are commonly drafted by the landlord, prospective tenants who are unfamiliar with certain terms and clauses may not realize the legal consequences of signing a lease. The *unconscionability* concept, founded in contract law, helps protect tenants from contracts in which they have signed away, without realizing it, important rights.

Basically, as applied to leases in some jurisdictions, the unconscionability concept follows the unconscionability provision of the Uniform Commercial Code (UCC). Under UCC 2–302, a court may declare an entire contract or any

of its clauses unconscionable and thus illegal, depending on the circumstances surrounding the transaction and the parties' relative bargaining positions. For example, in a residential lease, a clause claiming to absolve a landlord from responsibility for interruptions in such essential services as central heating or air conditioning will not shield the landlord from liability if the systems break down when they are needed most.

For Critical Analysis: *In landlord-tenant disputes, courts tend to be more protective of residential tenants than commercial tenants. Why is this?*

LEGAL REQUIREMENTS.   State or local law often dictates permissible lease terms. For example, a statute or ordinance might prohibit the leasing of a structure that is in a certain physical condition or is not in compliance with local building codes. Similarly, a statute may prohibit the leasing of property for a particular purpose. For instance, a state law might prohibit gambling houses. Thus, if a landlord and tenant intend that the leased premises be used only to house an illegal betting operation, their lease is unenforceable.

A property owner cannot legally discriminate against prospective tenants on the basis of race, color, national origin, religion, gender, or disability. Similarly, a tenant cannot legally promise to do something counter to laws prohibiting discrimination. A tenant, for example, cannot legally promise to do business only with members of a particular race. The public policy underlying these prohibitions is to treat all people equally.

Often, rental properties are leased by agents of the landowner. Recall from Chapter 16 that under the theory of *respondeat superior,* a principal (a landlord, with respect to leases) is liable for the wrongful actions of his or her agent if the actions occurred within the scope of employment. At issue in the following case is whether a landlord can be held liable for his agent's discrimination on the basis of sex against a woman who sought to rent a particular apartment.

Case 21.2 ● Walker v. Crigler

United States Court of Appeals,
Fourth Circuit, 1992.
976 F.2d 900.

HISTORICAL AND SOCIAL SETTING   *At common law, a landlord was free to rent, or refuse to rent, to anyone for any reason. For example, a landlord was not required to rent an apartment to someone with a considerable number of unpaid bills. Today, that rule still generally applies: a landlord does not need a particularly good reason to refuse to rent his or her property to someone. Over the last forty years, however, the federal government has recognized that*

(Continued)

Case 21.2—continued

persons have a right not to be denied a housing opportunity because of race, color, religion, gender, national origin, mental or physical disability, marital status, or the presence of children. Some states protect against discrimination on the basis of other characteristics as well, such as age.

BACKGROUND AND FACTS Darlene Walker, a single parent with one son, was looking for an apartment in Falls Church, Virginia. A real estate agent, John Moore, was assisting her in her search and took Walker to view an apartment owned by Frank Whitesell III and managed by Constance Crigler. Walker liked the apartment because it was near a school for her son and near transportation, and Moore called Crigler and told her that he had an applicant for the apartment. Crigler told Moore, and later Walker, that she would never rent to a woman in any circumstances. Walker asked Crigler if she was speaking for the owner, and Crigler said that she was. Walker sued Crigler and Whitesell in a federal district court for violating federal laws prohibiting discrimination in housing. The trial court found Crigler liable for damages in the amount of $5,000 but held that Whitesell was not liable for Crigler's actions, because he had previously instructed her, in writing, not to discriminate illegally against any potential renters. Walker appealed. (Shortly after the appeal was filed, Crigler filed for Chapter 7 bankruptcy, and a few months later the $5,000 judgment against her was discharged.)

IN THE WORDS OF THE COURT . . .
MURNAGHAN, Circuit Judge.

* * * *

* * * The evidence is sufficient to support the conclusion that Whitesell specifically intended that Crigler not discriminate. * * * However, * * * Whitesell could not insulate himself from liability for sex discrimination in regard to living premises owned by him and managed for his benefit merely by relinquishing the responsibility for preventing such discrimination to another party. * * *

* * * *

* * * Just as we feel no qualms in holding a property owner responsible for paying property taxes, meeting health code safety requirements, or ensuring that other responsibilities to protect the public are met, and we refuse to allow the owner to avoid these responsibilities with an assertion that he had conferred the duty to another, we must hold those who benefit from the sale and rental of property to the public to the specific mandates of anti-discrimination law if the goal of equal housing opportunity is to be reached.

DECISION AND REMEDY The U.S. Court of Appeals for the Fourth Circuit reversed the trial court's decision on this issue. Whitesell was ordered to pay $5,000 in damages to Walker.

FOR CRITICAL ANALYSIS—ETHICAL CONSIDERATION *For what policy reasons do courts impose liability on landlords for their agents' actions?*

Rights and Duties

The rights and duties of landlords and tenants generally pertain to four broad areas of concern—the possession, use, and maintenance of leased property and, of course, rent.

POSSESSION. Possession involves both the obligation of the landlord to deliver possession to the tenant at the beginning of the lease term and the right of the tenant to obtain possession and retain it until the lease expires.

The covenant of quiet enjoyment mentioned previously also applies to leased premises. Under this covenant, the landlord promises that during the lease term, neither the landlord nor anyone having a superior title to the property will disturb the tenant's use and enjoyment of the property. This covenant forms the essence of the landlord-tenant relationship, and if it is breached, the tenant can terminate the lease and sue for damages.

If the landlord deprives the tenant of the tenant's possession of the leased property or interferes with the tenant's use or enjoyment of it, an **eviction** occurs. An eviction occurs, for example, when the landlord changes the lock and refuses to give the tenant a new key. A **constructive eviction** occurs when the landlord wrongfully performs or fails to perform any of the undertakings the lease requires, thereby making the tenant's further use and enjoyment of the property exceedingly difficult or impossible. Examples of constructive eviction include a landlord's failure to provide heat in the winter, light, or other essential utilities.

Eviction A landlord's act of depriving a tenant of possession of the leased premises.

Constructive Eviction A form of eviction that occurs when a landlord fails to perform adequately any of the undertakings (such as providing heat in the winter) required by the lease, thereby making the tenant's further use and enjoyment of the property exceedingly difficult or impossible.

Implied Warranty of Habitability An implied promise by a landlord that rented residential premises are fit for human habitation—that is, in a condition that is safe and suitable for people to live in.

USE AND MAINTENANCE OF THE PREMISES.   If the parties do not limit by agreement the uses to which the property may be put, the tenant may make any use of it, as long as the use is legal and reasonably relates to the purpose for which the property is adapted or ordinarily used and does not injure the landlord's interest.

The tenant is responsible for any damages to the premises that he or she causes, intentionally or negligently, and the tenant may be held liable for the cost of returning the property to the physical condition it was in at the lease's inception. Unless the parties have agreed otherwise, the tenant is not responsible for ordinary wear and tear and the property's consequent depreciation in value.

Usually, the landlord must comply with state statutes and city ordinances that delineate specific standards for the construction and maintenance of buildings. Typically, these codes contain structural requirements common to the construction, wiring, and plumbing of residential and commercial buildings. In some jurisdictions, landlords of residential property are required by statute to maintain the premises in good repair.

A tenant looks over his apartment. Should these premises be considered habitable?

IMPLIED WARRANTY OF HABITABILITY.   The **implied warranty of habitability** requires a landlord who leases residential property to deliver the premises to the tenant in a habitable condition—that is, in a condition that is safe and suitable for people to live in—at the beginning of a lease term and to maintain them in that condition for the lease's duration. Some state legislatures have enacted this warranty into law. In other jurisdictions, courts have based the warranty on the existence of a landlord's statutory duty to keep leased premises in good repair, or they have simply applied it as a matter of public policy.

Generally, this warranty applies to major, or *substantial,* physical defects that the landlord knows or should know about and has had a reasonable time to repair—for example, a large hole in the roof. An unattractive or annoying feature, such as a crack in the wall, may be unpleasant, but unless the crack is a structural defect or affects the residence's heating capabilities, it is probably not sufficiently substantial to make the place uninhabitable. At issue in the following case is whether specific conditions in an apartment basement constituted a violation of the implied warranty of habitability.

Case 21.3 ● Weingarden v. Eagle Ridge Condominiums

Toledo Municipal Court,
Lucas County, Ohio, 1995.
71 Ohio Misc.2d 7,
653 N.E.2d 759.

HISTORICAL AND SOCIAL SETTING *Landlord-tenant law grew out of medieval property law. From the Middle Ages until 1970, a lease was held to convey to a tenant primarily an interest in land—the value of a lease was the land itself. In truth, however, the value of a lease for an apartment is that it gives someone a place to live. The tenant has little interest in the land. He or she wants secure walls, windows, and doors, and adequate heat, light, ventilation, and plumbing. U.S. courts began to recognize this truth in 1970 and subsequently revolutionized landlord-tenant law.*

Today, anyone who leases an apartment expects it to be habitable.

BACKGROUND AND FACTS Don Weingarden notified his landlord, Eagle Ridge Condominiums, that his apartment basement leaked when it rained or when snow melted. The water soaked the carpeting and caused the growth of mildew; this rendered the basement—which was one-third of the apartment—useless and spread odor throughout the apartment. For these and other reasons, Weingarden vacated the premises before the end of the term. When his security deposit was not returned, Weingarden filed a suit in an Ohio state court against Eagle Ridge.

IN THE WORDS OF THE COURT . . .
THOMAS J. OSOWIK, Judge.
    * * * *
    * * * [T]he leaking basement, resulting in thoroughly soaked carpeting and resultant mildew and its odors did constitute a condition that would affect the habitability of the apartment. * * * [T]he apartment was rented to the plaintiff with a carpeted basement, leading the tenant to believe that the basement was indeed a habitable part of the unit. Further, whenever it would rain or even when the snow melted, the leak was substantial. That continuing condition and the resultant mildew made the basement uninhabitable. * * * The basement represented approximately one third of the apartment.
    * * * [T]his breach of the warranty of habitability resulted in a constructive eviction of the tenant.

DECISION AND REMEDY The Ohio trial court ruled in Weingarden's favor and awarded him one-third of the amount of each month's rent (the basement was one-third of the apartment) plus his security deposit, less an amount for an unpaid utility bill.

FOR CRITICAL ANALYSIS—ETHICAL CONSIDERATION *What policy reasons justify imposing an implied warranty of habitability on landlords?*

RENT. *Rent* is the tenant's payment to the landlord for the tenant's occupancy or use of the landlord's real property. Generally, the tenant must pay the rent even if he or she refuses to occupy the property or moves out, as long as the refusal or the move is unjustifiable and the lease is in force.

Under the common law, destruction by fire or flood of a building leased by a tenant did not relieve the tenant of the obligation to pay rent and did not permit the termination of the lease. Today, however, state statutes have altered the common law rule. If the building burns down, apartment dwellers in most states are not continuously liable to the landlord for the payment of rent.

International Perspective

Unlike the law in the United States governing landlord-tenant relationships, much of which evolved under the common law, English landlord-tenant law has been created, to a great extent, by statute. English law traditionally adhered to the principle of *caveat tenant* ("let the tenant beware"). In other words, tenants had little recourse against landlords who refused to keep the leased premises in good repair. In 1985, however, the English Parliament enacted the Landlord and Tenant Act. The act sets forth details related to the landlord's obligations to maintain and repair leased premises. The act also requires that leased premises be fit for human habitation, a concept similar to the implied warranty of habitability in some U.S. jurisdictions (discussed elsewhere in this chapter). Although the English Landlord and Tenant Act applies mainly to dwellings rented for very low rates, it has improved, to some extent, the rights of all tenants in that country.

For Critical Analysis: *Given that tenants in the United States have traditionally had rights under the common law, why has it been necessary to regulate landlord-tenant relationships in the United States so extensively by statutory law?*

> **NOTE** Options that may be available to a tenant on a landlord's breach of the implied warranty of habitability include repairing the defect and deducting the amount from the rent, canceling the lease, and suing for damages.

In some situations, such as when a landlord breaches the implied warranty of habitability, a tenant is allowed to withhold rent as a remedy. When rent withholding is authorized under a statute (sometimes referred to as a "rent-strike" statute), the tenant must usually put the amount withheld into an *escrow account.* This account is held in the name of the depositor (in this case, the tenant) and an *escrow agent* (in this case, usually the court or a government agency), and the funds are returnable to the depositor if the third person (in this case, the landlord) fails to fulfill the escrow condition. Generally, the tenant may withhold an amount equal to the amount by which the defect rendering the premises unlivable reduces the property's rental value. How much that is may be determined in different ways, and the tenant who withholds more than is legally permissible is liable to the landlord for the excessive amount withheld.

Transferring Rights to Leased Property

Either the landlord or the tenant may wish to transfer his or her rights to the leased property during the term of the lease.

TRANSFERRING THE LANDLORD'S INTEREST.   Just as any other real property owner can sell, give away, or otherwise transfer his or her property, so can a landlord—who is, of course, the leased property's owner. If complete title to the leased property is transferred, the tenant becomes the tenant of the new owner. The new owner may collect subsequent rent but must abide by the terms of the existing lease agreement.

TRANSFERRING THE TENANT'S INTEREST.   The tenant's transfer of his or her entire interest in the leased property to a third person is an *assignment of the lease.* A lease assignment is an agreement to transfer all rights, title, and interest in the lease to the assignee. It is a complete transfer. Many leases require that the assignment have the landlord's written consent, and an assignment that lacks consent can be avoided (nullified) by the landlord. A landlord who knowingly accepts rent from the assignee, however, will be held to have waived the requirement. An assignment does not terminate a tenant's liabilities under a lease agreement, however, because the tenant may assign rights but not duties. Thus, even though the assignee of the lease is required to pay rent, the original tenant is not released from the contractual obligation to pay the rent if the assignee fails to do so.

The tenant's transfer of all or part of the premises for a period shorter than the lease term is a **sublease**. The same restrictions that apply to an assignment of the tenant's interest in leased property apply to a sublease. To illustrate, a student named Derek leases an apartment for a two-year period. Although Derek had planned on attending summer school, he is offered a job in Europe for the summer months and accepts. Because he does not wish to pay three months' rent for an unoccupied apartment, Derek subleases the apartment to Steven (the sublessee). (Derek may have to obtain his landlord's consent for this sublease if the lease requires it.) Steven is bound by the same terms of the lease as Derek, but as in a lease assignment, Derek remains liable for the obligations under the lease if Steven fails to fulfill them.

Sublease A lease executed by the lessee of real estate to a third person, conveying the same interest that the lessee enjoys but for a shorter term than that held by the lessee.

Land-Use Control

Property owners—even those who possess the entire bundle of rights set out earlier in this chapter—cannot do with their property whatever they wish. The rights of every property owner are subject to certain conditions and limitations.

There are three sources of land-use control. First, the law of torts (see Chapter 8) places on the owners of land obligations to protect the interests of individuals who come on the land and the interests of the owners of nearby land. Second, landowners may agree with others to restrict or limit the use of their property. Such agreements may "run with the land" when ownership is transferred to others. Thus, one who acquires real property with actual or *constructive* (imputed by law) notice of a restriction may be bound by an earlier, voluntary agreement to which he or she was not a party.

Third, controls are imposed by the government. Land use is subject to regulation by the state within whose political boundaries the land is located. Most states authorize control over land use through various planning boards and zoning authorities at a city or county level. The federal government does not engage in land-use control under normal circumstances, except with respect to federally owned land.[8] The federal government does influence state and local regulation, however, through the allocation of federal funds. Stipulations on land use may be a condition to the states' receiving such funds.

Sources of Public Control

The states' power to control the use of land through legislation is derived from their *police power* and the doctrine of *eminent domain*. Under their police

8. Federal (and state) laws concerning environmental matters such as air and water quality, the protection of endangered species, and the preservation of natural wetlands are also a source of land-use control. Some of these laws were discussed in Chapter 20.

Eminent Domain The power of a government to take land for public use from private citizens for just compensation.

power, state governments enact legislation that promotes the health, safety, and welfare of their citizens. This legislation includes land-use controls. The power of **eminent domain** is the government's authority to take private property for public use or purpose without the owner's consent. Typically, this is accomplished through a judicial proceeding to obtain title to the land.

Police Power

As an exercise of its police power,[9] a state can regulate the use of land within its jurisdiction. A few states control land use at the state level. Hawaii, for instance, employs a statewide land-use classification scheme. Some states have a land-permit process that operates in conjunction with local control. Florida, for example, uses such a scheme in certain areas of "critical environmental concern" to permit or prohibit development on the basis of available roads, sewers, and so on. Vermont also utilizes a statewide land-permit scheme.

Usually, however, a state authorizes its city or county governments to regulate the use of land within their local jurisdictions. A state confers this power through *enabling legislation*. Enabling legislation normally requires local governments to devise *general plans* before imposing other land-use controls. Enabling acts also typically authorize local bodies to enact *zoning laws* to regulate the use of land and the types of and specifications for structures. Local planning boards may regulate the development of subdivisions, in which private developers subdivide tracts of land and construct commercial or residential units for resale to others. Local governments may also enact growth-management ordinances to control development in their jurisdictions.

General Plan A comprehensive document that local jurisdictions are often required by state law to devise and implement as a precursor to specific land-use regulations.

GOVERNMENT PLANS.   Most states require that land-use laws follow a local government's general plan. A **general plan** is a comprehensive, long-term scheme dealing with the physical development, and in some cases redevelopment, of a city or community. It addresses such concerns as types of housing, protection of natural resources, provision of public facilities and transportation, and other issues related to land use. A plan indicates the direction of growth in a community and the contributions that private developers must make toward providing such public facilities as roads. If a proposed use is not authorized by the general plan, the plan may be amended to permit the use. (A plan may also be amended to preclude a proposed use.)

Even when a proposed use complies with a general plan, it may not be allowed. Most jurisdictions have requirements in addition to those in the general plan. These requirements are then included in specific plans—also called special, area, or community plans. Specific plans typically pertain to only a portion of a jurisdiction's area. For example, a specific plan may concern a downtown area subject to redevelopment efforts, an area with special environmental concerns, or an area with increased public transportation needs arising from population growth.

Zoning The division of a city by legislative regulation into districts and the application in each district of regulations having to do with structural and architectural designs of buildings and prescribing the use to which buildings within designated districts may be put.

ZONING LAWS.   In addition to complying with a general plan and any specific plans, a particular land use must comply with zoning laws. The term **zoning** refers to the dividing of an area into districts to which specific land-use regu-

9.   As pointed out in Chapter 5, the police power of a state encompasses the right to regulate private activities to protect or promote the public order, health, safety, morals, and general welfare.

lations apply. A typical zoning law consists of a zoning map and a zoning ordinance. The zoning map indicates the characteristics of each parcel of land
within an area and divides that area into districts. The zoning ordinance specifies the restrictions on land use within those districts.

Zoning ordinances generally include two types of restrictions. One type
pertains to the kind of land use—such as commercial versus residential—to
which property within a particular district may be put. The second type dictates the engineering features and architectural design of structures built
within that district.

Use Restrictions   Districts are typically zoned for residential, commercial,
industrial, or agricultural use. Each district may be further subdivided for
degree or intensity of use. For example, a residential district may be subdivided to permit a certain number of apartment buildings and a certain number of units in each building. Commercial and industrial districts are often
zoned to permit *heavy* or *light* activity. Heavy activity might include the operation of large factories. Light activity might include the operation of professional office buildings or small retail shops. Zoning that specifies the use to
which property may be put is referred to as **use zoning.**

Structural Restrictions   Restrictions known as *bulk regulations* cover such
details as minimum floor-space requirements and minimum lot-size restrictions. For example, a particular district's minimum floor-space requirements
might specify that a one-story building contain a minimum of 1,240 square
feet of floor space, and minimum lot-size restrictions might specify that each
single-family dwelling be built on a lot that is at least one acre in size. Referred
to collectively as **bulk zoning,** these regulations also dictate *setback* (the distance between a building and a street, sidewalk, or other boundary) and the
height of buildings, with different requirements for buildings in different areas.

Restrictions related to structure may also be concerned with such matters
as architectural control, the overall appearance of a community, and the
preservation of historic buildings. An ordinance may require that all proposed
construction be approved by a design review board composed of local architects. A community may restrict the size and placement of outdoor advertising, such as billboards and business signs. A property owner may be prohibited from tearing down or remodeling a historic landmark or building. In
challenges against these types of restrictions, the courts have generally upheld
the regulations.[10]

Variances   A **zoning variance** allows property to be used or structures to be
built in some way that varies from the restrictions of a zoning ordinance. A
variance may exempt property from a use restriction to allow, for example, a
bakery shop in a residential area. Or a variance may exempt a building from
a height restriction so that, for example, a two-story house can be built in a
district in which houses are otherwise limited to one floor. Some jurisdictions
do not permit variances from use restrictions.

Variances are normally granted by local adjustment boards. In general, a
property owner must meet three criteria to obtain a variance:

1. The owner must find it impossible to realize a reasonable return on the land
   as currently zoned.

Use Zoning Zoning
classifications within a particular
municipality that may be
distinguished based on the uses to
which the land is to be put.

Bulk Zoning Zoning
regulations that restrict the
amount of structural coverage
on a particular parcel of land.

Zoning Variance The granting
of permission by a municipality
or other public board to a
landowner to use his or her
property in a way that does not
strictly conform with the zoning
regulations so as to avoid
causing the landowner undue
hardship.

---

10.   See, for example, *Penn Central Transportation Co. v. New York City,* 438 U.S. 104, 98
S.Ct. 2646, 57 L.Ed.2d 631 (1978).

2. The adverse effect of the zoning ordinance must be particular to the party seeking the variance and not have a similar effect on other owners in the same zone.
3. Granting the variance must not substantially alter the essential character of the zoned area.

Perhaps the most important of these criteria is whether the variance would substantially alter the character of the area. Courts are more lenient about the other requirements when reviewing decisions of adjustment boards. As the following case illustrates, courts also tend to defer to the discretion of such boards unless there has been a clear abuse of authority.

Case 21.4 ● Allegheny West Civic Council, Inc. v. Zoning Board of Adjustment of the City of Pittsburgh

Supreme Court of Pennsylvania, 1997.
689 A.2d 225.

BACKGROUND AND FACTS Irwin Associates, Inc., contracted to sell, for $431,500, a vacant lot in an area in Pittsburgh, Pennsylvania, zoned for residential use. The deal collapsed when it was learned that the lot was contaminated with petroleum hydrocarbon and benzene in excess of state and federal guidelines. Estimated clean-up costs were $2.5 million to $3 million, with additional annual

monitoring costs of $10,000 to $20,000. Irwin asked the Pittsburgh Zoning Board of Adjustment for a variance to use the property as a parking lot. Allegheny West Civic Council wanted residential housing in the area and opposed Irwin's request. The board concluded that Irwin's proposed use would not be detrimental to the neighborhood and granted the variance. Allegheny West appealed to a Pennsylvania state court, which affirmed the board's decision. Ultimately, the case was appealed to the state supreme court.

IN THE WORDS OF THE COURT . . .
NIGRO, Justice.
* * * *

Irwin Associates' environmental consultant testified that the contamination exceeded state and federal guidelines and that a building on the property may be a health hazard because vapors could accumulate inside. Its real estate financing expert testified that it was unlikely that a financial institution would lend money for a construction project on the property because it would expose itself to potential liability for [clean-up] costs. Irwin Associates' president testified that the relatively small size of the lot precluded other permitted uses not involving improvements. The environmental consultant estimated that the [clean-up] cost would be $2.5 [million] to $3 million and annual monitoring costs would be $10,000 to $20,000. There is thus substantial evidence that Irwin Associates cannot use the property for a permitted purpose or can only conform it for a permitted purpose at a prohibitive cost. Furthermore, * * * there is evidence that the property is now without value as zoned. The local property assessment board assigned the property a fair market value of zero.

The Zoning Board did not abuse its discretion * * * in granting the variance.

(Continued)

Case 21.4—continued

DECISION AND REMEDY   The Supreme Court of Pennsylvania affirmed the board's decision to grant the variance. The variant use would not harm the character of the neighborhood, and denying the variance would create unnecessary hardship for the property owner.

FOR CRITICAL ANALYSIS—ECONOMIC CONSIDERATION   *What might have happened to neighboring property values if the variance had not been granted?*

SUBDIVISION REGULATIONS.   When subdividing a parcel of land into smaller plots, a private developer must comply not only with local zoning ordinances but also with local subdivision regulations. Subdivision regulations are different from zoning ordinances, although they may be administered by the same local agencies that oversee the zoning process. In the design of a subdivision, the local authorities may demand, for example, the allocation of space for a public park or school or may require a developer to construct streets to accommodate a specific level of traffic.

GROWTH-MANAGEMENT ORDINANCES.   To prevent population growth from racing ahead of the community's ability to provide necessary public services, local authorities may enact a growth-management ordinance to limit, for example, the number of residential building permits. A property owner may thus be precluded from constructing a residential building on his or her property even if the area is zoned for the use and the proposed structure complies with all other requirements. A growth-management ordinance may prohibit the issuance of residential building permits for a specific period of time, until the occurrence of a specific event (such as a decline in the total number of residents in the community), or on the basis of the availability of necessary public services (such as the capacity for drainage in the area or the proximity of hospitals and police stations).

LIMITATIONS ON THE EXERCISE OF POLICE POWER.   The government's exercise of its police power to regulate the use of land is limited in at least three ways. Two of these limitations arise under the Fourteenth Amendment to the Constitution. The third limitation arises under the Fifth Amendment and requires that, under certain circumstances, the government must compensate an owner who is deprived of the use of his or her property.

Due Process and Equal Protection   A government cannot regulate the use of land in a way that violates either the due process clause or the equal protection clause of the Fourteenth Amendment. A government may be deemed to violate the due process clause if it acts arbitrarily or unreasonably. Thus, there must be a *rational basis* for classifications that are imposed on property. Any classification that is reasonably related to the health or general welfare of the public is deemed to have a rational basis.

Under the equal protection clause, land-use controls cannot be discriminatory. A zoning ordinance is discriminatory if it affects one parcel of land in a way in which it does not affect surrounding parcels and if there is no rational basis for the difference. For example, classifying a single parcel in a way that does not accord with a general plan is discriminatory. Similarly, a zoning ordinance cannot be racially discriminatory. For example, a community may not zone itself to exclude all low-income housing if the intention is to exclude minorities.

A view of the ocean from a public park. If this had once been private property, why would the government have been prohibited from taking it for public use without paying the owner?

Just Compensation   Under the Fifth Amendment, private property may not be taken for a public purpose without the payment of just compensation.[11] If government restrictions on a landowner's property rights are overly burdensome, the regulation may be deemed a taking. A taking occurs when a regulation denies an owner the ability to use his or her property for any reasonable income-producing or private purpose for which it is suited. This requires the government to pay the owner.

Suppose Perez purchases a large tract of land with the intent to subdivide and develop it into residential properties. At the time of the purchase, there are no zoning laws restricting use of the land. After Perez has taken significant steps to develop the property, the county attempts to zone the tract "public parkland only." If this prohibits Perez from developing any of the land, it will be deemed a taking. If the county does not fairly compensate Perez, the regulation will be held unconstitutional and void.

The distinction between an ordinance that merely restricts land use and an outright taking is crucial. A restriction is simply an exercise of the state's police power; even though it limits a property owner's land use, the owner generally need not be compensated for the limitation. An ordinance that completely deprives an owner of use or benefit of property, or an outright governmental taking of property, however, must be compensated.

The United States Supreme Court has held that restrictions do not constitute a taking of an owner's property if they "substantially advance legitimate state interests" and do not "den[y] an owner economically viable use of his land."[12] It is not clear, however, exactly what constitutes a "legitimate state

> "[A] strong public desire to improve the public condition is not enough to warrant achieving the desire by a shorter cut than . . . paying for the change."
>
> Oliver Wendell Holmes, Jr., 1841–1935 (Associate justice of the United States Supreme Court, 1902–1932)

---

11.   Although the Fifth Amendment pertains to actions taken by the federal government, the Fourteenth Amendment has been interpreted as extending this limitation to state actions.
12.   *Agins v. Tiburon*, 447 U.S. 255, 100 S.Ct. 2138, 65 L.Ed. 2d 106 (1980).

interest" or when particular restrictions "substantially advance" that interest. Furthermore, the term "economically viable use" has not yet been clearly defined. One of the issues in the following case was whether the focus should be on the value of the land or the use to which it could be put.

Case 21.5 ● Del Monte Dunes at Monterey, Ltd. v. City of Monterey

United States Court of Appeals, Ninth Circuit, 1996. 95 F.3d 1422.

BACKGROUND AND FACTS The owners of ocean-front property in the City of Monterey, California, applied to the city several times for a permit to build a residential development. Del Monte Dunes at Monterey, Limited, bought the property and continued to seek a permit. Each time, the city denied use of more of the property, until no part remained available for any use that would be inconsistent with leaving the property in its natural state. Del Monte sold the property to the state for $800,000 more than it had paid for the property and filed a suit against the city in a federal district court. Del Monte claimed in part that the restrictions on use were an unconstitutional taking. The court awarded Del Monte nearly $1.5 million in damages, and the city appealed, arguing in part that because Del Monte sold the property to the state for more than it had paid, there must have been economically viable uses for the property.

IN THE WORDS OF THE COURT . . .
WALLACE, Circuit Judge:

* * * *

* * * The fact that [a property owner] received some money from the government in return for his property does not establish as a matter of law that economically viable uses for his property remain or that a taking did not occur.

Focusing the economically viable use inquiry solely on market value or on the fact that a landowner sold his property for more than he paid could inappropriately allow external economic forces, such as inflation, to affect the takings inquiry. * * * [O]ur focus is primarily on use, not value.

* * * *

Del Monte contended that the City denied it all economically viable use of the Dunes by requiring it to leave the property in its natural state. * * * . In support of its argument, Del Monte presented evidence establishing that the City progressively denied use of portions of the Dunes until no part remained available for a use inconsistent with leaving the property in its natural state.

* * * *

* * * [T]his evidence, viewed in the light most favorable to Del Monte, supports the jury's finding that the City's actions denied all economically viable use of the Dunes * * * .

DECISION AND REMEDY The U.S. Court of Appeals for the Ninth Circuit affirmed the jury's award. The restrictions on the property's use amounted to an unconstitutional taking, and Del Monte was entitled to damages.

FOR CRITICAL ANALYSIS—ETHICAL CONSIDERATION *Would it have been fair to Del Monte not to award damages?*

International Perspective

Like the U.S. Constitution, the German constitution places restraints on government's ability to take private property for public use. The German constitution first affirmatively establishes the right of the government to take private property for public use and then requires some payment to the landowner for the property that is taken. The German constitution also states that private-property owners have a duty to use their property for the public good.

For Critical Analysis: *Why might a government choose not to pay its citizens for property that is taken?*

Eminent Domain

As noted above, governments have an inherent power to take property for public use or purpose without the consent of the owner. This is the power of eminent domain, and it is very important in the public control of land use.

Every property owner holds his or her interest in land subject to a superior interest. Just as in medieval England the king was the ultimate landowner, so in the United States the government retains an ultimate ownership right in all land. This right, known as eminent domain, is sometimes referred to as the *condemnation power* of the government to take land for public use. It gives to the government a right to acquire possession of real property in the manner directed by the Constitution and the laws of the state whenever the public interest requires it. Property may not be taken for private benefit, but only for public use.

For example, when a new public highway is to be built, the government must decide where to build it and how much land to condemn. After the government determines that a particular parcel of land is necessary for public use, it brings a judicial proceeding to obtain title to the land.

Under the Fifth Amendment, although the government may take land for public use, it must pay fair and just compensation for it. Thus, in the previous highway example, after the proceeding to obtain title to the land, there is a second proceeding in which the court determines the *fair value* of the land. Fair value is usually approximately equal to market value.

In an attempt to preserve the natural beauty and resources of the land, environmental laws have increasingly prohibited private parties from using certain lands (wetlands and coastal lands, for example) in specific ways. Does imposing such limitations on landowners' rights constitute a taking by the government? This question is explored in this chapter's *Inside the Legal Environment.*

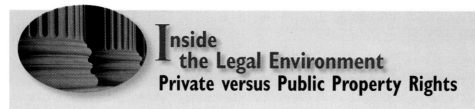

Inside the Legal Environment
Private versus Public Property Rights

Environmental regulations and other legislation to control land use are prevalent throughout the United States. Generally, these laws reflect the public's interest in preserving the beauty and natural resources of the land and in allowing the public to have access to and enjoy limited natural resources, such as coastal areas. Although few would disagree with the rationale underlying these laws, the owners of the private property directly affected by the laws may feel that they should be compensated for the limitation imposed on their right to do as they wish with their land. Several cases have been brought by private-property owners who allege that regulations limiting their control over their own land essentially constitute a taking of private-property rights in the public interest. Therefore, the private-property owners should receive the just compensation guaranteed under the Fifth Amendment.

For example, in one case a New Jersey property developer, Loveladies Harbor, Inc., owned fifty-one acres of land and planned to construct thirty-five single-family homes on fifty of the acres. A significant portion of the land (twelve and a half acres) consisted of wetlands that would need to be filled. Loveladies sought a permit from the Army Corps of Engineers to fill these wetlands, as required under the Clean Water Act (see Chapter 20). The Corps denied the permit, and ultimately Loveladies brought an action alleging that the refusal to allow it to develop the twelve and a half acres constituted a compensable taking under the Fifth Amendment.

The trial court held that when the Corps denied the permit to fill the wetlands, a taking had occurred. In affirming the trial court's decision, the federal appellate court phrased the essential question in the case as follows: "[W]hen the Government fulfills its obligation to preserve and protect the public interest, may the cost of obtaining that public benefit fall solely upon the affected property owner, or is it to be shared by the community at large[?]" The court, adopting the view of an increasing number of other courts, concluded that the expense should be borne by the public.[a]

For years, courts evaluating similar claims brought by private-property owners alleging regulatory takings generally sided with the public authorities and held that no compensable takings had occurred. Beginning in the 1980s, however, the tide began to turn, and the courts now give a little more weight to the interests of private-property owners.[b] This trend was bolstered by a United States Supreme Court ruling in 1994 in which the Court held that the city of Tigard, Oregon (a Portland suburb), could not require a property owner to dedicate a portion of her property for public use without compensation.[c]

For Critical Analysis: *Why are courts more willing today than in the past to consider the rights of private-property owners in regard to alleged regulatory takings?*

_____

a. *Loveladies Harbor, Inc. v. United States,* 28 F.3d 1171 (Fed. Cir. 1994).

b. See, for example, *Bell v. Town of Wells,* 557 A.2d 168 (Me. 1989); *Nollan v. California Coastal Commission,* 483 U.S. 825, 107 S.Ct. 3141, 97 L.Ed.2d 677 (1987); and *Lucas v. South Carolina Coastal Council,* 505 U.S. 1003, 112 S.Ct. 2886, 120 L.Ed.2d 798 (1992).
c. *Dolan v. City of Tigard,* 512 U.S. 374, 114 S.Ct. 2309, 129 L.Ed.2d 304 (1994).

The just compensation requirement was at the heart of the following case, in which the court considered a claim for compensation based, in part, on the public's perception of a health risk.

Case 21.6 ● Criscuola v. Power Authority of the State of New York

Court of Appeals of New York, 1993.
81 N.Y.2d 649,
621 N.E.2d 1195,
602 N.Y.S.2d 588.

BACKGROUND AND FACTS Joseph Criscuola owned property in Delaware County in the state of New York. To run a high-voltage power line through the county, the Power Authority of the State of New York (PASNY) acquired an easement across Criscuola's property and the property of his neighbors, through the state's power of eminent domain. In a proceeding to determine how much Criscuola and his neighbors were to be paid, the property owners sought, among other compensation, an amount represent-ing "cancerphobia" and the public's perception that exposure to electromagnetic emissions from power lines poses a health risk. The owners argued that this perception reduced the market value of their property—that the power line meant they would not be able to sell their property except at a low price. The court held that the owners had failed to prove that the public's "cancerphobia" was reasonable and denied the claim. On appeal, the owners contended that they did not have to prove that such fears were reasonable to recover compensation in an eminent domain proceeding.

IN THE WORDS OF THE COURT . . .
BELLACOSA, Judge.

* * * *

* * * The issue in a just compensation proceeding is whether or not the market value has been adversely affected. This consequence may be present even if the public's fear is unreasonable. Whether the danger is a scientifically genuine or verifiable fact should be irrelevant to the central issue of its market value impact. * * * Logic and fairness * * * dictate that any loss of market value proven with a reasonable degree of probability should be compensable, regardless of its source. If no one will buy a residential lot because it has a high voltage line across it, the lot is a total loss even though the owner has the legal right to build a house on it. If buyers can be found, but only at half the value it had before the line was installed, the owner has suffered a 50% loss. * * *

* * * *

We, of course, do not hold that claimants are relieved from giving any proof to establish their claims and just compensation damages. * * * This standard protects, as a countermeasure, the legitimate * * * concern against spurious claims and unjust encroachments against the public treasury. Some credible, tangible evidence that a fear is prevalent must be presented to prove the adverse market value impact. * * *

To add the extra component of reasonableness, as PASNY urges, * * * is not supportable or necessary. Thus, while a personal or quirky fear or perception is not proof enough, the public's or the market's relatively more prevalent perception should suffice, scientific certitude or reasonableness notwithstanding.

DECISION AND REMEDY The New York Court of Appeals reversed the decision of the lower court and remanded the case for a further determination of the amount that the property owners were to be compensated.

FOR CRITICAL ANALYSIS—POLITICAL CONSIDERATION *How does the requirement of just compensation affect the flexibility of government to enact land-use regulations?*

Ethical Perspective

Homeowners, particularly in high-crime areas, sometimes face a difficult—and expensive—situation. Police officers in pursuit of a wrong-doer may damage the homes of innocent persons in the process. The ethical question here is who should assume responsibility for these damages, the government or the innocent homeowners? Some homeowners have alleged that the reduction in the value of their property constitutes a compensable taking on the part of the government. Is it? According to at least one court, the answer is yes. The case involved a Minnesota homeowner whose house was severely damaged by the police when they attempted to capture a suspect who had entered and hidden himself in the home. To force the suspect out of the house, the police and a SWAT team fired rounds of tear gas into the home and threw grenades as well. The Supreme Court of Minnesota held that the damages constituted a taking and that the homeowner should be compensated for the damages to her home.[a]

In another case, however, the court held differently. The owner of a California convenience store had to spend $275,000 to repair the damages caused by police officers who were trying to capture a robbery suspect. The Supreme Court of California held that the damages were not a compensable taking. It held that the takings clause was not designed to compensate innocent persons for damages resulting from "routine efforts to enforce the criminal laws."[b]

For Critical Analysis: *What might be the effect on society if courts routinely held that damage to property owned by innocent persons was a compensable taking?*

---

a.   *Wegner v. Milwaukee Mutual Insurance Co.,* 479 N.W.2d 38 (Minn. 1991).
b.   *Customer Co. v. City of Sacramento,* 10 Cal.4th 368, 895 P.2d 900, 41 Cal.Rptr.2d 658 (1995).

Key Terms

Chapter Summary
Land-Use Control and Real Property

THE NATURE OF REAL PROPERTY (See pages 578–579.)	Real property (also called real estate or realty) is immovable. It includes land, subsurface and air rights, plant life and vegetation, and fixtures.

(Continued)

Chapter Summary, continued

OWNERSHIP OF REAL PROPERTY (See pages 579–582.)	1. **Fee simple absolute**—The most complete form of ownership.
	2. **Fee simple defeasible**—Ownership in fee simple that can end if a specified event or condition occurs.
	3. **Life estate**—An estate that lasts for the life of a specified individual; ownership rights in a life estate are subject to the rights of the future-interest holder.
	4. **Future interest**—A residuary interest not granted by the grantor in conveying an estate to another for life, for a specified period of time, or on the condition that a specific event does or does not occur. The grantor may retain the residuary interest (which is then called a reversionary interest) or transfer ownership rights in the future interest to another (the interest is then referred to as a remainder).
	5. **Nonpossessory interest**—An interest that involves the right to use real property but not to possess it. Easements, profits, and licenses are nonpossessory interests.
TRANSFER OF OWNERSHIP (See pages 582–586.)	1. **By deed**—When real property is sold or transferred as a gift, title to the property is conveyed by means of a deed. A deed must meet specific legal requirements. A *warranty deed* warrants the most extensive protection against defects of title. A *quitclaim deed* conveys to the grantee whatever interest the grantor had; it warrants less than any other deed. A deed may be recorded in the manner prescribed by *recording statutes* in the appropriate jurisdiction to give third parties notice of the owner's interest.
	2. **By will or inheritance**—If the owner dies after having made a valid will, the land passes as specified in the will. If the owner dies without having made a will, the heirs inherit according to state inheritance statutes.
	3. **By adverse possession**—When a person possesses the property of another for a statutory period of time (three to thirty years, with ten years being the most common), that person acquires title to the property, provided the possession is actual and exclusive, open and visible, continuous and peaceable, and hostile and adverse (without the permission of the owner).
	4. **By eminent domain**—The government can take land for public use, with just compensation, when the public interest requires the taking.
LEASEHOLD ESTATES (See pages 586–587.)	A leasehold estate is an interest in real property that is held only for a limited period of time, as specified in the lease agreement. Types of tenancies relating to leased property include the following:
	1. **Tenancy for years**—Tenancy for a period of time stated by express contract.
	2. **Periodic tenancy**—Tenancy for a period determined by the frequency of rent payments; automatically renewed unless proper notice is given.
	3. **Tenancy at will**—Tenancy for as long as both parties agree; no notice of termination is required.
	4. **Tenancy at sufferance**—Possession of land without legal right.
LANDLORD-TENANT RELATIONSHIPS (See pages 587–593.)	1. **Lease agreement**—The landlord-tenant relationship is created by a lease agreement. State or local laws may dictate whether the lease must be in writing and what lease terms are permissible.
	2. **Rights and duties**—The rights and duties that arise under a lease agreement generally pertain to the following areas: a. Possession—The tenant has an exclusive right to possess the leased premises, which must be available to the tenant at the agreed-on time. Under the

(Continued)

Chapter Summary, continued

LANDLORD-TENANT RELATIONSHIPS—continued (See pages 587–593.)	covenant of quiet enjoyment, the landlord promises that during the lease term neither the landlord nor anyone having superior title to the property will disturb the tenant's use and enjoyment of the property. b. Use and maintenance of the premises—Unless the parties agree otherwise, the tenant may make any legal use of the property. The tenant is responsible for any damage that he or she causes. The landlord must comply with laws that set specific standards for the maintenance of real property. The implied warranty of habitability requires that a landlord furnish and maintain residential premises in a habitable condition (that is, in a condition safe and suitable for human life). c. Rent—The tenant must pay the rent as long as the lease is in force, unless the tenant justifiably refuses to occupy the property or withholds the rent because of the landlord's failure to maintain the premises properly. 3. **Transferring rights to leased property—** a. If the landlord transfers complete title to the leased property, the tenant becomes the tenant of the new owner. The new owner may then collect the rent but must abide by the existing lease. b. Generally, tenants may assign their rights (but not their duties) under a lease contract to a third person. Tenants may also sublease leased property to a third person, but the original tenant is not relieved of any obligations to the landlord under the lease. In either case, the landlord's consent may be required.
LAND-USE CONTROL— PRIVATE CONTROL (See page 593.)	1. **The law of torts**—Owners are obligated to protect the interests of those who come on the land and those who own nearby land. 2. **Private agreements**—Owners may agree with others to limit the use of their property.
LAND-USE CONTROL— GOVERNMENT POLICE POWER (See pages 593–600.)	1. **Government plans**—Most states require that local land-use laws follow a general plan. 2. **Zoning laws**—Laws that divide an area into districts to which specific land-use regulations apply. Districts may be zoned for residential, commercial, industrial, or agricultural use. Within all districts there may be minimum lot-size requirements, structural restrictions, and other bulk zoning regulations. A variance allows for the use of property in ways that vary from the restrictions. 3. **Subdivision regulations**—Laws directing the dedication of specific plots of land to specific uses within a subdivision. 4. **Growth-management ordinances**—Limits on, for example, the number of residential building permits. 5. **Limits on the police power:** a. Due process and equal protection—Land-use controls cannot be arbitrary, unreasonable, or discriminatory. b. Just compensation—Private property taken for a public purpose requires payment of just compensation. "Taking" for a public purpose includes enacting overly burdensome regulations.
LAND-USE CONTROL— EMINENT DOMAIN (See pages 600–603.)	1. **Condemnation power**—Governments have the inherent power to take property for public use without the consent of the owner. 2. **Limits on the power of eminent domain**—Private property taken for a public purpose requires payment of just compensation.

For Review

1. What can a person who holds property in fee simple absolute do with the property? Can a person who holds property as a life estate do the same?

2. What are the requirements for acquiring property by adverse possession?

3. What is a leasehold estate? What types of leasehold estates, or tenancies, can be created when real property is leased?

4. What are the respective duties of the landlord and tenant concerning the use and maintenance of leased property? Is the tenant responsible for all damages that he or she causes, intentionally or negligently?

5. What limitations may be imposed on the rights of property owners?

Questions and Case Problems

21–1. Tenant's Rights and Responsibilities. You are a student in college and plan to attend classes for nine months. You sign a twelve-month lease for an apartment. Discuss fully each of the following situations.

  a. You have a summer job in another town and wish to assign the balance of your lease (three months) to a fellow student who will be attending summer school. Can you do so?

  b. You are graduating in May. The lease will have three months remaining. Can you terminate the lease without liability by giving a thirty-day notice to the landlord?

21–2. Property Ownership. Antonio is the owner of a lakeside house and lot. He deeds the house and lot "to my wife, Angela, for life, then to my son, Charles." Given these facts, answer the following questions:

  a. Does Antonio have any ownership interest in the lakeside house after making these transfers? Explain.

  b. What is Angela's interest called? Is there any limitation on her rights to use the property as she wishes?

  c. What is Charles's interest called? Why?

21–3. Property Ownership. Lorenz was a wanderer twenty-two years ago. At that time, he decided to settle down on an unoccupied, three-acre parcel of land that he did not own. People in the area indicated to him that they had no idea who owned the property. Lorenz built a house on the land, got married, and raised three children while living there. He fenced in the land, placed a gate with a sign above it that read "Lorenz's Homestead," and had trespassers removed. Lorenz is now confronted by Joe Reese, who has a deed in his name as owner of the property. Reese, claiming ownership of the land, orders Lorenz and his family off the property. Discuss who has the better "title" to the property.

21–4. Deeds. Wiley and Gemma are neighbors. Wiley's lot is extremely large, and his present and future use of it will not involve the entire area. Gemma wants to build a single-car garage and driveway along the present lot boundary. Because of ordinances requiring buildings to be set back fifteen feet from an adjoining property line, and because of the placement of her existing structures, Gemma cannot build the garage. Gemma contracts to purchase ten feet of Wiley's property along their boundary line for $3,000. Wiley is willing to sell but will give Gemma only a quitclaim deed, whereas Gemma wants a warranty deed. Discuss the differences between these deeds as they would affect the rights of the parties if the title to this ten feet of land later proved to be defective.

21–5. Subdivision Regulations. Suppose that as a condition of a developer's receiving approval for constructing a new residential community, the local authorities insist that the developer dedicate, or set aside, land for a new hospital. The hospital would serve not only the proposed residential community but also the rest of the city. If the developer challenges the condition in court, under what standard might the court invalidate the condition?

21–6. Growth-Management Ordinances. To prevent population growth from racing ahead of the local government's ability to provide adequate police and fire protection, as well as road development for the increase in traffic, the local planning board imposes an ordinance limiting the issuance of residential building permits to one thousand per year for the next three years. A property developer who owns several tracts zoned for residential housing and whose development plans comply with all other existing ordinances challenges the ban in court. Will she succeed? Discuss all the relevant issues. What difference would it make if the developer had already expended considerable resources and taken the last step toward approval of the development project?

21–7. The Lease Contract.   Christine Callis formed a lease agreement with Colonial Properties, Inc., to lease property in a shopping center in Montgomery, Alabama. Callis later alleged that before signing the lease agreement, she had told a representative of Colonial that she wanted to locate in a shopping center that would attract a wealthy clientele, and the representative had assured her that no discount stores would be allowed to lease space in the shopping center. The written lease agreement, which Callis signed, contained a clause stating that "[n]o representation, inducement, understanding or anything of any nature whatsoever made, stated or represented on Landlord's behalf, either orally or in writing (except this Lease), has induced Tenant to enter into this lease." The lease also stipulated that Callis would not conduct any type of business commonly called a discount store, surplus store, or other similar business. Later, Colonial did, in fact, lease space to discount stores, and Callis sued Colonial for breach of the lease contract. Will Callis succeed in her claim? Discuss fully. [*Callis v. Colonial Properties, Inc.,* 597 So.2d 660 (Ala. 1991)]

21–8. Taking.   Richard and Jaquelyn Jackson owned property in a residential subdivision near an airport operated by the Metropolitan Knoxville Airport Authority in Blount County, Tennessee. The Airport Authority considered extending a runway near the subdivision and undertook a study that found that the noise, vibration, and pollution from aircraft using the extension would render the Jacksons' property incompatible with residential use. The airport built the extension, bringing about the predicted results, and the Jacksons filed a suit against the Airport Authority, alleging a taking of their property. The Airport Authority responded that there was no taking because there were no direct flights over the Jacksons' property. In whose favor will the court rule, and why? [*Jackson v. Metropolitan Knoxville Airport Authority,* 922 S.W.2d 860 (Tenn. 1996)]

21–9. Limitations on Police Power.   John and Florence Dolan owned the A-Boy West Hardware store in downtown Tigard, Oregon. Wanting to expand the store and its parking lot, the Dolans applied to the city for a permit. Under the local zoning regulations, the city could attach conditions to downtown development to provide for projected public needs. The city told the Dolans that they could expand if they would dedicate a portion of their property for the improvement of a storm drainage system and dedicate an additional strip of land as a pedestrian and bicycle path. The dedication would involve about 10 percent of the Dolans' property. The Dolans sought a variance, which the city denied, and the Dolans appealed. The city claimed that there was a sufficient connection between the expansion of the store and

the dedication requirements, because the expansion would increase traffic to the area and would also increase storm runoff. The Dolans conceded that there would be increases but contended that the increases would not be enough to justify taking 10 percent of their property. The Dolans claimed that the city's condition was an uncompensated taking of their property in violation of the Fifth Amendment. How should the court rule? Discuss fully. [*Dolan v. City of Tigard,* 512 U.S. 374, 114 S.Ct. 2309, 129 L.Ed.2d 304 (1994)]

A Question of Ethics and Social Responsibility

21–10.   Lorenz and his wife purchased a home in Florissant, Missouri. Although the title to the property did not indicate it, the home had been designated as a landmark building. Lorenz later sought a variance that would have allowed him to make certain building changes, such as the installation of vinyl siding on the home. The local council denied the request. Lorenz later learned that the Weslings, an elderly couple whose home was also designated as a landmark building, had been granted a variance similar to the one Lorenz had sought. Lorenz argued that the discrepancy demonstrated that the council's decision had been arbitrary and capricious. The council members contended that they were within their discretion in allowing the Weslings' variance because of the Weslings' advanced age and because the Weslings had apparently been unaware of the ordinance at the time they made their modifications. On review, a court upheld the council's actions as being a proper exercise of discretion. [*Lorenz v. City of Florissant,* 787 S.W.2d 776 (Mo.App. 1990)]

1. Were the Weslings and Lorenz "similarly situated," as Lorenz argued? Lorenz offered evidence that he, too, suffered from physical hardship, but that evidence was contradicted by other evidence. Nonetheless, should the council have limited its inquiry and based its decision solely on property-related issues?

2. Given that the underlying rationale of all zoning and other forms of land-use control is the well-being of the community, do you agree that the council did what was ethically right by allowing special consideration for the Weslings? Alternatively, was Lorenz forced to bear a disproportionate share of the burden by being denied an identical variance? After all, the city could have uniformly enforced the ordinance and simply used tax dollars collected from the community to pay for a change in the structure of the Weslings' home so as to comply with the zoning ordinance. In this way, the landmarks would have been conserved *and* the Weslings would have been protected from hardship.

For Critical Analysis

21–11. Real property law dates back hundreds of years. What changes have occurred in society, including business and technological changes, that have affected the development and application of real property law? (Hint: Was airspace an issue three hundred years ago?)

INTERACTING WITH The Internet

■ Cornell Law University's Legal Information Institute has links to state statutes governing property for several of the states. To access these statutes, go to

http://fatty.law.cornell.edu/topics/state_statutes.html

■ Homes and Communities is a Web site offered by the U.S. Department of Housing and Urban Development. Information of interest to both consumers and businesses is available at this site, which can be accessed at

http://www.hud.gov/

■ The Internet Law Library of the House of Representatives offers extensive links to sources of law relating to real estate. Go to

http://law.house.gov/home.htm

CHAPTER 22

Promoting Competition

Contents

Chapter Objectives

After reading this chapter, you should be able to . . .

1. Explain the purpose of antitrust laws, and identify the major federal antitrust statutes.

2. Summarize the types of activities prohibited by Sections 1 and 2 of the Sherman Act, respectively.

3. Indicate why the Clayton Act was passed, and describe the types of activities prohibited by this act.

4. Describe how the antitrust laws are enforced.

5. Name several exemptions to the antitrust laws.

Antitrust Laws Laws protecting commerce from unlawful restraints.

Today's antitrust laws are the direct descendants of common law actions intended to limit *restraints on trade* (agreements between firms that have the effect of reducing competition in the marketplace). Such actions date to the fifteenth century in England. In America, concern over monopolistic practices arose following the Civil War with the growth of large corporate enterprises and their attempts to reduce or eliminate competition. To thwart competition they legally tied themselves together in *trusts,* legal entities in which trustees hold title to property for the benefit of others. The most powerful of these trusts, the Standard Oil trust, is discussed in this chapter's *Landmark in the Legal Environment.*

Many states attempted to control such monopolistic behavior by enacting statutes outlawing the use of trusts. That is why all of the laws that regulate economic competition today are referred to as **antitrust laws.** At the national level, the government recognized the problem in 1887 and passed the Interstate Commerce Act. Congress passed the Sherman Antitrust Act in 1890. In 1914, Congress passed the Clayton Act and the Federal Trade Commission Act to further curb anticompetitive or unfair business practices. Since their passage, the 1914 acts have been amended by Congress to broaden and strengthen their coverage.

This chapter examines these major antitrust statutes, focusing particularly on the Sherman Act and the Clayton Act, as amended, and the types of activities prohibited by those acts. Remember in reading this chapter that the basis of antitrust legislation is the desire to foster competition. Antitrust legislation was initially created—and continues to be enforced—because of our belief that competition leads to lower prices, generates more product information, and results in a better distribution of wealth between consumers and producers. As Oliver Wendell Holmes, Jr., indicated in the opening quotation, free competition is worth more to our society than the cost we pay for it. The cost is, of course, government regulation of business behavior.

The Sherman Antitrust Act

In 1890, Congress passed "An Act to Protect Trade and Commerce against Unlawful Restraints and Monopolies"—commonly known as the Sherman Antitrust Act or, more simply, as the Sherman Act. The Sherman Act was and remains one of the government's most powerful weapons in the struggle to maintain a competitive economy. Because of the act's significance, we examine its passage more closely in this chapter's *Landmark in the Legal Environment.*

Major Provisions of the Sherman Act

Sections 1 and 2 contain the main provisions of the Sherman Act:

1: Every contract, combination in the form of trust or otherwise, or conspiracy, in restraint of trade or commerce among the several States, or with foreign nations, is hereby declared to be illegal [and is a felony punishable by fine and/or imprisonment].

2: Every person who shall monopolize, or attempt to monopolize, or combine or conspire with any other person or persons, to monopolize any part of the trade or commerce among the several States, or with foreign nations, shall be deemed guilty of a felony [and is similarly punishable].

Landmark in the Legal Environment
The Sherman Antitrust Act of 1890

The author of the Sherman Antitrust Act of 1890, Senator John Sherman, was the brother of the famed Civil War general and a recognized financial authority. Sherman had been concerned for years with the diminishing competition within American industry. This concern led him to introduce into Congress in 1888, in 1889, and again in 1890 bills designed to destroy the large combinations of capital that were, he felt, creating a lack of balance within the nation's economy. He told Congress that the Sherman Act "does not announce a new principle of law, but applies old and well-recognized principles of the common law."[a]

The common law regarding trade regulation was not always consistent. Certainly it was not very familiar to the legislators of the Fifty-first Congress of the United States. The public concern over large business integrations and trusts was familiar, however. By 1890, the Standard Oil trust had become the foremost petroleum manufacturing and marketing combination in the United States. Streamlined, integrated, and centrally and efficiently controlled, its monopoly over the industry could not be disputed. Standard Oil controlled 90 percent of the U.S. market for refined petroleum products, and small

manufacturers were incapable of competing with such an industrial leviathan.

The increasing consolidation occurring in American industry, and particularly the Standard Oil trust, did not escape the attention of the American public. In March 1881, Henry Demarest Lloyd, a young journalist from Chicago, published an article in the *Atlantic Monthly* entitled "The Story of a Great Monopoly," which discussed the success of the Standard Oil Company. The article brought to the public's attention for the first time the fact that the petroleum industry in America was dominated by one firm—Standard Oil. Lloyd's article, which was so popular that the issue was reprinted six times, marked the beginning of the American public's growing awareness of, and concern over, the growth of monopolies, a concern that eventually prompted Congress to pass the Sherman Act in 1890.

In the pages that follow, we look closely at the major provisions of this act. Generally, the act prohibits business combinations and conspiracies that restrain trade and commerce, as well as certain monopolistic practices.

For Critical Analysis: *Is monopoly power (the ability to control a particular market) necessarily harmful to society's interests?*

___
a. 21 Congressional Record 2456 (1890).

These two sections of Sherman Act are quite different. Violation of Section 1 requires two or more persons, as a person cannot contract or combine or conspire alone. Thus, the essence of the illegal activity is *the act of joining together*. Section 2 applies both to several people who have joined together and to individual persons, because it specifies "[e]very person who . . . ." Thus, unilateral conduct can result in a violation of Section 2.

The cases brought to court under Section 1 of the Sherman Act differ from those brought under Section 2. Section 1 cases are often concerned with finding an agreement (written or oral) that leads to a restraint of trade. Section 2 cases deal with the structure of a monopoly that already exists in the marketplace. The term **monopoly** is generally used to describe a market in which there is a single or a limited number of sellers. Whereas Section 1 focuses on agreements that are restrictive—that is, agreements that have a wrongful purpose—Section 2 looks at the so-called misuse of **monopoly power** in the marketplace. Monopoly power exists when a firm has an extremely great amount of **market power**—the power to affect the market price of its product. We return to a discussion of these two sections of the Sherman Act after we look at the act's jurisdictional requirements.

Monopoly A term generally used to describe a market in which there is a single seller or a limited number of sellers.

Monopoly Power The ability of a monopoly to dictate what takes place in a given market.

Market Power The power of a firm to control the market price of its product. A monopoly has the greatest degree of market power.

Jurisdictional Requirements

Because Congress can regulate only interstate commerce, the Sherman Act applies only to restraints that affect interstate commerce. As discussed in Chapter 5, courts have construed the meaning of *interstate commerce* broadly, bringing even local activities within the regulatory power of the national government. In regard to the Sherman Act, courts have generally held that any activity that substantially affects interstate commerce is covered by the act. The Sherman Act also extends to nationals abroad who are engaged in activities that have an effect on U.S. foreign commerce. (The extraterritorial application of U.S. antitrust laws is discussed in Chapter 24.)

Section 1 of the Sherman Act

The underlying assumption of Section 1 of the Sherman Act is that society's welfare is harmed if rival firms are permitted to join in an agreement that consolidates their market power or otherwise restrains competition. The types of trade restraints that Section 1 of the Sherman Act prohibits generally fall into two broad categories: *horizontal restraints* and *vertical restraints*. Some restraints are so blatantly and substantially anticompetitive that they are deemed *per se* **violations**—illegal *per se* (on their face, or inherently)—under Section 1. Other agreements, however, even though they result in enhanced market power, do not *unreasonably* restrain trade. Under what is called the **rule of reason,** anticompetitive agreements that allegedly violate Section 1 of the Sherman Act are analyzed with the view that they may, in fact, constitute reasonable restraints on trade.

Per Se Violations versus the Rule of Reason

The need for a rule-of-reason analysis of some agreements in restraint of trade is obvious—if the rule of reason had not been developed, virtually any business agreement could conceivably be held to violate the Sherman Act. Justice Louis Brandeis effectively phrased this sentiment in *Chicago Board of Trade v. United States,* a case decided in 1918:

> Every agreement concerning trade, every regulation of trade, restrains. To bind, to restrain, is of their very essence. The true test of legality is whether the restraint imposed is such as merely regulates and perhaps thereby promotes competition or whether it is such as may suppress or even destroy competition.[1]

When analyzing an alleged Section 1 violation under the rule of reason, a court will consider several factors. These factors include the purpose of the agreement, the parties' power to implement the agreement to achieve that purpose, and the effect or potential effect of the agreement on competition. Yet another factor that a court might consider is whether the parties could have relied on less restrictive means to achieve their purpose.

The dividing line between agreements that constitute *per se* violations and agreements that should be judged under a rule of reason is seldom clear. More-

Per Se Violation A type of anticompetitive agreement—such as a horizontal price-fixing agreement—that is considered to be so injurious to the public that there is no need to determine whether it actually injures market competition; rather, it is in itself (*per se*) a violation of the Sherman Act.

Rule of Reason A test by which a court balances the positive effects (such as economic efficiency) of an agreement against its potentially anticompetitive effects. In antitrust litigation, many practices are analyzed under the rule of reason.

---

1.   246 U.S. 231, 38 S.Ct. 242, 62 L.Ed. 683 (1918).

over, in some cases, the United States Supreme Court has stated that it is apply-ing a *per se* rule, and yet a careful reading of the Court's analysis suggests that the Court is weighing benefits against harms under a rule of reason. Some have termed this a "soft," or "limited," *per se* rule. Others have called it a "narrow" rule of reason. Perhaps the most that can be said with certainty is that although the distinction between the two rules seems clear in theory, in the actual applica-tion of antitrust laws, the distinction has not always been so clear.

Section 1—Horizontal Restraints

The term **horizontal restraint** is encountered frequently in antitrust law. A hor-izontal restraint is any agreement that in some way restrains competition between rival firms competing in the same market. In the following subsec-tions, we look at several types of horizontal restraints.

PRICE FIXING.   Any agreement among competitors to fix prices constitutes a *per se* violation of Section 1. Perhaps the definitive case regarding **price-fixing agreements** remains the 1940 case of *United States v. Socony-Vacuum Oil Co.*[2] In that case, a group of independent oil producers in Texas and Louisiana were caught between falling demand due to the Great Depression of the 1930s and increasing supply from newly discovered oil fields in the region. In response to these conditions, a group of the major refining companies agreed to buy "distress" gasoline (excess supplies) from the independents so as to dispose of it in an "orderly manner." Although there was no explicit agreement as to price, it was clear that the purpose of the agreement was to limit the supply of gasoline on the market and thereby raise prices.

The United States Supreme Court recognized the dangerous effects that such an agreement could have on open and free competition. The Court held that the asserted reasonableness of a price-fixing agreement is never a defense; any agreement that restricts output or artificially fixes price is a *per se* viola-tion of Section 1. The rationale of the *per se* rule was best stated in what is now the most famous portion of the Court's opinion—footnote 59. In that footnote, Justice William O. Douglas compared a freely functioning price sys-tem to a body's central nervous system, condemning price-fixing agreements as threats to "the central nervous system of the economy."

GROUP BOYCOTTS.   A **group boycott** is an agreement by two or more sellers to boycott, or refuse to deal with, a particular person or firm. Such group boy-cotts have been held to constitute *per se* violations of Section 1 of the Sherman Act. Section 1 has been violated if it can be demonstrated that the boycott or joint refusal to deal was undertaken with the intention of eliminating compe-tition or preventing entry into a given market. Some boycotts, such as group boycotts against a supplier for political reasons, may be protected under the First Amendment right to freedom of expression, however.

HORIZONTAL MARKET DIVISION.   It is a *per se* violation of Section 1 of the Sherman Act for competitors to divide up territories or customers. For exam-ple, manufacturers A, B, and C compete against each other in the states of

Horizontal Restraint Any agreement that in some way restrains competition between rival firms competing in the same market.

Price-Fixing Agreement An agreement between competitors in which the competitors agree to fix the prices of products or services at a certain level; prohibited by the Sherman Act.

Group Boycott The refusal to deal with a particular person or firm by a group of competitors; prohibited by the Sherman Act.

---

2.   310 U.S. 150, 60 S.Ct. 811, 84 L.Ed.2d 1129 (1940).

Kansas, Nebraska, and Iowa. By agreement, A sells products only in Kansas; B sells only in Nebraska; and C sells only in Iowa. This concerted action reduces marketing costs and allows all three (assuming there is no other competition) to raise the price of the goods sold in their respective states. The same violation would take place if A, B, and C simply agreed that A would sell only to institutional purchasers (such as school districts, universities, state agencies and departments, and municipalities) in all three states, B only to wholesalers, and C only to retailers.

In the following case, after a partnership's dissolution, the former partners agreed to restrict future advertising to certain geographical regions. At issue is whether the agreement constituted a *per se* violation of Section 1 of the Sherman Act.

Case 22.1 ● Blackburn v. Sweeney

United States Court of Appeals, Seventh Circuit, 1995.
53 F.3d 825.

HISTORICAL AND SOCIAL SETTING

Disagreements over money often lead to the breakup of partnerships and other business associations—because money is the most common reason for going into business. Perhaps the most common mistake of partners—including lawyers who practice law together—is failing to adopt the common-sense approach of putting their partnership agreement in writing when business begins. It is the wrong time to attempt to come to an agreement after relations have become hostile, especially if the partnership has already dissolved.

BACKGROUND AND FACTS Thomas Blackburn, Raymond Green, Charles Sweeney, and Daniel Pfeiffer practiced law together as partners, relying on advertising to attract clients. When they came to a disagreement over the use of partnership funds, they split into separate partnerships—Blackburn and Green, and Sweeney and Pfeiffer. After the split, they negotiated and signed an agreement that restricted, for an indefinite time, the geographical area within which each partnership could advertise. Less than a year later, the Blackburn firm filed a suit in a federal district court against the Sweeney firm, alleging in part that the restriction on advertising was a *per se* violation of the Sherman Act. The court ruled in favor of Sweeney, and Blackburn appealed.

IN THE WORDS OF THE COURT . . .
CUMMINGS, Circuit Judge.
  * * * *

  * * * The purpose of the advertising Agreement was, as testified to by defendant Sweeney, to "really trade markets * * * . We, in effect, said that'll be your market." Both parties in this case * * * rely heavily on advertising as their primary source of clients. * * * [T]he reciprocal Agreement to limit advertising to different geographical regions was intended to be, and sufficiently approximates an agreement to allocate markets so that the *per se* rule of illegality applies.

DECISION AND REMEDY The U.S. Court of Appeals for the Seventh Circuit reversed the ruling of the lower court and remanded the case for the entry of a judgment in favor of the Blackburn firm.

FOR CRITICAL ANALYSIS—ETHICAL CONSIDERATION *Why didn't the court see the agreement to limit advertising as a reasonable covenant not to compete?*

TRADE ASSOCIATIONS.   Businesses in the same general industry or profession frequently organize trade associations to pursue common interests. A trade association's activities may include facilitating exchanges of information, representing members' business interests before governmental bodies, conducting advertising campaigns, and setting regulatory standards to govern the industry or profession. Generally, the rule of reason is applied to many of these horizontal actions.

For example, if a court finds that a trade association practice or agreement that restrains trade is sufficiently beneficial both to the association and to the public, it may deem the restraint reasonable. Other trade association agreements may have such substantially anticompetitive effects that the court will consider them to be in violation of Section 1 of the Sherman Act. In *National Society of Professional Engineers v. United States*,[3] for example, it was held that the society's code of ethics—which prohibited members from discussing prices with a potential customer until after the customer had chosen an engineer—was a Section 1 violation. The United States Supreme Court found that this ban on competitive bidding was "nothing less than a frontal assault on the basic policy of the Sherman Act."

JOINT VENTURES.   Joint ventures undertaken by competitors are also subject to antitrust laws. A *joint venture* is an undertaking by two or more individuals or firms for a specific purpose. If a joint venture does not involve price fixing or market divisions, the agreement will be analyzed under the rule of reason. Whether the venture will then be upheld under Section 1 depends on an overall assessment of the purposes of the venture, a strict analysis of the potential benefits relative to the likely harms, and—in some cases—an assessment of whether there are less restrictive alternatives for achieving the same goals.[4]

---

3.   453 U.S. 679, 98 S.Ct. 1355, 55 L.Ed.2d 637 (1978).
4.   See, for example, *United States v. Morgan*, 118 F.Supp. 621 (S.D.N.Y. 1953). This case is often cited as a classic example of how to judge joint ventures under the rule of reason.

A retail store displays a well-known designer's clothing. Is an agreement between the manufacturer and an independent retailer to sell the clothing at a certain price considered a violation of the Sherman Act?

Section 1—Vertical Restraints

Vertical Restraint Any restraint on trade created by agreements between firms at different levels in the manufacturing and distribution process.

A **vertical restraint** of trade is one that results from an agreement between firms at different levels in the manufacturing and distribution process. In contrast to horizontal relationships, which occur at the same level of operation, vertical relationships encompass the entire chain of production: the purchase of inventory, basic manufacturing, distribution to wholesalers, and eventual sale of a product at the retail level. For some products, these distinct phases may be carried out by different firms. If a single firm may carry out two or more of the different functional phases involved in bringing a product to the final consumer, the firm is considered to be a **vertically integrated firm.**

Vertically Integrated Firm A firm that carries out two or more functional phases (manufacture, distribution, retailing, and so on) of a product.

Even though firms operating at different functional levels are not in direct competition with one another, they are in competition with other firms. Thus, agreements between firms standing in a vertical relationship do significantly affect competition. Some vertical restraints are *per se* violations of Section 1; others are judged under the rule of reason.

Resale Price Maintenance Agreement An agreement between a manufacturer and a retailer in which the manufacturer specifies the minimum retail price of its products. Resale price maintenance agreements are illegal *per se* under the Sherman Act.

RESALE PRICE MAINTENANCE AGREEMENTS. An agreement between a manufacturer and a distributor or retailer in which the manufacturer specifies what the retail prices of its products must be is referred to as a **resale price maintenance agreement.** Resale price maintenance agreements, which are also known as *fair trade agreements,* were authorized for many years under *fair trade laws.* At issue in the following case is whether an agreement that set a maximum price for the resale of products supplied by a wholesaler to a dealer constituted price fixing in violation of Section 1 of the Sherman Act.

Case 22.2 ● State Oil Co. v. Khan

Supreme Court of the United States, 1997.
522 U.S. 3,
118 S.Ct.275,
139 L.Ed.2d 199.

BACKGROUND AND FACTS Barkat Khan leased a gas station under a contract with State Oil Company, which also agreed to supply gas to Khan for resale. Under the contract, State Oil would set a suggested retail price and sell gas to Khan for 3.25 cents per gallon less than that price. Khan could sell the gas at a higher price, but he would then be required to pay State Oil the difference (which would equal the entire profit Khan realized from raising the price). Khan failed to pay some of the rent due under the lease, and State Oil terminated the contract. Khan filed a suit in a federal district court against State Oil, alleging, among other things, price fixing in violation of the Sherman Act. The court ruled in State Oil's favor, and Khan appealed. The U.S. Court of Appeals for the Seventh Circuit reversed this judgment, and State Oil appealed to the United States Supreme Court.

IN THE WORDS OF THE COURT . . .
Justice O'CONNOR delivered the opinion of the Court.
* * * *

* * * Our analysis is * * * guided by our general view that the primary purpose of the antitrust laws is to protect interbrand competition. * * *

(Continued)

Case 22.2—continued

[C]ondemnation of practices resulting in lower prices to consumers is especially costly because cutting prices in order to increase business often is the very essence of competition.

* * * [W]e find it difficult to maintain that vertically-imposed maximum prices could harm consumers or competition to the extent necessary to justify their *per se* invalidation. * * *

* * * *

* * * [T]he *per se* rule * * * could in fact exacerbate problems related to the unrestrained exercise of market power by monopolist-dealers. Indeed, both courts and antitrust scholars have noted that [the *per se*] rule may actually harm consumers and manufacturers. * * *

* * * *

* * * [V]ertical maximum price fixing, like the majority of commercial arrangements subject to the antitrust laws, should be evaluated under the rule of reason. In our view, rule-of-reason analysis can effectively identify those situations in which vertical maximum price fixing amounts to anticompetitive conduct.

DECISION AND REMEDY   The United States Supreme Court vacated the decision of the appellate court and remanded the case. In doing so, the Supreme Court held that vertical price-fixing is not a *per se* violation of the Sherman Act but should be evaluated under the rule of reason.

FOR CRITICAL ANALYSIS—ECONOMIC CONSIDERATION   *Should all "commercial arrangements subject to the antitrust laws" be evaluated under the rule of reason?*

TERRITORIAL OR CUSTOMER RESTRICTIONS.   In arranging for the distribution of its product, a manufacturing firm often wishes to insulate dealers from direct competition with other dealers selling the product. To this end, it may institute territorial restrictions, or it may attempt to prohibit wholesalers or retailers from reselling the product to certain classes of buyers, such as competing retailers. There may be legitimate, procompetitive reasons for imposing such territorial or customer restrictions. For example, a computer manufacturer may wish to prevent a dealer from cutting costs and undercutting rivals by providing computers without promotion or customer service, while relying on nearby dealers to provide these services. This is an example of the "free rider" problem.

Vertical territorial and customer restrictions are judged under a rule of reason. The following case, *Continental T.V., Inc. v. GTE Sylvania, Inc.,* overturned the United States Supreme Court's earlier stance, which had been set out in *United States v. Arnold, Schwinn & Co.*[5] In *Schwinn*, the Court had held vertical territorial and customer restrictions to be *per se* violations of Section 1 of the Sherman Act. The *Continental* case has been heralded as one of the most important antitrust cases since the 1940s. It marked a definite shift from rigid characterization of these kinds of vertical restraints to a more flexible, economic analysis of the restraints under the rule of reason.

---

5.   388 U.S. 365, 87 S.Ct. 1856, 18 L.Ed.2d 1249 (1967).

Case 22.3 ● Continental T.V., Inc. v. GTE Sylvania, Inc.

Supreme Court of the United States, 1977.
433 U.S. 36,
97 S.Ct. 2549,
53 L.Ed.2d 568.

HISTORICAL AND SOCIAL SETTING *Since the passage of the antitrust laws around the turn of the century, the courts have been skeptical of any business action that appeared to restrain commerce, having long agreed that the "heart of our national economic policy [is] faith in the value of competition."[a] In determining what is or is not permitted under the antitrust laws, the courts have sometimes applied a rigid standard to business conduct. The trend, however, has been to establish a flexible standard, rather than a rigid one, particularly in regard to conduct that is considered to have procompetitive benefits. Under a flexible standard, a business practice that is considered a criminal offense in one decade may be judged a corporate virtue in the next. In the mid-1970s, for example, the United States Supreme Court began to qualify or overrule many of its previous decisions that prohibited certain business practices as per se violations of the antitrust laws. The Court appeared to be focusing on economic considerations, such as consumer* welfare,[b] *economic efficiency,[c] and interbrand versus intrabrand competition.*

BACKGROUND AND FACTS GTE Sylvania, Inc., a manufacturer of television sets, adopted a franchise plan that limited the number of franchises granted in any given geographical area and that required each franchise to sell only Sylvania products from the location or locations at which they were franchised. A franchise did not constitute an exclusive territory, and Sylvania retained sole discretion to increase the number of retailers in an area, depending on the success or failure of existing retailers in developing their market. Continental T.V., Inc., was a retailer under Sylvania's franchise plan. Shortly after Sylvania proposed a new franchise that would compete with Continental, Sylvania terminated Continental's franchise, and a suit was brought in a federal district court for money owed. Continental claimed that Sylvania's vertically restrictive franchise system violated Section 1 of the Sherman Act. The district court held for Continental, and Sylvania appealed. The appellate court reversed the trial court's decision. Continental appealed to the United States Supreme Court.

---

a. *Standard Oil Co. v. Federal Trade Commission,* 340 U.S. 231, 71 S.Ct. 240, 95 L.Ed. 239 (1951).

b. *Reiter v. Sonotone Corp.,* 442 U.S. 330, 99 S.Ct. 2326, 60 L.Ed.2d 931 (1979).

c. *Broadcast Music, Inc. v. Columbia Broadcasting System, Inc.,* 441 U.S. 1, 99 S.Ct. 1551, 60 L.Ed.2d 1 (1979).

IN THE WORDS OF THE COURT . . .

Mr. Justice POWELL delivered the opinion of the Court.

* * * *

Vertical restrictions reduce intrabrand competition by limiting the number of sellers of a particular product competing for the business of a given group of buyers. * * *

Vertical restrictions promote interbrand competition by allowing the manufacturer to achieve certain efficiencies in the distribution of his products. * * * Established manufacturers can use them to induce retailers to engage in promotional activities or to provide service and repair facilities necessary to the efficient marketing of their products. * * * The availability and quality of such services affect a manufacturer's goodwill and the competitiveness of his product. * * *

* * * *

* * * When anticompetitive effects are shown to result from particular vertical restrictions they can be adequately policed under the rule of reason * * * .

(Continued)

Case 22.3—continued

DECISION AND REMEDY   The United States Supreme Court upheld the appellate court's reversal of the district court's decision. Sylvania's vertical system, which was not price restrictive, did not constitute a *per se* violation of Section 1 of the Sherman Act.

FOR CRITICAL ANALYSIS—ECONOMIC CONSIDERATION   *Could the same argument made by the Court in this case (as to the effect of restrictions on market efficiency) be made in regard to resale price maintenance agreements (fair trade laws)?*

REFUSALS TO DEAL.   As discussed previously, joint refusals to deal (group boycotts) are subject to close scrutiny under Section 1 of the Sherman Act. A single manufacturer acting unilaterally, however, is generally free to deal, or not to deal, with whomever it wishes. In vertical arrangements, even though a manufacturer cannot set retail prices for its products, it can refuse to deal with retailers or dealers that cut prices to levels substantially below the manufacturer's suggested retail prices. In *United States v. Colgate & Co.,*[6] for example, the United States Supreme Court held that a manufacturer's advance announcement that it would not sell to price cutters was not a violation of the Sherman Act.

There are instances, however, in which a unilateral refusal to deal violates antitrust laws. These instances involve offenses proscribed under Section 2 of the Sherman Act and occur only if (1) the firm refusing to deal has—or is likely to acquire—monopoly power and (2) the refusal is likely to have an anticompetitive effect on a particular market.

Section 2 of the Sherman Act

Section 1 of the Sherman Act proscribes certain concerted, or joint, activities that restrain trade. In contrast, Section 2 condemns "every person who shall monopolize, or attempt to monopolize." There are two distinct types of behavior that are subject to sanction under Section 2: *monopolization* and *attempts to monopolize.* A tactic that may be involved in either offense is **predatory pricing.** Predatory pricing involves an attempt by one firm to drive its competitors from the market by selling its product at prices substantially *below* the normal costs of production; once the competitors are eliminated, the firm will attempt to recapture its losses and go on to earn very high profits by driving prices up far above their competitive levels.

Predatory Pricing The pricing of a product below cost with the intent to drive competitors out of the market.

Monopolization

In *United States v. Grinnell Corp.,*[7] the United States Supreme Court defined the offense of **monopolization** as involving the following two elements: "(1) the possession of monopoly power in the relevant market and (2) the willful acquisition or maintenance of the power as distinguished from growth or development as a consequence of a superior product, business acumen, or historic accident." A violation of Section 2 requires that both these elements—monopoly power and an intent to monopolize—be established.

Monopolization The possession of monopoly power in the relevant market and the willful acquisition or maintenance of the power, as distinguished from growth or development as a consequence of a superior product, business acumen, or historic accident. A violation of Section 2 of the Sherman Act requires that both of these elements be established.

---

6. 250 U.S. 300, 39 S.Ct. 465, 63 L.Ed. 992 (1919).
7. 384 U.S. 563, 86 S.Ct. 1698, 16 L.Ed.2d 778 (1966).

MONOPOLY POWER.   The Sherman Act does not define *monopoly*. In economic parlance, monopoly refers to control by a single entity. It is well established in antitrust law, however, that a firm may be a monopolist even though it is not the sole seller in a market. Additionally, size alone does not determine whether a firm is a monopoly. For example, a "mom and pop" grocery located in an isolated desert town is a monopolist if it is the only grocery serving that particular market. Size in relation to the market is what matters, because monopoly involves the power to affect prices and output. *Monopoly power,* as mentioned earlier in this chapter, exists when a firm has an extremely great amount of market power. If a firm has sufficient market power to control prices and exclude competition, that firm has monopoly power.

As difficult as it is to define market power precisely, it is even more difficult to measure it. Courts often use the so-called **market-share test**[8]—a firm's percentage share of the "relevant market"—in determining the extent of the firm's market power. A firm may be considered to have monopoly power if its share of the relevant market is 70 percent or more. This is merely a rule of thumb, however; it is not a binding principle of law. In some cases, a smaller share may be held to constitute monopoly power.[9]

The relevant market consists of two elements: (1) a relevant product market and (2) a relevant geographical market. What should the relevant product market include? No doubt, it must include all products that, although produced by different firms, have identical attributes, such as sugar. Products that are not identical, however, may sometimes be substituted for one another. Coffee may be substituted for tea, for example. In defining the relevant product market, the key issue is the degree of interchangeability between products. If one product is a sufficient substitute for another, the two products are considered to be part of the same product market.

The second component of the relevant market is the geographical boundaries of the market. For products that are sold nationwide, the geographical boundaries of the market encompass the entire United States. If a producer and its competitors sell in only a limited area (one in which customers have no access to other sources of the product), then the geographical market is limited to that area. A national firm may thus compete in several distinct areas and have monopoly power in one area but not in another. (See this chapter's *Inside the Legal Environment* for a further discussion of the concept of relevant market.)

THE INTENT REQUIREMENT.   Monopoly power, in and of itself, does not constitute the offense of monopolization under Section 2 of the Sherman Act. The offense also requires an intent to monopolize. A dominant market share may be the result of business acumen or the development of a superior product. It may simply be the result of historical accident. In these situations, the acquisition of monopoly power is not an antitrust violation. Indeed, it would be counter to society's interest to condemn every firm that acquired a position of power because it was well managed, efficient, and marketed a product desired

---

Market-Share Test   The primary measure of monopoly power. A firm's market share is the percentage of a market that the firm controls.

"A rule of such a nature as to bring all trade or traffic into the hands of one company, or one person, and to exclude all others, is illegal."

Sir Edward Coke, 1552–1634
(British jurist and legal scholar)

KEEP IN MIND Section 2 of the Sherman Act essentially condemns the act of monopolizing, not the possession of monopoly power.

---

8.   Other measures of market power have been devised, but the market-share test is the most widely used.
9.   This standard was first articulated by Judge Learned Hand in *United States v. Aluminum Co. of America,* 148 F.2d 416 (2d Cir. 1945). A 90 percent share was held to be clear evidence of monopoly power. Anything less than 64 percent, said Justice Hand, made monopoly power doubtful, and anything less than 30 percent was clearly not monopoly power.

Inside the Legal Environment
Relevant Market versus Trade Area

One of the difficulties in analyzing alleged violations of Section 2 of the Sherman Act is determining the relevant market. For example, consider a case that was brought by Gilbert Bathke and other gasoline retailers (the plaintiffs) located in small Iowa communities against Casey's General Stores, Inc. During the 1980s, Casey's, a multistate retailer of gasoline and other goods, had begun to lose profits to its competitors. In an attempt to increase its sales, Casey's directed its stores that were losing sales to reduce gas prices. The plaintiffs claimed that Casey's price reductions amounted to predatory pricing in violation of, among other laws, Section 2 of the Sherman Act.

One of the central issues in the case concerned Casey's share of the relevant geographical market. The plaintiffs contended that the relevant geographical market consisted of the small towns in which Casey's operated its stores. After all, contended the plaintiffs, consumers preferred to buy their gasoline in the towns in which they lived, and gasoline retailers' trade came mostly from in-town customers. The court held, however, that the plaintiffs had

failed to produce "evidence on a critical question: where those gasoline consumers could practically turn for alternatives."

The court pointed out that a geographical market "is determined by inquiring into the 'commercial realities' faced by consumers." Essentially, the question is not where consumers go for their gasoline but where they *could* go. Evidence of consumers' actual habits is not enough, said the court, to establish the relevant geographical market. To demonstrate the "logic and necessity of applying such a requirement in this case," the court illustrated the difference between a "trade area" and a "relevant market."

"Consider the following illustration," stated the court. "Fifteen miles outside of City A is a small town, Town B, which contains a single shoe store, Smith's Clothing. The only people who ever shop in Smith's Clothing are residents of Town B. When Smith's is accused of monopolization, the plaintiffs argue that Town B defines the relevant geographic market, since all of the store's customers come from there. In that case, Smith's market share is 100%. But further inquiry shows the

following. Last year 800 residents of Town B purchased shoes. 400 of them purchased from Smith's Clothing, and the other 400 purchased from the numerous shoe stores in City A. Note that this conclusion is absolutely consistent with the proposition that Smith's 'trade area' is Town B. . . . In sum, 'trade area' considers the extent to which customers will travel in order to do business at Smith's. 'Relevant market' considers the extent to which customers will travel in order to avoid doing business at Smith's."

The court concluded that the plaintiffs' evidence, at best, demonstrated only the "trade area" of Casey's stores. The plaintiffs looked at the issue "only from the perspective of Casey's rivals, not from the perspective of the consumer. This is not the correct approach to use in antitrust cases."[a]

For Critical Analysis: *How can plaintiffs in antitrust cases similar to this one obtain evidence concerning where consumers can "practically turn for alternatives"?*

a. *Bathke v. Casey's General Stores, Inc.,* 64 F.3d 340 (8th Cir. 1995).

by consumers. If, however, a firm possesses market power as a result of carrying out some purposeful act to acquire or maintain that power through anticompetitive means, then it is in violation of Section 2. In most monopolization cases, intent may be inferred from evidence that the firm had monopoly power and engaged in anticompetitive behavior.

Attempts to Monopolize

Section 2 also prohibits **attempted monopolization** of a market. Any action challenged as an attempt to monopolize must have been specifically intended to exclude competitors and garner monopoly power. In addition, the attempt

Attempted Monopolization
Any actions by a firm to eliminate competition and gain monopoly power.

must have had a "dangerous" probability of success—only *serious* threats of monopolization are condemned as violations. The probability cannot be dangerous unless the alleged offender possesses some degree of market power. In the following case, the United States Supreme Court summarizes the requirements that a plaintiff must meet to demonstrate that the defendant has attempted to monopolize a market.

Case 22.4 ● Spectrum Sports, Inc. v. McQuillan

Supreme Court of the United States, 1993.
506 U.S. 447,
113 S.Ct. 884,
122 L.Ed.2d 247.

HISTORICAL AND SOCIAL SETTING *Plastics are synthetic materials derived principally from petroleum. Because they are light, easy to clean, durable, and can be made strong, plastics are used in place of many natural substances. Most plastics are what are called polymers, made up of long chains of identical molecules. Bakelite was the world's first polymer. Bakelite was developed in 1909 and used originally in electrical insulation. Sorbothane is an elastic polymer with characteristics that make it useful in a variety of products.*

BACKGROUND AND FACTS BTR, Inc., owns the patent rights to sorbothane. In 1980, BTR granted Shirley and Larry McQuillan the distribution rights to sorbothane. In 1981, BTR split the rights between the McQuillans and Spectrum Sports, Inc. Over the next two years, BTR further undercut the McQuillans' once-exclusive rights. Finally, BTR refused to accept their orders, and the McQuillans' business failed. They filed a suit in a federal district court against BTR and Spectrum for, among other things, attempted monopolization in violation of the Sherman Act. The jury found in favor of the McQuillans, and the court ruled accordingly. BTR and Spectrum appealed, and the appellate court affirmed. The defendants appealed to the United States Supreme Court.

IN THE WORDS OF THE COURT . . .
Justice WHITE delivered the opinion of the Court.
* * * *

* * * [T]o demonstrate attempted monopolization a plaintiff must prove (1) that the defendant has engaged in predatory or anticompetitive conduct with (2) a specific intent to monopolize and (3) a dangerous probability of achieving monopoly power. In order to determine whether there is a dangerous probability of monopolization, * * * it [is] necessary to consider the relevant market and the defendant's ability to lessen or destroy competition in that market.
* * * *

* * * The purpose of the [Sherman] Act is not to protect businesses from the working of the market; it is to protect the public from the failure of the market. The law directs itself not against conduct which is competitive, even severely so, but against conduct which unfairly tends to destroy competition itself. * * * The concern that [Section] 2 might be applied so as to further anticompetitive ends is plainly not met by inquiring only whether the defendant has engaged in "unfair" or "predatory" tactics. * * *
* * * *

* * * In this case, [the jury inferred] specific intent and dangerous probability of success from the defendants' predatory conduct, without any proof of the relevant market or of a realistic probability that the defendants could achieve monopoly power in that market.

(Continued)

Case 22.4—continued

DECISION AND REMEDY   The United States Supreme Court reversed the decision of the appellate court and remanded the case.

FOR CRITICAL ANALYSIS—ECONOMIC CONSIDERATION   *Is predatory conduct always anticompetitive?*

The Clayton Act

▼ In 1914, Congress attempted to strengthen federal antitrust laws by enacting the Clayton Act. The Clayton Act was aimed at specific anticompetitive or monopolistic practices that the Sherman Act did not cover. The substantive provisions of the act deal with four distinct forms of business behavior, which are declared illegal but not criminal. With regard to each of the four provisions, the act's prohibitions are qualified by the general condition that the behavior is illegal only if it substantially tends to lessen competition or tends to create monopoly power. The major offenses under the Clayton Act are set out in Sections 2, 3, 7, and 8 of the act.

> **"The commerce of the world is conducted by the strong, and usually it operates against the weak."**
>
> Henry Ward Beecher, 1813–1887
> (American abolitionist leader)

Section 2—Price Discrimination

Section 2 of the Clayton Act prohibits **price discrimination,** which occurs when a seller charges different prices to competitive buyers for identical goods. Because businesses frequently circumvented Section 2 of the act, Congress strengthened this section by amending it with the passage of the Robinson-Patman Act in 1936.

Price Discrimination Setting prices in such a way that two competing buyers pay two different prices for an identical product or service.

As amended, Section 2 prohibits price discrimination that cannot be justified by differences in production costs, transportation costs, or cost differences due to other reasons. To violate Section 2, the seller must be engaged in interstate commerce, and the effect of the price discrimination must be to substantially lessen competition or create a competitive injury. Under the Robinson-Patman Act, a seller is prohibited from reducing a price to one buyer below the price charged to that buyer's competitor.

An exception is made if the seller can justify the price reduction by demonstrating that he or she charged the lower price temporarily and in good faith to meet another seller's equally low price to the buyer's competitor. To be predatory, a seller's pricing policies must also include a reasonable prospect of the seller's recouping its losses.[10]

Section 3—Exclusionary Practices

Under Section 3 of the Clayton Act, sellers or lessors cannot sell or lease goods "on the condition, agreement or understanding that the . . . purchaser or lessee thereof shall not use or deal in the goods . . . of a competitor or competitors of the seller." In effect, this section prohibits two types of vertical agreements

---

10.   See, for example, *Brooke Group, Ltd. v. Brown & Williamson Tobacco Corp.,* 509 U.S. 209, 113 S.Ct. 2578, 125 L.Ed.2d 168 (1993), in which the Supreme Court held that a seller's price-cutting policies could not be predatory "[g]iven the market's realities"—the size of the seller's market share, the expanding output by other sellers, plus other factors.

involving exclusionary practices—exclusive-dealing contracts and tying arrangements.

EXCLUSIVE-DEALING CONTRACTS.   A contract under which a seller forbids a buyer to purchase products from the seller's competitors is called an **exclusive-dealing contract.** A seller is prohibited from making an exclusive-dealing contract under Section 3 if the effect of the contract is "to substantially lessen competition or tend to create a monopoly."

The leading exclusive-dealing decision was made by the Supreme Court in the case of *Standard Oil Co. of California v. United States.*[11] In this case, the then-largest gasoline seller in the nation made exclusive-dealing contracts with independent stations in seven western states. The contracts involved 16 percent of all retail outlets, whose sales were approximately 7 percent of all retail sales in that market. The Court noted that the market was substantially concentrated because the seven largest gasoline suppliers all used exclusive-dealing contracts with their independent retailers and together controlled 65 percent of the market. Looking at market conditions after the arrangements were instituted, the Court found that market shares were extremely stable, and entry into the market was apparently restricted. Thus, the Court held that Section 3 of the Clayton Act had been violated, because competition was "foreclosed in a substantial share" of the relevant market.

TYING ARRANGEMENTS.   When a seller conditions the sale of a product (the tying product) on the buyer's agreement to purchase another product (the tied product) produced or distributed by the same seller, a **tying arrangement,** or *tie-in sales agreement,* results. The legality of a tie-in agreement depends on many factors, particularly the purpose of the agreement and the agreement's likely effect on competition in the relevant markets (the market for the tying product and the market for the tied product). In 1936, for example, the United States Supreme Court held that International Business Machines and Remington Rand had violated Section 3 of the Clayton Act by requiring the purchase of their own machine cards (the tied product) as a condition to the leasing of their tabulation machines (the tying product). Because only these two firms sold completely automated tabulation machines, the Court concluded that each possessed market power sufficient to "substantially lessen competition" through the tying arrangements.[12]

Section 3 of the Clayton Act has been held to apply only to commodities, not to services. Tying arrangements, however, also can be considered agreements that restrain trade in violation of Section 1 of the Sherman Act. Thus, those cases involving tying arrangements of services have been brought under Section 1 of the Sherman Act. Traditionally, the courts have held tying arrangements brought under the Sherman Act to be illegal *per se.* In recent years, however, courts have shown a willingness to look at factors that are important in a rule-of-reason analysis. This is another example of the "soft" *per se* rule referred to earlier in this chapter.

Exclusive-Dealing Contract
An agreement under which a seller forbids a buyer to purchase products from the seller's competitors.

Tying Arrangement An agreement between a buyer and a seller in which the buyer of a specific product or service becomes obligated to purchase additional products or services from the seller.

---

11.   37 U.S. 293, 69 S.Ct. 1051, 93 L.Ed. 1371 (1949).
12.   *International Business Machines Corp. v. United States,* 298 U.S. 131, 56 S.Ct. 701, 80 L.Ed. 1085 (1936).

What if a tying arrangement affects only one customer? Can the arrangement nonetheless violate Section 1 of the Sherman Act? The following case addresses this issue.

Case 22.5 ● Datagate, Inc. v. Hewlett-Packard Co.

United States Court of Appeals
Ninth Circuit, 1995.
60 F.3d 1421.

HISTORICAL AND TECHNOLOGICAL SETTING

Military investment in the 1940s fueled the growth of the electronics industry. Computers made at this time weighed several tons and required the space of a warehouse to store operating components. With the advent of smaller components in the 1960s, computers and other technological equipment became more compact. The Hewlett-Packard Company (HP) produced the first hand-held scientific calculator in 1972. In the decades since then, the growth of the electronics and computer industries has seemed unstoppable. Today, HP makes a variety of electronic products, including computer hardware and software.

BACKGROUND AND FACTS   Datagate, Inc., provided repair service for computer hardware made by the Hewlett-Packard Company (HP). HP offered the same service. HP also offered support for those who used its software, but the company refused to provide software support to those who did not buy its hardware service. Datagate filed a suit in a federal district court against HP, claiming in part that HP's practice constituted an illegal tying arrangement. The arrangement had been imposed on only one HP customer, Rockwell International, but the Rockwell hardware service contract was worth $100,000 per year. The court held that one customer was not enough and entered a judgment in favor of HP. Datagate appealed.

IN THE WORDS OF THE COURT . . .
BEEZER, Circuit Judge:
  * * * *

[One of the] elements [that] must be satisfied to establish that a tying arrangement is illegal *per se* [is that] the tying arrangement affects a not insubstantial volume of commerce. * * *
  * * * *
  * * * The * * * requirement can be satisfied by the foreclosure of a single purchaser, so long as the purchaser represents a "not insubstantial" dollar-volume of sales.
  * * * *
  * * * [T]he Rockwell hardware service contract at issue was worth approximately $100,000 per year. * * *
  This amount is sufficient.

DECISION AND REMEDY   The U.S. Court of Appeals for the Ninth Circuit reversed the decision of the lower court and remanded the case for trial.

FOR CRITICAL ANALYSIS—ECONOMIC CONSIDERATION   *Did Rockwell International have an alternative to the tying arrangement required by HP?*

Section 7—Mergers

Under Section 7 of the Clayton Act, a person or business organization cannot hold stock and/or assets in another business "where the effect . . . may be to substantially lessen competition." Section 7 is the statutory authority for preventing mergers that could result in monopoly power or a substantial lessening

> **"Combinations are no less unlawful because they have not as yet resulted in restraint."**
>
> Hugo L. Black, 1886–1971 (Associate justice of the United States Supreme Court, 1937–1971)

Market Concentration The percentage of a particular firm's market sales in a relevant market area.

Horizontal Merger A merger between two firms that are competing in the same marketplace.

of competition in the marketplace. Section 7 applies to three types of mergers: horizontal mergers, vertical mergers, and conglomerate mergers. We discuss each type of merger in the following subsections.

A crucial consideration in most merger cases is **market concentration.** Determining market concentration involves allocating percentage market shares among the various companies in the relevant market. When a small number of companies share a larger part of the market, the market is concentrated. For example, if the four largest grocery stores in Chicago accounted for 80 percent of all retail food sales, the market clearly would be concentrated in those four firms. Competition, however, is not necessarily diminished solely as a result of market concentration, and other factors will be considered in determining whether a merger will violate Section 7. One factor of particular importance in evaluating the effects of a merger is whether the merger will make it more difficult for potential competitors to enter the relevant market.

HORIZONTAL MERGERS.   Mergers between firms that compete with each other in the same market are called **horizontal mergers.** If a horizontal merger creates an entity with anything other than a small percentage market share, the merger will be presumed illegal. This is because of the United States Supreme Court's interpretation that Congress, in amending Section 7 of the Clayton Act in 1950, intended to prevent mergers that increase market concentration.[13] Three other factors that the courts also consider in analyzing the legality of a horizontal merger are overall concentration of the relevant market, the relevant market's history of tending toward concentration, and whether the apparent design of the merger is to establish market power or to restrict competition.

The Federal Trade Commission (FTC) and the Department of Justice (DOJ) have established guidelines indicating which mergers will be challenged.

---

13.   *Brown Shoe v. United States,* 370 U.S. 294, 82 S.Ct. 1502, 8 L.Ed.2d 510 (1962).

International Perspective

U.S. firms involved in mergers in other countries may find themselves subject to the antitrust laws of those countries. In India, for example, the government regulates any company that has a market share in excess of 25 percent and may bar mergers and other practices that are deemed contrary to the public interest. Taiwan prohibits mergers when the total resulting market share of the firms would exceed 33 percent.

In Germany, a company with more than 20 percent of a major market segment must inform the relevant government agency of this fact, and acquisitions or mergers that would cause undesirable market concentration can be prohibited. Mergers of particularly large companies in European nations are also subject to regulations issued by the European Union. A 1989 regulation gave the European Commission the authority to approve or reject mergers between firms with annual sales exceeding a specified threshold amount.

Other countries may have little or no regulation in respect to mergers. In Egypt, for example, private firms are generally not subject to antitrust restrictions on mergers and acquisitions.

For Critical Analysis: *If firms from different countries are contemplating a merger, what other differences in the law of the two countries—that is, other than different antitrust laws—should be considered?*

Under the guidelines, the first factor to be considered in determining whether a merger will be challenged is the degree of concentration in the relevant market. In determining market concentration, the FTC and DOJ employ what is known as the **Herfindahl-Hirschman Index (HHI)**. The HHI is the sum of the squares of the percentage market shares of the firms in the relevant market. For example, if there are four firms with shares of 30 percent, 30 percent, 20 percent, and and 20 percent, respectively, then the HHI equals 2,600 (30^2 + 30^2 + 20^2 + 20^2 = 2,600). If the premerger HHI is less than 1,000, then the market is unconcentrated, and the merger will not likely be challenged. If the premerger HHI is between 1,000 and 1,800, the industry is moderately concentrated, and the merger will be challenged only if it increases the HHI by 100 points or more. If the premerger HHI is greater than 1,800, the market is highly concentrated. In a highly concentrated market, a merger that produces an increase in the HHI between 50 and 100 points raises significant competitive concerns. Mergers that produce an increase in the HHI of more than 100 points in a highly concentrated market are deemed likely to enhance the market power of the surviving corporation. Thus, any attempted merger by the above four firms would be challenged by the FTC or the DOJ.

The FTC and the DOJ will also look at a number of other factors, including the ease of entry into the relevant market, economic efficiency, the financial condition of the merging firms, the nature and price of the product or products involved, and so on. If a firm is a leading one—having at least a 35 percent share and twice that of the next leading firm—any merger with a firm having as little as a 1 percent share will be challenged.

Herfindahl-Hirschman Index (HHI) An index of market power used to calculate whether a merger of two corporations will result in sufficient monopoly power to violate antitrust laws.

VERTICAL MERGERS.   A **vertical merger** occurs when a company at one stage of production acquires a company at a higher or lower stage of production. An example of a vertical merger is a company merging with one of its suppliers or retailers. Courts in the past have almost exclusively focused on "foreclosure" in assessing vertical mergers. Foreclosure occurs because competitors of the merging firms lose opportunities to either sell or buy products from the merging firms.

For example, in *United States v. E. I. du Pont de Nemours & Co.,*[14] du Pont was challenged for acquiring a considerable amount of General Motors (GM) stock. In holding that the transaction was illegal, the United States Supreme Court noted that stock acquisition would enable du Pont to prevent other sellers of fabrics and finishes from selling to GM, which then accounted for 50 percent of all auto fabric and finishes purchases.

Today, whether a vertical merger will be deemed illegal generally depends on several factors, including market concentration, barriers to entry into the market, and the apparent intent of the merging parties. Mergers that do not prevent competitors of either of the merging firms from competing in a segment of the market will not be condemned as "foreclosing" competition and are legal.

Vertical Merger The acquisition by a company at one stage of production of a company at a higher or lower stage of production (such as a company merging with one of its suppliers or retailers).

CONGLOMERATE MERGERS.   There are three general types of **conglomerate mergers:** market-extension, product-extension, and diversification mergers. A market-extension merger occurs when a firm seeks to sell its product in a new

Conglomerate Merger A merger between firms that do not compete with each other because they are in different markets (as opposed to horizontal and vertical mergers).

---

14.   353 U.S. 586, 77 S.Ct. 872, 1 L.Ed.2d 1057 (1957).

market by merging with a firm already established in that market. A product-extension merger occurs when a firm seeks to add a closely related product to its existing line by merging with a firm already producing that product. For example, a manufacturer might seek to extend its line of household products to include floor wax by acquiring a leading manufacturer of floor wax. Diversification occurs when a firm merges with another firm that offers a product or service wholly unrelated to the first firm's existing activities. An example of a diversification merger is an automobile manufacturer's acquisition of a motel chain. The following classic case involves a product-extension conglomerate merger.

Case 22.6 ● Federal Trade Commission v. Procter & Gamble Co.

Supreme Court of the United States, 1967.
386 U.S. 568,
87 S.Ct. 1224,
18 L.Ed.2d 303.

COMPANY PROFILE   *The Procter & Gamble Company (P&G) started in 1837 in Cincinnati, Ohio, when William Procter and James Gamble merged their candle-making and soap-making businesses. In 1878, P&G, which had by then become one of the largest companies in the city of Cincinnati, introduced The White Soap. The White Soap's appeal was that it floated. Renamed Ivory in 1882, the soap was advertised as "99 and 44/100ths percent pure." The advertising campaign for Ivory was one of the first to advertise directly to the consumer. Between 1930 and 1959, P&G became the largest seller of packaged consumer goods in the United States. The company has introduced or acquired more than 160 products under such familiar brand names as Bounce, Charmin, Cheer, Crest, Crisco, Duncan Hines, Folgers Coffee, Hawaiian Punch, Head & Shoulders, Icy Hot, Old Spice, Safeguard, Spic and Span, Tide, and Vicks.*

BACKGROUND AND FACTS   P&G, a large and diversified producer of high-turnover household products, acquired Clorox Chemical Company. At the time, Clorox was the leading manufacturer of household bleach in a highly concentrated market. Purex, the major competitor, did not sell its product in some markets, primarily in the northeastern and mid-Atlantic states. P&G's large advertising budget, along with other factors, allowed it to enjoy economic advantages in advertising its products. The Federal Trade Commission (FTC) brought an action against P&G, claiming that P&G's acquisition of Clorox substantially lessened competition in the market for liquid bleach and thus violated Section 7 of the Clayton Act. Arguing that the merger prevented other bleach products from entering the market, thereby eliminating potential competitors, the FTC ordered P&G to divest itself of (give up) the Clorox Chemical Company. P&G appealed. The appellate court reversed the FTC order and directed that the FTC's complaint be dismissed. The FTC appealed to the United States Supreme Court.

IN THE WORDS OF THE COURT . . .
Mr. Justice DOUGLAS delivered the opinion of the Court.
    * * * *

At the time of the acquisition, Clorox was the leading manufacturer of household liquid bleach, with 48.8% of the national sales * * * . The industry is highly concentrated; in 1957, Clorox and Purex accounted for almost 65% of the Nation's household liquid bleach sales, and, together with four other firms, for almost 80%. * * *
    * * * *

Since all liquid bleach is chemically identical, advertising and sales promotion are vital. * * *
    * * * *

* * * [T]he substitution of Procter with its huge assets and advertising advantages for the already dominant Clorox would dissuade new entrants and discourage active competition from the firms already in the industry due to fear of retaliation by Procter.

(Continued)

Case 22.6—continued

DECISION AND REMEDY The United States Supreme Court upheld the FTC order that Procter & Gamble divest itself of the Clorox Company.

FOR CRITICAL ANALYSIS—POLITICAL CONSIDERATION *How should a court determine when potential competition is sufficiently injured to require that a corporate acquisition be prevented?*

Section 8—Interlocking Directorates

Section 8 of the Clayton Act deals with *interlocking directorates*—that is, the practice of having individuals serve as directors on the boards of two or more competing companies simultaneously. Specifically, no person may be a director in two or more competing corporations at the same time if either of the corporations has capital, surplus, or undivided profits aggregating more than $14.73 million or competitive sales of $1.473 million or more. The threshold amounts are adjusted each year by the Federal Trade Commission (FTC). (The amounts given here are those announced by the FTC in 1998.)

The Federal Trade Commission Act

The Federal Trade Commission Act was enacted in 1914, the same year the Clayton Act was written into law. Section 5 is the sole substantive provision of the act. It provides, in part, as follows: "Unfair methods of competition in or affecting commerce, and unfair or deceptive acts or practices in or affecting commerce are hereby declared illegal." Section 5 condemns all forms of anticompetitive behavior that are not covered under other federal antitrust laws. The act also created the Federal Trade Commission to implement the act's provisions.

> **CONTRAST** Section 5 of the Federal Trade Commission Act is broader than the other antitrust laws. It covers virtually all anticompetitive behavior, including conduct that does not violate either the Sherman Act or the Clayton Act.

Enforcement of Antitrust Laws

The federal agencies that enforce the federal antitrust laws are the U.S. Department of Justice (DOJ) and the Federal Trade Commission (FTC). The DOJ can prosecute violations of the Sherman Act as either criminal or civil violations. Violations of the Clayton Act are not crimes, and the DOJ can enforce that statute only through civil proceedings. The various remedies that the DOJ has asked the courts to impose include **divestiture** (making a company give up one or more of its operating functions) and dissolution. The DOJ might force a group of meat packers, for example, to divest itself of control or ownership of butcher shops.

The FTC also enforces the Clayton Act (but not the Sherman Act) and has sole authority to enforce violations of Section 5 of the Federal Trade Commission Act. FTC actions are effected through administrative orders, but if a firm violates an FTC order, the FTC can seek court sanctions for the violation.

A private party can sue for treble damages and attorneys' fees under Section 4 of the Clayton Act if the party is injured as a result of a violation of any of the federal antitrust laws, except Section 5 of the Federal Trade Commission Act. In some instances, private parties may also seek injunctive relief to prevent

> **Divestiture** The act of selling one or more of a company's parts, such as a subsidiary or plant; often mandated by the courts in merger or monopolization cases.

> **NOTE** In a suit under the Federal Trade Commission Act, a private party can obtain damages, but not treble damages.

antitrust violations. The courts have determined that the ability to sue depends on the directness of the injury suffered by the would-be plaintiff. Thus, a person wishing to sue under the Sherman Act must prove (1) that the antitrust violation either caused or was a substantial factor in causing the injury that was suffered and (2) that the unlawful actions of the accused party affected business activities of the plaintiff that were protected by the antitrust laws.

In recent years, more than 90 percent of all antitrust actions have been brought by private plaintiffs. One reason for this is, of course, that successful plaintiffs may recover three times the damages that they have suffered as a result of the violation. Such recoveries by private plaintiffs for antitrust violations have been rationalized as encouraging people to act as "private attorneys general" who will vigorously pursue antitrust violators on their own initiative.

Exemptions from Antitrust Laws

There are many legislative and constitutional limitations on antitrust enforcement. Most statutory and judicially created exemptions to the antitrust laws apply to the following areas or activities:

1. *Labor.* Section 6 of the Clayton Act generally permits labor unions to organize and bargain without violating antitrust laws. Section 20 of the Clayton Act specifies that strikes and other labor activities are not violations of any law of the United States. A union can lose its exemption, however, if it combines with a nonlabor group rather than acting simply in its own self-interest.
2. *Agricultural associations and fisheries.* Section 6 of the Clayton Act (along with the Capper-Volstead Act of 1922) exempts agricultural cooperatives from the antitrust laws. The Fisheries Cooperative Marketing Act of 1976 exempts from antitrust legislation individuals in the fishing industry who

Janet Reno, the Attorney General of the United States, is the head of the U.S. Department of Justice (DOJ). Who, besides the DOJ, can enforce the antitrust laws?

International Perspective

As mentioned earlier in this chapter, the reach of U.S. antitrust laws extends beyond the territorial borders of the United States. The U.S. government (the DOJ or the FTC) and private parties may bring an action against a foreign party that has violated Section 1 of the Sherman Act, and the FTC act may also be applied to foreign trade. Foreign mergers, if Section 7 of the Clayton Act applies, may also be brought within the jurisdiction of U.S. courts.

The 1994 revision of the Antitrust Enforcement Guidelines for International Operations (the guidelines are jointly created by the DOJ and the FTC) provides as follows: "Anti-competitive conduct that affects U.S. domestic or foreign commerce may violate the U.S. antitrust laws regardless of where such conduct occurs or the nationality of the parties involved." Before U.S. courts will exercise jurisdiction and apply antitrust laws to actions occurring in other countries, however, normally it must be shown that the alleged violation had a *substantial effect* on U.S. commerce. (See Chapter 24 for a further discussion of the extraterritorial application of U.S. antitrust laws.)

For Critical Analysis: *Should U.S. business firms operating within the United States similarly be subject to the antitrust laws of other countries?*

collectively catch, produce, and prepare for market their products. Both exemptions allow members of such co-ops to combine and set prices for a particular product, but they do not allow them to engage in exclusionary practices or restraints of trade directed at competitors.

3. *Insurance.* The McCarran-Ferguson Act of 1945 exempts the insurance business from the antitrust laws whenever state regulation exists. This exemption does not cover boycotts, coercion, or intimidation on the part of insurance companies.

4. *Foreign trade.* Under the provisions of the 1918 Webb-Pomerene Act, American exporters may engage in cooperative activity to compete with similar foreign associations. This type of cooperative activity may not, however, restrain trade within the United States or injure other American exporters. The Export Trading Company Act of 1982 broadened the Webb-Pomerene Act by permitting the Department of Justice to certify properly qualified export trading companies. Any activity within the scope described by the certificate is exempt from public prosecution under the antitrust laws.

5. *Professional baseball.* In 1922, the United States Supreme Court held that professional baseball was not within the reach of federal antitrust laws because it did not involve "interstate commerce."[15] (See the *Ethical Perspective* below on this topic.)

6. *Oil marketing.* The 1935 Interstate Oil Compact allows states to determine quotas on oil that will be marketed in interstate commerce.

7. *Cooperative research and production.* Cooperative research among small business firms is exempt under the Small Business Administration Act of 1958, as amended. Research or production of a product, process, or service by joint ventures consisting of competitors is exempt under special federal legislation, including the National Cooperative Research Act of 1984 and the National Cooperative Production Amendments of 1993.

8. *Joint efforts by businesspersons to obtain legislative or executive action.* This is often referred to as the *Noerr-Pennington doctrine.*[16] For example, video producers might jointly lobby Congress to change the copyright laws, or a video-rental company might sue another video-rental firm, without being held liable for attempting to restrain trade. Though selfish rather than purely public-minded conduct is permitted, there is an exception: an action will not be protected if it is clear that the action is "objectively baseless in the sense that no reasonable [person] could reasonably expect success on the merits" and it is an attempt to make anticompetitive use of government processes.[17]

9. *Other exemptions.* Other activities exempt from antitrust laws include activities approved by the president in furtherance of the defense of our nation (under the Defense Production Act of 1950, as amended); state actions, when the state policy is clearly articulated and the policy is actively supervised by the state;[18] and activities of regulated industries (such as the

> **NOTE** State actions include the regulation of public utilities, whose rates may be set by the states in which they do business.

15. *Federal Baseball Club of Baltimore, Inc. v. National League of Professional Baseball Clubs,* 259 U.S. 200, 42 S.Ct. 465, 66 L.Ed. 898 (1922).
16. See *United Mine Workers of America v. Pennington,* 381 U.S. 657, 89 S.Ct. 1585, 14 L.Ed.2d 626 (1965), and *Eastern Railroad Presidents Conference v. Noerr Motor Freight, Inc.,* 365 U.S. 127, 81 S.Ct. 523, 5 L.Ed.2d 464 (1961).
17. *Professional Real Estate Investors, Inc. v. Columbia Pictures Industries, Inc.,* 508 U.S. 49, 113 S.Ct. 1920, 123 L.Ed.2d 611 (1993).
18. See *Parker v. Brown,* 347 U.S. 341, 63 S.Ct. 307, 87 L.Ed. 315 (1943).

Ethical Perspective

The fact that baseball remains exempt from antitrust laws not only seems unfair to many but also defies logic: Why is an exemption made for baseball but not for other professional sports? This perfectly reasonable question has been asked innumerable times, and the answer is always the same: baseball is exempt because the United States Supreme Court, in 1922, said that it was. The Court held that baseball is not subject to antitrust laws because baseball leagues' activities did not involve interstate commerce—and thus did not meet the requirement for federal jurisdiction.

Under modern interpretations of what constitutes interstate commerce, the Court's decision in the 1922 case would clearly be erroneous. Nonetheless, based on that decision, professional baseball continues to retain its extraordinary status as the only professional sport exempt from antitrust laws.

For Critical Analysis: *How can you explain professional baseball's continued exempt status under the antitrust laws?*

communication and banking industries) when federal commissions, boards, or agencies (such as the Federal Communications Commission and the Federal Maritime Commission) have primary regulatory authority.

Key Terms

antitrust laws 610
attempted monopolization 621
conglomerate merger 627
divestiture 629
exclusive-dealing contract 624
group boycott 613
Herfindahl-Hirschman Index (HHI) 627
horizontal merger 626

horizontal restraint 613
market concentration 626
market power 611
market-share test 620
monopolization 619
monopoly 611
monopoly power 611
per se violation 612
predatory pricing 619
price discrimination 623

price-fixing agreement 613
resale price maintenance agreement 616
rule of reason 612
tying arrangement 624
vertical merger 627
vertical restraint 616
vertically integrated firm 616

Chapter Summary
Promoting Competition

SHERMAN ANTITRUST ACT (1890)
(See pages 610–623.)

1. Major provisions—

   a. Section 1—Prohibits contracts, combinations, and conspiracies in restraint of trade.
      (1) Horizontal restraints subject to Section 1 include price-fixing agreements, group boycotts (joint refusals to deal), horizontal market division, trade association agreements, and joint ventures.
      (2) Vertical restraints subject to Section 1 include resale price maintenance agreements, territorial or customer restrictions, and refusals to deal.

   b. Section 2—Prohibits monopolies and attempts to monopolize.

(Continued)

Chapter Summary, continued

SHERMAN ANTITRUST ACT (1890)—continued (See pages 610–623.)	2. **Jurisdictional requirements**—The Sherman Act applies only to activities that have a significant impact on interstate commerce.
	
	3. **Interpretative rules—**
	  a. *Per se* rule—Applied to restraints on trade that are so inherently anticompetitive that they cannot be justified and are deemed illegal as a matter of law.
	  b. Rule of reason—Applied when an anticompetitive agreement may be justified by legitimate benefits. Under the rule of reason, the lawfulness of a trade restraint will be determined by the purpose and effects of the restraint.

CLAYTON ACT (1914) (See pages 623–629.)	The major provisions are as follows:
	
	1. **Section 2**—As amended in 1936 by the Robinson-Patman Act, prohibits price discrimination that substantially lessens competition and prohibits a seller engaged in interstate commerce from selling to two or more buyers goods of similar grade and quality at different prices when the result is a substantial lessening of competition or the creation of a competitive injury.
	
	2. **Section 3**—Prohibits exclusionary practices, such as exclusive-dealing contracts and tying arrangements, when the effect may be to substantially lessen competition.
	
	3. **Section 7**—Prohibits mergers when the effect may be to substantially lessen competition or to tend to create a monopoly.
	  a. Horizontal mergers—The acquisition by merger or consolidation of a competing firm engaged in the same relevant market. Will be unlawful only if a merger results in the merging firms' holding a disproportionate share of the market, resulting in a substantial lessening of competition, and if the merger does not enhance consumer welfare by increasing efficiency of production or marketing.
	  b. Vertical mergers—The acquisition by a seller of one of its buyers or vice versa. Will be unlawful if the merger prevents competitors of either merging firm from competing in a segment of the market that otherwise would be open to them, resulting in a substantial lessening of competition.
	  c. Conglomerate mergers—The acquisition of a noncompeting business.

FEDERAL TRADE COMMISSION ACT (1914) (See page 629.)	4. **Section 8**—Prohibits interlocking directorates. Prohibits unfair methods of competition; established and defined the powers of the Federal Trade Commission.
ENFORCEMENT OF ANTITRUST LAWS (See pages 629–630.)	Antitrust laws are enforced by the Department of Justice, by the Federal Trade Commission, and in some cases by private parties, who may be awarded treble damages and attorneys' fees.
EXEMPTIONS FROM ANTITRUST LAWS (See pages 630–632.)	1. Labor unions (under Section 6 of the Clayton Act of 1914). 2. Agricultural associations and fisheries (under Section 6 of the Clayton Act of 1914, the Capper-Volstead Act of 1922, and the Fisheries Cooperative Marketing Act of 1976). 3. Insurance—when state regulation exists (under the McCarran-Ferguson Act of 1945). 4. Export trading companies (under the Webb-Pomerene Act of 1918 and the Export Trading Company Act of 1982).

(Continued)

Chapter Summary, continued

EXEMPTIONS FROM
ANTITRUST LAWS—
continued
(See pages 630–632.)

5. Professional baseball (by a 1922 judicial decision).

6. Oil marketing (under the Interstate Oil Compact of 1935).

7. Cooperative research and production (under various acts, including the Small Business Administration Act of 1958, as amended, the National Cooperative Research Act of 1984, and the National Cooperative Production Amendments of 1993).

8. Joint efforts by businesspersons to obtain legislative or executive action (under the *Noerr-Pennington* doctrine).

9. Other activities, including certain national defense actions, state actions, and actions of certain regulated industries.

For Review

1. What is a monopoly? What is market power? How do these concepts relate to each other?

2. What type of activity is prohibited by Section 1 of the Sherman Act? What type of activity is prohibited by Section 2 of the Sherman Act?

3. What are the four major provisions of the Clayton Act, and what types of activities do these provisions prohibit?

4. What federal agencies enforce the federal antitrust laws?

5. Name four activities that are exempt from the antitrust laws.

Questions and Case Problems

22–1. Sherman Act.   An agreement that is blatantly and substantially anticompetitive is deemed a *per se* violation of Section 1 of the Sherman Act. Under what rule is an agreement analyzed if it appears to be anticompetitive but is not a *per se* violation? In making this analysis, what factors will a court consider?

22–2. Antitrust Laws.   Allitron, Inc., and Donovan, Ltd., are interstate competitors selling similar appliances, principally in the states of Indiana, Kentucky, Illinois, and Ohio. Allitron and Donovan agree that Allitron will no longer sell in Ohio and Indiana and that Donovan will no longer sell in Kentucky and Illinois. Have Allitron and Donovan violated any antitrust laws? If so, which law? Explain.

22–3. Antitrust Laws.   The partnership of Alvaredo and Parish is engaged in the oil-wellhead service industry in the states of New Mexico and Colorado. The firm presently has about 40 percent of the market for this service. Webb Corp. competes with the Alvaredo-Parish partnership in the same state area. Webb has approximately 35 percent of the market. Alvaredo and Parish acquire the stock and assets of the Webb Corp. Do the antitrust laws prohibit the type of action undertaken by Alvaredo and Parish? Discuss fully.

22–4. Horizontal Restraints.   Jorge's Appliance Corp. was a new retail seller of appliances in Sunrise City. Because of its innovative sales techniques and financing, Jorge's caused a substantial loss of sales from the appliance department of No-Glow Department Store, a large chain store with a great deal of buying power. No-Glow told a number of appliance manufacturers that if they continued to sell to Jorge's, No-Glow would discontinue its large volume of purchases from them. The manufacturers immediately stopped selling appliances to Jorge's. Jorge's filed suit against No-Glow and the manufacturers, claiming that their actions constituted an antitrust violation. No-Glow and the manufacturers were able to prove that Jorge's was a small retailer with a small portion of the market. They claimed that because the relevant market was not substantially affected, they were not guilty of restraint of trade. Discuss fully whether there was an antitrust violation.

22–5. Exclusionary Practices.   Instant Foto Corp. is a manufacturer of photography film. At the present time, Instant Foto has approximately 50 percent of the market.

Instant Foto advertises that the purchase price for Instant Foto film includes photo processing by Instant Foto Corp. Instant Foto claims that its film processing is specially designed to improve the quality of photos taken with Instant Foto film. Is Instant Foto's combination of film purchase and film processing an antitrust violation? Explain.

22–6. Sherman Act, Section 2. For some time, the four major and independently owned downhill skiing facilities in Aspen, Colorado—Ajax, Aspen Highlands, Buttermilk, and Snowmass—offered an "all-Aspen" skiing ticket that could be used at any of the four facilities. The proceeds of the all-Aspen ticket sales were distributed to the four facilities in proportion to the number of skiers using each one. By 1977, Aspen Skiing Co. had acquired ownership of Ajax, Buttermilk, and Snowmass. The company discontinued the all-Aspen ticket, offering instead a ticket that could be used by skiers only at its three facilities. As a result of Aspen Skiing Co.'s activities, Aspen Highlands's share of the skiing market declined from 20 percent in 1977 to only 11 percent by 1981. Aspen Highlands brought an action against Aspen Skiing Co., alleging that the latter had monopolized the Aspen skiing market and that its discontinuation of the all-Aspen ticket sales constituted an intentional attempt to misuse that power in violation of Section 2 of the Sherman Act. Aspen Skiing Co. claimed that its actions represented nothing more than a refusal to participate in a cooperative venture with a competitor and therefore could not possibly be illegal under antitrust laws. Which party will prevail in court, and why? [*Aspen Skiing Co. v. Aspen Highlands Skiing Corp.*, 472 U.S. 585, 105 S.Ct. 2847, 86 L.Ed.2d 467 (1985)]

22–7. Sherman Act, Section 1. Hartwell and Business Electronics Corp. were both authorized by Sharp Electronics Corp. to sell Sharp electronic products in the Houston, Texas, area. Business Electronics continuously sold Sharp products at below suggested retail prices. Hartwell complained to Sharp Electronics about its rival's price-cutting tactics, and Sharp Electronics eventually terminated Business Electronics's dealership. Business Electronics brought an action, claiming that Sharp and Hartwell had conspired together to create a vertical restraint of trade that was illegal *per se* under Section 1 of the Sherman Act. Does Sharp's termination of Business Electronics's dealership constitute a *per se* violation of Section 1, or should the rule of reason apply? Discuss fully. [*Business Electronics Corp. v. Sharp Electronics Corp.*, 485 U.S. 717, 108 S.Ct. 1515, 99 L.Ed.2d 806 (1988)]

22–8. Sherman Act, Section 1. Harcourt Brace Jovanovich Legal and Professional Publications (HBJ), the nation's largest provider of bar review materials and lecture services, began offering a Georgia bar review course in 1976. It was in direct, and often intense, competition with BRG of Georgia, Inc., the other main provider of bar review courses in Georgia, from 1977 to 1979. In early 1980, HBJ and BRG entered into an agreement that gave

BRG the exclusive right to market HBJ's materials in Georgia and to use its trade name, Bar/Bri. The parties agreed that HBJ would not compete with BRG in Georgia and that BRG would not compete with HBJ outside of Georgia. Immediately after the 1980 agreement, the price of BRG's course was increased from $150 to over $400. Jay Palmer, a former law student, brought an action against the two firms, alleging that the 1980 agreement violated Section 1 of the Sherman Act. What will the court decide? Discuss fully. [*Palmer v. BRG of Georgia, Inc.*, 498 U.S. 46, 111 S.Ct. 401, 112 L.Ed.2d 349 (1990)]

22–9. Clayton Act. Ford Motor Co. purchased Autolite Co., a manufacturer of spark plugs. Ford, Chrysler, and General Motors together produced 90 percent of American automobiles. The spark plug market was dominated by Champion (50 percent), General Motors (30 percent), and Autolite (15 percent). Ford had planned to begin manufacturing its own spark plugs but decided to buy Autolite instead. Following Ford's purchase of Autolite, Champion was the only independent spark plug manufacturer, and five years after Ford's acquisition of Autolite, Champion's share of the spark plug market had been reduced from 50 percent to about 33 percent. The United States brought an action against Ford, claiming that its acquisition of Autolite violated Section 7 of the Clayton Act because it substantially lessened competition in the spark plug market. Did Ford's acquisition of Autolite violate Section 7 of the Clayton Act by foreclosing a sufficiently large segment of the spark plug market to competition? Discuss fully. [*Ford Motor Co. v. United States*, 405 U.S. 562, 92 S.Ct. 1142, 31 L.Ed.2d 492 (1972)]

22–10. Tying Arrangements. Eastman Kodak Co. has about a 20 percent share of the highly competitive market for high-volume photocopiers and microfilm equipment and controls nearly the entire market for replacement parts for its equipment (which are not interchangeable with parts for other manufacturers' equipment). Prior to 1985, Kodak sold replacement parts for its equipment without significant restrictions. As a result, a number of independent service organizations (ISOs) purchased Kodak parts to use when repairing and serv-icing Kodak copiers. In 1985, Kodak changed its policy to prevent the ISOs from competing with Kodak's own service organizations. It ceased selling parts to ISOs and refused to sell replacement parts to its customers unless they agreed not to have their equipment serviced by ISOs. In 1987, Image Technical Services, Inc., and seventeen other ISOs sued Kodak, alleging that Kodak's policy was a tying arrangement in violation of Section 1 of the Sherman Act. Assuming that Kodak does not have market power in the market for photocopying and microfilm equipment, does Kodak's restrictive policy constitute an illegal tying arrangement? Does it violate antitrust laws in any way? Discuss fully. [*Eastman Kodak Co. v. Image Technical Services, Inc.*, 504 U.S. 451, 112 S.Ct. 2072, 119 L.Ed.2d 265 (1992)]

22–11. Robinson-Patman Act. Stelwagon Manufacturing Co. agreed with Tarmac Roofing Systems, Inc., to promote and develop a market for Tarmac's products in the Philadelphia area. In return, Tarmac promised not to sell its products to other area distributors. In 1991, Stelwagon learned that Tarmac had been selling its products to Stelwagon's competitors—the Standard Roofing Co. and the Celotex Corp.—at substantially lower prices. Stelwagon filed a suit against Tarmac in a federal district court. What is the principal factor in determining whether Tarmac violated the Robinson-Patman Act? Did Tarmac violate the act? [*Stelwagon Manufacturing Co. v. Tarmac Roofing Systems, Inc.,* 63 F.3d 1267 (3d Cir. 1995)]

22–12. Antitrust Laws. Great Western Directories, Inc. (GW), is an independent publisher of telephone directory Yellow Pages. GW buys information for its listings from Southwestern Bell Telephone Co. (SBT). Southwestern Bell Corp. owns SBT and Southwestern Bell Yellow Pages (SBYP), which publishes a directory in competition with GW. In June 1988, in some markets, SBT raised the price for its listing information, and SBYP lowered the price for advertising in its Yellow Pages. GW feared that these companies would do the same thing in other local markets, and it would then be too expensive to compete in those markets. Because of this fear, GW left one market and declined to compete in another. Consequently, SBYP had a monopoly in those markets. GW and another independent publisher filed a suit in a federal district court against Southwestern Bell Corp. What antitrust law, if any, did Southwestern Bell Corp. violate? Should the independent companies be entitled to damages? [*Great Western Directories, Inc. v. Southwestern Bell Telephone Co.,* 74 F.3d 613 (5th Cir. 1996)]

A Question of Ethics and Social Responsibility

22–13. A group of lawyers in the District of Columbia regularly acted as court-appointed attorneys for indigent defendants in District of Columbia criminal cases. At a meeting of the Superior Court Trial Lawyers Association (SCTLA), the attorneys agreed to stop providing this representation until the district increased their compensation. Their subsequent boycott had a severe impact on the district's criminal justice system, and the District of Columbia gave in to the lawyers' demands for higher pay. After the lawyers had returned to work, the Federal Trade Commission filed a complaint against the SCTLA and four of its officers and, after an investigation, ruled that the SCTLA's activities constituted an illegal group boycott in violation of antitrust laws. [*Federal Trade Commission v. Superior Court Trial Lawyers Association,* 493 U.S. 411, 110 S.Ct. 768, 107 L.Ed.2d 851 (1990)]

1. The SCTLA obviously was aware of the negative impact its decision would have on the district's criminal justice system. Given this fact, do you think the lawyers behaved ethically?
2. On appeal, the SCTLA claimed that its boycott was undertaken to publicize the fact that the attorneys were underpaid and that the boycott thus constituted an expression protected by the First Amendment. Do you agree with this argument?
3. Labor unions have the right to strike when negotiations between labor and management fail to result in agreement. Is it fair to prohibit members of the SCTLA from "striking" against their employer, the District of Columbia, simply because the SCTLA is a professional organization and not a labor union?

For Critical Analysis

22–14. Critics of antitrust law claim that in the long run, competitive market forces will eliminate private monopolies unless they are fostered by government regulation. Do you agree with these critics? Why or why not?

INTERACTING WITH
The Internet

■ The Antitrust Division of the U.S. Department of Justice is online at

http://www.usdoj.gov/

■ If you use the Yahoo browser, you can get valuable information about antitrust law by accessing

http://www.yahoo.com/Government/Law/

■ To see the American Bar Association's Web page on antitrust law, go to

http://www.abanet.org/antitrust

■ Go to West's Legal Studies Home Page at

http://www.westbuslaw.com

There you will find a variety of legal resources. Visit us often!

Investor Protection

Contents

Chapter Objectives

After reading this chapter, you should be able to . . .

1. Define what is meant by the term *securities*.
2. Describe the purpose and provisions of the Securities Act of 1933.
3. Explain the purpose and provisions of the Securities Exchange Act of 1934.
4. Identify federal laws that specifically regulate investment companies.
5. Point out some of the features of state securities laws.

> **"It shall be unlawful for any person in the offer or sale of any security . . . to engage in any transaction, practice, or course of business which operates or would operate as a fraud or deceit upon the purchase."**
>
> Securities Act of 1933, Section 17

Security Generally, a stock certificate, bond, note, debenture, warrant, or other document given as evidence of an ownership interest in a corporation or as a promise of repayment by a corporation.

After the great stock market crash of 1929, various studies showed a need for regulating securities markets. Basically, legislation for such regulation was enacted to provide investors with more information to help them make buying and selling decisions about **securities**—generally defined as any documents evidencing corporate ownership (stock) or debts (bonds)—and to prohibit deceptive, unfair, and manipulative practices. Today, the sale and transfer of securities are heavily regulated by federal and state statutes and by government agencies.

This chapter will discuss the nature of federal securities regulations and their effects on the business world. First, though, it is necessary to understand the paramount role played by the Securities and Exchange Commission (SEC) in the regulation of federal securities laws. Because of its importance in this area, we examine the origin and functions of the SEC in this chapter's *Landmark in the Legal Environment*.

Securities Act of 1933

The Securities Act of 1933[1] was designed to prohibit various forms of fraud and to stabilize the securities industry by requiring that all essential information concerning the issuance of securities be made available to the investing public. Essentially, the purpose of this act is to require disclosure.

What Is a Security?

Section 2(1) of the Securities Act states that securities include the following:

> [A]ny note, stock, treasury stock, bond, debenture, evidence of indebtedness, certificate of interest or participation in any profit-sharing agreement, collateral-trust certificate, preorganization certificate or subscription, transferable share, investment contract, voting-trust certificate, certificate of deposit for a security, fractional undivided interest in oil, gas, or other mineral rights, or, in general, any interest or instrument commonly known as a "security," or any certificate of interest or participation in, temporary or interim certificate for, receipt for, guarantee of, or warrant or right to subscribe to or purchase, any of the foregoing.[2]

Generally, the courts have interpreted Section 2(1) of the Securities Act to mean that a security exists in any transaction in which a person (1) invests (2) in a common enterprise (3) reasonably expecting profits (4) derived *primarily* or *substantially* from others' managerial or entrepreneurial efforts.[3]

For our purposes, it is probably most convenient to think of securities in their most common forms—stocks and bonds issued by corporations. Bear in mind, however, that securities can take many forms and have been held to include whiskey, cosmetics, worms, beavers, boats, vacuum cleaners, muskrats, and cemetery lots, as well as investment contracts in condominiums, franchises, limited partnerships, oil or gas or other mineral rights, and farm animals accompanied by care agreements.

Registration Statement

Section 5 of the Securities Act of 1933 broadly provides that if a security does not qualify for an exemption, that security must be *registered* before it is

---

1.   15 U.S.C. Sections 77–77aa.
2.   15 U.S.C. Section 77b(1). Amendments in 1982 added stock options.
3.   *SEC v. W. J. Howey Co.*, 328 U.S. 293, 66 S.Ct. 1100, 90 L.Ed. 1244 (1946).

Landmark in the Legal Environment
The Securities and Exchange Commission

The creation of the Securities and Exchange Commission (SEC) was a direct result of the stock market crash of October 29, 1929. The crash and the ensuing economic depression caused the public to focus on the importance of securities markets in the economic well-being of the nation. The feverish trading in securities during the preceding decade became the subject of widespread attention, and numerous reports circulated concerning the purportedly speculative and manipulative trading that occurred in the stock market.

As a result, in 1931, the Senate passed a resolution calling for an extensive investigation of securities trading. The investigation led, ultimately, to the passage by Congress of the Securities Act of 1933, which is also known as the *truth-in-securities* bill. In the following year, Congress passed the Securities Exchange Act. This 1934 act created the Securities and Exchange Commission as an independent regulatory agency whose function was to administer the 1933 and 1934 acts. Its major responsibilities in this respect are as follows:

1. Requiring disclosure of facts concerning offerings of securities listed on national securities exchanges and of certain securities traded over the counter (OTC).

2. Regulating the trade in securities on the thirteen national and regional securities exchanges and in the over-the-counter markets.
3. Investigating securities fraud.
4. Regulating the activities of securities brokers, dealers, and investment advisers and requiring their registration.
5. Supervising the activities of mutual funds.
6. Recommending administrative sanctions, injunctive remedies, and criminal prosecution against those who violate securities laws. (The SEC can bring enforcement actions for civil violations of federal securities laws. The Fraud Section of the Criminal Division of the Department of Justice prosecutes criminal violations.)

Since its creation, the SEC's regulatory functions have gradually been increased by legislation granting it authority in different areas. We look at the expanding powers of the SEC later in the chapter.

For Critical Analysis: *What is the source of the national government's authority to regulate the securities industry?*

---

offered to the public either through the mails or through any facility of interstate commerce, including securities exchanges. Issuing corporations must file a *registration statement* with the SEC. Investors must be provided with a *prospectus* that describes the security being sold, the issuing corporation, and the investment or risk attaching to the security. In principle, the registration statement and the prospectus supply sufficient information to enable unsophisticated investors to evaluate the financial risk involved.

> **BE AWARE** Federal securities laws do not supersede state securities laws.

CONTENTS OF THE REGISTRATION STATEMENT.   The registration statement must include the following:

1. A description of the significant provisions of the security offered for sale, including the relationship between that security and the other capital securities of the registrant. Also, the corporation must disclose how it intends to use the proceeds of the sale.
2. A description of the registrant's properties and business.
3. A description of the management of the registrant and its security holdings; remuneration; and other benefits, including pensions and stock options. Any interests of directors or officers in any material transactions with the corporation must be disclosed.

4. A financial statement certified by an independent public accounting firm.

5. A description of pending lawsuits.

In 1996, the SEC undertook steps to simplify corporate securities–offering procedures that will make it easier for small businesses to raise capital. Generally, the SEC intends to eliminate many of its regulations and required forms, and streamline the disclosure process, so that requirements will be easier to understand. The SEC may also create broader exemptions from registration requirements for small businesses (exemptions under the 1933 act will be discussed shortly).

OTHER REQUIREMENTS.   Before filing the registration statement and the prospectus with the SEC, the corporation is allowed to obtain an underwriter— a company that agrees to purchase the new issue of securities for resale to the public. There is a twenty-day waiting period (which can be accelerated by the SEC) after registration before the sale can take place. During this period, oral offers between interested investors and the issuing corporation concerning the purchase and sale of the proposed securities may take place; very limited written advertising is allowed. At this time, the so-called **red herring** prospectus may be distributed. It gets its name from the red legend printed across it stating that the registration has been filed but has not become effective.

After the waiting period, the registered securities can be legally bought and sold. Written advertising is allowed in the form of a **tombstone ad,** so named because historically the format resembles a tombstone. Such ads simply tell the investor where and how to obtain a prospectus. Normally, any other type of advertising is prohibited.

VIOLATIONS.   As mentioned, the SEC has the power to investigate and bring civil enforcement actions against companies that violate federal securities laws, including the Securities Act of 1933. Criminal violations are prosecuted by the Department of Justice. When the SEC was formed, Congress intended that the SEC also would rely on private lawsuits as a supplement to its efforts to enforce securities laws. Thus, private parties, such as shareholders, can bring suits against those who violate federal securities laws. (See the *Inside the Legal Environment* later in this chapter for a discussion of shareholder class-action suits.)

Registration violations of the 1933 act are not treated lightly. In the following classic case, purchasers of the corporation's bonds (bonds represent the borrowing of money by firms) sued BarChris Construction Corporation under Section 11 of the Securities Act of 1933. Section 11 imposes liability when a registration statement contains material false statements or material omissions.

> **DON'T FORGET** The purpose of the Securities Act of 1933 is disclosure— the SEC does not consider whether a security is worth the investment.

Red Herring A preliminary prospectus that can be distributed to potential investors after the registration statement (for a securities offering) has been filed with the Securities and Exchange Commission. The name derives from the red legend printed across the prospectus stating that the registration has been filed but has not become effective.

Tombstone Ad An advertisement, historically in a format resembling a tombstone, of a securities offering. The ad informs potential investors of where and how they may obtain a prospectus.

Case 23.1 ⬤ Escott v. BarChris Construction Corp.

United States District Court,
Southern District of New York, 1968.
283 F.Supp. 643.

HISTORICAL AND TECHNOLOGICAL SETTING   *Automatic pin-setting equipment became widely available to bowling*

alleys in the early 1950s. Partly because of this development, bowling became the leading U.S. indoor sport. Not all lanes in older bowling alleys could accommodate the new equipment. Business was good for those who built new facilities. Because the buyers of the new alleys could not always pay cash, the builders would sometimes accept

(Continued)

Case 23.1—continued

a promissory note for most of the price. Ordinarily, the builders' suppliers would not accept promises to pay in the future, however, but insisted on cash. For these reasons, the builders were often in need of capital.

BACKGROUND AND FACTS BarChris Construction Corporation was an expanding company that built bowling alleys and was in constant need of cash to finance its operations. In 1961, BarChris issued securities, in the form of bonds, after filing the appropriate registration statement with the Securities and Exchange Commission. By early 1962, the company's financial difficulties had become insurmount-

able, and BarChris defaulted on the interest due on the bonds one month after petitioning for bankruptcy. Purchasers of the BarChris bonds sued BarChris in a federal district court, alleging that BarChris had violated Section 11 of the Securities Act of 1933. The plaintiffs challenged the accuracy of the registration statement filed with the Securities and Exchange Commission and charged that the text of the prospectus was false and that material information had been omitted. There were three categories of defendants: BarChris and all of the signers of the registration statement, the underwriters, and BarChris's auditors.

IN THE WORDS OF THE COURT . . .
McLEAN, District Judge.

* * * *

* * * A material fact [is] * * * a fact which if it had been correctly stated or disclosed would have deterred or tended to deter the average prudent investor from purchasing the securities in question.

The average prudent investor is not concerned with minor inaccuracies or with errors as to matters which are of no interest to him. The facts which tend to deter him from purchasing a security are facts which have an important bearing upon the nature or condition of the issuing corporation or its business.

Judged by this test, there is no doubt that many of the misstatements and omissions in this prospectus were material. This is true of all of them which relate to the state of affairs in 1961, i.e., the overstatement of sales and gross profit for the first quarter, the understatement of contingent liabilities as of April 30, the overstatement of orders on hand and the failure to disclose the true facts with respect to officers' loans, customers' delinquencies, application of proceeds and the prospective operation of several alleys.

DECISION AND REMEDY The federal district court held BarChris Construction Corporation and all the signers of the registration statement for the bonds, the underwriters, and the corporation's auditors liable.

FOR CRITICAL ANALYSIS—SOCIAL CONSIDERATION *Under what common law theory might a buyer sue a seller for the seller's failure to disclose material facts about the goods being sold?*

Exempt Securities

A number of specific securities are exempt from the registration requirements of the Securities Act of 1933. These securities—which can also generally be resold without being registered—include the following:[4]

1. All bank securities sold prior to July 27, 1933.
2. Commercial paper, if the maturity date does not exceed nine months.
3. Securities of charitable organizations.
4. Securities resulting from a corporate reorganization issued for exchange with the issuer's existing security holders and certificates issued by

---

4. 15 U.S.C. Section 77c.

trustees, receivers, or debtors in possession under the bankruptcy laws (bankruptcy is discussed in Chapter 14).

5. Securities issued exclusively for exchange with the issuer's existing security holders, provided no commission is paid (for example, stock dividends and stock splits).

6. Securities issued to finance the acquisition of railroad equipment.

7. Any insurance, endowment, or annuity contract issued by a state-regulated insurance company.

8. Government-issued securities.

9. Securities issued by banks, savings and loan associations, farmers' cooperatives, and similar institutions subject to supervision by governmental authorities.

10. In consideration of the "small amount involved,"[5] an issuer's offer of up to $5 million in securities in any twelve-month period (including up to $1.5 million in nonissuer resales).

> **Be Aware** The issuer of an exempt security does not have to disclose the same information that other issuers do.

For the last exemption, under Regulation A,[6] the issuer must file with the SEC a notice of the issue and an offering circular, which must also be provided to investors before the sale. This is a much simpler and less expensive process than the procedures associated with full registration. Companies are allowed to "test the waters" for potential interest before preparing the offering circular. To *test the waters* means to determine potential interest without actually selling any securities or requiring any commitment on the part of those who are interested. Small-business issuers (companies with less than $25 million in annual revenues and less than $25 million in outstanding voting stock) can also use an integrated registration and reporting system that uses simpler forms than the full registration system.

Exhibit 23–1 summarizes the securities and transactions (discussed next) that are exempt from the registration requirements under the Securities Act of 1933 and SEC regulations.

Exempt Transactions

An issuer of securities that are not exempt under one of the categories listed above can avoid the high cost and complicated procedures associated with registration by taking advantage of certain transaction exemptions. An offering may qualify for more than one exemption. These exemptions are very broad, and thus most sales occur without registration. The exemptions are available only in the transaction in which the securities are issued, however (except for securities issued under Rule 504, which will be discussed shortly). A resale may be made only after registration (unless the resale qualifies as an exempt transaction).

REGULATION D. The SEC's Regulation D contains four separate exemptions from registration requirements for limited offers (offers that involve either a small amount of money or are made in a limited manner). Regulation D provides that any of these offerings made during any twelve-month period are exempt from the registration requirements.

---

5. 15 U.S.C. Section 77c(b).
6. 17 C.F.R. Sections 230.251–230.263.

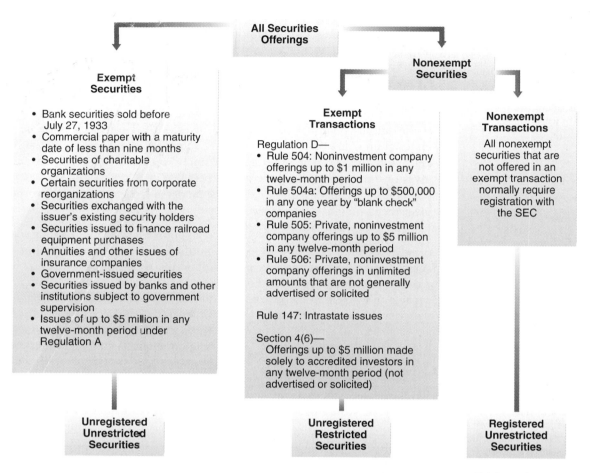

All Securities Offerings

Exempt Securities

- Bank securities sold before July 27, 1933
- Commercial paper with a maturity date of less than nine months
- Securities of charitable organizations
- Certain securities from corporate reorganizations
- Securities exchanged with the issuer's existing security holders
- Securities issued to finance railroad equipment purchases
- Annuities and other issues of insurance companies
- Government-issued securities
- Securities issued by banks and other institutions subject to government supervision
- Issues of up to $5 million in any twelve-month period under Regulation A

Nonexempt Securities

Exempt Transactions

Regulation D—
- Rule 504: Noninvestment company offerings up to $1 million in any twelve-month period
- Rule 504a: Offerings up to $500,000 in any one year by "blank check" companies
- Rule 505: Private, noninvestment company offerings up to $5 million in any twelve-month period
- Rule 506: Private, noninvestment company offerings in unlimited amounts that are not generally advertised or solicited

Rule 147: Intrastate issues

Section 4(6)—
Offerings up to $5 million made solely to accredited investors in any twelve-month period (not advertised or solicited)

Nonexempt Transactions

All nonexempt securities that are not offered in an exempt transaction normally require registration with the SEC

Unregistered Unrestricted Securities

Unregistered Restricted Securities

Registered Unrestricted Securities

■ **Exhibit 23–1**
Exemptions under the 1933 Securities Act

Rule 504 Noninvestment company offerings up to $1 million in any twelve-month period are exempt.[7] In contrast to investment companies (discussed later in this chapter), noninvestment companies are firms that are not engaged primarily in the business of investing or trading in securities.

Rule 504a Offerings up to $500,000 in any one year by so-called blank check companies—companies with no specific business plans except to locate and acquire presently unknown businesses or opportunities—are exempt if no general solicitation or advertising is used; the SEC is notified of the sales; and precaution is taken against nonexempt, unregistered resales.[8] The limits on advertising and unregistered resales do not apply if the offering is made solely in states that provide for registration and disclosure and the securities are sold in compliance with those provisions.[9]

7. 17 C.F.R. Section 230.504. Rule 504 is the exemption currently used by most small businesses, but that could change under new SEC Rule 1001. This rule permits, under certain circumstances, "testing the waters" for offerings of up to $5 million *per transaction*. These offerings, however, can be made only to "qualified purchasers" (knowledgeable, sophisticated investors).

8. Precautions to be taken against nonexempt, unregistered resales include asking the investor whether he or she is buying the securities for others; before the sale, disclosing to each purchaser in writing that the securities are unregistered and thus cannot be resold, except in an exempt transaction, without first being registered; and indicating on the certificates that the securities are unregistered and restricted.

9. 17 C.F.R. Section 230.504a.

Accredited Investors In the context of securities offerings, "sophisticated" investors, such as banks, insurance companies, investment companies, the issuer's executive officers and directors, and persons whose income or net worth exceeds certain limits.

Rule 505   Private, noninvestment company offerings up to $5 million in any twelve-month period are exempt, regardless of the number of **accredited investors** (banks, insurance companies, investment companies, the issuer's executive officers and directors, and persons whose income or net worth exceeds certain limits), so long as there are no more than thirty-five unaccredited investors; no general solicitation or advertising is used; the SEC is notified of the sales; and precaution is taken against nonexempt, unregistered resales. If the sale involves *any* unaccredited investors, *all* investors must be given material information about the offering company, its business, and the securities before the sale. The issuer is not required to believe that each unaccredited investor "has such knowledge and experience in financial and business matters that he is capable of evaluating the merits and the risks of the prospective investment."[10]

Rule 506   Private offerings in unlimited amounts that are not generally solicited or advertised are exempt if the SEC is notified of the sales; precaution is taken against nonexempt, unregistered resales; and the issuer believes that each unaccredited investor has sufficient knowledge or experience in financial matters to be capable of evaluating the investment's merits and risks. There may be no more than thirty-five unaccredited investors, although there may be an unlimited number of accredited investors. If there are *any* unaccredited investors, the issuer must provide to *all* purchasers material information about itself, its business, and the securities before the sale.[11]

This exemption is perhaps most important to those firms that want to raise funds through the sale of securities without registering them. It is often referred to as the *private placement* exemption, because it exempts "transactions not involving any public offering."[12] This provision applies to private offerings to a limited number of persons who are sufficiently sophisticated and in a sufficiently strong bargaining position to be able to assume the risk of the investment (and who thus have no need for federal registration protection), as well as to private offerings to similarly situated institutional investors.

KEEP IN MIND An investor can be "sophisticated" by virtue of his or her education and experience or by investing through a knowledgeable, experienced representative.

RULE 147—INTRASTATE ISSUES.   Also exempt are intrastate transactions involving purely local offerings.[13] This exemption applies to most offerings that are restricted to residents of the state in which the issuing company is organized and doing business. For nine months after the last sale, virtually no resales may be made to nonresidents, and precautions must be taken against this possibility. These offerings remain subject to applicable laws in the state of issue.

SECTION 4(6).   Under Section 4(6) of the Securities Act of 1933, an offer made *solely* to accredited investors is exempt if its amount is not more than $5 million. Any number of accredited investors may participate, but no unaccredited investors may do so. No general solicitation or advertising may be used; the SEC must be notified of all sales; and precaution must be taken against nonexempt, unregistered resales (because these are restricted securities and may be resold only by registration or in an exempt transaction).[14]

---

10.   17 C.F.R. Section 230.505.
11.   17 C.F.R. Section 230.506.
12.   15 U.S.C. Section 77d(2).
13.   15 U.S.C. Section 77c(a)(11); 17 C.F.R. Section 230.147.
14.   15 U.S.C. Section 77d(6).

RESALES. Most securities can be resold without registration (although some resales may be subject to certain restrictions, which were discussed previously in connection with specific exemptions). The Securities Act of 1933 provides exemptions for resales by most persons other than issuers or underwriters. Resales of restricted securities acquired under Rule 504a, Rule 505, Rule 506, or Section 4(6), however, trigger the registration requirements unless the party selling them complies with Rule 144 or Rule 144A. These rules are sometimes referred to as "safe harbors."

Rule 144   Rule 144 exempts restricted securities from registration on resale if there is adequate current public information about the issuer, the person selling the securities has owned them for at least two years, they are sold in certain limited amounts in unsolicited brokers' transactions, and the SEC is given notice of the resale.[15] "Adequate current public information" consists of the reports that certain companies are required to file under the Securities Exchange Act of 1934.

Rule 144A   Securities that at the time of issue are not of the same class as securities listed on a national securities exchange or quoted in a U.S. automated interdealer quotation system may be resold under Rule 144A.[16] They may be sold only to a qualified institutional buyer (an institution, such as an insurance company, an investment company, or a bank, that owns and invests at least $100 million in securities). The seller must take reasonable steps to ensure that the buyer knows that the seller is relying on the exemption under Rule 144A. A sample restricted stock certificate is shown in Exhibit 23–2.

> **CONTRAST** Securities do not have to be held for two years to be exempt from registration on a resale under Rule 144A, as they do under Rule 144.

Securities Exchange Act of 1934

The Securities Exchange Act of 1934 provides for the regulation and registration of securities exchanges; brokers; dealers; and national securities associations, such as the National Association of Securities Dealers (NASD). The SEC regulates the markets in which securities are traded by maintaining a continuous disclosure system for all corporations with securities on the securities exchanges and for those companies that have assets in excess of $10 million and five hundred or more shareholders. These corporations are referred to as Section 12 companies, because they are required to register their securities under Section 12 of the 1934 act.

The act regulates proxy solicitation for voting (proxies are discussed in Chapter 15) and allows the SEC to engage in market surveillance to regulate undesirable market practices such as fraud, market manipulation, misrepresentation, and stabilization. (*Stabilization* is a market-manipulating technique by which securities underwriters bid for securities to stabilize the prices of securities during their issuance.)

Section 10(b), SEC Rule 10b-5, and Insider Trading

Section 10(b) is one of the most important sections of the Securities Exchange Act of 1934. This section proscribes the use of "any manipulative or deceptive device or contrivance in contravention of such rules and regulations as the

---

15.   17 C.F.R. Section 230.144.
16.   17 C.F.R. Section 230.144A.

■ Exhibit 23-2—A Sample Restricted Stock Certificate

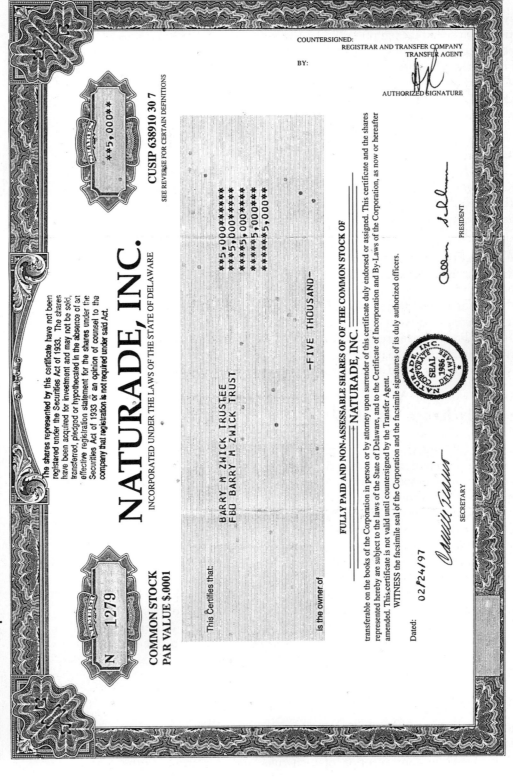

[SEC] may prescribe." Among the rules that the SEC has promulgated pursuant to the 1934 act is **SEC Rule 10b-5,** which prohibits the commission of fraud in connection with the purchase or sale of any security.

One of the most important purposes of Section 10(b) and SEC Rule 10b-5 relates to so-called **insider trading.** Because of their positions, corporate directors and officers often obtain advance inside information that can affect the future market value of the corporate stock. Obviously, their positions can give them a trading advantage over the general public and shareholders. The 1934 Securities Exchange Act defines inside information and extends liability to officers and directors for taking advantage of such information in their personal transactions when they know that it is unavailable to the persons with whom they are dealing.

Section 10(b) of the 1934 act and SEC Rule 10b-5 cover not only corporate officers, directors, and majority shareholders but also any persons having access to or receiving information of a nonpublic nature on which trading is based.[17] Those found liable under SEC Rule 10b-5 have a right to seek reimbursement from persons or entities that may have shared responsibility for the violations, including accountants, attorneys, and corporations.[18]

DISCLOSURE UNDER SEC RULE 10b-5. Any material omission or misrepresentation of material facts in connection with the purchase or sale of a security may violate not only Section 11 of the Securities Act of 1933 but also the antifraud provisions of Section 10(b) and SEC Rule 10b-5 of the 1934 act. The

SEC Rule 10b-5 A rule of the Securities and Exchange Commission that makes it unlawful, in connection with the purchase or sale of any security, to make any untrue statement of a material fact or to omit a material fact if such omission causes the statement to be misleading.

Insider Trading The purchase or sale of securities on the basis of information that has not been made available to the public.

> **"There are three kinds of lies: lies, damned lies, and statistics."**
>
> Benjamin Disraeli, 1804–1881
> (British prime minister, 1868, 1874–1880)

---

17. Note that a private cause of action under Section 10(b) and SEC Rule 10b-5 cannot be brought against accountants, attorneys, and others who "aid and abet" violations of the act. Only the SEC can bring actions against so-called aiders and abettors. See *Central Bank of Denver, N.A. v. First Interstate Bank of Denver, N.A.,* 511 U.S. 164, 114 S.Ct. 1439, 128 L.Ed.2d 119 (1994).
18. *Musick, Peeler & Garrett v. Employers Insurance of Wausau,* 508 U.S. 286, 113 S.Ct. 2085, 124 L.Ed.2d 194 (1993).

International Perspective

Traditionally, Germany has resisted any legal prohibition against insider trading. Instead, insider trading was regulated by voluntary guidelines that were included in employment contracts with banks and stock corporations. The guidelines prohibited trading by corporate insiders but were not consistently enforced. Generally, German banks and stock companies contended that moral codes were more effective than legal prohibitions in controlling insider trading.

German attitudes toward insider trading began to change in the early 1990s, however, in the wake of insider-trading scandals. In 1994, Germany made insider trading a criminal offense, thus bringing that country in line with other European nations. Germany now has a government agency, similar to the SEC, that regulates insider trading, and German business firms are changing the ways in which they traditionally have disseminated information. For example, in the past, companies frequently disclosed their sales and earnings information to various securities analysts. They also often sent copies of their annual reports to members of the press days before the announcement of the information in the reports at news conferences.

For Critical Analysis: *How can you explain the fact that, relative to the United States, Germany waited so long to create a securities regulation agency?*

key to liability (which can be civil or criminal) under Section 10(b) and SEC Rule 10b-5 is whether the insider's information is *material*. The following are some examples of material facts calling for a disclosure under the rule:

1. A new ore discovery.
2. Fraudulent trading in the company stock by a broker-dealer.
3. A dividend change (whether up or down).
4. A contract for the sale of corporate assets.
5. A new discovery (process or product).
6. A significant change in the firm's financial condition.

Courts have struggled with the problem of when information becomes public knowledge. Clearly, when inside information becomes public knowledge, all insiders should be allowed to trade without disclosure. The courts have suggested that insiders should refrain from trading for a "reasonable waiting period" when the news is not readily translatable into investment action. Presumably, this gives the news time to filter down to, and to be evaluated by, the investing public.

The following is one of the landmark cases interpreting SEC Rule 10b-5. The SEC sued Texas Gulf Sulphur Company for issuing a misleading press release. The release underestimated the magnitude and the value of a mineral discovery. The SEC also sued several of Texas Gulf Sulphur's directors, officers, and employees under SEC Rule 10b-5 for purchasing large amounts of the corporate stock prior to the announcement of the corporation's rich ore discovery.

Case 23.2 ● SEC v. Texas Gulf Sulphur Co.

United States Court of Appeals,
Second Circuit, 1968.
401 F.2d 833.

HISTORICAL AND ENVIRONMENTAL SETTING   *No court has ever held that every buyer or seller is entitled to all of the information relating to all of the circumstances in every stock transaction. By the mid-1950s, however, significant understatement of the value of the assets of a company had been held to be materially misleading.[a] In 1957, the Texas Gulf Sulphur Company (TGS) began exploring for minerals in eastern Canada. In March 1959, aerial geophysical surveys were conducted over more than fifteen thousand square miles of the area. The operations revealed numerous and extraordinary variations in the conductivity of the rock, which indicated a remarkable concentration of commercially exploitable minerals. One site of such variations was near Timmins, Ontario. On October 29 and 30, 1963, a ground survey of the site near Timmins indicated a need to drill for further evaluation.*

BACKGROUND AND FACTS   Texas Gulf Sulphur Company drilled a hole on November 12, 1963, that appeared to yield a core with an exceedingly high mineral content. TGS kept secret the results of the core sample. Officers and employees of the company made substantial purchases of TGS's stock or accepted stock options after learning of the ore discovery, even though further drilling was necessary to establish whether there was enough ore to be mined commercially. On April 11, 1964, an unauthorized report of the mineral find appeared in the newspapers. On the following day, April 12, TGS issued a press release that played down the discovery and stated that it was too early to tell whether the ore finding would be a significant one. Later on, TGS announced a strike of at least twenty-five million tons of ore, substantially driving up the price of TGS stock. The SEC brought suit in a federal district court against the officers and employees of TGS for violating the insider-trading prohibition of SEC Rule 10b-5. The officers and employees argued that the prohibition did not apply. They reasoned that the information on which they had traded was not material, as the mine had not been commercially proved. The court held that most of the defendants had not violated SEC Rule 10b-5, and the SEC appealed.

───────────
a.   *Speed v. Transamerica Corp.*, 99 F.Supp. 808 (D.Del. 1951).

(Continued)

Case 23.2—continued

IN THE WORDS OF THE COURT . . .
WATERMAN, Circuit Judge.

* * * *

* * * [W]hether facts are material within Rule 10b-5 when the facts relate to a particular event and are undisclosed by those persons who are knowledgeable thereof will depend at any given time upon a balancing of both the indicated probability that the event will occur and the anticipated magnitude of the event in light of the totality of the company activity. Here, * * * knowledge of the possibility, which surely was more than marginal, of the existence of a mine of the vast magnitude indicated by the remarkably rich drill core located rather close to the surface (suggesting mineability by the less expensive openpit method) within the confines of a large anomaly (suggesting an extensive region of mineralization) might well have affected the price of TGS stock and would certainly have been an important fact to a reasonable * * * investor in deciding whether he should buy, sell, or hold. After all, this first drill core was "unusually good and * * * excited the interest and speculation of those who knew about it."

* * * *

* * * [A] major factor in determining whether the * * * discovery was a material fact is the importance attached to the drilling results by those who knew about it. * * * [T]he timing by those who knew of it of their stock purchases and their purchases of short-term calls [rights to buy shares at a specified price within a specified time period]—purchases in some cases by individuals who had never before purchased calls or even TGS stock—virtually compels the inference that the insiders were influenced by the drilling results.

* * * *

We hold, therefore, that all transactions in TGS stock or calls by individuals apprised of the drilling results * * * were made in violation of Rule 10b-5.

DECISION AND REMEDY   The U.S. Court of Appeals for the Second Circuit ruled in favor of the SEC. All of the trading by insiders who knew of the mineral find violated Rule 10b-5.

FOR CRITICAL ANALYSIS—ECONOMIC CONSIDERATION   *Who is hurt by insider trading?*

APPLICABILITY OF SEC RULE 10b-5.   SEC Rule 10b-5 applies in virtually all cases concerning the trading of securities, whether on organized exchanges, in over-the-counter markets, or in private transactions. The rule covers notes, bonds, certificates of interest and participation in any profit-sharing agreement, agreements to form a corporation, and joint-venture agreements; in short, it covers just about any form of security. It is immaterial whether a firm has securities registered under the 1933 act for the 1934 act to apply.

Although SEC Rule 10b-5 is applicable only when the requisites of federal jurisdiction—such as the use of the mails, of stock exchange facilities, or of any instrumentality of interstate commerce—are present, virtually no commercial transaction can be completed without such contact. In addition, the states have corporate securities laws, many of which include provisions similar to SEC Rule 10b-5.

Ethical Perspective

Clearly, SEC Rule 10b-5 has broad applicability. As will be discussed shortly, the rule covers not only corporate insiders but even "outsiders"—those who receive and trade on tips received from insiders. Investigating and prosecuting violations of SEC Rule 10b-5 is costly, both for the government and for those convicted of insider trading.

Some people doubt that such extensive regulation is necessary and even contend that insider trading should be legal. Would there be any benefit from the legalization of insider trading? To evaluate this question, review the facts in *SEC v. Texas Gulf Sulphur Co.* (Case 23.2 in this chap-

ter). If insider trading were legal, the discovery of the ore sample would probably have caused many more company insiders to purchase stock. Consequently, the price of Texas Gulf's stock would have increased fairly quickly. These increases presumably would have attracted the attention of outside investors, who would have learned sooner that something positive had happened to the company and would thus have had the opportunity to purchase the stock. The higher demand for the stock would have more quickly translated into higher prices for the stock and hence, perhaps, a more efficient capital market.

For Critical Analysis: *How would you argue against the legalization of insider trading?*

OUTSIDERS AND SEC RULE 10b-5.   The traditional insider-trading case involves true insiders—corporate officers, directors, and majority shareholders who have access to (and trade on) inside information. Increasingly, liability under Section 10(b) of the 1934 act and SEC Rule 10b-5 has been extended to include certain "outsiders"—those who trade on inside information acquired *indirectly*. Two theories have been developed under which outsiders may be held liable for insider trading: the *tipper/tippee theory* and the *misappropriation theory*.

Tipper/Tippee Theory   Anyone who acquires inside information as a result of a corporate insider's breach of his or her fiduciary duty can be liable under SEC Rule 10b-5. This liability extends to **tippees** (those who receive "tips" from insiders) and even remote tippees (tippees of tippees).

Tippee A person who receives inside information.

The key to liability under this theory is that the inside information be obtained as a result of someone's breach of a fiduciary duty to the corporation whose shares are involved in the trading. Unless there is a breach of a duty not to disclose inside information, the disclosure was in exchange for personal benefit, and the tippee knows of this breach (or should know of it) and benefits from it, there is no liability under this theory.[19]

Misappropriation Theory   Liability for insider trading may also be established under the misappropriation theory. This theory holds that if an individual wrongfully obtains (misappropriates) inside information and trades on it for his or her personal gain, then the individual should be held liable because, in essence, the individual stole information rightfully belonging to another.

The misappropriation theory significantly extends the reach of SEC Rule 10b-5 to outsiders who would not ordinarily be deemed fiduciaries of the corporations in whose stock they trade. Courts will normally hold, however, that some fiduciary duty to some lawful possessor of material nonpublic information must have been violated and some harm to the defrauded party must have

---

19.   See, for example, *Chiarella v. United States,* 445 U.S. 222, 100 S.Ct. 1108, 63 L.Ed.2d 348 (1980); and *Dirks v. SEC,* 463 U.S. 646, 103 S.Ct. 3255, 77 L.Ed.2d 911 (1983).

occurred for liability to exist. For example, suppose that an employee of a printing shop that handles takeover bids learns of a takeover and trades on the information. Clearly, the employee has no fiduciary duty to the shareholders of either corporation involved in the takeover. The employee does, however, have a duty of loyalty to his or her employer—who lawfully possesses material nonpublic information.[20]

The following case raises the question of whether, for the tippee to be held liable under SEC Rule 10b-5, the tipper must have known that his or her breach of a fiduciary obligation would lead to the tippee's trading on the misappropriated information.

---

20. Note that in contrast to several other federal circuit courts of appeals, the U.S. Court of Appeals for the Fourth Circuit has refused to impose liability under the misappropriation theory for SEC Rule 10b-5 violations. See *United States v. Bryan,* 58 F.3d 933 (4th Cir. 1994).

Case 23.3 ● United States v. Libera

United States Court of Appeals, Seventh Circuit, 1993.
989 F.2d 596.

COMPANY PROFILE *Two weeks before the stock market crash in October 1929, the McGraw-Hill Book Company started* Business Week *magazine. In the first issue, the editors expressed concern about the health of the U.S. economy. This view was contrary to current opinion but certainly proved correct—the stock market crash occurred two weeks later and heralded the start of the Great Depression. Today,* Business Week *is one of the top U.S. business magazines. It is available, as are most of McGraw-Hill's magazines and other products, in multimedia versions.*

BACKGROUND AND FACTS R. R. Donnelley & Sons Company operates a printing plant that prints *Business Week* (owned by McGraw-Hill, Inc.). McGraw-Hill and Donnelley had a policy of keeping the contents of each issue confidential until 5:00 P.M. on Thursday, because the contents could affect the price of particular stocks and, before release, were regarded as inside information by the Securities and Exchange Commission. William Dillon observed that trading in stocks mentioned favorably in the magazine often began increasing on the Wednesday before publication and continued through the next Monday. Dillon, recognizing the value of receiving advance copies of *Business Week,* sought out Donnelley employees who would give him copies on Thursday mornings. Dillon, Benjamin Libera, and Francis Sablone used the information to trade regularly on Thursday mornings in the securities reported in *Business Week.* When their scheme was discovered, Dillon pleaded guilty to certain criminal charges and testified against Libera and Sablone, who were convicted of violations of Section 10(b) under the misappropriation theory. Libera and Sablone appealed, arguing that they could not be liable for insider trading unless the tipper (in this case, the Donnelly employees who gave them advance copies) knew that the breach of a fiduciary obligation would lead to the tippee's trading on the misappropriated information.

IN THE WORDS OF THE COURT . . .
WINTER, Circuit Judge.
* * * *

* * * [T]he misappropriation theory requires the establishment of two elements: (i) a breach by the tipper of a duty owed to the owner of the nonpublic information; and (ii) the tippee's knowledge that the tipper had breached the duty. We believe these two elements, without more, are sufficient for tippee liability. The tipper's knowledge that he or she was breaching a duty to the owner of confidential information suffices to establish the tipper's expectation that the breach will lead to some kind of a

(Continued)

Case 23.3—continued

misuse of the information. This is so because it may be presumed that the tippee's interest in the information is, in contemporary jargon, not for nothing. To allow a tippee to escape liability solely because the government cannot prove to a jury's satisfaction that the tipper knew exactly what misuse would result from the tipper's wrongdoing would not fulfill the purpose of the misappropriation theory, which is to protect property rights in information. Indeed, such a requirement would serve no purpose other than to create a loophole for such misuse.

DECISION AND REMEDY   The U.S. Court of Appeals for the Seventh Circuit affirmed the convictions of Libera and Sablone.

FOR CRITICAL ANALYSIS—SOCIAL CONSIDERATION   *From whom was the information misappropriated?*

Technology and Securities Laws

We have stressed elsewhere how technological advances have affected business practices as well as the law governing those practices. Not surprisingly, technology is also affecting practices in the securities industry—and securities law. More than ever before, today's investors have access to information that can help them make informed decisions. Information on the Internet, for example, ranges from the data concerning the financial performance of various companies to securities laws and regulations. (See *Interacting with the Internet* at the end of this chapter.)

As might be expected, the online era has opened the door to new forms of fraud. Officials in several states are undertaking investigations into numerous on-line schemes perpetrated via electronic "investor bulletin boards." For example, a purported investment adviser or stockbroker might offer his or her investment services to Internet users. Then, once the investor sends funds to invest, the scam artist walks off with the money. Securities officials in some states are planning to establish their own bulletin boards to warn users of these problems and answer questions concerning investments.

An interesting question raised by the extensive amount of on-line information available to investors is whether a court can reasonably assume that investors should know about that information. In other words, do investors have a duty to "surf the Net"? At least one court—the U.S. Court of Appeals for the Seventh Circuit—has suggested that they do. The case involved allegations by Whirlpool Financial Corporation that GN Holdings, Inc., had violated securities laws by issuing a misleading financial fore-

cast in connection with a securities offering. GN contended that the suit was barred by the statute of limitations. (Under federal securities laws, a plaintiff must file a claim within one year from the time that the cause of action accrues. Normally, an action under securities laws accrues when the plaintiff is put on notice of the fraud.) The question before the court was whether Whirlpool had been put on notice that GN's representations were misleading more than a year before Whirlpool filed its claim.

The court held that Whirlpool had constructive notice of the fraud the moment that the information needed to discover the fraud (discrepancies between GN's financial projections and the actual results) was in the public domain. Information in the public domain included information available on the Internet. The court stated that "with the advent of the 'information superhighway,' federal and state legislation and regulations, as well as information regarding industry trends, are easily accessed. A reasonable investor is presumed to have information available in the public domain, and therefore Whirlpool is imputed with constructive knowledge of this information." The court concluded, based on the date of Whirlpool's constructive notice, that Whirlpool's action against GN was barred by the statute of limitations.[a]

For Critical Analysis: *How might the "information superhighway" affect securities trading and regulation in the future?*

---

a.   *Whirlpool Financial Corp. v. GN Holdings, Inc.*, 67 F.3d 605 (7th Cir. 1995).

Insider Reporting and Trading—Section 16(b)

Officers, directors, and certain persons holding large amounts of stock[21] of Section 12 corporations (corporations that are required to register their securities under Section 12 of the 1934 act) must file reports with the SEC concerning their ownership and trading of the corporations' securities.[22] To discourage such insiders from using nonpublic information about their companies for their personal benefit in the stock market, Section 16(b) of the 1934 act provides for the recapture by the corporation of all profits realized by an insider on any purchase and sale or sale and purchase of the corporation's stock within any six-month period.[23] It is irrelevant whether the insider actually uses inside information; all such *short-swing* profits must be returned to the corporation.

Section 16(b) applies not only to stock but to warrants, options, and securities convertible into stock. In addition, the courts have fashioned complex rules for determining profits. Corporate insiders are wise to seek competent counsel prior to trading in the corporation's stock. Exhibit 23–3 on page 654 compares the effects of SEC Rule 10b-5 and Section 16(b).

People resort to various tactics to avoid liability under Section 16(b). These tactics include creative forms for the exchange of money for stock, as illustrated by the following case.

---

21. Those stockholders owning 10 percent of the class of equity securities registered under Section 12 of the 1934 act.
22. 15 U.S.C. Section 78*l*.
23. When a decline is predicted in the market for a particular stock, one can realize profits by "selling short"—selling at a high price and repurchasing later at a lower price to cover the "short sale." The short seller typically has to borrow the stock in the meantime (and pay interest on the borrowed stock).

Case 23.4 ● Tristar Corp. v. Freitas

United States District Court,
Eastern District of New York, 1994.
867 F.Supp. 149.

HISTORICAL AND ETHICAL SETTING *Between 1932 and 1934, the Senate Banking Committee held hearings on the securities markets. It discovered widespread fraud and abuse in securities financing and market practices. This discovery helped to propel the securities acts through Congress. The most important aspect of these acts is their requirement of full disclosure. All important information about a company, its securities, and the transaction must be disclosed. The parties can then make a free choice to deal (or not to deal) based on that information. Because of this unregulated freedom to deal, it is vital that the disclosed information be truthful and complete.*

BACKGROUND AND FACTS Ross Freitas and Carolyn Kenner were officers and directors of the Tristar Corporation. They were also Tristar shareholders, as they had bought Tristar stock between February 2 and June 15, 1989. Meanwhile, on May 31, they agreed to transfer their Tristar shares to Starion International, Ltd. Under a contract titled "Periodic Loan Agreement," Freitas and Kenner gave their shares to Starion's attorney. Starion paid Freitas and Kenner in periodic installments. With each payment, the attorney gave a block of the stock to Starion. When Tristar learned of the deal, the firm filed a suit in a federal district court against Freitas and Kenner, under Section 16(b), to obtain their profits. Tristar filed a motion for summary judgment.

(Continued)

Case 23.4—continued

IN THE WORDS OF THE COURT . . .
DEARIE, District Judge.
    *   *   *   *

    *   *   * As a general rule, a sale occurs when "the insider has incurred an 'irrevocable liability' to dispose of the stock so that his 'rights and obligations' have become fixed."

    The Court has examined the Loan Agreement and finds that on May 31, 1989 defendants did in fact "contract to sell or otherwise dispose of" the Agreement Shares within the meaning of [S]ection 16(b). The Court is persuaded that the Loan Agreement has the ordinary indicia [signs or indications] of an installment sales contract. * * * A common-sense assessment of the mechanics of the Loan Agreement reveals that all of the Agreement Shares were committed on May 31, 1989.

DECISION AND REMEDY The federal district court ruled in Tristar's favor. The court set for trial the issue of how much money Freitas and Kenner should pay to Tristar.

FOR CRITICAL ANALYSIS—ECONOMIC CONSIDERATION *Had the shares of stock simply been used as collateral, would this case have been decided differently?*

■ **Exhibit 23–3**
Comparison of Coverage, Application, and Liabilities under SEC Rule 10b-5 and Section 16(b)

	SEC RULE 10b-5	SECTION 16(b)
What is the subject matter of the transaction?	Any security (does not have to be registered)	Any security (does not have to be registered)
What transactions are covered?	Purchase or sale	Short-swing purchase and sale or short-swing sale and purchase
Who is subject to liability?	Virtually anyone with inside information under a duty to disclose—including officers, directors, controlling stockholders, and tippees	Officers, directors, and certain 10 percent stockholders
Is omission or misrepresentation necessary for liability?	Yes	No
Are there any exempt transactions?	No	Yes, there are a variety of exemptions
Is direct dealing with the party necessary?	No	No
Who may bring an action?	A person transacting with an insider, the SEC, or a purchaser or seller damaged by a wrongful act	A corporation or a shareholder by derivative action

Insider-Trading Sanctions

The Insider Trading Sanctions Act of 1984 permits the SEC to bring suit in a federal district court against anyone violating or aiding in a violation of the 1934 act or SEC rules by purchasing or selling a security while in the possession of material nonpublic information.[24] The violation must occur on or through the facilities of a national securities exchange or through a broker or dealer. Transactions connected with a public offering by an issuer of securities are excepted.

The Insider Trading and Securities Fraud Enforcement Act of 1988 extended the class of persons who may be subject to civil liability for insider-trading violations and gave the SEC authority to award **bounty payments** (rewards given by government officials for acts beneficial to the state) to persons providing information leading to the prosecution of insider-trading violations. The act also gave the SEC rulemaking authority to require specific policies and procedures in order to prevent insider trading, in addition to increasing the criminal penalties for violations. Maximum jail terms were increased from five to ten years, and fines were increased to $1 million for individuals and $2.5 million for partnerships and corporations.[25] Neither act has any effect on other actions the SEC or private investors may take.

In imposing sanctions for insider trading, the court may assess as a penalty as much as triple the profits gained or the loss avoided by the guilty party. For purposes of the act, profit or loss is defined as "the difference between the purchase or sale price of the security and the value of that security as measured by the trading price of the security at a reasonable period of time after public dissemination of the nonpublic information."[26] The following case provides an example, in a securities fraud case, of the computation of "avoided losses"—that is, the amount of the loss a violator avoids by selling his or her stock before a disclosure of negative information about a company.

Bounty Payment
A reward (payment) given to a person or persons who perform a certain service—such as informing legal authorities of illegal actions.

---

24. 15 U.S.C. Section 78u–1(a)(1).
25. 15 U.S.C. Section 78ff(a).
26. 15 U.S.C. Section 78u–1(d)(5)(f).

Case 23.5 ● SEC v. Patel

United States Court of Appeals,
Second Circuit, 1995.
61 F.3d 137.

HISTORICAL AND SOCIAL SETTING *A drug cannot be copyrighted or trademarked, but it can be patented. (Patents are discussed in Chapter 11.) When a drug's patent expires, the patented product falls into the public domain, and the patent owner is no longer protected against infringement. Other pharmaceutical manufacturers can make and market the drug as a "generic" drug. A generic drug is one that is produced without a brand name but that is identical to a product with a brand name. Generic drugs are cheaper than their brand-name counterparts.*

BACKGROUND AND FACTS In November 1987, Par Pharmaceutical, Inc., submitted to the Food and Drug Administration (FDA) an application for a new generic drug. The application falsely stated that the drug had been tested as required. Ratilal Patel, an officer and director of Par Pharmaceutical, knew that the application contained false information and subsequently (in early 1988) sold 75,000 shares of his stock in Par Pharmaceutical at a price of

(Continued)

Case 23.5—continued

approximately $21 per share. In 1988 and 1989, Par Pharmaceutical became the target of investigations and indictments for various improprieties, including bribery. By Friday, July 21, 1989, the price of Par stock was $10 per share. On Monday, July 24, Par Pharmaceutical publicly disclosed the facts about the falsified drug application. On Tuesday, the price of Par Pharmaceutical stock dropped to $7.125 per share. The SEC filed a suit in a federal district court against Patel, alleging that he had violated securities laws. The court ordered Patel to, among other things, pay the amount of the loss he avoided by selling his stock before the announcement of the false FDA application. The court computed the amount based on the difference between the price of Par Pharmaceutical stock on July 21 and the price on July 25. Patel appealed, contending in part that the earlier investigations and indictments had affected the price of the stock.

IN THE WORDS OF THE COURT . . .
MINER, Circuit Judge.
* * * *

* * * While calculations of this nature are not capable of exactitude, * * * any "risk of uncertainty [in calculating disgorgement] should fall on the wrongdoer whose illegal conduct created that uncertainty." Applying this principle, we find that the district court was eminently reasonable in its approach to the issue of avoided losses in this case. There certainly was a rational basis for the court to conclude that the earlier negative announcements had been fully taken into account by the market and that the July 24, 1989 disclosure alone accounted for the 28.75% decline identified as of July 25.

DECISION AND REMEDY   The U.S. Court of Appeals for the Second Circuit affirmed this part of the lower court's decision.

FOR CRITICAL ANALYSIS—SOCIAL CONSIDERATION   *What penalty, among those that a court can impose, might a corporate officer and director consider worse than paying out "avoided losses"?*

Proxy Statements

Section 14(a) of the Securities Exchange Act of 1934 regulates the solicitation of proxies from shareholders of Section 12 companies. The SEC regulates the content of proxy statements, which (as discussed in Chapter 15) are statements sent to shareholders by corporate officials who are requesting authority to vote on behalf of the shareholders in a particular election on specified issues. Whoever solicits a proxy must fully and accurately disclose in the proxy statement all of the facts that are pertinent to the matter on which the shareholders are to vote. SEC Rule 14a-9 is similar to the antifraud provisions of SEC Rule 10b-5. Remedies for violation are extensive; they range from injunctions that prevent a vote from being taken to monetary damages.

The Expanding Powers of the SEC

In recent years, Congress has expanded significantly the SEC's powers. For example, to further curb securities fraud, the Securities Enforcement Remedies and Penny Stock Reform Act of 1990 amended existing securities laws to expand greatly the types of securities violation cases that SEC administrative law judges can hear and the SEC's enforcement options. The act also provides that courts may bar persons who have engaged in securities fraud from serving as officers and directors of publicly held corporations.

Inside the Legal Environment
Curbing Class-Action Securities-Fraud Suits

Traditionally, the SEC has encouraged companies to disclose quantitative, forward-looking information—such as financial forecasts—to investors in prospectuses and other documents in connection with securities offerings. Ironically, one of the effects of SEC Rule 10b-5 is to deter such disclosure. To understand why, consider an example. A company announces that its projected earnings in a certain time period will be X amount. It turns out that the forecast was wrong. The earnings are in fact much lower, and the price of the company's stock is affected—negatively. The shareholders then bring a class-action suit against the company's managers, alleging that the directors violated SEC Rule 10b-5 by disclosing misleading financial information.

In many class-action suits, the accused managers are innocent of any intentional fraud; they simply made mistaken forecasts. The cost of such mistakes can be high, however, if the managers are sued for securities fraud. Rather than risk being sued—and risk potential liability under SEC Rule 10b-5—for publicizing misleading or deceptive financial information, many

companies understandably prefer to say less, rather than more, about their future prospects.

In part because of the controversy over so many class-action suits, in 1995 Congress passed the Private Securities Litigation Reform Act. The act provides, among other things, a "safe harbor" for publicly held companies that make forward-looking statements, such as financial forecasts. Those who make such statements are protected against liability for securities fraud as long as the statements are accompanied by "meaningful cautionary statements identifying important factors that could cause actual results to differ materially from those in the forward-looking statement." The act also deters class-action suits in other ways, such as by limiting attorneys' fees in class actions.

Critics of the legislation—including trial lawyers, consumer groups, and a number of others—contend that the safe harbor in essence gives corporate managers a "license to lie" about the companies' future prospects. Opponents of the law also believe that other provisions of the act, such as those that in effect make

it more difficult for plaintiffs to bring a claim of securities fraud, will make it harder for investors to recover for losses caused by fraud. The full effect of the legislation on investors and corporate decision makers depends, of course, on how the courts interpret and apply the act.

A United States Supreme Court decision in 1996 may also curb the extent of class-action suits alleging securities fraud, or at least alter the legal options available to shareholders. In *Matsushita Electric Industrial Co. v. Lawrence Epstein*,[a] the Court held that state-court settlements of class-action securities suits will be respected by federal courts. In other words, plaintiffs who are unsatisfied with a state-court settlement are barred from bringing the same suit in a federal forum in order to obtain better results.

For Critical Analysis: *How do class-action securities-fraud suits benefit society? Does the 1995 legislation go too far in curbing shareholders' rights?*

a. 516 U.S. 367, 116 S.Ct. 873, 134 L.Ed.2d 6 (1996).

The 1990 Securities Acts Amendments authorized the SEC to seek sanctions against those who violate foreign securities laws. These amendments increase the ability of the SEC to cooperate in international securities law enforcement. Under the Market Reform Act of 1990, the SEC can suspend trading in securities in the event that the prices rise and fall excessively in a short period of time.

Regulation of Investment Companies

Investment companies, and mutual funds in particular, grew rapidly after World War II. **Investment companies** act on behalf of many smaller shareholders by buying a large portfolio of securities and professionally managing

Investment Company A company that acts on behalf of many smaller shareholders/owners by buying a large portfolio of securities and professionally managing that portfolio.

A stockbroker checks investments with a computer. What restrictions does the SEC place on a broker's investment activities?

Mutual Fund A specific type of investment company that continually buys or sells to investors shares of ownership in a portfolio.

NOTE Congress intended the federal securities laws to protect the public from unethical business practices.

that portfolio. A **mutual fund** is a specific type of investment company that continually buys or sells to investors shares of ownership in a portfolio. Such companies are regulated by the Investment Company Act of 1940,[27] which provides for SEC regulation of their activities. The act was expanded by the 1970 amendments to the Investment Company Act. Further minor changes were made in the Securities Act Amendments of 1975 and in later years.

The 1940 act requires that every investment company register with the SEC and imposes restrictions on the activities of these companies and persons connected with them. For the purposes of the act, an investment company is defined as any entity that (1) is engaged primarily "in the business of investing, reinvesting, or trading in securities" or (2) is engaged in such business and has more than 40 percent of its assets in investment securities. Excluded from coverage by the act are banks, insurance companies, savings and loan associations, finance companies, oil and gas drilling firms, charitable foundations, tax-exempt pension funds, and other special types of institutions, such as closely held corporations.

All investment companies must register with the SEC by filing a notification of registration. Each year, registered investment companies must file reports with the SEC. To safeguard company assets, all securities must be held in the custody of a bank or stock exchange member, and that bank or stock exchange member must follow strict procedures established by the SEC.

No dividends may be paid from any source other than accumulated, undistributed net income. Furthermore, there are some restrictions on investment activities. For example, investment companies are not allowed to purchase securities on the margin (pay only part of the total price, borrowing the rest), sell short (sell shares not yet owned), or participate in joint trading accounts.

State Securities Laws

Today, all states have their own corporate securities laws, or "blue sky laws," that regulate the offer and sale of securities within individual state borders.[28] (The phrase *blue sky laws* dates to a 1917 decision by the United States Supreme Court in which the Court declared that the purpose of such laws was to prevent "speculative schemes which have no more basis than so many feet of 'blue sky.'")[29] Article 8 of the Uniform Commercial Code, which has been adopted by all of the states, also imposes various requirements relating to the purchase and sale of securities. State securities laws apply only to intrastate transactions. Since the adoption of the 1933 and 1934 federal securities acts, the state and federal governments have regulated securities concurrently. Issuers must comply with both federal and state securities laws, and exemptions from federal law are not exemptions from state laws.

There are differences in philosophy among state statutes, but certain features are common to all state blue sky laws. Typically, state laws have disclosure requirements and antifraud provisions, many of which are patterned after Section 10(b) of the Securities Exchange Act of 1934 and SEC Rule 10b-5. State

---

27.   15 U.S.C. Sections 80a–1 to 80a–64.
28.   These laws are catalogued and annotated in the Commerce Clearing House's *Blue Sky Law Reporter,* a loose-leaf service.
29.   *Hall v. Geiger-Jones Co.,* 242 U.S. 539, 37 S.Ct. 217, 61 L.Ed. 480 (1917).

laws also provide for the registration or qualification of securities offered or issued for sale within the state and impose disclosure requirements. Unless an applicable exemption from registration is found, issuers must register or qualify their stock with the appropriate state official, often called a *corporations commissioner*. Additionally, most state securities laws regulate securities brokers and dealers. The Uniform Securities Act, which has been adopted in part by several states, was drafted to be acceptable to states with differing regulatory philosophies.

Key Terms

accredited investor 644
bounty payment 655
insider trading 647
investment company 657

mutual fund 658
red herring 640
SEC Rule 10b-5 647
security 638

tippee 650
tombstone ad 640

Chapter Summary
Investor Protection

THE SECURITIES ACT OF 1933 (See pages 638–645.)	Prohibits fraud and stabilizes the securities industry by requiring disclosure of all essential information relating to the issuance of stocks to the investing public.
	1. **Registration requirements**—Securities, unless exempt, must be registered with the SEC before being offered to the public through the mails or any facility of interstate commerce (including securities exchanges). The *registration statement* must include detailed financial information about the issuing corporation; the intended use of the proceeds of the securities being issued; and certain disclosures, such as interests of directors or officers and pending lawsuits.
	2. **Prospectus**—A *prospectus* must be provided to investors, describing the security being sold, the issuing corporation, and the risk attaching to the security.
	3. **Exemptions**—The SEC has exempted certain offerings from the requirements of the Securities Act of 1933. Exemptions may be determined on the basis of the size of the issue, whether the offering is private or public, and whether advertising is involved. Exemptions are summarized in Exhibit 23–1.
THE SECURITIES EXCHANGE ACT OF 1934 (See pages 645–656.)	Provides for the regulation and registration of securities exchanges, brokers, dealers, and national securities associations (such as the NASD). Maintains a continuous disclosure system for all corporations with securities on the securities exchanges and for those companies that have assets in excess of $10 million and five hundred or more shareholders (Section 12 companies).
	1. **SEC Rule 10b-5 [under Section 10(b) of the 1934 act]**—
	a. Applies to insider trading by corporate officers, directors, majority shareholders, and any persons receiving information not available to the public who base their trading on this information.
	b. Liability for violation can be civil or criminal.
	c. May be violated by failing to disclose "material facts" that must be disclosed under this rule.

(Continued)

Chapter Summary, continued

THE SECURITIES EXCHANGE ACT OF 1934—continued (See pages 645–656.)	d. Applies in virtually all cases concerning the trading of securities—a firm does not have to have its securities registered under the 1933 act for the 1934 act to apply. e. Applies only when the requisites of federal jurisdiction (such as use of the mails, stock exchange facilities, or any facility of interstate commerce) are present. 2. **Insider trading [under Section 16(b) of the 1934 act]**—To prevent corporate officers and directors from taking advantage of inside information (information not available to the investing public), the 1934 act requires officers, directors, and shareholders owning 10 percent or more of the issued stock of a corporation to turn over to the corporation all short-term profits (called short-swing profits) realized from the purchase and sale or sale and purchase of corporate stock within any six-month period. 3. **Proxies [under Section 14(a) of the 1934 act]**—The SEC regulates the content of proxy statements sent to shareholders by corporate managers of Section 12 companies who are requesting authority to vote on behalf of the shareholders in a particular election on specified issues. Section 14(a) is essentially a disclosure law, with provisions similar to the antifraud provisions of SEC Rule 10b-5.
REGULATION OF INVESTMENT COMPANIES (See pages 657–658.)	The Investment Company Act of 1940 provides for SEC regulation of investment company activities. It was altered and expanded by the amendments of 1970 and 1975.
STATE SECURITIES LAWS (See pages 658–659.)	All states have corporate securities laws *(blue sky laws)* that regulate the offer and sale of securities within state borders; designed to prevent "speculative schemes which have no more basis than so many feet of 'blue sky.'" States regulate securities concurrently with the federal government.

For Review

1. What is the essential purpose of the Securities Act of 1933? What is the essential purpose of the Securities Exchange Act of 1934?

2. What is a registration statement? What must it include? What is a prospectus?

3. Basically, what constitutes a *security* under the Securities Act of 1933?

4. What is SEC Rule 10b-5? What is the key to liability under this rule? To what kinds of transactions does SEC Rule 10b-5 apply?

5. Name two theories under which "outsiders" can be held liable for violating SEC Rule 10b-5.

Questions and Case Problems

23–1. Registration Requirements. Langley Brothers, Inc., a corporation incorporated and doing business in Kansas, decides to sell no-par common stock worth $1 million to the public. The stock will be sold only within the state of Kansas. Joseph Langley, the chairman of the board, says the offering need not be registered with the SEC. His brother, Harry, disagrees. Who is right? Explain.

23–2. Registration Requirements. Huron Corp. had 300,000 common shares outstanding. The owners of these outstanding shares lived in several different states. Huron decided to split the 300,000 shares two for one. Will Huron Corp. have to file a registration statement and prospectus on the 300,000 new shares to be issued as a result of the split? Explain.

23–3. Definition of a Security. The W. J. Howey Co. (Howey) owned large tracts of citrus acreage in Lake County, Florida. For several years, it planted about five hundred acres annually, keeping half of the groves itself and offering the other half to the public to help finance additional development. Howey-in-the-Hills Service, Inc., was a service company engaged in cultivating and developing these groves, including the harvesting and marketing of the crops. Each prospective customer was offered both a land sales contract and a service contract, after being told that it was not feasible to invest in a grove unless service arrangements were made. Of the acreage sold by Howey, 85 percent was sold with a service contract with Howey-in-the-Hills Service. Howey did not register with the SEC or meet the other administrative requirements that issuers of securities must fulfill. The SEC sued to enjoin Howey from continuing to offer the land sales and service contracts. Howey responded that no SEC violation existed, because no securities had been issued. Evaluate the definition of a security given in this chapter, and then determine which party should prevail in court, Howey or the SEC. [*SEC v. W. J. Howey Co.,* 328 U.S. 293, 66 S.Ct. 1100, 90 L.Ed. 1244 (1946)]

23–4. Definition of a Security. U.S. News & World Report, Inc., set up a profit-sharing plan in 1962 that allotted to certain employees specially issued stock known as bonus or anniversary stock. The stock was given to the employees for past services and could not be traded or sold to anyone other than the corporate issuer, U.S. News. This special stock was issued only to employees and for no other purpose than as bonuses. Because there was no market for the stock, U.S. News hired an independent appraiser to estimate the fair value of the stock so that the employees could redeem the shares. Charles Foltz and several other employees held stock through this plan and sought to redeem the shares with U.S. News, but Foltz disputed the value set by the appraisers. Foltz sued U.S. News for violation of securities regulations. What defense would allow U.S. News to resist successfully Foltz's claim? [*Foltz v. U.S. News & World Report, Inc.,* 627 F.Supp. 1143 (D.D.C. 1986)]

23–5. Short-Swing Profits. Emerson Electric Co. purchased 13.2 percent of Dodge Manufacturing Co.'s stock in an unsuccessful takeover attempt in June 1967. Less

than six months later, when Dodge merged with Reliance Electric Co., Emerson decided to sell its shares. To avoid being subject to the short-swing profit restrictions of Section 16(b) of the Securities Exchange Act of 1934, Emerson decided on a two-step selling plan. First, it sold off sufficient shares to reduce its holdings to 9.96 percent [owners with less than 10 percent are exempt from Section 16(b)], and then it sold the remaining stock—all within a six-month period. Emerson in this way succeeded in avoiding Section 16(b) requirements. Reliance demanded that Emerson return the profits made on both sales. Emerson sought a declaratory judgment from the court that it was not liable, arguing that because at the time of the second sale it had not owned 10 percent of Dodge stock, Section 16(b) did not apply. Does Section 16(b) of the Securities Exchange Act of 1934 apply to Emerson's transactions, and is Emerson liable to Reliance for its profits? Discuss fully. [*Reliance Electric Co. v. Emerson Electric Co.,* 404 U.S. 418, 92 S.Ct. 596, 30 L.E.2d 575 (1972)]

23–6. SEC Rule 10b-5. Energy Resource Group, Inc. (ERG), entered into a written agreement with Ivan West by which West was to find an investor willing to purchase ERG stock. West later formed a partnership, called Investment Management Group (IMG), with Don Peters and another person. According to the terms of the partnership agreement, West's consulting work for ERG was excluded from the work of the IMG partnership. West learned through his consulting position with ERG that ERG was to be acquired by another corporation for $6.00 per share. At the time West learned of the acquisition, ERG stock was trading at $3.50 per share. Apparently, Peters learned of the acquisition from papers on West's desk in the IMG office and then shared the information with Ken Mick, his stockbroker. Mick then encouraged several clients to buy ERG stock prior to the public announcement of the acquisition. Mick, in return for leaking this inside information to clients, received a special premium from the enriched investors. Mick then paid a portion of the premium to Peters. The SEC brought an action against Peters for violating SEC Rule 10b-5. Under what theory might Peters be held liable for insider trading in violation of SEC Rule 10b-5? Discuss fully. [*SEC v. Peters,* 735 F.Supp. 1505 (D.Kans. 1990)]

23–7. Securities Fraud. William Gotchey owned 50 percent of the shares of First American Financial Consultants, Inc. (FAFC), an investment company registered with the SEC. In the fall of 1987, Paul Hatfield, a client of FAFC, spoke with Gotchey about investing. As a result of their conversations, Hatfield invested $5,000 with FAFC. In December, Hatfield told Gotchey that he wished to invest $20,000, $15,000 of which he wished to place in a secure investment. Gotchey told Hatfield that he would place this $15,000 in mortgage-backed securities to be invested through a mortgage company. For a time, Hatfield received interest payments from FAFC, purportedly from the mortgage-backed investment. He also received statements confirming that the investment had been made. In fact, Gotchey had deposited the entire $20,000 in an FAFC bank account. When Hatfield did not receive the interest payment due at the beginning of July 1988, he confronted Gotchey. Gotchey responded by asking Hatfield to sign an agreement whereby FAFC would repay the $15,000 in monthly installments over ten years. Hatfield refused. Gotchey did not account for the $15,000, and Hatfield received no interest payments after June 1988. Has Gotchey violated Section 10(b) of the Securities Exchange Act? Why or why not? [*SEC v. Gotchey,* 981 F.2d 1251 (4th Cir. 1992)]

23–8. SEC Rule 10b-5. Danny Cherif worked for a Chicago bank from 1979 until 1987, when his position was eliminated because of an internal reorganization. Cherif, through a forged memo to the bank's security department, caused his magnetic identification (ID) card—which he had received as an employee to allow him to enter the bank building—to remain activated after his employment was terminated. Cherif used his ID card to enter the building at night to obtain confidential financial information regarding extraordinary business transactions, such as tender offers. During 1988 and 1989, Cherif made substantial profits by using this information in securities trading. Eventually, Cherif's activities were investigated by the SEC, and he was charged with violating Section 10(b) and SEC Rule 10b-5 by misappropriating and trading on inside information in violation of his fiduciary duties to his former employer. Cherif argued that the SEC had wrongfully applied the misappropriation theory to his activities, because as a former employee, he no longer had a fiduciary duty to the bank. Will the court agree with Cherif? Discuss fully. [*SEC v. Cherif,* 933 F.2d 403 (7th Cir. 1991)]

23–9. SEC Rule 10b-5. In early 1985, FMC Corp. made plans to buy some of its own stock as part of a restructuring of its balance statement. Unknown to FMC management, the brokerage firm FMC employed—Goldman, Sachs & Co.—disclosed information on the stock purchase that found its way to Ivan Boesky. FMC was one of the seven major corporations in whose stock Boesky allegedly traded using inside information. Boesky made purchases of FMC's stock between February 18 and February 21, 1986, and between March 12 and April 4, 1986. Boesky's purchases amounted to a substantial portion of the total volume of FMC stock traded during these periods. The price of FMC stock increased from $71.25 on February 20, 1986, to $97.00 on April 25, 1986. As a result, FMC paid substantially more for the repurchase of its own stock than anticipated. When FMC discovered Boesky's knowledge of its recapitalization

plan, FMC sued Boesky for the excess price it had paid—approximately $220 million. Discuss whether FMC should recover under Section 10(b) of the Securities Exchange Act and SEC Rule 10b-5. [*In re Ivan F. Boesky Securities Litigation,* 36 F.3d 255 (2d Cir. 1994)]

23–10. SEC Rule 10b-5. Louis Ferraro was the chairman and president of Anacomp, Inc. In June 1988, Ferraro told his good friend Michael Maio that Anacomp was negotiating a tender offer for stock in Xidex Corp. Maio passed on the information to Patricia Ladavac, a friend of both Ferraro and Maio. Maio and Ladavac immediately purchased shares in Xidex stock. On the day that the tender offer was announced—an announcement that caused the price of Xidex shares to increase—Maio and Ladavac sold their Xidex stock and made substantial profits (Maio made $211,000 from the transactions, and Ladavac gained $78,750). The SEC brought an action against the three individuals, alleging that they had violated, among other laws, SEC Rule 10b-5. Maio and Ladavac claimed that they had done nothing illegal. They argued that they had no fiduciary duty either to Anacomp or to Xidex, and therefore they had no duty to disclose or abstain from trading in the stock of those corporations. Had Maio and Ladavac violated SEC Rule 10b-5? Discuss fully. [*SEC v. Maio,* 51 F.3d 623 (7th Cir. 1995)]

23–11. Definition of a Security. Life Partners, Inc. (LPI), facilitates the sale of life insurance policies that are owned by persons suffering from AIDS (acquired immune deficiency syndrome) to investors at a discount. The investors pay LPI, and LPI pays the policyholder. Typically, the policyholder, in turn, assigns the policy to LPI, which also obtains the right to make LPI's president the beneficiary of the policy. On the policyholder's death, LPI receives the proceeds of the policy and pays the investor. In this way, the terminally ill sellers secure much-needed income in the final years of life, when employment is unlikely and medical bills are often staggering. The SEC sought to enjoin (prevent) LPI from engaging in further transactions on the ground that the investment contracts were securities, which LPI had failed to register with the SEC in violation of securities laws. Do the investment contracts meet the definition of a security discussed in this chapter? Discuss fully. [*SEC v. Life Partners, Inc.,* 87 F.3d 536 (D.C.Cir. 1996)]

A Question of Ethics and Social Responsibility

23–12. Susan Waldbaum was a niece of the president and controlling shareholder of Waldbaum, Inc. Susan's mother (the president's sister) told Susan that the company was going to be sold at a favorable price and that a tender offer was soon to be made. She told Susan not to tell anyone except her husband, Keith Loeb, about the sale. (Loeb did not work for the company and was never brought into the family's inner circle, in which family members discussed confidential business information.) The next day, Susan told her husband of the sale and cautioned him not to tell anyone, because "it could possibly ruin the sale." The day after he learned of the sale, Loeb told Robert Chestman, his broker, about the sale, and Chestman purchased shares of the company for both Loeb and himself. Chestman was later convicted by a jury of, among other things, trading on misappropriated inside information in violation of SEC Rule 10b-5. [*United States v. Chestman*, 947 F.2d 551 (2d Cir. 1991)]

    1. On appeal, the central question was whether Chestman had acquired the inside information about the tender offer as a result of an insider's breach of a fiduciary duty. Could Loeb—the "tipper" in this case—be considered an insider?

    2. If Loeb was not an insider, did he owe any fiduciary (legal) duty to his wife or his wife's family to keep the information confidential? Would it be fair of the court to impose such a legal duty on Loeb?

For Critical Analysis

23–13. Do you think that the tipper/tippee and misappropriation theories extend liability under SEC Rule 10b-5 too far? Why or why not?

Unit V—Cumulative Hypothetical Problem

23–14. Business Ethics. Falwell Motors, Inc., is a large corporation that manufactures automobile batteries.

    1. The Federal Trade Commission (FTC) learns that one of the retail stores that sells Falwell's batteries engages in deceptive advertising practices. What actions can the FTC take against the retailer?

    2. For years, Falwell has shipped the toxic waste created by its manufacturing process to a waste-disposal site in the next county. The waste site has become contaminated by leakage from toxic waste containers delivered to the site by other manufacturers. Can Falwell be held liable for clean-up costs, even though its containers were not the ones that leaked? If so, what is the extent of its liability?

    3. Falwell faces stiff competition from Alchem, Inc., another battery manufacturer. To acquire control over Alchem, Falwell makes a tender offer to Alchem's shareholders. If Falwell succeeds in its attempt and Alchem is merged into Falwell, will the merger violate any antitrust laws? Suppose the merger falls through. The vice president of Falwell's battery division and the president of Alchem agree to divide up the market between them, so they will not have to compete for customers. In this agreement legal? Explain.

    4. One of Falwell's employees learns that Falwell is contemplating a takeover of a rival. The employee tells her husband about the possibility. The husband calls their broker, who purchases shares in the target corporation for the employee and her husband, as well as for himself. Has the employee violated any securities law? Has her husband? Has the broker? Explain.

INTERACTING WITH
The Internet

■ The Web site for the Securities and Exchange Commission (SEC) is called EDGAR, for Electronic Data Gathering Analysis and Retrieval system. Corporate financial information in the EDGAR database—including initial public offerings, proxy statements, annual corporate reports, registration statements, and other documents filed with the SEC—is available to the public. The site also contains information about the SEC's operations, the statutes it implements, its proposed and final rules, and its enforcement actions. To access EDGAR, go to

http://www.sec.gov/edgarhp.htm

■ The Center for Corporate Law at the University of Cincinnati College of Law examines all of the acts discussed in this chapter. Go to

http://www.law.uc.edu/CCL/

■ To find the Securities Act of 1933, go to

http://www.law.uc.edu/CCL/33Act/index.html

■ To examine the Securities Exchange Act of 1934, go to

http://www.law.uc.edu/CCL/34Act/index.html

■ For information on investor protection and securities fraud, including answers to frequently asked questions on the topic of securities fraud, go to

http://www.securitieslaw.com

The International Environment

Unit
Outline

CHAPTER 24

The Regulation of International Transactions

Contents

Chapter Objectives

After reading this chapter, you should be able to . . .

1. Identify and discuss some basic principles and doctrines that frame international business transactions.

2. Describe some ways in which U.S. businesspersons do business internationally.

3. Explain how parties to international contracts protect against various risks through contractual clauses and letters of credit.

4. Discuss how specific types of international business activities are regulated by governments.

5. Give examples of the extraterritorial application of certain U.S. laws.

Since ancient times, independent peoples and nations have traded their goods and wares with one another. In other words, international business transactions are not unique to the modern world, because people have always found that they can benefit from exchanging goods with others, as suggested by President Woodrow Wilson's statement in the opening quotation. What is new in our time is that, particularly since World War II, business has become increasingly *multinational*. It is not uncommon, for example, for a U.S. corporation to have investments or manufacturing plants in a foreign country, or for a foreign corporation to have operations within the United States.

Transacting business on an international level is considerably different from transacting business within the boundaries of just one nation. Buyers and sellers face far greater risks in the international marketplace than they do in a domestic context because the laws governing these transactions are more complex and uncertain. For example, the Uniform Commercial Code will govern many disputes that arise between U.S. buyers and sellers of goods unless they have provided otherwise in their contracts. What happens, however, if a U.S. buyer breaches a contract formed with a British seller? What law will govern the dispute—British or American? What if an investor owns substantial assets in a developing nation and the government of that nation decides to nationalize—assert its ownership over—the property? What recourse does the investor have against the actions of a foreign government? Questions such as these, which normally do not arise in a domestic context, can become critical in international business dealings.

Because the exchange of goods, services, and ideas on a global level is now a common phenomenon, it is important for the student of business law to be familiar with the laws pertaining to international business transactions. In this chapter, we first examine the legal context of international business transactions. We then look at some selected areas relating to business activities in a global context, including international sales contracts, civil dispute resolution, letters of credit, and investment protection. We conclude the chapter with a discussion of the application of certain U.S. laws in a transnational setting.

> "Our interests are those of the open door—a door of friendship and mutual advantage. This is the only door we care to enter."
>
> Woodrow Wilson, 1856–1924
> (Twenty-eighth president of the United States, 1913–1921)

A merchant checks the quality of goods. If a dispute arises, concerning the quality of these goods, between this merchant and a merchant in another country, what law governs the dispute?

International Principles and Doctrines

▼ Recall from our discussion of international law in Chapter 1 that *international law* is a body of written and unwritten laws that are observed by otherwise independent nations and that govern the acts of individuals as well as states. We also discussed in that chapter the major sources of international law, including international customs, treaties between nations, and international organizations and conferences. Here, we look at some other legal principles and doctrines that have evolved over time and that the courts of various nations have employed—to a greater or lesser extent—to resolve or reduce conflicts that involve a foreign element. The three important legal principles and doctrines discussed in the following sections are based primarily on courtesy and respect and are applied in the interests of maintaining harmonious relations among nations.

The Principle of Comity

Under what is known as the principle of **comity**, one nation will defer and give effect to the laws and judicial decrees of another country, as long as those laws

Comity A deference by which one nation gives effect to the laws and judicial decrees of another nation. This recognition is based primarily on respect.

and judicial decrees are consistent with the law and public policy of the accommodating nation. This recognition is based primarily on courtesy and respect. For example, assume that a Swedish seller and an American buyer have formed a contract, which the buyer breaches. The seller sues the buyer in a Swedish court, which awards damages. The buyer's assets, however, are in the United States and cannot be reached unless the judgment is enforced by a U.S. court of law. In this situation, if it is determined that the procedures and laws applied in the Swedish court were consistent with U.S. national law and policy, a court in the United States will likely defer to (and enforce) the foreign court's judgment.

The Act of State Doctrine

Act of State Doctrine A doctrine that provides that the judicial branch of one country will not examine the validity of public acts committed by a recognized foreign government within its own territory.

The **act of state doctrine** is a judicially created doctrine that provides that the judicial branch of one country will not examine the validity of public acts committed by a recognized foreign government within its own territory. This doctrine is premised on the theory that the judicial branch should not "pass upon the validity of foreign acts when to do so would vex the harmony of our international relations with that foreign nation."[1]

The act of state doctrine can have important consequences for individuals and firms doing business with, and investing in, other countries. For example, this doctrine is frequently employed in cases involving expropriation or confiscation. **Expropriation** occurs when a government seizes a privately owned business or privately owned goods for a proper public purpose and awards just compensation. When a government seizes private property for an illegal purpose or without just compensation, the taking is referred to as a **confiscation**. The line between these two forms of taking is sometimes blurred because of differing interpretations of what is illegal and what constitutes just compensation.

Expropriation The seizure by a government of privately owned business or personal property for a proper public purpose and with just compensation.

Confiscation A government's taking of privately owned business or personal property without a proper public purpose or an award of just compensation.

To illustrate: Tim Flaherty, an American businessperson, owns a mine in Brazil. The government of Brazil seizes the mine for public use and claims that the profits that Tim has realized from the mine in *preceding years* constitute just compensation. Tim disagrees, but the act of state doctrine may prevent Tim's recovery in a U.S. court of law.

When applicable, both the act of state doctrine and the doctrine of sovereign immunity (to be discussed shortly) tend to immunize foreign nations from the jurisdiction of U.S. courts. What this means is that firms or individuals who own property overseas often have little legal protection against government actions in the countries in which they operate. The applicability of the act of state doctrine is at issue in the following case.

---

1. *Libra Bank, Ltd. v. Banco Nacional de Costa Rica, S.A.,* 570 F.Supp. 870 (S.D.N.Y. 1983).

Case 24.1 ● W. S. Kirkpatrick & Co. v. Environmental Tectonics Corp., International

Supreme Court of the United States, 1990.
493 U.S. 400,
110 S.Ct. 701,
107 L.Ed.2d 816.

HISTORICAL AND POLITICAL SETTING *Once a colony of Great Britain, Nigeria gained its independence in 1960,* *which was also the year of the first meeting of the Organization of Petroleum Exporting Countries (OPEC). Nigeria, which possesses the greatest oil resources in Africa, later joined OPEC. In 1963, Nigeria became a federal republic, but between 1966 and 1979, the government changed hands four times in military coups. In 1975, the*

(Continued)

Case 24.1—continued

military announced that it would gradually return the government to civilian democratic rule, which finally occurred in 1979. Nigeria, benefiting from the increase in oil prices during the 1970s, began an intense program of modernization and construction. Among other problems that Nigeria has endured since its independence is internal corruption.

BACKGROUND AND FACTS In 1981, W. S. Kirkpatrick & Company learned that the Republic of Nigeria was interested in contracting for the construction and equipment of a medical center in Nigeria. Kirkpatrick, with the aid of a Nigerian citizen, secured the contract as a result of bribing Nigerian officials. Nigerian law prohibits both the payment and the receipt of bribes in connection with the awarding of government contracts, and the U.S. Foreign

Corrupt Practices Act of 1977 expressly prohibits U.S. firms and their agents from bribing foreign officials to secure favorable contracts. Environmental Tectonics Corporation, International (ETC), an unsuccessful bidder for the contract, learned of the bribery and sued Kirkpatrick in a U.S. federal court for damages. The district court granted summary judgment for Kirkpatrick, because resolution of the case in favor of ETC would require imputing to foreign officials an unlawful motivation (the obtaining of bribes) and accordingly might embarrass the Nigerian government or interfere with the conduct of U.S. foreign policy. ETC appealed, and the appellate court reversed the judgment of the district court. Kirkpatrick appealed to the United States Supreme Court.

IN THE WORDS OF THE COURT . . .
Justice SCALIA delivered the opinion of the Court.
* * * *

In every case in which we have held the act of state doctrine applicable, the relief sought * * * would have required a court in the United States to declare invalid the official act of a foreign sovereign performed within its own territory. * * * In the present case, by contrast, neither the claim nor any asserted defense requires a determination that Nigeria's contract with Kirkpatrick International was, or was not, effective.
* * * *

The short of the matter is this: Courts in the United States have the power, and ordinarily the obligation, to decide cases and controversies properly presented to them. The act of state doctrine does not establish an exception for cases and controversies that may embarrass foreign governments, but merely requires that, in the process of deciding, the acts of foreign [governments] taken within their own jurisdictions shall be deemed valid. That doctrine has no application to the present case because the validity of no foreign [government] act is at issue.

DECISION AND REMEDY The United States Supreme Court held that the act of state doctrine did not apply in this case and affirmed the judgment of the court of appeals.

FOR CRITICAL ANALYSIS—INTERNATIONAL CONSIDERATION
What does the United States have to gain by presuming the validity of the actions of foreign governments?

The Doctrine of Sovereign Immunity

Under certain conditions, the doctrine of **sovereign immunity** immunizes (protects) foreign nations from the jurisdiction of the U.S. courts. In 1976, Congress codified this rule in the Foreign Sovereign Immunities Act (FSIA). The FSIA exclusively governs the circumstances in which an action may be brought in the United States against a foreign nation, including attempts to attach a foreign nation's property.

Section 1605 of the FSIA sets forth the major exceptions to the jurisdictional immunity of a foreign state or country. A foreign state is not immune

Sovereign Immunity A doctrine that immunizes foreign nations from the jurisdiction of U.S. courts when certain conditions are satisfied.

from the jurisdiction of the courts of the United States when the state has "waived its immunity either explicitly or by implication" or when the action is "based upon a commercial activity carried on in the United States by the foreign state."[2]

Issues frequently arise as to what entities fall within the category of a foreign state. The question of what is a commercial activity has also been the subject of dispute. Under Section 1603 of the FSIA, a *foreign state* is defined to include both a political subdivision of a foreign state and an instrumentality of a foreign state. A *commercial activity* is broadly defined under Section 1603 to mean a commercial activity that is carried out by a foreign state within the United States. The act, however, does not define the particulars of what constitutes a commercial activity. Rather, it is left up to the courts to decide whether a particular activity is governmental or commercial in nature. (See this chapter's *Inside the Legal Environment* on page 672 for a further discussion of this issue.) In the following case, the court had to determine whether the defense of sovereign immunity was available under the FSIA.

---

2.   28 U.S.C. Section 1605(a)(1), (2).

Case 24.2 ● Eckert International, Inc. v. Government of the Sovereign Democratic Republic of Fiji

United States District Court,
Eastern District of Virginia, 1993.
834 F. Supp. 167.

BACKGROUND AND FACTS   In 1988, Eckert International, Inc., an American corporation, entered into a three-year contract with the government of Fiji to provide Fiji with public-relations consulting services in Washington, D.C., for annual payments of $250,000. In 1991, the contract was renewed without change for three more years. In 1992, Fiji's new prime minister terminated the contract and refused to pay Eckert for the remaining two years. Eckert sued Fiji in a U.S. district court for breach of contract. Fiji moved to dismiss the suit, asserting, among other things, that it was immunized from the jurisdiction of U.S. courts by the Foreign Sovereign Immunities Act (FSIA).

HISTORICAL AND POLITICAL SETTING   *A British colony for nearly a century, Fiji gained its independence in 1970. Ratu Sir Kamisese Mara became prime minister at the time of independence. In 1987, a coalition led by members of the Indian majority gained political power but was overthrown in October in a military coup led by native Fijian Sitivina Rambuka. Rambuka proclaimed Fiji a republic, and the nation withdrew from the British Commonwealth. A new constitution was adopted in 1990. In 1992, Rambuka replaced Mara as the head of government.*

IN THE WORDS OF THE COURT . . .
ELLIS, District Judge.
        *   *   *   *
        *   *   * [The FSIA's] "commercial activity" exception *   *   * differentiates between a foreign state's public acts performed in its sovereign capacity and a foreign state's private acts performed as a market participant. *   *   * [T]he focus in drawing the distinction between public and private acts must be on the nature of the act performed rather than on its purpose. *   *   *
        Measured by this standard, Fiji's act in entering into the 1991 contract was plainly a private act for the consulting contract is "inherently

(Continued)

Case 24.2—continued

commercial in nature" and is governed by the rules of the marketplace. Fiji's argument that its contract was governmental, rather than commercial, in nature because Eckert represented Fiji in its "political and diplomatic relationship" with the United States is unpersuasive. This reasoning mistakenly focuses on the contract's purpose, while ignoring its essentially commercial nature. Indeed, the 1991 contract and its predecessor are simply garden variety consulting contracts, no different from myriad other consulting contracts between organizations and lobbyists. * * * The FSIA neither permits nor contemplates * * * a misuse of sovereign immunity. To the contrary, where, as here, a foreign state has entered into an essentially commercial contract for the performance of consulting services, it may not claim sovereign immunity under the FSIA.

DECISION AND REMEDY The federal district court denied Fiji's motion to dismiss Eckert's claim.

FOR CRITICAL ANALYSIS—POLITICAL CONSIDERATION *Does the "commercial activities" exception to the FSIA conflict with the act of state doctrine?*

Doing Business Internationally

A U.S. domestic firm can engage in international business transactions in a number of ways. The simplest way to engage in international business transactions is to seek out foreign markets for domestically produced products or services. In other words, U.S. firms can look abroad for **export** markets for their goods and services. Alternatively, a U.S. firm can establish foreign production facilities so as to be closer to the foreign market or markets in which

Export To sell products to buyers located in other countries.

A worker sews a garment at a Levi's plant in Poland. Why would a U.S. domestic firm set up a manufacturing facility abroad?

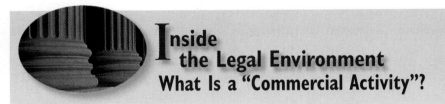

Inside the Legal Environment
What Is a "Commercial Activity"?

Unlike the economy of the United States, which is primarily controlled by private interests, the economies of many other countries, particularly developing nations, are often extensively controlled by government. This means that if a U.S. plaintiff sues a business or institution that is controlled by a foreign government, the foreign defendant may assert the defense of sovereign immunity under the Foreign Sovereign Immunities Act (FSIA) of 1976. In this situation, a U.S. court cannot exercise jurisdiction over the dispute unless the plaintiff can prove, among other things, that the defendant's actions constituted a "commercial activity." What, however, is a "commercial activity"?

Although the FSIA does not define this phrase with any precision, the United States Supreme Court has provided some guidance on the issue. For example, in *Saudi Arabia v. Nelson,*[a] the Court addressed the question of whether the Saudi Arabian government's allegedly wrongful arrest, imprisonment, and torture of an American employee of a

Saudi hospital constituted a commercial activity. The court concluded that it did not, holding that a state engages in commercial activity "where it exercises 'only those powers that can also be exercised by private citizens,' as distinct from those 'powers peculiar to sovereigns.'" The Court held that the alleged tortious actions of the Saudi government against the American employee were "sovereign" in character, and thus the Saudi government was immune from liability under the FSIA.

In 1995, the District of Columbia Court of Appeals applied this distinction between activities of a "sovereign character" and a "commercial character" in *Janini v. Kuwait University.*[b] The plaintiffs in the case were an American citizen, George Janini, and other former professors and employees of Kuwait University (KU). The plaintiffs were terminated from their positions when the government of Kuwait, following Iraq's invasion of Kuwait in August 1990, issued a decree stating, among other things, that "contracts concluded between the Government and those non-Kuwaiti workers who worked

for it . . . shall be considered automatically abrogated because of the impossibility of enforcement due to the Iraqi invasion."

The plaintiffs sued KU in a U.S. court, alleging that their termination breached their employment contracts, which required nine months' notice before termination. The plaintiffs sought back pay and other benefits to which they were entitled under their contracts. The question before the court was whether terminating the professors' positions constituted a commercial activity. The court held that it did. The court concluded that "there is nothing 'peculiarly sovereign' about unilaterally terminating an employment contract. Private parties often repudiate contracts in everyday commerce and may be held liable therefor. That the termination here may have been accomplished by a formal decree of abrogation does not affect its commercial nature."

For Critical Analysis: *In addition to finding that a government-controlled foreign defendant has engaged in a commercial activity, what other requirement must be met before a U.S. court can exercise jurisdiction over the defendant?*

a.   507 U.S. 349, 113 S.Ct. 1471, 123 L.Ed.2d 47 (1993).

b.   43 F.3d 1534, 310 U.S.App.D.C. 109 (D.C. Cir. 1995).

its products are sold. The advantages may include lower labor costs, fewer government regulations, and lower taxes and trade barriers. It is also possible to obtain business from abroad through the licensing of technology that has been developed and is owned by a domestic firm to an existing foreign company. Yet another way to expand abroad is by selling franchises to overseas entities. The presence of McDonald's, Burger King, and KFC franchises throughout the world attests to the popularity of franchising.

Exporting

The initial foray into international business by most U.S. companies is through exporting. Exporting can take two forms: direct exporting and indirect exporting. In *direct exporting,* a U.S. company signs a sales contract with a foreign purchaser that provides for the conditions of shipment and payment for the goods. (How payments are made in international transactions is discussed later in this chapter.) If business develops sufficiently in foreign countries, a U.S. corporation may develop a specialized marketing organization that, for example, sells directly to consumers in that country. Such *indirect exporting* can be undertaken by the appointment of a foreign agent or a foreign distributor.

FOREIGN AGENT.   When a U.S. firm desires a limited involvement in an international market, it will typically establish an *agency relationship* with a foreign firm. In an agency relationship (discussed in Chapter 16), one person (the agent) agrees to act on behalf of another (the principal). The foreign agent is thereby empowered to enter into contracts in the agent's country on behalf of the U.S. principal.

FOREIGN DISTRIBUTOR.   When a substantial market exists in a foreign country, a U.S. firm may wish to appoint a distributor located in that country. The U.S. firm and the distributor enter into a **distribution agreement,** which is a contract between the seller and the distributor setting out the terms and conditions of the distributorship—for example, price, currency of payment, availability of supplies, and method of payment. The terms and conditions primarily involve contract law. Disputes concerning distribution agreements may involve jurisdictional or other issues (discussed in detail later in this chapter). In addition, some **exclusive distributorships**—in which distributors agree to distribute only the sellers' goods—have raised antitrust problems.

Manufacturing Abroad

An alternative to direct or indirect exporting is the establishment of foreign manufacturing facilities. Typically, U.S. firms want to establish manufacturing plants abroad if they believe that by doing so they will reduce costs—particularly for labor, shipping, and raw materials—and thereby be able to compete more effectively in foreign markets. Apple Computer, IBM, General Motors, and Ford are some of the many U.S. companies that have established manufacturing facilities abroad. Foreign firms have done the same in the United States. Sony, Nissan, and other Japanese manufacturers have established U.S. plants to avoid import duties that the U.S. Congress may impose on Japanese products entering this country.

There are several ways in which an American firm can manufacture goods in other countries. They include licensing and franchising, as well as investing in a wholly owned subsidiary or a joint venture.

LICENSING.   It is possible for U.S. firms to license their technologies to foreign manufacturers. **Technology licensing** may involve a process innovation that lowers the cost of production, or it may involve a product innovation that generates a superior product. Technology licensing may be an attractive alternative to establishing foreign production facilities, particularly if the process or product innovation has been patented, because the patent protects—at least to some extent—against the possibility that the innovation might be pirated. Like any licensing agreement, a licensing agreement with a foreign-based firm calls for a payment of royalties on some basis—such as so many cents per unit produced or a certain percentage of profits from units sold in a particular geographical territory.

> **"Commerce is the great equalizer. We exchange ideas when we exchange fabrics."**
>
> R. G. Ingersoll, 1833–1899
> (American lawyer and orator)

Distribution Agreement A contract between a seller and a distributor of the seller's products setting out the terms and conditions of the distributorship.

Exclusive Distributorship A distributorship in which the seller and distributor of the seller's products agree that the distributor has the exclusive right to distribute the seller's products in a certain geographic area.

Technology Licensing Allowing another to use and profit from intellectual property (patents, copyrights, trademarks, innovative products or processes, and so on) for consideration. In the context of international business transactions, technology licensing is sometimes an attractive alternative to the establishment of foreign production facilities.

Ethical Perspective

The licensing of technology allows U.S. owners of intellectual property (such as patents, trademarks, and copyrights) to benefit from sales of their products in other countries. Much intellectual property, however, is "pirated"—that is, unauthorized copies of the property (such as a software program) are made and sold. In 1994, to protect intellectual property rights on a worldwide basis, more than one hundred nations signed the international agreement on Trade-Related Aspects of Intellectual Property Rights (TRIPS), which is administered by the World Trade Organization (WTO). These nations pledged to pass and enforce laws protecting patents, copyrights, and trademarks (see the *Landmark in the Legal Environment* in Chapter 11.)

The attempted enforcement of intellectual property rights on a worldwide basis, however, raises some ethical concerns. For example, in a developing country, the welfare of small business firms and consumers may be enhanced by the ability to purchase pirated (less expensive) copies of high-tech products. Although the owners of the pirated intellectual property lose out, it may be that the owners would have received nothing anyway—if no authorized copies (at higher prices) could have been sold in the poorer country. Furthermore, laws governing intellectual property rights are necessarily somewhat arbitrary. For example, if the United States grants copyright protection for a longer period of time than Japan, does this mean that U.S. law is "right" and Japanese law is "wrong"?

For Critical Analysis: *The piracy of another's property rights constitutes the crime of theft. Can this crime ever be justified?*

In certain circumstances, even in the absence of a patent, a firm may license the "know-how" associated with a particular manufacturing process—for example, a plant design or a secret formula. The foreign firm that agrees to sign the licensing agreement further agrees to keep the know-how confidential and to pay royalties. For example, the Coca-Cola Bottling Company licenses firms worldwide to use (and keep confidential) its secret formula for the syrup used in that soft drink, in return for a percentage of the income gained from the sale of Coca-Cola by those firms.

The licensing of technology benefits all parties to the transaction. Those who receive the license can take advantage of an established reputation for quality, and the firm that grants the license receives income from the foreign sales of the firm's products, as well as establishing a worldwide reputation. Additionally, once a firm's trademark is known worldwide, the demand for other products manufactured or sold by that firm may increase—obviously an important consideration.

FRANCHISING.   Franchising is a well-known form of licensing. Recall from Chapter 15 that a franchise can be defined as an arrangement in which the owner of a trademark, trade name, or copyright (the franchisor) licenses another (the franchisee) to use the trademark, trade name, or copyright—under certain conditions or limitations—in the selling of goods or services in exchange for a fee, usually based on a percentage of gross or net sales. Examples of international franchises include McDonald's, the Coca-Cola Bottling Company, Holiday Inn, Avis, and Hertz.

INVESTING IN A WHOLLY OWNED SUBSIDIARY OR A JOINT VENTURE.   One way to expand into a foreign market is to establish a wholly owned subsidiary

> **BE AWARE** A foreign manufacturer who is licensed to make and sell goods with a U.S. firm's trademark or name in a foreign country may attempt to sell those goods in the United States in direct competition with the U.S. firm. Such goods are known as "gray market" goods.

A Mobil station operates on Hainan Island in China. What benefits can a U.S. domestic firm realize from selling a franchise to an overseas entity?

firm in a foreign country. The European subsidiary would likely take the form of the *société anonyme* (S.A.), which is similar to a U.S. corporation. In German-speaking nations, it would be called an *Aktiengesellschaft* (A.G.). When a wholly owned subsidiary is established, the parent company, which remains in the United States, retains complete ownership of all the facilities in the foreign country, as well as complete authority and control over all phases of the operation.

The expansion of a U.S. firm into international markets can also take the form of a joint venture. In a joint venture, the U.S. company owns only part of the operation; the rest is owned either by local owners in the foreign country or by another foreign entity. In a joint venture, all of the firms involved share responsibilities, as well as profits and liabilities.

Commercial Contracts in an International Setting

Like all commercial contracts, an international contract should be in writing. The sample form shown in Exhibit 24–1 illustrates the typical terms and conditions that might be contained in an international contract. *(For an example of an actual international sales contract, refer back to the fold-out contract in Chapter 13.)*

Language and legal differences among nations can create special problems for parties to international contracts when disputes arise. It is possible to avoid these problems by including in a contract special provisions designating the official language of the contract, the legal forum (court or place) in which disputes under the contract will be settled, and the substantive law that will be applied in settling any disputes. Parties to international contracts should also indicate in their contracts what acts or events will excuse the parties from performance under the contract and whether disputes under the contract will be arbitrated or litigated.

RECALL The interpretation of the words in a contract can be the basis for a dispute even when both parties communicate in the same language.

International Perspective

In 1995, France implemented a law making the use of the French language mandatory in certain legal documents. Documents relating to securities offerings, such as prospectuses, for example, must be written in French. So must instruction manuals and warranties for goods and services offered for sale in France. Additionally, all agreements entered into with French state or local authorities, with entities controlled by state or local authorities, and with private entities carrying out a public service (such as providing utilities) must be written in French. The law has posed problems for some businesspersons because certain legal terms or phrases in documents governed by, say, U.S. or English law, have no equivalent terms or phrases in the French legal system.

For Critical Analysis: *How might language differences affect the meaning of certain terms or phrases in an international contract?*

Choice of Language

Choice-of-Language Clause A clause in a contract designating the official language by which the contract will be interpreted in the event of a future disagreement over the contract's terms.

A deal struck between a U.S. company and a company in another country normally involves two languages. The complex contractual terms involved may not be understood by one party in the other party's language. Typically, many phrases in one language are not readily translatable into another. To make sure that no disputes arise out of this language problem, an international sales contract should have a **choice-of-language clause** designating the official language by which the contract will be interpreted in the event of disagreement.

Choice of Forum

Forum-Selection Clause A provision in a contract designating the court, jurisdiction, or tribunal that will decide any disputes arising under the contract.

When several countries are involved, litigation may be sought in courts in different nations. There are no universally accepted rules regarding the jurisdiction of a particular court over subject matter or parties to a dispute. Consequently, parties to an international transaction should always include in the contract a **forum-selection clause** indicating what court, jurisdiction, or tribunal will decide any disputes arising under the contract. It is especially important to indicate specifically what court will have jurisdiction. The forum does not necessarily have to be within the geographical boundaries of either of the parties' nations.

Choice of Law

Choice-of-Law Clause A clause in a contract designating the law (such as the law of a particular state or nation) that will govern the contract.

A contractual provision designating the applicable law—such as the law of Germany or England or California—is called a **choice-of-law clause.** Every international contract typically includes a choice-of-law clause. At common law (and in European civil law systems), parties are allowed to choose the law that will govern their contractual relationship provided that the law chosen is the law of a jurisdiction that has a substantial relationship to the parties and to the international business transaction.

Under Section 1–105 of the Uniform Commercial Code, parties may choose the law that will govern the contract as long as the choice is "reasonable."

Article 6 of the United Nations Convention on Contracts for the International Sale of Goods, however, imposes no limitation on the parties in their choice of what law will govern the contract. The 1986 Hague Convention on the Law Applicable to Contracts for the International Sale of Goods—often referred to as the Choice-of-Law Convention—allows unlimited autonomy in the choice of law. The Hague Convention indicates that whenever a choice of law is not specified in a contract, the governing law is that of the country in which the *seller's* place of business is located.

Force Majeure Clause

Every contract, particularly those involving international transactions, should have a *force majeure* clause. *Force majeure* is a French term meaning "impossible or irresistible force"—which sometimes is loosely identified as "an act of God." In international business contracts, *force majeure* clauses commonly stipulate that in addition to acts of God, a number of other eventualities (such as governmental orders or regulations, embargoes, or shortages of materials) may excuse a party from liability for nonperformance.

Force Majeure Clause A provision in a contract stipulating that certain unforeseen events—such as war, political upheavals, acts of God, or other events—will excuse a party from liability for nonperformance of contractual obligations.

Civil Dispute Resolution

International contracts frequently include arbitration clauses. By means of such clauses, the parties agree in advance to be bound by the decision of a specified third party in the event of a dispute, as discussed in Chapter 3. The third party may be a neutral entity (such as the International Chamber of Commerce), a panel of individuals representing both parties' interests, or some other group or organization. (For an example of an arbitration clause in an international contract, refer to Exhibit 24–1, *as well as to the fold-out exhibit in Chapter 13.*) The United Nations Convention on the Recognition and Enforcement of Foreign Arbitral Awards (often called the New York Convention) assists in the enforcement of arbitration clauses, as do provisions in specific treaties between nations. The New York Convention has been implemented in nearly one hundred countries, including the United States.

If no arbitration clause is contained in the sales contract, litigation may occur. If forum-selection and choice-of-law clauses are included in the con-

International Perspective

One of the reasons many businesspersons find it advantageous to include arbitration clauses in their international contracts is because arbitration awards are usually easier to enforce than court judgments. As mentioned, the New York Convention provides for the enforcement of arbitration awards in those countries that have signed the convention. Enforcement of court judgments, however, normally depends on the principle of comity and bilateral agreements providing for such enforcement. How the principle of comity is applied, however, varies from one nation to another, and many countries have not agreed, in bilateral agreements, to enforce judgments rendered in U.S. courts.

For Critical Analysis: *What might be some other advantages of arbitration in the context of international transactions? Are there any disadvantages?*

■ **Exhibit 24–1 Sample International Purchase Order Form (Front)—Caution:** This form contains a typical set of terms written from the buyer's point of view, but it is not applicable to all factual situations and the laws of all states. Terms and conditions of sale or purchase must be custom drafted to be appropriate for the type of business and type of goods involved.

Sample International Purchase Order Terms & Conditions*
The _____ Company, Inc.
International Terms and Conditions of Purchase

1. *Acceptance.* Acceptance of this order is expressly limited to the terms and conditions contained herein, including all terms and conditions set forth on the face hereof. Acceptance of this order by Seller may be made by signing and returning the attached acknowledgement copy hereof, by other express acceptance, or by shipment of goods hereunder. If Seller uses its own order acknowledgement or other form to accept this order, it is understood that said form shall be used for convenience only and any terms or conditions contained therein inconsistent with or in addition to those contained herein shall be of no force or effect whatsoever between the parties hereto.

2. *Warranty.* Seller warrants the goods covered by this Agreement and their packaging and labelling shall be in merchantable condition and shall be free from defects in workmanship and materials and shall be in conformity with the specifications, drawings, samples and descriptions attached hereto or referred to on the face hereof, if any. Seller warrants that the goods covered by this Agreement shall be fit for such particular purposes and uses, if any, as specified by BUYER or otherwise known to Seller. Seller warrants that the goods shall be free and clear of any lien or other adverse claim against title, and to the extent not manufactured to detailed designs furnished by BUYER shall be free from defects in design. All warranties contained herein shall survive inspection, test and acceptance by BUYER. Seller agrees, at its own costs and expense, to defend and hold BUYER harmless from and against any and all claims made against BUYER based upon, relating to, or arising out of any claimed defects in the goods or services ordered hereunder. Seller's warranties (and any consumer warranties, service policies, or similar undertakings of Seller) shall be enforceable by BUYER'S customers and any subsequent owner or operator of the goods as well as by BUYER.

3. *Shipping Instructions.* No charge shall be made to BUYER for draying and packaging unless authorized by BUYER. Merchandise shipped by freight or express shall be packed, marked and described and the carrier shall be selected, so as to obtain the lowest rate possible under freight or express classifications or regulations except when otherwise specified by BUYER, and penalties or increased charges due to failure so to do will be charged to Seller. The foregoing notwithstanding, Seller shall comply with all instructions of BUYER as to packaging, marking, shipping and insurance. Prior to passage of title to BUYER the goods shall be held by Seller without risk or expense to BUYER.

4. *Invoices, Other Documents and Charges.* Seller shall invoice in duplicate. Originals of all invoices, government and commercial bills of lading and air express receipts shall be air mailed to the Purchasing Department of BUYER when goods are shipped. Packing slips must accompany item number, and a complete description of its contents. Except as otherwise provided on the face hereof, the contract price includes all costs and charges to be paid or reimbursed to Seller by BUYER, including without limitation, all applicable taxes and duties and all charges for packing, loading and transportation. Transportation charges and taxes and duties, when applicable, and when agreed on the face hereof to be borne by BUYER shall be billed as separate items on Seller's invoices.

5. *Inspection—Nonconformity.* BUYER may inspect the goods and, with respect to nonconforming goods, may return them or hold them at the Seller's risk and expense, and may in either event charge the Seller with cost of transportation, shipping, unpacking, examining, repacking, reshipping, and other like expense. Promptly upon BUYER's written request, and without expense to BUYER, Seller agrees to replace or correct defects of any rejected goods or other goods not conforming to the warranty set forth above. In the event of failure of Seller to replace or correct defects in nonconforming goods promptly, BUYER after reasonable notice to Seller, may make such corrections or replace such goods and charge Seller for the costs incurred by BUYER in doing so. Time is of the essence in this transaction. In addition to its remedies of breach of contract, BUYER reserves the right to return any or all goods in unopened original packing to Seller if delivered to BUYER more than five (5) days after the delivery date shown in shipping instructions. If the delivery date shown in shipping instructions is revised by BUYER by notification to Seller, the such five (5) day period shall not commence to run until such revised delivery date. Also, BUYER reserves the right to refuse goods delivered contrary to instructions or not in recognized standard containers. BUYER shall be under no duty to inspect goods prior to BUYER's use or resale, and neither retention, use nor resale of such goods shall be construed to constitute an acceptance of goods not in compliance with the requirements of this order.

6. *Changes.* Unless agreed in writing by BUYER, Seller shall not purchase materials, or make material commitments, or production arrangements, in excess of the amount, or in advance of the time necessary to meet BUYER'S delivery schedule. BUYER shall have the right at any time to make changes in drawings, designs, specifications, materials, packaging, time and place of delivery and method of transportation. If any such changes cause an increase or decrease in the cost, or the time required for the performance, an equitable adjustment shall be made and this agreement shall be modified in writing accordingly. Seller agrees to accept any such changes subject to this paragraph. This right to an adjustment shall be deemed waived unless asserted within thirty (30) days after the change is ordered. BUYER reserves the right to terminate this order or any part hereof for its sole convenience. In the event of such termination, Seller shall immediately stop all work hereunder, and shall immediately cause any of its suppliers or subcontractors to cease such work. Seller shall be paid a reasonable termination charge consisting of a percentage of the order price reflecting the percentage of the work performed prior to the notice of termination. Such charge shall be Seller's only remedy for such termination. Seller shall not be paid for any work done after receipt of the notice of termination nor for any work done by Seller's suppliers or subcontractor which Seller could reasonable have avoided.

7. *Default.* BUYER may also terminate this order or any part hereof for cause in the event of any default by the Seller of if the Seller fails to comply with any of the terms and conditions of this offer. Late deliveries, deliveries of goods which are defective or which do not conform to this order, and failure to provide BUYER, upon request, reasonable assurances of future performance shall all be causes allowing BUYER to terminate this order for cause. In the event of termination for cause, BUYER shall not be liable to Seller for any amount and Seller shall be liable to BUYER for any and all damage sustained by reason of the default which gave rise to the termination.

*Copyright 1988, Barry A. Sanders. All rights reserved. Reprinted with permission. These sample terms and conditions were used in connection with a presentation with the 21st Annual Uniform Commercial Code Institute. Mr. Sanders is with Latham & Watkins in Los Angeles, California.

■ Exhibit 24–1—Continued—Sample International Purchase Order Form (Back)

8. *Indemnity.* Seller will defend and indemnify BUYER, upon demand, against all claims, actions, liability, damage, loss and expense (including investigative expense and attorney's fees incurred in litigation or because of threatened litigation) as the result of BUYER'S purchase and/or use of goods and arising or alleged to arise from patent, trademark or copyright infringement; unfair competition; the failure or alleged failure of the goods to comply with specifications or with any express or implied warranties of Seller; the alleged violation by such goods or in its manufacture or sale of any statute, ordinance, or administrative order, rule or regulation; defects, whether latent or patent, in material or workmanship; defective design; defective warnings or instructions; or Seller's negligence.

9. *Price Reduction.* Seller will give BUYER the benefit of any price reductions occurring before the specified shipping date or to actual time of shipment, whichever is later. Likewise, if Seller accepts this order as a commission merchant, Seller shall obtain for BUYER from the manufacturer of such goods the benefit of price reductions to the specified date or to actual time of shipment, whichever is later. Seller warrants that the price for the articles sold BUYER hereunder are not less favorable than those currently extended to any other customer for the same or similar articles in similar quantities.

10. *Information.* Seller shall consider all information furnished by BUYER to be confidential and shall not disclose any such information to any other person, or use such information itself for any purpose other than performing this order unless Seller obtains written permission from BUYER to do so. This confidential requirement shall also apply to drawings, specifications, or other documents prepared by Seller for BUYER in connection with this order. Seller shall provide confidential information only to those of its agents, servants and employees who have been informed of the requirements of this paragraph and have agreed to be bound by them. Upon completion or termination of this order, Seller shall make such disposition of all such information and items as may be directed by BUYER. Seller shall not advertise or publish the fact that BUYER has ordered goods from Seller nor shall any information relating to this order be disclosed without BUYER'S written permission. Unless otherwise agreed in writing, no commercial, financial or technical information disclosed in any manner or at any time by Seller to BUYER shall be deemed secret or confidential and Seller shall have no rights against BUYER with respect thereto except such rights as may exist under patent laws.

11. *Tools, Dies, Etc.* Seller agrees that the information, tools, jigs, dies, etc., drawings, patterns and specifications supplied or paid for by BUYER shall be and remain BUYER'S property, shall be used only on BUYER'S orders, and shall be held by Seller for BUYER unless directed otherwise. Seller will account for such items and keep them in good working condition and fully covered by insurance at all times without expense to BUYER. In the event Seller devises and incorporates any new features design into any goods made under this order, Seller grants to BUYER the right of reproduction of such goods, together with a royalty-free, nonexclusive, irrevocable license to use such new features of design.

12. *General Provisions.*

(a) Seller and BUYER shall be independent contractors. This transaction does not create a principal-agent or partnership relationship between them, and neither one may legally commit the other in any matter.

(b) BUYER may deduct from any payment due to Seller or set-off against any claim by Seller any amount which is due to BUYER by Seller for any reason, including, among other reasons, any excess transportation charges caused by deviations from BUYER'S shipping instructions or the shipping of partial shipments.

(c) Seller shall comply with all laws, regulations and policies applicable to it by any jurisdiction and shall obtain all permits needed to complete this transaction under the laws of the country from which the shipment is made, including among other things, any required export permits and Central Bank approvals.

(d) All billings and payments shall be made in U.S. Dollars.

(e) In the event the importation of the goods results in the assessment of a countervailing duty on BUYER as the importer, Seller shall reimburse such countervailing duty to BUYER, provided such reimbursement is permitted under U.S. laws and regulations.

(f) Goods ordered hereunder to be made with use of BUYER'S confidential information, BUYER'S designs, BUYER'S trademarks or tradenames or BUYER'S customer's trademarks or tradenames shall be furnished by Seller exclusively to BUYER. Any excess of such inventory shall be destroyed by Seller at its own expense.

(g) Seller warrants that it has accepted no gratuities of any kind from any employee of BUYER in connection with placement of this order.

(h) Seller shall cooperate fully with BUYER at Seller's expense in obtaining approvals of the goods requested by BUYER from certifying organizations such as Underwriters Laboratories.

(i) Any goods that are hazardous will be packaged, marked and shipped by Seller to comply with all U.S. federal, state and local regulations and will further comply with all special BUYER requirements. Seller shall furnish BUYER a Material Hazard Data Sheet covering all such goods.

(j) BUYER shall not be liable to Seller for any loss incurred by Seller due to strikes, riots, storms, fires, explosions, acts of God, war, embargo, government boycott or other governmental action or any other causes similar thereto beyond the reasonable control of BUYER. Any failure or delay in performance of any of the foregoing shall not be a default hereunder.

(k) BUYER may waive performance of any condition, but waiver by BUYER of a condition shall not be considered a waiver of that condition for succeeding performance. None of BUYER'S remedies hereunder shall exclude its pursuit of its other legal remedies.

(l) This document and any other documents mentioned on the face hereof, constitute the entire agreement between the parties on this subject. All prior representations, negotiations or arrangements on this subject matter are superseded by these terms and shall not form a basis for interpretation of these terms. All amendments to these terms must be agreed to in writing by BUYER.

(m) If any manufacturer's excise tax, value added tax or other tax measured by selling price is included in or added to the price of the goods paid by BUYER, then, in the event all or any part of that tax shall be refunded to Seller, Seller shall promptly remit such refund in full to BUYER.

(n) This order is nonassignable. Any attempt to assign without BUYER'S written consent is void.

(o) This transaction and all its terms shall be construed in accordance with and all disputes shall be governed by the laws of the State of _____, U.S.A., specifically including the provisions of the Uniform Commercial Code, as adopted by that state, and excluding the provisions of the Convention on the International Sale of Goods. Seller submits to the jurisdiction of the courts located in the State of _____ in the event of any proceedings therein in connection herewith.

(p) Any and all disputes arising between BUYER and Seller in connection with this transaction (other than actions for contribution or indemnity with respect to court actions involving third parties) shall be exclusively and finally decided by arbitration in _____ under the rules of the American Arbitration Association. The arbitration award shall be final and nonappealable. There shall be three arbitrators, one chosen by each party and the third chosen by the first two, or in the event of their failure to agree, by the _____ state court of general jurisdiction. The arbitrators shall reach their decision, and state it in writing with reason for it, within twelve months after the appointment of the third arbitrator.

(q) This order shall expire in thirty (30) days from the date of issuance by BUYER, unless earlier revoked by BUYER or accepted by Seller. ■

tract, the lawsuit will be heard by a court in the forum specified and decided according to that forum's law. If no forum and choice of law have been specified, however, legal proceedings will be more complex and attended by much more uncertainty. For example, litigation may take place in two or more countries, with each country applying its own choice-of-law rules to determine which substantive law will be applied to the particular transactions. Even if a plaintiff wins a favorable judgment in a lawsuit litigated in the plaintiff's country, there is no way to predict whether the court's judgment will be enforced by judicial bodies in the defendant's country. As discussed earlier in this chapter, under the principle of comity, the judgment may be enforced in the defendant's country, particularly if the defendant's country is the United States and the foreign court's decision is consistent with U.S. national law and policy. Other nations, however, may not be as accommodating as the United States in this respect.

Making Payment on International Transactions

Currency differences between nations and the geographical distance between parties to international sales contracts add a degree of complexity to international sales that does not exist within the domestic market. Because international contracts involve greater financial risks, special care should be taken in drafting these contracts to specify both the currency in which payment is to be made and the method of payment.

Monetary Systems

While it is true that our national currency, the U.S. dollar, is one of the primary forms of international money, any U.S. firm undertaking business transactions abroad must be prepared to deal with one or more other currencies. After all, just as a U.S. firm wants to be paid in U.S. dollars for goods and services sold abroad, so, too, does a Japanese firm want to be paid in Japanese yen for goods and services sold outside Japan. Both firms therefore must rely on the convertibility of currencies.

Foreign Exchange Market A worldwide system in which foreign currencies are bought and sold.

FOREIGN EXCHANGE MARKETS.   Currencies are convertible when they can be freely exchanged one for the other at some specified market rate in a **foreign exchange market.** Foreign exchange markets are a worldwide system for the buying and selling of foreign currencies. At any point in time, the foreign exchange rate is set by the forces of supply and demand in unrestricted foreign exchange markets. The foreign exchange rate is simply the price of a unit of one country's currency in terms of another country's currency. For example, if today's exchange rate is one hundred Japanese yen for one dollar, that means that anybody with one hundred yen can obtain one dollar, and vice versa.

Correspondent Bank A bank in which another bank has an account (and vice versa) for the purpose of facilitating fund transfers.

CORRESPONDENT BANKING.   Often, a U.S. company can deal directly with its domestic bank, which will take care of the international money flow problem. Commercial banks sometimes have **correspondent banks** in other countries. Correspondent banking is a major means of transferring funds internationally. Suppose, for example, that a customer of Citibank wishes to pay a bill in euros to a company in Paris. Citibank can draw a bank check payable in euros on its account in Crédit Lyonnais, a Paris correspondent bank, and then send it to the French company to which its customer owes the money. Alternatively, Citibank's customer can request a wire transfer of the funds to the French company. Citibank instructs Crédit Lyonnais by wire to pay the necessary amount in euros. The Clearinghouse Interbank Payment System (CHIPS) handles about 90 percent of both national and international interbank transfers of U.S. funds. In addition, the Society for Worldwide International Financial Telecommunications (SWIFT) is a communication system that provides banks with messages concerning transactions.

Letters of Credit

Because buyers and sellers engaged in international business transactions are often separated by thousands of miles, special precautions are frequently taken to ensure performance under the contract. Sellers want to avoid delivering goods for which they might not be paid. Buyers desire the assurance that sellers will not be paid until there is evidence that the goods have been shipped. Thus, **letters of credit** are frequently used to facilitate international business transactions. In a simple letter-of-credit transaction, the *issuer* (a bank) agrees to issue a letter of credit and to ascertain whether the *beneficiary* (seller) performs certain acts. In return, the *account party* (buyer) promises to reimburse the issuer for the amount paid to the beneficiary. There may also be an *advising bank* that transmits information, and a *paying bank* may be involved to expedite payment under the letter of credit. Exhibit 24–2 on page 682 summarizes the "life cycle" of a letter of credit.

> **Letter of Credit** A written instrument, usually issued by a bank on behalf of a customer or other person, in which the issuer promises to honor drafts or other demands for payment by third persons in accordance with the terms of the instrument.

Under a letter of credit, the issuer is bound to pay the beneficiary (seller) when the beneficiary has complied with the terms and conditions of the letter of credit. The beneficiary looks to the issuer, not to the account party (buyer), when it presents the documents required by the letter of credit. Typically, the letter of credit will require that the beneficiary deliver to the issuing bank a *bill of lading* to prove that shipment has been made. Letters of credit assure beneficiaries (sellers) of payment while at the same time assuring account parties (buyers) that payment will not be made until the beneficiaries have complied with the terms and conditions of the letter of credit.

THE VALUE OF A LETTER OF CREDIT. The basic principle behind letters of credit is that payment is made against the documents presented by the beneficiary and not against the facts that the documents purport to reflect. Thus, in a letter-of-credit transaction, the issuer does not police the underlying contract; a letter of credit is independent of the underlying contract between the buyer and the seller. Eliminating the need for banks (issuers) to inquire into whether or not actual conditions have been satisfied greatly reduces the costs of letters of credit. Moreover, the use of a letter of credit protects both buyers and sellers.

> **DON'T FORGET** A letter of credit is independent of the underlying contract between the buyer and the seller.

COMPLIANCE WITH A LETTER OF CREDIT. In a letter-of-credit transaction, generally at least three separate and distinct contracts are involved: the contract between the account party (buyer) and the beneficiary (seller); the contract between the issuer (bank) and the account party (buyer); and finally, the

■ **Exhibit 24–2**
The "Life Cycle" of a
Letter of Credit

	THE LETTER–OF–CREDIT PROCUREMENT CYCLE
Step 1	The buyer and seller agree on the terms of sale. The sales contract dictates that a letter of credit is to be used to finance the transaction.
Step 2	The buyer completes an application for a letter of credit and forwards it to his or her bank, which will issue the letter of credit.
Step 3	The issuing (buyer's) bank then forwards the letter of credit to a correspondent bank in the seller's country.
Step 4	The correspondent bank relays the letter of credit to the seller.
Step 5	Having received assurance of payment, the seller makes the necessary shipping arrangements.
Step 6	The seller prepares the documents required under the letter of credit and delivers them to the correspondent bank.
Step 7	The correspondent bank examines the documents. If it finds them in order, it sends them to the issuing bank and pays the seller in accordance with the terms of the letter of credit.
Step 8	The issuing bank, having received the documents, examines them. If they are in order, the issuing bank will charge the buyer's account and send the documents on to the buyer or his or her customs broker. The issuing bank also will reimburse the correspondent bank.
Step 9	The buyer or broker receives the documents and picks up the merchandise from the shipper (carrier).

SOURCE: National Association of Purchasing Management.

letter of credit itself, which involves the issuer (bank) and the beneficiary (seller). These contracts are separate and distinct, and the issuer's obligations under the letter of credit do not concern the underlying contract between the buyer and the seller. Rather, it is the issuer's duty to ascertain whether the documents presented by the beneficiary (seller) comply with the terms of the letter of credit.

If the documents presented by the beneficiary comply with the terms of the letter of credit, the issuer (bank) must honor the letter of credit. Sometimes, however, it is difficult to determine exactly what a letter of credit requires. Moreover, the courts are divided as to whether *strict* or *substantial* compliance with the terms of the letter of credit is required. Traditionally, courts required strict compliance with the terms of a letter of credit, but in recent years, some courts have moved to a standard of *reasonable* compliance.

If the issuing bank refuses to pay the seller (beneficiary) even though the seller has complied with all the requirements of the letter, the seller can bring an action to enforce payment. In the international context, the fact that the issuing bank may be thousands of miles distant from the seller's business location can pose difficulties for the seller—as the following case illustrates.

Case 24.3 ● Pacific Reliant Industries, Inc. v. Amerika Samoa Bank

United States Court of Appeals,
Ninth Circuit, 1990.
901 F.2d 735.

HISTORICAL AND POLITICAL SETTING *Originally inhabited by Polynesians, Samoa is a group of islands 2,610 miles south of Hawaii. In 1899, the islands were divided into Western Samoa and American Samoa by the Treaty of Berlin, which was signed by Great Britain, Germany, and the United States. Thus, the United States acquired American Samoa. In 1960, American Samoa adopted a constitution, which it revised in 1967, but it remains a non-self-governing, unincorporated territory of the United States. Its currency is the U.S. dollar, its languages are Samoan and English, and it is administered by the U.S. Department of the Interior. The population of American Samoa is less than fifty thousand.*

BACKGROUND AND FACTS Pacific Reliant Industries, Inc., an Oregon company, sold building materials to Paradise Development Company, a company located in American Samoa. Pacific was reluctant to make several large deliveries, totaling more than $1 million in value,

without some protection against nonpayment. Accordingly, representatives from Pacific, Paradise, and Amerika Samoa Bank (ASB) met in American Samoa on two occasions to discuss the supply contract and a letter of credit. Following these negotiations, ASB issued a letter of credit in favor of Pacific on Paradise's account. Later, alleging that ASB had wrongfully dishonored the letter of credit, Pacific brought suit in the U.S. district court for the district of Oregon against ASB to recover payment. The court dismissed the suit for lack of personal jurisdiction, holding that ASB lacked sufficient "minimum contacts" (see Chapter 3) with the state of Oregon to subject it to a lawsuit in that state.[a] Pacific appealed, contending that this case was not typical of other letter-of-credit cases because ASB had participated in forming the underlying contract, had had personal contact with the beneficiary (Pacific), and had known that Pacific would not extend credit or ship goods from Oregon without the letter of credit.

---

a. State law governs some cases that may be brought in a federal court because the parties to the case are citizens of different states or are aliens. In such a case, the federal court normally applies the law of the state in which the court is located.

IN THE WORDS OF THE COURT . . .
CANBY, Circuit Judge.
* * * *

Here, both the negotiations for the underlying contract and the letter of credit occurred in American Samoa. * * * ASB did not initiate the transactions between itself, Paradise, or Pacific. Nor did ASB take any significant actions in Oregon. ASB did not invoke the benefits and protections of Oregon law and could not reasonably have expected to be haled into court there. We conclude that ASB's conduct as an issuing bank of a letter of credit does not subject it to suit in Oregon * * * .

DECISION AND REMEDY The U.S Court of Appeals for the Ninth Circuit affirmed the lower court's ruling. Pacific could not bring suit against ASB in Oregon.

FOR CRITICAL ANALYSIS—POLITICAL CONSIDERATION *If a court could exercise jurisdiction over a nonresident corporation that did not have minimum contacts with the jurisdiction in which the suit was brought, what might result?*

Regulation of Specific Business Activities

▼ Doing business abroad can affect the economies, foreign policy, domestic politics, and other national interests of the countries involved. For this reason, nations impose laws to restrict or facilitate international business. Controls may also be imposed by international agreement. We discuss here how different types of international activities are regulated.

Samsung televisions are unloaded in Laredo, Texas. Why are quotas and tariffs placed on some imported goods?

NOTE   Most countries restrict exports for the same reasons: to protect national security, to project foreign policy, to prevent the spread of nuclear weapons, and to preserve scarce commodities.

"The notion dies hard that in some sort of way exports are patriotic but imports are immoral."

Lord Harlech (David Ormsley Gore), 1918–1985 (English writer)

Investing

Investing in foreign nations involves a risk that the foreign government may take possession of the investment property. Expropriation, as already mentioned, occurs when property is taken and the owner is paid just compensation for what is taken. This does not violate generally observed principles of international law. Confiscation occurs when property is taken and no (or inadequate) compensation is paid. International legal principles are violated when property is confiscated. Few remedies are available for confiscation of property by a foreign government. Claims are often resolved by lump-sum settlements after negotiations between the United States and the taking nation.

To counter the deterrent effect that the possibility of confiscation may have on potential investors, many countries guarantee that foreign investors will be compensated if their property is taken. A guaranty can take the form of national constitutional or statutory laws or provisions in international treaties. As further protection for foreign investments, some countries provide insurance for their citizens' investments abroad.

Export Restrictions and Incentives

The U.S. Constitution provides in Article I, Section 9, that "No Tax or Duty shall be laid on Articles exported from any State." Thus, Congress cannot impose any export taxes. Congress can, however, use a variety of other devices to control exports. Congress may set export quotas on various items, such as grain being sold abroad. Under the Export Administration Act of 1979,[3] restrictions can be imposed on the flow of technologically advanced products and technical data.

Devices to stimulate exports and thereby aid domestic businesses include export incentives and subsidies. The Revenue Act of 1971,[4] for example, gave tax benefits to firms marketing their products overseas through certain foreign sales corporations, exempting income produced by the exports. Under the Export Trading Company Act of 1982,[5] U.S. banks are encouraged to invest in export trading companies. An export trading company consists of exporting firms joined to export a line of goods. The Export-Import Bank of the United States provides financial assistance, which consists primarily of credit guaranties given to commercial banks that in turn loan funds to U.S. exporting companies.

Import Restrictions

All nations have restrictions on imports, and the United States is no exception. Restrictions include strict prohibitions, quotas, and tariffs. Under the Trading with the Enemy Act of 1917,[6] for example, no goods may be imported from nations that have been designated enemies of the United States. Other laws prohibit the importation of illegal drugs, books that urge insurrection against the United States, and agricultural products that pose dangers to domestic crops or animals.

QUOTAS AND TARIFFS.   Quotas are limits on the amounts of goods that can be imported. Tariffs are taxes on imports. A tariff is usually a percentage of the

---

3.   50 U.S.C. Sections 2401–2420.
4.   26 U.S.C. Sections 991–994.
5.   15 U.S.C. Sections 4001, 4003.
6.   12 U.S.C. Section 95a.

value of the import, but it can be a flat rate per unit (for example, per barrel of oil). Tariffs raise the prices of goods, which causes some consumers to purchase less expensive, domestically manufactured goods.

DUMPING. The United States has specific laws directed at what it sees as unfair international trade practices. **Dumping,** for example, is the sale of imported goods at "less than fair value." "Fair value" is usually determined by the price of those goods in the exporting country. Foreign firms that engage in dumping in the United States hope to undersell U.S. businesses to obtain a larger share of the U.S. market. To prevent this, an extra tariff—known as an antidumping duty—may be assessed on the imports.

Dumping The selling of goods in a foreign country at a price below the price charged for the same goods in the domestic market.

MINIMIZING TRADE BARRIERS. Restrictions on imports are also known as trade barriers. The elimination of trade barriers is sometimes seen as essential to the world's economic well-being. To minimize trade barriers among nations, most of the world's leading trade nations abide by the General Agreement on Tariffs and Trade (GATT), which became the World Trade Organization (WTO) in 1995. (See Chapter 11 for a discussion of GATT and the WTO in respect to intellectual property rights.) Under Article I of GATT, each member country is required to grant **most-favored-nation status** to other member countries. This article obligates each member to treat other members at least as well as it treats that country that receives its most favorable treatment with regard to imports or exports.

Most-Favored-Nation Status A status granted in an international treaty by a provision stating that the citizens of the contracting nations may enjoy the privileges accorded by either party to citizens of the most favored nations. Generally, most-favored-nation clauses are designed to establish equality of international treatment.

Various regional trade agreements, or associations, also help to minimize trade barriers between nations. The European Union (EU), for example, attempts to minimize or remove barriers to trade among European member countries. The EU is the result of negotiations undertaken by European nations since the 1950s. By 1997, the EU had become a single integrated European trading unit made up of fifteen European nations. Another important regional trade agreement is the North American Free Trade Agreement (NAFTA). NAFTA, which became effective on January 1, 1994, created a regional trading unit consisting of Mexico, the United States, and Canada. The primary goal of NAFTA is to eliminate tariffs among these three countries on substantially all goods over a period of fifteen to twenty years.

Bribing Foreign Officials

Giving cash or in-kind benefits to foreign government officials to obtain business contracts and other favors is often considered normal practice. To reduce such bribery by representatives of U.S. corporations, Congress enacted the Foreign Corrupt Practices Act (FCPA) in 1977.[7] This act and its implications for American businesspersons engaged in international business transactions are discussed in detail in the *Landmark in the Legal Environment* in Chapter 2.

U.S. Laws in a Global Context

The internationalization of business raises questions of the extraterritorial effect of a nation's laws—that is, the effect of the country's laws outside the country. To what extent do U.S. domestic laws affect other nations' businesses?

---

7. 15 U.S.C. Sections 78m–78ff.

To what extent are U.S. businesses affected by domestic laws when doing business abroad? The following subsections discuss these questions in the context of U.S. antitrust law. We also look at the extraterritorial application of U.S. laws prohibiting employment discrimination.

U.S. Antitrust Laws

U.S. antitrust laws (discussed in Chapter 22) have a wide application. They may *subject* persons in foreign nations to their provisions, as well as *protect* foreign consumers and competitors from violations committed by U.S. citizens. Consequently, *foreign persons,* a term that by definition includes foreign governments, may sue under U.S. antitrust laws in U.S. courts.

Section 1 of the Sherman Act provides for the extraterritorial effect of the U.S. antitrust laws. The United States is a major proponent of free competition in the global economy, and thus any conspiracy that has a substantial effect on U.S. commerce is within the reach of the Sherman Act. The violation may even occur outside the United States, and foreign governments as well as persons can be sued for violations of U.S. antitrust laws. Before U.S. courts will exercise jurisdiction and apply antitrust laws, it must be shown that the alleged violation had a *substantial effect* on U.S. commerce. U.S. jurisdiction is automatically invoked, however, when a *per se* violation occurs.[8] A *per se* violation may consist of resale price fixing and tying, or tie-in, contracts. If a domestic firm, for example, joins a foreign cartel to control the production, price, or distribution of goods, and this cartel has a *substantial restraining effect* on U.S. commerce, a *per se* violation may exist. Hence, both the domestic firm and the foreign cartel may be sued for violation of the U.S. antitrust laws. Likewise, if foreign firms doing business in the United States enter into a price-fixing or other anticompetitive agreement to control a portion of U.S. markets, a *per se* violation may exist.

An alleged conspiracy on the part of Japanese television manufacturers to gain control of the electronic products market in the United States—in possible violation of the Sherman Act and other antitrust and tariff legislation—was considered by the United States Supreme Court in the following case.

---

8.   Certain types of restrictive contracts, such as price-fixing agreements, are deemed inherently anticompetitive and thus in restraint of trade as a matter of law. When such a restrictive contract is entered into, there is said to be a *per se* violation of the antitrust laws. See Chapter 22.

Case 24.4 ● Matsushita Electric Industrial Co. v. Zenith Radio Corp.

Supreme Court of the United States, 1986.
475 U.S. 574,
106 S.Ct. 1348,
89 L.Ed.2d 538.

HISTORICAL AND ECONOMIC SETTING *Zenith Electronics Corporation began broadcasting with the first all-electronic television station, W9XZV, in 1939. In 1948, Zenith intro-*

duced its first television sets. By 1960, there were twenty-seven U.S. companies manufacturing television sets. The technology improved, and sales increased. By 1980, virtually every American home had a television set, and many had two or three. During the 1970s, however, some of the companies that based their products entirely on U.S. technology had begun losing their market shares to foreign

(Continued)

Case 24.4—continued

competition. During the early 1980s, purchases of television sets manufactured by U.S. companies fell dramatically. While other U.S. manufacturers ceased selling television sets or sold their brands to foreign companies, Zenith fought its foreign competitors in the marketplace, in Congress, and in the United States Supreme Court. (Note that today, Zenith is no longer a U.S. manufacturer.)

BACKGROUND AND FACTS   Zenith Radio Corporation and several other U.S. manufacturers of television sets filed suit in a U.S. federal district court, alleging that Matsushita Electric Industrial Company and other Japanese firms had violated U.S. antitrust laws. Zenith and the other U.S. firms contended that the Japanese firms had "illegally conspired to drive American firms from the consumer electronic products market" by means of a "scheme to raise, fix and maintain artificially high prices for television receivers sold by [Matsushita and others] in Japan and, at

the same time, to fix and maintain low prices for television receivers exported to and sold in the United States." The alleged conspiracy began, according to Zenith, in 1953. The American firms claimed that the Japanese were engaged in a "predatory pricing" arrangement whereby the losses sustained by selling at such low prices in the United States were offset by monopoly profits obtained in Japan. Once the Japanese gained control over an overwhelming portion of the American market for electronic products, their monopoly power would enable them to recover their losses by charging artificially high prices in the United States as well. The district court granted summary judgment in favor of the Japanese firms, and the case was appealed. The appellate court reversed the judgment of the district court, and the case was appealed to the United States Supreme Court.

IN THE WORDS OF THE COURT . . .
Justice POWELL delivered the opinion of the Court.

*   *   *   *

*   *   * Two decades after their conspiracy is alleged to have commenced, [the Japanese firms] appear to be far from achieving [their alleged] goal: the two largest shares of the retail market in television sets are held by RCA and *   *   * Zenith, not by any of the [alleged conspirators]. Moreover, those shares, which together approximate 40% of sales, did not decline appreciably during the 1970's. [Japanese firms'] collective share rose rapidly during this period, from one-fifth or less of the relevant markets to close to 50%. Neither the District Court nor the Court of Appeals found, however, that [their] share presently allows them to charge monopoly prices; to the contrary, [the U.S. firms] contend that the conspiracy is ongoing—that [the Japanese firms] are still artificially depressing the market price in order to drive Zenith out of the market. *   *   *

The alleged conspiracy's failure to achieve its ends in the two decades of its asserted operation is strong evidence that the conspiracy does not in fact exist.

DECISION AND REMEDY   The United States Supreme Court reversed the decision of the court of appeals and remanded the case.

FOR CRITICAL ANALYSIS—ECONOMIC CONSIDERATION   *Why should the United States apply its antitrust laws to business firms owned by citizens or the government of another nation?*

Discrimination Laws

As explained in Chapter 17, there are laws in the United States prohibiting discrimination on the basis of race, color, national origin, religion, sex, age, and disability. These laws, as they affect employment relationships, generally apply extraterritorially. Since 1984, for example, the Age Discrimination in Employment Act (ADEA) of 1967 has covered U.S. employees working abroad for U.S. employers. The Americans with Disabilities Act of 1990, which requires employers to accommodate the needs of workers with disabilities, also applies to U.S. nationals working abroad for U.S. firms.

For some time, it was uncertain whether the major U.S. law regulating discriminatory practices in the workplace, Title VII of the Civil Rights Act of 1964, applied extraterritorially. The Civil Rights Act of 1991 addressed this issue. The act provides that Title VII applies extraterritorially to all U.S. employees working for U.S. employers abroad. Generally, U.S. employers must abide by U.S. discrimination laws *unless* to do so would violate the laws of the country in which their workplaces are located. This "foreign laws exception" allows employers to avoid being subjected to conflicting laws.

What happens if a Japanese firm doing business in the United States allegedly discriminates against U.S. employees in favor of Japanese citizens, which is permitted under a treaty between the United States and Japan? Is discrimination on the basis of citizenship the same thing as discrimination on the basis of national origin? These questions were addressed in the following case.

Case 24.5 ● Fortino v. Quasar Co., A Division of Matsushita Electric Corp. of America

United States Court of Appeals,
Seventh Circuit, 1991.
950 F.2d 389.

HISTORICAL AND ECONOMIC SETTING   *Motorola, Inc., manufactured automobile radios, police radios, and walkie-talkies before and during World War II, which ended in 1945. In the early years of television, Motorola marketed the first television sets priced under $200. By the 1970s, however, Motorola had begun losing its share of the television market to Japanese manufacturers, and in 1974, the company sold its Quasar television manufacturing facilities in Franklin Park, Illinois, to Matsushita Electric Industrial Company, which is based in Osaka, Japan. Matsushita made more than a million television sets in the Quasar plant in 1988. The next year, Matsushita appointed an American, who had worked for Quasar before its sale by Motorola, to Matsushita's second highest executive position in North America.*

BACKGROUND AND FACTS   In 1953, the United States and Japan entered into a Treaty of Friendship, Commerce, and Navigation. The treaty provides, among other things, that

Japanese companies doing business in the United States and U.S. companies doing business in Japan have the right to choose citizens of their own nations as executives for their firms. Quasar Company, doing business in the United States as a subsidiary of the Japanese company Matsushita Electric Industrial Company, employed U.S. workers and management personnel but was largely controlled by executives of Matsushita. After Matsushita suffered a $20 million loss in 1985, Matsushita executives restructured Quasar and cut its work force dramatically. Of eighty-nine managers working for the company, sixty-six were fired. None of the company's ten Japanese executives was laid off, and some of them received raises. John Fortino and two other American executives who had been fired (the plaintiffs) sued Quasar in a U.S. district court for, among other things, discriminating against them on the basis of national origin in violation of Title VII. Quasar defended by asserting that discrimination on the basis of citizenship, as allowed under the Treaty of Friendship, Commerce, and Navigation, did not violate Title VII. The trial court held for the American executives, and Quasar appealed.

IN THE WORDS OF THE COURT . . .
POSNER, Circuit Judge.
    *   *   *   *
    *   *   * [Title VII] protects Americans of non-Japanese origin from discrimination in favor of persons of Japanese origin. Title VII does not,

(Continued)

Case 24.5—continued

however, forbid discrimination on grounds of citizenship. Of course, especially in the case of a homogeneous country like Japan, citizenship and national origin are highly correlated; almost all citizens of Japan were born there. * * * By virtue of the treaty, "foreign businesses clearly have the right to choose citizens of their own nation as executives because they are such citizens." That right would be empty if the subsidiary could be punished for treating its citizen executives differently from American executives on the ground that, since the former were of Japanese national origin and the latter were not, it was discriminating on the basis of national origin. Title VII would be taking back from the Japanese with one hand what the treaty had given them with the other. This collision is avoided by holding national origin and citizenship separate.

DECISION AND REMEDY The U.S. Court of Appeals for the Seventh Circuit reversed the trial court's decision. The plaintiffs had no cause of action under Title VII.

FOR CRITICAL ANALYSIS—ETHICAL CONSIDERATION *What fundamental policies are in conflict in this case?*

Key Terms

act of state doctrine   668
choice-of-language clause   676
choice-of-law clause   676
comity   667
confiscation   668
correspondent bank   680
distribution agreement   673

dumping   685
exclusive distributorship   673
export   671
expropriation   668
force majeure clause   677
foreign exchange market   680

forum-selection clause   676
letter of credit   681
most-favored-nation status   685
sovereign immunity   669
technology licensing   673

Chapter Summary
The Regulation of International Transactions

INTERNATIONAL PRINCIPLES AND DOCTRINES (See pages 667–671.)	1. **The principle of comity**—Under this principle, nations give effect to the laws and judicial decrees of other nations for reasons of courtesy and international harmony.
	2. **The act of state doctrine**—A doctrine under which American courts avoid passing judgment on the validity of public acts committed by a recognized foreign government within its own territory.
	3. **The doctrine of sovereign immunity**—When certain conditions are satisfied, foreign nations are immune from U.S. jurisdiction under the Foreign Sovereign Immunities Act of 1976. Exceptions are made (a) when the foreign state has "waived its immunity either explicitly or by implication" or (b) when the action is "based upon a commercial activity carried on in the United States by the foreign state."

(Continued)

Chapter Summary, continued

DOING BUSINESS INTERNATIONALLY (See pages 671–675.)	Ways in which U.S. domestic firms engage in international business transactions include (a) exporting, which may involve foreign agents or distributors, and (b) manufacturing abroad through licensing arrangements, franchising operations, wholly owned subsidiaries, or joint ventures.
COMMERCIAL CONTRACTS IN AN INTERNATIONAL SETTING (See pages 675–680.)	Choice-of-language, forum-selection, and choice-of-law clauses are often included in international business contracts to reduce the uncertainties associated with interpreting the language of the agreement and dealing with legal differences. *Force majeure* clauses are included in most domestic and international contracts. They commonly stipulate that certain events, such as floods, fire, accidents, labor strikes, and shortages, may excuse a party from liability for nonperformance of the contract. Arbitration clauses are also frequently found in international contracts.
MAKING PAYMENT ON INTERNATIONAL TRANSACTIONS (See pages 680–683.)	1. **Currency conversion**—Because nations have different monetary systems, payment on international contracts requires currency conversion at a rate specified in a foreign exchange market. 2. **Correspondent banking**—Correspondent banks facilitate the transfer of funds from a buyer in one country to a seller in another. 3. **Letters of credit**—Letters of credit facilitate international transactions by ensuring payment to sellers and ensuring to buyers that payment will not be made until the sellers have complied with the terms of the letters of credit. Typically, compliance occurs when a bill of lading is delivered to the issuing bank.
REGULATION OF SPECIFIC BUSINESS ACTIVITIES (See pages 683–685.)	In the interests of their economies, foreign policies, domestic policies, or other national priorities, nations impose laws that restrict or facilitate international business. Such laws regulate foreign investments; exporting and importing activities; and in the United States, the bribery of foreign officials to obtain favorable contracts. The General Agreement on Tariffs and Trade (now the World Trade Organization) attempts to minimize trade barriers among nations, as do regional trade agreements, including the European Union and the North American Free Trade Agreement.
U.S. LAWS IN A GLOBAL CONTEXT (See pages 685–689.)	1. **Antitrust laws**—U.S. antitrust laws may be applied beyond the borders of the United States. Any conspiracy that has a substantial effect on commerce within the United States may be subject to the Sherman Act, even if the violation occurs outside the United States. 2. **Discrimination laws**—The major U.S. laws prohibiting employment discrimination, including Title VII of the Civil Rights Act of 1964, the Age Discrimination in Employment Act of 1967, and the Americans with Disabilities Act of 1990, cover U.S. employees working abroad for U.S. firms—*unless* to apply the U.S. laws would violate the laws of the host country.

For Review

1. What is the principle of comity, and why do courts deciding disputes involving a foreign law or judicial decree apply this principle?

2. What is the act of state doctrine? In what circumstances is this doctrine applied?

3. A foreign nation is not immune from the jurisdiction of U.S. courts if the nation waives its immunity. Under the Foreign Sovereign Immunities Act

of 1976, on what other basis might a foreign state be considered subject to the jurisdiction of U.S. courts?

4. In what circumstances will U.S. antitrust laws be applied extraterritorially?

5. Do U.S. laws prohibiting employment discrimination apply in all circumstances to U.S. employees working for U.S. employers abroad?

Questions and Case Problems

24–1. Letters of Credit. James Reynolds entered into an agreement to purchase dental supplies from Tooth-Tech, Inc. Reynolds also secured a letter of credit from Central Bank to pay for the supplies. Tooth-Tech placed sixty crates of dental supplies on board a steamship and received in return the invoices required under the letter of credit. The purchaser, Reynolds, subsequently learned that Tooth-Tech, Inc., had filled the sixty crates with rubbish, not dental supplies. Given the fact that an issuer's obligation under a letter of credit is independent of the underlying contract between the buyer and the seller, would the issuer be required to pay the seller in this situation? Explain.

24–2. Sovereign Immunity. Texas Trading & Milling Corp. and other companies brought an action for breach of contract against the Federal Republic of Nigeria and its central bank. Nigeria, a rapidly developing and oil-rich nation, had overbought huge quantities of cement from Texas Trading and others. Unable to accept delivery of the cement, Nigeria repudiated the contract, alleging immunity under the Foreign Sovereign Immunities Act of 1976. Because the buyer of the cement was the Nigerian government, did the doctrine of sovereign immunity remove the dispute from the jurisdiction of U.S. courts? [*Texas Trading & Milling Corp. v. Federal Republic of Nigeria,* 647 F.2d 300 (2d Cir. 1981)]

24–3. Letters of Credit. The Swiss Credit Bank issued a letter of credit in favor of Antex Industries to cover the sale of 92,000 electronic integrated circuits manufactured by Electronic Arrays. The letter of credit specified that the chips would be transported to Tokyo by ship. Antex shipped the circuits by air. Payment on the letter of credit was dishonored because the shipment by air did not fulfill the precise terms of the letter of credit. Should a court compel payment? Explain. [*Board of Trade of San Francisco v. Swiss Credit Bank,* 728 F.2d 1241 (9th Cir. 1984)]

24–4. Act of State Doctrine. Sabbatino, an American, contracted with a Cuban corporation that was largely owned by U.S. residents to buy Cuban sugar. When the Cuban government expropriated the corporation's property and rights in retaliation against a U.S. reduction of the Cuban sugar quota, Sabbatino entered into a new contract to make payment for the sugar to Banco Nacional de Cuba, a government-owned Cuban bank. Sabbatino refused to make the promised payment, and Banco subsequently filed an action in a U.S. district court seeking to recover payment for the sugar. The issue was whether the act of state doctrine should apply when a foreign state violates international law. (If the doctrine were applied, the Cuban government's action would be presumed valid, and thus Banco's claim would be legitimate.) Should the act of state doctrine be applied in these circumstances? Discuss. [*Banco Nacional de Cuba v. Sabbatino,* 376 U.S. 398, 84 S.Ct. 923, 11 L.Ed.2d 804 (1964)]

24–5. Antitrust Claims. Billy Lamb and Carmon Willis (the plaintiffs) were tobacco growers in Kentucky. Phillip Morris, Inc., and B.A.T. Industries, PLC, routinely purchased tobacco not only from Kentucky but also from producers in several foreign countries. In 1982, subsidiaries of Phillip Morris and B.A.T. (the defendants) entered into an agreement with La Fundacion Del Niño (the Children's Foundation) of Caracas, Venezuela, headed by the wife of the president of Venezuela. The agreement provided that the two subsidiaries would donate a total of approximately $12.5 million to the Children's Foundation, and in exchange, the subsidiaries would obtain price controls on Venezuelan tobacco, elimination of controls on retail cigarette prices in Venezuela, tax deductions for the donations, and assurances that existing tax rates applicable to tobacco companies would not be increased. The plaintiffs brought an action, alleging that the Venezuelan arrangement was an inducement designed to restrain trade in violation of U.S. antitrust laws. Such an arrangement, the plaintiffs contended, would result in the artificial depression of tobacco prices to the detriment of domestic tobacco growers, while ensuring lucrative retail prices for tobacco products sold abroad. The trial court held that the plaintiffs' claim was barred by the act of state doctrine. What will result on appeal? Discuss. [*Lamb v. Phillip Morris, Inc.,* 915 F.2d 1024 (6th Cir. 1990)]

24–6. Sovereign Immunity. The Bank of Jamaica, which is wholly owned by the government of Jamaica, contracted with Chisholm & Co. in January 1981 for Chisholm to arrange for lines of credit from various U.S. banks and to obtain $50 million in credit insurance from the Export-Import Bank of the United States. This Chisholm successfully did, but subsequently the Bank of Jamaica refused the deals arranged by Chisholm, and the bank refused to pay Chisholm for its services. Chisholm sued the bank in a federal district court for breach of an implied contract. The bank moved to dismiss the case, claiming, among other things, that it was immune from the jurisdiction of U.S. courts under the doctrine of sovereign immunity. What factors will the court consider in deciding whether the bank is immune from the jurisdiction of U.S. courts under the doctrine of sovereign immunity? Will the court agree? Discuss fully. [*Chisholm & Co. v. Bank of Jamaica*, 643 F.Supp. 1393 (S.D.Fla. 1986)]

24–7. Forum-Selection Clauses.   Royal Bed and Spring Co., a Puerto Rican distributor of furniture products, entered into an exclusive distributorship agreement with Famossul Industria e Comercio de Moveis Ltda., a Brazilian manufacturer of furniture products. Under the terms of the contract, Royal Bed was to distribute in Puerto Rico the furniture products manufactured by Famossul in Brazil. The contract contained choice-of-forum and choice-of-law clauses, which designated the judicial district of Curitiba, State of Paraná, Brazil, as the judicial forum and the Brazilian Civil Code as the law to be applied in the event of any dispute. Famossul terminated the exclusive distributorship and suspended the shipment of goods without just cause. Under Puerto Rican law, forum-selection clauses providing for foreign venues are not enforced as a matter of public policy. In what jurisdiction should Royal Bed bring suit? Discuss fully. [*Royal Bed and Spring Co. v. Famossul Industria e Comercio de Moveis Ltda.*, 906 F.2d 45 (5th Cir. 1990)]

24–8. Sovereign Immunity.   Reed International Trading Corp., a New York corporation, agreed to sell down jackets to Alink, a Russian business. Alink referred Reed to the Bank for Foreign and Economic Affairs of the Russian Federation for payment and gave Reed a letter of credit payable in New York. When Reed tried to collect, the bank refused to pay. Reed (and others) filed a suit in a federal district court against the bank (and others). The bank qualified as a "sovereign" under the Foreign Sovereign Immunities Act and thus claimed in part that it was immune from suit in U.S. courts. On what basis might the court hold that the bank was not immune? Explain. [*Reed International Trading Corp. v. Donau Bank, A.G.*, 866 F.Supp. 750 (S.D.N.Y. 1994)]

A Question of Ethics and Social Responsibility

24–9.   Ronald Riley, an American citizen, and Council of Lloyd's, a British insurance corporation with its principal place of business in London, entered into an agreement in 1980 that allowed Riley to underwrite insurance through Lloyd's. The agreement provided that if any dis-

pute arose between Lloyd's and Riley, the courts of England would have exclusive jurisdiction, and the laws of England would apply. Over the next decade, some of the parties insured under policies that Riley underwrote experienced large losses, for which they filed claims. Instead of paying his share of the claims, Riley filed a lawsuit in a U.S. district court against Lloyd's and its managers and directors (all British citizens or entities), seeking, among other things, rescission of the 1980 agreement. Riley alleged that the defendants had violated the Securities Act of 1933, the Securities Exchange Act of 1934, and Rule 10b-5. The defendants asked the court to enforce the forum-selection clause in the agreement. Riley argued that if the clause was enforced, he would be deprived of his rights under the U.S. securities laws. The court held that the parties were to resolve their dispute in England. [*Riley v. Kingsley Underwriting Agencies, Ltd.*, 969 F.2d 953 (10th Cir. 1992)]

1. Did the court's decision fairly balance the rights of the parties? How would you argue in support of the court's decision in this case? How would you argue against it?

2. Should the fact that an international transaction may be subject to laws and remedies different from or less favorable than those of the United States be a valid basis for denying enforcement of forum-selection and choice-of-law clauses?

3. All parties to this litigation other than Riley were British. Should this fact be considered by the court in deciding this case?

Case Briefing Assignment

24–10.   Examine Case A.10 [*Trans-Orient Marine Corp. v. Star Trading & Marine*, Inc., 731 F.Supp. 619 (S.D.N.Y. 1990)] in Appendix A. The case has been excerpted there in great detail. Review and then brief the case, making sure that you include answers to the following questions in your brief.

1. What specific circumstances led to this lawsuit?

2. What was the central international legal issue addressed by the court?

3. How did the court distinguish a "succession of state" from a "succession of government," and what was the effect of the distinction on executory contracts of the state?

4. What "seminal decision" on this issue was referred to by the court? On what other cases did the court rely in its reasoning?

For Critical Analysis

24–11.   Business cartels and monopolies that are legal in some countries may engage in practices that violate U.S. antitrust laws. In view of this fact, what are some of the implications of applying U.S. antitrust laws extraterritorially?

INTERACTING WITH The Internet

■ An index of Internet resources related to international law, including international treaties and conventions, has been published on the Web by the International Law Society of the University of Arizona College of Law at

http://aruba.ccit.arizona.edu/~rdespeld/ils.html

■ An extensive collection of URLs offering access to various international organizations is offered by the Villanova Center for Information Law and Policy at

http://www.vcilp.org/

■ Cornell Law School's Legal Information Institute publishes the text of the opinions of the International Court of Justice (World Court) in both English and French. The Cornell site also contains information on the court and links to selected international law sites. You can find this site at

http://www.law.cornell.edu/icj/

■ You might be interested in the information on foreign policy and international issues compiled by the U.S. Information Agency (USIA). You can find the USIA's site at

http://www.usia.gov/

■ For information on the World Intellectual Property Organization Arbitration Center, go to

http://www.wto.org

CHAPTER 25

The Legal Environment in Other Nations

Contents

Chapter Objectives

After reading this chapter, you should be able to . . .

1. Describe cultural differences among nations that can complicate efforts to do business abroad.
2. List differences between the common law and civil law legal systems.
3. Discuss different contract laws that exist in various nations.
4. Identify some of the employment laws that differ among nations.
5. Describe the government of the European Union.

As the world economy enters a new era, it is more important than ever, as the quotation alongside indicates, to think—and do business—with a global perspective. When doing business abroad, a company needs to be aware of how both international law and national law will affect its business activities. **International law** is that body of law that governs relations among or between nations. International customs, treaties, and organizations are all part of the international legal environment of business, which was discussed in Chapter 24. **National law**, in contrast, is the law of a particular nation, such as the United States, Japan, Germany, or Brazil.

In this chapter, we examine and compare the traditions and legal systems of various nations, as well as specific legal concepts and principles relating to selected areas of substantive law. While it is obviously impossible to discuss here all of the laws of every nation, the following pages will indicate how a variety of nations deal with some of the important issues facing U.S. businesspersons doing business overseas or conducting business transactions with foreign enterprises.

> **"Don't overlook the importance of worldwide thinking. A company that keeps its eye [only] on Tom, Dick, and Harry is going to miss Pierre, Hans, and Yoshio."**
>
> Al Ries, 1929–
> (Chairman, Trout & Ries, Inc., advertising agency)

International Law The law that governs relations among nations. International customs and treaties are generally considered to be two of the most important sources of international law.

National Law Law that pertains to a particular nation (as opposed to international law).

Doing Business Abroad

The ability to conduct business successfully in a foreign nation requires not only a knowledge of that nation's laws but also some familiarity with its cultural system, economy, and business climate. In this section, we look at some of the ways in which cultural and structural differences can affect transnational business operations.

Language and Communication

A crucial part of doing business abroad is understanding the local culture and how it differs from that of the United States. One obvious cultural difference among nations is language. Language differences have occasionally confounded efforts to do business abroad. The following is a list of just a few problems that American businesses have suffered because of language problems:

- Rolls-Royce changed the name of its "Silver Mist" in Germany, because in that country, *mist* translates as "manure."
- In Japan, Esso had difficulty selling gasoline in part because *Esso* sounds like the Japanese word for stalled car.
- Pepsi's "Come Alive with Pepsi" campaign was translated in Taiwan as "Pepsi brings your ancestors back from the grave."
- An airline in Brazil advertised plush "rendezvous lounges" on jets; in Brazil, *rendezvous* implies a special room for making love.
- The Chevy Nova did not go over very well in Spanish-speaking countries because in Spanish *no va* means "it does not go" or "it will not go."

The meaning of nonverbal language (body movements, gestures, facial expressions, and the like) also varies from culture to culture. In the United States, for example, a nod of the head indicates "yes," while in some countries, such as Greece, the same gesture means "no." Similarly, Americans usually indicate "no" by moving the head from side to side, while in India, for example, the same movement means "I'm listening. Please continue."

A college graduate. What legal factors should this graduate consider when applying to work in countries other than the United States?

Colors and Numbers

Colors also are associated with different meanings in different countries. For example, green is the national color of Egypt, but in Malaysia, green is associated with disease. The same is true for numbers. For example, the number 4 represents bad luck in Japan and Korea.

Perceptions of Time

A frequent source of cultural clashes abroad involves time. For many Americans, punctuality is crucial. In some foreign countries, businesspersons have a more flexible attitude toward time, and Americans seem excessively hurried. Northern Europeans tend to regard time in the same way as U.S. citizens do, but in Latin America, the Middle East, and parts of Asia, meetings may start late and last a long time.

Management Styles

Researchers have identified certain differences in management style across the continents. The American manager employs a direct, pragmatic, and competitive style. The Latin American manager is more humanistic and indirect, even though Latin American business firms are generally more hierarchical and authoritarian than firms in the United States. The Asian manager is more like the Latin American manager in that Asian management techniques are more indirect and designed to avoid confrontation. The European manager is more like the American, although there are substantial differences in management style between Northern European and Mediterranean nations, with the latter being somewhat less competitive and more family oriented.

Ethics

Given the varied cultures and religions of the world's nations, one might expect frequent conflicts in ethics between foreign and United States businesspersons. In fact, many of the most important ethical precepts are common to virtually all countries. There are some important ethical differences, however. In Islamic countries, for example, the consumption of alcohol and certain foods is forbidden by the Koran (the sacred book of the Islamic religion, which lies at the heart of Islamic law). It would be thoughtless and imprudent to invite a Saudi Arabian business contact out for a drink. Two notable differences in regard to ethics involve the legitimacy of certain side payments, or gift giving, and the role of women.

GIFT GIVING OR BRIBERY?   In many foreign nations, gift giving is a common practice among contracting companies or between companies and government. To Americans, such gift giving may look suspiciously like an unethical (and possibly illegal) bribe. This has been an important source of friction in international business, particularly after the U.S. Congress passed the Foreign Corrupt Practices Act (FCPA) in 1977 (discussed in Chapter 2). The act prohibits American business firms from offering side payments to foreign officials to secure favorable contracts. Payments to minor government officials—to facilitate necessary paperwork relating to a transaction, for example—are not prohibited by the FCPA.

Often, government workers in other countries are paid very little, and the government assumes that these workers will obtain extra income by receiving "grease payments" (to grease the wheels of the bureaucratic machine). Before an American company makes any kind of side payment, it should be sure that it understands local practice. Even when some payment is expected, the form or amount of the payment (if it is too excessive, for example) may violate the ethical rules of the foreign nation itself.

When a businessperson is presented with a gift in his or her official position as a corporate officer, the businessperson may face a dilemma. The company may itself prohibit the receipt of such gifts, for fear of being charged with favoritism by its other employees, yet rejecting the gift may seriously offend the giver. There may be some alternative, though, such as accepting the gift and quietly turning it over to the company or a charity.

Oprah Winfrey, one of the most successful businesspersons in the United States. Could she have had the same success in other countries?

WOMEN IN BUSINESS. The role played by women in other countries may present some difficult ethical problems for firms doing business internationally. Equal employment opportunity is a fundamental public policy in the United States, and Title VII of the Civil Rights Act of 1964 (discussed in Chapter 17) prohibits discrimination against women in the employment context. Some other countries, however, largely reject any professional role for women, which may cause difficulties for American women conducting business transactions in those countries.

For example, when the World Bank sent a delegation including women to negotiate with the Central Bank of Korea, the Koreans were surprised and offended. They thought that the presence of women meant that the Koreans were not being taken seriously. (This problem might have been cured simply by some advance communication.) In Islamic nations, women are expected to avoid exposing their arms or legs in public. While American women may find it difficult to respect this custom, it may be necessary for them to do so if they wish to succeed in business transactions conducted in those nations.

Comparative Legal Systems

▼ When doing business in a foreign nation, a company generally subjects itself to the jurisdiction and laws of that nation. Therefore, a wise businessperson will be familiar with the legal systems of foreign nations in which he or she conducts commercial transactions. The legal systems of foreign nations differ, in widely varying degrees, from that of the United States.

Constitutional Foundations

The foundation of a country's legal system is set forth in a governing document that is usually referred to as the nation's constitution. Most nations have several branches of government to exercise legislative, executive, and judicial powers. These systems differ considerably. For example, Taiwan has five independent branches of government. Some nations, including the United States, have federal systems, in which government powers are divided between national and provincial governments. Other nations have **unitary systems,** in which governing authority is concentrated in the hands of a central government and there are no independent local governing units.

> **"I [get] along pretty good in all these foreign countries, for I have a theory that it's their country and they got a right to run it like they want to."**
>
> Will Rogers, 1879–1935
> (American
> actor and humorist)

Unitary System A centralized governmental system in which local or subdivisional governments exercise only those powers given to them by the central government.

In the United States, the Constitution is a single document setting forth powers and rights. The United Kingdom has no single document but considers as its constitution a series of fundamental documents, including the Magna Carta, the Bill of Rights of 1689, and others. One important resulting difference is that British courts have no power to strike down a law as unconstitutional. In the United States, if the United States Supreme Court finds that an act of Congress violates the Constitution, the act will be declared illegal (see the discussion of judicial review in Chapter 3). In the United Kingdom, however, courts cannot invalidate laws passed by Parliament. French courts also lack the power of judicial review of legislative action, although a special constitutional council can invalidate laws. In Germany, laws can be reviewed for constitutionality but only in a special court, and the cases can only be brought by a government body, not individuals. India's constitution is a single document that grants to the courts the power of judicial review over statutory enactments. India also has a supreme court but lacks a fully independent judiciary.

Some nations have specialized commercial law courts to deal with business disputes (in the United States, some jurisdictions are establishing similar courts). France established such courts in 1807, and most nations with commercial codes have done likewise. The United Kingdom also has special commercial courts overseen by judges with expertise in business law.

Common Law and Civil Law Systems

Legal systems around the globe generally are divided into *common law* and *civil law* systems.

COMMON LAW SYSTEMS.   As discussed in Chapter 1, in a common law system, the courts independently develop the rules governing certain areas of law, such as torts and contracts. These common law rules apply to all areas not covered by statutory law. Although the common law doctrine of *stare decisis* obligates judges to follow precedential decisions in their jurisdictions, courts may modify or even overturn precedents when deemed necessary. Additionally, if there is no case law to guide a court, the court may create a new rule of law. Common law systems exist today in countries that were once a part of the British Empire (such as Australia, India, and the United States).

CIVIL LAW SYSTEMS.   In contrast to Great Britain and the other common law countries, most of the European nations base their legal systems on Roman civil law, or "code law." The term *civil law,* as used here, refers not to civil as opposed to criminal law but to *codified law*—an ordered grouping of legal principles enacted into law by a legislature or other governing body. In a **civil law system,** the only official source of law is a statutory code. Courts are required to interpret the code and apply the rules to individual cases, but courts may not depart from the code and develop their own laws. In theory, the law code will set forth all the principles needed for the legal system.

Civil Law System A system of law derived from that of the Roman Empire and based on a code rather than case law; the predominant system of law in the nations of continental Europe and the nations that were once their colonies.

The best-known example of civil law is the French Napoleonic Code, or *Code Napoléon,* some provisions of which are presented in Exhibit 25–1. This legal system was developed in 1804 by Napoléon Bonaparte, after he became emperor of France. The Napoleonic Code survives to this day, although it has been amended by subsequent French governments. Other significant early law codes are the Spanish Commercial Code of 1885, the Japanese Commercial Code of 1890, and the German Commercial Code of 1900.

■ Exhibit 25–I
Excerpts from the *Code Napoléon*

Code Napoléon

TITLE III.
OF CONTRACTS OR CONVENTIONAL OBLIGATIONS
IN GENERAL

Decreed the 7th of February 1804. Promulgated the 17th of the same Month.

CHAPTER I.

Preliminary Regulations.

1101.

A contract is an agreement that binds one or more persons, towards another or several others,
to give, to do, or not to do something.

* * * *

CHAPTER II.

Of Conditions essential to the Validity of Agreements.

1108.

Four conditions are essential to the validity of an agreement:
The consent of the party who binds himself;
His capacity to contract;
A certain object forming the matter of the contract;
A lawful cause in the bond.

Section I.

Of Consent

1109.

There can be no valid consent if such consent has been given by mistake, or has been extorted
through violence or surreptitiously obtained by fraud.

1110.

Mistake is not a cause for annulling the agreement except when it occurs in the very
substance of the thing which is the object thereof.

It is not a cause for nullity when it occurs only in the person with whom it is intended to contract,
unless the consideration of such person were the principal cause of the agreement.

SOURCE: *The French Civil Code* (Baton Rouge, La.: Claitor's Book Store, 1960 [Reprint]), pp. 302–305.

Today, civil law systems are followed in most of the continental European countries, as well as in the Latin American, African, and Asian countries that were once colonies of the continental European nations. Japan and South Africa also have civil law systems. Ingredients of the civil law system are found in the Islamic courts of predominantly Muslim countries. In the United States, the state of Louisiana, because of its historical ties to France, has, in part, a civil law system. The legal systems of Puerto Rico, Québec, and Scotland are similarly characterized as having elements of the civil law system. Exhibit 25–2 lists some of the nations that use common law systems and some that use civil law systems.

LEGAL SYSTEMS COMPARED.   Common law and civil law systems are not wholly distinct. For example, although the United States has a common law system, crimes are defined by statute as in civil law systems. Civil law systems

CIVIL LAW	COMMON LAW
Argentina	Australia
Austria	Bangladesh
Brazil	Canada
Chile	Ghana
China	India
Egypt	Israel
Finland	Jamaica
France	Kenya
Germany	Malaysia
Greece	New Zealand
Indonesia	Nigeria
Iran	Singapore
Italy	United Kingdom
Japan	United States
Mexico	Zambia
Poland	
South Korea	
Sweden	
Tunisia	
Venezuela	

■ **Exhibit 25–2**
The Legal Systems of Nations

Sharia Civil law principles of some Middle Eastern countries that are based on the Islamic directives that follow the teachings of the prophet Mohammed.

also may allow considerable room for judges to develop law. Civil law codes cannot be so precise as to address *every* contested issue, so the judiciary must interpret the codes.

Furthermore, there are significant differences among common law countries. The judges of different common law nations have produced differing common law principles. Thus, although the United States and India both derived their legal traditions from England, the common law principles governing contract law differ in some respects between the two countries. Similarly, the laws of nations that have civil law systems vary considerably. For example, the French code tends to set forth general principles of law, while the German code is far more specific and runs to thousands of sections. In some Middle Eastern countries, codes are grounded in the religious law of Islam, called *sharia*. The religious basis of these codes makes them far more difficult to alter.

Judges and Procedures

Judges play similar roles in virtually all countries: their primary function is the resolution of litigation. The characteristics and qualifications of judges, which are typically set forth in the nation's constitution, can vary widely, however. The U.S. judge normally does not actively participate in a trial, but many foreign judges involve themselves closely in the proceedings, such as by questioning witnesses. Because U.S. federal judges serve for life and cannot be removed by impeachment except in extreme cases (such as when a judge accepts a bribe), their decisions are less likely to be influenced by politics than may be the case in other countries. In India, for example, judges issuing rulings contrary to the prime minister's views have been transferred or demoted on occasion.

The procedures employed in resolving cases also vary substantially from country to country. A knowledge of a nation's legal procedures is important for a person conducting business transactions in that nation. For example, an American businessperson was on trial in Saudi Arabia for assaulting and slandering a co-worker, an offense for which he might have been jailed or deported. He initially was required to present two witnesses to his version of events, but he had only one. Fortunately, he became aware that he could "demand the oath." In this procedure, he swore before God that he had neither kicked nor slandered the complainant. After taking the oath, he was promptly adjudged not guilty, as lying under oath is one of the most serious sins under Islamic law. Had he failed to demand the oath, he almost certainly would have been found guilty.

Lawyers and Litigation

The role of lawyers, too, differs from country to country. In the United States, an attorney is required by canons of ethics to serve as a "zealous" advocate for his or her client's interests. In contrast, lawyers in the People's Republic of China are obligated first to further the interests of the government and not necessarily the interests of their clients. Attitudes regarding the function of lawyers also vary. For example, while it is not unusual for American businesspersons to include lawyers and accountants on their negotiating teams, in foreign settings, the presence of these professionals may imply that one is planning some deception.

Tort litigation tends to be more extensive and significant in common law systems than in civil law systems. Indeed, some have blamed America's alleged litigiousness in part on our common law system. Of course, many other factors, such as cultural and business traditions, also affect the legal climate for business. For example, citizens and businesses in some nations, such as Japan, are less disposed to go to court than are their counterparts in the United States.

The total number of lawyers in a country undoubtedly has some effect on litigation, though the vast majority of lawyers do not work directly on lawsuits and do not even appear in court. It is widely believed that the United States has more lawyers (as a percentage of the population) than any other country in the world except Iceland. Comparisons are difficult, however, because there is no uniform global definition of *lawyer*. In Sweden, for example, virtually anyone may serve as a lawyer, without meeting state-mandated educational and other requirements. Exhibit 25–3 shows the number of lawyers in various nations as a percentage of the population.

National Laws Compared

Certain legal principles are essential to a complex society, and virtually all nations have laws governing torts, contracts, employment, and other areas. Even when the basic principles are fundamentally similar (as in contract law), there are significant variations in the practical application and effect of these laws. This section summarizes some of the similarities and differences among national laws relating to torts, contracts, and employment relationships.

Of course, U.S. businesspersons contemplating any international business transaction should become familiar with the specific legal requirements of the particular country or countries involved. Relevant laws may include those discussed in this section as well as laws governing such areas as corporations, corporate securities, intellectual property, environmental protection, and unfair business practices.

Tort Law

Tort law, which allows persons to recover damages for harms or injuries caused by the wrongful actions of others, may vary widely among the nations. Common law nations have developed a body of judge-made law regarding what kinds of actions constitute negligence or some other tort that permits recovery. Civil law nations must authorize such recovery in their codes. (This chapter's *Inside the Legal Environment* discusses how the civil law codes of several nations define what constitutes a tort.) Even when the statutory language is similar, the application of tort law varies among nations. For example, which party has the burden of proof in a tort lawsuit differs among countries. In the United States, the burden of proof is on the plaintiff. In Russia, the defendant has the burden of proving that he or she was not at fault.

FAILURE TO ACT. National tort laws vary considerably with respect to liability for omissions, or failures to act. In some situations, a failure to act will not be regarded as a tort. For example, in the United States, tort law imposes no "duty to rescue," and a person normally is not liable for failing to rescue

NUMBER OF LAWYERS PER 100,000 CITIZENS	
Iceland	400
United States	311
Israel	295
Venezuela	254
Mexico	153
England	145
Germany	103
Singapore	74
Sweden	29
Guyana	17
Japan	12
Kenya	7
Iran	4
Indonesia	3

SOURCE: Based on information from Euromoney Publications, *The International Financial Law Review 1000* (1993).

■ **Exhibit 25–3**
Number of Lawyers per 100,000 Citizens

Inside the Legal Environment
Civil Code Tort Definitions

The following definitions[a] of which acts constitute torts show that even among countries with similar legal systems, the law is different. Even when the definitions are similar, the law may be applied differently.

Brazil: He who, by a voluntary act or omission, by negligence or carelessness, violates another's right, or causes him harm, is bound to compensate for the damage.

Egypt: Every culpable act that causes damage to another obliges the person who did it to compensate for it.

The Netherlands: Every unlawful act by which damage is caused to another obliges the person by whose fault the damage occurred to compensate for it.

Spain: He who by act or omission causes damage to another, either by fault or negligence, is obliged to compensate for the damage caused.

Tunisia: Every act a person does without lawful justification that causes willful and voluntary damage—material or moral—to another obliges the person who did it to compensate for the aforesaid damage, when it is shown that the act is the direct cause.

Uruguay: Every unlawful act a person does which causes damage to another imposes on the person whose malice, fault, or negligence brought it about the obligation to compensate for it. When the unlawful act was done maliciously, i.e., with the intention of causing harm—it amounts to a delict [an intentional tort, discussed in Chapter 8, or a crime], when the intention to cause harm is not present, the unlawful act amounts to a quasi-delict [a tort or a crime caused by negligence]. In either case, the unlawful act can be negative or positive according to whether the breach of duty consists of an act or omission.

For Critical Analysis: *Why are these definitions different?*

a. Andre Tunc, *International Encyclopedia of Comparative Law,* Vol. XI, Chapter 2, pp. 5–6.

---

another person in distress. German law is basically similar. In some countries, though, the failure to rescue another in distress is regarded as negligence.

DAMAGES.   National tort laws also differ in the way in which damages in tort cases are calculated. For example, Swiss law and Turkish law permit a court to reduce damages if an award of full damages would cause undue hardship for a party who was found negligent. In some nations of northern Africa, different amounts of damages are awarded depending on the type of tortious action committed and the degree of intent involved. In the United States, the calculation of actual (compensatory) damages does not depend on whether the tort was negligent or intentional.

STATUTES OF LIMITATIONS.   Statutes of limitations (deadlines for filing a lawsuit) in other countries also vary and tend to be longer than in the United States. In the United States, state statutes of limitations for tort cases typically run two to three years. In Italy, however, the plaintiff has five years after the tort's commission during which to bring suit. The general French limitations period is ten years.

PRODUCT LIABILITY.   A growing area of the law in many nations is product liability. As was discussed in Chapter 10, in the United States, product liability may be imposed on sellers and manufacturers of products based on the tort

Ethical Perspective

In the United States, product manufacturers are charged with a high duty of care to all product users. Manufacturers that purchase component parts for their products from other suppliers cannot avoid liability for injuries caused by those defective components. In the United States, if a case involved facts similar to those in Case 25.1, both the manufacturer of the defective component part and the manufacturer of the finished product would be subject to liability. Ultimately, tort liability, including product liability, is based on a society's perception of what is fair and just.

For Critical Analysis: *Why does this perception vary from one society to another?*

---

theories of negligence and strict liability, as well as under warranty theory. Generally, a U.S. manufacturer will be liable for an injury caused by a defective product even though the injury resulted from a defect in a component purchased by the manufacturer from another firm, or supplier. Although other nations also impose product liability on manufacturers and sellers, under some nations' laws, a manufacturer will not be held liable for a defectively designed component purchased from a supplier. The following case illustrates how the German Federal Supreme Court dealt with this issue.

Case 25.1 ● Re Product Liability (Case VI ZR 103/89)

Bundesgerichtshof [German Federal Supreme Court], 1991.
[1991] ECC 204.
[Translated from the German.]

HISTORICAL AND SOCIAL SETTING *In 1989, the communist government of East Germany was pressured, in part by the failure of its economic system and the increasing emigration of its people (5,000 to 10,000 a day), to open its borders to the West. The East German government collapsed in January 1990. East and West Germany unified their economic and monetary systems in July. Forty-five years of pent-up consumer demand in East Germany produced a temporary economic boom. Today, Germany is Western Europe's wealthiest nation.*

BACKGROUND AND FACTS The plaintiff purchased an exerciser called the Souplex-Expander from a retail store. The exerciser was manufactured by one company (K-AG), but another company (K-KG) had supplied plastic handle molds for the machine. While the plaintiff was exercising, one of the handles broke, and the expander flew upward, striking the plaintiff in the eye and causing her to lose all sight in that eye. The trial court held that K-KG was liable for damages, including damages for pain and suffering, but found that K-AG was not liable. On appeal, the court reversed and held that K-AG was also liable for these damages. K-AG appealed to the German Federal Supreme Court.

IN THE WORDS OF THE COURT . . .
DECISION
   * * * *

(a) The appeal[s] court made no findings to the effect that the defendant [K-AG] was aware of the dangerous nature of the handle. It evidently proceeded on the basis that the defendant was in a position to find out about the matter, since it explained that the defendant, because of its special

(Continued)

Case 25.1—continued

knowledge in the field of processing plastics, was not entitled to rely on the molds supplied to it by K-KG being suitable for producing safe and unbreakable handles. This Court cannot agree with that conclusion to such a degree of generality. The [appeals court] is right in objecting that none of the parties to the case has made any submissions to the effect that the defendant had a special knowledge of the weak points in synthetic components under stress. * * *

(b) In the present case the defendant also had no special cause to scrutinize the design of the expander handles inasmuch as the authorized testing office of the Rh-Technical Standards Association had tested the equipment, including the handle produced by the defendant, in accordance with section 3(4) of the Technical Equipment (Safety) Act and granted it the "GS" ("Safety Test") mark, and the B-Technical Standards association had assessed it as "good" after testing it. It is true that a manufacturer who designs his products himself is not exempted from liability for design faults therein solely because a testing institution has examined it and not found defects of the relevant sort. But the position is different for other enterprises that are brought in at various stages of the production process or of the distribution of industrial products; they have lower duties of care in relation to design risks than the actual manufacturer and designer of the product.

DECISION AND REMEDY   The German Federal Supreme Court reversed the appellate court and reinstated the verdict in favor of K-AG.

FOR CRITICAL ANALYSIS—ECONOMIC CONSIDERATION   *Should results in cases such as this influence companies' decisions about where they do business?*

Contract Law

Because international business transactions typically involve contracts, businesspersons should familiarize themselves with the contract law of the countries in which they do business. To a degree, the United Nations Convention on Contracts for the International Sale of Goods (CISG) has simplified matters for parties to international sales contracts. As of 1998, thirty-eight countries had ratified or acceded to the CISG, including the United States, Canada, Mexico, some Central and South American countries, and most of the European nations. Four other nations have signed the CISG and have indicated that they intend to ratify it.

Essentially, the CISG is to international sales contracts what the Uniform Commercial Code (UCC) is to domestic sales contracts in the United States. Recall from Chapter 1 that Article 2 of the UCC has been adopted by all of the states except Louisiana as the statutory law governing contracts for the sale of goods. The UCC applies when the parties to a contract for a sale of goods have failed to specify in writing some important term concerning price, delivery, or the like. Similarly, if the parties to international transactions fail to specify in writing the precise terms of a contract, the CISG will be applied.

For many transactions, however, the CISG may not be applicable. For one thing, the CISG applies only to transactions involving firms in countries that have signed the convention, or agreement, and parties (in nonsignatory

International Perspective

In a comparative study of the product liability laws of the United States and ten other countries, Donald G. Gifford, dean of the College of Law of West Virginia University, noted that in many of the foreign countries, victims of injuries caused by defective products need not always go to court to be compensated. Their medical expenses are often covered by national health-insurance programs or some combination of private and public health insurance. Gifford also found that in many nations, workers' compensation systems are more extensive, covering more injuries than are covered by U.S. workers' compensation laws.[a] Although many countries impose strict liability for injuries relating to defective products and inherently dangerous activities, such as travel by trains, automobiles, and aircraft, injured claimants cannot recover under strict liability laws for expenses already paid by entitlement programs, such as those just mentioned.

Additionally, in contrast to the United States, many European countries do not allow punitive damages, class-action lawsuits, or contingency fees. (Recall from Chapter 4 that lawyers who charge their clients on a contingency-fee basis receive a specified percentage—such as 30 percent—of whatever the court awards the client as damages.) All of these features of our legal system tend to encourage litigation.

While European businesses who do not deal in the U.S. marketplace may be isolated by their legal systems from product liability litigation to a certain extent, any foreign business firm that manufactures products marketed in the United States is potentially subject to product liability under U.S. laws for defective products that injure American consumers. For example, if a French firm manufactures a toy that is distributed in the United States and is deemed to be unreasonably dangerous by a U.S. court, the French firm may be held liable for damages, including punitive damages.

For Critical Analysis: *Why do U.S. businesses face more product liability suits than business firms in any other nation?*

a. For a discussion of this study, see *American Bar Association Journal*, June 1992, p.42.

---

nations) that have stipulated in their contracts that the CISG will govern any dispute. When transactions involve firms in countries that are not signatory to the CISG, the contract parties need to determine which nation's law will govern any disputes that may arise under the contract. Additionally, even when the CISG would apply, it applies only if the parties have not agreed otherwise in their contract. For example, parties may agree in their contract that German law or U.S. law or some other nation's law will govern any contract dispute that arises. For these reasons, the contract laws of individual nations remain important to businesspersons involved in international contracts.

BASIC CONTRACT REQUIREMENTS IN THE UNITED STATES.   A *contract* is an agreement that can be enforced in court. As was discussed in Chapters 12 and 13, in the United States, under the common law of contracts, several requirements must be met for a contract to be valid. The common law of contracts also applies to contracts for the sale of goods, except when the UCC (the statutory law governing sales contracts) has modified common law requirements.

One requirement is *agreement,* which is commonly divided into two events: offer and acceptance. One party, the *offeror,* offers to enter into a contract with another party, the *offeree.* Once the offer is accepted, a valid contract is created—providing the other requirements for a contract are met. Another requirement is *consideration*—each party must give something of legally sufficient value (such as money) to the other party, or the contract will fail. Other requirements include *legality* (the contract must not be contrary to the law or to public policy) and *capacity* (the parties must have the mental capacity to enter into a binding contract). Additionally, the parties' assent to the terms of the contract must be genuine, and certain contracts must be in writing to be enforceable.

Generally, the laws of other nations have similar requirements. There are some important differences, though, particularly with respect to specific aspects of the requirements of agreement, consideration, and legality. Other differences relate to remedies for breach of contract and defenses that can be raised to avoid liability for failing to perform a contract.

AGREEMENT—OFFER AND ACCEPTANCE.   The requirements of offer and acceptance are common among countries, although what is considered an offer varies by jurisdiction. In the United States, an offer, once made, normally can be revoked (canceled, or taken back) by the offeror at any time prior to the offer's acceptance. Many nations, however, require that an offer must remain open for some minimum period of time. For example, the German Civil Code, which has detailed provisions governing offer and acceptance, requires that a written contractual offer must be held open for a reasonable time, unless the offer specifically states otherwise. Unlike those in the United States, oral contractual offers (those made in person or by telephone) in Germany must be accepted immediately, or they terminate.

Mexico has some special rules for offer and acceptance. If a time for acceptance is not stated in an offer, the offer is deemed to be held open for three days, plus whatever time is necessary for the offer and acceptance to be sent through the mails. If acceptance is desired sooner, the offeror must state the time for acceptance in the offer.

In the United States, a contract's terms must be sufficiently definite that the parties (and a court) can determine whether the contract has been formed or not (see Chapter 12). For contracts for the sale of goods, however, the UCC has substantially relaxed common law requirements in respect to definiteness of contract terms (see Chapter 13). Mexico also has adopted a commercial code, which, like the UCC, liberalizes the traditional requirements of definiteness in mercantile transactions. Under contract law in some countries, such as Saudi Arabia, however, there are strict requirements about the definiteness of a contract's terms. If the terms of an offer are too vague or indefinite, acceptance of that offer normally will not create a valid contract.

CONSIDERATION.   In contrast to contract law in the United States, contract law in most civil law countries does not require consideration in order for a contract to be legally binding on the parties. German law, for example, does not require the exchange of consideration. An agreement to make a gift may thus be enforceable by the donee (the gift's recipient). In the United States, because consideration is required for a valid contract, promises to make gifts normally are not enforceable (because the donee does not give consideration for the gift).

In other countries, however, such as Saudi Arabia, consideration is required. Similarly, in India, consideration normally is required, although some contracts may be lawful even when the consideration consists of "past consideration" (that is, consideration that consists of an action that occurred in the past). As you read in Chapter 12, in the United States past consideration is no consideration.

LEGALITY. In most nations of the world, as in the United States, contracts to perform illegal acts are void and unenforceable—that is, they are not recognized by the courts as valid contracts. Islamic law, for example, prohibits the consumption of alcohol or pork products. Thus, in Islamic countries, contracts for the sale of those goods are illegal and unenforceable.

In some nations, such as China, certain types of contracts require formal approval by the central government or the relevant provincial government. Failure to obtain such approval will void, or nullify, the contract.

REMEDIES FOR BREACH OF CONTRACT. The types of remedies available for breach of contract vary widely throughout the world. In many countries, as in the United States, the normal remedy is damages—money given to the non-breaching party to compensate that party for the losses incurred owing to the breach (see Chapter 1). The calculation of damages resulting from a breach of contract, however, may differ from one country to another, just as does the calculation of damages under tort law.

National contract laws also differ as to whether and when equitable remedies, such as specific performance (discussed in Chapter 13), will be granted. Germany's typical remedy for a breach of contract is specific performance, which means that the party must go forward and perform the contract. Damages are available only after certain procedures have been employed to seek performance. In contrast, in the United States, the equitable remedy of specific performance will usually not be granted unless the remedy at law (money damages) is inadequate and the subject matter of the contract is unique.

DEFENSES. As in the United States, contract law in most nations allows parties to defend against contractual liability by claiming that certain requirements for contract formation have not been met. For example, many nations, including the United States, have laws requiring that certain types of contracts

A worker in an assembly plant. What are the legal advantages and disadvantages of contracting with workers as a foreign employer?

must be in writing. If such contracts are not in writing, they will not be enforced. In Saudi Arabia, the law strongly encourages parties to put all contracts in writing, and any written contract should be formally witnessed by two males or a male and a female. In that country, it may be difficult to enforce an oral contract.

Another common defense is the assertion that a contract was entered into because of fraud or duress, and thus genuineness of assent to the contract's terms was lacking. In some countries, a party may claim that a contract was not formed because the consideration supporting the contract was inadequate—that is, not *enough* value or money was given in exchange for a contractual promise. Indian courts, for example, look to the adequacy of consideration when determining whether the parties' assent to the contract was truly genuine and therefore whether the contract should be enforced. In the United States, in contrast, courts rarely inquire into the adequacy of consideration. Normally, only in cases in which the consideration is so grossly inadequate as to "shock the conscience of the court" will a court refuse to enforce a contract on this basis.

Employment Law

Employment law is particularly important in many foreign nations. The United States traditionally left the details of the employment relationship to a negotiation between the employer and the employee. Under the common law *employment-at-will* doctrine, employers were free to hire and fire employees "at will," meaning that an employee could be fired for any reason or no reason at all. Today, this common law doctrine is less applicable in the United States, because the workplace is regulated extensively by federal and state statutory law. Employment relationships in other nations also are subject to government regulation.

Abus de Droit A doctrine developed in the French courts. The doctrine modified employment at will and protected workers exercising their rights from wrongful discharge and other employer abuses.

MODIFICATIONS OF THE AT-WILL DOCTRINE.   Many other countries, like the United States, have modified their traditional at-will employment rules. In France, for example, the concept of employment at will can be traced back to the original Napoleonic Code. Over the years, the French have modified this doctrine considerably. French courts developed the doctrine of **abus de droit** (abuse of rights), which prohibited employers from firing workers for illness, pregnancy, unionization, political beliefs, the exercise of certain rights, or even personal dislike. French courts also began requiring employers to follow customary procedures before terminating workers. French employee-discharge laws were codified in the Dismissal Law of 1973, which also established procedural requirements that employers must follow when discharging workers (to be discussed shortly).

Under the Polish labor code, employment continues to be predominantly "at will." Either party may terminate the employment relationship at any time. Advance notice is generally required, however, and notice requirements vary, depending on the length of the worker's tenure with the employer. An employer may terminate an employee immediately and without notice if the worker has committed a criminal offense, lost a license or other employment qualification, seriously breached his or her duties, or failed to appear regularly at the job site. An employer cannot immediately discharge an employee for the last reason if the employee's absence was due to child-care needs, infectious disease, or entitled sick leave.

WAGES AND BENEFITS.   One of the reasons U.S. businesspersons decide to establish business operations, such as factories, in other countries is to cut production costs by taking advantage of lower wage rates. As you can see in Exhibit 25–4 on page 711, hourly labor costs in manufacturing vary significantly from country to country.

Although workers' wages may be lower in some countries than in the United States, typically workers in other countries have many paid holidays plus vacation time. In addition, employers in other countries may be subject to a variety of requirements not found in the United States.

In Mexico, for example, workers have a right to an annual bonus equal to fifteen days' salary and paid at the end of the year. Mexican law requires a minimum amount of paid vacation time (six days in the first year of employment) and also requires that companies give workers a 25 percent bonus above their ordinary pay rates during those vacations. For example, if a worker's ordinary pay is $200 per week, the vacation pay is $250 per week. Mexican employers also must periodically give training courses to workers. In some countries, such as Egypt, fringe benefits for employees account for as much as 40 percent of an employer's payroll costs.

INCOME SECURITY AND WORKERS' COMPENSATION.   Many countries, like the United States, have laws providing for social security and unemployment benefits. The specifics of these programs vary from country to country. Many nations also have some form of workers' compensation laws, much like state workers' compensation laws in the United States (discussed in Chapter 16). These laws compensate employees who are injured on the job. Rules define the nature and scope of workers' compensation and limit it to work-related injuries. In the following case, the issue before the Hong Kong court was whether a worker's death occurred in the course of employment.

Case 25.2 ● Fong Fung-Ying and Attorney General

Hong Kong
Court of Appeal, 1984.
Civil Appeal No. 111 of 1984.

BACKGROUND AND FACTS   A worker agreed to pick up some of his oxyacetylene welding and cutting equipment at the office of his supervisor at around 8:00 A.M. When his colleagues did not arrive, the worker and his supervisor went to a restaurant and drank wine until 8:50 A.M. The worker left the restaurant and went to a public lavatory in the same block as his office. He was stabbed and killed in the lavatory. His heirs sought to recover for his death under workers' compensation laws. The lower court held that the heirs could not recover under these laws because at the time of his death the worker was not acting in the course of employment. The heirs appealed.

IN THE WORDS OF THE COURT . . .
SIR ALAN HUGGINS, V.P.
* * * *

Obviously it cannot be right to say that, because a visit to the lavatory might in some circumstances be incidental to the deceased's employment, the deceased was in the course of his employment on every occasion on which

(Continued)

Case 25.2—continued

he went to that lavatory during working hours. There are two matters to be considered[:] (1) the purpose for which he went there and (2) the circumstances in which he went there. He might have gone there to place a bet with a book-maker, or merely to avoid working, and that would clearly not have been "in the course of" the employment. Of course, one could conceive of numerous possible alternative purposes, and if he went there on another frolic of his own he would have been no more in the course of his employment than he was during his visit to the restaurant. Is it a reasonable and proper assumption on the balance of probabilities that he went there to relieve himself, or was it for the claimant to adduce some evidence to show that that was his intention? * * *

It now being accepted that on the day in question the deceased's visit to the restaurant was not incidental to his employment, it follows that if he had gone from the restaurant to the lavatory with the intention of returning thereafter to the restaurant to continue his unauthorized break, that would equally not have been in the course of his employment.

DECISION AND REMEDY The Hong Kong Court of Appeal concluded that the survivors bore the burden of proving that the deceased was acting in the course of his employment. Because they were unable to meet this burden, the court dismissed their appeal.

FOR CRITICAL ANALYSIS—SOCIAL CONSIDERATION *Would the result in this case have been the same if it had involved a U.S. employer and an American employee, and been heard in a U.S. court?*

EQUAL EMPLOYMENT OPPORTUNITY. National laws around the globe vary widely with respect to equal employment opportunity. In the United States, employers are prohibited from discriminating against employees or job applicants on the basis of race, color, national origin, gender, religion, age, or disability. U.S. laws prohibiting discrimination on these bases also apply to all U.S. employees working for U.S. employers abroad. Generally, a U.S. employer must abide by U.S. laws prohibiting employment discrimination *unless* to do so would violate the laws of the country in which the employer's workplace is located. This "foreign laws exception" usually allows U.S. employers abroad to avoid being subjected to conflicting laws.

Some other countries also prohibit discriminatory practices. For example, in Indonesia, the Ministry of Manpower, which implements employment laws and regulations, prohibits discrimination in the workplace. Mexican law forbids employers from discriminating against employees on the basis of race, religion, or gender. The Japanese constitution prohibits discrimination based on race, religion, nationality, or gender.

In contrast, some countries, such as Egypt and Turkey, have no laws requiring equal employment opportunity. In Argentina, racial, religious, or other discrimination is not a political issue or a practice prohibited by law. Similarly, in Brazil, equal opportunity is not a factor in employment relationships.

Generally, in those countries that do prohibit employment discrimination, employers retain some flexibility in hiring and firing managerial personnel. In Mexico, for example, employers traditionally have been allowed to hire and fire "confidential" employees—managerial employees—at their discretion. In Italy, workers classified as managers are also less protected by the law.

EMPLOYMENT TERMINATION. In many countries, employers find it difficult, and often quite costly, to discharge unwanted or unneeded employees. Employment laws may prohibit the firing of employees for discriminatory reasons, and other laws may also come into play. For example, in France, if an employment contract is for an indefinite term, the employer can fire the worker only for genuine and serious cause or for economic reasons. The law also establishes procedural requirements. Before terminating a worker for cause, the employer must undertake a conciliatory session with labor court mediators. The employer has the burden of proving to the labor court that the cause of the dismissal was serious.

In Egypt, employers commonly use fixed-period employment contracts, which are automatically terminated at the end of the contract period. If an employee continues to work after the end of the contract period and no new contract is created, the employment contract becomes indefinite. It is very difficult to discharge an employee with an indefinite contract. The employee must first commit a serious offense, whereupon the employer must submit a proposal for termination to a committee consisting of representatives of the union, the employer, and the government. Employees may appeal adverse decisions of this committee.

Taiwanese law places clear restrictions on the termination of employment. An employer must provide a reason for discharging an employee. An employer may discharge an employee with advance notice and severance pay for a number of economic reasons or if the worker is incapable of performing the assigned work. The amount of notice and severance pay depends on the worker's tenure with the company. Employers may fire employees without notice or severance pay only for causes such as violence, imprisonment, extensive absenteeism, or lying on a job application should the lie cause the employer to suffer actual harm.

The legal requirements for terminating employment in France, Egypt, and Taiwan are representative of those in many other nations around the world. In practice, employers often circumvent these requirements by offering generous severance benefits to employees to encourage them to resign. Thus, employment termination laws may add substantially to the cost of conducting business abroad.

HOURLY LABOR COSTS IN MANUFACTURING, SELECTED COUNTRIES
(IN U.S. DOLLARS)

Germany	31.88
Japan	23.66
France	19.34
United States	17.20
Italy	16.48
Canada	16.03
Australia	14.40
Britain	13.77
Spain	12.70
South Korea	7.28
Singapore	7.28
Taiwan	5.82
Hong Kong	4.82
Brazil	4.28
Chile	3.63
Poland	2.09
Hungary	1.70
Argentina	1.67
Malaysia	1.59
Mexico	1.51
Czech Republic	1.30
Philippines	.71
Russia	.60
Thailand	.46
Indonesia	.30
China	.25
India	.25

SOURCE: *The Economist,* November 2, 1996, p.77.

■ **Exhibit 25–4**
Hourly Labor Costs in Manufacturing in Selected Countries (in U.S. Dollars)

The European Union

The European Union (EU) arose out of the 1957 Treaty of Rome, which created the Common Market, a free trade zone comprising the nations of Belgium, France, West Germany, Italy, the Netherlands, and Luxembourg. Since 1957, more nations have been added, and the powers of the EU have grown. The EU has added Austria, Denmark, Finland, Greece, Ireland, Portugal, Spain, Sweden, and the United Kingdom to the original Common Market countries. Some Eastern European nations have applied for membership. Some believe that the result will eventually be a "United States of Europe."

The EU has its own governing authorities. One is the Council of Ministers, which coordinates economic policies and includes one representative from each nation. The EU also has a commission that proposes regulations to the council and an elected assembly, which oversees the commission. The community has its own court, the European Court of Justice, which can review each nation's court decisions and is the ultimate authority on EU law.

> "A day will come when . . . all of you nations of the [European] continent, will, without losing your distinctive qualities, be blended into a . . . European fraternity."
>
> Victor Hugo, 1802–1885
> (French poet, novelist, and dramatist)

The EU has gone far toward creating a new body of law to govern all of the member nations, although some of the EU's efforts to create uniform laws have been confounded by nationalism. The council and the commission issue regulations, or directives, that define the EU law in various areas, and these requirements normally are binding on member states. EU directives govern such issues as environmental law, anticompetitive practices, and laws governing corporations. The EU directive on product liability, for example, states that a "producer of an article shall be liable for damage caused by a defect in the article, whether or not he knew or could have known of the defect." Liability extends to anyone who puts a trademark or other identifying feature on the article, and liability may not be excluded, even by contract.

Development of the EU has complicated European business law. A company now must consider international regulations, as well as the rules of the country of operation. This effect is illustrated by the following case.

Case 25.3 ● Alsatel-Société Alsacienne et Lorraine de Télécommunications et d'Electronique v. S.A. Novasam

Court of Justice of the European Communities, 1988.
Eur. Comm. Rep. 5987.
[Translated from the French.]

HISTORICAL AND POLITICAL SETTING *Alsace-Lorraine is an area in northeastern France, west of the Rhine River, consisting of the French regions of Alsace and Lorraine. Between the fifth and eighteenth centuries, Alsace-Lorraine was part of the German Empire. France acquired parts of the area by cession or seizure at different times before 1800, but at the end of the nineteenth century, it was again conquered by Germany. The area reverted to France in 1919, was retaken by Germany in 1940, and was liberated by the Allies in World War II, after which it was returned to France.*

BACKGROUND AND FACTS Alsatel-Société Alsacienne et Lorraine de Télécommunications et d'Electronique brought a claim against S.A. Novasam, a temporary employment agency. Novasam had terminated three contracts for the rental of telephone installations. A fifteen-year contract with Alsatel had bound Novasam to deal exclusively with Alsatel for any changes in service, extension of service, additional lines, or other modifications of the installations. The price of such modifications was to be set by Alsatel. Novasam's termination breached this contract under traditional contract law principles, but Novasam claimed that the contract was invalid under Article 86 of the EU treaty, which prohibits a company from abusing its dominant position or market power. The national court in France submitted the issue to the European Court of Justice for clarification.

IN THE WORDS OF THE COURT . . .
JUDGMENT:
  * * * *

Although the obligation imposed on customers to deal exclusively with the installer as regards any modification of the installation may be justified by the fact that the equipment remains the property of the installer, the fact that the price of the supplements to the contract entailed by those modifications is not determined but is unilaterally fixed by the installer and the automatic renewal of the contract for a 15-year term if as a result of those modifications the rental is increased by more than 25% may constitute unfair trading conditions prohibited as abusive practices by Article 86 of the treaty if all the conditions for the application of that provision are met.

(Continued)

Case 25.3—continued

The first condition for the application of that provision is that trade between member states must be affected. * * * That condition would be satisfied, in particular, if the contractual clauses referred to above had the effect of restricting imports of telephone equipment from other member states, thereby partitioning the market. There is nothing in the documents before the court which suggests that such is the case. However, it is for the national court to make the necessary findings of fact in that regard.

The second condition laid down by Article 86 is that there must be a dominant position within the common market or in a substantial part of it. The court has defined such a dominant position as a position of economic strength enjoyed by an undertaking which enables it to hinder the maintenance of effective competition on the relevant market by allowing it to behave to an appreciable extent independently of its competitors and customers.

* * * *

There is nothing in the documents before the court that suggests that plaintiff enjoys a dominant position throughout France. The only fact * * * with regard to the plaintiff's economic strength is the large share it holds of the regional market.

A finding of that kind is insufficient to establish that the undertaking in question occupies a dominant position.

DECISION AND REMEDY The Court of Justice of the European Communities formally ruled that "Article 86 of the [EU] treaty must be interpreted as meaning that contractual practices, even if abusive ones, on the part of an undertaking supplying telephone installations which has a large share of a regional market in a member state do not fall within the prohibition in that article where that undertaking does not occupy a dominant position in the relevant market, in this case the domestic market in telephone installations."

FOR CRITICAL ANALYSIS—TECHNOLOGICAL CONSIDERATION *How might the rapid changes in technology affect the application of law across national boundaries?*

Expanding Business Opportunities Abroad

▼ International business transactions have always been attended by more risk than is normally involved in domestic transactions. Since the end of the Cold War following the dissolution of the Soviet Union in 1991, though, the economic climate for business has improved around the globe. In the past, a business involved in overseas investments and operations faced the risk that a socialist government might come into power and nationalize the company, with or without compensation. While the risk of nationalization is still present today, the danger is far less. Additionally, in the past, some countries restricted the ability of U.S. companies to repatriate their profits (take the profits back to the United States), but these restrictions are also disappearing.

Conversely, many countries are now privatizing companies that had been nationalized and run by the government. **Privatization** occurs when a company purchases an entire business that has been operated by the government or

> "[A]s the state of the world changes, and new governments are formed, it seems to be wise from time to time to make new laws."
>
> Millard Fillmore, 1800–1874 (Thirteenth president of the United States, 1850–1853)

Privatization The replacement of government-provided products and services by private firms.

moves into competition in a field previously monopolized by the government. For example, Argentina is privatizing its mineral-extractive industries as well as its communications, transportation, and energy industries. Argentina also has eliminated most of the restrictions that it had placed on foreign investment and is eliminating most price controls.

The movement toward privatization is at different stages in other nations. France has gradually undertaken a denationalization program. India is still relatively socialized and requires government approval for much foreign investment. Government approval has become much easier to obtain, however. Egypt offers many investment incentives unavailable elsewhere.

The trend toward privatization has created significant opportunities for businesspersons. It has also created new opportunities for contracting on the basis of price, rather than politics. Other developments that have expanded international business opportunities were examined in Chapter 24, in the context of the international legal environment of business.

Key Terms

abus de droit 708	national law 695	*sharia* 700
civil law system 698	privatization 713	unitary system 697
international law 695		

Chapter Summary
The Legal Environment in Other Nations

COMPARATIVE LEGAL SYSTEMS	
CONSTITUTIONAL FOUNDATIONS (See pages 697–698.)	1. The foundation of a nation's legal system is its constitution.
	2. Most constitutions establish more than one branch of government to exercise legislative, executive, and judicial powers.
COMMON LAW AND CIVIL LAW SYSTEMS (See pages 698–701.)	1. **Common law systems**—Based on case law. Exist in countries that were once part of the British Empire.
	2. **Civil law systems**—Based on codes (statutes). Most European nations and their colonies have civil law systems.
COMPARATIVE LAWS	
TORTS (See pages 701–704.)	Tort law varies widely among nations. Rules regarding when a lawsuit can be filed, damages, and standards and burdens of proof are different. Even the codes in civil law systems differ in their definitions of what constitutes a "tort."
CONTRACTS (See pages 704–708.)	1. The United Nations Convention on Contracts for the International Sale of Goods (CISG) has internationalized some contract law. Contracting parties can agree to apply other law to their disputes, however.
	2. Similarities among the contract laws of all nations include the requirements of offer and acceptance and principles relating to fraud, illegality, and oral contracts.

(Continued)

Chapter Summary, continued

CONTRACTS—continued (See pages 704–708.)	3. Differences include what is considered an offer, whether consideration is required, and rules on damages and other remedies.
EMPLOYMENT (See pages 708–711.)	Most countries have restrictions on an employer's freedom to hire and fire employees. Some countries provide that an employee may be discharged without notice only for good cause (such as excessive absenteeism).
EUROPEAN UNION (See pages 711–713.)	The European Union (EU) is a free trade zone consisting of fifteen European nations. The EU has its own governing authorities, including a council and a commission that issue regulations binding on member nations. The EU also has a European Court of Justice, which is the ultimate authority on EU law.

For Review

1. What cultural differences affect the way in which business is done in other countries?

2. What are some of the similarities and differences between common law and civil law legal systems?

3. How do tort laws differ among nations?

4. How does contract law differ among nations?

5. What are some of the different employment laws in various countries?

Questions and Case Problems

25–1. Ethical Codes of Conduct. A considerable ethical controversy surrounds multinational enterprises (MNEs), which are often beyond the reach of national laws. For ethical or public-relations purposes, some MNEs have established internal codes of conduct to govern their behavior toward customers and other populations. Suppose that you were called on to draft such a code for an MNE. What provisions would you include?

25–2. Comparative Employment Laws. Assume that you are president of a manufacturing company that intends to expand overseas. Shipping costs and tariffs for your product are uniformly low. Your manufacturing process, however, is highly labor intensive. How would the employment laws of various nations influence your decision on where to situate a new manufacturing plant?

25–3. Women and Business. Joe Henderson is the president of an Asian branch of a U.S. bank. His top vice president is a woman, Betty Carter. He would like to take her with him to an important meeting at which he will undertake loan negotiations with a huge company. He has been advised, however, that he will lose respect in the eyes of the overseas company—and perhaps the com-

pany's business—if she accompanies him. He talks with her, and she informs him that she does not mind deferring to men at social activities, if local customs demand such deference, but that at the business meetings, she will expect business as usual and will not alter her behavior simply because she is a woman. What should Henderson do? Discuss.

25–4. Legal Systems. As China and formerly communist nations move toward free enterprise, they must develop a new set of business laws. If you could start from scratch, what kind of business law system would you adopt, a civil law system or a common law system? What kind of business regulations would you impose?

25–5. Ethics and Exporting. AgriChem is a U.S. firm that manufactures pesticides. AgriChem's main product is an effective insecticide called Rodeo. The U.S. Environmental Protection Agency has banned Rodeo because it has the potential to cause cancer. AgriChem has huge inventories of Rodeo that no longer can be sold in the United States. There is a substantial market for Rodeo in many Latin American countries, however, and American law permits the pesticide's export. Moreover, the Latin American countries permit its sale. Should AgriChem export Rodeo for sale in these countries?

25–6. Bribery of Foreign Officials. The Foreign Corrupt Practices Act of 1977 prohibits any U.S. corporation from paying foreign government officials to gain favorable business contracts. UsOil seeks to drill and produce oil and natural gas from a new field found in a foreign nation. The minister of the interior in that nation makes it clear, however, that he will consider granting drilling rights only to companies that make a major contribution to his family-run "charity." Should UsOil make this payment in order to obtain access to the market?

25–7. Doing Business Abroad. You are the human resources director for a major American conglomerate. Your company decides that it wants to expand its international presence considerably and asks you to develop a training program for managers. The aim of this training program is to develop managers who can operate effectively in foreign nations. What components would you include in such a program?

25–8. Employment Discrimination. Radio Free Europe and Radio Liberty (RFE/RL), a U.S. corporation doing business in Germany, employs more than three hundred U.S. citizens at its principal place of business in Munich, Germany. The concept of mandatory retirement is deeply embedded in German labor policy, and a contract formed in 1982 between RFE/RL and a German labor union contained a clause that required workers to be retired when they reached the age of sixty-five. When William Mahoney and other American employees (the plaintiffs) reached the age of sixty-five, RFE/RL terminated their employment as required under its contract with the labor union. The plaintiffs sued RFE/RL for discriminating against them on the basis of age, in violation of the Age Discrimination in Employment Act of 1967. Will the plaintiffs succeed in their suit? Discuss fully. [*Mahoney v. RFE/RL, Inc.,* 47 F.3d 447 (D.C. Cir. 1995)]

For Critical Analysis

25–9. In what ways can a nation's legal environment encourage foreign companies to do business in that country? What are the advantages and disadvantages of encouraging foreign investment?

Unit Six—Cumulative Hypothetical Problem

25–10. JB Mediquip, Inc., is a U.S. manufacturer of hospital equipment. JB does business throughout the world and has manufacturing plants in several other countries.

1. JB forms a contract with a business firm in Pardum, a foreign country, to purchase components for certain equipment that JB manufactures. The contract includes a choice-of-language clause, a choice-of-law clause, and a forum-selection clause. What do these clauses provide for, and what are their legal effects?

2. JB agrees to sell fifty hospital beds to a health-care facility operated on a military base in Zamboria, a foreign country. The health-care facility is owned and operated by the Zamborian government. JB ships the beds, but the health-care facility refuses to pay for them. To recover the price of the beds, JB sues the health-care facility in a U.S. district court. Zamboria moves to dismiss JB's action, contending that a U.S. court cannot exercise jurisdiction over the matter. On what ground might Zamboria base its assertion? Is Zamboria correct?

3. Many of the employees in JB's plant in Algoton, a foreign country, are American citizens. JB blatantly discriminates against the female employees in regard to salary and promotions. Several female employees sue JB in a U.S. court, alleging gender-based discrimination in violation of Title VII of the Civil Rights Act of 1964. JB contends that such discrimination is not illegal in Algoton, and therefore its actions are not illegal. Is JB correct? Explain.

INTERACTING WITH The Internet

■ The International Law Society of the University of Arizona College of Law has an online collection of various resources relating to international law, as well as to the national laws of some other countries. You can access this collection by going to

http://aruba.ccit.arizona.edu/~rdespeld/ils.html

■ To obtain information on the environmental laws of other countries, you can access the Australian Center for Environmental Law at

http://www.law.usyd.edu.au/~acel

■ If you are interested in learning about Russia's rules and regulations governing business, access Rules and Regulations in Russia at

http://www.spb.su/rulesreg/

■ Decisions from the English House of Lords, the final court of appeal in Britain, are now available on the Web. The site also provides general information on the judicial function of the House of Lords, including its jurisdiction and procedures. If you would like to learn more about the British civil and criminal justice system or to find decisions on certain types of cases, go to

http://www.parliament.the-stationery-office.co.uk/pa/ld/ldjudinf.htm

■ The Library of Congress's Global Legal Information Network has information on the national laws of more than thirty-five countries, as well as a comprehensive Guide to Law Online. You can access this site at

http://lcweb2.loc.gov/glin/lawhome.html

Briefing Cases— Instructions and Selected Cases

How to Brief a Case

To fully understand the law with respect to business, you need to be able to read and understand court decisions. To make this task easier, you can use a method of case analysis that is called briefing. There is a fairly standard procedure that you can follow when you "brief" any court case. You must first read the case opinion carefully. When you feel you understand the case, you can prepare a brief of it.

Although the format of the brief may vary, typically it will present the essentials of the case under headings such as those listed below.

1. **Citation.** Give the full citation for the case, including the name of the case, the date it was decided, and the court that decided it.
2. **Facts.** Briefly indicate (a) the reasons for the lawsuit; (b) the identity and arguments of the plaintiff(s) and defendant(s), respectively; and (c) the lower court's decision—if appropriate.
3. **Issue.** Concisely phrase, in the form of a question, the essential issue before the court. (If more than one issue is involved, you may have two—or even more—questions here.)
4. **Decision.** Indicate here—with a "yes" or "no," if possible—the court's answer to the question (or questions) in the Issue section above.
5. **Reason.** Summarize as briefly as possible the reasons given by the court for its decision (or decisions) and the case or statutory law relied on by the court in arriving at its decision.

When you prepare your brief, be sure that you include all of the important facts. The basic format is illustrated below in the briefed version of the sample court case that was presented in Chapter 1 in Exhibit 1–6. We have also annotated the briefed version to indicate the kind of information that is contained in each section.

Briefed Sample Court Case

EVANS v. FEDERAL EXPRESS CORP.
United States Court of Appeals
First Circuit, 1998.
133 F.3d 137.

FACTS Federal Express hired Michael Evans at the beginning of 1989 as a part-time freight handler. In 1991, Evans' supervisor Kenneth Pierce approved a four-week leave of absence for Evans to enter a residential drug-treatment program for cocaine abuse. At the hospital, Evans learned about alcoholism, and when he left, he joined an Alcoholics Anonymous program. Over the next three years, Evans was repeatedly absent from work without advance notice to his employer. After twice receiving written warnings, Evans asked for a leave of absence to enter a treatment program for alcohol abuse. Pierce refused. Two days later, Evans again was absent from work. Subsequently, under a threat of discharge, he quit. He filed a complaint against Federal Express, charging that he had been discriminated against on the basis of a disability—alcoholism. The federal district court that heard the case granted a summary judgment in favor of Federal Express. Evans appealed.

ISSUE Was Evans entitled to a second leave as a "reasonable accommodation" for his disability?

DECISION No. The U.S. Court of Appeals for the First Circuit affirmed the decision of the lower court.

REASON The Appellate court explained that "Massachusetts defines handicap to mean 'a physical or mental impairment which substantially limits one or more major life activities of a person' * * *. [A]lcoholism constitutes a 'handicap' under the Massachusetts statute." But, said the court, Evans' "claim rests on the view that in his circumstances a second leave to treat alcoholism was an obilgatory reasonable accommodation." An "element in the reasonableness equation is likelihood of success * * *. Evans had already made one effort to deal with alcoholism at the time of his cocaine treatment and had not succeeded. It is one thing to say that further treatment made medical sense, and quite another to say that the law required the company to retain Evans through a succession of efforts." The court acknowledged that after Evans left Federal Express, "he did undergo treatment and now holds down a job; but the company is entitled to be judged on what it knew at the time or could reasonably foresee (and for all we know the shock of the discharge is what helped Evans shape up)."

Review of Sample Court Case

CITATION The name of the case is *Evans v. Federal Express Corp.* The petitioner (the one bringing the appeal) is Michael Evans, and the respondent (the one against whom the appeal is taken) is Federal Express Corporation.

The case was decided by the U.S. Court of Appeals for the First Circuit in 1998. The citation is the Federal Reporter. The volume and page numbers of the reporter are left blank because the opinion has not yet been published in the reporter.

FACTS The *Facts* section identifies the parties to the lawsuit—the petitioner and the respondent—and describes the events leading up to the lawsuit and its appeal. Because this is an appeal, the decision of the lower court is included as a part of the facts of the case.

ISSUE The *Issue* section presents the central issue (or issues) to be decided by the court. In this case, the issue before the court was whether an employer is required to grant an employee repeated leaves of absence for treatment for substance abuse.

DECISION The *Decision* section, as the term indicates, contains the court's decision on the issue or issues before it. The decision reflects the opinion of the majority of the judges or justices hearing the case. Decisions by appellate courts are frequently phrased in reference to the lower court's decision. That is, the appellate court may "affirm"

the lower court's ruling or "reverse" it. In this particular case, the appellate court affirmed the decision of the lower court.

REASON The *Reason* section indicates what relevant laws and judicial principles were applied in forming the conclusion arrived at in the case at bar ("before the court"). In this case, the relevant law included a state statute that required "reasonable accommodation" for persons with disabilities. The court concluded that it was not a "reasonable accommodation" to require an employer to grant repeated leaves of absence to an employee for treatment for a substance-abuse disability.

SELECTED CASES FOR BRIEFING

Court opinions can run from a few pages to hundreds of pages in length. For reasons of space, only the essential parts of the opinions are presented in the cases that follow. A series of three asterisks indicates that a portion of the text—other than citations and footnotes—has been omitted. Four asterisks indicate the omission of at least one paragraph.

• •

Case A.1

Reference: Problem 4–12

RODRIGUEZ de QUIJAS v.
SHEARSON/AMERICAN EXPRESS, INC.
United States Supreme Court, 1989.
490 U.S. 477,
109 S.Ct. 1917,
104 L.Ed.2d 526.

KENNEDY, Justice.

The question here is whether a predispute agreement to arbitrate claims under the Securities Act of 1933 is unenforceable, requiring resolution of the claims only in a judicial forum.

I

Petitioners are individuals who invested about $400,000 in securities. They signed a standard customer agreement with the broker, which included a clause stating that the parties agreed to settle any controversies "relating to [the] accounts" through binding arbitration that complies with ~specified procedures. The agreement to arbitrate these controversies is unqualified, unless it is found to be unenforceable under federal or state law. * * * The investments turned sour, and petitioners eventually sued respondent and its broker-agent in charge of the accounts, alleging that their money was lost in unauthorized and fraudulent transactions. In their complaint they pleaded various violations of federal and state law, including claims under § 12(2) of the Securities Act of 1933, * * * and claims under three sections of the Securities Exchange Act of 1934.

The District Court ordered all the claims to be submitted to arbitration except for those raised under § 12(2) of the Securities Act. It held that the latter claims must proceed in the court action under our clear holding on the point in

Wilko v. Swan, 346 U.S. 427, 74 S.Ct. 182, 98 L.Ed. 168 (1953). The District Court reaffirmed its ruling upon reconsideration, and also entered a default judgment against the broker, who is no longer in the case. The Court of Appeals reversed, concluding that the arbitration agreement is enforceable because this Court's subsequent decisions have reduced Wilko to "obsolescence." * * *

II

The Wilko case, decided in 1953, required the Court to determine whether an agreement to arbitrate future controversies constitutes a binding stipulation "to waive compliance with any provision" of the Securities Act, which is nullified by § 14 of the Act. * * * The Court considered the language, purposes, and legislative history of the Securities Act, and concluded that the agreement to arbitrate was void under § 14. But the decision was a difficult one in view of the competing legislative policy embodied in the Arbitration Act, which the Court described as "not easily reconcilable," and which strongly favors the enforcement of agreements to arbitrate as a means of securing "prompt, economical and adequate solution of controversies." * * *

It has been recognized that Wilko was not obviously correct, for "the language prohibiting waiver of 'compliance with any provision of this title' could easily have been read to relate to substantive provisions of the Act without including the remedy provisions." * * * The Court did not read the language this way in Wilko, however, and gave two reasons. First, the Court rejected the argument that "arbitration is merely a form of trial to be used in lieu of a trial at law." * * * The Court found instead that § 14 does not permit waiver of "the right to select the judicial forum" in favor of arbitration, * * * because "arbitration lacks the certainty of a suit at law under the Act to enforce [the buyer's] rights," * * *. Second, the Court concluded that the Securities Act was intended to protect buyers of securities, who often do not deal at arm's length and on equal terms with sellers, by offering them "a wider choice of courts and venue" than is enjoyed by participants in other business transactions, making "the right to select the judicial forum" a particularly valuable feature of the Securities Act. * * *

* * * The shift in the Court's views on arbitration away from those adopted in Wilko is shown by the flat statement in [a prior case]: "By agreeing to arbitrate a statutory claim, a party does not forgo the substantive rights afforded by the statute; it only submits to their resolution in an arbitral, rather than a judicial, forum." * * * To the extent that Wilko rested on suspicion of arbitration as a method of weakening the protections afforded in the substantive law to would-be complainants, it has fallen far out of step with our current strong endorsement of the federal statutes favoring this method of resolving disputes.

Once the outmoded presumption of disfavoring arbitration proceedings is set to one side, it becomes clear that the right to select the judicial forum and the wider choice of courts are not such essential features of the Securities Act that § 14 is properly construed to bar any waiver of these provisions. Nor are they so critical that they cannot be waived under the rationale that the Securities Act was intended to place buyers of securities on an equal footing with sellers. Wilko identified two different kinds of provisions in the Securities Act that would advance this objective. Some are substantive, such as placing on the seller the burden of proving lack of scienter when a buyer alleges fraud. * * * Others are procedural. The specific procedural improvements highlighted in Wilko are the statute's broad venue provisions in the federal courts; the existence of nationwide service of process in the federal courts; the extinction of the amount-in-controversy requirement that had applied to fraud suits when they were brought in federal courts under diversity jurisdiction rather than as a federal cause of action; and the grant of concurrent jurisdiction in the state and federal courts without possibility of removal.

There is no sound basis for construing the prohibition in § 14 on waiving "compliance with any provision" of the Securities Act to apply to these procedural provisions. Although the first three measures do facilitate suits by buyers of securities, the grant of concurrent jurisdiction constitutes explicit authorization for complainants to waive those protections by filing suit in state court without possibility of removal to federal court. These measures, moreover, are present in other federal statutes which have not been interpreted to prohibit enforcement of predispute agreements to arbitrate. * * * [T]he party opposing arbitration carries the burden of showing that Congress intended in a separate statute to preclude a waiver of judicial remedies, or that such a waiver of judicial remedies inherently conflicts with the underlying purposes of that other statute. * * * But as Justice Frankfurter said in dissent in Wilko, so it is true in this case: "There is nothing in the record before us, nor in the facts of which we can take judicial notice, to indicate that the arbitral system . . . would not afford the plaintiff the rights to which he is entitled." * * *

The language quoted above from § 2 of the Arbitration Act also allows the courts to give relief where the party opposing arbitration presents "well-supported claims that the agreement to arbitrate resulted from the sort of fraud or overwhelming economic power that would provide grounds 'for the revocation of any contract.' " * * * This avenue of relief is in harmony with the Securities Act's concern to protect buyers of securities by removing "the disadvantages under which buyers labor" in their dealings with sellers. * * *

III

We now conclude that Wilko was incorrectly decided and is inconsistent with the prevailing uniform construction of other federal statutes governing arbitration agreements in the setting of business transactions. Although we are normally and properly reluctant to overturn our decisions construing statutes, we have done so to achieve a uniform interpretation of similar statutory language * * * and to correct a seriously erroneous interpretation of statutory language that would undermine congressional policy as expressed in other legislation, * * * Both purposes would be served here by overruling the Wilko decision. In this case, for example, petitioners' claims under the 1934 Act were subjected to arbitration, while their claim under the 1933 Act was not permitted to go to arbitration, but was required to proceed in court. That result makes little sense for similar claims, based on similar facts, which are supposed to arise within a single federal regulatory scheme. In addition, the inconsistency * * * undermines the essential rationale for a harmonious construction of the two statutes, which is to discourage litigants from manipulating their allegations merely to cast their claims under one of the securities laws rather than another. For all of these reasons, therefore, we overrule the decision in Wilko.

The judgment of the Court of Appeals is AFFIRMED.

Case A.2

Reference: Problem 5–12

AUSTIN v. BERRYMAN
United States Court of Appeals,
Fourth Circuit, 1989.
878 F.2d 786.

MURNAGHAN, Circuit Judge:

We have before us for *en banc* [by the whole court] reconsideration an appeal taken from an action success-fully brought by Barbara Austin in the United States District Court for the Western District of Virginia against the Virginia Employment Commission, challenging a denial of unemployment compensation benefits. * * * In brief, Austin charged, inter alia [among other things], that the denial of her claim for unemployment benefits, based on a Virginia statute specifically precluding such benefits for any individual who voluntarily quits work to join his or her spouse in a new location, was an unconstitutional infringement upon the incidents of marriage protected by the fourteenth amendment and an unconstitutional burden on her first amendment right to the free exercise of her religion. Her religion happened to command that she follow her spouse wherever he might go and the sincerity of her religious belief was not questioned. The district court found in Austin's favor and awarded injunctive relief and retroactive benefits.

On appeal, Judge Sprouse, writing for a panel majority, found that the denial of benefits did not implicate Austin's Fourteenth Amendment rights, but that it did unconstitutionally burden Austin's right to the free exercise of her religion. The panel also found, however, that any award of retroactive benefits was barred by the Eleventh Amendment. One panel member concurred with the panel majority as to the Fourteenth and Eleventh Amendment issues, but dissented as to the existence of a free exercise violation. The panel opinion now, of course, has been vacated by a grant of rehearing *en banc*.

After careful consideration of the additional arguments proffered by both sides, the Court, en banc, is convinced that the panel majority correctly concluded that denying Austin unemployment benefits did not infringe upon fundamental marital rights protected by the Fourteenth Amendment. To this extent, we adopt the majority panel opinion. We also find, however, that the denial of benefits did not unconstitutionally burden Austin's first amendment right to the free exercise of her religion. We are persuaded that the views expressed on the First Amendment, free exercise of religion claim in the opinion dissenting in part from the panel majority are correct, and we hereby adopt that opinion as that of the en banc court. As we find that Austin is not entitled to any relief, we need not address whether the Eleventh Amendment bars an award of retroactive benefits.

The decisive consideration, as we see it, is that the proximate cause of Austin's unemployment is geographic distance, not her religious beliefs. There is no conflict between the circumstances of work and Austin's religious precepts. Austin's religious beliefs do not "require" her "to refrain from the work in question." Austin is unable to work simply because she is now too far removed from her employer to make it practical. In striking contrast, if one, for genuine religious beliefs, moves to a new residence in order to continue to live with a spouse, and that residence is not geographically so removed as to preclude regular attendance at the worksite, no unemployment, and hence no unemployment benefits, will arise. That amounts to proof that extent of geographical non-propinquity, not religious belief, led to Austin's disqualification for unemployment benefits.

Austin voluntarily decided to quit her job and join her spouse in a new geographic location 150 miles away. Virginia has stated that every individual who follows such a course, no matter what the reason, religious or nonreligious, is disqualified for unemployment benefits. To craft judicially a statutory exception only for those individuals who profess Austin's religious convictions, particularly in the absence of a direct conflict between a given employment practice and a religious belief, would, in our view, result in a subsidy to members of a particular religious belief, impermissible under the Establishment Clause.

Accordingly, the judgment of the district court is REVERSED.

....

Case A.3

Reference: Problem 8–13

BURLINGHAM v. MINTZ
Supreme Court of Montana, 1995.
891 P.2d 527.

HUNT, Justice.
* * * *

On March 21, 1990, Candance Burlingham visited Dr. Mintz for a check-up and teeth cleaning. Dr. Mintz determined that she needed further treatment. Dr. Mintz also determined that Candance suffered from temporomandibular joint (TMJ) pain. On April 20, 1990, Candance returned to Dr. Mintz for treatment of her upper left rear molar. After applying a local anesthetic, Dr. Mintz noted that Candance had difficulty keeping her mouth open. To help keep her mouth open, Dr. Mintz placed a bite block between Candance's jaws. A bite block is a rubber coated tapered device with a serrated surface to keep it in place. The bite block was left in for approximately 45 minutes to one hour while Dr. Mintz completed the work. Later that day Candance began to suffer severe TMJ pain which did not abate. Dr. Mintz filled several more of Candance's teeth over the next few months, although he was hindered by her TMJ pain. In October 1990, Dr. Mintz referred Candance to a * * * specialist [in Kalispell, Montana,] who attempted, without success, to relieve Candance's pain. Eventually, Candance underwent restorative arthroscopic surgery in Spokane, Washington, to alleviate her TMJ pain.

On September 18, 1992, appellants filed suit alleging that Dr. Mintz's negligence caused Candance's TMJ injury. Appellants' first standard of care expert, Dr. James McGivney, was deposed on June 11, 1993. On August 12, 1993, appellants filed a motion asking the District Court to qualify Dr. McGivney as an **expert** [a person whose professional training or experience qualifies him or her to testify on a particular subject]. * * *

On February 8, 1994, the District Court denied appellants' motion[,] finding that Dr. McGivney, a suburban St. Louis dentist, was not familiar with the standards of practice or medical facilities available in Eureka, Montana, in a similar locality in Montana, or a similar locality anywhere in the country. The District Court granted appellants until the end of February to find another expert.
* * * *

On June 7, 1994, respondent filed a motion for summary judgment, arguing that appellants were not able to present expert testimony to meet their burden of proof to establish * * * a violation by respondent of his standard of care.

The District Court granted respondent's motion. Appellants appeal from the order granting summary judgment.

* * * *

The District Court concluded that appellants' proposed experts had no idea of the standards of practice in Eureka, Montana, in a similar locality in Montana, or in a similar place anywhere else in the country. A review of the testimony of respondent's and appellants' standard of care experts reveals little, if any, contradictory testimony as to the applicable standard of care for a dentist treating a patient suffering from TMJ pain in Eureka, Montana, or any other community in the country. Respondent's first standard of care expert testified that, with the exception of limited specialties, the same standard of care that applies to dentists in San Francisco and Kalispell, applies to dentists in Eureka. He agreed that the standard of care required in the diagnosis of and the treatment decisions regarding TMJ pain would be the same in San Francisco,

Kalispell, and Eureka. Respondent's second standard of care expert testified that in non-emergency situations the standard of care for dentists in Eureka is the same as the non-emergency standard of care anywhere else in the United States.

* * * *

We conclude that appellants' standard of care experts were familiar with the applicable non-emergency standard of care for dentists in Eureka if, by either direct or indirect knowledge, they were familiar with the applicable non-emergency standard of care for dentists in their communities, regardless of size or location. As a result, we hold that the District Court erred by excluding appellants' standard of care experts.

* * * *

* * * We reverse the summary judgment and remand this case to the District Court for further proceedings.

• •

Case A.4

Reference: Problem 13–12

POTTER v. OSTER
Supreme Court of Iowa, 1988.
426 N.W.2d 148.

NEUMAN, Justice.

This is a suit in equity brought by the plaintiffs to rescind an installment land contract based on the seller's inability to convey title. The question on appeal is whether, in an era of declining land values, returning the parties to the status quo works an inequitable result. We think not. Accordingly, we affirm the district court judgment for rescission and restitution.

The facts are largely undisputed. Because the case was tried in equity, our review is de novo. We give weight to the findings of the trial court, particularly where the credibility of witnesses is concerned, but we are not bound thereby.

The parties, though sharing a common interest in agribusiness, present a study in contrasts. We think the disparity in their background and experience is notable insofar as it bears on the equities of the transaction in issue. Plaintiff Charles Potter is a farm laborer and his wife, Sue, is a homemaker and substitute teacher. They have lived all their lives within a few miles of the real estate in question. Defendant Merrill Oster is an agricultural journalist and recognized specialist in land investment strategies. He owns Oster Communications, a multimillion dollar publishing concern devoted to furnishing farmers the latest in commodity market analysis and advice on an array of farm issues.

In May 1978, Oster contracted with Florence Stark to purchase her 160-acre farm in Howard County, Iowa, for $260,000 on a ten-year contract at seven percent interest. Oster then sold the homestead and nine acres to Charles and Sue Potter for $70,000. Potters paid $18,850 down and executed a ten-year installment contract for the bal-

ance at 8.5% interest. Oster then executed a contract with Robert Bishop for the sale of the remaining 151 acres as part of a package deal that included the sale of seventeen farms for a sum exceeding $5.9 million.

These back-to-back contracts collapsed like dominoes in March 1985 when Bishop failed to pay Oster and Oster failed to pay Stark the installments due on their respective contracts. Stark commenced forfeiture proceedings [proceedings to retake the property because Oster failed to perform a legal obligation—payment under the contract—and thus forfeited his right to the land]. Potters had paid every installment when due under their contract with Oster and had included Stark as a joint payee [one of two or more payees—persons to whom checks or notes are payable; see Chapter 25] with Oster on their March 1, 1985, payment. But they were financially unable to exercise their right to advance the sums due on the entire 160 acres in order to preserve their interest in the nine acres and homestead. As a result, their interest in the real estate was forfeited along with Oster's and Bishop's and they were forced to move from their home in August 1985.

Potters then sued Oster to rescind their contract with him, claiming restitution damages for all consideration paid. * * *

Trial testimony * * * revealed that the market value of the property had decreased markedly since its purchase. Expert appraisers valued the homestead and nine acres between $27,500 and $35,000. Oster himself placed a $28,000 value on the property; Potter $39,000. Evidence was also received placing the reasonable rental value of the property at $150 per month, or a total of $10,800 for the six-year Potter occupancy.

The district court concluded the Potters were entitled to rescission of the contract and return of the consideration paid including principal and interest, cost of improvements, closing expenses, and taxes for a total of $65,169.37. From this the court deducted $10,800 for six years' rental, bringing the final judgment to $54,369.37.

On appeal, Oster challenges the judgment. * * * [H]e claims Potters had an adequate remedy at law for damages which should have been measured by the actual economic loss sustained * * * .

* * * *

Rescission is a restitutionary remedy which attempts to restore the parties to their positions at the time the contract was executed. The remedy calls for a return of the land to the seller, with the buyer given judgment for payments made under the contract plus the value of improvements, less reasonable rental value for the period during which the buyer was in possession. The remedy has long been available in Iowa to buyers under land contracts when the seller has no title to convey.

Rescission is considered an extraordinary remedy, however, and is ordinarily not available to a litigant as a matter of right but only when, in the discretion of the court, it is necessary to obtain equity. Our cases have established three requirements that must be met before rescission will be granted. First, the injured party must not be in default. Second, the breach must be substantial and go to the heart of the contract. Third, remedies at law must be inadequate.

The first two tests are easily met in the present case. Potters are entirely without fault in this transaction. They tendered their 1985 installment payment to Oster before the forfeiture, and no additional payments were due until 1986. On the question of materiality, Oster's loss of equitable title [ownership rights protected in equity] to the homestead by forfeiture caused not only substantial, but total breach of his obligation to insure peaceful possession [an implied promise made by a landowner, when selling or renting land, that the buyer or tenant will not be evicted or disturbed by the landowner or a person having a lien or superior title] and convey marketable title under the Oster-Potter contract.

Only the third test—the inadequacy of damages at law—is contested by Oster on appeal. * * *

Restoring the status quo is the goal of the restitutionary remedy of rescission. Here, the district court accomplished the goal by awarding Potters a sum representing all they had paid under the contract rendered worthless by Oster's default. Oster contends that in an era of declining land values, such a remedy goes beyond achieving the status quo and results in a windfall to the Potters. Unwilling to disgorge the benefits he has received under the unfulfilled contract, Oster would have the court shift the "entrepreneural risk" [the risk assumed by one who initiates, and provides or controls the management of, a business enterprise] of market loss to the Potters by limiting their recovery to the difference between the property's market value at breach ($35,000) and the contract balance ($27,900). In other words, Oster claims the court should have awarded * * * damages. * * *

* * * *

* * * [L]egal remedies are considered inadequate when the damages cannot be measured with sufficient certainty. Contrary to Oster's assertion that Potters' compensation should be limited to the difference between the property's fair market value and contract balance at time of breach, * * * damages are correctly calculated as the difference between contract price and market value at the time for performance. Since the time of performance in this case would have been March 1990, the market value of the homestead and acreage cannot be predicted with any certainty, thus rendering such a formulation inadequate.

Most importantly, the fair market value of the homestead at the time of forfeiture is an incorrect measure of the benefit Potters lost. It fails to account for the special value Potters placed on the property's location and residential features that uniquely suited their family. For precisely this reason, remedies at law are presumed inadequate for breach of a real estate contract. Oster has failed to overcome that presumption here. His characterization of the transaction as a mere market loss for Potters, compensable by a sum which would enable them to make a nominal down payment on an equivalent homestead, has no legal or factual support in this record. * * *

* * * *

In summary, we find no error in the trial court's conclusion that Potters were entitled to rescission of the contract and return of all benefits allowed thereunder, less the value of reasonable rental for the period of occupancy * * * .

AFFIRMED.

• •

Case A.5   *Reference: Problem 14–11*

HAWLEY v. CEMENT INDUSTRIES, INC.
United States Court of Appeals, Eleventh Circuit, 1995. 51 F.3d 246.

PER CURIAM:

* * * *

In September 1990, Appellant Phillip E. Hawley ("Appellant") filed a Chapter 7 bankruptcy petition, claiming less than $20,000 in assets. In a signed statement dated June 15, 1989, Appellant listed his total assets at $13,822,477, total liabilities at $1,876,814, and total net worth at $11,945,663. Later in 1990, one of Appellant's creditors, Cement Industries, Inc. ("Appellee"), filed an adversary proceeding pursuant to 11 U.S.C. s 727(a)(5), urging the court to deny Appellant's discharge based on his failure to satisfactorily explain the loss of his assets between the filings of his financial statement and his bankruptcy petition.

Section 727(a)(5) of the Bankruptcy Code provides as follows: * * * ["](a) the court shall grant the debtor a discharge, unless— * * * the debtor has failed to explain satisfactorily, before determination of denial of discharge under this paragraph, any loss of assets or deficiency of assets to meet the debtor's liabilities.["]

* * * *

The bankruptcy court denied Appellant's discharge, observing that the Appellant, a "sophisticated and experienced businessman," had been unable to present documentation to explain the discrepancy between the value of his assets as listed in 1989 and the value he had listed in his bankruptcy petition in 1990. The court found a "complete lack of documentation to support the Debtor's loss of assets" and determined that "when examining the totality of the circumstances, this Court finds a pattern which leads this Court to conclude that the Debtor has not satisfactorily explained the loss or diminution of his assets."

The Appellant appealed to the district court. The district court affirmed and adopted the opinion of the bankruptcy court "as fully as if copied verbatim." The district court dismissed the appeal and Appellant then appealed to this Court * * * .

* * * *

* * * Appellant argues that Appellee failed to carry its burden in showing that Appellant's explanations for the loss of his assets were unsatisfactory. In its [Section] 727(a)(5) action, Appellee had the initial burden of proving its objection to Appellant's discharge. Appellee sus-

tained this burden by showing the vast discrepancies between Appellant's 1989 financial statement and his 1990 Chapter 7 schedules. Once the party objecting to the discharge establishes the basis for its objection, the burden then shifts to the debtor "to explain satisfactorily the loss." "To be satisfactory, 'an explanation' must convince the judge." "Vague and indefinite explanations of losses that are based on estimates uncorroborated by documentation are unsatisfactory." Obviously, Appellant's explanations did not "convince the judge." The bankruptcy judge clearly found Appellant's testimony and complete lack of documentation unconvincing. Upon review of the record, we find that the bankruptcy judge did not clearly err in finding that Appellant's explanation of his loss of more than $13 million in assets over the course of fifteen months was too vague and indefinite to be "satisfactory." Therefore, the judgment of the district court is AFFIRMED.

....

Case A.6

Reference: Problem 15–12

MASCHMEIER v. SOUTHSIDE PRESS, LTD.
Court of Appeals of Iowa, 1989.
435 N.W.2d 377.

HABHAB, Judge.

Defendant Kenneth E. Maschmeier and Charlotte A. Maschmeier created a corporation, Southside Press, Ltd., that did business at 1220 Second Avenue North in Council Bluffs. This building is owned by Kenneth and Charlotte and was leased by them to the corporation.

Kenneth and Charlotte are the majority shareholders, with each having 1300 shares. They are the only officers and directors of the corporation.

They gifted to their two sons [Marty and Larry] each 1200 shares of stock. All the parties were employed by Southside Press until the summer of 1985 when, because of family disagreements, Marty and Larry were terminated as employees. * * *

The parents on August 2, 1985, created a new corporation, Southside Press of the Midlands, Ltd. They are its only officers and directors. As individuals they terminated the lease of their building * * * with Southside and leased the same premises to Midlands. In addition, Kenneth, as president of Southside, entered into a lease with himself as president of Midlands whereby the printing equipment and two of the vehicles were leased to Midlands for $22,372 per year for five years, with an option to buy such assets at the end of the lease term at their fair market value but not to exceed $20,000. In addition, the inventory and two other vehicles owned by Southside were sold by it to Midlands. Notwithstanding the fact that a substantial part of the assets of Southside had been disposed of, the parents still received an annual salary from it of more than $20,000.

After Marty and Larry's employment with Southside had terminated, each obtained employment with other

printing companies in the same metropolitan area. The family disagreement continued. All stockholders were employed by companies that were competitive to Southside. Ultimately, the parents, as majority shareholders, offered to buy the sons' shares of stock for $20 per share. Their sons felt that this amount was inadequate. Thus, this lawsuit.

In 1985, Southside Press had gross sales of more than $600,000. The trial court found that in 1985 the corporate assets had a fair market value of $160,745. Shareholders' equity was found to be $236,502.92, and divided by the number of shares equals $47.30 per share. The court found that the majority shareholders had been abusive and oppressive to the minority shareholders by wasting the corporate assets and leaving Southside Press only a shell of a corporation. The court ordered the majority shareholders to pay $47.30 per share to the sons, or $56,760 to each son, plus interest at the maximum legal rate from the date of the filing of the petition.

* * * *

* * * [D]efendants state that the shares were valued at $20 pursuant to the corporate bylaws and should be enforced as an agreement of the shareholders. * * *

* * * *

Whenever a situation exists which is contrary to the principles of equity and which can be redressed within the scope of judicial action, a court of equity will devise a remedy to meet the situation though no similar relief has been granted before. The district court has the power to liquidate a corporation under [Iowa Code] section 496A.94(1). This statute also allows the district court to fashion other equitable relief.

It is contended that, in order for the trial court to have properly invoked the powers under section 496A.94(1), it had to find either the majority shareholders were oppressive in their conduct towards the minority shareholders, or that the majority shareholders misapplied or wasted corporate assets.

* * * The alleged oppressive conduct by those in control of a close corporation must be analyzed in terms of "fiduciary duties" owed by majority shareholders to the minority shareholders and "reasonable expectations" held by minority shareholders in committing capital and labor to the particular enterprise, in light of the predicament in which minority shareholders in a close corporation can be placed by a "freeze-out" situation.

* * * The trial court found * * * here [that] the majority shareholders attempted to "freeze out" or "squeeze out" the minority shareholders by terminating their employment and not permitting them to participate in the business.

* * * *

We concur with the trial court's findings that the majority shareholders acted oppressively toward the minority shareholders and wasted corporate assets. In this respect, we further determine that the trial court properly invoked Iowa Code section 496A.94 when it fashioned the remedy requiring the majority shareholders to purchase the shares of the minority.

But that does not resolve the problem[.] * * * The appellant challenges the method fashioned by the trial court in fixing the value of the stock and payment thereof by asserting it should be governed by the bylaws.

The articles of incorporation of Southside vested in the directors of the corporation the "authority to make provisions in the Bylaws of the corporation restricting the transfer of shares of this corporation." This the board of directors did when they adopted the following bylaw that relates to restrictions on the transferability of stock. * * *

* * * *

Section 3 [of the corporate bylaws] is a restriction on stock transfer. If a shareholder intends to sell his stock, he must first offer it to the corporation at a price "agreed upon by the shareholders at each annual meeting." The shareholders must agree on the value of the stock and if they are unable to do so, each has a right to select an appraiser and the appraisers shall appoint another and in this instance the five appraisers are to act as a Board of Appraisers to value the stock.

* * * Since none of the shareholders requested appraisers, we deem this, as the trial court did, to be a waiver. We concur with this statement from the trial court's ruling: "All parties have left the Court with the burden of evaluating the corporate stock."

* * * *

We agree with the defendants that a contractual formula price is enforceable even if the formula price is less than its fair market value. But here the parties were unable to agree to a price, i.e., at the last meeting of the stockholders. Thus the trial court was called upon to do so.

Courts have generally held that no one factor governs the valuation of shares; but that all factors, such as market value, asset value, future earning prospects, should be considered. In this case, the parties relied rather heavily on what is referred to in the record as book value (shareholders' equity) in arriving at stock value. The trial court likewise used shareholder equity but adjusted that amount by the present day fair market value of corporate assets.

* * * *

We determine that under the circumstances here the valuation per share as fixed by the trial court and the method it employed in arriving at value is fair and reasonable. However, we further conclude that the amount Larry and Marty are to receive must be reduced by the total amount of loans made to them as they appear on the corporate books.

* * * *

We affirm and modify.

....

Case A.7

Reference: Problem 24–11

TRANS-ORIENT MARINE CORP. v. STAR TRADING & MARINE, INC.

United States District Court, Southern District of New York, 1990.
731 F.Supp. 619.

WILLIAM C. CONNER, District Judge:

Defendant Republic of the Sudan moves this Court to dismiss the complaint for failure to state a claim or for summary judgment. It claims that the new Republic of the Sudan, as successor state, is not liable for the alleged breach of a five-year exclusive agency contract entered into by the prior sovereign state of Sudan. Defendant further asserts that a fundamental change in circumstances relieves it of any prior contractual obligations.

FACTS

Plaintiff's cause of action for breach of contract arises from an alleged five-year exclusive agency agreement to represent the Sudan in the United States P.L. 480 program [an agricultural trade development and assistance program]. The alleged October 14, 1983 agreement was effective from October 1, 1984 through September 30, 1989. In April 1985, a military coup deposed the then head of state, declaring a state of emergency and suspending the constitution. A twelve-month transitional military regime followed, which was then replaced by a civilian coalition government. The name of the state was changed from the Sudan to the Republic of Sudan. In June 1989, there was another military coup in which the present military regime overthrew the former civilian administration and suspended the constitution. Both parties agree that the Republic of the Sudan is a foreign sovereign state.

On January 3 and 4, 1985, the then Sudanese government sent letters advising plaintiff that a new agent, CIDCO, had been appointed to handle the contracts under P.L. 480 and that CIDCO would select the shipping agent. This alleged termination of the then-executory contract did not provide the one-year termination notice required under the original contract. Since January 1985, the Sudan has awarded CIDCO a continuing series of contracts to handle the wheat and wheat flour transportation under P.L. 480, in alleged violation of plaintiff's exclusive agency contract. No additional facts are relevant to the present motion.

DISCUSSION

The present Sudanese government asserts that it is not liable for the contractual obligations of the prior sovereign, pointing to the two military coups of 1985 and 1989 to sustain its position that both the 1985 military regime and the present administration are successor states and that there has been a fundamental change in circumstances. Plaintiff contends that neither the 1985 regime nor the present regime is a successor state but that they represent mere changes in government which do not relieve the present regime from the prior government's contractual obligations. Plaintiff further argues that even if either regime is a successor state, they have ratified the prior government's contract. For the following reasons, summary judgment is denied.

Whether a new administration may terminate the executory portions of its predecessor's contracts is based on the succession of state theory. International law sharply distinguishes the succession of state, which may create a discontinuity of statehood, from a succession of government, which leaves statehood unaffected. It is generally accepted that a change in government, regime or ideology has no effect on that state's international rights and obligations because the state continues to exist despite the change. * * *

However, where one sovereign succeeds another, and a new state is created, the rights and obligations of the successor state are affected. The rule with regard to contracts with private foreign individuals involves a balancing of competing interests. While the successor state is permitted to terminate existing contracts originally executed by the former sovereign and the private party, the successor state is liable to that party only for any amount due him as of the date of the change of sovereignty. But if the contract is totally executory, the successor state is released from the contract.

The Restatement of Foreign Relations Law describes a successor state to include: a state that wholly absorbs another state, that takes over part of the territory of another state, that becomes independent of another state of which it had formed a part, or that arises because of the dismemberment of the state of which it had been a part.

Careful study of defendant's submission reveals that the state of Sudan has not (1) wholly absorbed or been wholly absorbed by another state; (2) partly taken over or been partly taken over by another state; (3) become independent from another state of which it had formed a part; or (4) arisen out of dismemberment of a state of which it had been a part since the date of plaintiff's contract. Under the Restatement's definition, the state of Sudan has remained the same entity since its independence in 1956. Defendant's own exhibit in support of its motion substantiates that only a change in government was effected by the two military coups * * *.

Accordingly, the only changes in the Sudan since its independence in 1956 have been in the government, with seven distinct successive administrations. But there has been only one state.

Defendant unpersuasively emphasizes various aspects of the relevant transitions to reflect the creation of a new state: that the transitions resulted by way of military coups as opposed to routine, constitutional processes, the re-naming of the nation, the suspension of the constitu-tion, the closing of the borders and the declaration of a state of emergency. Treatises, as well as applicable case law, demonstrate that such features do not effect a succession of state. * * *

Furthermore, the Restatement's comparative chart in a Recognition of States section illustrates that a change in government by armed force or fraud, as well as institution of another regime following a civil war, leaves "no question of the existence of the state." It offers as contemporary examples of mere changes in government: Pinochet's 1973 ouster of Allende in Chile, Franco's 1936–39 takeover of Spain, and the Communist revolution in China.

The seminal decision on the distinction between a succession of state versus a change in government is the U. S. Supreme Court decision in *The Sapphire*. In *The Sapphire*, the Supreme Court considered whether a lawsuit begun by the French Emperor, Napoleon III, was abated by the overthrow of the Emperor during the course of litigation. In holding that the action was not extinguished, the Supreme Court stated that, "on the [Emperor's] deposition the sovereignty does not change, but merely the person or persons in whom it resides. . . . A change in such representative works no change in the national sovereignty or its rights."

* * * *

* * * In *United States v. National City Bank of New York*, the district court held the post-revolutionary State of Russia liable on the treasury notes of the pre-revolutionary state. Similarly, in *Jackson v. People's Republic of China*, the district court determined that the People's Republic, as successor government to the Imperial Chinese Government, was successor to its obligations, specifically, payment of principal due on the prior government-issued bonds. The law is clear that the obligations of a state are unaffected by a mere change in government. It is of no consequence that the Sudan allegedly breached an executory contract. The distinction between executed and executory contracts only applies where there has been a succession of state. The military coups of 1985 and 1989 did not effect a succession of state of the Sudan but merely changed the state's governing body, leaving the state's obligations undisturbed.

Defendant's alternative claim that a fundamental change of circumstances has occurred since October, 1983 relieving it of any prior contractual obligations is unsubstantiated. Defendant presents no explanation as to what "circumstances constituted an essential basis of the consent of the parties to be bound by the agreement" or what changes have "radically transform[ed] the extent of obligations still to be performed under the agreement." Having failed to demonstrate a fundamental change in circumstances, the present government is therefore contractually obligated to plaintiff under the October 14, 1983 five-year extension of agency contract if its predecessor indeed breached that agreement.

CONCLUSION

For the reasons discussed above, summary judgment is denied.

SO ORDERED.

The Constitution of the United States

PREAMBLE

We the People of the United States, in Order to form a more perfect Union, establish Justice, insure domestic Tranquility, provide for the common defence, promote the general Welfare, and secure the Blessings of Liberty to ourselves and our Posterity, do ordain and establish this Constitution for the United States of America.

ARTICLE I

Section 1. All legislative Powers herein granted shall be vested in a Congress of the United States, which shall consist of a Senate and House of Representatives.

Section 2. The House of Representatives shall be composed of Members chosen every second Year by the People of the several States, and the Electors in each State shall have the Qualifications requisite for Electors of the most numerous Branch of the State Legislature.

No Person shall be a Representative who shall not have attained to the Age of twenty five Years, and been seven Years a Citizen of the United States, and who shall not, when elected, be an Inhabitant of that State in which he shall be chosen.

Representatives and direct Taxes shall be apportioned among the several States which may be included within this Union, according to their respective Numbers, which shall be determined by adding to the whole Number of free Persons, including those bound to Service for a Term of Years, and excluding Indians not taxed, three fifths of all other Persons. The actual Enumeration shall be made within three Years after the first Meeting of the Congress of the United States, and within every subsequent Term of ten Years, in such Manner as they shall by Law direct. The Number of Representatives shall not exceed one for every thirty Thousand, but each State shall have at Least one Representative; and until such enumeration shall be made, the State of New Hampshire shall be entitled to chuse three, Massachusetts eight, Rhode Island and Providence Plantations one, Connecticut five, New York six, New Jersey four, Pennsylvania eight, Delaware one, Maryland six, Virginia ten, North Carolina five, South Carolina five, and Georgia three.

When vacancies happen in the Representation from any State, the Executive Authority thereof shall issue Writs of Election to fill such Vacancies.

The House of Representatives shall chuse their Speaker and other Officers; and shall have the sole Power of Impeachment.

Section 3. The Senate of the United States shall be composed of two Senators from each State, chosen by the Legislature thereof, for six Years; and each Senator shall have one Vote.

Immediately after they shall be assembled in Consequence of the first Election, they shall be divided as equally as may be into three Classes. The Seats of the Senators of the first Class shall be vacated at the Expiration of the second Year, of the second Class at the Expiration of the fourth Year, and of the third Class at the Expiration of the sixth Year, so that one third may be chosen every second Year; and if Vacancies happen by Resignation, or otherwise, during the Recess of the Legislature of any State, the Executive thereof may make temporary Appointments until the next Meeting of the Legislature, which shall then fill such Vacancies.

No Person shall be a Senator who shall not have attained to the Age of thirty Years, and been nine Years a Citizen of the United States, and who shall not, when elected, be an Inhabitant of that State for which he shall be chosen.

The Vice President of the United States shall be President of the Senate, but shall have no Vote, unless they be equally divided.

The Senate shall chuse their other Officers, and also a President pro tempore, in the Absence of the Vice President, or when he shall exercise the Office of President of the United States.

The Senate shall have the sole Power to try all Impeachments. When sitting for that Purpose, they shall be on Oath or Affirmation. When the President of the United States is tried, the Chief Justice shall preside: And no Person shall be convicted without the Concurrence of two thirds of the Members present.

Judgment in Cases of Impeachment shall not extend further than to removal from Office, and disqualification to hold and enjoy any Office of honor, Trust, or Profit under the United States: but the Party convicted shall nevertheless be liable and subject to Indictment, Trial, Judgment, and Punishment, according to Law.

Section 4. The Times, Places and Manner of holding Elections for Senators and Representatives, shall be prescribed in each State by the Legislature thereof; but the Congress may at any time by Law make or alter such Regulations, except as to the Places of chusing Senators.

The Congress shall assemble at least once in every Year, and such Meeting shall be on the first Monday in December, unless they shall by Law appoint a different Day.

Section 5. Each House shall be the Judge of the Elections, Returns, and Qualifications of its own Members, and a Majority of each shall constitute a Quorum to do Business; but a smaller Number may adjourn from day to day, and may be authorized to compel the Attendance of absent Members, in such Manner, and under such Penalties as each House may provide.

Each House may determine the Rules of its Proceedings, punish its Members for disorderly Behavior, and, with the Concurrence of two thirds, expel a Member.

Each House shall keep a Journal of its Proceedings, and from time to time publish the same, excepting such Parts as may in their Judgment require Secrecy; and the Yeas and Nays of the Members of either House on any question shall, at the Desire of one fifth of those Present, be entered on the Journal.

Neither House, during the Session of Congress, shall, without the Consent of the other, adjourn for more than three days, nor to any other Place than that in which the two Houses shall be sitting.

Section 6. The Senators and Representatives shall receive a Compensation for their Services, to be ascertained by Law, and paid out of the Treasury of the United States. They shall in all Cases, except Treason, Felony and Breach of the Peace, be privileged from Arrest during their Attendance at the Session of their respective Houses, and in going to and returning from the same; and for any Speech or Debate in either House, they shall not be questioned in any other Place.

No Senator or Representative shall, during the Time for which he was elected, be appointed to any civil Office under the Authority of the United States, which shall have been created, or the Emoluments whereof shall have been increased during such time; and no Person holding any Office under the United States, shall be a Member of either House during his Continuance in Office.

Section 7. All Bills for raising Revenue shall originate in the House of Representatives; but the Senate may propose or concur with Amendments as on other Bills.

Every Bill which shall have passed the House of Representatives and the Senate, shall, before it become a Law, be presented to the President of the United States; If he approve he shall sign it, but if not he shall return it, with his Objections to the House in which it shall have originated, who shall enter the Objections at large on their Journal, and proceed to reconsider it. If after such Reconsideration two thirds of that House shall agree to pass the Bill, it shall be sent together with the Objections, to the other House, by which it shall likewise be reconsidered, and if approved by two thirds of that House, it shall become a Law. But in all such Cases the Votes of both Houses shall be determined by Yeas and Nays, and the Names of the Persons voting for and against the Bill shall be entered on the Journal of each House respectively. If any Bill shall not be returned by the President within ten Days (Sundays excepted) after it shall have been presented to him, the Same shall be a Law, in like Manner as if he had signed it, unless the Congress by their Adjournment prevent its Return in which Case it shall not be a Law.

Every Order, Resolution, or Vote, to which the Concurrence of the Senate and House of Representatives may be necessary (except on a question of Adjournment) shall be presented to the President of the United States; and before the Same shall take Effect, shall be approved by him, or being disapproved by him, shall be repassed by two thirds of the Senate and House of Representatives, according to the Rules and Limitations prescribed in the Case of a Bill.

Section 8. The Congress shall have Power To lay and collect Taxes, Duties, Imposts and Excises, to pay the Debts and provide for the common Defence and general Welfare of the United States; but all Duties, Imposts and Excises shall be uniform throughout the United States;

To borrow Money on the credit of the United States;

To regulate Commerce with foreign Nations, and among the several States, and with the Indian Tribes;

To establish an uniform Rule of Naturalization, and uniform Laws on the subject of Bankruptcies throughout the United States;

To coin Money, regulate the Value thereof, and of foreign Coin, and fix the Standard of Weights and Measures;

To provide for the Punishment of counterfeiting the Securities and current Coin of the United States;

To establish Post Offices and post Roads;

To promote the Progress of Science and useful Arts, by securing for limited Times to Authors and Inventors the exclusive Right to their respective Writings and Discoveries;

To constitute Tribunals inferior to the supreme Court;

To define and punish Piracies and Felonies committed on the high Seas, and Offenses against the Law of Nations;

To declare War, grant Letters of Marque and Reprisal, and make Rules concerning Captures on Land and Water;

To raise and support Armies, but no Appropriation of Money to that Use shall be for a longer Term than two Years;

To provide and maintain a Navy;

To make Rules for the Government and Regulation of the land and naval Forces;

To provide for calling forth the Militia to execute the Laws of the Union, suppress Insurrections and repel Invasions;

To provide for organizing, arming, and disciplining, the Militia, and for governing such Part of them as may be employed in the Service of the United States, reserving to the States respectively, the Appointment of the Officers, and the Authority of training the Militia according to the discipline prescribed by Congress;

To exercise exclusive Legislation in all Cases whatsoever, over such District (not exceeding ten Miles square) as may, by Cession of particular States, and the Acceptance of Congress, become the Seat of the Government of the United States, and to exercise like Authority over all Places purchased by the Consent of the Legislature of the State in which the Same shall be, for the Erection of Forts, Magazines, Arsenals, dock-Yards, and other needful Buildings;—And

To make all Laws which shall be necessary and proper for carrying into Execution the foregoing Powers, and all other Powers vested by this Constitution in the Government of the United States, or in any Department or Officer thereof.

Section 9. The Migration or Importation of such Persons as any of the States now existing shall think proper to admit, shall not be prohibited by the Congress prior to the Year one thousand eight hundred and eight, but a Tax or duty may be imposed on such Importation, not exceeding ten dollars for each Person.

The privilege of the Writ of Habeas Corpus shall not be suspended, unless when in Cases of Rebellion or Invasion the public Safety may require it.

No Bill of Attainder or ex post facto Law shall be passed.

No Capitation, or other direct, Tax shall be laid, unless in Proportion to the Census or Enumeration herein before directed to be taken.

No Tax or Duty shall be laid on Articles exported from any State.

No Preference shall be given by any Regulation of Commerce or Revenue to the Ports of one State over those of another: nor shall Vessels bound to, or from, one State be obliged to enter, clear, or pay Duties in another.

No Money shall be drawn from the Treasury, but in Consequence of Appropriations made by Law; and a regular Statement and Account of the Receipts and Expenditures of all public Money shall be published from time to time.

No Title of Nobility shall be granted by the United States: And no Person holding any Office of Profit or Trust under them, shall, without the Consent of the Congress, accept of any present, Emolument, Office, or Title, of any kind whatever, from any King, Prince, or foreign State.

Section 10. No State shall enter into any Treaty, Alliance, or Confederation; grant Letters of Marque and Reprisal; coin Money; emit Bills of Credit; make any Thing but gold and silver Coin a Tender in Payment of Debts; pass any Bill of Attainder, ex post facto Law, or Law impairing the Obligation of Contracts, or grant any Title of Nobility.

No State shall, without the Consent of the Congress, lay any Imposts or Duties on Imports or Exports, except what may be absolutely necessary for executing its inspection Laws: and the net Produce of all Duties and Imposts, laid by any State on Imports or Exports, shall be for the Use of the Treasury of the United States; and all such Laws shall be subject to the Revision and Controul of the Congress.

No State shall, without the Consent of Congress, lay any Duty of Tonnage, keep Troops, or Ships of War in time of Peace, enter into any Agreement or Compact with another State, or with a foreign Power, or engage in War, unless actually invaded, or in such imminent Danger as will not admit of delay.

ARTICLE II

Section 1. The executive Power shall be vested in a President of the United States of America. He shall hold his Office during the Term of four Years, and, together with the Vice President, chosen for the same Term, be elected, as follows:

Each State shall appoint, in such Manner as the Legislature thereof may direct, a Number of Electors, equal to the whole Number of Senators and Representatives to which the State may be entitled in the Congress; but no Senator or Representative, or Person holding an Office of Trust or Profit under the United States, shall be appointed an Elector.

The Electors shall meet in their respective States, and vote by Ballot for two Persons, of whom one at least shall not be an Inhabitant of the same State with themselves. And they shall make a List of all the Persons voted for, and of the Number of Votes for each; which List they shall sign and certify, and transmit sealed to the Seat of the Government of the United States, directed to the President of the Senate. The President of the Senate shall, in the Presence of the Senate and House of Representatives, open all the Certificates, and the Votes shall then be counted. The Person having the greatest Number of Votes shall be the President, if such Number be a Majority of the whole Number of Electors appointed; and if there be more than one who have such Majority, and have an equal Number of Votes, then the House of Representatives shall immediately chuse by Ballot one of them for President; and if no Person have a Majority, then from the five highest on the List the said House shall in like Manner chuse the President. But in chusing the President, the Votes shall be taken by States, the Representation from each State having one Vote; A quorum for this Purpose shall consist of a Member or Members from two thirds of the States, and a Majority of all the States shall be necessary to a Choice. In every Case, after the Choice of the President, the Person having the greater Number of Votes of the Electors shall be the Vice President. But if there should remain two or more who have equal Votes, the Senate shall chuse from them by Ballot the Vice President.

The Congress may determine the Time of chusing the Electors, and the Day on which they shall give their Votes; which Day shall be the same throughout the United States.

No person except a natural born Citizen, or a Citizen of the United States, at the time of the Adoption of this Constitution, shall be eligible to the Office of President; neither shall any Person be eligible to that Office who shall not have attained to the Age of thirty five Years, and been fourteen Years a Resident within the United States.

In Case of the Removal of the President from Office, or of his Death, Resignation or Inability to discharge the Powers and Duties of the said Office, the same shall devolve on the Vice President, and the Congress may by Law provide for the Case of Removal, Death, Resignation or Inability, both of the President and Vice President, declaring what Officer shall then act as President, and such Officer shall act accordingly, until the Disability be removed, or a President shall be elected.

The President shall, at stated Times, receive for his Services, a Compensation, which shall neither be increased nor diminished during the Period for which he shall have been elected, and he shall not receive within that Period any other Emolument from the United States, or any of them.

Before he enter on the Execution of his Office, he shall take the following Oath or Affirmation: "I do solemnly swear (or affirm) that I will faithfully execute the Office of President of the United States, and will to the best of my Ability, preserve, protect and defend the Constitution of the United States."

Section 2. The President shall be Commander in Chief of the Army and Navy of the United States, and of the Militia of the several States, when called into the actual Service of the United States; he may require the Opinion, in writing, of the principal Officer in each of the executive Departments, upon any Subject relating to the Duties of their respective Offices, and he shall have Power to grant Reprieves and Pardons for Offenses against the United States, except in Cases of Impeachment.

He shall have Power, by and with the Advice and Consent of the Senate to make Treaties, provided two thirds of the Senators present concur; and he shall nominate, and by and with the Advice and Consent of the Senate, shall appoint Ambassadors, other public Ministers and Consuls, Judges of the supreme Court, and all other Officers of the United States, whose Appointments are not herein otherwise provided for, and which shall be established by Law; but the Congress may by Law vest the Appointment of such inferior Officers, as they think proper, in the President alone, in the Courts of Law, or in the Heads of Departments.

The President shall have Power to fill up all Vacancies that may happen during the Recess of the Senate, by granting Commissions which shall expire at the End of their next Session.

Section 3. He shall from time to time give to the Congress Information of the State of the Union, and recommend to their Consideration such Measures as he shall judge necessary and expedient; he may, on extraordinary Occasions, convene both Houses, or either of them, and in Case of Disagreement between them, with Respect to the Time of Adjournment, he may adjourn them to such Time as he shall think proper; he shall receive Ambassadors and other public Ministers; he shall take Care that the Laws be faithfully executed, and shall Commission all the Officers of the United States.

Section 4. The President, Vice President and all civil Officers of the United States, shall be removed from Office on Impeachment for, and Conviction of, Treason, Bribery, or other high Crimes and Misdemeanors.

ARTICLE III

Section 1. The judicial Power of the United States, shall be vested in one supreme Court, and in such inferior Courts as the Congress may from time to time ordain and establish. The Judges, both of the supreme and inferior Courts, shall hold their Offices during good Behaviour, and shall, at stated Times, receive for their Services a Compensation, which shall not be diminished during their Continuance in Office.

Section 2. The judicial Power shall extend to all Cases, in Law and Equity, arising under this Constitution, the Laws of the United States, and Treaties made, or which shall be made, under their Authority;—to all Cases affecting Ambassadors, other public Ministers and Consuls;—to all Cases of admiralty and maritime Jurisdiction;—to Controversies to which the United States shall be a Party;—to Controversies between two or more States;—between a State and Citizens of another State;—between Citizens of different States;—between Citizens of the same State claiming Lands under Grants of different

States, and between a State, or the Citizens thereof, and foreign States, Citizens or Subjects.

In all Cases affecting Ambassadors, other public Ministers and Consuls, and those in which a State shall be a Party, the supreme Court shall have original Jurisdiction. In all the other Cases before mentioned, the supreme Court shall have appellate Jurisdiction, both as to Law and Fact, with such Exceptions, and under such Regulations as the Congress shall make.

The Trial of all Crimes, except in Cases of Impeachment, shall be by Jury; and such Trial shall be held in the State where the said Crimes shall have been committed; but when not committed within any State, the Trial shall be at such Place or Places as the Congress may by Law have directed.

Section 3. Treason against the United States, shall consist only in levying War against them, or, in adhering to their Enemies, giving them Aid and Comfort. No Person shall be convicted of Treason unless on the Testimony of two Witnesses to the same overt Act, or on Confession in open Court.

The Congress shall have Power to declare the Punishment of Treason, but no Attainder of Treason shall work Corruption of Blood, or Forfeiture except during the Life of the Person attainted.

ARTICLE IV

Section 1. Full Faith and Credit shall be given in each State to the public Acts, Records, and judicial Proceedings of every other State. And the Congress may by general Laws prescribe the Manner in which such Acts, Records and Proceedings shall be proved, and the Effect thereof.

Section 2. The Citizens of each State shall be entitled to all Privileges and Immunities of Citizens in the several States.

A Person charged in any State with Treason, Felony, or other Crime, who shall flee from Justice, and be found in another State, shall on Demand of the executive Authority of the State from which he fled, be delivered up, to be removed to the State having Jurisdiction of the Crime.

No Person held to Service or Labour in one State, under the Laws thereof, escaping into another, shall, in Consequence of any Law or Regulation therein, be discharged from such Service or Labour, but shall be delivered up on Claim of the Party to whom such Service or Labour may be due.

Section 3. New States may be admitted by the Congress into this Union; but no new State shall be formed or erected within the Jurisdiction of any other State; nor any State be formed by the Junction of two or more States, or Parts of States, without the Consent of the Legislatures of the States concerned as well as of the Congress.

The Congress shall have Power to dispose of and make all needful Rules and Regulations respecting the Territory or other Property belonging to the United States; and nothing in this Constitution shall be so construed as to Prejudice any Claims of the United States, or of any particular State.

Section 4. The United States shall guarantee to every State in this Union a Republican Form of Government, and shall protect each of them against Invasion; and on Application of the Legislature, or of the Executive (when the Legislature cannot be convened) against domestic Violence.

ARTICLE V

The Congress, whenever two thirds of both Houses shall deem it necessary, shall propose Amendments to this Constitution, or, on the Application of the Legislatures of two thirds of the several States, shall call a Convention for proposing Amendments, which, in either Case, shall be valid to all Intents and Purposes, as part of this Constitution, when ratified by the Legislatures of three fourths of the several States, or by Conventions in three fourths thereof, as the one or the other Mode of Ratification may be proposed by the Congress; Provided that no Amendment which may be made prior to the Year One thousand eight hundred and eight shall in any Manner affect the first and fourth Clauses in the Ninth Section of the first Article; and that no State, without its Consent, shall be deprived of its equal Suffrage in the Senate.

ARTICLE VI

All Debts contracted and Engagements entered into, before the Adoption of this Constitution shall be as valid against the United States under this Constitution, as under the Confederation.

This Constitution, and the Laws of the United States which shall be made in Pursuance thereof; and all Treaties made, or which shall be made, under the Authority of the United States, shall be the supreme Law of the Land; and the Judges in every State shall be bound thereby, any Thing in the Constitution or Laws of any State to the Contrary notwithstanding.

The Senators and Representatives before mentioned, and the Members of the several State Legislatures, and all executive and judicial Officers, both of the United States and of the several States, shall be bound by Oath or Affirmation, to support this Constitution; but no religious Test shall ever be required as a Qualification to any Office or public Trust under the United States.

ARTICLE VII

The Ratification of the Conventions of nine States shall be sufficient for the Establishment of this Constitution between the States so ratifying the Same.

AMENDMENT I [1791]

Congress shall make no law respecting an establishment of religion, or prohibiting the free exercise thereof; or abridging the freedom of speech, or of the press; or the right of the people peaceably to assembly, and to petition the Government for a redress of grievances.

AMENDMENT II [1791]

A well regulated Militia, being necessary to the security of a free State, the right of the people to keep and bear Arms, shall not be infringed.

AMENDMENT III [1791]

No Soldier shall, in time of peace be quartered in any house, without the consent of the Owner, nor in time of war, but in a manner to be prescribed by law.

AMENDMENT IV [1791]

The right of the people to be secure in their persons, houses, papers, and effects, against unreasonable searches and seizures, shall not be violated, and no Warrants shall issue, but upon probable cause, supported by Oath or affirmation, and particularly describing the place to be searched, and the persons or things to be seized.

AMENDMENT V [1791]

No person shall be held to answer for a capital, or otherwise infamous crime, unless on a presentment or indictment of a Grand Jury, except in cases arising in the land or naval forces, or in the Militia, when in actual service in time of War or public danger; nor shall any person be subject for the same offence to be twice put in jeopardy of life or limb; nor shall be compelled in any criminal case to be a witness against himself, nor be deprived of life, liberty, or property, without due process of law; nor shall private property be taken for public use, without just compensation.

AMENDMENT VI [1791]

In all criminal prosecutions, the accused shall enjoy the right to a speedy and public trial, by an impartial jury of the State and district wherein the crime shall have been committed, which district shall have been previously ascertained by law, and to be informed of the nature and cause of the accusation; to be confronted with the witnesses against him; to have compulsory process for obtaining witnesses in his favor, and to have the Assistance of Counsel for his defence.

AMENDMENT VII [1791]

In Suits at common law, where the value in controversy shall exceed twenty dollars, the right of trial by jury shall be preserved, and no fact tried by jury, shall be otherwise re-examined in any Court of the United States, than according to the rules of the common law.

AMENDMENT VIII [1791]

Excessive bail shall not be required, nor excessive fines imposed, nor cruel and unusual punishments inflicted.

AMENDMENT IX [1791]

The enumeration in the Constitution, of certain rights, shall not be construed to deny or disparage others retained by the people.

AMENDMENT X [1791]

The powers not delegated to the United States by the Constitution, nor prohibited by it to the States, are reserved to the States respectively, or to the people.

AMENDMENT XI [1798]

The Judicial power of the United States shall not be construed to extend to any suit in law or equity, commenced or prosecuted against one of the United States by

Citizens of another State, or by Citizens or Subjects of any Foreign State.

AMENDMENT XII [1804]

The Electors shall meet in their respective states, and vote by ballot for President and Vice-President, one of whom, at least, shall not be an inhabitant of the same state with themselves; they shall name in their ballots the person voted for as President, and in distinct ballots the person voted for as Vice-President, and they shall make distinct lists of all persons voted for as President, and of all persons voted for as Vice-President, and of the number of votes for each, which lists they shall sign and certify, and transmit sealed to the seat of the government of the United States, directed to the President of the Senate;—The President of the Senate shall, in the presence of the Senate and House of Representatives, open all the certificates and the votes shall then be counted;—The person having the greatest number of votes for President, shall be the President, if such number be a majority of the whole number of Electors appointed; and if no person have such majority, then from the persons having the highest numbers not exceeding three on the list of those voted for as President, the House of Representatives shall choose immediately, by ballot, the President. But in choosing the President, the votes shall be taken by states, the representation from each state having one vote; a quorum for this purpose shall consist of a member or members from two-thirds of the states, and a majority of all states shall be necessary to a choice. And if the House of Representatives shall not choose a President whenever the right of choice shall devolve upon them, before the fourth day of March next following, then the Vice-President shall act as President, as in the case of the death or other constitutional disability of the President.—The person having the greatest number of votes as Vice-President, shall be the Vice-President, if such number be a majority of the whole number of Electors appointed, and if no person have a majority, then from the two highest numbers on the list, the Senate shall choose the Vice-President; a quorum for the purpose shall consist of two-thirds of the whole number of Senators, and a majority of the whole number shall be necessary to a choice. But no person constitutionally ineligible to the office of President shall be eligible to that of Vice-President of the United States.

AMENDMENT XIII [1865]

Section 1.   Neither slavery nor involuntary servitude, except as a punishment for crime whereof the party shall have been duly convicted, shall exist within the United States, or any place subject to their jurisdiction.

Section 2.   Congress shall have power to enforce this article by appropriate legislation.

AMENDMENT XIV [1868]

Section 1.   All persons born or naturalized in the United States, and subject to the jurisdiction thereof, are citizens of the United States and of the State wherein they reside. No State shall make or enforce any law which shall abridge the privileges or immunities of citizens of the United States; nor shall any State deprive any person of life, liberty, or property, without due process of law; nor

deny to any person within its jurisdiction the equal protection of the laws.

Section 2.   Representatives shall be apportioned among the several States according to their respective numbers, counting the whole number of persons in each State, excluding Indians not taxed. But when the right to vote at any election for the choice of electors for President and Vice President of the United States, Representatives in Congress, the Executive and Judicial officers of a State, or the members of the Legislature thereof, is denied to any of the male inhabitants of such State, being twenty-one years of age, and citizens of the United States, or in any way abridged, except for participation in rebellion, or other crime, the basis of representation therein shall be reduced in the proportion which the number of such male citizens shall bear to the whole number of male citizens twenty-one years of age in such State.

Section 3.   No person shall be a Senator or Representative in Congress, or elector of President and Vice President, or hold any office, civil or military, under the United States, or under any State, who having previously taken an oath, as a member of Congress, or as an officer of the United States, or as a member of any State legislature, or as an executive or judicial officer of any State, to support the Constitution of the United States, shall have engaged in insurrection or rebellion against the same, or given aid or comfort to the enemies thereof. But Congress may by a vote of two-thirds of each House, remove such disability.

Section 4.   The validity of the public debt of the United States, authorized by law, including debts incurred for payment of pensions and bounties for services in suppressing insurrection or rebellion, shall not be questioned. But neither the United States nor any State shall assume or pay any debt or obligation incurred in aid of insurrection or rebellion against the United States, or any claim for the loss or emancipation of any slave; but all such debts, obligations and claims shall be held illegal and void.

Section 5.   The Congress shall have power to enforce, by appropriate legislation, the provisions of this article.

AMENDMENT XV [1870]

Section 1.   The right of citizens of the United States to vote shall not be denied or abridged by the United States or by any State on account of race, color, or previous condition of servitude.

Section 2.   The Congress shall have power to enforce this article by appropriate legislation.

AMENDMENT XVI [1913]

The Congress shall have power to lay and collect taxes on incomes, from whatever source derived, without apportionment among the several States, and without regard to any census or enumeration.

AMENDMENT XVII [1913]

Section 1.   The Senate of the United States shall be composed of two Senators from each State, elected by the people thereof, for six years; and each Senator shall have one vote. The electors in each State shall have the qualifications requisite for electors of the most numerous branch of the State legislatures.

Section 2. When vacancies happen in the representation of any State in the Senate, the executive authority of such State shall issue writs of election to fill such vacancies: Provided, That the legislature of any State may empower the executive thereof to make temporary appointments until the people fill the vacancies by election as the legislature may direct.

Section 3. This amendment shall not be so construed as to affect the election or term of any Senator chosen before it becomes valid as part of the Constitution.

AMENDMENT XVIII [1919]

Section 1. After one year from the ratification of this article the manufacture, sale, or transportation of intoxicating liquors within, the importation thereof into, or the exportation thereof from the United States and all territory subject to the jurisdiction thereof for beverage purposes is hereby prohibited.

Section 2. The Congress and the several States shall have concurrent power to enforce this article by appropriate legislation.

Section 3. This article shall be inoperative unless it shall have been ratified as an amendment to the Constitution by the legislatures of the several States, as provided in the Constitution, within seven years from the date of the submission hereof to the States by the Congress.

AMENDMENT XIX [1920]

Section 1. The right of citizens of the United States to vote shall not be denied or abridged by the United States or by any State on account of sex.

Section 2. Congress shall have power to enforce this article by appropriate legislation.

AMENDMENT XX [1933]

Section 1. The terms of the President and Vice President shall end at noon on the 20th day of January, and the terms of Senators and Representatives at noon on the 3d day of January, of the years in which such terms would have ended if this article had not been ratified; and the terms of their successors shall then begin.

Section 2. The Congress shall assemble at least once in every year, and such meeting shall begin at noon on the 3d day of January, unless they shall by law appoint a different day.

Section 3. If, at the time fixed for the beginning of the term of the President, the President elect shall have died, the Vice President elect shall become President. If the President shall not have been chosen before the time fixed for the beginning of his term, or if the President elect shall have failed to qualify, then the Vice President elect shall act as President until a President shall have qualified; and the Congress may by law provide for the case wherein neither a President elect nor a Vice President elect shall have qualified, declaring who shall then act as President, or the manner in which one who is to act shall be selected, and such person shall act accordingly until a President or Vice President shall have qualified.

Section 4. The Congress may by law provide for the case of the death of any of the persons from whom the House of Representatives may choose a President whenever the right of choice shall have devolved upon them, and for the case of the death of any of the persons from whom the Senate may choose a Vice President whenever the right of choice shall have devolved upon them.

Section 5. Sections 1 and 2 shall take effect on the 15th day of October following the ratification of this article.

Section 6. This article shall be inoperative unless it shall have been ratified as an amendment to the Constitution by the legislatures of three-fourths of the several States within seven years from the date of its submission.

AMENDMENT XXI [1933]

Section 1. The eighteenth article of amendment to the Constitution of the United States is hereby repealed.

Section 2. The transportation or importation into any State, Territory, or possession of the United States for delivery or use therein of intoxicating liquors, in violation of the laws thereof, is hereby prohibited.

Section 3. This article shall be inoperative unless it shall have been ratified as an amendment to the Constitution by conventions in the several States, as provided in the Constitution, within seven years from the date of the submission hereof to the States by the Congress.

AMENDMENT XXII [1951]

Section 1. No person shall be elected to the office of the President more than twice, and no person who has held the office of President, or acted as President, for more than two years of a term to which some other person was elected President shall be elected to the office of President more than once. But this Article shall not apply to any person holding the office of President when this Article was proposed by the Congress, and shall not prevent any person who may be holding the office of President, or acting as President, during the term within which this Article becomes operative from holding the office of President or acting as President during the remainder of such term.

Section 2. This article shall be inoperative unless it shall have been ratified as an amendment to the Constitution by the legislatures of three-fourths of the several States within seven years from the date of its submission to the States by the Congress.

AMENDMENT XXIII [1961]

Section 1. The District constituting the seat of Government of the United States shall appoint in such manner as the Congress may direct:

A number of electors of President and Vice President equal to the whole number of Senators and Representatives in Congress to which the District would be entitled if it were a State, but in no event more than the least populous state; they shall be in addition to those appointed by the states, but they shall be considered, for the purposes of the election of President and Vice

THE CONSTITUTION OF THE UNITED STATES A-17

President, to be electors appointed by a state; and they shall meet in the District and perform such duties as provided by the twelfth article of amendment.

Section 2. The Congress shall have power to enforce this article by appropriate legislation.

AMENDMENT XXIV [1964]

Section 1. The right of citizens of the United States to vote in any primary or other election for President or Vice President, for electors for President or Vice President, or for Senator or Representative in Congress, shall not be denied or abridged by the United States, or any State by reason of failure to pay any poll tax or other tax.

Section 2. The Congress shall have power to enforce this article by appropriate legislation.

AMENDMENT XXV [1967]

Section 1. In case of the removal of the President from office or of his death or resignation, the Vice President shall become President.

Section 2. Whenever there is a vacancy in the office of the Vice President, the President shall nominate a Vice President who shall take office upon confirmation by a majority vote of both Houses of Congress.

Section 3. Whenever the President transmits to the President pro tempore of the Senate and the Speaker of the House of Representatives his written declaration that he is unable to discharge the powers and duties of his office, and until he transmits to them a written declaration to the contrary, such powers and duties shall be discharged by the Vice President as Acting President.

Section 4. Whenever the Vice President and a majority of either the principal officers of the executive departments or of such other body as Congress may by law provide, transmit to the President pro tempore of the Senate and the Speaker of the House of Representatives their written declaration that the President is unable to dis-

charge the powers and duties of his office, the Vice President shall immediately assume the powers and duties of the office as Acting President.

Thereafter, when the President transmits to the President pro tempore of the Senate and the Speaker of the House of Representatives his written declaration that no inability exists, he shall resume the powers and duties of his office unless the Vice President and a majority of either the principal officers of the executive department or of such other body as Congress may by law provide, transmit within four days to the President pro tempore of the Senate and the Speaker of the House of Representatives their written declaration that the President is unable to discharge the powers and duties of his office. Thereupon Congress shall decide the issue, assembling within forty-eight hours for that purpose if not in session. If the Congress, within twenty-one days after receipt of the latter written declaration, or, if Congress is not in session, within twenty-one days after Congress is required to assemble, determines by two-thirds vote of both Houses that the President is unable to discharge the powers and duties of his office, the Vice President shall continue to discharge the same as Acting President; otherwise, the President shall resume the powers and duties of his office.

AMENDMENT XXVI [1971]

Section 1. The right of citizens of the United States, who are eighteen years of age or older, to vote shall not be denied or abridged by the United States or by any State on account of age.

Section 2. The Congress shall have power to enforce this article by appropriate legislation.

AMENDMENT XXVII [1992]

No law, varying the compensation for the services of the Senators and Representatives, shall take effect, until an election of Representatives shall have intervened.

The Administrative Procedure Act of 1946
[EXCERPTS]

Section 551. Definitions

For the purpose of this subchapter—

* * * *

(4) "rule" means the whole or a part of an agency statement of general or particular applicability and future effect designed to implement, interpret, or prescribe law or policy or describing the organization, procedure, or practice requirements of an agency and includes the approval or prescription for the future of rates, wages, corporate or financial structures or reorganizations thereof, prices, facilities, appliances, services or allowances therefor or of valuations, costs, or accounting, or practices bearing on any of the foregoing[.]

* * * *

Section 552. Public Information; Agency Rules, Opinions, Orders, Records, and Proceedings

(a) Each agency shall make available to the public information as follows:

(1) Each agency shall separately state and currently publish in the Federal Register for the guidance of the public—

(A) descriptions of its central and field organization and the established places at which, the employees * * * from whom, and the methods whereby, the public may obtain information, make submittals or requests, or obtain decisions;

* * * *

(C) rules of procedure, descriptions of forms available or the places at which forms may be obtained, and instructions as to the scope and contents of all papers, reports, or examinations;

(D) substantive rules of general applicability adopted as authorized by law, and statements of general policy or interpretations of general applicability formulated and adopted by the agency[.]

* * *

* * * *

Section 552b. Open Meetings

* * * *

(j) Each agency subject to the requirements of this section shall annually report to Congress regarding its compliance with such requirements, including a tabulation of the total number of agency meetings open to the public, the total number of meetings closed to the public, the reasons for closing such meetings, and a description of any litigation brought against the agency under this section, including any costs assessed against the agency in such litigation * * *.

* * * *

Section 553. Rule Making

* * * *

(b) General notice of proposed rule making shall be published in the Federal Register, unless persons subject thereto are named and either personally served or otherwise have actual notice thereof in accordance with law. * * *

(c) After notice required by this section, the agency shall give interested persons an opportunity to participate in the rule making through submission of written data, views, or arguments with or without opportunity for oral presentation. * * *

* * * *

Section 554. Adjudications

* * * *

(b) Persons entitled to notice of an agency hearing shall be timely informed of—

(1) the time, place, and nature of the hearing;

(2) the legal authority and jurisdiction under which the hearing is to be held; and

(3) the matters of fact and law asserted.

* * * *

(c) The agency shall give all interested parties opportunity for—

(1) the submission and consideration of facts, arguments, offers of settlement, or proposals of adjustment when time, the nature of the proceeding, and the public interest permit; and

(2) to the extent that the parties are unable so to determine a controversy by consent, hearing and decision on notice * * *.

* * * *

Section 555. Ancillary Matters

* * * *

(c) Process, requirement of a report, inspection, or other investigative act or demand may not be issued, made, or enforced except as authorized by law. A person compelled to submit data or evidence is entitled to retain or, on payment of lawfully prescribed costs, procure a copy or transcript thereof, except that in a nonpublic investigatory proceeding the witness may for good cause be limited to inspection of the official transcript of his testimony.

* * * *

(e) Prompt notice shall be given of the denial in whole or in part of a written application, petition, or other request of an interested person made in connection with any agency proceeding. * * *

Section 556. Hearings; Presiding Employees; Powers and Duties; Burden of Proof; Evidence; Record as Basis of Decision

* * * *

(b) There shall preside at the taking of evidence—

(1) the agency;

(2) one or more members of the body which comprises the agency; or

(3) one or more administrative law judges * * *.

* * * *

(c) Subject to published rules of the agency and within its powers, employees presiding at hearings may—

(1) administer oaths and affirmations;

(2) issue subpoenas authorized by law;

(3) rule on offers of proof and receive relevant evidence;

(4) take depositions or have depositions taken when the ends of justice would be served;

(5) regulate the course of the hearing;

(6) hold conferences for the settlement or simplification of the issues by consent of the parties or by the use of alternative means of dispute resolution as provided in subchapter IV of this chapter;

(7) inform the parties as to the availability of one or more alternative means of dispute resolution, and encourage use of such methods;

* * * *

(9) dispose of procedural requests or similar matters;

(10) make or recommend decisions in accordance with * * * this title; and

(11) take other action authorized by agency rule consistent with this subchapter.

* * * *

Section 702. Right of Review

A person suffering legal wrong because of agency action * * * is entitled to judicial review thereof. An action in a court of the United States seeking relief other than money damages and stating a claim that an agency or an officer or employee thereof acted or failed to act in an official capacity or under color of legal authority shall not be dismissed nor relief therein be denied on the ground that it is against the United States or that the United States is an indispensable party. The United States may be named as a defendant in any such action, and a judgment or decree may be entered against the United States: Provided, [t]hat any mandatory or injunctive decree shall specify the [f]ederal officer or officers (by name or by title), and their successors in office, personally responsible for compliance. * * *

* * * *

Section 704. Actions Reviewable

Agency action made reviewable by statute and final agency action for which there is no other adequate remedy in a court are subject to judicial review. A preliminary, procedural, or intermediate agency action or ruling not directly reviewable is subject to review on the review of the final agency action.

Uniform Commercial Code [EXCERPTS]

Article 2
SALES

Part 1 Short Title, General Construction and Subject Matter

§ 2—101. Short Title.

This Article shall be known and may be cited as Uniform Commercial Code—Sales.

§ 2—102. Scope; Certain Security and Other Transactions Excluded From This Article.

Unless the context otherwise requires, this Article applies to transactions in goods; it does not apply to any transaction which although in the form of an unconditional contract to sell or present sale is intended to operate only as a security transaction nor does this Article impair or repeal any statute regulating sales to consumers, farmers or other specified classes of buyers.

§ 2—103. Definitions and Index of Definitions.

(1) In this Article unless the context otherwise requires

(a) "Buyer" means a person who buys or contracts to buy goods.

(b) "Good faith" in the case of a merchant means honesty in fact and the observance of reasonable commercial standards of fair dealing in the trade.

(c) "Receipt" of goods means taking physical possession of them.

(d) "Seller" means a person who sells or contracts to sell goods.

(2) Other definitions applying to this Article or to specified Parts thereof, and the sections in which they appear are:

"Acceptance". Section 2—606.
"Banker's credit". Section 2—325.
"Between merchants". Section 2—104.
"Cancellation". Section 2—106(4).
"Commercial unit". Section 2—105.
"Confirmed credit". Section 2—325.
"Conforming to contract". Section 2—106.
"Contract for sale". Section 2—106.
"Cover". Section 2—712.
"Entrusting". Section 2—403.

"Financing agency". Section 2—104.
"Future goods". Section 2—105.
"Goods". Section 2—105.
"Identification". Section 2—501.
"Installment contract". Section 2—612.
"Letter of Credit". Section 2—325.
"Lot". Section 2—105.
"Merchant". Section 2—104.
"Overseas". Section 2—323.
"Person in position of seller". Section 2—707.
"Present sale". Section 2—106.
"Sale". Section 2—106.
"Sale on approval". Section 2—326.
"Sale or return". Section 2—326.
"Termination". Section 2—106.

(3) The following definitions in other Articles apply to this Article:

"Check". Section 3—104.
"Consignee". Section 7—102.
"Consignor". Section 7—102.
"Consumer goods". Section 9—109.
"Dishonor". Section 3—507.
"Draft". Section 3—104.

(4) In addition Article 1 contains general definitions and principles of construction and interpretation applicable throughout this Article.

§ 2—104. Definitions: "Merchant"; "Between Merchants"; "Financing Agency".

(1) "Merchant" means a person who deals in goods of the kind or otherwise by his occupation holds himself out as having knowledge or skill peculiar to the practices or goods involved in the transaction or to whom such knowledge or skill may be attributed by his employment of an agent or broker or other intermediary who by his occupation holds himself out as having such knowledge or skill.

(2) "Financing agency" means a bank, finance company or other person who in the ordinary course of business makes advances against goods or documents of title or who by arrangement with either the seller or the buyer intervenes in ordinary course to make or collect payment due or claimed under the contract for sale, as by purchasing or paying the seller's draft or making advances against it or by merely taking it for collection whether or not documents of title accompany the draft. "Financing agency" includes also a bank or other person who similarly intervenes between persons who are in the position of seller and buyer in respect to the goods (Section 2—707).

(3) "Between merchants" means in any transaction with respect to which both parties are chargeable with the knowledge or skill of merchants.

§ 2—105. **Definitions: Transferability; "Goods"; "Future" Goods; "Lot"; "Commercial Unit".**

(1) "Goods" means all things (including specially manufactured goods) which are movable at the time of identification to the contract for sale other than the money in which the price is to be paid, investment securities (Article 8) and things in action. "Goods" also includes the unborn young of animals and growing crops and other identified things attached to realty as described in the section on goods to be severed from realty (Section 2—107).

(2) Goods must be both existing and identified before any interest in them can pass. Goods which are not both existing and identified are "future" goods. A purported present sale of future goods or of any interest therein operates as a contract to sell.

(3) There may be a sale of a part interest in existing identified goods.

(4) An undivided share in an identified bulk of fungible goods is sufficiently identified to be sold although the quantity of the bulk is not determined. Any agreed proportion of such a bulk or any quantity thereof agreed upon by number, weight or other measure may to the extent of the seller's interest in the bulk be sold to the buyer who then becomes an owner in common.

(5) "Lot" means a parcel or a single article which is the subject matter of a separate sale or delivery, whether or not it is sufficient to perform the contract.

(6) "Commercial unit" means such a unit of goods as by commercial usage is a single whole for purposes of sale and division of which materially impairs its character or value on the market or in use. A commercial unit may be a single article (as a machine) or a set of articles (as a suite of furniture or an assortment of sizes) or a quantity (as a bale, gross, or carload) or any other unit treated in use or in the relevant market as a single whole.

§ 2—106. **Definitions: "Contract"; "Agreement"; "Contract for Sale"; "Sale"; "Present Sale"; "Conforming" to Contract; "Termination"; "Cancellation".**

(1) In this Article unless the context otherwise requires "contract" and "agreement" are limited to those relating to the present or future sale of goods. "Contract for sale" includes both a present sale of goods and a contract to sell goods at a future time. A "sale" consists in the passing of title from the seller to the buyer for a price (Section 2—401). A "present sale" means a sale which is accomplished by the making of the contract.

(2) Goods or conduct including any part of a performance are "conforming" or conform to the contract when they are in accordance with the obligations under the contract.

(3) "Termination" occurs when either party pursuant to a power created by agreement or law puts an end to the contract otherwise than for its breach. On "termination" all obligations which are still executory on both sides are discharged but any right based on prior breach or performance survives.

(4) "Cancellation" occurs when either party puts an end to the contract for breach by the other and its effect is the same as that of "termination" except that the cancelling party also retains any remedy for breach of the whole contract or any unperformed balance.

§ 2—107. **Goods to Be Severed From Realty: Recording.**

(1) A contract for the sale of minerals or the like (including oil and gas) or a structure or its materials to be removed from realty is a contract for the sale of goods within this Article if they are to be severed by the seller but until severance a purported present sale thereof which is not effective as a transfer of an interest in land is effective only as a contract to sell.

(2) A contract for the sale apart from the land of growing crops or other things attached to realty and capable of severance without material harm thereto but not described in subsection (1) or of timber to be cut is a contract for the sale of goods within this Article whether the subject matter is to be severed by the buyer or by the seller even though it forms part of the realty at the time of contracting, and the parties can by identification effect a present sale before severance.

(3) The provisions of this section are subject to any third party rights provided by the law relating to realty records, and the contract for sale may be executed and recorded as a document transferring an interest in land and shall then constitute notice to third parties of the buyer's rights under the contract for sale.

Part 2 **Form, Formation and Readjustment of Contract**

§ 2—201. **Formal Requirements; Statute of Frauds.**

(1) Except as otherwise provided in this section a contract for the sale of goods for the price of $500 or more is not enforceable by way of action or defense unless there is some writing sufficient to indicate that a contract for sale has been made between the parties and signed by the party against whom enforcement is sought or by his authorized agent or broker. A writing is not insufficient because it omits or incorrectly states a term agreed upon but the contract is not enforceable under this paragraph beyond the quantity of goods shown in such writing.

(2) Between merchants if within a reasonable time a writing in confirmation of the contract and sufficient against the sender is received and the party receiving it has reason to know its contents, its satisfies the requirements of subsection (1) against such party unless written notice of objection to its contents is given within ten days after it is received.

(3) A contract which does not satisfy the requirements of subsection (1) but which is valid in other respects is enforceable

>(a) if the goods are to be specially manufactured for the buyer and are not suitable for sale to others in the ordinary course of the seller's business and the seller, before notice of repudiation is received and under circumstances which reasonably indicate that the goods are for the buyer, has made either a substantial beginning of their manufacture or commitments for their procurement; or

>(b) if the party against whom enforcement is sought admits in his pleading, testimony or otherwise in court that a contract for sale was made, but the contract is not enforceable under this provision beyond the quantity of goods admitted; or

>(c) with respect to goods for which payment has been made and accepted or which have been received and accepted (Sec. 2—606).

§ 2—202. Final Written Expression: Parol or Extrinsic Evidence.

Terms with respect to which the confirmatory memoranda of the parties agree or which are otherwise set forth in a writing intended by the parties as a final expression of their agreement with respect to such terms as are included therein may not be contradicted by evidence of any prior agreement or of a contemporaneous oral agreement but may be explained or supplemented

(a) by course of dealing or usage of trade (Section 1—205) or by course of performance (Section 2—208); and

(b) by evidence of consistent additional terms unless the court finds the writing to have been intended also as a complete and exclusive statement of the terms of the agreement.

§ 2—203. Seals Inoperative.

The affixing of a seal to a writing evidencing a contract for sale or an offer to buy or sell goods does not constitute the writing a sealed instrument and the law with respect to sealed instruments does not apply to such a contract or offer.

§ 2—204. Formation in General.

(1) A contract for sale of goods may be made in any manner sufficent to show agreement, including conduct by both parties which recognizes the existence of such a contract.

(2) An agreement sufficient to constitute a contract for sale may be found even though the moment of its making is undetermined.

(3) Even though one or more terms are left open a contract for sale does not fail for indefiniteness if the parties have intended to make a contract and there is a reasonably certain basis for giving an appropriate remedy.

§ 2—205. Firm Offers.

An offer by a merchant to buy or sell goods in a signed writing which by its terms gives assurance that it will be held open is not revocable, for lack of consideration, during the time stated or if no time is stated for a reasonable time, but in no event may such period of irrevocability exceed three months; but any such term of assurance on a form supplied by the offeree must be separately signed by the offeror.

§ 2—206. Offer and Acceptance in Formation of Contract.

(1) Unless other unambiguously indicated by the language or circumstances

>(a) an offer to make a contract shall be construed as inviting acceptance in any manner and by any medium reasonable in the circumstances;

>(b) an order or other offer to buy goods for prompt or current shipment shall be construed as inviting acceptance either by a prompt promise to ship or by the prompt or current shipment of conforming or nonconforming goods, but such a shipment of nonconforming goods does not constitute an acceptance if the seller seasonably notifies the buyer that the shipment is offered only as an accommodation to the buyer.

(2) Where the beginning of a requested performance is a reasonable mode of acceptance an offeror who is not notified of acceptance within a reasonable time may treat the offer as having lapsed before acceptance.

§ 2—207. Additional Terms in Acceptance or Confirmation.

(1) A definite and seasonable expression of acceptance or a written confirmation which is sent within a reasonable time operates as an acceptance even though it states terms additional to or different from those offered or agreed upon, unless acceptance is expressly made conditional on assent to the additional or different terms.

(2) The additional terms are to be construed as proposals for addition to the contract. Between merchants such terms become part of the contract unless:

>(a) the offer expressly limits acceptance to the terms of the offer;

>(b) they materially alter it; or

>(c) notification of objection to them has already been given or is given within a reasonable time after notice of them is received.

(3) Conduct by both parties which recognizes the existence of a contract is sufficient to establish a contract for sale although the writings of the parties do not otherwise establish a contract. In such case the terms of the particular contract consist of those terms on which the writings of the parties agree, together with any supplementary terms incorporated under any other provisions of this Act.

§ 2—208. **Course of Performance or Practical Construction.**

(1) Where the contract for sale involves repeated occasions for performance by either party with knowledge of the nature of the performance and opportunity for objection to it by the other, any course of performance accepted or acquiesced in without objection shall be relevant to determine the meaning of the agreement.

(2) The express terms of the agreement and any such course of performance, as well as any course of dealing and usage of trade, shall be construed whenever reasonable as consistent with each other; but when such construction is unreasonable, express terms shall control course of performance and course of performance shall control both course of dealing and usage of trade (Section 1—205).

(3) Subject to the provisions of the next section on modification and waiver, such course of performance shall be relevant to show a waiver or modification of any term inconsistent with such course of performance.

§ 2—209. **Modification, Rescission and Waiver.**

(1) An agreement modifying a contract within this Article needs no consideration to be binding.

(2) A signed agreement which excludes modification or rescission except by a signed writing cannot be otherwise modified or rescinded, but except as between merchants such a requirement on a form supplied by the merchant must be separately signed by the other party.

(3) The requirements of the statute of frauds section of this Article (Section 2—201) must be satisfied if the contract as modified is within its provisions.

(4) Although an attempt at modification or rescission does not satisfy the requirements of subsection (2) or (3) it can operate as a waiver.

(5) A party who has made a waiver affecting an executory portion of the contract may retract the waiver by reasonable notification received by the other party that strict performance will be required of any term waived, unless the retraction would be unjust in view of a material change of position in reliance on the waiver.

§ 2—210. **Delegation of Performance; Assignment of Rights.**

(1) A party may perform his duty through a delegate unless otherwise agreed or unless the other party has a substantial interest in having his original promisor perform or control the acts required by the contract. No delegation of performance relieves the party delegating of any duty to perform or any liability for breach.

(2) Unless otherwise agreed all rights of either seller or buyer can be assigned except where the assignment would materially change the duty of the other party, or increase materially the burden or risk imposed on him by his con-

tract, or impair materially his chance of obtaining return performance. A right to damages for breach of the whole contract or a right arising out of the assignor's due performance of his entire obligation can be assigned despite agreement otherwise.

(3) Unless the circumstances indicate the contrary a prohibition of assignment of "the contract" is to be construed as barring only the delegation to the assignee of the assignor's performance.

(4) An assignment of "the contract" or of "all my rights under the contract" or an assignment in similar general terms is an assignment of rights and unless the language or the circumstances (as in an assignment for security) indicate the contrary, it is a delegation of performance of the duties of the assignor and its acceptance by the assignee constitutes a promise by him to perform those duties. This promise is enforceable by either the assignor or the other party to the original contract.

(5) The other party may treat any assignment which delegates performance as creating reasonable grounds for insecurity and may without prejudice to his rights against the assignor demand assurances from the assignee (Section 2—609).

Part 3 **General Obligation and Construction of Contract**

§ 2—301. **General Obligations of Parties.**

The obligation of the seller is to transfer and deliver and that of the buyer is to accept and pay in accordance with the contract.

§ 2—302. **Unconscionable Contract or Clause.**

(1) If the court as a matter of law finds the contract or any clause of the contract to have been unconscionable at the time it was made the court may refuse to enforce the contract, or it may enforce the remainder of the contract without the unconscionable clause, or it may so limit the application of any unconscionable clause as to avoid any unconscionable result.

(2) When it is claimed or appears to the court that the contract or any clause thereof may be unconscionable the parties shall be afforded a reasonable opportunity to present evidence as to its commercial setting, purpose and effect to aid the court in making the determination.

§ 2—303. **Allocations or Division of Risks.**

Where this Article allocates a risk or a burden as between the parties "unless otherwise agreed", the agreement may not only shift the allocation but may also divide the risk or burden.

§ 2—304. **Price Payable in Money, Goods, Realty, or Otherwise.**

(1) The price can be made payable in money or otherwise. If it is payable in whole or in part in goods each party is a seller of the goods which he is to transfer.

(2) Even though all or part of the price is payable in an interest in realty the transfer of the goods and the seller's obligations with reference to them are subject to this Article, but not the transfer of the interest in realty or the transferor's obligations in connection therewith.

§ 2—305. Open Price Term.

(1) The parties if they so intend can conclude a contract for sale even though the price is not settled. In such a case the price is a reasonable price at the time for delivery if

(a) nothing is said as to price; or

(b) the price is left to be agreed by the parties and they fail to agree; or

(c) the price is to be fixed in terms of some agreed market or other standard as set or recorded by a third person or agency and it is not so set or recorded.

(2) A price to be fixed by the seller or by the buyer means a price for him to fix in good faith.

(3) When a price left to be fixed otherwise than by agreement of the parties fails to be fixed through fault of one party the other may at his option treat the contract as cancelled or himself fix a reasonable price.

(4) Where, however, the parties intend not to be bound unless the price be fixed or agreed and it is not fixed or agreed there is no contract. In such a case the buyer must return any goods already received or if unable so to do must pay their reasonable value at the time of delivery and the seller must return any portion of the price paid on account.

§ 2—306. Output, Requirements and Exclusive Dealings.

(1) A term which measures the quantity by the output of the seller or the requirements of the buyer means such actual output or requirements as may occur in good faith, except that no quantity unreasonably disproportionate to any stated estimate or in the absence of a stated estimate to any normal or otherwise comparable prior output or requirements may be tendered or demanded.

(2) A lawful agreement by either the seller or the buyer for exclusive dealing in the kind of goods concerned imposes unless otherwise agreed an obligation by the seller to use best efforts to supply the goods and by the buyer to use best efforts to promote their sale.

§ 2—307. Delivery in Single Lot or Several Lots.

Unless otherwise agreed all goods called for by a contract for sale must be tendered in a single delivery and payment is due only on such tender but where the circumstances give either party the right to make or demand delivery in lots the price if it can be apportioned may be demanded for each lot.

§ 2—308. Absence of Specified Place for Delivery.

Unless otherwise agreed

(a) the place for delivery of goods is the seller's place of business or if he has none his residence; but

(b) in a contract for sale of identified goods which to the knowledge of the parties at the time of contracting are in some other place, that place is the place for their delivery; and

(c) documents of title may be delivered through customary banking channels.

§ 2—309. Absence of Specific Time Provisions; Notice of Termination.

(1) The time for shipment or delivery or any other action under a contract if not provided in this Article or agreed upon shall be a reasonable time.

(2) Where the contract provides for successive performances but is indefinite in duration it is valid for a reasonable time but unless otherwise agreed may be terminated at any time by either party.

(3) Termination of a contract by one party except on the happening of an agreed event requires that reasonable notification be received by the other party and an agreement dispensing with notification is invalid if its operation would be unconscionable.

§ 2—310. Open Time for Payment or Running of Credit; Authority to Ship Under Reservation.

Unless otherwise agreed

(a) payment is due at the time and place at which the buyer is to receive the goods even though the place of shipment is the place of delivery; and

(b) if the seller is authorized to send the goods he may ship them under reservation, and may tender the documents of title, but the buyer may inspect the goods after their arrival before payment is due unless such inspection is inconsistent with the terms of the contract (Section 2—513); and

(c) if delivery is authorized and made by way of documents of title otherwise than by subsection (b) then payment is due at the time and place at which the buyer is to receive the documents regardless of where the goods are to be received; and

(d) where the seller is required or authorized to ship the goods on credit the credit period runs from the time of shipment but post-dating the invoice or delaying its dispatch will correspondingly delay the starting of the credit period.

§ 2—311. Options and Cooperation Respecting Performance.

(1) An agreement for sale which is otherwise sufficiently definite (subsection (3) of Section 2—204) to be a contract is not made invalid by the fact that it leaves particulars of performance to be specified by one of the parties. Any such specification must be made in good faith and within

limits set by commercial reasonableness.

(2) Unless otherwise agreed specifications relating to assortment of the goods are at the buyer's option and except as otherwise provided in subsections (1)(c) and (3) of Section 2—319 specifications or arrangements relating to shipment are at the seller's option.

(3) Where such specification would materially affect the other party's performance but is not seasonably made or where one party's cooperation is necessary to the agreed performance of the other but is not seasonably forthcoming, the other party in addition to all other remedies

  (a) is excused for any resulting delay in his own performance; and

  (b) may also either proceed to perform in any reasonable manner or after the time for a material part of his own performance treat the failure to specify or to cooperate as a breach by failure to deliver or accept the goods.

§ 2—312. **Warranty of Title and Against Infringement; Buyer's Obligation Against Infringement.**

(1) Subject to subsection (2) there is in a contract for sale a warranty by the seller that

  (a) the title conveyed shall be good, and its transfer rightful; and

  (b) the goods shall be delivered free from any security interest or other lien or encumbrance of which the buyer at the time of contracting has no knowledge.

(2) A warranty under subsection (1) will be excluded or modified only by specific language or by circumstances which give the buyer reason to know that the person selling does not claim title in himself or that he is purporting to sell only such right or title as he or a third person may have.

(3) Unless otherwise agreed a seller who is a merchant regularly dealing in goods of the kind warrants that the goods shall be delivered free of the rightful claim of any third person by way of infringement or the like but a buyer who furnishes specifications to the seller must hold the seller harmless against any such claim which arises out of compliance with the specifications.

§ 2—313. **Express Warranties by Affirmation, Promise, Description, Sample.**

(1) Express warranties by the seller are created as follows:

(a) Any affirmation of fact or promise made by the seller to the buyer which relates to the goods and becomes part of the basis of the bargain creates an express warranty that the goods shall conform to the affirmation or promise.

(b) Any description of the goods which is made part of the basis of the bargain creates an express warranty that the goods shall conform to the description.

(c) Any sample or model which is made part of the basis

of the bargain creates an express warranty that the whole of the goods shall conform to the sample or model.

(2) Iary to the creation of an express warranty that the seller use formal words such as "warrant" or "guarantee" or that he have a specific intention to make a warranty, but an affirmation merely of the value of the goods or a statement purporting to be merely the seller's opinion or commendation of the goods does not create a warranty.

§ 2—314. **Implied Warranty: Merchantability; Usage of Trade.**

(1) Unless excluded or modified (Section 2—316), a warranty that the goods shall be merchantable is implied in a contract for their sale if the seller is a merchant with respect to goods of that kind. Under this section the serving for value of food or drink to be consumed either on the premises or elsewhere is a sale.

(2) Goods to be merchantable must be at least such as

  (a) pass without objection in the trade under the contract description; and

  (b) in the case of fungible goods, are of fair average quality within the description; and

  (c) are fit for the ordinary purposes for which such goods are used; and

  (d) run, within the variations permitted by the agreement, of even kind, quality and quantity within each unit and among all units involved; and

  (e) are adequately contained, packaged, and labeled as the agreement may require; and

  (f) conform to the promises or affirmations of fact made on the container or label if any.

(3) Unless excluded or modified (Section 2—316) other implied warranties may arise from course of dealing or usage of trade.

§ 2—315. **Implied Warranty: Fitness for Particular Purpose.**

Where the seller at the time of contracting has reason to know any particular purpose for which the goods are required and that the buyer is relying on the seller's skill or judgment to select or furnish suitable goods, there is unless excluded or modified under the next section an implied warranty that the goods shall be fit for such purpose.

§ 2—316. **Exclusion or Modification of Warranties.**

(1) Words or conduct relevant to the creation of an express warranty and words or conduct tending to negate or limit warranty shall be construed wherever reasonable as consistent with each other; but subject to the provisions of this Article on parol or extrinsic evidence (Section 2—202) negation or limitation is inoperative to the extent that such construction is unreasonable.

(2) Subject to subsection (3), to exclude or modify the implied warranty of merchantability or any part of it the language must mention merchantability and in case of a

writing must be conspicuous, and to exclude or modify any implied warranty of fitness the exclusion must be by a writing and conspicuous. Language to exclude all implied warranties of fitness is sufficient if it states, for example, that "There are no warranties which extend beyond the description on the face hereof."

(3) Notwithstanding subsection (2)

(a) unless the circumstances indicate otherwise, all implied warranties are excluded by expressions like "as is", "with all faults" or other language which in common understanding calls the buyer's attention to the exclusion of warranties and makes plain that there is no implied warranty; and

(b) when the buyer before entering into the contract has examined the goods or the sample or model as fully as he desired or has refused to examine the goods there is no implied warranty with regard to defects which an examination ought in the circumstances to have revealed to him; and

(c) an implied warranty can also be excluded or modified by course of dealing or course of performance or usage of trade.

(4) Remedies for breach of warranty can be limited in accordance with the provisions of this Article on liquidation or limitation of damages and on contractual modification of remedy (Sections 2—718 and 2—719).

§ 2—317. **Cumulation and Conflict of Warranties Express or Implied.**

Warranties whether express or implied shall be construed as consistent with each other and as cumulative, but if such construction is unreasonable the intention of the parties shall determine which warranty is dominant. In ascertaining that intention the following rules apply:

(a) Exact or technical specifications displace an inconsistent sample or model or general language of description.

(b) A sample from an existing bulk displaces inconsistent general language of description.

(c) Express warranties displace inconsistent implied warranties other than an implied warranty of fitness for a particular purpose.

§ 2—318. **Third Party Beneficiaries of Warranties Express or Implied.**

Note: If this Act is introduced in the Congress of the United States this section should be omitted. (States to select one alternative.)

ALTERNATIVE A

A seller's warranty whether express or implied extends to any natural person who is in the family or household of his buyer or who is a guest in his home if it is reasonable to expect that such person may use, consume or be affected by the goods and who is injured in person by breach of the warranty. A seller may not exclude or limit the operation of this section.

ALTERNATIVE B

A seller's warranty whether express or implied extends to any natural person who may reasonably be expected to use, consume or be affected by the goods and who is injured in person by breach of the warranty. A seller may not exclude or limit the operation of this section.

ALTERNATIVE C

A seller's warranty whether express or implied extends to any person who may reasonably be expected to use, consume or be affected by the goods and who is injured by breach of the warranty. A seller may not exclude or limit the operation of this section with respect to injury to the person of an individual to whom the warranty extends. As amended 1966.

§ 2—319. **F.O.B. and F.A.S. Terms.**

(1) Unless otherwise agreed the term F.O.B. (which means "free on board") at a named place, even though used only in connection with the stated price, is a delivery term under which

(a) when the term is F.O.B. the place of shipment, the seller must at that place ship the goods in the manner provided in this Article (Section 2—504) and bear the expense and risk of putting them into the possession of the carrier; or

(b) when the term is F.O.B. the place of destination, the seller must at his own expense and risk transport the goods to that place and there tender delivery of them in the manner provided in this Article (Section 2—503);

(c) when under either (a) or (b) the term is also F.O.B. vessel, car or other vehicle, the seller must in addition at his own expense and risk load the goods on board. If the term is F.O.B. vessel the buyer must name the vessel and in an appropriate case the seller must comply with the provisions of this Article on the form of bill of lading (Section 2—323).

(2) Unless otherwise agreed the term F.A.S. vessel (which means "free alongside") at a named port, even though used only in connection with the stated price, is a delivery term under which the seller must

(a) at his own expense and risk deliver the goods alongside the vessel in the manner usual in that port or on a dock designated and provided by the buyer; and

(b) obtain and tender a receipt for the goods in exchange for which the carrier is under a duty to issue a bill of lading.

(3) Unless otherwise agreed in any case falling within subsection (1)(a) or (c) or subsection (2) the buyer must seasonably give any needed instructions for making delivery, including when the term is F.A.S. or F.O.B. the loading

berth of the vessel and in an appropriate case its name and sailing date. The seller may treat the failure of needed instructions as a failure of cooperation under this Article (Section 2—311). He may also at his option move the goods in any reasonable manner preparatory to delivery or shipment.

(4) Under the term F.O.B. vessel or F.A.S. unless otherwise agreed the buyer must make payment against tender of the required documents and the seller may not tender nor the buyer demand delivery of the goods in substitution for the documents.

§ 2—320. C.I.F. and C. & F. Terms.

(1) The term C.I.F. means that the price includes in a lump sum the cost of the goods and the insurance and freight to the named destination. The term C. & F. or C.F. means that the price so includes cost and freight to the named destination.

(2) Unless otherwise agreed and even though used only in connection with the stated price and destination, the term C.I.F. destination or its equivalent requires the seller at his own expense and risk to

(a) put the goods into the possession of a carrier at the port for shipment and obtain a negotiable bill or bills of lading covering the entire transportation to the named destination; and

(b) load the goods and obtain a receipt from the carrier (which may be contained in the bill of lading) showing that the freight has been paid or provided for; and

(c) obtain a policy or certificate of insurance, including any war risk insurance, of a kind and on terms then current at the port of shipment in the usual amount, in the currency of the contract, shown to cover the same goods covered by the bill of lading and providing for payment of loss to the order of the buyer or for the account of whom it may concern; but the seller may add to the price the amount of the premium for any such war risk insurance; and

(d) prepare an invoice of the goods and procure any other documents required to effect shipment or to comply with the contract; and

(e) forward and tender with commercial promptness all the documents in due form and with any indorsement necessary to perfect the buyer's rights.

(3) Unless otherwise agreed the term C. & F. or its equivalent has the same effect and imposes upon the seller the same obligations and risks as a C.I.F. term except the obligation as to insurance.

(4) Under the term C.I.F. or C. & F. unless otherwise agreed the buyer must make payment against tender of the required documents and the seller may not tender nor the buyer demand delivery of the goods in substitution for the documents.

§ 2—321. C.I.F. or C. & F.: "Net Landed Weights"; "Payment on Arrival"; Warranty of Condition on Arrival.

Under a contract containing a term C.I.F. or C. & F.

(1) Where the price is based on or is to be adjusted according to "net landed weights", "delivered weights", "out turn" quantity or quality or the like, unless otherwise agreed the seller must reasonably estimate the price. The payment due on tender of the documents called for by the contract is the amount so estimated, but after final adjustment of the price a settlement must be made with commercial promptness.

(2) An agreement described in subsection (1) or any warranty of quality or condition of the goods on arrival places upon the seller the risk of ordinary deterioration, shrinkage and the like in transportation but has no effect on the place or time of identification to the contract for sale or delivery or on the passing of the risk of loss.

(3) Unless otherwise agreed where the contract provides for payment on or after arrival of the goods the seller must before payment allow such preliminary inspection as is feasible; but if the goods are lost delivery of the documents and payment are due when the goods should have arrived.

§ 2—322. Delivery "Ex-Ship".

(1) Unless otherwise agreed a term for delivery of goods "ex-ship" (which means from the carrying vessel) or in equivalent language is not restricted to a particular ship and requires delivery from a ship which has reached a place at the named port of destination where goods of the kind are usually discharged.

(2) Under such a term unless otherwise agreed

(a) the seller must discharge all liens arising out of the carriage and furnish the buyer with a direction which puts the carrier under a duty to deliver the goods; and

(b) the risk of loss does not pass to the buyer until the goods leave the ship's tackle or are otherwise properly unloaded.

§ 2—323. Form of Bill of Lading Required in Overseas Shipment; "Overseas".

(1) Where the contract contemplates overseas shipment and contains a term C.I.F. or C. & F. or F.O.B. vessel, the seller unless otherwise agreed must obtain a negotiable bill of lading stating that the goods have been loaded on board or, in the case of a term C.I.F. or C. & F., received for shipment.

(2) Where in a case within subsection (1) a bill of lading has been issued in a set of parts, unless otherwise agreed if the documents are not to be sent from abroad the buyer may demand tender of the full set; otherwise only one part of the bill of lading need be tendered. Even if the agreement expressly requires a full set

(a) due tender of a single part is acceptable within the provisions of this Article on cure of improper delivery (subsection (1) of Section 2—508); and

(b) even though the full set is demanded, if the documents are sent from abroad the person tendering an incomplete set may nevertheless require payment upon furnishing an indemnity which the buyer in good faith deems adequate.

(3) A shipment by water or by air or a contract contemplating such shipment is "overseas" insofar as by usage of trade or agreement it is subject to the commercial, financing or shipping practices characteristic of international deep water commerce.

§ 2—324. "No Arrival, No Sale" Term.

Under a term "no arrival, no sale" or terms of like meaning, unless otherwise agreed,

(a) the seller must properly ship conforming goods and if they arrive by any means he must tender them on arrival but he assumes no obligation that the goods will arrive unless he has caused the non-arrival; and

(b) where without fault of the seller the goods are in part lost or have so deteriorated as no longer to conform to the contract or arrive after the contract time, the buyer may proceed as if there had been casualty to identified goods (Section 2—613).

§ 2—325. "Letter of Credit" Term; "Confirmed Credit".

(1) Failure of the buyer seasonably to furnish an agreed letter of credit is a breach of the contract for sale.

(2) The delivery to seller of a proper letter of credit suspends the buyer's obligation to pay. If the letter of credit is dishonored, the seller may on seasonable notification to the buyer require payment directly from him.

(3) Unless otherwise agreed the term "letter of credit" or "banker's credit" in a contract for sale means an irrevocable credit issued by a financing agency of good repute and, where the shipment is overseas, of good international repute. The term "confirmed credit" means that the credit must also carry the direct obligation of such an agency which does business in the seller's financial market.

§ 2—326. Sale on Approval and Sale or Return; Consignment Sales and Rights of Creditors.

(1) Unless otherwise agreed, if delivered goods may be returned by the buyer even though they conform to the contract, the transaction is

(a) a "sale on approval" if the goods are delivered primarily for use, and

(b) a "sale or return" if the goods are delivered primarily for resale.

(2) Except as provided in subsection (3), goods held on approval are not subject to the claims of the buyer's creditors until acceptance; goods held on sale or return are subject to such claims while in the buyer's possession.

(3) Where goods are delivered to a person for sale and such person maintains a place of business at which he deals in goods of the kind involved, under a name other than the name of the person making delivery, then with respect to claims of creditors of the person conducting the business the goods are deemed to be on sale or return. The provisions of this subsection are applicable even though an agreement purports to reserve title to the person making delivery until payment or resale or uses such words as "on consignment" or "on memorandum". However, this subsection is not applicable if the person making delivery

(a) complies with an applicable law providing for a consignor's interest or the like to be evidenced by a sign, or

(b) establishes that the person conducting the business is generally known by his creditors to be substantially engaged in selling the goods of others, or

(c) complies with the filing provisions of the Article on Secured Transactions (Article 9).

(4) Any "or return" term of a contract for sale is to be treated as a separate contract for sale within the statute of frauds section of this Article (Section 2—201) and as contradicting the sale aspect of the contract within the provisions of this Article on parol or extrinsic evidence (Section 2—202).

§ 2—327. Special Incidents of Sale on Approval and Sale or Return.

(1) Under a sale on approval unless otherwise agreed

(a) although the goods are identified to the contract the risk of loss and the title do not pass to the buyer until acceptance; and

(b) use of the goods consistent with the purpose of trial is not acceptance but failure seasonably to notify the seller of election to return the goods is acceptance, and if the goods conform to the contract acceptance of any part is acceptance of the whole; and

(c) after due notification of election to return, the return is at the seller's risk and expense but a merchant buyer must follow any reasonable instructions.

(2) Under a sale or return unless otherwise agreed

(a) the option to return extends to the whole or any commercial unit of the goods while in substantially their original condition, but must be exercised seasonably; and

(b) the return is at the buyer's risk and expense.

§ 2—328. Sale by Auction.

(1) In a sale by auction if goods are put up in lots each lot is the subject of a separate sale.

(2) A sale by auction is complete when the auctioneer so announces by the fall of the hammer or in other customary manner. Where a bid is made while the hammer is falling in acceptance of a prior bid the auctioneer may in

his discretion reopen the bidding or declare the goods sold under the bid on which the hammer was falling.

(3) Such a sale is with reserve unless the goods are in explicit terms put up without reserve. In an auction with reserve the auctioneer may withdraw the goods at any time until he announces completion of the sale. In an auction without reserve, after the auctioneer calls for bids on an article or lot, that article or lot cannot be withdrawn unless no bid is made within a reasonable time. In either case a bidder may retract his bid until the auctioneer's announcement of completion of the sale, but a bidder's retraction does not revive any previous bid.

(4) If the auctioneer knowingly receives a bid on the seller's behalf or the seller makes or procures such as bid, and notice has not been given that liberty for such bidding is reserved, the buyer may at his option avoid the sale or take the goods at the price of the last good faith bid prior to the completion of the sale. This subsection shall not apply to any bid at a forced sale.

Part 4   Title, Creditors and Good Faith Purchasers

§ 2—401.   **Passing of Title; Reservation for Security; Limited Application of This Section.**

Each provision of this Article with regard to the rights, obligations and remedies of the seller, the buyer, purchasers or other third parties applies irrespective of title to the goods except where the provision refers to such title. Insofar as situations are not covered by the other provisions of this Article and matters concerning title became material the following rules apply:

(1) Title to goods cannot pass under a contract for sale prior to their identification to the contract (Section 2—501), and unless otherwise explicitly agreed the buyer acquires by their identification a special property as limited by this Act. Any retention or reservation by the seller of the title (property) in goods shipped or delivered to the buyer is limited in effect to a reservation of a security interest. Subject to these provisions and to the provisions of the Article on Secured Transactions (Article 9), title to goods passes from the seller to the buyer in any manner and on any conditions explicitly agreed on by the parties.

(2) Unless otherwise explicitly agreed title passes to the buyer at the time and place at which the seller completes his performance with reference to the physical delivery of the goods, despite any reservation of a security interest and even though a document of title is to be delivered at a different time or place; and in particular and despite any reservation of a security interest by the bill of lading

   (a) if the contract requires or authorizes the seller to send the goods to the buyer but does not require him to deliver them at destination, title passes to the buyer at the time and place of shipment; but

   (b) if the contract requires delivery at destination, title passes on tender there.

(3) Unless otherwise explicitly agreed where delivery is to be made without moving the goods,

   (a) if the seller is to deliver a document of title, title passes at the time when and the place where he delivers such documents; or

   (b) if the goods are at the time of contracting already identified and no documents are to be delivered, title passes at the time and place of contracting.

(4) A rejection or other refusal by the buyer to receive or retain the goods, whether or not justified, or a justified revocation of acceptance revests title to the goods in the seller. Such revesting occurs by operation of law and is not a "sale".

§ 2—402.   **Rights of Seller's Creditors Against Sold Goods.**

(1) Except as provided in subsections (2) and (3), rights of unsecured creditors of the seller with respect to goods which have been identified to a contract for sale are subject to the buyer's rights to recover the goods under this Article (Sections 2—502 and 2—716).

(2) A creditor of the seller may treat a sale or an identification of goods to a contract for sale as void if as against him a retention of possession by the seller is fraudulent under any rule of law of the state where the goods are situated, except that retention of possession in good faith and current course of trade by a merchant-seller for a commercially reasonable time after a sale or identification is not fraudulent.

(3) Nothing in this Article shall be deemed to impair the rights of creditors of the seller

   (a) under the provisions of the Article on Secured Transactions (Article 9); or

   (b) where identification to the contract or delivery is made not in current course of trade but in satisfaction of or as security for a pre-existing claim for money, security or the like and is made under circumstances which under any rule of law of the state where the goods are situated would apart from this Article constitute the transaction a fraudulent transfer or voidable preference.

§ 2—403.   **Power to Transfer; Good Faith Purchase of Goods; "Entrusting".**

(1) A purchaser of goods acquires all title which his transferor had or had power to transfer except that a purchaser of a limited interest acquires rights only to the extent of the interest purchased. A person with voidable title has power to transfer a good title to a good faith purchaser for value. When goods have been delivered under a transaction of purchase the purchaser has such power even though

   (a) the transferor was deceived as to the identity of the purchaser, or

   (b) the delivery was in exchange for a check which is later dishonored, or

   (c) it was agreed that the transaction was to be a "cash sale", or

(d) the delivery was procured through fraud punishable as larcenous under the criminal law.

(2) Any entrusting of possession of goods to a merchant who deals in goods of that kind gives him power to transfer all rights of the entruster to a buyer in ordinary course of business.

(3) "Entrusting" includes any delivery and any acquiescence in retention of possession regardless of any condition expressed between the parties to the delivery or acquiescence and regardless of whether the procurement of the entrusting or the possessor's disposition of the goods have been such as to be larcenous under the criminal law.

(4) The rights of other purchasers of goods and of lien creditors are governed by the Articles on Secured Transactions (Article 9), Bulk Transfers (Article 6) and Documents of Title (Article 7).

Part 5   Performance

§ 2—501. Insurable Interest in Goods; Manner of Identification of Goods.

(1) The buyer obtains a special property and an insurable interest in goods by identification of existing goods as goods to which the contract refers even though the goods so identified are non-conforming and he has an option to return or reject them. Such identification can be made at any time and in any manner explicitly agreed to by the parties. In the absence of explicit agreement identification occurs

(a) when the contract is made if it is for the sale of goods already existing and identified;

(b) if the contract is for the sale of future goods other than those described in paragraph (c), when goods are shipped, marked or otherwise designated by the seller as goods to which the contract refers;

(c) when the crops are planted or otherwise become growing crops or the young are conceived if the contract is for the sale of unborn young to be born within twelve months after contracting or for the sale of crops to be harvested within twelve months or the next normal harvest season after contracting whichever is longer.

(2) The seller retains an insurable interest in goods so long as title to or any security interest in the goods remains in him and where the identification is by the seller alone he may until default or insolvency or notification to the buyer that the identification is final substitute other goods for those identified.

(3) Nothing in this section impairs any insurable interest recognized under any other statute or rule of law.

§ 2—502. Buyer's Right to Goods on Seller's Insolvency.

(1) Subject to subsection (2) and even though the goods have not been shipped a buyer who has paid a part or all of the price of goods in which he has a special property under the provisions of the immediately preceding section may on making and keeping good a tender of any unpaid portion of their price recover them from the seller if the seller becomes insolvent within ten days after receipt of the first installment on their price.

(2) If the identification creating his special property has been made by the buyer he acquires the right to recover the goods only if they conform to the contract for sale.

§ 2—503. Manner of Seller's Tender of Delivery.

(1) Tender of delivery requires that the seller put and hold conforming goods at the buyer's disposition and give the buyer any notification reasonably necessary to enable him to take delivery. The manner, time and place for tender are determined by the agreement and this Article, and in particular

(a) tender must be at a reasonable hour, and if it is of goods they must be kept available for the period reasonably necessary to enable the buyer to take possession; but

(b) unless otherwise agreed the buyer must furnish facilities reasonably suited to the receipt of the goods.

(2) Where the case is within the next section respecting shipment tender requires that the seller comply with its provisions.

(3) Where the seller is required to deliver at a particular destination tender requires that he comply with subsection (1) and also in any appropriate case tender documents as described in subsections (4) and (5) of this section.

(4) Where goods are in the possession of a bailee and are to be delivered without being moved

(a) tender requires that the seller either tender a negotiable document of title covering such goods or procure acknowledgment by the bailee of the buyer's right to possession of the goods; but

(b) tender to the buyer of a non-negotiable document of title or of a written direction to the bailee to deliver is sufficient tender unless the buyer seasonably objects, and receipt by the bailee of notification of the buyer's rights fixes those rights as against the bailee and all third persons; but risk of loss of the goods and of any failure by the bailee to honor the non-negotiable document of title or to obey the direction remains on the seller until the buyer has had a reasonable time to present the document or direction, and a refusal by the bailee to honor the document or to obey the direction defeats the tender.

(5) Where the contract requires the seller to deliver documents

(a) he must tender all such documents in correct form, except as provided in this Article with respect to bills of lading in a set (subsection (2) of Section 2—323); and

(b) tender through customary banking channels is sufficient and dishonor of a draft accompanying the documents constitutes non-acceptance or rejection.

§ 2—504. Shipment by Seller.

Where the seller is required or authorized to send the goods to the buyer and the contract does not require him to deliver them at a particular destination, then unless otherwise agreed he must

(a) put the goods in the possession of such a carrier and make such a contract for their transportation as may be reasonable having regard to the nature of the goods and other circumstances of the case; and

(b) obtain and promptly deliver or tender in due form any document necessary to enable the buyer to obtain possession of the goods or otherwise required by the agreement or by usage of trade; and

(c) promptly notify the buyer of the shipment.

Failure to notify the buyer under paragraph (c) or to make a proper contract under paragraph (a) is a ground for rejection only if material delay or loss ensues.

§ 2—505. Seller's Shipment under Reservation.

(1) Where the seller has identified goods to the contract by or before shipment:

(a) his procurement of a negotiable bill of lading to his own order or otherwise reserves in him a security interest in the goods. His procurement of the bill to the order of a financing agency or of the buyer indicates in addition only the seller's expectation of transferring that interest to the person named.

(b) a non-negotiable bill of lading to himself or his nominee reserves possession of the goods as security but except in a case of conditional delivery (subsection (2) of Section 2—507) a non-negotiable bill of lading naming the buyer as consignee reserves no security interest even though the seller retains possession of the bill of lading.

(2) When shipment by the seller with reservation of a security interest is in violation of the contract for sale it constitutes an improper contract for transportation within the preceding section but impairs neither the rights given to the buyer by shipment and identification of the goods to the contract nor the seller's powers as a holder of a negotiable document.

§ 2—506. Rights of Financing Agency.

(1) A financing agency by paying or purchasing for value a draft which relates to a shipment of goods acquires to the extent of the payment or purchase and in addition to its own rights under the draft and any document of title securing it any rights of the shipper in the goods including the right to stop delivery and the shipper's right to have the draft honored by the buyer.

(2) The right to reimbursement of a financing agency which has in good faith honored or purchased the draft under commitment to or authority from the buyer is not impaired by subsequent discovery of defects with reference to any relevant document which was apparently regular on its face.

§ 2—507. Effect of Seller's Tender; Delivery on Condition.

(1) Tender of delivery is a condition to the buyer's duty to accept the goods and, unless otherwise agreed, to his duty to pay for them. Tender entitles the seller to acceptance of the goods and to payment according to the contract.

(2) Where payment is due and demanded on the delivery to the buyer of goods or documents of title, his right as against the seller to retain or dispose of them is conditional upon his making the payment due.

§ 2—508. Cure by Seller of Improper Tender or Delivery; Replacement.

(1) Where any tender or delivery by the seller is rejected because non-conforming and the time for performance has not yet expired, the seller may seasonably notify the buyer of his intention to cure and may then within the contract time make a conforming delivery.

(2) Where the buyer rejects a non-conforming tender which the seller had reasonable grounds to believe would be acceptable with or without money allowance the seller may if he seasonably notifies the buyer have a further reasonable time to substitute a conforming tender.

§ 2—509. Risk of Loss in the Absence of Breach.

(1) Where the contract requires or authorizes the seller to ship the goods by carrier

(a) if it does not require him to deliver them at a particular destination, the risk of loss passes to the buyer when the goods are duly delivered to the carrier even though the shipment is under reservation (Section 2—505); but

(b) if it does require him to deliver them at a particular destination and the goods are there duly tendered while in the possession of the carrier, the risk of loss passes to the buyer when the goods are there duly so tendered as to enable the buyer to take delivery.

(2) Where the goods are held by a bailee to be delivered without being moved, the risk of loss passes to the buyer

(a) on his receipt of a negotiable document of title covering the goods; or

(b) on acknowledgment by the bailee of the buyer's right to possession of the goods; or

(c) after his receipt of a non-negotiable document of title or other written direction to deliver, as provided in subsection (4)(b) of Section 2—503.

(3) In any case not within subsection (1) or (2), the risk of loss passes to the buyer on his receipt of the goods if the seller is a merchant; otherwise the risk passes to the buyer on tender of delivery.

(4) The provisions of this section are subject to contrary agreement of the parties and to the provisions of this

Article on sale on approval (Section 2—327) and on effect of breach on risk of loss (Section 2—510).

§ 2—510. **Effect of Breach on Risk of Loss.**

(1) Where a tender or delivery of goods so fails to conform to the contract as to give a right of rejection the risk of their loss remains on the seller until cure or acceptance.

(2) Where the buyer rightfully revokes acceptance he may to the extent of any deficiency in his effective insurance coverage treat the risk of loss as having rested on the seller from the beginning.

(3) Where the buyer as to conforming goods already identified to the contract for sale repudiates or is otherwise in breach before risk of their loss has passed to him, the seller may to the extent of any deficiency in his effective insurance coverage treat the risk of loss as resting on the buyer for a commercially reasonable time.

§ 2—511. **Tender of Payment by Buyer; Payment by Check.**

(1) Unless otherwise agreed tender of payment is a condition to the seller's duty to tender and complete any delivery.

(2) Tender of payment is sufficient when made by any means or in any manner current in the ordinary course of business unless the seller demands payment in legal tender and gives any extension of time reasonably necessary to procure it.

(3) Subject to the provisions of this Act on the effect of an instrument on an obligation (Section 3—802), payment by check is conditional and is defeated as between the parties by dishonor of the check on due presentment.

§ 2—512. **Payment by Buyer Before Inspection.**

(1) Where the contract requires payment before inspection non-conformity of the goods does not excuse the buyer from so making payment unless

(a) the non-conformity appears without inspection; or

(b) despite tender of the required documents the circumstances would justify injunction against honor under the provisions of this Act (Section 5—114).

(2) Payment pursuant to subsection (1) does not constitute an acceptance of goods or impair the buyer's right to inspect or any of his remedies.

§ 2—513. **Buyer's Right to Inspection of Goods.**

(1) Unless otherwise agreed and subject to subsection (3), where goods are tendered or delivered or identified to the contract for sale, the buyer has a right before payment or acceptance to inspect them at any reasonable place and time and in any reasonable manner. When the seller is required or authorized to send the goods to the buyer, the inspection may be after their arrival.

(2) Expenses of inspection must be borne by the buyer but may be recovered from the seller if the goods do not conform and are rejected.

(3) Unless otherwise agreed and subject to the provisions of this Article on C.I.F. contracts (subsection (3) of Section 2—321), the buyer is not entitled to inspect the goods before payment of the price when the contract provides

(a) for delivery "C.O.D." or on other like terms; or

(b) for payment against documents of title, except where such payment is due only after the goods are to become available for inspection.

(4) A place or method of inspection fixed by the parties is presumed to be exclusive but unless otherwise expressly agreed it does not postpone identification or shift the place for delivery or for passing the risk of loss. If compliance becomes impossible, inspection shall be as provided in this section unless the place or method fixed was clearly intended as an indispensable condition failure of which avoids the contract.

§ 2—514. **When Documents Deliverable on Acceptance; When on Payment.**

Unless otherwise agreed documents against which a draft is drawn are to be delivered to the drawee on acceptance of the draft if it is payable more than three days after presentment; otherwise, only on payment.

§ 2—515. **Preserving Evidence of Goods in Dispute.**

In furtherance of the adjustment of any claim or dispute

(a) either party on reasonable notification to the other and for the purpose of ascertaining the facts and preserving evidence has the right to inspect, test and sample the goods including such of them as may be in the possession or control of the other; and

(b) the parties may agree to a third party inspection or survey to determine the conformity or condition of the goods and may agree that the findings shall be binding upon them in any subsequent litigation or adjustment.

Part 6 **Breach, Repudiation and Excuse**

§ 2—601. **Buyer's Rights on Improper Delivery.**

Subject to the provisions of this Article on breach in installment contracts (Section 2—612) and unless otherwise agreed under the sections on contractual limitations of remedy (Sections 2—718 and 2—719), if the goods or the tender of delivery fail in any respect to conform to the contract, the buyer may

(a) reject the whole; or

(b) accept the whole; or

(c) accept any commercial unit or units and reject the rest.

§ 2—602. **Manner and Effect of Rightful Rejection.**

(1) Rejection of goods must be within a reasonable time

after their delivery or tender. It is ineffective unless the buyer seasonably notifies the seller.

(2) Subject to the provisions of the two following sections on rejected goods (Sections 2—603 and 2—604),

(a) after rejection any exercise of ownership by the buyer with respect to any commercial unit is wrongful as against the seller; and

(b) if the buyer has before rejection taken physical possession of goods in which he does not have a security interest under the provisions of this Article (subsection (3) of Section 2—711), he is under a duty after rejection to hold them with reasonable care at the seller's disposition for a time sufficient to permit the seller to remove them; but

(c) the buyer has no further obligations with regard to goods rightfully rejected.

(3) The seller's rights with respect to goods wrongfully rejected are governed by the provisions of this Article on Seller's remedies in general (Section 2—703).

§ 2—603. Merchant Buyer's Duties as to Rightfully Rejected Goods.

(1) Subject to any security interest in the buyer (subsection (3) of Section 2—711), when the seller has no agent or place of business at the market of rejection a merchant buyer is under a duty after rejection of goods in his possession or control to follow any reasonable instructions received from the seller with respect to the goods and in the absence of such instructions to make reasonable efforts to sell them for the seller's account if they are perishable or threaten to decline in value speedily. Instructions are not reasonable if on demand indemnity for expenses is not forthcoming.

(2) When the buyer sells goods under subsection (1), he is entitled to reimbursement from the seller or out of the proceeds for reasonable expenses of caring for and selling them, and if the expenses include no selling commission then to such commission as is usual in the trade or if there is none to a reasonable sum not exceeding ten per cent on the gross proceeds.

(3) In complying with this section the buyer is held only to good faith and good faith conduct hereunder is neither acceptance nor conversion nor the basis of an action for damages.

§ 2—604. Buyer's Options as to Salvage of Rightfully Rejected Goods.

Subject to the provisions of the immediately preceding section on perishables if the seller gives no instructions within a reasonable time after notification of rejection the buyer may store the rejected goods for the seller's account or reship them to him or resell them for the seller's account with reimbursement as provided in the preceding section. Such action is not acceptance or conversion.

§ 2—605. Waiver of Buyer's Objections by Failure to Particularize.

(1) The buyer's failure to state in connection with rejec-

tion a particular defect which is ascertainable by reasonable inspection precludes him from relying on the unstated defect to justify rejection or to establish breach

(a) where the seller could have cured it if stated seasonably; or

(b) between merchants when the seller has after rejection made a request in writing for a full and final written statement of all defects on which the buyer proposes to rely.

(2) Payment against documents made without reservation of rights precludes recovery of the payment for defects apparent on the face of the documents.

§ 2—606. What Constitutes Acceptance of Goods.

(1) Acceptance of goods occurs when the buyer

(a) after a reasonable opportunity to inspect the goods signifies to the seller that the goods are conforming or that he will take or retain them in spite of their nonconformity; or

(b) fails to make an effective rejection (subsection (1) of Section 2—602), but such acceptance does not occur until the buyer has had a reasonable opportunity to inspect them; or

(c) does any act inconsistent with the seller's ownership; but if such act is wrongful as against the seller it is an acceptance only if ratified by him.

(2) Acceptance of a part of any commercial unit is acceptance of that entire unit.

§ 2—607. Effect of Acceptance; Notice of Breach; Burden of Establishing Breach After Acceptance; Notice of Claim or Litigation to Person Answerable Over.

(1) The buyer must pay at the contract rate for any goods accepted.

(2) Acceptance of goods by the buyer precludes rejection of the goods accepted and if made with knowledge of a non-conformity cannot be revoked because of it unless the acceptance was on the reasonable assumption that the non-conformity would be seasonably cured but acceptance does not of itself impair any other remedy provided by this Article for non-conformity.

(3) Where a tender has been accepted

(a) the buyer must within a reasonable time after he discovers or should have discovered any breach notify the seller of breach or be barred from any remedy; and

(b) if the claim is one for infringement or the like (subsection (3) of Section 2—312) and the buyer is sued as a result of such a breach he must so notify the seller within a reasonable time after he receives notice of the litigation or be barred from any remedy over for liability established by the litigation.

(4) The burden is on the buyer to establish any breach with respect to the goods accepted.

(5) Where the buyer is sued for breach of a warranty or other obligation for which his seller is answerable over

(a) he may give his seller written notice of the litigation. If the notice states that the seller may come in and defend and that if the seller does not do so he will be bound in any action against him by his buyer by any determination of fact common to the two litigations, then unless the seller after seasonable receipt of the notice does come in and defend he is so bound.

(b) if the claim is one for infringement or the like (subsection (3) of Section 2—312) the original seller may demand in writing that his buyer turn over to him control of the litigation including settlement or else be barred from any remedy over and if he also agrees to bear all expense and to satisfy any adverse judgment, then unless the buyer after seasonable receipt of the demand does turn over control the buyer is so barred.

(6) The provisions of subsections (3), (4) and (5) apply to any obligation of a buyer to hold the seller harmless against infringement or the like (subsection (3) of Section 2—312).

§ 2—608. Revocation of Acceptance in Whole or in Part.

(1) The buyer may revoke his acceptance of a lot or commercial unit whose non-conformity substantially impairs its value to him if he has accepted it

(a) on the reasonable assumption that its nonconformity would be cured and it has not been seasonably cured; or

(b) without discovery of such non-conformity if his acceptance was reasonably induced either by the difficulty of discovery before acceptance or by the seller's assurances.

(2) Revocation of acceptance must occur within a reasonable time after the buyer discovers or should have discovered the ground for it and before any substantial change in condition of the goods which is not caused by their own defects. It is not effective until the buyer notifies the seller of it.

(3) A buyer who so revokes has the same rights and duties with regard to the goods involved as if he had rejected them.

§ 2—609. Right to Adequate Assurance of Performance.

(1) A contract for sale imposes an obligation on each party that the other's expectation of receiving due performance will not be impaired. When reasonable grounds for insecurity arise with respect to the performance of either party the other may in writing demand adequate assurance of due performance and until he receives such assurance may if commercially reasonable suspend any performance for which he has not already received the agreed return.

(2) Between merchants the reasonableness of grounds for insecurity and the adequacy of any assurance offered shall be determined according to commercial standards.

(3) Acceptance of any improper delivery or payment does not prejudice the party's right to demand adequate assurance of future performance.

(4) After receipt of a justified demand failure to provide within a reasonable time not exceeding thirty days such assurance of due performance as is adequate under the circumstances of the particular case is a repudiation of the contract.

§ 2—610. Anticipatory Repudiation.

When either party repudiates the contract with respect to a performance not yet due the loss of which will substantially impair the value of the contract to the other, the aggrieved party may

(a) for a commercially reasonable time await performance by the repudiating party; or

(b) resort to any remedy for breach (Section 2—703 or Section 2—711), even though he has notified the repudiating party that he would await the latter's performance and has urged retraction; and

(c) in either case suspend his own performance or proceed in accordance with the provisions of this Article on the seller's right to identify goods to the contract notwithstanding breach or to salvage unfinished goods (Section 2—704).

§ 2—611. Retraction of Anticipatory Repudiation.

(1) Until the repudiating party's next performance is due he can retract his repudiation unless the aggrieved party has since the repudiation cancelled or materially changed his position or otherwise indicated that he considers the repudiation final.

(2) Retraction may be by any method which clearly indicates to the aggrieved party that the repudiating party intends to perform, but must include any assurance justifiably demanded under the provisions of this Article (Section 2—609).

(3) Retraction reinstates the repudiating party's rights under the contract with due excuse and allowance to the aggrieved party for any delay occasioned by the repudiation.

§ 2—612. "Installment Contract"; Breach.

(1) An "installment contract" is one which requires or authorizes the delivery of goods in separate lots to be separately accepted, even though the contract contains a clause "each delivery is a separate contract" or its equivalent.

(2) The buyer may reject any installment which is nonconforming if the non-conformity substantially impairs the value of that installment and cannot be cured or if the non-conformity is a defect in the required documents; but if the non-conformity does not fall within subsection (3) and the seller gives adequate assurance of its cure the buyer must accept that installment.

(3) Whenever non-conformity or default with respect to one or more installments substantially impairs the value of

the whole contract there is a breach of the whole. But the aggrieved party reinstates the contract if he accepts a non-conforming installment without seasonably notifying of cancellation or if he brings an action with respect only to past installments or demands performance as to future installments.

§ 2—613. Casualty to Identified Goods.

Where the contract requires for its performance goods identified when the contract is made, and the goods suffer casualty without fault of either party before the risk of loss passes to the buyer, or in a proper case under a "no arrival, no sale" term (Section 2—324) then

(a) if the loss is total the contract is avoided; and

(b) if the loss is partial or the goods have so deteriorated as no longer to conform to the contract the buyer may nevertheless demand inspection and at his option either treat the contract as voided or accept the goods with due allowance from the contract price for the deterioration or the deficiency in quantity but without further right against the seller.

§ 2—614. Substituted Performance.

(1) Where without fault of either party the agreed berthing, loading, or unloading facilities fail or an agreed type of carrier becomes unavailable or the agreed manner of delivery otherwise becomes commercially impracticable but a commercially reasonable substitute is available, such substitute performance must be tendered and accepted.

(2) If the agreed means or manner of payment fails because of domestic or foreign governmental regulation, the seller may withhold or stop delivery unless the buyer provides a means or manner of payment which is commercially a substantial equivalent. If delivery has already been taken, payment by the means or in the manner provided by the regulation discharges the buyer's obligation unless the regulation is discriminatory, oppressive or predatory.

§ 2—615. Excuse by Failure of Presupposed Conditions.

Except so far as a seller may have assumed a greater obligation and subject to the preceding section on substituted performance:

(a) Delay in delivery or non-delivery in whole or in part by a seller who complies with paragraphs (b) and (c) is not a breach of his duty under a contract for sale if performance as agreed has been made impracticable by the occurrence of a contingency the nonoccurrence of which was a basic assumption on which the contract was made or by compliance in good faith with any applicable foreign or domestic governmental regulation or order whether or not it later proves to be invalid.

(b) Where the causes mentioned in paragraph (a) affect only a part of the seller's capacity to perform, he must allocate production and deliveries among his customers but may at his option include regular customers not then under contract as well as his own requirements for further manufacture. He may so allocate in any manner which is fair and reasonable.

(c) The seller must notify the buyer seasonably that there will be delay or non-delivery and, when allocation is required under paragraph (b), of the estimated quota thus made available for the buyer.

§ 2—616. Procedure on Notice Claiming Excuse.

(1) Where the buyer receives notification of a material or indefinite delay or an allocation justified under the preceding section he may by written notification to the seller as to any delivery concerned, and where the prospective deficiency substantially impairs the value of the whole contract under the provisions of this Article relating to breach of installment contracts (Section 2—612), then also as to the whole,

(a) terminate and thereby discharge any unexecuted portion of the contract; or

(b) modify the contract by agreeing to take his available quota in substitution.

(2) If after receipt of such notification from the seller the buyer fails so to modify the contract within a reasonable time not exceeding thirty days the contract lapses with respect to any deliveries affected.

(3) The provisions of this section may not be negated by agreement except in so far as the seller has assumed a greater obligation under the preceding section.

Part 7 Remedies

§ 2—701. Remedies for Breach of Collateral Contracts Not Impaired.

Remedies for breach of any obligation or promise collateral or ancillary to a contract for sale are not impaired by the provisions of this Article.

§ 2—702. Seller's Remedies on Discovery of Buyer's Insolvency.

(1) Where the seller discovers the buyer to be insolvent he may refuse delivery except for cash including payment for all goods theretofore delivered under the contract, and stop delivery under this Article (Section 2—705).

(2) Where the seller discovers that the buyer has received goods on credit while insolvent he may reclaim the goods upon demand made within ten days after the receipt, but if misrepresentation of solvency has been made to the particular seller in writing within three months before delivery the ten day limitation does not apply. Except as provided in this subsection the seller may not base a right to reclaim goods on the buyer's fraudulent or innocent misrepresentation of solvency or of intent to pay.

(3) The seller's right to reclaim under subsection (2) is subject to the rights of a buyer in ordinary course or other good faith purchaser under this Article (Section 2—403).

Successful reclamation of goods excludes all other remedies with respect to them.

§ 2—703. Seller's Remedies in General.

Where the buyer wrongfully rejects or revokes acceptance of goods or fails to make a payment due on or before delivery or repudiates with respect to a part or the whole, then with respect to any goods directly affected and, if the breach is of the whole contract (Section 2—612), then also with respect to the whole undelivered balance, the aggrieved seller may

(a) withhold delivery of such goods;

(b) stop delivery by any bailee as hereafter provided (Section 2—705);

(c) proceed under the next section respecting goods still unidentified to the contract;

(d) resell and recover damages as hereafter provided (Section 2—706);

(e) recover damages for non-acceptance (Section 2—708) or in a proper case the price (Section 2—709);

(f) cancel.

§ 2—704. Seller's Right to Identify Goods to the Contract Notwithstanding Breach or to Salvage Unfinished Goods.

(1) An aggrieved seller under the preceding section may

(a) identify to the contract conforming goods not already identified if at the time he learned of the breach they are in his possession or control;

(b) treat as the subject of resale goods which have demonstrably been intended for the particular contract even though those goods are unfinished.

(2) Where the goods are unfinished an aggrieved seller may in the exercise of reasonable commercial judgment for the purposes of avoiding loss and of effective realization either complete the manufacture and wholly identify the goods to the contract or cease manufacture and resell for scrap or salvage value or proceed in any other reasonable manner.

§ 2—705. Seller's Stoppage of Delivery in Transit or Otherwise.

(1) The seller may stop delivery of goods in the possession of a carrier or other bailee when he discovers the buyer to be insolvent (Section 2—702) and may stop delivery of carload, truckload, planeload or larger shipments of express or freight when the buyer repudiates or fails to make a payment due before delivery or if for any other reason the seller has a right to withhold or reclaim the goods.

(2) As against such buyer the seller may stop delivery until

(a) receipt of the goods by the buyer; or

(b) acknowledgment to the buyer by any bailee of the goods except a carrier that the bailee holds the goods for the buyer; or

(c) such acknowledgment to the buyer by a carrier by reshipment or as warehouseman; or

(d) negotiation to the buyer of any negotiable document of title covering the goods.

(3) (a) To stop delivery the seller must so notify as to enable the bailee by reasonable diligence to prevent delivery of the goods.

(b) After such notification the bailee must hold and deliver the goods according to the directions of the seller but the seller is liable to the bailee for any ensuing charges or damages.

(c) If a negotiable document of title has been issued for goods the bailee is not obliged to obey a notification to stop until surrender of the document.

(d) A carrier who has issued a non-negotiable bill of lading is not obliged to obey a notification to stop received from a person other than the consignor.

§ 2—706. Seller's Resale Including Contract for Resale.

(1) Under the conditions stated in Section 2—703 on seller's remedies, the seller may resell the goods concerned or the undelivered balance thereof. Where the resale is made in good faith and in a commercially reasonable manner the seller may recover the difference between the resale price and the contract price together with any incidental damages allowed under the provisions of this Article (Section 2—710), but less expenses saved in consequence of the buyer's breach.

(2) Except as otherwise provided in subsection (3) or unless otherwise agreed resale may be at public or private sale including sale by way of one or more contracts to sell or of identification to an existing contract of the seller. Sale may be as a unit or in parcels and at any time and place and on any terms but every aspect of the sale including the method, manner, time, place and terms must be commercially reasonable. The resale must be reasonably identified as referring to the broken contract, but it is not necessary that the goods be in existence or that any or all of them have been identified to the contract before the breach.

(3) Where the resale is at private sale the seller must give the buyer reasonable notification of his intention to resell.

(4) Where the resale is at public sale

(a) only identified goods can be sold except where there is a recognized market for a public sale of futures in goods of the kind; and

(b) it must be made at a usual place or market for public sale if one is reasonably available and except in the case of goods which are perishable or threaten to decline in value speedily the seller must give the buyer reasonable notice of the time and place of the resale; and

(c) if the goods are not to be within the view of those

attending the sale the notification of sale must state the place where the goods are located and provide for their reasonable inspection by prospective bidders; and

(d) the seller may buy.

(5) A purchaser who buys in good faith at a resale takes the goods free of any rights of the original buyer even though the seller fails to comply with one or more of the requirements of this section.

(6) The seller is not accountable to the buyer for any profit made on any resale. A person in the position of a seller (Section 2—707) or a buyer who has rightfully rejected or justifiably revoked acceptance must account for any excess over the amount of his security interest, as hereinafter defined (subsection (3) of Section 2—711).

§ 2—707. **"Person in the Position of a Seller".**

(1) A "person in the position of a seller" includes as against a principal an agent who has paid or become responsible for the price of goods on behalf of his principal or anyone who otherwise holds a security interest or other right in goods similar to that of a seller.

(2) A person in the position of a seller may as provided in this Article withhold or stop delivery (Section 2—705) and resell (Section 2—706) and recover incidental damages (Section 2—710).

§ 2—708. **Seller's Damages for Non-Acceptance or Repudiation.**

(1) Subject to subsection (2) and to the provisions of this Article with respect to proof of market price (Section 2—723), the measure of damages for non-acceptance or repudiation by the buyer is the difference between the market price at the time and place for tender and the unpaid contract price together with any incidental damages provided in this Article (Section 2—710), but less expenses saved in consequence of the buyer's breach.

(2) If the measure of damages provided in subsection (1) is inadequate to put the seller in as good a position as performance would have done then the measure of damages is the profit (including reasonable overhead) which the seller would have made from full performance by the buyer, together with any incidental damages provided in this Article (Section 2—710), due allowance for costs reasonably incurred and due credit for payments or proceeds of resale.

§ 2—709. **Action for the Price.**

(1) When the buyer fails to pay the price as it becomes due the seller may recover, together with any incidental damages under the next section, the price

(a) of goods accepted or of conforming goods lost or damaged within a commercially reasonable time after risk of their loss has passed to the buyer; and

(b) of goods identified to the contract if the seller is unable after reasonable effort to resell them at a reasonable price or the circumstances reasonably indicate that such effort will be unavailing.

(2) Where the seller sues for the price he must hold for the buyer any goods which have been identified to the contract and are still in his control except that if resale becomes possible he may resell them at any time prior to the collection of the judgment. The net proceeds of any such resale must be credited to the buyer and payment of the judgment entitles him to any goods not resold.

(3) After the buyer has wrongfully rejected or revoked acceptance of the goods or has failed to make a payment due or has repudiated (Section 2—610), a seller who is held not entitled to the price under this section shall nevertheless be awarded damages for non-acceptance under the preceding section.

§ 2—710. **Seller's Incidental Damages.**

Incidental damages to an aggrieved seller include any commercially reasonable charges, expenses or commissions incurred in stopping delivery, in the transportation, care and custody of goods after the buyer's breach, in connection with return or resale of the goods or otherwise resulting from the breach.

§ 2—711. **Buyer's Remedies in General; Buyer's Security Interest in Rejected Goods.**

(1) Where the seller fails to make delivery or repudiates or the buyer rightfully rejects or justifiably revokes acceptance then with respect to any goods involved, and with respect to the whole if the breach goes to the whole contract (Section 2—612), the buyer may cancel and whether or not he has done so may in addition to recovering so much of the price as has been paid

(a) "cover" and have damages under the next section as to all the goods affected whether or not they have been identified to the contract; or

(b) recover damages for non-delivery as provided in this Article (Section 2—713).

(2) Where the seller fails to deliver or repudiates the buyer may also

(a) if the goods have been identified recover them as provided in this Article (Section 2—502); or

(b) in a proper case obtain specific performance or replevy the goods as provided in this Article (Section 2—716).

(3) On rightful rejection or justifiable revocation of acceptance a buyer has a security interest in goods in his possession or control for any payments made on their price and any expenses reasonably incurred in their inspection, receipt, transportation, care and custody and may hold such goods and resell them in like manner as an aggrieved seller (Section 2—706).

§ 2—712. **"Cover"; Buyer's Procurement of Substitute Goods.**

(1) After a breach within the preceding section the buyer

may "cover" by making in good faith and without unreasonable delay any reasonable purchase of or contract to purchase goods in substitution for those due from the seller.

(2) The buyer may recover from the seller as damages the difference between the cost of cover and the contract price together with any incidental or consequential damages as hereinafter defined (Section 2—715), but less expenses saved in consequence of the seller's breach.

(3) Failure of the buyer to effect cover within this section does not bar him from any other remedy.

§ 2—713. Buyer's Damages for Non-Delivery or Repudiation.

(1) Subject to the provisions of this Article with respect to proof of market price (Section 2—723), the measure of damages for non-delivery or repudiation by the seller is the difference between the market price at the time when the buyer learned of the breach and the contract price together with any incidental and consequential damages provided in this Article (Section 2—715), but less expenses saved in consequence of the seller's breach.

(2) Market price is to be determined as of the place for tender or, in cases of rejection after arrival or revocation of acceptance, as of the place of arrival.

§ 2—714. Buyer's Damages for Breach in Regard to Accepted Goods.

(1) Where the buyer has accepted goods and given notification (subsection (3) of Section 2—607) he may recover as damages for any non-conformity of tender the loss resulting in the ordinary course of events from the seller's breach as determined in any manner which is reasonable.

(2) The measure of damages for breach of warranty is the difference at the time and place of acceptance between the value of the goods accepted and the value they would have had if they had been as warranted, unless special circumstances show proximate damages of a different amount.

(3) In a proper case any incidental and consequential damages under the next section may also be recovered.

§ 2—715. Buyer's Incidental and Consequential Damages.

(1) Incidental damages resulting from the seller's breach include expenses reasonably incurred in inspection, receipt, transportation and care and custody of goods rightfully rejected, any commercially reasonable charges, expenses or commissions in connection with effecting cover and any other reasonable expense incident to the delay or other breach.

(2) Consequential damages resulting from the seller's breach include

(a) any loss resulting from general or particular requirements and needs of which the seller at the time of contracting had reason to know and which could not reasonably be prevented by cover or otherwise; and

(b) injury to person or property proximately resulting from any breach of warranty.

§ 2—716. Buyer's Right to Specific Performance or Replevin.

(1) Specific performance may be decreed where the goods are unique or in other proper circumstances.

(2) The decree for specific performance may include such terms and conditions as to payment of the price, damages, or other relief as the court may deem just.

(3) The buyer has a right of replevin for goods identified to the contract if after reasonable effort he is unable to effect cover for such goods or the circumstances reasonably indicate that such effort will be unavailing or if the goods have been shipped under reservation and satisfaction of the security interest in them has been made or tendered.

§ 2—717. Deduction of Damages From the Price.

The buyer on notifying the seller of his intention to do so may deduct all or any part of the damages resulting from any breach of the contract from any part of the price still due under the same contract.

§ 2—718. Liquidation or Limitation of Damages; Deposits.

(1) Damages for breach by either party may be liquidated in the agreement but only at an amount which is reasonable in the light of the anticipated or actual harm caused by the breach, the difficulties of proof of loss, and the inconvenience or nonfeasibility of otherwise obtaining an adequate remedy. A term fixing unreasonably large liquidated damages is void as a penalty.

(2) Where the seller justifiably withholds delivery of goods because of the buyer's breach, the buyer is entitled to restitution of any amount by which the sum of his payments exceeds

(a) the amount to which the seller is entitled by virtue of terms liquidating the seller's damages in accordance with subsection (1), or

(b) in the absence of such terms, twenty per cent of the value of the total performance for which the buyer is obligated under the contract or $500, whichever is smaller.

(3) The buyer's right to restitution under subsection (2) is subject to offset to the extent that the seller establishes

(a) a right to recover damages under the provisions of this Article other than subsection (1), and

(b) the amount or value of any benefits received by the buyer directly or indirectly by reason of the contract.

(4) Where a seller has received payment in goods their reasonable value or the proceeds of their resale shall be treated as payments for the purposes of subsection (2); but if the seller has notice of the buyer's breach before reselling goods received in part performance, his resale is subject to the conditions laid down in this Article on resale by an aggrieved seller (Section 2—706).

§ 2—719. **Contractual Modification or Limitation of Remedy.**

(1) Subject to the provisions of subsections (2) and (3) of this section and of the preceding section on liquidation and limitation of damages,

> (a) the agreement may provide for remedies in addition to or in substitution for those provided in this Article and may limit or alter the measure of damages recoverable under this Article, as by limiting the buyer's remedies to return of the goods and repayment of the price or to repair and replacement of nonconforming goods or parts; and

> (b) resort to a remedy as provided is optional unless the remedy is expressly agreed to be exclusive, in which case it is the sole remedy.

(2) Where circumstances cause an exclusive or limited remedy to fail of its essential purpose, remedy may be had as provided in this Act.

(3) Consequential damages may be limited or excluded unless the limitation or exclusion is unconscionable. Limitation of consequential damages for injury to the person in the case of consumer goods is prima facie unconscionable but limitation of damages where the loss is commercial is not.

§ 2—720. **Effect of "Cancellation" or "Rescission" on Claims for Antecedent Breach.**

Unless the contrary intention clearly appears, expressions of "cancellation" or "rescission" of the contract or the like shall not be construed as a renunciation or discharge of any claim in damages for an antecedent breach.

§ 2—721. **Remedies for Fraud.**

Remedies for material misrepresentation or fraud include all remedies available under this Article for non-fraudulent breach. Neither rescission or a claim for rescission of the contract for sale nor rejection or return of the goods shall bar or be deemed inconsistent with a claim for damages or other remedy.

§ 2—722. **Who Can Sue Third Parties for Injury to Goods.**

Where a third party so deals with goods which have been identified to a contract for sale as to cause actionable injury to a party to that contract

(a) a right of action against the third party is in either party to the contract for sale who has title to or a security interest or a special property or an insurable interest in the goods; and if the goods have been destroyed or converted a right of action is also in the party who either bore the risk of loss under the contract for sale or has since the injury assumed that risk as against the other;

(b) if at the time of the injury the party plaintiff did not bear the risk of loss as against the other party to the contract for sale and there is no arrangement between them for disposition of the recovery, his suit or settlement is, subject to his own interest, as a fiduciary for the other party to the contract;

(c) either party may with the consent of the other sue for the benefit of whom it may concern.

§ 2—723. **Proof of Market Price: Time and Place.**

(1) If an action based on anticipatory repudiation comes to trial before the time for performance with respect to some or all of the goods, any damages based on market price (Section 2—708 or Section 2—713) shall be determined according to the price of such goods prevailing at the time when the aggrieved party learned of the repudiation.

(2) If evidence of a price prevailing at the times or places described in this Article is not readily available the price prevailing within any reasonable time before or after the time described or at any other place which in commercial judgment or under usage of trade would serve as a reasonable substitute for the one described may be used, making any proper allowance for the cost of transporting the goods to or from such other place.

(3) Evidence of a relevant price prevailing at a time or place other than the one described in this Article offered by one party is not admissible unless and until he has given the other party such notice as the court finds sufficient to prevent unfair surprise.

§ 2—724. **Admissibility of Market Quotations.**

Whenever the prevailing price or value of any goods regularly bought and sold in any established commodity market is in issue, reports in official publications or trade journals or in newspapers or periodicals of general circulation published as the reports of such market shall be admissible in evidence. The circumstances of the preparation of such a report may be shown to affect its weight but not its admissibility.

§ 2—725. **Statute of Limitations in Contracts for Sale.**

(1) An action for breach of any contract for sale must be commenced within four years after the cause of action has accrued. By the original agreement the parties may reduce the period of limitation to not less than one year but may not extend it.

(2) A cause of action accrues when the breach occurs, regardless of the aggrieved party's lack of knowledge of the breach. A breach of warranty occurs when tender of delivery is made, except that where a warranty explicitly extends to future performance of the goods and discovery of the breach must await the time of such performance the cause of action accrues when the breach is or should have been discovered.

(3) Where an action commenced within the time limited by subsection (1) is so terminated as to leave available a remedy by another action for the same breach such other action may be commenced after the expiration of the time limited and within six months after the termination of the first action unless the termination resulted from voluntary discontinuance or from dismissal for failure or neglect to prosecute.

(4) This section does not alter the law on tolling of the statute of limitations nor does it apply to causes of action which have accrued before this Act becomes effective.

The National Labor Relations Act of 1935 [EXCERPTS]

* * * *

§ 157. Right of Employees as to Organization, Collective Bargaining, etc.

Employees shall have the right to self-organization, to form, join, or assist labor organizations, to bargain collectively through representatives of their own choosing, and to engage in other concerted activities for the purpose of collective bargaining or other mutual aid or protection, and shall also have the right to refrain from any or all of such activities except to the extent that such right may be affected by an agreement requiring membership in a labor organization as a condition of employment as authorized in section 158(a)(3) of this title.

§ 158. Unfair Labor Practices

(a) Unfair labor practices for an employer

It shall be an unfair labor practice for an employer—

(1) to interfere with, restrain, or coerce employees in the exercise of the rights guaranteed in section 157 of this title;

(2) to dominate or interfere with the formation or administration of any labor organization or contribute financial or other support to it: Provided, [t]hat subject to rules and regulations made and published by the Board pursuant to section 156 of this title, an employer shall not be prohibited from permitting employees to confer with him during working hours without loss of time or pay;

(3) by discrimination in regard to hire or tenure of employment or any term or condition of employment to encourage or discourage membership in any labor organization: Provided, [t]hat nothing in this subchapter, or in any other statute of the United States, shall preclude an employer from making an agreement with a labor organization (not established, maintained, or assisted by any action defined in this subsection as an unfair labor practice) to require as a condition of employment membership therein on or after the thirtieth day following the beginning of such employment or the effective date of such agreement, whichever is the later, (i) if such labor organization is the representative of the employees as provided in section 159(a) of this title, in the appropriate collective-bargaining unit covered by such agreement when made, and (ii) unless following an election held as provided in section 159(e) of this title within one year preceding the effective date of such agreement, the Board shall have certified that at least a majority of the employees eligible to vote in such election have voted to rescind the authority of such labor organization to make such an agreement: Provided further, [t]hat no employer shall justify any discrimination against an employee for nonmembership in a labor organization (A) if he has reasonable grounds for believing that such membership was not available to the employee on the same terms and conditions generally applicable to other members, or (B) if he has reasonable grounds for believing that membership was denied or terminated for reasons other than the failure of the employee to tender the periodic dues and the initiation fees uniformly required as a condition of acquiring or retaining membership;

(4) to discharge or otherwise discriminate against an employee because he has filed charges or given testimony under this subchapter;

(5) to refuse to bargain collectively with the representatives of his employees, subject to the provisions of section 159(a) of this title.

(b) Unfair labor practices by labor organization

It shall be an unfair labor practice for a labor organization or its agents—

(1) to restrain or coerce (A) employees in the exercise of the rights guaranteed in section 157 of this title: Provided, [t]hat this paragraph shall not impair the right of a labor organization to prescribe its own rules with respect to the acquisition or retention of membership therein; or (B) an employer in the selection of his representatives for the purposes of collective bargaining or the adjustment of grievances;

(2) to cause or attempt to cause an employer to discriminate against an employee in violation of subsection (a)(3) of this section or to discriminate against an employee with respect to whom membership in such organization has been denied or terminated on some ground other than his failure to tender the periodic dues and the initiation fees uniformly required as a condition of acquiring or retaining membership;

(3) to refuse to bargain collectively with an employer, provided it is the representative of his employees subject to the provisions of section 159(a) of this title;

(4) (i) to engage in, or to induce or encourage any individual employed by any person engaged in commerce or in an industry affecting commerce to engage in, a strike or a refusal in the course of his employment to use, manufacture, process, transport, or otherwise handle or work on any goods, articles, materials, or commodities or to perform any services; or (ii) to threaten, coerce, or restrain any person engaged in commerce or in an industry affecting commerce[.] * * *

(5) to require of employees covered by an agreement authorized under subsection (a)(3) of this section the payment, as a condition precedent to becoming a member of such organization, of a fee in an amount which the Board finds excessive or discriminatory under all the circumstances. In making such a finding, the Board shall consider, among other relevant factors, the practices and customs of labor organizations in the particular industry, and the wages currently paid to the employees affected;

(6) to cause or attempt to cause an employer to pay or deliver or agree to pay or deliver any money or other thing of value, in the nature of an exaction, for services which are not performed or not to be performed; and

(7) to picket or cause to be picketed, or threaten to picket or cause to be picketed, any employer where an object thereof is forcing or requiring an employer to recognize or bargain with a labor organization as the representative of his employees, or forcing or requiring the employees of an employer to accept or select such labor organization as their collective bargaining representative[.] * * *

(c) *Expression of views without threat of reprisal or force or promise of benefit*

The expressing of any views, argument, or opinion, or the dissemination thereof, whether in written, printed, graphic, or visual form, shall not constitute or be evidence of an unfair labor practice under any of the provisions of this subchapter, if such expression contains no threat of reprisal or force or promise of benefit.

(d) *Obligation to bargain collectively*

For the purposes of this section, to bargain collectively is the performance of the mutual obligation of the employer and the representative of the employees to meet at reasonable times and confer in good faith with respect to wages, hours, and other terms and conditions of employment, or the negotiation of an agreement, or any question arising thereunder, and the execution of a written contract incorporating any agreement reached if requested by either party, but such obligation does not compel either party to agree to a proposal or require the making of a concession: Provided, [t]hat where there is in effect a collective-bargaining contract covering employees in an industry affecting commerce, the duty to bargain collectively shall also mean that no party to such contract shall terminate or modify such contract, unless the party desiring such termination or modification—

(1) serves a written notice upon the other party to the contract of the proposed termination or modification sixty days prior to the expiration date thereof, or in the event such contract contains no expiration date, sixty days prior to the time it is proposed to make such termination or modification;

(2) offers to meet and confer with the other party for the purpose of negotiating a new contract or a contract containing the proposed modifications;

(3) notifies the Federal Mediation and Conciliation Service within thirty days after such notice of the existence of a dispute, and simultaneously therewith notifies any State or Territorial agency established to mediate and conciliate disputes within the State or Territory where the dispute occurred, provided no agreement has been reached by that time; and

(4) continues in full force and effect, without resorting to strike or lock-out, all the terms and conditions of the existing contract for a period of sixty days after such notice is given or until the expiration date of such contract, whichever occurs later[.] * * *

The Sherman Act of 1890 [EXCERPTS]

Section 1. Every contract, combination in the form of trust or otherwise, or conspiracy, in restraint of trade or commerce among the several States, or with foreign nations, is declared to be illegal. Every person who shall make any contract or engage in any combination or conspiracy hereby declared to be illegal shall be deemed guilty of a felony, and, on conviction thereof, shall be punished by fine not exceeding $10,000,000 if a corporation, or, if any other person, $350,000, or by imprisonment not exceeding three years, or by both said punishments, in the discretion of the court.

Section 2. Every person who shall monopolize, or attempt to monopolize, or combine or conspire with any other person or persons, to monopolize any part of the trade or commerce among the several States, or with foreign nations, shall be deemed guilty of a felony, and, on conviction thereof, shall be punished by fine not exceeding $10,000,000 if a corporation, or, if any other person, $350,000, or by imprisonment not exceeding three years, or by both said punishments, in the discretion of the court.

Section 3. Every contract, combination in form of trust or otherwise, or conspiracy, in restraint of trade or commerce in any Territory of the United States or of the District of Columbia, or in restraint of trade or commerce between any such Territory and another, or between any such Territory or Territories and any State or States or the District of Columbia, or with foreign nations, or between the District of Columbia and any State or States or foreign nations, is declared illegal. Every person who shall make any such contract or engage in any such combination or conspiracy, shall be deemed guilty of a felony, and, on conviction thereof, shall be punished by fine not exceeding $10,000,000 if a corporation, or, if any other person,

$350,000, or by imprisonment not exceeding three years, or by both said punishments, in the discretion of the court.

* * * *

Section 7. Every combination, conspiracy, trust, agreement, or contract is declared to be contrary to public policy, illegal, and void when the same is made by or between two or more persons or corporations, either of whom, as agent or principal, is engaged in importing any article from any foreign country into the United States, and when such combination, conspiracy, trust, agreement, or contract is intended to operate in restraint of lawful trade, or free competition in lawful trade or commerce, or to increase the market price in any part of the United States of any article or articles imported or intended to be imported into the United States, or of any manufacture into which such imported article enters or is intended to enter. Every person who shall be engaged in the importation of goods or any commodity from any foreign country in violation of this section, or who shall combine or conspire with another to violate the same, is guilty of a misdemeanor, and on conviction thereof in any court of the United States such person shall be fined in a sum not less than $100 and not exceeding $5,000, and shall be further punished by imprisonment, in the discretion of the court, for a term not less than three months nor exceeding twelve months.

Section 8. The word "person", or "persons", wherever used in sections 1 to 7 of this title shall be deemed to include corporations and associations existing under or authorized by the laws of either the United States, the laws of any of the Territories, the laws of any State, or the laws of any foreign country.

The Clayton Act of 1914
[EXCERPTS]

Section 3. That it shall be unlawful for any person engaged in commerce, in the course of such commerce, to lease or make a sale or contract for sale of goods, wares, merchandise, machinery, supplies, or other commodities, whether patented or unpatented, for use, consumption, or resale within the United States or * * * other place under the jurisdiction of the United States, or fix a price charged therefor, or discount from, or rebate upon, such price, on the condition, agreement, or understanding that the lessee or purchaser thereof shall not use or deal in the goods, wares, merchandise, machinery, supplies, or other commodities of a competitor or competitors of the lessor or seller, where the effect of such lease, sale, or contract for sale or such condition, agreement, or understanding may be to substantially lessen competition to tend to create a monopoly in any line of commerce.

Section 4. That any person who shall be injured in his business or property by reason of anything forbidden in the antitrust laws may sue therefor in any district court of the United States in the district in which the defendant resides or is found, or has an agent, without respect to the amount in controversy, and shall recover threefold the damages by him sustained, and the cost of suit, including a reasonable attorney's fee.

Section 4A. Whenever the United States is hereafter injured in its business or property by reason of anything forbidden in the antitrust laws it may sue therefor in the United States district court for the district in which the defendant resides or is found or has an agent, without respect to the amount in controversy, and shall recover actual damages by it sustained and the cost of suit.

Section 4B. Any action to enforce any cause of action under sections 4 or 4A shall be forever barred unless commenced within four years after the cause of action accrued. No cause of action barred under existing law on the effective date of this act shall be revived by this Act.

* * * *

Section 6. That the labor of a human being is not a commodity or article of commerce. Nothing contained in the antitrust laws shall be construed to forbid the existence and operation of labor, agricultural or horticultural organizations, instituted for the purposes of mutual help, and not having capital stock or conducted for profit, or to forbid or restrain individual members of such organizations from lawfully carrying out the legitimate objects thereof; nor shall such organizations or the members thereof, be held or construed to be illegal combinations or conspiracies in restraint of trade, under the antitrust laws.

Section 7. That no person engaged in commerce shall acquire, directly or indirectly, the whole or any part of the stock or other share capital and no corporation subject to the jurisdiction of the Federal Trade Commission shall acquire the whole or any part of the assets of another corporation engaged also in commerce, where in any line of commerce in any section of the country, the effect of such acquisition may be substantially to lessen competition, or to tend to create a monopoly.

No person shall acquire, directly or indirectly, the whole or any part of the stock or other share capital and no corporation subject to the jurisdiction of the Federal Trade Commission shall acquire the whole or any part of the assets of one or more corporations engaged in commerce, where in any line of commerce in any section of the country, the effect of such acquisition, of such stocks or assets, or of the use of such stock by the voting or granting of proxies or otherwise, may be substantially to lessen competition, or to tend to create a monopoly.

This section shall not apply to persons purchasing such stock solely for investment and not using the same by voting or otherwise to bring about, or in attempting to bring about, the substantial lessening of competition * * * .

Section 8. * * * No person at the same time shall be a director in any two or more corporations any one of which has capital, surplus, and undivided profits aggregating more than $1,000,000 engaged in whole or in part in commerce, * * * if such corporations are or shall have been theretofore, by virtue of their business and location of operation, competitors, so that the elimination of competition by agreement between them would constitute a violation of any of the provisions of the antitrust laws. * * *

The Federal Trade Commission Act of 1914 [EXCERPTS]

Section 5.

(a)(1) Unfair methods of competition in or affecting commerce, and unfair or deceptive acts or practices in or affecting commerce, are hereby declared unlawful.

(2) The Commission is hereby empowered and directed to prevent persons, partnerships, or corporations from using unfair methods of competition in or affecting commerce and unfair or deceptive acts or practices in or affecting commerce.

(1) Any person, partnership, or corporation who violates an order of the Commission after it has become final, and while such order is in effect, shall forfeit and pay to the United States a civil penalty of not more than $10,000 for each violation, which shall accrue to the United States and may be recovered in a civil action brought by the Attorney General of the United States. Each separate violation of such an order shall be a separate offense, except that in the case of a violation through continuing failure to obey or neglect to obey a final order of the Commission, each day of continuance of such failure or neglect shall be deemed a separate offense. In such actions, the United States district courts are empowered to grant mandatory injunctions and such other and further equitable relief as they deem appropriate in the enforcement of such final orders of the Commission.

The Robinson-Patman Act of 1936 [EXCERPTS]

Section 2. Discrimination in Price, Services, or Facilities—Price; Selection of Customers

(a) It shall be unlawful for any person engaged in commerce, in the course of such commerce, either directly or indirectly, to discriminate in price between different purchasers of commodities of like grade and quality, where either or any of the purchases involved in such discrimination are in commerce, where such commodities are sold for use, consumption, or resale within the United States or any Territory thereof or the District of Columbia or any insular possession or other place under the jurisdiction of the United States, and where the effect of such discrimination may be substantially to lessen competition or tend to create a monopoly in any line of commerce, or to injure, destroy, or prevent competition with any person who either grants or knowingly receives the benefit of such discrimination, or with customers of either of them; Provided, That nothing herein contained shall prevent differentials which make only due allowance for differences in the cost of manufacture, sale, or delivery resulting from the differing methods or quantities in which such commodities are to such purchasers sold or delivered: Provided, however, That the Federal Trade Commission may, after due investigation and hearing to all interested parties, fix and establish quantity limits, and revise the same as it finds necessary, as to particular commodities or classes of commodities, where it finds that available purchasers in greater quantities are so few as to render differentials on account thereof unjustly discriminatory or promotive of monopoly in any line of commerce; and the foregoing shall then not be construed to permit differentials based on differences in quantities greater than those so fixed and established: And provided further, That nothing herein contained shall prevent persons engaged in selling goods, wares, or merchandise in commerce from selecting their own customers in bona fide transactions and not in restraint of trade: And provided further, That nothing herein contained shall prevent price changes from time to time where in response to changing conditions affecting the market for or the marketability of the goods concerned, such as but not limited to actual or imminent deterioration of perishable goods, obsolescence of seasonal goods, distress sales under court process, or sales in good faith in discontinuance of business in the goods concerned.

Burden of Rebutting Prima-Facie Case of Discrimination

(b) Upon proof being made, at any hearing on a complaint under this section, that there has been discrimination in price or services or facilities furnished, the burden of rebutting the prima-facie case thus made by showing justification shall be upon the person charged with a violation of this section, and unless justification shall be affirmatively shown, the Commission is authorized to issue an order terminating the discrimination: Provided, however, That nothing herein contained shall prevent a seller rebutting the prima-facie case thus made by showing that his [or her] lower price or the furnishing of services or facilities to any purchaser or purchasers was made in good faith to meet an equally low price of a competitor, or the services or facilities furnished by a competitor.

Payment or Acceptance of Commission, Brokerage, or Other Compensation

(c) It shall be unlawful for any person engaged in commerce, in the course of such commerce, to pay or grant, or to receive or accept, anything of value as a commission, brokerage, or other compensation, or any allowance or discount in lieu thereof, except for services rendered in connection with the sale or purchase of goods, wares, or merchandise, either to the other party to such transaction or to an agent, representative, or other intermediary therein where such intermediary is acting in fact for or in behalf, or is subject to the direct or indirect control, of any party to such transaction other than the person by whom such compensation is so granted or paid.

Payment for Services or Facilities for Processing or Sale

(d) It shall be unlawful for any person engaged in commerce to pay or contract for the payment of anything of value to or for the benefit of a customer of such person in the course of such commerce as compensation or in consideration for any services or facilities furnished by or through such customer in connection with the processing, handling, sale or offering for sale of any products or commodities manufactured, sold, or offered for sale by such person, unless such payment or consideration is available on proportionally equal terms to all other customers competing in the distribution of such products or commodities.

Furnishing Services or Facilities for Processing, Handling, etc.

(e) It shall be unlawful for any person to discriminate in favor of one purchaser against another purchaser or purchasers of a commodity bought for resale, with or without processing, by contracting to furnish or furnishing, or by contributing to the furnishing of, any services or facilities connected with the processing, handling, sale, or offering for sale of such commodity so purchased upon terms not accorded to all purchasers on proportionally equal terms.

Knowingly Inducing or Receiving Discriminatory Price

(f) It shall be unlawful for any person engaged in commerce, in the course of such commerce, knowingly to induce or receive a discrimination in price which is prohibited by this section.

Section 3. Discrimination in Rebates, Discounts, or Advertising Service Charges; Underselling in Particular Localities; Penalties

It shall be unlawful for any person engaged in commerce, in the course of such commerce, to be a party to, or assist in, any transaction of sale, or contract to sell, which discriminates to his [or her] knowledge against competitors of the purchaser, in that, any discount, rebate, allowance, or advertising service charge is granted to the purchaser over and above any discount, rebate, allowance, or advertising service charge available at the time of such transaction to said competitors in respect of a sale of goods of like grade, quality, and quantity; to sell, or contract to sell, goods in any part of the United States at prices lower than those exacted by said person elsewhere in the United States for the purpose of destroying competition, or eliminating a competitor in such part of the United States; or, to sell, or contract to sell, goods at unreasonably low prices for the purpose of destroying competition or eliminating a competitor.

Any person violating any of the provisions of this section shall, upon conviction thereof, be fined not more than $5,000 or imprisoned not more than one year, or both.

Securities Act of 1933
[EXCERPTS]

Definitions

Section 2. When used in this title, unless the context requires—

(1) The term "security" means any note, stock, treasury stock, bond, debenture, evidence of indebtedness, certificate of interest or participation in any profit-sharing agreement, collateral-trust certificate, preorganization certificate or subscription, transferable share, investment contract, voting-trust certificate, certificate of deposit for a security, fractional undivided interest in oil, gas, or other mineral rights, any put, call, straddle, option, or privilege on any security, certificate of deposit, or group or index of securities (including any interest therein or based on the value thereof), or any put, call, straddle, option, or privilege entered into on a national securities exchange relating to foreign currency, or, in general, any interest or participation in, temporary or interim certificate for, receipt for, guarantee of, or warrant or right to subscribe to or purchase, any of the foregoing.

Exempted Securities

Section 3. (a) Except as hereinafter expressly provided the provisions of this title shall not apply to any of the following classes of securities:

* * * *

(2) Any security issued or guaranteed by the United States or any territory thereof, or by the District of Columbia, or by any State of the United States, or by any political subdivision of a State or Territory, or by any public instrumentality of one or more States or Territories, or by any person controlled or supervised by and acting as an instrumentality of the Government of the United States pursuant to authority granted by the Congress of the United States; or any certificate of deposit for any of the foregoing; or any security issued or guaranteed by any bank; or any security issued by or representing an interest in or a direct obligation of a Federal Reserve Bank. * * *

(3) Any note, draft, bill of exchange, or banker's acceptance which arises out of a current transaction or the proceeds of which have been or are to be used for current transactions, and which has a maturity at the time of issuance of not exceeding nine months, exclusive of days of grace, or any renewal thereof the maturity of which is likewise limited;

(4) Any security issued by a person organized and operated exclusively for religious, educational, benevolent, fraternal, charitable, or reformatory purposes and not for pecuniary profit, and no part of the net earnings of which inures to the benefit of any person, private stockholder, or individual;

* * * *

(11) Any security which is a part of an issue offered and sold only to persons resident within a single State or Territory, where the issuer of such security is a person resident and doing business within, or, if a corporation, incorporated by and doing business within, such State or Territory.

(b) The Commission may from time to time by its rules and regulations and subject to such terms and conditions as may be described therein, add any class of securities to the securities exempted as provided in this section, if it finds that the enforcement of this title with respect to such securities is not necessary in the public interest and for the protection of investors by reason of the small amount involved or the limited character of the public offering; but no issue of securities shall be exempted under this subsection where the aggregate amount at which such issue is offered to the public exceeds $5,000,000.

Exempted Transactions

Section 4. The provisions of section 5 shall not apply to—

(1) transactions by any person other than an issuer, underwriter, or dealer.

(2) transactions by an issuer not involving any public offering.

(3) transactions by a dealer (including an underwriter no longer acting as an underwriter in respect of the security involved in such transactions), except—

(A)   transactions taking place prior to the expiration of forty days after the first date upon which the security was bona fide offered to the public by the issuer or by or through an underwriter.

(B)   transactions in a security as to which a registration statement has been filed taking place prior to the expiration of forty days after the effective date of such registration statement or prior to the expiration of forty days after the first date upon which the security was bona fide offered to the public by the issuer or by or through an underwriter after such effective date, whichever is later (excluding in the computation of such forty days any time during which a stop order issued under section 8 is in effect as to the security), or such shorter period as the Commission may specify by rules and regulations or order, and

(C) transactions as to the securities constituting the whole or a part of an unsold allotment to or subscription by such dealer as a participant in the distribution of such securities by the issuer or by or through an underwriter.

With respect to transactions referred to in clause (B), if securities of the issuer have not previously been sold pursuant to an earlier effective registration statement the applicable period, instead of forty days, shall be ninety days, or such shorter period as the Commission may specify by rules and regulations or order.

(4) brokers' transactions, executed upon customers' orders on any exchange or in the over-the-counter market but not the solicitation of such orders.

* * * *

(6) transactions involving offers or sales by an issuer solely to one or more accredited investors, if the aggregate offering price of an issue of securities offered in reliance on this paragraph does not exceed the amount allowed under Section 3(b) of this title, if there is no advertising or public solicitation in connection with the transaction by the issuer or anyone acting on the issuer's behalf, and if the issuer files such notice with the Commission as the Commission shall prescribe.

Prohibitions Relating to Interstate Commerce and the Mails

Section 5. (a) Unless a registration statement is in effect as to a security, it shall be unlawful for any person, directly or indirectly—

(1) to make use of any means or instruments of transportation or communication in interstate commerce or of the mails to sell such security through the use or medium of any prospectus or otherwise; or

(2) to carry or cause to be carried through the mails or in interstate commerce, by any means or instruments of transportation, any such security for the purpose of sale or for delivery after sale.

(b) It shall be unlawful for any person, directly or indirectly—

(1) to make use of any means or instruments of transportation or communication in interstate commerce or of the mails to carry or transmit any prospectus relating to any security with respect to which a registration statement has been filed under this title, unless such prospectus meets the requirements of section 10, or

(2) to carry or to cause to be carried through the mails or in interstate commerce any such security for the purpose of sale or for delivery after sale, unless accompanied or preceded by a prospectus that meets the requirements of subsection (a) of section 10.

(c) It shall be unlawful for any person, directly, or indirectly, to make use of any means or instruments of transportation or communication in interstate commerce or of the mails to offer to sell or offer to buy through the use or medium of any prospectus or otherwise any security, unless a registration statement has been filed as to such security, or while the registration statement is the subject of a refusal order or stop order or (prior to the effective date of the registration statement) any public proceeding of examination under section 8.

Securities Exchange Act of 1934 [EXCERPTS]

Definitions and Application of Title

Section 3. (a) When used in this title, unless the context otherwise requires—

* * * *

(4) The term "broker" means any person engaged in the business of effecting transactions in securities for the account of others, but does not include a bank.

(5) The term "dealer" means any person engaged in the business of buying and selling securities for his own account, through a broker or otherwise, but does not include a bank, or any person insofar as he buys or sells securities for his own account, either individually or in some fiduciary capacity, but not as part of a regular business.

* * * *

(7) The term "director" means any director of a corporation or any person performing similar functions with respect to any organization, whether incorporated or unincorporated.

(8) The term "issuer" means any person who issues or proposes to issue any security; except that with respect to certificates of deposit for securities, voting-trust certificates, or collateral-trust certificates, or with respect to certificates of interest or shares in an unincorporated investment trust not having a board of directors or the fixed, restricted management, or unit type, the term "issuer" means the person or persons performing the acts and assuming the duties of depositor or manager pursuant to the provisions of the trust or other agreement or instrument under which such securities are issued; and except that with respect to equipment-trust certificates or like securities, the term "issuer" means the person by whom the equipment or property is, or is to be, used.

(9) The term "person" means a natural person, company, government, or political subdivision, agency, or instrumentality of a government.

Regulation of the Use of Manipulative and Deceptive Devices

Section 10. It shall be unlawful for any person, directly or indirectly, by the use of any means or instrumentality of interstate commerce or of the mails, or of any facility of any national securities exchange—

(a) To effect a short sale, or to use or employ any stop-loss order in connection with the purchase or sale, of any security registered on a national securities exchange, in contravention of such rules and regulations as the Commission may prescribe as necessary or appropriate in the public interest or for the protection of investors.

(b) To use or employ, in connection with the purchase or sale of any security registered on a national securities exchange or any security not so registered, any manipulative or deceptive device or contrivance in contravention of such rules and regulations as the Commission may prescribe as necessary or appropriate in the public interest or for the protection of investors.

Title VII of the Civil Rights Act of 1964
[EXCERPTS]

Section 703. Unlawful Employment Practices. (a) It shall be an unlawful employment practice for an employer—

(1) to fail or refuse to hire or to discharge any individual, or otherwise to discriminate against any individual with respect to his compensation, terms, conditions, or privileges of employment, because of such individual's race, color, religion, sex, or national origin; or

(2) to limit, segregate, or classify his employees or applicants for employment in any way which would deprive or tend to deprive any individual of employment opportunities or otherwise adversely affect his status as an employee, because of such individual's race, color, religion, sex, or national origin.

(b) It shall be an unlawful employment practice for an employment agency to fail or refuse to refer for employment, or otherwise to discriminate against, any individual because of his race, color, religion, sex, or national origin, or to classify or refer for employment any individual on the basis or his race, color, religion, sex, or national origin.

(c) It shall be an unlawful employment practice for a labor organization—

(1) to exclude or to expel from its membership, or otherwise to discriminate against, any individual because of his race, color, religion, sex, or national origin;

(2) to limit, segregate, or classify its membership or applicants for membership, or to classify or fail or refuse to refer for employment any individual, in any way which would deprive or tend to deprive any individual of employment opportunities, or would limit such employment opportunities or otherwise adversely affect his status as an employee or as an applicant for employment, because of such individual's race, color, religion, sex, or national origin; or

(3) to cause or attempt to cause an employer to discriminate against an individual in violation of this section.

(d) It shall be an unlawful employment practice for any employer, labor organization, or joint labor-management committee controlling apprenticeship or other training or retraining, including on-the-job training programs to discriminate against any individual because of his race, color, religion, sex, or national origin in admission to, or employment in, any program established to provide apprenticeship or other training.

(e) Notwithstanding any other provision of this subchapter—

(1) it shall not be an unlawful employment practice for an employer to hire and employ employees, for an employment agency to classify, or refer for employment any individual, for a labor organization to classify its membership or to classify or refer for employment any individual, or for an employer, labor organization, or joint labor-management committee controlling apprenticeship or other training or retraining programs to admit or employ any individual in any such program, on the basis of his religion, sex, or national origin in those certain instances where religion, sex, or national origin is a bona fide occupational qualification reasonably necessary to the normal operation of that particular business or enterprise, and

(2) it shall not be an unlawful employment practice for a school, college, university, or other educational institution or institution of learning to hire and employ employees of a particular religion if such school, college, university, or other educational institution or institution of learning is, in whole or in substantial part, owned, supported, controlled, or managed by a particular religion or by a particular religious corporation, association, or society, or if the curriculum of such school, college, university, or other educational institution or institution of learning is directed toward the propagation of a particular religion.

(f) As used in this subchapter, the phrase "unlawful employment practice" shall not be deemed to include any action or measure taken by an employer, labor organization, joint labor-management committee, or employment agency with respect to an individual who is a member of the Communist Party of the United States or of any other organization required to register as a Communist-action or Communist-front organization. * * *

(g) Notwithstanding any other provision of this subchapter, it shall not be an unlawful employment practice for an employer to fail or refuse to hire and employ any individual for any position, for an employer to discharge any individual from any position, or for an employment agency to fail or refuse to refer any individual for employment in any position, or for a labor organization to fail or refuse to refer any individual for employment in any position, if—

(1) the occupancy of such position, or access to the premises in or upon which any part of the duties of such position is performed or is to be performed, is subject to any requirement imposed in the interest of the national security of the United States * * * and

(2) such individual has not fulfilled or has ceased to fulfill that requirement.

(h) Notwithstanding any other provision of this subchapter, it shall not be an unlawful employment practice for an employer to apply different standards of compensation, or different terms, conditions, or privileges of employment pursuant to a bona fide seniority or merit system, or a system which measures earnings by quantity or quality of production or to employees who work in different locations, provided that such differences are not the result of an intention to discriminate because of race, color, religion, sex, or national origin, nor shall it be an unlawful employment practice for an employer to give and act upon the results of any professionally developed ability test provided that such test, its administration or action upon the results is not designed, intended or used to discriminate because of race, color, religion, sex, or national origin. * * *

(j) Nothing contained in this subchapter shall be interpreted to require any employer, employment agency, labor organization, or joint labor management committee subject to this subchapter to grant preferential treatment to any individual or to any group because of the race, color, religion, sex, or national origin of such individual or group on account of an imbalance which may exist with respect to the total number or percentage of persons of any race, color, religion, sex, or national origin employed by any employer, referred or classified for employment by any employment agency or labor organization, or admitted to, or employed in, any apprenticeship or other training program, in comparison with the total number or percentage of persons of such race, color, religion, sex, or

national origin in any community, State, section, or other area, or in the available work force in any community, State, section, or other area.

* * * *

Section 704. **Other Unlawful Employment Practices.** (a) It shall be an unlawful employment practice for an employer to discriminate against any of his employees or applicants for employment, for an employment agency, or joint labor-management committee controlling apprenticeship or other training or retraining, including on-the-job training programs, to discriminate against any individual, or for a labor organization to discriminate against any member thereof or applicant for membership, because he has opposed any practice made an unlawful employment practice by this subchapter, or because he has made a charge, testified, assisted, or participated in any manner in an investigation, proceeding, or hearing under this subchapter.

(b) It shall be an unlawful employment practice for an employer, labor organization, employment agency, or joint labor-management committee controlling apprenticeship or other training or retraining, including on-the-job training programs, to print or publish or cause to be printed or published any notice or advertisement relating to employment by such an employer or membership or any classification or referral for employment by such a labor organization, or relating to any classification or referral for employment by such an employment agency, or relating to admission to, or employment in, any program established to provide apprenticeship or other training by such a joint-labor-management committee, indicating any preference, limitation, specification, or discrimination, based on race, color, religion, sex, or national origin, except that such a notice or advertisement may indicate a preference, limitation, specification, or discrimination based on religion, sex or national origin when religion, sex, or national origin is a bona fide occupational qualification for employment.

The Civil Rights Act of 1991 [EXCERPTS]

Section 3. **Purposes.**

The purposes of this Act are—

(1) to provide appropriate remedies for intentional discrimination and unlawful harassment in the workplace;

(2) to codify the concepts of "business necessity" and "job related" enunciated by the Supreme Court in Griggs v. Duke Power Co., 401 U.S. 424 (1971), and in the other Supreme Court decisions prior to Wards Cove Packing Co. v. Atonio, 490 U.S. 642 (1989);

(3) to confirm statutory authority and provide statutory guidelines for the adjudication of disparate impact suits under title VII of the Civil Rights Act of 1964 (42 U.S.C. 2000e et seq.); and

(4) to respond to recent decisions of the Supreme Court by expanding the scope of relevant civil rights statutes in order to provide adequate protection to victims of discrimination.

Section 101. **Prohibition against All Racial Discrimination in the Making and Enforcement of Contracts.**

Section 1977 of the Revised Statutes (42 U.S.C. 1981) is amended * * * by adding at the end the following new subsections:

(b) For purposes of this section, the term "make and enforce contracts" includes the making, performance, modification, and termination of contracts, and the enjoyment of all benefits, privileges, terms, and conditions of the contractual relationship.

(c) The rights protected by this section are protected against impairment by nongovernmental discrimination and impairment under color of State law.

Section 102. **Damages in Cases of Intentional Discrimination.**

The Revised Statutes are amended by inserting after section 1977 (42 U.S.C.1981) the following new section:

Section 1977A. **Damages in Cases of Intentional Discrimination in Employment.**

(a) Right of Recovery.—

(1) Civil Rights.—In an action brought by a complaining party under section 706 or 717 of the Civil Rights Act of 1964 (42 U.S.C. 2000e-5) against a respondent who engaged in unlawful intentional discrimination (not an employment practice that is unlawful because of its disparate impact) prohibited under section 703, 704, or 717 of the Act (42 U.S.C. 2000e-2 or 2000e-3), and provided that the complaining party cannot recover under section 1977 of the Revised Statutes (42 U.S.C. 1981), the complaining party may recover compensatory and punitive damages as allowed in subsection (b), in addition to any relief authorized by section 706(g) of the Civil Rights Act of 1964, from the respondent.

* * * *

(b) Compensatory and Punitive Damages.—

(1) Determination of Punitive Damages.—A complaining party may recover punitive damages under this section against a respondent (other than a government, government agency or political subdivision) if the complaining party demonstrates that the respondent engaged in a discriminatory practice or discriminatory practices with malice or with reckless indifference to the federally protected rights of an aggrieved individual.

(2) Exclusions from Compensatory Damages.— Compensatory damages awarded under this section shall not include backpay, interest on backpay, or any other type of relief authorized under section 706(g) of the Civil Rights Act of 1964.

(3) Limitations.—The sum of the amount of compensatory damages awarded under this section for future pecuniary losses, emotional pain, suffering, inconvenience, mental anguish, loss of enjoyment of life, and other nonpecuniary losses, and the amount of punitive damages awarded under this section, shall not exceed, for each complaining party—

(A) in the case of a respondent who has more than 14 and fewer than 101 employees in each of 20 or more calendar weeks in the current or preceding calendar year, $50,000;

(B) in the case of a respondent who has more than 100 and fewer than 201 employees in each of 20 or more calendar weeks in the current or preceding calendar year, $100,000; and

(C) in the case of a respondent who has more than 200 and fewer than 501 employees in each of 20 or more calendar weeks in the current or preceding calendar year, $200,000; and

(D) in the case of a respondent who has more than 500 employees in each of 20 or more calendar weeks in the current or preceding calendar year, $300,000.

* * * *

Section 105. **Burden of Proof in Disparate Impact Cases.**

(a) Section 703 of the Civil Rights Act of 1964 (42 U.S.C. 2000e-2) is amended by adding at the end the following new [subsections to 703(k)(1)]—

(A) An unlawful employment practice based on disparate impact is established under this title only if—

(i) a complaining party demonstrates that a respondent uses a particular employment practice that causes a disparate impact on the basis of race, color, religion, sex, or national origin and the respondent fails to demonstrate that the challenged practice is job related for the position in question and consistent with business necessity; or

(ii) the complaining party makes the demonstration described in subparagraph (C) with respect to an alternative employment practice and the respondent refuses to adopt such alternative employment practice.

* * * *

(C) The demonstration referred to by subparagraph (A)(ii) shall be in accordance with the law as it existed on June 4, 1989, with respect to the concept of "alternative employment practice."

* * * *

Section 107. **Clarifying Prohibition against Impermissible Consideration of Race, Color, Religion, Sex, or National Origin in Employment Practices.**

(a) In General.—Section 703 of the Civil Rights Act of 1964 (42 U.S.C. 2000e-2) (as amended by sections 105 and 106) is further amended by adding at the end the following new subsection:

(m) Except as otherwise provided in this title, an unlawful employment practice is established when the complaining party demonstrates that race, color, religion, sex, or national origin was a motivating factor for any employment practice, even though other factors also motivated the practice.

* * * *

Section 109. **Protection of Extraterritorial Employment.**

(a) Definition of Employee.—Section 701(f) of the Civil Rights Act of 1964 (42 U.S.C. 2000e(f)) and section 101(4) of the Americans with Disabilities Act of 1990 (42 U.S.C. 12111(4)) are each amended by adding at the end the following: "With respect to employment in a foreign country, such term includes an individual who is a citizen of the United States."

Americans with Disabilities Act of 1990 [EXCERPTS]

Title I—EMPLOYMENT

Sec. 101. Definitions.

As used in this title: * * *

(8) **Qualified individual with a disability.**—The term "qualified individual with a disability" means an individual with a disability who, with or without reasonable accommodation, can perform the essential functions of the employment position that such individual holds or desires. For the purposes of this title, consideration shall be given to the employer's judgment as to what functions of a job are essential, and if an employer has prepared a written description before advertising or interviewing applicants for the job, this description shall be considered evidence of the essential functions of the job.

(9) **Reasonable accommodation.**—The term "reasonable accommodation" may include—

(A) making existing facilities used by employees readily accessible to and usable by individuals with disabilities; and

(B) job restructuring, part-time or modified work schedules, reassignment to a vacant position, acquisition or modification of equipment or devices, appropriate adjustment or modifications of examinations, training materials or policies, the provision of qualified readers or interpreters, and other similar accommodations for individuals with disabilities.

(10) **Undue Hardship.**—

(A) **In general.**—The term "undue hardship" means an action requiring significant difficulty or expense, when considered in light of the factors set forth in subparagraph (B).

(B) **Factors to be considered.**—In determining whether an accommodation would impose an undue hardship on a covered entity, factors to be considered include—

(i) the nature and cost of accommodation needed under this Act;

(ii) the overall financial resources of the facility or facilities involved in the provision of the reasonable accommodation; the number of persons employed at such facility; the effect on expenses and resources, or the impact otherwise of such accommodation upon the operation of the facility;

(iii) the overall financial resources of the covered entity; the overall size of the business of a covered entity with respect to the number of its employees; the number, type, and location of its facilities; and

(iv) the type of operation or operations of the covered entity, including the composition, structure, and functions of the workforce of such entity; the geographic separateness, administrative, or fiscal relationship of the facility or facilities in question to the covered entity.

Sec. 102. Discrimination.

(a) **General Rule.**—No covered entity shall discriminate against a qualified individual with a disability because of the disability of such individual in regard to job application procedures, the hiring, advancement, or discharge of employees, employee compensation, job training, and other terms, conditions, and privileges of employment.

(b) **Construction.**—As used in subsection (a), the term "discriminate" includes—

(1) limiting, segregating, or classifying a job applicant or employee in a way that adversely affects the opportunities or status of such applicant or employee because of the disability of such applicant or employee;

(2) participating in a contractual or other arrangement or relationship that has the effect of subjecting a covered entity's qualified applicant or employee with a disability to the discrimination prohibited by this title (such relationship includes a relationship with an employment or referral agency, labor union, an organization providing fringe benefits to an employee of the covered entity, or an organization providing training and apprenticeship programs);

(3) utilizing standards, criteria, or methods of administration—

(A) that have the effect of discrimination on the basis of disability; or

(B) that perpetuate the discrimination of others who are subject to common administrative control;

(4) excluding or otherwise denying equal jobs or benefits to a qualified individual because of the known disability of an individual with whom the qualified individual is known to have a relationship or association;

(5)

(A) not making reasonable accommodations to the known physical or mental limitations of an otherwise qualified individual with a disability who is an applicant or employee, unless such covered entity can demonstrate that the accommodation would impose an undue hardship on the operation of the business of such covered entity; or

(B) denying employment opportunities to a job applicant or employee who is an otherwise qualified individual with a disability, if such denial is based on the need of such covered entity to make reasonable accommodation to the physical or mental impairments of the employee or applicant;

(6) using qualification standards, employment tests or other selection criteria that screen out or tend to screen out an individual with a disability or a class of individuals with disabilities unless the standard, test or other selection criteria, as used by the covered entity, is shown to be job-related for the position in question and is consistent with business necessity; and

(7) failing to select and administer tests concerning employment in the most effective manner to ensure that, when such test is administered to a job applicant or employee who has a disability that impairs sensory, manual, or speaking skills, such test results accurately reflect the skills, aptitude, or whatever other factor of such applicant or employee that such test purports to measure, rather than reflecting the impaired sensory, manual, or speaking skills of such employee or applicant (except where such skills are the factors that the test purports to measure). * * *

Sec. 104. Illegal Use of Drugs and Alcohol. * * *

(b) **Rules of Construction.**—Nothing in subsection (a) shall be construed to exclude as a qualified individual with a disability an individual who—

(1) has successfully completed a supervised drug rehabilitation program and is no longer engaging in the illegal use of drugs, or has otherwise been rehabilitated successfully and is no longer engaging in such use;

(2) is participating in a supervised rehabilitation program and is no longer engaging in such use; or

(3) is erroneously regarded as engaging in such use, but is not engaging in such use; except that it shall not be a violation of this Act for a covered entity to adopt or administer reasonable policies or procedures, including but not limited to drug testing, designed to ensure that an individual described in paragraph (1) or (2) is no longer engaging in the illegal use of drugs. * * *

Sec. 107. Enforcement.

(a) Powers, Remedies, and Procedures.—The powers, remedies, and procedures set forth in sections 705, 706, 707, 709, and 710 of the Civil Rights Act of 1964 (42 U.S.C. 2000e-4, 2000e-5, 2000e-6, 2000e-8, and 2000e-9) shall be the powers, remedies, and procedures this title provides to the Commission, to the Attorney General, or to any person alleging discrimination on the basis of disability in violation of any provision of this Act, or regulations promulgated under section 106, concerning employment.

(b) Coordination.—The agencies with enforcement authority for actions which allege employment discrimination under this title and under the Rehabilitation Act of 1973 shall develop procedures to ensure that administrative complaints filed under this title and under the Rehabilitation Act of 1973 are dealt with in a manner that avoids duplication of effort and prevents imposition of inconsistent or conflicting standards for the same requirements under this title and the Rehabilitation Act of 1973. The Commission, the Attorney General, and the Office of Federal Contract Compliance Programs shall establish such coordinating mechanisms (similar to provisions contained in the joint regulations promulgated by the Commission and the Attorney General at part 42 of title 28 and part 1691 of title 29, Code of Federal Regulations, and the Memorandum of Understanding between the Commission and the Office of Federal Contract Compliance Programs dated January 16, 1981 (46 Fed. Reg. 7435, January 23, 1981)) in regulations implementing this title and Rehabilitation Act of 1973 not later than 18 months after the date of enactment of this Act.

Sec. 108. Effective Date.

This title shall become effective 24 months after the date of enactment.

The Uniform Partnership Act

(Adopted in forty-nine states [all of the states except Louisiana], the District of Columbia, the Virgin Islands, and Guam. The adoptions by Alabama and Nebraska do not follow the official text in every respect, but are substantially similar, with local variations.)

The Act consists of 7 Parts as follows:

I. Preliminary Provisions

II. Nature of Partnership

III. Relations of Partners to Persons Dealing with the Partnership

IV. Relations of Partners to One Another

V. Property Rights of a Partner

VI. Dissolution and Winding Up

VII. Miscellaneous Provisions

An Act to make uniform the Law of Partnerships

Be it enacted, etc.:

Part I   Preliminary Provisions

Sec. 1. Name of Act

This act may be cited as Uniform Partnership Act.

Sec. 2. Definition of Terms

In this act, "Court" includes every court and judge having jurisdiction in the case.

"Business" includes every trade, occupation, or profession.

"Person" includes individuals, partnerships, corporations, and other associations.

"Bankrupt" includes bankrupt under the Federal Bankruptcy Act or insolvent under any state insolvent act.

"Conveyance" includes every assignment, lease, mortgage, or encumbrance.

"Real property" includes land and any interest or estate in land.

Sec. 3. Interpretation of Knowledge and Notice

(1) A person has "knowledge" of a fact within the meaning of this act not only when he has actual knowledge thereof, but also when he has knowledge of such other facts as in the circumstances shows bad faith.

(2) A person has "notice" of a fact within the meaning of this act when the person who claims the benefit of the notice:

(a) States the fact to such person, or

(b) Delivers through the mail, or by other means of communication, a written statement of the fact to such person or to a proper person at his place of business or residence.

Sec. 4. Rules of Construction

(1) The rule that statutes in derogation of the common law are to be strictly construed shall have no application to this act.

(2) The law of estoppel shall apply under this act.

(3) The law of agency shall apply under this act.

(4) This act shall be so interpreted and construed as to effect its general purpose to make uniform the law of those states which enact it.

(5) This act shall not be construed so as to impair the obligations of any contract existing when the act goes into effect, nor to affect any action or proceedings begun or right accrued before this act takes effect.

Sec. 5. Rules for Cases Not Provided for in This Act.

In any case not provided for in this act the rules of law and equity, including the law merchant, shall govern.

Part II   Nature of Partnership

Sec. 6. Partnership Defined

(1) A partnership is an association of two or more persons to carry on as co-owners a business for profit.

(2) But any association formed under any other statute of this state, or any statute adopted by authority, other than the authority of this state, is not a partnership under this act, unless such association would have been a partnership in this state prior to the adoption of this act; but this act shall apply to limited partnerships except in so far as the statutes relating to such partnerships are inconsistent herewith.

Sec. 7. Rules for Determining the Existence of a Partnership

In determining whether a partnership exists, these rules shall apply:

(1) Except as provided by Section 16 persons who are not partners as to each other are not partners as to third persons.

(2) Joint tenancy, tenancy in common, tenancy by the entireties, joint property, common property, or part ownership does not of itself establish a partnership, whether such co-owners do or do not share any profits made by the use of the property.

(3) The sharing of gross returns does not of itself establish a partnership, whether or not the persons sharing them have a joint or common right or interest in any property from which the returns are derived.

(4) The receipt by a person of a share of the profits of a business is prima facie evidence that he is a partner in the business, but no such inference shall be drawn if such profits were received in payment:

    (a) As a debt by installments or otherwise,

    (b) As wages of an employee or rent to a landlord,

    (c) As an annuity to a widow or representative of a deceased partner,

    (d) As interest on a loan, though the amount of payment vary with the profits of the business,

    (e) As the consideration for the sale of a good-will of a business or other property by installments or otherwise.

Sec. 8. Partnership Property

(1) All property originally brought into the partnership stock or subsequently acquired by purchase or otherwise, on account of the partnership, is partnership property.

(2) Unless the contrary intention appears, property acquired with partnership funds is partnership property.

(3) Any estate in real property may be acquired in the partnership name. Title so acquired can be conveyed only in the partnership name.

(4) A conveyance to a partnership in the partnership name, though without words of inheritance, passes the entire estate of the grantor unless a contrary intent appears.

Part III Relations of Partners to Persons Dealing with the Partnership

Sec. 9. Partner Agent of Partnership as to Partnership Business

(1) Every partner is an agent of the partnership for the purpose of its business, and the act of every partner, including the execution in the partnership name of any instrument, for apparently carrying on in the usual way the business of the partnership of which he is a member binds the partnership, unless the partner so acting has in fact no authority to act for the partnership in the particular matter, and the person with whom he is dealing has knowledge of the fact that he has no such authority.

(2) An act of a partner which is not apparently for the carrying on of the business of the partnership in the usual way does not bind the partnership unless authorized by the other partners.

(3) Unless authorized by the other partners or unless they have abandoned the business, one or more but less than all the partners have no authority to:

    (a) Assign the partnership property in trust for creditors or on the assignee's promise to pay the debts of the partnership,

    (b) Dispose of the good-will of the business,

    (c) Do any other act which would make it impossible to carry on the ordinary business of a partnership,

    (d) Confess a judgment,

    (e) Submit a partnership claim or liability to arbitration or reference.

(4) No act of a partner in contravention of a restriction on authority shall bind the partnership to persons having knowledge of the restriction.

Sec. 10. Conveyance of Real Property of the Partnership

(1) Where title to real property is in the partnership name, any partner may convey title to such property by a conveyance executed in the partnership name; but the partnership may recover such property unless the partner's act binds the partnership under the provisions of paragraph (1) of section 9, or unless such property has been conveyed by the grantee or a person claiming through such grantee to a holder for value without knowledge that the partner, in making the conveyance, has exceeded his authority.

(2) Where title to real property is in the name of the partnership, a conveyance executed by a partner, in his own name, passes the equitable interest of the partnership, provided the act is one within the authority of the partner under the provisions of paragraph (1) of section 9.

(3) Where title to real property is in the name of one or more but not all the partners, and the record does not disclose the right of the partnership, the partners in whose name the title stands may convey title to such property, but the partnership may recover such property if the partners' act does not bind the partnership under the provisions of paragraph (1) of section 9, unless the purchaser or his assignee, is a holder for value, without knowledge.

(4) Where the title to real property is in the name of one or more or all the partners, or in a third person in trust for the partnership, a conveyance executed by a partner in the

partnership name, or in his own name, passes the equitable interest of the partnership, provided the act is one within the authority of the partner under the provisions of paragraph (1) of section 9.

(5) Where the title to real property is in the names of all the partners a conveyance executed by all the partners passes all their rights in such property.

Sec. 11. Partnership Bound by Admission of Partner

An admission or representation made by any partner concerning partnership affairs within the scope of his authority as conferred by this act is evidence against the partnership.

Sec. 12. Partnership Charged with Knowledge of or Notice to Partner

Notice to any partner of any matter relating to partnership affairs, and the knowledge of the partner acting in the particular matter, acquired while a partner or then present to his mind, and the knowledge of any other partner who reasonably could and should have communicated it to the acting partner, operate as notice to or knowledge of the partnership, except in the case of a fraud on the partnership committed by or with the consent of that partner.

Sec. 13. Partnership Bound by Partner's Wrongful Act

Where, by any wrongful act or omission of any partner acting in the ordinary course of the business of the partnership or with the authority of his co-partners, loss or injury is caused to any person, not being a partner in the partnership, or any penalty is incurred, the partnership is liable therefor to the same extent as the partner so acting or omitting to act.

Sec. 14. Partnership Bound by Partner's Breach of Trust

The partnership is bound to make good the loss:

(a) Where one partner acting within the scope of his apparent authority receives money or property of a third person and misapplies it; and

(b) Where the partnership in the course of its business receives money or property of a third person and the money or property so received is misapplied by any partner while it is in the custody of the partnership.

Sec. 15. Nature of Partner's Liability

All partners are liable

(a) Jointly and severally for everything chargeable to the partnership under sections 13 and 14.

(b) Jointly for all other debts and obligations of the partnership; but any partner may enter into a separate obligation to perform a partnership contract.

Sec. 16. Partner by Estoppel

(1) When a person, by words spoken or written or by conduct, represents himself, or consents to another representing him to any one, as a partner in an existing partnership or with one or more persons not actual partners, he is liable to any such person to whom such representation has been made, who has, on the faith of such representation, given credit to the actual or apparent partnership, and if he has made such representation or consented to its being made in a public manner he is liable to such person, whether the representation has or has not been made or communicated to such person so giving credit by or with the knowledge of the apparent partner making the representation or consenting to its being made.

(a) When a partnership liability results, he is liable as though he were an actual member of the partnership.

(b) When no partnership liability results, he is liable jointly with the other persons, if any, so consenting to the contract or representation as to incur liability, otherwise separately.

(2) When a person has been thus represented to be a partner in an existing partnership, or with one or more persons not actual partners, he is an agent of the persons consenting to such representation to bind them to the same extent and in the same manner as though he were a partner in fact, with respect to persons who rely upon the representation. Where all the members of the existing partnership consent to the representation, a partnership act or obligation results; but in all other cases it is the joint act or obligation of the person acting and the persons consenting to the representation.

Sec. 17. Liability of Incoming Partner

A person admitted as a partner into an existing partnership is liable for all the obligations of the partnership arising before his admission as though he had been a partner when such obligations were incurred, except that this liability shall be satisfied only out of partnership property.

Part IV   Relations of Partners to One Another

Sec. 18. Rules Determining Rights and Duties of Partners

The rights and duties of the partners in relation to the partnership shall be determined, subject to any agreement between them, by the following rules:

(a) Each partner shall be repaid his contributions, whether by way of capital or advances to the partnership property and share equally in the profits and surplus remaining after all liabilities, including those to partners, are satisfied; and must contribute towards the losses, whether of capital or otherwise, sustained by the partnership according to his share in the profits.

(b) The partnership must indemnify every partner in respect of payments made and personal liabilities reasonably incurred by him in the ordinary and proper conduct of its business, or for the preservation of its business or property.

(c) A partner, who in aid of the partnership makes any payment or advance beyond the amount of capital which he agreed to contribute, shall be paid interest from the date of the payment or advance.

(d) A partner shall receive interest on the capital contributed by him only from the date when repayment should be made.

(e) All partners have equal rights in the management and conduct of the partnership business.

(f) No partner is entitled to remuneration for acting in the partnership business, except that a surviving partner is entitled to reasonable compensation for his services in winding up the partnership affairs.

(g) No person can become a member of a partnership without the consent of all the partners.

(h) Any difference arising as to ordinary matters connected with the partnership business may be decided by a majority of the partners; but no act in contravention of any agreement between the partners may be done rightfully without the consent of all the partners.

Sec. 19. Partnership Books

The partnership books shall be kept, subject to any agreement between the partners, at the principal place of business of the partnership, and every partner shall at all times have access to and may inspect and copy any of them.

Sec. 20. Duty of Partners to Render Information

Partners shall render on demand true and full information of all things affecting the partnership to any partner or the legal representative of any deceased partner or partner under legal disability.

Sec. 21. Partner Accountable as a Fiduciary

(1) Every partner must account to the partnership for any benefit, and hold as trustee for it any profits derived by him without the consent of the other partners from any transaction connected with the formation, conduct, or liquidation of the partnership or from any use by him of its property.

(2) This section applies also to the representatives of a deceased partner engaged in the liquidation of the affairs of the partnership as the personal representatives of the last surviving partner.

Sec. 22. Right to an Account

Any partner shall have the right to a formal account as to partnership affairs:

(a) If he is wrongfully excluded from the partnership business or possession of its property by his co-partners,

(b) If the right exists under the terms of any agreement,

(c) As provided by section 21,

(d) Whenever other circumstances render it just and reasonable.

Sec. 23. Continuation of Partnership beyond Fixed Term

(1) When a partnership for a fixed term or particular undertaking is continued after the termination of such term or particular undertaking without any express agreement, the rights and duties of the partners remain the same as they were at such termination, so far as is consistent with a partnership at will.

(2) A continuation of the business by the partners or such of them as habitually acted therein during the term, without any settlement or liquidation of the partnership affairs, is prima facie evidence of a continuation of the partnership.

Part V   Property Rights of a Partner

Sec. 24. Extent of Property Rights of a Partner

The property rights of a partner are (1) his rights in specific partnership property, (2) his interest in the partnership, and (3) his right to participate in the management.

Sec. 25. Nature of a Partner's Right in Specific Partnership Property

(1) A partner is co-owner with his partners of specific partnership property holding as a tenant in partnership.

(2) The incidents of this tenancy are such that:

(a) A partner, subject to the provisions of this act and to any agreement between the partners, has an equal right with his partners to possess specific partnership property for partnership purposes; but he has no right to possess such property for any other purpose without the consent of his partners.

(b) A partner's right in specific partnership property is not assignable except in connection with the assignment of rights of all the partners in the same property.

(c) A partner's right in specific partnership property is not subject to attachment or execution, except on a claim against the partnership. When partnership property is attached for a partnership debt the partners, or any of them, or the representatives of a deceased partner, cannot claim any right under the homestead or exemption laws.

(d) On the death of a partner his right in specific partnership property vests in the surviving partner or partners, except where the deceased was the last surviving partner, when his right in such property vests in his legal representative. Such surviving partner or partners, or the legal representative of the last surviving partner, has no right to possess the partnership property for any but a partnership purpose.

(e) A partner's right in specific partnership property is not subject to dower, curtesy, or allowances to widows, heirs, or next of kin.

Sec. 26. Nature of Partner's Interest in the Partnership

A partner's interest in the partnership is his share of the profits and surplus, and the same is personal property.

Sec. 27. Assignment of Partner's Interest

(1) A conveyance by a partner of his interest in the

partnership does not of itself dissolve the partnership, nor, as against the other partners in the absence of agreement, entitle the assignee, during the continuance of the partnership, to interfere in the management or administration of the partnership business or affairs, or to require any information or account of partnership transactions, or to inspect the partnership books; but it merely entitles the assignee to receive in accordance with his contract the profits to which the assigning partner would otherwise be entitled.

(2) In case of a dissolution of the partnership, the assignee is entitled to receive his assignor's interest and may require an account from the date only of the last account agreed to by all the partners.

Sec. 28. Partner's Interest Subject to Charging Order

(1) On due application to a competent court by any judgment creditor of a partner, the court which entered the judgment, order, or decree, or any other court, may charge the interest of the debtor partner with payment of the unsatisfied amount of such judgment debt with interest thereon; and may then or later appoint a receiver of his share of the profits, and of any other money due or to fall due to him in respect of the partnership, and make all other orders, directions, accounts and inquiries which the debtor partner might have made, or which the circumstances of the case may require.

(2) The interest charged may be redeemed at any time before foreclosure, or in case of a sale being directed by the court may be purchased without thereby causing a dissolution:

    (a) With separate property, by any one or more of the partners, or

    (b) With partnership property, by any one or more of the partners with the consent of all the partners whose interests are not so charged or sold.

(3) Nothing in this act shall be held to deprive a partner of his right, if any, under the exemption laws, as regards his interest in the partnership.

Part VI   Dissolution and Winding up

Sec. 29. Dissolution Defined

The dissolution of a partnership is the change in the relation of the partners caused by any partner ceasing to be associated in the carrying on as distinguished from the winding up of the business.

Sec. 30. Partnership not Terminated by Dissolution

On dissolution the partnership is not terminated, but continues until the winding up of partnership affairs is completed.

Sec. 31. Causes of Dissolution

Dissolution is caused:

(1) Without violation of the agreement between the partners,

    (a) By the termination of the definite term or particular undertaking specified in the agreement,

    (b) By the express will of any partner when no definite term or particular undertaking is specified,

    (c) By the express will of all the partners who have not assigned their interests or suffered them to be charged for their separate debts, either before or after the termination of any specified term or particular undertaking,

    (d) By the expulsion of any partner from the business bona fide in accordance with such a power conferred by the agreement between the partners;

(2) In contravention of the agreement between the partners, where the circumstances do not permit a dissolution under any other provision of this section, by the express will of any partner at any time;

(3) By any event which makes it unlawful for the business of the partnership to be carried on or for the members to carry it on in partnership;

(4) By the death of any partner;

(5) By the bankruptcy of any partner or the partnership;

(6) By decree of court under section 32.

Sec. 32. Dissolution by Decree of Court

(1) On application by or for a partner the court shall decree a dissolution whenever:

    (a) A partner has been declared a lunatic in any judicial proceeding or is shown to be of unsound mind,

    (b) A partner becomes in any other way incapable of performing his part of the partnership contract,

    (c) A partner has been guilty of such conduct as tends to affect prejudicially the carrying on of the business,

    (d) A partner willfully or persistently commits a breach of the partnership agreement, or otherwise so conducts himself in matters relating to the partnership business that it is not reasonably practicable to carry on the business in partnership with him,

    (e) The business of the partnership can only be carried on at a loss,

    (f) Other circumstances render a dissolution equitable.

(2) On the application of the purchaser of a partner's interest under sections 28 or 29 [should read 27 or 28];

    (a) After the termination of the specified term or particular undertaking,

    (b) At any time if the partnership was a partnership at will when the interest was assigned or when the charging order was issued.

Sec. 33. General Effect of Dissolution on Authority of Partner

Except so far as may be necessary to wind up partnership affairs or to complete transactions begun but not then finished, dissolution terminates all authority of any partner to act for the partnership,

(1) With respect to the partners,

    (a) When the dissolution is not by the act, bankruptcy or death of a partner; or

    (b) When the dissolution is by such act, bankruptcy or death of a partner, in cases where section 34 so requires.

(2) With respect to persons not partners, as declared in section 35.

Sec. 34. Rights of Partner to Contribution from Copartners after Dissolution

Where the dissolution is caused by the act, death or bankruptcy of a partner, each partner is liable to his copartners for his share of any liability created by any partner acting for the partnership as if the partnership had not been dissolved unless

(a) The dissolution being by act of any partner, the partner acting for the partnership had knowledge of the dissolution, or

(b) The dissolution being by the death or bankruptcy of a partner, the partner acting for the partnership had knowledge or notice of the death or bankruptcy.

Sec. 35. Power of Partner to Bind Partnership to Third Persons after Dissolution

(1) After dissolution a partner can bind the partnership except as provided in Paragraph (3).

    (a) By any act appropriate for winding up partnership affairs or completing transactions unfinished at dissolution;

    (b) By any transaction which would bind the partnership if dissolution had not taken place, provided the other party to the transaction

        (I) Had extended credit to the partnership prior to dissolution and had no knowledge or notice of the dissolution; or

        (II) Though he had not so extended credit, had nevertheless known of the partnership prior to dissolution, and, having no knowledge or notice of dissolution, the fact of dissolution had not been advertised in a newspaper of general circulation in the place (or in each place if more than one) at which the partnership business was regularly carried on.

(2) The liability of a partner under paragraph (1b) shall be satisfied out of partnership assets alone when such partner had been prior to dissolution

    (a) Unknown as a partner to the person with whom the contract is made; and

    (b) So far unknown and inactive in partnership affairs that the business reputation of the partnership could not be said to have been in any degree due to his connection with it.

(3) The partnership is in no case bound by any act of a partner after dissolution

(a) Where the partnership is dissolved because it is unlawful to carry on the business, unless the act is appropriate for winding up partnership affairs; or

(b) Where the partner has become bankrupt; or

(c) Where the partner has no authority to wind up partnership affairs; except by a transaction with one who

    (I) Had extended credit to the partnership prior to dissolution and had no knowledge or notice of his want of authority; or

    (II) Had not extended credit to the partnership prior to dissolution, and, having no knowledge or notice of his want of authority, the fact of his want of authority has not been advertised in the manner provided for advertising the fact of dissolution in paragraph (1bII).

(4) Nothing in this section shall affect the liability under Section 16 of any person who after dissolution represents himself or consents to another representing him as a partner in a partnership engaged in carrying on business.

Sec. 36. Effect of Dissolution on Partner's Existing Liability

(1) The dissolution of the partnership does not of itself discharge the existing liability of any partner.

(2) A partner is discharged from any existing liability upon dissolution of the partnership by an agreement to that effect between himself, the partnership creditor and the person or partnership continuing the business; and such agreement may be inferred from the course of dealing between the creditor having knowledge of the dissolution and the person or partnership continuing the business.

(3) Where a person agrees to assume the existing obligations of a dissolved partnership, the partners whose obligations have been assumed shall be discharged from any liability to any creditor of the partnership who, knowing of the agreement, consents to a material alteration in the nature or time of payment of such obligations.

(4) The individual property of a deceased partner shall be liable for all obligations of the partnership incurred while he was a partner but subject to the prior payment of his separate debts.

Sec. 37. Right to Wind Up

Unless otherwise agreed the partners who have not wrongfully dissolved the partnership or the legal representative of the last surviving partner, not bankrupt, has the right to wind up the partnership affairs; provided, however, that any partner, his legal representative or his assignee, upon cause shown, may obtain winding up by the court.

Sec. 38. Rights of Partners to Application of Partnership Property

(1) When dissolution is caused in any way, except in contravention of the partnership agreement, each partner, as against his co-partners and all persons claiming through them in respect of their interests in the partnership, unless

otherwise agreed, may have the partnership property applied to discharge its liabilities, and the surplus applied to pay in cash the net amount owing to the respective partners. But if dissolution is caused by expulsion of a partner, bona fide under the partnership agreement and if the expelled partner is discharged from all partnership liabilities, either by payment or agreement under section 36(2), he shall receive in cash only the net amount due him from the partnership.

(2) When dissolution is caused in contravention of the partnership agreement the rights of the partners shall be as follows:

(a) Each partner who has not caused dissolution wrongfully shall have,

(I) All the rights specified in paragraph (1) of this section, and

(II) The right, as against each partner who has caused the dissolution wrongfully, to damages for breach of the agreement.

(b) The partners who have not caused the dissolution wrongfully, if they all desire to continue the business in the same name, either by themselves or jointly with others, may do so, during the agreed term for the partnership and for that purpose may possess the partnership property, provided they secure the payment by bond approved by the court, or pay to any partner who has caused the dissolution wrongfully, the value of his interest in the partnership at the dissolution, less any damages recoverable under clause (2a II) of the section, and in like manner indemnify him against all present or future partnership liabilities.

(c) A partner who has caused the dissolution wrongfully shall have:

(I) If the business is not continued under the provisions of paragraph (2b) all the rights of a partner under paragraph (1), subject to clause (2a II), of this section,

(II) If the business is continued under paragraph (2b) of this section the right as against his co-partners and all claiming through them in respect of their interests in the partnership, to have the value of his interest in the partnership, less any damages caused to his co-partners by the dissolution, ascertained and paid to him in cash, or the payment secured by bond approved by the court, and to be released from all existing liabilities of the partnership; but in ascertaining the value of the partner's interest the value of the good-will of the business shall not be considered.

Sec. 39. Rights Where Partnership Is Dissolved for Fraud or Misrepresentation

Where a partnership contract is rescinded on the ground of the fraud or misrepresentation of one of the parties thereto, the party entitled to rescind is, without prejudice to any other right, entitled,

(a) To a lien on, or right of retention of, the surplus of the partnership property after satisfying the partnership liabilities to third persons for any sum of money paid by him for the purchase of an interest in the partnership and for any capital or advances contributed by him; and

(b) To stand, after all liabilities to third persons have been satisfied, in the place of the creditors of the partnership for any payments made by him in respect of the partnership liabilities; and

(c) To be indemnified by the person guilty of the fraud or making the representation against all debts and liabilities of the partnership.

Sec. 40. Rules for Distribution

In settling accounts between the partners after dissolution, the following rules shall be observed, subject to any agreement to the contrary:

(a) The assets of the partnership are:

(I) The partnership property,

(II) The contributions of the partners necessary for the payment of all the liabilities specified in clause (b) of this paragraph.

(b) The liabilities of the partnership shall rank in order of payment, as follows:

(I) Those owing to creditors other than partners,

(II) Those owing to partners other than for capital and profits,

(III) Those owing to partners in respect of capital,

(IV) Those owing to partners in respect of profits.

(c) The assets shall be applied in the order of their declaration in clause (a) of this paragraph to the satisfaction of the liabilities.

(d) The partners shall contribute, as provided by section 18(a) the amount necessary to satisfy the liabilities; but if any, but not all, of the partners are insolvent, or, not being subject to process, refuse to contribute, the other partners shall contribute their share of the liabilities, and, in the relative proportions in which they share the profits, the additional amount necessary to pay the liabilities.

(e) An assignee for the benefit of creditors or any person appointed by the court shall have the right to enforce the contributions specified in clause (d) of this paragraph.

(f) Any partner or his legal representative shall have the right to enforce the contributions specified in clause (d) of this paragraph, to the extent of the amount which he has paid in excess of his share of the liability.

(g) The individual property of a deceased partner shall be liable for the contributions specified in clause (d) of this paragraph.

(h) When partnership property and the individual properties of the partners are in possession of a court for distribution, partnership creditors shall have priority on partnership property and separate creditors on individual property, saving the rights of lien or secured creditors as heretofore.

(i) Where a partner has become bankrupt or his estate is insolvent the claims against his separate property shall rank in the following order:

(I) Those owing to separate creditors,

(II) Those owing to partnership creditors,

(III) Those owing to partners by way of contribution.

Sec. 41. Liability of Persons Continuing the Business in Certain Cases

(1) When any new partner is admitted into an existing partnership, or when any partner retires and assigns (or the representative of the deceased partner assigns) his rights in partnership property to two or more of the partners, or to one or more of the partners and one or more third persons, if the business is continued without liquidation of the partnership affairs, creditors of the first or dissolved partnership are also creditors of the partnership so continuing the business.

(2) When all but one partner retire and assign (or the representative of a deceased partner assigns) their rights in partnership property to the remaining partner, who continues the business without liquidation of partnership affairs, either alone or with others, creditors of the dissolved partnership are also creditors of the person or partnership so continuing the business.

(3) When any partner retires or dies and the business of the dissolved partnership is continued as set forth in paragraphs (1) and (2) of this section, with the consent of the retired partners or the representative of the deceased partner, but without any assignment of his right in partnership property, rights of creditors of the dissolved partnership and of the creditors of the person or partnership continuing the business shall be as if such assignment had been made.

(4) When all the partners or their representatives assign their rights in partnership property to one or more third persons who promise to pay the debts and who continue the business of the dissolved partnership, creditors of the dissolved partnership are also creditors of the person or partnership continuing the business.

(5) When any partner wrongfully causes a dissolution and the remaining partners continue the business under the provisions of section 38(2b), either alone or with others, and without liquidation of the partnership affairs, creditors of the dissolved partnership are also creditors of the person or partnership continuing the business.

(6) When a partner is expelled and the remaining partners continue the business either alone or with others, without liquidation of the partnership affairs, creditors of the dissolved partnership are also creditors of the person or partnership continuing the business.

(7) The liability of a third person becoming a partner in the partnership continuing the business, under this section, to the creditors of the dissolved partnership shall be satisfied out of partnership property only.

(8) When the business of a partnership after dissolution is continued under any conditions set forth in this section the creditors of the dissolved partnership, as against the separate creditors of the retiring or deceased partner or the representative of the deceased partner, have a prior right to any claim of the retired partner or the representative of the deceased partner against the person or partnership continuing the business, on account of the retired or deceased partner's interest in the dissolved partnership or on account of any consideration promised for such interest or for his right in partnership property.

(9) Nothing in this section shall be held to modify any right of creditors to set aside any assignment on the ground of fraud.

(10) The use by the person or partnership continuing the business of the partnership name, or the name of a deceased partner as part thereof, shall not of itself make the individual property of the deceased partner liable for any debts contracted by such person or partnership.

Sec. 42. Rights of Retiring or Estate of Deceased Partner When the Business Is Continued

When any partner retires or dies, and the business is continued under any of the conditions set forth in section 41 (1, 2, 3, 5, 6), or section 38(2b) without any settlement of accounts as between him or his estate and the person or partnership continuing the business, unless otherwise agreed, he or his legal representative as against such persons or partnership may have the value of his interest at the date of dissolution ascertained, and shall receive as an ordinary creditor an amount equal to the value of his interest in the dissolved partnership with interest, or, at his option or at the option of his legal representative, in lieu of interest, the profits attributable to the use of his right in the property of the dissolved partnership; provided that the creditors of the dissolved partnership as against the separate creditors, or the representative of the retired or deceased partner, shall have priority on any claim arising under this section, as provided by section 41(8) of this act.

Sec. 43. Accrual of Actions

The right to an account of his interest shall accrue to any partner, or his legal representative, as against the winding up partners or the surviving partners or the person or partnership continuing the business, at the date of dissolution, in the absence of any agreement to the contrary.

Part VII   Miscellaneous Provisions

Sec. 44. When Act Takes Effect

This act shall take effect on the ___ day of ___ one thousand nine hundred and ___.

Sec. 45. Legislation Repealed

All acts or parts of acts inconsistent with this act are hereby repealed.

The Revised Uniform Partnership Act
[EXCERPTS]

Article 2.

GENERAL PROVISIONS

* * * *

§ 201. Partnership as Entity.

A partnership is an entity.

* * * *

§ 203. Partnership Property.

Property transferred to or otherwise acquired by a partnership is property of the partnership and not of the partners individually.

§ 204. When Property is Partnership Property.

(a) Property is partnership property if acquired in the name of:

(1) the partnership; or

(2) one or more partners with an indication in the instrument transferring title to the property of the person's capacity as a partner or of the existence of a partnership but without an indication of the name of the partnership.

(b) Property is acquired in the name of the partnership by a transfer to:

(1) the partnership in its name; or

(2) one or more partners in their capacity as partners in the partnership, if the name of the partnership is indicated in the instrument transferring title to the property.

(c) Property is presumed to be partnership property if purchased with partnership assets, even if not acquired in the name of the partnership or of one or more partners with an indication in the instrument transferring title to the property of the person's capacity as a partner or of the existence of a partnership.

(d) Property acquired in the name of one or more of the partners, without an indication in the instrument transferring title to the property of the person's capacity as a partner or of the existence of a partnership and without use of partnership assets, is presumed to be separate property, even if used for partnership purposes.

Article 3.

RELATIONS OF PARTNERS TO PERSONS DEALING WITH PARTNERSHIP

* * * *

§ 302. Transfer of Partnership Property.

(a) Subject to the effect of a statement of partnership authority under Section 303:

(1) Partnership property held in the name of the partnership may be transferred by an instrument of transfer executed by a partner in the partnership name.

(2) Partnership property held in the name of one or more partners with an indication in the instrument transferring the property to them of their capacity as partners or of the existence of a partnership, but without an indication of the name of the partnership, may be transferred by an instrument of transfer executed by the persons in whose name the property is held.

(3) A partnership may recover property transferred under this subsection if it proves that execution of the instrument of transfer did not bind the partnership under Section 301, unless the property was transferred by the initial transferee or a person claiming through the initial transferee to a subsequent transferee who gave value without having notice that the person who executed the instrument of initial transfer lacked authority to bind the partnership.

(b) Partnership property held in the name of one or more persons other than the partnership, without an indication in the instrument transferring the property to them of their capacity as partners or of the existence of a partnership, may be transferred free of claims of the partnership or the partners by the persons in whose name the property is held to a transferee who gives value without having notice that it is partnership property.

(c) If a person holds all of the partners' interests in the partnership, all of the partnership property vests in that person. The person may execute a document in the name of the partnership to evidence vesting of the property in that person and may file or record the document.

* * * *

§ 306. Partner's Liability.

All partners are liable jointly and severally for all obligations of the partnership unless otherwise agreed by the claimant or provided by law.

§ 307. Actions by and Against Partnership and Partners.

(a) A partnership may sue and be sued in the name of the partnership.

(b) An action may be brought against the partnership and any or all of the partners in the same action or in separate actions.

(c) A judgment against a partnership is not by itself a judgment against a partner. A judgment against a partnership may not be satisfied from a partner's assets unless there is also a judgment against the partner.

(d) A judgment creditor of a partner may not levy execution against the assets of the partner to satisfy a judgment based on a claim against the partnership unless:

(1) a judgment based on the same claim has been obtained against the partnership and a writ of execution on the judgment has been returned unsatisfied in whole or in part;

(2) an involuntary case under Title 11 of the United States Code has been commenced against the partnership and has not been dismissed within 60 days after commencement, or the partnership has commenced a voluntary case under Title 11 of the United States Code and the case has not been dismissed;

(3) the partner has agreed that the creditor need not exhaust partnership assets;

(4) a court grants permission to the judgment creditor to levy execution against the assets of a partner based on a finding that partnership assets subject to execution are clearly insufficient to satisfy the judgment, that exhaustion of partnership assets is excessively burdensome, or that the grant of permission is an appropriate exercise of the court's equitable powers; or

(5) liability is imposed on the partner by law or contract independent of the existence of the partnership.

(e) This section applies to any partnership liability or obligation resulting from a representation by a partner or purported partner under Section 308.

* * * *

Article 5.

TRANSFEREES AND CREDITORS OF PARTNER

§ 501. **Partner's Interest in Partnership Property not Transferable.**

A partner is not a co-owner of partnership property and has no interest in partnership property which can be transferred, either voluntarily or involuntarily.

* * * *

Article 6.

PARTNER'S DISSOCIATION

§ 601. **Events Causing Partner's Dissociation.**

A partner is dissociated from a partnership upon:

(1) receipt by the partnership of notice of the partner's express will to withdraw as a partner or upon any later date specified in the notice;

(2) an event agreed to in the partnership agreement as causing the partner's dissociation;

(3) the partner's expulsion pursuant to the partnership agreement;

(4) the partner's expulsion by the unanimous vote of the other partners if:

(i) it is unlawful to carry on the partnership business with that partner;

(ii) there has been a transfer of all or substantially all of that partner's transferable interest in the partnership, other than a transfer for security purposes, or a court order charging the partner's interest, which has not been foreclosed;

(iii) within 90 days after the partnership notifies a corporate partner that it will be expelled because it has filed a certificate of dissolution or the equivalent, its charter has been revoked, or its right to conduct business has been suspended by the jurisdiction of its incorporation, there is no revocation of the certificate of dissolution or no reinstatement of its charter or its right to conduct business; or

(iv) a partnership that is a partner has been dissolved and its business is being wound up;

(5) on application by the partnership or another partner, the partner's expulsion by judicial determination because:

(i) the partner engaged in wrongful conduct that adversely and materially affected the partnership business;

(ii) the partner willfully or persistently committed a material breach of the partnership agreement or of a duty owed to the partnership or the other partners under Section 404; or

(iii) the partner engaged in conduct relating to the partnership business which makes it not reasonably practicable to carry on the business in partnership with the partner;

(6) the partner's:

(i) becoming a debtor in bankruptcy;

(ii) executing an assignment for the benefit of creditors;

(iii) seeking, consenting to, or acquiescing in the appointment of a trustee, receiver, or liquidator of that partner or of all or substantially all of that partner's property; or

(iv) failing, within 90 days after the appointment, to have vacated or stayed the appointment of a trustee, receiver, or liquidator of the partner or of all or substantially all of the partner's property obtained without the partner's consent or acquiescence, or failing within 90 days after the expiration of a stay to have the appointment vacated;

(7) in the case of a partner who is an individual:

(i) the partner's death;

(ii) the appointment of a guardian or general conservator for the partner; or

(iii) a judicial determination that the partner has otherwise become incapable of performing the partner's duties under the partnership agreement;

(8) in the case of a partner that is a trust or is acting as a partner by virtue of being a trustee of a trust, distribution of the trust's entire transferable interest in the partnership, but not merely by reason of the substitution of a successor trustee;

(9) in the case of a partner that is an estate or is acting as a partner by virtue of being a personal representative of an estate, distribution of the estate's entire transferable interest in the partnership, but not merely by reason of the substitution of a successor personal representative; or

(10) termination of a partner who is not an individual, partnership, corporation, trust, or estate.

* * * *

Article 7.

PARTNER'S DISSOCIATION WHEN BUSINESS NOT WOUND UP

§ 701. Purchase of Dissociated Partner's Interest.

(a) If a partner is dissociated from a partnership without resulting in a dissolution and winding up of the partnership business under Section 801, the partnership shall cause the dissociated partner's interest in the partnership to be purchased for a buyout price determined pursuant to subsection (b).

(b) The buyout price of a dissociated partner's interest is the amount that would have been distributable to the dissociating partner under Section 808(b) if, on the date of dissociation, the assets of the partnership were sold at a price equal to the greater of the liquidation value or the value based on a sale of the entire business as a going concern without the dissociated partner and the partnership were wound up as of that date. In either case, the selling price of the partnership assets must be determined on the basis of the amount that would be paid by a willing buyer to a willing seller, neither being under any compulsion to buy or sell, and with knowledge of all relevant facts. Interest must be paid from the date of dissociation to the date of payment.

(c) Damages for wrongful dissociation under Section 602(b), and all other amounts owing, whether or not presently due, from the dissociated partner to the partnership, must be offset against the buyout price. Interest must be paid from the date the amount owed becomes due to the date of payment.

(d) A partnership shall indemnify a dissociated partner against all partnership liabilities incurred before the dissociation, except liabilities then unknown to the partnership, and against all partnership liabilities incurred after the dissociation, except liabilities incurred by an act of the dissociated partner under Section 702. For purposes of this subsection, a liability not known to a partner other than the dissociated partner is not known to the partnership.

(e) If no agreement for the purchase of a dissociated partner's interest is reached within 120 days after a written demand for payment, the partnership shall pay, or cause to be paid, in cash to the dissociated partner the amount the partnership estimates to be the buyout price and accrued interest, reduced by any offsets and accrued interest under subsection (c).

(f) If a deferred payment is authorized under subsection (h), the partnership may tender a written offer to pay the amount it estimates to be the buyout price and accrued interest, reduced by any offsets under subsection (c), stating the time of payment, the amount and type of security for payment, and the other terms and conditions of the obligation.

(g) The payment or tender required by subsection (e) or (f) must be accompanied by the following:

(1) a statement of partnership assets and liabilities as of the date of dissociation;

(2) the latest available partnership balance sheet and income statement, if any;

(3) an explanation of how the estimated amount of the payment was calculated; and

(4) written notice that the payment is in full satisfaction of the obligation to purchase unless, within 120 days after the written notice, the dissociated partner commences an action to determine the buyout price, any offsets under subsection (c), or other terms of the obligation to purchase.

(h) A partner who wrongfully dissociates before the expiration of a definite term or the completion of a particular undertaking is not entitled to payment of any portion of the buyout price until the expiration of the term or completion of the undertaking, unless the partner establishes to the satisfaction of the court that earlier payment will not cause undue hardship to the business of the partnership. A deferred payment must be adequately secured and bear interest.

(i) A dissociated partner may maintain an action against the partnership, pursuant to Section 406(b)(2)(ii), to determine the buyout price of that partner's interest, any offsets under subsection (c), or other terms of the obligation to purchase. The action must be commenced within 120 days after the partnership has tendered payment or an offer to pay or within one year after written demand for payment if no payment or offer to pay is tendered. The court shall determine the buyout price of the dissociated partner's interest, any offset due under subsection (c), and accrued interest, and enter judgment for any additional payment or refund. If deferred payment is authorized under subsection (h), the court shall also determine the security for payment and other terms of the obligation to purchase. The court may assess reasonable attorney's fees and the fees and expenses of appraisers or other experts for a party to the action, in amounts the court finds equitable, against a party that the court finds acted arbitrarily, vexatiously, or not in good faith. The finding may be based on the partnership's failure to tender payment or an offer to pay or to comply with subsection (g).

The Uniform Limited Liability Company Act
[EXCERPTS]

[ARTICLE] 2.

ORGANIZATION

Section 201. **Limited liability company as legal entity.**

A limited liability company is a legal entity distinct from its members.

Section 202. **Organization.**

(a) One or more persons may organize a limited liability company, consisting of one or more members, by delivering articles of organization to the office of the [Secretary of State] for filing.

(b) Unless a delayed effective date is specified, the existence of a limited liability company begins when the articles of organization are filed.

(c) The filing of the articles of organization by the [Secretary of State] is conclusive proof that the organizers satisfied all conditions precedent to the creation of a limited liability company.

Section 203. **Articles of organization.**

(a) Articles of organization of a limited liability company must set forth:

(1) the name of the company;

(2) the address of the initial designated office;

(3) the name and street address of the initial agent for service of process;

(4) the name and address of each organizer;

(5) whether the company is to be a term company and, if so, the term specified;

(6) whether the company is to be manager-managed, and, if so, the name and address of each initial manager; and

(7) whether one or more of the members of the company are to be liable for its debts and obligations under Section 303(c).

(b) Articles of organization of a limited liability company may set forth:

(1) provisions permitted to be set forth in an operating agreement; or

(2) other matters not inconsistent with law.

(c) Articles of organization of a limited liability company

may not vary the nonwaivable provisions of Section 103(b). As to all other matters, if any provision of an operating agreement is inconsistent with the articles of organization:

(1) the operating agreement controls as to managers, members, and members' transferees; and

(2) the articles of organization control as to persons, other than managers, members and their transferees, who reasonably rely on the articles to their detriment.

* * * *

Section 208. **Certificate of existence or authorization.**

(a) A person may request the [Secretary of State] to furnish a certificate of existence for a limited liability company or a certificate of authorization for a foreign limited liability company.

(b) A certificate of existence for a limited liability company must set forth:

(1) the company's name;

(2) that it is duly organized under the laws of this State, the date of organization, whether its duration is at-will or for a specified term, and, if the latter, the period specified;

(3) if payment is reflected in the records of the [Secretary of State] and if nonpayment affects the existence of the company, that all fees, taxes, and penalties owed to this State have been paid;

(4) whether its most recent annual report required by Section 211 has been filed with the [Secretary of State];

(5) that articles of termination have not been filed; and

(6) other facts of record in the office of the [Secretary of State] which may be requested by the applicant.

(c) A certificate of authorization for a foreign limited liability company must set forth:

(1) the company's name used in this State;

(2) that it is authorized to transact business in this State;

(3) if payment is reflected in the records of the [Secretary of State] and if nonpayment affects the authorization of the company, that all fees, taxes, and penalties owed to this State have been paid;

(4) whether its most recent annual report required by

Section 211 has been filed with the [Secretary of State];

(5) that a certificate of cancellation has not been filed; and

(6) other facts of record in the office of the [Secretary of State] which may be requested by the applicant.

(d) Subject to any qualification stated in the certificate, a certificate of existence or authorization issued by the [Secretary of State] may be relied upon as conclusive evidence that the domestic or foreign limited liability company is in existence or is authorized to transact business in this State.

* * * *

[ARTICLE] 3.

RELATIONS OF MEMBERS AND MANAGERS TO PERSONS DEALING WITH LIMITED LIABILITY COMPANY

* * * *

Section 303.   **Liability of members and managers.**

(a) Except as otherwise provided in subsection (c), the debts, obligations, and liabilities of a limited liability company, whether arising in contract, tort, or otherwise, are solely the debts, obligations, and liabilities of the company. A member or manager is not personally liable for a debt, obligation, or liability of the company solely by reason of being or acting as a member or manager.

(b) The failure of a limited liability company to observe the usual company formalities or requirements relating to the exercise of its company powers or management of its business is not a ground for imposing personal liability on the members or managers for liabilities of the company.

(c) All or specified members of a limited liability company are liable in their capacity as members for all or specified debts, obligations, or liabilities of the company if:

(1) a provision to that effect is contained in the articles of organization; and

(2) a member so liable has consented in writing to the adoption of the provision or to be bound by the provision.

* * * *

[ARTICLE] 4.

RELATIONS OF MEMBERS TO EACH OTHER AND TO LIMITED LIABILITY COMPANY

* * * *

Section 404.   **Management of limited liability company.**

(a) In a member-managed company:

(1) each member has equal rights in the management and conduct of the company's business; and

(2) except as otherwise provided in subsection (c) or in Section 801(b)(3)(i), any matter relating to the business

of the company may be decided by a majority of the members.

(b) In a manager-managed company:

(1) each manager has equal rights in the management and conduct of the company's business;

(2) except as otherwise provided in subsection (c) or in Section 801(b)(3)(i), any matter relating to the business of the company may be exclusively decided by the manager or, if there is more than one manager, by a majority of the managers; and

(3) a manager:

(i) must be designated, appointed, elected, removed, or replaced by a vote, approval, or consent of a majority of the members; and

(ii) holds office until a successor has been elected and qualified, unless the manager sooner resigns or is removed.

(c) The only matters of a member or manager-managed company's business requiring the consent of all of the members are:

(1) the amendment of the operating agreement under Section 103;

(2) the authorization or ratification of acts or transactions under Section 103(b)(2)(ii) which would otherwise violate the duty of loyalty;

(3) an amendment to the articles of organization under Section 204;

(4) the compromise of an obligation to make a contribution under Section 402(b);

(5) the compromise, as among members, of an obligation of a member to make a contribution or return money or other property paid or distributed in violation of this [Act];

(6) the making of interim distributions under Section 405(a), including the redemption of an interest;

(7) the admission of a new member;

(8) the use of the company's property to redeem an interest subject to a charging order;

(9) the consent to dissolve the company under Section 801(b)(2);

(10) a waiver of the right to have the company's business wound up and the company terminated under Section 802(b);

(11) the consent of members to merge with another entity under Section 904(c)(1); and

(12) the sale, lease, exchange, or other disposal of all, or substantially all, of the company's property with or without goodwill.

(d) Action requiring the consent of members or managers under this [Act] may be taken without a meeting.

(e) A member or manager may appoint a proxy to vote or otherwise act for the member or manager by signing an appointment instrument, either personally or by the member's or manager's attorney-in-fact.

The General Agreement on Tariffs and Trade of 1994 [EXCERPTS]

Part I

FINAL ACT EMBODYING THE RESULTS OF THE URUGUAY ROUND OF MULTILATERAL TRADE NEGOTIATIONS

1. Having met in order to conclude the Uruguay Round of Multilateral Trade Negotiations, the representatives of the Governments and of the European Communities, members of the Trade Negotiations Committee * * *, *agree* that the Agreement Establishing the Multilateral Trade Organization and the Ministerial Decisions and Declarations * * * embody the results of their negotiations and form an integral part of this Final Act.

　 *　 *　 *　 *

Part II

AGREEMENT ESTABLISHING THE MULTILATERAL TRADE ORGANIZATION

The *Parties* to this Agreement,

Recognizing that their relations in the field of trade and economic endeavour should be conducted with a view to raising standards of living, ensuring full employment and a large and steadily growing volume of real income and effective demand, and expanding the production and trade in good and services, while allowing for the optimal use of the world's resources in accordance with the objective of sustainable development, seeking both to protect and preserve the environment and enhance the means for doing so in a manner consistent with their respective needs and concerns at different levels of economic development,

Recognizing further that there is need for positive efforts designed to ensure that developing countries * * * secure a share in the growth in international trade commensurate with the needs of their economic development,

Being desirous of contributing to these objectives by entering into reciprocal and mutually advantageous arrangements directed to the substantial reduction of tariffs and other barriers to trade and to the elimination of discriminatory treatment in international trade relations,

Resolved, therefore, to develop an integrated, more viable and durable multilateral trading system encompassing the General Agreement on Tariffs and Trade, the results of the past trade liberalization efforts, and all of the results of the Uruguay Round of multilateral trade negotiations,

Determined to preserve the basic principles and to further the objectives underlying this multilateral trading system,

Agree as follows:

　 *　 *　 *　 *

The Multilateral Trade Organization [MTO] * * * is hereby established.

　 *　 *　 *　 *

[The] MTO shall facilitate the implementation, administration, operation, and further the objectives, of this Agreement and of the Multilateral Trade Agreements, and shall also provide the framework for the implementation, administration and operation of the Plurilateral Trade Agreements.

　 *　 *　 *　 *

[Except] as otherwise provided for under this Agreement or the Multilateral Trade Agreements, the MTO shall be guided by the decisions, procedures and customary practices followed by the contracting parties of the GATT 1947 and the bodies established in the framework of the GATT 1947.

　 *　 *　 *　 *

AGREEMENT ON AGRICULTURE

　 *　 *　 *　 *

2. In accordance with the Mid-Term Review Agreement that government measures of assistance, whether direct or indirect, to encourage agricultural and rural development are an integral part of the development programmes of developing countries, investment subsidies which are generally available to agriculture in developing country Members and agricultural input subsidies generally available to low-income or resource poor producers in developing country Members shall be exempt from domestic support reduction commitments that would otherwise be applicable to such measures, as shall domestic support to producers in developing country Members to encourage diversification from growing illicit narcotic crops. * * *

　 *　 *　 *　 *

AGREEMENT ON TEXTILES AND CLOTHING

　 *　 *　 *　 *

1. Members agree that circumvention by transshipment, rerouting, false declaration concerning country or place of

origin, and falsification of official documents, frustrates the implementation of this Agreement to integrate the textiles and clothing sector into the GATT 1994. Accordingly, Members should establish the necessary legal provisions and/or administrative procedures to address and take action against such circumvention. Members further agree that, consistent with their domestic laws and procedures, they will cooperate fully to address problems arising from circumvention.

* * * *

2. Safeguard action may be taken * * * when, on the basis of a determination by a Member, it is demonstrated that a particular product is being imported into its territory in such increased quantities as to cause serious damage, or actual threat thereof, to the domestic industry producing like and/or directly competitive products. Serious damage or actual threat thereof must demonstrably be caused by such increased quantities in total imports of that product and not by such other factors as technological changes or changes in consumer preference.

* * * *

AGREEMENT ON
TECHNICAL BARRIERS TO TRADE
* * * *

2.2 Members shall ensure that technical regulations are not prepared, adopted or applied with a view to or with the effect of creating unnecessary obstacles to international trade. For this purpose, technical regulations shall not be more trade-restrictive than necessary to fulfil a legitimate objective, taking account of the risks non-fulfilment would create. Such legitimate objectives [include] national security requirements; the prevention of deceptive practices; protection of human health or safety, animal or plant life or health, or the environment. In assessing such risks, relevant elements of consideration [include] * * * available scientific and technical information, related processing technology or intended end uses of products.

* * * *

AGREEMENT ON IMPLEMENTATION OF
ARTICLE VI OF GATT 1994
* * * *

2.1 For the purpose of this Agreement a product is to be considered as being dumped, i.e., introduced into the commerce of another country at less than its normal value, if the export price of the product exported from one country to another is less than the comparable price, in the ordinary course of trade, for the like product when destined for consumption in the exporting country.

* * * *

3.5 It must be demonstrated that the dumped imports are * * * causing injury within the meaning of this Agreement. The demonstration of a causal relationship between the dumped imports and the injury to the domestic industry shall be based on an examination of all rele-

vant evidence before the authorities. The authorities shall also examine any known factors other than the dumped imports which at the same time are injuring the domestic industry, and the injuries caused by these other factors must not be attributed to the dumped imports. Factors which may be relevant in this respect include * * * the volume and prices of imports not sold at dumping prices, contraction in demand or changes in the patterns of consumption, trade restrictive practices of and competition between the foreign and domestic producers, developments in technology and the export performance and productivity of the domestic industry.

* * * *

9.2 When an anti-dumping duty is imposed in respect of any product, such anti-dumping duty shall be collected in the appropriate amounts in each case, on a non-discriminatory basis on imports of such product from all sources found to be dumped and causing injury, except as to imports from those sources from which price undertakings under the terms of this Agreement have been accepted. The authorities shall name the supplier or suppliers of the product concerned. If, however, several suppliers from the same country are involved, and it is impracticable to name all of these suppliers, the authorities may name the supplying country concerned. If several suppliers from more than one country are involved, the authorities may name either all the suppliers involved, or, if this is impracticable, all the supplying countries involved.

* * * *

AGREEMENT ON
PRESHIPMENT INSPECTION
* * * *

12. User Members shall ensure that preshipment inspection entities do not request exporters to provide information regarding:

(a) manufacturing data related to patented, licensed or undisclosed processes, or to processes for which a patent is pending;

(b) unpublished technical data other than necessary to demonstrate compliance with technical regulations or standards;

(c) internal pricing, including manufacturing costs;

(d) profit levels;

(e) the terms of contracts between exporters and their suppliers unless it is not otherwise possible for the entity to conduct the inspection in question. In such cases, the entity shall only request the information necessary for this purpose.

* * * *

AGREEMENT ON SUBSIDIES
AND COUNTERVAILING MEASURES
* * * *

3.1 Except as provided in the Agreement on Agriculture,

the following subsidies * * * shall be prohibited:

(a) subsidies contingent, in law or in fact, whether solely or as one of several other conditions, upon export performance * * * ;

(b) subsidies contingent, whether solely or as one of several other conditions, upon the use of domestic over imported goods.

* * * *

AGREEMENT ON SAFEGUARDS

* * * *

2. A Member may apply a safeguard measure to a product only if that Member has determined * * * that such product is being imported into its territory in such increased quantities, absolute or relative to domestic production, and under such conditions as to cause or threaten to cause serious injury to the domestic industry that produces like or directly competitive products.

* * * *

8. Safeguard measures shall be applied only to the extent as may be necessary to prevent or remedy serious injury and to facilitate adjustment. * * *

* * * *

12. The total period of application of a safeguard measure including the period of application of any provisional measure, the period of initial application and any extension thereof, shall not exceed eight years.

* * * *

19. Safeguard measures shall not be applied against a product originating in a developing country Member as long as its share of imports of the product concerned in the importing Member does not exceed 3 [percent], provided that, developing country Members with less than 3 [percent] import share collectively account for not more than 9 [percent] of total imports of the product concerned.

* * * *

GENERAL AGREEMENT ON TRADE IN SERVICES

* * * *

1. With respect to any measure covered by this Agreement, each Member shall accord immediately and unconditionally to services and service suppliers of any other Member, treatment no less favourable than that it accords to like services and service suppliers of any other country.

* * * *

AGREEMENT ON TRADE-RELATED ASPECTS OF INTELLECTUAL PROPERTY RIGHTS, INCLUDING TRADE IN COUNTERFEIT GOODS

* * * *

1. Members shall ensure that enforcement procedures * * * are available under their national laws so as to permit effective action against any act of infringement of intellectual property rights covered by this Agreement, including expeditious remedies to prevent infringements and remedies which constitute a deterrent to further infringements. These procedures shall be applied in such a manner as to avoid the creation of barriers to legitimate trade and to provide for safeguards against their abuse.

2. Procedures concerning the enforcement of intellectual property rights shall be fair and equitable. They shall not be unnecessarily complicated or costly, or entail unreasonable time-limits or unwarranted delays.

* * * *

UNDERSTANDING ON RULES AND PROCEDURES GOVERNING THE SETTLEMENT OF DISPUTES

* * * *

2.1 The Dispute Settlement Body (DSB) * * * shall administer these rules and procedures and * * * the consultation and dispute settlement provisions of the covered agreements.

The North American Free Trade Agreement of 1993 [EXCERPTS]

Part One: **GENERAL PART**

Chapter One: **Objectives**

Article 101: **Establishment of the Free Trade Area**

The Parties to this Agreement * * * hereby establish a free trade area.

Article 102: **Objectives**

1. The objectives of this Agreement * * * are to: (a) eliminate barriers to trade in, and facilitate the cross-border movement of, goods and services between the territories of the Parties; (b) promote conditions of fair competition in the free trade area; (c) increase substantially investment opportunities in the territories of the Parties; (d) provide adequate and effective protection and enforcement of intellectual property rights in each Party's territory; (e) create effective procedures for the implementation and application of this Agreement, for its joint administration and for the resolution of disputes; and (f) establish a framework for further trilateral, regional and multilateral cooperation to expand and enhance the benefits of this Agreement.

* * * *

Part Two: **TRADE IN GOODS**

Chapter Three: **National Treatment and Market Access for Goods**

* * * *

Article 301: **National Treatment**

1. Each Party shall accord national treatment to the goods of another Party in accordance with Article III of the General Agreement on Tariffs and Trade (GATT) * * * .

2. [N]ational treatment shall mean, with respect to a state or province, treatment no less favorable than the most favorable treatment accorded by such state or province to any like, directly competitive or substitutable goods, as the case may be, of the Party of which it forms a part.

* * * *

Article 302: **Tariff Elimination**

1. Except as otherwise provided in this Agreement, no Party may increase any existing customs duty, or adopt any customs duty, on an originating good.

2. [E]ach Party shall progressively eliminate its customs duties on originating goods in accordance with its Schedule * * * .

* * * *

Article 316: **Consultations and Committee on Trade in Goods**

1. The Parties hereby establish a Committee on Trade in Goods, comprising representatives of each Party.

* * * *

3. The Parties shall convene at least once each year a meeting of their officials responsible for customs, immigration, inspection of food and agricultural products, border inspection facilities, and regulation of transportation for the purpose of addressing issues related to movement of goods through the Parties' ports of entry.

* * * *

Part Three: **TECHNICAL BARRIERS TO TRADE**

Chapter Nine: **Standards-Related Measures**

* * * *

Article 904:

Basic Rights and Obligations

Right to Take Standards-Related Measures

1. Each Party may * * * adopt, maintain or apply any standards-related measure, including any such measure relating to safety, the protection of human, animal or plant life or health, the environment or consumers, and any measure to ensure its enforcement or implementation. Such measures include those to prohibit the importation of a good of another Party or the provision of a service by a service provider of another Party that fails to comply with the applicable requirements of those measures or to complete the Party's approval procedures.

* * * *

Unnecessary Obstacles

4. No Party may prepare, adopt, maintain or apply any standards-related measure with a view to or with the effect of creating an unnecessary obstacle to trade between the Parties. An unnecessary obstacle to trade shall not be deemed to be created where: (a) the demonstrable purpose of the measure is to achieve a legitimate objective; and (b) the measure does not operate to exclude goods of another Party that meet that legitimate objective.

* * * *

Article 913: **Committee on Standards-Related Measures**

1. The Parties hereby establish a Committee on Standards-Related Measures, comprising representatives of each Party.

2. The Committee's functions shall include: (a) monitoring the implementation and administration of this Chapter * * * ; (b) facilitating the process by which the Parties make compatible their standards-related measures; (c) providing a forum for the Parties to consult on issues relating to standards-related measures * * * ; (d) enhancing cooperation on the development, application and enforcement of standards-related measures; and (e) considering non-governmental, regional and multilateral developments regarding standards-related measures, including under the GATT.

* * * *

Part Five: **INVESTMENT, SERVICES AND RELATED MATTERS**

Chapter Eleven: **Investment**

SECTION A—INVESTMENT

* * * *

Article 1102: **National Treatment**

* * * *

2. Each Party shall accord to investments of investors of another Party treatment no less favorable than that it accords, in like circumstances, to investments of its own investors with respect to the establishment, acquisition, expansion, management, conduct, operation, and sale or other disposition of investments.

* * * *

4. For greater certainty, no Party may: (a) impose on an investor of another Party a requirement that a minimum level of equity in an enterprise in the territory of the Party be held by its nationals, other than nominal qualifying shares for directors or incorporators of corporations; or (b) require an investor of another Party, by reason of its nationality, to sell or otherwise dispose of an investment in the territory of the Party.

* * * *

Part Six: **INTELLECTUAL PROPERTY**

Chapter Seventeen: **Intellectual Property**

Article 1701: **Nature and Scope of Obligations**

1. Each Party shall provide in its territory to the nationals of another Party adequate and effective protection and enforcement of intellectual property rights, while ensuring that measures to enforce intellectual property rights do not themselves become barriers to legitimate trade.

* * * *

Article 1705: **Copyright**
* * * *

2. Each Party shall provide to authors and their successors in interest those rights enumerated in the Berne Convention in respect of works covered by paragraph 1, including the right to authorize or prohibit: (a) the importation into the Party's territory of copies of the work made without the right holder's authorization; (b) the first public distribution of the original and each copy of the work by sale, rental or otherwise; (c) the communication of a work to the public; and (d) the commercial rental of the original or a copy of a computer program. Subparagraph (d) shall not apply where the copy of the computer program is not itself an essential object of the rental. Each Party shall provide that putting the original or a copy of a computer program on the market with the right holder's consent shall not exhaust the rental right.

* * * *

4. Each Party shall provide that, where the term of protection of a work, other than a photographic work or a work of applied art, is to be calculated on a basis other than the life of a natural person, the term shall be not less than 50 years from the end of the calendar year of the first authorized publication of the work or, failing such authorized publication within 50 years from the making of the work, 50 years from the end of the calendar year of making.

5. Each Party shall confine limitations or exceptions to the rights provided for in this Article to certain special cases that do not conflict with a normal exploitation of the work and do not unreasonably prejudice the legitimate interests of the right holder.

* * * *

Article 1706: **Sound Recordings**

1. Each Party shall provide to the producer of a sound recording the right to authorize or prohibit: (a) the direct or indirect reproduction of the sound recording; (b) the importation into the Party's territory of copies of the sound recording made without the producer's authorization; (c) the first public distribution of the original and each copy of the sound recording by sale, rental or otherwise; and (d) the commercial rental of the original or a copy of the sound recording, except where expressly

otherwise provided in a contract between the producer of the sound recording and the authors of the works fixed therein. Each Party shall provide that putting the original or a copy of a sound recording on the market with the right holder's consent shall not exhaust the rental right.

* * * *

Article 1708: Trademarks

* * * *

4. Each Party shall provide a system for the registration of trademarks, which shall include: (a) examination of applications; (b) notice to be given to an applicant of the reasons for the refusal to register a trademark; (c) a reasonable opportunity for the applicant to respond to the notice; (d) publication of each trademark either before or promptly after it is registered; and (e) a reasonable opportunity for interested persons to petition to cancel the registration of a trademark. A Party may provide for a reasonable opportunity for interested persons to oppose the registration of a trademark.

* * * *

7. Each Party shall provide that the initial registration of a trademark be for a term of at least 10 years and that the registration be indefinitely renewable for terms of not less than 10 years when conditions for renewal have been met.

* * * *

Article 1709: Patents

1. Subject to paragraphs 2 and 3, each Party shall make patents available for any inventions, whether products or processes, in all fields of technology, provided that such inventions are new, result from an inventive step and are capable of industrial application. For purposes of this Article, a Party may deem the terms "inventive step" and "capable of industrial application" to be synonymous with the terms "non-obvious" and "useful," respectively.

* * * *

Article 1711: Trade Secrets

1. Each Party shall provide the legal means for any person to prevent trade secrets from being disclosed to, acquired by, or used by others without the consent of the person lawfully in control of the information in a manner contrary to honest commercial practices, in so far as: (a) the information is secret in the sense that it is not, as a body

or in the precise configuration and assembly of its components, generally known among or readily accessible to persons that normally deal with the kind of information in question; (b) the information has actual or potential commercial value because it is secret; and (c) the person lawfully in control of the information has taken reasonable steps under the circumstances to keep it secret.

* * * *

Article 1714: Enforcement of Intellectual Property Rights: General Provisions

* * * *

3. Each Party shall provide that decisions on the merits of a case in judicial and administrative enforcement proceedings shall: (a) preferably be in writing and preferably state the reasons on which the decisions are based; (b) be made available at least to the parties in a proceeding without undue delay; and (c) be based only on evidence in respect of which such parties were offered the opportunity to be heard.

4. Each Party shall ensure that parties in a proceeding have an opportunity to have final administrative decisions reviewed by a judicial authority of that Party and, subject to jurisdictional provisions in its domestic laws concerning the importance of a case, to have reviewed at least the legal aspects of initial judicial decisions on the merits of a case. Notwithstanding the above, no Party shall be required to provide for judicial review of acquittals in criminal cases.

* * * *

Article 1717: Criminal Procedures and Penalties

1. Each Party shall provide criminal procedures and penalties to be applied at least in cases of willful trademark counterfeiting or copyright piracy on a commercial scale. Each Party shall provide that penalties available include imprisonment or monetary fines, or both, sufficient to provide a deterrent, consistent with the level of penalties applied for crimes of a corresponding gravity.

2. Each Party shall provide that, in appropriate cases, its judicial authorities may order the seizure, forfeiture and destruction of infringing goods and of any materials and implements the predominant use of which has been in the commission of the offense.

The Small Business Regulatory Enforcement Fairness Act of 1996
[EXCERPTS]

Section 801. **Congressional review**

(a)(1)(A) Before a rule can take effect, the Federal agency promulgating such rule shall submit to each House of the Congress * * * a report containing—(i) a copy of the rule; (ii) a concise general statement relating to the rule, including whether it is a major rule; and (iii) the proposed effective date of the rule.

* * * *

(C) Upon receipt of a report submitted under subparagraph (A), each House shall provide copies of the report to the chairman and ranking member of each standing committee with jurisdiction under the rules of the House of Representatives or the Senate to report a bill to amend the provision of law under which the rule is issued.

* * * *

(3) A major rule relating to a report submitted under paragraph (1) shall take effect on the latest of—

(A) the later of the date occurring 60 days after the date on which—(i) the Congress receives the report submitted under paragraph (1); or (ii) the rule is published in the *Federal Register*, if so published;

(B) if the Congress passes a joint resolution of disapproval * * * relating to the rule, and the President signs a veto of such resolution, the earlier date—(i) on which either House of Congress votes and fails to override the veto of the President; or (ii) occurring 30 session days after the date on which the Congress received the veto and objections of the President; or

(C) the date the rule would have otherwise taken effect, if not for this section (unless a joint resolution of disapproval * * * is enacted).

* * * *

(b)(1) A rule shall not take effect (or continue), if the Congress enacts a joint resolution of disapproval * * * .

* * * *

Section 657. **Oversight of regulatory enforcement**

* * * *

(b) (2) The [SBA Enforcement] Ombudsman shall—

(A) work with each agency with regulatory authority over small businesses to ensure that small business concerns that receive or are subject to an audit, on-site inspection, compliance assistance effort, or other enforcement related communication or contact by agency personnel are provided with a means to comment on the enforcement activity conducted by such personnel;

(B) establish means to receive comments from small business concerns regarding actions by agency employees conducting compliance or enforcement activities with respect to the small business concern * * * on a confidential basis * * * ;

(C) based on substantiated comments received from small business concerns and the [Regional Small Business Regulatory Fairness] Boards, annually report to Congress and affected agencies evaluating the enforcement activities of agency personnel including a rating of the responsiveness to small business of the various regional and program offices of each agency; [and]

(D) coordinate and report annually on the activities, findings and recommendations of the [Regional Small Business Regulatory Fairness] Boards to the Administrator [of the Small Business Adminstration] and to the heads of affected agencies[.]

* * * *

(c)(2) Each [Regional Small Business Regulatory Fairness] Board * * * shall—

(A) meet at least annually to advise the Ombudsman on matters of concern to small businesses relating to the enforcement activities of agencies[.]

Spanish Equivalents for Important Legal Terms in English

Abandoned property: bienes abandonados
Acceptance: aceptación; consentimiento; acuerdo
Acceptor: aceptante
Accession: toma de posesión; aumento; accesión
Accommodation indorser: avalista de favor
Accommodation party: firmante de favor
Accord: acuerdo; convenio; arregio
Accord and satisfaction: transacción ejecutada
Act of state doctrine: doctrina de acto de gobierno
Administrative law: derecho administrativo
Administrative process: procedimiento o metódo administrativo
Administrator: administrador (-a)
Adverse possession: posesión de hecho susceptible de proscripción adquisitiva
Affirmative action: acción afirmativa
Affirmative defense: defensa afirmativa
After-acquired property: bienes adquiridos con posterioridad a un hecho dado
Agency: mandato; agencia
Agent: mandatorio; agente; representante
Agreement: convenio; acuerdo; contrato
Alien corporation: empresa extranjera
Allonge: hojas adicionales de endosos
Answer: contestación de la demande; alegato
Anticipatory repudiation: anuncio

previo de las partes de su imposibilidad de cumplir con el contrato
Appeal: apelación; recurso de apelación
Appellate jurisdiction: jurisdicción de apelaciones
Appraisal right: derecho de valuación
Arbitration: arbitraje
Arson: incendio intencional
Articles of partnership: contrato social
Artisan's lien: derecho de retención que ejerce al artesano
Assault: asalto; ataque; agresión
Assignment of rights: transmisión; transferencia; cesión
Assumption of risk: no resarcimiento por exposición voluntaria al peligro
Attachment: auto judicial que autoriza el embargo; embargo

Bailee: depositario
Bailment: depósito; constitución en depósito
Bailor: depositante
Bankruptcy trustee: síndico de la quiebra
Battery: agresión; física
Bearer: portador; tenedor
Bearer instrument: documento al portador
Bequest or legacy: legado (de bienes muebles)
Bilateral contract: contrato bilateral
Bill of lading: conocimiento de embarque; carta de porte
Bill of Rights: declaración de derechos
Binder: póliza de seguro provisoria; recibo de pago a cuenta del precio
Blank indorsement: endoso en

blanco
Blue sky laws: leyes reguladoras del comercio bursátil
Bond: título de crédito; garantía; caución
Bond indenture: contrato de emisión de bonos; contrato del ampréstito
Breach of contract: incumplimiento de contrato
Brief: escrito; resumen; informe
Burglary: violación de domicilio
Business judgment rule: regla de juicio comercial
Business tort: agravio comercial

Case law: ley de casos; derecho casuístico
Cashier's check: cheque de caja
Causation in fact: causalidad en realidad
Cease-and-desist order: orden para cesar y desistir
Certificate of deposit: certificado de depósito
Certified check: cheque certificado
Charitable trust: fideicomiso para fines benéficos
Chattel: bien mueble
Check: cheque
Chose in action: derecho inmaterial; derecho de acción
Civil law: derecho civil
Close corporation: sociedad de un solo accionista o de un grupo restringido de accionistas
Closed shop: taller agremiado (emplea solamente a miembros de un gremio)
Closing argument: argumento al final
Codicil: codicilo
Collateral: guarantía; bien objeto de la guarantía real
Comity: cortesía; cortesía entre

naciones
Commercial paper: instrumentos negociables; documentos a valores commerciales
Common law: derecho consuetudinario; derecho común; ley común
Common stock: acción ordinaria
Comparative negligence: negligencia comparada
Compensatory damages: daños y perjuicios reales o compensatorios
Concurrent conditions: condiciones concurrentes
Concurrent jurisdiction: competencia concurrente de varios tribunales para entender en una misma causa
Concurring opinion: opinión concurrente
Condition: condición
Condition precedent: condición suspensiva
Condition subsequent: condición resolutoria
Confiscation: confiscación
Confusion: confusión; fusión
Conglomerate merger: fusión de firmas que operan en distintos mercados
Consent decree: acuerdo entre las partes aprobado por un tribunal
Consequential damages: daños y perjuicios indirectos
Consideration: consideración; motivo; contraprestación
Consolidation: consolidación
Constructive delivery: entrega simbólica
Constructive trust: fideicomiso creado por aplicación de la ley
Consumer protection law: ley para proteger el consumidor
Contract: contrato
Contract under seal: contrato formal o sellado
Contributory negligence: negligencia de la parte actora
Conversion: usurpación; conversión de valores
Copyright: derecho de autor
Corporation: sociedad anónima; corporación; persona jurídica
Co-sureties: cogarantes
Counterclaim: reconvención; contrademanda
Counteroffer: contraoferta
Course of dealing: curso de transacciones
Course of performance: curso de cumplimiento

Covenant: pacto; garantía; contrato
Covenant not to sue: pacto or contrato a no demandar
Covenant of quiet enjoyment: garantía del uso y goce pacífico del inmueble
Creditors' composition agreement: concordato preventivo
Crime: crimen; delito; contravención
Criminal law: derecho penal
Cross-examination: contrainterrogatorio
Cure: cura; cuidado; derecho de remediar un vicio contractual
Customs receipts: recibos de derechos aduaneros

Damages: daños; indemnización por daños y perjuicios
Debit card: tarjeta de dé bito
Debtor: deudor
Debt securities: seguridades de deuda
Deceptive advertising: publicidad engañosa
Deed: escritura; título; acta translativa de domino
Defamation: difamación
Delegation of duties: delegación de obligaciones
Demand deposit: depósito a la vista
Depositions: declaración de un testigo fuera del tribunal
Devise: legado; deposición testamentaria (bienes inmuebles)
Directed verdict: veredicto según orden del juez y sin participación activa del jurado
Direct examination: interrogatorio directo; primer interrogatorio
Disaffirmance: repudiación; renuncia; anulación
Discharge: descargo; liberación; cumplimiento
Disclosed principal: mandante revelado
Discovery: descubrimiento; producción de la prueba
Dissenting opinion: opinión disidente
Dissolution: disolución; terminación
Diversity of citizenship: competencia de los tribunales federales para entender en causas cuyas partes intervinientes son cuidadanos de distintos estados
Divestiture: extinción premature de derechos reales

Dividend: dividendo
Docket: orden del día; lista de causas pendientes
Domestic corporation: sociedad local
Draft: orden de pago; letrade cambio
Drawee: girado; beneficiario
Drawer: librador
Duress: coacción; violencia

Easement: servidumbre
Embezzlement: desfalco; malversación
Eminent domain: poder de expropiación
Employment discrimination: discriminación en el empleo
Entrepreneur: empresario
Environmental law: ley ambiental
Equal dignity rule: regla de dignidad egual
Equity security: tipo de participación en una sociedad
Estate: propiedad; patrimonio; derecho
Estop: impedir; prevenir
Ethical issue: cuestión ética
Exclusive jurisdiction: competencia exclusiva
Exculpatory clause: cláusula eximente
Executed contract: contrato ejecutado
Execution: ejecución; cumplimiento
Executor: albacea
Executory contract: contrato aún no completamente consumado
Executory interest: derecho futuro
Express contract: contrato expreso
Expropriation: expropriación

Federal question: caso federal
Fee simple: pleno dominio; dominio absoluto
Fee simple absolute: dominio absoluto
Fee simple defeasible: dominio sujeta a una condición resolutoria
Felony: crimen; delito grave
Fictitious payee: beneficiario ficticio
Fiduciary: fiduciaro
Firm offer: oferta en firme
Fixture: inmueble por destino, incorporación a anexación
Floating lien: gravamen continuado
Foreign corporation: sociedad extranjera; U.S. sociedad constituída en otro estado
Forgery: falso; falsificación

Formal contract: contrato formal
Franchise: privilegio; franquicia; concesión
Franchisee: persona que recibe una concesión
Franchisor: persona que vende una concesión
Fraud: fraude; dolo; engaño
Future interest: bien futuro

Garnishment: embargo de derechos
General partner: socio comanditario
General warranty deed: escritura translativa de domino con garantía de título
Gift: donación
Gift *causa mortis:* donación por causa de muerte
Gift *inter vivos:* donación entre vivos
Good faith: buena fe
Good faith purchaser: comprador de buena fe

Holder: tenedor por contraprestación
Holder in due course: tenedor legítimo
Holographic will: testamento ológrafico
Homestead exemption laws: leyes que exceptúan las casas de familia de ejecución por duedas generales
Horizontal merger: fusión horizontal

Identification: identificación
Implied-in-fact contract: contrato implícito en realidad
Implied warranty: guarantía implícita
Implied warranty of merchantability: garantía implícita de vendibilidad
Impossibility of performance: imposibilidad de cumplir un contrato
Imposter: imposter
Incidental beneficiary: beneficiario incidental; beneficiario secundario
Incidental damages: daños incidentales
Indictment: auto de acusación; acusación
Indorsee: endorsatario
Indorsement: endoso
Indorser: endosante
Informal contract: contrato no formal; contrato verbal
Information: acusación hecha por el ministerio público

Injunction: mandamiento; orden de no innovar
Innkeeper's lien: derecho de retención que ejerce el posadero
Installment contract: contrato de pago en cuotas
Insurable interest: interés asegurable
Intended beneficiary: beneficiario destinado
Intentional tort: agravio; cuasi-delito intenciónal
International law: derecho internaciónal
Interrogatories: preguntas escritas sometidas por una parte a la otra o a un testigo
Inter vivos **trust:** fideicomiso entre vivos
Intestacy laws: leyes de la condición de morir intestado
Intestate: intestado
Investment company: compañia de inversiones
Issue: emisión

Joint tenancy: derechos conjuntos en un bien inmueble en favor del beneficiario sobreviviente
Judgment *n.o.v.:* juicio no obstante veredicto
Judgment rate of interest: interés de juicio
Judicial process: acto de procedimiento; proceso jurídico
Judicial review: revisión judicial
Jurisdiction: jurisdicción

Larceny: robo; hurto
Law: derecho; ley; jurisprudencia
Lease: contrato de locación; contrato de alquiler
Leasehold estate: bienes forales
Legal rate of interest: interés legal
Legatee: legatario
Letter of credit: carta de crédito
Levy: embargo; comiso
Libel: libelo; difamación escrita
Life estate: usufructo
Limited partner: comanditario
Limited partnership: sociedad en comandita
Liquidation: liquidación; realización
Lost property: objetos perdidos

Majority opinion: opinión de la mayoría
Maker: persona que realiza u ordena; librador
Mechanic's lien: gravamen de constructor
Mediation: mediación; intervención

Merger: fusión
Mirror image rule: fallo de reflejo
Misdemeanor: infracción; contravención
Mislaid property: bienes extraviados
Mitigation of damages: reducción de daños
Mortgage: hypoteca
Motion to dismiss: excepción parentoria
Mutual fund: fondo mutual

Negotiable instrument: instrumento negociable
Negotiation: negociación
Nominal damages: daños y perjuicios nominales
Novation: novación
Nuncupative will: testamento nuncupativo

Objective theory of contracts: teoria objetiva de contratos
Offer: oferta
Offeree: persona que recibe una oferta
Offeror: oferente
Order instrument: instrumento o documento a la orden
Original jurisdiction: jurisdicción de primera instancia
Output contract: contrato de producción

Parol evidence rule: regla relativa a la prueba oral
Partially disclosed principal: mandante revelado en parte
Partnership: sociedad colectiva; asociación; asociación de participación
Past consideration: causa o contraprestación anterior
Patent: patente; privilegio
Pattern or practice: muestra o práctica
Payee: beneficiario de un pago
Penalty: pena; penalidad
Per capita: por cabeza
Perfection: perfeción
Performance: cumplimiento; ejecución
Personal defenses: excepciones personales
Personal property: bienes muebles
Per stirpes: por estirpe
Plea bargaining: regateo por un alegato
Pleadings: alegatos
Pledge: prenda
Police powers: poders de policia y

de prevención del crimen
Policy: póliza
Positive law: derecho positivo; ley positiva
Possibility of reverter: posibilidad de reversión
Precedent: precedente
Preemptive right: derecho de prelación
Preferred stock: acciones preferidas
Premium: recompensa; prima
Presentment warranty: garantía de presentación
Price discrimination: discriminación en los precios
Principal: mandante; principal
Privity: nexo jurídico
Privity of contract: relación contractual
Probable cause: causa probable
Probate: verificación; verificación del testamento
Probate court: tribunal de sucesiones y tutelas
Proceeds: resultados; ingresos
Profit: beneficio; utilidad; lucro
Promise: promesa
Promisee: beneficiario de una promesa
Promisor: promtente
Promissory estoppel: impedimento promisorio
Promissory note: pagaré; nota de pago
Promoter: promotor; fundador
Proximate cause: causa inmediata o próxima
Proxy: apoderado; poder
Punitive, or exemplary, damages: daños y perjuicios punitivos o ejemplares

Qualified indorsement: endoso con reservas
Quasi contract: contrato tácito o implícito
Quitclaim deed: acto de transferencia de una propiedad por finiquito, pero sin ninguna garantía sobre la validez del título transferido

Ratification: ratificación
Real property: bienes inmuebles
Reasonable doubt: duda razonable
Rebuttal: refutación
Recognizance: promesa; compromiso; reconocimiento
Recording statutes: leyes estatales sobre registros oficiales
Redress: reporación
Reformation: rectificación; reforma;

corrección
Rejoinder: dúplica; contrarréplica
Release: liberación; renuncia a un derecho
Remainder: substitución; reversión
Remedy: recurso; remedio; reparación
Replevin: acción reivindicatoria; reivindicación
Reply: réplica
Requirements contract: contrato de suministro
Rescission: rescisión
Res judicata: cosa juzgada; res judicata
Respondeat superior: responsabilidad del mandante o del maestro
Restitution: restitución
Restrictive indorsement: endoso restrictivo
Resulting trust: fideicomiso implícito
Reversion: reversión; sustitución
Revocation: revocación; derogación
Right of contribution: derecho de contribución
Right of reimbursement: derecho de reembolso
Right of subrogation: derecho de subrogación
Right-to-work law: ley de libertad de trabajo
Robbery: robo
Rule 10b-5: Regla 10b-5

Sale: venta; contrato de compreventa
Sale on approval: venta a ensayo; venta sujeta a la aprobación del comprador
Sale or return: venta con derecho de devolución
Sales contract: contrato de compraventa; boleto de compraventa
Satisfaction: satisfacción; pago
Scienter: a sabiendas
S corporation: S corporación
Secured party: acreedor garantizado
Secured transaction: transacción garantizada
Securities: volares; titulos; seguridades
Security agreement: convenio de seguridad
Security interest: interés en un bien dado en garantía que permite a quien lo detenta venderlo en caso de incumplimiento
Service mark: marca de

identificación de servicios
Shareholder's derivative suit: acción judicial entablada por un accionista en nombre de la sociedad
Signature: firma; rúbrica
Slander: difamación oral; calumnia
Sovereign immunity: immunidad soberana
Special indorsement: endoso especial; endoso a la orden de una person en particular
Specific performance: ejecución precisa, según los términos del contrato
Spendthrift trust: fideicomiso para pródigos
Stale check: cheque vencido
Stare decisis: acatar las decisiones, observar los precedentes
Statutory law: derecho estatutario; derecho legislado; derecho escrito
Stock: acciones
Stock warrant: certificado para la compra de acciones
Stop-payment order: orden de suspensión del pago de un cheque dada por el librador del mismo
Strict liability: responsabilidad unconditional
Summary judgment: fallo sumario

Tangible property: bienes corpóreos
Tenancy at will: inguilino por tiempo indeterminado (según la voluntad del propietario)
Tenancy by sufferance: posesión por tolerancia
Tenancy by the entirety: locación conyugal conjunta
Tenancy for years: inguilino por un término fijo
Tenancy in common: specie de copropiedad indivisa
Tender: oferta de pago; oferta de ejecución
Testamentary trust: fideicomiso testamentario
Testator: testador (-a)
Third party beneficiary contract: contrato para el beneficio del tercero-beneficiario
Tort: agravio; cuasi-delito
Totten trust: fideicomiso creado por un depósito bancario
Trade acceptance: letra de cambio aceptada
Trademark: marca registrada
Trade name: nombre comercial; razón social
Traveler's check: cheque del viajero
Trespass to land: ingreso no

authorizado a las tierras de otro
Trespass to personal property: violación de los derechos posesorios de un tercero con respecto a bienes muebles
Trust: fideicomiso; trust

Ultra vires: ultra vires; fuera de la facultad (de una sociedad anónima)
Unanimous opinion: opinión unámine
Unconscionable contract or clause: contrato leonino; cláusula leonino
Underwriter: subscriptor; asegurador
Unenforceable contract: contrato que no se puede hacer cumplir
Unilateral contract: contrato unilateral
Union shop: taller agremiado; empresa en la que todos los empleados son miembros del gremio o sindicato
Universal defenses: defensas legitimas o legales
Usage of trade: uso comercial
Usury: usura

Valid contract: contrato válido
Venue: lugar; sede del proceso
Vertical merger: fusión vertical de empresas
Voidable contract: contrato anulable
Void contract: contrato nulo; contrato inválido, sin fuerza legal
Voir dire: examen preliminar de un testigo a jurado por el tribunal para determinar su competencia
Voting trust: fideicomiso para ejercer el derecho de voto

Waiver: renuncia; abandono

Warranty of habitability: garantía de habitabilidad
Watered stock: acciones diluídos; capital inflado
White-collar crime: crimen administrativo
Writ of attachment: mandamiento de ejecución; mandamiento de embargo
Writ of *certiorari*: auto de avocación; auto de certiorari
Writ of execution: auto ejecutivo; mandamiento de ejecutión
Writ of mandamus: auto de mandamus; mandamiento; orden judicial

Glossary

Abus de droit A doctrine developed in the French courts. The doctrine modified employment at will and protected workers exercising their rights from wrongful discharge and other employer abuses.

Acceptance A voluntary act by the offeree that shows assent, or agreement, to the terms of an offer; may consist of words or conduct.

Accredited investors In the context of securities offerings, "sophisticated" investors, such as banks, insurance companies, investment companies, the issuer's executive officers and directors, and persons whose income or net worth exceeds certain limits.

Act of state doctrine A doctrine that provides that the judicial branch of one country will not examine the validity of public acts committed by a recognized foreign government within its own territory.

Actionable Capable of serving as the basis of a lawsuit.

Actual malice Real and demonstrable evil intent. In a defamation suit, a statement made about a public figure normally must be made with actual malice (with either knowledge of its falsity or a reckless disregard of the truth) for liability to be incurred.

Adhesion contract A "standard form" contract, such as that between a large retailer and a consumer, in which the stronger party dictates the terms.

Adjudicate To render a judicial decision. In the administrative process, the proceeding in which an administrative law judge hears and decides on issues that arise when an administrative agency charges a person or a firm with violating a law or regulation enforced by the agency.

Adjudication The act of rendering a judicial decision. In administrative process, the proceeding in which an administrative law judge hears and decides on issues that arise when an administrative agency charges a person or a firm with violating a law or regulation enforced by the agency.

Administrative agency A federal or state government agency established to perform a specific function. Administrative agencies are authorized by legislative acts to make and enforce rules to administer and enforce the acts.

Administrative law The body of law created by administrative agencies (in the form of rules, regulations, orders, and decisions) in order to carry out their duties and responsibilities.

Administrative law judge (ALJ) One who presides over an administrative agency hearing and who has the power to administer oaths, take testimony, rule on questions of evidence, and make determinations of fact.

Administrative process The procedure used by administrative agencies in the administration of law.

Adverse possession The acquisition of title to real property by occupying it openly, without the consent of the owner, for a period of time specified by a state statute. The occupation must be actual, open, notorious, exclusive, and in opposition to all others, including the owner.

Affirmative action Job-hiring policies that give special consideration to members of protected classes in an effort to overcome present effects of past discrimination.

Agency A relationship between two parties in which one party (the agent) agrees to represent or act for the other (the principal).

Agent A person who agrees to represent or act for another, called the principal.

Agreement A meeting of two or more minds in regard to the terms of a contract; usually broken down into two events—an offer by one party to form a contract, and an acceptance of the offer by the person to whom the offer is made.

Alien corporation A designation in the United States for a corporation formed in another country but doing business in the United States.

Alienation In real property law, a term used to define the process of transferring land out of one's possession (thus "alienating" the land from oneself).

Alternative dispute resolution (ADR) The resolution of disputes in ways other than those involved in the traditional judicial process. Negotiation, mediation, and arbitration are forms of ADR.

Answer Procedurally, a defendant's response to the plaintiff's complaint.

Anticipatory repudiation An assertion or action by a party indicating that he or she will not perform an obligation that the party is contractually obligated to perform at a future time.

Antitrust laws Laws protecting commerce from unlawful restraints.

Appropriate bargaining unit A designation based on job duties, skill levels, etc., of the proper entity that should be covered by a collective bargaining agreement.

Appropriation In tort law, the use by one person of another person's name, likeness, or other identifying characteristic without permission and for the benefit of the user.

Arbitration The settling of a dispute by submitting it to a disinterested third party (other than a court), who renders a decision that is (usually) legally binding.

Arbitration clause A clause in a contract that provides that, in case of a dispute, the parties will submit the dispute to arbitration rather than litigate the dispute in court.

Arbitrator A disinterested party who, by prior agreement of the parties submitting their dispute to arbitration, has the power to resolve the dispute and (generally) bind the parties.

Arson The malicious burning of another's dwelling. Some statutes have expanded this to include any real property regardless of ownership and the destruction of property by other means—for example, by explosion.

Articles of incorporation   The document filed with the appropriate governmental agency, usually the secretary of state, when a business is incorporated; state statutes usually prescribe what kind of information must be contained in the articles of incorporation.

Artisan's lien   A possessory lien given to a person who has made improvements and added value to another person's personal property as security for payment for services performed.

Assault   Any word or action intended to make another person fearful of immediate physical harm; a reasonably believable threat.

Assignment   The act of transferring to another all or part of one's rights arising under a contract.

Assumption of risk   A defense against negligence that can be used when the plaintiff is aware of a danger and voluntarily assumes the risk of injury from that danger.

Attachment   In the context of secured transactions, the process by which a security interest in the property of another becomes enforceable. In the context of judicial liens, a court-ordered seizure and taking into custody of property prior to the securing of a judgment for a past-due debt.

Attempted monopolization   Any actions by a firm to eliminate competition and gain monopoly power.

Attorney   A person who has received a law degree and has been licensed by one or more states to practice law.

Attorney-client privilege   Protected communications between an attorney and client made for the purpose of furnishing or obtaining professional legal advice or assistance. Courts and other government institutions cannot require diclosue of the comunications.

Authorization card   A card signed by an employee that gives a union permission to act on his or her behalf in negotiations with management once a majority of the employees has signed such cards.

Automatic stay   In bankruptcy proceedings, the suspension of

virtually all litigation and other action by creditors against the debtor or the debtor's property; the stay is effective the moment the debtor files a petition in bankruptcy.

Award   In the context of litigation, the amount of money awarded to a plaintiff in a civil lawsuit as damages. In the context of arbitration, the arbitrator's decision.

Bait-and-switch advertising   Advertising a product at a very attractive price (the "bait") and then informing the consumer, once he or she is in the store, that the advertised product is either not available or is of poor quality; the customer is then urged to purchase ("switched" to) a more expensive item.

Bankruptcy court   A federal court of limited jurisdiction that handles only bankruptcy proceedings. Bankruptcy proceedings are governed by federal bankruptcy law.

Battery   The unprivileged, intentional touching of another.

Beyond a reasonable doubt   The standard of proof used in criminal cases. If there is any reasonable doubt that a criminal defendant did not commit the crime with which he or she has been charged, then the verdict must be "not guilty."

Bilateral contract   A type of contract that arises when a promise is given in exchange for a return promise.

Bill of Rights   The first ten amendments to the U.S. Constitution.

Binder   A written, temporary insurance policy.

Binding authority   Any source of law that a court must follow when deciding a case. Binding authorities include constitutions, statutes, and regulations that govern the issue being decided, as well as court decisions that are controlling precedents within the jurisdiction.

Blue laws   State or local laws that prohibit the performance of certain types of commercial activities on Sunday.

Blue sky laws   State laws that regulate the offer and sale of securities.

Bona fide occupational qualification (BFOQ)   Identifiable characteristics reasonably necessary to the normal operation of a particular business. These characteristics can include gender, national origin, and religion, but not race.

Bounty payment   A reward (payment) given to a person or persons who perform a certain service—such as informing legal authorities of illegal actions.

Breach of contract   The failure, without legal excuse, of a promisor to perform the obligations of a contract.

Brief   A formal legal document submitted by the attorney for the appellant or the appellee (in answer to the appellant's brief) to an appellate court when a case is appealed. The appellant's brief outlines the facts and issues of the case, the judge's rulings or jury's findings that should be reversed or modified, the applicable law, and the arguments on the client's behalf.

Bulk zoning   Zoning regulations that restrict the amount of structural coverage on a particular parcel of land.

Bureaucracy   The organizational structure, consisting of government bureaus and agencies, through which the government implements and enforces the laws.

Burglary   The unlawful entry into a building with the intent to commit a felony. (Some state statutes expand this to include the intent to commit any crime.)

Business ethics   Ethics in a business context; a consensus of what constitutes right or wrong behavior in the world of business and the application of moral principles to situations that arise in a business setting.

Business invitees   Those people, such as customers or clients, who are invited onto business premises by the owner of those premises for business purposes.

Business judgment rule   A rule that immunizes corporate management from liability for actions that result in corporate losses or damages if the actions are undertaken in good faith and are within both the power of the corporation and the authority of management to make.

Business necessity A defense to allegations of employment discrimination in which the employer demonstrates that an employment practice that discriminates against members of a protected class is related to job performance.

Business tort The wrongful interference with another's business rights.

Case law The rules of law announced in court decisions. Case law includes the aggregate of reported cases that interpret judicial precedents, statutes, regulations, and constitutional provisions.

Categorical imperative A concept developed by the philosopher Immanuel Kant as an ethical guideline for behavior. In deciding whether an action is right or wrong, or desirable or undesirable, a person should evaluate the action in terms of what would happen if everybody else in the same situation, or category, acted the same way.

Causation in fact An act or omission without which an event would not have occurred.

Cease-and-desist order An administrative or judicial order prohibiting a person or business firm from conducting activities that an agency or court has deemed illegal.

Certification mark A mark used by one or more persons, other than the owner, to certify the region, materials, mode of manufacture, quality, or accuracy of the owner's goods or services. When used by members of a cooperative, association, or other organization, such a mark is referred to as a collective mark. Examples of certification marks include the "Good Housekeeping Seal of Approval" and "UL Tested."

Checks and balances The national government is composed of three separate branches: the executive, the legislative, and the judicial branches. Each branch of the government exercises a check upon the actions of the others.

Choice-of-language clause A clause in a contract designating the official language by which the contract will be interpreted in the event of a future disagreement over the contract's terms.

Choice-of-law clause A clause in a contract designating the law (such as the law of a particular state or nation) that will govern the contract.

Citation A reference to a publication in which a legal authority—such as a statute or a court decision—or other source can be found.

Civil law The branch of law dealing with the definition and enforcement of all private or public rights, as opposed to criminal matters.

Civil law system A system of law derived from that of the Roman Empire and based on a code rather than case law; the predominant system of law in the nations of continental Europe and the nations that were once their colonies. In the United States, Louisiana is the only state that has a civil law system.

Closed shop A firm that requires union membership by its workers as a condition of employment. The closed shop was made illegal by the Labor-Management Relations Act of 1947.

Collateral promise A secondary promise that is ancillary (subsidiary) to a principal transaction or primary contractual relationship, such as a promise made by one person to pay the debts of another if the latter fails to perform. A collateral promise normally must be in writing to be enforceable.

Collective bargaining The process by which labor and management negotiate the terms and conditions of employment, including working hours and workplace conditions.

Collective mark A mark used by members of a cooperative, association, or other organization to certify the region, materials, mode of manufacture, quality, or accuracy of the specific goods or services. Examples of collective marks include the labor union marks found on tags of certain products and the credits of movies, which indicate the various associations and organizations that participated in the making of the movies.

Comity A deference by which one nation gives effect to the laws and judicial decrees of another nation. This recognition is based primarily upon respect.

Commerce clause The provision in Article I, Section 8, of the U.S. Constitution that gives Congress the power to regulate interstate commerce.

Common law That body of law developed from custom or judicial decisions in English and U.S. courts, not attributable to a legislature.

Common situs picketing The illegal picketing of an entire construction site by workers who are involved in a labor dispute with a particular subcontractor.

Comparative negligence A theory in tort law under which the liability for injuries resulting from negligent acts is shared by all parties who were negligent (including the injured party), on the basis of each person's proportionate negligence.

Compensatory damages A money award equivalent to the actual value of injuries or damages sustained by the aggrieved party.

Complaint The pleading made by a plaintiff alleging wrongdoing on the part of the defendant; the document that, when filed with a court, initiates a lawsuit.

Computer crime Any act that is directed against computers and computer parts, that uses computers as instruments of crime, or that involves computers and constitutes abuse.

Concerted action Action by employees, such as a strike or picketing, with the purpose of furthering their bargaining demands or other mutual interests.

Concurrent jurisdiction Jurisdiction that exists when two different courts have the power to hear a case. For example, some cases can be heard in a federal or a state court.

Confiscation A government's taking of privately owned business or personal property without a proper public purpose or an award of just compensation.

Conglomerate merger A merger between firms that do not compete with each other because they are in different markets (as opposed to horizontal and vertical mergers).

Consent Voluntary agreement to a proposition or an act of another. A concurrence of wills.

Consequential damages Special damages that compensate for a loss that is not direct or immediate (for example, lost profits). The special damages must have been reasonably foreseeable at the time the breach or injury occurred in order for the plaintiff to collect them.

Consideration Generally, the value given in return for a promise. The consideration, which must be present to make the contract legally binding, must be something of legally sufficient value and bargained for and must result in a detriment to the promisee or a benefit to the promisor.

Constitutional law Law based on the U.S. Constitution and the constitutions of the various states.

Constructive eviction A form of eviction that occurs when a landlord fails to perform adequately any of the undertakings (such as providing heat in the winter) required by the lease, thereby making the tenant's further use and enjoyment of the property exceedingly difficult or impossible.

Consumer-debtor An individual whose debts are primarily consumer debts (debts for purchases made primarily for personal or household use).

Consumer law The body of statutes, agency rules, and judicial decisions protecting consumers of goods and services from dangerous manufacturing techniques, mislabeling, unfair credit practices, deceptive advertising, and so on. Consumer laws provide remedies and protections that are not ordinarily available to merchants or to businesses.

Contract An agreement that can be enforced in court; formed by two or more parties who agree to perform or to refrain from performing some act now or in the future.

Contractual capacity The threshold mental capacity required by the law for a party who enters into a contract to be bound by that contract.

Contributory negligence A theory in tort law under which a complaining party's own negligence contributed to or caused his or her injuries. Contributory negligence is an absolute bar to recovery in a minority of jurisdictions.

Conversion The wrongful taking, using, or retaining possession of personal property that belongs to another.

Conveyance The transfer of a title to land from one person to another by deed; a document (such as a deed) by which an interest in land is transferred from one person to another.

Copyright The exclusive right of "authors" to publish, print, or sell an intellectual production for a statutory period of time. A copyright has the same monopolistic nature as a patent or trademark, but it differs in that it applies exclusively to works of art, literature, and other works of authorship (including computer programs).

Corporate social responsibility The concept that corporations can and should act ethically and be accountable to society for their actions.

Corporate charter The document issued by a state agency or authority (usually the secretary of state) that grants a corporation legal existence and the right to function.

Corporation A legal entity formed in compliance with statutory requirements. The entity is distinct from its shareholders-owners.

Correspondent bank A bank in which another bank has an account (and vice versa) for the purpose of facilitating fund transfers.

Cost-benefit analysis A decision-making technique that involves weighing the costs of a given action against the benefits of the action.

Co-surety A joint surety; a person who assumes liability jointly with another surety for the payment of an obligation.

Counteradvertising New advertising that is undertaken pursuant to a Federal Trade Commission order for the purpose of correcting earlier false claims that were made about a product.

Counterclaim A claim made by a defendant in a civil lawsuit that in effect sues the plaintiff.

Counteroffer An offeree's response to an offer in which the offeree rejects the original offer and at the same time makes a new offer.

Cram-down provision A provision of the Bankruptcy Code that allows a court to confirm a debtor's Chapter 11 reorganization plan even though only one class of creditors has accepted it. To exercise the court's right under this provision, the court must demonstrate that the plan does not discriminate unfairly against any creditors and is fair and equitable.

Creditors' composition agreement An agreement formed between a debtor and his or her creditors in which the creditors agree to accept a lesser sum than that owed by the debtor in full satisfaction of the debt.

Crime A wrong against society proclaimed in a statute and, if committed, punishable by society through fines and/or imprisonment—and, in some cases, death.

Criminal law Law that defines and governs actions that constitute crimes. Generally, criminal law has to do with wrongful actions committed against society for which society demands redress.

Damages Money sought as a remedy for a breach of contract or for a tortious act.

Debtor in possession (DIP) In Chapter 11 bankruptcy proceedings, a debtor who is allowed to continue in possession of the estate in property (the business) and to continue business operations.

Deceptive advertising Advertising that misleads consumers, either by unjustified claims concerning a product's performance or by the omission of a material fact concerning the product's composition or performance.

Deed A document by which title to property (usually real property) is passed.

Defamation Anything published or publicly spoken that causes injury to another's good name, reputation, or character.

Default The failure to observe a promise or discharge an obligation. The term is commonly used to mean the failure to pay a debt when it is due.

Default judgment A judgment entered by a court against a defendant who has failed to appear in court to answer or defend against the plaintiff's claim.

Defendant One against whom a lawsuit is brought; the accused person in a criminal proceeding.

Defense That which a defendant offers and alleges in an action or suit as a reason why the plaintiff should not recover or establish what he or she seeks.

Deficiency judgment A judgment against a debtor for the amount of a debt remaining unpaid after collateral has been repossessed and sold.

Delegation doctrine A doctrine based on Article I, Section 8, of the U.S. Constitution, which has been construed to allow Congress to delegate some of its power to make and implement laws to administrative agencies.

Delegation of duties The act of transferring to another all or part of one's duties arising under a contract.

Depositary bank The first bank to receive a check for payment.

Deposition The testimony of a party to a lawsuit or a witness taken under oath before a trial.

Disaffirmance The legal avoidance, or setting aside, of a contractual obligation.

Discharge The termination of an obligation. In contract law, discharge occurs when the parties have fully performed their contractual obligations or when events, conduct of the parties, or operation of the law releases the parties from performance. In bankruptcy proceedings, the extinction of the debtor's dischargeable debts.

Discovery A phase in the litigation process during which the opposing parties may obtain information from

each other and from third parties prior to trial.

Disparagement of property An economically injurious falsehood made about another's product or property. A general term for torts that are more specifically referred to as slander of quality or slander of title.

Disparate-impact discrimination A form of employment discrimination that results from certain employer practices or procedures that, although not discriminatory on their face, have a discriminatory effect.

Disparate-treatment discrimination A form of employment discrimination that results when an employer intentionally discriminates against employees who are members of protected classes.

Distribution agreement A contract between a seller and a distributor of the seller's products setting out the terms and conditions of the distributorship.

Diversity of citizenship Under Article III, Section 2, of the Constitution, a basis for federal court jurisdiction over a lawsuit between (1) citizens of different states, (2) a foreign country and citizens of a state or of different states, or (3) citizens of a state and citizens or subjects of a foreign country. The amount in controversy must be more than $75,000 before a federal court can take jurisdiction in such cases.

Divestiture The act of selling one or more of a company's parts, such as a subsidiary or plant; often mandated by the courts in merger or monopolization cases.

Dividend A distribution to corporate shareholders of corporate profits or income, disbursed in proportion to the number of shares held.

Docket The list of cases entered on a court's calendar and thus scheduled to be heard by the court.

Document of title Paper exchanged in the regular course of business that evidences the right to possession of goods (for example, a bill of lading or a warehouse receipt).

Domain name The series of letters and symbols used to identify site

operators on the Internet; Internet "addresses."

Domestic corporation In a given state, a corporation that does business in, and is organized under the law of, that state.

Dominion Ownership rights in property, including the right to possess and control the property.

Double jeopardy A situation occurring when a person is tried twice for the same criminal offense; prohibited by the Fifth Amendment to the Constitution.

Dram shop act A state statute that imposes liability on the owners of bars and taverns, as well as those who serve alcoholic drinks to the public, for injuries resulting from accidents caused by intoxicated persons when the sellers or servers of alcoholic drinks contributed to the intoxication.

Due process clause The provisions of the Fifth and Fourteenth Amendments to the Constitution that guarantee that no person shall be deprived of life, liberty, or property without due process of law. Similar clauses are found in most state constitutions.

Dumping The selling of goods in a foreign country at a price below the price charged for the same goods in the domestic market.

Duress Unlawful pressure brought to bear on a person, causing the person to perform an act that he or she would not otherwise perform.

Duty of care The duty of all persons, as established by tort law, to exercise a reasonable amount of care in their dealings with others. Failure to exercise due care, which is normally determined by the "reasonable person standard," constitutes the tort of negligence.

Early neutral case evaluation A form of alternative dispute resolution in which a neutral third party evaluates the strengths and weakness of the disputing parties' positions; the evaluator's opinion forms the basis for negotiating a settlement.

Easement A nonpossessory right to use another's property in a manner established by either express or implied agreement.

Eighty-day cooling-off period A provision of the Taft-Hartley Act that allows federal courts to issue injunctions against strikes that might create a national emergency.

Embezzlement The fraudulent appropriation of money or other property by a person to whom the money or property has been entrusted.

Eminent domain The power of a government to take land for public use from private citizens for just compensation.

Employee committee Committee created by an employer and composed of representatives of management and nonunion employees to act together to improve workplace conditions.

Employment at will A common law doctrine under which either party may terminate an employment relationship at any time for any reason, unless a contract specifies otherwise.

Employment discrimination Treating employees or job applicants unequally on the basis of race, color, national origin, religion, gender, age, or disability; prohibited by federal statutes.

Enabling legislation A statute enacted by Congress that authorizes the creation of an administrative agency and specifies the name, composition, purpose, and powers of the agency being created.

Entrapment In criminal law, a defense in which the defendant claims that he or she was induced by a public official—usually an undercover agent or police officer—to commit a crime that he or she would otherwise not have committed.

Entrepreneur One who initiates and assumes the financial risks of a new enterprise and who undertakes to provide or control its management.

Environmental impact statement (EIS) A statement required by the National Environmental Policy Act for any major federal action that will significantly affect the quality of the environment. The statement must analyze the action's impact on the environment and explore alternative actions that might be taken.

Equal protection clause The provision in the Fourteenth Amendment to the Constitution that guarantees that no state will "deny to any person within its jurisdiction the equal protection of the laws." This clause mandates that the state governments treat similarly situated individuals in a similar manner.

Equitable principles and maxims General propositions or principles of law that have to do with fairness (equity).

Establishment clause The provision in the First Amendment to the Constitution that prohibits Congress from creating any law "respecting an establishment of religion."

Estate in property In bankruptcy proceedings, all of the debtor's legal and equitable interests in property presently held, wherever located, together with certain jointly owned property, property transferred in transactions voidable by the trustee, proceeds and profits from the property of the estate, and certain property interests to which the debtor becomes entitled within 180 days after filing for bankruptcy.

Ethics Moral principles and values applied to social behavior.

Eviction A landlord's act of depriving a tenant of possession of the leased premises.

Exclusionary rule In criminal procedure, a rule under which any evidence that is obtained in violation of the accused's constitutional rights guaranteed by the Fourth, Fifth, and Sixth Amendments, as well as any evidence derived from illegally obtained evidence, will not be admissible in court.

Exclusive distributorship A distributorship in which the seller and the distributor of the seller's products agree that the distributor has the exclusive right to distribute the seller's products in a certain geographic area.

Exclusive jurisdiction Jurisdiction that exists when a case can be heard only in a particular court or type of court.

Exclusive-dealing contract An agreement under which a seller forbids a buyer to purchase products from the seller's competitors.

Exculpatory clause A clause that releases a contractual party from liability in the event of monetary or physical injury, no matter who is at fault.

Executed contract A contract that has been completely performed by both parties.

Executive agency An administrative agency within the executive branch of government. At the federal level, executive agencies are those within the cabinet departments.

Executory contract A contract that has not as yet been fully performed.

Executory interest A future interest, held by a person other than the grantor, that or begins some time after the termination of the preceding estate.

Export To sell products to buyers located in other countries.

Express contract A contract in which the terms of the agreement are fully and explicitly stated in words, oral or written.

Express warranty A seller's or lessor's oral or written promise, ancillary to an underlying sales or lease agreement, as to the quality, description, or performance of the goods being sold or leased.

Expropriation The seizure by a government of privately owned business or personal property for a proper public purpose and with just compensation.

Family limited liability partnership A limited liability partnership in which the majority of the partners are related to one another. All of the partners must be natural persons, or persons acting in a fiduciary capacity for the benefit of natural persons.

Featherbedding A requirement that more workers be employed to do a particular job than are actually needed.

Federal form of government A system of government in which the states form a union and the sovereign power is divided between a central government and the member states.

Federal question A question that pertains to the U.S. Constitution, acts of Congress, or treaties. A federal question provides a basis for federal jurisdiction.

Fee simple An absolute form of property ownership entitling the property owner to use, possess, or dispose of the property as he or she chooses during his or her lifetime. Upon death, the interest in the property descends to the owner's heirs; a fee simple absolute.

Fee simple absolute An ownership interest in land in which the owner has the greatest possible aggregation of rights, privileges, and power. Ownership in fee simple absolute is limited absolutely to a person and his or her heirs; a fee simple absolute.

Fee simple defeasible An ownership interest in real property that can be taken away (by the prior grantor) upon the occurrence or nonoccurrence of a specified event.

Felony A crime—such as arson, murder, rape, or robbery—that carries the most severe sanctions, usually ranging from one year in a state or federal prison to the forfeiture of one's life.

Fiduciary As a noun, a person having a duty created by his or her undertaking to act primarily for another's benefit in matters connected with the undertaking. As an adjective, a relationship founded upon trust and confidence.

Final order The final decision of an administrative agency on an issue. If no appeal is taken, or if the case is not reviewed or considered anew by the agency commission, the administrative law judge's initial order becomes the final order of the agency.

Fixture A thing that was once personal property but that has become attached to real property in such a way that it takes on the characteristics of real property and becomes part of that real property.

Force majeure (pronounced mah-*zhure*) clause A provision in a contract stipulating that certain unforeseen events—such as war, political upheavals, acts of God, or other events—will excuse a party from liability for nonperformance of contractual obligations.

Foreign corporation In a given state, a corporation that does business in the state without being incorporated therein.

Foreign exchange market A worldwide system in which foreign currencies are bought and sold.

Forgery The fraudulent making or altering of any writing in a way that changes the legal rights and liabilities of another.

Formal contract A contract that by law requires for its validity a specific form, such as executed under seal.

Forum-selection clause A provision in a contract designating the court, jurisdiction, or tribunal that will decide any disputes arising under the contract..

Franchise Any arrangement in which the owner of a trademark, trade name, or copyright licenses another to use that trademark, trade name, or copyright, under specified conditions or limitations, in the selling of goods and services.

Franchisee One receiving a license to use another's (the franchisor's) trademark, trade name, or copyright in the sale of goods and services.

Franchisor One licensing another (the franchisee) to use his or her trademark, trade name, or copyright in the sale of goods or services.

Fraud Any misrepresentation, either by misstatement or omission of a material fact, knowingly made with the intention of deceiving another and on which a reasonable person would and does rely to his or her detriment.

Fraudulent misrepresentation (fraud) Any misrepresentation, either by misstatement or omission of a material fact, knowingly made with the intention of deceiving another and on which a reasonable person would and does rely to his or her detriment.

Free exercise clause The provision in the First Amendment to the Constitution that prohibits Congress from making any law "prohibiting the free exercise" of religion.

Future interest An interest in real property that is not at present possessory but will or may become possessory in the future.

Garnishment A legal process used by a creditor to collect a debt by seizing property of the debtor (such as wages) that is being held by a third party (such as the debtor's employer).

General partner In a limited partnership, a partner who assumes responsibility for the management of the partnership and liability for all partnership debts.

General plan A comprehensive document that local jurisdictions are often required by state law to devise and implement as a precursor to specific land-use regulations.

Good Samaritan statute A state statute that provides that persons who rescue or provide emergency services to others in peril—unless they do so recklessly, thus causing further harm—cannot be sued for negligence.

Grand jury A group of citizens called to decide, after hearing the state's evidence, whether a reasonable basis (probable cause) exists for believing that a crime has been committed and whether a trial ought to be held.

Group boycott The refusal to deal with a particular person or firm by a group of competitors; prohibited by the Sherman Act.

Guarantor A person who agrees to satisfy the debt of another (the debtor) only after the principal debtor defaults; a guarantor's liability is thus secondary.

Hearing A proceeding, less formal than a trieal, in which definite issues are considered, parties are allowed to present their case in a meaningful manner, witnesses are heard, and evidence is presented.

Herfindahl-Hirschman Index (HHI) An index of market power used to calculate whether a merger of two corporations will result in sufficient monopoly power to violate antitrust laws.

Homestead exemption A law permitting a debtor to retain the family home, either in its entirety or up to a specified dollar amount, free from the claims of unsecured creditors or trustees in bankruptcy.

Horizontal merger A merger between two firms that are competing in the same marketplace.

Horizontal restraint   Any agreement that in some way restrains competition between rival firms competing in the same market.

Hot-cargo agreement   An agreement in which employers voluntarily agree with unions not to handle, use, or deal in nonunion-produced goods of other employers; a type of secondary boycott explicitly prohibited by the Labor-Management Reporting and Disclosure Act of 1959.

Implied warranty   A warranty that the law derives by implication or inference from the nature of the transaction or the relative situation or circumstances of the parties.

Implied warranty of fitness for a particular purpose   A warranty that goods sold or leased are fit for a particular purpose. The warranty arises when any seller or lessor knows the particular purpose for which a buyer or lessee will use the goods and knows that the buyer or lessee is relying on the skill and judgment of the seller or lessor to select suitable goods.

Implied warranty of habitability   An implied promise by a landlord that rented residential premises are fit for human habitation—that is, in a condition that is safe and suitable for people to live in.

Implied warranty of merchantability   A warranty that goods being sold or leased are reasonably fit for the general purpose for which they are sold or leased, are properly packaged and labeled, and are of proper quality. The warranty automatically arises in every sale or lease of goods made by a merchant who deals in goods of the kind sold or leased.

Implied-in-fact contract   A contract formed in whole or in part from the conduct of the parties (as opposed to an express contract).

Impossibility of performance   A doctrine under which a party to a contract is relieved of his or her duty to perform when performance becomes impossible or totally impracticable (through no fault of either party).

Incidental beneficiary   A third party who incidentally benefits from a contract but whose benefit was not the reason the contract was formed; an incidental beneficiary has no rights in a contract and cannot sue to have the contract enforced.

Incidental damages   Damages resulting from a breach of contract, including all reasonable expenses incurred because of the breach.

Independent contractor   One who works for, and receives payment from, an employer but whose working conditions and methods are not controlled by the employer. An independent contractor is not an employee but may be an agent.

Independent regulatory agency   An administrative agency that is not considered part of the government's executive branch and is not subject to the authority of the president. Independent agency officials cannot be removed without cause.

Indictment (pronounced in-*dyte*-ment)   A charge by a grand jury that a named person has committed a crime.

Informal contract   A contract that does not require a specified form or formality in order to be valid.

Information   A formal accusation or complaint (without an indictment) issued in certain types of actions (usually criminal actions involving lesser crimes) by a law officer, such as a magistrate.

Initial order   In the context of administrative law, an agency's disposition in a matter other than a rulemaking. An administrative law judge's initial order becomes final unless it is appealed.

Innkeeper's lien   A possessory lien placed on the luggage of hotel guests for hotel charges that remain unpaid.

Insider trading   The purchase or sale of securities on the basis of "inside information" (information that has not been made available to the public) in violation of a duty owed to the company whose stock is being traded.

Intellectual property   Property resulting from intellectual, creative processes. Patents, trademarks, and copyrights are examples of intellectual property.

Intended beneficiary   A third party for whose benefit a contract is formed; an intended beneficiary can sue the promisor if such a contract is breached.

Intentional tort   A wrongful act knowingly committed.

Inter vivos trust   A trust created by the grantor (settlor) and effective during the grantor's lifetime; a trust not established by a will.

International law   The law that governs relations among nations. National laws, customs, treaties, and international conferences and organizations are generally considered to be the most important sources of international law.

Interrogatories   A series of written questions for which written answers are prepared and then signed under oath by a party to a lawsuit, usually with the assistance of the party's attorney.

Investment company   A company that acts on behalf of many smaller shareholders-owners by buying a large portfolio of securities and professionally managing that portfolio.

Joint tenancy   The joint ownership of property by two or more co-owners of property in which each co-owner owns an undivided portion of the property. Upon the death of one of the joint tenants, his or her interest automatically passes to the surviving joint tenants.

Judicial review   The process by which a court decides on the constitutionality of legislative enactments and actions of the executive branch.

Jurisdiction   The authority of a court to hear and decide a specific action.

Jurisprudence   The science or philosophy of law.

Justiciable controversy   A controversy that is not hypothetical or academic but real and substantial; a requirement that must be satisfied before a court will hear a case.

Larceny   The wrongful taking and carrying away of another person's personal property with the intent to permanently deprive the owner of the property. Some states classify larceny as either grand or petit, depending on the property's value.

Law A body of enforceable rules governing relationships among individuals and between individuals and their society.

Lease In real property law, a contract by which the owner of real property (the landlord, or lessor) grants to a person (the tenant, or lessee) an exclusive right to use and possess the property, usually for a specified period of time, in return for rent or some other form of payment.

Leasehold estate An estate in realty held by a tenant under a lease. In every leasehold estate, the tenant has a qualified right to possess and/or use the land.

Legacy A gift of personal property under a will.

Legal positivism A school of legal thought centered on the assumption that there is no law higher than the laws created by the government. Laws must be obeyed, even if they are unjust, to prevent anarchy.

Legal realism A school of legal thought of the 1920s and 1930s that generally advocated a less abstract and more realistic approach to the law, an approach that takes into account customary practices and the circumstances in which transactions take place. The school left a lasting imprint on American jurisprudence.

Legislative rule An administrative agency rule that carries the same weight as a congressionally enacted statute.

Letter of credit A written instrument, usually issued by a bank on behalf of a customer or other person, in which the issuer promises to honor drafts or other demands for payment by third persons in accordance with the terms of the instrument.

Levy The obtaining of money by legal process through the seizure and sale of property, usually done after a writ of execution has been issued.

Libel Defamation in written form.

License A revocable right or privilege of a person to come on another person's land.

Lien (pronounced leen) An encumbrance upon a property to satisfy a debt or protect a claim for payment of a debt.

Life estate An interest in land that exists only for the duration of the life of some person, usually the holder of the estate.

Limited liability company (LLC) A hybrid form of business enterprise that offers the limited liability of the corporation but the tax advantages of a partnership.

Limited liability limited partnership (LLLP) A limited liability partnership in which the liability of the general partner is, like the liability of the limited partner, limited to the amount of his or her investment in the firm.

Limited liability partnership A form of partnership that allows professionals to enjoy the tax benefits of a partnership while avoiding personal liability for the malpractice of other partners.

Limited partner In a limited partnership, a partner who contributes capital to the partnership but has no right to participate in the management and operation of the business. The limited partner assumes no liability for partnership debts beyond the capital contributed.

Limited partnership A partnership consisting of one or more general partners (who manage the business and are liable to the full extent of their personal assets for debts of the partnership) and one or more limited partners (who contribute only assets and are liable only to the extent of their contributions).

Liquidated damages An amount, stipulated in the contract, that the parties to a contract believe to be a reasonable estimation of the damages that will occur in the event of a breach.

Liquidation In regard to corporations, the process by which corporate assets are converted into cash and distributed among creditors and shareholders according to specific rules of preference. In regard to bankruptcy, the sale of all of the nonexempt assets of a debtor and the distribution of the proceeds to the

debtor's creditors. Chapter 7 of the Bankruptcy Code provides for liquidation bankruptcy proceedings.

Litigant A party to a lawsuit.

Litigation The process of resolving a dispute through the court system.

Lockout The closing of a plant to employees by an employer to gain leverage in collective bargaining negotiations.

Long arm statute A state statute that permits a state to obtain personal jurisdiction over nonresident defendants. A defendant must have certain "minimum contacts" with that state for the statute to apply.

Mailbox rule A rule providing that an acceptance of an offer becomes effective upon dispatch (upon being placed in a mailbox), if mail is, expressly or impliedly, an authorized means of communication of acceptance to the offeror.

Malpractice Professional misconduct or the lack of the requisite degree of skill as a professional. Negligence—the failure to exercise due care—on the part of a professional, such as a physician or an attorney, is commonly referred to as malpractice.

Market concentration A situation that exists when a small number of firms share the market for a particular good or service. For example, if the four largest grocery stores in Chicago accounted for 80 percent of all retail food sales, the market clearly would be concentrated in those four firms.

Market power The power of a firm to control the market price of its product. A monopoly has the greatest degree of market power.

Market-share liability A method of sharing liability among several firms that manufactured or marketed a particular product that may have caused plaintiff's injury. This form of liability sharing is used when the true source of the product is unidentifiable. Each firm's liability is proportionate to its respective share of the relevant market for the product. Market-share liability applies only if the injuring product is fungible, the true manufacturer is unidentifiable, and the unknown character of the manufacturer is not the plaintiff's fault.

Market-share test   The primary measure of monopoly power. A firm's market share is the percentage of a market that the firm controls.

Mechanic's lien   A statutory lien upon the real property of another, created to ensure payment for work performed and materials furnished in the repair or improvement of real property, such as a building.

Mediation   A method of settling disputes outside of court by using the services of a neutral third party, who acts as a communicating agent between the parties and assists the parties in negotiating a settlement.

Mediator   A person who attempts to reconcile the differences between two or more parties.

Mini-trial   A private proceeding in which each party to a dispute argues its position before the other side and vice versa. A neutral third party may be present and act as an adviser if the parties fail to reach an agreement.

Minimum wage   The lowest wage, either by government regulation or union contract, that an employer may pay an hourly worker.

Mirror image rule   A common law rule that requires, for a valid contractual agreement, that the terms of the offeree's acceptance adhere exactly to the terms of the offeror's offer.

Misdemeanor   A lesser crime than a felony, punishable by a fine or imprisonment for up to one year in other than a state or federal penitentiary.

Mitigation of damages   A rule requiring a plaintiff to have done whatever was reasonable to minimize the damages caused by the defendant.

Money laundering   Falsely reporting income that has been obtained through criminal activity as income obtained through a legitimate business enterprise—in effect, "laundering" the "dirty money."

Monopolization   The possession of monopoly power in the relevant market and the willful acquisition or maintenance of the power, as distinguished from growth or

development as a consequence of a superior product, business acumen, or historic accident.

Monopoly   A term generally used to describe a market in which there is a single seller or a limited number of sellers.

Monopoly power   The ability of a monopoly to dictate what takes place in a given market.

Mortgagee   Under a mortgage agreement, the creditor who takes a security interest in the debtor's property.

Mortgagor   Under a mortgage agreement, the debtor who gives the creditor a security interest in the debtor's property in return for a mortgage loan.

Most-favored-nation status   A status granted in an international treaty by a provision stating that the citizens of the contracting nations may enjoy the privileges accorded by either party to citizens of the most favored nations. Generally, most-favored-nation clauses are designed to establish equality of international treatment.

Motion for a directed verdict   In a jury trial, a motion for the judge to take the decision out of the hands of the jury and direct a verdict for the moving party on the ground that the other party has not produced sufficient evidence to support his or her claim.

Motion for a new trial   A motion asserting that the trial was so fundamentally flawed (because of error, newly discovered evidence, prejudice, or other reason) that a new trial is necessary to prevent a miscarriage of justice.

Motion for judgment N.O.V.   A motion requesting the court to grant judgment in favor of the party making the motion on the ground that the jury verdict against him or her was unreasonable and erroneous.

Motion for judgment on the pleadings   A motion by either party to a lawsuit at the close of the pleadings requesting the court to decide the issue solely on the pleadings without proceeding to trial. The motion will be granted only if no facts are in dispute.

Motion for summary judgment   A motion requesting the court to enter a judgment without proceeding to trial. The motion can be based on evidence outside the pleadings and will be granted only if no facts are in dispute.

Motion to dismiss   A pleading in which a defendant asserts that the plaintiff's claim fails to state a cause of action (that is, has no basis in law) or that there are other grounds on which a suit should be dismissed.

Multiple product order   An order issued by the Federal Trade Commission to a firm that has engaged in deceptive advertising by which the firm is required to cease and desist from false advertising not only in regard to the product that was the subject of the action but also in regard to all the firm's other products.

Mutual fund   A specific type of investment company that continually buys or sells to investors shares of ownership in a portfolio.

National law   Law that pertains to a particular nation (as opposed to international law).

Natural law   The belief that government and the legal system should reflect universal moral and ethical principles that are inherent in human nature. The natural law school is the oldest and one of the most significant schools of legal thought.

Necessaries   Necessities required for life, such as food, shelter, clothing, and medical attention; may include whatever is believed to be necessary to maintain a person's standard of living or financial and social status.

Negligence   The failure to exercise the standard of care that a reasonable person would exercise in similar circumstances.

Negligence *per se*   An act (or failure to act) in violation of a statutory requirement.

Negotiation   In regard to dispute settlement, a process in which parties attempt to settle their dispute informally, with or without attorneys to represent them.

No-par shares   Corporate shares that have no face value—that is, no specific dollar amount is printed on their face.

Nominal damages A small monetary award (often one dollar) granted to a plaintiff when no actual damage was suffered.

No-strike clause Provision in collective bargaining agreement that states the employees will not strike for any reason and labor disputes will be resolved by arbitration.

Notice-and-comment rulemaking A procedure in agency rulemaking that requires (1) notice, (2) opportunity for comment, and (3) a published draft of the final rule.

Novation The substitution, by agreement, of a new contract for an old one, with the rights under the old one being terminated. Typically, there is a substitution of a new person who is responsible for the contract and the removal of an original party's rights and duties under the contract.

Nuisance A common law doctrine under which persons may be held liable for using their property in a manner that unreasonably interferes with others' rights to use or enjoy their own property.

Objective theory of contracts A theory under which the intent to form a contract will be judged by outward, objective facts (what the party said when entering into the contract, how the party acted or appeared, and the circumstances surrounding the transaction) as interpreted by a reasonable person, rather than by the party's own secret, subjective intentions.

Offer A promise or commitment to perform or refrain from performing some specified act in the future.

Offeree A person to whom an offer is made.

Offeror A person who makes an offer.

Option contract A contract under which the offeror cannot revoke his or her offer for a stipulated time period, and the offeree can accept or reject the offer during this period without fear that the offer will be made to another person. The offeree must give consideration for the option

(the irrevocable offer) to be enforceable.

Order for relief A court's grant of assistance to a complainant. In bankruptcy proceedings, the order relieves the debtor of the immediate obligation to pay the debts listed in the bankruptcy petition.

Par-value shares Corporate shares that have a specific face value, or formal cash-in value, written on them, such as one dollar.

Partnership An agreement by two or more persons to carry on, as co-owners, a business for profit.

Past consideration An act done before the contract is made, which ordinarily, by itself, cannot be consideration for a later promise to pay for the act.

Patent A government grant that gives an inventor the exclusive right or privilege to make, use, or sell his or her invention for a limited time period. The word patent usually refers to some invention and designates either the instrument by which patent rights are evidenced or the patent itself.

Penalty A sum inserted into a contract, not as a measure of compensation for its breach but rather as punishment for a default. The agreement as to the amount will not be enforced, and recovery will be limited to actual damages.

***Per se* violation** A type of anticompetitive agreement—such as a horizontal price-fixing agreement—that is considered to be so injurious to the public that there is no need to determine whether it actually injures market competition; rather, it is in itself (*per se*) a violation of the Sherman Act.

Performance In contract law, the fulfillment of one's duties arising under a contract with another; the normal way of discharging one's contractual obligations.

Periodic tenancy A lease interest in land for an indefinite period involving payment of rent at fixed intervals, such as week to week, month to month, or year to year.

Persuasive authority Any legal authority or source of law that a

court may look to for guidance but on which it need not rely in making its decision. Persuasive authorities include cases from other jurisdictions and secondary sources of law.

Petition in bankruptcy The document that is filed with a bankruptcy court to initiate bankruptcy proceedings. The official forms required for a petition in bankruptcy must be completed accurately, sworn to under oath, and signed by the debtor.

Petty offense In criminal law, the least serious kind of criminal offense, such as a traffic or building-code violation.

Plaintiff One who initiates a lawsuit.

Plea bargaining The process by which a criminal defendant and the prosecutor in a criminal case work out a mutually satisfactory disposition of the case, subject to court approval; usually involves the defendant's pleading guilty to a lesser offense in return for a lighter sentence.

Pleadings Statements made by the plaintiff and the defendant in a lawsuit that detail the facts, charges, and defenses involved in the litigation; the complaint and answer are part of the pleadings.

Police powers Powers possessed by states as part of their inherent sovereignty. These powers may be exercised to protect or promote the public order, health, safety, morals, and general welfare.

Positive law The body of conventional, or written, law of a particular society at a particular point in time.

Potentially responsible party (PRP) A liable party under the Comprehensive Environmental Response, Compensation, and Liability Act (CERCLA). Any person who generated the hazardous waste, transported the hazardous waste, owned or operated a waste site at the time of disposal, or currently owns or operates a site may be responsible for some or all of the clean-up costs involved in removing the hazardous chemicals.

Precedent   A court decision that furnishes an example or authority for deciding subsequent cases involving identical or similar facts.

Predatory pricing   The pricing of a product below cost with the intent to drive competitors out of the market.

Preemption   A doctrine under which certain federal laws preempt, or take precedence over, conflicting state or local laws.

Preemptive rights   Rights held by shareholders that entitle them to purchase newly issued shares of a corporation's stock, equal in percentage to shares presently held, before the stock is offered to any outside buyers. Preemptive rights enable shareholders to maintain their proportionate ownership and voice in the corporation.

Preference   In bankruptcy proceedings, property transfers or payments made by the debtor that favor (give preference to) one creditor over others. The bankruptcy trustee is allowed to recover payments made both voluntarily and involuntarily to one creditor in preference over another.

Prenuptial agreement   An agreement made before marriage that defines each partner's ownership rights in the other partner's property. Prenuptial agreements must be in writing to be enforceable.

Preventive law   The law that an attorney practices when he or she plays the role of an adviser for a client, spotting possible legal problems and suggesting preventive measures before the problems harm the client.

Price discrimination   Setting prices in such a way that two competing buyers pay two different prices for an identical product or service.

Price-fixing agreement   An agreement between competitors in which the competitors agree to fix the prices of products or services at a certain level; prohibited by the Sherman Act.

Prima facie case   A case in which the plaintiff has produced sufficient evidence of his or her conclusion that the case can go to to a jury; a case in which the evidence compels the plaintiff's conclusion if the defendant produces no evidence to disprove it.

Primary source of law   A document that establishes the law on a particular issue, such as a constitution, a statute, an administrative rule, or a court decision.

Principal   In agency law, a person who agrees to have another, called the agent, act on his or her behalf.

Privilege   In tort law, the ability to act contrary to another person's right without that person's having legal redress for such acts. Privilege may be raised as a defense to defamation.

Privity of contract   The relationship that exists between the promisor and the promisee of a contract.

Probable cause   Reasonable grounds to believe the existence of facts warranting certain actions, such as the search or arrest of a person.

Probate court   A state court of limited jurisdiction that conducts proceedings relating to the settlement of a deceased person's estate.

Procedural law   Law that establishes the methods of enforcing the rights established by substantive law.

Product liability   The legal liability of manufacturers, sellers, and lessors of goods to consumers, users, and bystanders for injuries or damages that are caused by the goods.

Product misuse   A defense against product liability that may be raised when the plaintiff used a product in a manner not intended by the manufacturer. If the misuse is reasonably foreseeable, the seller will not escape liability unless measures were taken to guard against the harm that could result from the misuse.

Profit   In real property law, the right to enter upon and remove things from the property of another (for example, the right to enter onto a person's land and remove sand and gravel therefrom).

Promise   A declaration that something either will or will not happen in the future.

Promisee   A person to whom a promise is made.

Promisor   A person who makes a promise.

Promissory estoppel   A doctrine that applies when a promisor makes a clear and definite promise on which the promisee justifiably relies; such a promise is binding if justice will be better served by the enforcement of the promise.

Proximate cause   Legal cause; exists when the connection between an act and an injury is strong enough to justify imposing liability.

Proxy   In corporation law, a written agreement between a stockholder and another under which the stockholder authorizes the other to vote the stockholder's shares in a certain manner.

Puffery   A salesperson's often exaggerated claims concerning the quality of property offered for sale. Such claims involve opinions rather than facts and are not considered to be legally binding promises or warranties.

Punitive damages   Money damages that may be awarded to a plaintiff to punish the defendant and deter future similar conduct.

Quasi contract   A fictional contract imposed on parties by a court in the interests of fairness and justice; usually, quasi contracts are imposed to avoid the unjust enrichment of one party at the expense of another.

Quitclaim deed   A deed intended to pass any title, interest, or claim that the grantor may have in the property but not warranting that such title is valid. A quitclaim deed offers the least amount of protection against defects in the title.

Ratification   The act of accepting and giving legal force to an obligation that previously was not enforceable.

Real property   Land and everything attached to it, such as foliage and buildings.

Reasonable person standard   The standard of behavior expected of a hypothetical "reasonable person." The standard against which negligence is measured and that must be observed to avoid liability for negligence.

Recording statutes   Statutes that allow deeds, mortgages, and other real property transactions be recorded so as to provide notice to future purchasers or creditors of an existing claim on the property.

Red herring   A preliminary prospectus that can be distributed to potential investors after the registration statement (for a securities offering) has been filed with the Securities and Exchange Commission. The name derives from the red legend printed across the prospectus stating that the registration has been filed but has not become effective.

Reformation   A court-ordered correction of a written contract so that it reflects the true intentions of the parties.

Regulation Z   A set of rules promulgated by the Federal Reserve Board to implement the provisions of the Truth-in-Lending Act.

Release   A contract in which one party forfeits the right to pursue a legal claim against the other party.

Remainder   A future interest in property held by a person other than the original owner.

Remedy   The relief given to an innocent party to enforce a right or compensate for the violation of a right.

Reply   Procedurally, a plaintiff's response to a defendant's answer.

Res ipsa loquitur   A doctrine under which negligence may be inferred simply because an event occurred, if it is the type of event that would not occur in the absence of negligence. Literally, the term means "the facts speak for themselves."

Resale price maintenance agreement   An agreement between a manufacturer and a retailer in which the manufacturer specifies the minimum retail price of its products. Resale price maintenance agreements are illegal per se under the Sherman Act.

Rescission (pronounced reh-*sih*-zhen)   A remedy whereby a contract is canceled and the parties are returned to the positions they occupied before the contract was made; may be effected through the mutual consent of the parties, by their conduct, or by court decree.

Respondeat superior (pronounced ree-*spahn*-dee-uht soo-*peer*-ee-your)   In Latin, "Let the master respond." A doctrine under which a principal or an employer is held liable for the wrongful acts committed by agents or employees while acting within the scope of their agency or employment.

Restitution   An equitable remedy under which a person is restored to his or her original position prior to loss or injury, or placed in the position he or she would have been in had the breach not occurred.

Retained earnings   The portion of a corporation's profits that has not been paid out as dividends to shareholders.

Reversionary interest   A future interest in property retained by the original owner.

Revocation   In contract law, the withdrawal of an offer by an offeror; unless the offer is irrevocable, it can be revoked at any time prior to acceptance without liability.

Right of contribution   The right of a co-surety who pays more than his or her proportionate share upon a debtor's default to recover the excess paid from other co-sureties.

Right of first refusal   The right to purchase personal or real property—such as corporate shares or real estate—before the property is offered for sale to others.

Right of reimbursement   The legal right of a person to be restored, repaid, or indemnified for costs, expenses, or losses incurred or expended on behalf of another.

Right of subrogation   The right of a person to stand in the place of (be substituted for) another, giving the substituted party the same legal rights that the original party had.

Right-to-work law   A state law providing that employees are not to be required to join a union as a condition of obtaining or retaining employment.

Robbery   The act of forcefully and unlawfully taking personal property of any value from another; force or intimidation is usually necessary for an act of theft to be considered a robbery.

Rule of four   A rule of the United States Supreme Court under which the Court will not issue a writ of certiorari unless at least four justices approve of the decision to issue the writ.

Rule of reason   A test by which a court balances the positive effects (such as economic efficiency) of an agreement against its potentially anticompetitive effects. In antitrust litigation, many practices are analyzed under the rule of reason.

Rulemaking   The process undertaken by an administrative agency when formally adopting a new regulation or amending an old one. Rulemaking involves notifying the public of a proposed rule or change and receiving and considering the public's comments.

S corporation   A close business corporation that has met certain requirements as set out by the Internal Revenue Code and thus qualifies for special income-tax treatment. Essentially, an S corporation is taxed the same as a partnership, but its owners enjoy the privilege of limited liability.

Sales contract   A contract for the sale of goods under which the ownership of goods is transferred from a seller to a buyer for a price.

Scienter (pronounced sy-*en*-ter)   Knowledge by the misrepresenting party that material facts have been falsely represented or omitted with an intent to deceive.

Search warrant   An order granted by a public authority, such as a judge, that authorizes law-enforcement personnel to search particular premises or property.

SEC Rule 10b-5   A rule of the Securities and Exchange Commission that makes it unlawful, in connection with the purchase or sale of any security, to make any untrue statement of a material fact or to omit a material fact if such omission causes the statement to be misleading.

Secondary boycott   A union's refusal to work for, purchase from, or handle the products of a secondary employer, with whom the union has no dispute, for the purpose of forcing that employer to stop doing business with the primary employer, with whom the union has a labor dispute.

Secondary source of law   A publication that summarizes or interprets the law, such as a legal encyclopedia, a legal treatise, or an article in a law review.

Secured party   A lender, seller, or any other person in whose favor there is a security interest, including a person to whom accounts or chattel paper has been sold.

Security   Generally, a stock certificate, bond, note, debenture, warrant, or other document given as evidence of an ownership interest in a corporation or as a promise of repayment by a corporation.

Self-defense   The legally recognized privilege to protect one's self or property against injury by another. The privilege of self-defense protects only acts that are reasonably necessary to protect one's self or property.

Seniority system   In regard to employment relationships, a system in which those who have worked longest for the company are first in line for promotions, salary increases, and other benefits; they are also the last to be laid off if the work force must be reduced.

Service mark   A mark used in the sale or the advertising of services, such as to distinguish the services of one person from the services of others. Titles, character names, and other distinctive features of radio and television programs may be registered as service marks.

Severance pay   Funds in excess of normal wages or salaries paid to an employee upon termination of his or her employment with a company.

Sexual harassment   In the employment context, the granting of job promotions or other benefits in return for sexual favors or language or conduct that is so sexually offensive that it creates a hostile working environment.

Sharia   Civil law principles of some Middle Eastern countries that are based on the Islamic directives that follow the teachings of the prophet Mohammed.

Slander   Defamation in oral form.

Slander of quality (trade libel)   The publication of false information about another's product, alleging that it is not what its seller claims.

Slander of title   The publication of a statement that denies or casts doubt upon another's legal ownership of any property, causing financial loss to that property's owner.

Small claims courts   Special courts in which parties may litigate small claims (usually, claims involving $2,500 or less). Attorneys are not required in small claims courts, and in many states attorneys are not allowed to represent the parties.

Sole proprietorship   The simplest form of business, in which the owner is the business; the owner reports business income on his or her personal income tax return and is legally responsible for all debts and obligations incurred by the business.

Sovereign immunity   A doctrine that immunizes foreign nations from the jurisdiction of U.S. courts when certain conditions are satisfied.

Specific performance   An equitable remedy requiring exactly the performance that was specified in a contract; usually granted only when money damages would be an inadequate remedy and the subject matter of the contract is unique (for example, real property).

Standing to sue   The requirement that an individual must have a sufficient stake in a controversy before he or she can bring a lawsuit. The plaintiff must demonstrate that he or she either has been injured or threatened with injury.

Stare decisis **(pronounced *ster*-ay dih-*si*-ses)**   A common law doctrine under which judges are obligated to follow the precedents established in prior decisions.

Statute of Frauds   A state statute under which certain types of contracts must be in writing to be enforceable.

Statute of limitations   A federal or state statute setting the maximum time period during which a certain action can be brought or certain rights enforced.

Statutory law   The body of law enacted by legislative bodies (as opposed to constitutional law, administrative law, or case law).

Stock   An equity (ownership) interest in a corporation, measured in units of shares.

Stock certificate   A certificate issued by a corporation evidencing the ownership of a specified number of shares in the corporation.

Stop-payment order   An order by a bank customer to his or her bank not to pay or certify a certain check.

Strict liability   Liability regardless of fault. In tort law, strict liability may be imposed on defendants in cases involving abnormally dangerous activities, dangerous animals, or defective products.

Strike   An extreme action undertaken by unionized workers when collective bargaining fails; the workers leave their jobs, refuse to work, and (typically) picket the employer's workplace.

Sublease   A lease executed by the lessee of real estate to a third person, conveying the same interest that the lessee enjoys but for a shorter term than that held by the lessee.

Submission   An agreement by two or more parties to refer any disputes they may have under their contract to a disinterested third party, such as an arbitrator, who has the power to render a binding decision.

Substantive law   Law that defines, describes, regulates, and creates legal rights and obligations.

Summary jury trial (SJT)   A method of settling disputes in which a trial is held, but the jury's verdict is not binding. The verdict acts only as a guide to both sides in reaching an agreement during the mandatory negotiations that immediately follow the summary jury trial.

Summons   A document informing a defendant that a legal action has been commenced against him or her and that the defendant must appear in court on a certain date to answer the plaintiff's complaint. The document is delivered by a sheriff or any other person so authorized.

Supremacy clause   The provision in Article VI of the Constitution that provides that the Constitution, laws, and treaties of the United States are "the supreme Law of the Land." Under this clause, state and local laws that directly conflict with federal law will be rendered invalid.

Surety   A person, such as a cosigner on a note, who agrees to be primarily responsible for the debt of another.

Suretyship   An express contract in which a third party to a debtor-creditor relationship (the surety) promises to be primarily responsible for the debtor's obligation.

Taking   The taking of private property by the government for public use. Under the Fifth Amendment to the Constitution, the government may not take private property for public use without "just compensation."

Technology licensing   Allowing another to use and profit from intellectual property (patents, copyrights, trademarks, innovative products or processes, and so on) for consideration. In the context of international business transactions, technology licensing is sometimes an attractive alternative to the establishment of foreign production facilities.

Tenancy at sufferance   A type of tenancy under which one who, after rightfully being in possession of leased premises, continues (wrongfully) to occupy the property after the lease has been terminated. The tenant has no rights to possess the property and occupies it only because the person entitled to evict the tenant has not done so.

Tenancy at will   A type of tenancy under which either party can terminate the tenancy without notice; usually arises when a tenant who has been under a tenancy for years retains possession, with the landlord's consent, after the tenancy for years has terminated.

Tenancy by the entirety   The joint ownership of property by a husband and wife. Neither party can transfer his or her interest in the property without the consent of the other.

Tenancy for years   A type of tenancy under which property is leased for a specified period of time, such as a month, a year, or a period of years.

Tenancy in common   Co-ownership of property in which each party owns an undivided interest that passes to his or her heirs at death.

Tender   An unconditional offer to perform an obligation by a person who is ready, willing, and able to do so.

Third party beneficiary   One for whose benefit a promise is made in a contract but who is not a party to the contract.

Tippee   A person who receives inside information.

Tombstone ad   An advertisement, historically in a format resembling a tombstone, of a securities offering. The ad informs potential investors of where and how they may obtain a prospectus.

Tort   A civil wrong not arising from a breach of contract. A breach of a legal duty that proximately causes harm or injury to another.

Tortfeasor   One who commits a tort.

Toxic tort   Failure to use or to clean up properly toxic chemicals that cause harm to a person or society.

Trade dress   The image and overall appearance of a product—for example, the distinctive decor, menu, layout, and style of service of a particular restaurant. Basically, trade dress is subject to the same protection as trademarks.

Trade libel   The publication of false information about another's product, alleging it is not what its seller claims; also referred to as slander of quality.

Trade name   A term that is used to indicate part or all of a business's name and that is directly related to the business's reputation and goodwill. Trade names are protected under the common law (and under trademark law, if the name is the same as the firm's trademarked property).

Trade secrets   Information or processes that give a business an advantage over competitors who do not know the information or processes.

Trademark   A distinctive mark, motto, device, or implement that a manufacturer stamps, prints, or otherwise affixes to the goods it produces so that they may be identified on the market and their origins made known. Once a trademark is established (under the common law or through registration), the owner is entitled to its exclusive use.

Treaty   An agreement formed between two or more independent nations.

Trespass to land   The entry onto, above, or below the surface of land owned by another without the owner's permission or legal authorization.

Trespass to personal property   The unlawful taking or harming of another's personal property; interference with another's right to the exclusive possession of his or her personal property.

Tying arrangement   An agreement between a buyer and a seller in which the buyer of a specific product or service becomes obligated to purchase additional products or services from the seller.

U.S. trustee   A government official who performs certain administrative tasks that a bankruptcy judge would otherwise have to perform.

Unconscionable (pronounced un-*kon*-shun-uh-bul) contract (or unconscionable clause)   A contract or clause that is void on the basis of public policy because one party, as a result of his or her disproportionate bargaining power, is forced to accept terms that are unfairly burdensome and that unfairly benefit the dominating party.

Unenforceable contract   A valid contract rendered unenforceable by some statute or law.

Unilateral contract   A contract that results when an offer can only be accepted by the offeree's performance.

Union shop   A place of employment in which all workers, once employed, must become union members within a specified period of time as a condition of their continued employment.

Unitary system   A centralized governmental system in which local or subdivisional governments exercise only those powers given to them by the central government.

Unreasonably dangerous product   In product liability, a product that is defective to the point of threatening a consumer's health and safety. A product will be considered unreasonably dangerous if it is dangerous beyond the expectation of the ordinary consumer or if a less dangerous alternative was economically feasible for the manufacturer, but the manufacturer failed to produce it.

Use zoning   Zoning classifications within a particular municipality that may be distinguished based upon the uses to which the land is to be put.

Usury   Charging an illegal rate of interest.

Utilitarianism   An approach to ethical reasoning in which ethically correct behavior is not related to any absolute ethical or moral values but to an evaluation of the consequences of a given action on those who will be affected by it. In utilitarian reasoning, a "good" decision is one that results in the greatest good for the greatest number of people affected by the decision.

Valid contract   A contract that results when elements necessary for contract formation (agreement, consideration, legal purpose, and contractual capacity) are present.

Validation notice   An initial notice to a debtor from a collection agency informing the debtor that he or she has thirty days to challenge the debt and request verification.

Venue (pronounced *ven*-yoo)   The geographical district in which an action is tried and from which the jury is selected.

Vertical merger   The acquisition by a company at one stage of production of a company at a higher or lower stage of production (such as a company merging with one of its suppliers or retailers).

Vertical restraint   Any restraint on trade created by agreements between firms at different levels in the manufacturing and distribution process.

Vertically integrated firm   A firm that carries out two or more functional phases (manufacture, distribution, retailing, and so on) of a product.

Vesting   The creation of an absolute or unconditional right or power.

Void contract   A contract having no legal force or binding effect.

Voidable contract   A contract that may be legally avoided (canceled, or annulled) at the option of one of the parties.

Voir dire (pronounced vwahr-deehr)   A French phrase meaning "to speak the truth." In jury trials, the phrase refers to the process in which the attorneys question prospective jurors to determine whether they are biased or have any connection with a party of the action or with a prospective witness.

Warranty deed   A deed in which the grantor guarantees to the grantee that the grantor has title to the property conveyed in the deed, that there are no encumbrances on the property other than what the grantor has represented, and that the grantee will enjoy quiet possession of the property; a deed that provides the greatest amount of protection for the grantee.

Watered stock   Shares of stock issued by a corporation for which the corporation receives, as payment, less than the stated value of the shares.

Wetlands   Areas of land designated by government agencies (such as the Army Corps of Engineers or the Environmental Protection Agency) as protected areas that support wildlife and that therefore cannot be filled in or dredged by private contractors or parties.

Whistleblowing   An employee's disclosure to government, the press, or upper-management authorities that the employer is engaged in unsafe or illegal activities.

White-collar crime   Nonviolent crime committed by individuals or corporations to obtain a personal or business advantage.

Wildcat strike   A strike that is not authorized by the union that ordinarily represents the striking employees.

Workers' compensation laws   State statutes establishing an administrative procedure for compensating workers' injuries that s

Workout   An out-of-court agreement between a debtor and his or her creditors in which the parties work out a payment plan or schedule under which the debtor's debts can be discharged.

Writ of attachment   A court's order, prior to a trial to collect a debt, directing the sheriff or other officer to seize nonexempt property of the debtor; if the creditor prevails at trial, the seized property can be sold to satisfy the judgment.

Writ of certiorari (pronounced sur-shee-uh-*rah*-ree)   A writ from a higher court asking the lower court for the record of a case.

Writ of execution   A court's order, after a judgment has been entered against the debtor, directing the sheriff to seize (levy) and sell any of the debtor's nonexempt real or personal property. The proceeds of the sale are used to pay off the judgment, accrued interest, and costs of the sale; any surplus is paid to the debtor.

Wrongful discharge   An employer's termination of an employee's employment in violation of an employment contract or laws that protect employees.

Yellow dog contract   An agreement under which an employee promises his or her employer, as a condition of employment, not to join a union.

Zoning   The division of a city by legislative regulation into districts and the application in each district of regulations having to do with structural and architectural designs of buildings and prescribing the use to which buildings within designated districts may be put.

Zoning variance   The granting of permission by a municipality or other public board to a landowner to use his or her property in a way that does not strictly conform with the zoning regulations so as to avoid causing the landowner undue hardship.

Table of Cases

Index

Photo Credits

3 Portrait by Charles Sidney Hopkinson, Collection of the Supreme Court of the United States;   5 From the painting by Benjamin Ferrers in the National Portrait Gallery, photo: Corbis-Bettmann;   9 © Stacy Pick, Stock Boston;   15 Courtesy WestGroup;   17 ©Benaylouille Driss, Gamma Liaison, Inc.;   33 © Michael Newman, PhotoEdit;   38 © Photo Disc;   46 © Spencer Grant, PhotoEdit;   52 © Barbara Alper, Stock Boston;   54 © Comstock;   63 © PhotoEdit;   66 © Photo Disc;   69 © Corbis-Bettmann;   74 Courtesy Supreme Court of the United States;   80 © Ron Chappell, FPG;   92 © Jeff Greenberg, PhotoEdit;   94 Photo Disc;   98 © Tom McCathy, PhotoEdit;   115 © Stacy Pick, Stock Boston;   123 Photo Disc;   127 Telegraph Color Library, FPG;   130 © Matthew McVay, Tony Stone Images;   134 ©David Young-Wolff, PhotoEdit;   141, 145 © Tony Freeman, PhotoEdit;   147 © Bonnie Kamin, Photo Edit;   158 © Mark Richards, PhotoEdit;   166 Photo Disc;   177 © Chris Brown, Stock Boston;   193, 198, 201, 218, 223 Photo Disc;   226 © Richard Paisley, Stock Boston;   228, 234, 239 Photo Disc;   247 © Barbara J. Fiegles, Stock Boston;   249 © Amanda Merullo, Stock, Boston;   253 Photo Disc;   264 © Steve Leonard, Black Star;   269 Photo Disc;   271 © Tony Freeman, PhotoEdit;   280 © Michael Newman, PhotoEdit;   284 Photo Disc;   290 © Gary A. Conner, PhotoEdit;   296 © David Young-Wolff, PhotoEdit;   304 © Al Cook, Stock, Boston;   305 Ron Chappel, FPG;   313, 318, 348 Photo Disc;   357 Elizabeth Simpson, FPG;   362, 371, 381, 397, 399 Photo Disc;   406 Jim Erickson, The Stock Market;   407 Photo Disc;   415 Day Williams, Photo Researchers;   423 McIntyre, Photo Researchers;   427 Photo Disc;   446 Comstock;   447 Peter Pearson, Tony Stone Images;   451 Michael Newman, PhotoEdit;   460, 465, 476 Photo Disc;   481 Dennis Hallinan, FPG;   484, 489 Photo Disc;   498 Deborah Davis, PhotoEdit;   513 Jonathan Nourok, PhotoEdit;   529 Photo Disc;   531 Tony Freeman, PhotoEdit;   534 Photo Disc;   547 Photo Edit;   559 Photo Disc;   562 Michael Rosenfeld, Tony Stone Images;   568 Jack Dermid, Photo Researchers Inc.;   587 Tony Freeman, PhotoEdit;   590 Mark Richards PhotoEdit;   598 Photo Disc;   615 John Coletti, Stock Boston;   630 Theo Westebberger Gamma Liaison;   658 Art Montes de Oca, FPG;   667 Photo Disc;   671 Steven Weinberg, Tony Stone Images;   675 D. E. Cox, Tony Stone Images;   684 Bob Daemmrich, Stock Boston;   695 Photo Disc;   697 David Young-Wolff, Photo Edit;   707 Photo Disc